T0189301

Lecture Notes in Computer Science 12397

More information about this series at http://www.springer.com/series/7407

Igor Farkaš · Paolo Masulli ·
Stefan Wermter (Eds.)

Artificial Neural Networks and Machine Learning – ICANN 2020

29th International Conference on Artificial Neural Networks
Bratislava, Slovakia, September 15–18, 2020
Proceedings, Part II

 Springer

Editors
Igor Farkaš ⓘ
Department of Applied Informatics
Comenius University in Bratislava
Bratislava, Slovakia

Stefan Wermter ⓘ
Department of Informatics
University of Hamburg
Hamburg, Germany

Paolo Masulli ⓘ
Department of Applied Mathematics
and Computer Science
Technical University of Denmark
Kgs. Lyngby, Denmark

ISSN 0302-9743 ISSN 1611-3349 (electronic)
Lecture Notes in Computer Science
ISBN 978-3-030-61615-1 ISBN 978-3-030-61616-8 (eBook)
https://doi.org/10.1007/978-3-030-61616-8

LNCS Sublibrary: SL1 – Theoretical Computer Science and General Issues

This Springer imprint is published by the registered company Springer Nature Switzerland AG
The registered company address is: Gewerbestrasse 11, 6330 Cham, Switzerland

Preface

Research on artificial neural networks has progressed over decades, in recent years being fueled especially by deep learning that has proven to be data-greedy but efficient in solving various, mostly supervised tasks. Applications of artificial neural networks, especially related to artificial intelligence, influence our lives, reaching new horizons. Examples range from autonomous car driving, virtual assistants, and decision support systems, to healthcare data analytics, financial forecasting, and smart devices in our homes, just to name a few. These developments, however, also provide challenges, which were not imaginable previously, e.g., verification to prevent manipulation of voice, videos, or people's opinions during elections.

The International Conference on Artificial Neural Networks (ICANN) is the annual flagship conference of the European Neural Network Society (ENNS). This year, the special situation due to the COVID-19 pandemic influenced the planning of this conference in an unprecedented way. Based on the restrictions to travel and gatherings, as well as forecasts for the following months, it was not appropriate to decide for a large gathering such as ICANN to take place as a physical event in September 2020. Therefore, after a lot of consideration and discussions, the Organizing Committee, together with the Executive Committee of ENNS decided to postpone the physical meeting of ICANN 2020 and schedule next year's ICANN in September 2021 in Bratislava, Slovakia, since we also believe that a physical meeting has so many advantages compared to a virtual one.

Nevertheless, we decided to assist and do justice to the authors by disseminating their current work already completed for this year, running the paper selection and review process so that the successful submissions could appear online. Following a long-standing successful collaboration, the proceedings of ICANN are published as volumes within Springer's *Lecture Notes in Computer Science* series. The response to this year's call for papers resulted in an impressive number of 381 article submissions, of which almost all were long papers. After the official announcement that the conference would be postponed, 21 authors decided to withdraw their papers. The paper selection and review process that followed was decided during the online meeting of the Bratislava organizing team and the ENNS Executive Committee. The 20 Program Committee (PC) members agreed to review the long papers in stages. Stage one involved the review of 249 papers, of which 188 papers were selected for a stage-two review by independent reviewers. The majority of PC members had doctoral degrees (85%) and 70% of them were also professors. At the stage-two review, in total, 154 reviewers participated in the process, all having filled in an online questionnaire focusing on their areas of expertise, which significantly helped the general chair to properly assign papers to them. The reviewers were assigned one to three articles, but each article received three reports by the PC and reviewers, and these served as a major source for the final decision.

In total, 142 articles were accepted for the proceedings and the authors were requested to submit final versions. The acceptance rate was hence 37% when calculated from all initial submissions, or 57% when calculated from the initial papers selected for stage-two reviews. A list of PC members and reviewers, who agreed to publish their names, is included in these proceedings. With these procedures we tried to keep the quality of the proceedings high, while still having a critical mass of contributions reflecting the progress of the field. Overall, we hope that these proceedings will contribute to the dissemination of new results by the neural network community during these challenging times and that we can again have a physical ICANN in 2021.

We greatly appreciate the PC members and the reviewers for their invaluable work.

September 2020

Igor Farkaš
Paolo Masulli
Stefan Wermter

Organization

General Chairs

Igor Farkaš   Comenius University in Bratislava, Slovakia
L'ubica Beňušková   Comenius University in Bratislava, Slovakia

Organizing Committee Chairs

Kristína Malinovská   Comenius University in Bratislava, Slovakia
Alessandra Lintas   ENNS Lausanne, Switzerland

Honorary Chairs

Stefan Wermter   University of Hamburg, Germany
Věra Kůrková   Czech Academy of Sciences, Czech Republic

Program Committee

L'ubica Beňušková	Comenius University in Bratislava, Slovakia
Jérémie Cabessa	Panthéon-Assas University Paris II, France
Wlodek Duch	Nicolaus Copernicus University, Poland
Igor Farkaš	Comenius University in Bratislava, Slovakia
Juraj Holas	Comenius University in Bratislava, Slovakia
Věra Kůrková	Czech Academy of Sciences, Czech Republic
Tomáš Kuzma	Comenius University in Bratislava, Slovakia
Alessandra Lintas	University of Lausanne, Switzerland
Kristína Malinovská	Comenius University in Bratislava, Slovakia
Paolo Masulli	Technical University of Denmark, Denmark
Alessio Micheli	University of Pisa, Italy
Sebastian Otte	University of Tübingen, Germany
Jaakko Peltonen	University of Tampere, Finland
Antonio J. Pons	University of Barcelona, Spain
Martin Takáč	Comenius University in Bratislava, Slovakia
Igor V. Tetko	Technical University Munich, Germany
Matúš Tuna	Comenius University in Bratislava, Slovakia
Alessandro E. P. Villa	University of Lausanne, Switzerland
Roseli Wedemann	Rio de Janeiro State University, Brazil
Stefan Wermter	University of Hamburg, Germany

Communication Chair

Paolo Masulli   ENNS, Technical University of Denmark, Denmark

Reviewers

Argimiro Arratia   Polytechnic University of Catalonia, Spain
Andrá Artelt   Bielefeld University, Germany
Miguel Atencia   Universidad de Malaga, Spain
Cristian Axenie   Huawei German Research Center, Germany
Fatemeh Azimi   TU Kaiserslautern, Germany
Jatin Bedi   BITS Pilani, India
L'ubica Beňušková   Comenius University in Bratislava, Slovakia
Bernhard Bermeitinger   Universität St. Gallen, Switzerland
Yann Bernard   Inria, France
Jyostna Devi Bodapati   Indian Institute of Technology Madras, India
Nicolas Bougie   National Institute of Informatics, Japan
Evgeny Burnaev   Skoltech, Russia
Rüdiger Busche   Osnabrück University, Germany
Jérémie Cabessa   Panthéon-Assas University Paris II, France
Hugo Eduardo Camacho   Universidad Autónoma de Tamaulipas, Mexico
Antonio Candelieri   University of Milano-Bicocca, Italy
Siyu Cao   Beijing Jiaotong University, China
Antonio Carta   University of Pisa, Italy
Nico Cavalcanti   UFPE, Brazil
Gavneet Singh Chadha   South Westphalia University of Applied Sciences,
                               Germany
Shengjia Chen   Guangxi Normal University, China
Alessandro Di Nuovo   Sheffield Hallam University, UK
Tayssir Doghri   INRS, Canada
Haizhou Du   Shanghai University of Electric Power, China
Wlodzislaw Duch   Nicolaus Copernicus University, Poland
Ola Engkvist   AstraZeneca, Sweden
Manfred Eppe   University of Hamburg, Germany
Yuchun Fang   Shanghai University, China
Igor Farkaš   Comenius University in Bratislava, Slovakia
Oliver Gallitz   Technische Hochschule Ingolstadt, Germany
Jochen Garcke   University of Bonn, Germany
Dominik Geissler   Relayr GmbH, Germany
Claudio Giorgio   Catholic University of Milan, Italy
  Giancaterino
Francesco Giannini   University of Siena, Italy
Kathrin Grosse   CISPA Helmholtz Center for Information Security,
                               Germany
Philipp Grüning   University of Lübeck, Germany
Michael Guckert   Technische Hochschule Mittelhessen, Germany

Alberto Guillén	University of Granada, Spain
Song Guo	Nankai University, China
Simon Hakenes	Ruhr-Universität Bochum, Germany
Xiaoxu Han	Tianjin University, China
Martina Hasenjäger	Honda Research Institute Europe GmbH, Germany
Tieke He	Nanjing University, China
Raoul Heese	Fraunhofer ITWM, Germany
Xavier Hinaut	Inria, France
Juraj Holas	Comenius University in Bratislava, Slovakia
Junjie Huang	Chinese Academy of Sciences, China
Dania Humaidan	University of Tübingen, Germany
Nicolangelo Iannella	University of Oslo, Norway
Noman Javed	London School of Economics, UK
Shaoxiong Ji	Aalto University, Finland
Doreen Jirak	University of Hamburg, Germany
Renaud Jolivet	University of Geneva, Switzerland
Jan Kalina	Czech Academy of Sciences, Czech Republic
Izumi Karino	The University of Tokyo, Japan
John Kelleher	Technological University Dublin, Ireland
Matthias Kerzel	University of Hamburg, Germany
Adil Khan	Innopolis University, Russia
Matthias Kissel	Technical University of Munich, Germany
Atsushi Koike	National Institute of Technology, Japan
Stefanos Kollias	NTUA, Greece
Ekaterina Komendantskaya	Heriot–Watt University, UK
Petia Koprinkova-Hristova	IICT–BAS, Bulgaria
Irena Koprinska	The University of Sydney, Australia
Constantine Kotropoulos	Aristotle University of Thessaloniki, Greece
Adam Krzyzak	Concordia University, Canada
Věra Kůrková	Czech Academy of Sciences, Czech Republic
Sumit Kushwaha	Kamla Nehru Institute of Technology, India
Tomáš Kuzma	Comenius University in Bratislava, Slovakia
Nicolas Lachiche	University of Strasbourg, France
Wai Lam	The Chinese University of Hong Kong, Hong Kong
Yajie Li	Chinese Academy of Sciences, China
Mingxing Li	Guangxi Normal University, China
Mengdi Li	University of Hamburg, Germany
Boquan Li	Chinese Academy of Sciences, China
Jianfeng Li	Southwest University, China
Yang Lin	The University of Sydney, Australia
Alessandra Lintas	University of Lausanne, Switzerland
Yezheng Liu	Hefei University of Techonology, China
Vadim Liventsev	TU Eindhoven, The Netherlands
Viktor Liviniuk	University of California Irvine, USA
Nasrulloh Loka	Ghent University, Belgium
Shuai Lu	Jilin University, China

An Luo	South China University of Technology, China
Thomas Lymburn	The University of Western Australia, Australia
Kleanthis Malialis	University of Cyprus, Cyprus
Kristína Malinovská	Comenius University in Bratislava, Slovakia
Fragkiskos Malliaros	CentraleSupélec, France
Gilles Marcou	University of Strasbourg, France
Michael Marino	Universität Osnabrück, Germany
Paolo Masulli	Technical University of Denmark, Denmark
Guillaume Matheron	Institut des Systèmes Intelligents et de Robotique, France
Alessio Micheli	University of Pisa, Italy
Florian Mirus	BMW Group, Germany
Roman Neruda	Institute of Computer Science, ASCR, Czech Republic
Hasna Njah	University of Sfax, Tunisia
Mihaela Oprea	Petroleum-Gas University of Ploiesti, Romania
Christoph Ostrau	Bielefeld University, Germany
Sebastian Otte	University of Tübingen, Germany
Hyeyoung Park	Kyungpook National University Daegu Campus, South Korea
Jaakko Peltonen	Tampere University, Finland
Daniele Perlo	University of Turin, Italy
Vincenzo Piuri	University of Milan, Italy
Antonio Javier Pons Rivero	Universitat Politècnica de Catalunya, Spain
Mike Preuss	Universiteit Leiden, The Netherlands
Miloš Prágr	Czech Technical University, FEE, Czech Republic
Yili Qu	Sun Yat-Sen University, China
Laya Rafiee	Concordia University, Canada
Rajkumar Ramamurthy	Fraunhofer IAIS, Germany
Zuzana Rošťáková	Slovak Academy of Sciences, Slovakia
Frank Röder	University of Hamburg, Germany
Jun Sang	Chongqing University, China
Anindya Sarkar	Indian Institute of Technology, India
Yikemaiti Sataer	Southeast University, China
Simone Scardapane	Sapienza University of Rome, Italy
Jochen Schmidt	Rosenheim University of Applied Sciences, Germany
Cedric Schockaert	Paul Wurth Geprolux S.A., Luxembourg
Friedhelm Schwenker	University of Ulm, Germany
Andreas Sedlmeier	LMU Munich, Germany
Gabriela Šejnová	Czech Technical University in Prague, Czech Republic
Alexandru Serban	Radboud University, The Netherlands
Linlin Shen	Shenzhen University, China
Shashwat Shukla	Indian Institute of Technology Bombay, India
Caio Silva	Universidade Federal de Pernambuco, Brazil
Aleksander Smywiński-Pohl	AGH University of Science and Technology, Poland
Pouya Soltani Zarrin	IHP, Germany

Miguel Soriano	Institute for Cross-Disciplinary Physics and Complex Systems, Spain
Lea Steffen	FZI Research Center for Information Technology, Germany
Michael Stettler	University of Tübingen, Germany
Ruxandra Stoean	University of Craiova, Romania
Jérémie Sublime	ISEP, France
Chanchal Suman	IIT Patna, India
Xiaoqi Sun	Shanghai University, China
Alexander Sutherland	University of Hamburg, Germany
Zaneta Swiderska-Chadaj	Warsaw University of Technology, Poland
Rudolf Szadkowski	Czech Technical University in Prague, Czech Republic
Philippe Thomas	Université de Lorraine, France
Shiro Takagi	The University of Tokyo, Japan
Martin Takáč	Comenius University, Slovakia
Max Talanov	Kazan Federal University, Russia
Enzo Tartaglione	Università degli Studi Torino, Italy
Igor Tetko	Helmholtz Zentrum München, Germany
Juan-Manuel Torres-Moreno	Université d'Avignon, France
Jochen Triesch	Frankfurt Institute for Advanced Studies, Germany
Matúš Tuna	Comenius University in Bratislava, Slovakia
Takaya Ueda	Ritsumeikan University, Japan
Sagar Verma	CentraleSupélec, France
Ricardo Vigário	Universidade NOVA de Lisboa, Portugal
Alessandro E. P. Villa	University of Lausanne, Switzerland
Paolo Viviani	Noesis Solutions NV, Belgium
Shuo Wang	Monash University and CSIRO, Australia
Huiling Wang	Tampere University, Finland
Xing Wang	Ningxia University, China
Zhe Wang	Soochow University, China
Roseli Wedemann	Rio de Janeiro State University, Brazil
Baole Wei	Chinese Academy of Sciences, China
Feng Wei	York University, Canada
Yingcan Wei	The University of Hong Kong, Hong Kong
Martin Georg Weiß	Regensburg University of Applied Sciences, Germany
Thomas Wennekers	Plymouth University, UK
Marc Wenninger	Rosenheim Technical University of Applied Sciences, Germany
Stefan Wermter	University of Hamburg, Germany
John Wilmes	Brandeis University, USA
Christoph Windheuser	ThoughtWorks Inc., Germany
Moritz Wolter	University of Bonn, Germany
Changmin Wu	Ecole Polytechnique, France
Takaharu Yaguchi	Kobe University, Japan
Tsoy Yury	Solidware, South Korea

Contents – Part II

Neural Network Theory and Information Theoretic Learning

Normalization and Regularization Methods

Reinforcement Learning I

Reinforcement Learning II

Reinforcement Learning III

Spiking Neural Networks I

Spiking Neural Networks II

Text Understanding I

Text Understanding II

Unsupervised Learning

Contents – Part I

Cognitive Models

Convolutional Neural Networks and Kernel Methods

Deep Learning Applications I

Deep Learning Applications II

Explainable Methods

Few-Shot Learning

Generative Adversarial Network

Generative and Graph Models

Hybrid Neural-Symbolic Architectures

Image Processing

Medical Image Processing

Recurrent Neural Networks

Model Compression I

Fine-Grained Channel Pruning for Deep Residual Neural Networks

Siang Chen[1], Kai Huang[1(✉)], Dongliang Xiong[1], Bowen Li[1], and Luc Claesen[2]

[1] Institute of VLSI Design, Zhejiang University, Hangzhou, China
{11631032,huangk,xiongdl,11631033}@zju.edu.cn
[2] Engineering Technology - Electronics-ICT Department,
Hasselt University, 3590 Diepenbeek, Belgium
luc.claesen@uhasselt.be

Abstract. Pruning residual neural networks is a challenging task due to the constraints induced by cross layer connections. Many existing approaches assign channels connected by skip-connections to the same group and prune them simultaneously, limiting the pruning ratio on those troublesome filters. Instead, we propose a Fine-grained Channel Pruning (FCP) method that allows any channels to be pruned independently. To avoid the misalignment problem between convolution and skip connection, we always keep the residual addition operations alive. Thus we can obtain a novel efficient residual architecture by removing any unimportant channels without the alignment constraint. Besides classification, We further apply FCP on residual models for image super-resolution, which is a low-level vision task. Extensive experimental results show that FCP can achieve better performance than other state-of-the-art methods in terms of parameter and computation cost. Notably, on CIFAR-10, FCP reduces more than 78% FLOPs on ResNet-56 with no accuracy drop. Moreover, it achieves more than 48% FLOPs reduction on MSR-ResNet with negligible performance degradation.

Keywords: Channel pruning · Residual neural network · Efficient network structure

1 Introduction

Despite the superior performance of deep convolutional neural networks in machine learning, the massive computation and storage consumption prevents its deployment in resource constraint devices. Pruning is a promising way for convolutional neural network (CNN) model size compression by identifying and removing unnecessary neurons without significant performance degradation. Recent studies on neural network pruning can be divided into either non-structured [5] or structured pruning [21], the former prunes weight independently, thus always

Supported by the National Key R&D Program of China (2018YFB0904900, 2018YFB0904902).

© Springer Nature Switzerland AG 2020
I. Farkaš et al. (Eds.): ICANN 2020, LNCS 12397, pp. 3–14, 2020.
https://doi.org/10.1007/978-3-030-61616-8_1

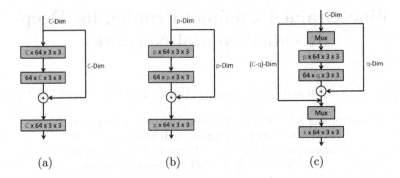

Fig. 1. An illustration of (**a**): baseline structure. (**b**): structure pruned by group strategy. (**c**): structure pruned by our fine-grained strategy. The red letter denotes the channel number. (Color figure online)

results in structures that are unfriendly for hardware acceleration, while the latter aims at removing parameters in units of filters which can take advantage of fast dense matrix multiplication [4]. Among the structured pruning methods, channel pruning (a.k.a filter pruning) [9] directly eliminates entire channels in each layer with no special hardware design required.

As the neural network becomes deeper and wider, it is a challenge to effectively train a very deep model. One good solution is residual learning [6], which leverages the shortcut connection between layers to reformulate the layers as learning residual information. The conception of residual learning has been widely used to design efficient neural network architectures. ResNet is one of the most popular residual architectures, which performs residual mapping by a shortcut and element-wise addition. Directly applying pruning methods to residual neural networks, however, brings some problems. Specifically, pruning filters of the last convolution in each basic block independently will lead to the misalignment between the skip connection and the corresponding output feature maps. Therefore, various works have been made to tackle these problems. [17] avoid pruning these troublesome layers. [16] prune pre-activation models by inserting an additional channel selection layer before the first convolution in each residual block. [13] apply the mixed block connection to avoid such problem. Recently, [3,4,22] all propose the Group Pruning for those layers connected by skip connections. Unfortunately, pruning in a group technique will lead to models shown in Fig. 1(b) such that all corresponding connections of one eliminated filter should be removed simultaneously, limiting the performance at especially high pruning ratios.

In this paper, we propose a novel Fine-grained Channel Pruning (FCP) approach as shown in Fig. 1(c), which solves the constraint that the pruning problem encounters when pruning residual neural networks. Instead of focusing on measuring the importance of filters, we insert gate function into all channels between layers, and transfer the problem of optimizing filter numbers into minimizing data transmissions. By paying attention on estimating the importance of each channel independently, we allow both input and output channels of convolutions to be pruned. The FCP method provides a larger search space for unimportant filter selections, thus can achieve a more fine-grained channel allocation between layers. Our contributions are summarized as follows:

(1) We analyze the pruning of residual neural network in detail and observe that the state-of-the-art group strategy is a coarse pruning that is still limited by the alinement constraint.
(2) We propose FCP to allow any channels between residual blocks to be pruned independently while keeping constant numbers of skip connections. By performing such pruning strategy, we can obtain a novel efficient residual network structure, of which connections can fully skip the residual building block.
(3) We demonstrate the effectiveness of FCP on both classification and image representation (super-resolution) tasks. The extensive experiments show that FCP can prune more parameters and FLOPs with less performance drop than state-of-the-art methods.

2 Related Work

Model pruning has shown great success in neural network compression by removing unimportant neurons with negligible performance degradation. Despite the deep compression of parameters, pruning individual weights [5] always leads to unstructured models, which makes it difficult to implement realistic speedup unless special software and hardware are designed. Therefore, many researches focus on filter pruning. [14] prune filters in each layer with small $l1$-norm magnitude. [16] impose sparsity-induced regularization on the scaling factor in batch normalization layers, and identify insignificant channels with small scaling factors. [8] prune the most replaceable filters containing redundant information by analyzing geometric median distance. Our work also falls into the category of channel pruning.

The problem of vanishing gradient prevents neural networks from becoming deeper to demonstrate higher performance. To address this problem, [6] apply element-wise addition on the feature maps between two residual blocks, which is known as ResNet. [10] connect each layer to every other layer in a feed-forward fashion, which fully exploits the advantages of skip connections and reduces the number of parameters as well. While the existence of skip connections makes it effective to train a very deep network, methods for pruning plain networks like VGG [19] and AlexNet [12] can not be applied to residual models directly: pruning the filters of each layer independently will result in misalignment of feature maps between residual blocks. [17] avoid this problem by only pruning the internal layers in residual blocks. [16] place a channel selection layer before the first convolution in each residual block to mask out insignificant channels, and leave the last convolution layer unpruned, which only works for pre-activation networks. [13] use a mixed block connectivity to avoid redundant computation.

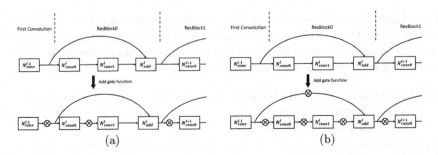

Fig. 2. Structures of ResBlock with node transformation before and after inserting the gate function (symbol ⊗). **(a)**: group pruning. **(b)**: our fine-grained pruning

Recently, [3,4,22] propose to assign the layers connected by pure skip connections into the same group, thus the filters in the same group can be pruned simultaneously. However, the above methods still can not remove each channel between residual blocks independently.

3   Approach

3.1   Rethinking Pruning Residual Neural Networks

To understand the relationship of channels between residual blocks more clearly in following sections, we first transform the operation on feature maps in the network into **Node**. Consider pruning two consecutive blocks in ResNet, as shown in Fig. 2(a) and 2(b). The structure consists of two basic Nodes:

1) **Node$_{add}$**: indicates the element-wise addition for channels of the same index from the output of the previous convolution and the corresponding skip connection, the operation can be defined as:

$$O_{add}^{l,c} = O_{conv1}^{l,c} + O_{conv}^{l-1,c} \tag{1}$$

where $O_{add}^{l,c}$ denotes the c-th output channel of Node$_{add}$ in l-th layer, $O_{conv1}^{l,c}$ denotes the c-th channel from the previous convolution.

2) **Node$_{conv}$**: indicates the regular convolution operation. Take the first convolution in ResBlock as an example:

$$O_{conv0}^{l+1,k} = \sum_{i=1}^{C} O_{add}^{l,c} * W^{l+1,c,k} \tag{2}$$

C is the total number of input channels, $O_{conv0}^{l+1,k}$ denotes the k-th output channel of convolution, $W_{l+1,c,k}$ denotes c-th input channel and k-th output channel weight. For representational simplicity, the kernel operation, bias term, BN and activation layers are not included in our formulation. Existing methods only estimate the importance of the output channel of convolutions as shown in Fig. 2(a), in order to allow all filters to be pruned, they regard the channel relationship as:

$$C(O_{conv}^{l-1}) = C(O_{add}^{l}) = C(O_{conv1}^{l}) = C(O_{conv1}^{l+1}) \tag{3}$$

$C(x)$ denotes the set of input channels in x. Based on Eq. (1) and Eq. (2), pruning these channels is under the constraint that the output channel number of the Node_{conv1}^{l}, channel number of skip connection and input channel of $\text{Node}_{conv0}^{l+1}$ should be maintained the same. Therefore, importance score for these filters in the group are accumulated together, which makes them harder to be pruned, and always results in dense connections between residual blocks and very few connections inner residual blocks especially for high pruning ratios. Instead, we consider the problem of pruning from the perspective of gating feature maps. Different from [22] that only add gates after convolutions, we try to insert gate function on each channel except the output channel of Node_{conv}^{l-1} as shown in Fig. 2(b), thus the operations for Node_{add}^{l} become:

$$
\begin{aligned}
O_{add}^{l,c} &= I_{add}^{l,c} + R_{add}^{l,c}, \\
I_{add}^{l,c} &= g_{add1}^{l,c} \times O_{conv1}^{l,c}, \\
R_{add}^{l,c} &= g_{add2}^{l,c} \times O_{conv}^{l-1,c}
\end{aligned}
\tag{4}
$$

while for $\text{Node}_{conv0}^{l+1}$:

$$
\begin{aligned}
O_{conv0}^{l+1,k} &= \sum_{c=1}^{C} I_{conv0}^{l+1,c} * W^{l+1,c,k}, \\
I_{conv0}^{l+1,c} &= g_{conv0}^{l+1,c} \times O_{add}^{l,c}
\end{aligned}
\tag{5}
$$

Here $g_{add}^{l,c}$ is the gate function for the corresponding channel, of which the value is 0 for masking. $I_{add}^{l,c}$ and $R_{add}^{l,c}$ is the c-th output channel of Node_{conv1}^{l} and the skip connection after the gate function respectively. According to Eq. (1) and Eq. (2), the channel relationship is actually:

$$C(O_{add}^{l}) = C(O_{conv}^{l-1}) \cup C(O_{conv1}^{l}) \tag{6}$$

$$C(I_{conv0}^{l+1}) = C(O_{add}^{l}) \times g_{conv0}^{l+1} \tag{7}$$

Combined with Eq. (5), the channel set of weights in each convolution only depends on input feature map for each Node, which means pruning the input of each Node equals to pruning filters. Note that here we only analyze the channels between residual block. For channels inner the residual block or in the plain neural network, we treat them as a special case without skip connections. Therefore the problem of pruning filters in residual neural network can be transformed into the optimization of feature map channels.

3.2   Channel Importance

The biggest difference between our approach and group pruning is that we prune each channel independently, therefore the problem arises on how to measure the importance of both input and output channel in normalization. Magnitude-based [8,14] or utilizing BN scaling factor [16] is not applicable for such pruning strategy, we leverage Taylor expansion [18] in this work, and extend this method to a more general one. Instead of only considering the output of each convolution, we multiply each channel between convolutions by a trainable scaling factor α, then we estimate the change in loss function caused by setting α to zero, thus we get the importance score of the corresponding channel:

$$IS(\alpha) = |\frac{\partial L}{\partial \alpha}\alpha| \tag{8}$$

which can be easily computed during back-propagation. Therefore, the gate function can be defined as:

$$g(\alpha) = \begin{cases} 0, & IS(\alpha) < T \\ \alpha, & otherwise \end{cases} \tag{9}$$

where T is a global threshold that depends on pruning ratio and is computed by sorting the importance score.

Note that we can also prune the R_{add} in the same way as in the other channels. We however do not prune R_{add}, there are three reasons: First and most important, keep constant numbers of residual connections can avoid the problem of misalignment for output channels of last convolution in each block. Second, in the case that I_{add} is pruned, R_{add} can still provide information for following layers, which retains the full capacity of network to some extent. Third, pruning R_{add} can not eliminate filters directly.

According to Eq. (8), the importance score is zero when gradient or α is zero, while the gradient depends on training process, we can induce more sparsity by adding a sparse constraint on α.

$$L_{FT} = L_D + \lambda \sum_{\alpha \in \Phi} |\alpha| \tag{10}$$

where L_D is the loss function on data, λ is the penalty.

To guarantee the importance score is accurate enough, we compute Eq. (8) of each channel by accumulating individual contribution in one epoch, and prune p percentage of the total channels each time besides zero scaling factors, then we fine-tune the network for T epochs based on the loss function Eq. (10). We iteratively conduct the prune and fine-tune step until meeting the compression requirement.

3.3   Analysis of Residual Neural Network

In this section, we analyze the possible efficient structures for ResNet pruned and reconstructed by our approach. For simplicity, we take two consecutive basic

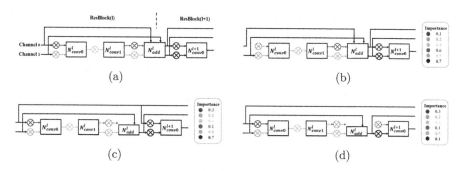

Fig. 3. Illustration of possible architectures pruned and reconstructed by FCP in channel-wise view, the dotted lines denote pruned channels. (**a**): structure before pruning. (**b**): only prune input channel. (**c**): only prune output channel. (**d**): prune both input and output channels

blocks with at most two channels for each convolution as examples in Fig. 3(a), a regular ResNet can be treated as a combination of replicated structures. Possible pruning for channels inter ResBlock can be summarized as follows:

1) Pruning I_{conv}. As shown in Fig. 3(b), we only remove the input channel 0 of Node^l_{conv0} while keeping the corresponding output channel of $\text{Node}^{l-1}_{conv1}$, $O^{l-1,c}_{add}$ will bypass through Node^l_{conv0} and connect to Node^l_{conv1} as a skip connection. We only need to store the pruned or the remaining channel indices to assure correct input channel feature maps flow into $\text{Node}^{l+1}_{conv0}$, which is negligible to the total amount of parameters.

2) Pruning I_{add}. We eliminate the output channels of weight in Node^l_{conv1}, but we do not prune I^{l+1}_{conv0} simultaneously so that the skip connection of channel 0 becomes a pure input for $\text{Node}^{l+1}_{conv0}$ in Fig. 3(c). Similarly, We should store the pruned or remaining channel index to exclude the pruned channel from addition operation.

3) Pruning both I_{conv} and I_{add}. We can remove the output channel of Node^l_{conv1} and the input channel of $\text{Node}^{l+1}_{conv0}$ as shown in Fig. 3(d). However, different from group pruning or pruning in plain neural networks, we allow the skip connection to bypass through $\text{Node}^{l+1}_{conv0}$ and connect to $\text{Node}^{l+1}_{conv1}$ directly.

4   Experiments

In this section, We demonstrate the benefits of FCP for ResNet on both classification and super-resolution tasks. For classification, we use two standard benchmarks: CIFAR-10 and CIFAR-100 [11]. CIFAR-10 contains 50000 training images and 10000 testing images of size 32×32, which are categorized into 10 different classes. CIFAR-100 is similar to CIFAR-10 but has 100 classes. For super-resolution, we conduct MSRResNet [20] on the DIV2K dataset [2], which contains 800 high-resolution images.

To compare with other state-of-the-art pruning methods for residual neural networks, we define different pruning levels as follows:

Skip. Only prunes the channels inner ResBlock.

In-only. Only prunes the input channels for the first convolution in each ResBlock.

Out-only. Only prunes the output channels for the last convolution in each ResBlock.

Group. This strategy prunes the channels connected by pure shortcut connections together.

4.1   Experimental Settings

Training Setting. For CIFAR-10 and CIFAR-100 datasets, we use the default parameter settings as [7]. For super-resolution on DIV2K dataset, we refer to the open-source platform BasicSR. The HR images are cropped into small images with size 480×480 by step 240, and the number of small images is 32208. The LR images with size 32×32 are randomly cropped from small images, then rotated by $90°$, $180°$, $270°$ and flip them horizontally. We optimize the weights via ADAM with batchsize $= 16$, $\beta_1 = 0.9$, $\beta_2 = 0.999$ and $\epsilon = 10^{-8}$. The initial learning rate is set to 2×10^{-4} and reduced to half every 500 epochs for 1500 epochs totally.

Pruning Setting. We prune models by following the Tick-Tock setup in [22]. All the networks are pruned 0.2% filters in each Tick stage for 10 epochs, followed by one Tock phase of 10 epochs for classification and 20 epochs for super-resolution, respectively. In the case of CIFAR-10 and CIFAR-100, the learning rate used in the Tick stage is set to 10^{-3}, we use the 1-cycle strategy to linearly increase the learning rate from 10^{-3} to 10^{-2} in the first half of the iteration, then linearly decrease it from 10^{-2} to 10^{-3}, sparse constraint λ is set to 10^{-3}. For DIV2K, the learning rate is set to 2×10^{-7} in the Tick stage, and increases from 2×10^{-7} to 2×10^{-5} in the first half of the iteration, and then linearly decreases from 2×10^{-7} to 2×10^{-5}. For fine-tuning stage, we use the same learning rate strategy as the Tock phase, the difference is that fine-tune epochs are 40 for classification and 125 for super resolution.

4.2   Results on Classification

CIFAR-10. Table 1 shows the results. Our FCP achieves a better performance than other state-of-the-art pruning methods for ResNet. For example, GBN [22] use the group strategy to prune ResNet-56 by 70.3% FLOPs with only 0.03% accuracy drop, we can however achieve no accuracy drop while pruning 7.75% more FLOPs and 5.44% more parameters. FPGM [8] prune ResNet-20 by 42.2% FLOPs with 1.11% accuracy drop, we can achieve even 0.09% better accuracy than baseline with more FLOPs pruned. Figure 4 shows the pruning result of ResNet-56 on CIFAR-10, active channel numbers between ResBlocks are not

Table 1. Comparison of pruning ResNet on CIFAR-10 and CIFAR-100

Dataset	Depth	Method	Baseline acc. (%)	Acc. ↓ (%)	Params ↓ (%)	Flops ↓ (%)
CIFAR-10	20	FPGM [8]	92.20	1.11	–	42.20
		GBN [22]	92.07	0.68	36.08	44.53
		Ours	92.07	**−0.09**	**36.62**	**48.46**
	32	FPGM [8]	92.63	0.32	–	41.50
		GBN [22]	93.22	0.46	35.93	44.59
		Ours	93.22	**0.10**	**38.70**	**52.10**
	56	He et al. [9]	92.80	1.00	–	50.00
		FPGM [8]	93.59	0.10	–	52.60
		GBN [22]	93.10	0.03	66.70	70.30
		Ours (60%)	93.10	**−0.37**	61.00	70.08
		Ours (78%)	93.10	0.00	**72.14**	**78.05**
	110	FPGM [8]	93.68	−0.16	–	52.30
		GBN [22]	94.02	−0.05	58.04	54.17
		Ours	94.02	**−0.24**	**58.89**	**68.01**
CIFAR-100	32	FPGM[8]	69.77	1.25	–	41.50
		GBN [22]	70.27	1.38	20.82	44.36
		Ours	70.27	**0.32**	**20.96**	**50.02**
	164	Li et al. [16]	76.63	0.54	–	50.60
		Ours	76.25	**−0.19**	**34.04**	**60.07**

limited to be the same, and some layers are even totally pruned to allow feature maps of previous layer directly flow into next layer.

CIFAR-100. As shown in Table 1, results on ResNet-32 and ResNet-164 demonstrate that FCP outperforms previous methods on CIFAR-100 again. For ResNet-164, there are few works on this pre-activation model which adds more constraints on pruning, but FCP can still reduce more than 60% FLOPs with a even 0.19% accuracy increase.

These results validate the effectiveness of FCP, which can produce a more compressed ResNet model with nearly the same or better performance compared to the original model.

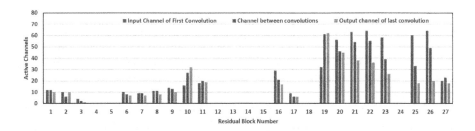

Fig. 4. Result of 70% FLOPs pruned by our method on ResNet-56-CIFAR-10

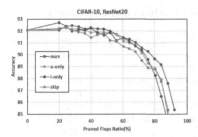
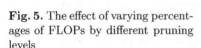

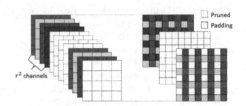

Fig. 5. The effect of varying percentages of FLOPs by different pruning levels

Fig. 6. Padding-and-Pruning strategy for the pixelshuffle layer

4.3   Comparison of Different Pruning Levels

To fairly validate the effectiveness of FCP at different pruning ratios, we compare different pruning levels using the same pruning criterion and settings in this paper.

Figure 5 shows the results. The skip strategy produces the smallest search space of channels and is more sensitive to pruning in most cases. Since in-only and out-only both can be treated as subsets of FCP, their results are similar. FCP is more fine-grained than the other three pruning levels, thus is more robust against pruning ratio and performs better especially at deeper pruning ratios.

4.4   Results on Super Resolution

In MSRResNet, upscaled features are generated by the pixelshuffle layer, which reshapes feature maps from $H \times W \times r^2 C$ to $rH \times rW \times C$ in a periodic way. Here the input image is assumed to be of size $H \times W \times C$, r is the scale factor. Thus there is a constraint on pruned channels of convolution before the pixelshuffle layer, we apply a novel padding-and-pruning approach to address this problem. As shown in Fig. 6, for each periodic r^2 channels with more than one channels remaining after pruning, we extend them to the original r^2 channel size by padding, and others are pruned away. Those padding channels will become blank pixels after the pixelshuffle layer, which means the final HR images consist of pixels directly from bilinear interpolation. This also makes sense that some pixels by bilinear interpolation may be good enough and convolutions for those pixels can be skipped.

We evaluate our pruned model on four standard benchmark datasets, including Set5, Set14, B100 and Manga109. Results are evaluated with PSNR and SSIM on Y channels of transformed YCbCr space. To show the effectiveness of FCP, we implement the state-of-the-art pruning methods: L1-norm based [14], FPGM [8], GBN [22].

Table 2 shows the parameters, FLOPs and performance for ×4 SR. FCP can reduce more parameters and FLOPs while maintaining higher PSNR and

Table 2. Quantitative results of evaluated methods for x4 SR

Method	Params	FLOPs	Set5	Set14	B100	Manga109
			PSNR/SSIM	PSNR/SSIM	PSNR/SSIM	PSNR/SSIM
Bicubic	–	–	28.63/0.8138	26.21/0.7087	26.04/0.6719	25.07/0.7904
EDSR	43090K	2894.5G	32.46/0.8968	28.80/0.7876	27.71/0.7420	31.02/0.9148
MSRResNet	1517K	146.0G	32.22/0.8952	28.63/0.7826	27.59/0.7357	30.48/0.9089
CARN	1592K	90.8G	32.13/0.8937	28.60/0.7806	27.58/0.7349	30.45/0.9073
Li et al. [14]	861K	78.69G	32.03/0.8931	28.54/0.7803	27.53/0.7346	30.23/0.9056
FPGM [8]	859K	83.94G	31.95/0.8917	28.48/0.7790	27.48/0.7332	30.03/0.9033
GBN [22]	863K	75.76G	32.09/0.8944	28.58/0.7815	27.56/0.7356	30.36/0.9075
Ours (60%)	973K	90.29G	32.18/0.8947	28.61/0.7823	27.58/0.7362	30.44/0.9084
Ours (50%)	799K	75.73G	32.15/0.8946	28.58/0.7816	27.57/0.7358	30.40/0.9080

SSIM on all datasets than other approaches. When compared to state-of-the-art models, we can achieve nearly 64% parameters and 62% computation cost of the baseline model with negligible performance drop, and SSIM on dataset B100 can be even better than original model. Our 60% pruned model performs better than CARN [1] on most of the datasets, but the parameters of our pruned model is 619K less. EDSR [15] optimizes performance by increasing network depth and width, but too much parameters and FLOPs limit the application on resource-constrained devices, while our pruned model has almost 54× reduction in model size and 38× reduction in computation cost. These results demonstrate that FCP can achieve better performance with a comparable compression ratio on pixel-level tasks.

5   Conclusion

In this paper, we propose a fine-grained channel pruning (FCP) approach for deep residual networks. Unlike previous works that prune in a group technique, we allow any channels between convolution layers to be pruned, our approach multiplies a scaling factor on each channel, then we compute the importance score based on Taylor expansion, finally we obtain the compact model by removing unimportant channels independently, which reveals a novel residual structure for efficient model design. Extensive experiments show that FCP outperforms other state-of-the-art filter pruning approaches on both classification and super-resolution tasks.

References

1. Ahn, N., Kang, B., Sohn, K.-A.: Fast, accurate, and lightweight super-resolution with cascading residual network. In: Ferrari, V., Hebert, M., Sminchisescu, C., Weiss, Y. (eds.) ECCV 2018. LNCS, vol. 11214, pp. 256–272. Springer, Cham (2018). https://doi.org/10.1007/978-3-030-01249-6_16
2. Bevilacqua, M., Roumy, A., Guillemot, C., Alberi-Morel, M.: Low-complexity single-image super-resolution based on nonnegative neighbor embedding. In: BMVC, pp. 1–10 (2012). https://doi.org/10.5244/C.26.135

3. Ding, X., Ding, G., Guo, Y., Han, J.: Centripetal SGD for pruning very deep convolutional networks with complicated structure. In: CVPR, pp. 4943–4953 (2019)
4. Gao, S., Liu, X., Chien, L., Zhang, W., Alvarez, J.M.: VACL: variance-aware cross-layer regularization for pruning deep residual networks. CoRR abs/1909.04485 (2019). http://arxiv.org/abs/1909.04485
5. Han, S., Pool, J., Tran, J., Dally, W.: Learning both weights and connections for efficient neural networks, pp. 1135–1143 (2015)
6. He, K., Zhang, X., Ren, S., Sun, J.: Deep residual learning for image recognition. In: CVPR, pp. 770–778 (2016). https://doi.org/10.1109/CVPR.2016.90
7. He, Y., Kang, G., Dong, X., Fu, Y., Yang, Y.: Soft filter pruning for accelerating deep convolutional neural networks. In: IJCAI, pp. 2234–2240 (2018). https://doi.org/10.24963/ijcai.2018/309
8. He, Y., Liu, P., Wang, Z., Hu, Z., Yang, Y.: Filter pruning via geometric median for deep convolutional neural networks acceleration. In: CVPR, pp. 4340–4349 (2019)
9. He, Y., Zhang, X., Sun, J.: Channel pruning for accelerating very deep neural networks. In: ICCV, pp. 1398–1406 (2017). https://doi.org/10.1109/ICCV.2017.155
10. Huang, G., Liu, Z., van der Maaten, L., Weinberger, K.Q.: Densely connected convolutional networks. In: CVPR, pp. 2261–2269 (2017). https://doi.org/10.1109/CVPR.2017.243
11. Krizhevsky, A.: Learning multiple layers of features from tiny images. Technical report (2009)
12. Krizhevsky, A., Sutskever, I., Hinton, G.E.: ImageNet classification with deep convolutional neural networks. In: NeurIPS, pp. 1106–1114 (2012)
13. Lemaire, C., Achkar, A., Jodoin, P.: Structured pruning of neural networks with budget-aware regularization. In: CVPR, pp. 9108–9116 (2019)
14. Li, H., Kadav, A., Durdanovic, I., Samet, H., Graf, H.P.: Pruning filters for efficient convnets. In: ICLR (2017)
15. Lim, B., Son, S., Kim, H., Nah, S., Lee, K.M.: Enhanced deep residual networks for single image super-resolution. In: CVPR Workshops, pp. 1132–1140 (2017). https://doi.org/10.1109/CVPRW.2017.151
16. Liu, Z., Li, J., Shen, Z., Huang, G., Yan, S., Zhang, C.: Learning efficient convolutional networks through network slimming. In: ICCV, pp. 2755–2763 (2017). https://doi.org/10.1109/ICCV.2017.298
17. Luo, J., Wu, J., Lin, W.: ThiNet: a filter level pruning method for deep neural network compression. In: ICCV, pp. 5068–5076 (2017). https://doi.org/10.1109/ICCV.2017.541
18. Molchanov, P., Mallya, A., Tyree, S., Frosio, I., Kautz, J.: Importance estimation for neural network pruning. In: CVPR, pp. 11264–11272 (2019)
19. Simonyan, K., Zisserman, A.: Very deep convolutional networks for large-scale image recognition. In: ICLR (2015). http://arxiv.org/abs/1409.1556
20. Wang, X., et al.: ESRGAN: enhanced super-resolution generative adversarial networks. In: Leal-Taixé, L., Roth, S. (eds.) ECCV 2018. LNCS, vol. 11133, pp. 63–79. Springer, Cham (2019). https://doi.org/10.1007/978-3-030-11021-5_5
21. Wen, W., Wu, C., Wang, Y., Chen, Y., Li, H.: Learning structured sparsity in deep neural networks. In: NeurIPS. pp. 2074–2082 (2016)
22. You, Z., Yan, K., Ye, J., Ma, M., Wang, P.: Gate decorator: global filter pruning method for accelerating deep convolutional neural networks. In: NeurIPS, pp. 2130–2141 (2019)

A Lightweight Fully Convolutional Neural Network of High Accuracy Surface Defect Detection

Yajie Li[1,2,3], Yiqiang Chen[1,2,3]([✉]), Yang Gu[1,3], Jianquan Ouyang[2], Jiwei Wang[1,3], and Ni Zeng[1,3]

[1] Institute of Computing Technology, Chinese Academy of Sciences, Beijing 100190, China
yqchen@ict.ac.cn
[2] Xiangtan University, Xiangtan 411105, China
[3] Beijing Key Laboratory of Mobile Computing and Pervasive Device, Beijing 100190, China

Abstract. Surface defect detection is an indispensable step in the production process. Recent researches based on deep learning have paid primarily attention to improving accuracy. However, it is difficult to apply in real situation, because of huge number of parameters and the strict hardware requirements. In this paper, a lightweight fully convolutional neural network, named LFCSDD, is proposed. The parameters of our model are 11x fewer than baselines at least, and obtain the accuracy of 99.72% and 98.74% on benchmark defect datasets, DAGM 2007 and KolektorSDD, respectively, outperforming all the baselines. In addition, our model can process the images with different sizes, which is verified on the RSDDs with the accuracy of 97.00%.

Keywords: Surface defect detection · Convolutional neural network · Lightweight

1 Introduction

The visual inspection of product surfaces plays a important role in the product quality control [25]. The visual inspection of product surfaces in most manufacturing processes depends mainly on human inspectors. Some studies [3,4,15,18] showed that human visual inspection is slow, expensive and erratic. And there are some difficulties in human visual inspection due to the diversity of surface defects and the complexity of the products. Machine learning methods are obviously the alternative to the human inspectors, since their characteristic of high precision and efficiency.

Machine learning methods can be divided into traditional machine learning methods and deep learning methods. For traditional machine learning methods, Song and Yan [19] used a method based on local binary patterns feature for hot-rolled steel strip surface defects. Shumin et al. [16] developed a method

© Springer Nature Switzerland AG 2020
I. Farkaš et al. (Eds.): ICANN 2020, LNCS 12397, pp. 15–26, 2020.
https://doi.org/10.1007/978-3-030-61616-8_2

based on histogram of oriented gradient features and SVM for fabric defect detection. Chondronasios et al. [2] proposed a method based on gray level co-occurrence matrix for surface defect classification of aluminum profiles. However, those approaches have certain limitations. Traditional machine learning methods are hard to apply in real life for complex defect situations, such as occlusion, object deformation and so on, because them extracted features are low level and not robust enough.

In recent years, deep learning has performed well in extracting image features [10]. Convolutional neural networks (CNNs) were designed to process images, which had high accuracy in visual inspection field and applied in actual production. Those methods based on deep learning can be mainly divided into two categories, namely: the methods based on image classification and the algorithms based on image segmentation. Wang et al. [25] proposed a fast and robust CNN model for discriminating defects and non-defects of products, which was focused on classification method. We refer this method as FRNet in the rest of this paper. Tao et al. [24] developed a novel cascaded autoencoder architecture for segmenting metallic defects. Cha et al. [1] modified and trained the Faster R-CNN to do real-time detection of various damages, which was based on segmenting images. Ren et al. [13] used a generic CNN-based approach to predict defects, classify images and segment damages of images. However, in order to pursue high precision and better performance, these algorithms based on CNN had the disadvantages of large number of parameters, high computational complexity and long training time, which introduced strict requirements for practical application conditions. These methods were not friendly to small and medium-sized enterprises with low hardware conditions and cannot be applied to mobile terminals, which made it difficult to be used on a large scale in the real environment.

In this study, we propose a lightweight fully convolutional network, named LFCSDD, to address the defect detection problem. We employ Inception-v3 structure [22] with different size of kernels to extract multi-scale image features and combine these representations to feed into a fully convolutional block with global pooling layer. The Inception model design can greatly reduce computing costs. And the aim of the fully convolutional block with a global pooling layer instead of a traditional fully-connected network is not only to reduce the number of network parameters and computational complexity of the model but also to allow our model process images with different sizes. The proposed lightweight model is proved to have high accuracy on some surface defect datasets, DAGM 2007 (availabled on the web[1]), KolektorSDD [23] and RSDDs [5].

The rest of this paper is organized as follows: the methodology is described in Sect. 2; the experiments is discussed in Sect. 3; the conclusion is presented in Sect. 4.

---

[1] https://hci.iwr.uni-heidelberg.de/node/3616.

2   Methodology

2.1   Model

To classify defective images and non-defective images correctly, we design a lightweight fully convolutional neural network, named LFCSDD. Due to the diversity and complexity of object defects, the first part of the model is two stacked Inception modules. In the Inception module, different branches have different receptive fields, which can identify a variety of defects. The second part is a fully convolutional block with max pooling operation. The last layer of model is a global average pooling layer to replace the fully-connected network, which can effectively reduce the number of parameters. The framework of LFCSDD is shown in the Fig. 1. For shorthand notation, the architecture can be denoted by Inception-v3(32) - Pool(2,2,2) - Inception-v3(64) - Pool(2,2,2)- Conv(3,3,64) - Pool(2,2,2) - Conv(3,3,128) - Pool(2,2,2) - Conv(3,3,512) - Conv(3,3,2) - Gap. The "Inception-v3(x)" stands for a Inception-v3 block, as shown in the Fig. 2, where x means the number of channels. The "Pool(x,y,z)" represents a pooling layer with a subsampling factor of $x \times y$ by stride z in both dimensions. The "Conv(x,y,z)" means a convolutional layer with z filters of kernel size of $(x \times y)$. The Gap represents a global average pooling operation. Then the details of Inception module and the fully convolutional block with global average pooling are explained separately.

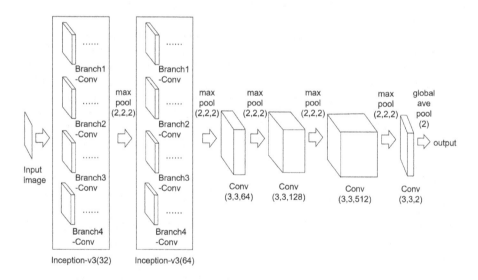

Fig. 1. The architecture of our network

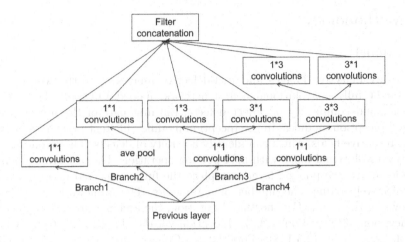

Fig. 2. The architecture of Inception-v3

2.2   Inception Module

The Inception module is a CNN architecture first proposed by Szegedy et al. [21], which is used in GooglLeNet (Inception-v1), followed by Inception-v2 [7], Inception-v3 [22] and Inception-ResNet [20]. The network with Inception model has been one of the best-performing models on ImageNet datasets [14] since its first introduction.

Inception module was originally proposed as an alternative to manually determining the type of filters in the convolutional layer. There are multiple branches in Inception, and each branch has receptive fields of different sizes, so that the model could learn features of different scales. The computational cost of Inception is also much lower than traditional deep convolutional neural networks such as VggNet [17] or its higher-performance successors [6]. This has made it feasible to utilize Inception networks in some scenarios where plentiful data needed to be processed at limited memory or computational capacity, for example in mobile vision settings [22]. Inception-v3, proposed by [22], is an architecture with fewer parameters, as shown in Fig. 2, because the computational cost saving increases dramatically by replacing any $n \times n$ convolution by a $1 \times n$ convolution followed by a $n \times 1$ convolution. And the 1×1 convolutions are used to reduce the computation and increase the activations per tile in a convolutional network, which makes train faster.

2.3   The Fully Convolutional Block with Global Average Pooling

The fully convolutional block is a good way to extract the high-level feature maps from multi-scale features. Global average pooling is used to address the large number of fully-connected layer parameters, which was first mentioned in the paper [12]. The result of this pooling operation is the global average of each feature graph, which can be used to replace the fully-connected layers as the output in the network without additional parameters.

3   Experiments

This part will discuss the experimental results. Datasets will be described in Subsect. 3.1. The training details will be presented in Subsect. 3.2. The evaluation metrics will be introduced in Subsect. 3.3. Specific experimental results will be presented in Subsect. 3.4, including the comparison of the performance and parameters of LFCSDD and some classical classification networks in different datasets, and the verification of the ability to classify images of different sizes on RSDDs.

3.1   Datasets

This paper evaluates our model on three surface defect datasets, DAGM 2007, KolektorSDD and RSDDs, which are previously used as benchmark datasets for surface defect detection. And their descriptions are as follows:

DAGM 2007. The dataset has six classes as shown in the Fig. 3(a), each containing 1,000 non-defective images and 150 defective images. The data processing method is as follows: we use a 128 * 128 pixel window to slide and cut the original 512 * 512 pixel images with the step size of 128 for non-defective images and the step size of 8 for defective images, because the number of non-defective images is greater than the number of defective images. For the clipped defect images, we keep the images with more than 80% defective parts and mix six types of images. The final training set contains 26414 defective images and 48064 non-defective images, and the test set contains 29597 defective images and 47936 non-defective images.

KolektorSDD. The Kolektor surface-defect dataset (KolektorSDD) is composed of 347 images without defects and 52 images with defects of electrical commutators from 50 physical defected electrical commutators (See Fig. 3(b)). 40 physical items are treated as training set, while the rest of 10 items are test set. The data processing method is as follows: we use a 128 * 128 pixel window to slide and cut the original 1408 * 512 pixel images with the step size of 128 for non-defective images and the step size of 8 for defective images. For the clipped defective images, we store the images containing more than 55% defective parts, because the defect is micro and the number of defective images in the dataset is small. The final training set contains 8,285 defective images and 7,674 non-defective images, and the test set contains 2,730 defective images and 1,704 non-defective images.

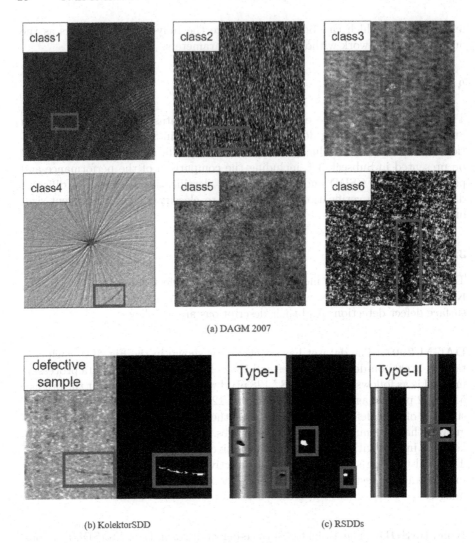

(a) DAGM 2007

(b) KolektorSDD   (c) RSDDs

Fig. 3. Datasets

RSDDs. The Rail surface discrete defects (RSDDs) dataset contains two types of dataset (See Fig. 3(c)). Type-I RSDDs dataset is the first type, which has 67 defective images with the size of 160 * 1000. Type-II RSDDs dataset is the second type, which has 128 defective images with the size of 55 * 1250. The processing method for this dataset is as follows: for the first dataset, cropping the original images to 160 * 160 size images generates the images containing more than 80% defective parts and the images without defective parts. Finally, we get 2,002 defective images and 2,312 non-defective images. For the second dataset, we crop the original images to 55 * 55 size images, as previously, and get 1498 defective images and 1858 non-defective images. 80% of these images are selected for the training set and the rest for the test set, randomly.

3.2 Training Details

The training details of LFCSDD are as follows. The learning is completed with 100 epochs and the batch-size is 300 for DAGM 2007, the same batch size for KolektorSDD and the batch-size is 100 for RSDDs because the three datasets have different sizes. The cross-entropy function is selected as the loss function of networks with adding the L2 regularization to avoid overfitting, where the rate of regularization is 0.000005. Adam [8] is used as the optimization algorithm to train the networks with learning rate decay method. The initial learning rate is 0.001 and decay parameter of the learning rate is 0.97. Inception modules use the RELU function as activation function, and other convolutional layers of LFCSDD choose the Leaky RELU function as activation function.

3.3 Evaluation Metrics

The evaluation metrics used in this paper include accuracy (Acc.), precision (Pre.), recall (Rec.) and area under the receiver operating characteristic curve [26] (AUC). Acc., Pre. and Rec. are calculated as follows:

$$Acc. = \frac{TP + TN}{TP + TN + FP + FN}, \tag{1}$$

$$Pre. = \frac{TP}{TP + FP}, \tag{2}$$

$$Rec. = \frac{TP}{TP + FN}, \tag{3}$$

where TP, FP, TN and FN represent the number of true positives, false positives, true negatives and false negatives, respectively.

3.4 Experiments Results

In this section, we compares our model with FRNet [25] and three classical classification networks, LeNet [11], AlexNet [9] and VggNet11 [17].

The Experiments Based on DAGM 2007. This part compares our model with baselines on DAGM 2007. The results are showed in Table 1, and the training situation is shown in the Fig. 4.

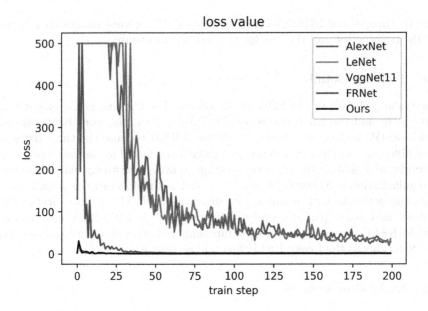

Fig. 4. The training convergence of the models on DAGM 2007

As shown in Table 1, our model gets the accuracy of 99.72%, the precision of 99.95%, the recall of 99.32% and the AUC of 99.99%, which achieves the best performance in four evaluation metrics compared to other models.

The Experiments Based on KolektorSDD. The results on KolektorSDD are shown in Table 2, and the training situation is shown in the Fig. 5.

Table 1. The results based on DAGM 2007

Model	Acc.(%)	Pre.(%)	Rec.(%)	AUC(%)
LeNet	97.13	98.46	93.95	99.13
AlexNet	93.15	99.59	82.40	94.06
VggNet11	97.69	99.83	94.11	99.39
FRNet	99.45	99.89	98.66	99.98
Ours	**99.72**	**99.95**	**99.32**	**99.99**

From the results of Table 2, our model has the accuracy of 98.74%, the precision of 99.59% the recall of 98.35% and the AUC of 99.94%. In addition, compared with other networks, our model gets the best performance on three evaluation metrics.

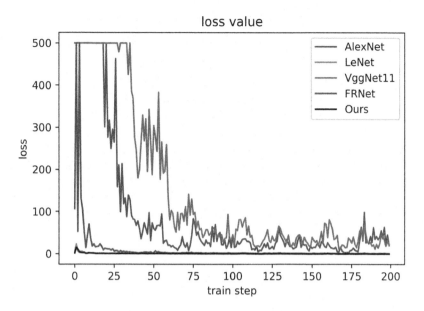

Fig. 5. The training convergence of the models on KolektorSDD

Table 2. The results based on KolektorSDD

Model	Acc.(%)	Pre.(%)	Rec.(%)	AUC(%)
LeNet	97.09	96.76	98.57	99.38
AlexNet	98.08	99.26	97.62	99.31
VggNet11	97.93	96.91	**99.82**	98.13
FRNet	97.74	96.66	99.78	99.89
Ours	**98.74**	**99.59**	98.35	**99.94**

As can be seen from Fig. 4 and Fig. 5, our model converges quickly. It can be concluded that our model is easy to train and well suited for transfer learning to fit more situations.

The Experiments Based on RSDDs Dataset. We also validate the performance of our approach on the RSDDs defect dataset when processing images of different sizes. RSDDs has two types of datasets, Type-I with an image size of 160 * 160 and Type-II with an image size of 55 * 55. Type-I and Type-II are mixed together as the third dataset, and its training set and test set contain images of two different sizes. The experimental results are shown in the Table 3.

Table 3 shows that our model has 97.00% accuracy, 98.05% precision, 95.18% recall, and 99.34% AUC on the mixed dataset, which surpasses the performance on datasets of other types. It can be concluded that LFCSDD can identify images of different sizes with high accuracy.

Table 3. The results based on RSDDs

Dataset	Acc.(%)	Pre.(%)	Rec.(%)	AUC(%)
Type-I	90.80	87.75	92.51	97.20
Type-II	94.38	91.94	95.64	97.35
Type-I + Type-II	**97.00**	**98.05**	**95.18**	**99.34**

The Number of Network Parameters. This part compares LFCSDD with FRNet, LeNet, AlexNet and VggNet11 on the number of network parameters. Parameter count is reported on DAGM 2007 (128 * 128 input size, 2 classes). The results are shown in Table 4, where percentage means the ratio of the number of LFCSDD parameters to the number of other models parameters.

Table 4. The parameter count of models

Model	Parameter count	Percentage(%)
LeNet	7,926,664	9.05
AlexNet	29,946,560	2.40
VggNet11	59,559,168	1.20
FRNet	34,882,240	2.06
Ours	**717,370**	\

The data in Table 4 show that the number of our model parameters is 717370, accounting for only 9.05% of Lenet, 2.40% of AlexNet, 1.20% of VggNet11 and 2.06% of FRNet. The fact that LFCSDD has the fewer number of parameters than others indicates that the improvements seen on DAGM 2007 and KolektorSDD come from a more efficient use of the model parameters.

4   Conclusions

In this paper, we propose a lightweight fully convolutional neural network, LFCSDD, of high accuracy surface defect detection. The network achieves the higher accuracy performance than LeNet, AlexNet, VggNet11 and FRNet on the DAGM 2007 and KolektorSDD. In addition, LFCSDD can process images of different sizes with high accuracy on RSDDs. And the most importantly, LFCSDD has the advantage of lightweight. Specifically, the number of parameters of our model is 11x fewer than LeNet, 41x fewer than AlexNet, 83x fewer than VggNet11 and 48x fewer than FRNet, which greatly saves memory. So LFCSDD reduces the requirement for hardware conditions and is easily applied to the mobile terminal and real-world factory testing environments.

Acknowledgement. This work is supported by the National Key Research and Development Plan of China (No. 2018YFC2000605).

References

1. Cha, Y.J., Choi, W., Suh, G., Mahmoudkhani, S., Büyüköztürk, O.: Autonomous structural visual inspection using region-based deep learning for detecting multiple damage types. Comput. Aided Civ. Infrastruct. Eng. **33**(9), 731–747 (2018)
2. Chondronasios, A., Popov, I., Jordanov, I.: Feature selection for surface defect classification of extruded aluminum profiles. Int. J. Adv. Manuf. Technol. **83**(1–4), 33–41 (2016)
3. Coren, S., Girgus, J.S., Day, R.: Visual spatial illusions: many explanations. Science **179**(4072), 503–504 (1973)
4. Day, R.H.: Visual spatial illusions: a general explanation. Science **175**(4028), 1335–1340 (1972)
5. Gan, J., Li, Q., Wang, J., Yu, H.: A hierarchical extractor-based visual rail surface inspection system. IEEE Sens. J. **17**(23), 7935–7944 (2017)
6. He, K., Zhang, X., Ren, S., Sun, J.: Delving deep into rectifiers: surpassing human-level performance on imagenet classification. In: Proceedings of the IEEE International Conference on Computer Vision, pp. 1026–1034 (2015)
7. Ioffe, S., Szegedy, C.: Batch normalization: Accelerating deep network training by reducing internal covariate shift. arXiv preprint arXiv:1502.03167 (2015)
8. Kingma, D.P., Ba, J.: Adam: A method for stochastic optimization. arXiv preprint arXiv:1412.6980 (2014)
9. Krizhevsky, A., Sutskever, I., Hinton, G.E.: Imagenet classification with deep convolutional neural networks. In: Advances in Neural Information Processing Systems, pp. 1097–1105 (2012)
10. LeCun, Y., Bengio, Y., Hinton, G.: Deep learning. Nature **521**(7553), 436–444 (2015)
11. LeCun, Y., Bottou, L., Bengio, Y., Haffner, P., et al.: Gradient-based learning applied to document recognition. Proc. IEEE **86**(11), 2278–2324 (1998)
12. Lin, M., Chen, Q., Yan, S.: Network in network. arXiv preprint arXiv:1312.4400 (2013)
13. Ren, R., Hung, T., Tan, K.C.: A generic deep-learning-based approach for automated surface inspection. IEEE Trans. Cybern. **48**(3), 929–940 (2017)
14. Russakovsky, O., et al.: Imagenet large scale visual recognition challenge. Int. J. Comput. Vis. **115**(3), 211–252 (2015)
15. Schoonard, J.W., Gould, J.D.: Field of view and target uncertainty in visual search and inspection. Hum. Factors **15**(1), 33–42 (1973)
16. Shumin, D., Zhoufeng, L., Chunlei, L.: Adaboost learning for fabric defect detection based on HOG and SVM. In: 2011 International Conference on Multimedia Technology, pp. 2903–2906. IEEE (2011)
17. Simonyan, K., Zisserman, A.: Very deep convolutional networks for large-scale image recognition. arXiv preprint arXiv:1409.1556 (2014)
18. Snyder, C.R.: Selection, inspection, and naming in visual search. J. Exp. Psychol. **92**(3), 428 (1972)
19. Song, K., Yan, Y.: A noise robust method based on completed local binary patterns for hot-rolled steel strip surface defects. Appl. Surf. Sci. **285**, 858–864 (2013)
20. Szegedy, C., Ioffe, S., Vanhoucke, V., Alemi, A.A.: Inception-v4, inception-ResNet and the impact of residual connections on learning. In: 31st AAAI Conference on Artificial Intelligence (2017)
21. Szegedy, C., et al.: Going deeper with convolutions. In: Proceedings of the IEEE Conference on Computer Vision and Pattern Recognition, pp. 1–9 (2015)

22. Szegedy, C., Vanhoucke, V., Ioffe, S., Shlens, J., Wojna, Z.: Rethinking the inception architecture for computer vision. In: Proceedings of the IEEE Conference on Computer Vision and Pattern Recognition, pp. 2818–2826 (2016)
23. Tabernik, D., Šela, S., Skvarč, J., Skočaj, D.: Segmentation-based deep-learning approach for surface-defect detection. J. Intell. Manuf. **31**(3), 759–776 (2019). https://doi.org/10.1007/s10845-019-01476-x
24. Tao, X., Zhang, D., Ma, W., Liu, X., Xu, D.: Automatic metallic surface defect detection and recognition with convolutional neural networks. Appl. Sci. **8**(9), 1575 (2018)
25. Wang, T., Chen, Y., Qiao, M., Snoussi, H.: A fast and robust convolutional neural network-based defect detection model in product quality control. Int. J. Adv. Manuf. Technol. **94**(9–12), 3465–3471 (2018)
26. Zweig, M.H., Campbell, G.: Receiver-operating characteristic (roc) plots: a fundamental evaluation tool in clinical medicine. Clin. Chem. **39**(4), 561–577 (1993)

Detecting Uncertain BNN Outputs on FPGA Using Monte Carlo Dropout Sampling

Tomoyuki Myojin[1,2]([✉]) [iD], Shintaro Hashimoto[1], and Naoki Ishihama[1]

[1] Japan Aerospace Exploration Agency, Tsukuba, Japan
{hashimoto.shintaro,ishihama.naoki}@jaxa.jp
[2] Hitachi, Ltd., Yokohama, Japan
tomoyuki.myojin.fs@hitachi.com

Abstract. Monte Carlo dropout sampling (MC Dropout), which approximates a Bayesian Neural Network, is useful for measuring the uncertainty in the output of a Deep Neural Network (DNN). However, because it takes a long time to sample DNN's output for calculating its distribution, it is difficult to apply it to edge computing where resources are limited. Thus, this research proposes a method of reducing a sampling time required for MC Dropout in edge computing by parallelizing the calculation circuit using FPGA. To apply MC dropout in an FPGA, this paper shows an efficient implementation by binarizing the neural network and simplifying dropout computation by pre-dropout and localizing parallel circuits. The proposed method was evaluated using the MNIST dataset and a dataset of satellite images of ships at sea captured. As a result, it was possible to reject approximately 60% of data which the model had not learned as "uncertain" on a classification identification problem of the image on an FPGA. Furthermore, for 20 units in parallel, the amount of increase in the circuit scale was only 2–3 times that of non-parallelized circuits. In terms of inference speed, parallelization of dropout circuits has achieved up to 3.62 times faster.

Keywords: Deep learning · FPGA · Binarized neural network · Uncertainty · Monte Carlo dropout sampling · SAR

1 Introduction

Image identification using deep learning has found wide use, especially in embedded edge computing. In embedded edge applications, power and computer resources are limited unlike computers with a powerful GPU, so a Deep Neural Network (DNN) requires power-saving features, real-time, and memory-saving. Despite these limitations, the DNNs requires reliability to provide high-quality systems and services in the edge computing application such as automobiles and satellites.

© Springer Nature Switzerland AG 2020
I. Farkaš et al. (Eds.): ICANN 2020, LNCS 12397, pp. 27–38, 2020.
https://doi.org/10.1007/978-3-030-61616-8_3

The reliability of the DNN can be further enhanced by determining the uncertainty in the output of the DNN using Monte Carlo Dropout Sampling (MC Dropout) [2,3]. Whereas the original dropout technique is used to obtain regularization by intentionally dropping neurons of the neural network during learning, MC Dropout also applies dropout at the time of inference and samples the output value of the DNN. This approximates a Bayesian Neural Network, which can calculate the distribution of output values. By evaluating the variance calculated from the output distribution, the uncertainty in the inference by the trained model can be measured. There are two types of DNN uncertainties: the uncertainty of the data itself, such as noise, and the model uncertainty. The former is called aleatoric uncertainty and the latter is called epistemic uncertainty [5], which can be measured by MC Dropout.

An example of measuring epistemic uncertainty will be described using a handwritten numerical classification task. MNIST is a well-known dataset of hand-drawn numerical images and has a variety of the digits from 0 to 9. Among them, there are two accepted ways of writing "7": one with a horizontal bar in the center and one without. In a particular linguistic sphere (e.g., in Japan), it is more common to write "7" without a horizontal bar. This paper calls the former 7_{bar} and the latter 7_{nobar}.

If 7_{bar} is inferred with the model $M_{7_{nobar}}$ trained on the dataset excluding 7_{bar}, the uncertainty in the prediction of 7_{bar} will be higher than that of 7_{nobar} (Table 1). Because 7_{bar} is unknown in the model $M_{7_{nobar}}$, the uncertainty of prediction (i.e., epistemic uncertainty) is high. Using this property makes possible to obtain a reliable inference by rejecting an inference result with a high uncertainty and classified as unreliable.

Table 1. Epistemic Uncertainties for the ($M_{7_{nobar}}$) model trained on dataset excluding 7_{bar} and for the ($M_{7_{bar}}$) model trained on dataset including 7_{bar}.

Input Image		
Variance for $M_{7_{nobar}}$	8.82×10^{-2}	9.14×10^{-10}
Variance for $M_{7_{bar}}$	4.66×10^{-13}	1.42×10^{-13}

MC Dropout has the advantage of being easy to implement because it is not necessary to change the network structure at the time of inference and learning. However, the disadvantage is that it requires multiple samplings during inference. According to Gal [3], it requires 20 samplings which means that the computation time is 20 times as long. In an environment with abundant computational resources or one that does need not operate in real time, this is not a problem.

However, in edge computing for embedded devices, computational resources and power supply are limited and there are many situations that require real-time computation. For example, in a task that identifies an object in a car, the time it takes to make inferences, or latency, is important. In another example, where power and computational resources are very limited, such as in outer space, it is necessary to have a power-saving and memory-saving DNN.

For this situation, inference using a DNN have been implemented in a Field Programmable Gate Array (FPGA) in recent years. In particular, a Binarized Neural Network (BNN), which represents the parameters of a Neural Network and/or the intermediate results of a calculation as a binary value instead of a floating point, has been realized in an FPGA [8,9].

This paper reports using MC Dropout in a BNN implemented on an FPGA, done in order to improve the reliability of inference results for edge computing for embedded devices. Parallelizing inferences on an FPGA ensures acceptable real-time performance. Experiments based on practical ship recognition using satellite images show that MC Dropout improves reliability in BNNs implemented on an FPGA.

The organization of this paper is shown below. Section 2 describes the method for measuring uncertainty using MC Dropout and rejecting unreliable judgments applied to image classification. Section 3 describes how to implement MC Dropout in an FPGA; three points are particularly important: (1) a method for constructing binarized neural network, (2) pre-dropout method that efficiently integrates dropout layer and activation layer, and (3) implementation of a circuit that parallelizes dropout. Section 4 evaluates the ability to reject uncertain results by MC Dropout implemented in FPGA and the overhead of inference time and circuit scale. In the evaluation, we use MNIST dataset and images of ships on the ocean captured by a satellite. Section 5 describes the evaluation results, and the Sect. 6 describes the conclusions of this paper.

2   Related Work

Gal [2,3] made a typical study of measuring uncertainty in DNNs using MC Dropout. Based on Gal's approach, we have measured the uncertainty in a DNN that performs object detection based on YOLOv3 using MC Dropout [7]. By rejecting the results identified as uncertain, this paper proposes a method to improve precision. The method would do this without adversely affecting recall improving reliability of identifying lunar craters from satellite images. Miller [6] adopted MC Dropout Sampling for object detection based on the SSD, and Feng [1] adopted it for Faster R-CNN. These methods target an object detection and do not address a classification problem. In addition, these methods do not take into account their use in edge computing.

Xilinx proposed a highly efficient implementation of a BNN on an FPGA using the simplified Batch Normalization by the FINN algorithm [9]. The BNN was implemented by high-level synthesis in the C language, does not require the use of a hardware description language such as VHDL and Verilog HDL, and has quite a low learning and development cost. Takamaeda et al. have also developed their own compiler NNgen to synthesize a model-specific hardware accelerator for deep neural [8]. NNgen generates a Verilog HDL source code from an input model definition written in Python. Hashimoto has developed an application that identifies the type and length of a ship from images captured by a satellite using a network based on the Xilinx FINN algorithm mentioned above [4]. This paper adopts the Xilinx FINN algorithm in consideration of its application to satellite images and its ease of implementation of parallelization.

3   Uncertainty of the DNN

3.1   Measuring Uncertainty with Monte Carlo Dropout

This section describes a method for measuring the uncertainty of inference results of a DNN. The DNN predicts the inference dataset in the inference phase using the optimal weights obtained in the learning phase from the learning dataset. Normally, the learning dataset and the inference dataset are independently and identically distributed, however, in some cases, the distribution of the inference dataset may differ from the learning dataset due to a lack in the learning dataset. If there is a shortage in the learning data set, it is not possible to obtain the optimum weights, resulting in bad inference results. In such a case, the model outputs an inference result with a high uncertainty for the inference dataset. Using the approximation of a deep Bayesian neural network using MC Dropout, it is possible to measure the uncertainty of the model for inference data. This uncertainty is called epistemic uncertainty.

Dropout is a regularization method to prevent over-fitting by probabilistically disabling neurons in the network and is usually used only during learning. By using dropout during inference, the network will generate a different result each time it is inferred. Inference results using MC Dropout are derived by the following.

$$\bar{y}(x) \approx \frac{1}{N_{mc}} \sum^{N_{mc}} y_{drop}(x) \tag{1}$$

where y_{drop} is output of the network that is dropped out, x is input to the network and N_{mc} is the number of times of sampling needed to get distribution. Because the neurons to drop out are randomly selected, $y_{drop}(x)$ will have different results for each sampling. Since the output of MC Dropout is a random variable, the expected value of the output can be obtained by calculating the average value. From another point of view, $\bar{y}$ can also be regarded as the ensemble output of slightly different networks generated by dropout. The variance of inference results is represented by the following.

$$var(x) \approx \frac{1}{N_{mc}} \sum^{N_{mc}} (y_{drop}(x) - \bar{y}(x))^2 \tag{2}$$

The value of this variance represents the uncertainty. Kendall et al. reported that this epistemic uncertainty tends to increase if the data set is intentionally reduced [5]. Thus, inferring an unlearned dataset for the model increases uncertainty.

By using this property, when inferring unlearned or unknown data, the result is unreliable and can be rejected as if the model is indistinguishable. This can be expressed by the following equation.

$$y_{reliable}(x) = \begin{cases} \bar{y}(x) & (var_y(x) < thresholds) \\ unknown & (var_y(x) \geq thresholds) \end{cases} \tag{3}$$

If the uncertainty is less than the threshold, the inference result is adopted as is, and if it is above the threshold, the inference result is rejected as "unknown." There are several ways to determine the threshold, e.g., based on the uncertainty at the time of inferring the learning data, or determined empirically.

3.2   Rejecting Uncertain Judgment in Classification

This section describes how to reject judgment of DNN based on uncertainty. In this section, we use the handwritten digit classification problem. MNIST, which is widely used as a dataset of handwritten digits, has almost 70,000 images of digits from 0 to 9. There are 7,293 numeral 7s; of these, 938 are with a horizontal bar (7_{bar}), 6,355 are without a horizontal bar (7_{nobar}).

Where only 7_{nobar} is used in a particular linguistic sphere, the model cannot correctly identify 7_{bar}, and the accuracy will be low. Moreover, the model may classify 7_{bar} as 7 with a high confidence. However, since this model does not learn that "7_{bar} is 7," it is not desirable to classify 7_{bar} as 7.

In such a case, by determining whether the prediction result is reliable using uncertainty, it is possible to prevent 7_{bar} from being classified as 7. If the value of uncertainty is greater than or equal to a certain value, it provides the option of identifying "Unknown," that is, no number. As a result, it is possible to prevent the wrong identification with a high confidence even though not learning, and it is a great help to improve the reliability of the identification.

Figure 1 shows the distribution of uncertainty when both the model $M_{7_{nobar}}$ learned in a dataset that does not contain 7_{bar} and the model $M_{7_{bar}}$ learned in a dataset that contains 7_{bar} identifies the 7_{bar} as 7. Despite the low uncertainty of $M_{7_{bar}}$, $M_{7_{nobar}}$ shows high uncertainty. By rejecting the identification result if the uncertainty is above a certain value, the accuracy is expected to be improved.

4   Uncertainty of BNN on FPGA

4.1   Binarized Neural Network

As described above, it is possible to improve the reliability of a DNN by using uncertainty. However, MC Dropout has the disadvantage that it takes a lot of computation time. MC Dropout requires at least 20 samplings of the identification result to obtain the variance of the identification result. This sampling is not a serious problem in a large-scale computer with abundant computer resources or an application that does not require real-time performance. Although, it can

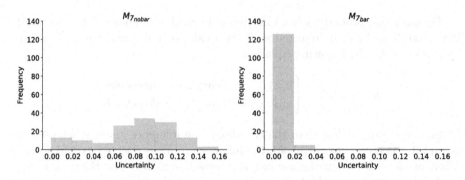

Fig. 1. Distribution of uncertainty when both the model $M_{7_{nobar}}$ learned in a dataset that does not contain 7_{bar} and the model $M_{7_{bar}}$ learned in a dataset that contains 7_{bar} identifies the 7_{bar} as '7' ($n = 136$).

be a problem in situations where computer resources are limited or in real-time is required, such as automobiles.

Therefore, the research found a method to calculate uncertainty without compromising real-time performance. The method uses parallel computing using the characteristics of FPGA in edge computing with an FPGA to utilize MC Dropout. To realize MC Dropout on an FPGA, a network was designed to include dropout for the FPGA, improved the calculation by pre-dropout, and parallelized dropout.

First, the paper will show the network implemented in an FPGA. Since an FPGA does not have enough memory or computational resources compared with GPGPU, a binarized neural network (BNN) was used; it replaces inputs, outputs, and weights from floating-point values to binary values. While the implementation of BNN by various methods has been proposed, implementation by the FINN algorithm was used for the implementation and the computational cost. FINN is an implementation of the BNN proposed by Xilinx, which achieves advanced parallelization in BNN. The network that was implemented for this paper was based on FINN and is shown in Fig. 2.

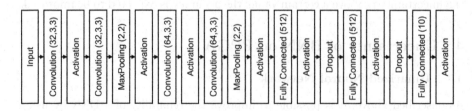

Fig. 2. Network architecture based on FINN algorithm

This network has several convolutional layers, max pooling layer, fully connected layers, and activation layers. The activation layer activate neuron upon reaching a special threshold. This special threshold is a unique feature of FINN that reduces the amount of computation by simultaneously performing batch regularization and activation. If the output value of a neuron is above the threshold, the output of the neuron is activated.

4.2 Pre-dropout

This section describes how to implement dropout efficiently on an FPGA. When implementing dropout, there is usually a dropout layer behind a fully connected layer and an activation layer, which removes the neurons probabilistically (Fig. 3). However, if the neurons to be deleted are determined stochastically every time during inference, the computation time increases accordingly. Therefore, a pre-dropout method was developed that can perform dropout at the same time as activation by the threshold described above.

The pre-dropout method is described below (Fig. 4). First, set the part of the threshold that is chosen at random in advance to the maximum, and create a set of this thresholds corresponding to the number of samplings. Next, infer according to the threshold during the inference phase. If the threshold is the maximum value, neurons are always inactive, which allows for probabilistic neuron inactivation. Finally, by switching the set of thresholds for each sampling, it is possible to obtain an output distribution such as MC Dropout. Since it is necessary to prepare a set of thresholds only for the number of samplings, it will use more memory. However, since the memory capacity for thresholds is not large, there is no problem in practice.

4.3 Localization of Parallelization

The following network was created to efficiently parallelize MC Dropout with a DNN on an FPGA. The conceptual diagram of a parallelized circuit is shown in Fig. 5. Since dropout applies only to the fully connected layer following the convolution layer; the calculation result of the convolution layer upstream from it is the same for each sampling. Therefore, process is continued up to the convolution layer common to each sampling, locally parallelizing the processing behind the convolution layer. First, N_{mc} groups of fully connected layer circuits are prepared for a group of convolutional layer circuits. Then, after replicating the results of the convolution layer by the N_{mc}, input respectively in the fully connected layer circuit. Finally, all the output results from the fully connected layer circuit are received, obtained as an inference result of N_{mc} times. Using the average and variance of these results, we obtain inference results and uncertainty.

5   Evaluation

To confirm the effectiveness of the proposed method, evaluation was done using two types of dataset. The first is the MNIST dataset of handwritten number images, which is widely used as an evaluation dataset for DNNs that classify

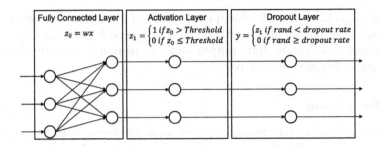

Fig. 3. Dropout without pre-dropout method

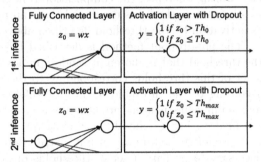

Fig. 4. Dropout with pre-dropout method

handwritten numbers. The second is the dataset of the ship captured images by the satellite, Advanced Land Observing Satellite 2 (ALOS-2), which was developed and launched by Japan Aerospace Exploration Agency. ALOS-2 has a L-band synthetic-aperture radar (SAR) sensor, which can capture images of ships on the ocean. Label data indicating the type of ship was created based on the information from the AIS (Automatic Identification System) using the latitude and longitude of the captured ship image. Figure 6 shows ship images.

To evaluate uncertainty for these two datasets, a part of data was chosen as "unknown" data to be detected. For the MNIST dataset, special labels were given to the 7 with a horizontal bar (7_{bar}), which is considered to be unknown data. The presence or absence of a horizontal bar was determined manually by eye. For the Ship SAR dataset, special labels were attached to ships longer than a certain length. Unknown data are removed from the learning dataset but included in the test dataset. This operation on the dataset can determine uncertainty about the dataset that is unknown to the model. The number of data and labels contained in the dataset are shown in Tables 2 and 3. An image in the MNIST dataset is 28×28 pixels, and an image in the Ship SAR dataset is 60×60 pixels.

Using these datasets, models are learned with the Theano Python library on GPU, which is NVIDIA TITAN V. After learning, the parameters of the weights and batch regularization are converted based on the algorithm of FINN.

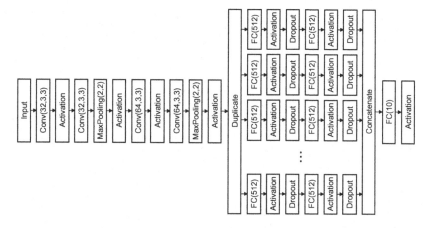

Fig. 5. Parallelization of dropout

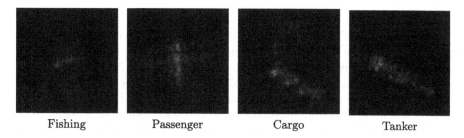

Fishing   Passenger   Cargo   Tanker

Fig. 6. Ship images captured by ALOS-2 with synthetic-aperture radar (SAR) sensor

The model used for the MNIST dataset is shown in Fig. 2 and the model used for the Ship SAR dataset is shown in Fig. 7. Since the input image size of Ship SAR dataset is larger than MNIST dataset, convolutional layers were added to the Ship SAR model. Since the image size of Ship SAR is larger than MNIST, a convolutional layer was added to the Ship SAR model. For the inference phase, Xilinx Zynq-7000 SoC ZC706 was used, which has 19.1 Mbit Block RAM, 218.6k Look-Up Tables and 437k Flip-Flops, whose size is assumed to be mounted on satellite.

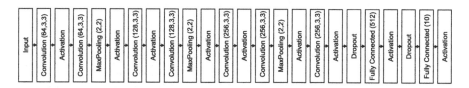

Fig. 7. Network architecture used for the Ship SAR dataset

Table 2. MNIST dataset

Label	Train	Test
0	5,923	980
1	6,742	1,135
2	5,958	1,032
3	6,131	1,010
4	5,842	982
5	5,421	892
6	5,918	958
7 (7_{nobar})	5,463	892
8	5,851	974
9	5,040	1,009
Unknown (7_{bar})	802	136

Table 3. Ship SAR dataset

Label	Train	Test
Fishing	187	34
Passenger	55	15
Cargo	1,170	178
Tanker	486	82
Unknown (Length > 265 m)	32	227

The viewpoints of evaluation are the rejection performance, circuit scale, and inference speed. The rejection performance is evaluated by two scores, Uncertainty Recall and Uncertainty Precision, especially defined for the experiment. Uncertainty Recall is the number that MC Dropout can reject as uncertain for a given input image that should be uncertain. Uncertainty Precision is a number that was unquestionably uncertain in the inference results determined to be uncertain by MC Dropout. The equations used to calculate these are shown in Eqs. 4 and 5.

$$Uncertainty\ Recall = \frac{|\{x \in U \mid var(x) \geq thresholds\}|}{|\{x \in U\}|} \tag{4}$$

$$Uncertainty\ Precision = \frac{|\{x \in U \mid var(x) \geq thresholds\}|}{|\{x \in X \mid var(x) \geq thresholds\}|} \tag{5}$$

where, all sets of input are X, the set of inputs that are uncertain is U, and the threshold to determine that it is uncertain is *thresholds*. The circuit scale measures the increase in circuit scale when compared without MC Dropout. Inference speed is measured time it takes to infer 20 samples compared to the case of not using MC Dropout.

6   Result

The evaluation results for the rejection performance are shown in Table 4. Threshold refers to the threshold values above which are considered to be uncertain. Each thresholds are selected so that Uncertainty Recall is maximized. In the MNIST dataset, Uncertainty Recall was 0.67 and Uncertainty Precision was 0.33 without binarization on a GPU. On the other hand, Uncertainty Recall was 0.66 and Uncertainty Precision was 0.50 with binarization on an FPGA. In the

Ship SAR dataset, Uncertainty Recall was 0.68 and Uncertainty Precision was 0.11 without binarization on a GPU. On the other hand, Uncertainty Recall was 0.63 and Uncertainty Precision was 0.15 with binarization on an FPGA. In both cases, the binary networks on the FPGA performed almost as well as the floating-point networks on the GPU. This result demonstrates that MC Dropout is useful for improving the reliability of edge computing using an FPGA because a BNN can obtain sufficient rejection performance.

Next, Table 5 shows the results of the overhead evaluation by MC Dropout. In the circuit of the MNIST model, utilization of block RAM, Flip-Flops, and Look-Up Table increased about two to three times for a parallelism of 20, and the Ship SAR model had almost the same results. From result, it is clear that the amount of increase in the circuit scale is sufficiently suppressed for the increase in the degree of parallelism by the local parallelization method. When the frequency of parallelism was 20, it took 9.341 ms to infer a image with the MNIST model whereas it takes 16.880 ms when the parallelism is 1, and it took 21.138 ms to infer an image with the Ship SAR model whereas it takes 76.540 ms when the parallelism is 1. Therefore, by parallelization, the MNIST model achieves about 1.81 times faster speeds, and the Ship SAR model achieves about 3.62 times faster speeds.

Table 4. Rejection performance

Dataset	Hardware	Threshold	Uncertainty recall	Uncertainty precision
MNIST	GPU (floating-point)	1.0×10^{-2}	0.67	0.33
MNIST	FPGA (binary)	8.0×10	0.66	0.50
Ship SAR	GPU (floating-point)	1.0×10^{-2}	0.68	0.11
Ship SAR	FPGA (binary)	7.1×10	0.63	0.15

Table 5. Utilization of circuit and inference time for sampling

Model	Frequency of parallel	Utilization of circuit			Inference time for 20 samples
		Block RAM	Flip-Flops	Look-Up Table	
MNIST	1	23%	9%	11%	16.880 ms
MNIST	20	72%	24%	28%	9.341 ms
Ship SAR	1	31%	11%	13%	76.540 ms
Ship SAR	20	93%	20%	23%	21.138 ms

7   Conclusion

This paper proposed a method to reject uncertain judgment results using MC dropout on an FPGA to improve the reliability of a DNN used in edge computing.

To implement MC dropout on an FPGA, it was necessary to binarize a neural network, to include a simplified dropout layer via the pre-dropout method, and to localize parallelized parts of a circuit. The evaluation showed that, using the proposed method with the MNIST and Ship SAR dataset, approximately 60% of unlearned data were rejected as "uncertain" on the FPGA. Furthermore, even if the parallelism had a frequency of 20, the circuit scale would only increase to about 2–3 times that of non-parallelized circuits. The inference speed of the parallelized circuits was achieved up to 3.62 times faster that of non-parallelized circuits. Therefore, the proposed method was able to improve the reliability of a DNN by detecting uncertain judgments implementing MC Dropout on an FPGA using edge computing.

References

1. Feng, D., Rosenbaum, L., Dietmayer, K.: Towards safe autonomous driving: capture uncertainty in the deep neural network for Lidar 3D vehicle detection. In: 2018 21st International Conference on Intelligent Transportation Systems (ITSC) (2018). https://doi.org/10.1109/itsc.2018.8569814
2. Gal, Y., Ghahramani, Z.: Bayesian convolutional neural networks with Bernoulli approximate variational inference. In: 4th International Conference on Learning Representations (ICLR) Workshop Track (2016)
3. Gal, Y., Ghahramani, Z.: Dropout as a Bayesian approximation: representing model uncertainty in deep learning. In: Proceedings of the 33rd International Conference on International Conference on Machine Learning, ICML 2016, vol. 48, pp. 1050–1059. JMLR.org (2016)
4. Hashimoto, S., Sugimoto, Y., Hamamoto, K., Ishihama, N.: Ship classification from SAR images based on deep learning. In: Arai, K., Kapoor, S., Bhatia, R. (eds.) Intell. Syst. Appl., vol. 868, pp. 18–34. Springer, Cham (2019). https://doi.org/10.1007/978-3-030-01054-6_2
5. Kendall, A., Gal, Y.: What uncertainties do we need in Bayesian deep learning for computer vision? pp. 5574–5584. Curran Associates, Inc. (2017)
6. Miller, D., Dayoub, F., Milford, M., Sünderhauf, N.: Evaluating merging strategies for sampling-based uncertainty techniques in object detection. arXiv:1809.06006 [cs.CV] (2018)
7. Myojin, T., Hashimoto, S., Mori, K., Sugawara, K., Ishihama, N.: Improving reliability of object detection for lunar craters using Monte Carlo dropout. In: Tetko, I.V., Kůrková, V., Karpov, P., Theis, F. (eds.) ICANN 2019. LNCS, vol. 11729, pp. 68–80. Springer, Cham (2019). https://doi.org/10.1007/978-3-030-30508-6_6
8. Takamaeda, S.: NNgen/nngen (February 2020). https://github.com/NNgen/nngen
9. Umuroglu, Y., et al.: FINN: a framework for fast, scalable binarized neural network inference. In: Proceedings of the 2017 ACM/SIGDA International Symposium on Field-Programmable Gate Arrays, FPGA 2017, pp. 65–74. Association for Computing Machinery, New York, NY, USA (2017). https://doi.org/10/ggmnh6

Neural Network Compression
via Learnable Wavelet Transforms

Moritz Wolter[1,2(✉)], Shaohui Lin[3], and Angela Yao[3]

[1] Institute for Computer Science, University of Bonn, Bonn, Germany
`wolter@cs.uni-bonn.de`
[2] Fraunhofer Center for Machine Learning and SCAI, Sankt Augustin, Germany
[3] School of Computing, National University of Singapore, Singapore, Singapore
`{linsh,ayao}@comp.nus.edu.sg`

Abstract. Wavelets are well known for data compression, yet have rarely been applied to the compression of neural networks. This paper shows how the fast wavelet transform can be used to compress linear layers in neural networks. Linear layers still occupy a significant portion of the parameters in recurrent neural networks (RNNs). Through our method, we can learn both the wavelet bases and corresponding coefficients to efficiently represent the linear layers of RNNs. Our wavelet compressed RNNs have significantly fewer parameters yet still perform competitively with the state-of-the-art on synthetic and real-world RNN benchmarks (Source code is available at https://github.com/v0lta/Wavelet-network-compression). Wavelet optimization adds basis flexibility, without large numbers of extra weights.

Keywords: Wavelets · Network compression

1 Introduction

Deep neural networks are routinely used in many artificial intelligence applications of computer vision, natural language processing, speech recognition, etc. However, the success of deep networks has often been accompanied by significant increases in network size and depth. Network compression aims to reduce the computational footprint of deep networks so that they can be applied on embedded, mobile, and low-range hardware. Compression methods range from quantization [1–3], pruning [4,5], to (low-rank) decomposition of network weights [6,7].

Early methods [4,6] separated compression from the learning; compression is performed after network training and then followed by fine-tuning. Such a multi-stage procedure is both complicated and may degrade performance. Ideally, one should integrate compression into the network structure itself; this has the dual benefit of learning less parameters and also ensures that the compression can be accounted for during learning. The more direct form of integrated compression and learning has been adopted in recent approaches [8,9], typically by enforcing a fixed structure on the weight matrices. Specifically, the structure must lend

© Springer Nature Switzerland AG 2020
I. Farkaš et al. (Eds.): ICANN 2020, LNCS 12397, pp. 39–51, 2020.
https://doi.org/10.1007/978-3-030-61616-8_4

itself to some form of efficient projection or decomposition in order to have a compression effect, *e.g.* via circulant projections or tensor train decompositions. Maintaining such a structure throughout learning, however, can be challenging, especially using only the first-order gradient descent algorithms favoured in deep learning. Typically, constrained optimization requires managing active and inactive constraints, and or evaluating the Karush-Kuhn-Tucker conditions, all of which can be very expensive. We therefore must enforce weight structure differently.

One way to simplify the learning is to fix the projection bases *a priori* *e.g.* to sinusoids, as per the Fourier transform, or rectangular functions, as per the Walsh-Hadamard transform (WHT) and its derivative the Fastfood transform [10]. The latter has been used to compress the linear layers of Convolutional Neural Networks (CNNs) [9,11]. As it relies on non-local basis functions, the Fastfood transform has a complexity of $O(n \log n)$ for projecting a signal of length n. More importantly, however, using fixed bases limits the network flexibility and generalization power. Since the choice of basis functions determines the level of sparsity when representing data, the flexibility to choose a (more compact) basis could bring significant compression gains. We advocate the use of wavelets as an alternative for representing the weight matrices of linear layers. Using wavelets offers us two key advantages. Firstly, we can apply the fast wavelet transform (FWT), which has only a complexity of $O(n)$ for projection and comes with a large selection of possible basis functions. Secondly, we can build upon the product filter approach for wavelet design [12] to directly integrate the learning of wavelet bases as a part of training CNNs or RNNs. Learning the bases gives us added flexibility in representing their weight matrices.

Motivated by these advantages, we propose a new linear layer which directly integrates the FWT into its formulation so layer weights can be represented as sparse wavelet coefficients. Furthermore, rather than limit ourselves to predefined wavelets as basis functions, we learn the bases directly as a part of network training. Specifically, we adopt the product filter approach to wavelet design. We translate the two hard constraints posed by this approach into soft objectives, which serve as novel wavelet loss terms. By combining these terms with standard learning objectives, we can successfully learn linear layers by using only the wavelet transform, its inverse, diagonal matrices and a permutation matrix. As the re-parametrisation is differentiable, it can be trained end-to-end using standard gradient descent. Our linear layer is general; as we later show in the experiments, it can be applied in both CNNs and RNNs. We focus primarily on gated recurrent units (GRUs), as they typically contain large and dense weight matrices for computing the cell's state and gate values. Our wavelet-RNNs are compressed by design and have significantly fewer parameters than standard RNNs, yet still remain competitive in performance. Our main contributions can be summarized as follows:

- We propose a novel method of *learning FWT basis functions* using modern deep learning frameworks by incorporating the constraints of the product filter approach as soft objectives. By learning local basis functions, we are

able to reduce the computational cost of the transform to $O(n)$ compared to existing $O(n \log n)$ methods that use fixed non-local basis functions.
- Based on this method, we propose an efficient linear layer which is compressed by design through its wavelet-based representation. This linear layer can be used flexibly in both CNNs and RNNs and allow for large feature or state sizes without the accompanying parameter blow-up of dense linear layers.
- Extensive experiments explore the effect of efficient wavelet-based linear layers on the various parts of the GRU cell machinery. Our approach demonstrates comparable compression performance compared to state-of-the-art model compression methods.

2   Related Work

2.1   Structured Efficient Linear Transforms

Our proposed approach can be considered a structured efficient linear transform, which replaces unstructured dense matrices with efficiently structured ones. There are several types of structures, derived from fast random projections [10], circulant projections [13,14], tensor train (TT) decompositions [8,15,16], low-rank decompositions [6,17,18].

One of the main difficulties in using structured representation is maintaining the structure throughout learning. One line of work avoids this by simply doing away with the constraints during the learning phase. For example, low-rank decompositions [6,17,18] split the learned dense weights into two low-rank orthogonal factors. The low-rank constraint then gradually disappears during the fine-tuning phase. The resulting representation is uncontrolled, and must trade off between the efficiency of the low rank and effectively satisfying the fine-tuning objective. In contrast, our proposed soft constraints can be applied jointly with the learning objective, and as such, not only does not require fine-tuning, but can ensure structure throughout the entire learning process.

Within the group of structured efficient linear transforms, the one most similar to the FWT that we are using is the Fastfood transform [11]. The fastfood transform is applied to reparameterize linear layers as a combination of 5 types of matrices: three random diagonal matrices, a random permutation matrix and a Walsh-Hadamard matrix. However, these three diagonal matrices are fixed after random initialization, resulting in a non-adaptive transform. Its fixed nature limits the representation power. As a remedy, [9] proposed an adaptive version in which the three diagonal matrices are optimized through standard backpropagation. Nevertheless, the approach still uses a fixed Walsh-Hadamard basis which may limit the generalization and flexibility of the linear layer. In contrast to the adaptive Fastfood transform, our method is more general and reduces computational complexity.

2.2   Compressing Recurrent Neural Networks

Compressing recurrent cells can be highly challenging; the recurrent connection forces the unit to be shared across all time steps in a sequence so minor changes in the unit can have a dramatic change in the output. To compress RNNs, previous approaches have explored pruning [19–21], quantization [22] and structured linear transforms [15,16,23,24].

The use of structured efficient linear transforms for compressing RNNs has primarily focused on using tensor decompositions, either via tensor train decomposition [15,16] or block-term tensor decomposition [24]. The tensor decomposition replaces linear layers with tensors with a lower number of weights and operations than the original matrix. Tensor train decomposition can compress the input-to-hidden matrix in RNNs, but requires the restricted setting on the hyperparameters (e.g. ranks and the restrained order of core tensors) making the compressed models sensitive to parameter selection [15]. Pan et al. [23] employ low-rank tensor ring decomposition to alleviate the strict constraints in tensor train decomposition. However, these methods need to approximate the matrix-vector operation by tensor-by-tensor multiplication, where the dense weights and input vectors are reshaped into higher-order tensors. This requires additional reshaping time and generates feature-agnostic representations during training. In contrast, our method shows more flexibility and efficiency performing on the fast wavelet transform, whose bases satisfy with wavelet design using soft objectives.

2.3 Wavelets in Machine Learning

A body of works using wavelets in machine learning exists. A group of publications is exploring how wavelets can be used to process weighted graphs trough wavelet-autoencoders [25] or convolutions with wavelet-constraints [26]. In deep learning wavelets have been used e.g. as input features [27] or as a tool for weight representation. The latter category includes the definition of convolution filters in the wavelet domain [28]. We define a new wavelet based structured efficient linear transform which replaces large dense layers. Using our new transform greatly reduces network size as we show in the experimental section.

3   Method

3.1   Fast Wavelet Transform

The wavelet transform projects signals into a multi-resolution spectral domain defined by the wavelet basis of choice. The wavelets themselves are oscillating basis functions derived from scaling and translating a prototypical mother wavelet function such as the Haar, Mexican hat, Daubechies, etc. We refer the curious reader to the excellent primer [12] for a thorough treatment on the topic. For our purposes, we can consider the wavelet transform as being analogous to the Fourier transform. Similarly, wavelets are akin to sinusoids, with a key distinction however, that wavelets are localized basis functions, i.e. are not infinite.

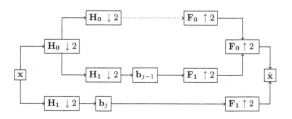

Fig. 1. Efficient wavelet signal analysis and synthesis following a tree structure. [12]. **H** denotes analysis filters and **F** stands for synthesis filters. Up ($\uparrow$) and down ($\downarrow$)-sampling by a factor of two is written as the arrow followed by the factor. Filtering and sampling can be accomplished jointly in deep learning frameworks by using strided convolutions for analysis and strided transposed convolutions for synthesis. In place of the dotted arrow more scale-levels can be included.

Similar to the fast Fourier transform, there exists a fast wavelet transform $\mathcal{W}$ and an inverse $\mathcal{W}^{-1}$ which can be expressed as matrix multiplications [12]:

$$\mathcal{W}(\mathbf{x}) = \mathbf{A}\mathbf{x} = \mathbf{b}, \tag{1}$$

$$\mathcal{W}^{-1}(\mathbf{b}) = \mathbf{S}\mathbf{b} = \mathbf{x}. \tag{2}$$

Given a signal $\mathbf{x}$ indexed by n, the forward wavelet transform yields coefficients b_{jk} in vector $\mathbf{b}$, which projects $\mathbf{x}$ onto the wavelet basis $\mathbf{A}$. Matrices $\mathbf{A}$ and $\mathbf{S}$ are referred to as analysis (or forward) and synthesis (or backward) matrices respectively. They are inverses of each other, *i.e.* $\mathbf{A} = \mathbf{S}^{-1}$, and allow for reconstruction of the signal from the wavelet coefficients. The double indices jk of b_{jk} denote the scale j and time k positions of each coefficient. Coefficients b_{jk} can be found by recursively convolving $\mathbf{x}$ with the analysis filters $\mathbf{h}_0$ and $\mathbf{h}_1$ with a stride of 2. This process is depicted in Fig. 1. The number of scales (6 in our case) is chosen depending on the problem. As a result of the strided convolution, the number of time steps is halved after each scale step. By working backwards through the scales, one can reconstruct $\hat{\mathbf{x}}$ from b_{jk} through transposed convolutions with the synthesis filters $\mathbf{f}_0$ and $\mathbf{f}_1$.

3.2   Learning Wavelet Bases

Typically, wavelets basis functions are selected from a library of established wavelets, *e.g.* as the rectangular functions of Haar wavelet, or arbitrarily designed by hand by the practitioner. Based on the product filter approach, designed wavelets must fulfill conditions of perfect reconstruction and alias cancellation [12]. Given filters $\mathbf{h}$ and $\mathbf{f}$ as well as their z-transformed counterparts $H(z) = \sum_n \mathbf{h}(n)z^{-n}$ and $F(z)$ respectively, the reconstruction condition can be expressed as

$$H_0(z)F_0(z) + H_1(z)F_1(z) = 2z^l, \tag{3}$$

and the anti-aliasing condition as

$$H_0(-z)F_0(z) + H_1(-z)F_1(z) = 0. \tag{4}$$

For the perfect reconstruction condition in Eq. 3, the center term z^l of the resulting z-transformed expression must be a two; all other coefficients should be zero. l denotes the power of the center. To enforce these constraints in a learnable setting, we can design corresponding differentiable loss terms which we call a wavelet loss. Instead of working in the z−space, we leverage the equivalence of polynomial multiplication and coefficient convolution ($*$) and reformulate Eq. 3 as:

$$\mathcal{L}_{pr}(\theta_w) = \sum_{k=0}^{N} \left[(\mathbf{h}_0 * \mathbf{f}_0)_k + (\mathbf{h}_1 * \mathbf{f}_1)_k - \mathbf{0}_{2,k} \right]^2, \tag{5}$$

where $\mathbf{0}_2$ is a zero vector with a two at z^l in its center. This formulation amounts to a measure of the coefficient-wise squared deviation from the perfect reconstruction condition. For alias cancellation, we observe that Eq. 4 is satisfied if $F_0(z) = H_1(-z)$ and $F_1(z) = -H_0(-z)$ and formulate our anti-aliasing loss as:

$$\mathcal{L}_{ac}(\theta_w) = \sum_{k=0}^{N} \left(f_{0,k} - (-1)^k h_{1,k} \right)^2 + \left(f_{1,k} + (-1)^k h_{0,k} \right)^2. \tag{6}$$

This formulation leads to the common alternating sign pattern, which we will observe later. We refer to the sum of the two terms in Eqs. 5 and 6 as a wavelet loss. It can be added to standard loss functions in the learning of neural networks.

3.3   Efficient Wavelet-Based Linear Layers

To use the wavelet-based linear layer, we begin by decomposing the weight matrices $\mathbf{W}$ as follows:

$$\mathbf{W} = \mathbf{D}\mathcal{W}^{-1}\mathbf{G}\mathbf{\Pi}\mathcal{W}\mathbf{B}, \tag{7}$$

where $\mathbf{D}, \mathbf{G}, \mathbf{B}$ are diagonal learnable matrices of size $n \times n$, and $\mathbf{\Pi} \in \{0,1\}^{n \times n}$ is a random permutation matrix, which stays fixed during training. We use identity matrices as initialization for $\mathbf{D}, \mathbf{G}, \mathbf{B}$. $\mathcal{W}$ and $\mathcal{W}^{-1}$ denote the wavelet transform and it's inverse, which can also be optimized during training. This approach is similar to [9], which relies on the fast Welsh-Hadamard transform. $\mathbf{D}, \mathbf{G}, \mathbf{B}$ and $\mathbf{\Pi}$ can be evaluated in $O(n)$ [29]. The fast wavelet transform requires only $O(n)$ steps instead of the $O(n \ln n)$ used by the non-local fast Fourier and fast Welsh-Hadamard transforms [12]. This is asymptotically faster than the transforms used in [9,29], who work with fixed Welsh-Hadamard and Fourier transforms. Non square cases where the number of inputs is larger than n can be handled by concatenating square representations with tied wavelet weights [9].

We can replace standard weights in linear layers with the decomposition described above, and learn the matrices in Eq. 7 using the wavelet loss as defined in Eq. 5 and 6 jointly with the standard network objective. Given the network parameters θ and all filter coefficients θ_w we minimize:

$$\min(\mathcal{L}(\theta)) = \min[(\mathcal{L}_o(\theta)) + \mathcal{L}_{pr}(\theta_w) + \mathcal{L}_{ac}(\theta_w)], \tag{8}$$

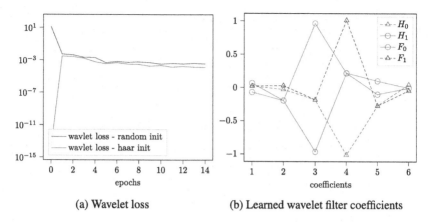

(a) Wavelet loss   (b) Learned wavelet filter coefficients

Fig. 2. (a) Wavelet loss sum of a randomly and Haar initialized wavelet array. In both cases, filter values converge to a product filter as indicated by trend of the wavelet loss towards zero . (b) Learned wavelet filter coefficients. Coefficients have been initialized at random. After training, the effects of the alias cancellation constraint are prominently visible. We must have $F_0(z) = H_1(-z)$ and $F_1(z) = -H_0(-z)$ for alias to cancel itself. Inserting $(-z)$ into the coefficient polynomial leads to a minus sign at odd powers. Additional multiplication with (-1) shifts it to even powers. Alias cancellation therefore imposes an alternating sign pattern. When F_0 and H_1 share the same sign F_1 and H_0 do not and vice versa.

where $\mathcal{L}_o(\theta)$ the original loss function (*e.g.* cross-entropy loss) of the uncompressed network, and $\mathcal{L}_{pr}(\theta_w) + \mathcal{L}_{ac}(\theta_w)$ the extra terms for the learnable wavelet basis.

Our wavelet-based linear layer can be applied to fully-connected layers in CNNs and RNNs. For example, suppose we are given a gated recurrent unit (GRU) as follows:

$$\mathbf{g}_r = \sigma(\mathbf{W}_r \mathbf{h}_{t-1} + \mathbf{V}_r \mathbf{x}_t + \mathbf{b}_r), \tag{9}$$

$$\mathbf{g}_z = \sigma(\mathbf{W}_z \mathbf{h}_{t-1} + \mathbf{V}_z \mathbf{x}_t + \mathbf{b}_z), \tag{10}$$

$$\mathbf{z}_t = \mathbf{W}(\mathbf{g}_r \odot \mathbf{h}_{t-1}) + \mathbf{V}\mathbf{x}_t + \mathbf{b}, \tag{11}$$

$$\mathbf{h}_t = \mathbf{g}_z \odot \tanh(\mathbf{z}_t) + (1 - \mathbf{g}_z) \odot \mathbf{h}_{t-1}, \tag{12}$$

where $\sigma(\cdot)$ and $\tanh(\cdot)$ are sigmoid and tanh activation functions, $\mathbf{z}_t$ is the candidate hidden layer values, $\mathbf{h}_t$ is the hidden layer state at the t-th time, and $\mathbf{g}_r, \mathbf{g}_z$ are the reset and update gates, respectively. $\odot$ denotes element-wise multiplication. $\mathbf{V}$, $\mathbf{V}_r$ and $\mathbf{V}_z$ are the input weights. We can learn efficient gating units by applying the representation from Eq. 7 to the recurrent weight matrices $\mathbf{W}$, $\mathbf{W}_r$ and $\mathbf{W}_z$. The recurrent weight matrices are of size $n_h \times n_h$ and are typically the largest matrices in a GRU and learning efficient versions of them can reduce the number of network parameters up to 90%.

Table 1. Experimental results on the MNIST digit-recognition. We work with a LeNet architecture as proposed in previous work. In comparison to the Fastfood approach [9] we obtain comparable performance with slightly fewer parameters. The size of our learnable-wavelet compression layer is set to 800.

Net	Error	Parameters	Reduction
LeNet-5	0.87%	431K	-
LeNet-fastfood	0.71%	39K	91%
LeNet-random	1.67%	36K	92%
LeNet-wavelet	0.74%	36K	92%

4   Experiments

We evaluate the effectiveness of our linear layer in both CNNs and RNNs. For CNNs, we select LeNet-5 on MNIST digit recognition classification benchmark [30] as a baseline. For RNNs, we test several GRU models on sequence learning tasks including the copy-memory and adding problem [31], sequential MNIST and Penn-Treebank (PTB) character modelling [32].

4.1   MNIST-Digit Recognition

We first apply our efficient wavelet layers to the MNIST digit recognition problem [30]. MNIST has 60K training and 10K test images with a size of 28×28 from 10 classes. We train using an Adadelta optimizer for 14 epochs using a learning rate of 1. The adaptive Fastfood transform is replaced with our proposed learnable-wavelet compression layer. In this feed-forward experiment, we apply dropout to the learned diagonal matrices $\mathbf{D}, \mathbf{G}, \mathbf{B}$ in Eq. 7.

We start by randomly initializing the wavelet array, consisting of 6 parameters per filter, with values drawn from the uniform distribution $\mathcal{U}^1_{-1}$. In this case, the initial condition is not a valid product filter so the wavelet loss is initially very large, as shown in Fig. 2a. However, as this loss term decreases as the random values in the wavelet array start to approximately satisfy the conditions of Eq. 3 and Eq. 4. Correspondingly, the accuracy also rises. With the random initialization we achieve a recognition accuracy of 98.33% with only 36k parameters. We visualize the learned filters in Fig. 2b. The alias cancellation condition causes an alternating sign pattern. Whenever F_0 and H_1 have the the same sign F_1 and H_0 do not and vice versa. As we observe high recognition rates and small wavelet loss values, we are confident that we have learned valid wavelet basis functions.

Inspired by the Welsh-Hadamard matrix, we also test with a zero-padded Haar wavelet as a initialization; this should ensure a valid FWT at all times. In this case, the initial wavelet loss is very small as shown in Fig. 2a, as we already start with a valid wavelet that perfectly satisfies conditions 3 and 4. However, as learning progresses, the condition is no longer satisfied, hence the jump in the

Table 2. RNN compression results on the adding and memory problems, exploring the impact of our efficient wavelet-based linear layer at various locations in the GRU. On the adding problem all tested variants are functional. Compressing the state and reset equations has virtually no effect on performance. Compressing the update gate leads to a working cell, but cells with a compressed update gate perform significantly worse. Note that on the adding problem, predicting a sum of 1 regardless of the input leads to an mse of 0.167. On the copy-memory benchmark, replacing the the state and reset weight matrices with our efficient wavelet version is possible without significant performance losses. A state size of 512 was used for all models. The expected cross entropy for a random guess is 0.12 with n=8.

	Reduced	Adding problem			Copy-memory problem		
		mse-loss	Accuracy	Weights	ce-loss	Accuracy	Weights
GRU	-	4.9e−4	99.23%	792K	4.8e−5	99.99%	808K
Wave-GRU	z_t	3.0e−4	99.45%	531K	2.4e−3	99.1%	548K
Wave-GRU	g_r	1.1e−4	99.96%	531K	3.7e−5	99.98%	548K
Wave-GRU	g_z	4.4e−4	97.78%	531K	1.1e−1	21.63%	548K
Wave-GRU	g_r, g_z	0.9e−4	99.85%	270K	3.7e−2	73.63%	288K
Wave-GRU	z_t, g_r	3.0e−4	98.56%	270K	2.4e−3	99.05%	288K
Wave-GRU	z_t, g_z	1.1e−3	92.64%	270K	1.2e−1	12.67%	288K
Wave-GRU	z_t, g_r, g_z	1.0e−3	91.64%	10K	1.2e−1	16.84%	27K
Ff-GRU	z_t, g_r, g_z	1.3e−3	85.99%	10K	1.2e−1	16.44%	27K

loss, before the gradual decrease once again. In Table 1, we compare our result to the Fastfood transform [9]. Our method achieves a comparable result with a higher parameter reduction rate of 92% (*vs.* 91%).

To explore the effect of our method on recurrent neural networks, we consider the challenging copy-memory and adding tasks as benchmarks [31].

The copy memory benchmark consists out of a sequence of 10 numbers, T zeros, a marker and 10 more zeros. The tested cell observes the input sequence. It must learn to reproduce the original input sequence after the marker. The numbers in the input sequence are drawn from $\mathcal{U}_0^n$. Element $n+1$ marks the point where to reproduce the original sequence. We choose to work with n=8 in our experiments and use a cross entropy loss. Accuracy is defined as the percentage of correctly memorized integers. For the adding problem, T random numbers are drawn from $\mathcal{U}_0^1$ out of which two are marked. The two marks are randomly placed in the first and second half of the sequence. After observing the entire sequence, the network should produce the sum of the two marked elements. A mean squared error loss function is used to measure the difference between the true and the expected sum. We count a sum as correct if $|\hat{y} - y| < 0.05$. We test on GRU cells with a state size of 512. T is set to 150 for the adding problem. Optimization uses a learning rate of 0.001 and Root Mean Square Propagation (RMSProp).

48   M. Wolter et al.

Table 3. RNN compression results on the sequential MNIST and Penn-Treebank benchmarks. On the sequential MNIST benchmark (a), the pattern here reflects what we saw on the adding and copy-memory benchmarks. Touching the update gate has a negative impact. All other equations can be compressed. our method (WaveGRU-64) achieves a comparable performance, compared to [15]. In (b) we show results for the best performing architectures on the Penn-Treebank data set, we compare to a TCN as proposed in [33]. We can compress the GRU cells state and reset equations without a significant drop in performance.

(a) Sequential MNIST					(b) Penn-Treebank			
	reduced	loss	accuracy	weights		reduced	loss	bpc	weights
GRU	-	6.49e-2	100%	795K	TCN	-	0.916	1.322	2,221K
Wave-GRU	z_t	8.98e-2	98%	534K	GRU	-	0.925	1.335	972K
Wave-GRU	g_r	6.06e-2	100%	534K	Wave-GRU	z_t	0.97	1.399	711K
Wave-GRU	g_z	1.82	26%	534K	Wave-GRU	g_r	0.925	1.335	711K
Wave-GRU	g_r, g_z	1.33	46%	274K	Wave-GRU	z_t, g_r	0.969	1.398	450K
Wave-GRU	z_t, g_r	9.48e-2	98%	274K					
Wave-GRU	z_t, g_z	1.60	34%	274K					
Wave-GRU	z_t, g_z, g_r	1.52	36%	13K					
WaveGRU-64	z_t, g_r	0.127	96.4%	4.9K					
TT-GRU	-	-	98.3%	5.1K					

We first explore the effect of our efficient wavelet layer on the reset g_r and update g_z equations (Eq. 9, 10) as well as the state z_t equation (Eq. 11). As shown in Table 2, We observed that efficient representations of the state and reset equations has little impact on performance, while significantly reducing the weights. In the combined case, our method has 2.8× less parameters than dense weight matrices with only 0.91% accuracy drop in copy memory problem. For the adding problem, our method achieves a factor of 2.9× reduction with only 0.67% accuracy drop. When incorporating this into multiple weight matrices, we find that using the efficient representation is problematic for the update matrix W_z next state computation. We found that compressing the update gate has a large impact on the performance, especially the combination with state compression. The update mechanism plays an important role for stability and should not be compressed. Compared to the Fastfood transform [9], our method is better at compressing entire cells. It achieves higher accuracy with the same number of weights both in adding problem and copy memory problem. For example, in adding problem, our method achieves a higher accuracy of 91.64% (*vs.* 85.99%) with the same number of weights, compared to the Fastfood transform [9].

Sequential-MNIST. The sequential MNIST benchmark dataset has previously been described in Sect. 4.1. A gray-scale image with a size of 28×28 is interpreted as a sequence of 784 pixels. The entire sequence is an input to the GRU, which will generate a classification score. We select a GRU with a hidden size of 512 as our baseline and an RMSProp optimizer with a learning rate of 0.001.

Results of our method are shown in Table 3a. Similar to the results of Table 2, we also observe that having efficient representations for the state and reset gate matrices work well, but compressing the update gate adversely impacts the results. Compared to only state compression, the combination of state and reset compression achieves a higher compression rate of 2.9× (vs. 1.5×), without the accuracy drop. We also compare to the tensor train approach used in [15]. We apply the efficient wavelet layer only on the reset and state weight matrices and reduce the cell size to 64. Our approach does reasonably well with fewer parameters.

Penn Treebank Character Modelling. We verify our approach on the Penn-Treebank (PTB) character modelling benchmark [32]. We split the dataset into training, validation and test sequences, which contains 5,059K training characters, 396K validation characters and 446K testing characters. Given an input sequence of 320 characters, the model should predict the next character. We work with a GRU of size 512 trained using an Adam optimizer with an initial learning rate of 0.005. Training is done using a cross entropy loss in addition to the wavelet loss, and results are reported using bits per character (bpc), where lower bpc is better. In Table 3b, we show results for a temporal convolutional network (TCN) [33], a vanilla GRU cell as well as state, reset and state reset compression, which we found to be successfully earlier. We confirm that our wavelet-based compression method can be used to compress reset gate and cell state without significant performance loss.

5   Conclusion

We presented a novel wavelet based efficient linear layer which demonstrates competitive performance within convolutional and recurrent network structures. On the MNIST digit recognition benchmark, we show state of the art compression results as well as convergence from randomly initialized filters. We explore RNN compression and observe comparable performance on the sequential MNIST task. In a gated recurrent unit we can compress the reset and state equations without a significant impact on performance. The update gate equation was hard to compress, in particular in combination with the state equation. Joint update gate and reset gate equation compression generally worked better than update and state compression. We conclude that the update mechanism plays the most important role within a GRU-cell, followed by the state equation and finally the reset gate. Results indicate that selective compression can significantly reduce cell parameters while retaining good performance. Product filters are only one way of wavelet design, alternative methods include lifting or spectral factorization approaches. We look forward to exploring some of these in the future. Efficient implementation of the FWT on GPUs is no simple matter. We hope this paper will spark future work on highly optimized implementations.

Acknowledgements. Research was supported by the Deutsche Forschungsgemeinschaft (DFG, German Research Foundation) project YA 447/2-1 (FOR 2535 Anticipating Human Behavior) and by the National Research Foundation Singapore under its NRF Fellowship Programme [NRF-NRFFAI1-2019-0001].

References

1. Courbariaux, M., Bengio, Y., David, J.-P.: BinaryConnect: training deep neural networks with binary weights during propagations. In: NIPS (2015)
2. Rastegari, M., Ordonez, V., Redmon, J., Farhadi, A.: XNOR-Net: imagenet classification using binary convolutional neural networks. In: Leibe, B., Matas, J., Sebe, N., Welling, M. (eds.) ECCV 2016. LNCS, vol. 9908, pp. 525–542. Springer, Cham (2016). https://doi.org/10.1007/978-3-319-46493-0_32
3. Han, S., Mao, H., Dally, W.J.: Deep compression: compressing deep neural network with pruning, trained quantization and Huffman coding. In 4th: International Conference on Learning Representations, ICLR 2016 (2016)
4. Han, S., Pool, J., Tran, J., Dally, W.: Learning both weights and connections for efficient neural networks. In: NIPS (2015)
5. Lin, S., Ji, R., Li, Y., Wu, Y., Huang, F., Zhang, B.: Accelerating convolutional networks via global & dynamic filter pruning. In: IJCAI (2018)
6. Denton, E.L., Zaremba, W., Bruna, J., LeCun, Y., Fergus, R.: Exploiting linear structure within convolutional networks for efficient evaluation. In: NIPS (2014)
7. Lin, S., Ji, R., Guo, X., Li, X.: Towards convolutional neural networks compression via global error reconstruction. In: IJCAI (2016)
8. Novikov, A., Podoprikhin, D., Osokin, A., Vetrov, D.P.: Tensorizing neural networks. In: NIPS (2015)
9. Yang, Z., et al.: Deep fried convnets. In: ICCV (2015)
10. Ailon, N., Chazelle, B.: The fast Johnson-Lindenstrauss transform and approximate nearest neighbors. SIAM J. Comput. **39**(1), 302–322 (2009)
11. Le, Q., Sarlós, T., Smola, A.: Fastfood-approximating kernel expansions in loglinear time. In: ICML, vol. 85 (2013)
12. Strang, G., Nguyen, T.: Wavelets and Filter Banks. SIAM, Philadelphia (1996)
13. Cheng, Y., Yu, F.X., Feris, R.S., Kumar, S., Choudhary, A., Chang, S.F.: An exploration of parameter redundancy in deep networks with circulant projections. In: ICCV (2015)
14. Araujo, A., Negrevergne, B., Chevaleyre, Y., Atif, J.: Training compact deep learning models for video classification using circulant matrices. In: Leal-Taixé, L., Roth, S. (eds.) ECCV 2018. LNCS, vol. 11132, pp. 271–286. Springer, Cham (2019). https://doi.org/10.1007/978-3-030-11018-5_25
15. Tjandra, A., Sakti, S., Nakamura, S.: Compressing recurrent neural network with tensor train. In: IJCNN. IEEE (2017)
16. Yang, Y., Krompass, D., Tresp, V.: Tensor-train recurrent neural networks for video classification. In: ICML. JMLR. org (2017)
17. Denil, M., Shakibi, B., Dinh, L., Ranzato, M.A., De Freitas, N.: Predicting parameters in deep learning. In: NIPS, pp. 2148–2156 (2013)
18. Jaderberg, M., Vedaldi, A., Zisserman, A.: Speeding up convolutional neural networks with low rank expansions. In: Proceedings of the British Machine Vision Conference. BMVA Press (2014)
19. Wen, W., et al.: Learning intrinsic sparse structures within long short-term memory. In: International Conference on Learning Representations (2018)

20. Narang, S., Elsen, E., Diamos, G., Sengupta, S.: Exploring sparsity in recurrent neural networks. In: ICLR (2017)
21. Wang, T., Fan, L., Wang, H.: Simultaneously learning architectures and features of deep neural networks. In: Tetko, I.V., Kůrková, V., Karpov, P., Theis, F. (eds.) ICANN 2019. LNCS, vol. 11728, pp. 275–287. Springer, Cham (2019). https://doi.org/10.1007/978-3-030-30484-3_23
22. Wang, Z., Lin, J., Wang, Z.: Accelerating recurrent neural networks: a memory-efficient approach. IEEE Trans. Very Large Scale Integr. (VLSI) Syst. **25**(10), 2763–2775 (2017)
23. Pan, Y., et al.: Compressing recurrent neural networks with tensor ring for action recognition. In: AAAI (2019)
24. Ye, J., et al.: Learning compact recurrent neural networks with block-term tensor decomposition. In: CVPR (2018)
25. Rustamov, R., Guibas, L.J.: Wavelets on graphs via deep learning. In: Advances in Neural Information Processing Systems (2013)
26. Bruna, J., Zaremba, W., Szlam, A., Lecun, Y.: Spectral networks and locally connected networks on graphs. In: International Conference on Learning Representations (ICLR 2014), CBLS, April 2014 (2014)
27. Lan-lan Chen, Yu., Zhao, J.Z., Zou, J.: Automatic detection of alertness/drowsiness from physiological signals using wavelet-based nonlinear features and machine learning. Expert Syst. Appl. **42**(21), 7344–7355 (2015)
28. Cotter, F., Kingsbury, N.: Deep learning in the wavelet domain. arXiv preprint arXiv:1811.06115 (2018)
29. Arjovsky, M., Shah, A., Bengio, Y.: Unitary evolution recurrent neural networks. In: ICML (2016)
30. LeCun, Y., et al.: Gradient-based learning applied to document recognition. Proc. IEEE **86**(11), 2278–2324 (1998)
31. Hochreiter, S., Schmidhuber, J.: Long short-term memory. Neural Comput. **9**(8), 1735–1780 (1997)
32. Marcus, M., Santorini, B., Marcinkiewicz, M.A.: Building a large annotated corpus of English: The Penn Treebank (1993)
33. Bai, S., Kolter, J.Z., Koltun, V.: An empirical evaluation of generic convolutional and recurrent networks for sequence modeling. arXiv:1803.01271 (2018)

Fast and Robust Compression of Deep Convolutional Neural Networks

Jia Wen[1], Liu Yang[1(✉)], and Chenyang Shen[2]

[1] College of Intelligence and Computing, Tianjin University, Tianjin 300350, China
{wenjia,yangliuyl}@tju.edu.cn
[2] Department of Radiation Oncology, University of Texas
Southwestern Medical Center, Dallas, TX 75390, USA
chenyang.shen@utsouthwestern.edu

Abstract. Deep convolutional neural networks (CNNs) currently demonstrate the state-of-the-art performance in several domains. However, a large amount of memory and computing resources are required in the commonly used CNN models, posing challenges in training as well as deploying, especially on those devices with limited computational resources. Inspired by the recent advancement of random tensor decomposition, we introduce a Hierarchical Framework for Fast and Robust Compression (HFFRC), which significantly reduces the number of parameters needed to represent a convolution layer via a fast low-rank Tucker decomposition algorithm, while preserving its expressive power. In the merit of randomized algorithm, the proposed compression framework is robust to noises in parameters. In addition, it is a general framework that any tensor decomposition method can be easily adopted. The efficiency and effectiveness of the proposed approach have been demonstrated via comprehensive experiments conducted on the benchmarks CIFAR-10 and CIFAR-100 image classification datasets.

Keywords: Deep convolutional neural networks · Random Tucker decomposition · Model compression

1 Introduction

Deep convolutional neural networks (CNNs) have demonstrated state-of-the-art performance in a wide range of applications, such as image classification [24], object detection [19], and face recognition [13]. The performance of CNNs heavily relies on deeper and wider network architecture, yielding to large network sizes which brings memory and computational concerns. For instance, VGG-16 model [21] has 14.71 million parameters and 15.36 billion floating point operations (FLOPs) when applying on ImageNet dataset. Therefore, CNNs are often trained and deployed on high-performance computational devices, such as graphics processing units (GPUs), to achieve satisfactory efficiency. It is particularly challenging to develop and deploy large-scale CNNs for devices with limited computational resources, such as mobile phones, wearable and IoT devices, etc., as requested in many modern applications.

© Springer Nature Switzerland AG 2020
I. Farkaš et al. (Eds.): ICANN 2020, LNCS 12397, pp. 52–63, 2020.
https://doi.org/10.1007/978-3-030-61616-8_5

Specifically, a CNN is often constructed with multiple layers of linear operations, including convolution, fully connection, followed by nonlinear activations. It was found that significant redundancy exists among the network parameters defining these linear operations [2,5]. In this regard, compression schemes which can substantially suppress model size will be useful to eliminate the redundancy while maintaining its satisfactory performance. So far, four types of strategies have been proposed to compress CNNs. One of the most intuitive strategies is quantization, which refers to compress the original network by reducing the number of bits of parameters [3,25]. However, most of these quantization methods must require specially designed hardware to achieve theoretical acceleration. Besides, light-weight networks [20,22] have been developed, which consist of compact modules. However, they have to be trained from scratch and need expert's knowledge to design the network architecture. Some pruning methods have also been put forward to simply remove unimportant parameters according to different criteria [8,14,17]. But in fact different priori assumptions are often needed for different criteria, which are hard to evaluate if it's right or not. The last type of approaches is called low-rank methods [1,9,11], which replaces the original network parameters of each layer with a low-rank approximation. It reconstructs the important parameters through the data itself, instead of setting the standard artificially. Hence, we mainly focus on the low-rank approximation method in this study.

Low-rank approximation is often realized by seeking for low-rank representations to accurately approximate a matrix or tensor via decomposition. Ma et al. proposed the matrix decomposition method with sparse low-rank constraint (MD-SL) [15]. However, a 4-way tensor is reshaped to a matrix, which loses the structural characteristics of the original convolutional layer. Some tensor decomposition methods have also been successfully applied to the model compression of neural networks [23,26,28]. Nevertheless, they aim at designing new model architectures of tensor format instead of decomposing pre-trained models. Specifically to approximate convolutional layers, two widely employed tensor decomposition methods Candecomp/Parafac (CP) and Tucker decomposition are used for the compression. Lebedev et al. proposed to compress convolutional neural networks using CP-decomposition with tensor power method (CP-TPM) [11]. Astrid et al. developed non-linear least-squares based CP decomposition (CP-NLS) to decompose CNNs [1]. Kim et al. implemented Tucker decomposition for CNNs compression [9].

One obvious drawback of tensor decomposition is its low computational efficiency [30]. To address this issue, random tensor decomposition algorithms [16,29] have been developed. These methods perform low-rank decomposition by projecting the original tensor using random basis of lower dimension. As a non-iterative scheme, it is highly efficient in computation and is able to achieve comparable performance to other decomposition methods when projecting to a relatively high dimensional space. However, its performance may degrade substantially if further reducing the dimension of random projection, but a decomposition of lower rank is often desired in many real applications.

Besides, randomized algorithms have been demonstrated robust to noises compared to deterministic methods by introducing some random factors [6,27], which is also a big advantage in noisy real applications.

Motivated by the aforementioned advancements and also being aware of the existing issues, we propose to develop a hierarchical compression framework that integrates tensor random projection with Tucker decomposition to compress CNNs. We first utilize random projection technique to decompose the original tensor to a tensor of intermediate size, which effectively reduce the dimension while preserving most of the information in original tensor. Further decomposition (Tucker decomposition in this study) on the intermediate tensor is then performed to efficiently achieve the desired compression ratio while accurately model the most essential information embedded in the intermediate tensor, and hence a satisfactory low-rank approximation of original tensor is expected. The proposed scheme balances the computational efficiency and decomposition performance by innovatively integrating the random projection and Tucker decomposition. Besides that, benefit from the character of random projection, the noises in parameter can be removed through decomposition. The major contributions of this work have been summarized as follows:

1. We proposed a novel hierarchical compression framework consists of two-layer compression, i.e. tensor random projection and Tucker decomposition, which is suitable for fast and reliable parameter compression of large-scale CNNs.
2. It is robust to the noises appears in the parameters which can get the core weights and remove the noisy weights at the same time through the random projection and Tucker decomposition.
3. The proposed hierarchical scheme is a general framework that can be easily adapted to other tensor decomposition methods.

The rest of this paper is organized as follows. In Sect. 2, we describe the proposed HFFRC. The experimental results are reported in Sect. 3, followed by the conclusion in Sect. 4.

2   Proposed Method

As the convolutional layers take the majority of memory usage and computation cost in large-scale CNNs, the proposed hierarchical compression framework mainly focus on the compression of convolutional layers of CNNs. To achieve our goal, we establish a three-step pipeline: 1) obtain a pre-trained CNN; 2) perform decomposition on convolutional layers; and 3) fine-tune the decomposed network. On account of the first and third steps are performed via standard CNN training scheme, we will focus on introducing the second step, i.e. hierarchical tensor decomposition (Fig. 1.), in the following sections. We will first introduce the tensor formulation of the convolutional layers and then present the proposed method in details.

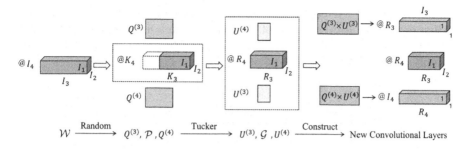

Fig. 1. The framework of hierarchical compression of a convolutional layer via random projection and Tucker decomposition. @ means the size of the 4-th dimension of a 4-way tensor.

2.1 Convolutional Kernel Tensor

In a deep CNN model, the parameter of the l-th layer can be denoted by a tensor $\mathcal{W}^{(l)}, 1 \leq l \leq L$, where L denotes the total number of convolutional layers. The main task is to decompose it for reducing parameters and computation complexity. We select one layer to illustrate how to decompose the parameters, and the superscript (l) in $\mathcal{W}^{(l)}$ is omitted to simplify the symbols, that is $\mathcal{W} \in \mathbb{R}^{I_1 \times I_2 \times I_3 \times I_4}$. It represents a 4-way tensor of a single convolutional layer, where $I_1 = I_2$ denotes the kernel size, I_3 denotes the number of input channels of the current layer and I_4 denotes the number of output channels. In each layer, the convolution operation maps an input tensor $\mathcal{X} \in \mathbb{R}^{H \times D \times I_3}$ to the output tensor $\mathcal{X}' \in \mathbb{R}^{H' \times D' \times I_4}$ by $\mathcal{W}$, which can be expressed as:

$$\mathcal{X}'_{h',d',t} = \sum_{i=1}^{I_1} \sum_{j=1}^{I_2} \sum_{s=1}^{I_3} \mathcal{W}_{i,j,s,t} \mathcal{X}_{h_i,d_j,s}, \tag{1}$$

where $h' = (h_i + b - i)/\triangle + 1$ and $d' = (d_j + b - j)/\triangle + 1$. b and $\triangle$ represent zero-padding size and stride, respectively. In a CNN, there are many layers and each layer consists of numerous parameters. Our goal is to decompose the parameters $\mathcal{W}$ of each layer, and then replace the original weights with the corresponding low-rank approximation.

2.2 Hierarchical Tensor Decomposition

Tensor Random Projection. The solution of Tucker decomposition is mainly through SVD algorithm. However, performing SVD is prohibitive for very large-scale problems. To solve this issue, randomness-based tensor decomposition has drawn researcher's attention [29,30]. The random technology is a powerful computation acceleration technique which has been proposed and studied for decades. It has been proven to be fast and efficient to perform, and effective in reducing the size of tensor. Therefore, we adopt the random projection to obtain a smaller tensor before Tucker decomposition for further compression.

More specifically, tensor random projection (TRP) method aims to process random projection at every mode of the tensor, then a much smaller sub-tensor is obtained which reserves most of the properties of the original tensor. The TRP is simply formulated as follows:

$$
\begin{aligned}
\hat{W} &= W \times_1 Q^{(1)}(Q^{(1)})^T \times_2 \cdots \times_N Q^{(N)}(Q^{(N)})^T \\
&= \underbrace{[W \times_1 (Q^{(1)})^T \times_2 \cdots \times_N (Q^{(N)})^T]}_{\mathcal{P}} \times_1 Q^{(1)} \times_2 \cdots \times_N Q^{(N)}
\end{aligned}
\tag{2}
$$

where $\times_n$ is the mode-n tensor production, $\{Q^{(n)}\}_{n=1}^N$ are the orthogonal matrices, and $\mathcal{P}$ is the projected tensor. $\mathcal{P}$ is much smaller than the original tensor and captures information about the interaction between different modes.

To obtain the orthogonal matrices $Q^{(n)}$, we first create a random matrix following the Gaussian distribution $M^{(n)} \in \mathbb{R}^{\Pi_{i=1,i\neq n}^N I_i \times K_n}$, where K_n is the dimension after random projection. Then a random projection $Y^{(n)} = (W^{(n)})^T M^{(n)}$ can be obtained along each mode, where $W^{(n)} \in \mathbb{R}^{\Pi_{i=1,i\neq n}^N I_i \times I_n}$ is the mode-n unfolding of tensor $\mathcal{W}$. At last, QR decomposition on $Y^{(n)}$ can be performed to get $Q^{(n)}$ and the random projected tensor can be computed via $\mathcal{P} \leftarrow W \times_n (Q^{(n)})^T$.

Specifically, for a 4-way tensor representing a convolutional layer, we keep mode-1 and mode-2 which are associated with spatial dimensions unchanged because they are often of small dimensions ($I_1 = I_2$ is typically 3 or 5 and hence we set $I_1 = I_2 = K_1 = K_2$). After random projection, we can get the projected tensor $\mathcal{P}$ and two orthogonal matrices $Q^{(3)}$, $Q^{(4)}$, where $\mathcal{P} \in \mathbb{R}^{K_1 \times K_2 \times K_3 \times K_4}$, and $Q^{(3)} \in \mathbb{R}^{I_3 \times K_3}$, $Q^{(4)} \in \mathbb{R}^{I_4 \times K_4}$. And then they will be employed to calculate the desired low-rank approximation of the original large-scale tensor.

Tucker Decomposition. We then apply the Tucker decomposition to further decompose $\mathcal{P}$ into a smaller core tensor multiplied by a matrix along each mode. Specifically, we again keep the mode-1 and mode-2 untouched and perform decomposition for the other modes. As such the tensor is decomposed as:

$$
\mathcal{P}_{i,j,s,t} = \sum_{r_3=1}^{R_3} \sum_{r_4=1}^{R_4} \mathcal{G}_{i,j,r_3,r_4} U^{(3)}_{s,r_3} U^{(4)}_{t,r_4},
\tag{3}
$$

In this equation, $\mathcal{G} \in \mathbb{R}^{K_1 \times K_2 \times R_3 \times R_4}$ is the core tensor, $U^{(3)} \in \mathbb{R}^{K_3 \times R_3}$, $U^{(4)} \in \mathbb{R}^{K_4 \times R_4}$ is the factor matrices and can be regarded as the principal components in each mode. R_3, R_4 are called the tensor ranks. Usually, the ranks are much smaller than the dimension of original tensor $\mathcal{P}$. Then we recalculate the factor matrixes using $U^{(3)} \leftarrow Q^{(3)} U^{(3)}$, $U^{(4)} \leftarrow Q^{(4)} U^{(4)}$. Finally, Tucker approximation of ordinary convolutional kernel is obtained, which is $\hat{W} = [\![\mathcal{G}; U^{(3)}, U^{(4)}]\!]$ with ranks R_3 and R_4.

Compared with original Tucker decomposition, our method implements decomposition in a hierarchical style. It can reduce computational complexity while preserving most of the essential information. Different from the pure random projection, the orthogonal matrixes lost by projection is recalculated with the factor matrixes to minimize the loss of information as much as possible. Besides, some useless information is got rid of after random projection, which can remove noises to some extent and make the model more robust.

2.3   Constructing New Layers

The core tensor $\mathcal{G}$ and factors $U^{(3)}$ and $U^{(4)}$ can be used to build the new convolutional layers replacing the original convolution layer. More specifically, the convolution operation of the new convolution layer (1) can be preformed via the following three steps:

$$\mathcal{Z}_{h,d,r_3} = \sum_{s=1}^{K_3} U^{(3)}_{s,r_3} \mathcal{X}_{h,d,s} \tag{4}$$

$$\mathcal{Z}'_{h',d',r_4} = \sum_{i=1}^{K_1} \sum_{j=1}^{K_2} \sum_{r_3=1}^{R_3} \mathcal{G}_{i,j,r_3,r_4} \mathcal{Z}_{h_i,d_j,r_3} \tag{5}$$

$$\mathcal{X}'_{h',d',t} = \sum_{r_4=1}^{R_4} U^{(4)}_{t,r_4} \mathcal{Z}'_{h',d',r_4} \tag{6}$$

The aforementioned process of hierarchical decomposition can then be repeated for all convolutional layers of a CNN.

2.4   Complexity Analysis

After decomposition from $\mathcal{W}$ to $\mathcal{G}$ and factors $[U^{(n)}]$, the number of parameters are compressed from $\prod_{i=1}^{4} I_i$ to $\prod_{i=1}^{4} R_i + \sum_{i=1}^{4} I_i \times R_i$. With random Tucker decomposition, compression ratio of parameters Υ and FLOPs Ψ to the uncompressed model are given by:

$$\Upsilon = \frac{\prod_{i=1}^{4} I_i}{I_3 R_3 + K_1 K_2 R_3 R_4 + I_4 R_4} \tag{7}$$

$$\Psi = \frac{(\prod_{i=1}^{4} I_i) H' D'}{I_3 R_3 H D + K_1 K_2 R_3 R_4 H' D' + I_4 R_4 H' D'} \tag{8}$$

3   Experiments

In this section, we demonstrate the effectiveness of our HFFRC method via several experiments.

3.1   Datasets

The proposed HFFRC was tested on two types of representative networks: simple CNNs (VGG-16 [21] on CIFAR-10 [10]) and Residual networks (ResNet-50 [7] on CIFAR-100 [10]). CIFAR-10 dataset contains 50,000 training images and 10,000 testing images, which are categorized into 10 classes. CIFAR-100 dataset contains the same images with CIFAR-10, except it has 100 classes containing 600 images each, which means it is more difficult to classify.

3.2 Baseline Methods and Evaluation

In the experiments, we compare the proposed algorithm with the following compression methods: CP-TPM [1], CP-NLS [11], Tucker [9] are three methods based on low-rank tensor decomposition; MD-SL [15] is a method based on sparse and low-rank matrix decomposition.

We report four metrics for evaluation, including compression rate for parameters (CRP) and compression rate for FLOPs (CRF), time for solving approximation of the model (Time) and accuracy drop compared to original uncompressed model(Acc ↓). Larger CRP and CRF values mean that more parameters are compressed, and less ones are left in the neural networks.

3.3 Hyper-parameters Setting

In our experiments, the hyper-parameters contain ranks (R_3, R_4) and random projection size (K_3, K_4) of each layer. The rank determines the compression rate of model, but solving it is NP-hard. Therefore, supposing the parameter of a certain layer is $\mathcal{W} \in \mathbb{R}^{I_1 \times I_2 \times I_3 \times I_4}$, we introduce two strategies to determine it: 1) Empirical Variational Bayesian Matrix Factorization (EVBMF) [18]. It is a global analytic solution through Bayesian inference, which can automatically find matrix rank according to data itself. 2) Percentage of the original tensor's dimension. For example, the dimension of a weight tensor is $3 \times 3 \times 32 \times 64$, then we set the rank as (16,32), which is 50% of original dimensions. The other hyper-parameter random projection size is determined by $K_n = I_n - v(I_n - R_n)$, where v is a hyper-parameter called weakening factor, and $0 \leq v \leq 1$, resulting in $R_n \leq K_n \leq I_n$.

3.4 Experiments on VGG-16

VGG-16 is a high-capacity network originally designed for the ImageNet dataset [4]. We use the modified version of the model on CIFAR-10 described in [12]. In detail, it consists of 13 convolutional layers and 2 fully connected layers with batch normalization layers, in which the fully connected layers do not occupy large portions of parameters due to the small input size and less hidden units.

We first train a VGG-16 model from scratch to obtain the baseline (accuracy is 0.9370). Then we implement our method on all convolutional layers of the pretrained model. Then a fine-tuning is needed for 100 epochs to recover the accurary. The performance comparison with other previous works is presented in Table 1. For fairness, we reproduced all of the methods on the same platform, and we fixed two compression ratios to test the performance of all methods. For the first ratio, the rank is set to 25% of each layer's dimension. For the second setting, the rank of HFFRC is determined via EVBMF. After building the compressed neural networks, we retrain the compressed model with the training set to recover the accuracy drop. And all other methods are tested on the same compression ratio.

Table 1. Result comparison on VGG-16 with CIFAR-10

CRP	CRF	Method	Time(s)	Acc↓
1.00	1.00	VGG-16	-	-
5.57	4.01	CP-TPM	839.52	0.0175
		CP-NLS	864.89	0.0178
		Tucker	17.15	0.0058
		MD-SL	1213.24	0.0050
		HFFRC	**10.96**	**0.0028**
7.35	7.93	CP-TPM	801.55	0.0242
		CP-NLS	812.32	0.0241
		Tucker	7.64	0.0094
		MD-SL	1028.02	**0.0066**
		HFFRC	**6.97**	0.0072

Table 2. Comparison before and after our compression on all convolutional layers

Method	Param(M)	FLOP(G)	Acc↓
VGG-16	14.99	0.628	-
HFFRC	2.04	0.079	0.0072
Resnet50	23.71	2.606	-
HFFRC	13.70	1.560	0.0068

The results show that our method can achieve 5.57× compression on parameters and 4.01× compression on FLOPs, with a negligible drop on accuracy (0.0028). In the case of higher compression ratio, despite the performance degradation, the accuracy reduction (0.0072) is acceptable compared to the compression ratio 7.35×. The number of parameters and FLOPs before and after our compression on all convolutional layers are compared in Table 2. We can see that in the case of not much performance degradation, the number of parameters and FLOPs are much less than that in the original network. For CP-TPM and CP-NLS, the time is more than 80 times of our method, and the accuracy is lower. For MD-SL, although it can get better accuracy results, it takes a long consuming time. Both the time and accuracy of our method outperform Tucker method, which means that the hierarchical strategy with random Tucker decomposition is better than Tucker. In general, experimental results show that our method can achieve less performance degradation, while greatly reducing the time complexity.

3.5 Experiments on Resnet-50

Resnet-50 is an efficient neural network, which has been widely used in various applications. We use a more challenging classification dataset, CIFAR-100 to test it. Similarly, we first train a Resnet-50 model from scratch to obtain the baseline, which has an accuracy of 0.7820. Then decomposition and fine-tuning for 100 epochs are implemented on it. On account of MD-SL is not tested on Resnet in its work, we did not compare with it. We adjust the rank of CP-TPM, CP-NLS, Tucker and the proposed HFFRC to achieve almost the same compression rate of parameters and FLOPs (CRP is 1.73 and CRF is 1.67). From Table 3, we can see that our method can achieve comparable accuracy with CP-TPM, CP-NLS, but has great advantage in the evaluation criterion Time.

Table 3. Result comparison on Resnet-50 with CIFAR-100

Method	Time(s)	Acc↓
CP-TPM	255.87	0.0067
CP-NLS	241.56	**0.0054**
Tucker	3.20	0.0073
HFFRC	**2.82**	0.0068

3.6 Effect of Hierarchical Decomposition on CIFAR-10

In order to better understand the proposed hierarchical decomposition, we fix the overall compression ratios as 50% and 75% and investigate the performance of the proposed scheme with different selections of intermediate tensor dimension. The hyper-parameter v defined in Sect. 3.3 is used as an indicator for dimension reduction achieved by random projection. Note that $v = 0$ indicates case of using Tucker decomposition only, while $v = 1$ stands for relying on random projection only for decomposition. The results are shown in Fig. 2. As we can see in both cases the computational time generally decreases when v increases. As we expected, the performance of proposed hierarchical decomposition is comparable, or even slightly better than using Tucker decomposition only when a relatively small v is chosen. In general, the proposed hierarchical decomposition obtains a better balance between computational time and accuracy compared to using random decomposition or Tucker decomposition only.

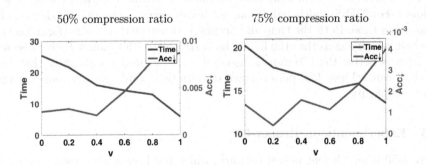

Fig. 2. Effect of hierarchical decomposition

3.7 Results on CIFAR-10 with Salt and Pepper Noises

The quality of the weights plays an important role in the whole training process. To illustrate the robustness of our method, we respectively add 20% and 30% salt and pepper noises into a pre-trained VGG-16 model. Then HFFRC and Tucker are used to compress it. The retraining process using CIFAR-10 dataset after decomposition of HFFRC and Tucker are shown in Fig. 3, the performances of these two methods both decrease with the increase of noises. However, HFFRC can remove noises to some extent from the original tensor during random projection, resulting better performance than Tucker.

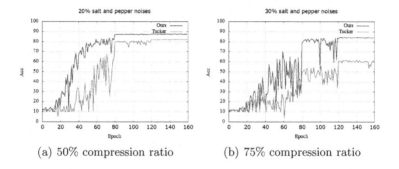

(a) 50% compression ratio   (b) 75% compression ratio

Fig. 3. Performance comparison under different percentages of noises

4 Conclusion

In order to compress the convolutional layers in deep CNNs, we have proposed a novel hierarchical scheme integrating random projection and Tucker decomposition. Our method enables to compress the large number of parameters in the network while maintaining the performance of CNNs, such that the compressed network can easily be implemented on resource-limited devices. Extensive experiments on popular CNNs for classification showed that the proposed HFFRC can get similar level of accuracy under larger compression ratio, while it achieved better balancing between performance and computational efficiency compared to random projection or Tucker decomposition only.

Acknowledgements. This work was supported in part by the National Natural Science Foundation of China under Grant 61732011 and Grant 61702358, in part by the Beijing Natural Science Foundation under Grant Z180006, in part by the Key Scientific and Technological Support Project of Tianjin Key Research and Development Program under Grant 18YFZCGX00390, and in part by the Tianjin Science and Technology Plan Project under Grant 19ZXZNGX00050.

References

1. Astrid, M., Lee, S.I.: CP-decomposition with tensor power method for convolutional neural networks compression. In: 2017 IEEE International Conference on Big Data and Smart Computing, pp. 115–118. IEEE (2017). https://doi.org/10.1109/BIGCOMP.2017.7881725
2. Ba, J., Caruana, R.: Do deep nets really need to be deep? In: Advances in Neural Information Processing Systems, pp. 2654–2662 (2014)
3. Balevi, E., Andrews, J.G.: Autoencoder-based error correction coding for one-bit quantization. IEEE Trans. Commun. (2020). https://doi.org/10.1109/tcomm.2020.2977280
4. Deng, J., Dong, W., Socher, R., Li, L.J., Li, K., Fei-Fei, L.: Imagenet: a large-scale hierarchical image database. In: 2009 IEEE Conference on Computer Vision and Pattern Recognition, pp. 248–255. IEEE (2009). https://doi.org/10.1109/CVPR.2009.5206848
5. Denil, M., Shakibi, B., Dinh, L., Ranzato, M., De Freitas, N.: Predicting parameters in deep learning. In: Advances in Neural Information Processing Systems, pp. 2148–2156 (2013). https://doi.org/10.14288/1.0165555
6. Erichson, N.B., Manohar, K., Brunton, S.L., Kutz, J.N.: Randomized CP tensor decomposition. arXiv preprint arXiv:1703.09074 (2017)
7. He, K., Zhang, X., Ren, S., Sun, J.: Deep residual learning for image recognition. In: Proceedings of the IEEE Conference on Computer Vision and Pattern Recognition, pp. 770–778 (2016). https://doi.org/10.1109/CVPR.2016.90
8. He, Y., Zhang, X., Sun, J.: Channel pruning for accelerating very deep neural networks. In: Proceedings of the IEEE International Conference on Computer Vision, pp. 1389–1397 (2017). https://doi.org/10.1109/iccv.2017.155
9. Kim, Y.D., Park, E., Yoo, S., Choi, T., Yang, L., Shin, D.: Compression of deep convolutional neural networks for fast and low power mobile applications. arXiv preprint arXiv:1511.06530 (2015)
10. Krizhevsky, A., et al.: Learning multiple layers of features from tiny images. Technical report, Citeseer (2009)
11. Lebedev, V., Ganin, Y., Rakhuba, M., Oseledets, I., Lempitsky, V.: Speeding-up convolutional neural networks using fine-tuned CP-decomposition. arXiv preprint arXiv:1412.6553 (2014)
12. Li, H., Kadav, A., Durdanovic, I., Samet, H., Graf, H.P.: Pruning filters for efficient convnets. arXiv preprint arXiv:1608.08710 (2016)
13. Liu, W., Wen, Y., Yu, Z., Li, M., Raj, B., Song, L.: Sphereface: deep hypersphere embedding for face recognition. In: Proceedings of the IEEE Conference on Computer Vision and Pattern Recognition, pp. 212–220 (2017). https://doi.org/10.1109/cvpr.2017.713
14. Luo, J.H., Wu, J., Lin, W.: Thinet: a filter level pruning method for deep neural network compression. In: Proceedings of the IEEE International Conference on Computer Vision, pp. 5058–5066 (2017). https://doi.org/10.1109/ICCV.2017.541
15. Ma, Y., et al.: A unified approximation framework for compressing and accelerating deep neural networks. In: 2019 IEEE 31st International Conference on Tools with Artificial Intelligence (ICTAI), pp. 376–383. IEEE (2019). https://doi.org/10.1109/ICTAI.2019.00060
16. Minster, R., Saibaba, A.K., Kilmer, M.E.: Randomized algorithms for low-rank tensor decompositions in the tucker format. SIAM J. Math. Data Sci. 2(1), 189–215 (2020). https://doi.org/10.1137/19m1261043

17. Molchanov, P., Mallya, A., Tyree, S., Frosio, I., Kautz, J.: Importance estimation for neural network pruning. In: Proceedings of the IEEE Conference on Computer Vision and Pattern Recognition, pp. 11264–11272 (2019). https://doi.org/10.1109/CVPR.2019.01152

18. Nakajima, S., Sugiyama, M., Babacan, S.D., Tomioka, R.: Global analytic solution of fully-observed variational bayesian matrix factorization. J. Mach. Learn. Res. **14**, 1–37 (2013). https://doi.org/10.1016/j.imavis.2012.11.001

19. Redmon, J., Farhadi, A.: Yolov3: an incremental improvement. arXiv preprint arXiv:1804.02767 (2018)

20. Sandler, M., Howard, A., Zhu, M., Zhmoginov, A., Chen, L.C.: Mobilenetv 2: inverted residuals and linear bottlenecks. In: Proceedings of the IEEE Conference on Computer Vision and Pattern Recognition, pp. 4510–4520 (2018). https://doi.org/10.1109/CVPR.2018.00474

21. Simonyan, K., Zisserman, A.: Very deep convolutional networks for large-scale image recognition. arXiv preprint arXiv:1409.1556 (2014)

22. Tan, M., Le, Q.V.: Efficientnet: rethinking model scaling for convolutional neural networks. arXiv preprint arXiv:1905.11946 (2019)

23. Tjandra, A., Sakti, S., Nakamura, S.: Compressing recurrent neural network with tensor train. In: 2017 International Joint Conference on Neural Networks, pp. 4451–4458. IEEE (2017). https://doi.org/10.1109/ijcnn.2017.7966420

24. Wang, F., et al.: Residual attention network for image classification. In: Proceedings of the IEEE Conference on Computer Vision and Pattern Recognition, pp. 3156–3164 (2017). https://doi.org/10.1109/CVPR.2017.683

25. Wang, K., Liu, Z., Lin, Y., Lin, J., Han, S.: Haq: hardware-aware automated quantization with mixed precision. In: Proceedings of the IEEE Conference on Computer Vision and Pattern Recognition, pp. 8612–8620 (2019). https://doi.org/10.1109/CVPR.2019.00881

26. Wang, W., Sun, Y., Eriksson, B., Wang, W., Aggarwal, V.: Wide compression: tensor ring nets. In: Proceedings of the IEEE Conference on Computer Vision and Pattern Recognition, pp. 9329–9338 (2018). https://doi.org/10.1109/cvpr.2018.00972

27. Wang, Y., Tung, H.Y., Smola, A.J., Anandkumar, A.: Fast and guaranteed tensor decomposition via sketching. In: Advances in Neural Information Processing Systems, pp. 991–999 (2015)

28. Ye, J., et al.: Learning compact recurrent neural networks with block-term tensor decomposition. In: Proceedings of the IEEE Conference on Computer Vision and Pattern Recognition, pp. 9378–9387 (2018). https://doi.org/10.1109/cvpr.2018.00977

29. Yuan, L., Li, C., Cao, J., Zhao, Q.: Randomized tensor ring decomposition and its application to large-scale data reconstruction. In: IEEE International Conference on Acoustics, Speech and Signal Processing, pp. 2127–2131 (2019). https://doi.org/10.1109/ICASSP.2019.8682197

30. Zhou, G., Cichocki, A., Xie, S.: Decomposition of big tensors with low multilinear rank. arXiv preprint arXiv:1412.1885 (2014)

Model Compression II

Pruning Artificial Neural Networks: A Way to Find Well-Generalizing, High-Entropy Sharp Minima

Enzo Tartaglione$^{(\boxtimes)}$, Andrea Bragagnolo, and Marco Grangetto

Computer Science Department, University of Torino, 10149 Turin, TO, Italy
{enzo.tartaglione,andrea.bragagnolo}@unito.it

Abstract. Recently, a race towards the simplification of deep networks has begun, showing that it is effectively possible to reduce the size of these models with minimal or no performance loss. However, there is a general lack in understanding why these pruning strategies are effective. In this work, we are going to compare and analyze pruned solutions with two different pruning approaches, one-shot and gradual, showing the higher effectiveness of the latter. In particular, we find that gradual pruning allows access to narrow, well-generalizing minima, which are typically ignored when using one-shot approaches. In this work we also propose PSP-entropy, a measure to understand how a given neuron correlates to some specific learned classes. Interestingly, we observe that the features extracted by iteratively-pruned models are less correlated to specific classes, potentially making these models a better fit in transfer learning approaches.

Keywords: Pruning · Sharp minima · Entropy · Post synaptic potential · Deep learning

1 Introduction

Artificial neural networks (ANNs) are nowadays one of the most studied algorithm used to solve a huge variety of tasks. Their success comes from their ability to learn from examples, not requiring any specific expertise and using very general learning strategies. The use of GPUs (and, recently, TPUs) for training ANNs gave a decisive kick to their large-scale deploy.

However, many deep models share a common obstacle: the large number of parameters, which allows their successful training [1,4], determines in turn a large number of operations at inference time, preventing efficient deployment to mobile and cheap embedded devices.

In order to address this problem, a number of approaches have been proposed, like defining new, more efficient models [10]. Recently, a race to shrink the size of these ANN models has begun: the so-called *pruning strategies* are indeed able to remove (or *prune*) non-relevant parameters from pre-trained models, reducing

© Springer Nature Switzerland AG 2020
I. Farkaš et al. (Eds.): ICANN 2020, LNCS 12397, pp. 67–78, 2020.
https://doi.org/10.1007/978-3-030-61616-8_6

the size of the ANN model, yet keeping a high generalization capability. On this topic, a very large amount of strategies have been proposed [6,14,19,21] from which we can identify two main classes:

- one-shot strategies: parameters are pruned using very fast, greedy approaches;
- gradual strategies: slower, potentially they can achieve higher *compression rates* (or in other words, they promise to prune more parameters at the cost of higher computational complexity).

In such a rush, however, an effort into a deeper understanding on potential properties of such sparse architectures has been mostly set aside: is there a specific reason for which we are able to prune many parameters with minimal or no generalization loss? Are one-shot strategies enough to match gradual pruning approaches? Is there any hidden property behind these sparse architectures?

In this work, we first compare one-shot pruning strategies to their gradual counterparts, investigating the benefits of having a much more computationally-intensive sparsifying strategy. Then, we shine a light on some local properties of minima achieved using the two different pruning strategies and finally, we propose *PSP-entropy*, a measure on the state of ReLU-activated neurons, to be used as an analysis tool to get a better understanding for the obtained sparse ANN models.

The rest of this paper is organized as follows. Section 2 reviews the importance of network pruning and the most relevant literature. Next, in Sect. 3 we discuss the relevant literature around local properties of minima for ANN models. Then, in Sect. 4 we propose PSP-entropy, a metric to measure how much a neuron specializes in identifying features belonging to a sub-set of classes learned at training time. Section 5 provides our findings on the properties for sparse architectures and finally, in Sect. 6, we draw the conclusions and identify further directions for future research.

2   State of the Art Pruning Techniques

In the literature it is possible to find a large number of pruning approaches, some old-fashioned [12] and others more recent [9,13,17]. Among the latter, many sub-categories can be identified. Ullrich et al. introduce what they call *soft weight sharing*, through which is possible to introduce redundancy in the network and reduce the amount of stored parameters [23]. Other approaches are based on parameters regularization and pruning: for example, Louizos et al. use an L_0 proxy regularization; Tartaglione et al., instead, define the importance of a parameter via a sensitivity measure used as regularization [21]. Other approaches are dropout-based, like *sparse variational dropout*, proposed by Molchanov et al. leveraging on a Bayesian interpretation of Gaussian dropout and promoting sparsity in the ANN model [17].

Overall, as stated in Sect. 1, most of the proposed pruning techniques can be divided in two macro classes. The first is defined by approaches based on *gradual pruning* [15,19,25], in which the network is, at the same time, trained and pruned following some heuristic approach, spanning a large number of pruning iterations. One among these, showing the best performances, is LOBSTER, where parameters are gradually pruned according to their local contribution to the loss [19]. The second class, instead, includes all the techniques based on *one-shot pruning* [6,9,16]: here the pruning procedure consists of three stages:

1. a large, over-parametrized network is normally trained to completion;
2. the network is then pruned using some kind of heuristic (e.g. magnitude thresholding) to satisfaction (the percentage of remaining parameters is typically an hyper-parameter);
3. the pruned model is further fine-tuned to recover the accuracy lost due to the pruning stage.

A recent work by Frankle and Carbin [6] proposed the *lottery ticket hypothesis*, which is having a large impact on the research community. They claim that from an ANN, early in the training, it is possible to extract a sparse sub-network on a one-shot fashion: such sparse network, when trained, can match the accuracy of the original model. In a follow-up, Renda et al. propose a retraining approach that replaces the fine-tuning step with *weight rewinding*: after pruning, the remaining parameters are reset to their initial values and the pruned network is trained again. They also argue that using the initial weights values is fundamental to achieve competitive performance, which is degraded when starting from a random initialization [18].

On the other hand, Liu et al. show that, even when retraining a pruned sub-network using a new random initialization, they are able to reach an accuracy level comparable to its dense counterpart; challenging one of the conjectures proposed alongside the lottery ticket hypothesis [14].

3   Local Properties of Minima

In the previous section we have explored some of the most relevant pruning strategies. All of them rely on state-of-the-art optimization strategies: applying very simple optimizing heuristics to minimize the loss function, like for example SGD [2,26], it is nowadays possible to succeed in training ANNs on huge datasets. These problems are typically over-parametrized, and the dimensionality of the deep model trained can be efficiently reduced with almost no performance loss [21]. Furthermore, minimizing non-convex objective functions is typically supposed to make the trained architecture stuck into local minima. However, the empirical evidence shows that something else is happening under the hood: understanding it is in general of interest in order to improve the learning strategies.

Goodfellow et al. observed there is essentially no loss barrier between a generic random initialization for the ANN model and the final configuration [8]. Such a phenomena has also been observed on larger architectures by Draxler et al. [5]. These works lay as basis for the "lottery ticket hypothesis" papers. However, a secondary yet relevant observation in [8] stated that there is a loss barrier between different ANN configurations showing similar generalization capabilities. Later, it was shown that typically a low loss path between well-generalizing solutions to the same learning problem can be found [20]. From this brief discussion it is evident that a general approach on how to better characterize such minima has yet to be found.

Keskar et al. showed why we should prefer small batch methods to large batch ones: they correlate the stochasticity introduced by small-batch methods to the sharpness of the reached minimum [11]. In general, they observe that the larger the batch, the sharper the reached minimum. Even more interestingly, they observe that the sharper the minimum, the worse the generalization of the ANN model. In general, there are many works supporting the hypothesis that flat minima generalize well, and this has been also the strength for a significant part of the current research [3,11]. However, in general this does not necessarily mean that no sharp minimum generalizes well, as we will see in Subsect. 5.2.

4 Towards a Deeper Understanding: An Entropy-Based Approach

In this section we propose PSP-entropy, a metric to evaluate the dependence of the output for a given neuron in the ANN model to the target classification task. The proposed measure will allow us to better understand the effect of pruning.

4.1 Post-synaptic Potential

Let us define the output of the given i-th neuron at the l-th layer as

$$y_{l,i} = \varphi\left[f(\mathbf{y}_{l-1}, \theta_{l,i})\right] \tag{1}$$

where $\mathbf{y}_{l-1}$ is the input of such neuron, $\theta_{l,i}$ are the parameters associated to it, $f(\cdot)$ is some affine function and $\varphi(\cdot)$ is the activation function, we can define its *post-synaptic potential* (PSP) [22] as

$$z_{l,i} = f(\mathbf{y}_{l-1}, \theta_{l,i}) \tag{2}$$

Typically, deep models are ReLU-activated: here on, let us consider the activation function for all the neurons in hidden layers as $\varphi(\cdot) = \text{ReLU}(\cdot)$. Under such assumption it is straightforward to identify two distinct regions for the neuron activation:

- $z_{l,i} \leq 0$: the output of the neuron will be exactly zero $\forall z_{l,i} \leq 0$;
- $z_{l,i} > 0$: there is a linear dependence of the output to $z_{l,i}$.

Hence, let us define

$$\varphi'(z) = \begin{cases} 0 & z \leq 0 \\ 1 & z > 0 \end{cases} \tag{3}$$

Intuitively, we understand that if two neurons belonging to the same layer, for the same input, share the same $\varphi'(z)$, then they are linearly-mappable to one equivalent neuron:

- $z_{l,i} \leq 0$, $z_{l,j} \leq 0$: one of them can be simply removed;
- $z_{l,i} > 0$, $z_{l,j} > 0$: they are equivalent to a linear combination of them.

In this work we are not interested in using this approach towards structured pruning: in the next section we are going to formulate a metric to evaluate the degree of disorder in the post synaptic potentials. The aim of such measure will be to have an analytical tool to give us a broader understanding on the behavior of the neurons in sparse architectures.

4.2   PSP-Entropy for ReLU-Activated Neurons

In the previous section we have recalled the concept of post-synaptic potential. Some interesting concepts have been also introduced for ReLU-activated networks: we can use its value to approach the problem of *binning* the state of a neuron, according to $\varphi'(z_{l,i})$. Hence, we can construct a binary random process that we can rank according to its entropy. To this end, let us assume we set as input of our ANN model two different patterns, $\mu_{c,1}$ and $\mu_{c,2}$, belonging to the same class c (for those inputs, we aim at having the same target at the output of the ANN model). Let us consider the PSP $z_{l,i}$ (where l is an hidden layer):

- if $\varphi'(z_{l,i}|\mu_{c,1}) = \varphi'(z_{l,i}|\mu_{c,2})$ we can say there is *low PSP entropy*;
- if $\varphi'(z_{l,i}|\mu_{c,1}) \neq \varphi'(z_{l,i}|\mu_{c,2})$ we can say there is *high PSP entropy*.

We can model an entropy measure for PSP:

$$H(z_{l,i}|c) = - \sum_{t=\{0,1\}} p\left[\varphi'(z_{l,i}) = t|c\right] \cdot \log_2 \left\{p\left[\varphi'(z_{l,i}) = t|c\right]\right\} \tag{4}$$

where $p[\varphi'(z_{l,i}) = t|c]$ is the probability $\varphi'(z_{l,i}) = t$ when presented an input belonging to the c-th class. Since we typically aim at solving a multi-class problem, we can model an overall entropy for the neuron as

$$H(z_{l,i}) = \sum_c H(z_{l,i}|c) \tag{5}$$

It is very important to separate the contributions of the entropy according to the c-th target class since we expect the neurons to catch relevant features being highly-correlated to the target classes. Equation (5) provides us very important information towards this end: the lower its value the more it specializes for some specific classes.

The formulation in (5) is very general and it can be easily extended to higher-order entropy, i.e. entropy of sets of neurons whose state correlates for the same classes. Now we are ready to use this metrics to shed further light to the findings in Sect. 5.

5 Experiments

For our test, we have decided to compare the state-of-the-art one-shot pruning proposed by Frankle and Carbin [6] to one of the top-performing gradual pruning strategies, LOBSTER [19]. Towards this end, we first obtain a sparse network model using LOBSTER; the non-pruned parameters are then re-initialized to their original values, according to the lottery ticket hypothesis [6]. Our purpose here is to determine whether the lottery ticket hypothesis applies also to the sparse models obtained using high-performing gradual pruning strategies.

As a second experiment, we want to test the effects of different, random initialization while keeping the achieved sparse architecture. According to Liu et al., this should lead to similar results to those obtained with the original initialization [14]. Towards this end, we tried 10 different new starting configurations. As a last experiment, we want to assess how important is the structure originating from the pruning algorithm in reaching competitive performances after re-initialization: for this purpose, we randomly define a new pruned architecture with the same number of pruned parameters as those found via LOBSTER. Also in this case, 10 different structures have been tested.

We decided to experiment with different architectures and datasets commonly employed in the relevant literature: LeNet-300 and LeNet-5-caffe trained on MNIST, LeNet-5-caffe trained on Fashion-MNIST [24] and ResNet-32 trained on CIFAR-10.[1] For all our trainings we used the SGD optimization method with standard hyper-parameters and data augmentation, as defined in the papers of the different compared techniques [6,14,19].

5.1 One-Shot vs Gradual Pruning

In Fig. 1 we show, for different percentages of pruned parameters, a comparison between the test accuracy of models pruned using the LOBSTER technique and the models retrained following the approaches we previously defined.

We can clearly identify a low compression rate regime in which the re-initialized model is able to recover the original accuracy, validating the lottery ticket hypothesis. On the other hand, when the compression rate rises (for example when we remove more than 95% of the LeNet-300 model's parameters, as observed in Fig. 1a), the re-training approach strives in achieving low classification errors.

As one might expect, other combinations of dataset and models might react differently. For example, LeNet-300 is no longer able to reproduce the original performance when composed of less then 5% of the original parameters. On the other hand, LeNet-5, when applied on MNIST, is able to achieve an accuracy of around 99.20% even when 98% of its parameters are pruned away (Fig. 1b). This does not happen when applied on a more complex dataset like Fashion-MNIST, where removing 80% of the parameters already leads to performance degradation

---

[1] https://github.com/akamaster/pytorch_resnet_cifar10

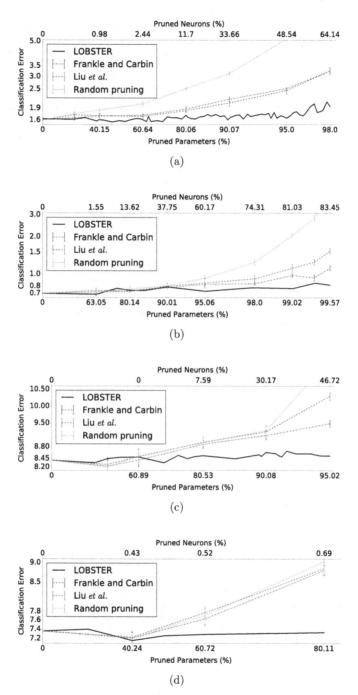

Fig. 1. Test set error for different compression rates: LeNet-300 trained on MNIST (a), LeNet-5 trained on MNIST (b), LeNet-5 trained on Fashion-MNIST (c) and ResNet-32 trained on CIFAR-10 (d).

(Fig. 1c). Such a gap becomes extremely evident when we re-initialize an even more complex architecture like ResNet-32 trained on CIFAR-10 (Fig. 1d).

From the reported results, we observe that the original initialization is not always important: the error gap between a randomly initialized model and a model using the original weights' values is minor, with the latter being slightly better. Furthermore, they both fail in recovering the performance for high compression rates.

5.2   Sharp Minima Can Also Generalize Well

In order to study the sharpness of local minima, let us focus, for example, on the results obtained on LeNet-5 trained on MNIST. We choose to focus our attention on this particular ANN model since, according to the state-of-the-art and coherently to our findings, we observe the lowest performance gap between gradual and one-shot pruning (as depicted in Fig. 1b); hence, it is a more challenging scenario to observe qualitative differences between the two approaches. However, we remark that all the observations for such a case apply also to the other architectures/datasets explored in Subsect. 5.1.

In order to obtain the maps in Fig. 2, we follow the approach proposed by [8] and we plot the loss for the ANN configurations between two reference ones: in our, case, we compare a solution found with gradual pruning (G) and one-shot (1-S). Then, we take a random orthogonal direction to generate a 2D map. Figure 2a shows the loss on the training set between iterative and one-shot pruning for the highest compression rate (99.57% of pruned parameters as shown in Fig. 1b). According to our previous findings, we see that iterative pruning lies in a lower loss region. Here, we show also the plot of the top-5 Hessian eigenvalues (all positive), in Fig. 2b, using the efficient approach proposed in [7]. Very

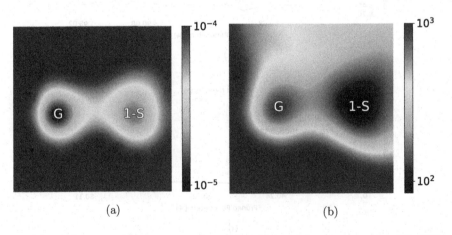

(a)   (b)

Fig. 2. Results of LeNet-5 trained on MNIST with the highest compression (99.57%): (a) plots the loss in the training set and (b) plots the magnitude of the top-5 largest hessian eigenvalues. G is the solution found with gradual learning while 1-S is the best one-shot solution (Frankle and Carbin).

interestingly, we observe that the solution proposed by iterative pruning lies in a narrower minimum than the one found using the one-shot strategy, despite generalizing slightly better. With this, we do not claim that narrower minima generalize well: gradual pruning strategies enable access to a *subset of well-generalizing narrow minima*, showing that not all the narrow minima generalize worse than the wide ones. This finding raises warnings against second order optimization, which might favor the research of flatter, wider minima, ignoring well-generalizing narrow minima. These non-trivial solutions are naturally found using gradual pruning which cannot be found using one-shot approaches, which on the contrary focus their effort on larger minima. In general, the sharpness of these minima explains why, for high compression rates, re-training strategies fail in recovering the performance, considering that it is in general harder to access this class of minima.

5.3 Study on the Post Synaptic Potential

In Subsect. 5.2 we have observed that, as a result, iterative strategies focus on well-generalizing sharp minima. Is there something else yet to say about those?

Let us inspect the average magnitude values of the PSPs for the different found solutions: towards this end, we could plot the average of their L2 norm values (z^2). As a first finding, gradually-pruned architectures naturally have lower PSP L2-norm values, as we observe in Fig. 3. None of the used pruning strategies explicitly minimize the term in z^2: they naturally drive the learning towards such regions. However, the solution showing better generalization capabilities shows lower z^2 values. Of course, there are regions with even lower z^2 values; however, according to Fig. 2a, they should be excluded since they correspond to high-loss values (not all the low z^2 regions are low-loss). If we look at the PSP-entropy formulated in (5), we observe something interesting: gradual and one-shot pruning show comparable first-order entropies, as shown in Fig. 4a.[2] It is interesting to see that there are also lower entropy regions which

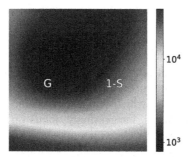

Fig. 3. L2 norm of PSP values for LeNet-5 trained on MNIST with 99.57% of pruned parameters.

---

[2] The source code for PSP-entropy is available at https://github.com/EIDOSlab/PSP-entropy.git.

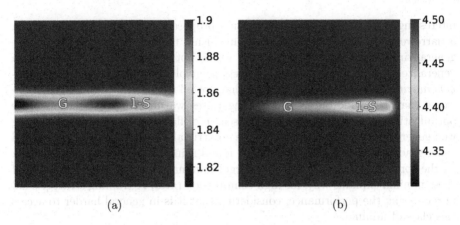

(a)   (b)

Fig. 4. Results on LeNet-5 trained on MNIST with 99.57% of pruned parameters. (a) plots the first order PSP-entropy, while (b) shows the second-order PSP entropy.

however correspond to higher loss values, according to Fig. 2a. When we move to higher-order entropies, something even more interesting happens: gradual pruning shows higher entropy than one-shot, as depicted in Fig. 4b (displaying the second order entropy). In such a case, having a lower entropy means having more groups of neurons specializing to specific patterns which correlate to the target class; on the contrary, having higher entropy yet showing better generalization performance results in having more general features, more agnostic towards a specific class, which still allow a correct classification performed by the output layer. This counter-intuitive finding has potentially-huge applications in transfer learning and domain adaptation, where it is critical to extract more general features, not very specific to the originally-trained problem.

6   Conclusion

In this work we have compared one-shot and gradual pruning on different state-of-the-art architectures and datasets. In particular, we have focused our attention in understanding potential differences and limits of both approaches towards achieving sparsity in ANN models.

We have observed that one-shot strategies are very efficient to achieve moderate sparsity at a lower computational cost. However, there is a limit to the maximum achievable sparsity, which can be overcome using gradual pruning. The highly-sparse architectures, interestingly, focus on a subset of sharp minima which are able to generalize well, which pose some questions to the potential sub-optimality of second-order optimization in such scenarios. This explains why we observe that one-shot strategies fail in recovering the performance for high compression rates. More importantly, we have observed, contrarily to what it could be expected, that highly-sparse gradually-pruned architectures are able to extract general features non-strictly correlated to the trained classes, making them unexpectedly, potentially, a good match for transfer-learning scenarios.

Future works include a quantitative study on transfer-learning for sparse architectures and PSP-entropy maximization-based learning.

References

1. Ba, J., Caruana, R.: Do deep nets really need to be deep? In: Advances in Neural Information Processing Systems, pp. 2654–2662 (2014)
2. Bottou, L.: Large-scale machine learning with stochastic gradient descent. In: Lechevallier, Y., Saporta, G. (eds.) Proceedings of COMPSTAT'2010, pp. 177–186. Springer, Heidelberg (2010). https://doi.org/10.1007/978-3-7908-2604-3_16
3. Chaudhari, P., Choromanska, A., et al.: Entropy-SGD: biasing gradient descentinto wide valleys. In: International Conference on Learning Representations, ICLR 2017 (2017)
4. Denton, E.L., Zaremba, W., Bruna, J., LeCun, Y., Fergus, R.: Exploiting linear structure within convolutional networks for efficient evaluation. In: Advances in Neural Information Processing Systems, pp. 1269–1277 (2014)
5. Draxler, F., Veschgini, K., Salmhofer, M., Hamprecht, F.: Essentially no barriers in neural network energy landscape. In: Dy, J., Krause, A. (eds.) Proceedings of the 35th International Conference on Machine Learning. Proceedings of Machine Learning Research, PMLR, Stockholmsmässan, Stockholm Sweden, 10–15 July 2018, vol. 80, pp. 1309–1318 (2018). http://proceedings.mlr.press/v80/draxler18a.html
6. Frankle, J., Carbin, M.: The lottery ticket hypothesis: finding sparse, trainable neural networks (2019). https://www.scopus.com/inward/record.uri?eid=2-s2.0-85069453436&partnerID=40&md5=fd1a2b2384d79f66a49cc838a76343d3
7. Golmant, N., Yao, Z., Gholami, A., Mahoney, M., Gonzalez, J.: pytorch-hessian-eigentings: efficient PyTorch Hessian eigendecomposition (October 2018). https://github.com/noahgolmant/pytorch-hessian-eigenthings
8. Goodfellow, I.J., Vinyals, O., Saxe, A.M.: Qualitatively characterizing neural network optimization problems. In: International Conference on Learning Representations, ICLR 2015 (2015)
9. Han, S., Pool, J., Tran, J., Dally, W.: Learning both weights and connections for efficient neural network. In: Advances in Neural Information Processing Systems, pp. 1135–1143 (2015)
10. Howard, A.G., et al.: MobileNets: Efficient convolutional neural networks for mobile vision applications. arXiv preprint arXiv:1704.04861 (2017)
11. Keskar, N.S., Mudigere, D., Nocedal, J., Smelyanskiy, M., Tang, P.T.P.: On large-batch training for deep learning: Generalization gap and sharp minima. arXiv preprint arXiv:1609.04836 (2016)
12. LeCun, Y., Denker, J.S., Solla, S.A.: Optimal brain damage. In: Advances in Neural Information Processing Systems, pp. 598–605 (1990)
13. Li, H., Kadav, A., Durdanovic, I., Samet, H., Graf, H.P.: Pruning filters for efficient ConvNets. In: International Conference on Learning Representations, ICLR 2017 (2017)
14. Liu, Z., Sun, M., Zhou, T., Huang, G., Darrell, T.: Rethinking the value of network pruning. In: International Conference on Learning Representations, ICLR 2019 (2019)
15. Louizos, C., Welling, M., Kingma, D.P.: Learning sparse neural networks through l_0 regularization. In: International Conference on Learning Representations, ICLR 2018 (2018)

16. Luo, J.H., Wu, J., Lin, W.: ThiNet: a filter level pruning method for deep neural network compression. In: Proceedings of the IEEE International Conference on Computer Vision, pp. 5058–5066 (2017)
17. Molchanov, D., Ashukha, A., Vetrov, D.: Variational dropout sparsifies deep neural networks. In: 34th International Conference on Machine Learning, ICML 2017, vol. 5, pp. 3854–3863 (2017). https://www.scopus.com/inward/record.uri?eid=2-s2.0-85048506601&partnerID=40&md5=c352a4786ef977ccea7e397bd7469f14
18. Renda, A., Frankle, J., Carbin, M.: Comparing rewinding and fine-tuning in neural network pruning. arXiv preprint arXiv:2003.02389 (2020)
19. Tartaglione, E., Bragagnolo, A., Grangetto, M., Lepsøy, S.: Loss-based sensitivity regularization: towards deep sparse neural networks (2020). https://iris.unito.it/retrieve/handle/2318/1737767/608158/ICML20.pdf
20. Tartaglione, E., Grangetto, M.: Take a ramble into solution spaces for classification problems in neural networks. In: Ricci, E., Rota Bulò, S., Snoek, C., Lanz, O., Messelodi, S., Sebe, N. (eds.) ICIAP 2019. LNCS, vol. 11751, pp. 345–355. Springer, Cham (2019). https://doi.org/10.1007/978-3-030-30642-7_31
21. Tartaglione, E., Lepsøy, S., Fiandrotti, A., Francini, G.: Learning sparse neural networks via sensitivity-driven regularization. In: Advances in Neural Information Processing Systems, pp. 3878–3888 (2018)
22. Tartaglione, E., Perlo, D., Grangetto, M.: Post-synaptic potential regularization has potential. In: Tetko, I.V., Kůrková, V., Karpov, P., Theis, F. (eds.) ICANN 2019. LNCS, vol. 11728, pp. 187–200. Springer, Cham (2019). https://doi.org/10.1007/978-3-030-30484-3_16
23. Ullrich, K., Welling, M., Meeds, E.: Soft weight-sharing for neural network compression. In: 5th International Conference on Learning Representations - Conference Track Proceedings, ICLR 2017 (2019). https://www.scopus.com/inward/record.uri?eid=2-s2.0-85071003624&partnerID=40&md5=dc00c36113f775ff4a6978b86543814d
24. Xiao, H., Rasul, K., Vollgraf, R.: Fashion-MNIST: a novel image dataset for benchmarking machine learning algorithms. CoRR abs/1708.07747 (2017). http://arxiv.org/abs/1708.07747
25. Zhu, M., Gupta, S.: To prune, or not to prune: exploring the efficacy of pruning for model compression. In: International Conference on Learning Representations, ICLR 2018 (2018)
26. Zinkevich, M., Weimer, M., Li, L., Smola, A.J.: Parallelized stochastic gradient descent. In: Advances in Neural Information Processing Systems, pp. 2595–2603 (2010)

Log-Nets: Logarithmic Feature-Product Layers Yield More Compact Networks

Philipp Grüning$^{(\boxtimes)}$, Thomas Martinetz, and Erhardt Barth

Institute for Neuro- and Bioinformatics, University of Lübeck, Lübeck, Germany
gruening@inb.uni-luebeck.de
https://www.inb.uni-luebeck.de

Abstract. We introduce Logarithm-Networks (Log-Nets), a novel bio-inspired type of network architecture based on logarithms of feature maps followed by convolutions. Log-Nets are capable of surpassing the performance of traditional convolutional neural networks (CNNs) while using fewer parameters. Performance is evaluated on the Cifar-10 and ImageNet benchmarks.

Keywords: Bio-inspired networks · Deep Learning · Efficient coding · Compact networks

1 Introduction

While deep CNNs have been very successful with many different and increasingly deep architectures, ideas of how to move forward beyond just 'deeper and larger' are rather rare. While some hope to make progress by adopting a more formal approach, e.g., Bayesian networks [22], others are convinced that progress can be made by further adopting principles from human vision [7,20]. We share this latter view, especially when it is supported by formal considerations, and propose a novel bio-inspired principle for the design of deep networks.

Current CNNs are based on models of visual processing in the primary visual cortex (V1), where the visual input is represented by orientation-selective simple- and complex cells. In applications, the corresponding linear filters are either handcrafted, learned in an unsupervised way, or learned by backpropagation. From a signal-processing perspective, such representations make sense, because they reduce the entropy of natural images, an insight that has led to the most advanced image-compression standards.

However, some cells in V1, and the majority of cells in the Brodmann area 18 (V2), are end-stopped in addition to being orientation sensitive [10]. While most cells do not respond to regions of uniform intensity (0D regions), end-stopped cells also suppress straight patterns (1D regions). In a world of horizontal rectangles, some simple cells would represent the horizontal edges, others the vertical edges and end-stopped cells would represent only the corners. From a signal-processing perspective, end-stopping makes sense because 2D regions

© Springer Nature Switzerland AG 2020
I. Farkaš et al. (Eds.): ICANN 2020, LNCS 12397, pp. 79–91, 2020.
https://doi.org/10.1007/978-3-030-61616-8_7

(such as corners and junctions) are the most informative regions, and it has been proven that 2D regions are unique [17]. Moreover, 2D regions are rare in natural images, which makes end-stopped representations both sparse and unique, i.e., efficient [1,34].

A major problem with models of end-stopped cells is that they have to be non-linear [33]. The standard model of an end-stopped cell is based on products of simple cell outputs, with simple cells of different orientations [33]. From this, we draw inspiration for the here proposed architecture. Such product terms are required for end-stopping but could be generated by non-linearities other than explicit multiplications. We will consider an alternative in this paper. In more general terms, what is needed are AND type combinations of simple cell responses. In our above example world of rectangles, the corner would be defined by "horizontal edge AND vertical edge," or, in general, the presence of more than just one orientation.

Multiple layers of convolutions and ReLUs could, in principle, also generate product terms (AND combinations) required for end-stopping, but one would assume that this would require a larger network with more parameters compared to a network that allows for direct AND combinations. The results presented in this paper offer indirect proof that this might be the case since the Log-Nets tend to be more compact at equal, or even better, performance compared to ReLU-Nets.

The more general view is that large networks could, in principle, learn to approximate complex non-linear functions, but if useful non-linearities are enabled directly, the network will be more efficient, i.e., more compact.

1.1 Related Work

The desire to find more efficient networks that keep their outstanding performance while being able to fit on small, e.g. mobile, devices has led to an active research field in architecture and layer-design. Well known networks such as the MobileNetV2 [21] employ depthwise separable convolutions and inverted residual layers. These types of layers are also used in the EfficientNet [26], which refutes the notion that a higher number of parameters is the best way to increase generalization [9], by combining network depth, width, and resolution in a smart way. This architecture, and many similar ones, are inspired by several search algorithms [25,28,31] that attempt to find a good trade-off between efficiency and accuracy. Another approach to gain efficiency is the reduction of parameters by pruning the weights of the network [5,16]. Moreover, changing the structure of network connections and using grouped convolutions can yield more efficient networks [35].

Only a few research papers exist that investigate second or higher-order non-linearities in CNNs. Zoumpourlis et al. [36] use quadratic terms in the first layer of a wide-ResNet [32] and can improve the test error compared to the original wide-ResNet. This is inspired by Volterra's Theory [29], and multiplicative interactions are supposed to provide selectivity and invariance. Further use of quadratic features can be found in earlier works such as those of Bergstra et al. [2], and Berkes and Wiscott [3]. Poon and Domingos use sum-product networks for image completion [19].

In this work, we explore the potential of product terms to model non-linearities that are more complex than simple ReLUs. We assume that these product terms may enable the network to learn more efficient representations.

2 Methods

The above AND combinations needed for efficient coding can be typically modeled via product terms. However, computing products of inputs in a neural network architecture can be a challenging task, since those operations are computationally expensive and move away from the typical regime of convolution and pooling layers. Yet, it is possible to compute products across various inputs implicitly, while still using convolutions: this is done by computing the logarithm of the signal, applying convolution in this *log-space* and re-transforming the signal back via exponentiation. We designed a layer that implements this idea, that we refer to as *Log-Layer*. This layer is incorporated in a larger architecture that we denote *Log-Block*. The term *Log-Net* refers to the overall architecture using mainly Log-Blocks.

2.1 Convolution in Log-Space

Our approach makes use of the rule of logarithmic addition:

$$\alpha log(x) + \beta log(y) = log(x^\alpha \cdot y^\beta). \tag{1}$$

Accordingly, if we compute the logarithm of an input tensor $x \in \mathbb{R}^{h \times w \times d_0}$ and convolve with a kernel $w \in \mathbb{R}^{k \times k \times d_0 \times d_1}$, we essentially compute a large product:

$$log(y_{(i,j,m)}) = \sum_{a,b,n} log(x_{(i+a,j+b,n)}) w_{(a,b,n,m)} \tag{2}$$

$$= log(\prod_{a,b,n} x_{(i+a,j+b,n)}^{w_{(a,b,n,m)}}); \tag{3}$$

with $a, b \in \{-k/2, \ldots, k/2\}$, $i \in \{1, \ldots, h\}$, $j \in \{1, \ldots, w\}$, $n \in \{1, \ldots, d_0\}$, and $m \in \{1, \ldots, d_1\}$.

This results in a second-order layer with many degrees of freedom. Figure 1 illustrates how particular pixel positions can suppress each other, a mechanism that can only be realized by convolution layers if a certain width and depth is given. Figure 2 shows how a 1×1 convolution in log-space can implement an orientation-selective operation: such a layer can efficiently model neurons that only produce a large output if all filters in a certain subset (e.g. specific different orientations) are activated, which is an essential requirement for end-stopped cells.

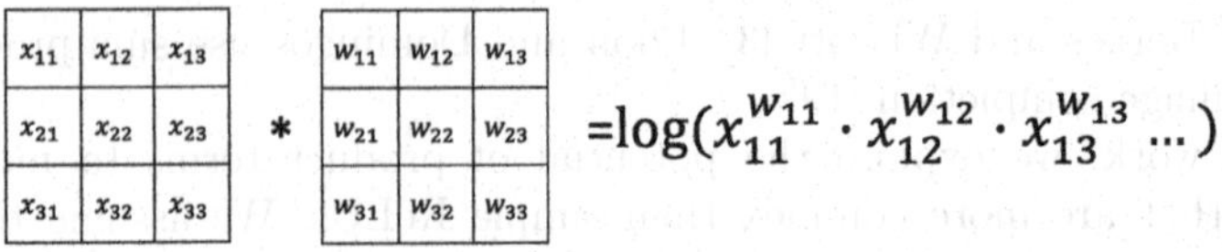

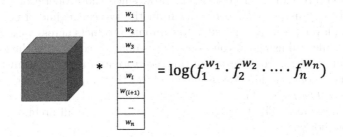

Fig. 1. Log-Filter Example 1: multiplicative combination of pixel values. The input signal, $(x_{11}, x_{12}, \ldots)$ is first transformed into log-space. Subsequently, it is convolved with the filter on the right. Using the rule in Eq. 1, a large product is computed, which can be transformed back to the original input-space by exponentiation. This approach allows for highly non-linear activations and sparse signals since, for example, single pixel values can compress the entire output.

Fig. 2. Log-Filter Example 2: the selection of feature maps can be realized via 1×1 convolutions. As in the example of Fig. 1, the input tensor (blue cube) of shape $h \times w \times n$ is transformed to the log-space and back. Using a 1×1 convolution in the log-space yields a product of exponentially-weighted feature maps $f_i^{w_i}, i = 1, \ldots, n$. This structure can model a neuron that is only excited if multiple orientations are activated, a typical property of end-stopped cells. (Color figure online)

2.2   Log-Layers

Using highly non-linear terms such as products, logarithms, and exponentials with gradient descent and backpropagation is not an easy task. The unconstrained multiplication of terms can yield very large activations or signals that are multiplied by zeros. Thus, leading to either exploding or vanishing gradients and unstable training behavior. Regarding the products of features, note that we are not interested in the actual value of the multiplication, but rather we want to employ the selective property of the operation. Accordingly, we rely heavily on the use of scaling operations, such as Batch Normalization, as well as ReLUs and offsets to avoid unstable training.

The left structure in Fig. 3 presents the processing chain of a Log-Layer: first of all, all negative values are discarded by a ReLU, and an offset of .5 is added to the signal. This is, of course, due to the fact that the logarithm of negative values is not defined, and the output reaches negative infinity when the input converges to 0. We use the base-2 logarithm, and with this signal cutoff, the resulting output is in $[-1, \infty]$. As a next step, the actual convolution is computed. Hereafter, we apply Batch Normalization to limit the output magnitude since exponentiation is subsequently applied. Here, we do not train any additional re-scaling weights that are commonly used in Batch Normalization. Hence, the output has zero mean and a standard deviation of 1. After exponentiation, we apply another Batch Normalization. This time, the motivation is similar to the use of Batch Normalization in typical CNNs, e.g., reducing the covariate shift (for more information see Ioffe and Szegedy [12]).

2.3 Log-Block: Convolution Blocks with Subsequent Log-Layers

When using a Log-Net, we focused on the orientation-selective aspect of Log-Layers. To model this, Log-Layers need to be combined with typical *convolution blocks* (convolution, Batch Normalization, and ReLU). We use Log-Layers with a kernel size of 1 that model the multiplication of feature maps, as described in the example of Fig. 2. Note that, the suppression according to pixel positions (see example in Fig. 1) is not modeled here. However, we evaluated 3×3 Log-Layers with depthwise separable convolutions in a hybrid architecture with the experiment described in Subsect. 3.3.

2.4 Shallow Architectures

As we have seen, AND operations on oriented filters are beneficial for efficient coding. In principle, such AND operations could result from repeated convolutions followed by ReLU non-linearities but would lead to wider and deeper networks. A network with Log-Layers could implement the required non-linearities with fewer layers and would result in shallower networks. However, we need to ensure that the architecture's size of the receptive field, which mainly depends on the number of convolutions and pooling operations, is large enough. Otherwise, a shallow Log-Net may not be able to cover the necessary context to encode the image effectively. To this end, we use a multi-scale structure that is shown in Fig. 3 on the right. The input is processed in parallel by two convolution blocks that differ in the pooling layer's position. The left block resembles the typical CNN architecture, where the convolution block is applied first, and then the output is pooled. On the right side, the pooling operation is done before the convolution. Essentially, the right path of the architecture allows for increasing the receptive field by the factor of 2. After applying the Log-Layers, both paths are again mixed via a 1×1 convolution.

3 Experiments

To test the assumption that fewer, highly non-linear layers can replace deeper networks based on simple convolutions, we conducted several experiments on the ImageNet [4] and Cifar-10 [13] benchmarks. Additionally, we evaluated a hybrid network in Subsect. 3.3 that combines Log-Blocks in the early layers and uses convolutions in later stages of the architecture.

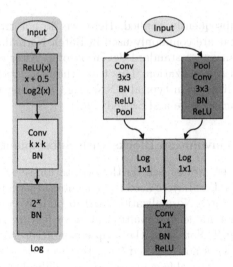

Fig. 3. Structure of the Log-Layer (left) and Log-Block (right): left side: before computing a convolution with kernel size k, we transform the input to the log2-space, making sure that the minimum value is not below -1. Subsequently, the convolution is computed. Via Batch Normalization (BN), the output is normalized to zero mean and a standard deviation of 1, since large values can otherwise increase quickly in the exponentiation of the signal (2^x). Hereafter, we employ another Batch Normalization at the end of the layer output, as it is commonly used in Deep Learning architectures. Right side: in order to increase the receptive field quickly, we use a parallel structure, where one path is directly downscaled by max-pooling. The paths are later concatenated and linearly mixed by a 1×1 convolution block.

3.1 Log-Layers on ImageNet

Compared to a regular convolution, Log-Layers do not increase the number of computations by much, and we assume that shallower networks are feasible. Accordingly, we tested a lightweight architecture on ImageNet. We used the proposed parallel architecture (see Subsect. 2.4) to increase the receptive fields in the network. The network consisted of 4 Log-Blocks (see Subsect. 2.1). The input dimensions of each block and layer are presented in Table 1. The initial feature dimension was 64. We trained the network for 100 epochs using the Adam optimizer and a batch size of 256. Every 33 steps, we reduced the initial learning rate of 0.001 by a factor of 10. Furthermore, we used a weight decay of 0.00001. We adopted the data augmentation code from the fast.ai Github repository [8].

3.2 Log-Layers on Cifar-10

We evaluated similar architectures on Cifar-10, each architecture being parametrized by the number of layers and the initial feature dimension (e.g., the Network in Table 1 has 4 layers with an initial feature dimension of 64). We tested a model with 2 layers and an initial feature dimension of 128, comprising

Table 1. Architecture of the Log-Net trained on ImageNet: the model contained 4 Log-Blocks (see Fig. 3 on the right) and a starting feature dimension of 64. Within the Log-Block, max-pooling was applied, and after each Log-Block, the number of features was doubled. We used a 1×1 convolution block to map the output of the 4th block to the feature dimension 256. Subsequently, global average pooling was applied, followed by a linear layer.

Input	Layer/block
$224^2 \times 3$	Log-Block
$112^2 \times 64$	Log-Block
$56^2 \times 128$	Log-Block
$28^2 \times 256$	Log-Block
$14^2 \times 512$	Log-Block
$7^2 \times 1024$	Conv-block 1×1
$7^2 \times 256$	Glob-avg-pool
256	Linear
1000	Softmax

500k trainable parameters; 3 models with 3 layers and an initial feature dimension of 32, 64, and 128, with 162k, 570k and 2.1M parameters, respectively; and we tested a model with 4 layers and an initial feature dimension of 64, with 2.2M parameters. Each model was trained for 120 epochs with the Adam optimizer and a batch size of 128. Each 40th step, the initial learning rate of 0.001 was reduced by a factor of 10. We compared our results to the ALL-CNN-C net from Springenberg et al. [23] and a smaller version of the EfficientNet [15,26]. For each model, we evaluated the minimal test error over all training epochs.

3.3 Layer Substitution

In the above-described experiments, we propose architectures that almost entirely consist of Log-Layers. However, the biological motivation of using product terms to code end-stopped signals mainly justifies using those multiplications in the early stages of the visual processing chain. Thus, in later, more semantic stages, this design principles may be less helpful. Accordingly, we tested whether a hybrid model with product terms in rather early layers followed by convolution blocks could be a better approach. The starting point of our hybrid models is based on the SimpleNet [6] architecture. We substituted its first block with different alternatives. Here, the term first block denotes all convolutions located before the first max-pooling layer. Its input dimension was $32 \times 32 \times 3$ and it returned a tensor with the shape $32 \times 32 \times 128$. We compared models with four different first blocks:

0) The original block. Containing 4 convolutions (and ReLu and Batch Normalization) with output dimensions 64, 128, 128, and 128, respectively.

1) The *Log-Block-Depthwise* contained a 1×1 convolution that expanded the 3-dimensional input to 18 dimensions, followed by a depthwise separable convolution with kernel size 3 yielding a tensor with 18 feature maps. After Batch Normalization, a Log-Layer ($k = 3$) plus ReLU was applied with output dimension 128. This design choice was inspired by the inverted residual layer presented in the MobileNetV2 [21].

2) We used a single Convolution Block (input dimension 3 to output dimension 128).

3) We used 2 Convolution Blocks in sequence, with input dimension 3 to output dimension 128 for the first block and input dimension 128 to output dimension 128 for the second block.

We compared the average test errors over 4 runs with different starting seeds (different initial weights and batch-order during training). The experiments were conducted on the same machine equipped with a GeForce RTX 2080 GPU, using PyTorch [18].

4   Results

On ImageNet, our network yielded a training accuracy of 0.63 and a validation accuracy of 0.66 with 2.59M parameters.

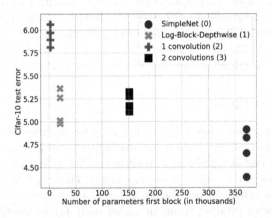

Fig. 4. Results for substituting the first block of the SimpleNet: x-axis shows the number of parameters of the modified first block. For each network, 4 runs were performed by varying the randomly drawn weights and the batch order. Results for the original SimpleNet architecture are shown on the right (blue dots). The Log-Block-Depthwise (green crosses) achieved comparable results while reducing the number of parameters by a factor of 17. Simple convolutions (red pluses) yielded inferior results with an only slightly lower number of parameters. The mean error of Double Convolutions (5.34, black squares) was slightly worse than the mean error of the Log-Block-Depthwise (5.25) while having a higher number of parameters. (Color figure online)

Table 2. Results on Cifar-10. We compared several Log-Nets, varying in size, and being parametrized by the number of layers and the first feature dimension. We compared these models to other state-of-the-art networks. For the ALL-CNN-C, we could not reproduce the results presented in the paper (9.08 vs. 13.06).

# layers	f-dim	# parameters (k)	Type	Error (%)
3	32	161	Log-Net	12.89
2	128	491	Log-Net	11.25
3	64	570	Log-Net	10.53
N/A	N/A	1369	ALL-CNN-C [23]	9.08
N/A	N/A	1369	ALL-CNN-C (ours)	13.06
3	128	2133	Log-Net	8.78
4	64	2211	Log-Net	10.03
N/A	N/A	2912	Efficient-net	9.17

The Cifar-10 results are listed in Table 2. Here, the EfficientNet based model achieved a test error of 9.17 with 2.91M parameters. The All-CNN-C network we trained achieved a test error of 13.06 with 1.36M parameters. With a test error of 8.78, the Log-Net with 3 Layers, an initial feature dimension of 128, and 2.1M parameters yielded the best result in this comparison.

The results of the substitution experiments (Subsect. 3.3) are given in Table 3. In addition to the mean test error, the mean training and inference time for one epoch on the training- and test set respectively are presented. The plot in Fig. 4 shows the Cifar-10 test error of each run on the y-axis and the parameter sizes of the different first blocks on the x-axis. With a test error of 5.25, our proposed Log-Block-Depthwise outperforms blocks consisting of simple convolutions. The original SimpleNet architecture yielded the best result with 4.79.

Table 3. Results for SimpleNet substitution: test error mean values and standard deviation of 4 runs varying by the random seed. Furthermore, the mean ($\pm$ standard deviation) training and inference time for one epoch on the training- and test set respectively are shown.

Name	Block #parameters	Mean $\pm$ Std	Mean train time (sec)	Mean val time (sec)
SimpleNet (0)	371k	4.79 $\pm$ 0.21	24.71 $\pm$ 0.16	2.09 $\pm$ 0.14
Log-Block-Depthwise (1)	21k	5.25 $\pm$ 0.21	14.70 $\pm$ 0.22	1.44 $\pm$ 0.14
1 convolution (2)	3k	6.10 $\pm$ 0.10	12.71 $\pm$ 0.18	1.37 $\pm$ 0.09
2 convolutions (3)	151k	5.34 $\pm$ 0.06	17.30 $\pm$ 0.13	1.72 $\pm$ 0.01

5   Discussion

We introduced Log-Nets as a new, bio-inspired design principle for deep networks. The main building block of the network, the Log-Layer, transforms its
input into the log-space, applies convolution, and transforms the output back
by exponentiation. In this way, the product terms required for efficient coding
(end-stopped cells) are computed implicitly. Our results show that Log-Nets
often perform better than the state of the art, especially when performance is
related to the size of the network, and more shallow and compact architectures
are possible.

Despite being a demanding dataset, shallow Log-Nets can yield good results
on ImageNet. However, the rather high training error indicates that our model
cannot completely learn based on the entire training set. Nevertheless, the top-1
accuracy of 66% is better than the accuracy of the AlexNet [14] (62.5%) while
the number of parameters of the Log-Net is smaller by a factor of 23. However, our results obtained on ImageNet may be further improved, since we did
not yet perform any optimization of the hyperparameters. Figure 5 lists the top
contenders on the ImageNet benchmark with less than 5M parameters, showing
that our model reaches a viable result.

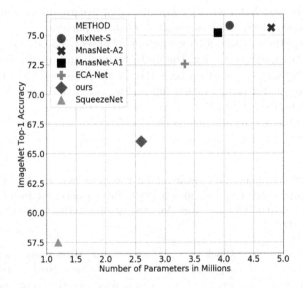

Fig. 5. ImageNet top-1 accuracy of state-of-the-art networks with less than 5 million
parameters [11, 25, 27, 30] (results taken from [24]).

On the Cifar-10 benchmark, our Log-Nets yielded better results when compared to two state-of-the-art models. With almost 800 thousand parameters less
(Log-Net with 3 layers and an initial feature dimension of 128), we outperformed
the tested EfficientNet architecture (8.76 vs. 9.17). Apparently, Log-Nets do need

a certain minimum depth, which is not surprising since a certain receptive field size needs to be achieved. Interestingly though, a wide network seems to be better than a deep network. While our networks did outperform other architectures of similar size, larger networks still achieved even better results on Cifar-10, for example, the SimpleNet (see Table 3). We were not able to reproduce the results of the ALL-CNN-C architecture, where the authors claim a test error of 9.08. Our architectures outperformed the ALL-CNN-C (13.06) as evaluated by us. In the EfficientNet paper, the test error of 1.9 was obtained by using a network pretrained on ImageNet. We did not use pretraining here and compared Log-Nets with the performance of the EfficientNet without pretraining. Note that, networks that perform very well on ImageNet will not necessarily perform equally well on the Cifar-10 dataset when trained from scratch.

We have shown that the complexity of the SimpleNet architecture can be further reduced without significant loss in performance, by replacing the first block of four convolutions with our Log-Block-Depthwise (see Table 3). Here, the Log-Net with Log-Layers performed very well although the number of parameters was reduced by a factor of 17. Furthermore, as shown in Fig. 4, the test errors of the Log-Nets were comparable to the errors of the SimpleNet while being obtained with smaller networks. Remarkably, simply reducing the number of convolutions did not yield a similar effect. Furthermore, our hybrid network based on the Log-Block-Depthwise significantly decreased the training- and test time. Hence, the Log-Block is a simple yet effective plug-and-play module that can be used to shrink any type of well-performing CNN. Accordingly, a viable alternative architecture can be built and tested quickly for time-critical and memory-critical applications. In conclusion, we presented a Log-Net architecture and a hybrid architecture, both employing Log-Layers. Our experiments demonstrate the benefits of this novel bio-inspired design principle: due to the more shallow architecture of the Log-Nets, fewer parameters are needed to obtain results comparable to the state of the art on Cifar-10 and ImageNet. When using implicit multiplications in the log space, the number of parameters in the first layer can be further reduced substantially with only a minimal loss in performance. We argue that ideas from biological vision are still a viable source of inspiration that, in our case, leads to smaller, more efficient networks. However, further research is needed to explore and evaluate the vast space of possible designs and configurations, which may lead to further future improvements.

References

1. Barth, E., Watson, A.B.: A geometric framework for nonlinear visual coding. Opt. Express **7**(4), 155–165 (2000)
2. Bergstra, J., Desjardins, G., Lamblin, P., Bengio, Y.: Quadratic polynomials learn better image features. Technical report, 1337 (2009)
3. Berkes, P., Wiskott, L.: On the analysis and interpretation of inhomogeneous quadratic forms as receptive fields. Neural Comput. **18**, 1868–1895 (2006)
4. Deng, J., Dong, W., Socher, R., Li, L.J., Li, K., Fei-Fei, L.: ImageNet: a large-scale hierarchical image database. In: CVPR 2009 (2009)

5. Frankle, J., Carbin, M.: The lottery ticket hypothesis: Finding sparse, trainable neural networks. arXiv preprint arXiv:1803.03635 (2018)
6. HasanPour, S.H., Rouhani, M., Fayyaz, M., Sabokrou, M.: Lets keep it simple, using simple architectures to outperform deeper and more complex architectures. arXiv preprint arXiv:1608.06037 (2016)
7. Hinton, G.F.: A parallel computation that assigns canonical object-based frames of reference. In: Proceedings of the 7th International Joint Conference on Artificial Intelligence, vol. 2, pp. 683–685 (1981)
8. Howard, J., et al.: fast.ai (2018). https://github.com/fastai/imagenet-fast/blob/master/imagenet_nv/fastai_imagenet.py
9. Huang, Y., et al.: GPipe: efficient training of giant neural networks using pipeline parallelism. In: Advances in Neural Information Processing Systems, pp. 103–112 (2019)
10. Hubel, D.H., Wiesel, T.N.: Receptive fields and functional architecture in two nonstriate visual areas (18 and 19) of the cat. J. Neurophysiol. 28(2), 229–289 (1965)
11. Iandola, F.N., Han, S., Moskewicz, M.W., Ashraf, K., Dally, W.J., Keutzer, K.: SqueezeNet: AlexNet-level accuracy with 50x fewer parameters and <0.5 mb model size. arXiv preprint arXiv:1602.07360 (2016)
12. Ioffe, S., Szegedy, C.: Batch normalization: accelerating deep network training by reducing internal covariate shift. In: International Conference on Machine Learning, pp. 448–456 (2015)
13. Krizhevsky, A., Nair, V., Hinton, G.: CIFAR-10 (Canadian Institute for Advanced Research). http://www.cs.toronto.edu/~kriz/cifar.html
14. Krizhevsky, A., Sutskever, I., Hinton, G.E.: ImageNet classification with deep convolutional neural networks. In: Advances in Neural Information Processing Systems, pp. 1097–1105 (2012)
15. kuangliu: pytorch-cifar (2020). https://github.com/kuangliu/pytorch-cifar/blob/master/models/efficientnet.py
16. Li, H., Kadav, A., Durdanovic, I., Samet, H., Graf, H.P.: Pruning filters for efficient convnets. arXiv preprint arXiv:1608.08710 (2016)
17. Mota, C., Barth, E.: On the uniqueness of curvature features. In: Baratoff, G., Neumann, H. (eds.) Dynamische Perzeption. Proceedings in Artificial Intelligence, Köln, vol. 9, pp. 175–178 (2000)
18. Paszke, A., et al.: PyTorch: an imperative style, high-performance deep learning library. In: Wallach, H., Larochelle, H., Beygelzimer, A., d'Alché-Buc, F., Fox, E., Garnett, R. (eds.) Advances in Neural Information Processing Systems, vol. 32, pp. 8024–8035. Curran Associates, Inc. (2019)
19. Poon, H., Domingos, P.: Sum-product networks: a new deep architecture. In: 2011 IEEE International Conference on Computer Vision Workshops (ICCV Workshops), pp. 689–690. IEEE (2011)
20. Sabour, S., Frosst, N., Hinton, G.E.: Dynamic routing between capsules. In: Advances in Neural Information Processing Systems, pp. 3856–3866 (2017)
21. Sandler, M., Howard, A., Zhu, M., Zhmoginov, A., Chen, L.C.: MobileNetV2: inverted residuals and linear bottlenecks. In: Proceedings of the IEEE Conference on Computer Vision and Pattern Recognition, pp. 4510–4520 (2018)
22. Shridhar, K., Laumann, F., Liwicki, M.: A comprehensive guide to Bayesian convolutional neural network with variational inference. arXiv preprint arXiv:1901.02731 (2019)
23. Springenberg, J., Dosovitskiy, A., Brox, T., Riedmiller, M.: Striving for simplicity: the all convolutional net. In: ICLR (workshop track) (2015)

24. Stojnic, R., Taylor, R.: ImageNet leaderboard (2020). https://paperswithcode.com/sota/image-classification-on-imagenet
25. Tan, M., et al.: MnasNet: platform-aware neural architecture search for mobile. In: Proceedings of the IEEE Conference on Computer Vision and Pattern Recognition, pp. 2820–2828 (2019)
26. Tan, M., Le, Q.: EfficientNet: rethinking model scaling for convolutional neural networks. In: International Conference on Machine Learning, pp. 6105–6114 (2019)
27. Tan, M., Le, Q.V.: MixConv: Mixed depthwise convolutional kernels. CoRR, abs/1907.09595 (2019)
28. Veniat, T., Denoyer, L.: Learning time/memory-efficient deep architectures with budgeted super networks. In: Proceedings of the IEEE Conference on Computer Vision and Pattern Recognition, pp. 3492–3500 (2018)
29. Volterra, V.: Theory of Functionals and of Integral and Integro-differential Equations. Dover Publications, Mineola, New York (1959)
30. Wang, Q., Wu, B., Zhu, P., Li, P., Zuo, W., Hu, Q.: ECA-Net: Efficient channel attention for deep convolutional neural networks. arXiv preprint arXiv:1910.03151 (2019)
31. Xie, L., Yuille, A.: Genetic CNN. In: Proceedings of the IEEE International Conference on Computer Vision, pp. 1379–1388 (2017)
32. Zagoruyko, S., Komodakis, N.: Wide residual networks. arXiv preprint arXiv:1605.07146 (2016)
33. Zetzsche, C., Barth, E.: Fundamental limits of linear filters in the visual processing of two-dimensional signals. Vis. Res. **30**, 1111–1117 (1990)
34. Zetzsche, C., Barth, E., Wegmann, B.: The importance of intrinsically two-dimensional image features in biological vision and picture coding. In: Watson, A.B. (ed.) Digital Images and Human Vision, pp. 109–38. MIT Press (October 1993)
35. Zhang, X., Zhou, X., Lin, M., Sun, J.: ShuffleNet: an extremely efficient convolutional neural network for mobile devices. In: Proceedings of the IEEE Conference on Computer Vision and Pattern Recognition, pp. 6848–6856 (2018)
36. Zoumpourlis, G., Doumanoglou, A., Vretos, N., Daras, P.: Non-linear convolution filters for CVV-based learning. In: Proceedings of the IEEE International Conference on Computer Vision, pp. 4761–4769 (2017)

Tuning Deep Neural Network's Hyperparameters Constrained to Deployability on Tiny Systems

Riccardo Perego[1] , Antonio Candelieri[2]([✉]) , Francesco Archetti[1] ,
and Danilo Pau[3]

[1] Department of Computer Science, Systems and Communication,
University of Milano-Bicocca, 20126 Milan, Italy
{riccardo.perego,francesco.archetti}@unimib.it
[2] Department of Economics, Management and Statistics,
University of Milano-Bicocca, 20126 Milan, Italy
antonio.candelieri@unimib.it
[3] System Research and Applications - STMicroelectronics, Agrate, Italy
danilo.pau@st.com

Abstract. Deep Neural Networks are increasingly deployed on tiny systems such as microcontrollers or embedded systems. Notwithstanding the recent success of Deep Learning, also enabled by the availability of Automated Machine Learning and Neural Architecture Search solutions, the computational requirements of the optimization of the structure and the hyperparameters of Deep Neural Networks usually far exceed what is available on tiny systems. Therefore, the deployability becomes critical when the learned model must be deployed on a tiny system. To overcome this critical issue, we propose a framework, based on Bayesian Optimization, to optimize the hyperparameters of a Deep Neural Network by dealing with black-box deployability constraints. Encouraging results obtained on a classification benchmark problem on a real microcontroller by STMicroelectronics are presented.

Keywords: Deep Neural Network · Hyperparameters optimization · Neural Architecture Search · Bayesian optimization

1 Introduction

In recent years Neural Architecture Search (NAS) has been gaining increasing attention in the Machine Learning (ML) community. NAS allows to generate novel Deep Neural Networks (DNNs) architectures offering better performances on many applications based on Deep Learning (DL), ranging from image/video analysis to Natural Language Processing (NLP). According to the recent literature, NAS can be implemented through different optimization strategies, such as Evolutionary Algorithms (AE) [1–4], Random Search [5], Reinforcement Learning [6–8] and Sequential Model-based Optimization (SMBO), also known as

© Springer Nature Switzerland AG 2020
I. Farkaš et al. (Eds.): ICANN 2020, LNCS 12397, pp. 92–103, 2020.
https://doi.org/10.1007/978-3-030-61616-8_8

Bayesian Optimization (BO) [9–11]. Besides, many AI companies have created and publicly shared Automated Machine Learning (AutoML) systems on cloud (e.g. Google AutoML tables[1], Amazon SageMaker[2] on AWS Cloud Computing) to make ML accessible to non-experts or to facilitate data scientists in reducing time and costs for training an accurate model given a new task [12].

It must be remarked that some recent BO works [11,13,14] represent the DNN architectures as a graph. Through this new graph representation, the BO process explores more efficiently a wider search space that includes DNN architecture with a variable number and type of layers.

Despite the amazing performances offered by the previous different strategies to search the optimal DNN architectures, in many cases the optimized DNN might require a significant amount of hardware resources [15,16]. Even more difficult, is the case when the optimized DNN is to be deployed on a *tiny* system, such as a microcontroller. This usually requires a further step: translating the DNN, which has been learned and stored in a high-level programming language, to a low-level language in order to run on the tiny systems. Therefore, the actual *deployability* of the DL model can be revealed only at the end of this translation-&-deployment step, making the deployability constraint black-box.

This paper presents how to implement a DNN's hyperparameter optimization (HPO) task under black-box deployability constraints, based on a SMBO approach dealing with black-box constraints, named SVM-CBO [17]. We have extended this framework and validated it on a classification benchmark problem on a real microcontroller by STMicroelectronics.

2   Problem Formulation

Searching for the optimal DNN architecture requires to minimize the following (black-box and expensive) loss function computed on k-fold cross validation:

$$\gamma^* = \arg\min_{\gamma \in \Gamma} \left(\frac{1}{k} \sum_{i=1}^{k} Loss(A_\gamma, D_{train}^{(i)}, D_{val}^{(i)}) \right) \tag{1}$$

Subject to:

$$c_t(\gamma) \leq t = 1, .., n_c \tag{2}$$

Where:

- A_γ is a ML algorithm with a specific hyperparameters configuration γ
- γ^* is the optimal hyperparameters configuration for A providing the lowest observed value of the validation loss
- *Loss* is the error metric to evaluate the performance of the ML algorithm with respect to a given hyperparameter configuration
- k is the number of folds of the k-fold cross-validation procedure

---

[1] https://cloud.google.com/automl-tables?hl=uk.
[2] https://aws.amazon.com/sagemaker/.

- $D_{train}^{(i)}$ and $D_{val}^{(i)}$ are, respectively, the i-th training and validation fold
- $\Gamma = \{\Gamma_1, ..., \Gamma_n\}$ is the set of hyperparameters configurations, where Γ_j represents the domain of a single hyperparameter γ_j
- c_t represents the t-th constraint that A_γ must satisfy
- n_c represents the total number of the constraints.

In this work 3 black-box constraints related to the deployability are considered. The first 2 are defined by the computational limits of the specific microcontroller used: *(i)* a maximum value for Read-Only Memory (ROM) and *(ii)* a maximum value for Random Access Memory (RAM). The third constraint is a metric named *X-Cross Accuracy*, that is a measure of the worsening in the loss function value from the original model to the translated-&-deployed one.

3   Proposed Approach SVM-CBO$_{RF}$

To solve the problem (1–2) this paper adopts a recent approach for global optimization of black-box function under black-box constraints, namely Support Vector Machine - Constrained Bayesian Optimization (SVM-CBO)[17]. The basic idea is to approximate the unknown feasible region - associated to the blackbox constraints - through a Support Vector Machine (SVM) classifier, with a radial basis function kernel [18] trained to distinguish between deployable and undeployable DNN's hyperparameters values.

Moreover, SVM-CBO can also deal with more complex problems, more specifically those settings characterized by a partially defined objective function [19]. Although it is not the case of this study, partial definition of the loss function can easily occur in ML/DL, for instance when some values of the hyperparameters lead to a crash (e.g., an out-of-memory error) and, consequently, to a premature termination of the learning task without any value of the loss function for that specific hyperparameters configuration. This issue is also known as *computability* or *trainability*: it is important to highlight that, for the application presented in this paper, *deployability* is a completely different issue. Indeed, given a hyperparameter configuration, the validation loss of the associated DNN could be *computable* but the resulting trained model could be *undeployable* on the tiny system. On the other hand, the not-computability of the loss function occurs in the case that the DNN model cannot be trained using that hyperparameters configuration: in this case, there is not any DNN model to deploy.

In a nutshell, SVM-CBO is composed of two different phases. In the first phase, the estimate of the feasible region is optimized, where the feasible region, in this work, is the portion of search space associated to hyperparameters values most probably leading to deployable DNNs models. In the second phase, a BO process is adopted, but limiting it to the estimated feasible region with the aim to optimize the loss function. A non-linear SVM classifier is used to approximate the feasible region and a probabilistic regression model, specifically a Random Forest [20], is used to approximate the objective function in the second phase of SVM-CBO. Indeed, according to the state of the art [21], RF is one of the best choices when the optimization problem is defined over a complex search space spanned by mixed and conditional variables, such as the hyperparameters of a DNN.

The new version of SVM-CBO, proposed in this paper, is named SVM-CBO$_{RF}$. We introduce some notations before the two algorithms described in Algorithms 1 and 2 for the two phases, respectively. Let $L_{1:m}$ denotes the set of hyperparameters configurations evaluated so far, that is $L_{1:m} = \{(\gamma^{(i)}, \mathcal{L}^{(i)})\}_{i=1,\ldots,m}$, with $\gamma^{(i)} \in \Gamma$ and $\mathcal{L}^{(i)}$ the associated validation losses (e.g., $\mathcal{L}^{(i)}$ is computed on a hold-out validation set or via k-fold cross validation). Furthermore, let $\Delta_{1:m}$ denotes the set storing the actual deployability of the model trained using the aforementioned hyperparameters configurations, that is $\Delta_{1:m} = \{(\gamma^{(i)}, \delta^{(i)})\}_{i=1,\ldots,m}$, with $\gamma^{(i)}$ as previously defined and $\delta^{(i)} \in \{+1, -1\}$ a label encoding the deployability or undeployability, respectively, of the model trained using the i-th hyperparameters configuration. In the case of partially defined objective functions, the original SVM-CBO [17] stores, in the first set, only the computable hyperparameters configurations, so the two sets are $L_{1:p}$ and $\Delta_{1:m}$, with $p \leq m$. Here, without any loss of generality, we consider the two sets having the same number of elements, m, and assign $\mathcal{L}^{(i)} = \emptyset$ in the case that the validation loss cannot be computed for the i-th hyperparameter configuration.

As follows, the two acquisition functions, used in the two phases of the SVM-CBO$_{RF}$ approach are presented.

3.1   Phase 1: Deployability Determination

In phase 1 of SVM-CBO$_{RF}$, the sampling of the most promising hyperparameters configuration is given by the minimization of the following acquisition function:

$$g_1(\gamma) = \left| \sum_{j=1}^{\nu} \alpha_j \delta^{(j)} k(\gamma^{(j)}, \gamma) \right| + \sum_{l=1}^{m} e^{-\frac{||\gamma^{(l)} - \gamma||^2}{2\ell^2}} \tag{3}$$

where the first addendum is the distance from the separation hypersurface defined by the SVM classifier, while the second addendum is a measure of *coverage* of the search space, depending on the m hyperparameters configurations evaluated so far. More precisely, ν and α_j are, respectively, the number of support vectors and the Lagrangian coefficients in the SVM classifier, $k(.,.)$ is the kernel function used by the SVM classifier – we suggest to use a Radial Basis Function kernel to model possible non-linear relations between the hyperparameters values and the deployability of the associated trained model. Then, ℓ is a parameter to model the coverage effect of each evaluated hyperparameters configuration: the larger ℓ the wider is the coverage associated to a hyperparameters configuration. In phase 1, the next hyperparameters configuration to evaluate is chosen by minimizing (3) on the overall search space, meaning that the next configuration must be closer to the SVM's separation hypersurface and far from previously evaluated configurations. Phase 1 is aimed at estimating the portion of search space related to hyperparameters configurations which should generate deployable DNN models. Let Ω denotes this portion of the search space which will be used in phase 2:

$$\Omega = \left\{ \gamma \in \Gamma : \sum_{j=1}^{\nu} \alpha_j \delta^{(j)} k\big(\gamma^{(j)}, \gamma\big) < 0 \right\} \tag{4}$$

Algorithm 1. Phase 1 of SVM-CBO$_{RF}$

---

input : m_0, M_1
output: L_M, Δ_M, SVM, $M_{p1} = m_0 + M_1$

initialization:
generate $\gamma^{(1)}, ..., \gamma^{(m_0)}$;
compute $\mathcal{L}^{(1)}, ..., \mathcal{L}^{(m_0)}$;
evaluate $\delta^{(1)}, ..., \delta^{(m_0)}$;

while $m < M_1$ **do**
> train an SVM classifier on $\Delta_{1:m}$;
> choose $\gamma^{(m+1)} = \min_{\gamma \in \Gamma} g_1(\gamma)$, with $g_1(\gamma)$ defined in (3);
> train and validate a DNN with $\gamma^{(m+1)}$ and compute $\mathcal{L}^{(m+1)}$;
> translate and deploy the trained DNN model to obtain $\delta^{(m+1)}$;
> update $L_{1:m+1} \leftarrow L_{1:m} \cup (\gamma^{(m+1)}, \mathcal{L}^{(m+1)})$;
> update $\Delta_{1:m+1} \leftarrow \Delta_{1:m} \cup (\gamma^{(m+1)}, \delta^{(m+1)})$;
> $m \leftarrow m + 1$;

end

3.2   Phase 2: BO Constrained to the Estimated Deployable Region

The phase 2 of SMV-CBO$_{RF}$ selects the next hyperparameters configuration to evaluate by the minimization of the following acquisition function:

$$g_2(\gamma) = \mu(\gamma) - \sqrt{\beta}\sigma(\gamma) \tag{5}$$

that is the well-known *Lower Confidence Bound* (LCB) [22], where $\mu(\gamma)$ and $\sigma(\gamma)$ are, respectively, the mean prediction and the associated uncertainty provided by a probabilistic surrogate model, and β is a parameter to manage the exploration-exploitation trade-off, for which a suitable scheduling with convergence proof is provided in [23]. The specificity of SVM-CBO, as well as SVM-CBO$_{RF}$, is that this minimization is performed only on the portion of the search space which is classified as deployable by the SVM classifier (instead of the entire search space).

4   Experimental Setting

4.1   Microcontroller STM32L476RGT6

The microcontroller device used to set up the hardware constraints is STM32L476RGT6[3] (Fig. 1) with ARM Cortex M4 80MHz, 1 Mbytes of ROM

---

[3] https://www.st.com/en/microcontrollers-microprocessors/stm32l476rg.html.

Algorithm 2. Phase 2 of SVM-CBO$_{RF}$

> **input** : M_{p1}, M_2, L_M, Δ_M, SVM
> **output:** $(\gamma^+, \mathcal{L}^+) \in L_{1:M} : \mathcal{L}^+ = \min\limits_{i=1,\dots,M}\{\mathcal{L}^{(i)}\}$ and $M = M_{p1} + M_2$
>
> **while** $m < M_2$ **do**
> > train a RF regressor on $L_{1:m}$;
> > choose $\gamma^{(m+1)} = \min\limits_{\gamma \in \Omega \subset \Gamma} g_2(\gamma)$, with $g_2(\gamma)$ as defined in (5);
> > train and validate a DNN with $\gamma^{(m+1)}$ and compute $\mathcal{L}^{(m+1)}$;
> > translate the trained DNN model and evaluate $\delta^{(m+1)}$;
> > update $L_{1:m+1} \leftarrow L_{1:m} \cup (\gamma^{(m+1)}, \mathcal{L}^{(m+1)})$;
> > update $\Delta_{1:m+1} \leftarrow \Delta_{1:m} \cup (\gamma^{(m+1)}, \delta^{(m+1)})$;
> > **if** $\delta^{(m+1)} = -1$ **then**
> > > re-train the SVM classifier on $\Delta_{1:m+1}$
> >
> > **end**
> > $m \leftarrow m + 1$;
> **end**

---

and 128 KBytes of RAM. STMicroelectronics, the manufacturer company of the adopted embedded device in the experiments, implemented a tool named STM32Cube.AI, which it creates a C-optimized version of any DNN that can be deployed on this kind of embedded devices.

Fig. 1. The Microcontroller adopted in this study

4.2 The Classification Learning Benchmark

The final aim of this study is to apply the proposed approach to optimize a Convolution Neural Network (CNN) for Human Activity Recognition (HAR) system, which also results deployable on the target microcontroller device described in the previous section. The CNN is available on a public Github repository[4]: the

---

[4] https://github.com/Shahnawax/HAR-CNN-Keras.

authors of this repository adopt, for training and testing the CNN architecture, the public human activities dataset proposed in [24] and available at the *UCI Machine Learning Repository* site under the name of *User Identification From Walking Activity Data Set*[5]. The authors of the repository divided the dataset of 24108 observations into a training set (19512 observations) and a test set (4596 observations). The dataset presents six different classes of human activities, which are: Downstairs, Jogging, Sitting, Standing, Upstairs, Walking. The observations are not well distributed among the classes: Downstairs with 9%, Jogging with 31.11%, Sitting with 5.53%, Standing with 4.59%, Upstairs with 10.96% and Walking with 38.81%. Authors of the repositorytake into account the same balance among classes to generate the test set. The CNN architecture available on the repository - the so-called baseline model - has an average accuracy of 92.09% on the test set.

Using the STM32Cube.AI tool, this CNN baseline model file (format '.h5') is reduced from its original dimension, that is 8.49 MBytes, to only 2.82 MBytes. However, the latter file dimension still does not satisfy the hardware requirements for loading and running the network on the target ST microcontroller.

4.3 Hyperparameters Optimization Setting

The search space considered in this study supports HPO for a given CNN architecture; it means that the numbers and types of layers remain the same during the whole optimization process. However, all other hyperparameters of the CNN layers are chosen via SVM-CBO$_{RF}$. Taking into account the CNN baseline architecture described in the previous section, the search space is spanned by the following hyperparameters. For convolutional layers, we considered the number of filters, the kernel size and the activation function. In addition, the pool size is considered as hyperparameter for the Max Pooling layer. Instead, for the dense

Table 1. Table reports the search space of HPO problem

Hyperparameter		Values
Conv2D	**Units**	[16, 32, 64, 128, 256]
	Activation	[ReLU, Sigmoid, SeLU, Tanh]
	Kernel Size	[1, 2]
MaxPooling	**Windows**	[1, 2]
Dropout		[0.1, 0.2, 0.3]
Dense	**Units**	[16, 32, 64, 128, 256]
	Activation	[ReLU, Sigmoid, SeLU, Tanh]
Optimizer		[Adam, SGD, RMSprop, Adagrad, Adadelta]

---

[5] http://archive.ics.uci.edu/ml/datasets/User+Identification+From+Walking+Acti vity.

layers we considered the number of units and the activation functions. Moreover, also the optimizer used to train the CNN model has been considered as hyperparameter, while its own hyperparameters, such as the *learning rate* and the *decay factor*, are fixed to the default values, as suggested by the DL library adopted, that is Keras[6]. Finally the whole search space is reported in Table 1.

Taking into account the hardware resources reported in Sect. 4.1, the constraints are represented by the amount of ROM (*leq* 128 kB) and RAM ($\leq$ 1990 kB) required for a specific CNN architecture to be saved and executed on the target microcontroller. Also another constraint is considered, which is X-Cross Accuracy measure. As previously mentioned, it is calculated by STM32Cube.AI tool and quantifies the reduction of performance (in terms of accuracy) between the high-level language trained model and the one translated to run on the target microcontroller. An X-Cross Accuracy $\geq 95\%$ is an empirical constraint suggested by STMicroelectonics. This measure significantly depends on the type of compression applied by STM32Cube.AI to translate the CNN model. Indeed, the STMicroeletronics tool is able to perform a translation of the CNN model with three increasing levels of compression factors: $\times 1$, $\times 4$, and $\times 8$. These compression factors can reduce the size of weights parameters of a model. In this study, only the compression factor $\times 1$ and $\times 4$ are adopted, because they are enough to produce a good model with reasonably hardware resources needs for the target microcontroller.

Due to randomness in the initialization of both SVM-CBO$_{RF}$ and weights of the CNN, we performed 15 different runs for each compression factor considered. The fixed budget for each experiment was 100 configurations to evaluate, where each evaluation requires, given the hyperparameters configuration, to train the CNN on the training set and validate the corresponding model on the test set. More precisely, the budget of each experiment is allocatd as follows:

- **10 initial configurations** chosen through Latin Hypercube Sampling (LHS) to initialize the SVM classifier
- **60 configurations** for the phase 1 (**Algorithm 1**)
- **30 configurations evaluations** for the phase 2 (**Algorithm 2**)

A single experiment required more than 2 h to be executed. The loss function adopted to train the CNN is the *Categorical Cross Entropy*, which is strictly connected to the Accuracy metric for the classification task type. In the next section, the performances of the optimal CNNs identified through SVM-CBO$_{RF}$ are compared against the CNN baseline, both in terms of Accuracy and hardware resources required to run them on the target microcontroller.

5   Results

Results are summarized in Table 2, comparing the optimal CNNs identified by SVM-CBO$_{RF}$ against the baseline model on Github. It is important to remark that Accuracy on the test set is the metric we have optimized, while RAM, ROM

---

[6] https://keras.io/.

and XCROSS Accuracy were used to define our deployability constraints. We have also computed MACC (Multiply-ACCumulated operations), which quantifies the logical complexity of the translated model. In this study it was just analyzed *ex-post*, as a further indicator of the CNN models complexity, in the future we plan to include it as a further constraint or objective to minimize.

As far as the compression factor ×1 is concerned, the optimal CNN models identified by SVM-CBO$_{RF}$ (over 15 different experiments) show, on average, an increase in terms of accuracy and a significant reduction in terms of required hardware resources on the target microcontroller. Also in the case of compression factor ×4, the optimal CNN models identified by SVMCBO$_{RF}$ show better performance than the baseline model. However, in this case, the reduction in terms of required hardware resources is less relevant. Anyway, this means that SVM-CBO$_{RF}$ was able to identify more accurate CNN models requiring approximately the same amount of hardware resources of the baseline model.

Applying statistical tests to analyse results in Table 2 does not provide any robust conclusion, since we should compare the baseline model against a sample of only 15 optimized models with respect to four variables together (i.e., Accuracy on test set, RAM, ROM and XCROSS Accuracy). Thus, we have reported here the most relevant descriptive statistics, that is the number of CNN models identified by SVM-CBO$_{RF}$, over 15 different runs, which are considered better than the baseline model (i.e., having higher Accuracy on test set, lower or equal RAM and ROM, and XCROSS Accuracy ≥ 95%). More precisely, we obtained: 12 better models out of 15 (80% of runs) in the case of compression factor ×1 and 9 better models out of 15 (60% of runs) in the case of compression ×4. Summarizing, one has a good chance to identify a better model within few runs of SVM-CBO$_{RF}$.

Table 2. Comparison between the baseline CNN and the optimal models identified by SVM-CBO$_{RF}$

Measures	Compression factor ×1		Compression factor ×4	
	Baseline	SVM-CBO$_{RF}$	Baseline	SVM-CBO$_{RF}$
Accuracy on test set	92.09	92.44 ± 0.64	92.07	92.93 ± 0.55
RAM	24.57	9.75 ± 5.11	24.57	15.56 ± 7.92
ROM	2955.80	688.30 ± 144.42	794.13	546.31 ± 283.34
XCROSS accuracy	100.00	100.00 ± 0.00	99.98	99.70 ± 0.53
MACC	874970	269327 ± 83895	874970	784767.33 ± 318078

In addition, Fig. 2 reports the behaviour of the Accuracy on the test set, averaged over the 15 experiments and with respect to the iterations of the optimization process. In both charts, the red dotted line represents the best average accuracy achieved at a given iteration, while the solid black lines represent the standard deviation measured over the 15 experiments. The vertical blue and green lines indicate the start of phase 1 and phase 2 of SVM-CBO$_{RF}$, respectively. When the compression factor $\times 4$ is applied, SVM-CBO$_{RF}$ efficiently explores the search space in phase 1, while in phase 2 it quickly converges to an optimal solution which is quite similar over all experiments. This behaviour could occur when an optimal solution is close to the boundary of the deployable region, a quite common situation in real-life applications where constraints limit any otherwise possible improvement of the objective function. On the contrary, when compression $\times 1$ is considered,

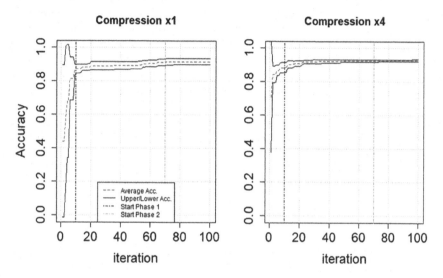

Fig. 2. Results of the average accuracy obtained from the experiments with different compression factors

6   Conclusions and Perspectives

Preliminary results of this study prove that the proposed SVM-CBO$_{RF}$, extending Bayesian Optimization to deal with black-box (deployability) constraints, is an efficient approach to search for accurate Deep Neural Networks to be run on tiny devices with limited hardware resources, such as microcontrollers.

Our idea is that the proposed constrained approach is more well suited for tiny Machine Learning applications with respect to multi-objective optimization approaches recently proposed for resource-efficient AutoML and/or NAS on large scale (e.g., cloud-based) platforms [15,16]. SVM-CBO$_{RF}$ is designed to search for the most accurate model given the hardware limitations of the tiny device, while multi-objective optimization is useful to search for a suitable trade-off between accuracy and resource-efficiency. As resulted from our experiments, the hardware resources of the tiny device limit any possible improvement in terms of accuracy for the DL model. Indeed, it is quite common, in real-life applications, that optimal solutions are close or exactly on the boundary of the region delimited by the constraints, therefore, approximating this region (i.e, phase 1 of SVM-CBO$_{RF}$) will make the constrained optimization process (i.e., phase 2 of SVM-CBO$_{RF}$) more effective and efficient than performing multi-objective optimization.

The study focused only on HPO of a given DNN architectures, this is its main limitation. Ongoing research activities are devoted to extend the approach to also include architecture search as well as to include further constraints and/or objectives, such as MACC.

Finally, it is important to remark that the proposed SVM-CBO$_{RF}$ approach does not depend on - and does not replace - any techniques for model compression or pruning. They can be in any case applied before to deploy the model identified by SVM-CBO$_{RF}$ and then verify if deployabilty constraints are satisfied. More interesting, we are planning future research activities, along with STMicroelectronics, to further extend SVM-CBO$_{RF}$ to also include the optimization of the hyperparameters related to model compression and pruning techniques.

Acknowledgements. We greatly acknowledge the DEMS Data Science Lab of the Department of Economics Management and Statistics (DEMS) for supporting this work by providing computational resources.

We want to thank STMicroelectronics company that provided us MCUs for the experiments and the valid support from its community.

References

1. Angeline, P.J., Saunders, G.M., Pollack, J.B.: An evolutionary algorithm that constructs recurrent neural networks. IEEE Trans. Neural Netw. **5**(1), 54–65 (1994)
2. Miikkulainen, R., et al.: Evolving deep neural networks. arXiv:1703.00548, March 2017
3. Suganuma, M., Shirakawa, S., Nagao, T.: A genetic programming approach to designing convolutional neural network architectures. In: Genetic and Evolutionary Computation Conference (2017)
4. Bianco, S., Buzzelli, M., Ciocca, G., Schettini, R.: Neural architecture search for image saliency fusion. Inf. Fusion **57**, 89–101 (2020)
5. Liu, H., Simonyan, K., Vinyals, O., Fernando, C., Kavukcuoglu, K.: Hierarchical representations for efficient architecture search. In: International Conference on Learning Representations (2018b)
6. Baker, B., Gupta, O., Naik, N., Raskar, R.: Designing neural network architectures using reinforcement learning. In: International Conference on Learning Representations (2017a)
7. Zhong, Z., Yan, J., Wu, W., Shao, J., Liu, C.L.: Practical block-wise neural network architecture generation. In: Proceedings of the IEEE Conference on Computer Vision and Pattern Recognition, pp. 2423–2432 (2018a)
8. Zoph, B., Le, Q.V.: Neural architecture search with reinforcement learning. In: International Conference on Learning Representations (2017)
9. Jin, H., Song, Q., Hu, X.: Auto-keras: an efficient neural architecture search system. In: Proceedings of the 25th ACM SIGKDD International Conference on Knowledge Discovery & Data Mining, pp. 1946–1956, July 2019

10. Zela, A., Klein, A., Falkner, S., Hutter, F.: Towards automated deep learning: efficient joint neural architecture and hyperparameter search. In: ICML 2018 Workshop on AutoML (AutoML 2018) (2018)
11. Kandasamy, K., Neiswanger, W., Schneider, J., Poczos, B., Xing, E.: Neural architecture search with Bayesian optimisation and optimal transport. arXiv:1802.07191, February 2018
12. Archetti, F., Candelieri, A.: Bayesian Optimization and Data Science. SO. Springer, Cham (2019). https://doi.org/10.1007/978-3-030-24494-1
13. Oh, C., Tomczak, J., Gavves, E., Welling, M.: Combinatorial Bayesian optimization using the graph cartesian product. In: Advances in Neural Information Processing Systems, pp. 2910–2920 (2019)
14. Baptista, R., Poloczek, M.: Bayesian optimization of combinatorial structures. arXiv preprint arXiv:1806.08838 (2018)
15. Elsken, T., Metzen, J. H., Hutter, F.: Efficient multi-objective neural architecture search via lamarckian evolution. arXiv preprint arXiv:1804.09081 (2018)
16. Dong, J.-D., Cheng, A.-C., Juan, D.-C., Wei, W., Sun, M.: DPP-Net: device-aware progressive search for pareto-optimal neural architectures. In: Ferrari, V., Hebert, M., Sminchisescu, C., Weiss, Y. (eds.) ECCV 2018. LNCS, vol. 11215, pp. 540–555. Springer, Cham (2018). https://doi.org/10.1007/978-3-030-01252-6_32
17. Antonio, C.: Sequential model based optimization of partially defined functions under unknown constraints. J. Global Optim. 1–23 (2019). https://doi.org/10.1007/s10898-019-00860-4
18. Saunders, C., Stitson, M.O., Weston, J., Bottou, L., Smola, A.: Support vector machine-reference manual (1998)
19. Candelieri, A., Galuzzi, B., Giordani, I., Perego, R., Archetti, F.: Optimizing partially defined black-box functions under unknown constraints via sequential model based optimization: an application to pump scheduling optimization in water distribution networks. In: Matsatsinis, N.F., Marinakis, Y., Pardalos, P. (eds.) LION 2019. LNCS, vol. 11968, pp. 77–93. Springer, Cham (2020). https://doi.org/10.1007/978-3-030-38629-0_7
20. Geurts, P., Ernst, D., Wehenkel, L.: Extremely randomized trees. Mach. Learn. **63**(1), 3–42 (2006)
21. Hutter, F., Hoos, H.H., Leyton-Brown, K.: Sequential model-based optimization for general algorithm configuration. In: Coello, C.A.C. (ed.) LION 2011. LNCS, vol. 6683, pp. 507–523. Springer, Heidelberg (2011). https://doi.org/10.1007/978-3-642-25566-3_40
22. Srinivas, N., Krause, A., Kakade, S.M., Seeger, M.: Gaussian process optimization in the bandit setting: no regret and experimental design. arXiv preprint arXiv:0912.3995 (2009)
23. Srinivas, N., Krause, A., Kakade, S.M., Seeger, M.W.: Information-theoretic regret bounds for Gaussian process optimization in the bandit setting. IEEE Trans. Inf. Theor. **58**(5), 3250–3265 (2012)
24. Casale, P., Pujol, O., Radeva, P.: Personalization and user verification in wearable systems using biometric walking patterns. Pers. Ubiquit. Comput. **16**(5), 563–580 (2012)

Obstacles to Depth Compression
of Neural Networks

Will Burstein and John Wilmes[✉]

Brandeis University, Waltham, MA, USA
{wburstein,wilmes}@brandeis.edu

Abstract. Massive neural network models are often preferred over smaller models for their more favorable optimization landscapes during training. However, since the cost of evaluating a model grows with the size, it is desirable to obtain an equivalent compressed neural network model before deploying it for prediction. The best-studied tools for compressing neural networks obtain models with broadly similar architectures, including the depth of the model. No guarantees have been available for obtaining compressed models with substantially reduced depth. In this paper, we present fundamental obstacles to any algorithm achieving depth compression of neural networks. In particular, we show that depth compression is as hard as learning the input distribution, ruling out guarantees for most existing approaches. Furthermore, even when the input distribution is of a known, simple form, we show that there are no *local* algorithms for depth compression.

1 Introduction

Perhaps the clearest trend of the past decade of deep learning has been the ever-increasing size of neural network (NN) models, fueled by advances in hardware acceleration, larger datasets, and improved optimization techniques.

It may be practical to train models on datacenter scale computational resources, but it is still desirable to obtain models that can be deployed to more modest hardware for inference tasks. In particular, for inference tasks on individual user data where low latency is important, deploying models onto smartphones or similarly constrained hardware may be necessary. Even in cases where inference tasks can be performed within data centers, the cost of evaluating a model, including its environmental impact, may still be significant if many real-time inference requests must be satisfied.

While small models are desirable at the time of inference, there are equally good reasons at training time for the rapid growth in scale of neural network models. Although depth-3 neural networks are already "universal models" in terms of their representational power, much deeper networks are empirically observed to have desirable optimization characteristics. In practice, good generalization performance is often easier to elicit from massive, very deep neural network models.

© Springer Nature Switzerland AG 2020
I. Farkaš et al. (Eds.): ICANN 2020, LNCS 12397, pp. 104–115, 2020.
https://doi.org/10.1007/978-3-030-61616-8_9

In order to combine the benefits of massively overparameterized models at training time with the computational efficiency of smaller models for inference, it is therefore desirable to convert large models to smaller ones before deployment. This is the task of model compression.

A classic approach to model compression task is pruning, i.e., zeroing out entries in the weight matrices of a NN. Some of the earliest work on this idea used information about second derivatives of the NN to find appropriate weights to trim [17,23]. A simpler idea is to simply drop all entries in the weight matrices below some threshold, and then retrain the network (keeping all dropped entries zero) [16]. A more sophisticated approach is to incorporate the pruning into the training [34]. A second but conceptually related approach to model compression is via low-rank factorization. Following the observation that many neural networks trained on real-world data have approximately low-rank weight matrices [8], several works have sought to compress NNs by replacing weight matrices with low-rank approximations [9,19,32].

Both the pruning and low-rank factorization approaches preserve the overall network architecture while reducing the complexity of the weight matrices, as measured in terms of either their sparsity or rank. These techniques can therefore reduce the number of parameters in the model, providing some improvement in the cost of inference, but they leave the depth of the network unchanged. Unfortunately, the depth of a network is a crucial hyperparameter for determining the cost of inference. Evaluation of a single layer of a neural network is amenable to parallelization, and graphics hardware is particularly good at accelerating this computation. By contrast, evaluating a deep neural network is inherently sequential.

Thus, algorithms for neural network model compression that substantially reduce depth are highly desirable. Unfortunately, depth compression has been much less studied than pruning or low-rank compression techniques. The workhorse technique is a specialization of the "student–teacher" learning framework. In this approach, a pretrained "teacher" network is used to train a "student" network with an entirely different architecture [1,4]. The teacher network gives access to finer features than the ultimate network output, such as the relative certainties the teacher network assigns to possible outputs [18], or the intermediate-layer representations [27]. However, provable guarantees for the accuracy of student networks relative to their teachers remain elusive.

The goal of this paper is to initiate the study of provable guarantees for depth compression. We obtain the first nontrivial lower bounds for the problem, illustrating two fundamental obstacles to any depth compression algorithm. First, we give a general reduction from the problem of depth compression to the problem of learning the input distribution. This allows us to lift distribution-learning lower bounds to the setting of depth compression. Second, even when the input distribution is known and well-behaved, we rule out a natural class of divide-and-conquer approaches for depth compression, showing that "local" algorithms cannot in general achieve any nontrivial compression guarantees.

Our ultimate goal is for positive algorithmic guarantees, and the present results are motivated by the philosophy that lower bounds can serve as a guideposts for what may be algorithmically feasible. Indeed, our lower bounds outline a set of plausible assumptions under which provable guarantees for depth compression may be achieved (see Sect. 5).

2   Learning and Compression

Let $f : \mathbb{R}^n \to \mathbb{R}^k$ be a map, and let $\mathcal{H}$ be a family of maps $h : \mathbb{R}^n \to \mathbb{R}^k$ (the hypothesis space). An $(\varepsilon, \mathcal{H})$-*compression* of f over a distribution D on $\mathbb{R}^n$ is a map $h \in \mathcal{H}$ which is ε-close to f in mean-squared error, i.e., such that $\mathbb{E}_{x \sim D} \| f(x) - h(x) \|^2 < \varepsilon$.[1] Let $\mathcal{D}$ be a family of distributions on $\mathbb{R}^n$. A (randomized) algorithm for the $(f, \mathcal{H}, \mathcal{D})$ **compression problem** takes as input the explicit neural network representation of f, and some number m of samples from a fixed but unknown distribution $D \in \mathcal{D}$, and produces a map $h : \mathbb{R}^n \to \mathbb{R}^k$, with the guarantee that for any $\varepsilon > 0$ if $m \geq \text{poly}(1/\varepsilon, 1/\delta, \text{size}(f))$ then h is an $(\varepsilon, \mathcal{H})$-compression of f over D. Where h is a random variable of the samples and the algorithm's internal randomness. The algorithm is *efficient* if it runs in time $\text{poly}(1/\varepsilon, 1/\delta, \text{size}(f))$. We will study $(f, \mathcal{H}, \mathcal{D})$ compression problems where f is an explicit deep neural network model and $\mathcal{H}$ is a family of much shallower neural networks.

Thus, the compression problem is similar to a PAC learning problem, with the additional explicit input of an improper[2] representation f of the target concept, and with the distribution-free assumption relaxed. There are well known examples where proper learning is NP-hard, although improper learning is tractable— for example, 3-term DNFs can be efficiently learned improperly as 3-term CNFs, but are NP-hard to learn properly. Here, we consider a different problem: both proper and improper learning may be hard, but transforming an improper model into a proper model (the compression problem) may still be tractable. As a simple example, learning noisy parities from random samples is widely believed to be hard, but with query access (as from some improper representation), the parity can be recovered using the Goldreich-Levin algorithm. The additional input of an improper representation is therefore essential to the complexity of the compression problem, and hardness results for learning do not directly transfer to the compression setting. Nevertheless, we will show in this paper how hardness results for learning can be used to obtain hardness results for neural network depth compression problems.

In order to have a sensible compression problem, in addition to bounding the depth of networks in $\mathcal{H}$, we must insist that their *total size* be bounded by some polynomial in the size of f. The most obvious measure of neural network size is

---

[1] In typical applications, f itself will be an approximation of some concept g known only through labeled examples, and the real goal is find an approximation of g in $\mathcal{H}$. To simplify our discussion, we will not attempt to find a compression of f which approximates this concept g better than f does itself, and so g can be safely ignored.

[2] "Improper" in the sense of not belonging to the hypothesis class $\mathcal{H}$.

perhaps the total number of neurons. However, we will instead use a finer-grained measurement that accounts for the magnitude of the weights in the network:

Definition 1. *Let $d \geq 1$, $\Lambda > 0$. Define $\mathrm{NN}_{\Lambda,d}$ to be the set of d-layer neural networks using 1-Lipschitz activation functions and with each weight matrix W having Frobenius norm bounded by Λ. That is, $f : \mathbb{R}^n \to \mathbb{R}^k$ belongs to $\mathrm{NN}_{\Lambda,d}$ if there exist integers $\ell_0, \ldots, \ell_d$ with $\ell_0 = n$ and $\ell_d = k$, and maps $g_i : \mathbb{R}^{\ell_{i-1}} \to \mathbb{R}^{\ell_i}$ for $1 \leq i \leq d$ of the form $g_i(x) = \sigma(Wx + b)$, where $W \in \mathbb{R}^{\ell_i \times \ell_{i-1}}$ satisfies $\|W\|_F \leq \Lambda$, and $b \in \mathbb{R}^{\ell_i}$, and $\sigma : \mathbb{R} \to \mathbb{R}$ is a 1-Lipschitz map applied component-wise, such that*

$$f = g_d \circ g_{d-1} \circ \cdots \circ g_1.$$

The maps g_i are called the layers of f.

For example, a neural network $f : \mathbb{R}^n \to \mathbb{R}$ with ReLU activations, a single hidden layer of m neurons, and bounded entries in its weight matrices, would belong to $\mathrm{NN}_{O(mn),2}$.

We will give lower bounds for compression problems conditioned on well-known complexity hypotheses, as well as unconditionally in the statistical query framework, which we now review. For computational problems over a distribution D (e.g., supervised learning of a concept), classical algorithms receive as input some number of samples from D. Often, these samples are used only to estimate the means of various random variables over the distribution D: for example, training a neural network by gradient descent requires labeled examples only in order to estimate the expected gradient at various points in parameter space. When an algorithm is formulated so that it does not require any access to D other than to query the expected value of bounded random variables over the distribution, it is called a *statistical query (SQ)* algorithm. The study of SQ algorithms was initiated be Kearns in 1993 [20], and has become an extremely powerful tool for algorithmic analysis [2,6,10,14]. The vast majority of computational problems known to admit efficient algorithms in fact admit efficient SQ algorithms. Unconditional lower bounds for SQ algorithms are also available, in particular characterizing the complexity of learning neural network models [29,33].

Formally, given some distribution D over a set X, let $\mathrm{vSTAT}_D(\tau)$ be an oracle that, when presented with query $\phi : X \to [0,1]$, returns a value v satisfying $|\sqrt{v} - \sqrt{\mathrm{E}_{x \sim D}(\phi(x))}| < \tau$ [12]. A statistical query algorithm for a computational problem over a distribution D is a randomized algorithm that accesses D only via queries to an oracle $\mathrm{vSTAT}_D(\tau)$. Simulating $\mathrm{vSTAT}_D(\tau)$ by estimating $\mathrm{E}_{x \sim D}(\phi(x))$ from samples in general requires $\Omega(1/\tau)$ samples from D. We therefore define the *total complexity* of a statistical query algorithm using the $\mathrm{vSTAT}_D(\tau)$ oracle to be $\max\{1/\tau, d\}$ where d is the number of queries performed by the algorithm.

Theorem 1. *For any $\Lambda, d > 2$ there exists $f \in \mathrm{NN}_{\Lambda,d}$ and a family $\mathcal{D}$ of distributions such that*

1. for every $D \in \mathcal{D}$, there exists a (lossless) $(0, \mathrm{NN}_{\Lambda,3})$-compression of f over D,
2. but the total complexity of $(f, \mathrm{NN}_{\Lambda,d-1}, \mathcal{D})$-compression is $\exp(\Omega(\Lambda))$.

Similar statements can be made for general (not necessarily SQ) algorithms, under some reasonable complexity hypotheses. For example, in the Learning Parities with Noise (LPN) problem, a learning algorithm is given access to examples $x \in \{\pm 1\}^n$ drawn from the uniform distribution on the hypercube, and labeled according to some unknown parity function $h : \{\pm 1\}^n \to \{\pm 1\}$, with these labels randomly flipped with noise rate η. The algorithm's task is to find a function which is ε-close to h. The problem is notoriously difficult and its intractability has been frequently assumed [3,13,21,22].

LPN Hypothesis. For any constants $0 < \eta, \varepsilon < 1/2$, there is no poly($n$)-time algorithm solving the LPN problem with noise rate η to accuracy ε.

Theorem 2. *For any $\varepsilon > 0$ and $\Lambda, d > 2$ there exists $f \in \mathrm{NN}_{\Lambda,d}$ and a family $\mathcal{D}$ of distributions such that, under the LPN hypothesis,*

1. *for every $D \in \mathcal{D}$, there exists a $(\varepsilon, \mathrm{NN}_{\Lambda,3})$-compression of f over D,*
2. *but $(f, \mathrm{NN}_{\Lambda,d-1}, \mathcal{D})$-compression does not admit a polynomial-time algorithm.*

The theorems above show that regardless of how the improper representation f is used, compression is hard unless the input distribution is known. When the distribution is known, compression algorithms that achieve guarantees beyond those available for standard supervised learning problems must rely nontrivially on the improper representation f.

Existing algorithms for NN depth compression make quite coarse use of the improper representation. One of the foundational works on model compression [4] proposes to compress massive ensemble models to smaller NN models simply by training the smaller model by gradient descent on data labeled by the ensemble model (along with a simple method for augmenting the set of unlabeled data in the case when insufficient unlabeled data is available). The same approach has empirically seen some success for compressing deep NN models to shallower architectures [1]. The most successful family of techniques has been the *knowledge distillation* approach of [18]. In its original formulation for classification problems, the deep representation f is assumed to have a final softmax layer; rather than training a shallow student network directly on labels generated from the outputs of f, the student is trained using mean squared error on the penultimate layer of f, representing the relative certainties f assigns to each category. This approach was extended in other works to train student models with different architectures on intermediate-layer features from the original model f [27], and beyond the classification setting [5].

None of these algorithms can succeed at compression without strong assumptions on the form of the improper representation f, and in particular they require f to have opaque regularization properties. Specifically, knowledge distillation and its cousins are empirically observed to work well for improper representations f obtained by training a deep neural network using gradient descent; without the "implicit bias" [15,24,30] imposed by the training of f, there is no reason to expect algorithmic guarantees for compression via knowledge distillation beyond the guarantees available for general learning problems.

Compression algorithms that work without strong assumptions on the regularization of f must instead make use of the detailed representation of f provided as input. This will not be an easy task. In the following Theorem 3, we will rule out natural divide-and-conquer approaches to making use of the improper representation f.

Let $f \in \mathrm{NN}_{\Lambda,d}$, and let $g_1, \ldots, g_d$ be the layers of f. For $1 \leq i \leq j \leq d$, the *slice* $f^{(i:j)}$ of f is the map $g_j \circ g_{j-1} \circ \cdots \circ g_i$. Given a distribution D on the input space of f, the distribution induced by D on the ith layer of f is the distribution of the random variable $f^{[1:i]}(x)$ over $x \sim D$.

Definition 2 (Locally compressible). *Let $f \in \mathrm{NN}_{\Lambda,d}$ and let D be a distribution on the input space of f. We say f is (ε, s, t)-locally compressible if for some $1 \leq i \leq d - t$ and $\Lambda' = \mathrm{poly}(\Lambda, d)$, there exists an $(\varepsilon, \mathrm{NN}_{\Lambda',s})$-compression of $f^{[i:i+t]}$ over the distribution induced by D on the ith layer of f.*

A natural divide-and-conquer approach for depth compression of a neural network would take some number of consecutive layers of the network, and replace those layers with a shallower (but perhaps wider) approximation. By iterating such an approach until no slice can be compressed, we might obtain a much shallower network. In the following theorem, we rule out such local algorithms by observing that there are arbitrarily deep networks admitting lossless (global) compressions, but which are locally incompressible.

Theorem 3. *There is some $c > 0$ such that for any $\Lambda, d > 3$, there is a neural network $f \in \mathrm{NN}_{\Lambda,d}$ and an input distribution D such that*

1. *f is not $(c, 2, 3)$-locally compressible over D,*
2. *but there exists a (lossless) $(0, \mathrm{NN}_{\Lambda(d-3),3})$-compression of f over D.*

3   Compression vs. Distribution Learning

Let D_0 be a probability distribution on $\mathbb{R}^n$. By a *family of η-perturbations of D_0* we mean a family $\mathcal{D}$ of distributions D given by random variables of the form $x + \eta s(x, D)v$, where $x \sim D_0$, $v \in \mathbb{R}^n$ is a fixed unit vector, and $s(x, D) \in \{\pm 1\}$ is a (deterministic) function of x and D, which for fixed D is measurable as a function of x with respect to D_0. Given such a family $\mathcal{D}$, we say a map $f : \mathbb{R}^n \to \mathbb{R}^k$ is a *Δ-separator* for $\mathcal{D}$ if it is measurable with respect to every distribution in $\mathcal{D}$ and $\|f(x + \eta v) - f(x - \eta v)\| \geq \Delta$ for all $x \in \mathrm{supp}(D_0)$.

A simple induction argument gives the following:

Proposition 1. *If $f \in \mathrm{NN}_{\Lambda,d}$ then f is Λ^d-Lipschitz.*

The following is the main technical lemma used in the proofs of Theorems 1 and 2. We denote by $\mathrm{D_{TV}}(D_1, D_2)$ the total variation distance between the distributions D_1 and D_2.

Lemma 1. *Let $\mathcal{D}$ be a family of η-perturbations of a distribution D_0 on $\mathbb{R}^n$, let f be a Δ-separator for $\mathcal{D}$, and let g be an $(\varepsilon, \mathrm{NN}_{\Lambda,d})$-compression of f over some (unknown) distribution $D \in \mathcal{D}$. Suppose $\eta\Lambda^d \leq \Delta/4$. There is an η-perturbation $\tilde{D}$ of D_0 satisfying $\mathrm{D_{TV}}(\tilde{D}, D) = 16\varepsilon/\Delta^2$ and an efficient algorithm that, given query access to f and g:*

1. *produces samples from $\tilde{D}$, given access to samples from D_0;*
2. *computes the probability density of points in $\mathbb{R}^n$ under $\tilde{D}$, given query access to the probability density of points under D_0.*

Proof. Let $v \in \mathbb{R}^n$ be the vector and $s : \mathbb{R}^n \times \mathcal{D} \to \{\pm 1\}$ the map characterizing $\mathcal{D}$ as a family of η-perturbations of D_0. Let $D \in \mathcal{D}$ and let $g \in \mathrm{NN}_{\Lambda,d}$ be a compression of f. Define the following map z on the support of D_0:

$$z(x_0) = \left\{ x + \eta v \; \|g(x_0) - f(x_0 + \eta v)\| < \|g(x_0) - f(x_0 - \eta v)\| x - \eta v \text{ otherwise} \right..$$

Let $\tilde{D}$ denote the distribution of $z(x_0)$, where $x_0 \sim D_0$.

We now argue that $\tilde{D}$ is close to D in total variation distance. Fix x in the support of D and let $x_0 = x - \eta s(x, D)v$. We have by Proposition 1 and the triangle inequality that

$$\|g(x_0) - f(x_0 + \eta s(x, D)v)\| \leq \|g(x_0) - g(x)\| + \|g(x) - f(x)\|$$
$$\leq \eta\Lambda^d + \|g(x) - f(x)\|.$$

Let $\theta = (\Delta/2 - \eta\Lambda^d)$ and suppose further that $\|g(x) - f(x)\| < \theta$, so that $\|g(x_0) - f(x)\| < \Delta/2$. In this case, by the triangle inequality and the fact that f is a Δ-separator,

$$\|g(x_0) - f(x_0 - \eta s(x, D)v)\| > \|f(x_0 + \eta v) - f(x_0 - \eta v)\| - \|g(x_0) - f(x)\|$$
$$> \Delta/2 > \|g(x_0) - f(x)\|.$$

So if $\|g(x) - f(x)\| < \theta$, we have $z(x_0) = x_0 + \eta s(x, D)v$. Hence,

$$\mathrm{D_{TV}}(D, \tilde{D}) \leq \Pr_{x_0 \sim D_0} (z(x_0) \neq x_0 + \eta s(x_0, D)v)$$
$$\leq \Pr_{x \sim D} (\|g(x) - f(x)\| \geq \theta)$$

so it suffices to bound this latter probability. We have by assumption that

$$\mathrm{E}_{x \sim D} (\|g(x) - f(x)\|^2) < \varepsilon.$$

So by Markov's inequality,

$$\Pr_{x \sim D} (\|g(x) - f(x)\| \geq \theta) = \Pr_{x \sim D} (\|g(x) - f(x)\|^2 \geq \theta^2) < \varepsilon/\theta^2 \leq 16\varepsilon/\Delta^2,$$

as desired.

It remains only to observe that $\tilde{D}$ admits an efficient sampling algorithm and probability density computation algorithm, given corresponding access to

D_0 and query access to f and g. Sampling from $\tilde{D}$ is the same as sampling x_0 from D_0 and computing $z(x_0)$, which requires one query of g and two of f. To compute probability densities $\tilde{p}$ under $\tilde{D}$, given probability densities p for D_0, we compute the density $\tilde{p}(x)$ at a point x as

$$\tilde{p}(x) = p(x - \eta v)\mathbf{1}(z(x - \eta v) = x) + p(x + \eta v)\mathbf{1}(z(x + \eta v) = x).$$

We denote by $\mathcal{P}_n$ the set of parity functions $h : \{\pm 1\}^n \to \{\pm 1\}$ on the n-dimensional Boolean hypercube. We recall two standard results concerning parities.

Lemma 2. *A parity function $h \in \mathcal{P}_n$ can be represented exactly by a neural network in $\mathrm{NN}(1,3)$ with $O(n)$ gates.*

Because the parities are pairwise uncorrelated, the set of parity functions has large "statistical dimension," from which it follows by a standard argument that the total complexity of any statistical algorithm for learning parities is also large. See, e.g., [12].

Lemma 3. *The total complexity of learning parities in $\mathcal{P}_n$ over the uniform distribution on the hypercube to within accuracy $\geq 3/4$ is $\exp(\Omega(n))$.*

Proof (Proof of Theorem 1). The theorem follows by applying Lemma 1 to an appropriate choice of map $f \in \mathrm{NN}_{\Lambda,d}$ and family $\mathcal{D}$ of distributions.

For some n to be defined, let $f : \mathbb{R}^{n+1} \to \mathbb{R}$ be given by the layer-d neural network with first layer

$$f_1(x_1, \ldots, x_{n+1}) = \Lambda x_{n+1}$$

and $f_i : \mathbb{R} \to \mathbb{R}$ given by $f_i(x) = \Lambda x$ for all $1 < i \leq d$. Clearly $f \in \mathrm{NN}_{\Lambda,d}$.

We now define $\mathcal{D}$ as a family of η-perturbations of a distribution. Let $\pi : \mathbb{R}^{n+1} \to \mathbb{R}^n$ be the projection onto the first n coordinates, $\pi(x_1, \ldots, x_{n+1}) = (x_1, \ldots, x_n)$. Let X be the embedding of the n-dimensional hypercube in $\mathbb{R}^{n+1}$ given by

$$X = \{x = (x_1, \ldots, x_n, 0) : \pi(x) \in \in \{\pm 1\}\}$$

and let D_0 be the uniform distribution on X. Let v be the standard basis vector $(0, \ldots, 0, 1) \in \mathbb{R}^{n+1}$. Let $\eta = \Lambda^{-d}$. For $h \in \mathcal{P}$, let D_h be the distribution of the random variable $x + \eta h(\pi(x))v$ where $x \sim D_0$. Let $\mathcal{D} = \{D_h : h \in \mathcal{P}\}$.

Thus, $\mathcal{D}$ is a family of η-perturbations of D_0. Furthermore, since $f(x + \eta v) - f(x - \eta v) = 2\eta \Lambda^d = 2$ for all $x \in \mathrm{supp}(D_0) = X$, we have that f is a Δ-separator for $\mathcal{D}$ where $\Delta = 2$.

To show the first claim of the theorem, that there is a $(0, \mathrm{NN}_{\Lambda,3})$-compression of f over any $D \in \mathcal{D}$, we first observe that for any $h \in \mathcal{P}$ and $x \in \mathrm{supp}(D_h)$, we have

$$f(x) = \Lambda^d \eta h(\pi(x)) = h(\pi(x)).$$

The claim then follows immediately from Lemma 2, for appropriate choice of $n = \Omega(\Lambda)$.

To bound the SQ complexity of the $(f, \mathrm{NN}_{\Lambda,d-1}, \mathcal{D})$-compression problem, we first suppose $g \in \mathrm{NN}_{\Lambda,d-1}$ is a $(1/16, \mathrm{NN}_{\Lambda,d-1})$-compression of f over some $D_h \in \mathcal{D}$. By Lemma 1, given inputs f and g, there is an efficient algorithm for estimating probabilities $\tilde{p}(x)$ of points under a distribution $\tilde{D}$, which is an η-perturbation of D_0 satisfying $\mathrm{D_{TV}}(\tilde{D}, \tilde{D}) < 1/4$. Since $\tilde{D}$ is an η-perturbation of D_0, its support includes exactly one of $x + \eta v$ and $x - \eta v$ for each $x \in X$. Let $\tilde{h}(x) = 1$ if $\tilde{p}(x + \eta v) > 0$ and $\tilde{h}(x) = -1$ otherwise. Then $\mathrm{Pr}_{x \sim D_0}(\tilde{h}(x) \neq h(x)) < 1/4$. In particular, given such a $g \in \mathrm{NN}_{\Lambda,d-1}$, we can learn h to within accuracy $3/4$ without any additional access to D_h. Hence, by Lemma 3, finding such a g has total complexity $\exp(\Omega(n)) = \exp(\Omega(\Lambda))$.

Proof (Proof of Theorem 2). The proof is essentially the same as for Theorem 1. We replace the parity functions with their noisy versions, with noise rate $\varepsilon/2$. A neural network computing the (non-noisy) parity, as from Lemma 2, will be an ε-approximation of the noisy parity with high probability. The result again follows by Lemma 1.

4   Local vs. Global Compression

The proof of Theorem 3 is a straightforward application of existing depth separation theorems for neural networks. Several versions of depth separations of 2-layer from 3-layer networks are known [7, 11, 28].

Theorem 4 (Eldan and Shamir [11, Theorem 1]). *There is a constant $c > 0$ such that for every n there is a probability distribution D on $\mathbb{R}^n$ and a map $g : \mathbb{R}^n \to \mathbb{R}$ with a neural network representation $g \in \mathrm{NN}_{\mathrm{poly}(n),3}$, such that if there exists a $(c, \mathrm{NN}_{\Lambda,2})$-compression of g, then $\Lambda = \exp(\Omega(n))$.*

Proof (Proof of Theorem 3). Let $c > 0$ be the constant, D be the distribution, and $g : \mathbb{R}^n \to \mathbb{R}$ be the neural network in $\mathrm{NN}_{\Lambda,3}$ with $\Lambda = \mathrm{poly}(n)$ given by Theorem 4. We define the network $f : \mathbb{R}^{n \times (d-3)} \to \mathbb{R}$ in $\mathrm{NN}_{\Lambda(d-3),d}$ using g as a gadget. Specifically, for $1 \leq i \leq d-3$, let $f^{(i)}(x) : \mathbb{R}^n \to \mathbb{R}$ be the network in $\mathrm{NN}_{\Lambda,d}$ be the network whose first i layers each compute the identity map on $\mathbb{R}^n$, whose $i+1$ through $i+3$ layers are identical to those of g, and whose subsequent $d-i-3$ layers each compute the identity map on $\mathbb{R}$. Let f be the neural network given by the product of the $f^{(i)}$ for $1 \leq i \leq d-3$. That is, the jth layer of f has as its input space the Cartesian product of the input spaces of the jth layers of the networks $f^{(i)}$ for $1 \leq i \leq d-3$, and similarly for the output spaces, and map computed on the jth layer is the Cartesian product of the maps of the jth layers of the networks $f^{(i)}$. The input distribution of f is D^{d-3}.

Clearly f has an exact representation in $\mathrm{NN}_{(d-3)\Lambda,3}$ as the Cartesian product of g with itself $d-3$ times, so a $(0, \mathrm{NN}_{(d-3)\Lambda,3})$-compression of f over D^{d-3} exists. We argue that f is not $(c, 2, 3)$-locally compressible over D^{d-3}. Letting $h = f^{(i)}$ be the ith constituent network of f, we have $h^{[i:i+3]} = g$. Furthermore, the distribution induced by D on the ith layer of h is simply D. Therefore by Theorem 4, there does not exist a $(c, \mathrm{NN}_{\mathrm{poly}(\Lambda),2})$-compression of $h^{[i:i+3]}$ over this distribution, for some absolute constant $c \geq 0$, and so the same is true of f. Hence, f is not $(c, 2, 3)$-locally compressible over D^{d-3}.

It is reasonable to conjecture that similar statements larger notions of local compressibility, e.g., $(c, 3, 5)$-local compression rather than $(c, 2, 3)$-local compression. Such results would similarly follow from depth separation theorems deeper neural networks. However, proving such separation theorems is a major open problem.

5   Outlook

Having established obstacles to neural network depth compression, we now consider whether these obstacles can indicate a path forward to positive algorithmic guarantees for depth compression.

The reduction from the compression problem to learning the input distribution presented in Sect. 3 relied heavily on the deep representation having a large Lipschitz parameter. This assumption is not entirely unreasonable, since deep neural network models trained "in the wild" indeed tend to have large Lipschitz parameters, as evidenced by their susceptibility to adversarially-perturbed inputs [31] (see also [26] for another manifestation of the non-Lipschitzness of deep networks). It is reasonable to ask whether depth compression might be easier, and algorithmic guarantees more accessible, under the assumption that the provided deep representation has a bounded Lipschitz parameter. Bounds on the Lipschitz parameter near the support of the input distribution are closely related to the robustness of a neural network model to adversarially-perturbed inputs. Previous work already finds a connection between depth compression and robustness to adversarial perturbations in the opposite direction, i.e., observing that knowledge distillation can be used as a defense against adversarial inputs [25].

A second approach would be to rely on regularization properties of real-world deep teacher networks in order to obtain algorithmic guarantees not for compression of arbitrary networks, but for the cases we are most interested in. The construction of Sect. 4 suggests that assumptions on the structure of the teacher network may be essential to obtaining positive guarantees. The empirical success of knowledge distillation for model compression suggests that deep teacher networks trained by gradient descent on real-world data distributions achieve some implicit bias in their intermediate-layer representations that is useful when training a shallower compressed model. As a first step, we ask whether algorithmic guarantees for knowledge distillation are possible in the classification setting when the underlying concept is separable and the teacher logits directly encode meaningful information about the distribution, such as the distance from a point to each of the classes.

References

1. Ba, J., Caruana, R.: Do deep nets really need to be deep? In: Advances in Neural Information Processing Systems (NIPS), pp. 2654–2662 (2014)
2. Blum, A., Frieze, A., Kannan, R., Vempala, S.: A polynomial-time algorithm for learning noisy linear threshold functions. Algorithmica **22**(1–2), 35–52 (1998)
3. Blum, A., Kalai, A., Wasserman, H.: Noise-tolerant learning, the parity problem, and the statistical query model. J. ACM (JACM) **50**(4), 506–519 (2003)
4. Buciluǎ, C., Caruana, R., Niculescu-Mizil, A.: Model compression. In: Proceedings of the 12th ACM SIGKDD International Conference on Knowledge Discovery and Data Mining, pp. 535–541 (2006)
5. Chen, G., Choi, W., Yu, X., Han, T., Chandraker, M.: Learning efficient object detection models with knowledge distillation. In: Advances in Neural Information Processing Systems, pp. 742–751 (2017)
6. Chu, C.T., et al.: Map-reduce for machine learning on multicore. In: Advances in Neural Information Processing Systems, pp. 281–288 (2007)
7. Daniely, A.: Depth separation for neural networks. In: Conference on Learning Theory, pp. 690–696 (2017)
8. Denil, M., Shakibi, B., Dinh, L., Ranzato, M., De Freitas, N.: Predicting parameters in deep learning. In: Advances in Neural Information Processing Systems (NIPS), pp. 2148–2156 (2013)
9. Denton, E.L., Zaremba, W., Bruna, J., LeCun, Y., Fergus, R.: Exploiting linear structure within convolutional networks for efficient evaluation. In: Advances in Neural Information Processing Systems (NIPS), pp. 1269–1277 (2014)
10. Dunagan, J., Vempala, S.: A simple polynomial-time rescaling algorithm for solving linear programs. Math. Program. **114**(1), 101–114 (2008)
11. Eldan, R., Shamir, O.: The power of depth for feedforward neural networks. In: Conference on Learning Theory, pp. 907–940 (2016)
12. Feldman, V.: A general characterization of the statistical query complexity. In: Conference on Learning Theory, pp. 785–830 (2017)
13. Feldman, V., Gopalan, P., Khot, S., Ponnuswami, A.K.: On agnostic learning of parities, monomials, and halfspaces. SIAM J. Comput. **39**(2), 606–645 (2009)
14. Feldman, V., Grigorescu, E., Reyzin, L., Vempala, S.S., Xiao, Y.: Statistical algorithms and a lower bound for detecting planted cliques. J. ACM (JACM) **64**(2), 1–37 (2017)
15. Gunasekar, S., Lee, J.D., Soudry, D., Srebro, N.: Implicit bias of gradient descent on linear convolutional networks. In: Advances in Neural Information Processing Systems, pp. 9461–9471 (2018)
16. Han, S., Pool, J., Tran, J., Dally, W.: Learning both weights and connections for efficient neural network. In: Advances in Neural Information Processing Systems (NIPS), pp. 1135–1143 (2015)
17. Hassibi, B., Stork, D.G., Wolff, G.J.: Optimal brain surgeon and general network pruning. In: Neural Networks, pp. 293–299 (1993)
18. Hinton, G., Vinyals, O., Dean, J.: Distilling the knowledge in a neural network. arXiv:1503.02531 (2015)
19. Jaderberg, M., Vedaldi, A., Zisserman, A.: Speeding up convolutional neural networks with low rank expansions. arXiv:1405.3866 (2014)
20. Kearns, M.J.: Efficient noise-tolerant learning from statistical queries. In: Proceedings of the 25th ACM Symposium on Theory of Computing (STOC), pp. 392–401 (1993)

21. Kiltz, E., Pietrzak, K., Venturi, D., Cash, D., Jain, A.: Efficient authentication from hard learning problems. J. Cryptol. **30**(4), 1238–1275 (2017)
22. Klivans, A., Kothari, P.: Embedding hard learning problems into Gaussian space. In: Approximation, Randomization, and Combinatorial Optimization. Algorithms and Techniques (APPROX/RANDOM 2014) (2014)
23. LeCun, Y., Denker, J.S., Solla, S.A.: Optimal brain damage. In: Advances in Neural Information Processing Systems (NIPS), pp. 598–605 (1990)
24. Neyshabur, B., Tomioka, R., Srebro, N.: In search of the real inductive bias: on the role of implicit regularization in deep learning. arXiv preprint arXiv:1412.6614 (2014)
25. Papernot, N., McDaniel, P., Wu, X., Jha, S., Swami, A.: Distillation as a defense to adversarial perturbations against deep neural networks. In: 2016 IEEE Symposium on Security and Privacy (SP), pp. 582–597 (2016)
26. Raghu, M., Poole, B., Kleinberg, J., Ganguli, S., Dickstein, J.S.: On the expressive power of deep neural networks. In: Proceedings of the 34th International Conference on Machine Learning, vol. 70, pp. 2847–2854 (2017)
27. Romero, A., Ballas, N., Kahou, S.E., Chassang, A., Gatta, C., Bengio, Y.: FitNets: hints for thin deep nets. arXiv:1412.6550 (2014)
28. Safran, I., Shamir, O.: Depth-width tradeoffs in approximating natural functions with neural networks. In: Proceedings of the 34th International Conference on Machine Learning, vol. 70, pp. 2979–2987 (2017)
29. Song, L., Vempala, S., Wilmes, J., Xie, B.: On the complexity of learning neural networks. In: Advances in Neural Information Processing Systems (NIPS), pp. 5520–5528 (2017)
30. Soudry, D., Hoffer, E., Nacson, M.S., Gunasekar, S., Srebro, N.: The implicit bias of gradient descent on separable data. J. Mach. Learn. Res. **19**(1), 2822–2878 (2018)
31. Szegedy, C., et al.: Intriguing properties of neural networks. arXiv:1312.6199 (2013)
32. Tai, C., Xiao, T., Zhang, Y., Wang, X., Weinan, E.: Convolutional neural networks with low-rank regularization. arXiv:1511.06067 (2015)
33. Vempala, S., Wilmes, J.: Gradient descent for one-hidden-layer neural networks: polynomial convergence and SQ lower bounds. In: Conference on Learning Theory, pp. 3115–3117 (2019)
34. Zhu, M., Gupta, S.: To prune, or not to prune: exploring the efficacy of pruning for model compression. arXiv:1710.01878 (2017)

Multi-task and Multi-label Learning

Multi-label Quadruplet Dictionary Learning

Jiayu Zheng, Wencheng Zhu, and Pengfei Zhu[(✉)]

College of Intelligence and Computing, Tianjin University, Tianjin 300350, China
{zhengjiayu,zhuwencheng,zhupengfei}@tju.edu.cn

Abstract. The explosion of the label space degrades the performance of the classic multi-class learning models. Label space dimension reduction (LSDR) is developed to reduce the dimension of the label space by learning a latent representation of both the feature space and label space. Almost all existing models adopt a two-step strategy, i.e., first learn the latent space, and then connect the feature space with the label space by the latent space. Additionally, the latent space lacks interpretability for LSDR. In this paper, motivated by cross-modal learning, we propose a novel one-step model, named Quadruplet Dictionary Learning (QDL), for multi-label classification with many labels. QDL models the latent space by the representation coefficients, which own preeminent recoverability, predictability and interpretability. By simultaneously learning two dictionary pairs, the feature space and label space are well bi-directly bridged and recovered by four dictionaries. Experiments on benchmark datasets show that QDL outperforms the state-of-the-art label space dimension reduction algorithms.

Keywords: Multi-label classification · Dictionary learning · Label space dimension reduction.

1 Introduction

Multi-label learning refers to the problem where each training sample is associated with more than one category. Multi-label classification tasks widely exist in many applications, e.g., text categorization [19], image annotation [12], information retrieval [24], bioinformatics [20], etc. An intuitive way for multi-label classification is to solve several independent single-label classification tasks without considering label correlations [24]. To exploit the label interdependency among multi-labels, great efforts are devoted and a large number of multi-label learning methods are developed [9]. Whereas, with the number of class labels increasing significantly, the traditional multi-class learning models become computationally impractical in the training process.

Label space dimension reduction (LSDR) is an efficient tool to handle the multi-label learning problem with many classes. Similar to dimension reduction in feature space, LSDR can be categorized into label selection and label

© Springer Nature Switzerland AG 2020
I. Farkaš et al. (Eds.): ICANN 2020, LNCS 12397, pp. 119–131, 2020.
https://doi.org/10.1007/978-3-030-61616-8_10

transformation as well. The label selection methods select a small subset of the most relevant labels from original labels by assuming that the label space can be approximatively represented by the subset. MOPLMS constructs a group-sparse regression model and conducts label selection by learning a label coefficient matrix [1]. ML-CSSP applies efficient randomized sampling schemes to select the columns of the label matrix [3]. By selecting the most informative and representative labels, the computation burden decreases without loss of prediction capability.

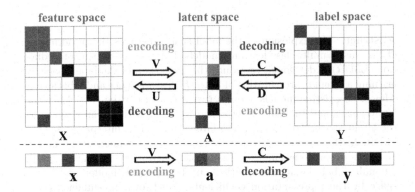

Fig. 1. The flowchart of quadruplet dictionary learning (QDL), **X**, **Y** and **A** denote the feature space, label space and latent space, respectively. **V** and **U** are the encoder and decoder for the feature space **X**. **D** and **C** are the encoder and decoder for the label space **Y**. Given a new sample **x**, its latent representation is obtained by the encoder **V** and then the prediction is conducted by the decoder **C**.

Owing to the high cost of direct transformation from the feature space to the label space, the label transformation methods learn a function to project the high-dimensional label space to a low-dimensional latent space [5,10,15,23]. As shown in Fig. 1, the key challenge for label transformation is how to connect the feature space **X** with the label space **Y** by the low-dimensional latent space **A**. For label transformation methods, we need to learn three indispensable variables, i.e, the encoder **D** that projects the label space **Y** to the latent space **A**, the encoder **V** that projects the feature space **X** to the latent space **A**, and the decoder **C** that reconstructs the decision space **Y** from the latent representation **A**. Given a query sample **x**, the prediction can be easily got by encoding the feature space with **V** and decoding latent representation **a** to the label space with **C**. Most existing label transformation methods first learn the encoders **D** and **V**. After the latent representation is got, the decoder **C** is then learned to recover the label space.

Until now, researchers have developed a large number of LSDR methods from the perspective of label transformation. Hsu et al. applied compressed sensing to encode the label space and use an iterative algorithm to reconstruct the labels [10]. Tai and Lin proposed a principal label space transformation (PLST) method by using singular value decomposition to pursue the encoding matrix [23]. In early works, they only learn the encoder for the label space and rarely take the correlation between the label space and the feature space into consideration. Sun et al. applied canonical correlation analysis (CCA) to maximize the correlation between the feature space and label space [22]. However, it's hard to design an appropriate decoder. Chen and Lin proposed a conditional principal label space transformation (CPLST) algorithm [5]. Although CPLST considers the recoverability of the label space, it ignores the predictability of the latent space. Lin et al. proposed a feature aware implicit embedding (FaIE) method by using both the recoverability of the original label space and the predictability of the latent space [15]. To exploit the nonlinear correlation of multiple labels, Li and Guo exploited kernel CCA to capture the nonlinear relationship among labels and introduced a nonlinear label transformation method [14]. For multi-label tasks with millions of labels, large-scale learning strategies (e.g., distributed learning) are introduced to improve the scalability problem [2].

If we consider the feature space and label space as two modalities, LSDR can be converted into a cross modal learning task. The existing works [5,14,22] actually use two projection matrices to get the latent space. For cross modal applications, e.g., image synthetic and image super-resolution, dictionary learning is widely used and achieves superior performance [11,17,27]. One dictionary is learned for each modality and the representation coefficients of different modalities are forced to be the same or connected by a linear projection matrix. The representation coefficients reflect the distribution of the samples on the corresponding dictionary atoms. Here, they are considered as the latent representation across different modalities. Hence, it is intuitive to exploit dictionary learning to get the latent space and realize LSDR.

Although numbers of label transformation methods are developed, they do not learn the encoders & decoders for the feature space and label space jointly. Thus, the correlation between two spaces and label dependency are not fully exploited. Additionally, the existing works lack interpretability of the latent space, which is also important for a machine learning model. In this paper, inspired by dictionary learning in cross modal tasks, we propose a novel quadruplet dictionary learning (QDL) model for label space dimension reduction. As shown in Fig. 1, we learn one dictionary pair $(\mathbf{U}, \mathbf{V})$ for the feature space $\mathbf{X}$, and the other dictionary pair $(\mathbf{C}, \mathbf{D})$ for the label space $\mathbf{Y}$, respectively. The synthetic dictionaries $\mathbf{U}$ and $\mathbf{C}$ are the decoders while the analysis dictionaries $\mathbf{V}$ and $\mathbf{D}$ are the encoders. By simultaneously learning the four dictionaries, the feature space and label space are bidirectionally connected and recovered. In the testing stage, the prediction can be directly obtained by the encoder (i.e., the analysis dictionary $\mathbf{V}$) and the decoder (i.e., the synthetic dictionary $\mathbf{C}$). The contributions of this paper are summarized as follows:

- A novel quadruplet dictionary learning (QDL) model is proposed for label space dimension reduction. Different from the current two-step strategies, QDL builds a bidirectional bridge between the feature space and label space, which can effectively utilize the correlation of the two spaces.

- QDL uses representation coefficients that reflect the distribution on the dictionary atoms as the latent space. The latent space is more predictive and explicable, and can well recover both the feature space and label space.
- Experiments on benchmark multi-label datasets with many classes show that QDL outperforms the state-of-the-art LSDR algorithms.

2   Quadruplet Dictionary Learning

2.1   Model

Let $\mathbf{X} \in \mathbb{R}^{d \times n}$ denote the feature matrix, where n is the number of instances and d is the dimension of the feature space. Then, the corresponding label matrix is $\mathbf{Y} \in \mathbb{R}^{c \times n}$, where c is the dimension of the label space. We assume that the dimension of the latent space is k $(k < d, c)$.

For label space dimension reduction, the key point is how to learn a latent space with excellent recoverability, predictability and interpretability. In addition, the correlation between the feature space and label space should be well exploited for latent space learning. Motivated by the dictionary learning techniques in cross modal learning, we considered the feature space and label space as two modalities.

Two dictionary pairs are introduced for the feature space and label space, respectively. The analysis and synthesis dictionaries of the feature space $\mathbf{X}$ are $\mathbf{V} \in \mathbb{R}^{k \times d}$ and $\mathbf{U} \in \mathbb{R}^{d \times k}$, respectively. The analysis and synthesis dictionaries of the label space $\mathbf{Y}$ are $\mathbf{D} \in \mathbb{R}^{k \times c}$ and $\mathbf{C} \in \mathbb{R}^{c \times k}$, respectively. By the analysis dictionaries, $\mathbf{X}$ and $\mathbf{Y}$ can be projected to the latent space, i.e., $\mathbf{VX}$ and $\mathbf{DY}$. Here $\mathbf{VX} = \mathbf{DY}$ is requested to exploit the correlation between $\mathbf{X}$ and $\mathbf{Y}$. Then the feature space and label space can be recovered by the synthesis dictionaries, i.e., $\mathbf{X} = \mathbf{UVX}$ and $\mathbf{Y} = \mathbf{CDY}$. The reconstruction errors should be minimized to ensure the recoverability of the latent space. According to analysis above, our QDL is formulated as follows:

$$
\min_{\mathbf{U},\mathbf{V},\mathbf{C},\mathbf{D}} \|\mathbf{X} - \mathbf{UVX}\|_F^2 + \|\mathbf{Y} - \mathbf{CDY}\|_F^2 \\
s.t.\ \mathbf{VX} = \mathbf{DY},\ \|\mathbf{u}_i\|_2^2 \leq 1, \|\mathbf{c}_i\|_2^2 \leq 1, i = 1, ..., k,
\tag{1}
$$

where $\mathbf{u}_i$ and $\mathbf{c}_i$ are the ith atoms of synthesis dictionaries $\mathbf{U}$ and $\mathbf{C}$. Actually, QDL implicitly uses label dependency when it learns the synthesis dictionary $\mathbf{C}$ in that $\mathbf{C}$ reflects the representative classes and other classes can be linearly reconstructed.

Here, the representation coefficient space is used as the latent space in that it has the following advantages: 1) *The feature space and label space can be well recovered by using the latent space*, i.e., $\mathbf{X} = \mathbf{UVX}$ and $\mathbf{Y} = \mathbf{CDY}$; 2) *The latent space has good predictability because the representation coefficients represent the distribution of the samples on the dictionaries $\mathbf{U}$ and $\mathbf{C}$*; 3) *Compared with the current LSDR models, the latent space in QDL is more explicable. $\mathbf{U}$ and $\mathbf{C}$ can be considered as a set of sample bases and label bases. Then the latent space is a new representation for $\mathbf{X}$ and $\mathbf{Y}$.*

Algorithm 1. Quadruplet Dictionary Learning

Input:

The data matrix $\mathbf{X} = [\mathbf{x}_1, \mathbf{x}_2, ..., \mathbf{x}_n] \in \mathbb{R}^{d \times n}$.

The label matrix $\mathbf{Y} = [\mathbf{y}_1, \mathbf{y}_2, ..., \mathbf{y}_n] \in \mathbb{R}^{c \times n}$.

The parameters λ;

Output:

The analysis and synthesis dictionaries of the feature space $\mathbf{V} \in \mathbb{R}^{k \times d}$ and $\mathbf{U} \in \mathbb{R}^{d \times k}$;

The analysis and synthesis dictionaries of the label space $\mathbf{D} \in \mathbb{R}^{k \times c}$ and $\mathbf{C} \in \mathbb{R}^{c \times k}$;

1: Initialize $\mathbf{A}$, $\mathbf{U}$, $\mathbf{V}$, $\mathbf{C}$ and $\mathbf{D}$.

2: **while**

3:    Update $\mathbf{A}$ by Eq.(4);

4:    Update $\mathbf{U}$ by Eq.(6);

5:    Update $\mathbf{V}$ by Eq.(9);

6:    Update $\mathbf{C}$ similar to Eq.(6);

7:    Update $\mathbf{D}$ similar to Eq.(9);

8: **until** It converges.

2.2 Optimization of QDL

We introduce $\mathbf{A}$ to relax the optimization objective in Eq. (1) and obtain the following problem:

$$\min_{\mathbf{A},\mathbf{U},\mathbf{V},\mathbf{C},\mathbf{D}} \left\{ \begin{array}{l} \|\mathbf{X} - \mathbf{U}\mathbf{A}\|_F^2 + \|\mathbf{Y} - \mathbf{C}\mathbf{A}\|_F^2 \\ +\lambda \left(\|\mathbf{V}\mathbf{X} - \mathbf{A}\|_F^2 + \|\mathbf{D}\mathbf{Y} - \mathbf{A}\|_F^2 \right) \end{array} \right\} \tag{2}$$
$$s.t. \ \|\mathbf{u}_i\|_2^2 \leq 1, \|\mathbf{c}_i\|_2^2 \leq 1, i = 1, 2, ..., k,$$

where λ is a parameter. The objective in Eq. (2) contains five subproblems and we iteratively update $\mathbf{A}$, $\mathbf{U}$, $\mathbf{V}$, $\mathbf{C}$ and $\mathbf{D}$. The optimization procedures are organized as follows:

Update Subproblem-A: To update relaxation variable $\mathbf{A}$, we fix other variables and neglect irrelevant items. The subproblem-$\mathbf{A}$ is acquired as follows:

$$\min_{\mathbf{A}} \left\{ \begin{array}{l} \|\mathbf{X} - \mathbf{U}\mathbf{A}\|_F^2 + \|\mathbf{Y} - \mathbf{C}\mathbf{A}\|_F^2 \\ +\lambda \left(\|\mathbf{V}\mathbf{X} - \mathbf{A}\|_F^2 + \|\mathbf{D}\mathbf{Y} - \mathbf{A}\|_F^2 \right) \end{array} \right\} \tag{3}$$

We set the derivative of Eq. (3) w.r.t $\mathbf{A}$ to 0 and have:

$$\mathbf{A} = \left(\mathbf{U}^T\mathbf{U} + \mathbf{C}^T\mathbf{C} + 2\lambda\mathbf{I} \right)^{-1} \left(\begin{array}{c} \mathbf{U}^T\mathbf{X} + \mathbf{C}^T\mathbf{Y} \\ +\lambda\mathbf{V}\mathbf{X} + \lambda\mathbf{D}\mathbf{Y} \end{array} \right) \tag{4}$$

where $\mathbf{I}$ is an identity matrix. The close solution of $\mathbf{A}$ is gotten in Eq. (4).

Update Subproblem-U: To update the synthesis dictionary $\mathbf{U}$, we fix $\mathbf{A}$ and omit unconcerned items. Then, we obtain the following subproblem:

$$\min_{\mathbf{U}} \|\mathbf{X} - \mathbf{U}\mathbf{A}\|_F^2 \tag{5}$$
$$s.t. \ \|\mathbf{u}_i\|_2^2 \leq 1, i = 1, 2, ..., k,$$

the optimization problem in Eq. (5) is well studied and the optimal solution can be achieved by using the Alternating Direction method Multipliers (ADMM) [4]. We introduce two variables $\mathbf{S}$, $\mathbf{T}$ and update the synthesis dictionary $\mathbf{U}$ as follows:

$$\begin{cases} \mathbf{U}^{t+1} = \arg\min_{\mathbf{U}} \|\mathbf{X}-\mathbf{U}^t\mathbf{A}\|_F^2 + \mu \|\mathbf{U}^t - \mathbf{T}^t + \mathbf{S}^t\|_F^2 \\ \mathbf{T}^{t+1} = \arg\min_{\mathbf{T}} \mu \|\mathbf{U}^{t+1} - \mathbf{T}^t + \mathbf{S}^t\|_F^2 \ s.t. \|\mathbf{h}_i\|_2^2 \le 1 \\ \mathbf{S}^{t+1} = \mathbf{S}^t + \mathbf{U}^{t+1} - \mathbf{T}^{t+1} \\ \mu = \rho\mu \end{cases} \tag{6}$$

where we set $\rho = 1.2$ and $\mu = 1$. The subproblem-$\mathbf{C}$ has similar optimization problem and solution as the subproblem-$\mathbf{U}$:

$$\min_{\mathbf{C}} \|\mathbf{Y} - \mathbf{CA}\|_F^2 \\ s.t. \ \|\mathbf{c}_i\|_2^2 \le 1, i = 1, 2, ..., k, \tag{7}$$

The optimization of Eq. (7) is the same as that of $\mathbf{U}$.

Update Subproblem-$\mathbf{V}$: To update the analysis dictionary $\mathbf{V}$, we fix $\mathbf{A}$ and ignore irrelevant items. Then we get the following optimization problem:

$$\min_{\mathbf{V}} \|\mathbf{VX} - \mathbf{A}\|_F^2 \tag{8}$$

Eq. (8) is the least-square problem and has the close solution:

$$\mathbf{V} = \mathbf{AX}^T \left(\mathbf{XX}^T + \varepsilon\mathbf{I}\right)^{-1} \tag{9}$$

where ε is a small number to avoid the bad condition number of matrix inversion (we set $\varepsilon = 10^{-6}$). The subproblem-$\mathbf{D}$ also has similar optimization problem and solution as the subproblem-$\mathbf{V}$:

$$\min_{\mathbf{V}} \|\mathbf{DY} - \mathbf{A}\|_F^2 \tag{10}$$

the close solution of $\mathbf{D}$ is $\mathbf{D} = \mathbf{AY}^T \left(\mathbf{YY}^T + \varepsilon\mathbf{I}\right)^{-1}$.

We iteratively update $\mathbf{A}$, $\mathbf{U}$, $\mathbf{V}$, $\mathbf{C}$ and $\mathbf{D}$ until objective function converges. Our algorithm QDL is summarized in **Algorithm 1**. Given a query sample $\mathbf{x}$, the label $\mathbf{y}$ of $\mathbf{x}$ can be predicted by $\mathbf{y} = \mathbf{CVx}$.

2.3 Time Complexity

In each iteration, we update $\mathbf{A}$, $\mathbf{U}$, $\mathbf{V}$, $\mathbf{C}$ and $\mathbf{D}$. The subproblem-$\mathbf{A}$, subproblem-$\mathbf{V}$ and subproblem-$\mathbf{D}$ have close solutions and the time complexities of three subproblems are $O(dk^2+ck^2+dkn+ckn)$, $O(dkn+d^2n+d^3)$ and $O(ckn+c^2n+c^3)$ respectively. We use ADMM to solve subproblem-$\mathbf{U}$ and subproblem-$\mathbf{C}$, the time complexities of these two subproblems are $O(dkn + d^2k + dk^2 + k^3)$ and $O(ckn + c^2k)$.

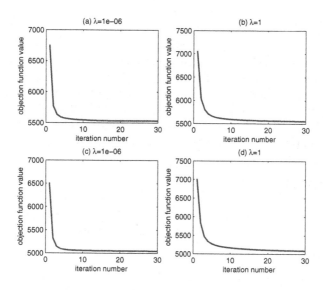

Fig. 2. The convergence curves on BIBTEX (a, b) and COREL5K (c, d) datasets with $\lambda = 1$ and $\lambda = 0.000001$

Table 1. Average Precision under 0.4 times of the dimension of the label space on benchmark datesets

DATA	BR	PLST	CPLST	FaIE	ML-CSSP	QDL
BIBTEX	0.0610	0.0638	0.0646	0.0639	0.0612	**0.1964**
CAL500	0.1480	0.1371	0.1431	0.1374	0.0175	**0.1823**
COREL5K	0.0184	0.0164	0.0174	0.0170	0.0175	**0.1474**
mediamill	0.0893	0.1012	0.1082	0.1007	0.1005	**0.5455**
espgame	0.0529	0.0614	0.0624	0.0619	0.0610	**0.0997**
iaprtc12	0.0731	0.0709	0.0721	0.0719	0.0705	**0.0844**
EURLex-4K	0.0026	0.0025	0.0025	0.0028	0.0027	**0.0061**

Table 2. AUC under 0.4 times of the dimension of the label space on benchmark datesets

DATA	BR	PLST	CPLST	FaIE	ML-CSSP	QDL
BIBTEX	0.5752	0.6659	0.6708	0.6685	0.6511	**0.7639**
CAL500	0.5983	0.6559	0.6646	0.6564	0.6533	**0.7013**
COREL5K	0.7140	0.7694	**0.7792**	0.7748	0.7749	0.7779
mediamill	0.4645	0.5459	0.5922	0.5494	0.5438	**0.7675**
espgame	0.5209	0.5729	0.5824	0.5768	0.5700	**0.6997**
iaprtc12	0.5354	0.5914	0.6005	0.5946	0.5870	**0.6641**
EURLex-4K	0.7537	0.7743	0.7737	0.7934	0.7915	**0.8298**

2.4 Convergence Analysis

The subproblem-**A**, subproblem-**V** and subproblem-**D** are convex and have close solutions. The subproblem-**U** and subproblem-**C** are solved by ADMM and guaranteed to obtain the optimal solutions. As the optimization problem in Eq. (2) is a bi-convex problem, it has been proved that the objective function converges finally [8]. Figure 2 presents the convergence curves on BIBTEX and COREL5K datasets with $\lambda = 1$ and $\lambda = 0.000001$. The numerical results show that our optimization approach can converge quickly in a few steps.

3 Experiments

In this section, we evaluate the performance of our algorithm on seven benchmark datasets and conduct comparison with several state-of-the-art algorithms.

3.1 Datasets and Comparison Methods

Seven benchmark datasets, including BIBTEX [13], CAL500 [25], COREL5K [6], mediamill [21], espgame [26], iaprtc12 [16] and EURLex-4K [2,18] are used in our experiment. For image datasets COREL5K, espgame and iaprtc12, we utilize the DenseSift features. If the number of samples is larger than 5000, we select 5000 samples randomly for training and testing. The label matrix is a binary matrix, where 1 means that the sample relates to this label and 0 means it does not belong to this class.

Meanwhile, we utilize BR [7], PLST [23], CPLST [5], ML-CSSP [3] and FaIE [15] to conduct performance comparsion in our experiment. BR is a label ranking method and is extended to handle the multi-label situation by using an artificial calibration label. PLST is a LSDR method. Similar to PCA, it learns a regression function from the feature space to the latent space. Unlike PLST, it considers both the prediction error and the encoding error. The prediction error is the same as CCA and the encoding error uses the reconstruction error in PLST. ML-CSSP is a label selection method. It reduces the problem to an efficient multi-label classification task by selecting important labels.

Table 3. Macro-F under 0.4 times of the dimension of the label space on benchmark datesets

DATA	BR	PLST	CPLST	FaIE	ML-CSSP	QDL
BIBTEX	0.0196	0.0471	0.0475	0.0473	0.0456	**0.1593**
CAL500	0.0928	0.2328	0.2320	0.2328	**0.2329**	0.2319
COREL5K	0.0086	0.0228	0.0228	0.0227	0.0226	**0.0361**
mediamill	0.0251	0.0753	0.0758	0.0753	0.0748	**0.0907**
espgame	0.0157	0.0404	0.0403	0.0402	0.0396	**0.0557**
iaprtc12	0.0205	0.0483	0.0485	0.0484	0.0477	**0.0525**
EURLex-4K	0.0015	0.0038	0.0037	0.0037	0.0037	**0.0044**

Table 4. Micro-F under 0.4 times of the dimension of the label space on benchmark datesets

DATA	BR	PLST	CPLST	FaIE	ML-CSSP	QDL
BIBTEX	0.0485	0.0478	0.0484	0.0483	0.0464	**0.1719**
CAL500	0.2326	0.2826	0.2908	0.2830	0.2795	**0.3374**
COREL5K	0.0273	0.0264	0.0283	0.0276	0.0273	**0.2268**
mediamill	0.0782	0.1032	0.1129	0.1039	0.1028	**0.5753**
espgame	0.0435	0.0439	0.0453	0.0446	0.0435	**0.0962**
iaprtc12	0.0578	0.0539	0.0554	0.0554	0.0534	**0.0682**
EURLex-4K	0.0058	0.0049	0.0049	0.0057	0.0056	**0.0078**

3.2 Parameter Setting

We use 5-fold cross validation on seven benchmark datasets to evaluate the performance of our algorithm. In each fold, we set 80% of samples as the training set and the remaining 20% of samples as the testing set. The average results of 5-fold cross validation are applied as the final results. Following the works [15], average precision, Micro-F1, Macro-F1 and average AUC are utilized as evaluation metrics. Since the four evaluation metrics have been studied in [28], we don't describe the metrics again. Similar to FaIE, the parameter λ in QDL is selected by cross-validation on the training set. The same as the work [5], we set the parameter of ridge regression as 0.1. The dimension of the latent space is set as $\{0.1, 0.2, 0.3, 0.4, 0.5\}$ times of the dimension of the label space respectively. We set the maximum number of iteration as 50.

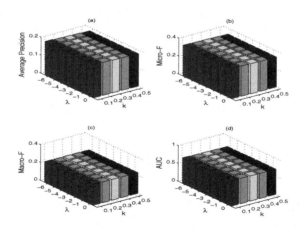

Fig. 3. Evaluation on CAL500 dataset with different λ and dimensions of the latent space

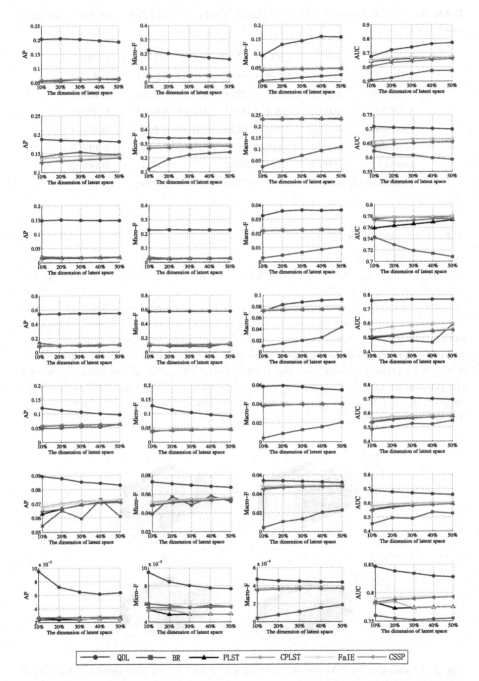

Fig. 4. The average precision, Micro-F, Macro-F and AUC on BIBTEX, CAL500, COREL5K, mediamill, espgame, iaprtc12 and EURLex-4K datasets for all comparison algorithms

3.3   Performance Comparison

We present the average precision, Micro-F, Macro-F and AUC on seven benchmark datasets in Fig. 4. In the figures, the horizontal axis represents the dimension of the latent space. The vertical axis represents the values of average precision, Micro-F, Macro-F and AUC. As shown, QDL achieves superior results in terms of the four evaluation metrics in comparison with other algorithms. For BIBTEX, mediamill, espgame, iaprtc12 and EURLex-4K, our algorithm achieves excellent results. For CAL500, our algorithm performs well in average precision, Micro-F and AUC. Our algorithm obtains similar results with PLST, CPLST, FaIE and ML-CSSP in Macro-F. For COREL5K, the CPLST performs best in AUC and is comparable with the performance of our algorithm. As the intrinsic dimension of latent space is much smaller than the feature and label space, the accuracies of QDL decrease with the dimension of latent space increasing for EURlex-4K. The results verify the effectiveness of QDL. QDL fully exploits the correlation between the feature space and label space by constructing a bidirectional bridge. Besides, by dictionary learning, the representation coefficients are used to model the latent space, which brings more predictability.

As the space of this paper is limited, we only show the values of the evaluation metrics when the dimension of the latent space is 0.4 times of the dimension of the label space in Tables 1, 2, 3 and 4. The best results are marked with bold face. We can observe that QDL obtains higher performance than other algorithms.

Next, we also investigated the parameter sensitivity of QDL. Figure 3 shows the evaluation on CAL500 dataset with different λ and dimensions of the latent space. The X-axis k represents the different dimensions of the latent space. The Y-axis represents the different values of λ and we take the logarithms (base 10) of parameters. It can be seen that QDL isn't sensitive to the parameter λ on CAL500 dataset. We find the same phenomenon on other datasets. Similar to dimension reduction in the feature space, we need to set the dimension of the latent space. As shown in Fig. 3, the performances of QDL change a little with different dimensions of the latent space.

4   Conclusions

In this paper, we proposed a novel quadruplet dictionary learning (QDL) model for multi-label classification with many classes. The feature space and label space are interconnected by two dictionary pairs, which can fully take advantage of the correlation between two spaces. By dictionary learning, QDL can recover both the feature space and label space, and therefore avoids information loss during label transformation. Experiments on seven multi-label datasets showed that QDL is superior to the existing label space dimension reduction methods for different dimensions of the latent space.

Acknowledge. This work was supported by the National Natural Science Foundation of China under Grants 61502332, 61876127 and 61732011, Natural Science Foundation of Tianjin under Grant 17JCZDJC30800, and Key Scientific and Technological Support Projects of Tianjin Key R&D Program under Grant 18YFZCGX00390 and Grant 18YFZCGX00680.

References

1. Balasubramanian, K., Lebanon, G.: The landmark selection method for multiple output prediction. In: ICML (2012)
2. Bhatia, K., Jain, H., Kar, P., Varma, M., Jain, P.: Sparse local embeddings for extreme multi-label classification. In: NIPS, pp. 730–738. Curran Associates, Inc. (2015)
3. Bi, W., Kwok, J.T.Y.: Efficient multi-label classification with many labels. In: ICML, vol. 3, pp. 405–413 (2013)
4. Boyd, S., Parikh, N., Chu, E., Peleato, B., Eckstein, J.: Distributed optimization and statistical learning via the alternating direction method of multipliers. Found. Trends® Mach. Learn. **3**(1), 1–122 (2011)
5. Chen, Y.N., Lin, H.T.: Feature-aware label space dimension reduction for multi-label classification. In: NIPS, pp. 1529–1537 (2012)
6. Duygulu, P., Barnard, K., de Freitas, J.F., Forsyth, D.A.: Object recognition as machine translation: learning a lexicon for a fixed image vocabulary. In: Heyden, A., Sparr, G., Nielsen, M., Johansen, P. (eds.) ECCV 2002. LNCS, vol. 2353, pp. 97–112. Springer, Berlin, Heidelberg (2002). https://doi.org/10.1007/3-540-47979-1_7
7. Fürnkranz, J., Hüllermeier, E., Mencía, E.L., Brinker, K.: Multilabel classification via calibrated label ranking. Mach. Learn. **73**(2), 133–153 (2008)
8. Gorski, J., Pfeuffer, F., Klamroth, K.: Biconvex sets and optimization with biconvex functions: a survey and extensions. Math. Methods Oper. Res. **66**(3), 373–407 (2007)
9. Guo, Y., Gu, S.: Multi-label classification using conditional dependency networks. In: IJCAI, pp. 1300–1305 (2011)
10. Hsu, D., Kakade, S., Langford, J., Zhang, T.: Multi-label prediction via compressed sensing. NIPS **22**, 772–780 (2009)
11. Huang, D.A., Frank Wang, Y.C.: Coupled dictionary and feature space learning with applications to cross-domain image synthesis and recognition. In: ICCV, pp. 2496–2503 (2013)
12. Kang, F., Jin, R., Sukthankar, R.: Correlated label propagation with application to multi-label learning. In: CVPR, vol. 2, pp. 1719–1726. IEEE (2006)
13. Katakis, I., Tsoumakas, G., Vlahavas, I.: Multilabel text classification for automated tag suggestion. In: ECML-PKDD, vol. 75 (2008)
14. Li, X., Guo, Y.: Multi-label classification with feature-aware non-linear label space transformation. In: IJCAI, pp. 3635–3642 (2015)
15. Lin, Z., Ding, G., Hu, M., Wang, J.: Multi-label classification via feature-aware implicit label space encoding. In: ICML, pp. 325–333 (2014)
16. Makadia, A., Pavlovic, V., Kumar, S.: A new baseline for image annotation. In: Forsyth, D., Torr, P., Zisserman, A. (eds.) ECCV 2008. LNCS, vol. 5304, pp. 316–329. Springer, Berlin, Heidelberg (2008). https://doi.org/10.1007/978-3-540-88690-7_24
17. Mandal, D., Biswas, S.: Generalized coupled dictionary learning approach with applications to cross-modal matching. TIP **25**(8), 3826–3837 (2016)
18. Mencia, E.L., Fürnkranz, J.: Efficient pairwise multilabel classification for large-scale problems in the legal domain. In: Daelemans, W., Goethals, B., Morik, K. (eds.) ECML PKDD 2008. LNCS, vol. 5212, pp. 50–65. Springer, Berlin, Heidelberg (2008). https://doi.org/10.1007/978-3-540-87481-2_4

19. Schapire, R.E., Singer, Y.: Boostexter: a boosting-based system for text categorization. Mach. Learn. **39**(2), 135–168 (2000)
20. Schietgat, L., Vens, C., Struyf, J., Blockeel, H., Kocev, D., Džeroski, S.: Predicting gene function using hierarchical multi-label decision tree ensembles. BMC Bioinf. **11**(1), 1 (2010)
21. Snoek, C.G., Worring, M., Van Gemert, J.C., Geusebroek, J.M., Smeulders, A.W.: The challenge problem for automated detection of 101 semantic concepts in multimedia. In: ACM Multimedia, pp. 421–430. ACM (2006)
22. Sun, L., Ji, S., Ye, J.: Canonical correlation analysis for multilabel classification: a least-squares formulation, extensions, and analysis. TPAMI **33**(1), 194–200 (2011)
23. Tai, F., Lin, H.T.: Multilabel classification with principal label space transformation. Neural Comput. **24**(9), 2508–2542 (2012)
24. Tsoumakas, G., Katakis, I., Vlahavas, I.: Mining multi-label data. In: Maimon, O., Rokach, L. (eds.) Data Mining and Knowledge Discovery Handbook, pp. 667–685. Springer, Boston, MA (2009). https://doi.org/10.1007/978-0-387-09823-4_34
25. Tsoumakas, G., Spyromitros-Xioufis, E., Vilcek, J., Vlahavas, I.: Mulan: a java library for multi-label learning. JMLR **12**, 2411–2414 (2011)
26. Von Ahn, L., Dabbish, L.: Labeling images with a computer game. In: Proceedings of the SIGCHI Conference on Human Factors in Computing Systems, pp. 319–326. ACM (2004)
27. Yang, J., Wang, Z., Lin, Z., Cohen, S., Huang, T.: Coupled dictionary training for image super-resolution. TIP **21**(8), 3467–3478 (2012)
28. Zhang, M.L., Zhou, Z.H.: A review on multi-label learning algorithms. TKDE **26**(8), 1819–1837 (2014)

Pareto Multi-task Deep Learning

Salvatore D. Riccio[1], Deyan Dyankov[2], Giorgio Jansen[3], Giuseppe Di Fatta[2],
and Giuseppe Nicosia[3,4(✉)]

[1] School of Mathematical Sciences, Queen Mary University of London, London, UK
[2] Department of Computer Science, University of Reading, Reading, UK
[3] Systems Biology Centre, University of Cambridge, Cambridge, UK
gn263@cam.ac.uk
[4] Department of Biomedical and Biotechnological Sciences, University of Catania,
Catania, Italy

Abstract. Neuroevolution has been used to train Deep Neural Networks
on reinforcement learning problems. A few attempts have been made to
extend it to address either multi-task or multi-objective optimization
problems. This research work presents the Multi-Task Multi-Objective
Deep Neuroevolution method, a highly parallelizable algorithm that can
be adopted for tackling both multi-task and multi-objective problems. In
this method prior knowledge on the tasks is used to explicitly define multiple utility functions, which are optimized simultaneously. Experimental
results on some Atari 2600 games, a challenging testbed for deep reinforcement learning algorithms, show that a single neural network with a
single set of parameters can outperform previous state of the art techniques. In addition to the standard analysis, all results are also evaluated
using the *Hypervolume indicator* and the *Kullback-Leibler divergence* to
get better insights on the underlying training dynamics. The experimental results show that a neural network trained with the proposed evolution strategy can outperform networks individually trained respectively
on each of the tasks.

Keywords: Multi-task learning · Multi-objective learning · Deep
Neuroevolution · Hypervolume · Kullback-Leibler divergence · Pareto
front · Evolution strategy · Atari 2600 games

1 Introduction

Deep Learning has successfully been adopted to solve many reinforcement learning problems. Recent results show the huge potential of this technique, with
impressive results that are far beyond human abilities [10,14,18]. The training of a Deep Neural Network (DNN) consists in changing its parameters to
minimize a defined cost function. The backpropagation algorithm [12] is used
in most applications to compute the gradient of the loss function for training
multilayer feedforward neural networks. Another possible algorithm to train a

---

S. D. Riccio and D. Dyankov—-These authors contributed equally to this work.

© Springer Nature Switzerland AG 2020
I. Farkaš et al. (Eds.): ICANN 2020, LNCS 12397, pp. 132–141, 2020.
https://doi.org/10.1007/978-3-030-61616-8_11

DNN is Deep Neuroevolution, a class of black-box algorithms inspired by biological evolution, which do not require the computation of the gradient. It was experimentally shown that networks trained with Deep Neuroevolution obtain results that can compete against gradient-descent deep learning algorithms in difficult reinforcement learning problems [3,5,8,13]. Population-based Neuroevolution algorithms can be adopted to find the optimal solution by exploring the space of both parameters and hyperparameters [9] as well as the best neural network architecture [15].

Deep Neuroevolution is a population-based algorithm, so it can be naturally extended to multi-task learning. Some works in this direction addressed multi-task learning [5,6], whereas other implemented a multi-objective strategy on a single task [17]. We propose a Deep Neuroevolution method for Multi-Task Multi-Objective problems, which is based on Evolution Strategy (MTMO-ES). This novel approach is used to optimize at the same time different tasks and different objectives with a single neural network associated with a single set of parameters. Multi-task learning aims at training a neural network to master multiple tasks simultaneously.

The proposed approach is tested on Atari 2600 games, a common benchmark for reinforcement learning algorithms. A network trained with MTMO-ES is shown to achieve better results than previous single-task single-objective deep reinforcement learning models trained individually on each task. A network trained for multi-task learning is expected to be inherently more general than one trained on a single task only.

Furthermore, we study the outcome of the network using two performance indices, the Kullback-Leibler divergence and the hypervolume indicator, that can be computed at each iteration, showing the underlying training dynamics. The rest of the paper is organized as follows: in Sect. 2 we discuss the theory behind the MTMO-ES algorithm. In Sect. 3 we present the analysis based on the hypervolume indicator and the Kullback-Leibler divergence, providing interesting insights of how to compute them for every iteration. Experimental results are shown in Sect. 4. Finally, conclusions are drawn in Sect. 5.

2 Multi-task Multi-Objective Evolution Strategy

The goal of deep learning algorithms is to train a network so that its parameter vector θ maximizes a specific utility function $u(\theta)$, which depends on the output obtained by the neural network associated with θ. For the sake of conciseness, u will be used instead of $u(\theta)$ unless otherwise stated. Such an optimization problem can be solved by Evolution Strategies (ES) [11], a class of nature-inspired black-box optimization methods [4]. In general, an Evolution Strategy algorithm works as follows. Starting from one or more parents, a number of offspring is generated using mutation, crossover, or other techniques. Offspring are typically evaluated on a cost function (fitness function) and a new set of parents are selected according to a chosen criterion for the next generation.

The aim of this work is to train a neural network with evolution strategy, so that the trained network achieves good performance in all tasks using a single set of parameters. The best parent, P, selected in the last iteration is the parameter vector of the trained network.

Offspring at iteration k are generated from a gaussian distribution centered in $\theta_P(k)$. To increase the robustness, we perform mirrored sampling (i.e., two offspring are generated symmetrically or mirrored with respect to their parent). In practice, each offspring is associated with another one that is symmetric with respect to the parent values $\theta_P(k)$. Evaluating the offspring allows to estimate the gradient without resorting to differentiation. This is useful especially when the rewards are sparse, which is a property that reinforcement learning problems commonly have. Multi-Task Multi-Objective based on Evolution Strategies (MTMO-ES) is based on this evolutionary approach and the details of the proposed method are described in the reminder of this section. At iteration 0, the parameter vector $\theta_P(0)$ (subscript P stands for Parent, whereas 0 is the iteration) is randomly initialized. In a single task, the new parent parameter vector can be computed at every iteration k as shown in Eq. (1):

$$\theta_P(k+1) = g(\theta_P(k), \nabla_\theta f(\theta(k))) \, , \, \theta(k) \in \Theta_k \tag{1}$$

where $\nabla_\theta f(\theta(k))$ is the gradient of the score function estimator, f is the distribution from which the chosen feature is obtained using $\theta(k)$, g is a chosen optimizer (e.g. Adam or stochastic gradient descent), and Θ_k is the set of offspring generated at iteration k. It is assumed that an utility u depends on the measured feature f for the single-task scenario. If there are two or more goals, the corresponding multi-objective optimization problem over $m \in \mathbb{N}$ goals is stated as $\mathrm{argmax}_\theta\{u_1(\theta), u_2(\theta), \ldots, u_m(\theta)\}$ We introduce a change to eq. (1) to address both the multi-task and the multi-objective problem. Let $\mathcal{T}$ be a finite set of chosen tasks (i.e.: $|\mathcal{T}| = t \in \mathbb{N}$), $\{u_1, u_2, \ldots, u_m\}$ is the set of goals, $\{f_1, f_2, \ldots, f_n\}$ is the set of measurable features. Every different task must be associated with at least one feature, so $t \leq n$. Note that, in general for a given i, f_i is not necessarily associated with τ_i. The association between features and tasks is explicitly defined. Let $\delta_{ij} = \{0,1\}$ be a binary variable that is 1 if and only if f_i is evaluated on task τ_j. It is also required that every feature f_i is associated with at most one task τ_j: $\sum_{j=1}^t \delta_{ij} = 1$, $\forall i \in \{1, \ldots, n\}$. Instead of computing only one gradient on one feature f_i evaluated on one task τ_j, we compute n gradients based on n features evaluated on t tasks. Every i-th gradient is then multiplied by a scalar α_i to obtain the overall Multi-Task Multi-Objective (MTMO-ES) gradient:

$$\theta_P(k+1) = g\left(\theta_P(k), \Sigma_{i=1}^n \alpha_i \nabla_\theta f_i(\theta(k))\right) \, , \, \theta(k) \in \Theta_k \tag{2}$$

$$\sum_{i=1}^n |\alpha_i| = 1 \, , \, \alpha_i \in \mathbb{R} \, \forall i \tag{3}$$

$$\sum_{i=1}^n |\alpha_i| \delta_{ij} = \frac{1}{t} \, , \, \forall j \in \{1, \ldots, t\} \tag{4}$$

It can be recognized that the MTMO-ES gradient is a linear combination of all single-task gradients. The condition in Eq. (3) is required to avoid a change in the modulus of the MTMO-ES gradient, provided that all single-task gradients are normalized. The condition in Eq. (4) avoids biases towards one of the tasks. In other terms, with Eq. (2)-(3) it is possible to rotate the final gradient accordingly to the measured features. This way it is possible to force the evolution of the vector θ towards a common direction that maximizes every goal. Before computing the gradient for every feature f_i, offspring scores are rank-normalized. Without this step, the network can get easily stuck in a local maximum within the first iterations [3]. The computation time required to compute every gradient in Eq. (2) is t times the one required for Eq. (1), because every mutation $\theta \in \Theta_k$ needs to be evaluated on every task. However, this algorithm can be easily parallelized exploiting the same approach implemented for the single-task algorithm [13]. With this formulation it is possible to address both multi-task and multi-objective learning at the same time using Evolution Strategies. It is also easy to minimize some goals and to maximize others. It is enough to associate with a negative α the features that have to be minimized.

3   Hypervolume and Kullback-Leibler Divergence

Hypervolume. Given a set of solutions Θ, its associated Pareto front is defined as the set P such that $P(\Theta) = \{\theta' \in \Theta \mid \nexists \theta \in \Theta : \theta \preceq \theta'\}$ where, using the standard notation, $\theta \preceq \theta'$ means that θ dominates the solution θ'. The hypervolume indicator [19] h is the volume between the Pareto front P and the reference point. This latter point is a parameter that must be carefully chosen to avoid distorted results [1]. In this work, the easiest and most natural choice is to select the origin as the reference point. The Pareto front can be computed at every iteration given the set of offspring Θ_k at iteration k. This means that also the hypervolume indicator h can be computed as a function of k. The difference between the maximum value of two different goals u_i and u_j can be high. To avoid biases in the hypervolume indicator, it is important to normalize each goal with respect to its maximum value over all iterations. This indicator shows how much effectively the network is learning to achieve good results on every goal. It can be analytically computed if $t = 2$. The computation is nontrivial for higher dimension and good estimations can be obtained with efficient algorithms [7].

Kullback-Leibler Divergence. Given two discrete distributions P and Q defined over the same support $\mathcal{X}$, the Kullback-Leibler divergence is described by eq. (5):

$$D_{KL}(P, Q) = \sum_{x \in \mathcal{X}} p(x) ln \frac{p(x)}{q(x)} \tag{5}$$

In this work, distributions P and Q are associated with a given goal u and they can change as a function of different samples of the set Θ. For hard reinforcement learning problems, those distributions are unknown and cannot be computed analytically. A viable approach is to exploit a frequentist approach, using relative frequencies on sampled values to get an estimate of $p(x)$ and $q(x)$. In

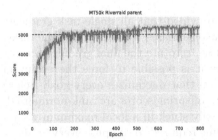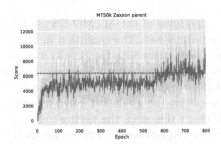

Fig. 1. Multi-task single-objective ES trained on River Raid and Zaxxon, evaluated on River Raid (left) and on Zaxxon (right) for 800 iterations. Elite mean scores, with minimum and maximum score per iteration. The dashed lines are the results obtained by ES single task as shown in [13]. The network trained with the new approach is able to perform better in both tasks, given that it is trained for a sufficient number of iterations.

practice, $\theta_P(k)$ is evaluated $N \in \mathbb{N}$ times to get N i.i.d. samples from $f(\theta_P(k))$. The interval from the minimum and the maximum values in all iterations is partitioned into $M \in \mathbb{N}$ subintervals with same length. Each subinterval is associated with the number of perturbations that have a score within the subinterval range. To overcome numerical issues coming from some subintervals having zero frequency, Laplace smoothing is applied to the data before computing D_{KL}. This smoothing technique consists in adding a small ϵ to each subinterval, followed by a normalization of P and Q to 1. The Kullback-Leibler divergence is computed using the distribution estimated at the current iteration k for P, and the one at a reference iteration $\bar{k}$ for Q. Some possible choices for $\bar{k}$ are the first iteration, the last iteration, or $\bar{k} = k - \Delta k$, where $\Delta k \in \mathbb{Z}$ is a fixed lag. The Kullback-Leibler divergence is also called information gain. It is a measure of the amount of information that the algorithm is able to extract going from Q to P [16]. When P and Q are identical, $D_{KL}(P, Q) = 0$. On the other hand, if for all $x \in \mathcal{X}$ $p(x) \neq 0$ and $q(x) = 0$, then the two distributions are disjointed. In this case, the D_{KL} will be large and it depends both on ϵ and on the distribution P. In practice, a large D_{KL} means that the two distributions are different, whereas a small value implies similar distributions.

4   Experimental Analysis and Results

All experiments are run on a single deep neural network. The architecture is the same used in [10], which consists of three convolutional layers, followed by a fully connected layer. The output layer is fully connected too, and each node is respectively associated with one out of the 18 valid actions. Our implementation is an extension of the work of Conti et al. [3] and inherits its parallelizability. Indeed, all simulations are run on a single machine using parallel GPU computing. Although the approach is general and can be applied to a large number of tasks, in this work we limited the analysis to scenarios with a few tasks for

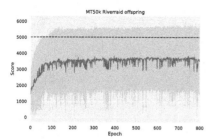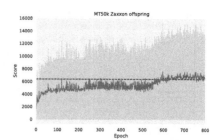

Fig. 2. Multi-task single-objective ES trained on River Raid and Zaxxon, evaluated on River Raid (left) and on Zaxxon (right) for 800 iterations. Offspring mean scores, with minimum and maximum score per iteration. The dashed lines are the mean elite scores obtained by ES single task in their respective game as shown in [13]. Interestingly, even the mean score obtained by Zaxxon offspring is slightly better than the mean elite score obtained with single-task ES.

the sake of simplicity. First, the multi-task approach is tested. The two Atari games Zaxxon and River Raid are chosen from OpenAI Gym [2] because they share similar game dynamics. Scores are compared with those obtained with a single-task ES approach (River Raid: 5009.0, Zaxxon: 6380.0) [13] and with IMPALA, a multi-task algorithm based on V-trace [6] (River Raid: 2850.15, Zaxxon: 6497.00). The mean of the scores obtained by the *parent candidate solutions* evaluated over 200 episodes is shown in Fig. 1. After an initial convergence toward a local minimum, the network is able to find new strategies and to outperform previous results on both tasks. Figure 2 shows the mean score obtained evaluating 5,000 offspring for every iteration. The range between minimum and

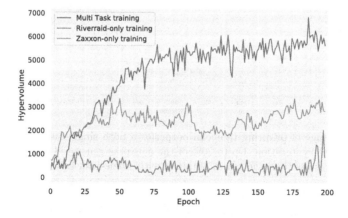

Fig. 3. Comparison between three training strategies: multi-task, single-task trained on one game, single-task trained on the other game. A network trained on a single task cannot master both games, whereas the network trained with the new approach is able to play well both games.

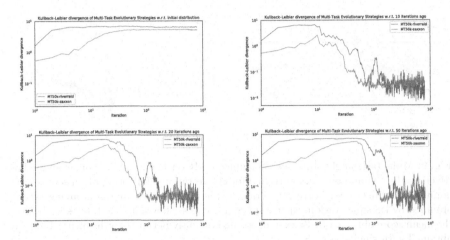

Fig. 4. D_{KL} computed on parent scores with respect to the first iteration (first row, left), to the previous 10 iterations (first row, right), to the previous 20 iterations (second row, left), to the previous 50 iterations (second row, right), shown as a log-log plot. $M = 100$ is the chosen number of subintervals. The index is computed separately on the two tasks, namely River Raid and Zaxxon. When the index is evaluated with respect to the first iteration, the two lines converge towards a value different from zero. Indeed, the sampled distribution obtained at iteration k diverges from the initial one for both tasks. When the index is evaluated using a fixed delay Δk, it is high for both tasks within the first hundred iterations, showing that the network is learning. Then the values decrease because the difference between the distributions becomes smaller.

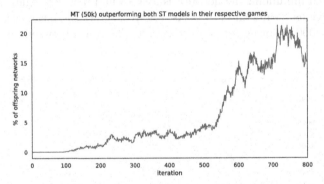

Fig. 5. Percentage of offspring that can outperform both single-task ES state-of-the-art scores for every iteration. Up to 20% of the networks generated for every iteration obtain better results than the scores obtained with single-task ES.

maximum value is large, which means that the algorithm is exploring new possible solutions at every iteration. We test other two runs, evaluating the score on both tasks for a single network trained with single-task single-objective ES. The hypervolume indicator is computed for three independent simulations. Results are shown in Fig. 3. This plot shows that the Pareto front obtained with the

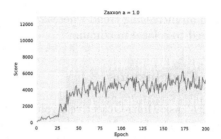

Fig. 6. Mean score obtained from 20 evaluations per iteration using single-task multi-objective ES on Zaxxon. The area shows the score range (from minimum to maximum) per iteration. The algorithm is maximizing both the score and the number of frames (left), compared with single-task single-objective ES where the only objective is the score (right). The score improves thanks to the additional requirement on the number of frames.

multi-task ES algorithm covers a larger area than the other two, which means that the new algorithm is finding strategies able to master both tasks at the same time. Using the single-task algorithm, the Pareto front moves along one of the two axes. With the multi-task algorithm, the direction of the Pareto front is common to both axes. The Kullback-Leibler divergence is then computed on parents score. All the results obtained using different lags Δk are plotted in Fig. 4. When the divergence is evaluated with respect to the initial distribution, we expect a convergence towards a large value. This is exactly the behavior showed in the figure, which means that the distribution at the end is completely different than the original one. When using a fixed lag Δk, an increasing smooth line shows that the network is changing its distribution faster and faster. This is usually followed by a negative slope, which means that the distribution is still changing, but slower than before. In the last iterations the line is noisy, showing that the two distributions have similar mean values, so the network is not really learning anymore. We also investigate how many strategies found during multi-task training are better in both tasks than the best elite score found with a single-task approach. This result is plotted in Fig. 5, which shows the percentage of the set of parameters per iteration that can outperform results obtained with single-task ES. It is notable that up to an impressive 20% (i.e.: around $1,000$) offspring during the last iterations are good candidates to be the next parent. Multi-task ES is able to find $2 - 3\%$ of offspring with outstanding results even in the first hundred iterations. Finally, single-task multi-objective ES is tested. We want to maximize the score of Zaxxon using two objectives: the score itself and the number of played frames. The idea is that explicitly forcing the network towards long-run strategies can help finding a better solution. The results of this new multi-objective strategy are compared with the ones of the single-objective ES strategy and the plots are shown in Fig. 6. Although the new method shows a slower improvement in the first iterations, at the end it achieves better results with an increasing trend whereas the single-objective version seems to have converged to a local maximum.

5 Conclusions

Multi-Task Multi-Objective Evolution Strategy (MTMO-ES) is a novel training algorithm for Deep Neural Networks that can simultaneously address both multi-task and multi-objective problems. Tests on some Atari 2600 games show that a neural network trained with this evolution strategy can obtain excellent results in more than one task or one objective, using only one set of parameters. It is indeed remarkable that a single network with a single set of parameters can outperform networks trained respectively on one task or one objective only. Thanks to its underlying structure, this algorithm can be easily parallelized using workers on many CPUs or GPUs. In principle, an arbitrarily large number of tasks can be chosen without affecting the total time required. In practice, the overhead will become not negligible after a certain number of tasks, and the algorithm will take longer. The hypervolume indicator and the Kullback-Leibler divergence, when computed at each iteration, can give useful insights on the learning dynamics. MTMO-ES is a general optimization method and does not require prior knowledge of the environment dynamics. For this reason, we believe it can be easily adopted in many diverse domains and obtain interesting results with relatively low implementation effort.

References

1. Auger, A., Bader, J., Brockhoff, D., Zitzler, E.: Theory of the hypervolume indicator: optimal μ-distributions and the choice of the reference point. In: FOGA, pp. 87–102 (2009)
2. Brockman, G., et al.: OpenAI Gym (2016). https://gym.openai.com
3. Conti, E., et al.: Improving exploration in evolution strategies for deep reinforcement learning via a population of novelty-seeking agents. In: NeurIPS 2018, Montreal, Canada (2018)
4. De Jong, K.: Evolutionary Computation - A Unified Approach. The MIT Press, Cambridge (2006)
5. Dyankov, D., Riccio, S.D., Di Fatta, G., Nicosia, G.: Multi-task learning by pareto optimality. In: Nicosia, G., Pardalos, P., Umeton, R., Giuffrida, G., Sciacca, V. (eds.) LOD 2019. LNCS, vol. 11943, pp. 605–618. Springer, Cham (2019). https://doi.org/10.1007/978-3-03037599-7_50
6. Espeholt, L., et al.: IMPALA: Scalable distributed deep-RL with importance weighted actor-learner architectures. In: Dy, J., Krause, A. (eds.) Proceedings of the 35th International Conference on Machine Learning, vol. 80, pp. 1407–1416 (2018)
7. Fonseca, C.M., Paquete, L., López-Ibáñez, M.: An improved dimension-sweep algorithm for the hypervolume indicator. In: 2006 IEEE International Conference on Evolutionary Computation, pp. 1157–1163 (2006)

8. Hausknecht, M., Lehman, J., Miikkulainen, R., Stone, P.: A neuroevolution app-roach to general Atari game playing. IEEE Trans. Comput. Intell. AI Games **6**, 355–366 (2014)

9. Jaderberg, M., et al.: Population based training of neural networks (2017). arXiv:1711.09846

10. Mnih, V., et al.: Human-level control through deep reinforcement learning. Nature **518**(7540), 529–533 (2015). https://doi.org/10.1038/nature14236

11. Rechenberg, I.: Evolutionsstrategie: optimierung technischer Systeme nach Prinzip-ien der biologischen Evolution. Ph.D. thesis, Technical University of Berlin, Depart-ment of Process Engineering (1971)

12. Rumelhart, D.E., Hinton, G.E., Williams, R.J.: Learning representations by back-propagating errors. Nature **323**, 533–536 (1986)

13. Salimans, T., Ho, J., Chen, X., Sidor, S., Sutskever, I.: Evolution Strategies as a Scalable Alternative to Reinforcement Learning. arXiv e-prints arXiv:1703.03864 (2017)

14. Silver, D., Hubert, T., Schrittwieser, J., Antonoglou, I., Lai, M., Guez, A., Lanctot, M., Sifre, L., Kumaran, D., Graepel, T., Lillicrap, T., Simonyan, K., Hassabis, D.: A general reinforcement learning algorithm that masters chess, shogi, and go through self-play. Science **362**, 1140–1144 (2018)

15. Stanley, K., Clune, J., Lehman, J., Miikkulainen, R.: Designing neural networks through neuroevolution. Nat. Mach. Intell. **1**, 24–35 (2019). https://doi.org/10.1038/s42256-018-0006-z

16. Stracquadanio, G., Nicosia, G.: Computational energy-based redesign of robust proteins. Comput. Chem. Eng. (2010). https://doi.org/10.1016/j.compchemeng.2010.04.005

17. Tan, T.G., Teo, J., On, C.: Single- versus multiobjective optimization for evolution of neural controllers in ms. Pac-Man. Int. J. Comput. Games Technol. 2013, 170914 (2013). https://doi.org/10.1155/2013/170914

18. Vinyals, O., et al.: Grandmaster level in starcraft ii using multi-agent reinforcement learning. Nature **575**, 350–354 (2019)

19. Zitzler, E., Thiele, L.: Multiobjective optimization using evolutionary algorithms - a comparative case study. In: A.E., E., T., B., M., S., HP., S. (eds.) Proceedings of the 30th International Conference on Machine Learning, vol. 1498, pp. 292–301 (1998)

Convex Graph Laplacian Multi-Task Learning SVM

Carlos Ruiz[1]([⊠]), Carlos M. Alaíz[1], and José R. Dorronsoro[1,2]

[1] Dept. Computer Engineering, Universidad Autónoma de Madrid, Madrid, Spain
carlos.ruizp@estudiante.uam.es, {carlos.alaiz,jose.dorronsoro}@uam.es
[2] Inst. Ing. Conocimiento, Universidad Autónoma de Madrid, Madrid, Spain

Abstract. Multi-Task Learning (MTL) goal is to achieve a better generalization by using data from different sources. MTL Support Vector Machines (SVMs) embrace this idea in two main ways: by using a combination of common and task-specific parts, or by fitting individual models adding a graph Laplacian regularization that defines different degrees of task relationships. The first approach is too rigid since it imposes the same relationship among all tasks. The second one does not have a clear way of sharing information among the different tasks. In this paper, we propose a model that combines both approaches. It uses a convex combination of a common model and of task specific models, where the relationships between these specific models are determined through a graph Laplacian regularization. We write the primal problem of this formulation and derive its dual problem, which is shown to be equivalent to a standard SVM dual using a particular kernel choice. Empirical results over different regression and classification problems support the usefulness of our proposal.

1   Introduction

Standard Machine Learning (ML) often seeks to minimize a fixed overall loss. This is the optimal goal when the training dataset is associated to a single homogeneous task, but less so when there might be somehow different subtasks underlying the common objective. If this is the case, it is natural to share the common task learning while allowing for specific learning procedures for the individual tasks. Among other advantages, this approach, known as Multi-Task Learning (MTL), complements data augmentation with task focusing, introduces inductive bias in the learning process and even performs implicit regularization. Starting with the work of R. Caruana [1], MTL has been applied to a large number of problems and under different underlying ML techniques.

Support Vector Machines (SVMs) are a natural choice for MTL. Although SVM models were originally formulated as linear models, the kernel trick allows to find the optimal hyperplane in a high-dimensional, even theoretically infinite space. Additionally, the ϵ-insensitive loss makes these models robust to noise in regression problems. Among the first approaches to SVM-based MTL is the Regularized Multi-Task Learning proposal in [2], where the primal problem for

© Springer Nature Switzerland AG 2020
I. Farkaš et al. (Eds.): ICANN 2020, LNCS 12397, pp. 142–154, 2020.
https://doi.org/10.1007/978-3-030-61616-8_12

linear SVM is expressed in a multi-task framework by introducing common and specific parts of each task model and penalizing these independently in the regularizer. This work is extended in [3], where a variety of kernel methods for multi-task problems with quadratic regularizers are reduced to solving a single-task problem using a multi-task kernel. This result is used in [4,5] for multi-task feature and structure learning. Also, multi-task regularizers with different goals have been proposed: for instance, in [6] the tasks are clustered, the intra-cluster distance is minimized while the inter-cluster distance is maximized. The ideas of Evgeniou *et al.* presented in [2] are extended in [7] to the use of multiple kernels for different tasks in regression, and they are generalized in [8] for classification and regression, addressing the use of task specific biases.

The initial approach, used in [2,8], is to consider the task models to be a sum of a common model and a task specific one, where a penalty μ controls the regularization balance between these common and specific parts. This is then transformed into a dual problem where μ is incorporated into the kernel matrix. With this formulation, the relationship between all tasks is assumed to be the same. The differences from the common model are all equally penalized, forcing the tasks to be equidistant to the common model. Other interesting approach shown in [3] and extended in [9] is to use a Graph Laplacian regularization, where the tasks are represented as nodes in a graph, and the distance between two task parameters is penalized according to the edge weight between those tasks. In this multi-task approximation, one can define different relations between the task pairs.

In this work we propose a new formulation, which we name Convex Graph Laplacian SVM-MTL, where the MTL models are a convex combination of common and specific components. A graph defines the relationships between the task-specific models, while the common model ensures the sharing of information across tasks. By using this formulation we can obtain the flexibility of using both different task relationships and the explicit shared information, represented in the common model. More precisely, our contributions in this work are:

- We introduce linear Convex Graph Laplacian MTL-SVMs.
- We extend this initial linear set-up to a multi-kernel setting where each component of the multi-task model can have its own kernel.
- We show numerically that our proposal gives competitive and often better results that either a single SVM model for all tasks, a combination of independent models, or Graph Laplacian MTL-SVMs.

The rest of the paper is organized as follows. In Sect. 2 we will briefly review previous formulations of the MTL and Graph MTL primal and dual problems and we present our approach in Sect. 3. We show our experimental results in Sect. 4, and the paper ends in Sect. 5, where we briefly discuss our results, offer some conclusions on them and present lines of further work.

2　Multi-Task Learning Support Vector Machine

We briefly review first standard SVMs. In order to show a more general result, we introduce a notation that allows to write Support Vector Classification (SVC) and Support Vector Regression (SVR) problems in a unified way. Following [10], consider a sample $S = \{(x_i, y_i, p_i),\ 1 \le i \le N\}$, where $y_i = \pm 1$, and a primal problem of the form

$$\underset{w,b,\xi}{\arg\min}\quad J(w, b, \xi) = C\sum_{n=1}^{N}\xi_i + \frac{1}{2}\|w\|^2 \tag{1}$$

$$\text{s.t.}\qquad y_i(w \cdot x_i + b) \ge p_i - \xi_i,\ \xi_i \ge 0,\ i = 1, \ldots, N.$$

It is easy to check [10] that for a classification sample $\{(x_i, y_i),\ 1 \le i \le M\}$, Problem (1) is equivalent to the SVC primal problem when choosing $N = M$ and $p_i = 1$ for all i. In a similar way, for a regression sample $\{(x_i, t_i),\ 1 \le i \le M\}$, Problem (1) is equivalent to the ϵ-insensitive SVR primal problem when we set $N = 2M$ and $y_i = 1$, $p_i = t_i - \epsilon$, $y_{M+i} = -1$, $p_{M+i} = -t_i - \epsilon$ for $i = 1, \ldots, M$. With this notation any result obtained for (1) will be valid for both SVC and SVR. The dual problem for this general formulation can be written as follows:

$$\underset{\alpha}{\arg\min}\quad \Theta(\alpha) = \alpha^{\mathsf{T}}Q\alpha - p^{\mathsf{T}}\alpha$$

$$\text{s.t.}\qquad 0 \le \alpha_i \le C,\ i = 1, \ldots, N,\ \sum_{i=1}^{N} y_i\alpha_i = 0, \tag{2}$$

where we use the vectors $\alpha^{\mathsf{T}} = (\alpha_1, \ldots, \alpha_N)$, $p^{\mathsf{T}} = (p_1, \ldots, p_N)$ and Q is the kernel matrix. To present our results in a compact way we will use this unified formulation in the rest of this work.

Turning our attention to Convex Multi-Task SVM, their formulation in [11] has the following primal problem:

$$\underset{w,v_r,b_r,\xi}{\arg\min}\quad J(w, v_r, b_r, \xi) = C\sum_{r=1}^{T}\sum_{i=1}^{N}\xi_i^r + \frac{1}{2}\|w\|^2 + \frac{1}{2}\sum_{r=1}^{T}\|v_r\|^2 \tag{3}$$

$$\text{s.t.}\qquad y_i^r\left(\lambda w \cdot x_i^r + (1-\lambda)v_r \cdot x_i^r + b_r\right) \ge p_i^r - \xi_i^r,$$

$$\xi_i^r \ge 0,\ i = 1, \ldots, n_r,\ r = 1, \ldots, T.$$

It can be shown that the dual problem of (3) is the following:

$$\underset{\alpha}{\arg\min}\quad \Theta(\alpha) = \alpha^{\mathsf{T}}\widehat{Q}\alpha - p^{\mathsf{T}}\alpha$$

$$\text{s.t.}\qquad 0 \le \alpha_i^r \le C,\ i = 1, \ldots, n_r,\ r = 1, \ldots, T,$$

$$\sum_{i=1}^{n_r} y_i\alpha_i^r = 0,\ r = 1, \ldots, T, \tag{4}$$

where $\widehat{Q}$ is the multi-task kernel matrix defined by the multi-task kernel $\widehat{k}$:

$$\widehat{k}(x_i^r, x_j^s) = \lambda^2 k(x_i^r, x_j^s) + (1-\lambda)^2\delta_{rs}k_r(x_i^r, x_j^s).$$

Here k and k_r are the common and task-specific kernels, and δ denotes the Kronecker delta function. Also, multiple equality constraints are included in (4), which are not compatible with the SMO algorithm used to solve the SVM dual. We will discuss below how to deal with this issue. One drawback of this approach is that every task-independent part is equally penalized. This implicitly assumes all models f_r to be equidistant to the common model f. This could be detrimental in those cases where not all the tasks are related in the same way.

Finally, another approach that can introduce different relations between tasks is the Graph Laplacian Multi-Task SVM introduced in [3]. Here the tasks are seen as nodes in a complete graph $\mathcal{G}$ and the edge weights A_{rs} control the relationship between the task nodes that they connect. The primal problem is defined as

$$\underset{v_r, b_r, \xi}{\arg\min} \quad J(v_r, b_r, \xi) = C \sum_{r=1}^{T} \sum_{i=1}^{N} \xi_i^r + \frac{\mu}{4} \sum_{r=1}^{T} \sum_{s=1}^{T} A_{rs} \|v_r - v_s\|^2 \tag{5}$$

$$\text{s.t.} \quad y_i^r (v_r \cdot x_i^r + b_r) \geq p_i^r - \xi_i^r, \ \xi_i^r \geq 0, \ i = 1, \ldots, n_r, \ r = 1, \ldots, T;$$

note that in this formulation no common part is shared across tasks. Moreover, consider the following extended vector $v \in \mathbb{R}^{T \times d}$ with $v^\mathsf{T} = (v_1^\mathsf{T}, \ldots, v_T^\mathsf{T})$ and the graph Laplacian $L = D - A$, where A is the graph weight matrix and D is the corresponding degree matrix, i.e., $D_{rs} = \delta_{rs} \sum_{q=1}^{T} A_{rq}$. Denoting by $\otimes$ the Kronecker product, it can be proved that

$$v^\mathsf{T} (L \otimes I_d) v = \frac{1}{2} \sum_{r=1}^{T} \sum_{s=1}^{T} A_{rs} \|v_r - v_s\|^2 . \tag{6}$$

Given this, and as shown in [3], the corresponding dual problem is

$$\underset{\alpha}{\arg\min} \quad \Theta(\alpha) = \alpha^\mathsf{T} \tilde{Q} \alpha - p^\mathsf{T} \alpha$$

$$\text{s.t.} \quad 0 \leq \alpha_i^r \leq C, \ i = 1, \ldots, n_r, \ r = 1, \ldots, T, \tag{7}$$

$$\sum_{i=1}^{n_r} y_i \alpha_i = 0, \ r = 1, \ldots, T,$$

where $\widetilde{Q}$ is the kernel matrix corresponding to the multi-task kernel $\widetilde{k}(x_i^r, x_j^s) = L_{rs}^+ k(x_i^r, x_j^s)$, and L^+ is the pseudo-inverse of the graph Laplacian matrix L. Notice that problem (7) is formally identical to (4), although using a different multi-task kernel.

We point out that in (5) only the distance between vectors is penalized, but the weight vector norms v_r are not regularized. This can lead to overfitting when the tasks are highly related. Also, the sharing of information is only made through the Graph Laplacian regularization term. To improve on this, we propose the Convex Graph Laplacian Multi-Task SVM described next.

3   Convex Graph Laplacian Multi-Task SVM

Convex Graph Laplacian Multi-Task SVM combines the two approaches above, working with a convex combination of a common component w and of specific models v_r. We also use both their individual regularizers and a Graph Laplacian regularization term. The multi-task models f_r are defined as $f_r = \lambda f + (1 - \lambda)g_r + b_r$ where f is the common model, g_r are the individual models, b_r are the bias terms and $\lambda \in [0, 1]$. Hence, this reduces to the common model by setting $\lambda = 1$, and to the individual models when $\lambda = 0$; in this last case we would have a Graph Laplacian model with additional individual weight regularization.

3.1 Convex Graph Laplacian Linear Multi-Task SVM

We consider first the case of the common and specific models being linear. More precisely, the primal problem is defined now as:

$$
\begin{aligned}
\underset{w,v_r,b_r,\xi}{\arg\min} \quad & J(w, v_r, b_r, \xi) = C \sum_{r=1}^{T} \sum_{i=1}^{N} \xi_i^r + \frac{1}{2} \|w\|^2 \\
& + \frac{1}{2} \sum_{r=1}^{T} \|v_r\|^2 + \frac{\mu}{4} \sum_{r=1}^{T} \sum_{s=1}^{T} A_{rs} \|v_r - v_s\|^2 \quad (8) \\
\text{s.t.} \quad & y_i^r \left(\lambda w \cdot x_i^r + (1 - \lambda)v_r \cdot x_i^r + b_r \right) \geq p_i^r - \xi_i^r, \\
& \xi_i^r \geq 0, \ i = 1, \ldots, n_r, \ r = 1, \ldots, T.
\end{aligned}
$$

We can write this primal problem in a more compact way as

$$
\begin{aligned}
\underset{w,v_r,b_r,\xi}{\arg\min} \quad & J(w, v, b_r, \xi) = C \sum_{r=1}^{T} \sum_{i=1}^{N} \xi_i^r + \frac{1}{2} \|w\|^2 + \frac{1}{2} v^\mathsf{T} (B \otimes I_d)v \\
\text{s.t.} \quad & y_i^r \left(\lambda w \cdot x_i^r + (1 - \lambda)v_r \cdot x_i^r + b_r \right) \geq p_i^r - \xi_i^r, \\
& \xi_i^r \geq 0, \ i = 1, \ldots, n_r, \ r = 1, \ldots, T.
\end{aligned} \quad (9)
$$

Here we have $v^\mathsf{T} = (v_1^\mathsf{T}, \ldots, v_T^\mathsf{T})$ and $B = (I_T + \mu L)$; also, $\otimes$ denotes again the Kronecker product, L is the Laplacian matrix of the task graph and I_d is the identity matrix of dimension d. To prove the equivalence between (8) and (9), we simply observe that

$$
v^\mathsf{T}(I_T \otimes I_d)v = \sum_{r=1}^{T} \|v_r\|^2, \ v^\mathsf{T}(L \otimes I_d)v = \frac{1}{2} \sum_{r=1}^{T} \sum_{s=1}^{T} A_{rs} \|v_r - v_s\|^2,
$$

and that the Kronecker product is bilinear. The second equality also uses (6). We derive next the dual problem corresponding to (9). Its Lagrangian is

$$
\begin{aligned}
\mathcal{L}(w, v, b_r, \xi, \alpha, \beta) = {} & C \sum_{r=1}^{T} \sum_{i=1}^{N} \xi_i^r + \frac{1}{2} \|w\|^2 + \frac{1}{2} v^\mathsf{T}(B \otimes I_d)v \\
& + \sum_{r=1}^{T} \sum_{i=1}^{n_r} \alpha_i^r p_i^r - \sum_{r=1}^{T} \sum_{i=1}^{n_r} \alpha_i^r \xi_i^r - \sum_{r=1}^{T} \sum_{i=1}^{n_r} \alpha_i^r y_i^r b_r \\
& - \lambda \sum_{r=1}^{T} \sum_{i=1}^{n_r} \alpha_i^r y_i^r w \cdot x_i^r - (1 - \lambda) \sum_{r=1}^{T} \sum_{i=1}^{n_r} \alpha_i^r y_i^r v_r \cdot x_i^r - \sum_{r=1}^{T} \sum_{i=1}^{n_r} \beta_i^r \xi_i^r.
\end{aligned} \quad (10)
$$

Taking derivatives with respect to the primal variables and equating them to zero, we obtain the stationary conditions, of which the one involving v becomes

$$v = (1 - \lambda)(B \otimes I_d)^{-1}\Psi\alpha, \tag{11}$$

where $\alpha^{\mathsf{T}} = (\alpha_1^1, \ldots, \alpha_{n_T}^T)$, and where the matrix Ψ of extended patterns is defined as:

$$\Psi = \begin{pmatrix} \Psi_1 & 0 & \cdots & 0 \\ 0 & \Psi_2 & \cdots & 0 \\ \vdots & \vdots & \ddots & \vdots \\ 0 & 0 & \cdots & \Psi_T \end{pmatrix}, \quad \Psi_r^{\mathsf{T}} = \begin{pmatrix} y_1^r(x_1^r)^{\mathsf{T}} \\ y_2^r(x_2^r)^{\mathsf{T}} \\ \vdots \\ y_{n_r}^r(x_{n_r}^r)^{\mathsf{T}} \end{pmatrix}.$$
$$\underset{(Td)\times N}{} \qquad \underset{n_r \times d}{}$$

Note that the inverse in (11) is well defined since $(B \otimes I_d)^{-1} = (B^{-1} \otimes I_d)$, and $B = I_T + \mu L$ is an invertible matrix. Using the stationary conditions, the Lagrangian becomes the function of α:

$$\mathcal{L}(\alpha) = -\frac{\lambda^2}{2}\sum_{r,s=1}^{\mathsf{T}}\sum_{i=1}^{n_r}\sum_{j=1}^{n_s}\alpha_i^r\alpha_j^s y_i^r y_j^s x_i^r x_j^s$$

$$-\frac{(1-\lambda)^2}{2}\sum_{r,s=1}^{\mathsf{T}}\sum_{i=1}^{n_r}\sum_{j=1}^{n_s}\alpha_i^r\alpha_j^s y_i^r y_j^s B_{rs}^{-1} x_i^r x_j^s + \sum_{r=1}^{T}\sum_{i=1}^{n_r}\alpha_i^r p_i^r,$$

and, therefore, we arrive at the dual problem:

$$\underset{\alpha}{\arg\min} \quad \Theta(\alpha) = \frac{1}{2}\sum_{r,s=1}^{\mathsf{T}}\sum_{i,j=1}^{n_r,n_s}\alpha_i^r\alpha_j^s y_i^r y_j^s \left[\lambda^2 + (1-\lambda)^2 B_{rs}^{-1}\right]x_i^r x_j^s - \sum_{r=1}^{T}\sum_{i=1}^{n_r}\alpha_i^r p_i^r$$

$$\text{s.t.} \qquad 0 \leq \alpha_i^r \leq C, \ i = 1, \ldots, n_r, \ r = 1, \ldots, T,$$

$$\sum_{i=1}^{n_r}\alpha_i^r y_i^r = 0, \ r = 1, \ldots, T. \tag{12}$$

Note that the quadratic part of the objective function has two different terms. The first one, corresponding to the common part, involves the dot products of all the points in the training set independently of their task, while the second term, which corresponds to the specific part, takes into account the task relationships via B_{rs}^{-1}. Once the dual problem is solved, the prediction of this multi-task model for a new point z from task $t \in \{1, \ldots, T\}$ can also be written as $f_t(z^t) = \lambda f(z^t) + (1-\lambda)g_t(z^t) + b_t$, where the f and g_t models are defined as:

$$f(z^{\mathsf{T}}) = \lambda\sum_{r=1}^{T}\sum_{i=1}^{n_r}\alpha_i^r y_i^r x_i^r \cdot z^t, \ g_t(z^{\mathsf{T}}) = (1-\lambda)\sum_{r=1}^{T}\sum_{i=1}^{n_r}\alpha_i^r y_i^r B_{rt}^{-1} x_i^r \cdot z^t.$$

3.2   Convex Graph Laplacian Kernel Multi-Task SVM

The above division in two differentiated parts is the starting point to extend the preceding linear discussion to a kernel setting, where we will work in different

Hilbert spaces for the common f and specific g_r model functions. We can observe this by extending (12) to the kernel case, which can be expressed as a standard SVM dual problem with an MTL kernel, namely

$$
\begin{aligned}
\arg\min_{\alpha} \quad & \Theta(\alpha) = \frac{1}{2}\alpha^\mathsf{T}\tilde{Q}\alpha - p\alpha \\
\text{s.t.} \quad & 0 \le \alpha_i^r \le C,\ i = 1,\ldots,n_r,\ r = 1,\ldots,T, \\
& \sum_{i=1}^{n_r} \alpha_i^r y_i^r = 0,\ r = 1,\ldots,T,
\end{aligned}
\tag{13}
$$

where the kernel matrix $\tilde{Q}$ is computed using the kernel function $\tilde{k}$ defined as:

$$
\tilde{k}(x_i^r, x_j^s) = \lambda^2 k(x_i^r, x_j^s) + (1-\lambda)^2 (I_T + \mu_2 L)_{rs}^{-1} k_g(x_i^r, x_j^s);
$$

here, k and k_g are the kernels corresponding to the common and specific parts respectively. When comparing (13) with the standard SVM dual (2), the differences are in the definition of the kernel matrix and the multiple equality constraints in (13), which have their origin at the multiple biases in (8). However, if we impose a single bias in all models, we have a dual problem that can be solved using the standard SMO algorithm.

Finally, we can write the kernel multi-task model prediction over a new pattern z^t from task t as $f_t(z^t) = \lambda f(z^t) + (1-\lambda)g_t(z^t) + b_t$, where

$$
f(z^t) = \lambda \sum_{r=1}^{T}\sum_{i=1}^{n_r} \alpha_i^r y_i^r k(x_i^r, z^t), \quad g_t(z^t) = (1-\lambda)\sum_{r=1}^{T}\sum_{i=1}^{n_r} \alpha_i^r y_i^r B_{rt}^{-1} k_g(x_i^r, z^t).
$$

4   Numerical Experiments

4.1   Datasets and Models

We test our method over eight different problems: majorca, tenerife, california, boston, abalone and crime for regression and landmine and binding for classification. In majorca and tenerife each task goal is to predict the photovoltaic production in these islands at different hours. In california and boston datasets the target is the price of houses and the tasks are defined using different location categories of these houses. In abalone we define three tasks: the prediction for male, female and infant specimens. The target in crime is to predict the number of crimes per 100 000 people in different cities of the U.S.; the prediction in each state is considered a task. For classification, in binding, the goal is to predict whether peptides will bind to a certain MHC molecule and each molecule represents a different task. In landmine the goal is the detection of landmines; each type of landmine defines a task. In Table 1 we can see the characteristics of the different datasets. We will compare the performance of our multi-task approach against four alternative models, described next. All of them are built using Gaussian kernels.

Table 1. Sample sizes, dimensions and number of tasks of the datasets used.

Dataset	Size	No. features	No. tasks	Avg. task size	Min. task size	Max. task size
majorca	15330	765	14	1095	1095	1095
tenerife	15330	765	14	1095	1095	1095
binding	32302	184	47	687	59	3089
landmine	14820	10	28	511	445	690
california	19269	9	5	3853	5	8468
boston	506	12	2	253	35	471
abalone	4177	8	3	1392	1307	1527
crime	1195	127	9	132	60	278

Common Task Learning SVM (CTL). A single SVM model is fitted on all the data, ignoring task information.

Independent Task learning SVM (ITL). Specific models are fitted for each task using only the tasks data; no cross-model learning takes place.

Convex Multi-Task learning SVM (cvxMTL). Here a convex combination between the common and the independent models is used. This multi-task approach uses both common and task-specific kernels.

Graph Laplacian MTL-SVM (GLMTL). This is the multi-task approach defined in [3]. It only uses specific models with a Graph Laplacian regularization term. In this approach, a single kernel is used for all tasks and there is no common part to be shared among the specific models.

Convex Graph Laplacian MTL-SVM (cvxGLMTL). This is our proposal, in which we use a convex combination of the common model and the specific models with their own regularizers to which we add a Graph Laplacian regularization.

4.2 Experimental Setup

Since each model taken has a different set of hyperparameters, their selection has been done in various ways. Model hyperparameters are basically chosen by cross-validation (CV) with some simplifications that we detail next. The three parameters of CTL, i.e., (C, ϵ, γ_c), are all chosen via CV and we do the same for the parameters $(C^r, \epsilon^r, \gamma_s^r)$ of each specific model in the ITL approach. For cvxMTL we will use the width γ_c selected for CTL and the specific widths γ_s^r obtained for ITL, whereas C, λ and ϵ are selected by CV. We use the γ_c selected for CTL in the GLMTL kernel and we select (C, ϵ, μ) by CV. For cvxGLMTL we use the γ_c from CTL in both the common and graph Laplacian kernels, the μ selected for GLMTL, and apply a CV procedure to select C, λ and, for regression, ϵ. In Table 2 we show the grids where the optimal values are searched and the procedure used to select each model's hyperparameters. Notice that only three hyperparameters per model are chosen by CV, to alleviate computational costs.

Table 2. Hyper-parameters, grids used to select them (when appropriate) and hyper-parameter selection method for each model.

	Grid	CTL	ITL	cvxMTL	GLMTL	cvxGLMTL
C	$\{4^k : -2 \leq k \leq 2\}$	CV	CV	CV	CV	CV
ϵ	$\{\frac{\sigma}{4^k} : 1 \leq k \leq 6\}$	CV	CV	CV	CV	CV
γ_c	$\{\frac{4^k}{d} : -2 \leq k \leq 3\}$	CV	-	CTL	CTL	CTL
γ_s	$\{\frac{4^k}{d} : -2 \leq k \leq 3\}$	-	CV	ITL	-	CTL
λ	$\{0.2k : 0 \leq k \leq 5\}$	-	-	CV	-	CV
μ	$\{4^k : -1 \leq k \leq 3\}$	-	-	-	CV	GLMTL

Cross-validation has been done in the following way. In majorca and tenerife, with time-dependent data, we have data for the years 2013, 2014 and 2015, which have been used for train, validation and test respectively. For the rest of the problems we have used a nested cross-validation scheme, using the inner CV to select the optimal hyperparameters and the outer folds to measure the fitness of our models. We work with 3 outer folds, using cyclically two thirds of the data for train and validation and keeping one third for test. We also use 3 inner folds, with 2 folds used for training and the remaining one for validation. These folds are selected randomly using the StratifiedKFold class of *Scikit-learn*; the stratification is made using the task labeling, so every fold has a similar task distribution. The regression CV score is the Mean Absolute Error (MAE), the natural measure for SVR fitness. The classification CV score is the F1 score, more informative than accuracy when we deal with unbalanced datasets. For all problems, we scale the data feature-wise into the [0, 1] interval and normalize the regression targets to have zero-mean and one-standard deviation. As mentioned before, the multiple biases of the multi-task approaches cvxMTL and cvxGLMTL imply the existence of multiple dual equality constraints. To avoid this and be able to apply the standard SMO algorithm, we use a simplified version of the MTL models in which a common bias is shared among all tasks.

Finally, for cvxGLMTL it is necessary to define a graph over the tasks. The weights of the edges connecting two tasks define the degree of relationship wanted or expected between them. This predefined graph information is included in the model through the Laplacian matrix regularization. Choosing a useful graph is not a trivial task and it may also be harmful when the prior information used does not match the characteristics of the data. In our experiments no prior information is given to the model, and we use a graph in which every task (node) is connected to all the others with the same constant weight. To normalize the Graph Laplacian regularization term we will use $A_{rs} = \frac{1}{T(T-1)}$.

4.3   Experimental Results

Table 3 shows the scores obtained in every problem considered. In the case of the regression tasks, we give both the MAE and R2 scores. Moreover, in Table 5 we

Table 3. Test MAE (top), and test R2 scores (bottom) in the regression problems.

	maj.	ten.	boston	california	abalone	crime
MAE						
CTL	5.265	5.786	2.254±0.035	41870.820 ± 76.723	1.483±0.039	0.078±0.001
ITL	5.119	5.341	2.779±0.134	37043.664 ± 371.549	1.488±0.038	0.082±0.006
cvxMTL	5.077	5.351	**2.228±0.006**	36848.971 ± 242.052	**1.466±0.028**	**0.074±0.003**
GLMTL	5.291	5.840	3.070±0.391	37123.515 ± 404.205	1.690±0.017	0.094±0.006
cvxGLMTL	**4.917**	**5.335**	2.230±0.038	**36720.854 ± 225.335**	1.467±0.026	**0.074±0.003**
R2						
CTL	0.831	0.902	0.843±0.044	0.638 ± 0.005	0.560±0.017	0.743± 0.022
ITL	0.843	0.904	0.776±0.017	0.696 ± 0.005	0.550±0.024	0.711±0.006
cvxMTL	0.845	**0.907**	0.850±0.045	0.700 ± 0.003	**0.566±0.013**	**0.755±0.016**
GLMTL	0.832	0.894	0.490±0.264	0.695 ± 0.007	0.366±0.027	0.596±0.033
cvxGLMTL	**0.849**	0.905	**0.852±0.046**	**0.702± 0.003**	**0.566±0.013**	0.752±0.016

Table 4. Test F1 score (left), and accuracy (right) in the classification problems.

	F1		Accuracy	
	landmine	binding	landmine	binding
CTL	0.106 ± 0.016	0.868 ± 0.002	0.942 ± 0.004	0.791 ± 0.003
ITL	0.183 ± 0.034	0.901 ± 0.000	0.942 ± 0.004	0.850 ± 0.000
cvxMTL	0.150 ± 0.023	0.906 ± 0.001	0.943 ± 0.004	0.858 ± 0.002
GLMTL	**0.227 ± 0.042**	0.896 ± 0.003	0.935 ± 0.002	0.844 ± 0.005
cvxGLMTL	0.163 ± 0.031	**0.908 ± 0.001**	**0.944 ± 0.004**	**0.862 ± 0.002**

show the p-values of the paired signed rank Wilcoxon tests we will perform. With these tests we can reject the null hypothesis, which states that the distribution of the differences of two related samples is symmetrical around zero. Given that there are several models to be compared, we proceed in the following manner: we first rank the models by their MAE score and, then, the absolute and quadratic error distributions of each model are compared using the Wilcoxon test with the immediately following model. With this, we can determine whether the error distributions of two consecutive models are significantly different. The rankings given in the Table show ties for those model pairs where the null hypothesis is rejected at the 5% significance level. It can be observed that, in terms of MAE, the proposed cvxGLMTL model obtains the best results in most regression problems and, even when cvxGLMTL does not achieve the smaller error, Table 5 shows that it is not significantly worse than the best model. Only for abalone the cvxMTL model obtains the significantly best result in terms of R2 scores.

In the case of classification, we show in Table 4 both accuracy and F1 score. We notice that in the landmine problem the accuracies obtained are high whereas the F1 scores are low, due to the unbalanced nature of the problem. In contrast, in binding, a balanced problem, both F1 score and accuracy have similar values.

Table 5. Top: Wilcoxon p-values of absolute errors of a regression model and the one following it in the MAE ranking and similar accuracy p values. Bottom: with the same scheme, p values of quadratic errors and the R2 score ranking and F1 scores.

	majorca		tenerife		boston		california		abalone		crime		classif.	
CTL	0.0000	(3)	0.0000	(4)	**0.2554**	(1)	0.0000	(4)	0.0002	(2)	0.0000	(2)	0.0277	(3)
ITL	0.8131	(2)	0.0035	(2)	0.0001	(2)	0.0318	(3)	0.2546	(2)	0.3995	(2)	**0.3454**	(1)
cvxMTL	0.0000	(2)	0.0000	(3)	-	(1)	0.0000	(2)	-	(1)	-	(1)	0.0277	(2)
GLMTL	0.4183	(3)	0.5962	(4)	0.0621	(2)	0.5658	(3)	0.0000	(3)	0.0000	(3)	-	(1)
cvxGLMTL	-	(1)	-	(1)	**0.4113**	(1)	-	(1)	**0.0771**	(1)	**0.6093**	(1)	**0.3454**	(1)
CTL	0.0032	(3)	0.0000	(2)	**0.1791**	(1)	0.0000	(4)	0.0016	(3)	0.0001	(2)	0.3454	(4)
ITL	0.6340	(2)	**0.5999**	(1)	0.0001	(2)	0.0035	(3)	0.3096	(3)	0.3972	(2)	0.0277	(3)
cvxMTL	0.0000	(2)	**0.0815**	(1)	-	(1)	0.0000	(2)	-	(1)	-	(1)	0.0431	(2
GLMTL	0.2040	(3)	0.7790	(2)	0.0384	(3)	0.6759	(3)	0.0000	(4)	0.0000	(3)	0.0277	(4)
cvxGLMTL	-	(1)	-	(1)	**0.2606**	(1)	-	(1)	0.0181	(2)	**0.7262**	(1)	-	(1)

Table 6. Train MAE in the regression problems (smallest values in bold face).

	maj.	ten.	boston	california	abalone	crime
MAE						
CTL	3.440	4.183	1.557 ± 0.198	40502.686 ± 222.209	1.434 ± 0.019	0.055 ± 0.006
ITL	3.590	3.914	1.883 ± 0.224	34403.940 ± 83.583	1.399 ± 0.025	0.050 ± 0.004
cvxMTL	3.649	3.921	1.522 ± 0.248	35061.556 ± 118.259	1.399 ± 0.027	0.055 ± 0.007
GLMTL	**2.630**	**3.728**	2.077 ± 0.447	**33984.568 ± 151.998**	1.594 ± 0.023	**0.038 ± 0.002**
cvxGLMTL	3.344	4.141	**1.516 ± 0.270**	34409.942 ± 101.472	**1.406 ± 0.023**	0.057 ± 0.007

Given the small number of accuracy or F1 values, the validity of applying a Wilcoxon test is not guaranteed. In any case and for illustration purposes, we have combined the score (either F1 or accuracy) obtained by the models in each one of the three CV outer folds of both landmine and binding problems. We thus obtain six paired samples which we use as inputs for the Wilcoxon test; we show the resulting p values and rankings in the last column of Table 5.

Finally, when comparing the two graph based MTL approaches, GLMTL performs quite well in the classification problems but less so in the regression ones. As a possible explanation we point out to Table 6, which shows the train MAEs of each regression model. Recall that GLMTL does not have an explicit weight regularization term and, thus, may be more susceptible of overfitting the training sample. This may be the case here since, as it can be seen, GLMTL has the smallest MAE in majorca, tenerife, california and crime. In these problems, where the tasks we consider may be more informative, it seems that GLMTL overfits on them and, hence, has worse test MAE values than cvxGLMTL.

5   Discussion and Conclusions

The Multi-Task learning paradigm incorporates data from multiple sources with the goal of achieving a better generalization than that of a common model or independent models per task. The idea is to make use of all the information, but at the same time refining each model for its particular task. Multi-Task Support Vector Machines are adapted into this framework usually in two ways: either a common part shared by all tasks and a task-specific part are combined, or a graph is defined over the tasks and an independent model is fitted for each task, while trying to be similar to the models of the most related tasks. The first approach imposes the same relationship between all the tasks, while the second one allows for different degrees of task relationships but loses the common part where the information is shared across tasks. In this work we have proposed a hybrid model that combines both approaches in a convex manner by incorporating both the common part and a graph which defines the task relationships. The numerical results over eight different problems show that our proposal performs better than both previous MTL approaches, and also better than either a global model or task-independent models, while the computational cost is similar. To finish, we mention two possible venues of further research that we are pursuing. The first one would be to learn the task relationship graph by exploring the data, instead of using predefined task relation values as we have done here. The second one would be to improve on using just a single convex combination parameter for all tasks by learning task specific λ values.

Acknowledgments. With partial support from Spain's grants TIN2016-76406-P and PID2019-106827GB-I00/AEI/10.13039/501100011033. Work supported also by the UAM–ADIC Chair for Data Science and Machine Learning. We thank Red Eléctrica de España for making available solar energy data and AEMET and ECMWF for access to the MARS repository. We also gratefully acknowledge the use of the facilities of Centro de Computación Científica (CCC) at UAM.

References

1. Caruana, R.: Multitask learning. Mach. Learn. **28**(1), 41–75 (1997)
2. Evgeniou, T., Pontil, M.: Regularized multi-task learning. In: Proceedings of the Tenth ACM SIGKDD International Conference on Knowledge Discovery and Data Mining, pp. 109–117. ACM (2004)
3. Evgeniou, T., Micchelli, C.A., Pontil, M.: Learning multiple tasks with kernel methods. J. Mach. Learn. Res. **6**, 615–637 (2005)
4. Argyriou, A., Evgeniou, T., Pontil, M.: Multi-task feature learning. In: Advances in Neural Information Processing Systems, pp. 41–48 (2007)
5. Argyriou, A., Pontil, M., Ying, Y., Micchelli, C.A.: A spectral regularization framework for multi-task structure learning. In: Advances in Neural Information Processing Systems, pp. 25–32 (2008)
6. Jacob, L., Vert, J.-P., Bach, F.R.: Clustered multi-task learning: a convex formulation. In: Advances in Neural Information Processing Systems, pp. 745–752 (2009)
7. Cai, F., Cherkassky, V.: SVM+ regression and multi-task learning. In: Proceedings of the 2009 International Joint Conference on Neural Networks, IJCNN 2009, pp. 503–509. IEEE Press, Piscataway (2009)
8. Cai, F., Cherkassky, V.: Generalized SMO algorithm for SVM-based multitask learning. IEEE Trans. Neural Netw. Learn. Syst. **23**(6), 997–1003 (2012)
9. Zhang, Y., Yeung, D.-Y.: A convex formulation for learning task relationships in multi-task learning. arXiv preprint arXiv:1203.3536 (2012)

10. Lin, C.-J.: On the convergence of the decomposition method for support vector machines. IEEE Trans. Neural Networks **12**(6), 1288–1298 (2001)
11. Ruiz, C., Alaíz, C.M., Dorronsoro, J.R.: A convex formulation of SVM-based multi-task learning. In: Pérez García, H., Sánchez González, L., Castejón Limas, M., Quintián Pardo, H., Corchado Rodríguez, E. (eds.) HAIS 2019. LNCS (LNAI), vol. 11734, pp. 404–415. Springer, Cham (2019). https://doi.org/10.1007/978-3-030-29859-3_35

Neural Network Theory
and Information Theoretic Learning

Prediction Stability as a Criterion
in Active Learning

Junyu Liu[1(✉)] , Xiang Li[2], Jiqiang Zhou[2], and Jianxiong Shen[3]

[1] Graduate School of Informatics, Kyoto University, Kyoto, Japan
liu.junyu.82w@st.kyoto-u.ac.jp
[2] Hikvision Research Institute, Hangzhou, China
[3] Institut de Robòtica i Informàtica Industrial, CSIC-UPC, Barcelona, Spain

Abstract. Recent breakthroughs made by deep learning rely heavily on a large number of annotated samples. To overcome this shortcoming, active learning is a possible solution. Besides the previous active learning algorithms that only adopted information after training, we propose a new class of methods named sequential-based method based on the information during training. A specific criterion of active learning called prediction stability is proposed to prove the feasibility of sequential-based methods. We design a toy model to explain the principle of our proposed method and pointed out a possible defect of the former uncertainty-based methods. Experiments are made on CIFAR-10 and CIFAR-100, and the results indicates that prediction stability was effective and works well on fewer-labeled datasets. Prediction stability reaches the accuracy of traditional acquisition functions like entropy on CIFAR-10, and notably outperformed them on CIFAR-100.

Keywords: Active learning · Classification · Prediction stability

1 Introduction

Recent breakthroughs made by deep learning heavily relied on Supervised Learning (SL) with large amount of annotated datasets [10,12]. But in the practical applications, large amount of labels are expensive and time-consuming [13]. Lack of labels is an important obstacle to adopt SL methods. To achieve similar accuracy to SL with less labels, (pool-based) active learning (AL) [11] has become a possible solution. These strategies have succeeded in many realms such as image processing [18] and natural language processing(NLP) [17].

The goal of active learning is to select the least number of typical samples and train the model to reach the same accuracy as one trained on all the samples. It's not difficult to find out that the core of active learning methods is the strategy of sample selection called acquisition function. Most of the previous works belong to the pool-based method, which selects a subset of samples

Junyu Liu did this work during his internship at the Hikvision Research Institute.

I. Farkaš et al. (Eds.): ICANN 2020, LNCS 12397, pp. 157–167, 2020.
https://doi.org/10.1007/978-3-030-61616-8_13

after a whole training process on the existing labeled dataset and then goes on [3,4,7,8,16,19]. Basing on the learning process of pool-based active learning, the samples selected are expected to be the ones with the most information. In many works, the selected samples were the most uncertain ones. The basic ideas included using confidence, max-entropy [16], mutual information [7], mean standard deviation [8] or variation-ratio [3] of samples as a measurement. Recent works of AL adopted strategies based on Bayesian Convolutional Neural Networks [4] and Generative Adversarial Nets (GAN) [19]. Although the principles of the networks were different from typical classification convolutional neural networks (CNN), the methods still generated or chose samples with the highest uncertainty. Another class of work selected samples by the expectation of model change. For instance, expected gradient length [15] choose samples expected to cause the largest gradients to the current model. After approximation of the algorithm, the selected samples were similar to adversarial examples [5]. Some works concentrate on exploring the typical samples of the whole dataset. For example, core-set [14] choose samples that are at the center of a neighbor area, and expect all the selected samples to cover the whole feature space.

Present active learning methods are different in strategy and implementation, but we can classify all the methods mentioned above as *spatial-based* ones. That is, although different methods concentrate on different parts of the AL process (prediction, model updating, etc.), the information took in to account all came from the prediction of the well-trained models before selection. The whole process was a flat one without information from the time course. Here we propose sequential-based methods, and as a verification of it, we propose a new criterion of sample selection in image classification called the *prediction stability*, which describes the oscillation of predictions across the epochs during training. Instead of starting from a well-trained model, this model also gathered information for the selection process while training the model. Among different epochs of a training process, the fluctuation of prediction on a sample is taken as the measure of uncertainty of the feature space around this sample. We designed a toy model to explain the principle of our proposed method and pointed out a possible defect of the former uncertainty-based methods. The results of our experiments also agreed with our assumption and prove the proposed method as an effective one.

The following parts of this paper are divided into 4 sections. The second section introduces the relation to prior work. The third is our methodology. The fourth section provides the experimental results. And the final part is the conclusion.

2   Relation to Prior Work

When comparing our proposed method with present AL algorithms mentioned in the introduction part, there are two major differences. First, our sequential-based method not only extracts features after training but also during the training process. Second, the previously proposed measures of the amount of information are based on more apparent criteria including uncertainty, the influence on the model and typical samples. They care more about the scales of the final predictions, but prediction stability is a new criterion to catch the indirect information of relative prediction changes.

3 Methodology

We can define the dataset of all samples as $X = \{x_i | i = 1...n\}$, with $X^L \subseteq X$ representing the labeled set containing n_l labels, and the complementary set $X^U = X \backslash X^L$ is the set of unlabeled n_u samples. The budget of AL is defined as B. For pool-based active learning, after initialization, in each round of AL, the model will select b samples from X^U for annotation and put the set of them $S \subseteq X^U$ into X^L, then the model is retrained on the new X^L set. This process repeats until the total number of selected samples reaches the budget. In previous works [7,8,16], the acquisition functions of subset S can be concluded as (1). In this equation, $f(\cdot)$ is the feature extracting function, and $g(\cdot)$ outputs the scores of samples.

$$S = \underset{S}{argmax}[\sum_{i=1}^{b} g(f(s_i))], s_i \in S \tag{1}$$

The previous spatial-based methods mentioned in the introduction part concentrate on the quality of final predictions. All the innovations focus on the measurements of the final prediction. Different from this kind of methods, we propose sequential-based methods that make use of the information during training. We'll prove the necessity of information during training later. Defining number of epochs in training as N_e, and $f_n(\cdot)$ as the $f(\cdot)$ function in n-th epoch, the acquisition function can be rewritten as Eq. 2.

$$S = \underset{S}{argmax}[\sum_{i=1}^{b} g(f_1(s_i), ..., f_{N_e}(s_i))], s_i \in S \tag{2}$$

As an application of sequential-based methods, we propose *prediction stability*, a new criterion of selecting the subset S in active learning. For implementation, we also adopt the common CNN model as the feature extractor and classifier. An important distinction with former spatial-based methods is that this criterion focuses not on the final scales of outputs, but the fluctuation of scales during training. As Fig. 1 shows, looking through the whole training process, features of samples like (a) tend to be relatively stable, but other samples like (b) oscillates from the beginning to the end. Instinct speculation is that samples like Fig. 1(b) should be selected for labeling. To do quantitative analysis, we test some common-used measures of fluctuation of data and choose the average variance of each unit of outputs across epochs as the measure of prediction stability. The diagrams in Fig. 1 also shows that, due to under-fitting, the former epochs of training are definitely to violate severely. Therefore only epochs in the later training process should be included in the calculation. After the experiment,

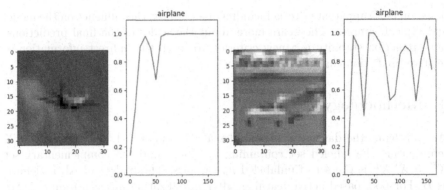

(a) Sample with high prediction stability (b) Sample with low prediction stability

Fig. 1. Example of samples with different prediction stability during training. The horizontal axis in the right diagrams is the index of epochs, and the vertical axis shows the scale of a unit of the output vector.

we find that the selected epochs are actually in the over-fitting area, which is relatively stable. Also, considering the time complexity, only several epochs are chosen in the end.

The definition of prediction stability can be written as Eq. 3:

$$g(x) = \sum_{c=1}^{C} var(f_{e_1}(x)_c, ..., f_{e_n}(x)_c) \tag{3}$$

Where C is the length of the output vectors by $f(\cdot)$, $f(x)_c$ is the c-th unit of output $f(x)$, and $\{e_1, e_2, ..., e_n\} = E$ is the set of index of selected epochs. The whole framework of prediction stability is displayed in Algorithm 1.

Algorithm 1. Prediction Stability

Input: CNN model M, dataset $X = \{x_i | i = 1...n\}$, initial sampling number k, number of epochs per training process N_e, set of index of selected epochs E, budget B, subset of samples selected each round S.

1: Generate first k samples randomly, and produce labels for them;
2: **repeat**
3:     **for** $i = 1 \rightarrow N_e$ **do**
4:         Train the model M on labeled samples;
5:         **if** $i \in E$ **then**
6:             Predict outputs P_i of M on unlabeled set.
7:     Get prediction stability of each image along selected epochs;
8:     Select top $|S|$ samples with lowest prediction stability, generate labels and put them into labeled sample pool;
9: **until** Reach the budget B

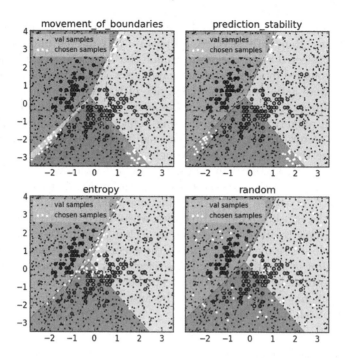

Fig. 2. Toy example applying different acquisition functions to iris dataset. The axes are the first two features (sepal length, sepal width) of the samples. Plains of different colors reflect the decision boundaries of each category (setosa, versicolor and verginica). Dashed lines are the one-against-all classifiers trained on the original iris dataset. Colored points are original samples of different categories in the iris dataset. The validation set consists of samples randomly generated around the original samples. White stars are samples selected from the validation set by different acquisition functions. The top-left image shows the changes of decision boundaries during training. The small patches are areas that belonged to different categories during training, and white stars are the same as those selected by prediction stability.

To help explain the principle of prediction stability, we made a toy example on the iris dataset [1,2], as demonstrated in Fig. 2. The main body of this example came from the sample code in the document of sklearn[1]. This task aimed to do a 3-class classification (setosa, versicolor and verginica). We adopted SVM-based multi-class stochastic gradient descent (SGD) linear-classifiers. For the convenience of visualization, the task was done on the first two features (sepal length, sepal width) of the iris dataset. The axes in Fig. 2 are the first two features of the samples, and therefore the plains are the feature space of the samples, which is the set of all the possible values of the samples. One class (setosa, blue points in Fig. 2) is linearly separable from the other two; the latter (versicolor and verginica) are not linearly separable from each other.

---

[1] https://scikit-learn.org/stable/auto_examples/linear_model/plot_sgd_iris.html.

The distribution of selected samples reflected the principle of different acquisition functions. Randomly selected samples roughly obeyed uniform distribution. Samples selected by entropy were around the T-crossing of three categories and were surrounded by samples of the training set. But for prediction stability, the samples were gathering at the outer side of the decision boundaries. During the training process, the decision boundaries between different categories were swinging roughly around the crossing point of the boundaries. The sway was within a sector-shaped area, like the small patches in the top-left image of Fig. 2. Because the boundary was a straight line, the outer part of the sector was influenced most by the change of the boundary, which was the area where the selected samples (white stars in the top images of Fig. 2) located.

The uncertainty-based acquisition functions tended to make finer-grained borders near the crossing of multi-categories, where the predicted probabilities of a sample to belong to different categories were close to each other. But as shown in this example, these methods sacrificed the accuracy at the feature space far from the training set. Rather, the samples selected by prediction stability, which located at the boundaries with the least number of training samples, were the ones the classifiers were of least certainty because no information about this area was obtained from the training data.

4   Experimental Results

4.1   Implementation Details

Datasets. CIFAR-10 and CIFAR-100 [9] were used for the evaluation of our proposed method. The samples of the two datasets are all 32×32 small image patches. Each dataset contains 50000 training samples and 10000 test samples respectively. The training and test samples are equally distributed into all categories. But the difference is that CIFAR-10 only has 10 classes, and CIFAR-100 contains 100 classes. Therefore, the number of samples in each class of CIFAR-10 is 10 times that of CIFAR-100.

Architecture Details. As for the model M for feature extraction, we employed ResNet-18 [6], which is a relatively deep architecture, and a popular choice among recent works on AL. This network mainly consists of the first convolution layer and the following 4 residual blocks. The implementation was based on an open-source framework[2]. The softmax outputs of the network, which were the final score vector of categories, were chosen as the output in this work.

All the models in this work were implemented on an NVIDIA TITAN Xp GPU. During training, the batch size was 128, and 164 epochs were utilized in each training process. In our experiments, for each dataset, a subset containing 1000 samples was selected for the first training process. Since biases of numbers among different classes in the initially labeled dataset might heavily influence

---

[2] https://github.com/bearpaw/pytorch-classification.git.

the selection after the first training process, an equal number of samples were randomly selected from each category of the dataset in the beginning. 1000 samples were selected and labeled after each training process, and the final size of the labeled dataset was 10000. To overcome the influence of random factors and get objective results, we generated 6 sets of initially labeled samples at first and did the first training processes of all the methods on the same 6 datasets. The final results of each method were the average of the six trails.

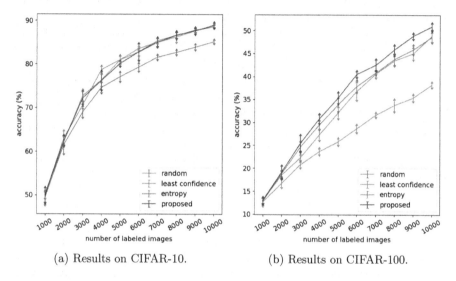

(a) Results on CIFAR-10.   (b) Results on CIFAR-100.

Fig. 3. Results on CIFAR-10 and CIFAR-100 (1 standard deviation; across 6 trials).

4.2   CIFAR-10

The results on CIFAR-10 is displayed by Fig. 3(a). Because the output features were the probability of all classes, entropy and least confidence (ranking by the largest score among categories for each sample) measure were calculated on the outputs directly. For the calculation of prediction stability, we finally selected 5 epochs starting from the last one with an interval of 5.

$$e_i = N_e - (i - 1) \times interval, i = 1, 2, 3, 4, 5 \tag{4}$$

The results showed that although information about the value of outputs was not included directly, the proposed prediction stability method still overwhelmed random selection, and achieved similar performance with acquisition functions like entropy and least confidence on CIFAR-10.

4.3 CIFAR-100

The performance of each method on CIFAR-100 is exhibited in Fig. 3(b). To perform prediction stability on CIFAR-100, the interval of epoch selection was set to 1. Previous works in the introduction part hardly reported their results on this dataset, but our results on CIFAR-100 showed different tendencies with CIFAR-10. Entropy and least confidence, especially the least confidence, suffered from deterioration of performance. The accuracy of both acquisition functions was lower than random selection. But our proposed method proves better performance and outperforms random selection.

We believe the better performance of our proposed model on CIFAR-100 than CIFAR-10 is caused by the number of training samples in the feature space. The major difference between the two datasets is CIFAR-100 has fewer samples in each class, which means the feature space of each class is more sparse and has fewer labels to distinguish the border. As shown in the toy model, the uncertainty-based method tends to make a fine-grained border around the labeled samples and ignore the unknown area of the feature space. Therefore it worked worse when there were less labeled samples. The result of the two datasets showed that prediction stability has a better capacity for fewer-labeled datasets.

4.4 Ablation Study

Measure of Prediction Stability. Experiments were made to test the performance of different measures of prediction stability, as displayed in Fig. 4. We tested the absolute increase among features of different epochs. This measure is represented by Eq. 5.

$$F(x) = \sum_{i=2}^{|E|} |f_{e_i}(x) - f_{e_{i-1}}(x)| \tag{5}$$

Taking the absolute increase as a measure led to a nearly 40% drop in performance. It suggests that it's not the tendency of change, but the distribution of output, that determines the performance of prediction stability.

Also, we tested the result of taking variance as the acquisition function but removed the softmax calculation. A deterioration of the result could also be observed clearly, which proved the necessity of the softmax layer's function of normalization. The output features of different samples were transferred into comparable probabilities, and therefore the differences in absolute scales of output features didn't influence the variances.

Interval of Epoch Selection. Experiments were made to test the influence of epoch selection on the results of prediction stability. The epoch selection process was based on Eq. 4. Results on the two datasets are different, as exhibited in Fig. 5. Although accuracy was slightly better when the interval equaled 5,

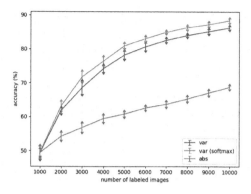

Fig. 4. Results on CIFAR-10 with different measure of prediction stability (1 standard deviation; across 6 trials).

CIFAR-10 was not sensitive to interval change. But in CIFAR-100, the accuracy declined as the interval of epoch increased. This happened may because the models trained on CIFAR-100 over-fitted at later epochs than CIFAR-10. That is, when the interval was 10, the result of some epochs of CIFAR-100 was still not in the relatively stable state and caused a decrease in accuracy.

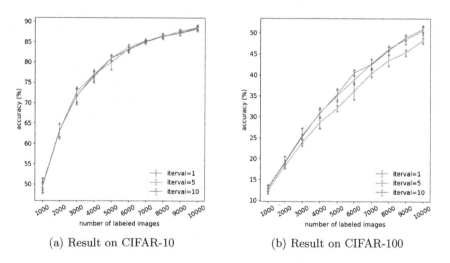

(a) Result on CIFAR-10   (b) Result on CIFAR-100

Fig. 5. Results on different intervals of prediction stability (1 standard deviation; across 6 trials).

5   Conclusion

In this paper, we proposed a new class of AL methods named sequential-based AL method. A new criterion, prediction stability was proposed as an application of the sequential-based method. We designed an example to demonstrate the principle of prediction stability and unveiled that the previous uncertainty-based methods tend to ignore unknown areas in the feature space. Testing results of prediction stability on CIFAR-10 and CIFAR-100 proved the feasibility of the sequential-based method class.

As for the future work, we will focus on fusing our proposed method with uncertainty-based AL methods, because the information extracted by two kinds of methods are complementary.

References

1. Dua, D., Graff, C.: UCI machine learning repository (2017). http://archive.ics.uci.edu/ml
2. Fisher, R.A.: The use of multiple measurements in taxonomic problems. Ann. Eugenics **7**(2), 179–188 (1936)
3. Freeman, L.C.: Elementary Applied Statistics: For Students in Behavioral Science. Wiley, New York (1965)
4. Gal, Y., Islam, R., Ghahramani, Z.: Deep Bayesian active learning with image data. In: Proceedings of the 34th International Conference on Machine Learning, vol. 70, pp. 1183–1192. JMLR.org (2017)
5. Goodfellow, I.J., Shlens, J., Szegedy, C.: Explaining and harnessing adversarial examples. Computer Science (2014)
6. He, K., Zhang, X., Ren, S., Sun, J.: Deep residual learning for image recognition. In: The IEEE Conference on Computer Vision and Pattern Recognition (CVPR) (2016)
7. Houlsby, N., Huszár, F., Ghahramani, Z., Lengyel, M.: Bayesian active learning for classification and preference learning. arXiv preprint arXiv:1112.5745 (2011)
8. Kampffmeyer, M., Salberg, A.B., Jenssen, R.: Semantic segmentation of small objects and modeling of uncertainty in urban remote sensing images using deep convolutional neural networks. In: Proceedings of the IEEE Conference on Computer Vision and Pattern Recognition Workshops, pp. 1–9 (2016)
9. Krizhevsky, A., Hinton, G., et al.: Learning multiple layers of features from tiny images. Technical report. Citeseer (2009)
10. Law, H., Deng, J.: CornerNet: detecting objects as paired keypoints. In: Ferrari, V., Hebert, M., Sminchisescu, C., Weiss, Y. (eds.) Computer Vision – ECCV 2018. LNCS, vol. 11218, pp. 765–781. Springer, Cham (2018). https://doi.org/10.1007/978-3-030-01264-9_45
11. Lewis, D.D., Gale, W.A.: A sequential algorithm for training text classifiers. In: Croft, B.W., van Rijsbergen, C.J. (eds.) SIGIR 1994, pp. 3–12. Springer, London (1994). https://doi.org/10.1007/978-1-4471-2099-5_1
12. Liu, J., et al.: An original neural network for pulmonary tuberculosis diagnosis in radiographs. In: Kůrková, V., Manolopoulos, Y., Hammer, B., Iliadis, L., Maglogiannis, I. (eds.) ICANN 2018. LNCS, vol. 11140, pp. 158–166. Springer, Cham (2018). https://doi.org/10.1007/978-3-030-01421-6_16
13. Qu, Z., Liu, J., Liu, Y., Guan, Q., Yang, C., Zhang, Y.: OrieNet: a regression system for latent fingerprint orientation field extraction. In: Kůrková, V., Manolopoulos, Y., Hammer, B., Iliadis, L., Maglogiannis, I. (eds.) ICANN 2018. LNCS, vol. 11141, pp. 436–446. Springer, Cham (2018). https://doi.org/10.1007/978-3-030-01424-7_43

14. Sener, O., Savarese, S.: Active learning for convolutional neural networks: a core-set approach. arXiv preprint arXiv:1708.00489 (2017)
15. Settles, B., Craven, M.: An analysis of active learning strategies for sequence labeling tasks. In: Proceedings of the Conference on Empirical Methods in Natural Language Processing, pp. 1070–1079. Association for Computational Linguistics (2008)
16. Shannon, C.E.: A mathematical theory of communication. Bell Syst. Tech. J. **27**(3), 379–423 (1948)
17. Tanguy, L., Tulechki, N., Urieli, A., Hermann, E., Raynal, C.: Natural language processing for aviation safety reports: from classification to interactive analysis. Comput. Ind. **78**, 80–95 (2016)
18. Zhou, Z., Shin, J., Zhang, L., Gurudu, S., Gotway, M., Liang, J.: Fine-tuning convolutional neural networks for biomedical image analysis: actively and incrementally. In: Proceedings of the IEEE Conference on Computer Vision and Pattern Recognition, pp. 7340–7351 (2017)
19. Zhu, J.J., Bento, J.: Generative adversarial active learning. arXiv preprint arXiv:1702.07956 (2017)

Neural Spectrum Alignment: Empirical Study

Dmitry Kopitkov$^{(\boxtimes)}$ ⓘ and Vadim Indelman$^{(\boxtimes)}$ ⓘ

^{1} Technion Autonomous Systems Program (TASP),
Technion - Israel Institute of Technology, 32000 Haifa, Israel
`dimkak@technion.ac.il`
^{2} Department of Aerospace Engineering, Technion - Israel Institute of Technology,
32000 Haifa, Israel
`vadim.indelman@technion.ac.il`

Abstract. Expressiveness and generalization of deep models was recently addressed via the connection between neural networks (NNs) and kernel learning, where first-order dynamics of NN during a gradient-descent (GD) optimization were related to *gradient similarity* kernel, also known as Neural Tangent Kernel (NTK) [9]. In the majority of works this kernel is considered to be time-invariant [9,13]. In contrast, we empirically explore these properties along the optimization and show that in practice *top* eigenfunctions of NTK align toward the target function learned by NN which improves the overall optimization performance. Moreover, these *top* eigenfunctions serve as basis functions for NN output - a function represented by NN is spanned almost completely by them for the entire optimization process. Further, we study how learning rate decay affects the *neural spectrum*. We argue that the presented phenomena may lead to a more complete theoretical understanding behind NN learning.

Keywords: Deep learning · Neural tangent kernel · Kernel learning

1 Introduction

Understanding expressiveness and generalization of deep models is essential for robust performance of NNs. Recently, the optimization analysis for a general NN architecture was related to *gradient similarity* kernel [9], whose properties govern NN expressivity level, generalization and convergence rate. Under various considered conditions [9,13], this NN kernel converges to its steady state and is invariant along the entire optimization, which significantly facilitates the analyses of Deep Learning (DL) theory [1,2,9,13].

Yet, in a typical realistic setting the *gradient similarity* kernel is far from being constant, as we empirically demonstrate in this paper. Particularly, during training its spectrum aligns towards the target function that is learned by NN, which improves the optimization convergence rate [1,15]. Furthermore, we

© Springer Nature Switzerland AG 2020
I. Farkaš et al. (Eds.): ICANN 2020, LNCS 12397, pp. 168–179, 2020.
https://doi.org/10.1007/978-3-030-61616-8_14

show that these *gradient similarity* dynamics can also explain the expressive superiority of deep NNs over more shallow models. Hence, we argue that understanding the *gradient similarity* of NNs beyond its time-invariant regime is a must for full comprehension of NN expressiveness power.

To encourage the onward theoretical research of the kernel, herein we report several strong empirical phenomena and trends of its dynamics. To the best of our knowledge, these trends neither were yet reported nor they can be explained by DL theory developed so far. To this end, in this paper we perform an empirical investigation of fully-connected (FC) NN, its *gradient similarity* kernel and the corresponding Gramian at training data points during the entire period of a typical learning process. Our main empirical contributions are:

(a) We show that Gramian serves as a NN memory, with its *top* eigenvectors changing to align with the learned target function. This improves the optimization performance since the convergence rate along kernel *top* eigenvectors is typically higher.

(b) During the entire optimization NN output is located inside a sub-space spanned by these *top* eigenvectors, making the eigenvectors to be a basis functions of NN.

(c) Deeper NNs demonstrate a stronger alignment, which may explain their expressive superiority. In contrast, shallow wide NNs with a similar number of parameters achieve a significantly lower alignment level and a worse optimization performance.

(d) We show additional trends in kernel dynamics as a consequence of learning rate decay, demonstrating that the information of the target function is spread along bigger number of *top* eigenvectors after each decay.

(e) Experiments over various FC architectures, real-world datasets, *supervised* and *unsupervised* learning algorithms and number of popular optimizers were performed. All experiments showed the mentioned above spectrum alignment.

The paper is structured as follows. In Sect. 2 we define necessary notations. In Sect. 3 we relate *gradient similarity* with Fisher information matrix (FIM) of NN and in Sect. 4 we provide more insight about NN dynamics on L2 loss example. In Sect. 5 the related work is described and in Sect. 6 we present our main empirical study. Conclusions are discussed in Sect. 7. Further, additional derivations and experiments are placed in Appendix [12].

2   Notations

Consider a NN $f_\theta(X) : \mathbb{R}^d \to \mathbb{R}$ with a parameter vector θ, a typical sample loss ℓ and an empirical loss L, training samples $D = \left[\mathcal{X} = \{X^i \in \mathbb{R}^d\}, \mathcal{Y} = \{Y^i \in \mathbb{R}\} \right]$, $i \in [1, \ldots, N]$ and loss gradient $\nabla_\theta L$:

$$L(\theta, D) = \frac{1}{N} \sum_{i=1}^{N} \ell \left[Y^i, f_\theta(X^i) \right], \quad \nabla_\theta L(\theta, D) = \frac{1}{N} \sum_{i=1}^{N} \ell' \left[Y^i, f_\theta(X^i) \right] \cdot \nabla_\theta f_\theta(X^i),$$

$$(1)$$

where $\ell'[Y, f_\theta(X)] \triangleq \nabla_{f_\theta} \ell[Y, f_\theta(X)]$. The above formulation can be extended to include *unsupervised* learning methods in [11] by eliminating labels $\mathcal{Y}$ from the equations. Further, techniques with a model $f_\theta(X)$ returning multidimensional outputs are out of scope for this paper, to simplify the formulation.

Consider a GD optimization with learning rate δ, where parameters change at each discrete optimization time t as $d\theta_t \triangleq \theta_{t+1} - \theta_t = -\delta \cdot \nabla_\theta L(\theta_t, D)$. Further, a model output change at any X according to first-order Taylor approximation is:

$$df_{\theta_t}(X) \triangleq f_{\theta_{t+1}}(X) - f_{\theta_t}(X) \approx -\frac{\delta}{N} \sum_{i=1}^{N} g_t(X, X^i) \cdot \ell'[Y^i, f_{\theta_t}(X^i)], \quad (2)$$

where $g_t(X, X') \triangleq \nabla_\theta f_{\theta_t}(X)^T \cdot \nabla_\theta f_{\theta_t}(X')$ is a *gradient similarity* - the dot-product of gradients at two different input points also known as NTK [9].

In this paper we mainly focus on optimization dynamics of f_θ at training points. To this end, define a vector $\bar{f}_t \in \mathbb{R}^N$ with i-th entry being $f_{\theta_t}(X^i)$. According to Eq. (2) the discrete-time evolution of f_θ at testing and training points follows:

$$df_{\theta_t}(X) \approx -\frac{\delta}{N} \cdot g_t(X, \mathcal{X}) \cdot \bar{m}_t, \quad d\bar{f}_t \triangleq \bar{f}_{t+1} - \bar{f}_t \approx -\frac{\delta}{N} \cdot G_t \cdot \bar{m}_t, \quad (3)$$

where $G_t \triangleq g_t(\mathcal{X}, \mathcal{X})$ is a $N \times N$ Gramian with entries $G_t(i, j) = g_t(X^i, X^j)$ and $\bar{m}_t \in \mathbb{R}^N$ is a vector with the i-th entry being $\ell'[Y^i, f_{\theta_t}(X^i)]$.

Likewise, denote eigenvalues of G_t, sorted in decreasing order, by $\{\lambda_i^t\}_{i=1}^N$, with $\lambda_{max}^t \triangleq \lambda_1^t$ and $\lambda_{min}^t \triangleq \lambda_N^t$. Further, notate the associated orthonormal eigenvectors by $\{\bar{v}_i^t\}_{i=1}^N$. Note that $\{\lambda_i^t\}_{i=1}^N$ and $\{\bar{v}_i^t\}_{i=1}^N$ also represent estimations of eigenvalues and eigenfunctions of the kernel $g_t(X, X')$ (see Appendix A for more details). Below we will refer to large and small eigenvalues and their associated eigenvectors by *top* and *bottom* terms respectively.

Equation (3) describes the first-order dynamics of GD learning, where $\bar{m}_t$ is a functional derivative of any considered loss L, and the global optimization convergence is typically associated with it becoming a zero vector, due to Euler-Lagrange equation of L. Further, G_t translates a movement in θ-space into a movement in a space of functions defined on $\mathcal{X}$.

3   Relation to Fisher Information Matrix

NN Gramian can be written as $G_t = A_t^T A_t$ where A_t is $|\theta| \times N$ Jacobian matrix with i-th column being $\nabla_\theta f_{\theta_t}(X^i)$. Moreover, $F_t = A_t A_t^T$ is known as the empirical FIM of NN[1] [10,14] that approximates the second moment of model gradients $\frac{1}{N} F_t \approx \mathbb{E}_X[\nabla_\theta f_{\theta_t}(X) \nabla_\theta f_{\theta_t}(X)^T]$. Since F_t is dual of G_t, both matrices share same non-zero eigenvalues $\{\lambda_i^t \neq 0\}$. Furthermore, for each λ_i^t the respectful eigenvector $\bar{\omega}_i^t$ of F_t is associated with appropriate $\bar{v}_i^t$ - they are left and right

---

[1] In some papers [17] FIM is also referred to as a Hessian of NN, due to the tight relation between F_t and the Hessian of the loss (see Appendix B for details).

singular vectors of A_t respectively. Moreover, change of θ_t along the direction $\bar{\omega}_i^t$ causes a change to $\bar{f}_t$ along $\bar{v}_i^t$ (see Appendix C for the proof). Therefore, spectrums of G_t and F_t describe principal directions in function space and θ-space respectively, according to which $\bar{f}_t$ and θ_t are changing during the optimization. Based on the above, in Sect. 5 we relate some known properties of F_t towards G_t.

4 Analysis of L2 Loss for Constant Gramian

To get more insight into Eq. (3), we will consider L2 loss with $\ell\left[Y^i, f_\theta(X^i)\right] = \frac{1}{2}\left[f_\theta(X^i) - Y^i\right]^2$. In such a case we have $\bar{m}_t = \bar{f}_t - \bar{y}$, with $\bar{y}$ being a vector of labels. Assuming G_t to be fixed along the optimization (see Sect. 5 for justification), NN dynamics can be written as:

$$\bar{f}_t = \bar{f}_0 - \sum_{i=1}^N \left[1 - \left[1 - \frac{\delta}{N}\lambda_i\right]^t\right] <\bar{v}_i, \bar{m}_0> \bar{v}_i, \tag{4}$$

$$\bar{m}_t = \sum_{i=1}^N \left[1 - \frac{\delta}{N}\lambda_i\right]^t <\bar{v}_i, \bar{m}_0> \bar{v}_i. \tag{5}$$

Full derivation and extension for dynamics at testing points appear in Appendices D-E. Under the stability condition $\delta < \frac{2N}{\lambda_{max}}$ that satisfies $\lim_{t\to\infty}\left[1 - \frac{\delta}{N}\lambda_i\right]^t = 0$, the above equations can be viewed as a transmission of a signal from $\bar{m}_0 = \bar{f}_0 - \bar{y}$ into our model $\bar{f}_t$. At each iteration $\bar{m}_t$ is decreased along each $\{\bar{v}_i : \lambda_i \neq 0\}$ and the same information decreased from $\bar{m}_t$ in Eq. (5) is appended to $\bar{f}_t$ in Eq. (4).

Hence, in case of L2 loss and for a constant Gramian matrix, conceptually GD transmits information packets from the residual $\bar{m}_t$ into our model $\bar{f}_t$ along each axis $\bar{v}_i$. Further, $s_i^t \triangleq 1 - |1 - \frac{\delta}{N}\lambda_i|$ governs a speed of information flow along $\bar{v}_i$. Importantly, note that for a high learning rate (i.e. $\delta \approx \frac{2N}{\lambda_{max}}$) the information flow is slow for directions $\bar{v}_i$ with both very large and very small eigenvalues, since in former the term $1 - \frac{\delta}{N}\lambda_i$ is close to -1 whereas in latter - to 1. Yet, along with the learning rate decay, performed during a typical optimization, s_i^t for very large λ_i is increased. However, the speed along a direction with small λ_i is further decreasing with the decay of δ. As well, in case $\lambda_{min} > 0$, at the convergence $t \to \infty$ we will get from Eqs. (4)–(5) the global minima convergence: $\bar{f}_\infty = \bar{f}_0 - \bar{m}_0 = \bar{y}$ and $\bar{m}_\infty = \bar{0}$.

Under the above setting, there are two important key observations. First, due to the restriction over δ in practice the information flow along small λ_i can be prohibitively slow in case a conditional number $\frac{\lambda_{max}}{\lambda_{min}}$ is very large. This implies that for a faster convergence it is desirable for NN to have many eigenvalues as close as possible to its λ_{max} since this will increase a number of directions in the function space where information flow is fast. Second, if $\bar{m}_0$ (or $\bar{y}$ if $\bar{f}_0 \approx 0$) is contained entirely within *top* eigenvectors, small eigenvalues will not affect the convergence rate at all. Hence, the higher alignment between $\bar{m}_0$ (or $\bar{y}$) and *top* eigenvectors may dramatically improve overall convergence rate. The above conclusions and their extensions towards the testing loss are proved in formal manner in [1,15] for two-layer NNs. Further, the generalization was also shown to be dependent on the above alignment.

In Sect. 6 we evaluate the above conclusions experimentally, showing them to be true. Moreover, we will demonstrate the exceptional alignment between $\bar{y}$ and *top* eigenvectors of G_t along the optimization process. Such behavior can further explain the expressiveness power of NNs.

5 Related Work

First-order NN dynamics can be understood by solving the system in Eq. (3). However, its solution is highly challenging due to two main reasons - non-linearity of $\bar{m}_t$ w.r.t. $\bar{f}_t$ (except for the L2 loss) and intricate and yet not fully known time-dependence of Gramian G_t. Although *gradient similarity* $g_t(X, X')$ and corresponding G_t achieved a lot of recent attention in DL community [9,13], their properties are still investigated mostly only for limits under which G_t becomes time-constant. In [9] $g_t(X, X')$ was proven to converge to Neural Tangent Kernel (NTK) in infinite width limit, while in [13] G_0 was shown to accurately explain NN dynamics when θ_t is nearby θ_0. The considered case of constant Gramian facilitates solution of Eq. (3), as demonstrated in Sect. 4, which otherwise remains intractable.

Yet, in practical-sized NNs the spectrum of G_t is neither constant nor it is similar to its initialization. Recent several studies explored its adaptive dynamics [3,18], with most works focusing on one or two layer NNs. Further, in [4,8] equations for NTK dynamics were developed for a general NN architecture. Likewise, in the Appendix F we derive similar dynamics for the Gramian G_t. Yet, the above derivations produce intricate equations and it is not straightforward to explain the actual behavior of G_t along the optimization, revealed in this paper. In Sect. 6 we empirically demonstrate that *top* spectrum of G_t drastically changes by aligning itself with the target function. To the best of our knowledge, the presented NN kernel trends were not investigated in such detail before.

Further, many works explore properties of FIM F_t both theoretically and empirically [6,10,15,17]. All works agree that in typical NNs only a small part of FIM eigenvalues are significantly strong, with the rest being negligibly small. According to Sect. 3 the same is also true about eigenvalues of G_t. Furthermore, in [1,15] authors showed that NN learnability strongly depends on alignment between labels vector $\bar{y}$ and *top* eigenvectors of G_t. Intuitively, it can be explained by fast convergence rate along $\bar{v}_i$ with large λ_i vs impractically slow one along directions with small λ_i, as was shortly described in Sect. 4. Due to most of the eigenvalues being very small, the alignment between $\bar{y}$ and *top* eigenvectors of G_t defines the optimization performance. Moreover, in [15] authors shortly noted the increased aforementioned alignment comparing ResNet convolutional NN before and after training. In Sect. 6 we empirically investigate this alignment for FC architecture, in comprehensive manner for various training tasks.

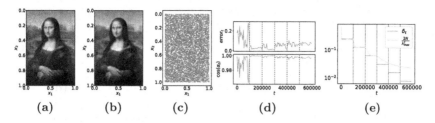

Fig. 1. (a) Mona Lisa target function for a regression task. (b) NN $f_\theta(X)$ at convergence. (c) 10^4 sampled training points. (d) Accuracy of first order dynamics in Eq. (3). Depicted is $error_t = \frac{\|d\tilde{f}_t - d\bar{f}_t\|}{\|d\tilde{f}_t\|}$, where $d\bar{f}_t = -\frac{\delta_t}{N} \cdot G_t \cdot \bar{m}_t$ is the first-order approximation of a real differential $d\tilde{f}_t \triangleq \bar{f}_{t+1} - \bar{f}_t$; $\cos(\alpha_t)$ is cosine of an angle between $d\tilde{f}_t$ and $d\bar{f}_t$. As observed, Eq. (3) explains roughly 90% of NN change. (e) Learning rate δ_t and its upper stability boundary $\frac{2N}{\lambda_{max}^t}$ along the optimization. We empirically observe a relation $\lambda_{max}^t \approx \frac{2N}{\delta_t}$.

Furthermore, the picture of information flow from Sect. 4 also explains what target functions are more "easy" to learn. The *top* eigenvectors of G_t typically contain low-frequency signal, which was discussed in [1] and proved in [2] for data uniformly distributed on a hypersphere. In its turn, this explains why low-frequency target functions are learned significantly faster as reported in [1,16,19]. We support findings of [2] also in our experiments below, additionally revealing that for a general case the eigenvectors/eigenfunctions of the *gradient similarity* are not spherical harmonics considered in [2].

6   Experiments

In this section we empirically study Gramian dynamics along the optimization process. Our main goal here is to illustrate the alignment nature of the *gradient similarity* kernel and verify various deductions made in Sect. 4 under a constant-Gramian setting for a real learning case. To do so in detailed and intuitive manner, we focus our experiments on 2D dataset where visualization of kernel eigenfunctions is possible. We perform a simple regression optimization of FC network via GD, where a learning setup is similar to common conventions applied by DL practitioners[2]. **All** empirical conclusions are also validated for high-dimensional real-world data, which we present in Appendix [12].

Setup. We consider a regression of the target function $y(X)$ with $X \in [0,1]^2 \subseteq \mathbb{R}^2$ depicted in Fig. 1a. This function is approximated via Leaky-Relu FC network and L2 loss, using $N = 10000$ training points sampled uniformly from $[0,1]^2$ (see Fig. 1c). Training dataset is normalized to an empirical mean 0 and a standard deviation 1. NN contains 6 layers with 256 neurons each, with $|\theta| = 264193$, that

---

[2] Related code can be accessed via a repository https://bit.ly/2kGVHhG.

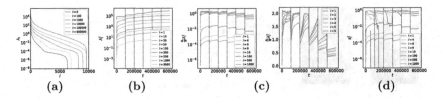

Fig. 2. (a) Eigenvalues $\{\lambda_i^t\}_{i=1}^N$ for different t. (b) Individual eigenvalues along t. (c) $\frac{\delta_t}{N}\lambda_i^t$ along time t, for various i. (d) The information flow speed $s_i^t = 1 - |1 - \frac{\delta}{N}\lambda_i|$ discussed in Sect. 4, for various i. For first 8 eigenvectors, roughly, this speed is increased at learning rate drop.

was initialized via Xavier initialization [5]. Such large NN size was chosen to specifically satisfy an over-parametrized regime $|\theta| \gg N$, typically met in DL community. Further, learning rate δ starts at 0.25 and is multiplied by 0.5 each 10^5 iterations, with the total optimization duration being $6 \cdot 10^5$. At convergence $f_\theta(X)$ gets very close to its target, see Fig. 1b. Additionally, in Fig. 1d we show that first-order dynamics in Eq. (3) describe around 90% of the change in NN output along the optimization, leaving another 10 for higher-order Taylor terms. Further, we compute G_t and its spectrum along the optimization, and thoroughly analyze them below.

Eigenvalues. In Figs. 2a–2b it is shown that each eigenvalue is monotonically increasing along t. Moreover, at learning rate decay there is an especial boost in its growth. Since $\frac{\delta_t}{N}\lambda_i^t$ also defines a speed of movement in θ-space along one of FIM eigenvectors (see Sect. 3), such behavior of eigenvalues suggests an existence of mechanism that keeps a roughly constant movement speed of θ within $\mathbb{R}^{|\theta|}$. To do that, when δ_t is reduced, this mechanism is responsible for increase of $\{\lambda_i^t\}_{i=1}^N$ as a compensation. This is also supported by Fig. 2c where each $\frac{\delta_t}{N}\lambda_i^t$ is balancing, roughly, around the same value along the entire optimization. Furthermore, in Fig. 1e it is clearly observed that an evolution of λ_{max}^t stabilizes[3] only when it reaches value of $\frac{2N}{\delta_t}$, further supporting the above hypothesis.

Neural Spectrum Alignment. Notate by $\cos\left[\alpha_t\left(\bar{\phi}, k\right)\right] \triangleq \sqrt{\frac{\sum_{i=1}^k <\bar{v}_i^t, \bar{\phi}>^2}{\|\bar{\phi}\|_2^2}}$ the cosine of an angle $\alpha_t\left(\bar{\phi}, k\right)$ between an arbitrary vector $\bar{\phi}$ and its projection to the sub-space of $\mathbb{R}^N$ spanned by $\{\bar{v}_i^t\}_{i=1}^k$. Further, $E_t(\bar{\phi}, k) \triangleq \cos^2\left[\alpha_t\left(\bar{\phi}, k\right)\right]$ can be considered as a *relative energy* of $\bar{\phi}$, the percentage of its energy $\|\bar{\phi}\|_2^2$ located inside $span\left(\{\bar{v}_i^t\}_{i=1}^k\right)$. In our experiments we will use $E_t(\bar{\phi}, k)$ as an alignment metric between $\bar{\phi}$ and $\{\bar{v}_i^t\}_{i=1}^k$. Further, we evaluate alignment of G_t with $\bar{y}$ instead of $\bar{m}_0$ since $\bar{f}_0$ is approximately zero in the considered FC networks.

---

[3] Trend $\lambda_{max}^t \rightarrow \frac{2N}{\delta_t}$ was consistent in FC NNs for a wide range of initial learning rates, number of layers and neurons, and various datasets (see Appendix [12]), making it an interesting venue for a future theoretical investigation

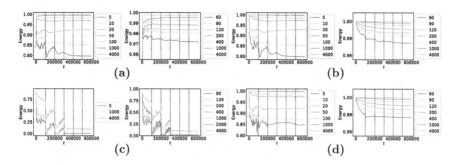

Fig. 3. (a) For different k, relative energy of the label vector $\bar{y}$ in *top* k eigenvectors of G_t, $E_t(\bar{y}, k)$, along the optimization time t. (b) Relative energy of NN output, $E_t(\bar{f}_t, k)$. (c) Relative energy of the residual, $E_t(\bar{m}_t, k)$. (d) Relative energy of NN output, $E_t(\bar{f}_t^{test}, k)$, with both G_t and $\bar{f}_t^{test}$ computed at 10^4 testing points. Dashed vertical lines depict time t at which learning rate δ was decayed (see Fig. 1e).

In Fig. 3a we depict relative energy of the label vector $\bar{y}$ in *top* k eigenvectors of G_t, $E_t(\bar{y}, k)$. As observed, 20 *top* eigenvectors of G_t contain 90% of $\bar{y}$ for almost all t. Similarly, 200 *top* eigenvectors of G_t contain roughly 98% of $\bar{y}$, with rest of eigenvectors being practically orthogonal w.r.t. $\bar{y}$. That is, G_t aligns its *top* spectrum towards the ground truth target function $\bar{y}$ almost immediately after training starts, which improves the convergence rate since the information flow is fast along *top* eigenvectors, as discussed in Sect. 4 and proved in [1,15].

Further, we can see that for $k < 400$ the relative energy $E_t(\bar{y}, k)$ is decreasing after each decay of δ, yet for $k > 400$ it keeps growing along the entire optimization. Hence, the *top* eigenvectors of G_t can be seen as NN memory that is learned/tuned toward representing the target $\bar{y}$, while after each learning rate drop the learned information is spread more evenly among a higher number of different *top* eigenvectors.

Likewise, in Fig. 3b we can see that NN outputs vector $\bar{f}_t$ is located entirely in a few hundreds of *top* eigenvectors. In case we consider G_t to be constant, such behavior can be explained by Eq. (3) since each increment of $\bar{f}_t$, $d\bar{f}_t$, is also located within *top* eigenvectors of G_t. Yet, for a general NN with a time-dependent kernel the theoretical justification for the above empirical observation is currently missing. Further, similar relation is observed also at points outside of $\mathcal{X}$ (see Fig. 3d), leading to the empirical conclusion that *top* eigenfunctions of *gradient similarity* $g_t(X, X')$ are the basis functions of NN $f_\theta(X)$.

Residual Dynamics. Further, a projection of the residual $\bar{m}_t$ onto *top* eigenvectors, shown in Fig. 3c, is decreasing along t, supporting Eq. (5). Particularly, we can see that at $t = 600000$ only 10% of $\bar{m}_t$'s energy is located inside *top* 4000 eigenvectors, and thus at the optimization end 90% of its energy is inside *bottom* eigenvectors. Moreover, in Fig. 4a we can observe that the projection of $\bar{m}_t$ along *bottom* 5000 eigenvectors almost does not change during the entire optimization. Thus, we empirically observe that the information located in the *bottom* spec-

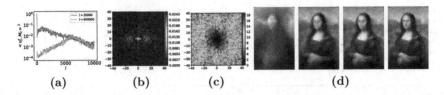

Fig. 4. (a) Spectral projections of the residual $\bar{m}_t$, $< \bar{v}_i^t, \bar{m}_t >^2$, at $t = 20000$ and $t = 600000$; (b) and (c) Fourier Transform of $\bar{m}_t$ at $t = 20000$ and $t = 600000$ respectively. The high frequency is observed to be dominant in (c). (d) a linear combination $\bar{f}_{t,k} \triangleq \sum_{i=1}^k < \bar{v}_i^t, \bar{f}_t > \bar{v}_i^t$ of first $k = \{10, 100, 200, 500\}$ eigenvectors at $t = 600000$. Each vector $\bar{f}_{t,k}$ was interpolated from training points $\{X^i\}_{i=1}^N$ to entire $[0,1]^2$ via a linear interpolation.

trum of G_t was not learned, even for a relatively long optimization process (i.e. 600000 iterations), which can be explained by slow convergence associated with *bottom* eigenvectors. Furthermore, since this spectrum part is also associated with high-frequency information [2], $\bar{m}_t$ at $t = 600000$ comprises mostly the noise, which is also evident from Figs. 4b–4c.

Moreover, we can also observe in Fig. 3c a special drop of $E_t(\bar{m}_t, k)$ at times of δ decrease. This can be explained by the fact that a lot of $\bar{m}_t$'s energy is trapped inside first several $\{\bar{v}_i^t\}$ (see $E_t(\bar{m}_t, 5)$ in Fig. 3c). When learning rate is decreased, the information flow speed $s_i^t \triangleq 1 - |1 - \frac{\delta_t}{N}\lambda_i^t|$, discussed in Sect. 4, is actually increasing for a few *top* eigenvectors (see Fig. 2d). That is, terms $\frac{\delta_t}{N}\lambda_i^t$, being very close to 2 before δ's decay, are getting close to 1 after, as seen in Fig. 2c. In its turn this accelerates the information flow along these first $\{\bar{v}_i^t\}$, as described in Eq. (4)–(5). Further, this leads also to a special descend of $E_t(\bar{m}_t, k)$ and of the training loss (see Fig. 7b below).

Eigenvectors. We further explore $\{\bar{v}_i^t\}$ in a more illustrative manner, to produce a better intuition about their nature. In Fig. 4d a linear combination of several *top* eigenvectors at $t = 600000$ is presented, showing that with only 100 vectors we can accurately approximate the NN output in Fig. 1b.

Furthermore, in Fig. 5 several eigenvectors are interpolated to entire $[0,1]^2$. We can see that *top* $\{\bar{v}_i^t\}$ obtained visual similarity with various parts of Mona Lisa image and indeed can be seen as basis functions of $f_\theta(X)$ depicted in Fig. 1b. Likewise, we also demonstrate the Fourier Transform of each $\bar{v}_i^t$. As observed, the frequency of the contained information is higher for smaller eigenvalues, supporting conclusions of [2]. More eigenvectors are depicted in Appendices I-N.

Likewise, in Fig. 6 same eigenvectors are displayed at $t = 20000$. At this time the visual similarity between each one of first eigenvectors and the target function in Fig. 1a is much stronger. This can be explained by the fact that the information about the target function within G_t is spread from first few towards higher number of *top* eigenvectors after each learning rate drop, as was described above. Hence, before the first drop at $t = 100000$ this information is mostly gathered within first few $\{\bar{v}_i^t\}$ (see also $E_t(\bar{y}, 10)$ in Fig. 3a).

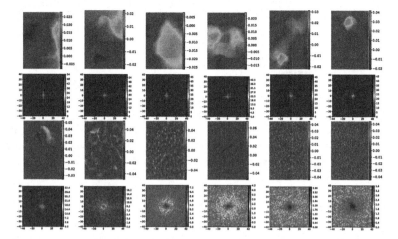

Fig. 5. Eigenvectors of Gramian G_t at $t = 600000$, and their Fourier Transforms (see the Appendix G for technical details). First two rows: from left-to-right, 6 first eigenvectors. Last two rows: 10-th, 100-th, 500-th, 1000-th, 2000-th and 4000-th eigenvectors. As observed, a frequency of signal inside of each eigenvector increases when moving from large to small eigenvalue.

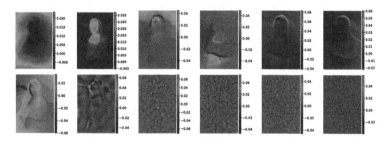

Fig. 6. First line: from left-to-right, 6 first eigenvectors of Gramian G_t at $t = 20000$. Second line: 10-th, 100-th, 500-th, 1000-th, 2000-th and 4000-th eigenvectors.

Alignment and NN Depth/Width. Here we further study how the width and the depth of NN affect the alignment between G_t and the ground truth signal $\bar{y}$. To this purpose, we performed the optimization under the identical setup, yet with NNs containing various numbers of layers and neurons. In Fig. 7a we can see that in deeper NN *top* eigenvectors of G_t aligned more towards $\bar{y}$ - the relative energy $E_t(\bar{y}, 400)$ is higher for a larger depth. This implies that more layers, and the higher level of non-linearity produced by them, yield a better alignment between G_t and $\bar{y}$. In its turn this allows NN to better approximate a given target function, as shown in Figs. 7b–7c, making it more expressive for a given task. Moreover, in evaluated 2-layer NNs, with an increase of neurons and parameters the alignment rises only marginally.

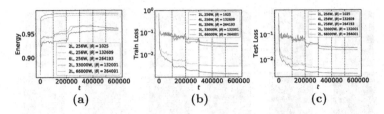

Fig. 7. (a) For NNs with a different number of layers **L** and number of neurons **W**, relative energy of labels $\bar{y}$ in *top* 400 eigenvectors of G_t, $E_t(\bar{y}, 400)$, along the optimization time t; (b) training loss and (c) testing loss of these models.

Scope of Analysis. The above empirical analysis was repeated under numerous different settings and can be found in Appendix [12]. We evaluated various FC architectures, with and without shortcuts between the layers and including various activation functions. Likewise, optimizers GD, stochastic GD and Adam were tested on problems of regression (L2 loss) and density estimation (noise contrastive estimation [7]). Additionally, various high-dimensional real-world datasets were tested, including MNIST and CIFAR100. All experiments exhibit the same alignment nature of kernel towards the learned target function. The results are also consistent with our previous experiments in [11].

7   Discussion and Conclusions

In this paper we empirically revealed that during GD *top* eigenfunctions of *gradient similarity* kernel change to align with the target function $y(X)$ learned by NN $f_\theta(X)$, and hence can be considered as a NN memory tuned during the optimization to better represent $y(X)$. This alignment is significantly higher for deeper NNs, whereas a NN width has only a minor effect on it. Moreover, the same *top* eigenfunctions represent a *neural spectrum* - the $f_\theta(X)$ is a linear combination of these eigenfunctions during the optimization. As well, we showed various trends of the kernel dynamics affected by learning rate decay. Same alignment behavior was observed for various *supervised* and *unsupervised* losses and high-dimensional datasets, optimized via several different optimizers. Likewise, several variants of FC architecture were evaluated. Since the above alignment is critical for a learning [1,2,15], the main question remains to how NN architecture and optimization hyper-parameters affect this spectrum, and what is their optimal configuration for learning a given function $y(X)$. We shall leave it for a future exciting research.

Acknowledgments. The authors thank Daniel Soudry and Dar Gilboa for discussions on dynamics of a Neural Tangent Kernel (NTK). This work was supported in part by the Israel Ministry of Science & Technology (MOST) and Intel Corporation. We gratefully acknowledge the support of NVIDIA Corporation with the donation of the Titan Xp GPU, which, among other GPUs, was used for this research.

References

1. Arora, S., Du, S.S., Hu, W., Li, Z., Wang, R.: Fine-grained analysis of optimization and generalization for overparameterized two-layer neural networks. arXiv preprint arXiv:1901.08584 (2019)
2. Basri, R., Jacobs, D., Kasten, Y., Kritchman, S.: The convergence rate of neural networks for learned functions of different frequencies. arXiv preprint arXiv:1906.00425 (2019)
3. Dou, X., Liang, T.: Training neural networks as learning data-adaptive kernels: Provable representation and approximation benefits. arXiv preprint arXiv:1901.07114 (2019)
4. Dyer, E., Gur-Ari, G.: Asymptotics of wide networks from Feynman diagrams. arXiv preprint arXiv:1909.11304 (2019)
5. Glorot, X., Bengio, Y.: Understanding the difficulty of training deep feedforward neural networks. In: Proceedings of the Thirteenth International Conference on Artificial Intelligence and Statistics, pp. 249–256 (2010)
6. Gur-Ari, G., Roberts, D.A., Dyer, E.: Gradient descent happens in a tiny subspace. arXiv preprint arXiv:1812.04754 (2018)
7. Gutmann, M., Hyvärinen, A.: Noise-contrastive estimation: a new estimation principle for unnormalized statistical models. In: Proceedings of the Thirteenth International Conference on Artificial Intelligence and Statistics, pp. 297–304 (2010)
8. Huang, J., Yau, H.T.: Dynamics of deep neural networks and neural tangent hierarchy. arXiv preprint arXiv:1909.08156 (2019)
9. Jacot, A., Gabriel, F., Hongler, C.: Neural tangent kernel: Convergence and generalization in neural networks. In: Advances in Neural Information Processing Systems (NIPS), pp. 8571–8580 (2018)
10. Karakida, R., Akaho, S., Amari, S.I.: Universal statistics of fisher information in deep neural networks: mean field approach. arXiv preprint arXiv:1806.01316 (2018)
11. Kopitkov, D., Indelman, V.: General probabilistic surface optimization and log density estimation. arXiv preprint arXiv:1903.10567 (2019)
12. Kopitkov, D., Indelman, V.: Neural spectrum alignment: empirical study - appendix. https://bit.ly/3aipgtl (2019)
13. Lee, J., Xiao, L., Schoenholz, S.S., Bahri, Y., Sohl-Dickstein, J., Pennington, J.: Wide neural networks of any depth evolve as linear models under gradient descent. arXiv preprint arXiv:1902.06720 (2019)
14. Ollivier, Y.: Riemannian metrics for neural networks I: feedforward networks. Inf. Infer.: J. IMA 4(2), 108–153 (2015)
15. Oymak, S., Fabian, Z., Li, M., Soltanolkotabi, M.: Generalization guarantees for neural networks via harnessing the low-rank structure of the Jacobian. arXiv preprint arXiv:1906.05392 (2019)
16. Rahaman, N., et al.: On the spectral bias of neural networks. arXiv preprint arXiv:1806.08734 (2018)
17. Sagun, L., Evci, U., Guney, V.U., Dauphin, Y., Bottou, L.: Empirical analysis of the hessian of over-parametrized neural networks. arXiv preprint arXiv:1706.04454 (2017)
18. Woodworth, B., Gunasekar, S., Lee, J., Soudry, D., Srebro, N.: Kernel and deep regimes in overparametrized models. arXiv preprint arXiv:1906.05827 (2019)
19. Zhang, J., Springenberg, J.T., Boedecker, J., Burgard, W.: Deep reinforcement learning with successor features for navigation across similar environments. arXiv preprint arXiv:1612.05533 (2016)

Nonlinear, Nonequilibrium Landscape Approach to Neural Network Dynamics

Roseli S. Wedemann[1]([✉]) [iD] and Angel R. Plastino[2] [iD]

[1] Instituto de Matemática e Estatística, Universidade do Estado do Rio de Janeiro,
Rua São Francisco Xavier 524, Rio de Janeiro, RJ 20550-900, Brazil
`roseli@ime.uerj.br`
[2] CeBio y Departamento de Ciencias Básicas, Universidad Nacional del Noroeste
de la Provincia de Buenos Aires, UNNOBA, Conicet,
Roque Saenz Peña 456, Junin, Argentina
`arplastino@unnoba.edu.ar`

Abstract. Distributions maximizing S_q entropies are not rare in Nature. They have been observed in complex systems in diverse fields, including neuroscience. Nonlinear Fokker-Planck dynamics constitutes one of the main mechanisms that can generate S_q-maximum entropy distributions. In the present work, we investigate a nonlinear Fokker-Planck equation associated with general, continuous, neural network dynamical models for associative memory. These models admit multiple applications in artificial intelligence, and in the study of mind, because memory is central to many, if not all, the processes investigated by psychology and neuroscience. We explore connections between the nonlinear Fokker-Planck treatment of network dynamics, and the nonequilibrium landscape approach to this dynamics discussed in [34]. We show that the nonequilibrium landscape approach leads to fundamental relations between the Liapunov function of the network model, the deterministic equations of motion (phase-space flow) of the network, and the form of the diffusion coefficients appearing in the nonlinear Fokker-Planck equations. This, in turn, leads to an H-theorem involving a free energy-like functional related to the S_q entropy. To illustrate these results, we apply them to the Cohen-Grossberg family of neural network models.

Keywords: Continuous neural network dynamics · Nonlinear
Fokker-Planck equations · Nonequilibrium landscape theory ·
Nonextensive thermostatistics · Cohen-Grossberg neural networks ·
Associative memory

1 Introduction

Neural network models for associative memory, such as the Hopfield model [10, 11], constitute promising descriptions of the physical and algorithmic counterparts of diverse mental phenomena, both normal and pathological. These models form a valuable tool for many applications in artificial intelligence and also for the

© Springer Nature Switzerland AG 2020
I. Farkaš et al. (Eds.): ICANN 2020, LNCS 12397, pp. 180–191, 2020.
https://doi.org/10.1007/978-3-030-61616-8_15

study of the mind, because memory is at the heart of many (if not all) of the processes investigated by psychiatry, psychoanalysis and neuroscience [4,12,23]. The applications of neural network models to neuroscience is based on the assumption that (associative) memory is codified in the brain neural network's architecture. Working within this theoretical paradigm we advanced, in recent years, associative memory neural network models for various phenomena, such as neurosis, creativity, and the interplay between conscious and unconscious mental activity [3,20,28,32,33]. In the memory models considered in [20,28,32,33], memories are retrieved according to the Tsallis-Stariolo, Generalized Simulated Annealing (GSA) algorithm [26], inspired on the S_q-thermostatistical formalism [25]. GSA includes, as a particular, limiting case, the standard Boltzmann Machine algorithm [10], based on the Boltzmann-Gibbs thermostatistics.

The S_q-thermostatistics (or nonextensive thermostatistics) is a theoretical framework based on the S_q, power-law, entropic measures, that has in recent years been successfully applied to the study of several types of complex systems [25]. The GSA scheme is of relevance, because it simulates a natural dynamics generating the S_q-maximum entropy distributions, within the context of neural networks with discrete states [20,28]. For example, for some network configurations, the avalanches occurring during the GSA, memory retrieval process obey S_q-maximum entropy (q-MaxEnt), power-law distributions [20]. These distributions, the hallmark of S_q-thermostatistics, have features that are consistent with many power-law distributions observed in theoretical, numerical studies [17], as well as in experimental research in neuroscience (see [1,20,22] and references therein). In particular, they are consistent with experimental data on the distribution of the time duration and spatial reach of signal propagation (captured by fMRI images), during brain stimulation [1,22]. Other features of our models [28,33] also exhibit power-law and q-MaxEnt behavior. These results motivate us to conduct further explorations of the use of concepts from S_q-thermostatistics, in connection with neural network models and their dynamical behavior. The present work belongs to this general line of enquiry.

With the aforementioned biological applications in mind, we shall consider networks of neurons admitting continuous state variables [5,11]. In the absence of noise, these networks constitute deterministic, continuous dynamical systems. The Fokker-Planck formalism permits us to take into account the effects of noise in the behavior of the networks [15,29–31]. An intriguing development that has been taking place in recent years concerns the so-called nonequilibrium, landscape theory of network, or network-like, dynamics [8,27,34]. This approach to the dynamics of complex systems is, in many cases, based on a Fokker-Planck description of the dynamical systems under consideration. Within this approach, the nonequilibrium behavior of the system, corresponding to time-dependent solutions of the associated Fokker-Planck equation, is analyzed in terms of an abstract potential landscape, and an associated phase-space flow, that involve the effects due to both the deterministic part of the dynamics (drift field) and the noisy part (diffusion term). So far, applications of this approach have considered only linear Fokker-Planck equations [8,27,34].

The aim of the present contribution is to explore a generalization of the nonequilibrium, landscape theory of neural networks [8, 27, 34], based on a nonlinear Fokker-Planck formalism associated with the nonextensive, entropic functional S_q. As an illustration of these developments, we shall apply them to the Cohen-Grossberg neural networks with continuous variables. The Cohen-Grossberg networks [5] constitute a generalization of the Hopfield model that, besides including this model as a particular instance, also include as special cases other important dynamical systems, such as the Lotka-Volterra systems in population dynamics and ecology [14].

In this work, we shall show how the generalization of the nonequilibrium landscape approach leads to dynamical structures, independent of the value of the Tsallis entropic parameter q, that elucidate the connection between the Liapunov function of the network dynamics, the drift field, and the (state-dependent) diffusion coefficients of the Fokker-Planck equations associated with the networks. These relations lead, in turn, to the formulation of an H-theorem for the nonlinear Fokker-Planck equation, and to the stationary solution, which has the form of a q-MaxEnt density. These developments shed light on possible mechanisms explaining the origin of q-MaxEnt, power-law densities. This type of densities has been observed in systems like brain networks, exhibiting long-range interactions and/or spatial disorder [25]. The present approach extends and generalizes the nonequilibrium, landscape formalism advanced in [34], incorporating the nonextensive, thermostatistical features corresponding to power-law, S_q entropic measures. Studies along this line may support the choice of different entropic measures for modelling complex networks such as the brain, as well as neural networks used in many applications of artificial intelligence [10, 22, 26]. When $q = 1$, the present formalism reduces to the one associated with Boltzmann entropy and the linear Fokker-Planck equation [34].

2 S_q-Generalized Thermostatistical Formalism

The S_q-thermostatistics (sometimes referred to as nonextensive thermostatistics) is a generalization of the Boltzmann-Gibbs (BG) thermostatistics. It admits a remarkable range of applications in various areas of science, particularly in connection with the study of complex systems [2, 24, 25]. This thermostatistics is associated with the power-law, Tsallis entropic functional [25]

$$S_q[P] = \frac{\kappa}{q-1} \int P(\boldsymbol{u}) \left[1 - \left(\frac{P(\boldsymbol{u})}{P_c} \right)^{q-1} \right] d^N \boldsymbol{u}, \tag{1}$$

where $P(\boldsymbol{u})$ (with $\boldsymbol{u} \in \Re^N$) is a probability density, and $q \in \Re$ is the Tsallis, entropic parameter. The constant κ determines the units in which we measure S_q, and the constant P_c has the same dimensions as $P(\boldsymbol{u})$. In the limit $q \to 1$, the Tsallis entropy S_q reduces to the BG logarithmic entropy, $S_{BG} = S_1 = -\kappa \int P \ln(P/P_c) d^N \boldsymbol{u}$. Here, we will work with the dimensionless density $\rho = P/P_c$, and set $\kappa P_c = 1$, yielding

$$S_q[\rho] = \frac{1}{(q-1)} \left(1 - \int \rho^q \, d^N \boldsymbol{u} \right). \tag{2}$$

Complex systems that present power-law behavior can often be described by the q-exponential function, that plays a central role in the S_q-thermostatistics and is defined, for $z \in \Re$, as

$$\exp_q(z) = \begin{cases} [1 + (1-q)z]^{\frac{1}{1-q}}, & \text{for } 1 + (1-q)z > 0, \\ 0, & \text{for } 1 + (1-q)z \le 0. \end{cases} \tag{3}$$

When $q \to 1$, (3) becomes the standard exponential function. We also use the alternative notation $\exp_q(z) = [1 + (1-q)z]_+^{1/(1-q)}$.

The constrained optimization of the entropic functional S_q (2) leads to q-MaxEnt densities expressed in terms of q-exponential functions [25]. The q-MaxEnt densities accurately describe experimental data in many areas. They are also observed in data arising from numerical simulations of a wide family of complex systems [20,24,25]. Nonextensive thermostatistics has thus been applied to fields as diverse as physics, astronomy, biology, biomedicine, psychology, cognition, computer science, machine learning and economics. It seems unlikely that there is a single mechanism generating the q-MaxEnt densities in all these scenarios. Probably, there is a family of mechanisms, or dynamical scenarios, leading to q-MaxEnt densities, and a few have already been identified. Among the most studied, we can mention (i) systems with long-range interactions [2] (ii) nonlinear dynamical systems at the edge of chaos (having weak chaos) [24], and (iii) systems governed by diffusion, Fokker-Planck, or reaction-diffusion equations with nonlinear, power-law, diffusion terms [6,7,9,13,18,19,21]. Systems described by nonlinear Fokker-Planck equations (NLFPEs) have been the focus of considerable attention in recent years. The study of these systems constitutes, among the diverse areas where the S_q-thermostatistics has been applied, the one most developed from the analytical point of view, and the one where the dynamical origin of the q-MaxEnt densities is better understood.

3 Nonlinear Fokker-Planck Dynamics, q-Statistics, and Nonequilibrium Landscapes for General Networks

We consider a neural network that, in the absence of noise (random perturbations), is a continuous, deterministic, dynamical system. At each instant t, the dynamical state of the network is described by the set of N phase-space variables $\{u_1, u_2, \cdots, u_N\}$. Variable u_i represents the state of neuron i and evolves according to a set of coupled, ordinary differential equations,

$$\frac{du_i}{dt} = K_i(u_1, u_2, \cdots, u_N), \quad i = 1, \ldots, N, \tag{4}$$

which can be expressed compactly, in vector notation, as $\frac{du}{dt} = \boldsymbol{K}(\boldsymbol{u})$, with $\boldsymbol{u}, \boldsymbol{K} \in \Re^N$. That is, the vector $\boldsymbol{u}$, representing the system's state, evolves according to the phase-space flux given by the vectorial field $\boldsymbol{K}$. As an example, consider the equations of motion of the continuous Hopfield neural network,

$$\tau_i \frac{du_i}{dt} = -u_i + \sum_{j=1}^{N} \omega_{ij} g(u_j), \tag{5}$$

for which $K_i(\boldsymbol{u}) = \frac{1}{\tau_i} \left[-u_i + \sum_{j=1}^{N} \omega_{ij} g(u_j) \right]$.

Instead of studying the evolution of one realization of the system, one can study the evolution of a statistical ensemble of copies of the system. This is the point of view of statistical mechanics, which in many practical situations, for very large N, is the only feasible one. The statistical ensemble is represented by a time-dependent probability density in phase space $\rho(u_1, \cdots, u_N, t)$, satisfying the Liouville equation $(\partial \rho / \partial t) + \boldsymbol{\nabla} \cdot (\rho \boldsymbol{K}) = 0$, which is a continuity equation in phase space. Here, $\boldsymbol{\nabla} = (\partial / \partial u_1, \dots, \partial / \partial u_N)$ is the N-dimensional $\boldsymbol{\nabla}$-operator. If the network under consideration evolves under the effects of noise, as happens in biological neural networks, the evolution is nondeterministic. To account for the effects of noise, one can add an extra diffusion-like term to the Liouville continuity equation, obtaining the linear Fokker-Planck equation (FPE)

$$\frac{\partial \rho}{\partial t} = D \nabla^2 \rho - \boldsymbol{\nabla} \cdot (\rho \boldsymbol{K}), \tag{6}$$

where D is a constant, reflecting the global diffusion features of the system's dynamics. The last term on the right hand side of (6) is called the *drift* term and $\boldsymbol{K}$ is referred to as the *drift* field, or alternatively, the phase-space flow.

A generalization of the linear FPE (6), incorporating nonlinear diffusion [9], is given by

$$\frac{\partial \rho}{\partial t} = D \nabla^2 [\rho^{2-q}] - \boldsymbol{\nabla} \cdot [\rho \boldsymbol{K}], \tag{7}$$

where q is a real parameter that, as we shall later see, coincides with Tsallis' entropic parameter in (1). Equation (7) is a generalization of evolution Eq. (6), and constitutes a versatile tool for the study of various phenomena in complex systems. The nonlinear diffusion term in the NLFPE can describe an ensemble of interacting particles, with the nonlinearity providing an effective description of the interactions [21]. Physical systems with spatial disorder and/or long-range interactions seem to be natural candidates for applying this formalism, and a considerable amount of work by the complex systems research community has been devoted recently to this line of enquiry [16,18,19,25]. Nonlinear Fokker-Planck dynamics can also arise as an approximate description of an underlying, more fundamental, linear evolution. In this contribution, we propose a nonlinear Fokker-Planck dynamics for neural network dynamical models, such as the Cohen-Grossberg one, as a possible phenomenological mechanism explaining or describing the origin of the q-MaxEnt, power-law distributions observed in some studies of brain neural networks. In recent works [15,29,30], we already considered some aspects of the nonlinear Fokker-Planck approach to neural network dynamics. Those efforts were centered on Hopfield neural networks, or on linear, neural-like networks devised to explore conceptual issues concerning the problem of synaptic asymmetries. Now we adopt a different perspective, exploring the relation between the nonlinear Fokker-Planck treatment of, and the nonequilibrium landscape approach to continuous, neural network dynamics.

Equation (7) can be rewritten in the form

$$\frac{\partial \rho}{\partial t} = D\boldsymbol{\nabla} \left[\left(\frac{2-q}{1-q} \right) \rho \, \boldsymbol{\nabla} \left(\rho^{1-q} \right) \right] - \boldsymbol{\nabla} \cdot [\rho \boldsymbol{K}] , \tag{8}$$

and both forms will reduce to (6) in the limit where $q \to 1$. The diffusion term in (8) describes homogeneous and isotropic diffusion, since the diffusion coefficient does not depend itself on the phase-space variables. When applying the Fokker-Planck formalism to the dynamics of networks, where noisy diffusion depends on local properties of synapses that convey the interaction between pairs of neurons, it is necessary to consider a more general scenario involving inhomogeneous and anisotropic diffusion. Consequently, we will consider the more general NLFPE

$$\frac{\partial \rho}{\partial t} = D \sum_{ij} \frac{\partial}{\partial u_i} \left\{ \left(\frac{2-q}{1-q} \right) G_{ij} \, \rho \, \frac{\partial}{\partial u_j} \rho^{(1-q)} \right\} - \sum_i \frac{\partial}{\partial u_i} (K_i \rho) , \tag{9}$$

where the matrix elements representing local diffusion, $G_{ij} = G_{ij}(\boldsymbol{u})$, depend on the phase-space variables. We shall now apply to the above nonlinear, evolution equation the landscape approach advocated in [8,27,34]. Following [34], we start with the stationary state NLFPE,

$$0 = D \sum_{ij} \frac{\partial}{\partial u_i} \left\{ \left(\frac{2-q}{1-q} \right) G_{ij} \, \rho \, \frac{\partial}{\partial u_j} \rho^{(1-q)} \right\} - \sum_i \frac{\partial}{\partial u_i} (K_i \rho) , \tag{10}$$

and introduce an appropriate ansatz for the stationary situation,

$$\rho(\boldsymbol{u}) = [1 - (1-q)W(\boldsymbol{u})]_+^{\frac{1}{1-q}} , \tag{11}$$

based on an abstract potential landscape $W(\boldsymbol{u})$. Note that this ansatz is based on the q-exponential function (3) naturally appearing in the S_q-formalism. In the standard case of linear FPEs, the ansatz (11) reduces to the ansatz $\rho(\boldsymbol{u}) = \exp(-W)$, employed in [34].

Calculating the derivatives in the two terms of Eq. (10), we obtain

$$\frac{\partial (K_i \rho)}{\partial u_i} = \rho \left(\frac{\partial K_i}{\partial u_i} - K_i \, \rho^{q-1} \frac{\partial W}{\partial u_i} \right) , \tag{12}$$

and

$$\frac{\partial}{\partial u_i} \left\{ \left(\frac{2-q}{1-q} \right) G_{ij} \, \rho \, \frac{\partial}{\partial u_j} \rho^{(1-q)} \right\} =$$
$$- (2-q) \left[\left(\rho \frac{\partial G_{ij}}{\partial u_i} - \rho^q G_{ij} \frac{\partial W}{\partial u_i} \right) \frac{\partial W}{\partial u_j} + \rho \, G_{ij} \frac{\partial^2 W}{\partial u_i \partial u_j} \right] . \tag{13}$$

Substituting (12) and (13) in (10) and factoring ρ^q, we obtain

$$\sum_i \left(\rho^{1-q} \frac{\partial K_i}{\partial u_i} - K_i \frac{\partial W}{\partial u_i} \right) =$$
$$D(2-q) \sum_{ij} \left(G_{ij} \frac{\partial W}{\partial u_i} \frac{\partial W}{\partial u_j} - \rho^{1-q} \frac{\partial G_{ij}}{\partial u_i} \frac{\partial W}{\partial u_j} - \rho^{1-q} G_{ij} \frac{\partial^2 W}{\partial u_i \partial u_j} \right). \quad (14)$$

Substituting (11) in (14), we have

$$\sum_i \left([1-(1-q)W] \frac{\partial K_i}{\partial u_i} - K_i \frac{\partial W}{\partial u_i} \right) = D(2-q) \times$$
$$\sum_{ij} \left\{ G_{ij} \frac{\partial W}{\partial u_i} \frac{\partial W}{\partial u_j} - [1-(1-q)W] \left(\frac{\partial G_{ij}}{\partial u_i} \frac{\partial W}{\partial u_j} + G_{ij} \frac{\partial^2 W}{\partial u_i \partial u_j} \right) \right\}. \quad (15)$$

The computations that follow will be considerably simplified if we express the above equation in terms of the re-scaled quantity $\tilde{W} = (2-q)W$. We shall first consider a regime of weak fluctuations, or weak noise, corresponding to $D \ll 1$. Analyzing the behavior of solutions of the FPE within that regime, we shall obtain a set of relations connecting the Liapunov function and the phase-space flow (drift field) of the network, and the diffusion coefficients. We shall show that these relations, in turn, imply important properties of the FPE that hold for arbitrary values of D.

If we expand $\tilde{W}(\boldsymbol{u})$ in a power series,

$$\tilde{W}(\boldsymbol{u}) = \frac{1}{D} \sum_{k=0}^{\infty} D^k \phi_k(\boldsymbol{u}), \quad (16)$$

substitute (16) in (15) and, considering the case of weak fluctuations ($D \ll 1$), keep the dominant terms proportional to D^{-1}, we obtain

$$D^{-1} \sum_i \left(-(1-q)\phi_0 \frac{\partial K_i}{\partial u_i} - K_i \frac{\partial \phi_0}{\partial u_i} \right) =$$
$$D^{-1} \sum_{ij} \left\{ G_{ij} \frac{\partial \phi_0}{\partial u_i} \frac{\partial \phi_0}{\partial u_j} + (1-q)\phi_0 \left(\frac{\partial G_{ij}}{\partial u_i} \frac{\partial \phi_0}{\partial u_j} + G_{ij} \frac{\partial^2 \phi_0}{\partial u_i \partial u_j} \right) \right\}. \quad (17)$$

The above Eq. (17) may be rewritten as

$$\sum_i \left(K_i \frac{\partial \phi_0}{\partial u_i} \right) = \boldsymbol{K} \cdot \nabla \phi_0 = -\sum_{ij} \left(G_{ij} \frac{\partial \phi_0}{\partial u_i} \frac{\partial \phi_0}{\partial u_j} \right)$$
$$- (1-q)\phi_0 \sum_i \left[\frac{\partial K_i}{\partial u_i} + \sum_j \left(\frac{\partial G_{ij}}{\partial u_i} \frac{\partial \phi_0}{\partial u_j} + G_{ij} \frac{\partial^2 \phi_0}{\partial u_i \partial u_j} \right) \right]. \quad (18)$$

Now, we derive a connection between the drift field, the diffusion parameters and ϕ_0, such that the above equation is satisfied. It is of special interest if that connection can be formulated as a q-independent structure, that holds for any value of the entropic parameter. It can be seen by inspection, that (18) is satisfied in a q-independent way if

$$\boldsymbol{K} \cdot \boldsymbol{\nabla} \phi_0 = - \sum_{ij} \left(G_{ij} \frac{\partial \phi_0}{\partial u_i} \frac{\partial \phi_0}{\partial u_j} \right) , \tag{19}$$

and

$$\sum_i \left[\frac{\partial K_i}{\partial u_i} + \sum_j \left(\frac{\partial G_{ij}}{\partial u_i} \frac{\partial \phi_0}{\partial u_j} + G_{ij} \frac{\partial^2 \phi_0}{\partial u_i \partial u_j} \right) \right] = 0. \tag{20}$$

The above pair of equations imply that

$$K_i = - \left(\sum_j G_{ij} \frac{\partial \phi_0}{\partial u_j} \right) + \varUpsilon_i , \tag{21}$$

where $\boldsymbol{\varUpsilon} = (\varUpsilon_i, \ldots \varUpsilon_N)$ is a divergenceless vector field that, at each point in phase space, is orthogonal to $\boldsymbol{\nabla} \phi_0$. That is,

$$\boldsymbol{\nabla} \cdot \boldsymbol{\varUpsilon} = 0, \quad \text{and} \quad \boldsymbol{\varUpsilon} \cdot \boldsymbol{\nabla} \phi_0 = 0. \tag{22}$$

When $q = 1$, Eq. (18) becomes the Hamilton-Jacobi-like equation derived in [34], for the linear FPE. When we consider the equations of motion (4) for one single realization of our network and (19), we have

$$\frac{d\phi_0(\boldsymbol{u})}{dt} = \boldsymbol{\nabla} \phi_0 \cdot \frac{d\boldsymbol{u}}{dt} = \boldsymbol{\nabla} \phi_0 \cdot \boldsymbol{K}$$
$$= - \sum_{i,j} G_{ij} \frac{\partial \phi_0}{\partial u_i} \frac{\partial \phi_0}{\partial u_j} \leq 0. \tag{23}$$

The last inequality holds, because the matrix $[G_{ij}]$ characterizing the diffusion term is definite positive. Equation (23) means that the quantity ϕ_0 is a Liapunov function (an energy landscape) of the network dynamics.

On the basis of the above results, we can obtain an H-theorem for a network Fokker-Planck dynamics governed by any evolution Eq. (9) that complies with (21–22). Introducing the free-energy like functional,

$$\mathcal{F} = D \int \left(\frac{\rho^{2-q} - \rho}{1 - q} \right) d^N \boldsymbol{u} + \int \phi_0 \rho \, d^N \boldsymbol{u} , \tag{24}$$

it follows from the FPE (9) and the conditions (21–22), that the above quantity satisfies the H-theorem,

$$\frac{d\mathcal{F}}{dt} = - \int \rho \sum_{ij} \left\{ G_{ij} \left[D \left(\frac{2-q}{1-q} \right) \frac{\partial \rho^{1-q}}{\partial u_i} - \frac{\partial \phi_0}{\partial u_i} \right] \right.$$
$$\left. \times \left[D \left(\frac{2-q}{1-q} \right) \frac{\partial \rho^{1-q}}{\partial u_j} - \frac{\partial \phi_0}{\partial u_j} \right] \right\} d^N \boldsymbol{u} \leq 0. \tag{25}$$

This H-theorem holds for any value of D, provided that the conditions (21–22) are satisfied. It is worth noting that the free-energy functional $\mathcal{F}$ can be expressed in terms of an S_q entropy: $\mathcal{F} = \langle \phi_0 \rangle - DS_{q^*}[\rho]$, where $q^* = 2 - q$ and $\langle \phi_0 \rangle = \int \phi_0 \rho \, d^N \boldsymbol{u}$. Moreover, under conditions (21–22), the stationary solution of (9) is $\rho_{\mathrm{st}}(\boldsymbol{u}) = \exp_q\left[-(1/D)(\alpha_0 + \phi_0(\boldsymbol{u}))\right]$. Choosing the constant α_0 appropriately one gets a normalized ρ_{st}.

4   Fokker-Planck Dynamics of the Cohen-Grossberg Continuous Neural Network

In the Cohen-Grossberg model of neural networks [5], the continuous state variables u_i, describing the state of each neuron i, evolve according to the set of N coupled, ordinary differential equations,

$$\frac{du_i}{dt} = a_i(u_i) \left[b_i(u_i) - \sum_{j=1}^{N} c_{ij} d_j(u_j) \right] = K_i(\boldsymbol{u}), \quad i = 1, \ldots, N, \qquad (26)$$

where the c_{ij}'s are constant weights, the $a_i(u_i)$'s, $b_i(u_i)$'s, and $d_i(u_i)$'s are appropriate functions of the state variables u_i, and it is assumed that $a_i(u_i)d'_i(u_i) \geq 0$. Different instances of the Cohen-Grossberg model correspond to different choices for the $a_i(u_i)$, $b_i(u_i)$, and $d_i(u_i)$ functions.

The Cohen-Grossberg model with symmetric weights, $c_{ij} = c_{ji}$, admits an *energy function* (also called Liapunov function), given by [5]

$$\Omega = -\sum_{i=1}^{N} \int_0^{u_i} b_i(\epsilon_i) d'_i(\epsilon_i) d\epsilon_i + \frac{1}{2} \sum_{j,k=1}^{N} c_{jk} d_j(u_j) d_k(u_k). \qquad (27)$$

Evaluating the partial derivatives of Ω with respect to the u_i's, and combining them with the equations of motion (26), it can be verified that these evolution equations can be rewritten, in terms of the partial derivatives of Ω and of the quantities $\frac{d}{du_i} d_i(u_i) = d'_i(u_i)$, as

$$\frac{du_i}{dt} = -\left[\frac{a_i(u_i)}{d'_i(u_i)}\right] \frac{\partial \Omega}{\partial u_i} = K_i(u_1, u_2, \ldots, u_N). \qquad (28)$$

The celebrated Hopfield model constitutes a special case of the Cohen-Grossberg one. In fact, if $a_i(u_i) = -1/\tau_i$, $b_i(u_i) = u_i$, $c_{ij} = \omega_{ij}$, and $d_i(u_i) = g(u_i)$, the evolution Eqs. (26) reduce to the equations of motion of the continuous Hopfield neural network (5). We thus see that the Hopfield model is obtained when having the a_i's all constant, the b_i's all linear, and the d_i's all equal to the same function $g(u_i)$.

Taking into account the form (28) of the equations of motion for the Cohen-Grossberg model, we see that the dynamics of this network is compatible with a FPE of the form (9), provided that

$$G_{ij}(\boldsymbol{u}) = \begin{cases} a_i(u_i)/d'_i(u_i), & \text{for } i = j, \\ 0, & \text{for } i \neq j. \end{cases} \qquad (29)$$

The concomitant Fokker-Planck equation for the Cohen-Grossberg model admits an H-theorem, $d\mathcal{F}/dt \leq 0$, with $\mathcal{F} = \langle \Omega \rangle - DS_{q^*}[\rho]$, and its stationary solution is of the form $\rho_{\text{st}}(\boldsymbol{u}) = \exp_q[-(1/D)(\alpha_0 + \Omega)(\boldsymbol{u})]$, with α_0 constant.

5   Concluding Remarks

We have investigated important relationships between the nonlinear Fokker-Planck treatment of network dynamics, on the one hand, and the nonequilibrium landscape approach to this dynamics, on the other one. In the research literature, the latter approach has so far been discussed only in connection with linear Fokker-Planck equations. In the present contribution, we have shown that this nonequilibrium landscape technique can be applied to nonlinear Fokker-Planck network dynamics, yielding interesting and relevant connections between the network's Liapunov function, the phase-space flow, and the structure of the diffusion term. These relationships allow the attainment of the H-theorem of the network's Fokker-Planck dynamics.

Our present considerations were motivated by the S_q maximum entropy, power-law distributions that have been observed in numerical simulations [20, 28] and in real data [1, 22], in the field of neuroscience. The study of dynamical mechanisms that produce these q-MaxEnt distributions is highly relevant, since the classical Boltzmann-Gibbs approach produces exponential distributions and does not account for observed power laws. This theoretical framework also supports the choice of different entropic measures for modelling and simulating complex networks such as the brain, as well as other neural network models in artificial intelligence [10, 22, 26]. Moreover, the results we have obtained and presented here may have wider implications. They constitute the first step in the exploration of the links between two major theoretical frameworks in the study of complex systems: nonextensive thermostatistics [25] and nonequilibrium landscape theory [8, 27, 34]. We have shown that ideas from each of these theories can profitably be related to ideas from the other one. We hope that our present contribution will motivate other researchers to further investigate the connections between these two theoretical approaches. Most probably, their common interface will be a fertile ground for new discoveries.

References

1. Beggs, J.M., Plenz, D.: Neuronal avalanches in neocortical circuits. J. Neurosci. **23**, 11167–11177 (2003). https://doi.org/10.1523/JNEUROSCI.23-35-11167.2003
2. Brito, S., da Silva, L.R., Tsallis, C.: Role of dimensionality in complex networks. Nature Sci. Rep. **6**, 27992.1–27992.8 (2016). https://doi.org/10.1038/srep27992
3. de Carvalho, L.A.V., Mendes, D.Q., Wedemann, R.S.: Creativity and delusions: the dopaminergic modulation of cortical maps. In: Sloot, P.M.A., Abramson, D., Bogdanov, A.V., Dongarra, J.J., Zomaya, A.Y., Gorbachev, Y.E. (eds.) ICCS 2003. LNCS, vol. 2657, pp. 511–520. Springer, Heidelberg (2003). https://doi.org/10.1007/3-540-44860-8_53

4. Cleeremans, A., Timmermans, B., Pasquali, A.: Consciousness and metarepresentation: a computational sketch. Neural Netw. **20**, 1032–1039 (2007). https://doi.org/10.1016/j.neunet.2007.09.011
5. Cohen, M.A., Grossberg, S.: Absolute stability of global pattern formation and parallel memory storage by competitive neural networks. IEEE Trans. Syst. Man. Cybern. **13**, 815–826 (1983). https://doi.org/10.1109/TSMC.1983.6313075
6. Czégel, D., Balogh, S., Pollner, P., Palla, G.: Phase space volume scaling of generalized entropies and anomalous diffusion scaling governed by corresponding nonlinear Fokker-Planck equations. Sci. Rep. **8**, 1883 (2018). https://doi.org/10.1038/s41598-018-20202-w
7. da Silva, P.C., da Silva, L.R., Lenzi, E.K., Mendes, R.S., Malacarne, L.C.: Anomalous diffusion and anisotropic nonlinear Fokker-Planck equation. Phys. A **342**(1), 16–21 (2004). https://doi.org/10.1016/j.physa.2004.04.054
8. Fang, X., Kruse, K., Lu, T., Wang, J.: Nonequilibrium physics in biology. Rev. Mod. Phys. **91**(4), 045004 (2019). https://doi.org/10.1103/RevModPhys.91.045004
9. Franck, T.D.: Nonlinear Fokker-Planck Equations: Fundamentals and Applications. Springer, Heidelberg (2005). https://doi.org/10.1007/b137680
10. Hertz, J.A., Krogh, A., Palmer, R.G., (eds.): Introduction to the Theory of Neural Computation. Lecture Notes, vol. 1. Perseus Books, Cambridge (1991)
11. Hopfield, J.J.: Neurons with graded responses have collective computational properties like those of two-state neurons. Proc. Natl. Acad. Sci. **81**, 3088–3092 (1984). https://doi.org/10.1073/pnas.81.10.3088
12. Kandel, E.: Psychiatry, Psychoanalysis, and the New Biology of Mind. American Psychiatric Publishing Inc., Washington (2005)
13. Lenzi, E.K., Lenzi, M.K., Ribeiro, H.V., Evangelista, L.R.: Extensions and solutions for nonlinear diffusion equations and random walks. Proc. Roy. Soc. A: Math. Phys. Eng. Sci. **475**(2231), 20190432 (2019). https://doi.org/10.1098/rspa.2019.0432
14. Lotka, A.J.: Elements of Mathematical Biology. Dover, New York (1956)
15. de Luca, V.T.F., Wedemann, R.S., Plastino, A.R.: Neuronal asymmetries and Fokker-Planck dynamics. In: Kůrková, V., Manolopoulos, Y., Hammer, B., Iliadis, L., Maglogiannis, I. (eds.) ICANN 2018. LNCS, vol. 11141, pp. 703–713. Springer, Cham (2018). https://doi.org/10.1007/978-3-030-01424-7_69
16. Martinez, S., Plastino, A.R., Plastino, A.: Nonlinear Fokker-Planck equations and generalized entropies. Phys. A **259**(1–2), 183–192 (1998). https://doi.org/10.1016/S0378-4371(98)00277-5
17. Papa, A.R.R., da Silva, L.: Earthquakes in the brain. Theory Biosci. **116**, 321–327 (1997)
18. Plastino, A.R., Plastino, A.: Non-extensive statistical mechanics and generalized Fokker-Planck equation. Phys. A **222**(1), 347–354 (1995). https://doi.org/10.1016/0378-4371(95)00211-1
19. Ribeiro, M.S., Nobre, F.D., Curado, E.M.F.: Classes of N-dimensional nonlinear Fokker-Planck equations associated to Tsallis entropy. Entropy **13**(11), 1928–1944 (2011). https://doi.org/10.3390/e13111928
20. Siddiqui, M., Wedemann, R.S., Jensen, H.J.: Avalanches and generalized memory associativity in a network model for conscious and unconscious mental functioning. Phys. A **490**, 127–138 (2018). https://doi.org/10.1016/j.physa.2017.08.011
21. Souza, A.M.C., Andrade, R.F.S., Nobre, F.D., Curado, E.M.F.: Thermodynamic framework for compact q-Gaussian distributions. Phys. A **491**, 153–166 (2018). https://doi.org/10.1016/j.physa.2017.09.013

22. Tagliazucchi, E., Balenzuela, P., Fraiman, D., Chialvo, D.R.: Criticality in large-scale brain fMRI dynamics unveiled by a novel point process analysis. Front. Physiol.—Fractal Physiol. **3**, 15 (2012). https://doi.org/10.3389/fphys.2012.00015

23. Taylor, J.G.: A neural model of the loss of self in schizophrenia. Schizophrenia Bull. **37**(6), 1229–1247 (2011). https://doi.org/10.1093/schbul/sbq033

24. Tirnakli, U., Borges, E.P.: The standard map: From Boltzmann-Gibbs statistics to Tsallis statistics. Nat. Sci. Rep. **6**, 23644.1–23644.8 (2016). https://doi.org/10.1038/srep23644

25. Tsallis, C.: Introduction to Nonextensive Statistical Mechanics, Approaching a Complex World. Springer, New York (2009). https://doi.org/10.1007/978-0-387-85359-8

26. Tsallis, C., Stariolo, D.A.: Generalized simulated annealing. Phys. A **233**, 395–406 (1996). https://doi.org/10.1016/S0378-4371(96)00271-3

27. Wang, J., Xu, L., Wang, E.: Potential landscape and flux framework of nonequilibrium networks: robustness, dissipation, and coherence of biochemical oscillations. Proc. Nat. Acad. Sci. **105**(34), 12271–12276 (2008). https://doi.org/10.1073/pnas.0800579105, https://www.pnas.org/content/105/34/12271

28. Wedemann, R.S., Donangelo, R., de Carvalho, L.A.V.: Generalized memory associativity in a network model for the neuroses. Chaos **19**(1), 015116 (2009). https://doi.org/10.1063/1.3099608

29. Wedemann, R.S., Plastino, A.R.: Asymmetries in synaptic connections and the nonlinear Fokker-Planck formalism. In: Villa, A.E.P., Masulli, P., Pons Rivero, A.J. (eds.) ICANN 2016. LNCS, vol. 9886, pp. 19–27. Springer, Cham (2016). https://doi.org/10.1007/978-3-319-44778-0_3

30. Wedemann, R.S., Plastino, A.R.: q-maximum entropy distributions and memory neural networks. In: Lintas, A., Rovetta, S., Verschure, P.F.M.J., Villa, A.E.P. (eds.) ICANN 2017. LNCS, vol. 10613, pp. 300–308. Springer, Cham (2017). https://doi.org/10.1007/978-3-319-68600-4_35

31. Wedemann, R.S., Plastino, A.R., Tsallis, C.: Curl forces and the nonlinear Fokker-Planck equation. Phys. Rev. E **94**(6), 062105 (2016). https://doi.org/10.1103/PhysRevE.94.062105

32. Wedemann, R.S., de Carvalho, L.A.V.: Some things psychopathologies can tell us about consciousness. In: Villa, A.E.P., Duch, W., Érdi, P., Masulli, F., Palm, G. (eds.) ICANN 2012. LNCS, vol. 7552, pp. 379–386. Springer, Heidelberg (2012). https://doi.org/10.1007/978-3-642-33269-2_48

33. Wedemann, R.S., de Carvalho, L.A.V., Donangelo, R.: Access to symbolization and associativity mechanisms in a model of conscious and unconscious processes. In: Samsonovich, A.V., Jóhannsdóttir, K.R. (eds.) Biologically Inspired Cognitive Architectures 2011, Frontiers in Artificial Intelligence and Applications, vol. 233, pp. 444–449. IOS Press, Amsterdam, Netherlands (2011). https://doi.org/10.3233/978-1-60750-959-2-444

34. Yan, H., Zhao, L., Hu, L., Wang, X., Wang, E., Wang, J.: Nonequilibrium landscape theory of neural networks. Proc. Nat. Acad. Sci. **110**(45), E4185–E4194 (2013). https://doi.org/10.1073/pnas.1310692110

Hopfield Networks for Vector Quantization

C. Bauckhage[1,2,3(✉)] [iD], R. Ramamurthy[1,3], and R. Sifa[1,3]

[1] Fraunhofer Center for Machine Learning, Sankt Augustin, Germany
[2] Computer Science, University of Bonn, Bonn, Germany
[3] Fraunhofer IAIS, Sankt Augustin, Germany
{c.bauckhage,r.ramamurthy,r.sifa}@iais.fraunhofer.de

Abstract. We consider the problem of finding representative prototypes within a set of data and solve it using Hopfield networks. Our key idea is to minimize the mean discrepancy between kernel density estimates of the distributions of data points and prototypes. We show that this objective can be cast as a quadratic unconstrained binary optimization problem which is equivalent to a Hopfield energy minimization problem. This result is of current interest as it suggests that vector quantization can be accomplished via adiabatic quantum computing.

1 Introduction

When dealing with n data points $\boldsymbol{x}_j \in \mathbb{R}^m$, vector quantization is to determine $k \ll n$ prototypes $\boldsymbol{w}_i \in \mathbb{R}^m$ which provide a compressed representation of the data (see Fig. 1). Since this has obvious applications in signal processing, data mining, or different stages of the pattern recognition pipeline, research on vector quantization has a venerable history and many algorithms in this arena have become established textbook material [6,10,11,15,16,22,23,26,28,29,31].

In this paper, we propose to quantize with respect to the mean discrepancy between a kernel density estimate of a set of data and a kernel density estimate of a set of prototypes and show how to accomplish this using Hopfield networks.

The mean discrepancy measures the similarity of two probability densities in terms of the squared distance between their embeddings in a reproducing kernel Hilbert space [17]. It is a popular loss function in deep generative modeling [2, 8,14,24,25] and can also serve as an objective in data clustering [20]. Curiously, however, the idea of *minimizing* mean discrepancies in order to align two samples seems to have been largely overlooked. While there exists a connection between mean discrepancies and information theoretic vector quantization [36], it appears not to have been used before.

Letting $MD^2(\mathcal{X}, \mathcal{W})$ denote the mean discrepancy between the distribution of points in a data set $\mathcal{X}$ and the distribution of prototypes in a codebook $\mathcal{W}$, our contributions in this paper are as follows:

© Springer Nature Switzerland AG 2020
I. Farkaš et al. (Eds.): ICANN 2020, LNCS 12397, pp. 192–203, 2020.
https://doi.org/10.1007/978-3-030-61616-8_16

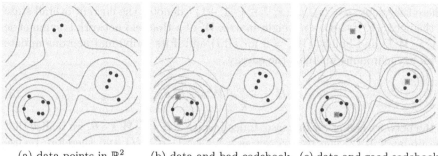

(a) data points in $\mathbb{R}^2$ (b) data and bad codebook   (c) data and good codebook

Fig. 1. A set $\mathcal{X}$ of 16 data points $\boldsymbol{x}_j$ (blue dots) and two codebooks $\mathcal{W}$ of 3 proto-types $\boldsymbol{w}_i$ (orange squares). Kernel density estimates for data points and prototypes are visualized in terms of isolines. The prototypes in (b) provide a sub-optimal representation as their density differs noticeable from the data density. The prototypes in (c) result from solving the mean discrepancy minimization problem in (1) using a Hopfield network; here, both densities are similar. (Color figure online)

We focus on a constrained form of the vector quantization problem where prototypes are required to coincide with data points, that is we aim at solving

$$\mathcal{W} = \underset{\mathcal{W}' \subset \mathcal{X}}{\operatorname{argmin}} \; MD^2(\mathcal{X}, \mathcal{W}')$$
$$\text{s.t.} \quad |\mathcal{W}'| = k \ll n. \tag{1}$$

Note that prototypes which coincide with actual data points are often easy to interpret and that methods which yield such prototypes are of increasing interest to analysts for whom explainability is a primary concern [5,9,13,30,33,34].

Given the subset selection problem in (1), we show how to cast it in terms of a quadratic binary optimization problem which can be rewritten as an energy minimization problem that can be solved by a Hopfield network.

Next, we recall basic aspects of Hopfield networks (Sect. 2) and present our ideas behind mean discrepancy minimization for vector quantization (Sect. 3). We then derive expressions for weights and biases of Hopfield networks that solve the above problem (Sect. 4) and practically verify their utility (Sect. 5). Finally, we discuss related work and implications of our results with regard to vector quantization by means of quantum computing (Sect. 6).

2   Hopfield Networks for Problem Solving

Hopfield networks are a venerable class of neurocomputing models [1,19] and well established textbook material [18,32]. They are recurrent neural networks of n fully connected neurons $s_1, \ldots, s_n$ each of which is a bipolar threshold unit

$$s_i = \operatorname{sign}(\boldsymbol{w}_i^\mathsf{T} \boldsymbol{s} - \theta_i) \tag{2}$$

where the vector $s = [s_1, \ldots, s_n]^\mathsf{T} \in \{-1, +1\}^n$ denotes the current overall state of the network. If the $n \times n$ weight matrix W of a Hopfield network is symmetric ($W = W^\mathsf{T}$) and hollow ($W_{ii} = 0$ for all i) and if its individual neurons update in an asynchronous manner, the energy

$$H = -\frac{1}{2} s^\mathsf{T} W s + \theta^\mathsf{T} s \tag{3}$$

of the network can never increase. Indeed, since $\nabla H = -Ws + \theta$, we realize that the updates in (2) can be written as $s_i = \mathrm{sign}(-e_i^\mathsf{T} \nabla H)$ and therefore realize a form of gradient descend on (3). As there are only finitely many, namely 2^n distinct overall states for the network to be in, this implies that it will reach a (local) energy minimum after finitely many steps [19].

Traditionally, this property of Hopfield networks has been most comonly used in the context of associative memories for pattern recogntion; however, Hopfield networks also allow for problem solving [32]. Here, the idea is to devise an energy function H whose minimizers

$$s^* = \operatorname*{argmin}_{s \in \{-1, +1\}^n} -\frac{1}{2} s^\mathsf{T} W s + \theta^\mathsf{T} s \tag{4}$$

encode solutions to the problem at hand. Below, we discuss how to accomplish this for the constrained vector quantization problem in (1).

3   Mean Discrepancy as a Vector Quantization Objective

In what follows, we assume that we are given a sample $\mathcal{X} = \{x_1, \ldots, x_n\}$ of n data points $x_j \in \mathbb{R}^m$ for which we seek a codebook $\mathcal{W} = \{w_1, \ldots, w_k\}$ of $k \ll n$ prototypes $w_i \in \mathbb{R}^m$.

Our basic idea is to consider probability density estimates of the distributions of the points in $\mathcal{X}$ and $\mathcal{W}$ and to use them to guide the selection of characteristic prototypes. In particular, we will consider common Parzen density estimates

$$p(x) = \frac{1}{n} \sum_{j=1}^{n} \phi(x, x_j) \tag{5}$$

$$q(x) = \frac{1}{k} \sum_{i=1}^{k} \phi(x, w_i) \tag{6}$$

for $\mathcal{X}$ and $\mathcal{W}$, respectively, where $\phi(\cdot, \cdot)$ is a Gaussian radial basis kernel.

Since the Gaussian kernel is an instance of a Mercer kernel, there must exist some feature map $\varphi : \mathbb{R}^m \to \mathbb{H}$ and a possibly infinite dimensional feature space $\mathbb{H}$ which, as a Hilbert space, is endowed with an inner product $\langle \cdot | \cdot \rangle_{\mathbb{H}} : \mathbb{H} \times \mathbb{H} \to \mathbb{R}$. Hence, the kernel density estimates in (5) and (6) can equivalently be written in terms of inner products of feature space vectors, namely

$$p(\boldsymbol{x}) = \frac{1}{n} \sum_{j=1}^{n} \left\langle \varphi(\boldsymbol{x}) \,\middle|\, \varphi(\boldsymbol{x}_j) \right\rangle_{\mathbb{H}} = \left\langle \varphi(\boldsymbol{x}) \,\middle|\, \frac{1}{n} \sum_{j=1}^{n} \varphi(\boldsymbol{x}_j) \right\rangle_{\mathbb{H}}$$

$$q(\boldsymbol{x}) = \frac{1}{k} \sum_{i=1}^{k} \left\langle \varphi(\boldsymbol{x}) \,\middle|\, \varphi(\boldsymbol{w}_i) \right\rangle_{\mathbb{H}} = \left\langle \varphi(\boldsymbol{x}) \,\middle|\, \frac{1}{k} \sum_{i=1}^{k} \varphi(\boldsymbol{w}_i) \right\rangle_{\mathbb{H}}$$

In other words, we have the important result that our kernel density estimates are feature space inner products

$$p(\boldsymbol{x}) = \left\langle \varphi(\boldsymbol{x}) \,\middle|\, \bar{\varphi}_{\mathcal{X}} \right\rangle_{\mathbb{H}} \tag{7}$$

$$q(\boldsymbol{x}) = \left\langle \varphi(\boldsymbol{x}) \,\middle|\, \bar{\varphi}_{\mathcal{W}} \right\rangle_{\mathbb{H}} \tag{8}$$

where we write

$$\bar{\varphi}_{\mathcal{X}} = \frac{1}{n} \sum_{j=1}^{n} \varphi(\boldsymbol{x}_j) \tag{9}$$

$$\bar{\varphi}_{\mathcal{W}} = \frac{1}{k} \sum_{i=1}^{k} \varphi(\boldsymbol{w}_i) \tag{10}$$

to denote the feature space sample means of the $\boldsymbol{x}_j$ and $\boldsymbol{w}_i$, respectively.

Next, we note that any details as to the particular shape of the density $p(\boldsymbol{x})$ in (5) depend on the elements of $\mathcal{X}$ and that specifics of the density $q(\boldsymbol{x})$ in (6) depend on the elements of $\mathcal{W}$. In (7) and (8), these dependencies have been completely moved into in the second factors of the respective inner products; the first factor $\varphi(\boldsymbol{x})$ is the same in both equations. This is then to say that all information as to specific properties of the two densities must be contained in the vectors $\bar{\varphi}_{\mathcal{X}}$ and $\bar{\varphi}_{\mathcal{W}}$, respectively. In other words, the mean vectors $\bar{\varphi}_{\mathcal{X}}$ and $\bar{\varphi}_{\mathcal{W}}$ fully characterize our density estimates $p(\boldsymbol{x})$ and $q(\boldsymbol{x})$; everything we could ever infer about their individual properties is implicitly captured by these feature space means. Hence, any difference between the two densities will cause the mean discrepancy

$$MD^2(\mathcal{X}, \mathcal{W}) = \left\| \bar{\varphi}_{\mathcal{X}} - \bar{\varphi}_{\mathcal{W}} \right\|_{\mathbb{H}}^2 \tag{11}$$

to exceed zero.

The expression in (11) therefore provides a minimization objective that can guide the search for an optimal codebook: Given $\mathcal{X}$ and an initial guess for $\mathcal{W}$, we may attempt to minimize MD^2 w.r.t. to $\mathcal{W}$ in order to determine an appropriate compressed representation of the data at hand. While this idea seems reasonable, it also seems infeasible. After all, we generally neither know the implicit feature map φ required to determine $\bar{\varphi}_{\mathcal{X}}$ and $\bar{\varphi}_{\mathcal{W}}$ nor how to compute distances in feature space $\mathbb{H}$. Next, we therefore show how to circumvent these issues.

4   Hopfield Networks for Mean Discrepancy Minimization

To solve the constrained quantization problem in (1) which requires $\mathcal{W} \subset \mathcal{X}$, we first modify our ansatz for $q(\boldsymbol{x})$. That is, instead of working with (6), we consider the following kernel density estimate of the distribution of the points in $\mathcal{W}$

$$q(\boldsymbol{x}) = \frac{1}{k} \sum_{j=1}^{n} \phi(\boldsymbol{x}, \boldsymbol{x}_j) \, z_j \tag{12}$$

where

$$z_j \in \{0,1\} \quad \text{and} \quad \sum_{j=1}^{n} z_j = k. \tag{13}$$

This modified model reflects the constraint that the sought after prototypes $\boldsymbol{w}_i \in \mathcal{W}$ are to coincide with certain data points $\boldsymbol{x}_j \in \mathcal{X}$. The n additional binary variables z_j indicate which of the data points are considered to be prototypes.

To derive a solution strategy for our problem, we first note that the squared feature space distance in (11) can be rewritten in terms of inner products

$$MD^2(\mathcal{X}, \mathcal{W}) = \left\langle \bar{\varphi}_{\mathcal{X}} \,\middle|\, \bar{\varphi}_{\mathcal{X}} \right\rangle_{\mathbb{H}} + \left\langle \bar{\varphi}_{\mathcal{W}} \,\middle|\, \bar{\varphi}_{\mathcal{W}} \right\rangle_{\mathbb{H}} - 2\left\langle \bar{\varphi}_{\mathcal{X}} \,\middle|\, \bar{\varphi}_{\mathcal{W}} \right\rangle_{\mathbb{H}} \tag{14}$$

When plugging our modified ansatz in (13) into (14), some algebra reveals that the mean discrepancy between $\mathcal{X}$ and $\mathcal{W}$ becomes

$$MD^2(\mathcal{X}, \mathcal{W}) = \frac{1}{n^2} \sum_{j=1}^{n} \sum_{l=1}^{n} \phi(\boldsymbol{x}_j, \boldsymbol{x}_l)$$

$$+ \frac{1}{k^2} \sum_{j=1}^{n} \sum_{l=1}^{n} z_j \, \phi(\boldsymbol{x}_j, \boldsymbol{x}_l) \, z_l$$

$$- \frac{2}{nk} \sum_{j=1}^{n} \sum_{l=1}^{n} \phi(\boldsymbol{x}_j, \boldsymbol{x}_l) \, z_l \tag{15}$$

which is to say that the mean discrepancy in (11) can be written entirely in terms of available ingredients, namely in terms of Gaussian kernels evaluated on elements of $\mathcal{X}$ and $\mathcal{W}$.

To cats (15) in a more concise form, we introduce a binary indicator vector $\boldsymbol{z} \in \{0,1\}^n$ and a kernel matrix $\boldsymbol{\Phi} \in \mathbb{R}^{n \times n}$ whose entries are $\Phi_{il} = \phi(\boldsymbol{x}_j, \boldsymbol{x}_l)$. This allows us to write

$$MD^2(\mathcal{X}, \mathcal{W}) = \frac{1}{n^2} \mathbf{1}^{\mathsf{T}} \boldsymbol{\Phi} \mathbf{1} + \frac{1}{k^2} \boldsymbol{z}^{\mathsf{T}} \boldsymbol{\Phi} \boldsymbol{z} - \frac{2}{nk} \mathbf{1}^{\mathsf{T}} \boldsymbol{\Phi} \boldsymbol{z} \tag{16}$$

where $\mathbf{1}$ denotes the n-dimensional vector of all ones.

Noting that the first term on the right of (16) is a constant independent of z, we find that our constrained MD^2-based vector quantization problem consists in solving

$$z^* = \operatorname*{argmin}_{z \in \{0,1\}^n} \frac{1}{k^2} z^\mathsf{T} \Phi z - \frac{2}{nk} \mathbf{1}^\mathsf{T} \Phi z \tag{17}$$
$$\text{s.t.} \quad \mathbf{1}^\mathsf{T} z = k$$

which we recognize as a constrained quadratic binary optimization problem.

Furthermore, since $\mathbf{1}^\mathsf{T} z = k$ implies $(\mathbf{1}^\mathsf{T} z - k)^2 = 0$, we observe that (17) is equivalent to

$$z^* = \operatorname*{argmin}_{z \in \{0,1\}^n} \frac{1}{k^2} z^\mathsf{T} \Phi z - \frac{2}{nk} \mathbf{1}^\mathsf{T} \Phi z + \lambda \left(\mathbf{1}^\mathsf{T} z - k \right)^2 \tag{18}$$

where $\lambda \in \mathbb{R}$ is a Lagrange multiplier. Written like this, our constrained vector quantization problem is thus revealed to be a quadratic unconstrained binary optimization problem (QUBO).

Continuing further, we observe that (18) can be rewritten as

$$\begin{aligned} z^* &= \operatorname*{argmin}_{z \in \{0,1\}^n} z^\mathsf{T} \left(\frac{1}{k^2} \Phi + \lambda \, \mathbf{1}\mathbf{1}^\mathsf{T} \right) z - \left(\frac{2}{nk} \Phi \mathbf{1} + \lambda \, 2 \, k \, \mathbf{1} \right)^\mathsf{T} z + const \\ &\equiv \operatorname*{argmin}_{z \in \{0,1\}^n} z^\mathsf{T} P \, z - p^\mathsf{T} z \end{aligned} \tag{19}$$

which now looks eerily similar to the Hopfield energy minimization problem in (4). Yet, (4) and (19) differ in that the former minimizes over bipolar vectors $s \in \{-1, +1\}^n$ whereas the latter minimizes over binary vectors $z \in \{0,1\}^n$. However, noting that bipolar and binary vectors are affinely isomorphic

$$s = 2z - 1 \quad \Leftrightarrow \quad z = \frac{s+1}{2}, \tag{20}$$

we have

$$\begin{aligned} z^\mathsf{T} P z - p^\mathsf{T} z &= \tfrac{1}{4} (s+1)^\mathsf{T} P (s+1) - \tfrac{1}{2} p^\mathsf{T} (s+1) \\ &= \tfrac{1}{4} s^\mathsf{T} P s + \tfrac{2}{4} \mathbf{1}^\mathsf{T} P s - \tfrac{1}{2} p^\mathsf{T} s + const \\ &= \tfrac{1}{4} s^\mathsf{T} P s + \tfrac{1}{2} \left(P \mathbf{1} - p \right)^\mathsf{T} s + const \\ &\equiv s^\mathsf{T} Q \, s + q^\mathsf{T} s + const \end{aligned} \tag{21}$$

In other words, we find the crucial result that the vector quantization problem in (1) can be cast as the problem of solving

$$s^* = \operatorname*{argmin}_{s \in \{-1,+1\}^n} s^\mathsf{T} Q s + q^\mathsf{T} s \tag{22}$$

where

$$Q = \frac{1}{4}\left(\frac{1}{k^2}\Phi + \lambda\, 11^\mathsf{T}\right) \tag{23}$$

$$q = \frac{1}{2}\left(\left(\frac{1}{k^2}\Phi + \lambda\, 11^\mathsf{T}\right)1 - \left(\frac{2}{nk}\Phi^\mathsf{T}1 + \lambda\, 2\, k\, 1\right)\right). \tag{24}$$

Once the vector s^* that solves this problem has been determined, its entries s_j^* equal to $+1$ indicate which elements x_j of $\mathcal{X}$ to select into the codebook $\mathcal{W}$.

To conclude our derivation, we note that, while (22) looks almost identical to the Hopfield energy minimization problem in (4), matrix Q is symmetric but *not* hollow. However, since it is easy to see that all its diagonal elements are constant multiples of 1, we have

$$s^\mathsf{T}Qs = s^\mathsf{T}\left(Q - \frac{\lambda}{4\,k^2}I\right)s + \frac{\lambda}{4\,k^2}s^\mathsf{T}Is = s^\mathsf{T}\left(Q - \frac{\lambda}{4\,k^2}I\right)s + const. \tag{25}$$

Hence, defining

$$W = -2\,Q - \frac{\lambda}{2\,k^2}I \tag{26}$$

$$\theta = q \tag{27}$$

we finally find that the vector quantization problem in (1) can be solved by a Hopfield network of n neurons whose weight matrix and bias vector are given by (26) and (27), respectively.

5   Practical Validation

In order to provide illustrative examples for the kind of solutions Hopfield networks find for the vector quantization problem in (1), this section presents prototypical results obtained from experimenting with three standard benchmark data sets: The MIT CBCL face database, the MNIST database of handwritten digits, and the MNIST-Fashion database.

In either case, we vectorized the designated training samples and normalized them to zero mean and unit variance before running vector quantization. In our experiments with Hopfield networks, we considered Gaussian kernels $\phi(x_j, x_l)$ with manually tuned variance or bandwidth parameters σ^2 and initialized the states of all neurons in the network to -1. For simple baseline comparisons, we considered MacQueen's algorithm [28] which solves an unconstrained vector quantization problem.

Tables 1, 2, and 3 show prototypical examples for the kinds of results we obtained. The first column in each table shows baseline results, all other columns show prototypes obtained from running Hopfield networks.

Looking at these results, we note that Hopfield networks with weight matrices and bias vectors computed from kernels of larger bandwidth tend to yield prototypes that resemble the ones produced by MacQueen's algorithm (this is easiest

Table 1. Prototypical results for the CBCL data set.

	MacQueen	Hopfield net, $\sigma^2 = 25$	Hopfield net, $\sigma^2 = 200$
$k = 16$			
$k = 49$			

Table 2. Prototypical results for the MNIST data set.

	MacQueen	Hopfield net, $\sigma^2 = 10$	Hopfield net, $\sigma^2 = 150$
$k = 16$			
$k = 49$			

to see in Tables 2 and 3). For smaller choices of the bandwidth parameter, however, our Hopfield networks yield prototypes less akin to local means. Especially in Tables 2 and 3 we see that Hopfield networks for mean discrepancy-based vec-

Table 3. Prototypical results for the MNIST fashion data set.

	MacQueen	Hopfield net, $\sigma^2 = 50$	Hopfield net, $\sigma^2 = 100$
$k = 16$			
$k = 49$			

tor quantization can therefore produce more diverse or varied prototypes than methods based on minimizing variances around local centroids. In practice, this behavior is often considered beneficial for data analysis as it provides a more comprehensive picture of the data under consideration [5,9,13,30,33,34].

6   Related Work

Many well established vector quantization techniques are indeed neurocomputing techniques [10,22,29,31]. Hopfield networks, too, have been considered in this context before. However, prior work such as in [12] focuses on simpler bipartition problems while contributions such as in [35] involve higher order Hopfield networks. The ideas brought forth in this paper therefore mark a middle ground as they show how to accomplish vector quantization for $k > 2$ using standard Hopfield networks.

Our idea of MD^2 minimization for vector quantization is related to information theoretic vector quantization (ITVQ) due to Principe and coworkes [23,31,36]. ITVQ, too, considers Gaussian kernel density estimates but allows for different variance parameters when estimating $p(x)$ and $q(x)$. Another difference is that ITVQ minimizes the Cuachy-Schwarz divergence of $p(x)$ and $q(x)$ rather than their mean discrepancy. One can, however, show that –for the case of Gaussian kernels– our ansatz in (5), (6) which considers the same variance parameter for $p(x)$ and $q(x)$ is a special case of ITVQ and thus inherits all its properties, in particular its mode seeking property [36]. However, unlike ITVQ, our MD^2-based approach is not restricted to Gaussian kernels. That is, we can theoretically and practically work with other kinds of (unimodal) kernels such as, say, the Laplacian and we will explore this possibility in future work.

The constrained vector quantization problem we set up in (1) also bears some resemblance to the k-medoids or p-medians problem. Yet, it differs in that our solution does not consider variances about local centroids but a comparatively simple quadratic unconstrained binary optimization problem (QUBO).

QUBOs are of considerable current interest as they can be solved on quantum computing devices [3,4,27]. Indeed, adiabatic quantum computers such as produced by D-Wave are especially tailored towards solving Ising energy minimization problems [7,21]. Since these generalize Hopfield energy minimization problems (as they do not require the weight matrix W to be hollow), we observe that everything a Hopfield network can do, an adiabatic quantum computer can do, too. However, while a Hopfield network may converge to a local minimum of its energy function and therefore to suboptimal solutions, an adiabatic quantum computer is (much) more likely to determine a globally optimal solution [4]. In addition, it will often achieve this quadratically faster than classically possible [4]. All of this provides further auspicious directions for future work as it suggests quantum computing solutions to the vector quantization problem.

7   Conclusion

This paper considered the problem of vector quantization by means of Hopfield networks.

Our key idea was to cast vector quantization as the problem of minimizing the mean discrepancy between kernel density estimates of the distributions of data points and prototypes. Focusing on the use case where prototypes are required to coincide with given data points, we showed that the objective of minimizing mean discrepancies can be cast as a quadratic unconstrained binary optimization problem. Further straightforward algebra then revealed this QUBO to be equivalent to a Hopfield energy minimization problem.

Experimental results on benchmark data showed that our Hopfield networks are well able to extract representative as well as meaningful prototypes that are often more diverse than those produced by common baseline methods.

The fact that this paper established that constrained vector quantization can be cast as a quadratic unconstrained binary optimization problem is of current interest because it suggests that quantum computers can accomplish vector quantization. This opens up new auspicious directions for future work in this venerable field.

Acknowledgments. This work is a joint effort of the Fraunhofer Research Center for Machine Learning (FZML) within the Cluster of Excellence Cognitive Internet Technologies (CCIT) and the Competence Center for Machine Learning Rhine-Ruhr (ML2R). ML2R is funded by the Federal Ministry of Education and Research (BMBF) of Germany (grant no. 01IS18038A). The authors gratefully acknowledge this support.

References

1. Amari, S.I.: Neural theory of association and concept-formation. Biol. Cybern. **26**(3), 175–185 (1977). https://doi.org/10.1007/BF00365229
2. Arbel, M., Binkowski, M., Sutherland, D., Gretton, A.: On gradient regularizers for MMD GANs. In: Proceeding NeurIPS (2019)
3. Bauckhage, C., Brito, E., Cvejoski, K., Ojeda, C., Sifa, R., Wrobel, S.: Ising models for binary clustering via adiabatic quantum computing. In: Pelillo, M., Hancock, E. (eds.) EMMCVPR 2017. LNCS, vol. 10746, pp. 3–17. Springer, Cham (2018). https://doi.org/10.1007/978-3-319-78199-0_1
4. Bauckhage, C., Sanchez, R., Sifa, R.: Problem solving with hopfield networks and adiabatic quantum computing. In: Proceedings IJCNN (2020)
5. Bauckhage, C., Sifa, R., Dong, T.: Prototypes within minimum enclosing balls. In: Tetko, I.V., Kůrková, V., Karpov, P., Theis, F. (eds.) ICANN 2019. LNCS, vol. 11731, pp. 365–376. Springer, Cham (2019). https://doi.org/10.1007/978-3-030-30493-5_36
6. Bauckhage, C., Thurau, C.: Adapting information theoretic clustering to binary images. In: Proceedings ICPR (2010)
7. Bian, Z., Chudak, F., Macready, W., Rose, G.: The Ising Model: Teaching an Old Problem New Tricks. Technical report, D-Wave Systems (2010)
8. Binkowski, M., Sutherland, D., Arbel, M., Gretton, A.: Demystifying MMD GANs. In: Proceedings ICLR (2018)
9. Caro, M., Aarva, A., Deringer, V., Csanyi, G., Laurila, T.: Reactivity of amorphous carbon surfaces: rationalizing the role of structural motifs in functionalization using machine learning. Chem. Mater. **30**(21), 7446–7455 (2018). https://doi.org/10.1021/acs.chemmater.8b03353
10. Cheng, Y.: Mean shift, mode seeking, and clustering. IEEE Trans. Pattern Anal. Mach. Intell. **17**(8), 767–776 (1995). https://doi.org/10.1109/34.400568
11. Dasgupta, S., Freund, Y.: Random projection trees for vector quantization. IEEE Trans. Inf. Theory **55**(7), 3229–3242 (2009). https://doi.org/10.1109/TIT.2009.2021326
12. Ding, C.: Data clustering: principal components, hopfield and self-aggregation networks. In: Proceedings IJCAI (2003)
13. Drachen, A., Sifa, R., Thurau, C.: The name in the game: patterns in character names and game tags. Entertain. Comput. **5**(1), 21–32 (2014). https://doi.org/10.1016/j.entcom.2014.02.001
14. Dziugaite, G., Roy, D., Ghahramani, Z.: Training generative neural networks via maximum mean discrepancy optimization. In: Proceedings UAI (2015)
15. Fukunaga, K., Hostelter, L.: The estimation of the gradient of a density function, with applications in pattern recognition. IEEE Trans. Inf. Theory **21**(1), 32–40 (1975). https://doi.org/10.1109/TIT.1975.1055330
16. Gersho, A., Gray, R.: Vector Quantization and Signal Compression. Springer, Heidelberg (1991)
17. Gretton, A., Borgwardt, K., Rasch, M.J., Schölkopf, B., Smola, A.: A kernel two-sample test. J. Mach. Learn. Res. **13**(25), 723–773 (2012)
18. Haykin, S.: Neural Networks and Learning Machines, 3rd edn. Prentice Hall (2008)
19. Hopfield, J.: Neural networks and physical systems with collective computational abilities. PNAS **79**(8), 2554–2558 (1982). https://doi.org/10.1073/pnas.79.8.2554

20. Jegelka, S., Gretton, A., Schölkopf, B., Sriperumbudur, B.K., von Luxburg, U.: Generalized clustering via kernel embeddings. In: Mertsching, B., Hund, M., Aziz, Z. (eds.) KI 2009. LNCS (LNAI), vol. 5803, pp. 144–152. Springer, Heidelberg (2009). https://doi.org/10.1007/978-3-642-04617-9_19

21. Johnson, M., et al.: Quantum annealing with manufactured spins. Nature **473**(7346), 194–198 (2011). https://doi.org/10.1038/nature10012

22. Kohonen, T.: Learning vector quantization. In: Self-Organizing Maps. Springer Series in Information Sciences, vol 30, pp. 175–189. Springer, Heidelberg (1995). https://doi.org/10.1007/978-3-642-97610-0_6

23. Lehn-Schioler, T., Hedge, A., Erdogmus, D., Principe, J.: Vector quantization using information theoretic concepts. Nat. Comput. **4**(1), 39–51 (2005). https://doi.org/10.1007/s11047-004-9619-8

24. Li, C.L., Chang, W.C., Cheng, Y., Tang, Y., Poczos, B.: MMD GAN: towards Deeper understanding of moment matching network. In: Proceedings NIPS (2017)

25. Li, Y., Swersky, K., Zemel, R.: Generative moment matching networks. In: Proceedings ICML (2015)

26. Linde, Y., Buzo, A., Gray, R.: An algorithm for vector quantizer design. IEEE Trans. Commun. **28**(1), 84–95 (1980). https://doi.org/10.1109/TCOM.1980.1094577

27. Lucas, A.: Ising formulations of many NP problems. Front. Phys. **2**, 5:1–5:15 (2014). https://doi.org/10.3389/fphy.2014.00005

28. MacQueen, J.: Some methods for classification and analysis of multivariate observations. In: Proceedings Berkeley Symposium on Mathematical Statistics and Probability (1967)

29. Martinetz, T., Berkovich, S., Schulten, K.: Neural-gas network for vector quantization and its application to time-series prediction. IEEE Trans. Neural Netw. **4**(4), 558–569 (1993). https://doi.org/10.1109/72.238311

30. Molina, A., Vergari, A., Di Mauro, N., Natarajan, S., Esposito, F., Kersting, K.: Mixed sum-product networks: a deep architecture for hybrid domains. In: Proceedings AAAI (2018)

31. Rao, S., Han, S., Principe, J.: Information theoretic vector quantization with fixed point updates. In: Proceedings IJCNN (2007)

32. Rojas, R.: Neural Networks - A Systematic Introduction. Springer, Heidelberg (1996)

33. Sifa, R.: An overview of Frank-Wolfe optimization for stochasticity constrained interpretable matrix and tensor factorization. In: Kůrková, V., Manolopoulos, Y., Hammer, B., Iliadis, L., Maglogiannis, I. (eds.) ICANN 2018. LNCS, vol. 11140, pp. 369–379. Springer, Cham (2018). https://doi.org/10.1007/978-3-030-01421-6_36

34. Sifa, R., Bauckhage, C.: Online k-Maxoids clustering. In: Proceedings DSAA (2017)

35. Soper, A.: A higher order hopfield network for vector quantisation. Neural Comput. Appl. **7**, 99–106 (1998). https://doi.org/10.1007/BF01414161

36. Xu, J.W., Paiva, A., Park, I., Principe, J.: A reproducing kernel Hilbert space framework for information-theoretic learning. IEEE Trans. Signal Process. **56**(12), 5891–5902 (2008). https://doi.org/10.1109/TSP.2008.2005085

Prototype-Based Online Learning on Homogeneously Labeled Streaming Data

Christian Limberg[1,2(✉)], Jan Philip Göpfert[1], Heiko Wersing[2],
and Helge Ritter[1]

[1] CoR-Lab, Bielefeld University,
Universitätsstraße 25, 33615 Bielefeld, Germany
{climberg,jgoepfert,helge}@techfak.uni-bielefeld.de
[2] HONDA Research Institute Europe GmbH,
Carl-Legien-Straße 30, 63073 Offenbach, Germany
heiko.wersing@honda-ri.de

Abstract. Algorithms in machine learning commonly require training
data to be independent and identically distributed. This assumption is
not always valid, e.g. in online learning, when data becomes available
in homogeneously labeled blocks, which can severely impede especially
instance-based learning algorithms. In this work, we analyze and visualize this issue, and we propose and evaluate strategies for Learning
Vector Quantization to compensate for homogeneously labeled blocks.
We achieve considerably improved results in this difficult setting.

Keywords: Incremental learning · Online learning · Classification ·
Learning Vector Quantization · Prototype-based models

1 Introduction

In machine learning, algorithms are commonly developed under the assumption
that data, specifically training data, is independent and identically distributed
(i. i. d.). Unfortunately, this is not always the case. Training (and test) data may
be subject to certain selection biases, which can negatively affect the performance of the trained model once deployed [3]. Furthermore, requirements and
the environment can change over time, which is referred to a concept drift, and
requires adaptive algorithms and strategies [2,12]. Online and lifelong-learning
approaches can often cope with these dynamic scenarios – however, another
problem emerges from how labeled data is obtained, especially when labels are
provided by human collaborators. To improve efficiency, modern interfaces allow
processing in homogeneously labeled batches [8]. Even when these are not the
result of deliberate design choices with respect to sampling and interface, the
nature of continuous processes is often such that data "happen" in batches. Take,
for example, a robot interacting with a teacher, learning to identify objects. The

© Springer Nature Switzerland AG 2020
I. Farkaš et al. (Eds.): ICANN 2020, LNCS 12397, pp. 204–213, 2020.
https://doi.org/10.1007/978-3-030-61616-8_17

robot's sensory input is available as a stream that relates information about a certain object for a certain uninterrupted time interval, before attention shifts to a different object [4,11]. Clearly, the resulting data is not i. i. d.

Instance-based classifiers are well suited for active learning tasks [9,10]. They deal with changing classes by naturally adapting to new, previously unseen data. Similarly, old data can be forgotten, if necessary, by simply removing it from memory. To aid interpretability, generalization, and computational efficiency, data is quantized in the form of prototypes, such as by the popular Generalized Learning Vector Quantization (GLVQ) [5,13] with its incremental learning rule. Computational efficiency is especially important in online scenarios, where speed is crucial and hardware may be limited.

In GLVQ, each prototype belongs to a certain class and is updated (i. e. moved around) incrementally, being attracted to data with the same label and repelled by data with different labels. For this process to yield desirable results, the data must not be queried in homogeneously labeled batches, as we explore in this work.

In Sect. 2 we revisit GLVQ and demonstrate with synthetic data how training with homogeneously labeled batches negatively impacts the classifier's performance. In Sect. 4.2 we evaluate a number of strategies on data sets to compensate for this problem; in Sect. 4.5 we then focus on data obtained during a user study. We conclude by summarizing our findings in Sect. 5.

2   Generalized Learning Vector Quantization (GLVQ)

As mentioned above, GLVQ [13] seeks prototypes $w_1, \ldots, w_m$ (where m does not need to remain fixed during training) that represent the training data well, such that an instance can be classified by assigning to it the label of the prototype closest to it. It does so by incrementally updating the positions of the prototypes. Given a training point x with label y, GLVQ selects the prototype w_1 (referred to as the winner) closest to x with the same label y and the prototype w_2 (referred to as the loser) closest to x with a different label. w_1 is then moved towards x; w_2 is moved away from it.

Specifically, let d_1 and d_2 denote the Euclidean distance from x to w_1 and w_2, respectively. With the relative distance function $\mu(x) = (d_1 - d_2)/(d_1 + d_2)$, the incremental update rule is then

$$w_1 \leftarrow w_1 + \alpha \cdot \frac{e^{\mu(x)}}{(1 + e^{\mu(x)})^2} \cdot \frac{d_2}{(d_1 + d_2)^2} \cdot (x - w_1) \tag{1}$$

$$w_2 \leftarrow w_2 - \alpha \cdot \frac{e^{\mu(x)}}{(1 + e^{\mu(x)})^2} \cdot \frac{d_1}{(d_1 + d_2)^2} \cdot (x - w_2), \tag{2}$$

where α is the learning rate.

It is this incremental pushing and pulling of the prototypes that makes GLVQ successful as long as the training data is i. i. d. When it is not, GLVQ fails in positioning prototypes appropriately.

3 Efficient Online Learning on Homogeneously Labeled Batches

As laid out by Sato and Yamada [13], performing the incremental proto-type according to Eqs. (1) and (2) follows a stochastic gradient descent. The monotonous updates that result from training on homogeneously labeled batches, however, do not lead to a desirable optimum. Let us explore and visualize a synthetic example that showcases the problem. In Fig. 1 we have data from four Gaussians, forming four clusters of points that are labeled accordingly. If the data were presented to GLVQ with four prototypes as i. i. d., it would quickly position the prototypes close to the cluster centers, forming appropriate decision boundaries between the four Gaussians.

If instead we present the training points to GLVQ in homogeneously labeled batches, we observe that, whilst for any given batch the winning prototype is

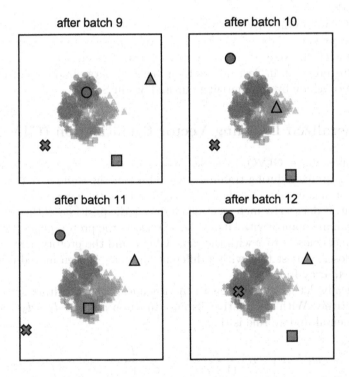

Fig. 1. Repeated training on points that share the same label results in bad prototypes from GLVQ. During batch 9, the blue class was trained; during batch 10 the orange; during batch 11 the green; and during batch 12 the red. Each class is represented by one prototype, and their positions (indicated by the big markers) after training on 50 samples of each class is displayed. Even though, after training on a each batch, the winning prototype is properly moved to the center of the respective class, all other prototypes are pushed away from their respective clusters. (Color figure online)

correctly pulled into the respective cluster, all other prototypes are pushed away from the marginal distribution.

The optimization-breaking prototype updated are due to Eq. (2). To compensate, we propose the following modifications to the update rule, before comparing them empirically in Sect. 4.

- Inhibit: Our problem arises from repeated, uninterrupted "loosing updates" according to Eq. (2). We can track and mitigate this directly by introducing an inhibitory factor γ that depends on the number s_i of such updates to the prototype w_i:

$$\gamma(s_i) = \frac{\phi_\sigma(s_i)}{\phi_\sigma(0)} \cdot (1 - \gamma_0) + \gamma_0 \,, \tag{3}$$

where ϕ_σ is the probability density function of the normal distribution around zero with variance σ. We require $0 < \gamma_0 < 1$ to ensure $\gamma(s_i) > \gamma_0 > 0$. We increment/decrement the counter s_i whenever prototype w_i receives a loosing/winning update, respectively. However, to ensure that "winning" only increases and never decreases $\gamma(s_i)$ we omit any decrements to s_i whenever s_i has a value of 0. We demonstrate the effect of different parameter choices in Fig. 2.

- Buffer: Conventionally, in non-online settings, training data order can be randomized to circumvent the problem we are facing. Depending on the concrete requirements of the scenario for which a classifier is to be deployed, it may be possible to delay training to a certain extent. When this is the case, we can store training data in a buffer and select from it randomly to relax the homogeneity of the labels within a batch[1]. This introduces two problems, as it increases memory consumption (which, as mentioned above, can be problematic precisely in online settings where limited hardware is an issue) as well as temporarily holding back the classifier from learning and adapting to new data. We propose to use a dynamic buffer, where with probability p_B an incoming training point is placed in the buffer, or used directly for training with probability $1 - p_B$.

- Soft Select: One of the advantages of LVQ is that it can flexibly work with different numbers of prototypes per class. This allows to mitigate some of the effects of the repeated "loosing updates" by distributing them between loosing prototypes. We probabilistically soften the updates by considering not just the nearest loosing prototype, but for each update selecting a prototype with a different label at random, where the probability is inversely proportional to its distance from the training point x.

For a given training point x, let $\mathcal{N}_x$ denote the set of prototypes that do not share the same label as x, and for prototype w_i let d_i denote the distance from x to w_i. Then, we set the probability p_i of selecting w_i to

$$p_i = \frac{\frac{1}{d_i}}{\sum_{w_j \in \mathcal{N}_i} \frac{1}{d_j}} = \left(d_i \cdot \sum_{w_j \in \mathcal{N}_i} \frac{1}{d_j} \right)^{-1} . \tag{4}$$

---

[1] This strategy is similar to *Experience Replay* [1] used in Reinforcement Learning.

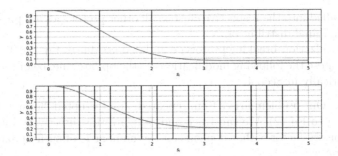

Fig. 2. Different inhibition functions γ for updating loosing prototype w^-. Decay steps s_i are displayed as vertical black lines. Upper function has parameters $\sigma = 1$, $\Delta s = 1$, $\gamma_0 = 0.05$. Bottom function has parameters $\sigma = 1$, $\Delta s = 0.3$, $\gamma_0 = 0.2$, making the decay rate smaller and having a minimum weight update of $w^- = w^- + 0.2\Delta w^-$

4   Experiments and Evaluation

4.1   Baselines

- GLVQ: The GLVQ approach as it is explained above.
- Winner Only: As above but the weight update of the loosing prototype is skipped by setting $\Delta w^- = 0$, so that only the winning prototype w^+ is updated.
- KNN: The k-nearest-Neighbors (KNN) classifier can be also seen as an LVQ variant that places always a prototype when training a sample. Because the prototypes are not moving, KNN should not be affected by block-wise training but requires a significant higher amount of memory and also more computation resources when classifying a sample, and thus is maybe not applicable in most online applications. A hyper-parameter of KNN when classifying a sample is k which defines the number of nearest neighbors to be considered.

4.2   Datasets

We trained all above-mentioned approaches on several real-world data sets. To allow a meaningful comparison between the approaches and baselines, we limit the number of prototypes per class to 5. We determined the best hyperparameters for strategies Inhibit and Buffer by conducting a grid search, where we noticed a wide range of well-performing parameter combinations. Approaches Soft Select and Winner Only are parameter-free in this regard. For Inhibit we found $\gamma_0 \in [0.1, 0.5]$ and $\sigma \in [2, 6]$ to yield desirable results. For Buffer the best performing buffer sizes are highly dependent on the number of classes in the data set and range from 150 to 800 samples, where for p_B comparably high values from 0.7 to 0.9 perform well. To increase stability, we performed 5-fold cross validation.

To simulate a block-correlated data stream, we sorted all samples in bins based of their class. We trained the defined approaches with blocks of 50 samples, cycling through the class bins in a round robin fashion. We are training the approaches for 500 of those blocks and evaluate the result based on this training. Samples were duplicated for data sets not containing enough samples per class to fulfill this requirement. For feature extraction of CIFAR, OUTDOOR, and CUPSNBOTTLES we used the deep convolutional net VGG16 [14] pretrained on *image net* data, and retained the output of the penultimate layer, which yields a 4096-dimensional, highly distinctive feature space. Since FASHION MNIST is only black and white, we ran a PCA on the pixel data to extract 100-dimensional features.

As an evaluation metric we use the mean accuracy over the whole training. We decided to use this performance measure since in most online learning applications not only the final performance of the model is important, but also the performance increase in earlier states of training. In our evaluation we score a hold out test set after each trained block and averaged over the complete training (see Table 1). KNN preformed best on all data sets, as expected. Beyond that, the approaches Inhibit and Buffer performed best. GLVQ has a significant lower performance than other approaches on all data sets but especially on CIFAR-10 and FASHION MNIST. Results for the latter were worst. This suggests, that a high dimensional feature representation from a CNN can compensate GLVQ's effects in negative weight update. Furthermore, a large number of classes seems to diminish the drift, when we compare CIFAR-100 to CIFAR-10, which may be because of the negative weight update shared between more loser prototypes. However, Inhibit and Buffer still perform better (see Fig. 3 for training runs on CIFAR-10).

4.3   Resource Demands

Let us now compare the approaches in terms of their computational and memory requirements. KNN is the most memory-heavy approach, requiring all training points to be stored, which can grow to arbitrarily large numbers. Classifying an input is computationally demanding because distances between each input point and each training point need to be calculated. GLVQ reduces this complexity to a set number of representatives per class, which makes it more efficient memory-wise as well as computationally – since data sets have a fixed number of classes and the update for moving a prototype (see Eqs. (1) and (2)) can be calculated efficiently.

All other approaches considered by us are variants of GLVQ, so they share the same foundation of complexity, with small differences. The baseline Winner Only is computationally even more effective because the update step for the loosing prototype (Eq. (2)) does not need to be calculated. Soft Select requires a little extra computation for selecting a weighted random loser prototype (Eq. (4)) – which we consider negligible because the distances to all prototypes have to be calculated anyway. Buffer requires storing a few extra samples, but the buffer size is usually substantially smaller than the entire training set (compared to

Table 1. Mean accuracies of the tested approaches. Each classifier was trained on 500 blocks of samples. Each block contained 50 samples of the same class. The table contains the average performance evaluated on a held-out test-set calculated after each block.

Data set	Classes	Inhibit	Buffer	Soft Select	GLVQ	Winner Only	KNN
CIFAR-10 [6]	10	71.18	69.08	63.76	37.07	69.14	74.78
CIFAR-100 [6]	100	42.73	42.00	40.37	38.35	41.52	44.32
FASHION MNIST [15]	10	73.28	71.73	43.93	13.66	73.33	81.46
CUPSNBOTTLES [7]	10	97.07	97.07	89.04	93.88	96.91	98.67
OUTDOOR [11]	50	92.26	92.24	88.60	89.62	91.65	94.93

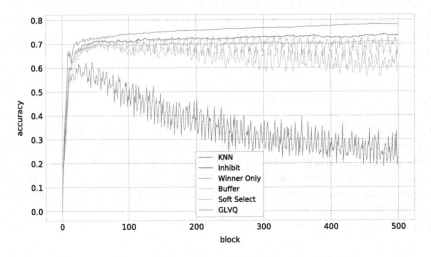

Fig. 3. Test accuracy for all approaches trained on up to 500 blocks from CIFAR-10. The performance drop of GLVQ under training conditions is visible in the red line. Upper baseline is KNN, which demands more resources compared to other approaches. KNN is followed by the approaches Inhibit, Winner Only and Buffer with a significant margin. The accuracy of GLVQ, Soft Select, and Buffer oscillates periodically, which signals the negative impact of training on homogeneously labeled blocks. (Color figure online)

KNN). Inhibit requires storing an extra integer s_i per prototype for counting the number of losses, and the update rule (see Eq. (3)) adds computation during training.

4.4 Relaxed Homogeneity

To soften the constraints of monotonic blocks which share the same label cleanly, we also want to evaluate all approaches and baselines in case of blocks which have a predominance of a common label, but have samples of other classes present. Therefore we introduce a homogeneity experiment parameter, which describes the percentage of other classes within all blocks. To give an example, with a homogeneity parameter of 80%, about 8% of the containing samples share the same label while the block has a 20% admixture of samples from other classes. The results of training all approaches on the CIFAR-10 data set with several homogeneity settings can be seen in Table 2.

Table 2. Final performance of the evaluated approaches after training for 500 blocks from CIFAR-10 with various homogeneity settings.

Homogeneity	Inhibit	Buffer	Soft Select	GLVQ	Winner Only	KNN
100%	71.18	69.08	63.76	37.07	69.14	74.78
80%	71.84	70.64	65.70	51.34	69.38	74.86
60%	72.02	71.67	66.88	62.04	69.26	74.79
40%	72.17	72.23	67.66	69.78	69.49	75.05
20%	71.95	72.48	68.38	72.36	69.33	75.09
0%	71.77	72.52	68.08	72.24	69.27	75.12

As expected, KNN is not affected by the trained blocks label distribution. The performance of GLVQ increases steadily with less homogeneity. This underlines again the reason for bad performance of GLVQ in this setting. While Buffer and Soft Select improved also with lesser homogeneity, the performance of Inhibit and Winner Only is not changing significantly with different homogeneity values.

4.5   User Study Label Data

In this part of the evaluation, we do not want to use artificial created blocks for training as before but rather consider more realistic label data we gathered within a user study for an earlier contribution [8]. In the user study a novel label interface was evaluated, which facilitates fast labeling of image data by selecting images in batches using a graphical 2D visualization. The evaluation of the interface was very promising. It produced a by far higher number of labels compared to classical "1-label-per-user-action" interfaces. Also the participants labeling errors decreased. This motivates the proposed labeling interface but also raises the need of a more efficient classifier (in the study we used KNN), which is also robust in terms of label blocks.

The interface uses an online classifier to query new samples. After labeling a batch, this classifier is then trained with all new samples. The updated classifier is then used to actively query new batches for further labeling actions. In the study the participants had to label 6 hard-to-distinguish classes from the OUTDOOR data set we evaluated before. By using the confidence estimation of a KNN classifier, since as we saw earlier it is not affected by the block-wise appearance of class labels, we were able to query the most beneficial samples for training KNN.

However, within the user study we also recorded all user actions (when and which samples were labeled and what class label was given). Reusing this label information of all 31 participants and combining it into one training, we simulate a crowd-sourced labeling task [16] for evaluating the proposed approaches together with the baselines. For producing more variety we shuffled the order of the participants 10 times and averaged the results (see Fig. 4).

Comparable to our former experiments, KNN performed also best on the label data acquired from the user study. Inhibit and Buffer followed on the next two ranks, again followed by Winner Only. GLVQ is also in this setting significantly worse, underlying the importance of the problem for human label data.

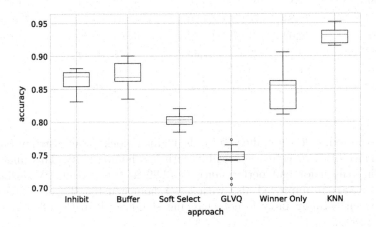

Fig. 4. All approaches were trained on real-world label data from a user study we did earlier. 31 participants have labeled a data set with a visualization user interface, which let them label multiple samples of one class with one user action. We combined all label information of all participants into one data stream to simulate a crowd-sourced label task.

5   Conclusion

This contribution proposed modified update rules for the widespread used GLVQ classifier to avoid instability under online learning with sequentially blocked/correlated data and explored the behavior of the modified algorithm for correlated data sequences derived from several popular benchmark data sets. On the tested data sets the approaches Inhibit and Buffer performed best. A further simulated crowd-sourced labeling task with actual human label data, further corroborated the findings of these benchmark experiments under conditions that are close to typical interactive real world labeling scenarios.

Inhibit and Buffer implement different ideas to maintain also for the case of sequentially correlated class labels the underlying rationale of GLVQ that there is a gain in classifier performance if also the loosing prototype w- is updated.

However, both `Inhibit` and `Buffer` only have a slight advantage compared to the `Winner Only` approach, which has the advantage that no hyper-parameter have to be defined. If computation- and memory-demands do not matter, we recommend to use `KNN` since it is not affected by correlated samples and has the highest performance in all experiments.

References

1. Adam, S., Busoniu, L., Babuska, R.: Experience replay for real-time reinforcement learning control Part C (Appl. Rev.). IEEE Trans. Syst. Man. Cybern. **42**(2), 201–212 (2011)
2. Göpfert, J.P., Hammer, B., Wersing, H.: Mitigating concept drift via rejection. In: Kůrková, V., Manolopoulos, Y., Hammer, B., Iliadis, L., Maglogiannis, I. (eds.) ICANN 2018. LNCS, vol. 11139, pp. 456–467. Springer, Cham (2018). https://doi.org/10.1007/978-3-030-01418-6_45
3. Huang, J., Smola, A.J., Gretton, A., Borgwardt, K.M., Schölkopf, B.: Correcting sample selection bias by unlabeled data. In: NIPS (2006)
4. Kirstein, S., Wersing, H., Körner, E.: A biologically motivated visual memory architecture for online learning of objects. Neural Netw. **21**(1), 65–77 (2008)
5. Kohonen, T.: Learning Vector quantization. In: Self-Organizing Maps. Springer Series in Information Sciences, vol. 30, pp. 175–189. Springer, Heidelberg (1995). https://doi.org/10.1007/978-3-642-97610-0_6
6. Krizhevsky, A., Hinton, G., et al.: Learning multiple layers of features from tiny images (2009)
7. Limberg, C.: CUPSNBOTTLES (2020). https://doi.org/10.21227/ywwz-cb26
8. Limberg, C., Krieger, K., Wersing, H., Ritter, H.: Active learning for image recognition using a visualization-based user interface. In: Tetko, I.V., Kůrková, V., Karpov, P., Theis, F. (eds.) ICANN 2019. LNCS, vol. 11728, pp. 495–506. Springer, Cham (2019). https://doi.org/10.1007/978-3-030-30484-3_40
9. Limberg, C., Wersing, H., Ritter, H.: Improving active learning by avoiding ambiguous samples. In: Kůrková, V., Manolopoulos, Y., Hammer, B., Iliadis, L., Maglogiannis, I. (eds.) ICANN 2018. LNCS, vol. 11139, pp. 518–527. Springer, Cham (2018). https://doi.org/10.1007/978-3-030-01418-6_51
10. Limberg, C., Wersing, H., Ritter, H.J.: Efficient accuracy estimation for instance-based incremental active learning. In: European Symposium on Artificial Neural Networks (ESANN), pp. 171–176, April 2018
11. Losing, V., Hammer, B., Wersing, H.: Interactive online learning for obstacle classification on a mobile robot. In: International Joint Conference on Neural Networks (IJCNN) pp. 1–8 (2015)
12. Losing, V., Hammer, B., Wersing, H.: Incremental on-line learning: a review and comparison of state of the art algorithms. Neurocomputing **275**, 1261–1274 (2018)
13. Sato, A., Yamada, K.: Generalized learning vector quantization. In: proceedings NIPS, pp. 423–429, (1995)
14. Simonyan, K., Zisserman, A.: Very deep convolutional networks for large-scale image recognition (2014). arXiv: 1409.1556
15. Xiao, H., Rasul, K., Vollgraf, R.: Fashion-MNIST: a novel image dataset for benchmarking machine learning algorithms. arXiv preprint arXiv:1708.07747 (2017)
16. Zhang, J., Wu, X., Sheng, V.S.: Learning from crowdsourced labeled data: a survey. Artif. Intell. Rev. **46**(4), 543–576 (2016). https://doi.org/10.1007/s10462-016-9491-9

Normalization and Regularization Methods

Neural Network Training with Safe Regularization in the Null Space of Batch Activations

Matthias Kissel[(⊠)], Martin Gottwald, and Klaus Diepold

Chair of Data Processing, Technical University of Munich, Munich, Germany
matthias.kissel@tum.de
https://www.ei.tum.de/ldv/

Abstract. We propose to formulate the training of neural networks with side optimization goals, such as obtaining structured weight matrices, as lexicographic optimization problem. The lexicographic order can be maintained during training by optimizing the side-optimization goal exclusively in the null space of batch activations. We call the resulting training method *Safe Regularization*, because the side optimization goal can be safely integrated into the training with limited influence on the main optimization goal. Moreover, this results in a higher robustness regarding the choice of regularization hyperparameters. We validate our training method with multiple real-world regression data sets with the side-optimization goal of obtaining sparse weight matrices.

Keywords: Neural network · Nullspace · Regularization

1 Introduction

In recent years, the trend for neural networks has been towards ever larger and deeper networks [12,25]. As the size of the network increases, so does the amount of storage required and the effort to propagate information through the network. These factors limit the use of large networks for specific applications, such as applications with real-time requirements or on mobile platforms [30].

A possible approach to make large networks applicable to environments with strict computational limitations or memory restrictions is to exploit structures in the weight matrices [21]. If the weight matrices are structured, the memory requirement and the computational resources required can be drastically reduced. The goal to have structured weight matrices after the training of the neural network can be integrated into the training as side-optimization goal. For example, Cheng et al. [2] imposed a circulant structure on weight matrices in order to speed up the information propagation through the network using Fast Fourier Transforms. Wen et al. [24] used group lasso regularization to learn low rank convolutional filters. One structure often pursued in literature is sparsity [19,23]. If the weight matrices of a neural network are sparse, only the

© Springer Nature Switzerland AG 2020
I. Farkaš et al. (Eds.): ICANN 2020, LNCS 12397, pp. 217–228, 2020.
https://doi.org/10.1007/978-3-030-61616-8_18

non-zero elements of the matrix have to be stored and used for the calculation of neural activations. Therefore, less memory and computation time is required.

The secondary goal of obtaining weight matrices with a certain structure is usually integrated into the training by specific regularization techniques [10,14]. A core difficulty of using existing regularization techniques, however, is the choice of suitable hyperparameters. A bad choice can lead to excessive influence of the regularization terms on the training, which in turn can worsen the performance regarding generalization. Hyperparameters are usually determined by heuristics, empirical experience or rules of thumb, whereby it cannot be guaranteed that the choice is optimal. This is especially a problem, because the choice of suitable hyperparameters depends strongly on the respective problem.

In this paper, we introduce a *Safe Regularization* technique, which minimizes the interference of the side optimization goal with the main goal of reducing the training loss. For that, we formulate the training of neural networks in combination with regularization as lexicographic optimization problem, whereas the regularization terms are considered as subordinate optimization goals. The lexicographic order of both optimization problems is ensured during the training by optimizing the subordinate goal exclusively in the null space of batch activations. These updates do not affect the gradient direction of the main goal. We call the presented training method *Safe Regularization*, because the influence of regularization terms on the main goal is minimized. The risk of worsening the training result by choosing inappropriate hyperparameters is drastically reduced.

Our proposed training method is not limited to existing regularization techniques. Rather, it opens up the possibility of integrating any desired side optimization target into the training of neural networks while minimizing the influence on the main optimization goal, namely the reduction of the training loss. We identified four major use cases of our method:

- Uncertain solution properties: The training of neural networks can be accelerated by incorporating knowledge about the solution into the training algorithm. However, there is a risk that the solution deteriorates in case that the considered property is not present. Our algorithm solves this problem by prioritizing the main objective over the secondary goal.
- Desired neural network design: It is often desired that the neural network has certain properties after training (for example, structures in the weight matrices of the network). However, it is usually not possible to estimate if the desired property is compatible with the problem. Our algorithm offers the possibility to guide the optimization towards solutions which have desired properties while limiting the danger of worsening the result.
- Unknown importance of the side objective: The hyperparameters for the side objective, such as regularization terms, are usually determined by a time-consuming search. Our algorithm reduces the sensitivity towards these parameters, so that the hyperparameter selection can be greatly simplified.
- Niche applications: Our algorithm inherently offers the possibility to learn lexicographic models, which is the goal of some niche applications (like learning lexicographic preference models).

The remainder of this paper is organized as follows. We first give an overview over existing methods using null spaces of neural networks and related training algorithms. Then, we define our method formally. In the subsequent Section, we compare our training method with standard regularization techniques using several real-world regression problems. Finally, we summarize our findings.

2   Literature Review

Several methods exist for exploiting null spaces during the training of artificial neural networks. For example, Potlapalli and Luo [17] proposed to train self-organizing maps by reducing errors in the null space of the weight vectors, instead of aligning the weights directly with the inputs. The goal is to reduce the bias of the weight vectors, which in turn increases the generalization abilities of the network. Similarly, Yoon et al. [28] proposed to perform classification with Convolutional Neural Networks in an alternative projection space. This space is constructed as a subset of the null space of training error vectors.

Other methods have been proposed to make use of the input null space of the neural network, to be precise, the null space of the input data matrix. Xu et al. [26] showed how to exploit the null space of the input data matrix to increase the privacy of data fed to classifiers. By that, private data can be *cleaned* before sending them to a company for further analysis. From a theoretical point of view, Goggin et al. [8] argued that neural networks are powerful predictors precisely because they can access the null space of the input data.

An interesting approach exploiting the null space of gradient updates has been proposed by Wang et al. [22]. Their Null Space Gradient Descent algorithm is applied to the online learning to rank problem for content-based image retrieval. The algorithm restricts the new exploratory search directions to be sampled in the null space of previously poorly performing gradients. Therefore, their exploration strategy results in more promising search directions compared to existing approaches. In contrast to this approach, we consider the null space of the presynaptic activations in neural networks, instead of the gradients for the updates directly. Moreover, we use the null space basis to directly calculate the appropriate descent directions for the side optimization problem.

Our proposed training algorithm exploits the null space of batch activations for the hidden layers during training. Similar optimization algorithms have been proposed in the field of constrained optimization [5,29]. In contrast to these approaches, we formulate our problem as lexicographic optimization problem and apply our algorithm to the domain of neural network training.

The training methods most related to *Safe Regularization* are algorithms using forward-backward splitting [4], also known as proximal gradient methods [9]. These methods split the weight update into two steps. The first step is an ordinary subgradient step aiming to reduce the considered training loss. The subsequent step aims to find weights which stay close to the interim weight vector while minimizing a regularization function. Our approach differs mainly in two aspects. Firstly, we restrict the updates of our side optimization goal to be in the null space of batch activations. This limits deviations in neural networks outputs directly, instead of only penalizing deviations of the neural networks weights. Secondly, our method is based on existing regularization techniques. In particular, we weight the importance of the side optimization problem with a hyperparameter as known from existing regularization techniques. This increases the comparability with existing methods.

3   Method: *Safe Regularization*

In this section we describe our proposed method *Safe Regularization* in detail. We use a similar notation as in [20] and introduce our method for the classic feed forward network because of ease of notation and generality. *Safe Regularization* is applicable to more complex architectures, for example Convolutional Networks.

We focus on regression problems where the data set consists of samples $x_i \in \mathbb{R}^m$ and target values $y_i \in \mathbb{R}^n$ with $i = 1, \ldots, T$. For training, all samples x_i and y_i are combined row-wise into matrices $X \in \mathbb{R}^{T \times m}$ and $Y \in \mathbb{R}^{T \times n}$, respectively. The matrices are processed in one forward pass through the network. We use the mean squared error as training and test loss, however, our method is not limited to a specific loss. The optimization problem is thus of the form

$$J: \mathcal{W} \to \mathbb{R} \quad J(\mathbf{W}) = \frac{1}{T} \sum_{i=0}^{T} \| \{F(\mathbf{W}, X) - Y\}_i \|^2, \tag{1}$$

where $\{\cdot\}_i$ denotes the i-th row of a matrix, $F(\mathbf{W}, x) := \Lambda_L(W_L, \cdot) \circ \ldots \circ \Lambda_1(W_1, \phi_0)$ is a feed forward network with parameters $\mathbf{W} \in \mathcal{W} := \mathbb{R}^{n_0 \times n_1} \times \ldots \times \mathbb{R}^{n_{L-1} \times n_L}$ and layer mappings $\Lambda_l(W_l, \phi_{l-1}) := \sigma(\phi_{l-1} \cdot W_l)$. Layer inputs are concatenated with a constant and matrices receive an extra column to represent a bias. The non-linearity $\sigma(\cdot)$ is applied element wise. In the network we have n_l units in each layer $l = 1, \cdots, L$, whereas L is the total number of layers. Due to the data set we further have $n_0 = m$ and $n_L = n$.

We consider training of neural networks as a lexicographic optimization problem, where the main objective is the reduction of the error J. Typically, one uses gradient descent

$$\mathbf{W}' \leftarrow \mathbf{W} - \alpha \cdot \nabla_{\mathbf{X}} J(\mathbf{X})|_{\mathbf{X}=\mathbf{W}}, \tag{2}$$

where α denotes a step size selected by state-of-the-art methods such as *Adam* [13]. The side optimization problem is represented as a second objective function $\tilde{J}: \mathcal{W} \to \mathbb{R}$ and also has to be minimized.

We introduce our method with the goal to find parameters $\hat{\mathbf{W}}'$, which not only minimize further the error J like $\mathbf{W}'$, but also posses a special property defined by $\tilde{J}$, for example sparsity. Weights which improve the side objective $\tilde{J}$ are marked with a tilde (cf. $\tilde{\mathbf{W}}$ in Fig. 1). We would like to emphasize that we do not impose any restrictions on the function $\tilde{J}$. Any side optimization which is representable as a differentiable objective $\tilde{J}$ can be used.

In *Safe Regularization* we look at weight matrices W_l of each layer l individually and consider a shift $\Delta W_l = \tilde{W}_l - W_l$, such that $\hat{W}'_l = W'_l + \Delta W_l$ is always a

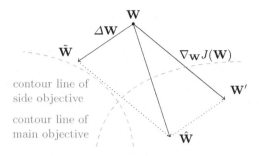

Fig. 1. An exemplary lexicographic optimization problem. The descent direction of the main objective is modified by a side goal. Dashed lines represent level sets of corresponding objectives.

descent direction for J, and whenever possible also for $\tilde{J}$. Similar to classic regularization techniques, the trajectories resulting from gradient descent dynamics are modified. Every time a step with respect to J (cf. Eq. (2)) is applied, the optimizer moves additionally in a direction defined by our side optimization problem. It is guided early on to regions, where the side objective is becoming small. A short sketch of the update directions is provided in Fig. 1. The side optimization problem can be formulated and solved in various ways. In our work, we obtain shift directions ΔW_l as gradients of a second objective $\tilde{J}: \mathcal{W} \to \mathbb{R}$, which result in update rules of the form

$$\mathbf{W}' \leftarrow \mathbf{W} - \alpha \cdot \nabla_{\mathbf{X}}\Big(J(\mathbf{X}) + \lambda\tilde{J}(\mathbf{W})\Big)\Big|_{\mathbf{X}=\mathbf{W}}. \tag{3}$$

By using different values for λ the strength of the side objective can be controlled. When choosing the ℓ_1 or ℓ_2 norm for $\tilde{J}$ we recover the well-known regularization strategies. However, to demonstrate the capabilities of *Safe Regularization*, we also use their squared ratio

$$\tilde{J}(W_l) = \lambda\frac{\ell_1^2(W_l)}{\ell_2^2(W_l)}, \tag{4}$$

which is a measure for the sparsity of a matrix and is used in various fields, for example in compressive sensing [15]. We include a factor λ directly in the definition of $\tilde{J}$, which plays the same role as in classic regularization. In the following, all expressions are for layer l, so we omit the index l whenever suitable.

For a current point W in the weight space we find weights $\hat{W}' = W' + \Delta W$, where W' is the result of Eq. (2), which decrease both J and $\tilde{J}$ by solving $\tilde{W} := \operatorname{argmin}_W \tilde{J}(W)$, for example via gradient descent

$$\tilde{W}' \leftarrow \tilde{W} - \beta \cdot \nabla_X \tilde{J}(X)\Big|_{X=\tilde{W}}, \tag{5}$$

starting from the initial value $\tilde{W} = W$. For the shift we have have $\Delta W = \tilde{W} - W$. If the iteration (5) is applied only a single time, as required for the later algorithm, we can define directly

$$\Delta W = -\beta \cdot \nabla_X \tilde{J}(X)\Big|_{X=W}. \tag{6}$$

Of course, naïvely manipulating W to shrink the value of $\tilde{J}$ would distract the main optimization problem. Hence, the core requirement in *Safe Regularization* is to modify weight matrices W_l' only in the null spaces of their respective layer input ϕ_{l-1}. This ensures the lexicographic ordering of the main and side optimization problems.

If one assumes that a shift ΔW is in the kernel of the layer input ϕ_{l-1}, i.e. $\Delta W_l \in \ker(\phi_{l-1})$, it follows immediately for all $l = 1, \dots, L$

$$\Lambda_l(\hat{W}_l', \phi_{l-1}) = \sigma\Big(\phi_{l-1}\hat{W}_l'\Big) = \sigma\Big(\phi_{l-1}W_l' + \underbrace{\phi_{l-1}\Delta W_l}_{=0}\Big) = \Lambda_l(W_l', \phi_{l-1}).$$

In other words the function represented by the neural network is not changed by the shift with respect to the training data batch. Optimizing $\tilde{J}$ can never manipulate the original update direction corresponding to the main objective.

Care must be taken concerning the existence of a null space. If there are n units in a layer together with a layer input $\phi_{l-1} \in \mathbb{R}^{T \times n_{l-1}}$, we know that the dimension of the null space satisfies $\dim \ker \phi = n - \text{rowrank}(\phi)$. For data sets with redundant samples it is possible that the row rank of X is smaller than the dimension of the data set, which results in an non-empty null space. However, after the first non-linearity is applied, the transformed data set has typically full row rank. To guarantee the existence of a sufficiently large null space, the second core idea in *Safe Regularization* is to use layers with more units than samples in X. In the batch learning setting, this implies that $n_l > T$ for $l = 1, \dots, L$.

We are currently working on extending the theoretical results to optimization algorithms using mini-batches. By that, the width of layers must only be larger than the mini-batch size, and thus the restrictive assumptions are greatly weakened. In the experiment section, we show empirically that the proposed algorithm already achieves very promising results also for the mini-batch setting.

Now that we have ensured the existence of a null space of the layer input ϕ, we can restrict the shift directions ΔW by projecting the gradient of Eq. (6) onto that space. This results in the true gradient for the considered sub space. For defining the projection, let A be a basis of the null space, i.e. $\text{span}(A) = \ker(\phi_{l-1})$, where $\ker(T)$ denotes the kernel of a matrix T. Different methods exists to calculate A. In our proof-of-concept implementation we use a singular value decomposition, which is computationally expensive. However, more efficient methods exist, for example randomized singular value decomposition or other subspace estimation techniques.

We now seek for coefficients ξ such that the point $A\xi$, which resides in the linear space defined by the columns of A, is closest to $\nabla_X \tilde{J}(X)\big|_{X=W}$ with respect to the Frobenius norm. That means we solve

$$\min_{\xi} \left\| A \cdot \xi - \beta \, \nabla_X \tilde{J}(X)\Big|_{X=W} \right\|_F^2. \tag{7}$$

Algorithm 1: Training with *Safe Regularization*

Input: Training Data $X, Y, \mathbf{W}_{init}$, hyperparameters
while not *converged* **do**
    for l **in** *1,...,L* **do**
        Find A s.t. $\text{span}(A) = \ker(\phi_{l-1})$
        $g_l = \nabla_X J(X)|_{X=W_l}$
        $\tilde{g}_l = A \cdot \text{pinv}(A) \cdot \nabla_X \tilde{J}(X)|_{X=W_l}$
        $W_l' = W_l - Adam(\alpha, g_l + \tilde{g}_l)$
    end
end

This linear least squares problem has the solution $\xi = A^\dagger \beta \, \nabla_X \tilde{J}(X)\big|_{X=W}$ with the pseudo inverse $A^\dagger = (A^\mathsf{T} A)^{-1} A^\mathsf{T}$, which defines a shift that resides in the null space as $\Delta W^{NS} = A\xi$. Finally, we can extend update rule (2) as depicted in Fig. 1 and yield

$$W_l' \leftarrow W_l - \alpha \cdot \nabla_X J(X)|_{X=W_l} - \Delta W_l^{NS}$$

$$W_l' \leftarrow W_l - \alpha \cdot \nabla_X J(X)|_{X=W_l} - \beta A(A^\mathsf{T} A)^{-1} A^\mathsf{T} \, \nabla_X \tilde{J}(X)\Big|_{X=W_l}. \quad (8)$$

For both step sizes α and β we use the same value α to reduce the search space of hyperparameters. An overview over the training method is given in Algorithm 1.

4 Experiments

We validate our training algorithm empirically. First, we analyze the performance of *Safe Regularization* for batch-wise gradient descent. Second, we show that our method achieves promising results even when mini-batches are used. We compare the performance for the Boston Housing data set and various regression problems selected from the UCI Machine Learning Repository [3]:

- *Boston Housing* [1,11]: The objective is to predict the median value of owner-occupied homes from features like the average number of rooms per dwelling.
- *Communities and Crime* [18]: This data set contains features about communities such as the age distribution of its population or the number of full time police officers (we use only features which are available for all communities). The aim is to predict the total number of violent crimes per population.
- *Concrete Compressive Strength* [27]: This data set was created to analyze the compressive strength of concrete based on features like the age of the concrete or its components (e.g. the amount of cement).
- *Yacht Hydrodynamics* [6,16]: The purpose of this data set is to find a connection between the residuary resistance of sailing yachts and geometric features of the yacht like the hull geometry coefficients.

We compare training results in terms of mean squared test error and regularization loss after training, which is a measure of how well the side-optimization goal has been achieved. The chosen side-optimization goal for our experiments is to obtain sparse neural network weight matrices by using Eq. (4) as regularizer. For all our experiments we report the mean and standard deviation of the squared prediction error over ten independent runs. The code as well as all hyperparameters will be available online. In all experiments we use neural networks with two hidden layers and Rectified Linear Units, *Glorot*-uniform weight initialization [7] (except for biases, which are initialized to zero), a convergence patience of 10 and *Adam* as step-size optimizer with standard parameters.

4.1   Training Using Batches

First, we compare the performance of *Safe Regularization* to standard regularization using batch-gradient updates. In order to ensure a sufficiently large null space, which can be used to pursue the side objective, the neural network must comprise of more units in each layer than data samples considered during training. Hence, we use 1000 units per layer for our experiments with the *Boston Housing* and *Yacht Hydrodynamics* data sets, and 2500 units per layer for the *Communities And Crime* and *Concrete Compressive Strength* data sets.

Figure 2 depicts the performance ratio (test error and regularization loss) of both methods for each regularization strengths λ. One can see, that in contrast to the standard regularization technique, the influence of the side objective on the main objective in terms of reducing the prediction error is limited for *Safe Regularization*. This results in comparable or smaller test errors for our proposed method for all considered data sets, especially for increasing regularization hyperparameter λ (the ratio is bigger than one). Furthermore, *Safe Regularization* is more robust with respect to selecting the hyperparameter λ. This can also be seen in the regularization loss after training for different λ. *Safe Regularization* leads to a more robust decrease in the regularization loss for increasing values of λ. However, with a proper λ, standard regularization is able to achieve a smaller regularization loss after training at the price of a worse test error.

To further illustrate the pursuit of the side objective, we illustrate histograms of weight magnitudes for both regularization methods at the end of training on the *Boston Housing* data set (Fig. 4). For sake of visualization, histograms are drawn as lines instead of bars. The histograms for *Safe Regularization* look qualitatively similar to those of standard regularization. This indicates that *Safe Regularization* can replace existing approaches to regularization. The strongest effect for both methods is that a single peak for $\lambda = 0$ is split into two smaller ones, indicating that weights matrices are more sparse than without regularization. For both methods the exact positions of the peaks depend on the value of λ and the peaks are differently pronounced. The difference is in how both methods pursue the side objective. Standard regularization clearly separates weights in two groups with different magnitudes for large λ. But as shown before, this

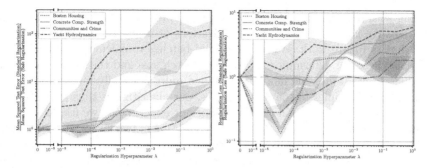

Fig. 2. Performance comparison between *Safe Regularization* and standard regularization with batch-wise training. The abscissa is split into two regions, the left uses a linear scaling and the right a logarithmic. This is required to visualize $\lambda = 0$. (left) The mean squared test error increases much stronger with increasing λ for standard regularization. (right) *Safe Regularization* leads to a more robust decrease in the regularization loss for increasing λ. However, with the correct choice of λ standard regularization is able to achieve a smaller regularization loss after training (at the price of a worse test error).

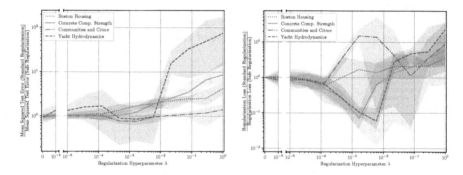

Fig. 3. The same comparison as in Fig. 2, but now using mini-batches. As before, the abscissa is split and has different scalings. (left) The dependence of the mean squared test error on λ for both methods is very similar to the results of batch-wise training. (right) The regularization loss for both methods shows roughly the same behavior as before, yet the effect is smaller.

comes at cost of larger test errors than *Safe Regularization* for too strong regularization. Finding the exact value for λ, where both the side objective and the test error are satisfied, is subject to tedious hyperparameter tuning. Our proposed *Safe Regularization* appears nearly independent of λ.

4.2 Training Using Mini-batches

For standard applications, the number of units in hidden layers of a neural network is usually smaller than the number of training samples in the data set. To use *Safe Regularization* for such problems, we look in this section empirically at training with mini-batches, which is a standard procedure for optimizing neural networks. We leave the theoretical implications of using mini-batches with our algorithm as future work. When using mini-batches to calculate gradients, the null space is solely determined by the mini-batch size and the number of units in hidden layers. Since the number of hidden units is usually much larger than the number of samples in the mini-batches, our algorithm is thus applicable to realistic real-world regression problems. For our experiments we use 32 samples per mini-batch and small neural networks consisting of two layers with 200 units.

Figure 3 shows the results of our algorithm on the introduced data sets compared to the standard training procedure using regularization terms. The reader sees a similar behavior as for batch-gradient training, but to slightly lesser extend. Furthermore, the optimal value for the hyperparameter λ moves to higher values for the standard training techniques. We regard this as confirmation that *Safe Regularization* can also lead to more robust behavior and lower test errors for training with mini-batches compared to standard regularization techniques. We would like to emphasize that this happens in the mini batch setting, even though we derive our method from a pure batch setting. As shown in Fig. 3 (left), our method achieves similar test errors for properly tuned standard regularization and clearly better errors for bad choices of λ. From Fig. 3 (right) we conclude that weights fulfill the side objective better than standard regularization for most values of λ and most of the data sets considered.

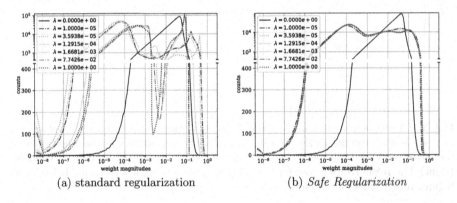

(a) standard regularization   (b) *Safe Regularization*

Fig. 4. Histograms of absolute weight values for different λ at the end of training on the *Boston Housing* data set. The ordinate has two distinct scales. The upper part is logarithmic to capture high counts ($>10^3$), while the lower part is linear to reveal trends with only low frequencies (<400). Both methods show qualitatively similar histograms for various λ, indicating that *Safe Regularization* can replace standard approaches. Compared to training without regularization $\lambda = 0$, both regularizer shift weight magnitudes towards smaller values for all chosen λ and additionally split the single peak for $\lambda = 0$ into two smaller ones. The important difference is the sensitiveness to the regularization strength λ. *Safe Regularization* demonstrates for all λ the same behavior, while the outcome of standard regularization depends strongly on the concrete choice. Both the position of peaks and the separation between them varies strongly with λ.

5   Conclusion

We showed how neural network training with regularization can be formulated as lexicographic optimization problem. Moreover, we demonstrated how the neural network can be optimized considering the lexicographic order, which we call *Safe Regularization*. The lexicographic ordering is ensured during training by performing updates for the side optimization problem exclusively in the null space of batch activations, which in turn guarantees that the update direction of the main objective is not corrupted.

Our training method prioritizes the main objective over the side objective, which results in smaller test errors after training. Nevertheless, the training is guided towards solutions that are also minimizing the side objective. In some cases they result in even smaller regularization loss after training compared to the results obtained with standard regularization. Furthermore, the influence of the regularization hyperparameter is reduced using our approach. *Safe Regularization* is more robust regarding hyperparameter selection. We were able to achieve similar results by using mini-batches instead of performing batch updates using the whole data set. This ensures the applicability to many regression tasks, in particular considering modern neural network architectures. Moreover, the proposed training method is not limited to a specific regularization technique, but rather allows to safely incorporate any suitable side objective into the training process. This opens up new possibilities for the training of neural networks, such as safe testing for certain structures in the regression problem.

References

1. Belsley, D.A., Kuh, E., Welsch, R.: Regression diagnostics: identifying influential data and sources of collinearity (1980)
2. Cheng, Y., Felix, X.Y., Feris, R.S., Kumar, S., Choudhary, A., Chang, S.F.: Fast neural networks with circulant projections. arXiv preprint arXiv:1502.03436 (2015)
3. Dua, D., Graff, C.: UCI machine learning repository (2017). http://archive.ics.uci.edu/ml
4. Duchi, J., Singer, Y.: Efficient online and batch learning using forward backward splitting. J. Mach. Learn. Res. **10**, 2899–2934 (2009)
5. Feppon, F., Allaire, G., Dapogny, C.: Null space gradient flows for constrained optimization with applications to shape optimization (2019)
6. Gerritsma, J., Onnink, R., Versluis, A.: Geometry, resistance and stability of the delft systematic yacht hull series. Int. Shipbuilding Prog. **28**(328), 276–297 (1981)
7. Glorot, X., Bengio, Y.: Understanding the difficulty of training deep feedforward neural networks. In: Proceedings of the Thirteenth International Conference on Artificial Intelligence and Statistics (2010)
8. Goggin, S.D., Gustafson, K.E., Johnson, K.M.: Accessing the null space with nonlinear multilayer neural networks. In: Science of Artificial Neural Networks (1992)
9. Goldstein, T., Studer, C., Baraniuk, R.: A field guide to forward-backward splitting with a FASTA implementation. arXiv preprint arXiv:1411.3406 (2014)
10. Goodfellow, I., Bengio, Y., Courville, A.: Deep Learning. MIT Press, Cambridge (2016)

11. Harrison Jr., D., Rubinfeld, D.L.: Hedonic housing prices and the demand for clean air. J. Environ. Econ. Manag. **5**(1), 81–102 (1978)
12. He, K., Zhang, X., Ren, S., Sun, J.: Deep residual learning for image recognition. In: Proceedings of the IEEE Conference on Computer Vision and Pattern Recognition (2016)
13. Kingma, D., Ba, J.: Adam: a method for stochastic optimization. In: International Conference on Learning Representations (2014)
14. Kukačka, J., Golkov, V., Cremers, D.: Regularization for deep learning: a taxonomy. arXiv preprint arXiv:1710.10686 (2017)
15. Lopes, M.E.: Estimating unknown sparsity in compressed sensing. In: Proceedings of the 30th International Conference on Machine Learning, vol. 28 (2013)
16. Ortigosa, I., Lopez, R., Garcia, J.: A neural networks approach to residuary resistance of sailing yachts prediction. In: Proceedings of the International Conference on Marine Engineering MARINE (2007)
17. Potlapalli, H., Luo, R.C.: Projection learning for self-organizing neural networks. IEEE Trans. Ind. Electron. **43**(4), 485–491 (1996)
18. Redmond, M., Baveja, A.: A data-driven software tool for enabling cooperative information sharing among police departments. Eur. J. Oper. Res. **141**(3), 660–678 (2002)
19. Scardapane, S., Comminiello, D., Hussain, A., Uncini, A.: Group sparse regularization for deep neural networks. Neurocomputing **241**, 81–89 (2017)
20. Shen, H.: Towards a mathematical understanding of the difficulty in learning with feedforward neural networks. In: The IEEE Conference on Computer Vision and Pattern Recognition (CVPR) (2018)
21. Sindhwani, V., Sainath, T., Kumar, S.: Structured transforms for small-footprint deep learning. In: Advances in Neural Information Processing Systems (2015)
22. Wang, H., Langley, R., Kim, S., McCord-Snook, E., Wang, H.: Efficient exploration of gradient space for online learning to rank. In: The 41st International ACM SIGIR Conference on Research & Development in Information Retrieval (2018)
23. Weigend, A.S., Rumelhart, D.E., Huberman, B.A.: Generalization by weight-elimination with application to forecasting. In: Advances in Neural Information Processing Systems (1991)
24. Wen, W., Wu, C., Wang, Y., Chen, Y., Li, H.: Learning structured sparsity in deep neural networks. In: Advances in Neural Information Processing Systems (2016)
25. Xie, D., Xiong, J., Pu, S.: All you need is beyond a good init: exploring better solution for training extremely deep convolutional neural networks with orthonormality and modulation. In: Proceedings of the IEEE Conference on Computer Vision and Pattern Recognition (2017)
26. Xu, K., Cao, T., Shah, S., Maung, C., Schweitzer, H.: Cleaning the null space: a privacy mechanism for predictors. In: Thirty-First AAAI Conference on Artificial Intelligence (2017)
27. Yeh, I.C.: Modeling of strength of high-performance concrete using artificial neural networks. Cem. Concr. Res. **28**(12), 1797–1808 (1998)
28. Yoon, S.W., Seo, J., Moon, J.: Meta learner with linear nulling. arXiv preprint arXiv:1806.01010 (2018)
29. Yuan, Y.: A null space algorithm for constrained optimization. In: Advances in Scientific Computing. Science Press, Beijing (2001)
30. Zhang, C., Patras, P., Haddadi, H.: Deep learning in mobile and wireless networking: a survey. IEEE Commun. Surv. Tutor. **21**(3), 2224–2287 (2019)

The Effect of Batch Normalization in the Symmetric Phase

Shiro Takagi[✉], Yuki Yoshida, and Masato Okada

The University of Tokyo, Kashiwanoha, Chiba 277-0882, Japan
`takagi@mns.k.u-tokyo.ac.jp`

Abstract. Learning neural networks has long been known to be difficult. One of the causes of such difficulties is thought to be the equilibrium points caused by the symmetry between the weights of the neural network. Such an equilibrium point is known to delay neural network training. However, neural networks have been widely used in recent years largely because of the development of methods that make learning easier. One such technique is batch normalization, which is empirically known to speed up learning. Therefore, if the equilibrium point due to symmetry truly affects the neural network learning, and batch normalization speeds up the learning, batch normalization should help escape from such equilibrium points. Therefore, we analyze whether batch normalization helps escape from such equilibrium points by a method called statistical mechanical analysis. By examining the eigenvalue of the Hessian matrix of the generalization error at the equilibrium point, we find that batch normalization delays escape from poor equilibrium points. This contradicts the empirically known finding of speeding up learning, and we discuss why we obtained this result.

Keywords: Neural network · Symmetric phase · Batch normalization

1 Introduction

A neural network is known as a model that has structural symmetries, i.e., the output can be the same value even if a specific weight value is replaced with another weight value. This symmetry creates a sequence of saddle points and local minima on the error surface in parameter space (hereafter, we call the equilibrium point a symmetric equilibrium point), and these equilibrium points are known to delay the learning of neural networks [2,3,9,11,33,38,40]. Due to this equilibrium point, training of the neural network can be divided into two phases: the symmetric phase, which is an early-stage training phase where training does not proceed because the neural network is trapped around the symmetric point, and the specialization phase, where the neural network escapes from the equilibrium point and begins to learn properly (see Sect. 3.1 for details). Therefore, the learning behavior of neural networks in the symmetry phase is thought to be a key to determining the difficulty in training neural networks.

© Springer Nature Switzerland AG 2020
I. Farkaš et al. (Eds.): ICANN 2020, LNCS 12397, pp. 229–240, 2020.
https://doi.org/10.1007/978-3-030-61616-8_19

Neural networks have been widely used in recent years because of the development of methods that facilitate learning. Batch normalization is one such technique, and it is known that it contributes to faster learning [4,7,18,23,26,34]. If batch normalization contributes to faster learning, it is expected to expedite escape from such a symmetric equilibrium point. Therefore, we analyze the eigenvalue of the Hessian matrix of the error at the symmetric equilibrium point to determine whether batch normalization actually helps escape from such a point. The Hessian matrix at a fixed point describes the local curvature of the loss surface at the point, which has a crucial influence on the learning speed of the model around the point; for example, if the absolute values of any negative eigenvalue are small, it will take long time to escape from the fixed point. This requires analytically computing the error and its dynamics. To that end, we derived the learning dynamics of a neural network with batch normalization by statistical mechanical analysis. The statistical mechanical analysis is a method to analytically derive the dynamics of the generalization error in the large limit of the input dimension and is well suitable for the analysis of the symmetric equilibrium point since it enables us to analytically study the learning behavior around the point.

2 Statistical Mechanical Analysis of Two-Layered Neural Network with Batch Normalization

2.1 Teacher-Student Learning

For the statistical mechanical analysis, we have to consider the learning under the framework of teacher-student learning [6,30,32,35,36]. Hence, we analyzed the training of a two-layered neural network by stochastic gradient descent (SGD) in the framework of teacher-student learning, where data used for training once are not used twice. Teacher-student learning refers to supervised learning assuming that both the learner and the true function are neural networks [6,32]. The true function is called a teacher network, and the learner is called a student network.

Consider the teacher network and student network with N input neurons and 1 output neuron. Each network has one hidden layer, and the number of hidden neurons is M for the teacher and K for the student. We assume that for each update, b new inputs $\boldsymbol{\xi}^u \in \mathbb{R}^N$ $(u = 1, ..., b)$ are used, where each component ξ_i^u $(i = 1, ..., N)$ of input data $\boldsymbol{\xi}^u$ is sampled i.i.d. from the distribution of expected value 0 and variance σ^2. Let the weight matrix of the first layer of the student network be $[\mathbf{J}_1, ..., \mathbf{J}_K]^T \in \mathbb{R}^{K \times N}$ and the weight vector of the second layer is $\mathbf{w} \in \mathbb{R}^K$, the weight matrix of the first layer of the teacher network is $[\mathbf{B}_1, ..., \mathbf{B}_M]^T \in \mathbb{R}^{M \times N}$ and the weight vector of the second layer is $\mathbf{v} \in \mathbb{R}^M$. The elements of the first-layer weight vector of the student and teacher are $J_{il} \in \mathbb{R} \overset{\text{iid}}{\sim} \mathcal{N}(0, 1/N)$, $B_{nl} \in \mathbb{R} \overset{\text{iid}}{\sim} \mathcal{N}(0, 1/N)$ $(1 \leq i \leq K, 1 \leq n \leq M, 1 \leq l \leq N)$. For simplicity, each element of the second-layer weight vector is assumed to be 1 in both networks, but it is simple to extend to the general case of learning weights. A neural network that fixes each element of the weight vector of the second layer to a constant is called a soft-committee machine. The activation function of the hidden layer is $\phi : \mathbb{R} \to \mathbb{R}$ and that of the output layer is an identity map. We use the square loss $\varepsilon = \frac{1}{2}(t^u - s^u)^2$ as the loss function.

2.2 Formulation for Statistical Mechanical Analysis

Here, we define the order parameters, which describe the global behavior of the system as $Q_{ij} = \mathbf{J}_i \cdot \mathbf{J}_j, R_{in} = \mathbf{J}_i \cdot \mathbf{B}_n, T_{nm} = \mathbf{B}_n \cdot \mathbf{B}_m$ [6,32].

In the limit of large degrees of freedom with the number of input elements $N \to \infty$, the time evolution differential equations of these parameters can be derived, depending on the activation function [6,32]. The generalized error ε_g, defined as the expected value of the training error with the distribution followed by $\boldsymbol{\xi}$, is a function of the order parameter. Therefore, by deriving the dynamics of the order parameter, the dynamics of the generalization error can also be derived. Since this method is based on statistical mechanics, we call it statistical mechanical analysis.

2.3 Statistical Mechanical Analysis of Neural Network with Batch Normalization

In batch normalization, each input $x_i^u = \mathbf{J}_i \cdot \boldsymbol{\xi}^u$ to each hidden neuron is normalized with the sample mean $\mu_{x_i} = \frac{1}{b} \sum_{u=1}^{b} x_i^u$ and sample standard deviation $\sigma_{x_i} = \sqrt{\frac{1}{b} \sum_{u=1}^{b}(x_i^u - \mu_{x_i})^2}$. Then, the normalized inputs are multiplied by the gain parameter g_i and added by the bias parameter β_i, which are learnable parameters: $g_i \frac{(x_i^u - \mu_{x_i})}{\sigma_{x_i}} + \beta_i$.

Here, we do not subtract the mean μ_{x_i} and do not add β_i, the error of which is negligible when the sample size b is large since x_i always follows the distribution of expected value 0. When b is large, the sample standard deviation for b inputs of each element of the hidden layer is $\sigma_{x_i} \approx \sqrt{\frac{1}{b}\sum_{u=1}^{b}(x_i^u)^2} \approx \sqrt{\langle (x_i^u)^2 \rangle} \approx \sqrt{\mathbf{J}_i^T \langle \boldsymbol{\xi}^u \boldsymbol{\xi}^{u^T} \rangle \mathbf{J}_i} = \sqrt{\sigma^2 ||\mathbf{J}_i||^2} = \sigma\sqrt{Q_{ii}}$. Note that $\langle \cdot \rangle$ is an operation that takes the expected value of the input $\boldsymbol{\xi}$. Hence, inputs to the hidden layer i are reparameterized as $\frac{g_i}{\sigma\sqrt{Q_{ii}}} x_i^u$. Then, the outputs of the student and teacher networks are

$$s^u = \sum_{i}^{K} w_i \phi \left(\frac{g_i}{\sigma\sqrt{Q_{ii}}} x_i^u \right) \in \mathbb{R}, \quad t^u = \sum_{n}^{M} v_n \phi \left(y_n^u \right) \in \mathbb{R}, \tag{1}$$

where $y_n^u = \mathbf{B}_n \cdot \boldsymbol{\xi}^u$. Note that $\frac{g_i}{\sigma\sqrt{Q_{ii}}} x_i^u$ and y_n^u follow Gaussian distribution of mean 0 since we assume that $N \to \infty$.

The update equations of the weights J_i and the gain parameter g_i by SGD are as follows:

$$J_i \leftarrow J_i - \frac{\eta}{N} \nabla \varepsilon = J_i + \frac{\eta}{Nb} \sum_{u=1}^{b} [(t^u - s^u) \cdot w_i] \, \phi'\left(\frac{g_i}{\sigma\sqrt{Q_{ii}}} x_i^u\right) \frac{g_i}{\sigma\sqrt{Q_{ii}}} \xi^u, \quad (2)$$

$$g_i \leftarrow g_i - \frac{\eta}{N} \nabla \varepsilon = g_i + \frac{\eta}{Nb} \sum_{u=1}^{b} [(t^u - s^u) \cdot w_i] \, \phi'\left(\frac{g_i}{\sigma\sqrt{Q_{ii}}} x_i^u\right) \frac{1}{\sigma\sqrt{Q_{ii}}} x_i^u, \quad (3)$$

where $\frac{\eta}{N}$ is the learning rate. Note that we assume that $\frac{g_i x_i^u}{\sigma\sqrt{Q_{ii}} Q_{ii}} J_i$ is negligible and omitted it from the update equation of J_i because $\frac{g_i x_i^u}{\sigma\sqrt{Q_{ii}} Q_{ii}} J_i \approx O(\frac{1}{\sqrt{N}})$, while $\frac{g_i}{\sigma\sqrt{Q_{ii}}} \xi^u \approx O(1)$ at initialization. Considering g_i as an order parameter, it is straightforward to derive the update equation of the order parameters. Here, we sum the update equations of the order parameters from time 0 to time Ndt, where Ndt is large enough but much smaller than N since dt is small. As a result, we can derive the dynamics of order parameters as follows:

$$\frac{dQ_{ij}}{dt} = \eta \left[\sum_{p=1}^{M} I_3(\hat{x}_i^u, \hat{x}_j^u, y_p^u) - \sum_{p=1}^{K} I_3(\hat{x}_i^u, \hat{x}_j^u, \hat{x}_p^u) + \sum_{p=1}^{M} I_3(\hat{x}_j^u, \hat{x}_i^u, y_p^u) - \sum_{p=1}^{K} I_3(\hat{x}_j^u, \hat{x}_i^u, \hat{x}_p^u) \right]$$

$$+ \frac{\eta^2}{b} \left[\sum_{p,q}^{K,K} I_4(\hat{x}_i^u, \hat{x}_j^v, \hat{x}_p^u, \hat{x}_q^v) + \sum_{p,q}^{M,M} I_4(\hat{x}_i^u, \hat{x}_j^v, y_p^u, y_q^v) \right.$$

$$\left. - \sum_{p,q}^{K,M} I_4(\hat{x}_i^u, \hat{x}_j^v, \hat{x}_p^u, y_q^v) - \sum_{p,q}^{M,K} I_4(\hat{x}_i^u, \hat{x}_j^v, y_p^u, \hat{x}_q^v) \right], \quad (4)$$

$$\frac{dR_{in}}{dt} = \eta \left[\sum_{p=1}^{M} I_3(\hat{x}_i^u, y_n^u, y_p^u) - \sum_{p=1}^{K} I_3(\hat{x}_i^u, y_n^u, \hat{x}_p^u) \right], \quad (5)$$

$$\frac{dg_i}{dt} = \eta \left[\sum_{p=1}^{M} I_3(\hat{x}_i^u, x_i^u, y_p^u) - \sum_{p=1}^{K} I_3(\hat{x}_i^u, x_i^u, \hat{x}_p^u) \right], \quad (6)$$

where $\hat{x}_i = \frac{g_i}{\sigma\sqrt{Q_{ii}}} x_i$ and $I_3(z_1, z_2, z_3) = \langle \phi'(z_1) z_2 \phi(z_3) \rangle$ and $I_4(z_1, z_2, z_3, z_4) = \langle \phi'(z_1)\phi'(z_2)\phi(z_3)\phi(z_4) \rangle$ can be calculated analytically when a set of random variables (z_1, z_2, z_3, z_4) follows a multivariate Gaussian distribution of the expected value $\mathbf{0}$ [6,30,32]. Note that $\langle \cdot \rangle$ means taking the expected value as of x and y, and the term $\frac{\eta^2}{b}$ is negligible when b is large. The generalization error can also be written as

$$\varepsilon_g = \frac{1}{2} \left[\sum_{p,q}^{M,M} I_2(y_p^u, y_q^u) + \sum_{p,q}^{K,K} I_2(\hat{x}_p^u, \hat{x}_q^u) - 2 \sum_{p,q}^{K,M} I_2(\hat{x}_p^u, y_q^u) \right], \quad (7)$$

where $I_2(z_1, z_2) = \langle \phi(z_1)\phi(z_2) \rangle$, which can also be calculated exactly. When the activation function is $\phi(x) = \mathrm{erf}(x/\sqrt{2})$ and b is assumed to be large, the dynamics of these order parameters and the generalization error are as follows:

$$\frac{dQ_{ij}}{dt} = \frac{2\eta}{\pi} [\mathcal{Q}_1 - \mathcal{Q}_2], \quad \frac{dR_{in}}{dt} = \frac{2\eta}{\pi} \frac{g_i}{\sigma\sqrt{Q_{ii}}} [\mathcal{R}], \quad \frac{dg_i}{dt} = \frac{2\eta}{\pi g_i} [\mathcal{G}], \quad (8)$$

where $\mathcal{Q}_1 = \mathcal{Q}_1(Q_{ij}, R_{in}, T_{nm})$, $\mathcal{Q}_2 = \mathcal{Q}_2(Q_{ij})$, $\mathcal{R} = \mathcal{R}(Q_{ij}, R_{in}, T_{nm})$, $\mathcal{G} = \mathcal{G}(Q_{ij}, R_{in}, T_{nm})$. The exact expressions of these functions are as follows:

$$\mathcal{Q}_1 = \sum_{p=1}^{M} \left[\frac{\left(R'_{jp}(1+Q'_{ii}) - Q'_{ij}R'_{ip}\right)}{(1+Q'_{ii})\sqrt{(1+Q'_{ii})(1+T'_{pp}) - R'^2_{ip}}} + \frac{\left(R'_{ip}(1+Q'_{jj}) - Q'_{ji}R'_{jp}\right)}{(1+Q'_{jj})\sqrt{(1+Q'_{jj})(1+T'_{pp}) - R'^2_{jp}}} \right],$$
$$\tag{9}$$

$$\mathcal{Q}_2 = \sum_{p=1}^{K} \left[\frac{\left(Q'_{jp}(1+Q'_{ii}) - Q'_{ij}Q'_{ip}\right)}{(1+Q'_{ii})\sqrt{(1+Q'_{ii})(1+Q'_{pp}) - Q'^2_{ip}}} + \frac{\left(Q'_{ip}(1+Q'_{jj}) - Q'_{ji}Q'_{jp}\right)}{(1+Q'_{jj})\sqrt{(1+Q'_{jj})(1+Q'_{pp}) - Q'^2_{jp}}} \right],$$
$$\tag{10}$$

$$\mathcal{R} = \sum_{p=1}^{M} \frac{\left(T'_{np}(1+Q'_{ii}) - R'_{in}R'_{ip}\right)}{(1+Q'_{ii})\sqrt{(1+Q'_{ii})(1+T'_{pp}) - R'^2_{ip}}} - \sum_{p=1}^{K} \frac{\left(R'_{pn}(1+Q'_{ii}) - R'_{in}Q'_{ip}\right)}{(1+Q'_{ii})\sqrt{(1+Q'_{ii})(1+Q'_{pp}) - Q'^2_{ip}}},$$
$$\tag{11}$$

$$\mathcal{G} = \sum_{p=1}^{M} \frac{\left(R'_{ip}(1+Q'_{ii}) - Q'_{ii}R'_{ip}\right)}{(1+Q'_{ii})\sqrt{(1+Q'_{ii})(1+T'_{pp}) - R'^2_{ip}}} - \sum_{p=1}^{K} \frac{\left(Q'_{ip}(1+Q'_{ii}) - Q'_{ii}Q'_{ip}\right)}{(1+Q'_{ii})\sqrt{(1+Q'_{ii})(1+Q'_{pp}) - Q'^2_{ip}}},$$
$$\tag{12}$$

$$\varepsilon_g = \frac{1}{\pi} \left[\sum_{p,q}^{M,M} \operatorname{asin}\left(\frac{T'_{pq}}{\sqrt{(1+T'_{pp})(1+T'_{qq})}} \right) \right.$$
$$\left. + \sum_{p,q}^{K,K} \operatorname{asin}\left(\frac{Q'_{pq}}{\sqrt{(1+Q'_{pp})(1+Q'_{qq})}} \right) - 2\sum_{p,q}^{K,M} \operatorname{asin}\left(\frac{R'_{pq}}{\sqrt{(1+Q'_{pp})(1+T'_{qq})}} \right) \right].$$
$$\tag{13}$$

Note that $Q'_{lk} = \frac{\sigma^2 g_l g_k}{\sigma_{x_l} \sigma_{x_k}} Q_{lk}$, $R'_{lk} = \frac{\sigma^2 g_l}{\sigma_{x_l}} R_{lk}$, $T'_{lk} = \sigma^2 T_{lk}$ for $(l, k) = (i, j, n, p, q)$.

3 Error Surface Near the Symmetric Equilibrium Point

3.1 Symmetric Phase

It is known that there are two phases in learning a two-layered neural network [31, 33, 41]. The first phase is called the symmetric phase, where the student network's weights cannot determine which weight of the teacher network they should specialize. This is because there are many parameters that can play the same role due to the symmetry of the neural network. As explained above, such symmetry delays training as the neural network is trapped around a symmetric equilibrium point.

However, as the learning progresses, the neural network gradually escapes from such an equilibrium point due to the small noise, and the weight vectors of the student network correspond to any of the weight vectors of the teacher network. This is the second phase, the specialization phase. In the specialization phase, the student network eventually learns the input/output structure of the teacher network completely. In this paper, we focus on the behavior of neural networks in the symmetric phase, especially around the symmetric equilibrium point.

3.2   Effect of Batch Normalization at the Symmetric Equilibrium Point

In the following, we consider the case where the number of hidden neurons in the student network and the teacher network is the same: $K = M$. In the symmetric phase, when the covariance matrix of the teacher's weight vectors is isotropic, that is, $T_{nm} = \delta_{nm}$, we can reduce the abovementioned order parameters into a smaller number of order parameters [33]. Note that δ_{nm} is a function that returns 1 when $n = m$ and 0 when $n \neq m$. The reduced order parameters are as follows:

$$Q_{ij} = \begin{cases} Q\,(i = j) \\ C\,(i \neq j) \end{cases}, \quad R_{in} = \begin{cases} R\,(i = n) \\ S\,(i \neq n) \end{cases}, \quad g_i = g.$$

Now, assume that the neural network is at the symmetric equilibrium point. The order parameters R, S, Q, C, and g at this equilibrium point are defined as R^*, S^*, Q^*, C^*, g^*, respectively. Owing to the symmetry between the parameters at the equilibrium point, the equations $Q^* = C^*, R^* = S^*$ hold. Since the relation of $Q^* = C^*$ is conserved up to the first-order terms in the perturbation expansion, the order parameters can be further reduced to four parameters, Q, R, S, and g, and we can derive the dynamics of these four order parameters.

Here, we assume that $Q = \frac{1}{g^2}$ because g is a parameter to scale the magnitude of the normalized input, so it is expected to have the opposite relationship with Q. In fact, we empirically confirmed that this holds through training. Then, the value of the order parameter at the symmetric equilibrium point is $R^* = S^* = \sqrt{\frac{K+(K-1)\tau}{\tau K}}$, $Q^* = \frac{K+(K-1)\tau}{\tau}$, $g^* = \sqrt{\frac{\tau}{K+(K-1)\tau}}$ by solving $\frac{dR}{dt} = \frac{dS}{dt} = \frac{dQ}{dt} = \frac{dg}{dt} = 0$. We represent a vector of order parameters by $\Omega = (R, S, Q, g)$ and the Hessian of the generalization error by $\nabla_\Omega \nabla_\Omega \varepsilon_g(\Omega) = H$. By estimating the eigenvalue of this Hessian matrix at the symmetric equilibrium point, we can understand the local topography of the error surface. This is because the eigenvalue of the Hessian is a quantity that describes how the perturbation affects the change in error when the parameter is slightly moved from the point where the eigenvalue is evaluated. When some eigenvalues of the Hessian are almost zero, there are directions in which adding a perturbation hardly affects the error since the Hessian is evaluated at the equilibrium point. In other words, the local error surface is flat. Conversely, when a large eigenvalue exists, the terrain is steep where positive eigenvalues imply that there are directions in which the error increases and negative eigenvalues are signs of directions in which the error decreases. Hence, when the absolute values of any negative eigenvalue are small, it is difficult to escape from this equilibrium point.

Therefore, we calculated the eigenvalues of the Hessian matrix numerically and examined the effect of batch normalization on the local shape of the error surface at the symmetric equilibrium point. Figures 1 and 2 plot the calculated eigenvalues as a function of the hidden layer width K and the input variance τ. Unless otherwise specified, the width of the hidden layer was $K = 2$ and the variance in the input was $\tau = 1$.

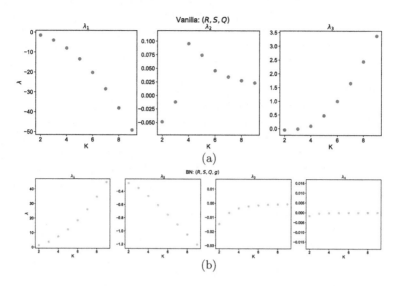

Fig. 1. Eigenvalue of the Hessian matrix for hidden layer K. The vertical axis λ indicates the magnitude of the eigenvalue, and the horizontal axis K indicates the number of hidden neurons. $\lambda_i(i = 1, .., 4)$ is the result for the ith eigenvalue. (a) Normal two-layered neural network without batch normalization. (b) When batch normalization is used. You can see that the absolute value of the negative eigenvalue is relatively smaller when batch normalization is added.

As shown in Fig. 1, when batch normalization is used, the direction where the eigenvalue becomes 0 appears for large K. In addition, the absolute value of the negative eigenvalue is smaller when batch normalization is used. Hence, it can be expected that the neural network takes a longer time to escape from the equilibrium point when batch normalization is added.

As shown in Fig. 2, a similar tendency was observed for input variance τ. In ordinary neural networks, the absolute value of the negative eigenvalue becomes very large as τ becomes large. In other words, escape from the equilibrium point is expected to be very easy. However, when batch normalization is used, a direction in which the eigenvalue is almost 0 appears as before, and a direction in which the error surface is flat is created. Additionally, the absolute value of the negative eigenvalue is clearly smaller than that of the vanilla neural network. Therefore, we can expect that escape from the equilibrium point will take a longer time when batch normalization is added.

To confirm this, we compare the time evolution of the generalization error of both the vanilla neural network and the batch normalization with large K and τ. The number of iterations is $20,000$, the hidden width is $K = M = 2$ and the input variance is $\tau = 1$ unless otherwise specified. Figure 3 shows the result. The neural network with batch normalization has a longer period when the generalization error hardly changes. This period corresponds to the period when the neural network is near the symmetric equilibrium point. Therefore, as

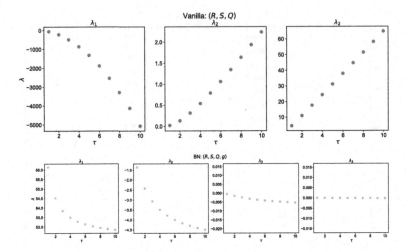

Fig. 2. The same as Fig. 1 except that the x axis is the input variance τ. As shown in Fig. 1, batch normalization decreases the absolute value of the negative eigenvalue.

expected, in both cases where the width of the hidden layer K and the input variance τ are large, the neural network with batch normalization takes more time to escape from the symmetric equilibrium point.

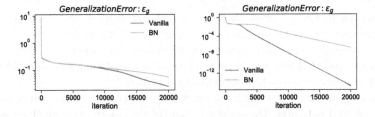

Fig. 3. Generalization error for large K and τ. Vanilla shows the result of a normal two-layered neural network, and BN shows the result when batch normalization is added. The generalization error is calculated not with the order parameter derived by statistical mechanics but with the result of numerical calculation calculated by updating the weights sequentially without using approximation. Note that $\eta = 1$, $N = 100$, $b = 100$, and the total number of iterations is 20,000.

4   Related Work

The symmetry of neural networks is thought to be a cause of the difficulty of training neural networks. The Hessian of the error surface in the output space of the neural network are known to have a singular point [1,10,37]. Previous studies show how this point delays training [2,3,9,11,33,38,40]. When students have extra parameters to express teachers, the global minimum is on the singular region, and it takes time to reach the solution [9]. Even when local minima and saddles are in singular regions, the neural network is attracted to the point, and training is delayed [33,39,40]. Our work is related to the second case.

Statistical mechanical analysis was invented and developed in the 1990s. Saad and Solla derived dynamics of the weight from the input layer to the hidden layer of the two-layered soft-committee machine [32]. Biehl and Schwarze studied the weight from the input layer to the hidden layer for a general two-layered neural network [6]. Yoshida et al. and Goldt et al. derived the learning dynamics of all weights of a general two-layered neural network [12,42]. We extended the analysis of the dynamics of the soft committee to a case with batch normalization.

Various discussions have focused on why batch normalization speeds up learning. Mitigating internal covariate shift [18], smoothing the error surface [20,34], decoupling length and direction optimization of weight vectors [23], allowing a larger learning rate [7], and adjusting the effective learning rate [4,26] might be reasons why batch normalization speeds up neural network training. Although Luo et al. analyzed the dynamics of batch normalization by statistical mechanical analysis [26], this is limited to the discussion of single-layer perceptrons. This is insufficient for our purpose since symmetric equilibrium points do not appear in a single-layer perceptron. Therefore, we derived the dynamics of a two-layered neural network.

5 Discussion

We derived the learning dynamics and generalization error of a two-layered neural network with batch normalization by statistical mechanical analysis. Using them, we analyzed the shape of the error surface in the parameter space around the equilibrium point caused by the symmetry of the network and found that, at least in the situation we considered, batch normalization delays escape from the equilibrium point. This contradicts the empirical fact that batch normalization speeds up the learning of neural networks. In the following, we consider the cause of this result.

The first possibility is to consider the infinitesimal learning rate. There are many studies that consider the small limit of the learning rate to analyze learning dynamics [8,19,27], and statistical mechanical analysis also relies on this assumption. In this method, it is difficult to discuss the finite size effect of learning rates. Since batch normalization is known to smooth the complicated error surface [7,34], it might be harder to escape with a small learning rate.

The second possibility is that the solution found in practical applications is the symmetric equilibrium point. In other words, it is possible that the network achieved a level of performance without completely breaking the symmetry between the parameters of the networks. In recent years, the learning of neural networks often uses networks with much greater expressive power for solving tasks, and it is well known that there are many parameters that are practically unused in such cases. In fact, a neural network is known to maintain high accuracy even when more than 90% of its weights are pruned [15,16,24,25]. This is partly because stochastic gradient descent implicitly regularizes neural networks, finding simple functions [5,14,28,29]. In addition, it is known that the solutions found by neural networks have a flat terrain in the vicinity of the error surface, which shows that the learning has been completed while maintaining symmetry. [17,21,22]. Furthermore, for example, Yoshida et al. argue that neural networks will not be trapped at the symmetric equilibrium point when neural networks have multiple outputs [42]. Additionally, Yoshida et al. and Goldt et al. claim that the statistical property of the data can mitigate delay learning due to the symmetric equilibrium point [13,43]. Although we find considerable evidence that neural networks can maintain high symmetry even after training, these are still speculations, and further study on these possibilities is left for future study.

References

1. Amari, S.: Natural gradient works efficiently in learning. Neural Comput. **10**(2), 251–276 (1998)
2. Amari, S., Ozeki, T., Karakida, R., Yoshida, Y., Okada, M.: Dynamics of learning in MLP: natural gradient and singularity revisited. Neural Comput. **30**(1), 1–33 (2018)
3. Amari, S., Park, H., Ozeki, T.: Singularities affect dynamics of learning in neuromanifolds. Neural Comput. **18**(5), 1007–1065 (2006)
4. Arora, S., Li, Z., Lyu, K.: Theorical analysis of auto rate-tuning by batch normalization. arXiv preprint arXiv:1812.03981 (2018)
5. Arpit, D., et al.: A closer look at memorization in deep networks. In: Proceedings of the 34th International Conference on Machine Learning (2017)
6. Biehl, M., Schwarze, H.: Learning by on-line gradient descent. J. Phys. A: Math. Gen. **28**(3), 643 (1995)
7. Bjorck, J., Gomes, G., Selman, B., Weinberger, K.Q.: Understanding batch normalization. In: Advances in Neural Information Processing Systems, vol. 31 (2018)
8. Chaudhari, P., Soatto, S.: Stochastic gradient descent performs variational inference, converges to limit cycles for deep networks. In: 6th International Conference on Learning Representations (2018)
9. Cousseau, F., Ozeki, T., Amari, S.: Dynamics of learning in multilayer perceptrons near singularities. IEEE Trans. Neural Netw. **19**(8), 1313–1328 (2008)
10. Fukumizu, K.: A regularity condition of the information matrix of a multilayer perception network. Neural Netw. **9**(5), 871–879 (1996)
11. Fukumizu, K., Amari, S.: Local minima and plateaus in hierarchical structures of multilayer perceptrons. Neural Netw. **13**, 317–327 (2000)
12. Goldt, S., Advani, M.S., Saxe, A.M., Krzakala, F., Zdeborova, L.: Dynamics of stochastic gradient descent for two-layer neural networks in the teacher-student setup. In: Advances in Neural Information Processing Systems, vol. 32 (2019)
13. Goldt, S., Mezard, M., Krzakala, F., Zdeborova, L.: Modelling the influence of data structure on learning in neural networks: the hidden manifold model. arXiv preprint arXiv:1909.11500 (2019)
14. Gunasekar, S., Woodworth, B.E., Bhojanapalli, S., Neyshabur, B., Srebro, N.: Implicit regularization in matrix factorization. In: Advances in Neural Information Processing Systems, vol. 30 (2017)

15. Han, S., Pool, J., Tran, J., Dally, W.: Learning both weights and connections for efficient neural network. In: Advances in Neural Information Processing Systems, vol. 28 (2015)
16. Hassibi, B., Stork, D.G.: Second order derivatives for network pruning: optimal brain surgeon. In: Advances in Neural Information Processing Systems, vol. 6 (1993)
17. Hochreiter, S., Schmidhuber, J.: Flat minima. Neural Comput. **9**(1), 1–42 (1997)
18. Ioffe, S., Szegedy, C.: Batch normalization: accelerating deep network training by reducing internal covariate shift. In: Proceedings of the 32nd International Conference on Machine Learning (2015)
19. Jastrzebski, S., et al.: Three factors influencing minima in SGD. arXiv preprint arXiv:1711.04623 (2017)
20. Karakida, R., Akaho, S., Amari, S.: The normalization method for alleviating pathological sharpness in wide neural networks. In: Advances in Neural Information Processing Systems, vol. 32 (2019)
21. Karakida, R., Akaho, S., Amari, S.: Universal statistics of fisher information in deep neural networks: mean field approach. In: Chaudhuri, K., Sugiyama, M. (eds.) Proceedings of Machine Learning Research, 16–18 April 2019, vol. 89, pp. 1032–1041. PMLR (2019)
22. Keskar, N.S., Mudigere, D., Nocedal, J., Smelyanskiy, M., Tang, P.T.P.: On large-batch training for deep learning: generalization gap and sharp minima. In: 5th International Conference on Learning Representations (2017)
23. Kohler, J., Daneshmand, H., Lucchi, A., Zhou, M., Neymeyr, K., Hofmann, T.: Exponential convergence rates for batch normalization: the power of length-direction decoupling in non-convex optimization. arXiv preprint arXiv:1805.10694 (2018)
24. LeCun, Y., Denker, J.S., Solla, S.A.: Optimal brain damage. In: Advances in Neural Information Processing Systems, vol. 3 (1990)
25. Li, H., Kadav, A., Durdanovic, I., Samet, H., Graf, H.P.: Pruning filters for efficient convnets. arXiv preprint arXiv:1608.08710 (2016)
26. Luo, P., Wang, X., Shao, W., Peng, Z.: Towards understanding regularization in batch normalization. arXiv preprint arXiv:1809.00846 (2018)
27. Mandt, S., Hoffman, M., Blei, D.: A variational analysis of stochastic gradient algorithms. In: Proceedings of the 33nd International Conference on Machine Learning (2016)
28. Neyshabur, B., Tomioka, R., Salakhutdinov, R., Srebro, N.: Geometry of optimization and implicit regularization in deep learning. arXiv preprint arXiv:1705.03071 (2017)
29. Neyshabur, B., Tomioka, R., Srebro, N.: In search of the real inductive bias: on the role of implicit regularization in deep learning. In: 3rd International Conference on Learning Representations (2015)
30. Riegler, P., Biehl, M.: On-line backpropagation in two-layered neural networks. J. Phys. A **28**, L507–L513 (1995)
31. Saad, D., Solla, S.A.: Dynamics of on-line gradient descent learning for multilayer neural networks. In: Advances in Neural Information Processing Systems, vol. 8 (1995)
32. Saad, D., Solla, S.A.: Exact solution for on-line learning in multilayer neural networks. Phys. Rev. Lett. **74**(41), 4337–4340 (1995)
33. Saad, D., Solla, S.A.: On-line learning in soft committee machines. Phys. Rev. E **52**(4), 4225–4243 (1995)

34. Santurkar, S., Tsipras, D., Ilyas, A., Mardy, A.: How does batch normalization help optimization? arXiv preprint arXiv:1805.11604 (2018)
35. Schwarze, H.: Learning a rule in a multilayer neural network. J. Phys. A **26**, 5781–5794 (1993)
36. Seung, H.S., Somopolinsky, H., Tishby, N.: Statistical mechanics of learning from examples. Phys. Rev. A **45**(8), 6056–6091 (1992)
37. Watanabe, S.: Algebraic geometrical methods for hierarchical learning machines. Neural Netw. **14**(8), 1049–1060 (2001)
38. Watanabe, S., Amari, S.: Learning coefficients of layered models when the true distribution mismatches the singularities. Neural Comput. **15**(5), 1011–1033 (2003)
39. Wei, H., Amari, S.: Dynamics of learning near singularities in radial basis function networks. Neural Netw. **21**(7), 989–1005 (2008)
40. Wei, H., Zhang, J., Cousseau, F., Ozeki, T., Amari, S.: Dynamics of learning in multilayer perceptrons near singularities. Neural Comput. **20**(3), 813–842 (2008)
41. West, A.H.L., Saad, D., Nabney, I.T.: The learning dynamics of a universal approximator. In: Advances in Neural Information Processing Systems, vol. 9 (1996)
42. Yoshida, Y., Karakida, R., Okada, M., Amari, S.: Statistical mechanical analysis of learning dynamics of two-layer perceptron with multiple output units. J. Phys. A **52**(18), 184002 (2019)
43. Yoshida, Y., Okada, M.: Data-dependence of plateau phenomenon in learning with neural network – statistical mechanical analysis. In: Advances in Neural Information Processing Systems, vol. 32 (2019)

Regularized Pooling

Takato Otsuzuki$^{(\boxtimes)}$, Hideaki Hayashi$^{(\boxtimes)}$ⓘ, Yuchen Zhengⓘ,
and Seiichi Uchidaⓘ

Kyushu University, Fukuoka, Japan
takato.otsuzuki@human.ait.kyushu-u.ac.jp, hayashi@ait.kyushu-u.ac.jp

Abstract. In convolutional neural networks (CNNs), pooling operations play important roles such as dimensionality reduction and deformation compensation. In general, max pooling, which is the most widely used operation for local pooling, is performed independently for each kernel. However, the deformation may be spatially smooth over the neighboring kernels. This means that max pooling is too flexible to compensate for actual deformations. In other words, its excessive flexibility risks canceling the essential spatial differences between classes. In this paper, we propose *regularized pooling*, which enables the value selection direction in the pooling operation to be spatially smooth across adjacent kernels so as to compensate only for actual deformations. The results of experiments on handwritten character images and texture images showed that regularized pooling not only improves recognition accuracy but also accelerates the convergence of learning compared with conventional pooling operations.

Keywords: Pooling operation · Convolutional neural networks · Deformation compensation

1 Introduction

Max pooling in convolutional neural networks (CNNs) is the operation used to select the maximum value in each kernel, as shown in Fig. 1(a). It plays several important roles in CNN-based image recognition. One is the dimensionality reduction of convolutional features; by using a max pooling operation with an appropriate stride length, we can reduce the size of the convolutional feature map and expect efficient computation as well as information aggregation. Another role is deformation compensation. Even if the convolutional features undergo local (i.e., small) spatial translations due to deformations in the input images, the reduced feature maps are invariant to the translations. Consequently, the CNN becomes robust to deformations in the input images.

This paper is motivated by the fact that the deformation compensation ability of the max pooling operation is excessive for actual deformations. Most of the actual deformations are topology-preserving, i.e., spatially continuous within each object region; if a part of an object shifts to a certain direction,

© Springer Nature Switzerland AG 2020
I. Farkaš et al. (Eds.): ICANN 2020, LNCS 12397, pp. 241–254, 2020.
https://doi.org/10.1007/978-3-030-61616-8_20

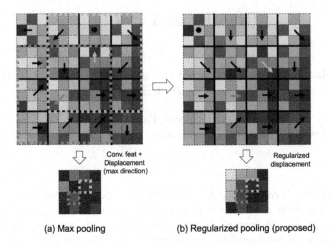

(a) Max pooling   (b) Regularized pooling (proposed)

Fig. 1. (a) Max pooling and (b) our regularized pooling. A darker color indicates a larger feature value. The arrow indicates the relative position of the selected value from the center of the kernel. In (a), the maximum value is determined at each kernel. In (b), the value selections in adjacent kernels are regularized (spatially smoothed) and, consequently, a non-maximum value can be selected. The dotted squares indicate the 3×3 window (i.e., $w = 3$) for smoothing the direction of selection. **Although the stride length is identical to kernel size $n = 3$ in this figure for a simpler illustration, our method can be realized in arbitrary conditions.** (Color figure online)

its neighboring part also shifts to a similar direction. However, since the value selection by max pooling is performed for each kernel independently, it not only compensates for intra-class topology-preserving deformations, but may also "over-compensate" for essential differences between similar classes.

Figure 1(a) illustrates the excessive flexibility of max pooling, where the kernel size n and the stride s are equally set at 3 for a simpler illustration. (In the later experiments, s was often smaller than n.) The arrow on the convolutional feature map shows directions of the maximum value (depicted as the darkest point) from the center of the kernel. The value selection is performed independently at each kernel and therefore the arrows point random directions in the map. If we consider that each arrow represents a local displacement, the arrows work as spatial warping to compensate for the deformations in the map. We can thus understand that these random directions do not fit to continuous deformations. In other words, the flexibility of the max pooling operation is excessive for the actual deformations.

The lower part of Fig. 1(a) shows the result of the max pooling operation. Due to the greedy selection of the maximum value at each kernel, the result of pooling consists mostly of large feature values (i.e., darker colors). However, the original convolutional feature map is not always large; it exhibits a trend that the upper-left side has smaller values and the lower-right side has larger values.

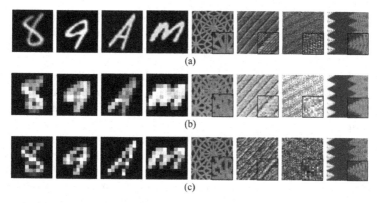

Fig. 2. (a) Original image and its results for (b) max pooling and (c) our regularized pooling. Both pooling operations are applied to a channel of the first convolution layer with the kernel size $n = 5$ and the stride $s = 5$. The window size w for the regularization is 3.

The result of max pooling no longer exhibits this trend. This means that max pooling easily overlooks small-valued but important parts and thus might ignore essential differences between similar classes.

Figures 2(a) and (b) show digit and texture images and their results when the max pooling operation is applied to their first convolutional feature map, respectively. The digit images have one or two holes ('8,' '9,' and 'A') or near-hole concave parts ('m'). These hole parts have smaller values and thus nearly disappear by the max pooling operation despite their importance for their discrimination. For example, the max pooling result of '8' might be confused with that of '5' (In fact, this '8' is misrecognized as '5' by a CNN with the max pooling operation). Texture images are composed of coarse and fine structures. Their fine structures are lost by max pooling, whereas the coarse ones are still preserved.

In this paper, we propose a *regularized pooling* operation, where the flexibility of the pooling operation is regularized to fit the characteristics of actual deformations. Figure 1(b) illustrates the proposed regularized pooling operation. The key idea is to smooth the value selection directions in the pooling operation. By taking the average of max value directions in the neighboring kernels in a window (the dotted squares in (a)), a non-maximum value can be selected and then over-compensation is suppressed. Note that, unlike average pooling, this regularization does not affect the feature values themselves; it only affects the selection of the value from the kernel.

Figure 2(c) shows the result of the regularized pooling operation (with the 3×3 window). The holes of digit images and fine structures of texture images are well preserved even after the pooling operations, compared with the max pooling operation (b). We can thus expect that our regularized pooling can avoid over-compensation and thus keep the separability among classes. It should be noted that this property will lead to a stable training process with a faster convergence because it will be possible to avoid local minima due to the over-compensation.

The main contributions of this paper are summarized as follows:

- We propose a regularized pooling operation whose capability in terms of deformation compensation fits the characteristics of actual deformations. To the best of authors' knowledge, this is the first proposal of the regularized pooling operation.
- Since the regularized pooling operation can avoid over-compensation and thus preserve essential inter-class differences, it has positive effects on both the training and testing steps. We experimentally show these effects; our regularized pooling operation accelerates the training step (i.e., provides quick convergence) and improves the recognition accuracy, especially by avoiding confusion between similar classes, such as '7' and '9' and 'a' and 'e.' In a qualitative study, we also observed that the proposed method can preserve important inter-class differences.
- We investigate when the proposed method is superior to max pooling using different datasets such as handwritten character image datasets and a texture image dataset. The experiment with texture images also shows the structure preservation capability of the regularized pooling operation.

2   Related Work

In recent years, many researchers have focused on pooling operations to improve the performance of deep learning-based architectures [5,7,12]. Pooling operations can reduce the dimension of the input features and render them to invariant to small shifts and deformations [17]. However, the spatial information lost in the traditional pooling layers causes problems that limit the learning capability of deep neural networks [4,16].

2.1   Traditional Pooling Operations

To handle the problems in the traditional pooling operations, many methods have been proposed to extend or improve them in different ways [8,14,24–26]. To solve the problems that the MP2-pooling (2×2 max pooling) reduces the size of the hidden layers quickly and the disjointed nature of the regions of pooling can limit generalization, Graham [8] proposed fractional max pooling (FMP) to reduce the size of the image by a factor of α with $1 < \alpha < 2$. Zhai et al. [26] proposed S3Pool, which extends standard max pooling by decomposing pooling into two steps: max pooling with stride one and a non-deterministic spatial downsampling step by randomly sampling rows and columns from a feature map. They observed that this general stochasticity acts as a strong regularizer, and can also be seen as performing implicit data augmentation by introducing distortions to the feature maps. To regularize CNN-based architectures, Yu et al. [25] proposed mixed pooling that was inspired by the random dropout [11] and DropConnect [23] methods. Similarly, Wei *et al.* [24] proposed an intermediate form between max and average pooling called polynomial pooling (P-pooling) to provide an optimally balanced and self-adjusted pooling strategy for semantic segmentation. To compensate for spatial information lost in the max pooling layer, Zheng *et al.* [28] extracted displacement directions from the max pooling layers and combined them with the original max pooling features to capture structural deformations in text recognition tasks.

2.2 Recent Pooling Operations

Considering the limitations of traditional pooling methods, many pooling operations and layers have recently been proposed to address problems in traditional pooling methods pertaining to specific applications such as image detection and classification [6,9,13,21], handwriting and text recognition [8,20,28], semantic segmentation [2,10,24], and other challenging computer vision tasks [1,19,21,27]. He *et al.* [9] introduced a spatial pyramid pooling (SPP) layer to remove the fixed-size constraint on the network, thereby making the network robust to object deformation. Kobayashi [13] proposed a trainable local pooling function guided by global features beyond local ones. The parameterized pooling form is derived from a probabilistic perspective to flexibly represent various types of pooling, and the parameters are estimated by using statistics of the input feature map. More recently, Gao *et al.* [6] proposed Local Importance-based Pooling (LIP) that can automatically enhance discriminative features during the downsampling procedure by learning adaptive importance weights based on the inputs. LIP solved the problem that the traditional downsampling layers can prevent discriminative details from being well preserved, which is crucial for the recognition and detection tasks.

Compared with prevalent pooling operations, the proposed regularized pooling considers spatial information and regulates the directions of pooling to be homogenized around the neighboring kernels. The advantage of the proposed method is that it compensates for deformations when the neighboring parts shift to random directions. In this way, the proposed method becomes more effective than conventional pooling methods at accelerating convergence.

3 Regularized Pooling

Figure 3 shows an overview of regularized pooling. Regularized pooling takes a convolutional feature map as its input and outputs a new feature map. Although the outline of the calculation is similar to that of max pooling, the main difference is that the direction to the maximum value in a kernel, called the displacement direction, is extracted and then revised by the displacement directions at the neighboring kernels.

Specifically, the displacement direction is first extracted from the input feature map by the max pooling operation. Assume that we can conduct the max pooling operations I times vertically and J times horizontally by

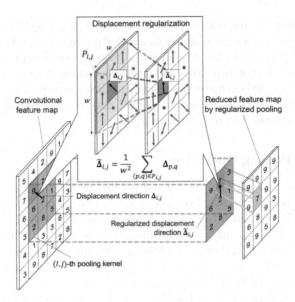

Fig. 3. Overview of the regularized pooling operation, where the pooling kernel size $n = 3$, smoothing window size $w = 3$, and stride $s = 1$. The direction from the center of the kernel to the maximum value, called the displacement direction $\Delta_{i,j}$, is first calculated for the (i,j)-th kernel. For example, in the red area of the figure, the direction from '2' to '9' is treated as the displacement direction $\Delta_{i,j}$. Displacement directions for the entire feature map are then regularized via smoothing. As shown in the blue area, the averaged displacement directions around the target pixel is treated as the regularized displacement direction $\widetilde{\Delta}_{i,j}$. Finally, the reduced feature map is calculated by extracting the pixel value in the kernel indicated by the direction of the regularized displacement direction. (Color figure online)

sliding an $n \times n$ kernel with the stride s^1. For the (i,j)-th pooling kernel ($i \in \{1,\ldots,I\}, j \in \{1,\ldots,J\}$), the displacement direction $\Delta_{i,j}$ is defined as the direction from the center of the kernel to the maximum value. The possible value for the element of $\Delta_{i,j}$, $(\Delta_{i,j})_k$ ($k = 1,2$), depends on the parity of n. For an odd n, $(\Delta_{i,j})_k \in \{-\frac{n-1}{2},\ldots,-1,0,1,\ldots,\frac{n-1}{2}\}$, whereas $(\Delta_{i,j})_k \in \{-\frac{n}{2},\ldots,-1,1,\ldots,\frac{n}{2}\}$ for an even n. The displacement directions are then regularized by considering the adjacent displacement directions. The regularization is based on spatial smoothing of the displacement directions. The regularized displacement direction $\widetilde{\Delta}_{i,j}$ is calculated as follows:

$$\widetilde{\Delta}_{i,j} = \frac{1}{w^2} \sum_{(p,q)\in P_{ij}} \Delta_{p,q}, \tag{1}$$

---

[1] To be specific, given a convolutional feature map of size $H \times W$ as input, $I = \lfloor (H-1)/s \rfloor + 1$ and $J = \lfloor (W-1)/s \rfloor + 1$ if we add a proper size of padding to the input.

where the odd integer w is the size of the smoothing window and $P_{ij} = \{\boldsymbol{\Delta}_{p,q} | p \in \{i - \frac{w-1}{2}, \ldots, i + \frac{w-1}{2}\}, q \in \{j - \frac{w-1}{2}, \ldots, j + \frac{w-1}{2}\}\}$. Finally, the output feature map is generated by using the regularized displacement directions. The pixel value in the (i, j)-th kernel indicated by the regularized displacement direction $\widetilde{\boldsymbol{\Delta}}_{i,j}$ is extracted as the (i, j)-th value of the reduced feature map.

Note that $\widetilde{\boldsymbol{\Delta}}_{i,j}$ can be a non-integer vector due to the smoothing in Eq. (1) while it should be an integer vector for the acquisition of a reduced feature map. Therefore, we quantize $\widetilde{\boldsymbol{\Delta}}_{i,j}$ if it is a non-integer. For an odd n, the element of $\widetilde{\boldsymbol{\Delta}}_{i,j}$ is rounded to the nearest integer[2]. For an even n, the element is rounded away from zero, so as not to be zero.

4   Experiment on Character Images

We first assessed the effectiveness of the regularized pooling operation by comparing it with traditional pooling operations. In particular, we verified that regularized pooling improves the convergence speed of learning through a comparison of performance profiles. Second, we qualitatively show that regularized pooling reduces the dimensionality of the input feature map while preserving detailed structures via example-based evaluation. Finally, we evaluate the effects of the kernel size, smoothing window size, and stride, which are important hyperparameters of regularized pooling.

4.1   Dataset

We evaluated our regularized pooling on two standard benchmark datasets of handwritten character images, MNIST [18] and EMNIST [3]. Character images often undergo various and severe deformations; however, those deformations are still continuous and topology-preserving so as not to spoil inter-class differences. Therefore, character images are the most suitable for understanding the characteristics of the proposed regularized pooling operation. MNIST is comprised of 28×28 handwritten digit images and split to $60,000$ training samples and $10,000$ test samples. EMNIST is comprised of uppercase and lowercase English alphabet letters with 37 classes (after several identifications between indistinguishable classes, such as 'o' and 'O') and $88,800$ for training and $14,800$ for test.

4.2   Experimental Setup

The network architecture used in this experiment is summarized in Table 1. In the table, "conv, 3×3, 64" represents a convolutional layer with a 3×3-sized 64-channel kernel. This network was based on VGG [22] with some convolutional blocks and fully connected layers removed to fit the network to the size of the input image. Two convolutional layers with a ReLU activation function were

---

[2] If the fraction part is exactly 0.5, it is rounded away from zero.

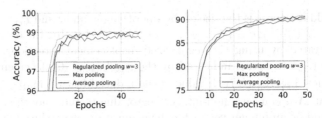

Fig. 4. Comparison of performance profiles among regularized pooling, max pooling, and average pooling on the MNIST (left) and EMNIST (right) datasets.

cascaded as a block, and a pooling layer was connected after the convolutional block. After repeating this convolutional and pooling connection three times, a fully-connected (FC) layer with a softmax activation was connected as the last layer. Dropout with a ratio of 0.25 was used for the last FC layer. Regularized pooling was applied to the first pooling layer. For comparison, we used max pooling and average pooling.

In all experiments, we calculated the average of five trials by changing the initial weights of the network when computing classification accuracy. To clarify the effect of pooling, all images were resized to 60×60. Zero-padding was not used in any pooling operation. We used the SGD optimizer for weight updating. The learning rate was 10^{-2} for MNIST and 10^{-4} for EMNIST. The number of learning epochs and the batch size were set to 50 and 100, respectively. We employed cross entropy as a loss function.

4.3 Performance Comparison with Traditional Pooling Methods

Figure 4 shows the comparison of performance profiles among regularized pooling, max pooling, and average pooling on the test datasets of MNIST and EMNIST. In this figure, the pooling kernel size n, smoothing window size w, and stride were set to $n = 5$, $w = 3$, and $s = 5$, respectively. Note that every line shows the average of five trials by changing the initial weights of the network.

These results confirmed that the learning convergence of regularized pooling is faster than those of max pooling and average pooling. Compared to max pooling, our regularized pooling could suppress the excessive deformation compensations and thus could avoid local minima due to them, especially the early training stages, when the feature values tend to have random-like values and the deformation compensation ability of max pooling is abused. Examples that support the above hypotheses are provided in the next subsection.

It is also very important that regularized pooling is better than average pooling. Regularized pooling still keeps important (large) feature values compared to average pooling. This is because feature values themselves are smoothed by average pooling, whereas they are not smoothed by our regularized pooling— regularized pooling just smooths the selection direction.

Table 1. Network architecture

Name	Output	Layer
conv1	60 × 60	conv, 3 × 3, 64
		conv, 3 × 3, 64
pool1	12 × 12	**regularized pool**, $n \times n$, or
		max pool, $n \times n$, or
		average pool, $n \times n$
conv2		conv, 3 × 3, 128
		conv, 3 × 3, 128
pool2	6 × 6	max pool, 2 × 2
conv3		conv, 3 × 3, 256
		conv, 3 × 3, 256
pool3	3 × 3	max pool, 2 × 2
FC	3 × 3	FC + softmax

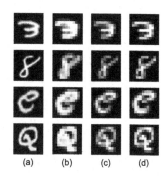

(a)   (b)   (c)   (d)

Fig. 5. Visualization of the feature maps after the pooling operation. (a) Original feature map. (b) Max pooling. (c) Average pooling. (d) Regularized pooling.

4.4   Qualitative Evaluation

We qualitatively evaluated the differences between regularized pooling and traditional pooling methods by visualizing the feature maps after the application of the pooling operations. The visualization examples are shown in Fig. 5. In max pooling, the shapes of the characters collapsed due to over-compensation. For example, the holes of '8' and 'Q' are filled with white pixels. In average pooling, the outlines of the characters are blurred although their shapes are preserved better than by max pooling. This is because average pooling considered the surrounding information by smoothing the feature values directly. Conversely, regularized pooling preserved both the shapes and the outlines of the characters better than max pooling and average pooling because it considers surrounding information by regularizing the deformation features, without directly smoothing the input feature maps.

We verified how the qualitative differences among the pooling methods in the above visualization affected recognition errors. Figure 6 shows the number of misrecognitions between certain class pairs along with the learning epochs. In Figs. 6(a) and 6(b), '7' and '9,' and 'a' and 'e,' are given as the pairs whose structural differences are subtle, i.e., confusing pairs. In addition, Figs. 6(c) and 6(d) show the misrecognitions between the pairs of '2' and '7,' and 'C' and 'O,' where there are clear structural differences in the handwritten images, i.e., easy pairs. For the confusing pairs, regularized pooling reduced misrecognitions compared with max pooling and average pooling, whereas there was no remarkable difference among the three pooling methods for the easy pairs. These results show that regularized pooling preserves the detailed structure of the input feature map by suppressing over-compensations and thus effectively distinguishes between class pairs with subtle structural differences.

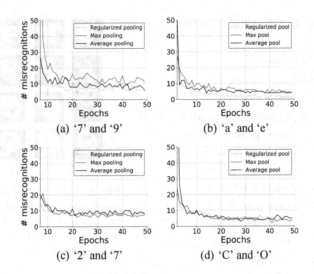

Fig. 6. The number of misrecognitions between specific class pairs. (a) and (b) are confusing pairs, and (c) and (d) are easy pairs.

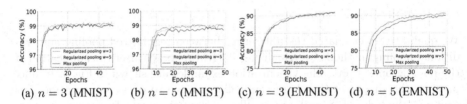

Fig. 7. Effects of the pooling kernel size n and smoothing window size w.

4.5   Effect of Hyperparameters

We evaluated the effect of the hyperparameters, i.e., the pooling kernel size n, smoothing window size w, and stride s. Figure 7 shows the performance profiles when n and w were varied to $n = 3$ and 5 and $w = 3$ and 5. The results by max pooling are also shown for comparison. These results suggest that the effect of n on the results is more significant than w. Moreover, the difference between regularized pooling and max pooling was clearer when n was larger. This is because the larger the value of n was, the stronger the effect of over-compensation due to max pooling was, whereas regularized pooling suppressed it.

The effect of the stride s is shown in Fig. 8. This figure summarizes the performance profiles of regularized pooling and max pooling on the MNIST dataset while s was varied to $s = 2, 3, 4,$ and 5. The result shows that regularized pooling showed faster convergence than max pooling at all s values, while a smaller stride s yielded better performance.

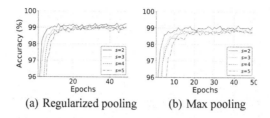

(a) Regularized pooling   (b) Max pooling

Fig. 8. Performance profiles when varying the stride s.

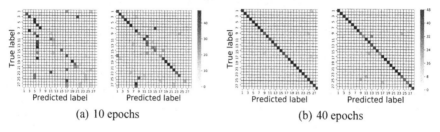

(a) 10 epochs   (b) 40 epochs

Fig. 9. Confusion matrix of texture recognition. Left: max pooling. Right: regularized pooling.

5   Experiment on Texture Images

In this experiment, we aimed to clarify the characteristics of regularized pooling by analyzing the results of classification for texture images with various structures. In particular, we reveal the kind of images for which regularized pooling is effective.

We used the Kylberg texture dataset [15] that contains 28 classes with 160 unique samples each ($112 \times 28 = 5376$ samples for training, $48 \times 28 = 1344$ samples for testing). Each sample is a grayscale image of size 576×576 pixels. We resized all images to 256×256 in the experiment. For weight updating, we used the Adam optimizer with parameters of 10^{-4}, $\beta_1 = 0.9$, and $\beta_2 = 0.99$. The batch size was set to 32. The network architecture and other experimental conditions were the same as in the experiments described in Sect. 4.

Figure 9 shows the confusion matrix on the test set obtained by using max pooling and regularized pooling at 10 and 40 epochs. According to Fig. 9(a), certain classes such as class 6, 19, 20, and 21 are almost completely correctly recognized in the early stage of learning. Example images from the improved classes by regularized pooling are shown in Fig. 10(a). The common feature of these images was that they had a periodic structure. Regularized pooling could retain this periodic structure to some extent and thus show superiority. In Fig. 9(b), however, several classes, such as class 10, 23, 26, and 27, were not correctly recognized by regularized pooling, even at the 40 epoch. Example images from these classes are shown in Fig. 10(b), and it can be seen that they are near-random patterns without any specific periodicity, i.e., no clear structure. These results demonstrated that regularized pooling is effective for patterns with a

(a) Improved classes, 6, 19, 20, and 21.

(b) Degraded classes, 10, 23, 26, and 27.

Fig. 10. Examples texture images from the improved and degraded classes.

periodic structure. This is because regularized pooling performs spatially continuous operations between adjacent kernels, and therefore preserves frequency information to some extent in the feature map after pooling.

6   Conclusion

We proposed regularized pooling, which enables a local pooling operation suitable for actual deformations. In the traditional max pooling operation, the value selection direction is determined as the maximum value position at each kernel independently. By considering it as a deformation compensation process, this independent strategy will cause over-compensation. In contrast, our regularized pooling operation smooths the value selection directions over the neighboring kernels to suppress over-compensation and thus stabilizes the training process. Through experiments on image recognition, we demonstrated that regularized pooling improves separability of similar classes and the convergence of learning compared with the conventional pooling methods.

In future work, we will further consider another strategy for smoothing the value selection directions, although we have shown that even simple average-based smoothing is already effective. For example, using an adaptive window size controlled by some spatial and/or channel-wise attention mechanisms will be a possible choice.

Acknowledgments. This work was supported by JSPS KAKENHI Grant Number JP17H06100 and JST ACT-I Grant Number JPMJPR18UO.

References

1. Aich, S., Stavness, I.: Global sum pooling: a generalization trick for object counting with small datasets of large images. In: Proceedings of CVPR Deep Vision Workshop (2019)
2. Bulo, S.R., Neuhold, G., Kontschieder, P.: Loss max-pooling for semantic image segmentation. In: Proceedings of CVPR, pp. 7082–7091 (2017)

3. Cohen, G., Afshar, S., Tapson, J., Van Schaik, A.: EMNIST: extending MNIST to handwritten letters. In: Proceedings of IJCNN, pp. 2921–2926 (2017)
4. Feng, J., Ni, B., Tian, Q., Yan, S.: Geometric l_p-norm feature pooling for image classification. In: Proceedings of CVPR, pp. 2609–2704 (2011)
5. Gao, Y., Beijbom, O., Zhang, N., Darrell, T.: Compact bilinear pooling. In: Proceedings of CVPR, pp. 317–326 (2016)
6. Gao, Z., Wang, L., Wu, G.: LIP: local importance-based pooling. In: Proceedings of ICCV, pp. 3355–3364 (2019)
7. Gong, Y., Wang, L., Guo, R., Lazebnik, S.: Multi-scale orderless pooling of deep convolutional activation features. In: Fleet, D., Pajdla, T., Schiele, B., Tuytelaars, T. (eds.) ECCV 2014. LNCS, vol. 8695, pp. 392–407. Springer, Cham (2014). https://doi.org/10.1007/978-3-319-10584-0_26
8. Graham, B.: Fractional max-pooling. arXiv preprint arXiv:1412.6071 (2014)
9. He, K., Zhang, X., Ren, S., Sun, J.: Spatial pyramid pooling in deep convolutional networks for visual recognition. IEEE Trans. Pattern Anal. Mach. Intell. **37**(9), 1904–1916 (2015)
10. He, Y., Chiu, W.C., Keuper, M., Fritz, M.: STD2P: RGBD semantic segmentation using spatio-temporal data-driven pooling. In: Proceedings of CVPR, pp. 4837–4846 (2017)
11. Hinton, G.E., Srivastava, N., Krizhevsky, A., Sutskever, I., Salakhutdinov, R.R.: Improving neural networks by preventing co-adaptation of feature detectors. arXiv preprint arXiv:1207.0580 (2012)
12. Husain, S.S., Bober, M.: REMAP: multi-layer entropy-guided pooling of dense CNN features for image retrieval. IEEE Trans. Image Process. **28**(10), 5201–5213 (2019)
13. Kobayashi, T.: Global feature guided local pooling. In: Proceedings of ICCV, pp. 3365–3374 (2019)
14. Kumar, A.: Ordinal pooling networks: for preserving information over shrinking feature maps. arXiv preprint arXiv:1804.02702 (2018)
15. Kylberg, G.: The kylberg texture dataset v. 1.0. External report (blue series) 35. Centre for Image Analysis, Swedish University of Agricultural Sciences and Uppsala University, Uppsala, Sweden (2011). http://www.cb.uu.se/~gustaf/texture/
16. Laptev, D., Savinov, N., Buhmann, J.M., Pollefeys, M.: TI-POOLING: transformation-invariant pooling for feature learning in convolutional neural networks. In: Proceedings of CVPR, pp. 289–297 (2016)
17. LeCun, Y., Bengio, Y., Hinton, G.: Deep learning. Nature **521**(7553), 436–444 (2015)
18. LeCun, Y., Bottou, L., Bengio, Y., Haffner, P., et al.: Gradient-based learning applied to document recognition. Proc. IEEE **86**(11), 2278–2324 (1998)
19. Liu, J.J., Hou, Q., Cheng, M.M., Feng, J., Jiang, J.: A simple pooling-based design for real-time salient object detection. In: Proceedings of CVPR, pp. 3917–3926 (2019)
20. Nguyen, D., Lu, S., Tian, S., Ouarti, N., Mokhtari, M.: A pooling based scene text proposal technique for scene text reading in the wild. Pattern Recogn. **87**, 118–129 (2019)
21. Saeedan, F., Weber, N., Goesele, M., Roth, S.: Detail-preserving pooling in deep networks. In: Proceedings of CVPR, pp. 9108–9116 (2018)
22. Simonyan, K., Zisserman, A.: Very deep convolutional networks for large-scale image recognition. In: Proceedings of ICLR (2015)
23. Wan, L., Zeiler, M., Zhang, S., Le Cun, Y., Fergus, R.: Regularization of neural networks using dropconnect. In: Proceedings of ICML, pp. 1058–1066 (2013)

24. Wei, Z., et al.: Building detail-sensitive semantic segmentation networks with polynomial pooling. In: Proceedings of CVPR, pp. 7115–7123 (2019)
25. Yu, D., Wang, H., Chen, P., Wei, Z.: Mixed pooling for convolutional neural networks. In: Miao, D., Pedrycz, W., Ślęzak, D., Peters, G., Hu, Q., Wang, R. (eds.) RSKT 2014. LNCS (LNAI), vol. 8818, pp. 364–375. Springer, Cham (2014). https://doi.org/10.1007/978-3-319-11740-9_34
26. Zhai, S., et al.: S3Pool: pooling with stochastic spatial sampling. In: Proceedings of CVPR, pp. 4970–4978 (2017)
27. Zhang, Y., Tang, S., Muandet, K., Jarvers, C., Neumann, H.: Local temporal bilinear pooling for fine-grained action parsing. In: Proceedings of CVPR, pp. 12005–12015 (2019)
28. Zheng, Y., Iwana, B.K., Uchida, S.: Mining the displacement of max-pooling for text recognition. Pattern Recogn. **93**, 558–569 (2019)

Reinforcement Learning I

Deep Recurrent Deterministic Policy Gradient for Physical Control

Lei Zhang[1], Shuai Han[2,3], Zhiruo Zhang[1], Lefan Li[1], and Shuai Lü[2,3(✉)] (iD)

[1] College of Software, Jilin University, Changchun 130012, China
{zhanglei1317,zhangzr2017,lilf5517}@mails.jlu.edu.cn
[2] College of Computer Science and Technology, Jilin University,
Changchun 130012, China
hanshuai18@mails.jlu.edu.cn, lus@jlu.edu.cn
[3] Key Laboratory of Symbolic Computation and Knowledge Engineering
(Jilin University), Ministry of Education, Changchun 130012, China

Abstract. The observable states play a significant role in Reinforcement Learning (RL), meanwhile, the performance of RL is strongly associated with the quality of inferred hidden states. It is a challenging task to accurately extract hidden states because they are often related to both environment's and agent's histories, and require numerous domain knowledge. In this work, we aim to leverage history information to improve the performance of agent. Firstly, we discuss that the neglect and usual process of history information are harmful to agent's performance. Secondly, we propose a novel model that combines the advantage of both supervised learning and RL. Specifically, we extend the framework of classical policy gradient and propose to extract history information using recurrent neural networks. Thirdly, we evaluate our model in simulated physical control environments, outperforming the state-of-the-art models and performing obviously better on more challenging tasks. Finally, we analyze the reasons and suggest possible approaches to extend and scale up the model.

Keywords: Reinforcement learning · Neural networks · Deep learning

1 Introduction

Reinforcement learning (RL) proposes a formal framework on which an agent depends to learn strategies by interacting with an environment through the gathering of experience [5]. Deep Reinforcement Learning (DRL) has attracted a lot of attention in recent years, since Deep Q-Network (DQN) [18] algorithm was proposed, which surpasses human experts on some popular Atari games. Neural networks, working as high-capacity function approximators, play a significantly important role in the proposal of DRL [17]. In a series of value-based models that are efficient in discrete action spaces, such as DQN, Double DQN [9], Dueling DQN [24], the observation of environment is in the form of frames, which

© Springer Nature Switzerland AG 2020
I. Farkaš et al. (Eds.): ICANN 2020, LNCS 12397, pp. 257–268, 2020.
https://doi.org/10.1007/978-3-030-61616-8_21

directly works as the input of the deep neural networks to represent the current state. It works efficiently in some simple stimulated environments, Atari games, for example. When many challenges are coming from continuous action spaces, however, the method that only one frame is used to infer state has a negative effect on the RL model, limiting the applicability of model-free DRL to real-world tasks.

Consider such a simple situation: when the agent is playing a table tennis competition with a human, it is difficult for the agent to judge whether the ball in the air is approaching to or departing from the agent itself with only one frame information. Therefore, it is necessary to make an observation sequence $(o_1, o_2, \cdots, o_n)$ to be the raw material of the inferred state. Through a particular process, the observation sequence can be transformed into a reliable inferred state, which means that more accurate and useful features of the current state can be extracted.

The most common and easiest approach is to cut an observation sequence in a fixed length and feed the subsequence into normal neural networks, such as linear or convolution network [18]. However, the elder observations and the younger ones usually contribute differently to inferring the current state. It is not the ideal method to treat each observation in sequence equally. To address this issue, some researchers have done a wealth of creative attempts in prior work. A hybrid approach named Recurrent Reinforcement Learning is proposed [14]; it combines recurrent neural networks (RNN) with deep Q-network and obtains a better performance but only in discrete action spaces. Another algorithm called Asynchronous Advantage Actor-Critic (A3C) actually has a Long Short-Term Memory (LSTM) [11] version which also utilizes RNN in their model [17]. Nevertheless, A3C is an on-policy model and has high sample complexity [8]. What's more, it usually runs in parallel which requires a huge computation. Hence, we wondered: *Whether it is possible to propose a model-free and off-policy RL algorithm that can use samples more efficiently?*

The answer is positive. We present a novel model-free RL model, called Deep Recurrent Deterministic policy gradient (DRD), which can robustly solve challenging problems coming from a variety of domains with continuous action spaces. DRD is based on Deep Deterministic Policy Gradient (DDPG) [16], the state-of-the-art Actor-Critic method, and employs an efficient RNN—LSTM to extract features and to infer the current state more effectively and precisely. We show an obvious improvement when it is compared with benchmarks in simulated physical control environments which are widely used in DRL community.

2   Background

In a standard RL setup, there is an agent interacting with an environment E in discrete timesteps, whose aim is to learn reward-maximizing behavior policy. At each timestep t, the agent receives an observation o_t, takes an action a_t and receives a reward r_t as well as a new observation o_{t+1}. In general, the process mentioned above belongs to the Markov Decision Process (MDP) which requires the state s_t rather than the observation o_t. Observation can hardly represent the state of current environment entirely, since it is usually part of the state in real world. In a lot of prior work, it has been assumed that the environment is fully-observed, i.e. $s_t = o_t$. It is obviously illogical and it is the main topic of our work, which will be discussed in next section. But we take the same assumption here in order to introduce the background more clearly.

An agent's behavior is selected through a policy $\pi : S \rightarrow \mathcal{P}(A)$, which maps a state to a probability distribution over the actions. The environment E is probably stochastic. A MDP includes a state space S, an action space A, an initial state distribution $p(s_1)$, transition dynamics $p(s_{t+1}|s_t, a_t)$, and reward function $r(s_t, a_t)$. A t-step interaction history can be written as $h_t = (s_1, a_1, r_1, s_2, \cdots, s_{t-1}, a_{t-1}, r_{t-1}, s_t)$. Since the reward depends on the action, and actually on the policy π, the goal of RL is to find a (near-)optimal policy π to maximize the discounted cumulative reward, $R_t = \sum_{i=t}^{T} \gamma^{(i-t)} r(s_i, a_i)$, for a given discount factor $\gamma \in (0, 1]$, which determines the priority of short-term rewards.

Many RL algorithms use action-value function to describe the expected return after taking an action a_t in state s_t when following a policy π:

$$Q^\pi(s_t, a_t) = \mathbb{E}_\pi[R_t|s_t, a_t] \tag{1}$$

In Q-learning, the action-value function can be learned by using temporal difference learning, an update rule based on the Bellman equation. The Bellman equation describes a fundamental relationship between the value of a state-action pair (s_t, a_t) and the value of the subsequent state-action pair (s_{t+1}, a_{t+1}):

$$Q^\pi(s_t, a_t) = r(s_t, a_t) + \gamma \mathbb{E}_\pi[Q^\pi(s_{t+1}, a_{t+1})] \tag{2}$$

In Deep Q-learning, a neural network is used as a Q-function approximator, $Q(s, a|\theta^Q)$, parameterized by θ^Q. Policy π is defined as greedy policy, $\pi = \max_a Q(s, a)$. Thus, it can be optimized by minimizing the loss:

$$L(\theta^Q) = \mathbb{E}_\pi[(Q^\pi(s_t, a_t|\theta^Q) - y_t)^2] \tag{3}$$

where

$$y_t = r(s_t, a_t) + \gamma Q^\pi(s_{t+1}, \pi(s_{t+1})|\theta^Q) \tag{4}$$

the process of parameters' updates is:

$$\theta^Q \leftarrow \theta^Q + (r(s_t, a_t) + \gamma(Q(s_{t+1}, \pi(s_{t+1})) - Q(s_t, a_t)))\nabla_\theta(Q(s_t, a_t|\theta^Q)) \tag{5}$$

In prior work, Q-learning algorithm combined with neural networks [18] is able to learn to play Atari directly from pixels. It is effective only in discrete action space, because its policy $\pi = \max_a Q(s, a)$ requires to compare the Q value of each action a which is impossible in continuous action spaces. To apply this idea to continuous action spaces, an Actor-Critic framework should be adopted.

In Actor-Critic framework, there are two neural networks playing as actor and critic respectively. The policy $\pi(s|\theta^\pi)$, known as the actor, selects a specific

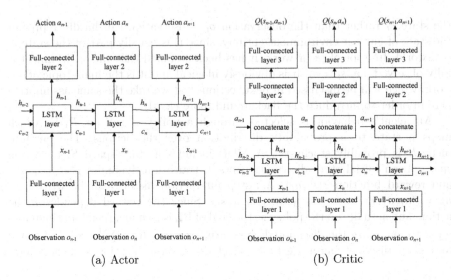

(a) Actor   (b) Critic

Fig. 1. The architecture of our model

action for each state deterministically, i.e. $\pi : S \to A$. The critic $Q(s, a|\theta^Q)$ is learned by using the Bellman equation as in Deep Q-learning. The actor is updated by taking the gradient of the $Q(s, \pi(a)|\theta^Q)$ of the critic. It is known as the deterministic policy gradient (DPG) algorithm [21]:

$$\nabla_{\theta^\pi}\pi = \mathbb{E}_\pi[\nabla_{a_t}Q(s_t, a_t|\theta^Q)\nabla_{\theta^\pi}\pi(s_t|\theta^\pi)] \tag{6}$$

3   Model

As mentioned above, single observation cannot indicate state entirely. We employ LSTM in both actor and critic so as to infer current state from observation sequence more comprehensively (see Fig. 1).

- In actor model, a fixed length observation sequence firstly enters a full-connected layer to increase their dimension and then the LSTM component extracts the current state features from the sequence. Finally, the following full-connected layer works as a policy and maps the state to the specific action.
- In critic model, the first two steps are the same as the actor's, the third step is to concatenate action and state features, and the Q-function approximator outputs the Q value according to the action and state.

In neural network training, a simple heuristic that rescaling gradient which enters the LSTM layer by $1/\sqrt{2}$ is utilized to mildly increase stability. Besides, gradients are clipped to make sure their norm less than or equal to 10, which is common in RNN training but not in DRL [1].

Neural networks are not all of DRL and many effective technologies have been widely used to address some typical RL problems, such as the inefficient use of data and the lack of exploration. We also add some effective technologies into our model to response to these problems:

1) An experience replay buffer the same as that in DQN [18] is used to break the samples' correlation, which exists because the samples are generated when agent explores sequentially in an environment. The samples which are randomly sampled from replay buffer can meet theoretical assumption of RL. Therefore, the agent can become more robust.

2) Like [18], we utilize a pair of target network $\pi^*(s|\theta^{\pi^*})$ and $Q^*(s, a|\theta^{Q^*})$ to improve the stability of learning. They are the copy of the actor and critic respectively in the beginning, and their weights are updated by some proportion τ at each timestep $\theta^* \leftarrow \tau\theta + (1 - \tau)\theta^*$, with $\tau \ll 1$. The Eq. 4 turns:

$$y_t = r(s_t, a_t) + \gamma Q^*(s_{t+1}, \pi^*(s_{t+1})) \tag{7}$$

where the actions are selected from a target actor network π^*, and expected Q values are computed from a target critic network $Q^*(s|\theta^{Q^*})$.

3) Inspired by DDPG [16], a noise process is adopted to balance exploration and learning. A noise sampled from a noise distribution is added to the action selected by actor.

$$a = \pi(s) + \mathcal{N} \tag{8}$$

where $\mathcal{N}$ has a lot of versions, Gaussian distribution, for example. The noise process adopted in our experiments is Ornstein-Uhlenbeck process, since it can provide efficient exploration in physical control problems with inertia.

As summarized in Algorithm 1, a general flow of the DRD algorithm proceeds as follow: two pairs of actor and critic networks are initialized with random parameters at first, and the target pair networks' parameters are the copy of the original pair. A replay buffer R implemented with a first-in-first-out queue is empty before training. In each episode, a random process $\mathcal{N}$ is also initialized in the beginning. At $1st$ timestep, the state s_1 is a list of n elements whose first $n - 1$ are all zero vectors and the last is the initial observation vector o_1 of the environment. Actor network selects an action a_1 according to the state s_1, and the action a_1 added with noise is executed by the agent. A reward r and a new observation vector o_2 can be obtained after action a_1. A new state s_2 is generated through removing the first element of previous state and adding o_2 at last. The tuple (s_1, a_1, r_1, s_2) is so-called experience which is stored in R. When R has enough experiences, a batch of experiences are sampled from it randomly, and the original networks are updated according to Eqs. 3, 6 and 7. After the updates of original networks, target networks are also updated softly. From $1st$ timestep to max timestep T, the agent interaction and networks update are repeated at each step. Not requiring any more knowledge about environment except for the

---

Algorithm 1. DRD Algorithm

1: Initialize critic network $Q(s, a|\theta^Q)$ and actor $\pi(s|\theta^\pi)$ with random parameters θ^Q and θ^π
2: Initialize target network Q^* and π^* with weights $\theta^{Q^*} \leftarrow \theta^Q$, $\theta^{\pi^*} \leftarrow \theta^\pi$
3: Initialize replay buffer R
4: **for** *episode* = 1 to M **do**
5:     Initialize a random process $\mathcal{N}$ for action exploration
6:     Receive initial observation state $s_1 = (0, 0, ..., 0, o_1)$
7:     **for** $t = 1$ to T **do**
8:         Select action $a_t = \pi(s_t|\theta^\pi) + \mathcal{N}_t$ according to the current policy and exploration noise
9:         Execute action a_t, receive reward r_t and new observation o_{t+1}, and get new state $s_{t+1} = (o_{t-n+2}, o_{t-n+1}, ..., o_t, o_{t+1})$
10:        Store transition (s_t, a_t, r_t, s_{t+1}) in R
11:        Sample a random mini-batch of N transitions (s_i, a_i, r_i, s_{i+1}) from R
12:        $y_i = r(s_i, a_i) + \gamma Q^*(s_{i+1}, \pi^*(s_{i+1}))$
13:        Update actor by using the sampled gradient:

$$\nabla_{\theta^\pi} \pi|_{s_i} \approx \frac{1}{N} \sum_{i=1}^{N} \nabla_a Q(s_i, \pi(s_i|\theta^\pi)|\theta^Q) \nabla_{\theta^\pi} \pi(s_i|\theta^\pi)$$

14:        Update critic by minimizing the loss: $L = \frac{1}{N} \sum_{i=1}^{N} (Q(s_i, a_i) - y_i)^2$
15:        Update the target networks:

$$\theta^{Q^*} \leftarrow \tau\theta^Q + (1 - \tau)\theta^{Q^*}$$

$$\theta^{\pi^*} \leftarrow \tau\theta^\pi + (1 - \tau)\theta^{\pi^*}$$

16:    **end for**
17: **end for**

---

shape of observation and action, it is a model-free RL algorithm consequently. Though it requires higher computation, the current environment state which has a significant impact on agent's performance can be inferred more accurately. Besides, with the experience buffer, data is utilized efficiently.

4   Results

To evaluate our model DRD[1], we measured its performance in simulated physical environments that contain various continuous control tasks using MuJoCo [22], interfaced through OpenAI Gym [2]. MuJoCo is a fast and accurate physics engine where the observation of the robots includes joint angles, joint velocities, the coordinates of the center of mass and others, and the controls are joint torques. It is designed for physical control optimization and has been a common and effective environment which is cited by a lot of the state-of-the-art policy

---

[1] Code available at https://github.com/cheunglei/drd.

gradient algorithms, such as DDPG [16], PPO [20], TRPO [19], and ACKTR [25]. The details of tasks in our evaluation are summarized in Table 1. Figure 2 is the screenshot of tasks. dim(a) is the number of action dimensions, and dim(o) is the number of observation dimensions. With the exception of InvertedPendulum and InvertedDoublePendulum, the goals of other tasks are to move forward as quickly as possible. Because of much higher degrees of freedom, these tasks are more challenging than the basic ones. Besides, excessive controls and falling over will be penalized. The episode is terminated when the z-coordinate of the body or the forward pitch of the body beyond a specific range [4].

Table 1. Descriptions of MuJoCo tasks

Task name	dim(a)	dim(o)	Brief description
HalfCheetah	6	17	The half-cheetah is a planar biped robot with 9 rigid links, including two legs and a torso, along with 6 actuated joints
Hopper	3	11	A planar monopod robot with a torso, a upper leg, a lower leg, and a foot is required to move through hopping
HumanoidStandup	17	376	The humanoid robot which has head, body, arms, and legs is required to stand up as soon as possible
InvertedPendulum	1	4	An inverted pendulum is mounted on a pivot point on a cart. Applying continuous horizontal forces on cart to make it move but keeping the pendulum upright
InvertedDoublePendulum	1	11	Extends the InvertedPendulum task by replacing the single-link pole by a two-link rigid structure. It makes the system more unstable so it is much more difficult
Walker2d	6	17	The walker is a planar biped robot with two legs and a torso. It is required to walk without falling

For our DRD, we use a linear network layer of 200 hidden nodes and a LSTM network layer of 300 hidden nodes respectively, with rectified linear units (ReLU) between layers for both the actor and critic, and a tanh unit following the output of the actor. However, the critic has one more layer of 400 hidden nodes to combine the state with the action. Both actor and critic network parameters are updated using Adam [13] at a learning rate of 10^{-3}. After each 100 rollout

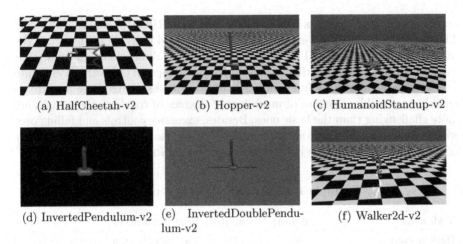

(a) HalfCheetah-v2   (b) Hopper-v2   (c) HumanoidStandup-v2

(d) InvertedPendulum-v2   (e) InvertedDoublePendu-   (f) Walker2d-v2
lum-v2

Fig. 2. Screenshot of MuJoCo environments

steps, the networks are trained with a mini-batch of a 64 transitions for 50 steps, which are sampled uniformly from a replay buffer containing the entire history of the agent. Note that the intersecting parameters owned by DDPG and our model are kept the same so as to eliminate the effects of parameter differences.

To diminish the influence of the initial parameters of the policy, we use a purely exploratory policy for the first 10,000 timesteps, except InvertedPendulum and InvertedDoublePendulum in which only for 2,000 timesteps. The capacity of replay buffer is 1 million timesteps, which means that all timesteps are stored to improve diversity of samples. The action noise process is Ornstein-Uhlenbeck process with $\theta = 0.15$, $\sigma = 0.3$, $dt = 10^{-2}$. Both target networks are updated with $\tau = 10^{-2}$ at each training step.

Each task is run for 1 million timesteps with evaluations every 2,000 timesteps, where each evaluation reports the average reward over 5 episodes with no exploration noise. Our results are collected over 5 random seeds of the network initialization and the Gym simulator.

We compare our algorithm against DDPG [16] as implemented by PyTorch according to the paper, as well as the state-of-the-art policy gradient algorithms ACKTR [25] and TRPO [19] implemented by OpenAI's baselines repository [3]. The learning curves are presented in Fig. 3 and results are summarized in Table 2. The shaded region represents half a standard deviation of the average evaluation over 5 trials. For visual clarity, they are smoothed uniformly. DRD matches or outperforms all other algorithms in final performance across all tasks.

When both the number of action dimensions and the number of observation dimensions are relatively larger, e.g. HalfCheetah, HumanoidStandup and Walker2d, our DRD performs better more obviously. There is no doubt that more observation information can lead to more specific state information, however, other algorithms are lack of the ability to effectively exploit observations while our DRD is expert here. Meanwhile, more action dimensions means more

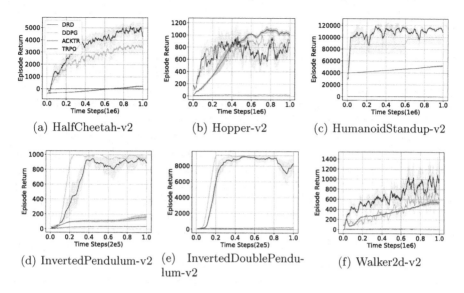

(a) HalfCheetah-v2   (b) Hopper-v2   (c) HumanoidStandup-v2

(d) InvertedPendulum-v2 (e) InvertedDoublePendu-   (f) Walker2d-v2
                              lum-v2

Fig. 3. Learning curves in some environments of MuJoCo

complex control strategy which is a challenge to different RL models, thus it can reflect the capability of different models more clearly. Our model is more suitable for those environments which are relatively more complex and have more state information. It is worth-noting that TRPO doesn't perform well in our experiments which adapt MuJoCo tasks version 2, although it matches ACKTR in MuJoCo tasks version 1 [6]. We can conclude that TRPO does not have a excellent adaptability to environment like our and other models.

Although in simple tasks, i.e. InvertedPendulum and InvertedDoublePendulum, the learning speed of DRD is affected slightly, the final results of those tasks almost do not decrease, which can be seen as a normal fluctuation. We believe the reason why its learning speed declines is that DRD considers history observations too much at the beginning of the trainings and it takes some time for DRD to adjust its weights of history and current observations.

Table 2. Max average return over 5 trials of 1 million timesteps ± standard deviation over trials

Task name	DDPG [16]	ACKTR [25]	TRPO [19]	DRD
HalfCheetah	4254.89	234.93	23.52	**5715.50 ± 569.71**
Hopper	1330.33	1096.6	20.36	**1666.48 ± 797.37**
HumanoidStandup	97374.80	52140.0	63.48	**128693.02 ± 10554.02**
InvertedPendulum	**1000.00**	161.3	34.24	1000.0 ± 0.0
InvertedDoublePendulum	**9358.93**	214.6	20.30	9350.54 ± 3.87
Walker2d	1425.33	553.2	17.98	**1711.03 ± 867.87**

5   Related Work

Network architecture is critical in DRL. By exploiting the feature extraction capabilities of deep neural networks (DNNs) to deal with high-dimensional state spaces, the combination of DNN with RL handles several major obstacles that hindered classical RL [7]. "How to take advantage of the advancement of DNN to strengthen DRL performance" is a hot topic in RL community.

Li et al. [14] proposed a hybrid approach that combines the strength of RNN with DQN to solve a customer relationship management task, where inferring a whole state is challenging while RNN is efficient. In order to acquire long-term profits in the dynamic financial markets, Li et al. [15] utilized the Stacked Denoising Auto Encoders (SDAEs) and LSTM as parts of the function approximator on a novel trading agent, which demonstrates significant improvement over the baselines. Being able to address the shortcomings that the agent relies on complete game screen to make each decision, Deep Recurrent Q-Network (DRQN) [10] not only seamlessly integrates information through time and replicates DQN's performance on standard Atari games through partial observations but also shows scaling performance as the observability increases.

Based on the conclusion that RNN can support meta-learning in a fully supervised context, Deep Meta-Reinforcement Learning is suggested by Wang et al. [23]. Its key concept is, to train a RNN which can implement its own, free-standing RL procedure through using normal DRL. As they illustrate, the RL procedure learned in secondary owns an adaptiveness and sample efficiency that the original RL procedure lacks.

We believe that our framework can be easily combined with other RL technologies such as distributed reinforcement learning or prioritized experience replay, because Recurrent Replay Distributed DQN (R2D2) [12] successfully trains recurrent RL agents built upon prioritized distributed replay. R2D2 becomes the first agent to exceed human-level performance in 52 of the 57 Atari games and matches the state-of-the-art on DMLab-30. Therefore, an evaluation of the distributed version of DRD is left for future work.

6   Conclusion

In this work, we focus on how to accurately infer hidden states through history sequence of observation. We prove that the neglect and usual process of history information will harm the agent's performance. We propose a novel model which combines the capability of LSTM to extract features from a sequence with the strength of the Actor-Critic framework to learn an optimal policy efficiently to extends DRL model in continuous action space domain. The experiments we conducted show an obvious improvement on the baseline. The analysis of results is consistent with the principle and intuition. Besides, figuring out relationship between the performance of DRD and the length of history sequence could be a part of future work.

Acknowledgments. This work was supported by the National Natural Science Foundation of China under Grant Nos. 61300049, 61763003; the National Key R&D Program of China under Grant No. 2017YFB1003103; and the Natural Science Research Foundation of Jilin Province of China under Grant Nos. 20180101053JC, 20190201193JC.

References

1. Bengio, Y., Boulanger-Lewandowski, N., Pascanu, R.: Advances in optimizing recurrent networks. In: 2013 IEEE International Conference on Acoustics, Speech and Signal Processing, pp. 8624–8628 (2013)
2. Brockman, G., et al.: OpenAI gym (2016). http://arxiv.org/abs/1606.01540
3. Dhariwal, P., et al.: OpenAI baselines (2017). https://github.com/openai/baselines
4. Duan, Y., Chen, X., Houthooft, R., Schulman, J., Abbeel, P.: Benchmarking deep reinforcement learning for continuous control. In: International Conference on Machine Learning, pp. 1329–1338 (2016)
5. François-Lavet, V., Henderson, P., Islam, R., Bellemare, M.G., Pineau, J., et al.: An introduction to deep reinforcement learning. Found. Trends Mach. Learn. **11**(3–4), 219–354 (2018)
6. Fujimoto, S., Hoof, H., Meger, D.: Addressing function approximation error in actor-critic methods. In: International Conference on Machine Learning, pp. 1582–1591 (2018)
7. Garnier, P., Viquerat, J., Rabault, J., Larcher, A., Kuhnle, A., Hachem, E.: A review on deep reinforcement learning for fluid mechanics (2019). http://arxiv.org/abs/1908.04127
8. Haarnoja, T., Zhou, A., Abbeel, P., Levine, S.: Soft actor-critic: off-policy maximum entropy deep reinforcement learning with a stochastic actor. In: International Conference on Machine Learning, pp. 1856–1865 (2018)
9. van Hasselt, H., Guez, A., Silver, D.: Deep reinforcement learning with double Q-learning. In: AAAI Conference on Artificial Intelligence, pp. 2094–2100 (2016)
10. Hausknecht, M.J., Stone, P.: Deep recurrent Q-learning for partially observable MDPs. In: 2015 AAAI Fall Symposia, pp. 29–37 (2015). http://www.aaai.org/ocs/index.php/FSS/FSS15/paper/view/11673
11. Hochreiter, S., Schmidhuber, J.: Long short-term memory. Neural Comput. **9**(8), 1735–1780 (1997)
12. Kapturowski, S., Ostrovski, G., Quan, J., Munos, R., Dabney, W.: Recurrent experience replay in distributed reinforcement learning. In: International Conference on Learning Representations (2019)
13. Kingma, D.P., Ba, J.: Adam: a method for stochastic optimization. In: International Conference on Learning Representations (2015)
14. Li, X., et al.: Recurrent reinforcement learning: a hybrid approach (2015). http://arxiv.org/abs/1509.03044
15. Li, Y., Zheng, W., Zheng, Z.: Deep robust reinforcement learning for practical algorithmic trading. IEEE Access **7**, 108014–108022 (2019)
16. Lillicrap, T.P., et al.: Continuous control with deep reinforcement learning. In: International Conference on Learning Representations (2016)
17. Mnih, V., et al.: Asynchronous methods for deep reinforcement learning. In: International Conference on Machine Learning, pp. 1928–1937 (2016)
18. Mnih, V., et al.: Human-level control through deep reinforcement learning. Nature **518**(7540), 529 (2015)

19. Schulman, J., Levine, S., Abbeel, P., Jordan, M., Moritz, P.: Trust region policy optimization. In: International Conference on Machine Learning, pp. 1889–1897 (2015)
20. Schulman, J., Wolski, F., Dhariwal, P., Radford, A., Klimov, O.: Proximal policy optimization algorithms (2017). http://arxiv.org/abs/1707.06347
21. Silver, D., Lever, G., Heess, N., Degris, T., Wierstra, D., Riedmiller, M.: Deterministic policy gradient algorithms. In: International Conference on Machine Learning, pp. 387–395 (2014)
22. Todorov, E., Erez, T., Tassa, Y.: MuJoCo: a physics engine for model-based control. In: 2012 IEEE/RSJ International Conference on Intelligent Robots and Systems, pp. 5026–5033 (2012)
23. Wang, J.X., et al.: Learning to reinforcement learn (2016). http://arxiv.org/abs/1611.05763
24. Wang, Z., Schaul, T., Hessel, M., Hasselt, H., Lanctot, M., Freitas, N.: Dueling network architectures for deep reinforcement learning. In: International Conference on Machine Learning, pp. 1995–2003 (2016)
25. Wu, Y., Mansimov, E., Grosse, R.B., Liao, S., Ba, J.: Scalable trust-region method for deep reinforcement learning using kronecker-factored approximation. In: Advances in Neural Information Processing Systems, pp. 5279–5288 (2017)

Exploration via Progress-Driven Intrinsic Rewards

Nicolas Bougie[1,2(✉)] and Ryutaro Ichise[2,1]

[1] The Graduate University for Advanced Studies, Sokendai, Tokyo, Japan
{nicolas-bougie,ichise}@nii.ac.jp
[2] National Institute of Informatics, Tokyo, Japan

Abstract. Traditional exploration methods in reinforcement learning rely on well-designed extrinsic rewards. However, many real-world scenarios involve sparse or delayed rewards. One solution inspired by curious behaviors in animals is to let the agent develop its own intrinsic rewards. In this paper we propose a novel end-to-end curiosity mechanism which uses learning progress as novelty bonus. We compare a policy-based and a visual-based progress bonus to move the agent towards hard-to-learn regions of the state space. We further leverage the agent's learning to identify the most critical regions, which results in more sample-efficient and global exploration strategies. We evaluate our method on a variety of benchmark environments, including Minigrid, Super Mario Bros., and Atari games. Experimental results show that our method outperforms prior approaches in most tasks in terms of exploration efficiency and average scores, especially for those featuring high-level exploration patterns or with deceptive rewards.

Keywords: Reinforcement learning · Exploration · Curiosity in reinforcement learning · Autonomous exploration

1 Introduction

Reinforcement learning (RL) provides a formalism for learning policies by interacting with an environment. Traditionally, it aims to learn an optimal policy that maximizes cumulative extrinsic rewards; it may be the distance to the goal or specifically designed for the task. Its combination with deep neural networks as function approximators has been used to obtain exciting results in environments with rich sensory inputs, complex goals, and challenging dynamics. Despite recent successes in a range of complex tasks such as Atari games [15] and robot control [12], it remains an open problem how to apply RL to environments with poorly-defined, sparse or deceptive rewards. To discover efficient exploration strategies, multiple heuristics such as entropy regularization [14] were introduced but did not yield significant improvements in sparse reward tasks.

Following similar behaviors of animals, one solution to this problem is to let the agent discover skills that will be useful later (i.e. curiosity-driven learning).

© Springer Nature Switzerland AG 2020
I. Farkaš et al. (Eds.): ICANN 2020, LNCS 12397, pp. 269–281, 2020.
https://doi.org/10.1007/978-3-030-61616-8_22

A number of curiosity measurement strategies have been proposed such as count-based exploration [17] or the use of information gain [8]. Some other approaches generate a bonus based on the inability to predict the future [18]; but tend to attract the agent to states with stochastic transitions due to hardly predictable environmental dynamics. Another line of work aims to predict the features of a fixed random neural network on the observation of the agent [3]. However, capturing complex visual features remains challenging. In spite of their ability to deal with local exploration and capture the consequences of short-term decisions, they tend to get stuck in local optima and can be computationally expensive. Furthermore, when using prediction errors as an intrinsic reward, the intrinsic reward may vanish quickly with additional visitations.

In this paper, we introduce a novel definition of curiosity that considers the agent's learning progress on a multi-step horizon as exploration bonus. To quantify the agent's learning progress in terms of "quantity" and "quality", we propose to measure the divergence between a parametric model (i.e. the current model) and prior models. We postulate that rewarding hard-to-learn regions of the state space is crucial to efficiently explore. By doing so, it drives the agent to seek more knowledge about such regions. A key idea in our work is to deal with high-level exploration by measuring progress on a multi-steps horizon scale. This allows us to overcome the known "vanishing curiosity" issues of prior work that use the absolute prediction error to guide exploration - curiosity rewards soon exhaust as the prediction becomes perfect or does not improve. To further improve the benefits of our method, we introduce a mechanism called *episodic-skills* to direct the focus on hard-to-learn regions/skills. In other words, we let the agent discover which skills are important in the environment and encourage the visits of states carrying information about them.

We benchmark our approach on a set of hard exploration tasks from Minigrid, Super Mario Bros., and Atari games. We compare our method with state-of-the-art curiosity methods. The experimental results show that our agent can escape from local optima in sparse or deceptive reward environments, to learn comparable or superior policies in most of the tasks. Results also demonstrate that progress-driven exploration is crucial in tasks with high-level exploration patterns and that our agent explores faster as compared to other techniques.

2 Related Work

Our method is related to *encouraging exploration* in RL. Most techniques can be grouped into three classes: goal-based, count-based, and curiosity-based exploration.

Goal conditioned learning [9] constructs a goal-conditioned policy to push the agent to acquire new skills and explore novel states. Namely, they optimize average reward with respect to a goal distribution. Universal value function approximators [20] samples a fixed goal at the beginning of each episode and rewards the agent when the current goal can be achieved. Nonetheless, selecting relevant goals remains an open problem. A solution [5] and its recent follow-up [16], proposed to generate increasingly difficult goals to drive the agent towards the final goal.

Another group of works keeps visit counts for states to favor exploration of rarely visited states [13]. To extend count-based exploration to continuous state spaces, a solution [17] is to train an observation density model to supply counts. Another technique [23] is to discretize the states by hashing and then apply a simple count-based strategy. However, one can expect these methods to be less effective when some *valuable* states require more attention - more visits.

This work belongs to the category of approaches that consider curiosity as exploration bonus. A method [18] relies on predicting environment dynamics using an inverse or a forward dynamic model. Another work uses prediction error in the feature space as a measure of the importance of states [3]. The exploration can also be motivated by introducing a new term in the loss function that measures state diversity [7]. In contrast, our work aims to learn intrinsic rewards by measuring the agent's learning progress. The crucial difference here, however, is that rather than simply estimating diversity, we measure the quantity and quality of the learning progress. Exploration bonus can also be based on maximizing information gain about the agent's knowledge of the environment [8]. Another work [6] guides exploration by maximizing an entropy objective. Episodic curiosity through reachability [19] uses the number of time-steps between two states as curiosity measure. Nonetheless, one problem with these approaches is that the curiosity exhausts quickly during training. Moreover, dealing only with local novelty makes it likely for agents to get stuck in undesirable local optima. In our paper, we introduce long-time horizon learning progress to overcome these pitfalls.

3   Method

We consider an agent performing actions in an environment. In this work we focus on tasks where extrinsic rewards provided by the environment are sparse or delayed - zero for most of the time steps. At each time step t, the agent collects an observation s_t, samples an action a_t from a set of actions A following a policy $\pi_{\theta_P}(s_t)$, and then receives an extrinsic reward r_t^e. We augment the task reward with an intrinsic exploration bonus r_t^i, $r_t = \alpha r_t^e + \beta r_t^i$, where α and β are hyperparameters to weight the importance of both rewards. The policy $\pi_{\theta_P}(s_t)$ is represented by a deep neural network and its parameters θ_P are optimized to maximize the sum of these two rewards, $\max_{\theta_P} \mathbb{E}_{\pi_{\theta_P}}[\sum_t r_t]$.

Our main contribution is a novel intrinsic reward based on the agent's learning progress. Since learning progress is non stationary, it is useful to normalize it by diving the original intrinsic reward by a running estimate of the standard deviations of the intrinsic rewards $\bar{R}_{ib}$. We can assign a curiosity bonus via:

$$r_t^i = \left[\frac{\bar{r}_t^i}{\sigma(\bar{R}_{ib})} \right] \tag{1}$$

where $\bar{r}_t^i$ is the progress-driven reward before normalization.

In the following section we present the key components of our progress-driven curiosity reward.

3.1   Progress-Driven Exploration

Progress-driven exploration is a method to motivate the agent to explore hard-
to-learn regions of the state space and develop novel strategies to escape local
optima induced by poorly defined or deceptive extrinsic rewards. To this end, we
aim to measure the agent's progress during training. We assume a parametric
model that given the current state s_t outputs a probability distribution which
can be interpreted as the *agent's knowledge* of s_t. In this work, we compare two
models: policy-based progress, and representation-based progress. We propose as
intrinsic motivation to measure the distance between the current distribution and
prior distributions. Concretely, we measure learning progress in terms of *quantity*
and *quality*. To deal with global exploration, i.e. exploring the consequences of
long-term decisions, we further propose to estimate progress at different time-
scales on a batch of observations.

This process drives the agent to gather unseen observations which would
maximize long-time horizon learning progress, while encouraging the revisit of
hard-to-learn state trajectories. Moreover, using progress instead of absolute prediction errors allows us to overcome the known "vanishing curiosity" shortcoming. Our exploration bonus remains large independently of the number of visits,
by adapting curiosity based on the agent's understanding of the world. In the
next section, we detail how is calculated the intrinsic reward for the *policy-based*
and the *representation-based* model.

Policy-Based Progress (PoBP). The policy-based progress model (PoBP)
works as follows. The agent fills an observation memory with the latest observations. At every time step, we estimate the probability distributions over actions
associated with the agent's policy and a set of recent policies for each observation. Given those distributions, we evaluate the agent's learning progress (along
the state trajectory stored in the memory) by measuring the distance between
the current policy and prior policies. Then we produce an intrinsic bonus to promote effective exploration strategies, based on learning progress. We describe
more details of each step below.

Let's consider a policy $\bar{\pi}_\theta(a|s)$ which quantifies the importance of an action
a in a state s. We first define the probability distribution over actions:

$$\pi_\theta(a|s) = \frac{e^{\bar{\pi}_\theta(a|s)}}{\sum_{z \in A} e^{\bar{\pi}_\theta(z|s)}} \tag{2}$$

Please note that this step is only performed when the policy does not estimate
a probability distribution over actions given a state. With a slight abuse of
notation, we refer to the probabilistic policy as π_θ.

We assume a batch $\Psi = \{s_1, ..., s_N\}$ of the N most recent observations and Ω
a set of M prior policies. To fill Ω, every K time steps we substitute the oldest
policy in memory with the current policy. By doing so, we can measure the
agent's learning progress at different time-scales. Note that at the beginning of
each episode the memory Ψ is empty. Policy-based progress can now be estimated

as the average distance between the current policy and previous policies over batch of observations:

$$\bar{r}_t^i = \frac{1}{|\Psi|} \sum_{s \in \Psi} \frac{1}{|\Omega|+1} \left[\sum_{\theta_{old} \in \Omega} [\eta D(\pi_{\theta_{old}}(s) || \pi_{uni}(s)) + \nu D(\pi_{\theta_{old}}(s) || \pi_\theta(s))] + \gamma D(\pi_\theta(s) || \pi_{uni}(s)) \right]$$

(3)

where π_θ is the current policy, $\pi_{\theta_{old}}$ refers to a prior policy, D is a distance function, π_{uni} is a fixed *uniform* policy - the probability distribution over the actions is uniform, and η, ν, γ are hyperparameters of our method. The first term, $D(\pi_{\theta_{old}}(s) || \pi_{uni}(s))$, measures the learning progress *quality* of prior policy $\pi_{\theta_{old}}$ - it encourages the policy to be as distant as possible to the uniform distribution, which quantifies whether some actions are certainly better than others. The second term, $D(\pi_{\theta_{old}}(s) || \pi_\theta(s))$ measures the *quantity* of learning progress; it is expressed in the distance between the current policy and a prior policy. The third term, $D(\pi_\theta(s) || \pi_{uni}(s))$, is the quality of the current policy.

The distance function D can be any distance measure such as KL-divergence or euclidean distance. Theoretically, the KL divergence would be a robust choice. We define the Kullback-Leibler (KL) divergence between two policies as:

$$D_{KL}(\pi(s) || \pi'(s)) = \sum_{a \in A} \pi(a|s) \log(\frac{\pi(a|s)}{\pi'(a|s)})$$

(4)

Although KL measure performs well in many tasks, performance can degrade in some environments with deceptive rewards. In such environments, encountering negative rewards can greatly deteriorate the quality of the learned policy, occasionally causing instability in the training phase. Instead, we propose to embrace the Jensen-Shannon (JS) divergence. We extend it to calculate the distance between two policies as the following:

$$D_{JS}(\pi(s) || \pi'(s)) = \frac{1}{2} D_{KL}(\pi(s) || \pi^*(s)) + \frac{1}{2} D_{KL}(\pi'(s) || \pi^*(s))$$

(5)

where $\pi^*(s) = \frac{1}{2}(\pi(s) + \pi'(s))$. We compare in Sect. 4.2 the impact of using KL-divergence or JS-divergence on our method.

Representation-Based (ReBP). The reconstruction-based model (ReBP) assesses learning progress based on the agent's understanding of the visual features of its environment. Instead of using the probability distribution over actions, we seek to measure the agent's progress to reconstruct the observations. This approach is motivated by the idea that, to accurately reconstruct a region of the state space, the agent needs to acquire good knowledge about the environment's dynamics and objects, by interacting with them (without the need to learn or model dynamics).

To do so, we propose to measure the quality of a variational autoencoder (VAE) [11] for encoding the latent representations in the data. We assume that an observation s of an agent is generated by a random latent process z. Learning

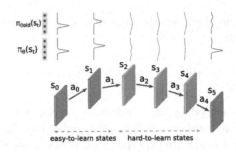

Fig. 1. Illustration of the idea of episodic skills. Some states (in green) should be given more weight because they are hard-to-learn. (Color figure online)

progress can be estimated by measuring the distance between the posterior distribution $p(z|s)$ after experiencing new observation and the prior $p(z)$. Several measures such as KL divergence can be used. However, computing the posterior distribution $p(z|s)$ is often intractable. Instead, we use a VAE with encoder parameters ϕ to model the approximate posterior distribution $q_\phi(z|s)$.

Formally, let $\Psi = \{s_1, ..., s_N\}$ be a set of observations and Ω a set of prior VAEs. Similarly to PoBP, every K time steps the oldest VAE is substituted with the current version. For online training of the VAE, we store the experience and make 5 epochs of training every 50,000 steps. We express the intrinsic reward as:

$$\bar{r}^i_t = \frac{1}{|\Psi|} \sum_{s \in \Psi} \frac{1}{|\Omega|+1} \left[\sum_{\phi_{old} \in \Omega} [\eta D_{KL}(q_{\phi_{old}}(z|s)\|p(z)) + \upsilon D_{KL}(q_{\phi_{old}}(z|s)\|q_\phi(z|s))] + \gamma D_{KL}(q_\phi(z|s)\|p(z)) \right] \tag{6}$$

As a result, the agent seeks out states as diverse as possible and in doing so increases the distance between $q_\phi(z|s)$ and $p(z)$ in average - agent's learning quality. In practice, $p(z)$ is specified as a standard normal distribution. On the other hand, it also favors to revisit state trajectories where the agent can improve its understanding by maximizing the distance (progress) between the current VAE $q_\phi(z|s)$ and prior VAE $q_{\phi_{old}}(z|s)$.

3.2 Episodic Skills

When performing informed exploration, we observed that 1) some states may need more attention because they are hard-to-learn or more task-relevant, 2) high-level exploration requires to balance the loss of easy immediate reward [3]. We propose a simple mechanism relying on an episodic memory to address all of these issues at once (Fig. 1). We call a "skill", sk, a sequence of T observations (i.e. a specific region of the state-space). In the absence of domain knowledge, a general-purpose choice is to set $T = N$. The key insight is to prioritize the agent's learning of important skills, which entails that they should be given more weight. Therefore, visiting a state should trigger a positive intrinsic reward not only because it is locally informative (i.e. progress along the current trajectory), but also because it is informative about previously encountered hard-to-learn skills. That is, visiting such a state enables progress in other skills.

Episodic Memory. The episodic memory stores a set of important skills $\{sk_1 : (s_1, .., s_T), ..., sk_C : (s_1, .., s_T)\}$ where s_1 is the initial state of the skill and s_T is the final state. It has a limited capacity of size C. We define an embedding function, later used to efficiently compare or measure a distance in the episodic memory. We can embed an observation s to a latent space, $\varphi(s)$. When employing *policy-based* progress, we use the representation extracted after passing the input through the sequence of convolutional layers of the policy network, whereas for *visual-based* progress, we use the mean of the VAE's encoder as the state encoding. Intuitively, we extend the above definition to skill embedding, $\varphi(sk) = (\varphi(s_1), .., \varphi(s_T))$.

Reward Calculation. During intrinsic reward calculation, we compute an exploration bonus independently for each skill sk, similarly to the *policy-based* or *representation-based* method. To avoid unstable behaviors, we weight each skill reward, $\bar{r}^i_{sk}$, as being proportional to the similarity with the current observation, s_t. This approach is justified by the common sense that progress on distant states is unlikely to be related to the exploration of the current state. The sum of the weighted bonus of each skill is added to the intrinsic reward:

$$\bar{r}^i_t += \mathbb{E}_{sk \sim M} \left[\alpha_{sk} \bar{r}^i_{sk} \right] \tag{7}$$

where α_{sk} is the similarity between $\varphi(s_t)$ and $\varphi(sk)$. In this work, we use the average pairwise cosine distance as similarity measure.

Memory Update. At the end of the episode, to decide if a skill should be added in memory, we first measure if the skill novelty is larger than a threshold $t_{novelty}$. Rather than operating directly in the state space, we utilize the cosine distance on skill embeddings to perform this check. This induces a discretization of the embedding space which guarantees to store skills as diverse as possible. Then, hard-to-learn skills are added to the memory if the bonus $\bar{r}^i_{sk}$ is less than t_{hl}. As a result, this process keeps skills for which the agent has poor knowledge and made little progress. When the capacity is exceeded we randomly substitute a skill with the new skill.

4 Experiments

In this section, we first evaluate our method trained on a fixed and randomly generated environments from the Minigrid [4] domain. Second, we compare *progress-driven exploration* against standard RL and intrinsic reward-based approaches on five Atari 2600 games [1] as well as Super Mario Bros [10], combining intrinsic rewards with sparse or deceptive extrinsic rewards. Third, we test the proposed method in the absence of any exploration bonus on Super Mario Bros. Finally, we provide an ablation study on Montezuma Revenge [1].

As our policy learning method, we use PPO with similar hyperparameters as in the original implementation of RND [3]. The input is passed through three

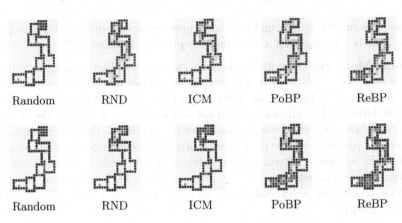

Fig. 2. State visitation heatmaps averaged over 10 runs for different models: random, RND, ICM, PPO+PoBP, and PPO+ReBP. The models are trained for 40 m frames on a fixed maze (top row) and on randomly generated mazes (bottom row) in Multi-RoomN10.

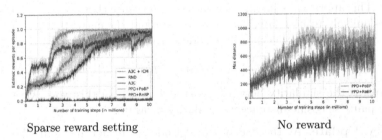

Fig. 3. Average extrinsic reward obtained with sparse reward setting (left) and maximum distance achieved with no extrinsic reward (right) in the Super Mario Bros environment. We run every algorithm with a repeat of 10 and show all runs. Mean and standard error of the mean over trials are plotted.

convolutional layers (for Minigrid) or four (other domains). We estimate learning progress on a batch of states of size $N = 6$ over $M = 4$ prior models. We utilize an episodic memory of capacity 15, and $t_{novelty} = 0.10$ (Minigrid) or $t_{novelty} = 0.25$. The frequency update K of the prior model buffer, Ψ, is set to 50,000. The value of η, ν, γ is 1.0,0.8,0.2 respectively for PoBP, and 1.0,1.0,0.2 for ReBP. If not specified differently, we employ the JS-divergence (Eq. 5) to measure the divergence between two policies. To combine r_t^e and r_t^i, we set the coefficient of extrinsic reward $\alpha = 2$, and $\beta = 1$.

4.1 Fixed Versus Randomly Generated Environments

To investigate the ability of our agent to learn from randomly generated environments and generalize to unseen appearances, we trained the models on a fixed maze and on randomly generated mazes from the MultiRoomN10 (Fig. 2) [4].

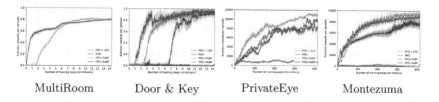

MultiRoom   Door & Key   PrivateEye   Montezuma

Fig. 4. Reward as a function of training step for a variety of hard exploration tasks. We run every algorithm with a repeat of 10.

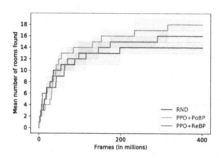

Fig. 5. Number of rooms found during the exploration phase in Montezuma's Revenge. We run every method 10 times.

Note that the maze used for the evaluation of the methods was fixed. It consists of a board divided into several rooms. To reach the final goal (red square), it requires to discover rooms and open doors. The environment is challenging due to its sparsity - the agent only receives a positive reward (+1) when it reaches the final goal. The observations are given in the form of grayscale images of size 84×84 of the visible cells surrounding the agent.

We compare PPO+PoBP and PPO+ReBP with three baselines: random agent, RND [3], and ICM [18]. A random policy can only explore the first room. We observe that ICM fails to efficiently explore the environments in both scenarios. While RND is able to solve the fixed maze task, it struggles in randomly generated mazes. On the other hand, our methods could learn efficient strategies to discover all the rooms. This suggests that progress-driven exploration allows generalization across the environments and is more robust to changes in randomly generated mazes.

4.2 Exploration with Sparse Extrinsic Rewards

We now report results in three sparse domains including Super Mario Bros (Fig. 3a), Minigrid (MultiRoom-N10-S4, Door & Key 16×16), and Atari games (Fig. 4). We observe that the gap between our approach and the others is increasing with the degree of sparsity. On Montezuma's revenge PPO+PoBP achieves state of the art performance. It is likely caused by its ability to discover more rooms than RND model (Fig. 5). Furthermore, when environments do not

Table 1. Mean score of our method and baselines on Atari games. We report the results achieved over total 600M timesteps of training, averaged over 10 seeds.

Method	Maximum Mean Score (at convergence)				
	Montezuma's Revenge	Private Eye	Gravitar	Pitfall	Seaquest
A2C [14]	22	650	2, 452	−25	1, 525
PPO [21]	2, 475	98	3, 438	−41	1, 785
RND [3]	8, 654	9, 026	4, 621	−2	3, 280
PPO+EC [19]	7, 022	6, 254	3, 521	−20	**3,485**
PPO+ICM [18]	554	773	4, 784	−13	2, 865
PPO+GoCu [2]	9, 123	10, 223	550	−2	2, 055
DeepCS [22]	3, 500	1, 105	881	−186	3, 343
Average Human [24]	4, 753	69, 571	3351	6, 464	20, 182
PPO+PoBP(KL-divergence)	**9,478**	10, 876	**5,112**	−1	2, 874
PPO+PoBP(JS-divergence)	9, 125	**11,124**	5, 069	**109**	2, 958
PPO+ReBP	8, 934	8, 598	4, 915	0	3, 165

involve complex dynamics such as Minigrid, representation-based models can quickly achieve high-performance, whereas on more challenging games, policy-based models outperform other approaches. Please note that PPO+PoBP(KL-divergence) is less ideal than PPO+PoBP(JS-divergence) in tasks with deceptive rewards. It might be related to the fact that the former is more affected by a deterioration of the policy. In other tasks, the choice of distance measure has a limited impact on the performance.

Next, we further consider more exploration bonus as baselines. We conduct experiments on tasks featuring complex control dynamics, sparse extrinsic rewards, or deceptive rewards. We selected five hard exploration Atari 2600 games [1]: Montezuma's Revenge, Private Eye, Gravitar, Pitfall, and Seaquest. In these games, a poor exploration strategy often results in a suboptimal policy - local optima. The results are shown in Table 1. In 4 out 5 games, our agents consistently exceed the performance of baselines techniques. Moreover, on Montezuma's Revenge and Gravitar, they could surpass average human performance as well as the previous state of the art. We observe that on Pitfall most algorithms fail to find any positive rewards, which entails that they cannot reinforce their policy. On the other hand, by using policy-based learning progress combined with JS-divergence, PPO+PoBP could achieve a positive score. On Seaquest our model's performance is comparable to that of the state of the art.

4.3   No Extrinsic Reward

For testing the good exploration coverage of our method, we trained our agent without any extrinsic reward from the environment. Our agent only receives a curiosity-based signal to reinforce its policy. We evaluate our approach in the Super Mario Bros environment [10]. Initially, this game is played using a joystick which requires pressing simultaneously multiple buttons. In our implementation, each combination of buttons is mapped to a unique action resulting in 12 pos-

Table 2. Reward in Montezuma's revenge with varying batch size N. Averages over 10 trials are reported after 600M steps of training.

Method	Maximum Mean Score (at convergence)					
	$N=2$	$N=6$	$N=8$	$N=10$	$N=15$	$N=20$
PPO+PoBP (KL-divergence)	7.553	9,478	9.521	8.620	5.231	5.787
PPO+PoBP (JS-divergence)	6.542	9,125	9.024	6.785	4.023	4.008
PPO+ReBP	6.989	9,125	7.568	5.874	2.210	2.087

Table 3. Score in Montezuma's revenge using different number of prior models M. Averages over 10 runs are shown after 600M steps.

Method	Maximum Mean Score (at convergence)				
	$M=2$	$M=3$	$M=4$	$M=6$	$M=8$
PPO+PoBP (KL-divergence)	7,254	8,452	9,478	8,767	3,571
PPO+PoBP (JS-divergence)	7,642	9,250	9,125	7,187	2,028
PPO+ReBP	6,988	7,125	8,934	6,245	3,698

sible actions. As can be seen in Fig. 3b, in order to remain curious the agent is pushed to explore distant regions of the state space, which entails that the overall state coverage increases over time. It highlights that in the absence of extrinsic rewards, our method provides indirect supervision for learning useful behaviors.

4.4 Ablation Study

Batch Size of Observations. Our technique relies on batch of last observations. One legitimate question is to study the impact of the batch size, N, on the performance of the algorithm. We conduct a study with N varying between 2 and 20. As shown in Table 2, when using $N = 6$ both models (PoBP, ReBP) can achieve high scores. We observed that *progress-driven exploration's* performance is reasonably robust to the choice of N, as long as $N \leq 8$. We can draw the observation that increasing N contributes positively to the capturing of global progress, by providing more information about the current observation.

Number of Prior Models. We report experiments showing the effect of increased number of prior models, M. Table 3 shows that agents trained with a larger number of prior models obtain higher mean returns after similar numbers of updates. On the other hand, when more than 6 prior policies are used, it tends to make progress-driven exploration unstable. We hypothesize that when using a large number of prior models, progress scores of the oldest models are much larger and therefore saturate the intrinsic rewards. The experimental results show that M = 4 is a reasonable choice in most domains.

5 Conclusion

In this paper, we present a new intrinsic reward formulation that encourages the exploration of hard-to-learn regions, based on the learning progress measured on the divergence of models. We compare a policy-based model with a representation-based model to evaluate progress. This enables us to overcome the known "vanishing curiosity" problem of prior work. Further benefits stem from giving more attention to important skills. We demonstrated the effectiveness of our approach and compared it against a number of baselines on Minigrid, Super Mario Bros., and Atari games. As a future work, we would like to use the current learning progress to drive exploration in new tasks in a few-shot style.

References

1. Bellemare, M.G., Naddaf, Y., Veness, J., Bowling, M.: The arcade learning environment: an evaluation platform for general agents. JAIR **47**, 253–279 (2013)
2. Bougie, N., Ichise, R.: Skill-based curiosity for intrinsically motivated reinforcement learning. Mach. Learn. **109**(3), 493–512 (2019). https://doi.org/10.1007/s10994-019-05845-8
3. Burda, Y., Edwards, H., Storkey, A., Klimov, O.: Exploration by random network distillation. arXiv preprint:1810.12894 (2018)
4. Chevalier-Boisvert, M., Willems, L., Pal, S.: Minimalistic gridworld environment for openAI gym (2018). https://github.com/maximecb/gym-minigrid
5. Florensa, C., Held, D., Geng, X., Abbeel, P.: Automatic goal generation for reinforcement learning agents. arXiv preprint:1705.06366 (2017)
6. Haarnoja, T., Zhou, A., Abbeel, P., Levine, S.: Soft actor-critic: off-policy maximum entropy deep reinforcement learning with a stochastic actor. arXiv preprint:1801.01290 (2018)
7. Hong, Z.W., Shann, T.Y., Su, S.Y., Chang, Y.H., Fu, T.J., Lee, C.Y.: Diversity-driven exploration strategy for deep reinforcement learning. In: NIPS (2018)
8. Houthooft, R., Chen, X., Duan, Y., Schulman, J., De Turck, F., Abbeel, P.: Variational information maximizing exploration. In: NIPS, pp. 1109–1117 (2016)
9. Kaelbling, L.P.: Learning to achieve goals. In: IJCAI, pp. 1094–1098 (1993)
10. Kauten, C.: Super mario bros for openAI gym. https://github.com/Kautenja/gym-super-mario-bros (2018)
11. Kingma, D.P., Welling, M.: Auto-encoding variational Bayes. In: ICLR (2014)
12. Lillicrap, T.P., et al.: Continuous control with deep reinforcement learning. arXiv preprint:1509.02971 (2015)
13. Machado, M., Bellemare, M., Bowling, M.: Count-based exploration with the successor representation. arXiv preprint:1807.11622 (2018)
14. Mnih, V., et al.: Asynchronous methods for DRL. In: ICML, pp. 1928–1937 (2016)
15. Mnih, V., et al.: Human-level control through deep reinforcement learning. Nature **518**(7540), 529 (2015)
16. Nair, A.V., Pong, V., Dalal, M., Bahl, S., Lin, S., Levine, S.: Visual reinforcement learning with imagined goals. In: ICML, pp. 9191–9200 (2018)
17. Ostrovski, G., Bellemare, M.G., van den Oord, A., Munos, R.: Count-based exploration with neural density models. In: ICML, pp. 2721–2730 (2017)
18. Pathak, D., Agrawal, P., Efros, A.A., Darrell, T.: Curiosity-driven exploration by self-supervised prediction. In: ICML (2017)
19. Savinov, N., et al.: Episodic curiosity through reachability. In: ICLR (2019)
20. Schaul, T., Horgan, D., Gregor, K., Silver, D.: Universal value function approximators. In: Proceedings of the International conference on Machine Learning (2015)
21. Schulman, J., Wolski, F., Dhariwal, P., Radford, A., Klimov, O.: Proximal policy optimization algorithms. arXiv preprint:1707.06347 (2017)

22. Stanton, C., Clune, J.: Deep curiosity search: intra-life exploration improves performance on challenging deep reinforcement learning problems. In: ICML (2019)
23. Tang, H., et al.: Exploration: a study of count-based exploration for deep reinforcement learning. In: NIPS, pp. 2753–2762 (2017)
24. Wang, Z., Schaul, T., Hessel, M., Van Hasselt, H., Lanctot, M., De Freitas, N.: Dueling network architectures for deep reinforcement learning. In: ICML (2016)

An Improved Reinforcement Learning Based Heuristic Dynamic Programming Algorithm for Model-Free Optimal Control

Jia Li, Zhaolin Yuan, and Xiaojuan Ban[✉]

Artificial Intelligence and 3D Visualization Lab,
University of Science and Technology Beijing, Beijing, China
banxj@ustb.edu.cn

Abstract. For complicated processing industrial area, model-free adaptive control in data-driven schema is a classic problem. This paper proposes an improved reinforcement learning (RL) based heuristic dynamic programming algorithm for optimal tracking control in industrial system. The proposed method designs a double neural networks framework and employs a gradient-based optimization schema to present the optimal control law. Inspired by the experience replay buffer in deep RL learning, historical system trajectories in short-term are also considered in the training phase which achieves the stabilization of network learning. An experimental study based on an simulated industrial device shows that the proposed method is superior to other algorithms in terms of time consumption and control accuracy.

Keywords: Heuristic dynamic programming · Optimal tracking control · Model-free · Reinforcement learning

1 Introduction

In modern complex process industrial production, optimizing control performance indicators is the primary task of different control algorithms and control systems. Due to the non-linear, multi-variable, and high-delay characteristics of most industrial machine, it is difficult for operators to maintain a stable target value. Deviation of target values will cause product quality degradation and increase industrial production costs. Research on the optimization control of industrial process control has been a hot issue in the industrial and academic circles. For industrial machine with clear mechanical structures and accurate dynamic models, model-based optimization control methods can be used, such as: real-time optimization (RTO) [1], model predictive control (MPC) [2] etc. However, there are some systems with complicated mechanical structures and difficult to observe some variables. Therefore, model-based methods are not suitable for the control of such complex industrial machine. Researchers have proposed data-driven control methods to control such model-free industrial machine.

© Springer Nature Switzerland AG 2020
I. Farkaš et al. (Eds.): ICANN 2020, LNCS 12397, pp. 282–294, 2020.
https://doi.org/10.1007/978-3-030-61616-8_23

Dai et al. [3] proposed a data driven optimization (DDO) control algorithm to solve the control problem of hematite grinding system. Wang et al. [4] used a data-driven adaptive evaluation method to solve the infinite range robust optimal control problem for continuous-time unknown nonlinear systems.

In recent years, great progress has been made in the use of adaptive dynamic programming (ADP) methods to solve industrial process control problems. Wei et al. [5] transformed the optimal tracking control of the coal gasification process into a two person zero-sum optimal control problem, and used an iterative ADP method to solve the problem. Jiang et al. [6] used the Interleaved Learning Policy Iteration (ILPL) to realize the optimization of the operation index of the flotation process, and obtained more than the traditional value iteration (VI), policy iteration (PI) algorithm for better control effect. Jiang et al. [7] combined RL with lifting technology to achieve optimal control of the dual-rate system at the machine and operation layers of the flotation process.

The above algorithms use the real-time data generated by the controlled system to train the neural network. This training method ignores the impact of historical trajectory data generated by the system on model learning in a short period of time. And on-line control of machine in industrial scenarios has high requirements on the real-time performance of the algorithm. The above methods rely on the neural network that represents the control strategy for the calculation of the control amount, and the training of the control network or action network will cause a large time overhead. In order to solve the above problems, this paper introduces the short-term experience replay technology [8,9] to train on the short-term system running track data. Experiments show that this technology effectively enhances the convergence stability of the algorithm and is universal in other ADP-based online control algorithms. At the same time, an iterative gradient optimization algorithm is proposed in this paper, which can solve the control input amount without an action network. Experiments show that this method can improve the control accuracy and reduce the time consumption in the model learning process.

The main contributions of this article are summarized as follows:

- A heuristic critic network value iteration (HCNVI) based on the ADP algorithm architecture is proposed. This algorithm can solve the optimal control input of the system only through evaluation network, model network and gradient optimization algorithm.
- A short-term experience playback technique suitable for critic network training is proposed. When training the evaluation network, the short-term system trajectory data is used together for model training. This method can effectively enhance the evaluation network convergence speed.
- The effectiveness of the HCNVI algorithm is verified by simulation experiments. The experimental results show that the proposed method is superior to other comparison methods in terms of time consumption and control accuracy.

2   HCNVI Algorithm for Online Control

For complex industrial systems, the primary goal of control is to make the target control value $\mathbf{y}(k)$ track its set point $\mathbf{y}^*(k)$ under control value $\mathbf{u}(k)$ and external noise $c(k)$. In addition, in order to ensure the safety of the industrial machine, the control inputs must meet certain restrictions. Based on the above index factors, the control problem of the system can be transformed into a constraint optimization Eq. (1),

$$\min_{u(k)} \quad J(k) = \sum_{l=k}^{\infty} \gamma^{l-k} U(k) \tag{1}$$
$$s.t. \quad \begin{array}{l} \mathbf{y}(k+1) = f(\mathbf{y}(k), \mathbf{u}(k), c(k)) \\ u_{i\,min} \le u_i(k) \le u_{i\,max}, i = 1, 2 \end{array}$$

$$U(k) = Q\left(\mathbf{y}(k) - \mathbf{y}^*(k)\right)^2 + \left(\mathbf{u}(k) - \frac{\mathbf{u}_{mid}}{2}\right)^T R\left(\mathbf{u}(k) - \frac{\mathbf{u}_{mid}}{2}\right) \tag{2}$$

$f(\cdot)$ is an unknown nonlinear function. $J(k)$ is a function of cumulative evaluation value of discount, which is used to evaluate the quality of the control strategy. Equation (2) is the utility function, which represents the utility to execute the control input $\mathbf{u}(k)$ in the current state $\mathbf{y}(k)$. $\gamma \in (0, 1]$ is a discount factor, which represents the proportion of the penalty value generated in the short-term control of the system in the cumulative penalty term. $Q > 0$, R is a symmetric positive definite matrix. $\mathbf{u}_{i\,min}$ and $\mathbf{u}_{i\,max}$ respectively represent the restrictions on $\mathbf{u}_i(k)$, $\mathbf{u}_{mid} = \frac{\mathbf{u}_{max} + \mathbf{u}_{min}}{2}$.

2.1   Theoretical Optimal Control Model

In this subsection, according to the definition of Eq. (1), the optimal control input $\mathbf{u}^*(k)$ under ideal conditions is solved. Equation (1) can be expressed in the form of the Bellman equation of Eq. (3),

$$J(k) = U(k) + \gamma \sum_{l=k+1}^{\infty} \gamma^{l-k-1} U(l) \tag{3}$$
$$= U(k) + \gamma J(k+1)$$

According to the Bellman optimal principle, the optimal evaluation function $J^*(k)$ at the k-th time satisfies the discrete Hamilton-Jacobi-Bellman equation,

$$J^*(k) = \min_{u_k} \{U(k) + \gamma J^*(k+1)\} \tag{4}$$

At the k-th time, the optimal control input $\mathbf{u}^*(k)$ can be expressed as follows,

$$u^*(k) = \arg\min_{u_k} \{U(k) + \gamma J^*(k+1)\} \tag{5}$$

Since $f(\cdot)$ in Eq. (1) is a complex nonlinear function, Eq. (4) cannot be solved directly, but Algorithm 1 can be used to solve the optimal value function and optimal control law in an iterative manner of value function, where $\boldsymbol{x}(k)$ is used to characterize the state of the system, $\boldsymbol{x}(k) = \left[\mathbf{y}(k), \boldsymbol{c}(k)^{\mathrm{T}}\right]^{\mathrm{T}}$. According to literature [10], it can be proved that when $i \to \infty$, the value function $V_i \to J^*$ and the control law $\boldsymbol{u}_i \to \boldsymbol{u}^*$.

2.2   Heuristic Critic Network Value Iterative Algorithm

The subsection will propose an iterative algorithm based on Algorithm 1. The algorithm can perform online learning based on the real-time monitoring data $\boldsymbol{x}(k)$ generated by the controlled system, and calculate a control input $\boldsymbol{u}(k)$ that satisfies the $\Omega_{\boldsymbol{u}}$ constraint by minimizing $J(k)$. The HCNVI algorithm contains two neural networks, named model network and critic network.

Algorithm 1. Value iteration algorithm

Initialization: Randomly define $V_0(\cdot)$

1: **for** $i = 0, 1, 2, ..., \infty$ **do**

2:    Strategy improvement

$$\boldsymbol{u}_i\,(k) = \arg\min_{\boldsymbol{u}_k \in \Omega_{\boldsymbol{u}}} U(y(k), \boldsymbol{u}(k)) + \gamma V_i(\boldsymbol{x}(k+1)) \tag{6}$$

3:    Strategy evaluation

$$V_{i+1}\,(\boldsymbol{x}(k)) = U(y(k), \boldsymbol{u}_i(k)) + \gamma V_i(\boldsymbol{x}(k+1)) \tag{7}$$

Critic Network. HCNVI uses a neural network called critic network to approximate the $V(\cdot)$ function in Algorithm 1. The neural network chooses a single hidden layer artificial neural network as follows,

$$\hat{J}(k) = W_{c2} \tanh\left(W_{c1}(\boldsymbol{x}(k))\right) \tag{8}$$

The internal parameters of W_{c1} and W_{c2} are initialized to random numbers between -1 and 1. The model uses online data generated during system control for network training. In order to ensure the real-time performance of the algorithm update, this paper uses a single-step temporal difference error (TD error) to calculate and evaluate the estimated error value of the network as,

$$e_c(k) = \hat{J}(k) - (\gamma \hat{J}(k+1) + U(k)) \tag{9}$$

The network loss function is $E_c(k) = e_c^2(k)$. By minimizing the loss function, the critic network can incrementally approach the critic function for the current control strategy according to the status signal and the utility value fed back by the controlled system. Use the chain rule to calculate the gradient of the loss value $E_c(k)$ to the network parameters,

$$\frac{\partial e_c^2(k)}{\partial W_{c2}} = 2e_c(k)\tanh(W_{c1}\boldsymbol{x}(k))^{\mathrm{T}}$$

$$\frac{\partial e_c^2(k)}{\partial W_{c1}} = 2e_c(k)[W_{c2}^{\mathrm{T}} \odot (1 - \tanh^2(W_{c1}\boldsymbol{x}(k)))]\boldsymbol{x}(k)^{\mathrm{T}} \tag{10}$$

Use gradient descent algorithm to train and update the critic network,

$$W_{ci}(k) = W_{ci}(k) - l_c\frac{\partial e_c^2(k)}{\partial W_{ci}(k)} \tag{11}$$

l_c is the learning rate. Because the external noise in the environment fluctuates continuously, the network needs to quickly converge according to the training data when the external noise $c(k)$ changes, and l_c needs to be set to a fixed value to maintain the learning ability.

Because the difference between different physical quantities is huge, the network will difficult to learn effectively. Therefore, the extremums in the offline data generated by the controlled system are used to normalize and shrink all training data using Eq. (12),

$$\bar{z} = \frac{2\,(z - z_{\min})}{z_{\max} - z_{\min}} - 1 \tag{12}$$

Model Network. Model network is designed to model the dynamic system, and predict the changes about system state in the next moment based on the current system state, external noise and control inputs. The network structure still uses a single hidden layer neural network. The model network is specifically defined as follows,

$$\hat{y}(k+1) = W_{m2}\tanh\left(W_{m1}(\phi(k))\right) \tag{13}$$

where $\phi(k) = \left[\boldsymbol{x}(k)^{\mathrm{T}}, \boldsymbol{u}(k)^{\mathrm{T}}\right]^{\mathrm{T}}$. All parameters in W_{m1} and W_{m2} are initialized to random numbers between -1 and 1. Train the model network by gradient descent method,

$$W_{mi}(k) = W_{mi}(k) - l_m\frac{\partial E_m(k)}{\partial W_{mi}(k)} \tag{14}$$

The loss function is defined as,

$$E_m(k) = \frac{1}{2}\boldsymbol{e}_m^{\mathrm{T}}(k)\boldsymbol{L}_m\boldsymbol{e}_m(k) \tag{15}$$

$$\boldsymbol{e}_m(k) = \hat{\mathbf{y}}(k+1) - \mathbf{y}(k+1) \tag{16}$$

For model networks, the training data is also scaled down using Eq. (12). The model network is trained offline. After the control task is started, the model network will no longer be adjusted.

Action Generation. Most ADP algorithms calculate the control input by establishing an action network, and use the evaluation network output value to update the parameters of the action network. The HCNVI method remove the action network based on the HDP algorithm architecture and directly use the critic network and model network to calculate the action. This method can make the controlled system converge more quickly when the environmental noise changes, and reduce the memory consumption and the training time consumption.

The process of calculating the control action $\boldsymbol{u}(k)$ using the critic network and model network is shown in Algorithm 2. In Eq. (18), when the cumulative

---

Algorithm 2. Calculate control action using iterative gradient descent algorithm

---

INPUT: k-th system state $\boldsymbol{x}(k) = [\mathbf{y}(k), \boldsymbol{c}(k)]$
OUTPUT: k-th action output $\boldsymbol{u}(k)$
1: Randomly select $\boldsymbol{u}_0 = [v_1, v_2]^{\mathrm{T}}$
2: $v_1 \sim U(-1, 1), v_2 \sim U(-1, 1)$
3: $i = 0$
4: **do**
5:    Predict the system state at the next moment with $\boldsymbol{u}_i$ as the control input

$$\hat{\mathbf{y}}(k+1) = W_{m2} \tanh \left(W_{m1}\left(\boldsymbol{x}(k), \boldsymbol{u}_i\right)\right) \tag{17}$$

6:    Let $\hat{\boldsymbol{x}}(k+1) = [\hat{\mathbf{y}}(k+1), \boldsymbol{c}(k)^{\mathrm{T}}]^{\mathrm{T}}$, estimated evaluation value of $k+1$-th time

$$\hat{J}(k+1) = W_{c2} \tanh \left(W_{c1}(\hat{\boldsymbol{x}}(k+1))\right) \tag{18}$$

7:    Calculate the evaluation value at the k-th time

$$\hat{J}(k) = U\left(\mathbf{y}_k, \boldsymbol{u}_i\right) + \gamma \hat{J}(k+1) \tag{19}$$

8:    Update $\boldsymbol{u}_i$ using gradient descent

$$\boldsymbol{u}_{i+1} = \boldsymbol{u}_i - l_u * \frac{\partial \hat{J}(k)}{\partial \boldsymbol{u}_i} \tag{20}$$

9:    Limit $\boldsymbol{u}_{i+1}$ to constraint $\Omega_{\boldsymbol{u}}$

$$\boldsymbol{u}_{i+1} = max([-1, -1]^{\mathrm{T}}, min([1, 1]^{\mathrm{T}}, \boldsymbol{u}_{i+1})) \tag{21}$$

10:    $i = i + 1$
11: **while** $\|\boldsymbol{u}_{i+1} - \boldsymbol{u}_i\| > \epsilon_a$ and $i < Na$
12: Anti-normalization$\boldsymbol{u}(k)$

$$\boldsymbol{u}(k) = \frac{\boldsymbol{u}(i+1) \odot (\boldsymbol{u}_{\max} - \boldsymbol{u}_{\min})}{2} + \boldsymbol{u}_{mid} \tag{22}$$

13: return $\boldsymbol{u}(k)$

---

discounted penalty at time $k+1$ is estimated, the external noise of the system at the next moment is unknown. However, since the feed noise in a real industrial environment changes continuously and there are few sudden changes, this model uses the noise $c(k)$ at the current moment as the noise $c(k+1)$ at the next moment.

2.3   Short-Term Experience Replay

In order to increase the accuracy and convergence speed of critic network training, the paper further proposes a short-term experience replay method to optimize the network training loss function and calculate the optimization gradient. The short-term experience replay method modifies the error value calculation Eq. (9) as,

$$e_c(k) = \frac{1}{L} \sum_{i=0}^{L-1} \hat{J}(\boldsymbol{x}(k-i)) - (U(k-i) + \gamma \hat{J}(\boldsymbol{x}(k-i+1))) \tag{23}$$

By storing the running trajectory data of the controlled system in the short-term during the training process, the short-term trajectory data can be used to jointly calculate and evaluate the loss value of the network and optimize the gradient direction.

HDP, DHP and the HCNVI algorithm proposed in this paper are online control algorithms modeled for value functions. The update of their strategy modules uses the model network as the medium to calculate the critic network output value $\hat{J}(k)$ for the control input $\boldsymbol{u}(k)$ gradient and update the action network based on this gradient or use Algorithm 2 to optimize $\boldsymbol{u}(k)$. Therefore, the accuracy of the $\boldsymbol{u}(k)$ gradient estimation greatly affects the update effect of the strategy module, and then affects the control effect and convergence speed of the entire control system. The gradient expression of $\boldsymbol{u}(k)$ is Eq. (24).

$$\nabla \boldsymbol{u}(k) = \gamma \frac{\partial \boldsymbol{x}(k+1)}{\partial \boldsymbol{u}(k)} \frac{\partial \hat{J}(k+1)}{\partial \boldsymbol{x}(k+1)} + \frac{\partial U(k)}{\partial \boldsymbol{u}(k)} \tag{24}$$

In the equation, $\frac{\partial \hat{J}(k+1)}{\partial \boldsymbol{x}(k+1)}$ is also called the co-state $\boldsymbol{\lambda}(k+1)$ at $(k+1)$ moment, which represents the gradient of the critic network output value to the system state. The model network can be trained using the system's offline data. When the amount of training data is sufficient, it can achieve extremely high accuracy. And it can be roughly considered that the estimation of $\frac{\partial \boldsymbol{x}(k+1)}{\partial \boldsymbol{u}(k)}$ is sufficiently accurate. $U(k)$ is determined as a utility function, and $\frac{\partial U(k)}{\partial \boldsymbol{u}(k)}$ is also determined. Therefore, the estimation error for $\nabla \boldsymbol{u}(k)$ mainly comes from the estimation error for the co-state $\boldsymbol{\lambda}(k+1)$.

For large industrial machine, the system runs slowly, and the system state does not change drastically in a short time, so $\boldsymbol{x}(k) \approx \boldsymbol{x}(k+1)$. The critic network has continuous and differentiable properties. Therefore, $\boldsymbol{\lambda}(k) \approx \boldsymbol{\lambda}(k+1)$ can be approximated. Similarly, due to the slow running process of the system, the distribution of system state parameters in the training data provided to the control model learning is very concentrated, and it can be approximated the Eq. (25).

$$\forall 1 \leq t < L, \|\boldsymbol{x}(k-t) - \boldsymbol{x}(t)\| < \delta \tag{25}$$

The formula shows that the system state $\boldsymbol{x}(k-t)$ are all in the area with $\boldsymbol{x}(k)$ as the center and δ as the radius in the short term. Using Eq. (9) and short-term L pieces of data for critic network training, the network can learn better in the neighborhood of $\boldsymbol{x}(k)$, and then estimate $\lambda(k)$ more accurately.

The specific process of applying HCNVI algorithm to industrial system control is Algorithm 3.

Algorithm 3. Using HCNVI Algorithm to Realize Online Control of Industrial machine

---

1: **Run** off-line data using thickener, train model network with equation (14)
2: $k = 0$
3: **while** k <T **do**
4:     Get $\mathbf{y}(k), \boldsymbol{c}(k)$ according to the controlled system
5:     **if** $k \geq 1$ **then**
6:         $i = 0$
7:         **do**
8:             Let $L = \min(L_c, k)$, solve $e_c(k)$ using Equation (23)
9:             Train critic network with equation (11)
10:             $i = i + 1$
11:         **while** $i < N_c$ and $e_c(k)^2 > \epsilon_c$
12:     Solve $\boldsymbol{u}(k)$ using Algorithm 2
13:     Apply $\boldsymbol{u}(k)$ to the controlled system and wait for T_d minutes
14:     $k = k + 1$

---

3   Simulation and Experiments

3.1   Thickener Simulation Model

Due to the high cost of control experiments in real industrial scenarios, this subsection builds thickener machine simulation model to verify the effectiveness of the proposed control algorithm. Thickener is a typical complex process industrial machine in mining field. The operation process has the characteristics of nonlinear, multivariable and high time delay. The model construction method refers to [11–16], the first-order rate of change of mud layer height $h(t)$ and underflow concentration $c_u(t)$ is derived:

$$\frac{dh(t)}{dt} = -\frac{W(t)\theta}{Ac_a^2(t)} * \frac{c_l(t)\left[u_t(t) + u_r(t)\right] - c_u(t)u_r(t)}{h(t) - c_a(t)\frac{W(t)\theta}{Ac_a^2(t)}} \tag{26}$$

$$\frac{dc_u(t)}{dt} = \frac{c_l(t)\left[u_t(t) + u_r(t)\right] - c_u(t)u_r(t)}{p\left(h(t) - c_a(t)\frac{W(t)\theta}{Ac_a^2(t)}\right)} \tag{27}$$

In this simulation model, the flocculant pump speed f_f and the underflow pump speed f_u are control inputs $\boldsymbol{u} = [f_u, f_f]^{\mathrm{T}}$, and the feed pump speed f_i and the feed concentration c_i are external interference amounts $\boldsymbol{c} = [f_i, c_i]^{\mathrm{T}}$. The underflow concentration c_u is the control system tracking variable $\boldsymbol{y} = c_u$. The ideal control system can drive y to track its set point y^* by adjusting u within a reasonable range under the constant fluctuation of the external interference amount c. According to the actual production situation, some variables are defined as follows: $\boldsymbol{u}_{\min} = [40, 30]$, $\boldsymbol{u}_{\max} = [120, 50]$, $y_{\min} = 280$, $y_{\max} = 1200$, $\boldsymbol{c}_{\min} = [40, 30]$, $\boldsymbol{c}_{\max} = [120, 50]$, $y^* = 680$.

Next in this section, experiments will be performed to verify the control effect of the HCNVI model under the input of Gaussian noise amount $\boldsymbol{c}(k)$ based on the thickener machine simulation, and compare with other algorithms.

3.2   Simulation of Thickener Control Under Gaussian Noise Input

In a real industrial scenario, the feed concentration and feed flow of the thickener fluctuate in real time. In the experiments in this section, the two noise quantities of the feed flow and feed concentration continue to fluctuate to simulate the environment of the thickener system in a real industrial scenario. The single-step increment of the noise input obeys the Gaussian distribution Eq. (28), and the fluctuation of the feed is shown in Fig. 1.

$$\begin{aligned}c(k+1) &= c(k) + \Delta c \\ \Delta c &\sim N(\mu = 0, \Sigma = \mathrm{diag}(0.6, 0.6))\end{aligned} \tag{28}$$

The HCNVI algorithm proposed in this paper is used for comparison experiments with the HDP and DHP algorithms. The simulation experiment parameters are as follows: Iteration round $T = 270$, simulation step $T_d = 120s$, $Q = 0.004$, $\gamma = 0.6$, $N_a = 4000$, $N_c = 500$, $\epsilon_c = 0.001$, $\epsilon_a = 0.0001$, $l_m = 0.01$, $l_c = 0.01$, $l_a = 0.009$, $l_u = 0.4$, $L_c = 2$, $L_m = [0.01, 3]$. Among them, the HDP and DHP algorithms also use short-term experience playback, and the playback point number L is 2. In the experiments, the critic network structure of HDP, DHP, and HCNVI is the same, and the network parameters are initialized to the same values. The experimental results are shown in Fig. 1.

Comparing the control performance of different control algorithms under continuous changes in environmental noise, it can be found that HCNVI can limit the underflow concentration within the around of set point, and the concentration amplitude is smaller than other algorithms. It can also be seen from the change curve of the utility value that compared with other algorithms, the utility value of the HCNVI algorithm is relatively small overall, and is almost zero in the late training period.

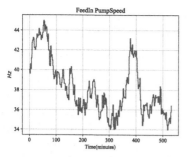

(a) The speed of feed pump varies in real time.

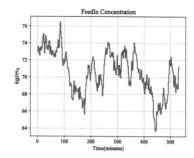

(b) The feed concentration varies in real time.

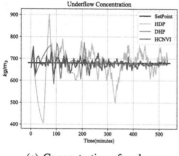

(c) Concentration of underflow.

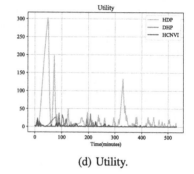

(d) Utility.

Fig. 1. (a), (b) are noise input in the simulation experiment. (c), (d) are the result of HCNVI and other ADP algorithms under fluctuate noisy input.

Table 1. Performance analysis between different control algorithms

Noise type	Stable noise input			Gaussian noise input		
Contrast indicators	MSE	MAE	IAE	MSE	MAE	IAE
HDP	414.182	141.854	7.246	6105.619	275.075	54.952
DHP	290.886	109.312	5.392	732.814	96.145	16.560
HCNVI	**44.445**	**66.604**	**3.867**	**307.618**	**76.176**	**12.998**

Table 1 shows the comparison results of underflow concentration control performance indexes of different algorithms in two noise inputs. The Stable noise is adding a step mutation to feed pump speed and feed concentration at a certain moment. Compared with other algorithms, the HCNVI algorithm can better control the underflow concentration stability near its set point, and it has better control of overall stability (represented by MSE and IAE) and control robustness (represented by MAE). In the process industry control scenario, the MAE index of the control system is particularly important. The severe fluctuations in the material properties of a certain process will cause subsequent fluctuations in the downstream material processing process, which seriously affects the stability of production and the quality of the final product. The advantage of the HCNVI algorithm on the MAE index confirms its applicability in process industry control problems.

In order to verify the effect of short-term experience replay technology on the performance of the control algorithm, this paper compares the control performance of HDP and HCNVI in the case of inexperienced playback and short-term experience playback ($L = 2$). The utility comparison results are shown in Fig. 2. By observing the change curve of the utility value in the case of inexperienced playback, it can be found that the curve fluctuates greatly. Compared with short-term experience replay, the control model without experience replay requires more iterations to make the system converge. The experimental results show that the short-term experience playback technology has a significant effect on improving the convergence speed of the control model, and it is universal for different ADP algorithms.

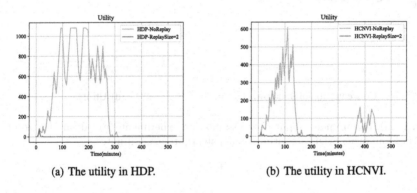

(a) The utility in HDP.　　　　　(b) The utility in HCNVI.

Fig. 2. The influence of short-term experience replay on HDP and HCNVI.

4　Conclusion

This paper proposes an adaptive control algorithm HCNVI based on RL. This algorithm solves the industrial machine control problem by constructing a model network for identifying the dynamic equations of the system and a critic network for estimating the cumulative discounted cost. This method can realize online learning and obtain better control effect by using only system output data and historical operation data when the controlled system is unknown. In addition, the short-term experience playback technology proposed in this paper can well enhance the stability of critic network training, and has good generality in other ADP algorithms.

According to the results of simulation experiments, it can be found that the HCNVI algorithm compared with other online ADP algorithms consumes less training time in the control problem of thickener simulation systems and obtain a better control effect. The reason is the simple structure of the HCNVI algorithm model and high learning agility. However, the HCNVI algorithm also has its own limitations. The feasibility of removing the action network is based on the slow and stable operation of large industrial machines. But when the controlled system is relatively complex and no longer has this characteristic, such as the system state quantity change process is not continuous or the system runs faster, it is difficult for HCNVI to rely on iterative algorithms to maintain the optimal control amount, and the control performance is likely to be degraded. How to make the HCNVI algorithm and other non-action network ADP algorithms applicable to such complex controlled systems, while optimizing training time consumption and ensuring its control performance and convergence speed, will be a very interesting research direction in the future.

Acknowledgments. This research was funded by the National Key Research and Development Program of China with grant number (No. 2019YFC0605300 and No. 2016YFB0700500), the National Natural Science Foundation of China with grant number (No. 61572075, No. 61702036 and No. 61873299) and Key Research Plan of Hainan Province (No. ZDYF2019009).

References

1. Shen, Y., Hao, L., Ding, S.X.: Real-time implementation of fault tolerant control systems with performance optimization. IEEE Trans. Ind. Electron. **61**(5), 2402–2411 (2014)
2. Kouro, S., Cortes, P., Vargas, R., Ammann, U., Rodriguez, J.: Model predictive control - a simple and powerful method to control power converters. IEEE Trans. Ind. Electron. **56**(6), 1826–1838 (2009)
3. Dai, W., Chai, T., Yang, S.X.: Data-driven optimization control for safety operation of hematite grinding process. IEEE Trans. Ind. Electron. **62**(5), 2930–2941 (2015)
4. Wang, D., Liu, D., Zhang, Q., Zhao, D.: Data-based adaptive critic designs for nonlinear robust optimal control with uncertain dynamics. IEEE Trans. Syst. Man Cybern. Syst. **46**(11), 1544–1555 (2016)
5. Wei, Q.-L., Liu, D.-R.: Adaptive dynamic programming for optimal tracking control of unknown nonlinear systems with application to coal gasification. IEEE Trans. Autom. Sci. Eng. **11**(4), 1020–1036 (2014)
6. Jiang, Y., Fan, J.-L., Chai, T.-Y., Li, J.-N., Lewis, L.F.: Data-driven flotation industrial process operational optimal control based on reinforcement learning. IEEE Trans. Ind. Inform. **14**(5), 1974–1989 (2017)
7. Jiang, Y., Fan, J.-L., Chai, T.-Y., Lewis, L.F.: Dual-rate operational optimal control for flotation industrial process with unknown operational model. IEEE Trans. Ind. Electron. **66**(6), 4587–4599 (2019)
8. Modares, H., Lewis, F.L.: Automatica integral reinforcement learning and experience replay for adaptive optimal control of partially-unknown constrained-input. Automatica **50**(1), 193–202 (2014)
9. Mnih, V., Silver, D., Riedmiller, M.: Playing atari with deep reinforcement learning. In: NIPS Deep Learning Workshop 2013, Lake Tahoe, USA NIPS, pp. 1–9 (2013)

10. Wang, D., Liu, D.-R., Wei, Q.-L., Zhao, D.-B., Jin, N.: Automatica optimal control of unknown nonaffine nonlinear discrete-time systems based on adaptive dynamic programming. Automatica **48**(8), 1825–1832 (2012)
11. Chai, T.-Y., Jia, Y., Li, H.-B., Wang, H.: An intelligent switching control for a mixed separation thickener process. Control Eng. Pract. **57**, 61–71 (2016)
12. Kim, B.H., Klima, M.S.: Development and application of a dynamic model for hindered-settling column separations. Miner. Eng. **17**(3), 403–410 (2004)
13. Wang, L.-Y., Jia, Y., Chai, T.-Y., Xie, W.-F.: Dual rate adaptive control for mixed separation thickening process using compensation signal based approach. IEEE Trans. Ind. Electron. 1 (2017)
14. Wang, M.: Design and development of model software of processes of slurry neutralization, sedimentation and separation. Northeastern University (2011)
15. Tang, M.-T.: Hydrometallurgical equipment. Central South University (2009)
16. Lin-Yan, W., Jian, L., Yao, J., Tian-You, C.: Dual-rate intelligent switching control for mixed separation thickening process. Acta Automatica Sinica **44**(2), 330–343 (2018)
17. Luo, B., Liu, D.-R., Huang, T.-W., Wang, D.: Model-free optimal tracking control via critic-only Q-learning. IEEE Trans. Neural Netw. Learn. Syst. **27**(10), 2134–2144 (2016)
18. Padhi, R., Unnikrishnan, N., Wang, X.-H., Balakrishnan, S.N.: A single network adaptive critic (SNAC) architecture for optimal control synthesis for a class of nonlinear systems. Neural Netw. **19**(10), 1648–1660 (2006)

PBCS: Efficient Exploration and Exploitation Using a Synergy Between Reinforcement Learning and Motion Planning

Guillaume Matheron$^{(\boxtimes)}$ (ID), Nicolas Perrin (ID), and Olivier Sigaud (ID)

Sorbonne Université, CNRS, Institut des Systèmes Intelligents et de Robotique, ISIR, 75005 Paris, France
guillaume_pub@matheron.eu

Abstract. The exploration-exploitation trade-off is at the heart of reinforcement learning (RL). However, most continuous control benchmarks used in recent RL research only require local exploration. This led to the development of algorithms that have basic exploration capabilities, and behave poorly in benchmarks that require more versatile exploration. For instance, as demonstrated in our empirical study, state-of-the-art RL algorithms such as DDPG and TD3 are unable to steer a point mass in even small 2D mazes. In this paper, we propose a new algorithm called "Plan, Backplay, Chain Skills" (PBCS) that combines motion planning and reinforcement learning to solve hard exploration environments. In a first phase, a motion planning algorithm is used to find a single good trajectory, then an RL algorithm is trained using a curriculum derived from the trajectory, by combining a variant of the Backplay algorithm and skill chaining. We show that this method outperforms state-of-the-art RL algorithms in 2D maze environments of various sizes, and is able to improve on the trajectory obtained by the motion planning phase.

Introduction

Reinforcement Learning (RL) algorithms have been used successfully to optimize policies for both discrete and continuous control problems with high dimensionality [23,25], but fall short when trying to solve difficult exploration problems [1,17,38]. On the other hand, motion planning (MP) algorithms such as RRT [22] are able to efficiently explore in large cluttered environments but, instead of trained policies, they output trajectories that cannot be used directly for closed loop control.

In this paper, we consider environments that present a hard exploration problem with a sparse reward. In this context, a *good trajectory* is one that reaches a state with a positive reward, and we say that an environment is *solved* when a

This work was partially supported by the French National Research Agency (ANR), Project ANR-18-CE33-0005 HUSKI.

I. Farkaš et al. (Eds.): ICANN 2020, LNCS 12397, pp. 295–307, 2020.
https://doi.org/10.1007/978-3-030-61616-8_24

controller is able to reliably reach a rewarded state. We illustrate our approach with 2D continuous action mazes as they facilitate the visual examination of the results, but we believe that this approach can be beneficial to many robotics problems.

If one wants to obtain closed loop controllers for hard exploration problems, a simple approach is to first use an MP algorithm to find a single good trajectory τ, then optimize and robustify it using RL. However, using τ as a stepping stone for an RL algorithm is not straightforward. In this article, we propose PBCS, an approach that fits the framework of Go-Explore [8], and is based on the Backplay algorithm [35] and skill chaining [20,21]. We show that this approach greatly outperforms both DDPG [23] and TD3 [14] on continuous control problems in 2D mazes, as well as approaches that use Backplay but no skill chaining.

PBCS has two successive phases. First, the environment is explored until a single good trajectory is found. Then this trajectory is used to create a curriculum for training DDPG. More precisely, PBCS progressively increases the difficulty through a backplay process which gradually moves the starting point of the environment backwards along the trajectory resulting from exploration. Unfortunately, this process has its own issues, and DDPG becomes unstable in long training sessions. Calling upon a skill chaining approach, we use the fact that even if Backplay eventually fails, it is still able to solve some subset of the problem. Therefore, a partial policy is saved, and the reminder of the problem is solved recursively until the full environment can be solved reliably.

In this article, we contribute an extension of the Go-Explore framework to continuous control environments, a new way to combine a variant of the Backplay algorithm with skill chaining, and a new state-space exploration algorithm.

1   Related Work

Many works have tried to incorporate better exploration mechanisms in RL, with various approaches.

Encouraging Exploration of Novel States. The authors of [43] use a count-based method to penalize states that have already been visited, while the method proposed by [2] reuses actions that have provided diverse results in the past. Some methods try to choose policies that are both efficient and novel [7,9,33,34], while some use novelty as the only target, entirely removing the need for rewards [10,19]. The authors of [3,31,41] train a forward model and use the unexpectedness of the environment step as a proxy for novelty, which is encouraged through reward shaping. Some approaches try to either estimate the uncertainty of value estimates [29], or learn bounds on the value function [5]. All these solutions try to integrate an exploration component within RL algorithms, while our approach separates exploration and exploitation into two successive phases, as in [6].

Using Additional Information About the Environment. Usually in RL, the agent can only learn about the environment through interactions. However, when additional information about the task at hand is provided, other methods are available. This information can take the form of expert demonstrations [13,18,21,27,30,35,37], or having access to a single rewarded state [12]. When a full representation of the environment is known, RL can still be valuable to handle the dynamics of the problem: PRM-RL [11] and RL-RRT [4] use RL as reachability estimators during a motion planning process.

Building on the Go-Explore Framework. To our knowledge, the closest approach to ours is the Go-Explore [8] framework, but in contrast to PBCS, Go-Explore is applied to discrete problems such as Atari benchmarks. In a first phase, a single valid trajectory is computed using an ad-hoc exploration algorithm. In a second phase, a learning from demonstration (LfD) algorithm is used to imitate and improve upon this trajectory. Go-Explore uses Backplay [35,37] as the LfD algorithm, with Proximal Policy Optimization (PPO) [40] as policy optimization method. Similar to Backplay, the authors of [16] have proposed Recall Traces, a process in which a backtracking model is used to generate a collection of trajectories reaching the goal.

The authors of [26] present an approach that is similar to ours, and also fits the framework of Go-Explore. In phase 1, they use a guided variant of RRT, and in phase 2 they use a learning from demonstration algorithm based on TRPO. Similarly, PBCS follows the same two phases as Go-Explore, with major changes to both phases. In the first phase, our exploration process is adapted to continuous control environments by using a different binning method, and different criteria for choosing the state to reset to. In the second phase, a variant of Backplay is integrated with DDPG instead of PPO, and seamlessly integrated with a skill chaining strategy and reward shaping.

The Backplay algorithm in PBCS is a deterministic variant of the one proposed in [35]. In the original Backplay algorithm, the starting point of each policy is chosen randomly from a subset of the trajectory, but in our variant the starting point is deterministic: the last state of the trajectory is used until the performance of DDPG converges (more details are presented in Sect. 3.2), then the previous state is chosen, and so on until the full trajectory has been exploited.

Skill Chaining. The process of *skill chaining* was explored in different contexts by several research papers. The authors of [20] present an algorithm that incrementally learns a set of skills using classifiers to identify changepoints, while the method proposed in [21] builds a skill tree from demonstration trajectories, and automatically detects changepoints using statistics on the value function. To our knowledge, our approach is the first to use Backplay to build a skill chain. We believe that it is more reliable and minimizes the number of changepoints because the position of changepoints is decided using data from the RL algorithm that trains the policies involved in each skill.

2   Background

Our work is an extension of the Go-Explore algorithm. In this section, we summarize the main concepts of our approach.

Reset-Anywhere. Our work makes heavy use of the ability to reset an environment to any state. The use of this primitive is relatively uncommon in RL, because it is not always readily available, especially in real-world robotics problems. However, it can be invaluable to speed up exploration of large state spaces. It was used in the context of Atari games by [18], proposed in [39] as VINE, and gained popularity with [37].

Sparse Rewards. Most traditional RL benchmarks only require very local exploration, and have smooth rewards guiding them towards the right behavior. Thus sparse rewards problems are especially hard for RL algorithms: the agent has to discover without any external signal a long sequence of actions leading to the reward. Most methods that have been used to help with this issue require prior environment-specific knowledge [36].

Maze Environments. Lower-dimension environments such as cliff walk [42] are often used to demonstrate fundamental properties of RL algorithms, and testing in these environments occasionally reveals fundamental flaws [24]. We deliberately chose to test our approach on 2D maze environments because they are hard exploration problems, and because reward shaping behaves very poorly in such environments, creating many local optima. Our results in Sect. 4 show that state-of-the-art algorithms such as DDPG and TD3 fail to solve even very simple mazes.

DDPG. Deep Deterministic Policy Gradient (DDPG) is a continuous action actor-critic algorithm using a deterministic actor that performs well on many control tasks [23]. However, DDPG suffers from several sources of instability. Our maze environments fit the analysis made by the authors of [32], according to whom the critic approximator may "leak" Q-value across walls of discontinuous environments. With a slightly different approach, [15] suggests that extrapolation error may cause DDPG to over-estimate the value of states that have never been visited or are unreachable, causing instability. More generally, the authors of [42] formalize the concept of "deadly triad", according to which algorithms that combine function approximation, bootstrapping updates and off-policy are prone to diverge. Even if the deadly triad is generally studied in the context of the DQN algorithm [25], these studies could also apply to DDPG. Finally, the authors of [24] show that DDPG can fail even in trivial environments, when the reward is not found quickly enough by the built-in exploration of DDPG.

3   Methods

Figure 1 describes PBCS. The algorithm is split in two successive phases, mirroring the Go-Explore framework. In a first phase, the environment is incrementally explored until a single rewarded state is found. In a second phase, a single trajectory provides a list of starting points, that are used to train DDPG on increasingly difficult portions of the full environment. Each time the problem becomes too difficult and DDPG starts to fail, training stops, and the trained agent is recorded as a local skill. Training then resumes for the next skill, with a new target state. This loop generates a set of skills that can then be chained together to create a controller that reaches the target reliably.

Notations

State Neighborhood. For any state $s \in S$, and $\epsilon > 0$, we define $B_\epsilon(s)$ as the closed ball of radius ϵ centered around s. Formally, this is the set $\{s' \in S \mid d(s, s') \le \epsilon\}$ where d is the L2 distance.

Skill Chaining. Skill chaining consists in splitting a complex task into simpler sub-tasks that are each governed by a different policy. Complex tasks can then be solved by executing each policy sequentially.

Formally, each task T_i has an activation condition $A_i \subset S$, and a policy $\pi_i : S \to A$. A *task chain* is a list of tasks $T_0 \ldots T_n$, which can be executed sequentially: the actor uses π_0 until the state of the system reaches a state $s \in A_1$, then it uses π_1, and so on until the end of the episode (which can be triggered by reaching either a terminal state or a predetermined maximum number of steps).

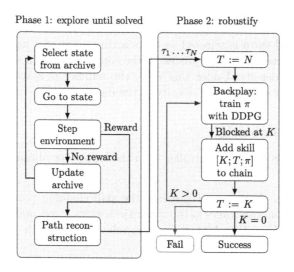

Fig. 1. Overview of PBCS. The red path is only used when testing the algorithm without skill chaining, otherwise the blue path is used. (Color figure online)

3.1 Phase 1: Explore Until Solved

In phase 1, PBCS explores to find a single path that obtains a non-zero reward in the environment. An archive keeps track of all the visited states. In this archive, states s are grouped in square state-space bins. A state-counter c_s is attached to each state, and a bin-counter c_b is attached to each bin. All counters are initialized to 0.

The algorithm proceeds in 5 steps, as depicted in Fig. 1:

1. **Select state from archive.** To select a state, the non-empty bin with the lowest counter is first selected, then from all the states in this bin, the state with the lowest counter is selected. Both the bin and state counters are then incremented.
2. **Go to state.** The environment is reset to the selected state. This assumes the existence of a "reset-anywhere" primitive, which can be made available in simulated environments.
3. **Step environment.** A single environment step is performed, with a random action.
4. **Update archive.** The newly-reached state is added to the archive if not already present.
5. **Termination of phase 1.** As soon as the reward is reached, the archive is used to reconstruct the sequence of states that led the agent from its initial state to the reward. This sequence $\tau_0 \ldots \tau_N$ is passed on to phase 2.

This process can be seen as a random walk with a constraint on the maximum distance between two states: in the beginning, a single trajectory is explored until it reaches a state that is too close to an already-visited state. When this happens, a random visited state is selected as the starting point of a new random walk. Another interpretation of this process is the construction of a set of states with uniform spatial density. Under this view, the number of states in each cell is used as a proxy for the spatial density of the distribution.

3.2 Phase 2: Robustify

Phase 2 of PBCS learns a controller from the trajectory obtained in phase 1.

Skill Chaining. Algorithm 1 presents the skill chaining process. It uses the `Backplay` function, that takes as input a trajectory $\tau_0 \ldots \tau_T$, and returns a policy π and an index $K < T$ such that running policy π repeatedly on a state from

---

Algorithm 1: Phase 2 of PBCS

    Input : $\tau_0 \ldots \tau_N$ the output of phase 1
    Output: $\pi_0 \ldots \pi_n$ a chain of policies with activation sets $A_0 \ldots A_n$
1 $T = N$
2 $n = 0$
3 while $T > 0$ **do**
4 $\pi_n, T = \texttt{Backplay}(\tau_0 \ldots \tau_T)$
5 $A_n = B_\epsilon(\tau_T)$
6 $n = n + 1$
7 end
8 Reverse lists $\pi_0 \ldots \pi_n$ and $A_0 \ldots A_n$

$B_\epsilon(\tau_K)$ always leads to a state in $B_\epsilon(\tau_T)$. The main loop builds a chain of skills that roughly follows trajectory τ, but is able to improve upon it. Specifically, activation sets A_n are centered around points of τ but policies π_n are constructed using a generic RL algorithm that optimizes the path between two activation sets. The list of skills is then reversed, because it was constructed backwards.

Backplay. The Backplay algorithm was originally proposed in [35]. More details on the differences between this original algorithm and our variant are available in Sect. 1.

The `Backplay` function (Algorithm 2) takes as input a section $\tau_0 \ldots \tau_T$ of the trajectory obtained in phase 1, and returns a (K, π) pair where K is an index on trajectory τ, and π is a policy trained to reliably attain $B_\epsilon(\tau_T)$ from $B_\epsilon(\tau_K)$. The policy π is trained using DDPG to reach $B_\epsilon(\tau_T)$ from starting point $B_\epsilon(\tau_K)$, where K is initialized to $T - 1$, and gradually decremented in the main loop.

At each iteration, the algorithm evaluates the feasibility of a skill with target $B_\epsilon(\tau_T)$, policy π and activation set $B_\epsilon(\tau_K)$. If the measured performance is 100% without any training (line 5), the current skill is saved and the starting point is decremented. Otherwise, a training loop is executed until performance stabilizes (line 8). This is performed by running Algorithm 3 repeatedly until no improvement over the maximum performance is observed α times in a row. We ran our experiments with $\alpha = 10$.

Then the performance of the skill is measured again (line 9), and three cases are handled:

- **The skill is always successful (line 10).** The current skill is saved and the index of the starting point is decremented.
- **The skill is never successful (line 13).** The last successful skill is returned.
- **The skill is sometimes successful.** The current skill is not saved, and the index of the starting point is decremented. In our maze environment, this happens when $B_\epsilon(\tau_K)$ overlaps a wall: in this case some states of $B_\epsilon(\tau_K)$ cannot reach the target no matter the policy.

Algorithm 2: The Backplay algorithm

Input : $(\tau_0 \ldots \tau_T)$ a state-space trajectory
Output: π_s a trained policy
         K_s the index of the starting point of the policy
1 $K = T - 1$
2 Initialize a DDPG architecture with policy π
3 **while** $K > 0$ **do**
4 | Test performance of π between $B_\epsilon(\tau_K)$ and $B_\epsilon(\tau_T)$ over β episodes
5 | **if** *performance* $= 100\%$ **then**
6 | | $\pi_s = \pi$, $K_s = K$
7 | **else**
8 | | Run **Train** (Algorithm 3) repeatedly until performance stabilizes.
9 | | Test performance of π between $B_\epsilon(\tau_K)$ and $B_\epsilon(\tau_T)$ over β episodes
10 | | **if** *performance* $= 100\%$ **then**
11 | | | $\pi_s = \pi$, $K_s = K$
12 | | **end**
13 | | **if** *performance* $= 0\%$ *and* K_s *exists* **then**
14 | | | **return** (K_s, π_s)
15 | | **end**
16 | **end**
17 | $K = K - 1$
18 **end**
19 **return** (K_s, π_s)

Reward Shaping. With reward shaping, we bypass the reward function of the environment, and train DDPG to reach any state τ_T. We chose to use the method proposed by [28]: we define a potential function in Eq. (1a), where $d(s, A_i)$ is the L2 distance between s and the center of A_i. We then define our shaped reward in Eq. (1b).

$$\Phi(s) = \frac{1}{d(s, A_i)} \tag{1a}$$

$$R_{\text{shaped}}(s, a, s') = \begin{cases} 10 & \text{if } s \in A_i \\ \Phi(s') - \Phi(s) & \text{otherwise.} \end{cases} \tag{1b}$$

Algorithm 3 shows how this reward function is used in place of the environment reward. This training function runs β episodes of up to max_steps steps each, and returns the fraction of episodes that were able to reach the reward. β is a hyperparameter that we set to 50 for our test.

Importantly, reaching a performance of 100% is not always possible, even with long training sessions, because the starting point is selected in $B_\epsilon(\tau_K)$, and some of these states may be inside obstacles for instance.

Algorithm 3: Training process with reward shaping

Input : τ_K the source state
τ_T the target state
Output: The average performance p

1 n = 0
2 **for** $i = 1 \ldots \beta$ **do**
3 $\quad$ $s \sim B_\epsilon(\tau_K)$
4 $\quad$ **for** $j = 1 \ldots max\_steps$ **do**
5 $\quad\quad$ $a = \pi(s) + \text{random noise}$
6 $\quad\quad$ $s' = \text{step}(s, a)$
7 $\quad\quad$ $r = \begin{cases} 10 & d(s', \tau_T) \le \epsilon \\ \frac{1}{d(s', \tau_T)} - \frac{1}{d(s, \tau_T)} & \text{otherwise} \end{cases}$
8 $\quad\quad$ DDPG.train(s, a, s', r)
9 $\quad\quad$ $s = s'$
10 $\quad\quad$ **if** $d(s', \tau_T) \le \epsilon$ **then**
11 $\quad\quad\quad$ n = n + 1
12 $\quad\quad\quad$ **break**
13 $\quad\quad$ **end**
14 $\quad$ **end**
15 **end**
16 $p = \frac{n}{\beta}$

---

4 Experimental Results

We perform experiments in continuous maze environments of various sizes. For a maze of size N, the state-space is the position of a point mass in $[0, N]^2$ and the action describes the speed of the point mass, in $[-0.1, 0.1]^2$. Therefore, the step function is simply $s' = s + a$, unless the $[s, s']$ segment intersects a wall. The only reward is -1 when hitting a wall and 1 when the target area is reached.

Our results are presented in Table 1. We first tested standard RL algorithms (DDPG and TD3), then PBCS, but without skill chaining (this was done by replacing the blue branch with the red branch in Fig. 1). When the full algorithm would add a new skill to the skill chain and continue training, this variant stops and fails. These results are presented in column "PBCS without skill chaining". Finally, the full version of PBCS with skill chaining is able to solve complex mazes up to 15×15 cells, by chaining several intermediate skills.

5 Discussion of Results

As expected, standard RL algorithms (DDPG and TD3) were unable to solve all but the simplest mazes. These algorithms have no mechanism for state-space exploration other than uniform noise added to their policies during rollouts. Therefore, in the best-case scenario they perform a random walk and, in the worst-case scenario, their actors may actively hinder exploration.

Table 1. Results of various algorithms on maze environments. For each test, the number of environment steps performed is displayed with a red background when the policy was not able to reach the target, and a green one when training was successful. In "Vanilla" experiments, the red paths represent the whole area explored by the RL algorithm. In "Backplay" experiments, the trajectory computed in phase 1 is displayed in red, and the "robustified" policy or policy chain is displayed in green. Activation sets A_i are displayed as purple circles.

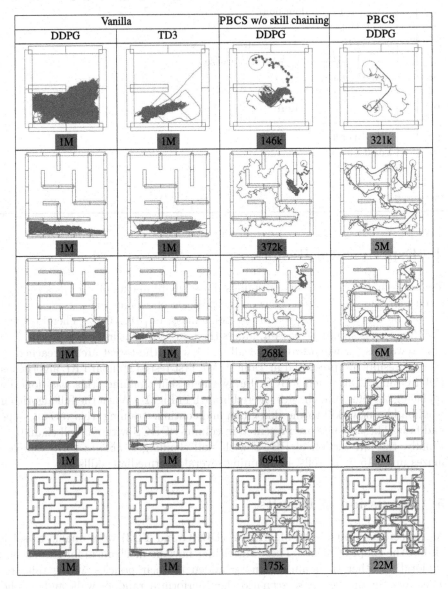

More surprisingly, PBCS without skill chaining is still unable to reliably solve mazes larger than 2 × 2. Although phase 1 always succeeds in finding a feasible trajectory τ, the robustification phase fails relatively early. We attribute these failures to well-known limitations of DDPG exposed in Sect. 2.

The full version of PBCS with skill chaining is able to overcome these issues by limiting the length of training sessions of DDPG, and is able to solve complex mazes up to 7 × 7, by chaining several intermediate skills.

6   Conclusion

The authors of Go-Explore identified state-space exploration as a fundamental difficulty on two Atari benchmarks. We believe that this difficulty is also present in many continuous control problems, especially in high-dimension environments. We have shown that the PBCS algorithm can solve these hard exploration, continuous control environments by combining a motion planning process with reinforcement learning and skill chaining. Further developments should focus on testing these hybrid approaches on higher dimensional environments that present difficult exploration challenges together with difficult local control, such as the Ant-Maze MuJoCo benchmark [44], and developing methods that use heuristics suited to continuous control in the exploration process, such as Quality-Diversity approaches [34].

References

1. Achiam, J., Knight, E., Abbeel, P.: Towards Characterizing Divergence in Deep Q-Learning. arXiv:1903.08894 (2019)
2. Benureau, F.C.Y., Oudeyer, P.Y.: Behavioral diversity generation in autonomous exploration through reuse of past experience. Front. Robot. AI **3**, 8 (2016)
3. Burda, Y., Edwards, H., Storkey, A., Klimov, O.: Exploration by Random Network Distillation. arXiv:1810.12894 (2018)
4. Chiang, H.T.L., Hsu, J., Fiser, M., Tapia, L., Faust, A.: RL-RRT: Kinodynamic Motion Planning via Learning Reachability Estimators from RL Policies. arXiv:1907.04799 (2019)
5. Ciosek, K., Vuong, Q., Loftin, R., Hofmann, K.: Better Exploration with Optimistic Actor-Critic. arXiv:1910.12807 (2019)
6. Colas, C., Sigaud, O., Oudeyer, P.Y.: GEP-PG: Decoupling Exploration and Exploitation in Deep Reinforcement Learning Algorithms. arXiv:1802.05054 (2018)
7. Cully, A., Demiris, Y.: Quality and Diversity Optimization: a unifying Modular Framework. IEEE Trans. Evol. Comput. 1 (2017)
8. Ecoffet, A., Huizinga, J., Lehman, J., Stanley, K.O., Clune, J.: Go-Explore: a New Approach for Hard-Exploration Problems. arXiv:1901.10995 (2019)
9. Erickson, L.H., LaValle, S.M.: Survivability: measuring and ensuring path diversity. In: 2009 IEEE International Conference on Robotics and Automation, pp. 2068–2073 (2009)
10. Eysenbach, B., Gupta, A., Ibarz, J., Levine, S.: Diversity is All You Need: Learning Skills without a Reward Function. arXiv:1802.06070 (2018)

11. Faust, A., et al.: PRM-RL: Long-range Robotic Navigation Tasks by Combining Reinforcement Learning and Sampling-based Planning. arXiv:1710.03937 (2018)
12. Florensa, C., Held, D., Wulfmeier, M., Zhang, M., Abbeel, P.: Reverse Curriculum Generation for Reinforcement Learning. arXiv:1707.05300 (2018)
13. Fournier, P., Sigaud, O., Colas, C., Chetouani, M.: CLIC: Curriculum Learning and Imitation for object Control in non-rewarding environments. arXiv:1901.09720 (2019)
14. Fujimoto, S., Hoof, H.v., Meger, D.: Addressing Function Approximation Error in Actor-Critic Methods. ICML (2018)
15. Fujimoto, S., Meger, D., Precup, D.: Off-Policy Deep Reinforcement Learning without Exploration. arXiv:1812.02900 (2018)
16. Goyal, A., et al.: Recall Traces: Backtracking Models for Efficient Reinforcement Learning. arXiv:1804.00379 (2019)
17. van Hasselt, H., Doron, Y., Strub, F., Hessel, M., Sonnerat, N., Modayil, J.: Deep Reinforcement Learning and the Deadly Triad. arXiv:1812.02648 (2018)
18. Hosu, I.A., Rebedea, T.: Playing Atari Games with Deep Reinforcement Learning and Human Checkpoint Replay. arXiv:1607.05077 (2016)
19. Knepper, R.A., Mason, M.T.: Path diversity is only part of the problem. In: 2009 IEEE International Conference on Robotics and Automation, pp. 3224–3229 (2009)
20. Konidaris, G., Barto, A.G.: Skill discovery in continuous reinforcement learning domains using skill chaining. In: Bengio, Y., et al. (eds.) Advances in Neural Information Processing Systems, vol. 22, pp. 1015–1023 (2009)
21. Konidaris, G., Kuindersma, S., Grupen, R., Barto, A.G.: Constructing skill trees for reinforcement learning agents from demonstration trajectories. In: Lafferty, J.D., et al. (eds.) Advances in Neural Information Processing Systems, vol. 23, pp. 1162–1170 (2010)
22. Lavalle, S.M.: Rapidly-Exploring Random Trees: A New Tool for Path Planning. Iowa State University, Technical report (1998)
23. Lillicrap, T.P., et al: Continuous control with deep reinforcement learning. arXiv:1509.02971 (2015)
24. Matheron, G., Perrin, N., Sigaud, O.: The problem with DDPG: understanding failures in deterministic environments with sparse rewards. arXiv:1911.11679 (2019)
25. Mnih, V., et al.: Playing Atari with Deep Reinforcement Learning. arXiv:1312.5602 (2013)
26. Morere, P., Francis, G., Blau, T., Ramos, F.: Reinforcement Learning with Probabilistically Complete Exploration. arXiv:2001.06940 (2020)
27. Nair, A., McGrew, B., Andrychowicz, M., Zaremba, W., Abbeel, P.: Overcoming Exploration in Reinforcement Learning with Demonstrations. arXiv:1709.10089 (2018)
28. Ng, A.Y., Harada, D., Russell, S.J.: policy invariance under reward transformations: theory and application to reward shaping. In: Proceedings of the Sixteenth International Conference on Machine Learning, ICML 1999, pp. 278–287 (1999)
29. Osband, I., Blundell, C., Pritzel, A., Van Roy, B.: Deep Exploration via Bootstrapped DQN. arXiv:1602.04621 (2016)
30. Paine, T.L., et al.: Making Efficient Use of Demonstrations to Solve Hard Exploration Problems. arXiv:1909.01387 (2019)
31. Pathak, D., Agrawal, P., Efros, A.A., Darrell, T.: Curiosity-driven Exploration by Self-supervised Prediction. arXiv:1705.05363 (2017)
32. Penedones, H., Vincent, D., Maennel, H., Gelly, S., Mann, T., Barreto, A.: Temporal Difference Learning with Neural Networks - Study of the Leakage Propagation Problem. arXiv:1807.03064 (2018)

33. Pugh, J.K., Soros, L.B., Szerlip, P.A., Stanley, K.O.: Confronting the challenge of quality diversity. In: Proceedings of the 2015 Annual Conference on Genetic and Evolutionary Computation, pp. 967–974, GECCO 2015. ACM, New York (2015)
34. Pugh, J.K., Soros, L.B., Stanley, K.O.: Quality diversity: a new frontier for evolutionary computation. Front. Robot. AI **3**, 40 (2016)
35. Resnick, C., Raileanu, R., Kapoor, S., Peysakhovich, A., Cho, K., Bruna, J.: Backplay: "Man muss immer umkehren'. arXiv:1807.06919 (2018)
36. Riedmiller, M., et al.: Learning by Playing - Solving Sparse Reward Tasks from Scratch. arXiv:1802.10567 (2018)
37. Salimans, T., Chen, R.: Learning Montezuma's Revenge from a Single Demonstration. arXiv:1812.03381 (2018)
38. Schaul, T., Quan, J., Antonoglou, I., Silver, D.: Prioritized Experience Replay. arXiv:1511.05952 (2015)
39. Schulman, J., Levine, S., Moritz, P., Jordan, M.I., Abbeel, P.: Trust Region Policy Optimization. arXiv:1502.05477 (2015)
40. Schulman, J., Wolski, F., Dhariwal, P., Radford, A., Klimov, O.: Proximal Policy Optimization Algorithms. arXiv:1707.06347 (2017)
41. Stadie, B.C., Levine, S., Abbeel, P.: Incentivizing Exploration In Reinforcement Learning With Deep Predictive Models. arXiv:1507.00814 (2015)
42. Sutton, R.S., Barto, A.G.: Reinforcement Learning: An Introduction. MIT Press, Cambridge (2018)
43. Tang, H., et al.: #Exploration: A Study of Count-Based Exploration for Deep Reinforcement Learning. arXiv:1611.04717 (2016)
44. Tassa, Y., et al.: DeepMind Control Suite. arXiv:1801.00690 (2018)

Understanding Failures of Deterministic Actor-Critic with Continuous Action Spaces and Sparse Rewards

Guillaume Matheron[✉][iD], Nicolas Perrin[iD], and Olivier Sigaud[iD]

Sorbonne Université, CNRS, Institut des Systèmes Intelligents et de Robotique,
ISIR, 75005 Paris, France
guillaume_pub@matheron.eu

Abstract. In environments with continuous state and action spaces, state-of-the-art actor-critic reinforcement learning algorithms can solve very complex problems, yet can also fail in environments that seem trivial, but the reason for such failures is still poorly understood. In this paper, we contribute a formal explanation of these failures in the particular case of sparse reward and deterministic environments. First, using a very elementary control problem, we illustrate that the learning process can get stuck into a fixed point corresponding to a poor solution, especially when the reward is not found very early. Then, generalizing from the studied example, we provide a detailed analysis of the underlying mechanisms which results in a new understanding of one of the convergence regimes of these algorithms.

1 Introduction

The Deep Deterministic Policy Gradient (DDPG) algorithm [11] is one of the earliest deep Reinforcement Learning (RL) algorithms designed to operate on potentially large continuous state and action spaces with a deterministic policy, and it is still one of the most widely used. However, it is often reported that DDPG suffers from instability in the form of sensitivity to hyper-parameters and propensity to converge to very poor solutions or even diverge. Various algorithms have improved stability by addressing well identified issues, such as the over-estimation bias in TD3 [7] but, because a fundamental understanding of the phenomena underlying these instabilities is still missing, it is unclear whether these ad hoc remedies truly address the source of the problem. Thus, better understanding why these algorithms can fail even in very simple environments is a pressing question.

To investigate this question, we introduce in Sect. 4 a very simple one-dimensional environment with a sparse reward function in which DDPG sometimes fails. Analyzing this example allows us to provide a detailed account of

This work was partially supported by the French National Research Agency (ANR), Project ANR-18-CE33-0005 HUSKI.

I. Farkaš et al. (Eds.): ICANN 2020, LNCS 12397, pp. 308–320, 2020.
https://doi.org/10.1007/978-3-030-61616-8_25

these failures. We then reveal the existence of a cycle of mechanisms operating in the sparse reward and deterministic case, leading to the quick convergence to a poor policy. In particular, we show that when the reward is not discovered early enough, these mechanisms can lead to a *deadlock* situation where neither the actor nor the critic can evolve anymore. Critically, this deadlock persists even when the agent is subsequently trained with rewarded samples.

The study of these mechanisms is backed-up with formal analyses in a simplified context where the effects of function approximation is ignored. Nevertheless, the resulting understanding helps analyzing the practical phenomena encountered when using actors and critics represented as neural networks.

2 Related Work

Issues when combining RL with function approximation have been studied for a long time [3,4,17]. In particular, it is well known that deep RL algorithms can diverge when they meet three conditions coined as the "deadly triad" [16], that is when they use (1) function approximation, (2) bootstrapping updates and (3) off-policy learning. However, these questions are mostly studied in the continuous state, discrete action case. For instance, several recent papers have studied the mechanism of this instability using DQN [12]. In this context, four failure modes have been identified from a theoretical point of view by considering the effect of a linear approximation of the deep-Q updates and by identifying conditions under which the approximate updates of the critic are contraction maps for some distance over Q-functions [1]. Meanwhile, [10] shows that, due to its stabilizing heuristics, DQN does not diverge much in practice when applied to the ATARI domain.

In contrast to these papers, here we study a failure mode specific to continuous action actor-critic algorithms. It hinges on the fact that one cannot take the maximum over actions, and must rely on the actor as a proxy for providing the optimal action instead. Therefore, the failure mode identified in this paper cannot be reduced to any of the ones that affect DQN. Besides, the formal analyses presented in this article show that the failure mode we are investigating does not depend on function approximation errors, thus it cannot be directly related to the deadly triad.

More related to our work, several papers have studied failure to gather rewarded experience from the environment due to poor exploration [5,6,14], but we go beyond this issue by studying a case where the reward is actually found but not properly exploited. Finally, like us the authors of [8] study a failure mode which is specific to DDPG-like algorithms, but the studied failure mode is different. They show under a batch learning regime that DDPG suffers from an *extrapolation error* phenomenon, whereas we are in the more standard incremental learning setting and focus on a deadlock resulting from the shape of the Q-function in the sparse reward case.

3   Background: Deep Deterministic Policy Gradient

The DDPG algorithm [11] is a deep RL algorithm based on the Deterministic Policy Gradient theorem [15]. It borrows the use of a replay buffer and target networks from DQN [13]. DDPG is an instance of the Actor-Critic model. It learns both an actor function π_ψ (also called policy) and a critic function Q_θ, represented as neural networks whose parameters are respectively noted ψ and θ.

The deterministic actor takes a state $s \in S$ as input and outputs an action $a \in A$. The critic maps each state-action pair (s, a) to a value in $\mathbb{R}$. The reward $r : S \times A \to \mathbb{R}$, the termination function $t : S \times A \to \{0, 1\}$ and the discount factor $\gamma < 1$ are also specified as part of the environment.

The actor and critic are updated using stochastic gradient descent on two losses L_ψ and L_θ. These losses are computed from mini-batches of samples $(s_i, a_i, r_i, t_i, s_{i+1})$, where each sample corresponds to a transition $s_i \to s_{i+1}$ resulting from performing action a_i in state s_i, with subsequent reward $r_i = r(s_i, a_i)$ and termination index $t_i = t(s_i, a_i)$.

Two target networks $\pi_{\psi'}$ and $Q_{\theta'}$ are also used in DDPG. Their parameters ψ' and θ' respectively track ψ and θ using exponential smoothing. They are mostly useful to stabilize function approximation when learning the critic and actor networks. Since they do not play a significant role in the phenomena studied in this paper, we ignore them in our formal analyses.

Equations (1) and (2) define L_ψ and L_θ:

$$L_\psi = -\sum_i Q_\theta\left(s_i, \pi_\psi\left(s_i\right)\right) \tag{1}$$

$$\begin{cases} \forall i, y_i = r_i + \gamma(1 - t_i)Q_{\theta'}\left(s_{i+1}, \pi_{\psi'}\left(s_{i+1}\right)\right) \\ L_\theta = \sum_i \left[Q_\theta\left(s_i, a_i\right) - y_i\right]^2. \end{cases} \tag{2}$$

Training for the loss given in (1) yields the parameter update in (3), with α the learning rate:

$$\psi \leftarrow \psi + \alpha \sum_i \frac{\partial \pi_\psi(s_i)}{\partial \psi}^T \nabla_a Q_\theta(s_i, a)|_{a=\pi_\psi(s_i)}. \tag{3}$$

As DDPG uses a replay buffer, the mini-batch samples are acquired using a behavior policy β which may be different from the actor π. Usually, β is defined as π plus a noise distribution, which in the case of DDPG is either a Gaussian function or the more sophisticated Ornstein-Uhlenbeck noise.

Importantly for this paper, the behavior of DDPG can be characterized as an intermediate between two extreme regimes:

- When the actor is updated much faster than the critic, the policy becomes greedy with respect to this critic, resulting into a behavior closely resembling that of the Q-LEARNING algorithm. When it is close to this regime, DDPG can be characterized as off-policy.

– When the critic is updated much faster than the actor, the critic tends towards $Q^\pi(s, a)$. The problems studied in this paper directly come from this second regime.

4   A New Failure Mode

In this section, we introduce a simplistic environment which we call 1D-TOY. It is a one-dimensional, discrete-time, continuous state and action problem, depicted in Fig. 1.

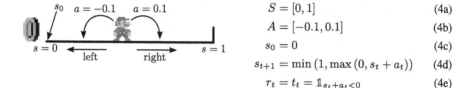

$$S = [0, 1] \tag{4a}$$
$$A = [-0.1, 0.1] \tag{4b}$$
$$s_0 = 0 \tag{4c}$$
$$s_{t+1} = \min\left(1, \max\left(0, s_t + a_t\right)\right) \tag{4d}$$
$$r_t = t_t = \mathbb{1}_{s_t + a_t < 0} \tag{4e}$$

Fig. 1. The 1D-TOY environment

Despite its simplicity, DDPG can fail on 1D-TOY. We first show that DDPG fails to reach 100% success. We then show that if learning a policy does not succeed soon enough, the learning process can get stuck. Besides, we show that the initial actor can be significantly modified in the initial stages before finding the first reward. We explain how the combination of these phenomena can result into a deadlock situation. We generalize this explanation to any deterministic and sparse reward environment by revealing and formally studying a undesirable cyclic process which arises in such cases. Finally, we explore the consequences of getting into this cyclic process.

4.1   Empirical Study

In all experiments, we set the maximum episode length N to 50, but the observed phenomena persist with other values.

Residual Failure to Converge Using Different Noise Processes. We start by running DDPG on the 1D-TOY environment. This environment is trivial as one infinitesimal step to the left is enough to obtain the reward, end the episode and succeed, thus we might expect a quick 100% success. However, the first attempt using an Ornstein-Uhlenbeck (OU) noise process shows that DDPG succeeds in only 94% of cases, see Fig. 2a.

These failures might come from an exploration problem. Indeed, at the start of each episode the OU noise process is reset to zero and gives little noise in the first steps of the episode. In order to remove this potential source of failure, we replace the OU noise process with an exploration strategy similar to ϵ-greedy

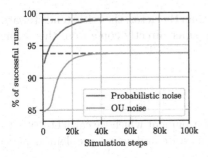 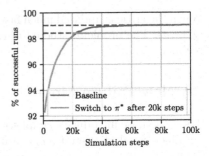

(a) Success rate of DDPG with Ornstein-Uhlenbeck (OU) and probabilistic noise. Even with probabilistic noise, DDPG fails on about 1% of the seeds.

(b) Comparison between DDPG with probabilistic noise and a variant in which the behavior policy is set to the optimal policy π^* after 20k steps.

Fig. 2. Success rate of variants of DDPG on 1D-TOY over learning steps (N = 10k).

which we call "probabilistic noise". For some $0 < p < 1$, with probability p, the action is randomly sampled (and the actor is ignored), and with probability $1 - p$ no noise is used and the raw action is returned. In our tests, we used $p = 0.1$. This guarantees at least a 5% chance of success at the first step of each episode, for any policy. Nevertheless, Fig. 2a shows that even with probabilistic noise, about 1% of seeds still fail to converge to a successful policy in 1D-TOY, even after 100k training steps. All the following tests are performed using probabilistic noise.

We now focus on these failures. On all failing seeds, we observe that the actor has converged to a saturated policy that always goes to the right $(\forall s, \pi(s) = 0.1)$. However, some mini-batch samples have non-zero rewards because the agent still occasionally moves to the left, due to the probabilistic noise applied during rollouts. The expected fraction of non-zero rewards is slightly more than 0.1%[1]. Fig. 3a shows the occurrence of rewards in minibatches taken from the replay buffer when training DDPG on 1D-TOY. After each rollout (episode) of n steps, the critic and actor networks are trained n times on minibatches of size 100. So for instance, a failed episode of size 50 is followed by a training on a total of 5000 samples, out of which we expect more than 5 in average are rewarded transitions.

The constant presence of rewarded transitions in the minibatches suggests that the failures of DDPG on this environment are not due to insufficient exploration by the behavior policy.

Correlation Between Finding the Reward Early and Finding the Optimal Policy. We have shown that DDPG can get stuck in 1D-TOY despite finding the reward regularly. Now we show that when DDPG finds the reward early in the training session, it is also more successful in converging to the optimal policy. On the

---

[1] 10% of steps are governed by probabilistic noise, of which at least 2% are the first episode step, of which 50% are steps going to the left and leading to the reward.

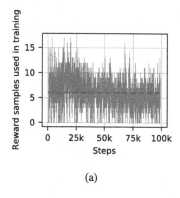

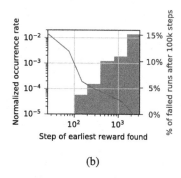

(a)

(b)

Fig. 3. (a) Number of rewards found in mini-batches during training. After a rollout of n steps, the actor and critic are both trained on n minibatches of size 100. The red dotted line indicates an average of 6.03 rewarded transitions present in these n minibatches. (b) In red, normalized probability of finding the earliest reward at this step. In blue, for each earliest reward bin, fraction of these episodes that fail to converge to a good actor after 100k steps. Note that when the reward is found after one or two episodes, the convergence to a successful actor is certain. (Color figure online)

other hand, when the first reward is found late, the learning process more often gets stuck with a sub-optimal policy.

From Fig. 3b, the early steps appear to have a high influence on whether the training will be successful or not. For instance, if the reward is found in the first 50 steps by the actor noise (which happens in 63% of cases), then the success rate of DDPG is 100%. However, if the reward is first found after more than 50 steps, then the success rate drops to 96%. Figure 3b shows that finding the reward later results in lower success rates, down to 87% for runs in which the reward was not found in the first 1600 steps. Therefore, we claim that there exists a critical time frame for finding the reward in the very early stages of training.

Spontaneous Actor Drift. At the beginning of each training session, the actor and critic of DDPG are initialized to represent respectively close-to-zero state-action values and close-to-zero actions. Besides, as long as the agent does not find a reward, it does not benefit from any utility gradient. Thus we might expect that the actor and critic remain constant until the first reward is found. Actually, we show that even in the absence of reward, training the actor and critic triggers non-negligible updates that cause the actor to reach a saturated state very quickly.

To investigate this, we use a variant of 1D-TOY called DRIFT where the only difference is that no rewarded or terminal transitions are present in the environment. We also use a stripped-down version of DDPG, removing rollouts and using random sampling of states and actions as minibatches for training.

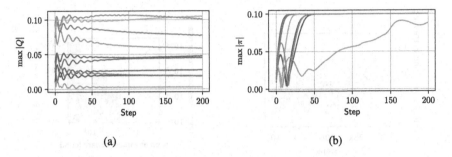

(a)   (b)

Fig. 4. Drift of $\max|Q|$ and $\max|\pi|$ in the DRIFT environment, for 10 different seeds. In the absence of reward, the critic oscillates briefly before stabilizing. However, the actor very quickly reaches a saturated state, at either $\forall s, \pi(s) = 0.1$ or -0.1.

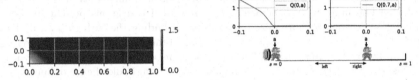

(a) Critic values in the deadlock configuration. The critic is non-zero only in the region that immediately leads to a reward $(s + a < 0)$

(b) Two snapshots of the critic for different states in a failed run. The high Q values in the $s + a < 0$ region are not propagated.

Fig. 5. Visualization of the critic in a failing run, in which the actor is stuck to $\forall s, \pi(s) = 0.1$.

Figure 4b shows that even in the absence of reward, the actor function drifts rapidly (notice the horizontal scale in steps) to a saturated policy, in a number of steps comparable to the "critical time frame" identified above. The critic also has a transitive phase before stabilizing.

In Fig. 4a, the fact that $\max_{s,a}|Q(s,a)|$ can increase in the absence of reward can seem counter-intuitive, since in the loss function presented in Eq. (2), $|y_i|$ can never be greater than $\max_{s,a}|Q(s,a)|$. However, it should be noted that the changes made to Q are not local to the minibatch points, and increasing the value of Q for one input (s, a) may cause its value to increase for other inputs too, which may cause an increase in the global maximum of Q. This phenomenon is at the heart of the over-estimation bias when learning a critic [7], but this bias does not play a key role here.

4.2   Explaining the Deadlock Situation for DDPG on 1D-TOY

Up to now, we have shown that DDPG fails about 1% of times on 1D-TOY, despite the simplicity of this environment. We have now collected the necessary elements to explain the mechanisms of this deadlock in 1D-TOY.

Figure 5 shows the value of the critic in a failed run of DDPG on 1D-TOY. We see that the value of the reward is not propagated correctly outside of the region in which the reward is found in a single step $\{(s,a) \mid s+a < 0\}$. The key of the deadlock is that once the actor has drifted to $\forall s, \pi(s) = 0.1$, it is updated according to $\nabla_a Q_\theta(s,a)|_{a=\pi_\psi(s)}$ (Eq. (3)). Figure 5b shows that for $a = \pi(s) = 0.1$, this gradient is zero therefore the actor is not updated. Besides, the critic is updated using $y_i = r(s_i, a_i) + \gamma Q(s_i', \pi(s_i'))$ as a target. Since $Q(s_i', 0.1)$ is zero, the critic only needs to be non-zero for directly rewarded actions, and for all other samples the target value remains zero. In this state the critic loss given in Eq. (2) is minimal, so there is no further update of the critic and no further propagation of the state-action values. The combination of the above two facts clearly results in a deadlock.

Importantly, the constitutive elements of this deadlock do not depend on the batches used to perform the update, and therefore do not depend on the experience selection method. We tested this experimentally by substituting the behavior policy for the optimal policy after 20k training steps. Results are presented in Fig. 2b and show that, once stuck, even when it is given ideal samples, DDPG stays stuck in the deadlock configuration. This also explains why finding the reward early results in better performance. When the reward is found early enough, $\pi(s_0)$ has not drifted too far, and the gradient of $Q(s_0, a)$ at $a = \pi(s_0)$ drives the actor back into the correct direction.

Note however that even when the actor drifts to the right, DDPG does not always fail. Indeed, because of function approximators the shape of the critic when finding the reward for the first time varies, and sometimes converges slowly enough for the actor to be updated before the convergence of the critic.

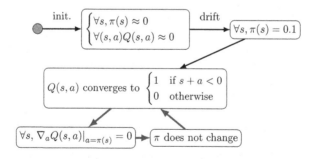

Fig. 6. Deadlock observed in 1D-TOY, represented as the cycle of red arrows. (Color figure online)

Figure 6 summarizes the above process. The entry point is represented using a green dot. First, the actor drifts to $\forall s, \pi(s) = 0.1$, then the critic converges to

Q^π which is a piecewise-constant function, which in turn means that the critic provides no gradient, therefore the actor is not updated (as seen in Eq. 3)[2].

4.3   Generalization

Our study of 1D-TOY revealed how DDPG can get stuck in this simplistic environment. We now generalize to the broader context of more general continuous action actor critic algorithms, including at least DDPG and TD3, and acting in any deterministic and sparse reward environment. The generalized deadlock mechanism is illustrated in Fig. 7 and explained hereafter in the idealized context of perfect approximators.

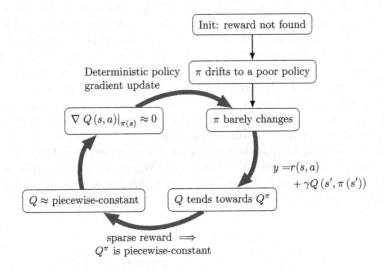

Fig. 7. A cyclic view of the undesirable convergence process in continuous action actor-critic algorithms, in the deterministic and sparse reward case. (Color figure online)

Entry Point: As shown in the previous section, before the behavior policy finds any reward, training the actor and critic can still trigger non-negligible updates that may cause the actor to quickly reach a poor state and stabilize. This defines our entry point in the process.

Q *Tends Towards* **Q^π** *:* A first step into the cycle is that, if the critic is updated faster than the policy, the update rule of the critic Q given in Eq. (2) makes Q converge to Q^π. Indeed, if π is fixed, Q is updated regularly via approximate dynamic programming with the Bellman operator for the policy π. Under strong assumptions, or assuming exact dynamic programming, it is possible to prove

---

[2] Note that Fig. 5 shows a critic state which is slightly different from the one presented in Fig. 6, due to the limitations of function approximators.

that the iterated application of this operator converges towards a unique function Q^π, which corresponds to the state-action value function of π as defined above [9].

$\mathbf{Q^\pi}$ *is Piecewise-Constant:* In a deterministic environment with sparse terminal rewards, Q^π is piecewise-constant because $V^\pi(s')$ only depends on two things: the (integer) number of steps required to reach a rewarded state from s', and the value of this reward state, which is itself piecewise-constant. Note that we can reach the same conclusion with non-terminal rewards, by making the stronger hypothesis on the actor that $\forall s, r(s, \pi(s)) = 0$. Notably, this is the case for the actor $\forall s, \pi(s) = 0.1$ on 1D-TOY.

Q is Approximately Piecewise-Constant and $\nabla_{\mathbf{a}}\mathbf{Q}(\mathbf{s}, \mathbf{a})|_{\mathbf{a}=\pi(\mathbf{s})} \approx \mathbf{0}$: Quite obviously, from Q^π is piecewise-constant and Q tends towards Q^π, we can infer that Q progressively becomes almost piecewise-constant as the cyclic process unfolds. Actually, the Q function is estimated by a function approximator which is never truly discontinuous. The impact of this fact is studied in Sect. 4.5. However, we can expect Q to have mostly flat gradients since it is trained to match a piecewise-constant function. We can thus infer that, globally, $\nabla_a Q(s, a)|_{a=\pi(s)} \approx 0$. And critically, the gradients in the flat regions far from the discontinuities give little information as to how to reach regions of higher values.

π *Barely Changes:* DDPG uses the deterministic policy gradient update, as seen in Eq. (3). This is an analytical gradient that does not incorporate any stochasticity, because Q is always differentiated exactly at $(s, \pi(s))$. Thus the actor update is stalled, even when the reward is regularly found by the behavior policy. This closes the loop of our process.

4.4   Consequences of the Convergence Cycle

As illustrated with the red arrows in Fig. 7, the more loops performed in the convergence process, the more the critic tends to be piecewise-constant and the less the actor tends to change. Importantly, this cyclic convergence process is triggered as soon as the changes on the policy drastically slow down or stop. What matters for the final performance is the quality of the policy reached before this convergence loop is triggered. Quite obviously, if the loop is triggered before the policy gets consistently rewarded, the final performance is deemed to be poor.

The key of this undesirable convergence cycle lies in the use of the deterministic policy gradient update given in Eq. (3). Actually, rewarded samples found by the exploratory behavior policy β tend to be ignored by the conjunction of two reasons. First, the critic is updated using $Q(s', \pi(s'))$ and not $Q(s, \beta(s))$, thus if π differs too much from β, the values brought by β are not properly propagated. Second, the actor being updated through (3), i.e. using the analytical gradient of the critic with respect to the actions of π, there is no room for considering other actions than that of π. Besides, the actor update involves only the state s of the sample taken from the replay buffer, and not the reward found from this sample $r(s, a)$ or the action performed. For each sample state s, the actor update is intended to make $\pi(s)$ converge to $\text{argmax}_a \, \pi(s, a)$ but the experience of different actions performed for identical or similar states is only available through $Q(s, \cdot)$, and in DDPG it is only exploited through the gradient of $Q(s, \cdot)$ at $\pi(s)$, so the process can easily get stuck in a local optimum, especially if the critic tends towards a piecewise-constant function, which as we have shown happens when the reward is sparse. Besides, since TD3 also updates the actor according to (3) and the critic according to (2), it is susceptible to the same failures as DDPG.

4.5   Impact of Function Approximation

We have just explained that when the actor has drifted to an incorrect policy before finding the reward, an undesirable convergence process should result in DDPG getting stuck to this policy. However, in 1D-TOY, we measured that the actor drifts to a policy moving to the right in 50% of cases, but the learning process only fails 1% of times. More generally, despite the issues discussed in this paper, DDPG has been shown to be efficient in many problems. This better-than-predicted success can be attributed to the impact of function approximation.

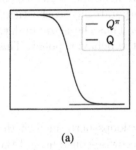
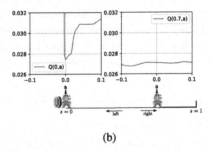

(a)   (b)

Fig. 8. (a) Example of a monotonous function approximator. (b) Simply changing the vertical scale of the graphs presented in Fig. 5b reveals that the function approximator is not perfectly flat, and has many unwanted local extrema. Specifically, continuously moving from $\pi(0) = 0.1$ to $\pi(0) < 0$ requires crossing a significant valley in $Q(0, a)$, while $\pi(0) = 0.1$ is a strong local maximum.

Figure 8a shows a case in which the critic approximates Q^π while keeping a monotonous slope between the current policy value and the reward. In this case, the actor is correctly updated towards the reward (if it is close enough to the discontinuity). This is the most often observed case, and naturally we expect approximators to smooth out discontinuities in target functions in a monotonous way, which facilitates gradient ascent. However, the critic is updated not only in state-action pairs where $Q^\pi(s, a)$ is positive, but also at points where $Q^\pi(s, a) = 0$, which means that the bottom part of the curve also tends to flatten. As this happens, we can imagine phenomena that are common when trying to approximate discontinuous functions, such as the overshoot observed in Fig. 8b. In this case, the gradient prevents the actor from improving.

5   Conclusion and Future Work

In RL, continuous action and sparse reward environments are challenging. In these environments, the fact that a good policy cannot be learned if exploration is not efficient enough to find the reward is well-known and trivial. In this paper, we have established the less trivial fact that, if exploration does find the reward consistently but not early enough, an actor-critic algorithm can get stuck into a configuration from which rewarded samples are just ignored. We have formally characterized the reasons for this situation, and we believe our work sheds new light on the convergence regime of actor-critic algorithms.

Our study was mainly built on a simplistic benchmark which made it possible to study the revealed deadlock situation in isolation from other potential failure modes such as exploration issues, the over-estimation bias, extrapolation error or the deadly triad. The impact of this deadlock situation in more complex environments is a pressing question. For this, we need to sort out and quantify the impact of these different failure modes. Using new tools such as the ones provided in [2], recent analyses of the deadly triad such as [1] as well as simple, easily visualized benchmarks and our own tools, for future work we aim to conduct deeper and more exhaustive analysis of all the instability factors of DDPG-like algorithms, with the hope to contribute in fixing them.

References

1. Achiam, J., Knight, E., Abbeel, P.: Towards characterizing divergence in deep q-learning. arXiv:1903.08894 (2019)
2. Ahmed, Z., Roux, N.L., Norouzi, M., Schuurmans, D.: Understanding the impact of entropy on policy optimization. arXiv:1811.11214 (2019)
3. Baird, L.C., Klopf, A.H.: Technical Report WL-TR-93-1147. Wright-Patterson AIr Force Base, Ohio, Wright Laboratory (1993)
4. Boyan, J.A., Moore, A.W.: Generalization in reinforcement learning: safely approximating the value function. In: Advances in Neural Information Processing Systems, pp. 369–376 (1995)
5. Colas, C., Sigaud, O., Oudeyer, P.Y.: GEP-PG: Decoupling Exploration and Exploitation in Deep Reinforcement Learning Algorithms. arXiv:1802.05054 (2018)
6. Fortunato, M., et al.: Noisy Networks for Exploration. arXiv:1706.10295 (2017)
7. Fujimoto, S., van Hoof, H., Meger, D.: Addressing Function Approximation Error in Actor-Critic Methods. ICML (2018)
8. Fujimoto, S., Meger, D., Precup, D.: Off-Policy Deep Reinforcement Learning without Exploration. arXiv:1812.02900 (2018)
9. Geist, M., Pietquin, O.: Parametric value function approximation: a unified view. In: ADPRL 2011, Paris, France, pp. 9–16 (2011)
10. van Hasselt, H., Doron, Y., Strub, F., Hessel, M., Sonnerat, N., Modayil, J.: Deep Reinforcement Learning and the Deadly Triad. arXiv:1812.02648 (2018)

11. Lillicrap, T.P., et al.: Continuous control with deep reinforcement learning. arXiv:1509.02971 (2015)
12. Mnih, V., et al.: Playing Atari with Deep Reinforcement Learning. arXiv:1312.5602 (2013)
13. Mnih, V., et al.: Human-level control through deep reinforcement learning. Nature **518**(7540), 529–533 (2015)
14. Plappert, M., et al.: Parameter space noise for exploration. arXiv preprint arXiv:1706.01905 (2017)
15. Silver, D., Lever, G., Heess, N., Degris, T., Wierstra, D., Riedmiller, M.: Deterministic policy gradient algorithms. In: International Conference on Machine Learning, pp. 387–395 (2014)
16. Sutton, R.S., Barto, A.G.: Reinforcement Learning: An Introduction. MIT Press, Cambridge (2018)
17. Tsitsiklis, J.N., Van Roy, B.: Analysis of temporal-difference learning with function approximation. In: Advances in Neural Information Processing Systems, pp. 1075–1081 (1997)

Reinforcement Learning II

Reinforcement Learning II

GAN-Based Planning Model in Deep Reinforcement Learning

Song Chen[1], Junpeng Jiang[1], Xiaofang Zhang[1,2(✉)], Jinjin Wu[1], and Gongzheng Lu[2]

[1] School of Computer Science and Technology, Soochow University, Suzhou, China
xfzhang@suda.edu.cn
[2] State Key Laboratory for Novel Software Technology, Nanjing University, Nanjing, China

Abstract. Deep reinforcement learning methods have achieved unprecedented success in many high-dimensional and large-scale space sequential decision-making tasks. In these methods, model-based methods rely on planning as their primary component, while model-free methods primarily rely on learning. However, the accuracy of the environmental model has a significant impact on the learned policy. When the model is incorrect, the planning process is likely to compute a suboptimal policy. In order to get a more accurate environmental model, this paper introduces the GAN-based Planning Model (GBPM) exploiting the strong expressive ability of Generative Adversarial Net (GAN), which can learn to simulate the environment from experience and construct implicit planning. The GBPM can be trained using real transfer samples experienced by the agent. Then, the agent can utilize the GBPM to produce simulated experience or trajectories so as to improve the learned policy. The GBPM can act as a role for experience replay so that it can be applied to both model-based and model-free methods, such as Dyna, DQN, ACER, and so on. Experimental results indicate that the GBPM can improve the data efficiency and algorithm performance on Maze and Atari 2600 game domain.

Keywords: Deep reinforcement learning · Model-based · Planning · Generative Adversarial Net

1 Introduction

Reinforcement learning methods [21,22] can be divided into model-based and model-free methods. The use of deep neural networks [8] combined with model-free reinforcement learning methods has made great progress in developing effective agents for a wide range of fields, where the original observations directly map to values or actions. For example, the Deep Q-Network (DQN) [10,11] has tackled many Atari games with complex visual input successfully. However, compared with model-based methods, a model-free approach fails to exploit the underlying sequential nature of decision-making [17], and thus it has no planning.

© Springer Nature Switzerland AG 2020
I. Farkaš et al. (Eds.): ICANN 2020, LNCS 12397, pp. 323–334, 2020.
https://doi.org/10.1007/978-3-030-61616-8_26

Model-based methods [5] rely on planning as their primary component, while model-free methods [4,19] primarily rely on learning. The key idea of model-based methods is to learn a model of the environment and then plan with this model. This learned model is used to evaluate and select among possible policies. As a sequence, model-based methods can support generalization to state samples that are not previously experienced and help to build the connection between present actions and future rewards. The most attractive advantage of model-based methods is that it can improve performance by increasing simulation steps.

In deep reinforcement learning, experience replay (ER) [1,6,10,11] is widely used to reduce sample correlation. Experience replay stores experience tuples which are sampled during training. The agent selects several transitions from the buffer and updates the value function. Experience replay can be viewed as a model-based RL method [13], where the buffer acts as a model of the environment. However, ER does not perform multi-step rollouts of hypothetical trajectories according to a model and it just replays previous agent-environment transitions. As a result, ER can avoid model errors, but it causes bias in updating.

In this paper, we introduce the GAN-based Planning Model (GBPM) exploiting the strong expressive ability of Generative Adversarial Net (GAN) [7], which can learn to simulate the environment from experience and construct implicit planning. The GBPM can get a more accurate model of the environment and it is data-efficient. During training, the GBPM can be trained by using real transfer samples the agent experienced and the agent can utilize the GBPM to produce simulated experiences or trajectories so as to polish the learned policy. An agent that uses the GBPM to implement two ways of planning: one is using simulated experience by the GBPM to improve policy, the other is using simulated experience by the GBPM to select an action for the current state.

The main contributions of this paper are: (1) This paper proposes a novel learnable model-based planning module for simulating the environment in RL. An agent can learn to construct a plan via the GAN-based Planning Model. (2) The GBPM can act as a role for experience replay so that it can be applied to both model-based and model-free methods. This paper integrates the GBPM into some deep reinforcement learning methods effectively, including Dyna [20, 21], DQN [11], and ACER [24]. (3) In this paper, comprehensive experiments are conducted to evaluate the algorithms integrated with GBPM, involving a maze solving problem and Atari 2600 games. The experiment results verify the improvement of algorithm performance in different state dimensions.

2   Related Work

Many effective work has focused on planning with model-based RL. The classic "Dyna" algorithm [21] learns a model of the environment, which is then used to train a policy. Tamar et al proposed the value iteration network (VIN) [23], which is a fully differentiable neural network with a planning module. It trains a deep CNN to plan via iterative rollouts implicitly. Similar to this work, David Silver et al presented the "Predictron" [18], which consists of a fully abstract model, represented by a Markov reward process, that can be rolled forward multiple "imagined" planning steps. The closest work to "Predictron" is "QMDP-net" [9], which is a neural network architecture for planning under partial observability. It combines the strengths of model-free learning and model-based planning. Similarly, Theophane Weber et al introduced Imagination-Augmented Agents (I2As) [15], which prescribes how a model should be used to arrive at a policy. It learns to interpret predictions from a learned environment model to construct implicit plans in arbitrary, by using the predictions as an additional context in deep policy networks. To prescribe how to construct a plan, Razvan Pascanu et al introduced the "Imagination-based Planner (IBP)" [14]. The IBP can learn to construct, evaluate, and execute plans and it can learn when to act versus when to imagine.

Many model-free reinforcement learning methods rely on experience replay. Experience replay can be viewed as a model-based RL method, where the buffer acts as a model of the environment. To improve the utilization of important samples, Schaul et al proposed a deep reinforcement learning with prioritized experience replay (PER) algorithm [16]. Wang et al presented an actor-critic DRL agent with experience replay (ACER) [24] and it adopts three innovations, including truncated importance sampling with bias correction, stochastic dueling network architectures, and efficient trust region policy optimization. To provide some of the benefits of both Dyna-style planning and ER, Pan et al developed a novel semi-parametric Dyna algorithm [13].

In this paper, with the strong expressive ability of GAN, we aim to propose a model that can learn to simulate the environment from experience and construct implicit planning. Furthermore, this model can act as a role for experience replay so that it can be applied to both model-based and model-free methods.

3   The GBPM Architecture

The GBPM is a model-based agent which learns from previous experience and can make effective planning about the future. We can get a more accurate model of the environment from the GBPM and it is data-efficient.

3.1   The GBPM Module

The architecture of the GBPM is shown in Fig. 1. The GBPM module is made up of GAN and it consists of a deep generative network model called Generator (G) and a deep discriminative network model called Discriminator (D). The Generator (G) and the Discriminator (D) are both deep network models.

In our work, the simulated model of the environment which is learned by the GBPM is used to predict the next state and the reward signals from the environment. In detail, the transition samples that agent experiences are considered as the training samples of the GBPM. The form of the transition samples is (s_t, a_t, r_t, s_{t+1}). The GBPM takes the tuple of (s_t, a_t) of transition samples as the noise input of the Generator (G). While the input of the Discriminator

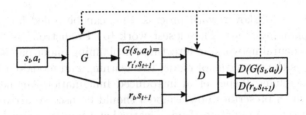

Fig. 1. The architecture of the GBPM.

(D) is the tuple of (r_t, s_{t+1}), that is the true reward and next state. As a result, the Generator (G) outputs the predicted reward and the next state according to the state and action in the time step t. This process can be described as $G(s_t, a_t) = r'_t, s'_{t+1}$. The Discriminator (D) outputs the probability of discriminating the newly generated transition sample that comes from the real sample.

During training, the generator and the discriminator take constantly confrontational training according to the actual transition samples. Thus, the GBPM can fit the environment better and implicit more accurately planning. Then the agent can take advantage of it to produce simulated experience or trajectories with the purpose of improving the learned policy.

The GBPM has an excellent ability for generalization. It can make accurate predictions of the future of agent. These generative samples may have been experienced by the agent, or perhaps the agent has never experienced. Therefore, the GBPM can effectively plan and guide the agent to improve its policy. In addition, the GBPM can replace the experience replay in some model-free methods. So it can be applied to both model-based and model-free methods.

3.2   Dyna with GBPM

Dyna is one of the classic model-based reinforcement learning algorithms. It is an integrated architecture for learning, planning and reacting. It is specifically designed for the situation in which the agent does not have complete knowledge of the effects of its actions on the environment.

Within a planning agent, real experience has at least two roles: it can be used to improve the model (to make it more accurately match the real environment), it is called model-learning. In our work, we use real experience to improve the GBPM. Real experience can also be used to directly improve the value function and policy using different kinds of reinforcement learning methods, such as Q-learning. In this case, it is called direct reinforcement learning.

DynaQ with the GBPM is a simple architecture integrating the major functions needed in an online planning agent. The overall architecture of DynaQ with the GBPM is shown in Fig. 2. The planning methods and the direct RL methods are both Q-learning. The agent interacts with the environment and produces real experience. We use it to train the GBPM and the GBPM can simulate the experience for planning.

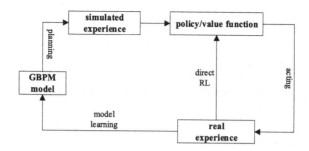

Fig. 2. The architecture of DynaQ with the GBPM.

3.3   DQN with GBPM

In order to improve the performance of the DQN on some tasks, the GBPM planning module is embedded to make DQN obtain the ability of planning.

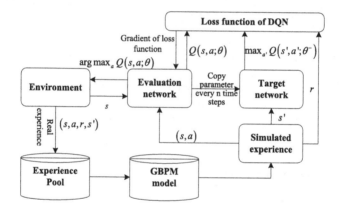

Fig. 3. The architecture of the DQN with the GBPM.

The complete training process of DQN with the GBPM is shown in Fig. 3. First of all, traditional DQN uses the experience replay mechanism. In our work, we replace the experience replay with the GBPM and still retain the use of the experience pool. We do not use the real experience to train the network but to learn a model of the environment with GAN, and it can produce simulated experience to train the network for planning. At each time step, the transferred samples $e_t = (s_t, a_t, r_t, s_{t+1})$ obtained by interacting the agent with the environment are stored in the experience pool $D = \{e_1, ..., e_t\}$. During training, each time a fixed number of transfer samples (mini-batch) are randomly selected from the experience pool to train the GBPM. Then the GBPM produces mini-batch simulated transition samples to update the parameters θ of the network with the Stochastic Gradient Descent algorithm.

3.4   ACER with GBPM

ACER is an actor-critic deep reinforcement learning algorithm with experience replay. Importance sampling is applied to control the variance and stability in ACER. It retrieves a trajectory $\{s_0, a_0, r_0, \mu(\cdot|s_0), ..., s_k, a_k, r_k, \mu(\cdot|s_k)\}$, where the actions have been sampled according to the behavior policy μ, from the memory of experience.

While in our work, ACER with the GBPM first samples a transition trajectory from the experience pool to train the GBPM and then it simulates a new trajectory according to the behavior policy μ. So the importance weighted policy gradient can be calculated by the simulated trajectory.

The rest of the ACER with the GBPM algorithm is exactly the same as ACER [24]. It estimates the action value function $Q^\pi(s_t, a_t)$ using Retrace [12] with multi-step estimation. To avoid high variance, importance weight truncation with bias correction is adopted in ACER. Moreover, ACER uses an efficient trust region policy optimization method which maintains an average policy network that represents a running average of past policies. In this paper, we embed a trainable planning module with GAN which can produce a simulated trajectory for training the network in the ACER.

4   Experiment

In this section, the performance of DynaQ and DynaQ-GBPM is compared on the Maze domain which is a simple maze that contains some obstacles [21]. Then the performance of DQN-GBPM and ACER-GBPM are evaluated on Atari games domain which is a discrete action domain.

4.1   Results on Maze Domain

Simple Maze. Our first experiment domain is a simple maze with some obstacles shown in Fig. 4. Each square can be considered as a state. The square with "S" is the start state and the square with "G" is the goal state.

In each state, there are four actions: up, down, right, and left, which take the agent deterministically to the corresponding neighboring states. When the agent moves to an obstacle or the edge of the maze, the agent remains where it is. The reward is zero on all transition, except those into the goal state, on which it is +1. After reaching the goal state, the agent returns to the start state to begin a new episode. This is a discounted and episodic task with $\gamma = 0.95$.

In this section, we first carry out an experiment in which DynaQ and DynaQ-GBPM agents are applied to the simple maze shown in Fig. 4. The average learning curves for the simple maze are shown in Fig. 5. The generator and the discriminator in the GBPM are both deep neural networks. The initial action values are zero, the step-size parameter is $\alpha = 0.1$ and the exploration parameter is $\epsilon = 0.1$. The planning step n of DynaQ and DynaQ-GBPM is 5. The curves show the number of steps taken by the agent to reach the goal in every episode, averaged over 30 repetitions of the environment.

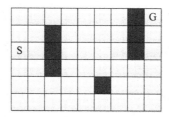

Fig. 4. The simple Maze domain.

Figure 5 shows that DynaQ-GBPM finds the solution to the goal faster than DynaQ. In DynaQ and DynaQ-GBPM, learning and planning are accomplished by exactly the same algorithm, operating on real experience for learning and on simulated experience for planning. However, the GBPM can simulate more accurate samples for the agent and can learn to fit the environment better. As the new experience is gained, the model is updated to match reality better. As the model changes, the planning process in DynaQ-GBPM will gradually compute a different way of behaving to match the new model.

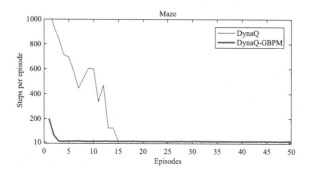

Fig. 5. Comparisons of DynaQ and DynaQ-GBPM for Simple Maze domain.

Blocking Maze. The second experiment domain is a blocking maze, which can be used to illustrate the existence of model error and then to check whether the agent can recover from the wrong model. The blocking maze is shown in Fig. 6. In Fig. 6(a), we can see that there is a short path from "S" to "G". Then after 1000 time steps, the position of the barrier has changed and the short path is "blocked". So we need to take a longer path along the left of the barrier from "S" to "G" which is shown in Fig. 6(b).

The graph of the average reward for DynaQ and DynaQ-GBPM is shown in Fig. 7. Both two agents find the short path within 1000 time steps, and the DynaQ-GBPM agent performs better than the DynaQ agent. After 1000 time

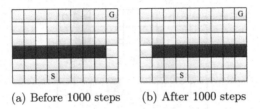

(a) Before 1000 steps   (b) After 1000 steps

Fig. 6. The Blocking Maze domain.

steps, the environment has changed. In this period, these two agents obtain no reward because they are wandering around behind the barrier. After a period of exploration, they are able to find the shortest path for a new optimal policy. The DynaQ-GBPM agent still performs better than the DynaQ agent and the gap between them gradually grows with increasing time step. So we can conclude that the DynaQ-GBPM agent easily understands the changes in the environment and can recover from the wrong model.

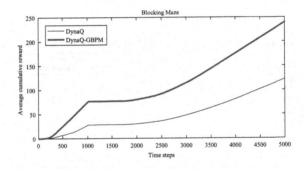

Fig. 7. Comparisons of DynaQ and DynaQ-GBPM for Blocking Maze domain.

4.2 Results on Atari Games Domain

The second experiment domain is the Atari 2600 game environment in the OpenAI Gym [2]. In this section, We compare the performance of DQN and DQN-GBPM, ACER and ACER-GBPM on four strategic Atari 2600 games.

DQN and DQN-GBPM. To compare the performance of DQN and DQN-GBPM, we use the same set of parameters in DQN [11]. The value network structure of DQN-GBPM is the same as DQN. The value network consists of three convolutional layers and two fully connected layers. The network architecture of the GBPM in DQN-GBPM is exactly the same as in infoGAN [3]. The generator consists of two fully connected layers and two convolutional layers. The discriminator is made up of two convolutional layers and two fully connected layers. The experiment conducts 200 independent training periods (Epoch) which includes 200000 steps parameter updating for each game.

We first compare the rewards of DQN, DQN-PER [16] and DQN-GBPM during each epoch of training the agent to play Atari 2600 games, including Seaquest, Amidar, Gravitar, and Alien. These four games have been widely used in recent related works. The DQN algorithm uses the normal experience replay which takes the samples from the experience pool with moderate probability. While the DQN-PER makes use of the prioritized experience replay which uses the time difference error of each sample as the criterion for evaluating the priority of samples. Different from these, the DQN-GBPM algorithm applies the GBPM to produce simulated experience.

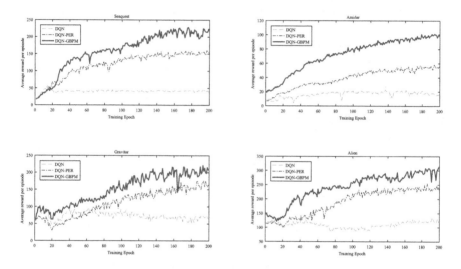

Fig. 8. Comparisons of DQN, DQN-PER and DQN-GBPM for Atari games

The results are shown in Fig. 8. It is indicated that DQN-GBPM outperforms DQN and DQN-PER on all of four Atari 2600 games. The GBPM can learn the real model of the environment based on the experience of the agent, so the DQN-GBPM algorithm gains the ability of planning and it can generalize to many states that the agent has never experienced. By contrast, the normal experience replay and the prioritized experience replay cannot express the environment model well, the performance of the DQN and DQN-PER algorithm is slightly worse than that of the DQN-GBPM algorithm.

ACER and ACER-GBPM. Most of the parameters used in the ACER and ACER-GBPM algorithms are identical in the experiment. The parameter settings are consistent with the parameter settings in the ACER algorithm [24].

When using experience replay, ACER gives each thread an experience pool with a capacity of 50000 samples. Moreover, ACER just uses real experience in the replay memory to generate sample trajectories for training. While ACER-GBPM produces a simulated sample trajectory for training using the GBPM environment model learned from real sample experience in the experience pool. The network architecture of the GBPM in ACER-GBPM is exactly the same as in DQN-GBPM. The experiment conducts 1,000 training periods (Epoch) and each Epoch includes 80,000 steps. Thus, a total of 80,000,000 steps are trained.

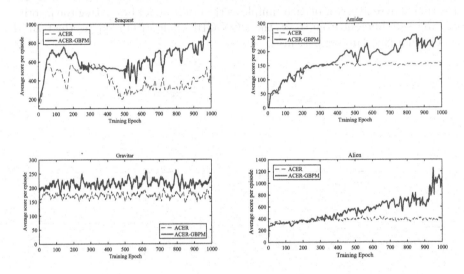

Fig. 9. Comparisons of ACER and ACER-GBPM for Atari games

We also compared the rewards of ACER and ACER-GBPM during each epoch of training the agent to play Atari 2600 games, including Seaquest, Amidar, Gravitar, and Alien. The results are shown in Fig. 9. ACER-GBPM outperforms ACER on all of four Atari 2600 games. Thus, we can conclude that the GBPM can learn the real model of the environment based on the experience of the agent and using the GBPM to produce simulated sample trajectories for training can improve the performance of the ACER algorithm.

5 Conclusion

In this paper, we have introduced the GAN-based Planning Model exploiting the strong expressive ability of GAN, which can learn to simulate the environment from experience and construct implicit planning. We have integrated the GBPM into some deep reinforcement learning methods effectively, like Dyna, DQN and ACER, endowing them the ability to learn model-based planning from GAN. A series of experiments on Maze and Atari 2600 game domains are conducted and empirical experiment results show that the GBPM does improve the performance of these algorithms.

In future work, how to improve the GBPM to make it more generalizable needs to be considered. Furthermore, how to embed the GBPM into other deep reinforcement learning algorithms based on planning, like Monte Carlo Tree Search is an interesting topic.

Acknowledgment. This work was supported in part by National Natural Science Foundation of China (61772263), Suzhou Technology Development Plan (SYG201807), and the Priority Academic Program Development of Jiangsu Higher Education Institutions.

References

1. Adam, S., Busoniu, L., Babuska, R.: Experience replay for real-time reinforcement learning control. IEEE Trans. Syst. Man Cybern. Part C (Appl. Rev.) **42**(2), 201–212 (2011). https://doi.org/10.1109/TSMCC.2011.2106494
2. Brockman, G., et al.: OpenAI gym. arXiv preprint arXiv:1606.01540 (2016)
3. Chen, X., Duan, Y., Houthooft, R., Schulman, J., Sutskever, I., Abbeel, P.: Info-GAN: interpretable representation learning by information maximizing generative adversarial nets. In: Advances in Neural Information Processing Systems, pp. 2172–2180 (2016)
4. Degris, T., Pilarski, P.M., Sutton, R.S.: Model-free reinforcement learning with continuous action in practice. In: 2012 American Control Conference (ACC), pp. 2177–2182. IEEE (2012). https://doi.org/10.1109/ACC.2012.6315022
5. Doya, K., Samejima, K., Katagiri, K.I., Kawato, M.: Multiple model-based reinforcement learning. Neural Comput. **14**(6), 1347–1369 (2002). https://doi.org/10.1162/089976602753712972
6. Foerster, J., et al.: Stabilising experience replay for deep multi-agent reinforcement learning. In: Proceedings of the 34th International Conference on Machine Learning, vol. 70, pp. 1146–1155. JMLR.org (2017)
7. Goodfellow, I., et al.: Generative adversarial nets. In: Advances in Neural Information Processing Systems, pp. 2672–2680 (2014)
8. Hinton, G., et al.: Deep neural networks for acoustic modeling in speech recognition: the shared views of four research groups. IEEE Sig. Process. Mag. **29**(6), 82–97 (2012). https://doi.org/10.1109/MSP.2012.2205597
9. Karkus, P., Hsu, D., Lee, W.S.: QMDP-Net: deep learning for planning under partial observability. In: Advances in Neural Information Processing Systems, pp. 4694–4704 (2017)
10. Mnih, V., et al.: Playing Atari with deep reinforcement learning. arXiv preprint arXiv:1312.5602 (2013)
11. Mnih, V., et al.: Human-level control through deep reinforcement learning. Nature **518**(7540), 529–533 (2015). https://doi.org/10.1038/nature14236
12. Munos, R., Stepleton, T., Harutyunyan, A., Bellemare, M.: Safe and efficient off-policy reinforcement learning. In: Advances in Neural Information Processing Systems, pp. 1054–1062 (2016)
13. Pan, Y., Zaheer, M., White, A., Patterson, A., White, M.: Organizing experience: a deeper look at replay mechanisms for sample-based planning in continuous state domains. arXiv preprint arXiv:1806.04624 (2018). https://doi.org/10.24963/ijcai.2018/666

14. Pascanu, R., et al.: Learning model-based planning from scratch. arXiv preprint arXiv:1707.06170 (2017)
15. Racanière, S., et al.: Imagination-augmented agents for deep reinforcement learning. In: Advances in Neural Information Processing Systems, pp. 5690–5701 (2017)
16. Schaul, T., Quan, J., Antonoglou, I., Silver, D.: Prioritized experience replay. arXiv preprint arXiv:1511.05952 (2015)
17. Shadlen, M.N., Shohamy, D.: Decision making and sequential sampling from memory. Neuron **90**(5), 927–939 (2016). https://doi.org/10.1016/j.neuron.2016.04.036
18. Silver, D., et al.: The predictron: end-to-end learning and planning. In: Proceedings of the 34th International Conference on Machine Learning, vol. 70, pp. 3191–3199. JMLR.org (2017)
19. Strehl, A.L., Li, L., Wiewiora, E., Langford, J., Littman, M.L.: PAC model-free reinforcement learning. In: Proceedings of the 23rd International Conference on Machine Learning, pp. 881–888 (2006). https://doi.org/10.1145/1143844.1143955
20. Sutton, R.S.: Dyna, an integrated architecture for learning, planning, and reacting. ACM SIGART Bull. **2**(4), 160–163 (1991). https://doi.org/10.1145/122344.122377
21. Sutton, R.S., Barto, A.G.: Reinforcement Learning: An Introduction. MIT Press, Cambridge (2018)
22. Sutton, R.S., Barto, A.G., et al.: Introduction to Reinforcement Learning, vol. 135. MIT Press, Cambridge (1998)
23. Tamar, A., Wu, Y., Thomas, G., Levine, S., Abbeel, P.: Value iteration networks. In: Advances in Neural Information Processing Systems, pp. 2154–2162 (2016)
24. Wang, Z., et al.: Sample efficient actor-critic with experience replay. arXiv preprint arXiv:1611.01224 (2016)

Guided Reinforcement Learning via Sequence Learning

Rajkumar Ramamurthy[(⊠)], Rafet Sifa, Max Lübbering,
and Christian Bauckhage

Fraunhofer IAIS, Sankt Augustin, Germany
{rajkumar.ramamurthy,rafet.sifa,max.lubbering,
christian.bauckhage}@iais.fraunhofer.de

Abstract. Applications of Reinforcement Learning (RL) suffer from high sample complexity due to sparse reward signals and inadequate exploration. Novelty Search (NS) guides as an auxiliary task, in this regard to encourage exploration towards unseen behaviors. However, NS suffers from critical drawbacks concerning scalability and generalizability since they are based off instance learning. Addressing these challenges, we previously proposed a generic approach using unsupervised learning to learn representations of agent behaviors and use reconstruction losses as novelty scores. However, it considered only fixed-length sequences and did not utilize sequential information of behaviors. Therefore, we here extend this approach by using sequential auto-encoders to incorporate sequential dependencies. Experimental results on benchmark tasks show that this sequence learning aids exploration outperforming previous novelty search methods.

Keywords: Reinforcement Learning · Exploration · Novelty Search · Representation learning · Sequence learning

1 Introduction

Reinforcement Learning (RL) is concerned with training of agents to learn any given task by interacting with an unknown environment. In combination with deep learning, they are successfully applied to a broad spectrum of complex tasks including playing games [13,27], navigating complex environments [12,30], and controlling robots [6,25]. However, current methods in RL face two major challenges such as sample inefficiency and inadequate exploration rendering them not suitable for real world applications. These challenges are attributed to the inherent nature of RL that is to deal with *sparse/deceptive rewards* and *exploration-exploitation dilemma*.

First, the learning is based on delayed and sparse reward signals that are available only in the goal states. In tasks that require longer episodes, propagating reward signals to previous actions poses a significant challenge of temporal

© Springer Nature Switzerland AG 2020
I. Farkaš et al. (Eds.): ICANN 2020, LNCS 12397, pp. 335–345, 2020.
https://doi.org/10.1007/978-3-030-61616-8_27

credit assignment. Even in dense reward settings, reward functions can be deceptive. For instance, consider a grid environment in which the agent is rewarded based on its distance to the goal position. Without adequate exploration, it may get stuck in deceptive walls, failing to reach the target. Further, the learning is typically done in an end-to-end fashion with deep neural networks, which also poses problem since the representation and policy are learnt simultaneously which would also require more training data.

Secondly, the RL agents has to deal with the   *exploration-exploitation* dilemma. ie. whether to pursue exploration or exploit the known policy to find better policies. Typically, exploration is still performed randomly using simple methods such as epsilon-greedy strategies, or Gaussian or Boltzmannian policies. Alternatively, exploration is also performed by perturbing weights of deep neural networks using black-box methods such as Evolution Strategies (ES) [22,23]. They have been found to scale better than traditional RL algorithms and have faster training wall-clock times. Nevertheless, a more directed exploration is desired due to the deceptiveness and sparseness of reward signals, which still demand a lot of training episodes.

Incorporating auxiliary tasks could be a powerful tool to address these concerns. These tasks are typically learnt simultaneously with primary RL goal and generate additional training signals when the reward signals are scarce. The main idea is to include an additional cost function in an unsupervised fashion as a form of multi-task learning. For instance, these auxiliary tasks include predicting terminal states [8], reward at next time steps [7] and depth maps from image observations [12]. However, incorporating an auxiliary task could be challenging [5] due to several reasons; the choice of a suitable auxiliary task for the original task and the weighting between the primary and auxiliary tasks has to be chosen appropriately, otherwise it would influence the primary objective and slow down the learning.

One approach that is tailored to solve these challenges is including Novelty Search [9,10] into RL objective [4]. The primary idea is to include an additional objective to encourage novel behaviors than observed in the past. This is achieved by incorporating a domain-specific behavioral characteristic (BC) that distinguish agent's behavior. BCs are generally designed by domain experts based on the given task and in this way, they are aligned with the reward objective. Classically, it is based on instance based learning and the novelty of a policy is computed as the distance to its k-nearest neighbors. This auxiliary task of novelty search has shown to improve exploration in several benchmark tasks.

However, such an approach has several drawbacks. First, it relies heavily on the storage of behaviors in an archive set upon which neighborhood models are applied to compute novelty scores. However, as complex tasks require storing a large number of policies with a high dimensional behavior characteristic, computing novelties becomes a computational bottleneck. Secondly, since only a limited set of policies can be stored in the archive set, it may not generalize well and is not robust to temporal variations.

In our previous work [20], we proposed a function approximation approach to address these concerns of scalability and generalizability pertaining to novelty search methods. In particular, we proposed to use sparse auto-encoders to learn representation of agent behaviors and to use reconstruction errors as novelty bonuses to policies. Yet, the sparse auto-encoders considered only fixed-length BCs and do not consider sequential information into account. In this paper, drawing on recent developments in machine translation and natural language processing, we propose to use a Recurrent Neural Network (RNN) based auto-encoders. Specifically, we use a Sequence-to-Sequence (shortly Seq-2-Seq) architecture to learn encodings of variable length BCs by utilizing sequential dependencies. Therefore, our main contribution is a simple and robust exploration approach to speed up learning along with an experimental evaluation against policy gradient and novelty search methods.

Related Work: Several methods have been proposed to improve sample efficiency and to promote directed exploration. However, the general theme of most approaches can be categorized mainly into (i) *reward shaping* which provide additional reward signals for intrinsic motivation [1,14,16] and curiosity [15,24] (ii) *auxiliary tasks* which incorporate additional objectives [7,8,12] into the RL objective to guide the policy learning In comparison, our approach can be seen as a hybrid approach; while incorporation of novelty objective falls under the category of auxiliary tasks, novelty scores can be seen as a form of reward shaping.

2   Preliminaries

We consider a Markov Decision Process (MDP) defined by the tuple $\langle S, A, T, R, \lambda \rangle$ where S is a set of states, A is a set of actions available to the agent, R is the reward function, T is the transition probability. In a standard RL setting, the agent observes o_t about the state s_t of the environment and performs an action a_t. On performing this action a_t, the environment moves to a new state s_{t+1} based on the transition function $T(s_{t+1}, s_t, a_t)$ and returns with a scalar reward based on the reward function $r_t = R(s_{t+1}, s_t, a_t)$. The actions are chosen using a policy function $\pi(s_t, a_t)$ which maps each state-action pair (s_t, a_t) to the probability of selecting the action in the particular state; Therefore, the goal is to find an optimal policy that maximizes the return discounted by $\lambda \in (0, 1)$ over a period of time T given as $G_T = \sum_{t=1}^{T} \lambda^{t-1} r_t$. For continuous high dimensional states and actions, the policy is approximated by a deep neural network π_θ with weights θ. In this case, the optimal policy is found by determining weights θ^* that maximize the expected cumulative reward $\theta^* = \text{argmax}_\theta \, \mathbb{E}_{\pi_\theta}[G_T]$. A variety of policy gradient methods [18,19,23,25,26] can be used to compute the optimal policy. Based on previous works, we consider Evolution Strategies [23] as it gives the flexibility to include novelty scores easily and parallelizable capabilities.

Evolution Strategies: Evolution strategies (ES) [21,22] are a class of black-box optimization procedures inspired by evolution. Let f be the objective function that acts on parameter θ. In RL, it is the cumulative reward obtained from the environment. ES maintains a multivariate gaussian distribution centered around the parameter with co-variance $\sigma^2 I$ (i.e.) $\theta \sim \mathcal{N}(0, \sigma^2 I)$. Given this, it aims to maximize the average objective of the entire population $\mathbb{E}_{\theta \sim \mathcal{N}(0, \sigma^2 I)}[F(\theta)]$.

At each iteration k, n perturbations are sampled from the distribution by adding gaussian noise to the current parameter θ (i.e. $\theta_k^i = \theta_k + \sigma \epsilon_i$ where $\epsilon_i \sim \mathcal{N}(0, I)$), $i = 0, 1, \ldots n$. Then the gradient is approximated by a sum of sampled perturbations weighted by their corresponding objective measurements

$$\nabla_{\theta_k} \mathbb{E}_{\epsilon \sim \mathcal{N}(0,I)}[F(\theta_k + \sigma \epsilon)] \approx \frac{1}{n\sigma} \sum_{i=1}^{n} F(\theta_k^i) \epsilon_i \qquad (1)$$

Novelty Search: Solving sparse/deceptive RL problems demand numerous interactions with environment. The main reason is that RL algorithms usually do not reward intermediate skills that lead to target skills. Novelty Search (NS) tackles this problem by directing the search towards policies with higher novelty instead of ones with higher cumulative reward. To distinguish policies, each policy π_θ (parameterized by a DNN with weights θ) is assigned a domain-dependent Behavior Characteristic (BC) denoted as $b(\pi_\theta)$. In continuous control tasks, it is typically a sequence of hand-designed features obtained during a roll out of the policy.

Classically, novelty search is performed through lazy learning using k-nearest neighbors. A set of fixed size known as archive set A stores observed policies and BCs. The novelty of a given parameterized policy $N(\theta, A)$ can be computed as the average distance to its K nearest neighbors. Given this metric, we can then use the ES framework as discussed above to drive the search process towards novel behaviors by taking a gradient step with respect to current policy parameters θ_k.

$$\nabla_{\theta_k} \mathbb{E}_{\epsilon \sim \mathcal{N}(0,I)}[N(\theta_k + \sigma \epsilon)] \approx \frac{1}{n\sigma} \sum_{i=1}^{n} N(\theta_k^i, A) \epsilon_i \qquad (2)$$

$$N(\theta, A) = \frac{1}{|K|} \sum_{i \in K} \|b(\pi_\theta) - b(i)\|^2 \qquad (3)$$

While novelty search alone can learn policies that would perform the given task, however it may ignore some aspects of reward functions when BC is not designed diligently. Therefore, novelty search is typically used to guide RL and can be incorporated in general to speed up the learning. With ES, it is straightforward to combine NS and RL objectives [4] using a weighted combination of objective as shown in the update rule in Eq. (4). The weight w for the RL objective is referred as "reward pressure" and it is initially set to 1.0 to purely pursue environment reward signals. Based on the learning progress, if the performance is not improved in few iterations k_{max}, the reward pressure w is decreased by δ_w. Similarly, when the performance is improved, then w is increased by δ_w

$$\boldsymbol{\theta}_{k+1} = \boldsymbol{\theta}_k + \alpha \frac{1}{n\sigma} \sum_{i=1}^{n} wF(\boldsymbol{\theta}_k^i)\epsilon_i + (1-w)N(\boldsymbol{\theta}_k^i, \boldsymbol{A})\epsilon_i \tag{4}$$

3   Sequence Learning of Agent Behaviors

Classic novelty search has several drawbacks. First, the policies are stored in an archive set, therefore to compute the novelty of a policy, its nearest neighbors must be retrieved first. Since complex tasks demand a large dimensional behavior characteristic and evaluate a large number of policies, finding nearest neighbors becomes a bottleneck computationally. Second, it may not generalize well to unseen behaviors as only a limited number of policies can be stored. To tackle this scalability and generalization issues, in our previous work [20], we proposed a general approach using sparse auto-encoders. The idea is to learn representation of agent behaviors and to use arising prediction error as a measure of novelty. By varying the sparsity levels, the generalization can be controlled.

However, the sparse auto-encoders [20] considered only fixed-length sequences; since it is a simple autoencoder, it does not recognize temporal dependencies between its input. Drawing on recent developments in natural language processing [29] and computer vision [28], it is beneficial to apply sequential autoencoders to model temporal dependencies. To that end, we propose to use Seq-2-Seq architecture that uses an RNN-based encoder to encode the given variable-length behavior sequence into a fixed-length context vector, followed by an RNN-based decoder reconstructs the behavior using the encoded context vector. The arising prediction error can be seen as a measure of novelty as new agent behaviors produce higher reconstruction errors.

In a nutshell, our system consists of two modules; a sequential autoencoder that provides novelty bonuses to policies and a policy learner module that trains a policy network that outputs action sequences to maximize the joint objective of cumulative reward and novelty.

Training: The sequential autoencoder consists of two RNNs: an encoder E with parameter with parameters ϕ_e and the decoder network D with parameters ϕ_d. The input to the model is BC of a policy which is a sequence of agent behaviors in the episode $\boldsymbol{b} = (\boldsymbol{b_1}, \boldsymbol{b_2}, \ldots \boldsymbol{b_T})$ where $b_i \in \mathbb{R}^N$. The encoder network reads in this sequence processing one element at a time. After the last element has been read, the final hidden state of the encoder network holds a representation of the entire agent behavior. Given this representation as input, the decoder network re-constructs the whole sequence by predicting one element at a time as $\boldsymbol{b}' = (\boldsymbol{b_1'}, \boldsymbol{b_2'}, \ldots \boldsymbol{b_T'})$. In particular, the decoder predicts the sequence in reverse order in order to keep the optimization tractable so that the network learns easily to predict low-order correlations. The two networks E and D are jointly trained to minimize the reconstruction loss L between the actual and the predicted sequences as in Eq. (5).

To encode diverse behaviors and to encourage generalizability, it is desired to enforce learning of sparse representations [20]. To this end, we follow [11] to retain only top k hidden units by setting rest of the units to zero. Further, to perform stable gradient updates, a fixed sized behavior buffer is used to store the behavior sequences. And, at each learning iteration, a mini-batch is sampled to perform the gradient descent.

$$L(\boldsymbol{b}, \boldsymbol{b'}) = \frac{1}{T} \sum_{i=1}^{T} \sum_{j=1}^{N} (\boldsymbol{b}_{ij} - \boldsymbol{b'}_{ij})^2 \tag{5}$$

Inference: During the inference, when a policy π_θ is given, a roll-out is performed and the behavior sequence $b(\pi_\theta)$ is collected. Then, the novelty bonus is compute by passing the behavior sequence to encoder-decoder networks to obtain the reconstruction error $N(\boldsymbol{\theta}) = L(b(\pi_\theta), b'(\pi_\theta))$.

4   Experimental Results

To evaluate our methods, we consider Mujoco continuous control tasks as they are a standard set of benchmark tasks. Particularly, we consider four tasks, namely Inverted Pendulum, Inverted Double Pendulum, Half Cheetah, and Hopper. The ES learner trains a policy network that is implemented as a multi-layer perceptron with two hidden layers, each containing 64 tanh neurons. At each time step, the observation vector is fed into the policy network, which then predicts an action vector denoting motor commands. For the training of the policy network, we use a learning rate of $\alpha = 0.1$. For generating the perturbations for ES, we sample 50 perturbations with a noise standard deviation $\sigma = 0.1$. However, for the inverted double pendulum, we use $\sigma = 0.01$ as its solutions are sensitive to perturbations. We use *pytorch-optimize* framework [17] which provides ES implementation that allows easy integration of multiple objective functions (reward and novelty).

Behavior Characterization: As discussed earlier, NS methods need a task-specific behavior characteristic to compute novelty scores. For the pendulum tasks, BC is a sequence of cart and pole positions. Similarly, for locomotive tasks, it is chosen to be the sequence of agent 2-D positions. Additionally, the agent positions are set relative to the start position, and the negative values are clipped to avoid agents to walk backward.

Sequential Auto-encoder: The autoencoder consists of encoder and decoder RNNs with Gated Recurrent Units (GRUs) [2] consisting of several layers. Additionally, the context vector from the encoder is subject to sparsity constraints. The encoder and decoder networks are jointly trained using Adam optimizer with a batch size of 100. For stable gradient updates, a behavior buffer of size 1000 is also maintained as in [20]. The behavior sequences are sampled based on the task to have the maximum sequence length of 50, and padding is not used, so that they are variable-length sequences. Other hyper-parameters such as learning rate, number of GRU units, and layers are obtained through formal search.

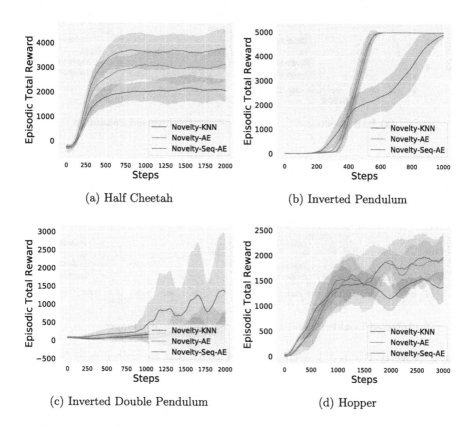

Fig. 1. **Pure Novelty Exploration:** Learning curves of agents that are trained using only novelty scores. We can observe that autoencoder based methods perform better than classic novelty search methods. More importantly, the sequential auto encoder approach performs better than plain auto encoder as it does not capture sequential dependencies

Baselines: To benchmark our approach, we consider two baselines. First, classic novelty search using k-nearest neighbors with $k = 10$ and an archive set of size 1000. In this case, the archive set is implemented as a FIFO so that only the recent behaviors are retained. The BC is a sequence of agent positions sub-sampled at intervals to have a fixed length of 50. Second, behavior auto encoder [20] is implemented as a feed-forward multi-layer perceptron with sparsity constraints. It is trained using Adam optimizer with learning rate of 0.001 and batch size of 100. The size of the behavior buffer is set to 1000 implemented the same

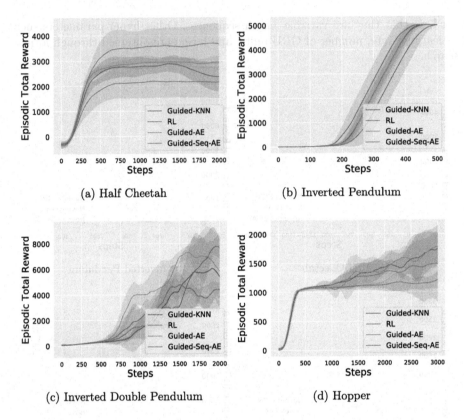

(a) Half Cheetah   (b) Inverted Pendulum

(c) Inverted Double Pendulum   (d) Hopper

Fig. 2. Novelty-Guided: Learning curves of agents that are trained using both novelty and reward scores. It is observed that the novelty guided methods perform better than ES. Particularly, sequential autoencoders performed better than other novelty guided methods.

way as in the archive set. The network architecture and sparsity levels are found through a formal grid search.

Discussion: We first test our methods on a pure novelty search setting by running with several random seeds. This can be achieved by setting the reward pressure w to 0. To benchmark, we compare against the baseline methods which use k-nearest neighbors and behavior autoencoders. Figure 1 shows the learning curves in the chosen tasks. Our important result is that the sequential autoencoders exhibit improvements over plain autoencoders, due to the incorporation of sequential dependencies, although the effects are not significant in some tasks. This is because the plain autoencoders are already high performing. In general, the representation learning of behaviors yields better performance than the classic novelty search.

Next, we apply our approach to a novelty-guided scenario by setting the reward pressure w to 1. In this way, initially, the policy is updated using only the environmental rewards. If the best performance stagnates more than $k_{max} = 50$, then reward pressure is decremented by a delta $\delta_w = 0.05$ so that novelty scores from the sequential auto encoder starts to guide the learning. Once the performance is improved, the reward pressure is incremented by the same delta. In this way, the importance of the auxiliary task can be adapted on the fly. As a pure RL baseline, we compare our solutions to ES, which considers only the environment rewards at any time. Figure 2 shows the summary of learning curves on chosen tasks. It is observed that the guided method using sequential autoencoders performs better than other guided methods that use k-nearest neighbors and plain autoencoders, in three out of four tasks. In general, all guided methods significantly improve upon the pure RL method, which shows the benefit of using auxiliary tasks. With respect to sparsity levels, in our grid search, we observed that sparse encodings yielded better results than dense ones, aligning with previous work [20]. In summary, our results suggest that learning of sequential dependencies helps encourage exploration.

5 Conclusion

In this paper, we proposed an unsupervised learning approach to act as an auxiliary task to guide RL. The results suggest the sequence prediction of agent behaviors performs better than simple reconstruction using plain autoencoders. Our work connects the idea of Novelty Search with Auxiliary tasks because it is generally tagged only as an approach to improve exploration. This connection opens up several opportunities; in addition to novelty search task, additional auxiliary tasks can also be devised. For instance, an expert's preference [3] obtained through human interaction can also be incorporated to guide the learning. Since ES offers easy integration of these additional objectives out of the box, we intend to focus our future work in this direction.

Acknowledgement. In parts, the authors of this work were supported by the Fraunhofer Research Center for Machine Learning (RCML) within the Fraunhofer Cluster of Excellence Cognitive Internet Technologies (CCIT). We gratefully acknowledges this support.

References

1. Bellemare, M.G., Srinivasan, S., Ostrovski, G., Schaul, T., Saxton, D., Munos, R.: Unifying Count-Based Exploration and Intrinsic Motivation. arXiv preprint arXiv:1606.01868 (2016)
2. Cho, K., et al.: Learning phrase representations using RNN encoder-decoder for statistical machine translation. arXiv preprint arXiv:1406.1078 (2014)
3. Christiano, P.F., Leike, J., Brown, T., Martic, M., Legg, S., Amodei, D.: Deep reinforcement learning from human preferences. In: Advances in Neural Information Processing Systems, pp. 4299–4307 (2017)
4. Conti, E., Madhavan, V., Such, F.P., Lehman, J., Stanley, K.O., Clune, J.: Improving Exploration in Evolution Strategies for Deep Reinforcement Learning via a Population of Novelty-Seeking Agents. arXiv preprint arXiv:1712.06560 (2017)

5. Du, Y., Czarnecki, W.M., Jayakumar, S.M., Pascanu, R., Lakshminarayanan, B.: Adapting Auxiliary Losses using Gradient Similarity. arXiv preprint arXiv:1812.02224 (2018)
6. Gu, S., Holly, E., Lillicrap, T., Levine, S.: Deep reinforcement learning for robotic manipulation with asynchronous off-policy updates. In: Proceedings of International Conference on Robotics and Automation (2017)
7. Jaderberg, M., et al.: Reinforcement Learning with Unsupervised Auxiliary Tasks. arXiv preprint arXiv:1611.05397 (2016)
8. Kartal, B., Hernandez-Leal, P., Taylor, M.E.: Terminal prediction as an auxiliary task for deep reinforcement learning. In: Proceedings of the AAAI Conference on Artificial Intelligence and Interactive Digital Entertainment (2019)
9. Lehman, J., Stanley, K.O.: Abandoning objectives: evolution through the search for novelty alone. Evol. Comput. **19**(2), 189–223 (2011)
10. Lehman, J., Stanley, K.O.: Evolving a diversity of virtual creatures through novelty search and local competition. In: Proceedings of International Conference on Genetic and Evolutionary Computation (2011)
11. Makhzani, A., Frey, B.: K-sparse autoencoders. arXiv preprint arXiv:1312.5663 (2013)
12. Mirowski, P., et al.: Learning to Navigate in Complex Environments. arXiv preprint arXiv:1611.03673 (2016)
13. Mnih, V., et al.: Human-level control through deep reinforcement learning. Nature **518**, 529–533 (2015)
14. Ostrovski, G., Bellemare, M.G., van den Oord, A., Munos, R.: Count-Based Exploration with Neural Density Models (2017)
15. Pathak, D., Agrawal, P., Efros, A.A., Darrell, T.: Curiosity-driven exploration by self-supervised prediction. In: Proceedings of International Conference on Machine Learning (2017)
16. Pathak, D., Gandhi, D., Gupta, A.: Self-Supervised Exploration via Disagreement. arXiv preprint arXiv:1906.04161 (2019)
17. Ramamurthy, R.: Pytorch-Optimize - A Black Box Optimization Framework. https://github.com/rajcscw/pytorch-optimize (2020)
18. Ramamurthy, R., Bauckhage, C., Sifa, R., Schücker, J., Wrobel, S.: Leveraging domain knowledge for reinforcement learning using MMC architectures. In: Tetko, I.V., Kůrková, V., Karpov, P., Theis, F. (eds.) ICANN 2019. LNCS, vol. 11728, pp. 595–607. Springer, Cham (2019). https://doi.org/10.1007/978-3-030-30484-3_48
19. Ramamurthy, R., Bauckhage, C., Sifa, R., Wrobel, S.: Policy learning using SPSA. In: Kůrková, V., Manolopoulos, Y., Hammer, B., Iliadis, L., Maglogiannis, I. (eds.) ICANN 2018. LNCS, vol. 11141, pp. 3–12. Springer, Cham (2018). https://doi.org/10.1007/978-3-030-01424-7_1
20. Ramamurthy, R., Sifa, R., Lübbering, M., Bauckhage, C.: Novelty-guided reinforcement learning via encoded behaviors. In: Proceedings of International Joint Conference on Neural Networks (2020)
21. Rechenberg, I.: Evolutionsstrategie: Optimierung technischer Systeme nach Prinzipien der biologischen Evolution. Ph.D. thesis, Technical University of Berlin, Department of Process Engineering (1971)
22. Rechenberg, I.: Evolutionsstrategien. In: Simulationsmethoden in der Medizin und Biologie (1978)
23. Salimans, T., Ho, J., Chen, X., Sutskever, I.: Evolution Strategies as a Scalable Alternative to Reinforcement Learning. arXiv:1703.03864 (2017)
24. Schmidhuber, J.: Formal theory of creativity, fun, and intrinsic motivation (1990–2010). IEEE Trans. Auton. Mental Dev. **2**, 230–247 (2010)

25. Schulman, J., Levine, S., Abbeel, P., Jordan, M., Moritz, P.: Trust region policy optimization. In: Proceedings of International Conference on Machine Learning (2015)
26. Silver, D., Lever, G., Heess, N., Degris, T., Wierstra, D., Riedmiller, M.: Deterministic policy gradient algorithms. In: Proceedings of International Conference on Machine Learning (2014)
27. Silver, D., et al.: Mastering the game of go without human knowledge. Nature **550**(7676), 354–359 (2017)
28. Srivastava, N., Mansimov, E., Salakhudinov, R.: Unsupervised learning of video representations using LSTMs. In: Proceedings of International Conference on Machine Learning (2015)
29. Sutskever, I., Vinyals, O., Le, Q.V.: Sequence to sequence learning with neural networks. In: Proceedings in Neural Information Processing Systems (2014)
30. Zhu, Y., et al.: Target-driven visual navigation in indoor scenes using deep reinforcement learning. In: Proceedings of International Conference on Robotics and Automation (2017)

Neural Machine Translation Based on Improved Actor-Critic Method

Ziyue Guo, Hongxu Hou$^{(\boxtimes)}$, Nier Wu, and Shuo Sun

College of Computer Science-College of Software,
Inner Mongolia University, Hohhot, China
guoziyue08@126.com, cshhx@imu.edu.cn, wunier04@126.com, sunshuo07@126.com

Abstract. Reinforcement learning based neural machine translation (NMT) is limited by the sparse reward problem which further affects the quality of the model, and the actor-critic method is mainly used to enrich the reward of the output fragments. But for low-resource agglutinative languages, it does not show significant results. To this end, we propose an novel actor-critic approach that provides additional affix-level rewards and also combines the traditional token-level rewards to guide the parameters update of the NMT model. In addition, for purpose of improving the decoding speed, we utilize an improved non-autoregressive model as the actor model to make it pay more attention to the translation quality while outputting in parallel. We achieve remarkable progress on two translation tasks, including the low-resource Mongolian-Chinese and the public NIST English-Chinese, while significantly shorting training time and accomplishing faster convergence.

Keywords: Non-autoregressive neural machine translation ·
Reinforcement Learning · Actor-Critic Method

1 Introduction

Most neural machine translation architectures (NMT) [2,12] are autoregressive models that sequentially generate target sequences. Among them, the model with the most excellent performance is the Transformer [13], which is completely based on the Attention Mechanism [2] and realizes the parallelization of the training process which highly reduce the delay of training phase. However, since there is no golden reference when decoding, it utilizes previous generated sequence to predict the target word which seriously affects the decoding efficiency. In recent years, Gu et al. [4] proposed non-autoregressive neural machine translation model (NAT) which utilizes Knowledge Distillation [5] method to assist training and realizes the parallelization of the decoding process while further significantly reduces the decoding delay. Subsequently, many works are improved on the basis of this model and to some extent alleviate the over-translation and under-translation problems of the non-autoregressive model without losing its fast decoding characteristic, such as [6,10,11] and [14].

© Springer Nature Switzerland AG 2020
I. Farkaš et al. (Eds.): ICANN 2020, LNCS 12397, pp. 346–357, 2020.
https://doi.org/10.1007/978-3-030-61616-8_28

In this paper, inspired by Wu [15], we apply the idea of Reinforcement Learning (RL) to our model by using the Actor-Critic algorithm [1] and accelerate the decoding speed by treating the NAT architecture as a actor model to iteratively optimize the generated translation. At the same time, considering that for the language with rich morphology, only the token-level rewards of traditional reinforcement learning cannot be used to obtain the sentence structure and deeper semantics of the tokens [3], so we propose to add additional affix-level rewards and in conjunction with original rewards to guide the parameters update. Moreover, so as to further improve the translation quality of the NAT model, we propose to add capsule network [8] layers in the encoder and decoder to replace the position encoding layer, which can extract deeper position information of the source sequence. We also utilize the Interpolation Knowledge Distillation [5] method to use the output of the autoregressive teacher model as the distilled data.

We verify the effectiveness of the proposed architecture on two machine translation tasks, including NIST English-Chinese and CCMT2019 Mongolian-Chinese, and further validate from different aspects such as model time consuming and the convergence of the loss function. For NIST English-Chinese, experiments show that our model has an average increase of 7.45 BLEU scores compared to the baseline NAT model. What's more remarkable is that compared to the baseline actor-critic model, the speed has increased by nearly 4 times, and at the same time the results are close to similar. Furthermore, so as to verify that the affix-level reward can further consider the grammar and semantic information between sentences, we also carry out ablation study on CCMT2019 Mongolian-Chinese, and finally obtained 27.98 BLEU with the decoding delay is only 179 ms.

2   Background

2.1   Non-autoregressive Neural Machine Translation

Under the condition of given source sequence $S = (s_1, ..., s_n)$ and target sequence $T = (t_1, ..., t_L)$, the autoregressive model (AT) simulates the conditional distribution of S and T by searching the maximum likelihood of the current predictive word based on the source sentence and the generated target sentence. The process has the following equation:

$$P_{AR}(T|S; \theta) = \prod_{l=1}^{L} P(t_l|t_1, ..., t_{l-1}, S; \theta) \tag{1}$$

where L represents the length of the target sentence and θ is a series of parameters of the model.

Such models are comprehensive used and have brilliant performance in neural sequence modeling. However, there is a large delay since the decoding phase needs to depend on the generated words. In order to improve the decoding speed, Gu et al. [4] propose a non-autoregressive neural machine translation model which breaks the order dependence characteristic of the traditional models and achieves parallelization of decoding by generating independent distributions of each target word simultaneously:

$$P_{NAR}(T|S;\theta) = P(L_y|S;\theta)) \prod_l P(t_l|S, L_y; \theta) \tag{2}$$

where L_y represents the predicted target sentence length.

2.2   Actor-Critic Based Neural Machine Translation

RL can be leveraged to bridge the gap between NMT training and inference by directly optimizing the evaluation indicators such as BLEU scores during training. Specifically, NMT model can be regarded as an agent that interacts with the environment and the agent will select an action from the vocabulary, that is a candidate word according to the policy (ie, the parameters of agent).

The reward is defined as $R(\hat{t}, t_l)$ in NMT by comparing generated sentence $\hat{t}$ with reference sentence t. It is a token-level reward and once the NMT model generates a complete target sequence, the overall final feed will be observed. The objective function is to maximize the expected reward:

$$L_{RL} = \sum_{l=1}^{L} E_{\hat{t} \sim p(\hat{t}|s_l)} R(\hat{t}, t_l) = \sum_{l=1}^{L} \sum_{\hat{t} \epsilon T} p(\hat{t}|s_l) R(\hat{t}, t_l) \tag{3}$$

where T is the space for all candidate translation sentences which is grows exponentially because of the large vocabulary size, and it is impossible to accurately maximize L_{RL}.

3   Approach

3.1   Actor Model

Encoder. As shown in Fig. 1, we utilize an improved non-autoregressive model as actor model to accelerate the decoding process. The features detected by all capsules in the Capsule Network [8] are encapsulated in the form of vector. We bring it into the NAT model based on the intuition: extracting more positional characteristics from the source sentence will benefit to the hidden layer states of the encoder and decoder. Inspired by this, we use the source word embedding e_i calculated by the self-attention layer as the input of each capsule:

$$c_j = \sum_i \alpha_{ij} F(e_i, w_{ij}) \tag{4}$$

where α is the coupling coefficient, w_{ij} is the weight matrix, $F(\cdot)$ denotes transformation function and we use feed-forward neural network to achieve. The output c_j contains in-depth position information in a vector manner.

Decoder Based on Capsule Network. Similar to the encoder side, we use the child capsule network layer to extract the source information more deeply. To comprehensively capture the overall information of the source, we introduce the parent capsule network layer to integrate the information of the M children capsules and map it to the representation suitable for the parent capsules, the process can be described as Eq. 5:

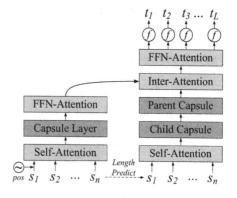

Fig. 1. The architecture of the improved actor model.

$$s_j = \sum_i^M F(c_{ij}, w_{ij}) \qquad (5)$$

Our Squashing function compresses the modulus of the input vector to $[0, 1)$. The parent capsule will update the status based on the input information flow:

$$p_j = Squash(s_j) = \frac{\|s_j\|^2}{1 + \|s_j\|^2} \cdot \frac{s_j}{\|s_j\|^2} \qquad (6)$$

Then integrate all of the children capsules to generate parent capsules representation $P = [p_1, p_2, ..., p_N]$ which containing the position information. The source sequence is encoded into N capsules, later iteratively determine what information will be fed to the Inter-Attention sub-layer:

$$Attention(Q_p, K_p, V_p) = softmax(\frac{Q_p K_p^T}{\sqrt{d_k}}) \cdot V_p \qquad (7)$$

where Q_p is the output of parent capsule network containing location information and K_p, V_p are the vectors from the encoder.

Providing the decoder with a source sequence that combines location information will assist the implementation of parallelization and make the generated translation have a favorable word order. We combine the extracted location relationship with the source information, then feed these directly to the attention layer to provide a stronger signal. All of the Q_p, K_p, V_p can be calculated by Eq. 8:

$$Emb(Q_p, K_p, V_p) = (e_1 + p_1, ..., e_n + p_n) \qquad (8)$$

where e_i means the initial input word embedding and p_i represents the position information perceived via capsule network.

Length Predictor. During training phase, there is no requirement to predict the target sentence length due to the exist of ground truth. However, for the sake of accomplishing parallel decoding, predicting the sentence length in advance will advantage the decoder to infer. We adopt a creative and persuasive equation to calculate:

$$L_y = \eta L_x + C \tag{9}$$

where C is an bias term and η represents the ratio between target length and source length in the training set. Then we predict the target sentence length from $[\alpha L_x - B, \alpha L_x + B]$, where B represents half of the searching window. Through this method, we can get multiple translation sentences of different lengths.

3.2   Critic Model

For the NMT method of RL, it is usually selects an action which is a candidate word from the lexical table according to the previously generated target words and source sequence. After generating the complete sequence $\hat{T} = \{\hat{t}_1, ..., \hat{t}_M\}$, the reward is calculated by comparing with the ground truth $T^* = \{t_1^*, ..., t_L^*\}$:

$$R(\hat{T}, T^*) = \sum_{m=1}^{M} r_m(\hat{t}_m; \hat{T}_{1,...,m-1}, T^*)) \tag{10}$$

where M is the length of the generated sequence $\hat{T}$ and $\hat{T}_{1,...,m-1}$ is the candidate sequence that has been generated. $R(\hat{T}, T^*)$ represents a token-level reward between the generated translation and the ground truth which can be optimized by iteratively updating.

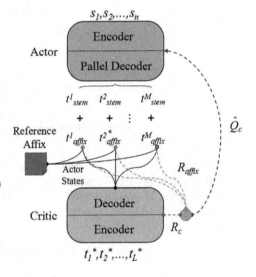

Fig. 2. The framework of improved actor-critic method.

Nevertheless, there is only one final reward for the complete candidate sequence generated. This sparseness of reward will affect the efficiency of the model. Bahdanau et al. [1] propose to utilize the intermediate rewards generated by the actor network to facilitate the learning of the critic network which is shown in Eq. 11:

$$r_l(\hat{t}, t_l^*) = R(\hat{t}_{1...l}, t^*) - R(\hat{t}_{1...l-1}, t^*) \tag{11}$$

However, the reward is only based on the morphological similarity of the actor model output and the reference translation, which does not show significant performance for low-resource languages.

To this end, we propose an improved method of actor-critic which provides additional affix-level rewards for such rich-forming languages. As shown in Fig. 2, we jointly train token-level rewards predicted by critic and additional affix similarity rewards introduced in this paper to iteratively optimize the generated translation. Specifically, due to the state of the generated translation may be confused, that is the problem of inaccurate additional components of words, so we add part-of-speech (POS) annotation to the output of the actor model. Then perform the segmentation of stems and affixs and calculate affix-level rewards based on the ground truth. In this way, according to the POS of the generated word, the semantic relationship of the sentence in which the word is located can be further obtained. In the experiment, we set a threshold when solving the affix similarity which is introduced in Sect. 4.2 specifically.

Critic model takes the golden reference as the input of the encoder and calculates the token-level value R_c and affix-level similarity reward R_{affix} between the candidate sequence generated by the actor model and the corresponding reference at each time step. The critic accumulates the learned single-step rewards and outputs the total reward Q_c eventually to guide the optimization of the actor model:

$$
\begin{aligned}
\hat{Q}_c &= \lambda R_c(\hat{T}, T^*) + (1 - \lambda) R_{affix}(\hat{T}, T^*) \\
&= \lambda \sum_{l=1}^{L} r_c(\hat{t}_l; t_l^*) + (1 - \lambda) \sum_{l=1}^{L} r_{affix}(\hat{t}_l; t_l^*)
\end{aligned}
\tag{12}
$$

where λ is hyper-parameter and $R_{affix}(\cdot)$ represents the additional affix similarity reward which we employ *cosine similarity* to measure it, as shown in Eq. 13:

$$
r_{affix} = \frac{\hat{t}_l \cdot t_l^*}{\|\hat{t}_l\| \, \|t_l^*\|}
\tag{13}
$$

3.3   Training

Objective Function. During the training phase, we utilize cross-entropy to calculate the loss of the non-autoregressive model with position awareness, as shown in Eq. 14:

$$
L_{NAT}(S; \theta) = - \sum_{l=1}^{L_y} \sum_{t_l} (log P_{NAT}(t_l | L_y, S) \cdot log P_{AT}(t_l | t_1, .., t_{l-1}, S; \theta))
\tag{14}
$$

Interpolation Knowledge Distillation. We employ Sequence-Level Interpolation Knowledge Distillation (SIKD) [5] to fine-tune which make the model simultaneously consider both the teacher's output and its golden reference for the same source. The loss function is shown in Eq. 15:

$$
L_{SIKD} = (1 - \xi) L_{NLL} + \xi L_{KD} = -(1 - \xi) log p(r|s) - \xi log p(\hat{r}|s)
\tag{15}
$$

where ξ is hyper-parameter, r is the golden reference and $\hat{r}$ is the distilled data from the teacher model. Then we expand the second intractable item:

$$\hat{t} = \underset{\hat{y} \in \Omega_k}{argmax sim}(\hat{r}, \hat{y})q(\hat{y}|s) \tag{16}$$

where sim is the similarity calculated by *Jaccard distance*, Ω_k is the K-best list from beam search which is close to $\hat{r}$ and has high probability under the guidance of teacher model, and $q(\cdot)$ represents the probability distribution of the teacher model (ie, the autoregressive model).

Reinforcement Learning. The reward of RL will be changed to the weighted sum of the original reward and the affix-level reward which is shown in Eq. 17:

$$L_{RL} = \sum_{l=1}^{L_y} E_{\hat{t} \sim p(\hat{t}|s_l)} \left[\lambda R_c(\hat{t}, t_l^*) + (1-\lambda)R_{affix}(\hat{t}, t_l^*) \right] \tag{17}$$

Joint Training. We fine-tune the non-autoregressive model with interpolation knowledge distillation and perform secondary training on the NAT-based actor model and critic model. The final training loss is shown in the Eq. 18:

$$L_{Total} = \beta(\alpha L_{NAT} + (1-\alpha)L_{SIKD}) + (1-\beta)L_{RL} \tag{18}$$

where α and β are hyper-parameters.

4   Experiments

4.1   Experimental Setting

Datasets. We utilize two machine translation tasks in our experiments: NIST English-Chinese (En-Zh)[1] and CCMT2019 Mongolian-Chinese (Mo-Zh). For NIST En-Zh, we use MT02 as validation set and employ MT03, MT04, MT05 and MT06 as test sets. Furthermore, we segment all datasets into sub-word units by byte pair encoder (BPE) algorithm [9] and use our own tools to divide CCMT2019 Mo-Zh task into stems and affixes.

Baseline. We use the synchronous decoding model proposed by Zhou et al. [16] as the teacher model to guide the training of the actor model. The following tasks are selected as baseline systems: Transformer [13] with state-of-the-art performance, NAT-FT model proposed by Gu et al. [4], NAT model by iterative refinement [6], NAT model for retrieving sequential information [10], NMT system with reinforcement learning [15] which denote as RL-NMT and actor-critic for sequence prediction model [1].

---

[1] https://www.ldc.upenn.edu/.

Model Setting. The parameter settings of our model are the same as described in Transformer [13]. The word vector dimension set to 278 and the number of hidden layer neurons set to 507, layer depth set to 5, the attention head set to 2 and the number of capsules is set to 6. We set the hyper-parameter ξ in Eq. 15 to 0.5, λ in Eq. 17 to 0.5, α to 0.6 and β to 0.5 in Eq. 18 based on experimental verification. Latency is computed as average per sentence decoding time on the full test set without mini-batching and we test it on two NIVDIA TITAN X.

Table 1. Experimental results of different models on the NIST English-Chinese dataset. Where "multinomial" indicates that multinomial sampling is utilized to make the data diverse, "shaping" represents that reward shaping is employed and "i" means the number of iterations. RF-C denotes Reinforce-Critic based on actor-critic algorithm, LL empresses log-likelihood training. In our model, NAT-CN indicates the NAT model with the addition of the capsule network layers, NAT-CN+AC means using the improved non-autoregressive model as the actor model, and "Total" represents combining all the methods mentioned in this article.

Models	NIST En-Zh						Latency
	Dev	MT03	MT04	MT05	MT06	Average	
Transformer	29.40	27.61	25.94	26.33	28.18	27.02	707 ms
RL-NMT(beam size = 4)	27.35	26.59	26.47	26.26	27.27	26.88	591 ms
RL-NMT(multinomial+shaping)	27.72	27.06	26.28	26.96	27.48	26.95	623 ms
NAT-FT	19.60	18.35	17.86	18.11	16.93	17.81	102 ms
NAT-IR($i = 10$)	20.13	19.32	18.02	18.98	18.23	18.64	398 ms
NAT-RSI	21.88	19.60	18.52	20.64	19.63	19.60	189 ms
Actor-Critic(RF-C+LL)	26.87	25.70	26.05	26.39	25.22	25.84	641 ms
Our model							
NAT-CN	20.85	21.03	19.99	20.98	21.42	20.86	78 ms
NAT-CN+AC	24.32	23.74	23.52	24.01	22.68	23.49	145 ms
NAT-CN+Total	26.76	24.35	25.67	26.02	24.98	25.26	163 ms

4.2 Results and Analysis

Main Results. We mainly perform experiments on the NIST English-Chinese dataset and the experiment results are shown in Table 1. Where "average" represents the average BLEU [7] score of test sets from MT03 to MT06.

For our improved NAT model with capsule network, the BLEU[2] score is increased 4.49 on the MT06 test set compared to the baseline NAT-FT model and the average BLEU score is increased 3.05 but the decoding delay is reduced 24 ms. When the improved NAT model is used as the actor model, the average BLEU score is 23.49 and the decoding delay is only 145 ms which is 4.42 times

---

[2] https://github.com/moses-smt/mosesdecoder/blob/master/scripts/generic/multi-bleu.perl.

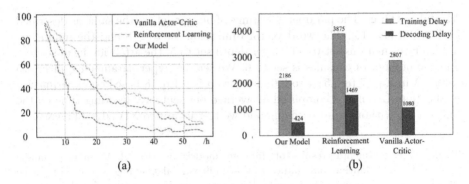

Fig. 3. (a) Graph of loss function for different models. (b) Diagram of training time for different models.

faster than the baseline actor-critic model. After combining all the methods, our model has an average increase of 7.45 BLEU scores compared to the NAT-FT model and the MT06 test set significantly improved 8.05 BLEU scores. It still has a certain degree of BLEU score difference when compared with Transformer, but our model has a speed increase of 4.34 times. It is worth noting that compared to the baseline actor-critic model, the speed is increased by about 4 times while achieving similar results.

Effect of Training Time. In order to verify the validity of our model, we also conduct experiments on the convergence of the loss function and the time consuming of the training process. We compare our model with the original actor-critic model [1] and the NMT model with RL [15]. As shown in Fig. 3(a), our model achieves faster convergence, and the curve gradually stabilizes after convergence. The training time of the different models are shown in

Table 2. Quality evaluation on CCMT2019 Mongolian-Chinese dataset. Where VR represents the vanilla token-level reward, SIKD is short for sentence-level interpolation knowledge distillation method, POS refers to part-of-speech tagging of tokens, and ASR is the proposed affix similarity reward.

Mo-Zh	Latency	BLEU	Promote
+VR	105 ms	25.31	–
+SIKD	148 ms	26.48	+1.17
+POS	166 ms	26.83	+1.52
+ASR	179 ms	27.98	+2.67

Fig. 3(b), our model is significantly lower than the other two models in terms of training delay and decoding delay. This is because we utilize non-autoregressive model as the actor model which can generate target tokens in parallel and greatly reduce translation latency.

Ablation Study. As shown in Table 2, we perform ablation study on different methods utilized in this paper on CCMT2019 Mongolian-Chinese dataset. When using the vanilla token-level reward only, the BLEU score is 25.31 and the decoding delay is only 105 ms. After combining the interpolation knowledge distillation method, the BLEU scores increased 1.17, and the part-of-speech tagging also brings an improvement of 0.35 BLEU scores. Since Mongolian is a kind of agglutinative language with rich word composition, we get 1.15 BLEU scores improvement when we combined the affix-level reward which is sufficient to prove that the calculation of affix-level reward further considers the sentence pattern and semantics between the generated translation and the golden reference. When combined all the methods, we get 27.98 BLEU scores which has a significant improvement of 2.67 compared to the baseline system, but the decoding delay is only 179 ms.

Effect of Affix Similarity Threshold a. We set a threshold when solving the affix similarity between the generated tokens and the reference tokens. If the value of similarity exceeds the threshold, the reward obtained will also increase to indicate that the status is normal, yet if it is lower than the threshold, the affix similarity reward will decrease which indicates that the state is more chaotic and the

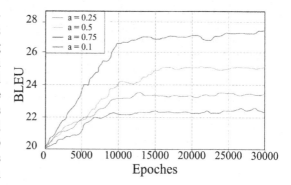

Fig. 4. Training curves for affix similarity with different threshold a.

parameters still need to be updated. When it is at a high level of affix similarity, the generated translation is generally consistent with golden reference in terms of pattern and the meaning of sentence, otherwise it is regarded as inconsistent. The choice of threshold is shown in Fig. 4, when $a = 0.75$ the system has the most stable and fastest BLEU improvement over time.

5 Conclusion

We propose a novel NAT model architecture which combines the pose transformation characteristics of the capsule network to obtain higher location features. We regard the improved NAT model as an actor model to greatly increase the decoding speed. Moreover, we combine the proposed affix-level reward with the original reward as the final feedback to optimize the translation generated by the actor in an iterative manner, thereby alleviating the reward sparse problem of reinforcement learning especially in low-resource languages. The experiments show that our model has significantly improved both in translation quality and decoding speed.

Our future work is to apply the proposed model to more machine translation tasks, especially for low-resource languages, and to explore methods that are more suitable for the characteristics of agglutinative languages.

References

1. Bahdanau, D., et al.: An actor-critic algorithm for sequence prediction. In: 5th International Conference on Learning Representations, ICLR 2017, Toulon, France, 24–26 April 2017, Conference Track Proceedings (2017). https://openreview.net/forum?id=SJDaqqveg

2. Bahdanau, D., Cho, K., Bengio, Y.: Neural machine translation by jointly learning to align and translate. In: 3rd International Conference on Learning Representations, ICLR 2015, San Diego, CA, USA, 7–9 May 2015, Conference Track Proceedings (2015). http://arxiv.org/abs/1409.0473

3. Choshen, L., Fox, L., Aizenbud, Z., Abend, O.: On the weaknesses of reinforcement learning for neural machine translation. In: 8th International Conference on Learning Representations, ICLR 2020, Addis Ababa, Ethiopia, 26–30 April 2020. OpenReview.net (2020). https://openreview.net/forum?id=H1eCw3EKvH

4. Gu, J., Bradbury, J., Xiong, C., Li, V.O.K., Socher, R.: Non-autoregressive neural machine translation. In: 6th International Conference on Learning Representations, ICLR 2018, Vancouver, BC, Canada, 30 April–3 May 2018, Conference Track Proceedings (2018)

5. Hinton, G.E., Vinyals, O., Dean, J.: Distilling the knowledge in a neural network. CoRR (2015). http://arxiv.org/abs/1503.02531

6. Lee, J., Mansimov, E., Cho, K.: Deterministic non-autoregressive neural sequence modeling by iterative refinement. In: Proceedings of the 2018 Conference on Empirical Methods in Natural Language Processing, Brussels, Belgium, 31 October 31–4 November 2018, pp. 1173–1182 (2018)

7. Papineni, K., Roukos, S., Ward, T., Zhu, W.: Bleu: a method for automatic evaluation of machine translation. In: Proceedings of the 40th Annual Meeting of the Association for Computational Linguistics, Philadelphia, PA, USA, 6–12 July 2002, pp. 311–318. ACL (2002). https://doi.org/10.3115/1073083.1073135. https://www.aclweb.org/anthology/P02-1040/

8. Sabour, S., Frosst, N., Hinton, G.E.: Dynamic routing between capsules. In: Advances in Neural Information Processing Systems 30: Annual Conference on Neural Information Processing Systems 2017, Long Beach, CA, USA, 4–9 December 2017, pp. 3856–3866 (2017)

9. Sennrich, R., Haddow, B., Birch, A.: Neural machine translation of rare words with subword units. In: Proceedings of the 54th Annual Meeting of the Association for Computational Linguistics, ACL 2016, Berlin, Germany, 7–12 August 2016, Volume 1: Long Papers. The Association for Computer Linguistics (2016). https://doi.org/10.18653/v1/p16-1162

10. Shao, C., Feng, Y., Zhang, J., Meng, F., Chen, X., Zhou, J.: Retrieving sequential information for non-autoregressive neural machine translation. In: Proceedings of the 57th Conference of the Association for Computational Linguistics, ACL 2019, Florence, Italy, 28 July–2 August 2019, pp. 3013–3024 (2019). https://www.aclweb.org/anthology/P19-1288/

11. Sun, Z., Li, Z., Wang, H., He, D., Lin, Z., Deng, Z.: Fast structured decoding for sequence models. In: Wallach, H.M., Larochelle, H., Beygelzimer, A., d'Alché-Buc, F., Fox, E.B., Garnett, R. (eds.) Advances in Neural Information Processing Systems 32: Annual Conference on Neural Information Processing Systems 2019, NeurIPS 2019, Vancouver, BC, Canada, 8–14 December 2019, pp. 3011–3020 (2019). http://papers.nips.cc/paper/8566-fast-structured-decoding-for-sequence-models

12. Sutskever, I., Vinyals, O., Le, Q.V.: Sequence to sequence learning with neural networks. In: Advances in Neural Information Processing Systems 27: Annual Conference on Neural Information Processing Systems 2014, Montreal, Quebec, Canada, 8–13 December 2014, pp. 3104–3112 (2014). http://papers.nips.cc/paper/5346-sequence-to-sequence-learning-with-neural-networks

13. Vaswani, A., et al.: Attention is all you need. In: Advances in Neural Information Processing Systems 30: Annual Conference on Neural Information Processing Systems 2017, Long Beach, CA, USA, 4–9 December 2017, pp. 5998–6008 (2017)

14. Wang, Y., Tian, F., He, D., Qin, T., Zhai, C., Liu, T.: Non-autoregressive machine translation with auxiliary regularization. In: The Thirty-Third AAAI Conference on Artificial Intelligence, AAAI 2019, The Ninth AAAI Symposium on Educational Advances in Artificial Intelligence, EAAI 2019, Honolulu, Hawaii, USA, 27 January–1 February 2019, pp. 5377–5384 (2019)

15. Wu, L., Tian, F., Qin, T., Lai, J., Liu, T.: A study of reinforcement learning for neural machine translation. In: Proceedings of the 2018 Conference on Empirical Methods in Natural Language Processing, Brussels, Belgium, 31 October–4 November 2018, pp. 3612–3621 (2018). https://www.aclweb.org/anthology/D18-1397/

16. Zhou, L., Zhang, J., Zong, C.: Synchronous bidirectional neural machine translation. TACL 91–105 (2019). https://transacl.org/ojs/index.php/tacl/article/view/1513

Neural Machine Translation Based on Prioritized Experience Replay

Shuo Sun, Hongxu Hou[✉], Nier Wu, and Ziyue Guo

College of Computer Science-College of Software,
Inner Mongolia University, Hohhot, China
sunshuo07@126.com, cshhx@imu.edu.cn, wunier04@126.com, guoziyue08@126.com

Abstract. Reward mechanism of reinforcement learning alleviates the inconsistency between training and evaluation in neural machine translation. However, the model still incapable to learn ideal parameters when rewards are sparse or a weak sampling strategy is adopted. Therefore, we propose a reinforcement learning method based on prioritized experience replay to deal with the problems. The model experiences are obtained through reinforcement learning. Then they are stored in a experience buffer and assigned priorities according to the value of experience. The experience with higher priority in buffer will be extracted by model to optimize the parameters during training phase. To verify the robustness of our method, we not only conduct experiments on English-German and Chinese-English, but also perform on agglutinative language Mongolian-Chinese. Experimental results show that our work consistently outperforms the baselines.

Keywords: Reinforcement learning · Prioritized experience replay · Agglutinative language

1 Introduction

Recently, neural machine translation (NMT) [1,4] has become increasingly popular due to its superior performance. Ordinary NMT is trained using maximum likelihood estimation (MLE) [2] that is to minimize the cross entropy loss between the generated token and the ground-truth token to make the model converge, which leads to the inconsistency of measurement in training and evaluation phase. Studies show that reinforcement learning (RL) can evaluate translation parameters intensively by adding rewards to a single token [14], the core of RL is minimum risk training (MRT) [11] that is to reduce the error accumulation and training risk caused by sampling error by maximizing token rewards.

However, when parameters are updated with maximum reward, the model still extracts experience by random sampling in next iteration, which makes model unable to fully learn the experience. It will cause algorithm instability or gradient dispersion and give up some rare experiences which are helpful and need replaying to learn in the future. Experience Replay [5] solves these problems and

© Springer Nature Switzerland AG 2020
I. Farkaš et al. (Eds.): ICANN 2020, LNCS 12397, pp. 358–368, 2020.
https://doi.org/10.1007/978-3-030-61616-8_29

it is applied to many reinforcement learning methods, such as DQN (Deep Q-Learning) [6], Nature DQN [3] and DDQN(Double DQN) [7], etc. These methods sample experiences with same probability in experience buffer and then calculate target Q value. However, the buffer is unable to distinguish which sample is more significant.

In this paper, to relief the reward sparseness in NMT and remedy the defect of the random sampling from experience buffer, we propose a reinforcement learning method based on prioritized experience replay [10], which extracts the most valuable experience when sampling to constantly update the model parameters. However, how to measure the value of experience is a significant problem. Temporal-Difference error (TD-error) can precisely solve the similarity between learning experience and expecting experience. As a result, we adopt TD-error as our priority measurement criterion. Meanwhile, due to the high complexity of traversing experience one by one from buffer, we utilize sum-tree to extract experience efficiently. Furthermore, we experiment on a low-resource translation task: Mongolian-Chinese. Through pre-processing, we learn additional information such as appended elements of agglutinative language and syntactic rules to enhance translation quality.

In summary, we mainly made the following contributions:

- It is the first time that prioritized experience replay is applied to neural machine translation. It can be applied to any end-to-end NMT systems.
- The case component analysis is incorporated into Mongolian-Chinese translation task when preprocessing the corpus, which improves the translation performance.
- We test two different NMT models: traditional RNNSearch and the best performing Transformer model in WMT16 English-German, LDC2014 Chinese-English and CCMT2019 Mongolian-Chinese translation tasks. Experimental results show that our method has excellent performance.

2   Reinforcement Learning Based Neural Machine Translation

Generic NMT models are based on an encoder decoder architecture. The encoder reads and encodes the source language sequence $X = (x_1, ..., x_n)$ into the context vector representation, and the decoder generates the corresponding target language sequence $\hat{Y} = (\hat{y}_1, ..., \hat{y}_m)$. Given H training sentence pairs $\left\{x^i, y^i\right\}_{i=1}^{H}$, at each timestep t, NMT is trained by maximizing likelihood estimation (MLE) and generates the target word $\hat{y}_t$ by maximum the probability of translation conditioned on the source sentence X. The training goal is to maximize:

$$L_{MLE} = \sum_{i=1}^{H} logp(\hat{y}^i|x^i) = \sum_{i=1}^{H} \sum_{t=1}^{m} logp(\hat{y}_t^i|\hat{y}_1^i...\hat{y}_{t-1}^i, x^i) \qquad (1)$$

where m indicates the length of sentence $\hat{y}^i$.

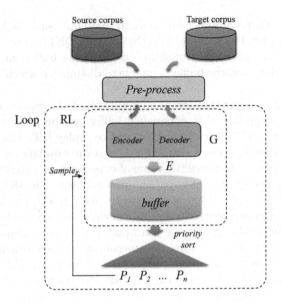

Fig. 1. The Illustration of the reinforcement learning for neural machine translation based on prioritized experience replay (referred to as RL-PER). The preprocessed bilingual data is sent to the reinforcement learning framework, and experience buffer stores experiences learned by NMT model. Utilize sum-tree to prioritize these experiences and extract the highest priority one to update network parameters.

According to [13], reinforcement learning enables NMT to evaluate the possible risks of tokens during model training and usually estimates the overall expectation by sampling $\hat{y}$ with policy $p(\hat{y}|x)$. NMT model can be viewed as an agent. Under the supervised $(p(\hat{y}_t|x_t))$ environment, the state at each time t is expressed as $(\hat{Y}_{1,...,t-1}, X)$ and action is generated a word $\hat{y}_t$. The training goal of RL is to maximize the expected reward:

$$L_{RL} = \sum_{i=1}^{H} R\left(\hat{y}_{env}^i, y^i\right), \hat{y}_{env}^i \sim p\left(\hat{y}|x^i\right), \forall_i \in [H]. \tag{2}$$

where $R(\hat{y}_{env}, y)$ is the final reward calculated by BLEU after generating the complete sentence $\hat{y}_{env}$ which is extracted from the environment. To increase stationarity, we combine the two samples linearly:

$$L_{COM} = \mu \times L_{MLE} + (1 - \mu) \times L_{RL} \tag{3}$$

where μ is the hyperparameter controlling the trade-off between MLE and RL objectives. L_{COM} is the strategy to stabilize RL training progress.

3 Approach

Our approach consists of three parts: pre-processing, experience learning and prioritized experience replay. Figure 1 shows the overall architecture.

3.1 Pre-processing

To obtain information such as stem-affixes, center word with the context, and structural relationships in agglutinative language, we combine the model computational complexity with the hard environment of the experiment and adopt ELMO[1] [9] to preprocess source and target word embedding, as shown in Fig. 2. The specific equation is as follows:

$$h_t = f\left(Wx_t + Uh_{t-1} + b\right) \quad (4)$$

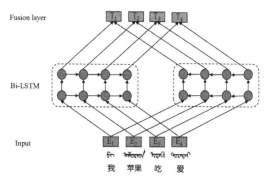

Fig. 2. Our pre-processing method.

$$ELMO_k = E\left(T_k; \Theta\right) = \gamma \sum_{j=0}^{L} s_j h_{k,j}^{LM} \quad (5)$$

where $T_k = \left\{ h_{k,j}^{LM} | j = 0, ...L \right\}$, and $h_{k,j}^{LM}$ represents the output of each layer of the Bi-LSTM. γ is used to control the size of the vector generated by the ELMO model, the parameter s indicates softmax-normalized weights.

The method alleviate the semantic knowledge problem which cannot be solved by grammatical knowledge when Mongolian words and sentences are generating at the present stage. From this, the model learns the relationship knowledge and additional component information of Mongolian corpus.

3.2 Experience Learning

Mnih et al. [6] applied experience replay to reinforcement learning and experience buffer is initially empty. The data which is obtained by reinforcement learning is stored in the form of memory unit (s_i, a_i, r_i, s_{i+1}). It makes the data of each step can be sampled multiple times and dramatically improves data efficiency,

---

[1] http://allennlp.org/elmo/ ELMO, which fully consider contextual information has shown certain potential in semantic learning. It has strong modeling capabilities, meanwhile, the parameters and complexity are relatively small, which is convenient for model construction and training.

breaks the correlation of training samples and alleviates the problem of sample distribution variation.

$$buffer_i = E\left(state_i, action_i, reward_i, state_{i+1}\right) \tag{6}$$

For an experience, *state* indicates the current state when predicting a word, i.e, $s_i : \left(T_{trg}^{1...i-1}, T_{src}\right)$, and *action* represents the next word predicted T_{trg}^i by policy $p\left(T_{trg}^i | T_{trg}^{i-1}, T_{src}^{1...j}, \theta\right)$, where T_{src} and T_{trg} are the outputs of the preprocessed model. To ease sparse reward, we employ the reward shaping to calculate *reward* that measure the similarity between the predicted next word and the groudtruth. The immediate reward at each time step t is defined as:

$$r_t\left(\hat{y}_t, y\right) = R\left(\hat{y}_{1...t}, y\right) - R\left(\hat{y}_{1...t-1}, y\right) \tag{7}$$

where $R\left(\hat{y}_{1...t}, y\right)$ is defined as the BLEU score of $\hat{y}_{1...t}$ respect to y. And $R\left(\hat{y}, y\right) = \sum_{i=1}^{k} r_t\left(\hat{y}, y\right)$, where k is the length of $\hat{y}$.

3.3   Prioritized Experience Replay

Traditional methods extract experiences with equal probability to update parameters iteratively. However, it ignores the respective importance of these experiences. To this end, we propose prioritized experience replay to solve the problems caused by weak sampling strategies in NMT. Those samples which can learn more information are given more weights and the significant experience is replayed at a higher frequency. Therefore, learning and sampling are faster and more efficient. Following we respectively introduce the experience value, priority of experience and extract method.

The Experience Value of RL-Based NMT. In RL-based NMT, the experience value is shown as:

$$Q_w(s_t, a_t) = Q_w(s_t, a_t) + \delta_t \tag{8}$$

where $Q_w(s_t, a_t)$ represent the value of current experience, δ_t is TD-error.

The goal of reinforcement learning is to minimize the TD-error, which means to minimize the difference between the learned parameters and the ideal parameters in each new timestep. Combining the peculiarity, we set TD-error as the index which experience can be sampled preferentially. The specific equation of TD-error:

$$\delta_t = r_{t+1} + \gamma max_a Q_w(s_{t+1}, a_{t+1}) - Q_w(s_t, a_t) \tag{9}$$

where Q is the predicted probability of the model and r is the reward of the predicted word in NMT. r_{t+1} represent current reward, $Q_w(s_{t+1}, a_{t+1})$ is the current Q value and $Q_w(s_t, a_t)$ indicate Q value of the previous round. The equation mainly refers to the value change after next update. If the error is large, it means the experience to update possesses has more information and the priority is higher. The method combines prediction and evaluation, which makes the model more stable.

The Priority of RL-Based NMT. Experience extraction of reinforcement learning is mainly divided into ranking priority experience extraction and probability priority experience extraction. We mainly apply probability priority experience extraction to prevent the network from over-fitting. It can ensure the experience that TD-error is zero still has the probability to be extracted. We initially set the priority of each experience as:

$$P(i) = \frac{p_i^\alpha}{\sum_{i=1}^k p_i^\alpha}, p_i = |\delta_t + \varepsilon| \tag{10}$$

where $p_i > 0$ is the priority of experience i. ε is a small constant so that some special edge examples with TD-error of 0 can also be extracted. k is the amount of experiences in the experience buffer. The exponent α determines how much prioritization is used, with $\alpha = 0$ corresponding to the uniform case.

Prioritized Experience Extraction. The process of obtaining each experience priority is as follows. First, we obtain Q and the corresponding TD-error through model training. Then we can know the initial priority $p(i)$ of each experience through TD-error. It alleviates overfitting problem of the model but traversing the entire priority experience buffer will inevitably cause the waste of a large number of resources and reduce the training speed. For this reason, we adopt the sum-tree to extract experience selectively.

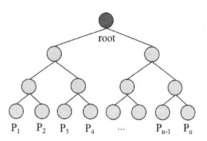

Fig. 3. The structure of Sum-Tree. Obtain the priority index from the root node, and judge the priority path by comparing the left and right child of each node until the data domain part corresponding to the leaf node is found to start training.

As shown in Fig. 3. Sum-Tree is a binary tree, the root node is the sum of all priorities, and the leaf nodes stores priority of each experience. The experience buffer is divided into several intervals, and a number is randomly selected from each interval. Starting from the root node, if the random number is larger than the left node, then go left way, otherwise the right way is taken and the priority of the left child is subtracted from this number. We extract the data domain corresponding to the found leaf node to start training. This method facilitates the accumulation and calculation of priorities, meanwhile reduces the time complexity of empirical sample insertion and sampling. The training objective function is:

$$L_{RL} = \sum_{i=1}^H R\left(\hat{y}_{buffer}^i, y^i\right), \hat{y}_{buffer}^i \sim p\left(\hat{y}|x^i\right), \forall_i \in [H] \tag{11}$$

Table 1. Evaluation of translation quality on LDC2014 Zh→En and WMT14 En→De tasks. Profiting from the priority experience replay strategy, our method achieved 43.08 and 28.23 BLEU scores on two translation tasks, which has a great improvement over the baselines.

Systems	LDC2014 Zh-En				WMT14 En-De
	MT14	MT15	MT16	AVE	Newstest2014
RNNSearch [1]	33.76	34.08	33.98	33.94	21.20
Transformer [12]	41.82	41.67	41.92	41.80	27.30
Transformer+RL [14]	41.96	42.13	41.97	42.02	27.25
Our work					
RNNSearch+RL-PER	35.46	35.73	35.65	**35.61(+1.67)**	**22.36(+1.16)**
Transformer+RL-PER	43.48	42.98	42.79	**43.08(+1.28)**	**28.23(+0.93)**

where $\hat{y}^i_{buffer}$ represents the sentence obtained from the experience buffer. After updating the parameters by training the extracted experience, TD-error will also be updated and so will the $P(i)$. All the father nodes corresponding to the P value in the sum-tree need updating. The experience with the highest priority will be re-extracted, then we can carry on new training until the model converges.

4 Experiment and Analysis

In this section, we respectively evaluate the three translation tasks of English-German, Chinese-English and Mongolian-Chinese to verify the effectiveness of the method we proposed in this paper.

4.1 Datasets

For the English-German translation task, we employ the WMT14 En-De dataset which contains 4.5 million sentence pairs. BPE is used to encode sentences, where the shared source-target vocabulary has approximately 37,000 tokens. Newstest2012/2013 are chosen for development set, Newstest2014 as test set.

For the Chinese-English translation tasks, LDC2014 corpus as a training set with a total of 1.6 million bilingual pairs. BPE is also used to preprocess the source languages and target languages, which includes 34500 English words and 28000 Chinese words. MT2013 as a development set and MT2014/2015/2016 as a test set.

For the Mongolian-Chinese translation tasks, we use CCMT2019 corpus for experiments. We randomly drawing 2000 sentences from the whole corpus. 1000 sentences are used as development set, and the other 1000 sentences as test set. The remaining corpus as our training set.

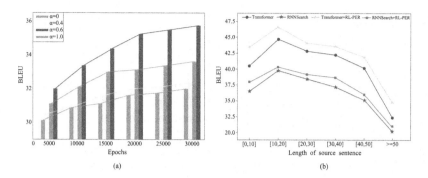

Fig. 4. (a): Result of different exponent α. (b): BLEU scores on test set of LDC2014 Zh→En over different length of source sentences.

4.2 Setting

In this paper, our model mainly adopts two different structures, Transformer-Big and RNNSearch. For Transformer-Big, following [12], we set $dropout = 0.1$, the dimension of the word embedding is set to 1024. Beam Search to sample the target token with beam size $K = 4$ and the length penalty $\alpha = 0.6$. A single model is obtained by averaging the last 20 checkpoints and we use adaptive methods to adjust the learning rate. For RNNSearch [1], it is a RNN-based encoder decoder framework with attention mechanism. We set the hidden layer nodes and word embedding dimensions of the encoder and decoder to 1024 and $dropout = 0$. The learning rate and checkpoint settings are consistent with the Transformer-Big. During testing, beam size $K = 4$ and $\alpha = 0$. For ELMO, set the word embedding dimension to 1024 and LSTM layers $L = 2$.

We utilize BLEU [8] to evaluate these translation tasks. All models are implemented in T2T tool and trained on two Titan XP GPUs. We stop training when the model does not improve on the tenth evaluation of the development set.

4.3 Main Results and Analysis

We mainly performed experiments on the LDC2014 Zh→En and WMT14 En→De data sets. The experimental results are shown in Table 1. Transformer and RNNSearch as our baseline systems, and we denote the work of [14] as Transformer+RL. It can be seen that on the Transformer model, our method improves 1.28 BLEU over the baseline on Zh→En, and the quality of En→De translation improves 0.93 BLEU. It is because our method incorporate prioritized experience replay to neural machine translation, which makes the reward more random and ease the issue of reward sparseness. Furthermore, the experience with a high priority will be extracted from the experience buffer to update the corresponding parameters when the model resampling, it enables the model performance more stabilize. The same advantage is also shown on the RNNSearch model. Compared with Transformer+RL, our method also improves 1.06 and 0.98 BLEU points on this two tasks separately.

4.4   Ablation Study

As shown in Table 2, we performed ablation study on different techniques utilized in this paper on dataset CWMT2019 Mongolian-Chinese. As aforementioned, we set Transformer and RNNSearch as our baselines. It can be seen that priority experience replay strategy plays a critical role, which is indispensable part of the method in this paper. Meanwhile, the pre-processing is also beneficial for enhancing performance. It can be verified that the effectiveness of preprocessing for Mongolian corpus by ana-

Table 2. BLEU scores on dataset CWMT2019 Mongolian→Chinese.

Mo-Zh	BLEU	Promote
RNNSearch	28.73	–
+Pre-processing	29.45	0.72
+RL-PER	29.76	1.03
Ensemble	30.69	1.96
Transformer	30.25	–
+Pre-processing	31.03	0.78
+RL-PER	31.57	1.32
Ensemble	32.26	2.01

lyzing case components since the method enables the model to learn more additional information of corpus. The ensemble study combines pre-processing with RL-PER to improve the performance of Mongolian-Chinese translation tasks, and received 30.69 and 32.26 BLEU scores on RNNSearch and Transformer models respectively.

4.5   Effect of Exponent α and Sentence Length

The choice of exponent α determines how much priority is used. As shown in Fig. 4(a), we performed four comparison experiments, α take values 0, 0.4, 0.6, and 1.0 on different epoches respectively. As aforementioned, when $\alpha = 0$, it is the traditional uniform sampling method for experience replay, this method ignores the respective importance of these experiences. When $\alpha = 0.4$ and $\alpha = 1.0$, the BLEU scores increases with the number of epoches, and model performs better than $\alpha = 0$. We can see that $\alpha = 0.6$ has a stable and rapid BLEU improvement over time.

To verify the performance of our method on long sentences, following [1], we divided the development set data and test set data of the Chinese-English task according to the sentence length. Figure 4(b) shows the BLEU scores for different sentence lengths. No matter on RNNSearch or Transformer, our work have outstanding behaviors continuously. It profits from when model resampling, the experience with a high priority will be extracted from the experience buffer to train the model, which accelerates convergence. This strong sampling strategy enables model to learn ideal model parameters.

5   Conclusion and Future Work

In this paper, we propose a novel reinforcement learning method that incorporates prioritized experience replay, each learned experience is stored in the experience buffer and the highest priority experience is extracted to guide the optimization of model parameters, thereby ease the problem of reward sparse and weak sampling strategy. Moreover, we also experiment on the Mongolian→Chinese. Additional information such as the appended elements and syntactic rules of agglutinative language are learned by pre-processing to improve translation quality. We validate the effectiveness of our method on RNNSearch and Transformer. Extensive experiments clearly show that our method has achieved significant improvements. In the future, we hope to apply our method to more NLP tasks, such as text summaries, question answering systems, etc.

References

1. Bahdanau, D., Cho, K., Bengio, Y.: Neural machine translation by jointly learning to align and translate. In: 3rd International Conference on Learning Representations, ICLR 2015, San Diego, CA, USA, 7–9 May 2015, Conference Track Proceedings (2015). http://arxiv.org/abs/1409.0473

2. Harris, C.M., Mandelbaum, J.: A note on convergence requirements for nonlinear maximum-likelihood estimation of parameters from mixture models. Comput. OR **12**(2), 237–240 (1985). https://doi.org/10.1016/0305-0548(85)90048-6

3. van Hasselt, H., Guez, A., Silver, D.: Deep reinforcement learning with double q-learning. In: Proceedings of the Thirtieth AAAI Conference on Artificial Intelligence, Phoenix, Arizona, USA, 12–17 February 2016, pp. 2094–2100 (2016). http://www.aaai.org/ocs/index.php/AAAI/AAAI16/paper/view/12389

4. He, D., et al.: Dual learning for machine translation. In: Advances in Neural Information Processing Systems 29: Annual Conference on Neural Information Processing Systems 2016, Barcelona, Spain, 5–10 December 2016, pp. 820–828 (2016). http://papers.nips.cc/paper/6469-dual-learning-for-machine-translation

5. Lin, L.J.: Self-improving reactive agents based on reinforcement learning, planning and teaching. Mach. Learn. **8**, 293–321 (1992). https://doi.org/10.1007/BF00992699

6. Mnih, V., et al.: Playing Atari with deep reinforcement learning. CoRR abs/1312.5602 (2013). http://arxiv.org/abs/1312.5602

7. Mnih, V., et al.: Human-level control through deep reinforcement learning. Nature **518**(7540), 529–533 (2015). https://doi.org/10.1038/nature14236

8. Papineni, K., Roukos, S., Ward, T., Zhu, W.: Bleu: a method for automatic evaluation of machine translation. In: Proceedings of the 40th Annual Meeting of the Association for Computational Linguistics, Philadelphia, PA, USA, 6–12 July 2002, pp. 311–318 (2002). https://www.aclweb.org/anthology/P02-1040/

9. Peters, M.E., et al.: Deep contextualized word representations. In: Proceedings of the 2018 Conference of the North American Chapter of the Association for Computational Linguistics: Human Language Technologies, NAACL-HLT 2018, New Orleans, Louisiana, USA, 1–6 June 2018, (Volume 1: Long Papers), pp. 2227–2237 (2018). https://www.aclweb.org/anthology/N18-1202/

10. Schaul, T., Quan, J., Antonoglou, I., Silver, D.: Prioritized experience replay. In: 4th International Conference on Learning Representations, ICLR 2016, San Juan, Puerto Rico, 2–4 May 2016, Conference Track Proceedings (2016). http://arxiv.org/abs/1511.05952

11. Shen, S., et al.: Minimum risk training for neural machine translation. In: Proceedings of the 54th Annual Meeting of the Association for Computational Linguistics, ACL 2016, Berlin, Germany, 7–12 August 2016, Volume 1: Long Papers (2016). https://www.aclweb.org/anthology/P16-1159/

12. Vaswani, A., et al.: Attention is all you need. In: Advances in Neural Information Processing Systems 30: Annual Conference on Neural Information Processing Systems 2017, Long Beach, CA, USA, 4–9 December 2017, pp. 5998–6008 (2017). http://papers.nips.cc/paper/7181-attention-is-all-you-need
13. Williams, R.J.: Simple statistical gradient-following algorithms for connectionist reinforcement learning. Mach. Learn. **8**, 229–256 (1992). https://doi.org/10.1007/BF00992696
14. Wu, L., Tian, F., Qin, T., Lai, J., Liu, T.: A study of reinforcement learning for neural machine translation. In: Proceedings of the 2018 Conference on Empirical Methods in Natural Language Processing, Brussels, Belgium, 31 October–4 November 2018, pp. 3612–3621 (2018). https://www.aclweb.org/anthology/D18-1397/

Improving Multi-agent Reinforcement Learning with Imperfect Human Knowledge

Xiaoxu Han[1,2], Hongyao Tang[1], Yuan Li[3(✉)], Guang Kou[2(✉)], and Leilei Liu[1]

[1] College of Intelligence and Computing, Tianjin University, Tianjin 300350, China
{xiaoxu.han,bluecontra,liuleilei}@tju.edu.cn
[2] Artificial Intelligence Research Center, National Innovation Institute of Defense
Technology, Beijing 100072, China
kg5188@163.com
[3] Academy of Military Sciences, Beijing 100091, China
yuan.li@nudt.edu.xn

Abstract. Multi-agent reinforcement learning has gained great success in many decision-making tasks. However, there are still some challenges such as low efficiency of exploration, significant time consumption, which bring great obstacles for it to be applied in the real world. Incorporating human knowledge into the learning process has been regarded as a promising way to ameliorate these problems. This paper proposes a novel approach to utilize imperfect human knowledge to improve the performance of multi-agent reinforcement learning. We leverage logic rules, which can be seen as a popular form of human knowledge, as part of the action space in reinforcement learning. During the trial-and-error, the value of rules and the original action will be estimated. Logic rules, therefore, can be selected flexibly and efficiently to assist the learning. Moreover, we design a new exploration way, in which rules are preferred to be explored at the early training stage. Finally, we make experimental evaluations and analyses of our approach in challenging StarCraftII micromanagement scenarios. The empirical results show that our approach outperforms the state-of-the-art multi-agent reinforcement learning method, not only in the performance but also in the learning speed.

Keywords: Multi-agent reinforcement learning · Logic rules · Exploration · StarCraftII

1 Introduction

Over the past few years, multi-agent reinforcement learning (MARL) has achieved significant progress in various tasks. However, there are still some problems that have not been solved. With the increase of agents, the policy space is dramatically expanded, and the simultaneous learning of multiple agents makes the environment non-stationary, which brings great difficulties to find a converged policy for each agent. Furthermore, due to the nature of reinforcement

© Springer Nature Switzerland AG 2020
I. Farkaš et al. (Eds.): ICANN 2020, LNCS 12397, pp. 369–380, 2020.
https://doi.org/10.1007/978-3-030-61616-8_30

learning (RL), learning from scratch, MARL algorithms learn good control policies only after millions of steps of very poor performance in simulation.

These problems are well-known and there has been much work focusing on them. An effective approach to these problems is leveraging human knowledge to guide learning, which can reduce the inefficient exploration of agents. In many tasks, humans usually have accumulated much useful experience, which should be well utilized. The way of combining human knowledge with RL has attracted much attention. A straightforward method [12] is to utilize logic rules in priority. If a rule is matched in any state, the agent will act following the rule without any judgment. The drawback of this approach resides in the excessive dependence on the quality of rules. In fact, human knowledge may be suboptimal. Therefore, how to improve learning with imperfect human knowledge has become a key problem. A natural idea is to balance the usage of human knowledge and the policy learned by trial-and-error by evaluating the value of the two action sources and reusing knowledge selectively during the learning process. [7,11] designed complicated mechanisms to calculate and update the confidence of knowledge and the learned policy, and the agent chooses actions from the two action sources accordingly. However, such a method increases the computational complexity, and it is inefficient to be applied in problems with large state space. Training additional action selector can also learn to select proper action source under a certain state. [2] trained a DQN model additionally to make decisions from knowledge-based policy or the policy learned by the A3C algorithm. Nevertheless, adding a network means increasing training difficulty and training time, contrary to the original intention of leveraging human knowledge.

In this paper, we propose a novel approach to improve MARL with high-level human knowledge represented in the form of logic rules. Different from previous methods that require designing complicated mechanisms to calculate confidences, we leverage the Q-value in RL as a uniform criterion to judge the value of rules and original actions. We expand the action space of RL with the selection of rules; once an extended action is chosen, its corresponding rule will be parsed and executed. Therefore, the Q-value of these two types of actions will be estimated and updated during the trial-and-error. In this way, agents have the ability to automatically balance the usage of rules and its own self-learned policy and utilize proper rules under certain states. Further, we find the traditional ϵ-greedy exploration cannot exploit the advantages of rules, so we propose Rule-Prioritized Exploration mechanism to accelerate learning by efficiently using the rules. Our approach can be easily combined with existing MARL algorithms to improve their performance. In this paper, we apply our method to QMIX [8], VDN [9], and IQL [10] and make experiments in challenging micromanagement scenarios of StarCraftII. The empirical results show that our approach achieves significant improvement in the performance of MARL algorithms.

2   Background and Related Work

2.1   Partially Observable Stochastic Games

In this paper we consider a *partially observable stochastic game* which can be defined as a tuple $\langle \mathcal{N}, \mathcal{S}, \mathcal{A}^1, \cdots, \mathcal{A}^n, \mathcal{T}, \mathcal{R}^1, \cdots, \mathcal{R}^n, \mathcal{O}^1, \cdots, \mathcal{O}^n \rangle$. $\mathcal{S}$ denotes the environmental information and the possible configurations of the environment. $\mathcal{A}_i$ is the set of available actions of agent i. $\mathcal{R}_i : \mathcal{S} \times \mathcal{A} \to \mathbb{R}$ is the reward function of agent i. $\mathcal{T} : \mathcal{S} \times \mathcal{A} \times \mathcal{S} \to [0, 1]$ is the transition function which defines transition probability between global states and $\mathcal{O}^i$ is the set of observation of agent i.

At each time step, each agent i chooses an action $a_i \in \mathcal{A}^i$, forming a joint action $\boldsymbol{a} = (a_1, a_2, \cdots, a_n)$. Policy $\pi_i : \mathcal{O}^i \times \mathcal{A}^i \to [0, 1]$ specifies the probability distribution over the action space of agent i. The goal of agent i is to learn the optimal policy π_i^* that maximizes the expected return with a discount factor γ: $E_{\pi_i}\{\sum_{t=0}^{\infty} \gamma^t r_t^i\}$. Let $\boldsymbol{\pi} = (\pi_1, \cdots, \pi_n)$ denote the joint policy of all agents. The state-action value function of an agent i under a joint policy $\boldsymbol{\pi}$ can be defined as $Q_i^{\boldsymbol{\pi}} = E_{\boldsymbol{\pi}}\{\sum_{t=0}^{\infty} \gamma^t r_t^i | \mathcal{O}, \mathcal{A}\}$.

2.2   MARL Algorithms

In this paper, we apply our approach to three representative MARL algorithms:

1. **IQL:** In this method, agents are trained independently and simultaneously in a common environment. The action-value function for each agent i is updated following (1). This method has a problem: each agent updates its policy independently, resulting in a non-stationary environment with no convergence guarantees even with infinite exploration.

$$Q_i(o_i, a_i) \leftarrow Q_i(o_i, a_i) + \alpha[r_i + \gamma max_a Q_i(o_i', a_i) - Q_i(o_i, a_i)] \qquad (1)$$

2. **VDN:** While each agent learns individual Q_i independently, VDN learns a centralized but factored Q_{tot}. VDN assumes the joint action-value function for the multi-agent system can be additively decomposed into value functions across agents, see Eq. (2).

$$Q_{tot}((o^1, o^2, ..., o^N), (a^1, a^2, ..., a^N)) = \sum_{i=1}^{N} Q_i(o^i, a^i) \qquad (2)$$

3. **QMIX:** Assuming that $\frac{\partial Q_{tot}}{\partial Q_i} \geq 0$, QMIX factors the joint action-value Q_{tot} into a monotonic non-linear combination of individual Q_i via a mixing network, as (3):

$$Q_{tot}((o^1, o^2, ..., o^N), (a^1, a^2, ..., a^N)) = M(Q_1(o^1, a^1), ..., Q_N(o^N, a^N)) \qquad (3)$$

Where M represents the monotonic function of Q_{tot} and individual value functions $Q_i(o^i, a^i)$. Such monotonic decomposition ensures that a global *argmax* performed on Q_{tot} yields the same result as a set of individual arg max operations performed on each individual Q_i.

2.3 Related Work

Different approaches to incorporating human knowledge into RL have been proposed. Some works consider improving the state representation in RL through embedding external knowledge. The knowledge graph has been used as a representation of high-dimensional information in RL. [1] expressed the entities and relationships in text-based adventure games as knowledge graphs. The sophisticated models developed for disposing domain knowledge had also been studied. [4] utilized the predication of dynamic models about the environment to improve the state representation for the policy network.

An important cluster of related research is Imitation Learning (IL), which aims to imitate expert behaviors from demonstration data. [6] introduced an adversarial training mechanism into IL, where the generator attempted to imitate expert and the discriminator distinguished between the fake sample and the expert sample. To address the 'cold start' problem, [5] leveraged a combinatorial loss function to pre-train neural network based on demonstration data and then updated the model with RL methods.

The form of human knowledge is not limited to the demonstrations but can be extended to logic rules. A wide range of expert systems making use of such rules have been developed, but many of them turn out to be ineffective. The main reason is that expert systems do not have the ability to learn. Several studies have been conducted in combining rules with RL. [3] leveraged rules to reduce the size of the state space by dividing state space into several patterns. Nevertheless, it is inefficient to classify all states, and the approach is only suitable for problems with extremely small state space. [13] interposed the training of DQN with a decaying probability to follow the rules. However, this approach cannot filter suboptimal rules so that it works only with high-quality rules.

3 Methodology

3.1 Extending Action Space with Rule Selection

Let $\Gamma = \{\Gamma_1, ... \Gamma_K\}$ represents the rule set consisting of K rules, which is shared among n agents. A mapping function set $F = \{f_1, ..., f_k, ..., f_K\}$, where the f_k represents a parsing map for rule Γ_k. The rule parsing map takes the current state as input and outputs the action to be performed under rule policy. For agent i with the length J of action space, $\dot{a}_i^j, 1 \leq j \leq J$ denotes agent's original actions. We extend the rule actions which are denoted with $\ddot{a}_i^k, 1 \leq k \leq K$ with the original action space. Thus, the action space of agent i becomes $a_i = \{\dot{a}_i^1, ... \dot{a}_i^J, \ddot{a}_i^1, ..., \ddot{a}_i^K\}$. Once a rule action $\ddot{a}_i^k$ is selected, the corresponding mapping function f_k will be triggered to find the corresponding action $\dot{a}_i^j \leftarrow f_k(\ddot{a}_i^k)$ under the rule policy Γ_k.

The rule actions and the original actions under certain states are both evaluated by the Q-value, which represents the expected cumulated reward from the current state to the final state by performing the current policy. Whether to use the original action or the rule action can be determined by Q_i, which is updated following Eq. (4), where o_i is the current local observation state and o_i' is the next observation state for agent i.

$$Q_i(o_i, \dot{a}_i) \leftarrow Q_i(o_i, \dot{a}_i) + \alpha[r_i + \gamma max_{\dot{a}_i} Q_i(o_i', \dot{a}_i) - Q_i(o_i, \dot{a}_i)], 1 \leq i \leq N$$
$$Q_i(o_i, \ddot{a}_i) \leftarrow Q_i(o_i, \ddot{a}_i) + \alpha[r_i + \gamma max_{\ddot{a}_i} Q_i(o_i', \ddot{a}_i) - Q_i(o_i, \ddot{a}_i)], 1 \leq i \leq N$$

(4)

3.2 Rule-Prioritized Exploration

A traditional exploration strategy is ϵ-greedy. In this method, exploration and exploitation divide the probability of choosing actions into two sections, and the probability of exploration ϵ is decaying during learning. During exploration, ϵ-greedy does not distinguish between actions, and the probability of each action being explored is uniform.

However, treating rule actions and original actions indiscriminately cannot exploit the advantages of rules. Therefore, we design a new mechanism, Rule-Prioritized Exploration, to distinguish the exploration of the rule action and the original action. To encourage agents to explore from rule actions, we define a parameter δ to balance the probability of choosing the rule actions and original actions. The probability interval of choosing action in our method is shown in Fig. 1. Notice that the probability for selecting rule actions is also decaying with the decline of ϵ, which means the agent explores rules preferentially at the early training process.

Fig. 1. The probability interval of Rule-Prioritized Exploration

The procedure of Rule-Prioritized Exploration is shown in Algorithm 1. Function $rand()$ is used to generate a random number. If it is in the range of 0 and $\epsilon * \delta$, the rule action is selected. If the number is in the range of $\epsilon * \delta$ and ϵ, an

---

Algorithm 1. Rule-Prioritized Exploration

Input: Exploration probability δ, ϵ, original action set $\{\dot{a}_i^j\}_{j=1}^J$, and rule action set $\{\ddot{a}_i^k\}_{k=1}^K$
Output: a
1: **if** $0 \leq rand() \leq \epsilon * \delta$ **then**
2:     a is sampled from $\{\dot{a}_i^j\}_{j=1}^J$
3: **else if** $\epsilon * \delta \leq rand() \leq \epsilon$ **then**
4:     a is sampled from $\{\ddot{a}_i^k\}_{k=1}^K$
5: **else if** $rand() \geq \epsilon$ **then**
6:     $a = argmax_{a'} Q(o, a')$
7: **end if**

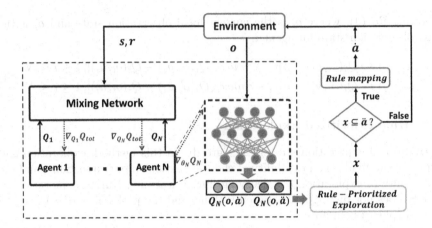

Fig. 2. The overall architecture of RMLPE-QMIX. Red dashed lines indicate the gradient flow. (Color figure online)

action (either a rule action or an original action) is randomly selected. In this way, the rule action is well used during the exploration. At last, if the number is bigger than ϵ, the action that maximizes Q_i will be chosen.

3.3   Rule Mixing Learning with Prioritized Exploration

We define the integration of the above two methods as Rule Mixing Learning with Prioritized Exploration method (RMLPE). Our approach can be easily applied to various MARL algorithms: the agents share a predefined rule set Γ, and rule actions are added in the action space of each agent. The Q-values for rule actions and original actions will be used to make decisions following at each time step, and updated under the network of agent i based on the feedback of the environment. To illustrate the whole procedure of RMLPE, we take QMIX as an example and show the architecture of the method combining RMLPE with QMIX (RMLPE-QMIX) in Fig. 2.

The network of agent i takes its local observation information o_i as input and outputs Q_i, which contains $Q_i(o_i, \dot{a}_i)$ and $Q_i(o_i, \ddot{a}_i)$. According to the rule prioritized exploration, agent i will select an action x. Then $x \in \{\dot{a}_i^1, ... \dot{a}_i^J\}$ or $x \in \{\ddot{a}_i^1, ..., \ddot{a}_i^K\}$ will be determined as presented in Algorithm 1. If x represents one of rule actions $\ddot{a}_i^k$, the mapping f_k will be triggered to figure out the corresponding executable primitive action $\dot{a}_i^j$ and execute. Otherwise, x will be executed directly. No matter x belongs to which kind of action source, the transition $\langle o_t, x, r, o_{t+1} \rangle$ will be stored in the replay buffer. The mixing network and decentralized network of each agent will be updated through sample transitions. The pseudocode of RMLPE is described in Algorithm 2.

Algorithm 2. Rule Mixing Learning with Prioritized Exploration

---

Input: Rule set Γ, MARL model, rule mapping function set F, the exploration probability δ and ϵ

Output: MARL model with RMLPE method

1: Initialize MARL model with random weights θ and the replay buffer D
2: **while** not done **do**
3:    **for** agent i **do**
4:       Get current observation o_i for each agent i
5:       Compute Q_i according to MARL models based on o_i and select an action x_i following *Rule-Prioritized Exploration*
6:       **if** $x_i \in \{\dot{a}_i^j\}_{j=1}^J$ **then**
7:          Execute x_i in the environment
8:       **end if**
9:       **if** $x_i \in \{\ddot{a}_i^k\}_{k=1}^K$ **then**
10:      Execute $f_k(x_i) \in \Gamma_i$ in the environment
11:      **end if**
12:      Get reward r_t and next observation o_{next}
13:      Store transition (o_t, x_t, r_t, o_{t+1}) in D
14:      Train MARL models (e.g., IQL, QMIX) with mini-batch samples from replay buffer D
15:    **end for**
16: **end while**

---

4 Experimental Setup

4.1 Environments

Our experiments are carried out on StarCraft Multi-Agent Challenge(SMAC), an open-source environment[1] for evaluating MARL approaches. SMAC contains various micromanagement combat scenarios in which each of the learning agents controls an individual army unit based only on local observations, and the opponent's units are controlled by the handcrafted heuristics.

We adopt two challenging combat scenarios: 5 Marines and 6 Marines ($5m$ v $6m$), 27 Marines and 30 Marines ($27m$ v $30m$). Both scenarios are asymmetric, in which the enemy army outnumbers the allied army by one or more units. The environment is partially observable: each unit has a certain sight range based on its local observation, and the information about allied or enemy units out of range cannot be received. The action space consists of the following set of discrete actions: *noop, stop, move[direction], attack[enemy id]*. The *attack[enemy id]* action is available only if the enemy is within shoot range. Figure 3 shows the screenshots of the scenarios.

4.2 Imperfect Rules

In our experiments, we leverage rules derived from human experience in firing strategy. The premise of firing is that there are enemies within the agent's shoot

---

[1] https://github.com/oxwhirl/smac.

(a) $5m$ v $6m$ (b) $27m$ v $30m$

Fig. 3. Screenshots of the combat scenrios in StarCraft II

range. The firing micromanagement of human players in combat games is: attack the nearest enemy or the enemy with the least hit points; attack an enemy with several companions to concentrate fire. Therefore, we incorporate the following rules into learning. For the third rule, we work out the number of allied units focusing fire on one enemy is 3, based on the firepower and hit points per unit.

1. IF *there are enemies within shoot range* THEN *attack the nearest enemy.*
2. IF *there are enemies within shoot range* THEN *attack the least hit points enemy.*
3. IF *there are enemies within shoot range* THEN *attack the enemy which is aimed by less than three allied units.*

These rules are imperfect for two reasons. Firstly, in a specific state, at most one of the three rules can take effect, which means these rules are mutually exclusive. Secondly, even if the condition of a rule is satisfied, it is merely an option as whether the rule is beneficial to the final performance is doubtful.

4.3   Experimental Settings

For the adopted scenarios in StarCraftII, the difficulty level of the opponent is set to be 7, *very difficult*. Besides, our proposed approaches share the same learning parameters with the original MARL algorithms. The shared learning setting is as follows: we use the RMSprop optimizer with a learning rate of 5×10^{-4}, and the discounting factor γ is set to 0.99. The ϵ is annealed linearly from 1.0 to 0.05 over 50k time steps and is kept constant for the rest of the learning. The replay buffer contains the most recent 5000 episodes and a batch of 32 episodes will be sampled for training. Due to the partially observable settings, the architecture of each agent is a *Deep Recurrent Q-networks* (DRQN) with a recurrent layer comprised of a GRU with a 64-dimensional hidden state.

5   Experimental Results

Combined with various famous MARL algorithms, including QMIX, VDN, and IQL, RMLPE is evaluated in several experiments. We firstly illustrate the improvements brought by RMLPE to three baseline algorithms. Then, we show RMLPE is capable of leveraging rules with different qualities to improve learning. Finally, we investigate the impact of the exploration ratio: δ.

The *test win rate* is leveraged as an indicator to evaluate the performance of methods. For each run of a method, we run 24 test episodes every 5000 training steps in which agents performing action selection greedily in a decentralized fashion. The percentage of episodes where the agents defeat all enemy units within the permitted time limit is referred to as the test win rate. Besides, all the experimental results are performed at least 5 runs with different seeds.

5.1 Improvement over Baselines

Figure 4 illustrates comparisons between RMLPE enabled and non-RMLPE enabled MARL algorithms in $5m$ v $6m$ and $27m$ v $30m$ scenarios. It is obvious that RMLPE improves the learning process of all the baseline MARL methods in two scenarios, at both the win rate and the learning speed. For the baseline algorithms, QMIX performs best, whereas IQL performs worst due to the non-stationary problem. To investigate the performance brought by pure rules, we design experiments where agents act following rules only. When the pre-condition of rules is satisfied, i.e., the conditions for firing are met, the agent will randomly select one rule to execute. In our design, the agents move toward the location of enemies. The performance of pure rules is presented in the dashed line in Fig. 4.

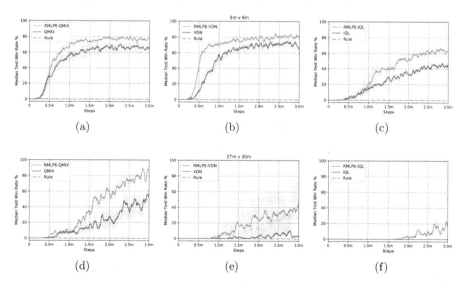

Fig. 4. Median win rate of different algorithms on two scenarios, [25%, 75%] percentile interval is shaded. (a), (b), (c) represent the comparisons of RMLPE-QMIX/VDN/IQL method and their baseline algorithms on the *hard* scenario: 5m v 6m. (d), (e), (f) show the results on the *super hard* scenario: 27m v 30m.

The results demonstrate that RMLPE can dramatically improve the learning process even with such poor performance rules.

5.2 Ability of Dealing with Imperfect Rules

To investigate the effectiveness of each rule in learning and to show RMLPE can optionally leverage uneven quality rules, we present the usage rate of rules during training. We record the number of times each rule is used for every 5000 train steps. The mean using frequency of rules in final 50k train steps is shown in Table 1, with the peak in bold. As we can see, most methods tend to use the second rule more frequently, indicating that RMLPE picks out the second rule which appears to be more effective in learning. As for the total rule usage, rules are used much less frequently in $27m$ v $30m$ than $5m$ v $6m$. Different dimensions of the action space between two scenarios cause this phenomenon. The action space in $27m$ v $30m$ is three times the size of $5m$ v $6m$, there are fewer times to choose rules as the action space gets bigger.

Table 1. Mean usage frequency of rules

Methods	5m v 6m				27m v 30m			
	Rule1	Rule2	Rule3	Total	Rule1	Rule2	Rule3	Total
RMLPE-QMIX	0.0667	**0.2830**	0.0392	0.3889	0.0537	**0.0730**	0.0536	0.1803
RMLPE-VDN	0.0762	**0.2850**	0.0432	0.4044	0.0158	**0.0270**	0.0899	0.1327
RMLPE-IQL	0.0464	**0.2800**	0.03852	0.3649	0.0045	0.0243	**0.0268**	0.0556

The curves in Fig. 5(a) show the mean using frequency of each rule during the training process of RMLPE-QMIX method in $5m$ v $6m$ scenario. In the beginning, all using frequencies increase significantly in both scenarios, due to the Rule-Prioritized Exploration. Then the using frequencies of *rule* 1 and *rule* 3 maintain a low level while that of *rule* 2 continues to increase quickly and converges at a high level. From the results of using frequency curve, we can find that *rule* 2 appears to the most useful rule for the training in $5m$ v $6m$. To further investigate the impact of each rule on training, we perform an experiment in which the rules in the RMLPE method are set to be *rule* 1, *rule* 2, *rule* 3 respectively and the results are shown in Fig. 5(b). It is obvious that in terms of contribution to the performance of RMLPE, *rule* 2 ranks top, *rule* 1 s and *rule* 3 third. These results illustrate that RMLPE can identify the useful rule from rule set and decide which rule should be applied under a different state.

5.3 Effect of the Exploration Ratio

The exploration parameter δ plays an important role in balancing the exploration between the rule action and the original action. In our experiments on combat tasks (see Fig. 4), we choose the best hyperparameters δ for each method independently. In this section, we make comparisons of the impact of different values

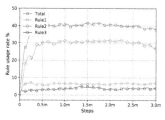

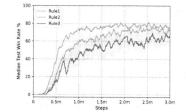

(a) Mean rule usage rate curve   (b) Median test win rate of only using one rule

Fig. 5. The mean rule usage rate curve and the median test win rate during the training of RMLPE-QMIX only with *rule 1/2/3* respectively in $5m$ v $6m$ scenario.

of δ (varying from 0.1 to 0.5) on the performance of RMLPE. Figure 6 depicts the final mean win rate of RMLPE method combined with three baseline algorithms for each exploration ratio δ. Comparing to the baseline algorithms (dashed line in Fig. 6), we find that RMLPE enabled algorithms beat all the baselines, with any exploration ratio. The proper value of δ varies with the MARL methods, and it should not be too big or too small for most algorithms. Therefore a suitable value interval of exploring rules exists for the different methods.

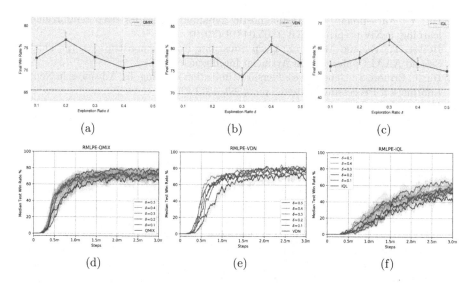

Fig. 6. The above figures: the median win rate in final 50k train steps for RMLPE-QMIX/VDN/IQL methods in $5m$ v $6m$ map, as a function of exploration ratio δ. The square markers for each ratio denote the mean win rate, and the error bars show [25%, 75%] percentile interval for the mean win rate. The dashed line represents the final win rate of the baseline MARL algorithms. (d), (e), (f) show the learning curves of RMLPE methods with different δ.

6   Conclusion

In this paper, we propose a novel approach called Rule Mixing Learning with Prioritized Exploration, RMLPE, to improve MARL by incorporating logic rules into the learning. The incorporated rules can be imperfect, that is, rules are not necessarily guaranteed to be effective under all circumstances. RMLPE can efficiently select useful rules and exploit them to facilitate learning by extending the action space with rules. A new exploration method is also proposed to accelerate learning in the early training stage. The evaluation of our methods is conducted on challenging StarCraftII micro scenarios and the results show RMLPE can greatly improve and accelerate the learning process of MARL methods even with suboptimal rules. In the future, it is worthwhile to investigate combining large-scale human knowledge with RL to solve more challenging problems.

References

1. Ammanabrolu, P., Riedl, M.O.: Playing text-adventure games with graph-based deep reinforcement learning. arXiv preprint arXiv:1812.01628 (2018)
2. Bougie, N., Ichise, R.: Deep reinforcement learning boosted by external knowledge. In: Proceedings of the 33rd Annual ACM Symposium on Applied Computing, pp. 331–338 (2018)
3. Bougie12, N., Ichise, R.: Rule-based reinforcement learning augmented by external knowledge
4. Du, Y., Narasimhan, K.: Task-agnostic dynamics priors for deep reinforcement learning. arXiv preprint arXiv:1905.04819 (2019)
5. Hester, T., Vecerik, M., et al.: Deep q-learning from demonstrations. In: Thirty-Second AAAI Conference on Artificial Intelligence (2018)
6. Ho, J., Ermon, S.: Generative adversarial imitation learning. In: Advances in Neural Information Processing Systems, pp. 4565–4573 (2016)
7. Moreno, D.L., Regueiro, C.V., et al.: Using prior knowledge to improve reinforcement learning in mobile robotics. In: Proceedings of the Towards Autonomous Robotics Systems, University of Essex, UK (2004)
8. Rashid, T., Samvelyan, M., et al.: QMIX: monotonic value function factorisation for deep multi-agent reinforcement learning. In: Proceedings of the 35th International Conference on Machine Learning, ICML 2018, pp. 4292–4301 (2018)
9. Sunehag, P., Lever, G., et al.: Value-decomposition networks for cooperative multi-agent learning based on team reward. In: Proceedings of the 17th International Conference on Autonomous Agents and Multiagent Systems, pp. 2085–2087 (2018)
10. Tan, M.: Multi-agent reinforcement learning: Independent vs. cooperative agents. In: Proceedings of the Tenth International Conference on Machine Learning, pp. 330–337 (1993)
11. Wang, Z., Taylor, M.E.: Interactive reinforcement learning with dynamic reuse of prior knowledge from human and agent demonstrations. In: Proceedings of the Twenty-Eighth International Joint Conference on Artificial Intelligence, IJCAI 2019, pp. 3820–3827. ijcai.org (2019)
12. Zhang, G., Li, Y., et al.: Efficient training techniques for multi-agent reinforcement learning in combat tasks. IEEE Access **7**, 109301–109310 (2019)
13. Zhang, H., Gao, Z., et al.: Faster and safer training by embedding high-level knowledge into deep reinforcement learning. arXiv preprint arXiv:1910.09986 (2019)

Reinforcement Learning III

Reinforcement Learning III

Adaptive Skill Acquisition in Hierarchical Reinforcement Learning

Juraj Holas$^{(\boxtimes)}$ and Igor Farkaš

Faculty of Mathematics, Physics and Informatics,
Comenius University in Bratislava, Bratislava, Slovakia
{juraj.holas,igor.farkas}@fmph.uniba.sk

Abstract. Reinforcement learning has become an established class of powerful machine learning methods operating online on sequential tasks by direct interaction with an environment instead of processing precollected training datasets. At the same time, the nature of many tasks with an inner hierarchical structure has evoked interest in hierarchical RL approaches that introduced the two-level decomposition directly into computational models. These methods are usually composed of lower-level controllers – *skills* – providing simple behaviors, and a high-level controller which uses the skills to solve the overall task. Skill discovery and acquisition remain principal challenges in hierarchical RL, and most of the relevant works have focused on resolving this issue by using pre-trained skills, fixed during the main learning process, which may lead to suboptimal solutions. We propose a universal pluggable framework of *Adaptive Skill Acquisition* (ASA), aimed to augment existing solutions by trying to achieve optimality. ASA can observe the high-level controller during its training and identify skills that it lacks to successfully learn the task. These missing skills are subsequently trained and integrated into the hierarchy, enabling better performance of the overall architecture. As we show in the pilot maze-type experiments, the identification of missing skills performs reasonably well, and embedding such skills into the hierarchy may significantly improve the performance of an overall model.

Keywords: Hierarchical Reinforcement Learning · Skill Acquisition · Adaptive model

1 Introduction

As an approach inspired by the knowledge acquisition process in humans and other animals, the Reinforcement Learning (RL) has gained significant interest in both research studies and practical applications. Despite the impressive progress in traditional or 'flat' RL in the recent years, these approaches still struggle to solve tasks involving several layers of abstraction. To render such problems

---

Supported by grant 1/0796/18 from Slovak Grant Agency for Science (VEGA).

I. Farkaš et al. (Eds.): ICANN 2020, LNCS 12397, pp. 383–394, 2020.
https://doi.org/10.1007/978-3-030-61616-8_31

tractable, a promising approach of *Hierarchical Reinforcement Learning* (HRL) was introduced in [22].

Introduction of hierarchy into the RL framework has the ability to accelerate the learning process in sequential decision-making tasks, as the agents on different levels of hierarchy can decompose the problems at hand into smaller subproblems. The common underlying feature of the ongoing research in HRL field is the usage of skills – actions that are temporally extended in time – forming an implicit or explicit hierarchy within the task. The top-level task represents the original problem at hand and is solved by RL (the core Markov decision process, MDP), while the lower level may be fixed, pre-trained, or solved by separate RL themselves (sub-MDPs).

In the simplest scenario, the set of skills can be hand-crafted and trained manually, as a series of independent RL agents [17,22]. Other methods use the pre-training phase to explore the nature of the environment and determine a useful set of skills to be trained [6,7,9,13–15]. Moving towards more universal solutions, we may observe HRL algorithms that are able to (semi-)automatically learn hierarchies [1,9,16,19,23]. These algorithms often construct and learn the hierarchy one level at a time in a bottom-up fashion, hence the higher-level policies are trained only when the lower-level ones have been fixed.

However, having the skill set fixed before training the higher level of a hierarchy can considerably limit the final performance, as discussed in [11]. First, the skills are trained either using a surrogate reward signal, or by the deconstruction of the state space in a pre-training phase, which leads to useful, yet not necessarily optimal set of skills. Subsequently, the top-level agent using these skills as actions may not be able to optimally learn the overall task. As an example, we can imagine a walking robot tasked to navigate through the maze, and provide it with two skills: walk forward and turn left, but no 'turn right' skill. The top-level controller can still learn a strategy to solve the maze with given skills, however it will be clearly suboptimal for cases where the robot should have turned right. This principle of *optimality under given hierarchy* must be accounted for when designing HRL architectures [22].

Research has also been performed on training the whole hierarchy at a time, especially in continuous state and action spaces. A number of papers on this topic are restricted for use with only Universal-MDP (which, despite its name, is a subset of MDP), limited only to spatial tasks [11,16,23]. Only a little work has been done on training the entire hierarchy in the continuous environment of a general MDP [12]. All of these approaches, however, rely on building a specialised hierarchical structure of abstract agents, and on using a tailored algorithm to train such a structure, which is not transferable to any other infrastructure. Hence, adapting their work into an existing model in order to improve its efficiency may not be feasible, and the complete replacement of the existing model may be necessary.

In this paper, we present a new approach called *Adaptive Skill Acquisition* in Hierarchical Reinforcement Learning, or ASA-HRL. It represents a pluggable component able to dynamically construct and integrate missing skills into any hierarchy of agents. The vast majority of HRL approaches fix the skill set prior to training the higher level of hierarchy, which, as discussed, can lead to imperfections within the hierarchy. We focus on the most common case of such imperfections – a useful skill that was not identified during lower-level training, and hence is missing from the skill set. While the top-level agent is being trained, ASA can automatically identify these missing skills, train them, and incorporate them into the hierarchy. The top-level agent then resumes its training with this enriched hierarchy, and can solve the core-MDP more efficiently.

The ASA approach is composed of three key steps: First, the missing skill is identified by self-observation of the top agent, by gathering statistics about the sequences of skills it invokes. Second, the identified skill is trained by traditional RL methods. Third and final step is to integrate the newly trained skill into the overall hierarchy, after which the training of top-level controller can continue.

2   Preliminaries

We define a *Markov Decision Process* (MDP) as a tuple $\langle S, A, P, p_0, R, \gamma \rangle$, where S is a set of states; A is a set of actions; $P : S \times A \times S \to [0,1]$ is a probability distribution describing the state transition; $p_0 : S \to [0,1]$ is a probability distribution of the initial state, $R : S \times A \to \mathbb{R}$ is a (possibly non-deterministic) reward function; $\gamma \in (0,1]$ is a reward discount factor. Traditional ('flat') RL aims to find an optimal policy $\pi : S \times A \to [0,1]$ that optimizes the expected overall discounted return $G(\pi) = \mathbb{E}_\pi[\sum_{t=0}^{T} \gamma^t R(s_t, a_t)]$, where $\mathbb{E}_\pi$ denotes the expected value if an agent follows a policy π.

In Hierarchical RL, we do not optimize a single policy π, but rather a set of policies on two (or more) levels. We have a set of skills – low-level policies $\pi_1^L, \ldots, \pi_n^L$ that act using the original actions: $\pi_i^L(s_t) = a_t$. On top of them we have a manager – high-level policy π^H. Its purpose is to decide which skill will be used in a given situation, and thus its high-level actions a_t^H are in fact invocations of skill policies: $\pi^H(s_t) = a_t^H \in \{\pi_1^L, \ldots, \pi_n^L\}$. In our paper we study variable-length sequences of such skill invocations, which we denote by $\delta = [a_t^H, \ldots, a_{t+k}^H]$.

3   Related Work

Building agents that can learn hierarchical policies is a longstanding problem in Reinforcement Learning. One of the most general approaches to define temporally extended hierarchies is the *Options framework* [22], upon which most of other research is built. However, most HRL approaches only work in discrete domains [2,4,7,13–15,22], and only recent ones can be applied to high-dimensional continuous domains [1,6,9,10], as we do in this work.

Numerous methods use a different reward signal for training the lower level, either in a form of a low-level target produced by a high-level agent [2,11,16], or by constructing a surrogate reward for each skill which may lead to more versatile skills [6,23]. Similarly to those, we also construct a specialised reward signal for each missing skill, so that each new skill fills in the specific gap in the skill set.

While the vast majority of research field focuses on strictly two-level hierarchies [1,2,6,7,9,10,13–15,22,23], some authors opted for more dynamical multi-level hierarchies, essentially forming a tree of skills [4]. Despite having tested ASA only on two levels, we designed it in a way that it could be in principle deployed on any level of general tree-like hierarchy.

A slight parallel to our approach can be found in Skill-chaining [9], a two-level HRL method that incrementally chains options backwards from the end goal state to the start state. Similarly to us, they also construct new skills based on their starting and target region. However, their algorithm is well suitable for near-linearly organized tasks, but should fail to achieve reasonable results if the environment features high branching factor, or if it is not bounded at all.

Closer to our work is the algorithm [21], which also allows for enrichment of the skill set by supplementing it with new ones. However, they require a hand-defined curriculum of tasks supported by pre-defined stochastic grammar from which the new skills are generated, which poses a fixed limit for capabilities of new skills. Our key advantage relative to their approach is that ASA is not bounded by a predefined set of possible skills, and thus can create a new skill that was not considered in advance.

4 Our Approach

We propose an approach named *Adaptive Skill Acquisition* (ASA) in hierarchical reinforcement learning. The novelty of this approach lies in an additional augmentation of existing pre-trained skills according to the needs of the agent.

In its core, ASA is an algorithm that enables the agent to *add new skills* if needed, in the midst of learning the core task. If an agent was presented with a set of pre-trained skills (as in [1,6,7,9,13,14,17,19,22]), it is possible that this set would not contain all skills necessary to solve the core task. In such case, ASA could dynamically add new ones that would cover the missing functionality.

The hierarchical architecture needed for ASA is based on the common features of almost all relevant research: a HRL system consisting of two layers[1], where the top layer learns the core task and the bottom layer employs a fixed number of pre-trained policies. These loose constraints enable the usage in various algorithms. In terms of MDP complexity, ASA is aimed to work in both discrete and continuous state spaces, as well as continuous action spaces in the lower level (the action space of a high-level agent is inherently discrete). The knowledge of the model, needed for UMDP (as in [11,16,23]), or other specificities are not presumed by ASA either. We thoroughly focus on working with sparse-reward environments which, though being much harder to solve, offer a greater research potential.

---

[1] ASA can be deployed on multiple levels of a multi-level hierarchy.

One of our core goals was to develop ASA as an independent pluggable component that can be adapted into any existing HRL model to enrich its capabilities without extensive re-work. The Adaptive Skill Acquisition approach consists of three key steps: identification, training, and integration; as presented in following sections. The identification and creation of a new skill can be adapted with virtually zero implementation changes. For the skill's integration into HRL hierarchy, we implemented several options that can be directly used or customized, and users can also easily create new ones that fit their specific architecture.

4.1   Identification of a Missing Skill

During learning the core task, the agent must be able to recognize the need for another skill. By means of self-observation, the agent will try to identify potentially sub-optimal sequences of high-level actions (skill invocations) that tend to occur significantly more often. Such sequences hint at a regularity in the core-MDP that was not discovered by the original skill building process, and is only modelled using the reoccurring sequence of pre-defined skills. This sequence will serve as a candidate for training a new skill, capable of solving the subtask in a more efficient way.

We denote $\delta = [a_t^H, \ldots, a_{t+k}^H]$ a sequence of high-level actions taken between timesteps t and $t + k$. Throughout the learning process, we collect the counts $C(\delta)$ for observed sequences, limiting the sequence length to a reasonable threshold. As mentioned, most frequent sequences are suitable candidates for detected inefficiencies. However, short sequences naturally have a tendency to appear more frequently in the data, hence we cannot simply take the sequence δ with greatest $C(\delta)$. Instead, we analytically compute a null-hypothesis count:

$$C_H(\delta) = (T - |\delta| + 1) \prod_{i=1}^{|\delta|} p(\delta_i)$$

where T denotes the length of the whole roll-out. The quantity $C_H(\delta)$ thus describes how many occurrences of the sequence δ are expected under a random 'null' policy. We use the empirical probability distribution of invoked skills for $p(\delta_i)$. The overall score (frequency) of the sequence is then computed as a ratio of two counts: $f(\delta) = C(\delta)/C_H(\delta)$. Every sequence with $f(\delta) > 1$ occurs more often than it would do under the null policy. Hence, the higher f-score the sequence gains, the more likely it is to execute the repeated non-optimal steps. By ranking the sequences using f-score, we can identify possible candidates for a new skill.

We implemented a customized data structure based on lexicographic trees to count the sequences in time-efficient way, and to retrieve our desired statistics. This way, the computational increase to the overall learning process was shrunk to a marginal level.

After having identified the sequence as a candidate for a new skill, we need to define the MDP problem that it represents. As the RL process is guided solely by the reward signal, we especially need to formulate a reward signal that will lead it. We adapted the approach by [9] of having the starting and target regions for each skill. As the sequences are being populated for the computation of $f(\delta)$, we also record the starting and ending states of each sequence. Thus, during training of the new skill based on sequence δ, the agent is spawned in one of δ's starting states, and is rewarded only upon reaching the corresponding target region. We intentionally train a skill using such sparse-reward environment, as we want to avoid any engineered bias caused by more complicated reward shaping.

4.2   Training of a New Skill

Next we can initiate the training process of a new skill. Using standard RL methods, we need to train a controller to solve MDP $\langle S, A, P, p'_0, R', \gamma \rangle$, where S, A, P, and γ are given by the environment, while p'_0 and R' were constructed during the skill identification. After complete MDP specification, the problem simplifies into a standard task of reinforcement learning. We employed TRPO [20] or Natural Policy Gradient [8] algorithm for training the new low-level agent.

4.3   Integration of a New Skill

After the new skill is ready, we can integrate it into an existing HRL architecture. This is the only step that is inherently approach-specific, i.e. it might need to be adjusted when ASA will be used in different architectures. Nevertheless, we focused on the most common implementation and created several options that can be directly employed.

All relevant recent approaches operate on a policy-optimization scheme stemming from actor–critic architecture, where both the action-selecting *actor* and the state-evaluating *critic* are implemented as neural networks. The architecture of an actor can vary from a simple multi-layer perceptron to convolutional neural network or recurrent models such as LSTM. However, its output always directly represents the action to be executed, either as a real-valued vector of actions (in continuous-action environments), or one-hot-encoded index of an action (i.e. classification in discrete-action environments).

The high-level actor in HRL architectures chooses from a discrete set of n actions (skills), forming a neural classifier. Adding an $(n + 1)$-th skill to the architecture essentially means extending the output vector of the actor network by one extra unit. The new output unit, of course, needs to have some initialised weights (and a bias, if used).

We tested several initialisation schemes to prepare weights for the new output unit, both uninformed (Table 1) and informed (Table 2):

Uninformed schemes construct the new weight vector in a random manner, not utilising any additional knowledge collected during training.

Informed schemes utilize the collected data in order to bootstrap the training of the agent, while keeping the computational complexity minimal. During the initialization we considered the existing weights of the output layer $[w_1, \ldots, w_n]$ for current n skills, the sequence of skill invocations $\delta = [a_t^H, \ldots, a_{t+k}^H]$, and the states s_t that occurred at the beginning of δ in different roll-outs. In the four

Table 1. Uninformed initialization schemes tested in ASA model.

#	Description
1	**Random initialisation:** As a baseline, we used randomized initialisation of both weights and bias, using the original weight initializator of the network. Mean and variation were adjusted to match the mean and variation of weights for previous n skills
2	**Random with bias boost:** Initialize weights randomly, again adjusting the mean and variation. However, bias was made significantly greater in order to intentionally increase activation of $(n+1)$-th unit. This should encourage natural exploration of new skill by the high-level RL agent

Table 2. Informed initialization schemes tested in ASA model.

#	Description	Coefficients
3	**Initial states' skills:** Combine the old weights w.r.t. probability of choosing the old skill in s_t	$c_i = P(a_t^H = \pi_i^L \mid s_t)$
4	**δ's skills:** Combine the old weights w.r.t. frequency of using the old skill in δ	$c_i \propto \sum_l^k [a_{t+l}^H = \pi_i^L]$ where $a_{t+l}^H \in \delta$
5	**Smoothed δ's skills:** New weights are computed as an exponentially smoothed average of skills used in δ (the first skill of δ has a greatest weight on average, the last one has the lowest)	$c_i \propto \sum_l^k \gamma^l [a_{t+l}^H = \pi^{L_i}]$ where $a_{t+l}^H \in \delta$
6	**δ's first skill:** Initialize weights by copying weights of skill that was used as first step of δ. Small noise is added to prevent the two skills from being chosen identically	no coefficients, $w_{n+1} = w_{a_t^H} + \epsilon$

informed schemes, the new weights vector is computed as a linear combination of the old weights: $w_{n+1} = \sum_{i=1}^n c_i w_i$. The coefficients of this combination are normalized to the unit sum: $\sum_{i=1}^n c_i = 1$.

All these schemes (except for random initialisation) were designed with a goal to increase the probability of choosing the newly trained skill in situations it has been trained for. This subsequently enhances the exploration of new skill, helping the top-level agent to adopt it quickly.

5 Experiments

We designed three experiments (Sect. 5.3) to answer the following questions:

- How much does adding a new skill help in training an overall task?
- How well does ASA identify and formulate a new skill?
- How do different skill integration schemes affect efficiency in an overall task?

5.1   Environment and Task Specification

We evaluated our approach on a continuous task of navigating through various mazes. We constructed a set of six different mazes, altering both the structure and difficulty of the maps, as shown in Fig. 1. In each episode, a map is chosen from this set randomly, and the agent is placed at its beginning. An episode ends upon successful reaching of the goal point (depicted by a green sphere), or after 100 high-level steps, yielding an unsuccessful run.

 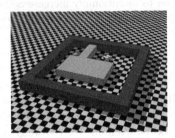

Fig. 1. Examples of mazes the agent had to navigate through. The green sphere designates the target position.

The agent is a simulated vacuum-cleaner-like robot, with continuous activation on both wheels. Robot's only observation is a LIDAR-like sensor, that shows a presence of objects and their distance in all directions, with a limited range radius (three times the robot's size). The agent does *not* have any information about its orientation (compass), or which maze it has been placed into.

As our primary goal is to focus on sparse-reward environments, the agent is given the reward of +1 only upon reaching the goal point. All other actions are uniformly penalised with −0.05 reward per step, giving the agent no information about its progress. Thus we operate in a randomised, continuous state- and action-space environment with sparse rewards, yielding a reasonably challenging task to face.

5.2   Implementation and Training Description

The HRL agent is constructed of a two-level hierarchy of trained agents. Initially it is given an imperfect set of locomotion skills, including ones to efficiently move a larger distance forward/backward, or turn left, but not a skill to turn right. Both the low-level and high-level controllers are trained using either Natural Policy Gradient [8] or TRPO [20], depending on experiment setup. The high-level policy is updated each *iteration* – a batch of 5000 high-level steps (≈80 episodes, on average). We use multi-layer perceptrons for both actor and critic networks, as well as trained policy-baseline function. The ASA project was implemented with a great help of *RL-Lab* [5] and *Garage* [3] frameworks. It is organised as modular and pluggable component that can be deployed into further works.

5.3   Results

Overall Performance: In experiment 1 we compared the performance of agents with engaged ASA and those without it, to appreciate the gain in performance caused by our approach. The evaluation metric is Average discounted reward, i.e. $G(\pi) = \mathbb{E}_\pi[\sum_{t=0}^{T} \gamma^t R(s_t, a_t)]$. As the agent is penalised for each step it takes, greater reward essentially indicates faster routes to the goal point. The results from each experiment were averaged over 8 trials with different random seeds.

Our approach significantly outperformed the baseline agent in various conditions. Figure 2a depicts the usage of full-stack approach, i.e. all three key steps (decision, training, integration) were performed by ASA. We trained the model either using TRPO or an older NPG algorithm, to demonstrate its usability with different methods. In Fig. 2b we forced the initialisation of a new skill in different iterations, leaving the skill formulation, training, and integration to ASA. As can be seen, regardless of the initiation point, we were able to identify the missing skill that helps to increase the efficiency.

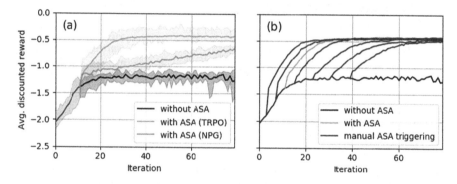

Fig. 2. Results after using ASA to train and integrate a new skill. New skill was added (a) according to ASA computation, or (b) at other times overriding ASA's decision.

Quality of Skill Identification: In experiment 2, we wanted to falsify the hypothesis that *any* added skill may cause an improvement. We manually designed an unprofitable skill policy, and let ASA integrate it into agent's hierarchy. As shown in Fig. 3, the performance with a bad skill initially dropped as the high-level agent tried to explore it, and eventually leveled out with the original performance when the agent learned to ignore it. This *lower bound* on a skill quality shows that ASA's identification of the missing skill is useful.

On the other side of the spectrum, we also wanted to state an *upper bound* on a skill quality to see how much room there is for ASA improvement. For this purpose we created an ideal skill that was missing in the hierarchy, and let ASA integrate it. As we saw in Fig. 2, the skill produced by ASA increased the

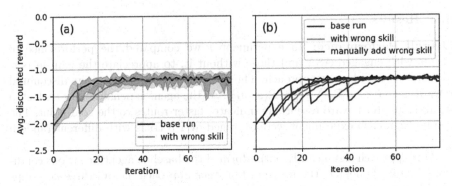

Fig. 3. Integration of a new skill that is intentionally badly manually designed, (a) at time of ASA decision, or (b) at other times.

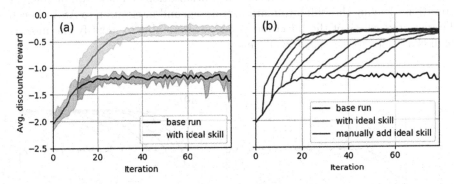

Fig. 4. Integration of an ideal new skill that was designed manually to optimally enrich the skill set, (a) at time of ASA decision, or (b) at other times.

average reward from -1.24 to -0.43. The ideal skill, however, could only raise it by a small amount to -0.32, as seen in Fig. 4. Such a result implies that the identification of a skill performed by ASA is sufficiently effective.

Integration Schemes: Next, in experiment 3 we aimed to compare the efficiency of skill integration schemes 1 to 6 described in Sect. 4.3. With the exception of random initialisation (scheme #1), all of these schemes were designed to boost the exploration of the new skill, and thus also the overall performance with an added skill. As shown in Fig. 5, usage of different integration schemes before (a) or at time when ASA decided to add new skill (b) had negligible effect on the reward gain or learning speed.

The only, yet still not very significant difference in learning speed can be observed between uninformed (#1,2) and informed (#4–6) schemes if we add a new skill much later, i.e. after the training of the imperfect hierarchy converged to a stable solution (Fig. 5c). By observing this phenomenon we found that the later we add a new skill, the more notable this difference is. We attribute this

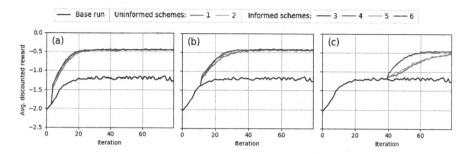

Fig. 5. Effect of using different integration schemes during the skill integration (a) in 4th iteration; (b) in 12th iteration (ASA decision); (c) in 40th iteration.

effect to the naturally decreased exploration in later stages of training, which is not supported by uninformed schemes in contrast to the informed ones.

6   Conclusion and Future Work

In this paper, we examined the option of adding new skills to (possibly suboptimal) HRL hierarchies. We proposed a framework of *Adaptive Skill Acquisition* that is able to dynamically detect that a skill is missing, formulate the task, train, and integrate new skill into any existing hierarchical architecture. Our results in continuous sparse-reward environments confirm that ASA can successfully recognize what skill is missing and that its integration can significantly improve the overall performance. However, we found that none of our proposed skill integration schemes outperformed the random one, even though all of them worked reasonably well. In future work, we plan to extend our pilot results by employing multiple RL tasks and more hierarchical architectures, confirm the intended reusability of our approach. We would also like to investigate whether employing pseudo-rehearsal [18] into integration scheme may increase the adaptation of a new skill.

References

1. Bacon, P.L., Harb, J., Precup, D.: The option-critic architecture. In: AAAI Conference on Artificial Intelligence (2017)
2. Bakker, B., Schmidhuber, J.: Hierarchical reinforcement learning with subpolicies specializing for learned subgoals. In: International Conference on Neural Networks and Computational Intelligence, pp. 125–130 (2004)
3. Garage contributors: Garage: a toolkit for reproducible reinforcement learning research (2019). https://github.com/rlworkgroup/garage
4. Dietterich, T.G.: Hierarchical reinforcement learning with the MAXQ value function decomposition. J. Artif. Intell. Res. **13**(1), 227–303 (2000)
5. Duan, Y., Chen, X., Houthooft, R., Schulman, J., Abbeel, P.: Benchmarking deep reinforcement learning for continuous control. In: International Conference on Machine Learning, pp. 1329–1338 (2016)

6. Florensa, C., Duan, Y., Abbeel, P.: Stochastic neural networks for hierarchical reinforcement learning. In: International Conference on Learning Representations (2017)
7. Goel, S., Huber, M.: Subgoal discovery for hierarchical reinforcement learning using learned policies. In: Florida AI Research Society Conference, pp. 346–350 (2003)
8. Kakade, S.M.: A natural policy gradient. In: Advances in Neural Information Processing Systems, pp. 1531–1538 (2002)
9. Konidaris, G., Barto, A.G.: Skill discovery in continuous reinforcement learning domains using skill chaining. In: Advances in Neural Information Processing Systems, pp. 1015–1023 (2009)
10. Kulkarni, T.D., Narasimhan, K., Saeedi, A., Tenenbaum, J.: Hierarchical deep reinforcement learning: integrating temporal abstraction and intrinsic motivation. In: Advances in Neural Information Processing Systems, pp. 3675–3683 (2016)
11. Levy, A., Konidaris, G., Platt, R., Saenko, K.: Learning multi-level hierarchies with hindsight. In: International Conference on Learning Representations (2019)
12. Li, A.C., Florensa, C., Clavera, I., Abbeel, P.: Sub-policy adaptation for hierarchical reinforcement learning. In: International Conference on Learning Representations (2020)
13. McGovern, A., Barto, A.G.: Automatic discovery of subgoals in reinforcement learning using diverse density. In: International Conference on Machine Learning, vol. 1, pp. 361–368 (2001)
14. McGovern, E.A., Barto, A.G.: Autonomous discovery of temporal abstractions from interaction with an environment. Ph.D. thesis, University of Massachusetts at Amherst (2002)
15. Menache, I., Mannor, S., Shimkin, N.: Q-cut—dynamic discovery of sub-goals in reinforcement learning. In: Elomaa, T., Mannila, H., Toivonen, H. (eds.) ECML 2002. LNCS (LNAI), vol. 2430, pp. 295–306. Springer, Heidelberg (2002). https://doi.org/10.1007/3-540-36755-1_25
16. Nachum, O., Gu, S.S., Lee, H., Levine, S.: Data-efficient hierarchical reinforcement learning. In: Advances in Neural Information Processing Systems, pp. 3303–3313 (2018)
17. Parr, R., Russell, S.J.: Reinforcement learning with hierarchies of machines. In: Advances in Neural Information Processing Systems, pp. 1043–1049 (1998)
18. Robins, A.: Catastrophic forgetting, rehearsal and pseudorehearsal. Connection Sci. 7(2), 123–146 (1995)
19. Schmidhuber, J.: Learning to generate sub-goals for action sequences. In: Artificial Neural Networks, pp. 967–972 (1991)
20. Schulman, J., Levine, S., Abbeel, P., Jordan, M., Moritz, P.: Trust region policy optimization. In: International Conference on Machine Learning, pp. 1889–1897 (2015)
21. Shu, T., Xiong, C., Socher, R.: Hierarchical and interpretable skill acquisition in multi-task reinforcement learning. In: International Conference on Learning Representations (2018)
22. Sutton, R.S., Precup, D., Singh, S.: Between MDPs and semi-MDPs: a framework for temporal abstraction in reinforcement learning. Artif. Intell. 112, 181–211 (1999)
23. Vezhnevets, A.S., et al.: Feudal networks for hierarchical reinforcement learning. In: International Conference on Machine Learning, pp. 3540–3549 (2017)

Social Navigation with Human Empowerment Driven Deep Reinforcement Learning

Tessa van der Heiden[1]($\boxtimes$), Florian Mirus[1]($\boxtimes$), and Herke van Hoof[2]($\boxtimes$)

[1] BMW Group, Landshuter Str. 26, 85716 Unterschleißheim, Germany
`tessa.heiden@bmw.de`, `florian.mirus@bmwgroup.de`
[2] University of Amsterdam, Science Park, Amsterdam 1098 XH, Netherlands
`h.c.vanhoof@uva.nl`

Abstract. Mobile robot navigation has seen extensive research in the last decades. The aspect of collaboration with robots and humans sharing workspaces will become increasingly important in the future. Therefore, the next generation of mobile robots needs to be socially-compliant to be accepted by their human collaborators. However, a formal definition of compliance is not straightforward. On the other hand, empowerment has been used by artificial agents to learn complicated and generalized actions and also has been shown to be a good model for biological behaviors. In this paper, we go beyond the approach of classical Reinforcement Learning (RL) and provide our agent with intrinsic motivation using empowerment. In contrast to self-empowerment, a robot employing our approach strives for the empowerment of people in its environment, so they are not disturbed by the robot's presence and motion. In our experiments, we show that our approach has a positive influence on humans, as it minimizes its distance to humans and thus decreases human travel time while moving efficiently towards its own goal. An interactive user-study shows that our method is considered more social than other state-of-the-art approaches by the participants.

Keywords: Reinforcement learning · Empowerment · Human-robot interaction

1 Introduction

Recent advances in sensor and control technologies have allowed the development of robots assisting people in domestic, industrial, and traffic environments. One key challenge in such settings, where humans and robots share the same workspace, is that the robot must plan safe, collision-free paths, which have to be socially compliant for the humans to accept robots as collaborators in the long run.

© Springer Nature Switzerland AG 2020
I. Farkaš et al. (Eds.): ICANN 2020, LNCS 12397, pp. 395–407, 2020.
https://doi.org/10.1007/978-3-030-61616-8_32

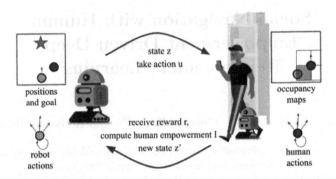

Fig. 1. Our social compliant robot (SCR) uses occupancy maps centered around each human to compute human empowerment, so it minimally disturbs people to pursue their goals.

However, moving and thereby interacting with people requires robots to follow specific unwritten social rules, for instance, politely keeping their distance [29], which depends not only on the situation [27] but also the social context and the people involved [23]. According to Kruse *et al.* [17], the three main requirements for a robot to navigate in a socially compliant way are *comfort*, *naturalness*, and *sociability*. Robots acting according to these rules will have a higher chance of acceptance by human users (Fig. 1).

Existing methods for social robot navigation either model social conventions between agents explicitly [22], or implicitly learn them through Imitation Learning (IL) [26], or even through Reinforcement Learning (RL) [4]. However, explicitly defining rules or reward functions for social navigation is not straightforward, while generating a sufficiently large body of training examples for imitation learning can be cumbersome or infeasible.

Empowerment [16] allows the agent to generate rewards by itself and offers a useful alternative. It is the channel capacity between actions and future states and maximizes an agent's influence on its near future. In contrast to self-empowerment, where a self-empowered agent will try to push others away to maximize its future rewards, an agent who strives for others' empowerment maintains the influence of them on their futures [24].

In this paper, we propose a novel approach to social robot navigation employing a combination of Reinforcement Learning (RL) and human empowerment to provide a robot with intrinsic motivation. An agent employing our approach strives for people's empowerment to minimize disturbance when pursuing their goals and respect people's personal space. Our contribution is to use the concept of human empowerment introduced by Salge and Polani [24] as an intrinsic reward function for RL for social navigation.

In an extensive evaluation in a simulation environment, we compare our method with state-of-the-art robotic navigation methods. Inspired by [17], we use two additional metrics to assess social behavior: the distance between human and robot and the robot's jerk. Additionally, we study the robot's influence on people and vice-versa by introducing two new metrics, the travel time and distance of humans and the robot. Last, we assess our approach in a user-study. Our experiments show that our approach can achieve socially compliant robot navigation by using human empowerment. Finally, our method applies to any multi-agent system that requires a robot to interact with humans in a socially compliant way, since it does not require a cost function.

2   Related Work

Many approaches have designed interaction models to enhance social awareness in robot navigation. We discuss these methods first and motivate the practicality of Deep Reinforcement Learning (DRL). We proceed by describing empowerment as a member of a family of intrinsic motivators for RL.

2.1   Social Navigation

The goals for social navigation can be divided into three main categories: *comfort*, *naturalness* and *sociability* [17]. Examples of *comfort* are respecting personal space, avoiding erratic behavior, and not interfering with the other's movement. *Naturalness* is mostly related to how similar a robot's motion is to human behavior, e.g., smooth and interpretable, while *sociability* is mainly associated with social conventions and etiquettes. Previous works have tried to create navigation frameworks satisfying all of those requirements. Well-engineered methods are the Social Force Model (SFM) [11], Interacting Gaussian Process (IGP) [30], Optimal Reciprocal Collision Avoidance (ORCA) [12] and Reciprocal Velocity Obstacles (RVO) [32]. Although all of these methods yield collision-free paths, they rely on manually engineered models with limited additional social characteristics.

In contrast to such model-based approaches, Deep Learning (DL) models have shown to produce more human-like paths [10]. For instance, Deep Neural Networks (DNNs) allow policies to better comply with humans' social rules [7]. Early works separate the prediction of the environment and the policy's planning task into two neural networks [2], which could cause the freezing robot problem since the predicted human motion could occupy all the available future space [30].

Imitation Learning (IL) and Inverse Reinforcement Learning (IRL) obtain policies directly from demonstrations [22], which requires an extensive data set due to the uncertainty of human motion. Alternatively, DRL aims to learn cooperative strategies by interacting with the environment [6]. However, the definition of a suitable cost function that encourages a robot to navigate socially is a challenging task. Even if a cost function might appear evident in some cases (e.g., collision-free and keeping distance to neighbors), it often has to be regularised to achieve smooth and risk-averse behavior.

2.2 Empowerment

Instead of shaping the reward function to achieve the desired behavior, an emerging field within RL focuses on intrinsic motivation [21]. There are many different ways to motivate an agent intrinsically, and one possible technique is called empowerment [15,25]. Empowerment was applied to teach agents task-independent behavior and training in settings with sparse rewards, such as stabilizing an inverted pendulum, learning a biped to walk [13]. Aubret *et al.* [1] provides a comprehensive survey of empowerment for RL.

Earlier approaches were only applicable in discrete state-action spaces, but recently [20] show efficient implementations for continuous settings. In our work, we will build upon these models.

3 Methodology

Our goal is to teach an agent on how to navigate its target in a socially compliant manner safely. A combination of two rewards can achieve these two objectives. In this section, we describe our agent and the two types of rewards.

We consider the system to be Markovian, where each next state x_{t+1} depends only on the current state x_t and agent's action u_t and no prior history. A value network model V_ϕ is trained to accurately approximate the optimal value function V^* that implicitly encodes social cooperation between agents and the empowerment of the people, see Eq. 1.

$$V^*(x_t) = \sum_{t=0}^{T} \gamma^t R_t(x_{t+1}, \pi^*(x_t)) \tag{1}$$

$R_t(\cdot)$ is the reward function and π^* is the optimal policy that maximizes the expected return, with discount factor $\gamma \in (0,1)$.

3.1 Reward for Safe Navigation

The first task of the agent is to reach its goal while avoiding collisions and keeping a comfortable distance to humans. We consider the number of humans in each episode to be fixed.

Equation 2 defines the environmental reward function $R_{t,e}(x_t, u_t^\pi)$ for this task with the robot's state denoted as x_t and its action with u_t^π. Similar to other DRL methods for social navigation [4–6] we award task accomplishments and penalize collisions or uncomfortable distances.

$$R_{t,e}(x_t, u_t^\pi) = \begin{cases} -.25 & \text{if } d_i < 0.01 \\ -0.1+\frac{d_i}{2} & \text{else if } 0.01 \leq d_i \leq 0.2 \\ 1 & \text{else if } d_g \leq 0.01 \\ 0 & \text{otherwise} \end{cases} \tag{2}$$

Here $d_g = \|\bar{p} - \bar{p}_g\|_2$ is the robot's distance to the goal during a time interval Δt and $d_i = \|\bar{p} - \bar{p}_i\|_2$ is the robot's distance to neighbor i. It gets rewarded when its current position $\bar{p}$ reaches the position of the goal $\bar{p}_g$, but penalized if its position is too close to another one's position $\bar{p}_i$.

The robot's own state, $\mathbf{x}$, consists of a 2D position vector $\bar{p} = [p_x, p_y]$ and 2D velocity vector $\bar{v} = [v_x, v_y]$. The human states are denoted by $\mathbf{X} = [X_1, X_2, ..., X_k]$, which is a concatenated vector of states of all k humans participating in the scene. Each entry is similar to the robot's state, namely, $X_i = [\bar{p}_i, \bar{v}_i]$. The final state of the robot is the concatenation of the state of the humans and robot, $x_t = [\mathbf{X}_t, \mathbf{x}_t]$. Its action is a desired velocity vector, $u_t^\pi = \bar{v}_d$.

3.2   Empowerment for Social Compliance

The robot's second task is to consider people in its neighborhood and respond to their intentions in a socially compliant manner. Designing a suitable reward function is a challenging task, among other things, due to the stochasticity in people's behaviors. This is where we use empowerment [15,25], an information-theoretic formulation of an agent's influence on its near future.

Human Empowerment. Empowerment in our case, motivates the robot to approach states in which its neighbors are most empowered. Now the robot aims to maximize the empowerment of another person rather than its own, which Salge and Polani [24] call *human empowerment* in contrast to *robot empowerment*. As a result, the robot will prevent obstructing the human, for example, by getting too close or by interfering with the human's actions, both of which Kruse *et al.* [17] defined as social skills.

Equation 3 describes the definition of empowerment ε being the maximal mutual information I for a state z_t [15]. It is the channel capacity between action u_t^ω and future state z_{t+1}, maximized over source policy ω. Policy ω is part of the human's decision making system.

$$\varepsilon(z_t) = \max_\omega I(z_{t+1}, u_t^\omega | z_t) = \max_\omega H(u_t^\omega | z_t) - H(u_t^\omega | z_t, z_{t+1}) \tag{3}$$

The right part defines the empowerment with entropies $H(\cdot)$. It corresponds to increasing the diversity of decisions, while at the same time limiting those decision that have no effect. Intuitively, the empowerment of the person reflects his or her ability to influence their future.

The human state z_t takes an ego-centric parameterization [5]. Each state is an occupancy grid map centered around the person, denoted with $\mathbf{g}_k$. It is a 3D tensor with dimensions $c \times r \times 3$, where c and r run over the height and width of the grid. Each entry contains the presence and velocity vector of a neighbor j at that location $\bar{e}_j = [1, v_x, v_y]$. The resulting state of the humans is a concatenated vector denoted by $z_t = [\mathbf{g}_1, \mathbf{g}_2, ..., \mathbf{g}_k]$ and action are continuous values in $\mathbb{R}^2$.

Estimating Empowerment with Neural Networks. To compute empowerment, we consider the mutual information defined by the Kullback-Leibler divergence [18] between the joint $p(z_{t+1}, u_t|z_t)$ and the product of the marginal distributions $p(z_{t+1}|z_t)$ and $\omega(u_t|z_t)$:

$$
\begin{aligned}
I &= D_{KL}(p(z_{t+1}, u_t|z_t) \parallel p(z_{t+1}|z_t)\omega(u_t|z_t)) \\
&= \iint p(z_{t+1}, u_t|z_t) \ln \frac{p(z_{t+1}, u_t|z_t)}{p(z_{t+1}|z_t)\omega(u_t|z_t)} dz_{t+1} du
\end{aligned} \tag{4}
$$

The main problem in the formulation in Eq. 4 is the intractability due to the integral of all future states. Since the introduction of empowerment [15,25] many have designed methods to deal with this. Recent works provide an efficient method to estimate a lower bound on empowerment $\hat{I}$, via variational methods [3,13,20].

$$
\hat{I} = \iint p(z_{t+1}, u_t|z_t) \ln \frac{q(u_t|z_t, z_{t+1})}{\omega(u_t|z_t)} dz_{t+1} du \tag{5}
$$

Instead of $p(z_{t+1}|z_t)$ a planning distribution $p(u_t|z_t, z_{t+1})$ is used, which is approximated with the variational approximation $q(u_t|z_t, z_{t+1})$ to obtain a lower bound. $\hat{I}$ can now be maximized over the parameters of the source, $\omega(u_t|z_t)$ and variational $q(u_t|z_t, z_{t+1})$ networks. $p(z_{t+1}|u_t, z_t)$ is a third neural network that computes the future state z_{t+1} from z_t and u_t^ω.

The gradient can be computed as follows, in which the joint parameters of $\omega(\cdot)$ and $q(\cdot)$ are denoted by θ:

$$
\frac{\partial}{\partial\theta}\hat{I} = \frac{\partial}{\partial\theta}\mathbb{E}_{p(z_{t+1}, u_t|z_t)}\left[\ln \frac{q(u_t|z_t, z_{t+1})}{\omega(u_t|z_t)}\right] \tag{6}
$$

Using Monte-Carlo integration to estimate the continuous case, we can obtain the following gradient:

$$
\frac{\partial}{\partial\theta}\hat{I} \approx \sum_{n=1}^{N} \frac{\partial}{\partial\theta}[\ln(q(u_t|z_t, z_{t+1})) - \ln(\omega(u_t|z_t))] \tag{7}
$$

We are free to choose any type of distribution for q. However, ω and p need to correspond to human policy and dynamics. Since human movement is not discrete, we model both $q(u_t|z_t, z_{t+1}) = \mathcal{N}(\mu_\theta, \sigma_\theta^2)$, $p(z_{t+1}|u_t, z_t) = \mathcal{N}(\mu_\psi, \sigma_\psi^2)$ and $\omega(u_t|z_t) = \mathcal{N}(\mu_\theta, \sigma_\theta^2)$ as Gaussian distributions, of which the mean and the variance are parameterised by deep neural networks, with parameters θ and ψ.

3.3 Training Procedure

The robot with policy π learns to safely navigate to its goal and achieve human empowered states. This is achieved by training a value network V_ϕ with the reward function combining the mutual information $\hat{I}_t(\cdot)$ and the environmental reward $R_{t,e}(\cdot)$. The hyper-parameter β is used to regulate the trade-off between social compliance and safety:

$$R_t(z_t, x_t, u_t^\omega, u_t^\pi) = (1 - \beta) \cdot I_t(z_{t+1}, u_t^\omega | z_t) + \beta \cdot R_{t,e}(x_t, u_t^\pi) \qquad (8)$$

A set of demonstrations from the ORCA policy is used to give the robot a head start. ORCA describes a deterministic control policy [32] and its demonstrations speed up learning, because experiences in which the robot reaches the goal are now part of the memory. Next, the behavior policy π collects samples of experience tuples $e_t = (z_t, x_t, u_t^\pi, r_{t,e}, z_{t+1}, x_{t+1})$ until a final state is reached. Random actions are selected with probability ϵ. Once these are collected, our hypothetical human policy ω together with q and p are used to estimate $\hat{I}_t$. Finally, the networks are trained with a random mini-batch obtained from the memory (e^b). The value network V_ϕ is optimized by the Temporal Difference Method (TDM) [28] with standard experience replay and fixed target network techniques [5, 6, 19].

$$y_t = r_{e,t}^{(b)} + \hat{I}_t^{(b)} + \gamma^t \hat{V}_{\hat{\phi}}(z_{t+1}^{(b)}, x_{t+1}^{(b)}), \quad \phi \leftarrow \phi - \lambda \nabla_\phi (y_t - V_\phi(z_t, x_t))^2 \qquad (9)$$

$\hat{V}_{\hat{\phi}}$ denotes the target network and y_t denotes the TD target that is used to update the value network. The networks ω_θ and q_θ updated through gradient ascent and p_ψ via gradient descent:

$$\theta \leftarrow \theta + \lambda \nabla_\theta \hat{I}_t, \quad \psi \leftarrow \psi - \lambda \nabla_\psi (z_{t+1}^{(b)} - p(u_t, z_t))^2 \qquad (10)$$

The behavior policy π uses the joined state x_t to navigate collision-free to its goal. p, q and ω take the occupancy grids centered around each human z_t as states for the computation of $\hat{I}_t$.

4 Experiments

We conduct three experiments to evaluate our proposed model. The first experiment compares our model against four existing state-of-the-art methods. The second experiment assess the social competences, based on the metrics defined by Kruse *et al.* [17]. The final experiment considers human subjects that evaluate the models in an interactive simulator.

4.1 Implementation Details

The simulator used in this work is from [6]. It starts and terminates an episode with five humans and the robot. The human's decisions are simulated by Berg *et al.* [31], which uses the ORCA policy [32] to calculate their actions. ORCA uses the optimal reciprocal assumption to avoid other agents. In Subsect. 4.4, another simulator is used to control the position of one human manually and terminates once the human reaches its goal. The code and videos can be found online[1].

We implemented the networks in PyTorch and trained them with a batch size of 100 for 10 000 episodes. For the value network, the learning rate is $\lambda_v = 0.001$ and the discount factor γ is 0.9. The exploration rate of the ϵ decays linearly from 0.5 to 0.1 in the first 5000 episodes and stays 0.1 for the remaining 5000 episodes. These values are the same as Chen et al. [6].

The parameter β is 0.25, because that gave the highest discomfort distance rate and success rate. The learning rates for the other networks are similar. The value network is trained with stochastic gradient descent, identical to Chen et al. [6]. The planning, source, and transition networks are trained with Adam [14], similar to [13].

4.2   State-of-the-Art Navigation Benchmark

Table 1 reports the rates of success, collision, the robot navigation time, discomfort distance, and the average discounted cumulative reward averaged over 500 episodes. **Success** is the rate of robot reaching its goal within a time limit of 20 s. **Collision** is the rate of the robot colliding with humans. **Discomfort distance** is the rate in which the distance between the robot and a human was smaller than 0.1. We compare our robot with four existing state-of-the-art methods, ORCA [31], Collision Avoidance with Deep Reinforcement Learning (CADRL) [5], Long Short Term Memory - Reinforcement Learning (LSTM-RL) [8] and Socially Attentive Reinforcement Learning (SARL) [6]. As can be seen, our Socially Compliant Robot (SCR) and SARL both outperform other baselines on the standard metrics. Next, we look more thoroughly into the performance of SCR and SARL.

Table 1. Both SCR and SARL outperform the other baselines, which can be seen by the best values (grey). ORCA does not have any collisions, because this is the central idea behind the method (*). The numbers are computed for 500 different test scenarios.

	Success rate %	Collision rate %	Robot time	Discomfort distance %	Reward
ORCA	0.99	.000*	12.3	0.00*	.284
CADRL	0.94	.035	10.8	0.10	.291
LSTM-RL	0.98	.022	11.3	0.05	.299
SARL	0.99	.002	10.6	0.03	.334
SCR (ours)	0.99	.001	10.9	0.03	.331

---

[1] https://github.com/tessavdheiden/SCR.

4.3   Influence of Robot on Humans and Vice-Versa

Table 2 shows travel times and distances of both humans and the robot. **Robot time** and **Human time** are the average navigation times of the agents to reach their goals. Keeping both low indicates that the robot does not disturb humans and moves quickly to its target. The path length of the robot, **Trav. distance**, is calculated to make sure that it moves without unnecessary detours. The simulator allows making the robot invisible to the humans, which is called the Invisible baseline (Invisible Baseline (IB)). This baseline serves as a testbed for validating the other policies' abilities in reasoning about the interactions with humans.

As humans do not observe the IB agent, they do not avoid it, meaning that the agent has to take additional detours to avoid humans. On the contrary, SARL has a low travel distance and time, but human travel times are highest. SARL has learned that humans avoid it and exploits this fact by directly taking the shortest route itself without considering others. The travel times of SCR and that of the humans are nearly the same. These numbers suggest that our method has learned to minimally disturb other people while moving to its own goal efficiently due to human empowerment.

Table 2. SCR moves efficiently to its target and doesn't disturb people as their travel times are low. SARL has learned that people avoid it, so the humans' travel times are higher than its own. The IB takes a considerable detour because people do not see it. Moreover, SCR has the lowest jerk $\left(\frac{m}{s^3}\right)$, since it avoids being close to a person and non-smooth behavior as this would lower the empowerment of its neighbors.

	Robot time	Trav. distance	Human time	Sep. distance	Jerk
IB	11.5	10.7	9.1	.85	.73
SARL	10.6	9.2	10.7	.41	.77
SCR (ours)	10.9	9.3	9.1	.43	.51

Next, we examine how we can evaluate social compliance further. Fong *et al.* [9] and Kruse *et al.* [17] state that people judge robots negatively if the separation distance between them is low and move non-smoothly. **Sep. distance** is the distance between a human and the robot and **Jerk** is the jerk of the robot $\left(\frac{m}{s^3}\right)$.

The reported numbers are in the last two columns of Table 2. Even though on average SCR and SARL are close to humans, they do not come closer than a distance of .1 m, see collision rate in Table 1. The IB and SARL move with a high jerk because their reward functions do not incorporate it. On the other hand, SCR has the lowest jerk because it avoids erratic behavior as that would lower humans' empowerment.

4.4 Human Evaluation

A successful navigation strategy can best be tested with real persons. To that end, 30 persons interacted with the robot and controlled the position of one human in the simulator (see footnote 1). The robot and humans start at 90° from each other and need to cross the center to reach their goals. The simulator terminates once the human reaches his/her goal. After that, subjects are asked to rate the social performance of the robot with a score from 1 to 10 (similar to the study performed by [26]). Figure 2 shows a boxplot with the evaluation scores for the three agents. A one-way repeated-measure analysis of variance (ANOVA) was conducted to determine significance, and a significant effect was obtained ($f(2,27) = 13.485$, $p < .01$). As can be seen in Fig. 2, both SARL and the IB have similar medians, but the samples of the baseline deviate more from the median. The IB started to move away from the human, even before the human started to move. SARL, on the other hand, moves directly to its own goal. SCR hast the highest score, which shows the potential of our method.

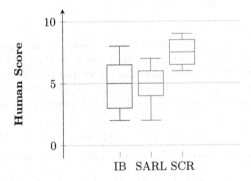

Fig. 2. The box plots summarize evaluation scores on three methods, IB, SARL and SARL (ours). Both the IB and SARL have almost the same median, but for the IB the humans' scores deviate more from the median. Our method obtains the highest score.

4.5 Qualitative Results

Figure 3 shows SARL and SCR navigating through a crowd of five people. The left figures shows SARL (a, b) and right SCR (c, d) at two different time steps. The trajectories indicate that SARL goes directly to its goal, while SCR waits at $t = 6$ (c). Moreover, at $t = 9.2$, SARL has reached its goal, but only two out of five humans reach theirs (b, purple and light blue stars). In contrast, SCR reaches its goal at $t = 10.5$, but all people reached their final destinations (d). SARL overtakes two people (a, red and green) and alters the path of another (a, blue). On the contrary, SCR lets them pass (c, red, green and blue). SARL uses occupancy maps to model the pairwise interaction between humans [6], so it cannot incorporate the robot's influence on each human. On the contrary, SCR uses empowerment maps for each human with high values in states in which it does not block anyone.

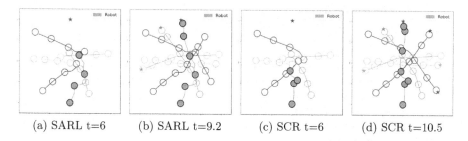

(a) SARL t=6   (b) SARL t=9.2   (c) SCR t=6   (d) SCR t=10.5

Fig. 3. SARL (a, b) and SCR (c, e) in a scene with 5 humans. The humans' destinations are the opposite of the x, y-axis' origin from their initial locations. SARL reaches its destination quickly, but only two out of five humans reach it (b, 2 stars). Two persons (red, blue) need to adjust their path to avoid the robot (orange). SCR waits at t=6 (c) and all humans reach their destination (d, 5 stars). (Color figure online)

5   Conclusion and Future Work

This paper proposed a reinforcement learning method for social navigation with intrinsic motivation using the empowerment of surrounding people. Our approach avoids the hard-coded reward signals and allows people nearby not to be disturbed by the robot. Our experiments show that our policy outperforms other methods on social characteristics. The influence of the robot's motion is hard to evaluate from artificial human motion alone and without actual humans interacting with the robot. Thus, we also compared the methods in an interactive simulator and obtained positive results. For future work, we would like to extend the model to deal with a variable amount of humans and with different policies. It would also be interesting to extend the method to incorporate the effect that (non-moving) objects have on humans.

References

1. Aubret, A., Matignon, L., Hassas, S.: A survey on intrinsic motivation in reinforcement learning. arXiv preprint arXiv:1908.06976 (2019)
2. Bansal, S., Tolani, V., Gupta, S., Malik, J., Tomlin, C.: Combining optimal control and learning for visual navigation in novel environments. arXiv preprint arXiv:1903.02531 (2019)
3. Burda, Y., Grosse, R., Salakhutdinov, R.: Importance weighted autoencoders. arXiv preprint arXiv:1509.00519 (2015)

4. Chen, Y., Everett, M., Liu, M., How, J.P.: Socially aware motion planning with deep reinforcement learning. In: 2017 IEEE/RSJ IROS, pp. 1343–1350. IEEE (2017)

5. Chen, Y., Liu, M., Everett, M., How, J.P.: Decentralized non-communicating multiagent collision avoidance with deep reinforcement learning. In: 2017 IEEE ICRA, pp. 285–292. IEEE (2017)

6. Chen, C., Liu, Y., Kreiss, S., Alahi, A.: Crowd-robot interaction: crowd-aware robot navigation with attention-based deep reinforcement learning. In: 2019 ICRA, pp. 6015–6022. IEEE (2019)

7. Cross, E., Hortensius, R., Wykowska, A.: From social brains to social robots: applying neurocognitive insights to human-robot interaction. Philos. Trans. Roy. Soc. London. Ser. B Biol. Sci. 374 (2019)

8. Everett, M., Chen, Y., How, J.P.: Motion planning among dynamic, decision-making agents with deep reinforcement learning. In: 2018 IEEE/RSJ IROS, pp. 3052–3059. IEEE (2018)

9. Fong, T., Nourbakhsh, I., Dautenhahn, K.: A survey of socially interactive robots. Robot. Auton. Syst. 42(3–4), 143–166 (2003)

10. Gu, T., Dolan, J.: Toward human-like motion planning in urban environments. In: 2014 IEEE Intelligent Vehicles Symposium Proceedings, pp. 350–355. IEEE (2014)

11. Helbing, D., Molnar, P.: Social force model for pedestrian dynamics. Phys. Rev. E 51(5), 4282 (1995)

12. Karamouzas, I., Heil, P., van Beek, P., Overmars, M.H.: A predictive collision avoidance model for pedestrian simulation. In: Egges, A., Geraerts, R., Overmars, M. (eds.) MIG 2009. LNCS, vol. 5884, pp. 41–52. Springer, Heidelberg (2009). https://doi.org/10.1007/978-3-642-10347-6_4

13. Karl, M., Soelch, M., Becker-Ehmck, P., Benbouzid, D., van der Smagt, P., Bayer, J.: Unsupervised real-time control through variational empowerment. arXiv preprint arXiv:1710.05101 (2017)

14. Kingma, D.P., Ba, J.: Adam: A method for stochastic optimization. arXiv preprint arXiv:1412.6980 (2014)

15. Klyubin, A.S., Polani, D., Nehaniv, C.L.: Empowerment: a universal agent-centric measure of control. In: 2005 IEEE Congress on Evolutionary Computation, vol. 1, pp. 128–135. IEEE (2005)

16. Klyubin, A.S., Polani, D., Nehaniv, C.: Empowerment: A universal agent-centric measure of control, vol. 1, pp. 128–135 (2005)

17. Kruse, T., Pandey, A.K., Alami, R., Kirsch, A.: Human-aware robot navigation: a survey. Robot. Autonomous Syst. 61(12), 1726–1743 (2013)

18. Kullback, S., Leibler, R.A.: On information and sufficiency. Ann. Math. Stat. 22(1), 79–86 (1951)

19. Mnih, V., et al.: Human-level control through deep reinforcement learning. Nature 518(7540), 529 (2015)

20. Mohamed, S., Rezende, D.J.: Variational information maximisation for intrinsically motivated reinforcement learning. In: NeurIPS, pp. 2125–2133 (2015)

21. Oudeyer, P., Kaplan, F., Hafner, V.V.: Intrinsic motivation systems for autonomous mental development. IEEE Trans. Evol. Comput. 11(2), 265–286 (2007)

22. Pfeiffer, M., Schwesinger, U., Sommer, H., Galceran, E., Siegwart, R.: Predicting actions to act predictably: Cooperative partial motion planning with maximum entropy models. In: 2016 IEEE/RSJ IROS, pp. 2096–2101. IEEE (2016)

23. Robicquet, A., Sadeghian, A., Alahi, A., Savarese, S.: Learning social etiquette: human trajectory understanding in crowded scenes. In: Leibe, B., Matas, J., Sebe, N., Welling, M. (eds.) ECCV 2016. LNCS, vol. 9912, pp. 549–565. Springer, Cham (2016). https://doi.org/10.1007/978-3-319-46484-8_33

24. Salge, C., Polani, D.: Empowerment as replacement for the three laws of robotics. Front. Robot. AI **4**, 25 (2017)

25. Salge, C., Glackin, C., Polani, D.: Empowerment–An Introduction. In: Prokopenko, M. (ed.) Guided Self-Organization: Inception. ECC, vol. 9, pp. 67–114. Springer, Heidelberg (2014). https://doi.org/10.1007/978-3-642-53734-9_4

26. Shiarlis, K., Messias, J., Whiteson, S.: Acquiring social interaction behaviours for telepresence robots via deep learning from demonstration. In: 2017 IEEE/RSJ International Conference on Intelligent Robots and Systems (IROS), pp. 37–42. IEEE (2017)

27. Sieben, A., Schumann, J., Seyfried, A.: Collective phenomena in crowds-where pedestrian dynamics need social psychology. PLoS One **12**(6), e0177328 (2017)

28. Sutton, R.S., Barto, A.G., et al.: Introduction to Reinforcement Learning, vol. 2. MIT Press, Cambridge (1998)

29. Templeton, A., Drury, J., Philippides, A.: Walking together: behavioural signatures of psychological crowds. Roy. Soc. Open Science **5**(7), 180172 (2018)

30. Trautman, P., Krause, A.: Unfreezing the robot: navigation in dense, interacting crowds. In: 2010 IEEE/RSJ IROS, pp. 797–803. IEEE (2010)

31. van den Berg, J., Guy, S.J., Snape, J., Lin, M.C., Manocha, D.: Rvo2 library: Reciprocal collision avoidance for real-time multi-agent simulation

32. Van den Berg, J., Lin, M., Manocha, D.: Reciprocal velocity obstacles for real-time multi-agent navigation. In: 2008 IEEE International Conference on Robotics and Automation, pp. 1928–1935. IEEE (2008)

Curious Hierarchical Actor-Critic Reinforcement Learning

Frank Röder[✉], Manfred Eppe[✉], Phuong D. H. Nguyen[✉],
and Stefan Wermter[✉]

Department of Informatics, Knowledge Technology Institute, Universität Hamburg,
Hamburg, Germany
{3roeder,eppe,pnguyen,wermter}@informatik.uni-hamburg.de

Abstract. Hierarchical abstraction and curiosity-driven exploration are two common paradigms in current reinforcement learning approaches to break down difficult problems into a sequence of simpler ones and to overcome reward sparsity. However, there is a lack of approaches that combine these paradigms, and it is currently unknown whether curiosity also helps to perform the hierarchical abstraction. As a novelty and scientific contribution, we tackle this issue and develop a method that combines hierarchical reinforcement learning with curiosity. Herein, we extend a contemporary hierarchical actor-critic approach with a forward model to develop a hierarchical notion of curiosity. We demonstrate in several continuous-space environments that curiosity can more than double the learning performance and success rates for most of the investigated benchmarking problems. We also provide our source code (https://github.com/knowledgetechnologyuhh/goal_conditioned_RL_baselines) and a supplementary video (https://www2.informatik.uni-hamburg.de/wtm/videos/chac_icann_roeder_2020.mp4).

1 Introduction

A general problem for reinforcement learning (RL) is sparse rewards. For example, tasks as simple as drinking water involve a complex sequence of motor commands, and only upon completion of this complex sequence, a reward is provided, which destabilizes the learning of value functions. Hierarchical reinforcement learning (HRL) partially alleviates this issue by decomposing difficult tasks into simpler subtasks, providing additional intrinsic rewards upon completion of the subtasks. Therefore, HRL is a major step towards human-like cognition [24] and decision-making [4]. There exists a considerable body of research demonstrating that hierarchical architectures provide a significant performance gain compared to non-hierarchical architectures by performing such abstractions [9,19,30].

However, HRL does not completely eliminate the problem of reward sparsity. By adding intrinsic rewards for achieving subtasks, it rather transforms the

---

F. Röder and M. Eppe—Equal contribution.

© Springer Nature Switzerland AG 2020
I. Farkaš et al. (Eds.): ICANN 2020, LNCS 12397, pp. 408–419, 2020.
https://doi.org/10.1007/978-3-030-61616-8_33

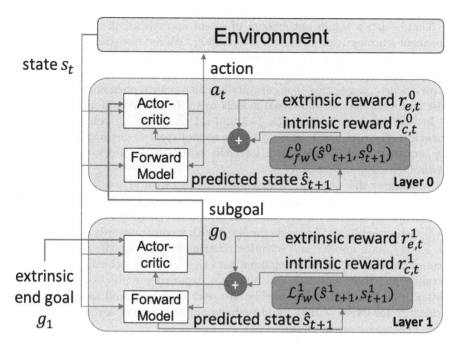

Fig. 1. The CHAC Architecture with two layers of hierarchy. A forward model is employed to compute the prediction error $\mathcal{L}_{fw}^{i}(\hat{s}_{t+1}^{i}, s_{t+1}^{i})$, which provides an additional curiosity-based reward $r_{c,t}^{i}$ for the layer i of hierarchy. This intrinsic reward is added to the extrinsic reward $r_{e,t}^{i}$ to train the actor-critic.

problem of reward sparsity into the problem of selecting the appropriate subgoals or subtasks. Learning the subgoal or subtask-selection still suffers from reward sparsity. So how can we improve the learning of subtask selection under sparse rewards?

Current RL literature offers two commonly used methods for overcoming rewards sparsity that we will investigate to address this question. The first method is hindsight experience replay (HER) [2]. The idea behind HER is to pretend in hindsight that the final state of a rollout was the goal of the rollout, regardless of whether it was actually the original one. This way, unsuccessful roll-outs get rewarded by considering in hindsight that they were successful. In recent work, Levy et al. [19] have successfully combined HER with a hierarchical actor-critic reinforcement learning approach, demonstrating a significant performance gain for several continuous-space environments. The second method to densify rewards is curiosity. Existing curiosity-based approaches in non-hierarchical reinforcement learning (e.g. [13,23]) provide additional rewards when the agent is surprised. Following research around Friston et al. [11], the notion of surprise is based on the prediction error of an agent's internal forward model. That is, the agent is surprised when its internal prediction of the world dynamics does not coincide with its actual dynamics.

There exists a significant amount of recent approaches on hierarchical reinforcement learning (e.g. [3,15,16,18,19,22,30]). We are also aware of significant recent improvements in curiosity-driven non-hierarchical reinforcement learning (e.g. [1,5,6,8,10,13,14,23,31]). However, despite significant evidence from Cognitive Sciences, suggesting that curiosity is a hierarchical phenomenon [24], there exist no functional computational models to verify this hypothesis.

In this paper, we address this lack and ask the following **central research question:** *To what extent can we alleviate reward-sparsity and improve the learning performance of hierarchical actor-critic reinforcement learning with a hierarchical curiosity mechanism?*

We address this question by extending the hierarchical actor-critic approach by Levy et al. [19] with a reward signal that fosters the agent's curiosity. We extend the approach with Friston et al.'s proposal to model surprise based on prediction errors [11] and provide the agent with intrinsic rewards if it is surprised (cf. Fig. 1). As a novelty and scientific contribution, we are the first to present a computational model that combines curiosity with hierarchical reinforcement learning, and that considers also hindsight experience replay as an additional method to overcome reward sparsity. We refer to our method as Curious Hierarchical Actor-Critic (CHAC) and evaluate our approach in several continuous-space benchmark environments.

2   Background and Related Work

Our research integrates hierarchical reinforcement learning with a curiosity and surprise mechanism inspired by the principle of active inference [11]. In the following, we provide the background of these mechanisms and methods.

2.1   Reinforcement Learning

Reinforcement learning (RL) involves a Markov Decision Process (MDP) to maximize the long-term expected reward. An MDP is defined as a tuple, $\langle S, A, R, T, \gamma \rangle$, where S is a set of states, A is a set of actions, $R : S \times A$ is a reward function, $T : S \times A \mapsto Pr(S) = p(s_{t+1}|s_t, a_t)$ is a transition probability of reaching state s_{t+1} from the current state s_t when executing action a_t, and $\gamma \in [0, 1)$ is a discount factor, indicating how much the agent prefers short-term to long-term rewards. In our setting, the agent takes actions drawn from a probability distribution over action, a policy, denoted $\pi(a|s) : S \mapsto A$. The goal of the agent is to take actions that maximize long-term expected reward. In this work, we employ the Deep Deterministic Policy Gradient (DDPG) algorithm [20] for the policy learning. DDPG is a model-free off-policy actor-critic algorithm, which combines the Deterministic Policy Gradient (DPG) algorithm [29] with Deep Q-network (DQN) [21]. This enables agent with DDPG to work in continuous space while learning with large, non-linear function approximators more stably and efficiently. In Sect. 3, we define how this non-hierarchical notion of reinforcement learning is extended to the hierarchical actor-critic case.

2.2 Curiosity-Driven Exploration

Friston et al. [11] describe surprise as "the improbability of sampling some signals, under a generative model of how those signals were caused.". Hence, curiosity can be achieved by maximizing surprise, i.e., by maximizing the probability of sampling signals that do not coincide with the predictions by the generative model [7,11][1].

A common method realizing this in practical reinforcement learning applications is to define a generative forward model $f_{fw} : S \times A \mapsto S$ that maps states and actions to successive states. One can then use the forward model to implement surprise as a function of the error between the successive states predicted by the model and the actual successive states. This strategy and derivatives thereof have been successfully employed in several non-hierarchical reinforcement learning approaches [1,5–7,10,13,14,23,27,28,31].

For example, Pathak et al. [23] propose an Intrinsic Curiosity Module, introducing an additional internal reward that is defined as the squared error of the predictions generated by a forward model. Similarly, Hafez et al. [13] implement surprise as the absolute error of a set of forward models, and Watters et al. [31] use the squared error as a reward signal.

3 Curious Hierarchical Actor-Critic

The hierarchical actor-critic (HAC) approach by Levy et al. [19] has shown great potential in continuous-space environments. At the same time, there exists extensive research [13,23] showing how curious agents striving to maximize their surprise can improve their learning performance. In the following, we describe how we combine both paradigms.

3.1 Hierarchical Actor-Critic

Hierarchical actor-critic (HAC) [19] is a framework that enables agents to learn a nested hierarchy of policies. It uses hindsight experience replay (HER) [2] to alleviate reward-sparsity. Each layer of the hierarchy learns to solve a subproblem defined by the spaces and a transition function of the layers below: It produces actions that are subgoals for the next lower level. The highest layer receives the current state and the overall extrinsic goal as input. The lowest layer produces motor commands that are executable by the agent in the environment. HAC involves the following three kinds of state transitions that implement HER in a hierarchical setting.

Hindsight Goal Transitions are akin to the transitions in the non-hierarchical HER method: After a rollout has completed, the agent pretends in hindsight that the actually achieved state was the goal state. They enable the critic function to

---

[1] Note that curiosity is a broad term and there exist other rich notions of curiosity [12]. However, for this paper we focus on the well-defined and established notion of curiosity as maximizing a function over prediction errors.

encounter at least one sparse reward after a sequence of actions. *Hindsight Action Transitions*: These additional state transitions are generated by pretending in hindsight that the action provided as subgoal to the low-level layer has been achieved. This alleviates the slow learning of a hierarchical layer due to the sparsity in achieving the subgoal provided by a higher level. As a result, HAC can learn multiple levels of policies in parallel, even if the lower-level policies are not yet fully trained. *Subgoal Testing Transitions* foster the generation of subgoals that are actually achievable by the low-level layer. They are used to test whether subgoals can be achieved and penalize a subgoal that could not be reached. Since difficult subgoals are penalized in the beginning of the training, but not anymore when the agent's performance has improved, subgoal testing mechanism provides HAC with a method to automatically generate a curriculum.

We build our approach on these transitions using the following formal framework: We define a hierarchy of k layers with each containing an actor-critic network and a replay buffer to store experiences. Here the RL setting (cf. Sect. 2.1) is expanded for hierarchical agents. Each layer Π_i of the hierarchy is described as a Universal Markov Decision Process (UMDP), an extension of MDP with an additional set of goals by applying universal value function approximator (UVFA) [26]. An UMDP is a tuple $\mathcal{U}_i = \langle \mathcal{S}_i, \mathcal{G}_i, \mathcal{A}_i, \mathcal{T}_i, \mathcal{R}_i, \gamma_i \rangle$ containing the state space $\mathcal{S}_i$, the goal space $\mathcal{G}_i$, the action space $\mathcal{A}_i$, the transition probability function $\mathcal{T}_i = p_i(s^i_{t+1}|a^i, s^i_t)$, the reward function $\mathcal{R}_i$, and the discount rate $\gamma_i \in [0, 1)$ for each layer i. The state space of each layer is identical to the original, namely $\mathcal{S}_i = \mathcal{S}$. The produced subgoals by the policy $\pi_i : \mathcal{S} \times \mathcal{G}_i \mapsto \mathcal{A}_i$ of each layer are within $\mathcal{S}$, and therefore $\mathcal{G}_i = \mathcal{S}$. The action space is equal to the goal space of the next lower layer, except the lowest one, thus $\mathcal{A}_i = \mathcal{S}$, $i > 0$. Only in the lowest layer, we execute the so-called primitive actions of the agent within the environment and therefore have $\mathcal{A}_0 = \mathcal{A}$ [19].

3.2   Combining Hierarchical Actor-Critic with Curiosity

To combine HAC with curiosity-based rewards, we implement a forward model based on a multi-layered perceptron that learns to predict the successive state $\hat{s}_{t+1}$ given the current state s_t and an action a_t at time t. Formally, this mapping is given as follows, with the model parameters θ:

$$f_{fw}(s_t, a_t; \theta) \Rightarrow \hat{s}_{t+1} \tag{1}$$

An action a^i_t produced by a policy π_i of the layer i (except the bottom layer, where $i = 0$) at time t is a subgoal for the subsequent level. We implement one forward model $f^i_{fw}(s_t, a^i_t; \theta^i)$ per layer. That is, we define a forward model not only for the primitive action $a^{i=0} \in \mathcal{A}$ in the lowest layer but also for the subgoal action $a^i \in \mathcal{A}_i = \mathcal{S}$ in the higher layers. The learning objective for training the forward model is to minimize the prediction loss, defined as:

$$\mathcal{L}^i_{fw}(\hat{s}^i_{t+1}, s^i_{t+1}) = \frac{(s^i_{t+1} - \hat{s}^i_{t+1})^2}{2}. \tag{2}$$

Similar to the approach by Pathak et al. [23], the forward model's error of the layer i is used to realize the curiosity-based bonus, denoted as $r_{c,t}^i$. We calculate the mean-squared-error as follows:

$$r_{c,t}^i = \frac{(s_{t+1}^i - \hat{s}_{t+1}^i)^2}{2} \tag{3}$$

The regular extrinsic rewards (from the environment) are defined in the range of $[-1, 0]$, hence we need to normalize the curiosity reward $r_{t,c}^i$ resulted of Eq. 3. The normalization of the curiosity reward is conducted with respect to the maximum and minimum values of the curiosity level in the whole history (stored in a buffer), $r_{c,max}^i$ and $r_{c,min}^i$ respectively, as follows:

$$r_{c,t}^i = \frac{r_{c,t}^i - r_{c,min}^i}{r_{c,max}^i - r_{c,min}^i} - 1 \tag{4}$$

In other words, if the prediction error is high, corresponding to high curiosity, the normalized value will be close to 0, otherwise, it is close to -1.

The total reward r_t^i at time t that layer i receive, given the extrinsic reward $r_{e,t}^i$ and the curiosity reward $r_{c,t}^i$, is controlled by the hyper-parameter η as follows:

$$r_t^i = \eta \cdot r_{e,t}^i + (1 - \eta) \cdot r_{c,t}^i \tag{5}$$

This part is crucial in determining the balance of changing the reward, since $r_t^i = r_{e,t}^i$ if $\eta = 1$, which is identical to HAC. We further elaborate on the different values of η in Sect. 4.

3.3   Architecture and Training

We implement the forward model (of each hierarchical layer i) as a multilayer perceptron (MLP), receiving the concatenated current state s_t and action a_t, to generate a prediction for the successor state $\hat{s}_{t+1}$ as output (cf. Eq. 1). For all experiments in this paper (see Sect. 4), we use an MLP with 3 hidden layers of size 256 (cf. Fig. 2) to learn the forward model from the agent's experiences. Experimentally, we found that this setting yields the best performance results. Following Levy et al. [19], we also realize the actor and critic networks with MLPs of 3 hidden layers of size 64.

Both the forward model and actor-critic are trained consecutively with a learning rate of 0.001 using the ADAM optimizer [17]. After each interaction episode, 1024 samples are randomly drawn from the replay buffer for training the network parameters of all components, including the forward model. The hyper-parameters used were either adapted from HAC [19] or fine-tuned with preliminary experiments.

Fig. 2. Forward model architecture

4 Experiments

We compare the performance of our framework in several goal-based environments with continuous state and action spaces. All environments provide a sparse extrinsic reward when the goal is reached. To evaluate our approach, we record the learning performance in terms of successful rollouts in relation to training rollouts. Therefore, we alternate training (with exploration using ϵ-greedy) and testing rollouts (without exploration) and measure the success rate as the average number of successful testing rollouts within a testing batch.

4.1 Environments

Our proposed approach is evaluated in the following simulated environments:

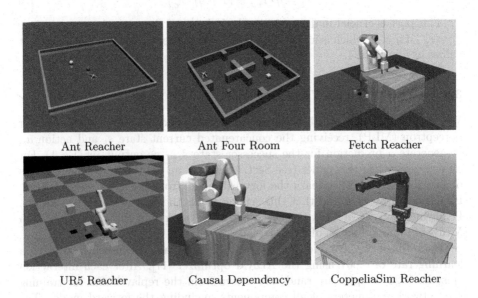

Fig. 3. Simulated environments for experiments

- *Ant reacher:* The *Ant reacher* environment (see Fig. 3a) consists of a four-legged robotic agent that must learn to walk to reach a target location. The action space is based on the joint angles of the limbs, and the observation space consists of the Cartesian locations and velocities of the body parts of the agent. The target location is random Cartesian coordinates of the agent's torso. The yellow and pink spheres in the figure indicate the end-goal and subgoal respectively.

- *Ant four rooms:* This environment is the same as *Ant reacher*, except that there are walls in the environments that the agent cannot pass (see Fig. 3b). The walls form four rooms that are connected by passages to transition from one room to another, increasing the difficulty compared to *Ant reacher*.
- *Fetch robot reacher:* This reacher environment (see Fig. 3c) is based on an inverse kinematics model that provides a 3D continuous action space. The task of the robot is to move the gripper to a target position (indicated in the figure by the black sphere), defined in terms of Cartesian coordinates.
- *UR5 reacher:* This environment consists of the first three DoFs (two shoulder joints and one elbow joint) of a UR5 robotic arm that must reach (feasible) random joint configurations indicated by yellow boxes in Fig. 3d. The action space is determined by the angles of the joints, and the state space consists of joint velocities angles.
- *Causal Dependency:* The robotic arm of this environment needs to address a simple causal dependency. This dependency is implemented by a button (blue button) that needs to be pressed before a target position (red button) can be reached (cf. Fig. 3e). The button press opens the lid over the target location so that the arm must first move towards the button and then towards the target location.
- *CoppeliaSim Reacher:* This environment is based upon the robot simulation CoppeliaSim [25] and is structured similarly to *Fetch robot reacher*, containing the same task. The task differs from the *Fetch robot reacher* in terms of its goal and observational space. It also makes use of inverse kinematics to reach a target location (red object) seen in Fig. 3f.

4.2 Results

Results from Fig. 4 reveal significant performance gains in terms of the learning progress for most of the investigated environments. For each environment, we use at least seven experiments to calculate the mean. For the shaded area, we use the standard deviation and sometimes apply a bit of smoothing. The benefit of curiosity differs depending on the task. Hence, we show up four values of η for each environment. For the ant environments (Fig. 4a and Fig. 4b), curiosity shows different effects. One assumption is that *Ant reacher* is an easier environment and curiosity-driven exploration is not as useful as it is in the more difficult *Ant four rooms*. For *Ant reacher*, the performance of HAC is quite similar to what CHAC is able to achieve. Both settle in at a mean success rate of 0.9 (cf. Fig. 4a). In *Ant four rooms*, the mean success rate of HAC is between 0.4 and 0.5. When using CHAC with curiosity and $\eta = 0.5$, the performance rises and achieves mean success rates between 0.65 and 0.8 (cf. Fig. 4b). Within the *Fetch reacher environment*, HAC cannot achieve success rates greater than 0.12. Using CHAC with $\eta \in \{0.25, 0.75\}$ improves the success rates roughly by

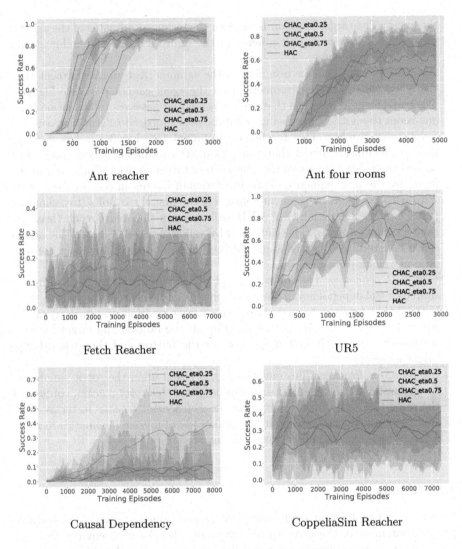

Fig. 4. Learning performance of the four environments

a factor of 2 (cf. Fig. 4c). The HAC-based UR5 agent achieves a different performance than reported in the paper of HAC [19][2]. However, CHAC speeds up learning by a factor of up to 1.67 with $\eta \in \{0.5, 0.75\}$ (cf. Fig. 4d). A performance gain is also achieved within the *Causal Dependency* environment. While HAC fails to learn a good policy, also CHAC struggles with most of its values of η. Both of them are not able to exceed a mean success rate of 0.12. Except with $\eta = 0.75$, CHAC shows up a mean success rate between 0.3 and 0.4 (cf. Fig. 4e),

---

[2] Our implementation contains a slightly different initialization and gain RPM values for the robot's joints. Nevertheless, the comparison is given.

resulting in a performance gain of more than 200%. The *CoppeliaSim Reacher* shows performance differences right from the start. Even if the training fluctuates, CHAC achieves an improvement roughly 1.5 times better than HAC with $\eta = 0.25$.

5 Conclusion

Curiosity and the ability to perform problem-solving in a hierarchical manner are two important features of human-level problem-solving and learning. As a novelty and scientific contribution, this paper presents the first computational approach that combines both features by extending hierarchical actor-critic reinforcement learning with a curiosity-enabled reward function. The level of curiosity is modeled by the prediction error of learnable forward models included in all hierarchical layers. Our experimental results provide significant evidence that curiosity improves hierarchical problem-solving. Specifically, using the success rate as evaluation metrics, we show that curiosity can more than double the learning performance for the proposed hierarchical architecture and benchmark problems.

Acknowledgements. Manfred Eppe, Phuong Nguyen, and Stefan Wermter acknowledge funding by the German Research Foundation (DFG) under the IDEAS project and the LeCAREbot project. We thank Andrew Levy for the productive communication and the publication of the original HAC code.

References

1. Alet, F., Schneider, M.F., Lozano-Perez, T., Kaelbling, L.P.: Meta-learning curiosity algorithms. In: International Conference on Learning Representations (ICLR), p. online (2020)
2. Andrychowicz, M., et al.: Hindsight experience replay. In: Conference on Neural Information Processing Systems (NeurIPS), pp. 5048–5058. Curran Associates, Inc. (2017)
3. Bacon, P.L., Harb, J., Precup, D.: The option-critic architecture. In: Conference on Artificial Intelligence (AAAI), pp. 1726–1734. AAAI Press (2017)
4. Botvinick, M., Weinstein, A.: Model-based hierarchical reinforcement learning and human action control. Philos. Trans. Roy. Soc. B: Biol. Sci. **369**(1655) (2014)
5. Burda, Y., Edwards, H., Pathak, D., Storkey, A., Darrell, T., Efros, A.A.: Large-scale study of curiosity-driven learning. In: International Conference on Learning Representations (ICLR), p. online (2019)
6. Burda, Y., Edwards, H., Storkey, A., Klimov, O.: Exploration by random network distillation. In: International Conference on Learning Representations (ICLR), p. online (2019)
7. Butz, M.V.: Toward a unified sub-symbolic computational theory of cognition. Front. Psychol. **7**, 925 (2016)
8. Colas, C., Fournier, P., Sigaud, O., Chetouani, M., Oudeyer, P.Y.: CURIOUS: intrinsically motivated modular multi-goal reinforcement learning. In: International Conference on Machine Learning (ICML), pp. 1331–1340 (2019)

9. Eppe, M., Nguyen, P.D.H., Wermter, S.: From semantics to execution: integrating action planning with reinforcement learning for robotic causal problem-solving. Front. Robot. AI **6** (2019)
10. Forestier, S., Oudeyer, P.Y.: Modular active curiosity-driven discovery of tool use. In: IEEE International Conference on Intelligent Robots and Systems, pp. 3965–3972. IEEE (2016)
11. Friston, K., Mattout, J., Kilner, J.: Action understanding and active inference. Biol. Cybern. **104**(1–2), 137–160 (2011)
12. Gottlieb, J., Oudeyer, P.Y.: Towards a neuroscience of active sampling and curiosity. Nat. Rev. Neurosci. **19**(12), 758–770 (2018)
13. Hafez, M.B., Weber, C., Wermter, S.: Curiosity-driven exploration enhances motor skills of continuous actor-critic learner. In: IEEE International Conference on Development and Learning and Epigenetic Robotics (ICDL-EpiRob), pp. 39–46. IEEE (2017)
14. Hester, T., Stone, P.: Intrinsically motivated model learning for developing curious robots. Artif. Intell. **247**, 170–86 (2017)
15. Jaderberg, M., et al.: Reinforcement learning with unsupervised auxiliary tasks. In: International Conference on Learning Representations (ICLR), p. online (2017)
16. Jiang, Y., Gu, S.S., Murphy, K.P., Finn, C.: Language as an abstraction forhierarchical deep reinforcement learning. In: Neural Information Processing Systems (NeurIPS), pp. 9419–9431. Curran Associates, Inc. (2019)
17. Kingma, D.P., Ba, J.L.: Adam: a method for stochastic optimization. In: International Conference on Learning Representations (ICLR), p. online (2015)
18. Kulkarni, T.D., Narasimhan, K., Saeedi, A., Tenenbaum, J.B.: Hierarchical deep reinforcement learning: integrating temporal abstraction and intrinsic motivation. In: Conference on Neural Information Processing Systems (NeurIPS), pp. 3675–3683 (2016)
19. Levy, A., Konidaris, G., Platt, R., Saenko, K.: Learning multi-level hierarchies with hindsight. In: International Conference on Learning Representations (ICLR), p. online (2019)
20. Lillicrap, T.P., et al.: Continuous control with deep reinforcement learning. In: International Conference on Learning Representations (ICLR), p. online (2016)
21. Mnih, V., et al.: Human-level control through deep reinforcement learning. Nature **518**(7540), 529–533 (2015)
22. Nachum, O., Gu, S.S., Lee, H., Levine, S.: Data-efficient hierarchical reinforcement learning. In: Conference on Neural Information Processing Systems (NeurIPS), pp. 3303–3313. Curran Associates, Inc. (2018)
23. Pathak, D., Agrawal, P., Efros, A.A., Darrell, T.: Curiosity-driven exploration by self-supervised prediction. In: International Conference on Machine Learning (ICML), pp. 2778–2787. PMLR (2017)
24. Pezzulo, G., Rigoli, F., Friston, K.J.: Hierarchical Active Inference: A Theory of Motivated Control (2018)
25. Rohmer, E., Singh, S.P.N., Freese, M.: Coppeliasim (formerly v-rep): a versatile and scalable robot simulation framework. In: Proceedings of the International Conference on Intelligent Robots and Systems (IROS) (2013)
26. Schaul, T., Horgan, D., Gregor, K., Silver, D.: Universal value function approximators. In: International Conference on Machine Learning (ICML), vol. 37, pp. 1312–1320. PMLR (2015)
27. Schillaci, G., Hafner, V.V., Lara, B.: Exploration behaviors, body representations, and simulation processes for the development of cognition in artificial agents. Front. Robot. AI **3**, 39 (2016)

28. Schmidhuber, J.: Formal theory of creativity, fun, and intrinsic motivation (1990–2010). IEEE Trans. Auton. Mental Dev. **2**(3), 230–247 (2010)
29. Silver, D., Lever, G., Hees, N., Degris, T., Wierstra, D., Riedmiller, M.: Deterministic policy gradient algorithms. In: International Conference on Machine Learning (ICML), vol. 32, pp. 387–395 (2014)
30. Vezhnevets, A.S., et al.: FeUdal networks for hierarchical reinforcement learning. In: International Conference on Machine Learning (ICML), vol. 70, pp. 3540–3549. PMLR (2017)
31. Watters, N., Matthey, L., Bosnjak, M., Burgess, C.P., Lerchner, A.: COBRA: Data-Efficient Model-Based RL through Unsupervised Object Discovery and Curiosity-Driven Exploration (2019)

Policy Entropy for Out-of-Distribution Classification

Andreas Sedlmeier[(✉)], Robert Müller, Steffen Illium,
and Claudia Linnhoff-Popien

LMU Munich, Munich, Germany
andreas.sedlmeier@ifi.lmu.de

Abstract. One critical prerequisite for the deployment of reinforcement learning systems in the real world is the ability to reliably detect situations on which the agent was not trained. Such situations could lead to potential safety risks when wrong predictions lead to the execution of harmful actions. In this work, we propose PEOC, a new policy entropy based out-of-distribution classifier that reliably detects unencountered states in deep reinforcement learning. It is based on using the entropy of an agent's policy as the classification score of a one-class classifier. We evaluate our approach using a procedural environment generator. Results show that PEOC is highly competitive against state-of-the-art one-class classification algorithms on the evaluated environments. Furthermore, we present a structured process for benchmarking out-of-distribution classification in reinforcement learning.

Keywords: Out-of-distribution classification · Policy entropy · Deep reinforcement learning

1 Introduction

In the last years, impressive results were achieved using deep reinforcement learning techniques in areas as diverse as robotics or real time strategy games. Despite these successes, systems built using these algorithms are still mostly deployed in controlled settings such as laboratory environments or video games. Reliability of such learning systems when faced with changing observations in a real-world setting is still an open problem. Being able to differentiate between states seen in training and non-encountered states can for example prevent silent and possibly critical failures of the learning system, caused by wrong predictions which lead to the execution of unfavorable actions. We model the out-of-distribution (OOD) detection problem as a one-class classification problem, where only the in-distribution states are available at training time. Having framed the problem this way, we propose PEOC, a new policy entropy based out-of-distribution classifier, which uses the policy entropy $H(\pi)$ as the classification score to detect OOD states. PEOC classifiers can be constructed based on various RL algorithms from the policy-gradient and actor-critic classes.

© Springer Nature Switzerland AG 2020
I. Farkaš et al. (Eds.): ICANN 2020, LNCS 12397, pp. 420–431, 2020.
https://doi.org/10.1007/978-3-030-61616-8_34

2 Preliminaries

2.1 Reinforcement Learning

In the standard reinforcement learning (RL) formulation [19], an agent interacts with an environment defined as an MDP $\mathcal{M}$ [16] by executing a sequence of actions $a_t \in \mathcal{A}, t = 0, 1, \ldots$ over a possibly infinite number of discrete time steps t. Each time step t, the agent is able to observe the state $s_t \in \mathcal{S}$ and to select an action $a_t \in \mathcal{A}$ according to it's policy π. After executing the action, the next state s_{t+1} is observed together with a scalar reward r_t. The agents goal's is to find a policy $\pi : \mathcal{S} \rightarrow \mathcal{A}$, which maximizes the expectation of return G_t at state s_t over a potentially infinite horizon: $R_t = \sum_{k=0}^{\infty} \gamma^k \cdot r_{t+k}$ where $\gamma \in [0, 1]$ is the discount factor.

There are two fundamental approaches to reinforcement learning (RL), value based and policy based algorithms. In value based RL one seeks to find the optimal state-value or action-value function typically through an objective function based on the bellman equation. The optimal policy is then given by always selecting the action with the highest value in the current state. In contrast, policy-based methods directly search for the optimal policy $\pi^*(a|s)$ with parameters θ. Modern deep RL approaches use neural networks to represent the policy or the value function and train by gradient descent on the parameters θ.

Both approaches have their strengths and weaknesses. Value based methods can be trained off-policy where data from all previous runs can be reused for learning, leading to more sample efficiency. Policy based methods only use data from runs from the most recent version of the policy. However, they tend to be more stable than their value based counterparts.

Actor-critic algorithms are hybrid methods that combine both approaches [14,17]. The actor selects actions, while the critic is an estimate of the value function used to criticize the actor's actions. In this work, we use proximal policy optimization (PPO) [17], an actor-critic algorithm that has proven successful in a wide variety of tasks ranging from robotics [2] to real time strategy games [4]. Due to the non-stationarity of the training data (experience collected while acting according to the current policy), RL algorithms are often very unstable. PPO aims to reduce this, by avoiding harsh changes in the policy's parameters. That is, the probability ratio

$$r_t(\theta) = \frac{\pi_\theta(a_t|s_t)}{\pi_{\theta_{old}}(a_t|s_t)} \tag{1}$$

between the old and the new policy, should not significantly differ from $r_t(\theta) = 1$. In addition, an entropy bonus (based on the policy which can be interpreted as a distribution over actions) is often added to the loss function to refrain the agent from being overly confident and encouraging exploration. While PPO supports both discrete and continuous action spaces, the evaluations in this work focus on the discrete case. In this case, the policy's entropy with n actions in some state s_t can be readily computed by

$$H(\pi(s_t)) = -\sum_{i=0}^{n} \pi(a_i|s_t) * \log \pi(a_i|s_t) \tag{2}$$

2.2 Out-of-Distribution Detection

Out-of-distribution (OOD) detection (also called novelty-, outlier- or anomaly-detection, depending on the specific setting and applied approach), is a thoroughly researched topic for low-dimensional settings. The various approaches can be categorized as belonging to density-based, probabilistic, distance-based, reconstruction-based or information theoretic classes. For an extensive survey on the topic of novelty detection with a focus on low-dimensional settings, see [15]. Further, it is important to differentiate between problems where samples from all classes are available at training time, versus problems where only samples of a single class are available. The work at hand falls into the latter category (sometimes called one-class classification) as no OOD states (states that were not encountered during training) are available at training time. While conventional out-of-distribution detection methods work reliably for low-dimensional settings, most break down with increasing dimensionality. This is an effect of the curse of dimensionality, as in high dimensional input spaces, data becomes sparse and the real outliers become indistinguishable from noise being present in irrelevant dimensions. For an in depth discussion of these effects and modern techniques, see e.g. [1].

With the rise of deep neural networks in the last years, new approaches were presented that try to tackle high-dimensional feature-spaces [11,12]. Still, most methods require access to training samples from all classes, and are not applicable to one-class classification problems. One exception are deep autoencoder (AE) based approaches that try to learn useful representations of the training data in an unsupervised fashion. AEs can be used to detect samples that were not part of the training data, by using the reconstruction error as the classification score [1].

2.3 Evaluation of Binary Classifiers

As we model the OOD detection problem as a one-class classification problem, it is important to correctly evaluate the performance of different classifiers. The basis of most approaches to evaluate the performance of a binary classifier is the classification score output by the classifier. Combined with a configurable threshold t, binary classification labels can be derived from these scores. Consequently, the amount of true positives (tp) and false positives (fp) reported by a classifier, when applied to a dataset, depends on the chosen threshold. A common choice to visualize this dependency is via a Receiver Operating Characteristic Curve (ROC). It plots the true positive rate $tpr(t)$ on the y-axis against the false positive rate $fpr(t)$ on the x-axis (see Fig. 4). When defining OOD samples as positives, the $tpr(t)$ (or recall) is defined as the percentage of ground-truth OOD samples correctly classified as OOD at threshold t. The $fpr(t)$ then is the percentage of falsely reported positives out of the ground-truth negatives. The ROC curve of a random classifier is the diagonal between $(0,0)$ and $(1,1)$, while the curve of a classifier with better performance than random lies above this diagonal. In addition to this visual evaluation, the area under the curve (ROC

AUC) can be computed. This is useful in order to compare the performance of different classifiers as well as repeated evaluation runs with different classifier configurations (or in our case, different environment configurations and repeated RL training runs).

3   Related Work

3.1   Out-of-distribution Detection in Deep RL

Recently, an epistemic uncertainty based approach to detect out-of-distribution states was proposed in [18]. The basic idea of the approach is that an agent's epistemic uncertainty is reduced for in-distribution situations (states encountered during training), and thus lower than for unencountered (OOD) situations. The author's approach can be combined with different uncertainty estimation approaches like deep ensembles or Monte-Carlo dropout. The goal of this work is closely related to the work at hand, as it also tries to build a classifier to detect OOD states in deep reinforcement learning. A limitation of the uncertainty based approach is that it is only applicable to value based reinforcement learning. Our proposed approach PEOC by difference is applicable to policy-gradient or actor-critic RL algorithms.

3.2   Entropy Regularization and Maximum Entropy RL

The approach presented in this work differs in its goal from related reinforcement learning approaches dealing with policy entropy. Most work considering policy entropy in RL is interested in using it during training, e.g. for exploration purposes during the learning phase. As such, the probability distribution underlying the policy is used to introduce stochasticity in the action selection process. One idea which can be categorized as entropy regularization initially proposed in [20] is to add the entropy of the policy $H(\pi)$ to the objective function in order to discourage premature convergence to local optima. This idea was later successfully applied to various reinforcement learning algorithms [14,17]. The extension of this idea, to not only find a policy with maximum entropy, but directly optimize the expectation of the entropy is called maximum entropy reinforcement learning [10]. It not only tries to optimize the policy entropy of visited states but also optimize the policy to seek out states that have high entropy.

Although we also focus on the policy entropy, the goal of our work is very different, as we are not trying to improve the learning performance of the RL algorithm. The question considered by the work at hand is whether the policy entropy can be used to detect OOD states after the learning phase has completed.

4   Policy Entropy for Out-of-Distribution Classification

This section presents a new type of policy based out-of-distribution classifier that can be applied in deep reinforcement learning settings, we call PEOC (Policy Entropy Out-of-distribution Classifier). We show how the policy entropy

$H(\pi)$ of a RL agent can be used to detect OOD states. PEOC classifiers can be constructed based on various RL algorithms from the policy-gradient and actor-critic classes. These types of algorithms use a stochastic policy π which is determined by a conditional probability distribution $p(a|s)$ defining the probability of taking action a in state s of the environment. The policy entropy $H(\pi)$ then quantifies how random the actions being taken by an agent following the policy are.

The goal of RL is to maximize the expected future return, which is achieved by finding the optimal (state-dependent) action-sequences. Assuming that optimal behavior in most cases means acting non-randomly, the idea of PEOC then boils down to the hypothesis that the entropy of the action distribution has to decrease for states encountered during training in order to act optimally. If this is the case, the policy entropy $H(\pi)$ can be used as the score of a binary classifier to detect OOD states.

Expressed more formally, a successful training process reduces $H(\pi(s_i))$ for states $s_i \in \mathbb{I}$, with $\mathbb{I}$ being the set of in-distribution data, i.e. the states encountered in training. All possible states that were not encountered in training, i.e. $s_o \notin \mathbb{I}$ define the set of out-of-distribution data $\mathbb{O}$. If the policy entropy of all states in the in-distribution set is smaller than the entropy of all states in the out-of-distribution set:

$$H(\pi(s_i)) < H(\pi(s_o)), \forall s_i \in \mathbb{I}, \forall s_o \in \mathbb{O} \tag{3}$$

a decision boundary exists that allows for a perfect separation of in- and out-of-distribution states, making it possible to construct a perfect classifier with $tpr = 1$, $fpr = 0$ as described in Sect. 2.3. In practice, the policy entropy distributions will most likely overlap, reducing the performance of a classifier constructed based on them. In the following chapters, we present experiments conducted following the process described in Sect. 5 to evaluate the performance, based on a reinforcement learning benchmark environment.

5   A Process for Benchmarking OOD Classification in Reinforcement Learning

In this section, we present a process for benchmarking out-of-distribution classification in reinforcement learning (Fig. 1). This process encompasses a complete pipeline starting with the training of reinforcement learning policies, over in- and out-of-distribution state sample collection, (non-policy based) benchmark classifier fitting, leading up to the final classifier performance evaluations.

The complete process can be repeated (n times) using different random seeds in order to average out variance in the classifier evaluation caused e.g. by random initialization of neural network weights or the level generators. We call one such run a *process-repeat*. When running more than one process-repeat, it is possible to compute some central estimator of the performance (e.g. median and standard-deviation of the AUC) over the process-repeats, and visualize the performance results using e.g. box-plots.

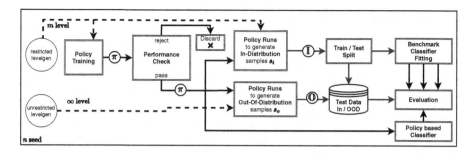

Fig. 1. A process for benchmarking OOD classification in reinforcement learning. The complete process can be repeated n times using different random seeds to average out variance in the classifier evaluation caused by random sampling.

For each process-repeat, *policy training* is performed on a different set of m levels for a fixed amount of timesteps. As optimizing policy performance of the learning algorithm is not the focus, it is possible to perform a policy selection step after training, as would be done in a real-world usecase, where only the best policies get deployed in production. The process continues only if the *policy performance check* is passed, e.g. policy performance in training converged near the maximum return of the environment. If not, the policy is *discarded* and the next process-repeat continues from the beginning.

If the policy performance check was passed, multiple *policy runs* are executed on the same set of m levels as in training (called IND runs). All states s_i encountered during these IND runs are collected and together constitute the set of in-distribution states $\mathbb{I}$. Separately, multiple *policy runs* are executed using the unrestricted level generator, so that each policy run uses a new level from the generator (called OOD runs). All states s_o encountered during these runs are collected and together constitute the set of OOD states $\mathbb{O}$. Figure 2 shows example states as generated during policy training, IND runs and OOD runs.

A *train/test split* is performed on the set of collected in-distribution states $\mathbb{I}$. Non-policy based *benchmark classifiers* are fitted only on the train part of the in-distribution states, in order to prevent overfitting. Policy based classifiers, like PEOC do not need a *fitting* step on the in-distribution data, as they are based on the policy network learned during the policy training phase. The test part of $\mathbb{I}$ is combined with the complete set $\mathbb{O}$ and constitutes the *test data*, on which all classifiers are evaluated. As for this evaluation, ground-truth labels (i.e. which set $\mathbb{I}$ or $\mathbb{O}$ a sample belongs to) are known, receiver operating characteristics of the classifiers can be calculated.

Note again, that this complete training & classifier evaluation process, as described above, can be repeated n times using different random seeds to compute some central estimators of the classifier performances.

6   Experimental Setup

6.1   Environments

Until recently, a lack of suitable benchmark environments made it difficult
to evaluate out-of-distribution classification performance in deep reinforcement
learning. Standard evaluation environments for deep reinforcement learning like
OpenAI Gym [5] or the arcade learning environment [3] are not suitable, as it
is necessary to create different in- and out-of-distribution state sets. In the last
two years, an increased research focus on generalization performance has lead
to the development of new benchmark environments that allow for a separation
of training- and test-environments [6,9,21]. Some of these environments are also
suitable to evaluate out-of-distribution classification performance.

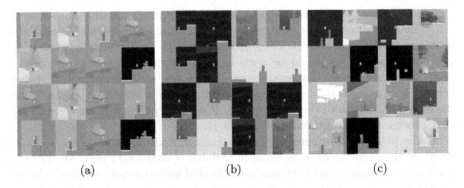

(a)   (b)   (c)

Fig. 2. Example states as generated during training/policy runs. Policy training and
IND runs (2a, 2b) are restricted to 4 different levels, resulting in different, restricted
sets of levels for each repeat. No seed restriction is applied to the level generator for
OOD runs (2c).

For our experiments, we chose the CoinRun [6] environment as the level
generator, as we deemed it's procedural level generation approach to be the
most suitable to evaluate the proposed PEOC approach. CoinRun is a simple
platform jump&run game, with discrete actions, where the agent has to collect
the coin at the far right side of the level. To do this, stationary obstacles, chasms
and moving enemies have to be avoided, to avert death. A state in the CoinRun
environment is a color image encoded as a vector of size $64 \times 64 \times 3$. Figure 2
shows example states of different levels as used for training and testing.

6.2   Evaluation Algorithms and Hyperparameters

We evaluate the performance of PEOC based on PPO2 as the RL algorithm.
For this, we make use of the PPO2 implementation from the OpenAI Baselines
package [7]. We combine PPO2 with an IMPALA Convolutional neural network

architecture [8], as good results were achieved with this in related work. The evaluated network consists of a convolutional sequence with depths $[16, 32, 32]$ followed by a max-pooling layer and 2 residual blocks.

We repeated the complete training & classifier evaluation process as described in Sect. 5 for 40 times using different level seeds. Each repeat, policy training was performed for 25×10^5 time steps. We store a snapshot of the policy after the first policy update as well as after the last policy update and call the classifiers constructed based on them PEOC-1 and PEOC-150 respectively. 8 policies passed the performance check, i.e. the return converged at the achievable maximum of 10. Policy IND runs are executed for a total of $\sim 30 \times 10^3$ steps, OOD runs for $\sim 10 \times 10^3$ steps. After performing a 2/1 train/test split on the in-distribution set, this results in an evenly distributed test set containing $\sim 20 \times 10^3$ in-and out-of-distribution samples on which the classifiers are evaluated. Parameters are summarized in Table 1.

Table 1. Training & evaluation parameters

# training & Classifier evaluation process repeats	40
# policies after perf. check	8
m level per repeat	4
Policy training steps, per repeat	25×10^5
RL Policy selection	return converges at 10
IND run steps, per repeat	30×10^3
OOD run steps, per repeat	10×10^3
Classifier train/test split	2/1

In order to benchmark the classification performance of PEOC, each repeat, 3 non-policy based state-of-the-art classifiers are fit on the train split of the in-distribution data: An autoencoder based approach, based on [1] and the SO-GAAL and MO-GAAL approaches as presented in [13]. We use the implementation and default hyperparameters as provided by [22] for all 3 classifiers.

7   Performance Results

Of the 40 process-repeats executed, 8 policies passed the policy performance check after 25×10^5 training steps, i.e. performance of the respective policy converged at 10, the maximum achievable return of the CoinRun environment. Figure 3 left shows mean and standard-deviation of the achieved return of these policies against the number of training updates. As expected, return performance increases, reflecting the discovery of increasingly successful policies. Policy entropy (Fig. 3 right) decreases over training progress, confirming the hypothesis that the entropy of the action distribution has to decrease for states encountered during training in order to act optimally.

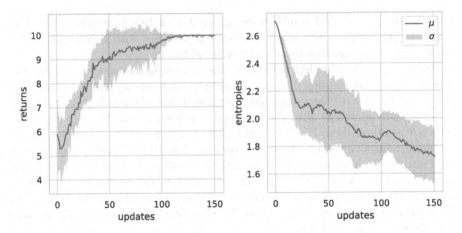

Fig. 3. Reward and policy entropy over training updates of the 8 policies that passed the performance check. The solid line and shaded regions represent the mean μ and standard deviation σ of the successful training runs, respectively.

Each of these policies was evaluated for 30×10^3 steps on the respective environments they were trained on, collecting 8 separate sets of in-distribution samples. For each of these, separate instances of the 3 benchmark classifiers were then fit on the train split of the respective in-distribution set, while testing of all classifiers was performed on the respective OOD set. The classification scores were then visualized in 8 separate ROC plots to compare the performance of the respective benchmark classifiers. In addition, the area under the curve (ROC AUC) was computed. Figure 4 shows that none of the classifiers reaches perfect classification results in any of the process-repeats. Still, some classifiers perform better than others. PEOC-1, i.e. the policy entropy based out-of-distribution classifier using the policy snapshot after the first update performs best across all process-repeats, when considering the area under the curve (AUC) with values ranging from 0.7056 to 0.7844. Even so, there are exceptions as can be seen in Fig. 4f, where the MO-GAAL classifier achieved the highest AUC of 0.7853. Apart from the raw AUC values, it becomes apparent from the ROC curves, that for some evaluations (e.g. AE in Fig. 4b), perfect $fpr = 0$ can be achieved while still classifying more than 40% of the OOD samples correctly. PEOC-150 mostly shows rather low performance, underperforming the other classifiers for most process-repeats. With an AUC varying between 0.5155 and 0.7605 the performance is not reliable in summary.

Using the ROC AUC values of all process-repeats, we compare the overall performance of the different classifiers, i.e. we summarize the 8 receiver operating characteristics for each classifier. Figure 5 shows this overall classifier performance in the form of a box-plot. Using the median ROC AUC as a central measures of classifier performance, PEOC-1 surpases the other classifiers with a value of 0.74. PEOC-150 shows a far lower median value of 0.63. The non-policy

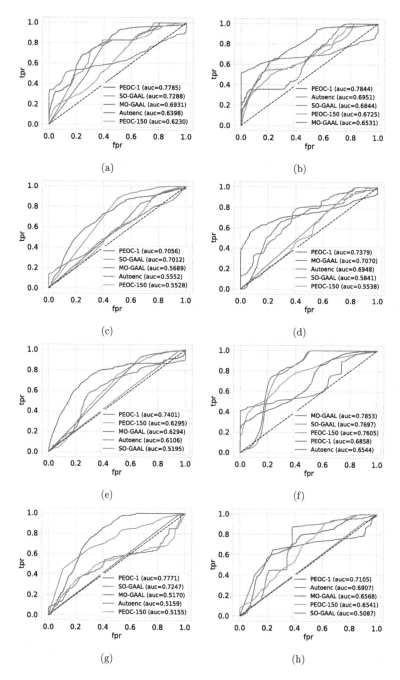

Fig. 4. ROC plots of the classifier evaluations of the 8 process-repeats. Each plot a)-h) shows the true-positive rate (*tpr*) against the false-positive rate (*fpr*) achieved by the classifier on the respective test data set.

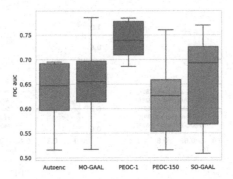

Fig. 5. Comparison of classifier performance based on ROC AUC values of 8 process-repeats.

based benchmark classifiers' median ROC AUC are 0.65 for the autoencoder, 0.69 for SO-GAAL and 0.65 for MO-GAAL.

8   Discussion and Future Work

In this work, we proposed PEOC, a policy entropy based out-of-distribution classifier as well as a structured process for benchmarking OOD classification in RL that can be reused for comparing different OOD classification approaches in the future. Performance evaluation results on the procedural CoinRun [6] environment show that PEOC-1 (using the policy after the first update) based on PPO2 as the RL algorithm, is highly competitive against state-of-the-art one-class classification algorithms, i.e. it reliably classifies out-of-distribution states.

Interestingly, using the final policy as the basis of the classifier did show inferior performance when compared to the policy after the first update. As to why this is the case, one hypothesis is that the convolutional layers of the policy network at first learn general features representing the states of the environment which seem to work well to differentiate in- from out-of-distribution states. With further progressing training, the network then concentrates on features relevant to policy performance optimization which might be less relevant for OOD detection. We aim to analyse this further using visualization approaches from the field of interpretable machine learning.

As our current evaluation was limited to only one policy-gradient based approach, i.e. PPO2, it will be interesting to see if the choice of RL algorithm has an influence on classifier performance. Another interesting question is the behaviour of PEOC when using a policy that successfully generalizes to unencountered states. Being able to differentiate between states seen in training, states the policy generalizes to and completely out-of-distribution states, where no generalization is possible, would be extremely valuable for deploying RL agents in the real world.

References

1. Aggarwal, C.C.: Outlier analysis. In: Aggarwal, C.C., et al. (eds.) Data Mining, pp. 237–263. Springer, Cham (2015). https://doi.org/10.1007/978-3-319-14142-8_8
2. Andrychowicz, O.M., Baker, et al.: Learning dexterous in-hand manipulation. Int. J. Robot. Res. **39**(1), 3–20 (2020)
3. Bellemare, M.G., Naddaf, Y., Veness, J., Bowling, M.: The arcade learning environment: an evaluation platform for general agents. J. Artif. Intell. Res. **47**, 253–279 (2013)
4. Berner, C., et al.: Dota 2 with large scale deep reinforcement learning. arXiv preprint arXiv:1912.06680 (2019)
5. Brockman, G., et al.: Openai gym (2016)
6. Cobbe, K., Hesse, C., Hilton, J., Schulman, J.: Leveraging procedural generation to benchmark reinforcement learning. arXiv preprint arXiv:1912.01588 (2019)
7. Dhariwal, P., et al.: Openai baselines (2017)
8. Espeholt, L., Soyer, H., Munos, R., et al.: IMPALA: scalable distributed deep-RL with importance weighted actor-learner architectures. CoRR (2018)
9. Farebrother, J., Machado, M.C., Bowling, M.: Generalization and regularization in DQN (2018)
10. Haarnoja, T., Tang, H., Abbeel, P., Levine, S.: Reinforcement learning with deep energy-based policies. In: Proceedings of the 34th International Conference on Machine Learning, vol. 70, pp. 1352–1361. JMLR. org (2017)
11. Hendrycks, D., Gimpel, K.: A Baseline for Detecting Misclassified and Out-of-Distribution Examples in Neural Networks. ArXiv e-prints, October 2016
12. Liang, S., Li, Y., Srikant, R.: Enhancing The Reliability of Out-of-distribution Image Detection in Neural Networks. ArXiv e-prints, June 2017
13. Liu, Y., et al.: Generative adversarial active learning for unsupervised outlier detection. IEEE Trans. Knowl. Data Eng. (2019)
14. Mnih, V., et al.: Asynchronous methods for deep reinforcement learning. CoRR (2016)
15. Pimentel, M.A., Clifton, D.A., Clifton, L., Tarassenko, L.: A review of novelty detection. Sig. Process. **99**, 215–249 (2014)
16. Puterman, M.L.: Markov Decision Processes: Discrete Stochastic Dynamic Programming. Wiley, Hoboken (2014)
17. Schulman, J., Wolski, F., et al.: Proximal policy optimization algorithms. CoRR (2017)
18. Sedlmeier, A., Gabor, T., Phan, T., Belzner, L., Linnhoff-Popien, C.: Uncertainty-based out-of-distribution classification in deep reinforcement learning, pp. 522–529 (2020)
19. Sutton, R.S., Barto, A.G.: Introduction to Reinforcement Learning, vol. 135. MIT Press, Cambridge (1998)
20. Williams, R.J., Peng, J.: Function optimization using connectionist reinforcement learning algorithms. Connection Sci. **3**(3), 241–268 (1991)
21. Zhang, C., Vinyals, O., Munos, R., Bengio, S.: A study on overfitting in deep reinforcement learning (2018)
22. Zhao, Y., Nasrullah, Z., Li, Z.: PyOD: a python toolbox for scalable outlier detection. J. Mach. Learn. Res. **20**(96), 1–7 (2019)

Reservoir Computing

Analysis of Reservoir Structure Contributing to Robustness Against Structural Failure of Liquid State Machine

Yuta Okumura and Naoki Wakamiya[(✉)][iD]

Graduate School of Information Science and Technology, Osaka University,
1-5 Yamadaoka, Suita, Osaka 565-0871, Japan
{yuta-o,wakamiya}@ist.osaka-u.ac.jp

Abstract. Attempts have been made to realize reservoir computing by using physical materials, but they assume the stable structure of a reservoir. However, in reality, a physical reservoir suffers from malfunctions, noise, and interferences, which cause failures of neurons and disconnection of synaptic connections. Consequently dynamics of system state changes and computation performance deteriorates. In this paper, we investigate structural properties contributing to the functional robustness of a reservoir. More specifically, we analyze the relationship between structural properties of a reservoir of a Liquid State Machine and the decrease in discrimination capability in a delayed readout task when experiencing failures of connections and neurons. We apply seven types of networks which have different structural properties to a reservoir. As a result, we revealed that high modularity, structural irregularity, and high clustering coefficient are most important for an LSM to be robust against random connection and neuron failures.

Keywords: Liquid State Machine · Robustness · Structural properties

1 Introduction

Reservoir computing is one of computation models of a neural network [11,12]. Input is given to a recurrent neural network, called a reservoir, which maps the input to a higher dimensional space as a dynamic state of the reservoir, and a simple readout unit translates the dynamics to a corresponding desired output. A unique feature which makes reservoir computing different from other neural networks is that learning or training is performed only on readout connections while a reservoir itself is kept unchanged.

For its simplicity and universal computational capability, reservoir computing has been attracting researchers. More specifically, since a reservoir can be any dynamical system as far as it exhibits sufficiently different dynamics for a given different input, which is called Separation Property [12], attempts have been

© Springer Nature Switzerland AG 2020
I. Farkaš et al. (Eds.): ICANN 2020, LNCS 12397, pp. 435–446, 2020.
https://doi.org/10.1007/978-3-030-61616-8_35

made to realize physical reservoir computing by using a soft material, laser, quantum, and electron as a reservoir [3,14,16,18]. In our research group, we apply a reservoir computing model to a wireless network called IWSN (Impulse-based Wireless Sensor Network) [8]. In IWSN, a wireless network plays the role of a reservoir, where wireless devices behave as neurons and exchange spike signals with devices in the range of radio signals. Information about sensing data and events is derived at a readout unit outside a network. Using a simple task, we confirmed observation of spiking activity of only 5 devices among 100 enables event detection with accuracy higher than 99% despite its simplicity and low-energy consumption [8]. Although the feasibility and performance of such physical reservoir computing are verified by experiments and simulations, they assume the stable structure of a reservoir.

However, in reality, as being a physical entity, a physical reservoir suffers from malfunctions, noise, and interferences, such as a failure of circuitry and disturbance of wireless communication. Even if a failure is not fatal and causes only a slight change in the structure of a reservoir, its dynamics can considerably change. As a result computation performance can easily deteriorate. The performance can be recovered by retraining, but it takes time and effort. For stable operation of a physical reservoir computing system, it is preferred that a reservoir itself is robust to structural changes.

Therefore, in this paper, we investigate structural properties contributing to functional robustness of a reservoir. More specifically, we investigate the relationship between structural properties of a reservoir and the decrease in discrimination capability in a delayed readout task when experiencing loss of connections and neurons. As a reservoir computation model, we adopt a Liquid State Machine. We apply seven types of networks which have different structural properties to a reservoir including connectome data of the cortex and the sub-cortical area of the human brain obtained by measurements. In evaluation, we use random connection failures and random neuron failures which are supposed to happen most frequently in physical reservoirs. The influence of failures can be different by the difference of structural properties of a reservoir. For example, It is said that a scale-free network is robust to random failures than other networks in the field of network science. However, it is only about connectivity and not about the dynamics. We also consider how to construct a robust structure in a physical reservoir computing system by taking our IWSN as an example.

In this paper, we explain experimental settings in Sect. 2. Next, we show results and discuss structural properties contributing robustness against structural failures in Sect. 3. Finally, we conclude this paper in Sect. 4.

2   Experimental Setting

2.1   Liquid State Machine

In this paper, we use Liquid State Machine as a reservoir computing model. A system is composed of two input units, one recurrent neural network as a reservoir, and one readout unit. Each of an input unit is individually connected

Table 1. Parameters of neuron model

parameter	value	
simulation time step Δt ms	0.1	
membrane time constant τ_m	0.03	
membrane resistance R MΩ	1	
initial membrane potential v_0 mV	random in $[13.5, 15]$	
threshold potential θ mV	15	
reset potential v_r mV	13.5	
constant current I_{con} nA	13.5	
excitatory rate R	0.8	
	excitatory	inhibitory
refractory period Δ^{abs} ms	3	2
from excitatory	30	60
synaptic weight w nA from inhibitory	-19	-19
from input	18	9
exponential decay time constant τ_s	0.003	0.006
transmission delay Δ^{ax} ms	1.5	0.8

to randomly chosen 30% of neurons of a reservoir. On the other hand, a readout
unit is connected from all neurons of a reservoir. With reference to [12], we use
Leaky Integrate & Fire (LIF) neurons to organize a reservoir, where 80% of
neurons are excitatory and the others are inhibitory. We also use a simplified
exponential decay model as a change of post-synapse potential by neuron fires
with reference to [7]. Table 1 summarizes the parameters used in this paper.

2.2   Reservoir Network Model

In this section, we describe generation models of a recurrent neural network of a
reservoir and measures of structural properties. Here, a neuron is called a node
and a synaptic connection is called a link.

To generate a reservoir having a variety of structure, we use seven types
of networks, including five generation models, i.e. distance-based Erdős-Rényi
(DB) [4,12], Barabási–Albert (BA) [1], Watts–Strogatz (WS) [19], Ring, and
Random, known in the complex network field, connectome obtained by measurement (Real) [9,10,17] and its generation model (HC) [2]. In any network
generation model, there should be at most only one link in the same direction
between the same pair of nodes. N is the number of nodes and E is the number
of links. Examples of generated networks are shown in Fig. 1.

In DB model, first, nodes are randomly distributed in a 3D space and next
two randomly chosen nodes is connected with the probability $p \propto \exp(-(d/\lambda)^2)$
where d is the Euclidean distance between nodes and λ is a parameter [12].
Repeat random selection of nodes and stochastic connection until the number of
links reaches E. Therefore, nodes in proximity are likely to be connected while
there exist a few long-range connections. Such distance-dependent connectivity
is quite natural in general and a neural network of the brain is considered to

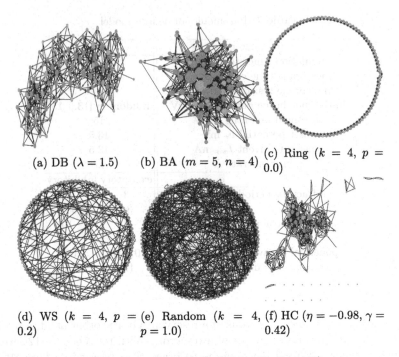

(a) DB ($\lambda = 1.5$)   (b) BA ($m = 5$, $n = 4$)   (c) Ring ($k = 4$, $p = 0.0$)

(d) WS ($k = 4$, $p = 0.2$)   (e) Random ($k = 4$, $p = 1.0$)   (f) HC ($\eta = -0.98$, $\gamma = 0.42$)

Fig. 1. Network examples ($N = 100$, $E = 400$)

follow a similar discipline. In BA model, first a complete graph of m nodes is generated and nodes are added one after another. A newly added node establishes links to n ($n \leq m$) nodes stochastically selected with probability $p_i = \frac{k_i}{\sum_j k_j}$. Here, k_i is the degree of node i, i.e. total number of incoming and outgoing links. It is known that a BA network has the scale-free property as its degree distribution follows a power law. WS model can generate a network with the small-world property. Small world property is characterized by the short average path length, along with the high clustering coefficient [19]. First, all nodes are arranged in a circular layout and each node is connected to the nearest $\frac{E}{N}$ nodes. The generated initial network is called a Ring model in this paper. Next, rewire each link with probability p by changing a destination node to a randomly chosen node from those unconnected from the origin node. We call a network generated with rewiring probability $p = 0.2$ as WS and one with $p = 1.0$ as Random. Note that Random is different from a general random network in the complex network field because the former guarantees every node has at least $\frac{E}{N}$ links resulting in more regular structure. Regarding Real model, we use the cerebral cortex and subcortical networks estimated from measurement of actual brains [10]. The data set contains 423 networks of healthy 22 to 35 year old male and female. A target area is divided into 1015 ROIs and one ROI (Regions of Interest) is regarded as one node. Links between ROIs are estimated based on high-quality functional- and high-angular resolution diffusion imaging (HARDI) MRI data. Finally, a

Table 2. Structural properties of evaluated networks

	DB	BA	Ring	WS	Random	Real	HC
Clustering coefficient	0.059	0.442	0.6	0.311	0.006	0.202	0.007
APL	5.526	2.375	80.400	5.383	4.240	5.620	4.453
Diameter	13.57	4.0	160.0	10.0	7.88	19.04	9.47
Betweenness centrality	3443	1099	63441	3501	2571	643	2702
Modularity	0.602	0.188	0.709	0.719	0.284	0.609	0.313
SWP	0.355	0.812	0.293	0.655	0.293	0.527	0.294
Recurrentness	0.954	1.0	1.0	1.000	0.993	0.251	0.979
The number of hub nodes	0	9.14	0	0	0	22.34	0
Variance in degree distribution	14.36	2425.6	0	1.78	4.97	106.06	10.87

model proposed in [2], which can generate a network similar to a human brain connectome, is called a human connectome (HC) model in this paper. First, HC generates several bidirectional links among N nodes. After that, a link is generated between a pair of nodes with probability which is determined based on distance and the degree of having the same nodes as common neighbors. As a result, a network is likely to have many triangle structures in which three nodes are mutually connected. Since networks of Real have about 800 nodes and 4000 links on average, parameters are set to have $N = 800$ and $E = 4000$ in all models. Regarding parameters, $m = 5$ and $n = 5$ in BA, $\lambda = 1.7$ in DB, $\eta = -0.98$, $\gamma = 0.42$, $\rho = \frac{E}{N(N-1)}$, and number of initial links is 62 in HC, respectively.

To quantify the structural properties of a reservoir, we use the following metrics: clustering coefficient [19], average path length (APL) [19], diameter, betweenness centrality [6], modularity [15], small world propensity (SWP) [13]. Because of space limitation, we do not explain their details here, but we should note that we use an average of all nodes as a measure of a reservoir regarding clustering coefficient and betweenness centrality, which are originally per-node measures. In addition, we use recurrentness, the number of hub nodes, and variance in the degree distribution. Recurrentness is the ratio of nodes having a return path. The number of hub nodes is the number of nodes whose degree is over 30. We use unbiased variance for variance in degree distribution.

Table 2 summarizes averages of 100 topologies generated for each model. Note that HC networks have different structural properties from Real. It is because HC model is designed for a network with $N \approx 100$ and the network density $\rho = \frac{E}{N(N-1)}$ is about 5%, which is different from the experimental setting where $N = 800$ and $\rho = 0.6\%$. As a result, HC is between DB and Random.

2.3   Delayed Readout Task

A delayed readout task is to classify an input after a certain period from when the input is given. We use a very simple two-class classification which can be

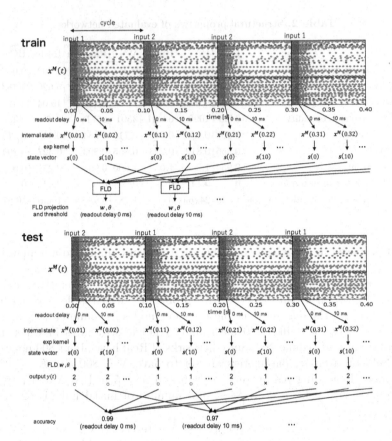

Fig. 2. Outline of delayed readout task

accomplished by using a simple linear discrimination algorithm at a readout unit (Fig. 2). The simplicity allows us to more directly evaluate the robustness of a reservoir without the influence of the implementation of a readout algorithm. As a readout algorithm, we adopt Fisher's linear discrimination [5].

We first set random initial membrane potential and run an LSM for 100 cycles of 100 ms. During the initial 10 ms of each cycle, a randomly chosen input unit fires at every Δt to give input to a reservoir. We obtain a series of firing activity (1 or 0) for all neurons in a reservoir for 100 cycles, which we use as training data.

Next, we apply an exponential kernel (Eq. (1)) to training data of each cycle for continuation.

$$s_i(t) = \int_0^t x_i(t-u)f(u)du \tag{1}$$

$$f(t) = \exp^{-\frac{t}{T_{decay}}} \tag{2}$$

Here, $x_i(t)$ is the firing activity of neuron i at time t, which is 1 if neuron i fires and 0 otherwise. T_{decay} is the time constant which is empirically assumed as $T_{decay} = 10$ ms in this paper. Then, to evaluate the discrimination accuracy of readout with delay of d ms ($0 \leq d \leq 90$), we obtain a state vector $s(d) = \{s_1(10 + d), s_2(10 + d), \ldots, s_N(10 + d)\}$ for each cycle. A set of state vectors is used to determine the projection direction w and the threshold θ of Fisher's linear discrimination (FLD) for each of the readout delay.

Then, test data of another 100 cycles are obtained using random initial membrane potentials and a random input sequence. By using the projection direction and the threshold determined on training data, discrimination is performed. Finally, by comparing the output with the actual input, the accuracy of discrimination is evaluated.

3   Results and Discussion

Figure 3 summarizes the average accuracy of 100 networks for each network model when experiencing random connection failure, i.e., removal of randomly chosen connections. The horizontal axis and the vertical axis represent the readout delay and the failure rate respectively. The color of each square represents the accuracy of the corresponding readout delay and failure rate. The upper right area has lower accuracy (blue squares) in all network models. We also notice that the blue area is the largest in BA and the smallest in DB. When there is no failure, most models have high accuracy (dark red squares) except for BA. For more direct comparison, Fig. 4a shows contours of 80% accuracy for all network models. Since accuracy monotonically decreases with larger readout delay and larger failure rate, a model with a contour in the upper right of Fig. 4a is considered robust against random connection failures.

DB is the most robust for having a contour in the most upper-right position. However, as the failure rate increases, the accuracy approaches those of other networks. Reasons for the high accuracy of DB are high modularity and irregular structure. High modularity means there are dense synaptic connections within each module while inter-module connections are rather sparse. Therefore, in contrast to a network of flat and homogeneous structure, modules have unique dynamics different from each other. Consequently, the dynamics of modules where input is given change more than the others, which enables a readout unit to distinguish between dynamics caused by different inputs. In addition, irregular structure contributes to generation of a variety of dynamics depending on different inputs. Structural irregularity here means high variance in the degree distribution. If all neurons have the identical degree, the influence of input uniformly propagates to the whole network independently of where input is given. This is a reason why the accuracy of Ring, which has the highest modularity, is slightly low when there is no failure. However, because of the high clustering coefficient, Ring can maintain connectivity facing connection failures and thus can achieve the second highest accuracy with high failure rate. The high clustering coefficient indicates there are many triangle structures. Even if one

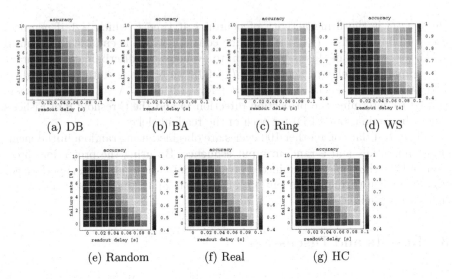

(a) DB   (b) BA   (c) Ring   (d) WS

(e) Random   (f) Real   (g) HC

Fig. 3. Accuracy in delayed readout task with random connection failures (Color figure online)

connection of a triangle is lost, three neurons composing the triangle are still connected. In other words, there are many detours in networks with the high clustering coefficient.

Real is also robust, because it keeps relatively higher accuracy than BA, HC, Random, and WS in most failure rates. Real has the second-highest accuracy when there is no failure because of high modularity and irregular structure. In addition, its relatively higher clustering coefficient contributes to robustness. Among the others, the accuracy of BA networks is significantly low. In BA networks, many neurons fire very frequently even when there is no input because very high-degree neurons are mutually connected and stimulate each other. Therefore, input does not cause a significant change in firing activity, i.e. dynamics, of a network and the accuracy becomes low. Random networks have high accuracy when there is no failure because random structure plays the role similar to an irregular structure. Random has low irregularity (small variance in degree distribution in Table 2), but the randomness of connection contributes to generation of a variety of dynamics. However, the low clustering coefficient makes Random fragile. HC has structural properties similar to Random, but HC has lower accuracy because HC has less randomness of connection because of its connection generation depending on the distance between neurons. WS has a higher clustering coefficient and higher modularity than Random, but its contour is close to that of Random. It is because the accuracy of WS when there is no failure is lower than that of Random due to its structural regularity. Ring has a lower accuracy than WS when there is no failure, but its doubled clustering coefficient makes Ring more robust. The above results suggest that modularity and structural irregularity are important together for high accuracy and clustering coefficient contributes to robustness by maintaining connectivity.

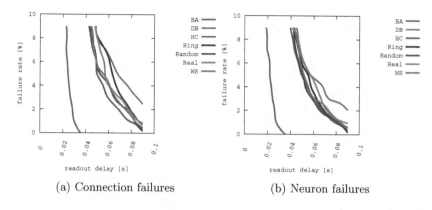

(a) Connection failures   (b) Neuron failures

Fig. 4. Contours of 80% accuracy with random failures

We also investigate the influence of random neuron failures, i.e. removal of randomly chosen neurons. Contours of 80% accuracy are shown in Fig. 4b. DB, Ring, and Real networks, which are robust against random connection failures, keep relatively higher accuracy than other models against random neuron failures, too. This result suggests the high clustering coefficient should also contribute to robustness against random neuron failures. However, accuracy is lower and contours of most models locate in lower-left positions than random connection failures. When a neuron is lost, its influence on multiple neurons completely disappears, which further affects the propagation of firing activity of remaining neurons. Consequently, network dynamics is more likely to change drastically in comparison to connection failure. Specifically, a decrease in accuracy is significant with DB, Ring, and Real. Because of their high modularity, neuron failure affects more in a module than in a flat network. For example, when a neuron fails in a Random network, 0.25% of connections are lost from a whole network. On the contrary, the loss of a neuron in a module results in a loss of 1.25% of connections from a module in a Ring network. As a result, dynamics of each module changes more drastically than in a flat network.

In summary, high modularity and irregular structure contribute to high accuracy when there is no failure and high clustering coefficient contributes to robustness against random failures by maintaining connectivity. Thus for a physical reservoir to achieve robustness against random failures, it is desired to construct a reservoir structure satisfying those properties. Since any physical reservoir can be modeled as a network, we think this finding applies to a variety of physical reservoir computing systems.

Finally we consider how to realize a robust physical reservoir using our IWSN as an example. In an IWSN, physical constraints prevent a network from having an arbitrary structure. For example, connections exist among all nearby wireless devices, because those devices within the range of radio signal propagation can communicate with each other. Thus a device cannot have many short-range connections and a few long-range connections simultaneously as a brain neural

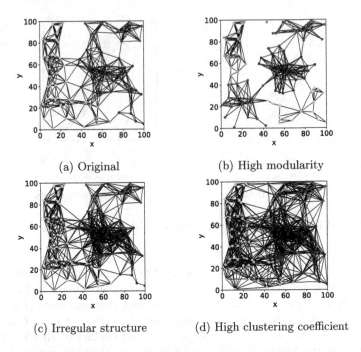

(a) Original

(b) High modularity

(c) Irregular structure

(d) High clustering coefficient

Fig. 5. Example topologies before and after structure control

network does. In addition, if devices are homogeneous regarding communication range, connections are always bi-directional while synaptic connections are directional. The degree and range of control which we can perform to achieve a desired network structure depend on system configuration, but here we assume that only the communication range is adjustable on each device. Since devices are equipped with an omnidirectional antenna, all nodes within the range of radio can receive signals, that is, a circular communication area is considered.

The high modularity of structure means that a network can be divided into modules where devices in a module are densely connected and devices belonging to different modules have a few connections. To achieve the high modularity, first, devices are divided into modules depending on their proximity. Then, the communication range is set large at devices near the center of a module and small at other devices by multiplying the communication range by parameter α, which is derived as $\alpha(d) = \frac{3}{2} - \frac{1}{1+\exp(\frac{1}{5}(8-d))}$. Here, d is the distance to the center of a module and constant parameters are determined empirically. Examples of networks before and after the adjustment are shown in Fig. 5a and Fig. 5b, respectively where modules are indicated by color. As shown, we can accomplish different connection density between intra- and inter-modules. The average modularity of random 10 networks increases from 0.596 to 0.703.

Similarly, we can improve the structural irregularity by multiplying communication range by $\beta(k) = \frac{1}{2} - \frac{1}{1+\exp(1+\frac{1}{5}(20-k))}$. Here, k is the degree, that is, the number of devices in the communication range before adjustment. The equation strengthens the variance of degree distribution by increasing the communication range in an area where devices are densely deployed and decreasing the range in a sparse area. As a result, the heterogeneity increases as shown in Fig. 5c. The average variance of 10 random networks increases from 50.19 to 162.28.

Furthermore, by simply increasing the communication range as shown in Fig. 5d, the clustering coefficient increases. In the figure, the communication range is changed from 20 to 30 at all devices. The increased communication range allows neighboring devices of a device to communicate with each other. As a result, the average clustering coefficient increases from 0.655 to 0.689. A reason why change is small is that IWSN inherently has the high clustering coefficient owing to proximity-based connection.

We should note here that improving certain structural properties sometimes sacrifices other properties. For example, extending communication range to have irregular structure or higher clustering coefficient often breaks modular structure by increasing inter-module connections. Therefore, careful design and control are required to achieve the desired structure which satisfies both high performance and high robustness.

4   Conclusion

In this paper, by applying seven types of networks having different structural properties as a reservoir and comparing their discrimination capability in facing random connection and neuron failures, we revealed that high modularity, structural irregularity, and high clustering coefficient are most important. As future work, we plan to evaluate robustness in other scenarios, such as simultaneous failures and cascading failures, and consider recovery mechanisms which enable a physical reservoir computing system can retrieve the performance by local and autonomous recovery. We also consider the construction of a robust reservoir in other types of physical reservoir computing systems to realize ambient reservoir computing.

Acknowledgements. This study was partly supported by JSPS KAKENHI Grant Number 16H01719. Data were provided in part by the Human Connectome Project, WU-Minn Consortium (Principal Investigators: David Van Essen and Kamil Ugurbil; 1U54MH091657) funded by the 16 NIH Institutes and Centers that support the NIH Blueprint for Neuroscience Research; and by the McDonnell Center for Systems Neuroscience at Washington University.

References

1. Albert, R., Barabási, A.L.: Statistical mechanics of complex networks. Rev. Modern Phys. **74**(1), 47 (2002)
2. Betzel, R.F., et al.: Generative models of the human connectome. Neuroimage **124**, 1054–1064 (2016)

3. Dale, M., Miller, J.F., Stepney, S.: Reservoir computing as a model for *in-materio* computing. In: Adamatzky, A. (ed.) Advances in Unconventional Computing. ECC, vol. 22, pp. 533–571. Springer, Cham (2017). https://doi.org/10.1007/978-3-319-33924-5_22

4. Erdos, P., Rényi, A.: On the evolution of random graphs. Publ. Math. Inst. Hungarian Acad. Sci. **5**(1), 17–60 (1960)

5. Fisher, R.A.: The use of multiple measurements in taxonomic problems. Ann. Eugenics **7**(7), 179–188 (1936)

6. Freeman, L.C.: A set of measures of centrality based on betweenness. Sociometry 35–41 (1977)

7. Gerstner, W., Kistler, W.M.: Spiking Neuron Models: Single Neurons, Populations, Plasticity. Cambridge University Press, Cambridge (2002)

8. Kamei, D., Wakamiya, N.: Analysis of LSM-based event detection in impulse-based wireless sensor networks. In: Proceedings of the 2018 International Symposium on Nonlinear Theory and Its Applications (NOLTA 2018), pp. 460–463 (2018)

9. Kerepesi, C., Szalkai, B., Varga, B., Grolmusz, V.: How to direct the edges of the connectomes: dynamics of the consensus connectomes and the development of the connections in the human brain. PLOS ONE **11**(6), e0158680 (2016)

10. Kerepesi, C., Szalkai, B., Varga, B., Grolmusz, V.: The braingraph.org database of high resolution structural connectomes and the brain graph tools. Cogn. Neurodyn. **11**(5), 483–486 (2017). https://doi.org/10.1007/s11571-017-9445-1

11. Lukoševičius, M., Jaeger, H.: Reservoir computing approaches to recurrent neural network training. Comput. Sci. Rev. **3**(3), 127–149 (2009)

12. Maass, W., Natschläger, T., Markram, H.: Real-time computing without stable states: a new framework for neural computation based on perturbations. Neural Comput. **14**(11), 2531–2560 (2002)

13. Muldoon, S.F., Bridgeford, E.W., Bassett, D.S.: Small-world propensity and weighted brain networks. Sci. Rep. **6**, 22057 (2016)

14. Nakajima, K., Hauser, H., Li, T., Pfeifer, R.: Information processing via physical soft body. Sci. Rep. **5**, 10487 (2015)

15. Newman, M.E., Girvan, M.: Finding and evaluating community structure in networks. Phys. Rev. E **69**(2), 026113 (2004)

16. Soriano, M.C., Massuti-Ballester, P., Yelo, J., Fischer, I.: Optoelectronic reservoir computing using a mixed digital-analog hardware implementation. In: Tetko, I.V., Kůrková, V., Karpov, P., Theis, F. (eds.) ICANN 2019. LNCS, vol. 11731, pp. 170–174. Springer, Cham (2019). https://doi.org/10.1007/978-3-030-30493-5_18

17. Szalkai, B., Kerepesi, C., Varga, B., Grolmusz, V.: High-resolution directed human connectomes and the consensus connectome dynamics. PLOS ONE **14**(4), e0215473 (2019)

18. Tanaka, G., et al.: Recent advances in physical reservoir computing: a review. Neural Netw. **115**, 110–123 (2019)

19. Watts, D.J., Strogatz, S.H.: Collective dynamics of 'small-world' networks. Nature **393**(6684), 440 (1998)

Quantifying Robustness and Capacity of Reservoir Computers with Consistency Profiles

Thomas Lymburn[1]([✉])[iD], Thomas Jüngling[1][iD], and Michael Small[1,2][iD]

[1] Complex Systems Group, Department of Mathematics and Statistics,
The University of Western Australia,
35 Stirling Highway, Crawley, WA 6009, Australia
thomas.lymburn@research.uwa.edu.au
[2] Mineral Resources, CSIRO, Kensington, WA 6151, Australia

Abstract. We study the consistency property in reservoir computers with noise. Consistency quantifies the functional dependence of a driven dynamical system on its input via replica tests. We characterise the high-dimensional profile of consistency in typical reservoirs subject to intrinsic and measurement noise. An integral of the consistency is introduced to measure capacity and act as an effective size of the reservoir. We observe a scaling law in the dependency of the consistency capacity on the noise amplitude and reservoir size, and demonstrate how this measure of capacity explains performance.

Keywords: Reservoir computing · Consistency correlation · Signal-to-noise ratio · Principal component analysis

1 Introduction

The interplay of signal and noise is a well-known concept in engineering, but is much less understood in nonlinear dynamical systems. Every physical system is naturally subject to some form of noise which may be relevant depending on the context. Recently, there has been growing interest in using physical versions of machine learning techniques, due to their potential for increased speed and efficiency. Thus the role of noise in the non-digital physical substrates is an important subject of investigation [18]. In particular, reservoir computing (RC) is a technique that employs a wide range of physical systems for computation [20] and therefore motivates the study of noise effects. In this paper we will apply the concept of consistency, a measure of functional dependence in drive-response systems, to RC. The basic idea of consistency is to drive a nonlinear dynamical system repeatedly with the same signal, and then compare the responses by means of cross-correlation [21]. Hence, the problem of modelling a sophisticated functional relationship is elegantly bypassed [17,19]. The relevance of consistency for RC has recently been highlighted [2,13]. We will employ

© Springer Nature Switzerland AG 2020
I. Farkaš et al. (Eds.): ICANN 2020, LNCS 12397, pp. 447–458, 2020.
https://doi.org/10.1007/978-3-030-61616-8_36

here a high-dimensional extension of the consistency measure to characterise the robustness and the signal processing capacity in reservoirs [12].

Throughout this work we will consider echo state networks (ESNs), a reservoir computing form of recurrent neural networks (RNN) [6,11]. An ESN is a dynamical system represented as a network. It is typically characterized by untrained and randomly generated weights in both the input and the reservoir. For a network of N nodes with a single input and output, we denote the weight matrices by $\mathbf{V} \in \mathbb{R}^N$, and $\mathbf{W} \in \mathbb{R}^{N \times N}$, respectively. The state vector $\mathbf{x}(t) \in \mathbb{R}^N$ of the network is updated according to

$$\mathbf{x}(t+1) = \tanh(\mathbf{W} \cdot \mathbf{x}(t) + \mathbf{V} \cdot u(t) + \boldsymbol{\beta}) , \tag{1}$$

where $u(t)$ is a scalar input sequence with $t \in \mathbb{Z}$ being discrete time, $\boldsymbol{\beta} \in \mathbb{R}^N$ is a vector of biases, and $\tanh(\cdot)$ is a commonly used activation function that is applied elementwise. Only the weights $\mathbf{R} \in \mathbb{R}^N$ of the linear readout $y(t) = \sum_i R_i x_i(t)$ are trained. Typically ridge regression is used to reproduce a target signal $z(t)$, leading to $\boldsymbol{R} = \mathrm{argmin}_{\mathbf{R}'} \sum_t \left(\sum_i R_i' x_i(t) - z(t) \right)^2 + \lambda \|\mathbf{R}'\|_2^2$ with λ the ridge parameter.

We apply the consistency measure to quantify the response of ESNs with various network structures. These structures are encoded in the connectivity matrix $\mathbf{W}$ which is usually set to be sparse and random in the typical ESN practise. Here, we will consider a ring (or lattice) structure, sparse random networks, and fully connected networks as reservoirs. In Sect. 2 we describe how to calculate a consistency profile of the high-dimensional reservoir trajectory. In Sect. 3 we add intrinsic and measurement noise to the ESNs and investigate the corresponding consistency profiles. In Sect. 4 we use the consistency profiles to obtain a measure of the network's computational capacity and effective size. We will investigate how this measure depends on the reservoir size and noise amplitude, and relate this to the performance of the reservoir.

2   Consistency Profiles

Consistency is a measure of functional dependence in the response of a system to a drive signal [21]. It is determined by driving a system repeatedly with a signal, or driving multiple replicas with an identical driving signal, each starting from different initial conditions. The agreement of the replicas is then measured with a pairwise cross-correlation, the *consistency correlation* [14]. Assuming ergodicity and long enough time series, and denoting the two scalar recordings of the replicas as $x(t)$ and $x'(t)$, the consistency correlation reads $\gamma^2 = \langle \overline{x}(t) \overline{x}'(t) \rangle_t$, where the bar denotes normalisation to zero mean and unit variance, and $\langle \cdot \rangle_t$ is a time average. A key result of consistency theory is that γ poses a fundamental limit on the correlation between the output of the system and any function of the input [9]. The implication of this result in the context of RC is that the performance measured in terms of cross-correlation between readout and target is limited by the consistency level [12]. However, while the readout of a reservoir computer may be scalar, the performance with respect to a general task is determined by its multivariate response time series. The functional dependence of which is characterised by a high-dimensional generalisation of the consistency correlation, which we call the *consistency profile* or the *consistency spectrum*. It is obtained by a method similar to principal component analysis (PCA) to determine an orthogonal set of characteristic directions with corresponding consistency correlations γ_k^2, where $k = 1...N$ and N is the dimension of the reservoir. We will briefly recall the theoretical framework of the consistency profile; for a more detailed discussion see Ref. [12].

The initial point of analysis is the stationary N-dimensional response trajectory of the reservoir, $\{x_i(t)\}_{i=1...N}$. We calculate the covariance matrix $[C_{xx}]_{ij} = \langle x_i(t)x_j(t)\rangle_t$ after normalizing to zero mean. Since C_{xx} is positive semi-definite, the eigendecomposition is given by $C_{xx} = Q\Sigma^2 Q^\top$. The columns of the orthogonal matrix Q are the directions of the principal components, and the diagonal entries of Σ^2 are their magnitudes, which are the variances in these directions. The transformation $T_\circ = Q\Sigma^{-1}Q^\top$ yields coordinates in which the reservoir response is isotropic, see Fig. 1. To ensure numerical stability of this transformation in the presence of rank deficiencies, we add a small regularization term $10^{-9} \times \mathbf{1}$ to C_{xx}, with $\mathbf{1}$ denoting the $N \times N$ identity matrix.

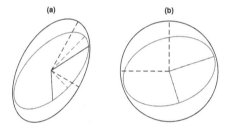

Fig. 1. An illustration of the PCA description of the consistent components (red) and full response (black). The directions of maximum and minimum consistency are shown in blue. Panel (a) shows the analysis in the original coordinates and panel (b) shows it in the normalized coordinates after the transform $T_\circ$. (Color figure online)

The concept of consistency is similar to the signal-to-noise ratio in signal processing, except that consistency is tailored to the response of nonlinear dynamical systems. The core idea is to decompose a signal from a driven dynamical system into a consistent component and an inconsistent component which are linearly independent, $x(t) = s(t) + n(t)$. The term $s(t)$ represents a function of the input signal, and $n(t)$ is noise that does not depend on the input. Given all quantities have zero mean, the consistency correlation is the ratio of variances $\gamma^2 = \langle s^2(t)\rangle_t/\langle x^2(t)\rangle_t$. Extending this result to the high-dimensional reservoir trajectory in the normalized coordinates $\mathbf{x}_\circ(t) = T_\circ\mathbf{x}(t)$, the covariance matrix of the consistent component is – under ergodicity and in the limit of long time series – equal to the cross-covariance matrix of two replica [12],

$$[C_c]_{ij} = \langle s_{\circ,i}(t)s_{\circ,j}(t)\rangle = \langle x_{\circ,i}(t)x'_{\circ,j}(t)\rangle . \tag{2}$$

The consistent (signal) components $s_o(t)$ form an ellipsoid within the isotropic full response $x_o(t)$. By performing the decomposition $C_c = Q_c G^2 Q_c^\top$ we obtain the principal components as the orthogonal set of consistency directions. The consistency profile is given by the diagonal elements γ_k^2 of the matrix G^2, where the index k enumerates the consistency components.

3   Noise in ESN

We will use the consistency profiles to measure how different network structures deal with noise. This will be done for three different network structures (Fig. 2), subject to either intrinsic i.i.d. noise according to Eq. (3), or observational i.i.d. noise as in Eq. (4) (with $x(t)$ from Eq. (1)). Each component of the noise is denoted as $\nu_i(t) \sim \mathcal{N}(0,1)$, and $\Omega > 0$ is the noise strength ('amplitude'). The driving signal $u(t)$ is set to be scalar Gaussian white noise. Other choices of stationary input signals are possible, like for example in Sect. 4.2, and will result in different consistency profiles. The noisy trajectories for each case are

$$\tilde{x}_{int}(t+1) = \tanh(W \cdot \tilde{x}_{int}(t) + V \cdot u(t) + \beta + \Omega \nu(t)) , \tag{3}$$

$$\tilde{x}_{obs}(t) = x(t) + \Omega \nu(t) . \tag{4}$$

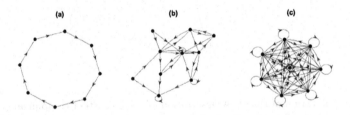

Fig. 2. Network types studied here. (a) ring topology, (b) sparse random connectivity and (c) fully connected.

The network types that we use as reservoirs are the unidirectional ring (Fig. 2(a)), sparsely connected random networks (Fig. 2(b)), and fully connected networks (Fig. 2(c)). For the sparse random networks, each potential directed link between pairs of nodes is drawn randomly with a probability of connection given by $p = 10/N$, which ensures that the average degree is 10 regardless of network size. Aside from the adjacency structure, all networks are generated with random internal weights drawn from a Gaussian distribution then scaled to achieve a spectral radius of one. The input connections are chosen uniformly from the interval $[-1, 1]$. All of these structures, including the simpler ring topology, are capable of performing nontrivial tasks [1,4,16].

Consistency profiles for these networks are shown in Fig. 3 for a selected network size of $N = 200$. There are no qualitative differences for other reservoir sizes over several orders of magnitude ($N < 2000$). For both forms of noise there is a wide range of consistency levels in the corresponding principal components. Some components are extremely sensitive to noise, while others maintain almost complete consistency for the displayed noise levels. These consistent components (directions in state space) explain how a reservoir computer can be robust to noise. We also note that there is a significant difference between the profiles of the ring topology and the more highly connected networks, with the ring topology being more robust to noise. We speculate that the remarkable agreement between the profiles of the sparsely connected and the fully connected networks might be related to the average shortest path length.

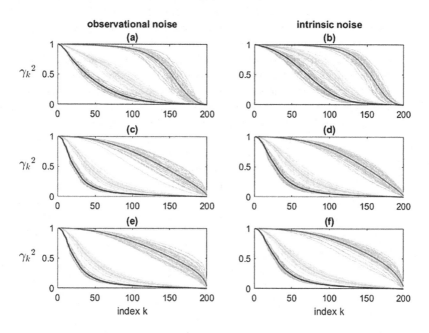

Fig. 3. The consistency profiles of ESNs with different structures when subject to observational and intrinsic noise. Panels (a-b) show the profiles of a ring network, (c-d) show a sparsely connected network and (e-f) show a fully connected network. The profiles for different noise levels are shown, with $\Omega = 0.01$ shown in red, $\Omega = 0.05$ in green and $\Omega = 0.1$ in blue. All networks have $N = 200$. (Color figure online)

4   Capacity

One way to assess the quality of an information processing system is to determine its capacity to compute a range of nonlinear functions. The more capacity a system has, the broader the range of functions it has access to in order to synthesise some target function, and thus the more accurate it may be. There is no unified measure of the capacity of an information processing system, though several have been proposed [3,5,7]. Here we will derive a capacity measure from the consistency profile, which is particularly useful in the presence of noise or chaos in the reservoir.

Given the typically linear readout, a naive measure of capacity of a fully consistent reservoir is given by the number of linearly independent functions in its response trajectory. This number is the rank of the covariance matrix of the multivariate time series and is limited by the number of nodes N. However, this simple capacity measure does not take into account the quality of the set of functions, nor does it apply in the presence of noise.

In the context of consistency, we will not investigate the suitability of the reservoir functions for a particular task, but instead measure how each function is attenuated by noise, and how this affects the performance in general. In the following, all quantities will be normalised to zero mean, and—unless stated otherwise—also to unit variance, to allow for compatibility with standard measures of correlation and covariance. A bias neuron will consequently not be introduced in addition to the reservoir activations. Moreover, all time series are considered to be stationary and sufficiently long to approximate limit values, and to leave aside discussion on statistical aspects including training, validation, and testing methodology. Let $z(t)$ be an arbitrary scalar target signal with $\langle z \rangle = 0$ and $\langle z^2 \rangle = 1$, and $u(t)$ the corresponding scalar input signal, with $\langle u \rangle = 0$ and $\langle u^2 \rangle = 1$, and $\langle \cdot \rangle$ being a time average. We further assume that the target depends on the input via a functional dependence $z(t) = \mathcal{F}[u](t)$, meaning that the present value of $z(t)$ can be completely determined by using the values of $u(t')$ for $t' \leq t$, eventually up to some maximum lag $t - t_m < t'$. Let the reservoir response to the input $u(t)$, including any form of noise, be $\{\tilde{x}_i(t)\}_{i=1...N}$ with $\langle \tilde{x}_i \rangle = 0$. Applying the normalisation $T_o = Q\Sigma^{-1}Q^\top$ from the PCA of $\tilde{\mathbf{x}}(t)$ yields the isotropic response $\mathbf{x}_o(t) = T_o\tilde{\mathbf{x}}(t)$. In these coordinates we calculate the cross-covariance matrix C_c to determine the consistent components. From the eigendecomposition $C_c = Q_c G^2 Q_c^\top$, we use the orthogonal transformation $\boldsymbol{\xi}(t) = Q_c^\top \mathbf{x}_o(t)$ to align the main axes of the consistent ellipsoid with our coordinate system. Let the consistent components be $\gamma_k s_k(t)$ with $\langle s_k \rangle = 0$ and $\langle s_k^2 \rangle = 1$, where the consistency correlations γ_k^2 are the diagonal elements of G^2 because of the previous normalisation procedure. Using the least-mean-squares expression for the readout vector $\mathbf{R}$ in the $\boldsymbol{\xi}$-coordinates, we find that $R_k = \gamma_k \langle s_k z \rangle$, because any correlation from the target can only stem from the consistent components. Denoting the correlations in R_k as $a_k = \langle s_k z \rangle$, we can write the output of the reservoir as

$$y(t) = \sum_k \gamma_k a_k \xi_k(t) . \tag{5}$$

The output has zero mean by construction, and the variance can be determined as $\langle y^2 \rangle = \sum_k \gamma_k^2 a_k^2$, using $\langle \xi_k \xi_l \rangle = \delta_{kl}$. From this, we can calculate the mean-square error (MSE) (which here is equal to the normalised MSE), and the cross-correlation C_{yz} with the target, as $\text{MSE} = 1 - \sum_k \gamma_k^2 a_k^2$ and $C_{yz}^2 = \sum_k \gamma_k^2 a_k^2$, respectively. The recurring expression here is the sum of consistency correlations

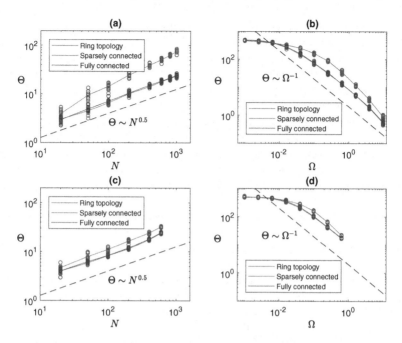

Fig. 4. Capacity for networks of different sizes noise amplitudes (b). Panels (a-b) are for observational noise and (c-d) are for intrinsic noise. For panels (a) and (c) the noise amplitude is fixed at $\Omega = 0.5$ and for panel (b) and (d) the network size is $N = 500$. The results are averaged across 10 different realisations of the network structures. Dependencies in (c) and (d) are truncated to display only the reliable range with respect to systematic errors from finite-size estimates.

γ_k^2 and squared target correlations a_k^2. Considering these in general to be independent, because the former is a measure of the reservoir response only whereas the latter depends on the task, we define the *consistency capacity* as

$$\Theta = \sum_{k=1}^{N} \gamma_k^2 = \mathrm{Tr}(C_c) \,. \tag{6}$$

The latter identity comes from the fact that the orthogonal transformation Q_c does not change the trace. By construction, the capacity is $0 \leq \Theta \leq N$. As the size of a network with full rank gives the number of functions it produces, this measure of capacity can be thought of as the effective network size for reservoirs with noise, or chaos acting as noise.

4.1   Capacity and Noise

We calculate numerically the capacity of ESNs with the different structures described above for a range of N and Ω, and for both intrinsic and observational noise. Figures 4(a)-(c) show the dependence of the capacity Θ on the reservoir size N for the three network types and fixed noise strength. The capacity increases monotonically with reservoir size, and a power law is indicated for all networks. The power-law exponent of the ring network appears to be slightly larger than that of the other two types, which behave remarkably similarly. All exponents are less than one, in agreement with the upper bound $\Theta \leq N$, while the majority are close to $\Theta \propto \sqrt{N}$. In Fig. 4(b)-(d), we show for a fixed size N the dependence of Θ on the noise strength Ω. While for vanishing noise the capacity is $\Theta = N$, it decays monotonically with increasing noise. A power-law scaling is indicated for moderate noise levels, most pronounced for the sparse random and the fully connected reservoirs. For observational noise, we show how this can be traced back to scaling behavior in the principal components of a noise free reservoir.

In the case of uniformly additive measurement noise, the consistency spectrum and capacity can be determined analytically. Let the fully consistent time series of a reservoir be $x_i(t)$, with $\langle x_i \rangle = 0$ for each i, and the noisy observations $\tilde{x}_i(t)$ according to Eq. (4). If the eigenvalues (or singular values) of the covariance matrix C_{xx} of the noise-free time series are known, here denoted as σ_k^2, the noise intensity is added to the variance of each of these signal components separately. Thus the covariance matrix of the noisy time series reads $C_{\tilde{x}\tilde{x}} = C_{xx} + \Omega^2 \mathbf{1}$. The consistency correlations follow then as the noise-free variance divided by the total variance for each of the original principal components independently

$$\gamma_k^2 = \frac{\sigma_k^2}{\sigma_k^2 + \Omega^2} \, . \tag{7}$$

It is worth mentioning that the noise amplitude can be related to the ridge parameter λ if regularisation is applied. For time series of length L, the identity $\lambda = \Omega^2 L$ holds. Thus if the coefficients a_i for $\lambda = 0$ are known, the ridge trace can be determined using the readout in Eq. (5) and the consistencies in Eq. (7).

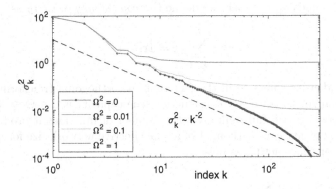

Fig. 5. Scaling of noise-free principal components of a sparse random network reservoir with $N = 300$ nodes, and interaction with additive measurement noise of strength Ω.

Figure 5 shows the principal components σ_k^2 for a noise-free reservoir of the sparse random type. A large part of the spectrum appears to scale with the power law $\sigma_k^2 \propto k^{-2}$. To our knowledge, this behavior has not previously been documented. We do not aim at a theory of this scaling here, but consider it as a phenomenological premise for the scope of our investigation. This implies a level of caution in the analysis given the uncertainty about the validity and range of the observed scaling behavior. In particular, the different reservoir types indicate deviations from the scaling behavior, which thus may be a specific property of a certain class of reservoirs. We also note that the detailed scaling depends on the type of input signal. Assuming the indicated power law holds strictly, we can apply Eq. (7). We set $\sigma_k = bk^{-1}$, with $b > 0$ depending on N, and calculate an infinite sum to account for the quickly decaying tail of the spectrum. We obtain $\Theta = (b\pi/2\Omega)\coth(b\pi/\Omega) - 1/2$. This expression contains two regimes. For $\Omega \ll b$, $\Theta \propto b/\Omega$, and for $\Omega \gg b$, $\Theta \propto b^2/\Omega^2$. The former reveals the power law indicated in Fig. 4(b). An intuitive explanation of how it emerges from the noise-free scaling $\sigma_k \propto k^{-1}$ is given as follows. By increasing the noise level Ω the signal components σ_k are successively covered by noise, as illustrated in Fig. 5. As long as the σ-spectrum is only partially covered, the spacing between the components determines the rate by which a noise increment translates into a change of capacity, such that the σ_k scaling determines the $\Theta(\Omega)$ scaling. The latter power law is not shown in the figures. It emerges when noise exceeds the largest signal component, σ_1, so that the above mechanism of successive component coverage ceases. Hence, in Eq. (7) all $\gamma_k^2 \approx \sigma_k^2/\Omega^2$, from which follows that $\Theta \propto \Omega^{-2}$. Note that the analytical model does not account for the case of vanishing noise $\Omega \to 0$, where the predicted capacity diverges instead of saturating to the reservoir size, $\Theta \to N$. This is due to the infinite sum approximation which requires $\gamma_k \to 0$ for large k and therefore is not valid as the reservoir becomes fully consistent. The model can be refined by truncating the sum, however, this does not lead to further insight.

Another observation from the noise-free principal components is a scaling with the reservoir size by $\sigma_k^2 \propto N$ (not shown). This is explained by the increased overall signal power due to the input weights vector $\mathbf{V} \in \mathbb{R}^N$, under the assumption that all nodes in the reservoir are highly correlated. In contrast, if the input power was kept constant, e.g. by setting the number of non-zero input weights to N_0 independently of N, the principal components would remain approximately the same throughout the scaling regime. Introducing the N-scaling in the analytical model by setting $b^2 \propto N$, we obtain $\Theta \propto \sqrt{N}$ in the moderate noise regime. This agrees with the observations in Fig. 4(a).

In summary, the scaling law $\Theta \propto \sqrt{N}/\Omega$ was derived using the observation $\sigma_k^2 \propto N/k^2$ from sparse random networks and measurement noise. It holds for this network type very well, especially for large reservoirs, but also for the fully connected network. The behavior of the ring reservoir deviates slightly, although the findings still agree well. Remarkably, the same behavior is indicated for intrinsic noise, even though this noise type is qualitatively different from the observational noise, for which the exact relationship Eq. (7) holds. We conclude

that the generating mechanisms are robust and explain a generic behavior of the
consistency capacity of reservoirs with noise.

4.2   Capacity and Performance

The size of a reservoir computer is known to be an important factor of its performance, with common practise being to create a reservoir as large as computationally feasible [10]. As the consistency capacity Θ gives a measure of the
effective size of a reservoir subject to noise, it is expected to have some predictive
power of the performance.

To confirm the relationship between performance and capacity, we apply our
reservoirs to a chaotic time series prediction task on which reservoir computers
are known to perform well [8,15]. We will predict the Lorenz system and measure
the relationship between capacity and the (normalised) MSE. The input is chosen
to be the X-variable such that $u(t) = X(t\,\Delta)$ and the target is the X-variable
τ time steps in the future, $z(t) = X((t + \tau)\Delta)$, where $\Delta = 0.1$ and $\tau = 11$,
corresponding to approximately one Lyapunov time. We will perform this task
for reservoirs with sizes $N \in [20, 300]$ and with both observational and intrinsic
noise with amplitudes $\Omega \in [0, 0.2]$.

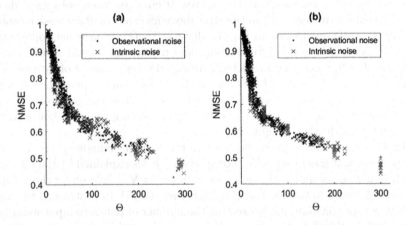

Fig. 6. Performance on the Lorenz prediction task given by NMSE for reservoirs of
various sizes with various levels of noise added, leading to a range of capacities. The
red data points correspond to the reservoirs without added noise. Panel (a) shows the
results for a ring network, panel (b) shows the results for a sparsely connected network. The results for the fully connected network are similar to the sparsely connected
network and not shown.

The results for ESNs with the ring topology and sparse random connectivity are shown in Figs. 6(a) and 6(b), respectively. Firstly, we notice that the
performance is monotonic with the capacity, with some variation due to the
different random realisations. Within that variation, all outcomes collapse to a

single curve. This implies that the consistency capacity is a valid predictor of performance. Second, there is a sharp drop in the NMSE as Θ increases from 0 to 50, after which the performance improves gradually. The implication is that a small fraction of the degrees of freedom are responsible for a significant portion of the reservoir's computation. Finally, the performance of the reservoirs with capacity reduced by noise is similar to the performance of a reservoir without noise but with similar Θ (assuming full rank, $\Theta = N$ for $\Omega = 0$, though large ring networks may have a rank-deficient response). This means that the effect of noise in a reservoir is equivalent to removing some of the degrees of freedom and reducing the reservoir size.

5   Conclusion

We have demonstrated how consistency profiles describe reservoir computers with different forms of noise. By doing so we have shown how reservoirs with noise may still perform useful computation, and that the simple degree-one ring network is more robust to noise than networks with higher degrees.

Beyond understanding robustness to noise, the consistency profiles can be used for a measure of the capacity of the reservoir. This capacity measure applies to reservoirs with and without noise, and can be thought of as the effective size of the reservoir. We find that the capacity measure scales as $\Theta \propto \sqrt{N}/\Omega$ and, regardless of the level or type of noise, serves as a performance predictor.

In this work we have only considered a small subset of network structures and Gaussian white noise. The consistency profile may provide interesting insights into the effect of scale-free topologies, local structures, different ESN hyperparameters and different forms of noise. We have also focused on the restricted training algorithm of reservoir computing. The consistency profile may give more insights into the functions produced by RNN with trained internal weights.

Acknowledgements. T.L. is supported by the Australian Government Research Training Program at The University of Western Australia. T.J. acknowledges fruitful discussions about the concept of consistency, as well as inspiring insights into the field of reservoir computing, with Ingo Fischer and members of the Nonlinear Photonics Group during his time at the IFISC (UIB-CSIC) in Palma de Mallorca. M.S. is supported by the Australian Research Council Discovery Project (Grant No. DP180100718).

References

1. Appeltant, L., et al.: Information processing using a single dynamical node as complex system. Nat. Commun. **2**, 468 (2011)
2. Bueno, J., Brunner, D., Soriano, M.C., Fischer, I.: Conditions for reservoir computing performance using semiconductor lasers with delayed optical feedback. Opt. Exp. **25**(3), 2401 (2017)
3. Carroll, T.L., Pecora, L.M.: Network structure effects in reservoir computers. Chaos **29**(8), 083130 (2019)

4. Dale, M., Dewhirst, J., O'Keefe, S., Sebald, A., Stepney, S., Trefzer, M.A.: The role of structure and complexity on reservoir computing quality. In: McQuillan, I., Seki, S. (eds.) UCNC 2019. LNCS, vol. 11493, pp. 52–64. Springer, Cham (2019). https://doi.org/10.1007/978-3-030-19311-9_6

5. Dambre, J., Verstraeten, D., Schrauwen, B., Massar, S.: Information processing capacity of dynamical systems. Sci. Rep. **2**, 514 (2012)

6. Jaeger, H.: The "echo state" approach to analysing and training recurrent neural networks-with an erratum note. German National Research Center for Information Technology GMD Technical Report **148** (2001)

7. Jaeger, H.: Short term memory in echo state networks. German National Research Center for Information Technology GMD Technical Report **152** (2002)

8. Jaeger, H., Haas, H.: Harnessing nonlinearity: predicting chaotic systems and saving energy in wireless communication. Science **304**(5667), 78 (2004)

9. Jüngling, T., Soriano, M.C., Oliver, N., Porte, X., Fischer, I.: Consistency properties of chaotic systems driven by time-delayed feedback. Phys. Rev. E **97**, 042202 (2018)

10. Lukoševičius, M.: A practical guide to applying echo state networks. In: Montavon, G., Orr, G.B., Müller, K.-R. (eds.) Neural Networks: Tricks of the Trade. LNCS, vol. 7700, pp. 659–686. Springer, Heidelberg (2012). https://doi.org/10.1007/978-3-642-35289-8_36

11. Lukoševičius, M., Jaeger, H.: Reservoir computing approaches to recurrent neural network training. Comput. Sci. Rev. **3**(3), 127 (2009)

12. Lymburn, T., Khor, A., Stemler, T., Corréa, D.C., Small, M., Jüngling, T.: Consistency in echo-state networks. Chaos **29**(2), 023118 (2019)

13. Nakayama, J., Kanno, K., Uchida, A.: Laser dynamical reservoir computing with consistency: an approach of a chaos mask signal. Opt. Exp. **24**(8), 8679 (2016)

14. Oliver, N., Jüngling, T., Fischer, I.: Consistency properties of a chaotic semiconductor laser driven by optical feedback. Phys. Rev. Lett. **114**, 123902 (2015)

15. Pathak, J., Hunt, B., Girvan, M., Lu, Z., Ott, E.: Model-free prediction of large spatiotemporally chaotic systems from data: a reservoir computing approach. Phys. Rev. Lett. **120**, 024102 (2018)

16. Rodan, A., Tino, P.: Minimum complexity echo state network. IEEE Trans. Neural Netw. **22**(1), 131 (2011)

17. Schumacher, J., Haslinger, R., Pipa, G.: Statistical modeling approach for detecting generalized synchronization. Phys. Rev. E **85**, 056215 (2012)

18. Semenova, N., Porte, X., Andreoli, L., Jacquot, M., Larger, L., Brunner, D.: Fundamental aspects of noise in analog-hardware neural networks. Chaos **29**(10), 103128 (2019)

19. Soriano, M.C., Van der Sande, G., Fischer, I., Mirasso, C.R.: Synchronization in simple network motifs with negligible correlation and mutual information measures. Phys. Rev. Lett. **108**, 134101 (2012)

20. Tanaka, G.: Recent advances in physical reservoir computing: a review. Neural Netw. **115**, 100 (2019)

21. Uchida, A., McAllister, R., Roy, R.: Consistency of nonlinear system response to complex drive signals. Phys. Rev. Lett. **93**, 244102 (2004)

Two-Step FORCE Learning Algorithm for Fast Convergence in Reservoir Computing

Hiroto Tamura[1,2(✉)] and Gouhei Tanaka[1,2]

[1] Graduate School of Engineering, The University of Tokyo, Tokyo 113-8656, Japan
{h-tamura,gtanaka}@g.ecc.u-tokyo.ac.jp
[2] International Research Center for Neurointelligence, The University of Tokyo, Tokyo 113-0033, Japan

Abstract. Reservoir computing devices are promising as energy-efficient machine learning hardware for real-time information processing. However, some online algorithms for reservoir computing are not simple enough for hardware implementation. In this study, we focus on the first order reduced and controlled error (FORCE) algorithm for online learning with reservoir computing models. We propose a two-step FORCE algorithm by simplifying the operations in the FORCE algorithm, which can reduce necessary memories. We analytically and numerically show that the proposed algorithm can converge faster than the original FORCE algorithm.

Keywords: Reservoir computing · FORCE learning · Edge computing · Nonlinear time series generation

1 Introduction

In recent years, the reservoir computing [2,6] has been attracting much attention as an efficient learning approach derived from studies on a special type of the recurrent neural networks (RNNs). In the standard RNN approach, all the connection weights are modified during training. On the other hand, in the reservoir computing, a large neural population called the reservoir has fixed and random recurrent connection weights, and only the readout weights from the reservoir to output units are modified during training. Thus, the learning cost of the reservoir computing is much less than that of the standard RNN, though their performance is comparable in many tasks [5].

On the other hand, the fixed connection weights of the reservoir are favorable for hardware implementation as adaptable devices are not required for this part. In fact, many attempts have been made for realizing physical reservoirs [11]. These techniques are promising for exploring machine learning hardware for real-time information processing. In most studies on physical reservoir computing, the

This work was partially supported by JSPS KAKENHI Grant Numbers JP20J13556 (HT), JP20K11882 (GT), and JST CREST Grant Number JPMJCR19K2, Japan.

I. Farkaš et al. (Eds.): ICANN 2020, LNCS 12397, pp. 459–469, 2020.
https://doi.org/10.1007/978-3-030-61616-8_37

focus has been how to efficiently implement the reservoir part and less attention has been paid to implementation of the readout part. However, particularly for real-time processing of stream data with a reservoir computer in edge computing [8], it is significant to improve the efficiency of the readout part implemented with a low-power device. This issue motivates us to develop a hardware-friendly simplified learning algorithm in the readout.

In this study, we focus on a powerful online learning method called the First Order Reduced and Controlled Error (FORCE) algorithm [10], which is suitable for a reservoir computing model with a feedback loop from output units to the reservoir. In general, training a reservoir computing model with the feedback of its own output is more difficult than training that without such a feedback loop. This is because in the former case, a change in the readout weights influences the reservoir dynamics and thus further modifications of the readout weights are necessary for stabilizing the states of the reservoir outputs. To address this difficulty, the FORCE algorithm was proposed. This algorithm can suppress the error between the target and the model output even from the early phase of the training (control phase), so that the modification of the readout weights does not affect the reservoir's dynamics until the convergence of the weights (learning phase). In recent years, the FORCE learning has been applied not only to reservoirs composed of rate-based neurons but also to reservoirs composed of spiking neurons [3,7,12].

Although the FORCE learning is a useful online learning rule, it is not straightforward to implement this rule in hardware except for general-purpose computer. This is because the FORCE learning requires complicated matrix operations and huge memories. Thus, in this study, we propose a simplified version of the FORCE algorithm called the two-step FORCE algorithm, which uses simpler operations and smaller memories than the original one. We also analytically and numerically show that, in spite of its simplicity, our algorithm can converge faster than the original FORCE algorithm.

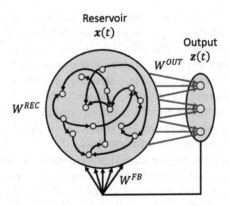

Fig. 1. Schematic diagram of a reservoir computing model with a feedback loop. The yellow points represent the reservoir neurons or output units, the black arrows represent the fixed internal connections, and the red arrows represent the output connections whose weights are modified during the training phase. (Color figure online)

2 Model

2.1 A Reservoir Computing Model with a Feedback Loop

As illustrated in Fig. 1, a reservoir computing model is composed of two parts: a reservoir and output units. The reservoir is a recurrent network of neurons with nonlinear activation function, connected with synaptic weights. The reservoir plays a role to generate complex dynamics. On the other hand, the readout extracts features from the reservoir state to produce a model output. This output is fed back into the reservoir through the feedback connections. In a time series generation task, the network is required to autonomously generate the output that approximates the desired target or teacher signal.

We assume a reservoir computing model represented by the following leaky integrator dynamics:

$$\tau \dot{\boldsymbol{x}} = -\boldsymbol{x} + W^{REC}\boldsymbol{y} + W^{FB}\boldsymbol{z}, \tag{1}$$

$$\boldsymbol{y} = \boldsymbol{\phi}(\boldsymbol{x}), \tag{2}$$

$$\boldsymbol{z} = W^{OUT}\boldsymbol{y}, \tag{3}$$

where $\tau \in \mathbb{R}$ denotes the time constant for the reservoir dynamics, $\boldsymbol{x}(t) := (x_1(t), \ldots, x_N(t))^{\mathrm{T}} \in \mathbb{R}^N$ ($N \in \mathbb{N}$: the number of the reservoir neurons) denotes the activities of the reservoir neurons at time $t \in \mathbb{R}$, $\boldsymbol{y}(t) \in \mathbb{R}^N$ denotes the outputs of the reservoir neurons, $\boldsymbol{\phi}(\boldsymbol{x}) = (\phi(x_1), \ldots, \phi(x_N))^{\mathrm{T}} := (\tanh(x_1), \ldots, \tanh(x_N))^{\mathrm{T}}$ denotes the nonlinear activation function, $\boldsymbol{z}(t) \in \mathbb{R}^M$ ($M \in \mathbb{N}$: the dimension of the model's output) is the output of the model. Hereafter, we denote the unit of continuous time $t \in \mathbb{R}$ by [sec].

On the other hand, $W^{REC} \in \mathbb{R}^{N \times N}, W^{FB} \in \mathbb{R}^{N \times M}$ and $W^{OUT} \in \mathbb{R}^{M \times N}$ are the connection weight matrices representing the synaptic strength. In the reservoir computing approach, W^{REC} and W^{FB} are fixed and only W^{OUT} is modified during the training phase. The entries of W^{REC} are sampled i.i.d. from the Gaussian distribution $\mathcal{N}(0, p^2/N)$ with the spectral radius p. The fraction of non-zero entries in W^{FB} is denoted by q with $0 \le q \le 1$. The non-zero qMN entries of W^{FB} are sampled i.i.d. from the uniform distribution $\mathcal{U}(-1, 1)$ and the rest of them are set at 0.

2.2 FORCE Learning Based on RLS

The detail of the FORCE algorithm [10] is introduced to help understand our proposed model. Here we consider the discrete-time dynamics and denote the output connection weight matrix W^{OUT} at time $n \in \mathbb{Z}$ by $W^{OUT}(n)$. The FORCE algorithm is based on the recursive least square (RLS) filter [1], and can be derived from the online minimization of the following loss function $\mathrm{Loss}(W^{OUT}(n))$ at each time n:

$$\mathrm{Loss}(W^{OUT}(n)) := \sum_{j=1}^{n} \|\boldsymbol{e}^-(j)\|^2, \tag{4}$$

where

$$e^-(j) := d(j) - W^{OUT}(j-1)y(j), \qquad (5)$$

and $d(j)$ denotes a desired target of the output at time j. The resulting update rule of $W^{OUT}(n)$ is described as follows:

$$s(n) := \frac{1}{1 + y^T(n)P(n-1)y(n)}, \qquad (6)$$

$$\Delta P(n) = -s(n)P(n-1)y(n)y^T(n)P(n-1), \qquad (7)$$

$$\Delta W^{OUT}(n) = s(n)e^-(n)P(n-1)y(n), \qquad (8)$$

where

$$\Delta W^{OUT}(n) := W^{OUT}(n) - W^{OUT}(n-1), \qquad (9)$$

$$\Delta P(n) := P(n) - P(n-1). \qquad (10)$$

The initial value of $P(n) \in \mathbb{R}^{N \times N}$ is given by:

$$P(0) = \frac{1}{\gamma}I, \qquad (11)$$

where $\gamma \in \mathbb{R}$ and $I \in \mathbb{R}^{N \times N}$ represents the identity matrix. $P(n)$ is a running estimate for the inverse of the auto-correlation matrix of the neuronal outputs $y(n')$ plus a regularization term:

$$P(n) = \left(\sum_{n'=1}^{n} y(n')y(n')^T + \gamma I \right)^{-1}, \qquad (12)$$

which stores the history of the activities of the reservoir neurons.

3   Results

3.1   Two-Step FORCE Learning

The FORCE learning is roughly separated into two phases: the control phase and learning phase [10]. In the control phase, W^{OUT} rapidly changes in order to suppress the error immediately. In the learning phase, following the control phase, W^{OUT} is subtly modified such that W^{OUT} can converge to a fixed value, while keeping the error small. However, in the original FORCE algorithm, these two phases are not explicitly separated.

In our two-step FORCE learning, on the other hand, we explicitly separate them and use a different updating rule in each phase. Moreover, with hardware implementation of the learning algorithm in mind, we define the continuous-time adaptive rule based on the continuous-time version of the RLS method [9].

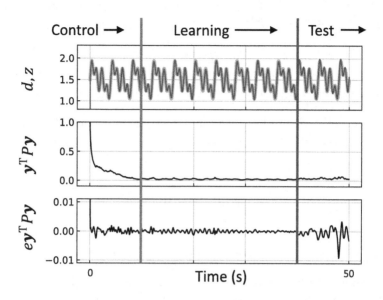

Fig. 2. Numerical simulation of the two-step FORCE learning. In the top panel, the orange curve represents the teacher signal $d(t)$ (generated by Eq. (23) in Appendix) and the blue curve represents the output $z(t)$. The bottom panel denotes $\dot{W}^{OUT}\boldsymbol{y}/\eta = \boldsymbol{e}\boldsymbol{y}^{\mathrm{T}}P\boldsymbol{y}$. The green line indicates the timing of switching from the control phase to the learning phase ($T_0 = 10.0\,\text{s}$), and the red line indicates the timing of the end of the training ($t = 40.0\,\text{s}$). (Color figure online)

In the control phase (for $t \leq T_0$), W^{OUT} is updated as follows:

$$\dot{P} = -\eta P\boldsymbol{y}\boldsymbol{y}^{\mathrm{T}}P, \tag{13}$$

$$\dot{W}^{OUT} = \eta \boldsymbol{e}\boldsymbol{y}^{\mathrm{T}}P, \tag{14}$$

where $\boldsymbol{e}(t) := \boldsymbol{d}(t) - \boldsymbol{z}(t)$ and $\eta > 0$ is a fixed learning rate.

In the learning phase (for $t > T_0$), we fix the value of $P(t)$ at $P_0 := P(T_0)$ and update the output weights as follows:

$$\dot{W}^{OUT} = \eta \boldsymbol{e}\boldsymbol{y}^{\mathrm{T}}P_0. \tag{15}$$

If $\|\dot{W}^{OUT}\boldsymbol{y}\| = \|\eta \boldsymbol{e}\boldsymbol{y}^{\mathrm{T}}P\boldsymbol{y}\|$ is sufficiently small, we switch from the control phase to the learning phase. Currently the timing of switching, T_0, is determined empirically, and how to choose an appropriate value of T_0 for ensuring the convergence of the algorithm is demonstrated in Sect. 3.4.

Figure 2 shows an example of the two-step FORCE learning for the periodic target $d(t) \in \mathbb{R}$. The figure indicates that, through the two-step FORCE learning, the model was successfully trained to autonomously generate the desired time series even after W^{OUT} is fixed (in the test phase).

3.2   Convergence Analysis

We here prove the convergence of the two-step FORCE algorithm in the learning phase (Eq. (15)) under an assumption.

We assume that $\|\eta e y^{\mathrm{T}} P_0 y\| \ll 1$ is achieved through the control phase, though it remains unknown how the RLS rule in the control (Eqs. (13)–(14)) achieves this condition.

Then, in the learning phase, we can express the dynamics of the output as follows:

$$
\begin{aligned}
\dot{z} = \dot{W}^{OUT} y + W^{OUT} \dot{y} \\
= \eta e y^{\mathrm{T}} P_0 y + W^{OUT} \dot{y} \\
\simeq W^{OUT} \dot{y}.
\end{aligned} \tag{16}
$$

Here, the change in W^{OUT} does not influence the dynamics of z and y, even though there is a feedback of z to the reservoir. This case is equivalent to the filtering problem with no feedback, and if the reservoir has sufficient complexity, the following assumption is satisfied during the learning phase:

$$
\exists W^{OUT*} \in \mathbb{R}^{M \times N} \text{ s.t. } W^{OUT*} y(t) = d(t) \text{ for } \forall t \geq T_0. \tag{17}
$$

Now we can define a Lyapunov candidate function (inspired by [4]) as follows:

$$
\begin{aligned}
V := \frac{1}{2} \mathrm{tr} \left(\tilde{W} P_0^{-1} \tilde{W}^{\mathrm{T}} \right) \\
= \frac{1}{2} \sum_{m=1}^{M} \tilde{w}_m^{\mathrm{T}} P_0^{-1} \tilde{w}_m \\
\geq 0,
\end{aligned} \tag{18}
$$

where $\tilde{W} := W^{OUT*} - W^{OUT}$, $\tilde{w}_m$ denotes the mth column of $\tilde{W}^{\mathrm{T}}$, and the last inequality holds because P_0^{-1} is positive definite from Eq. (13).

Since $e = \tilde{W} y$,

$$
\begin{aligned}
\dot{V} = \frac{1}{2} \mathrm{tr} \left(2 \tilde{W} P_0^{-1} \dot{\tilde{W}}^{\mathrm{T}} \right) \\
= \mathrm{tr} \left(\tilde{W} P_0^{-1} (-\dot{W}^{OUT})^{\mathrm{T}} \right) \\
= -\eta \mathrm{tr} \left(\tilde{W} P_0^{-1} (P_0 y e^{\mathrm{T}}) \right) \\
= -\eta \mathrm{tr} \left(\tilde{W} y y^{\mathrm{T}} \tilde{W}^{\mathrm{T}} \right) \\
= -\eta (\tilde{W} y)^{\mathrm{T}} (\tilde{W} y) \\
\leq 0.
\end{aligned} \tag{19}
$$

Furthermore, if $\tilde{W}$ is a zero matrix (i.e., $W^{OUT} = W^{OUT*}$), $V = \dot{V} = 0$ is achieved. Thus, in the learning phase, $\tilde{W} \to 0$ (i.e., $W^{OUT} \to W^{OUT*}$) holds.

3.3   Convergence Rate Comparison: Standard FORCE Algorithm vs. Two-Step FORCE Algorithm

If we use the rule in the control phase (Eqs. (13)–(14)) during the whole training (i.e., removing the learning phase), the situation is equivalent to the standard FORCE algorithm.

In this case, we can define the Lyapunov candidate function as

$$V := \frac{1}{2} \text{tr} \left(\tilde{W} P^{-1} \tilde{W}^{\text{T}} \right) \geq 0. \tag{20}$$

Using the following relation:

$$\begin{aligned} \dot{\overline{P^{-1}}} &= -P^{-1} \dot{P} P^{-1} \\ &= -P^{-1} (-\eta P \boldsymbol{y} \boldsymbol{y}^{\text{T}} P) P^{-1} \\ &= \eta \boldsymbol{y} \boldsymbol{y}^{\text{T}}, \end{aligned} \tag{21}$$

we obtain

$$\begin{aligned} \dot{V} &= \frac{1}{2} \text{tr} \left(2 \tilde{W} P^{-1} \dot{\tilde{W}}^{\text{T}} + \tilde{W} \dot{\overline{P^{-1}}} \tilde{W}^{\text{T}} \right) \\ &= \frac{1}{2} \text{tr} \left(2 \tilde{W} P^{-1} (-\dot{W}^{OUT})^{\text{T}} + \tilde{W} (\eta \boldsymbol{y} \boldsymbol{y}^{\text{T}}) \tilde{W}^{\text{T}} \right) \\ &= \frac{\eta}{2} \text{tr} \left(-2 \tilde{W} \boldsymbol{y} \boldsymbol{y}^{\text{T}} \tilde{W}^{\text{T}} + \tilde{W} \boldsymbol{y} \boldsymbol{y}^{\text{T}} \tilde{W}^{\text{T}} \right) \\ &= -\frac{\eta}{2} (\tilde{W} \boldsymbol{y})^{\text{T}} (\tilde{W} \boldsymbol{y}) \\ &\leq 0. \end{aligned} \tag{22}$$

If $\tilde{W}$ is a zero matrix, $V = \dot{V} = 0$ is achieved. Thus, also in this case, $\tilde{W} \to 0$ holds, and the convergence of the learning is guaranteed.

However, comparing Eq. (19) and Eq. (22), one can see that the update of P (Eq. (13)) in the learning phase makes the convergence of W^{OUT} slower. Therefore, the two-step FORCE algorithm converges faster than the standard FORCE algorithm in the learning phase, if the assumption $\|\eta e \boldsymbol{y}^{\text{T}} P_0 \boldsymbol{y}\| \ll 1$ is satisfied.

Figure 3 compares the convergence of the two-step FORCE algorithm and the standard one. This figure shows that W^{OUT} in the two-step FORCE algorithm converges faster than the standard one, and the error $\boldsymbol{d} - \boldsymbol{z}$ of the two-step FORCE algorithm in the test phase is smaller than that of the standard one. This result suggests the potential of the two-step FORCE learning.

3.4   Length of Control Phase T_0

The goal of the control phase is to find a matrix P_0 such that $\|\eta e(t) \boldsymbol{y}^{\text{T}}(t) P_0 \boldsymbol{y}(t)\| (= \|\dot{W}^{OUT} \boldsymbol{y}(t)\|) \ll 1$ for $\forall t > T_0$. However, how the RLS update rule (Eqs. (13)–(14)) achieves this condition remains unknown. Thus, how to choose an appropriate length of the control phase, T_0, is an issue to be considered.

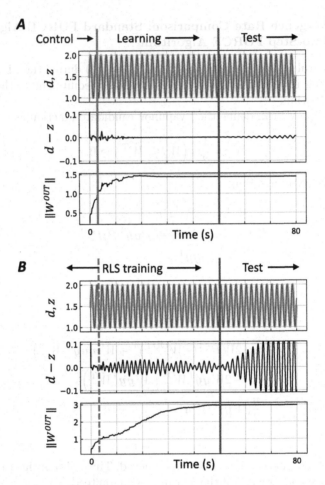

Fig. 3. Comparison of the convergence between two types of the FORCE learning rules. In the top panels, the orange curves represent the teacher signals $d(t)$ (generated by Eq. (24) in Appendix) and the blue curves represent the outputs of the reservoir $z(t)$. Red lines denote the timing of the end of the training ($t = 50.0\,\mathrm{s}$). **(A)** Two-step FORCE learning. (Switching time: $T_0 = 3.0\,\mathrm{s}$.) **(B)** Standard FORCE learning.

Nevertheless, there is a tendency in the relation between the teacher signal $d(t)$ and the appropriate T_0. For simplicity, we here consider 1-dim sinusoidal targets $d(t) \in \mathbb{R}$ with a common amplitude and a period T. Figure 4 indicates that the estimated minimum appropriate length T_0 monotonically increases with the period T of the input signal. This relation can be observed also for more complex periodic target cases (though the results are not shown here). Thus, we can estimate an appropriate value of T_0 from the period of $d(t)$ in periodic cases.

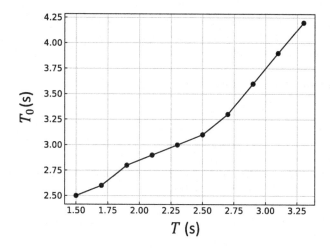

Fig. 4. The minimum appropriate length of the control phase T_0. The horizontal axis represents the period T of the sinusoidal target $d(t)$ (generated by Eq. (25) in Appendix), and the vertical axis represents the minimum length of the control phase T_0 which can keep the mean squared error smaller than 0.01.

4 Discussion

In this study, we have proposed the simplified version of the RLS-based FORCE algorithm called the two-step FORCE algorithm, aiming to apply the FORCE algorithm to efficient hardware implementation. Our two-step FORCE algorithm explicitly separates the training phase into two steps: the control phase (for suppressing the error and seeking the appropriate matrix P) and the learning phase (for the convergence of the readout weights W^{OUT}). As a result of the convergence analysis of the learning phase using the Lyapunov candidate function, we have proven that the two-step FORCE algorithm converges faster than the standard FORCE algorithm if we choose an appropriate timing of the switching from the control phase to the learning phase ($t = T_0$).

However, how to choose an appropriate length of the control phase T_0 remains unknown, because why the RLS update rule can achieve $\|\dot{W}^{OUT}\boldsymbol{y}\| = \|\eta e\boldsymbol{y}^{\mathrm{T}}P\boldsymbol{y}\| \ll 1$ remains unclear. Therefore, the theoretical analysis of the control phase is our important future work.

Although the learning phase occupies the most part of the training phase, the learning rule in the control phase still uses complicated matrix operations and the update of the matrix P requires a large memory. Thus, for hardware implementation of a reservoir computing model with the proposed learning algorithm, we can execute the control phase outside the circuit as a prior learning. To avoid this, we should develop a simpler learning rule in the control phase.

The current work focused on the reservoir computing model with a feedback from the outputs to the reservoir, but our two-step algorithm can also be directly applied to the reservoir without the feedback (which is not called the FORCE learning). This is because, without the feedback from the outputs, we can ignore the impact of the change in the readout weights on the dynamics of the reservoir and easily train these weights.

Acknowledgements. The authors thank Dr. K. Fujiwara for stimulating discussions.

Appendix

We used the parameters setting shown in Table 1 in all the simulations. Δt denotes the time step width used when we convert continuous-time systems into discrete-time systems. (i.e., the discrete time n corresponds to the continuous time $n\Delta t$.)

In Fig. 2, we used the following equation for the periodic teacher signal $d(t)$:

$$d(t) = 0.2 \cdot \left[\sin\left(\frac{2\pi t}{1.0}\right) + \sin\left(\frac{2\pi t}{2.0}\right) + \sin\left(\frac{2\pi t}{4.0}\right) \right] + 1.5. \tag{23}$$

In Fig. 3, we used the following equation for the periodic teacher signal $d(t)$:

$$d(t) = 0.5 \cdot \left[\sin\left(\frac{2\pi t}{2.0}\right) \right] + 1.5. \tag{24}$$

In Fig. 4, we used the following equation for the periodic teacher signal $d(t)$ with the variable period T:

$$d(t) = 0.5 \cdot \left[\sin\left(\frac{2\pi t}{T}\right) \right] + 1.5, \tag{25}$$

and we searched the minimum appropriate T_0 with the interval of 0.1 s.

Table 1. Model parameters common in all the simulations.

Parameter	Value
N	1000
M	1
τ	0.1 s
Δt	0.01 s
p	1.2 (Fig. 2), 0.8 (Fig. 3, Fig. 4)
q	0.2
γ	0.01
η	10.0

References

1. Haykin, S.: Adaptive Filter Theory. Prentice-Hall Inc., Upper Saddle River (1996)
2. Jaeger, H.: The "echo state" approach to analysing and training recurrent neural networks-with an erratum note. Bonn, Germany: German Natl. Res. Center Inf. Technol. GMD Tech. Rep. **148**(34), 13 (2001)
3. Kim, C.M., Chow, C.C.: Learning recurrent dynamics in spiking networks. elife **7**, e37124 (2018)
4. Ljung, L.: Analysis of recursive stochastic algorithms. IEEE Trans. Autom. Control **22**(4), 551–575 (1977)
5. Lukoševičius, M., Jaeger, H.: Reservoir computing approaches to recurrent neural network training. Comput. Sci. Rev. **3**(3), 127–149 (2009)
6. Maass, W., Natschläger, T., Markram, H.: Real-time computing without stable states: a new framework for neural computation based on perturbations. Neural Comput. **14**(11), 2531–2560 (2002)
7. Nicola, W., Clopath, C.: Supervised learning in spiking neural networks with force training. Nat. Commun. **8**(1), 1–15 (2017)
8. Shi, W., Cao, J., Zhang, Q., Li, Y., Xu, L.: Edge computing: vision and challenges. IEEE Internet Things J. **3**(5), 637–646 (2016)
9. Slotine, J.J.E., Li, W., et al.: Applied Nonlinear Control, vol. 199. Prentice Hall, Englewood Cliffs (1991)
10. Sussillo, D., Abbott, L.F.: Generating coherent patterns of activity from chaotic neural networks. Neuron **63**(4), 544–557 (2009)
11. Tanaka, G., et al.: Recent advances in physical reservoir computing: a review. Neural Netw. **115**, 100–123 (2019)
12. Thalmeier, D., Uhlmann, M., Kappen, H.J., Memmesheimer, R.M.: Learning universal computations with spikes. PLoS Comput. Biol. **12**(6), e1004895 (2016)

Morphological Computation of Skin Focusing on Fingerprint Structure

Akane Musha[1]([✉]) [iD], Manabu Daihara[1], Hiroki Shigemune[2],
and Hideyuki Sawada[1] [iD]

[1] Waseda University, Shinjuku-Ku, Tokyo, Japan
`musha@sawada.waseda.phys.ac.jp`, `sawada@waseda.jp`
[2] Shibaura Institute of Technology, Koto-Ku, Tokyo, Japan
`hshige@shibaura-it.ac.jp`

Abstract. When humans get tactile sensation, we touch an object with the skin and the stimuli are transmitted to the brain. The effect of the skin in tactile perception however has not been clarified yet, and sensors considering the skin functions are not introduced. In this research, we investigate the information processing performed by the skin against physical stimuli in touching an object from the viewpoint of morphological computation. We create a dynamical model that expresses the skin structure based on the spring and mass model, and show that the model contributes to the learning of temporal response against physical stimuli. In addition, we conduct an experiment to compare the learning performance of a finger model having fingerprints with a model without fingerprints. Frequency response against physical stimuli with different frequencies is examined, and the result shows that the performance of a model with fingerprints is better in the higher frequency range. The model with fingerprints also reflects the hardness of the human skin remarkably. These results are expected to help clarify the information processing ability of the human skin focusing on the fingerprint structure in response to external physical stimuli.

Keywords: Morphological computation · Reservoir computing · Fingerprints · Skin

1 Introduction

When we touch an object, we do not directly touch it with a tactile receptor as a sensor, but contract our skin to the object to obtain a tactile sensation. Tactile receptors lie under the skin and react to physical stimuli given to the skin. Human tactile mechanisms are currently being studied in various fields, and some functions have been realized as sensors for engineering applications. It is still difficult to reproduce the same tactile perception mechanisms as humans.

In this research, we focus on the morphological computational capabilities of human skin structure. As shown in Fig. 1, the human skin is structured as a stack of three layers of tissue with different hardness. In addition, the surface of the skin is covered with

I. Farkaš et al. (Eds.): ICANN 2020, LNCS 12397, pp. 470–481, 2020.
https://doi.org/10.1007/978-3-030-61616-8_38

fingerprints, and four different tactile receptors that receive particular physical stimuli are arranged at fixed positions under the skin. The received stimuli are transmitted to the brain through the nerve system, which are recognized as tactile sensation. Maeno et al. introduced a physical model of the human epidermal ridge, and studied the mechanical functions of tactile receptors using computer simulation [1]. Morphological computation is a research field that focuses on the structure of biological organs, and investigates the computational capability of the structure [2–4]. It has shown that the high-dimensional transient dynamics of a living organ contributes to the learning of time series data, since they provide a source of information about past stimuli [5]. Some previous studies introduced the dynamics of conical silicone to investigate the morphological computational capabilities of the organs [6–8]. The studies also suggested that each structure had a unique computational capability [7], which was similar to human skin in many ways.

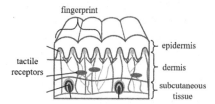

Fig. 1. Human skin structure

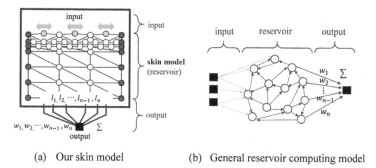

(a)   Our skin model   (b)   General reservoir computing model

Fig. 2. Structure of our skin model and general reservoir computing model

By imitating the structure of the human skin using a mechanical model, it would contribute to the learning of time series data to recognize tactile stimuli. We propose a morphological system considering the human skin structure as shown in Fig. 2, which illustrates the correspondence between general reservoir computing model [9] and our proposal. Our proposed model consists of three main layers: the input part, the middle part, and the output part. Here, the middle part is constructed with a skin model. For the first experiment in this research, we use this model to learn time series data and show that the model contributes to the learning performance. In the second experiment, input data having different frequency components are given to the model to investigate the frequency response of the different structures of the models. The results show that the fingerprint structure of the skin give effects to its physical properties. The results are expected to help clarify the information processing in the human skin.

2 Related Work

2.1 Morphological Computation Using Random Models

Hauser et al. introduced a dynamical system constructed by randomly arranging mass points and springs for learning time series data [10, 11]. They used the motion of a physical object with fixed parameters such as initial position and spring constants to determine the structure of the dynamical system. For the learning of the weights that determine the output values, the displacement of the mass points at each time in the learning phase is used. Then in the testing phase, the output is given by a linear summation using the weights and the motion of the dynamical system.

The results showed that with only simple linear calculations, a dynamical system with a random structure that could hold the influence of past inputs for a certain period of time had a role in helping to find parameters for learning time series data. By referring to the theorem and the proof provided by Boyd et al. [12], they concluded that a nonlinear, time invariant filter with fading memory could be emulated by using a dynamical system with a generic structure [10]. Furthermore, they also showed that the model with a feedback system was not limited to the emulation of filters with fading memory, but could be applied to a wide range of complex calculations [11].

2.2 Relationship Between Structure and Learning Performance

The relationship between the model structure and the learning performance was investigated by Yamanaka et al. using a simple dynamical model made of mass points and springs [13]. They firstly investigated the learning performance of a dynamical model when the size of the gravitational direction and the horizontal direction are changed. Then, they investigated the learning performance of the model by changing the spring constants and the damping coefficients of the springs, and compared the learning performance of the dynamical model with the Echo State Network.

These experimental results confirmed that the learning performance of dynamical models does not simply depend on the size of the model, but are related with the shape. Furthermore, the spring constant and the damping coefficient also affect the learning performance. The experiments comparing the learning performance of the Echo State Network and the dynamical model show that the Echo State Network is superior in accuracy, but the dynamical model is superior in the stability of learning.

3 Skin Model for Morphological Computation

3.1 Construction of the Skin Model

In this study, we pay attention to the physical properties of human skin as a reservoir, and propose a novel model of a reservoir with the characteristics of the skin by referring to the actual hardness and the physical structure. With the use of the reservoir model, we examine the information processing ability. The introduced models are shown in Fig. 3, where the human finger pad is reproduced to investigate the information processing of the skin when it touches an object.

As shown in Fig. 1, human skin consists of three layered organs, which are the hardest epidermis, the hard dermis, and the soft subcutaneous tissue. In addition, the surface of the skin is covered with fingerprints, and four kinds of tactile receptors that receive different stimuli are arranged at fixed positions inside the skin. The received stimuli are transmitted to the brain through the nerve system, which are recognized as tactile sensation.

We construct two models that imitate these structures by using the combination of mass points and springs. Figures 3(a) and (b) show the model with fingerprints and the model without fingerprints, respectively. Red, green and white circles present mass points, and lines connecting with mass points show springs. Two layers from the top take the function of the epidermis, and the further two layers present the role of the dermis. The rest three layers at the bottom are related to the function of the subcutaneous tissue. Here, the spring constants corresponding to the epidermis including the fingerprints are made hard, and gradually become soft from the dermis to the subcutaneous tissue, by referring to the structure of the actual human finger skin.

3.2 Physical Simulation of the Motion of Skin Model

We simulated the dynamics of the finger model when input force is applied to the surface of the skin. In this study, we investigate the information processing ability of the skin model against the physical stimuli applied to the skin when a finger touches an object. Here, we consider the situation when the force is applied to mass points colored in green simultaneously, and the physical response of the mass points is simulated.

The simulation is conducted by employing the following equations, and the implementation is performed using MATLAB.

$$P_x(t) = \Delta t\, v_x(t - \Delta t) + P_x(t - \Delta t) \tag{1}$$

$$v_x(t) = v_x(t - \Delta t) + \Delta t(F_x(t) + u(t)) \tag{2}$$

$$P_y(t) = \Delta t\, v_y(t - \Delta t) + P_y(t - \Delta t) \tag{3}$$

$$v_y(t) = v_y(t - \Delta t) + \Delta t\, F_y(t) \tag{4}$$

where $P_x(t)$ and $P_y(t)$ are the coordinates of a mass point in x- and y-dimensions, respectively, and $v_x(t)$ and $v_y(t)$ are the velocity of the mass points. Δt is the calculation time step. $F_x(t)$ and $F_y(t)$ are the sum of the forces applied from all the springs connecting to the mass point. As shown in Fig. 4, $u(t)$ represents the force given to the model, which is applied only to the mass points colored in green from outside. In this study, the force $u(t)$ given from outside is applied only in the horizontal direction as shown in Fig. 4(b).

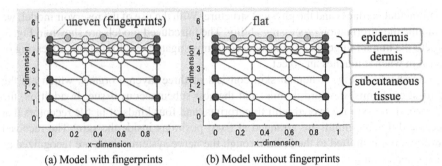

(a) Model with fingerprints   (b) Model without fingerprints

Fig. 3. Two finger skin models using mass and springs (Color figure online)

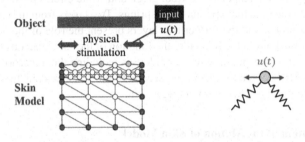

(a) Skin model and applied force   (b) Force application in horizontal direction

Fig. 4. Application of force to the skin model (Color figure online)

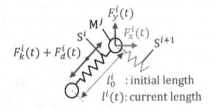

Fig. 5. Forces generated in a mass point M^j

Now we can consider a physical equation to the j-th mass point M^j as shown in Fig. 5. We suppose M^j receives the force $\mathbf{F}^i(t) = \left[F_x^i(t), F_y^i(t) \right]$ from the connecting i-th spring S^i, and the equations are described as follows.

$$F_k^i(t) = k_3^i \left(l^i(t) - l_0^i \right)^3 + k_1^i \left(l^i(t) - l_0^i \right) \tag{5}$$

$$F_d^i(t) = d_3^i \left(\frac{l^i(t) - l_0^i}{\Delta t} \right)^3 + d_1^i \frac{l^i(t) - l_0^i}{\Delta t} \tag{6}$$

where $F_k^i(t)$ is the force caused by the effect of the springs, and $F_d^i(t)$ is the force affected by the damping coefficients of the springs and the mass. In addition, l_0^i and $l^i(t)$ are the initial and current length of the spring S^i, respectively. k_3^i and k_1^i are the spring constants, and d_3^i and d_1^i are the damping coefficients, each for cubic term and linear term, respectively. We correspond the spring constants to the hardness of the skin, and also the damping coefficients to the damping of the skin motion in response to applied stimuli. We determine the spring constants and the damping coefficients by referring to the hardness of each layer presented in the study of Maeno et al. [14], so that the epidermis is the hardest, and the tissue becomes softened as it approaches the subcutaneous tissue. The values of k_1 and d_1 are set in the range from 4.25 to 102.56. In addition, we consider that linear terms contribute greatly to skin movement, and the constants k_3 and d_3 are set to 0.1 times of k_1 and d_1.

As shown in Fig. 5, the x-y component of the force applied to the mass points connecting to a spring $F_x^i(t)$ and $F_y^i(t)$ are defined by the following equations by employing the normalized spring direction vector $\mathbf{n} = \left[n_x^i(t), n_y^i(t) \right]$. In this case, the sign should be positive for the mass at the end of the force, and negative for the mass at the source.

$$F_x^i(t) = (\pm 1)\left(F_k^i(t) + F_d^i(t) \right) n_x^i(t) \tag{7}$$

$$F_y^i(t) = (\pm 1)\left(F_k^i(t) + F_d^i(t) \right) n_y^i(t) \tag{8}$$

Finally, the force that j-th mass point M^j receives from all the connecting springs $\mathbf{F}(t) = \left[F_x(t), F_y(t) \right]$ is obtained from the following equation.

$$\mathbf{F}(t) = \sum_{i=1}^{N} \mathbf{F}^i(t) \tag{9}$$

where N is the total number of springs connecting to M^j.

3.3 Learning of Dynamics Using the Correspondence of Model

For the learning of the time series data, the dynamics of the skin model is employed in this study. The lengths of all the springs in every time step store the time series data as the dynamics of the skin model.

Firstly we prepare the pairs of input data $\mathbf{u} = \{u(t)\}$ and the corresponding target data $\mathbf{O_T} = \{O_T(t)\}$, and let the models learn the relations between them. The prepared data are divided into two sets, a learning set and a testing set. The input $u(t)$ is given by the sinusoidal waves, and the target data is obtained by the following equations, which represents Volterra-type integral consisting of Gaussian kernel h_2.

$$O_T(t) = \iint h_2(\tau_1, \tau_2) u(t - \tau_1) u(t - \tau_2) d\tau_1 d\tau_2 \tag{10}$$

$$h_2(\tau_1, \tau_2) = \exp\left(-\left(\frac{(\tau_1 - \mu_1)^2}{2\sigma_1^2} + \frac{(\tau_2 - \mu_2)^2}{2\sigma_2^2} \right) \right) \tag{11}$$

where the integral intervals are set as $\tau_1, \tau_2 \in [0, 0.2]$. The values that characterize Gaussian kernel h_2 are set as $\sigma_1 = \sigma_2 = 0.05$, $\mu_1 = \mu_2 = 0.1$.

First in the learning phase, a matrix $\mathbf{L} \in \mathbb{R}^{S \times L}$ is defined by arranging the lengths of all the springs $l^i(t)$ in the finger model at every time step as follows,

$$
\mathbf{L} =
\begin{bmatrix}
l^1(t) & l^2(t) & \cdots & l^L(t) \\
l^1(t + \Delta t) & l^2(t + \Delta t) & \cdots & l^L(t + \Delta t) \\
\vdots & \vdots & \ddots & \vdots \\
l^1(t + S\Delta t) & l^2(t + S\Delta t) & \cdots & l^L(t + S\Delta t)
\end{bmatrix}
\tag{12}
$$

where S presents the total number of time steps in the learning phase, and L shows the total number of springs. The target data $\mathbf{O}_T \in \mathbb{R}^{S \times 1}$ is employed for the learning to determine the output weights $\mathbf{w}_{\text{out}} = \left[w_{out}^1, w_{out}^2, \ldots, w_{out}^L \right]^T$ by the following equation.

$$
\mathbf{w}_{\text{out}} = \mathbf{L}^\dagger \mathbf{O}_T
\tag{13}
$$

Since $\mathbf{L}$ is not a square matrix, we use the pseudoinverse matrix $\mathbf{L}^\dagger \in \mathbb{R}^{L \times S}$.

In the test of the performance, the output of the skin model $\mathbf{O} = \{O(t)\}$ is obtained by the following equation using the output weights determined by Eq. (13).

$$
O(t) = \sum_{i=1}^{L} w_{out}^i l^i(t)
\tag{14}
$$

The learning capability of the two models is compared by the *MSE* value as follows.

$$
MSE = \frac{1}{M} \sum_{t=1}^{M} (O_T(t) - O(t))^2
\tag{15}
$$

where M is the total number of time steps in the testing phase.

4 Experiments for the Verification of the Morphological Computation

4.1 Learning of Sinusoidal Input Signals

In this experiment, we investigate the learning performance of the skin model of different hardness by inputting sinusoidal data. In this experiment, we prepare three different models with different hardness: a standard model, a softer model, and a harder model. Compared to the standard model, the softer model has the 0.5 times smaller values of the spring constant and the damping coefficient. On the other hand, the harder model consists of the 1.5 times harder values.

Input time series data $u(t)$ are created by the multiplication of three sine waves as,

$$
u(t) = \sin(2\pi f_1 t) \cdot \sin(2\pi f_2 t) \cdot \sin(2\pi f_3 t)
\tag{16}
$$

where f_1, f_2 and f_3 are 2.11 Hz, 3.73 Hz and 4.33 Hz, respectively. The sampling interval is set to 0.001 s and the simulation time is set to 200,000 steps. The first 60,000 steps of simulation data are washout to use the stable data, and 140,000 step data are used for the learning. In addition, 15,000 step data immediately after the learning data are employed for testing.

The results are shown in Fig. 6. The left figures show the results of the skin model with fingerprints, and the right ones show the results without fingerprints. Three different hardness of skin are compared for verifying the temporal response against sinusoidal signals. The red solid lines show the target data, and the blue dotted lines present the output from the skin model. The output errors *MSE* are shown in Tables 1 and 2.

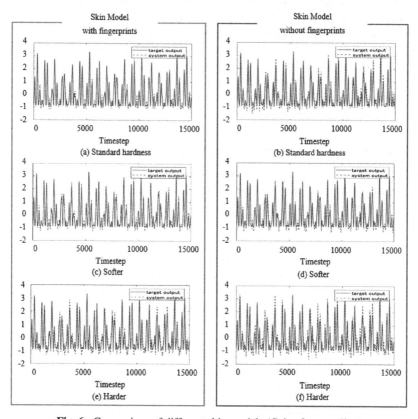

Fig. 6. Comparison of different skin models (Color figure online)

Table 1. MSE of the model with fingerprints

Standard model	2.55×10^{-2}
Softer model	2.98×10^{-2}
Harder model	1.32×10^{-1}

Table 2. MSE of the model without fingerprints

Standard model	1.14×10^{-1}
Softer model	5.44×10^{-2}
Harder model	2.11×10^{-1}

The results show that the output from the skin model could reproduce the target data successfully. This means that the proposed skin model contributes to the learning of time series data. By comparing the differences in the results with and without fingerprints, the model with fingerprints performed with smaller errors than the model without fingerprints. This fact indicates that the fingerprints may contribute to the learning ability. On the other hand, in the comparison of the results of different hardness, significant difference was not found among three models. The results of this experiment suggest that the actual human skin may perform the time series information processing against physical stimuli given from outside.

4.2 Response Analysis Against Different Frequencies

In this experiment, the response of the skin model against different frequencies is investigated. Two skin models with and without fingerprints are examined, and simple sinusoidal inputs $u(t)$ having different frequencies are given to the models.

$$u(t) = \sin(2\pi ft) \tag{17}$$

where f presents frequencies from 2 Hz to 198 Hz at every 4 Hz. The sampling interval is set to 0.001 s. We prepare 20 patterns of simulation time from 2,100 to 9,700, since the appropriate time for learning is different for each frequency. Washout from simulation data is also varied from 700 to 8,300 steps by considering the stability of the data. In addition, we prepare 20 patterns of testing time from 160 to 920 steps. To investigate the effect of hardness of the skin model, we conduct the same experiments for 5 models with different hardness as shown in Table 3 and Fig. 7. As shown in Table 3, the hardness of each model is given by changing the value of k_1 presented in Eq. (5).

Table 3. Parameter range of different hardness

Hardness Level	0.5	0.75	1	1.25	1.5
k_1 (epidermis)	15.7–51.28	23.54–76.92	31.38–102.56	39.23–128.2	47.07–153.84
k_1 (dermis)	5.6–40.39	8.4–60.59	11.2–80.78	14–100.98	16.8–121.17
k_1 (subcutaneous tissue)	2.13–8.76	3.19–13.14	4.25–17.52	5.31–21.9	6.38–26.28

The experimental results are shown in Figs. 8 and 9. Figure 8 shows the examples of outputs from two models having different hardness. Figures (a) and (b) present outputs from the softest models when sinusoidal input of 38 Hz is given. On the other hand, figures (c) and (d) show the outputs when sinusoidal input of 50 Hz is given. Both the soft and hard models with fingerprints are able to follow the target data even the input frequencies are different. The models without fingerprints cause the delay to sinusoidal inputs, especially the delay was greater for the input signal with 38 Hz.

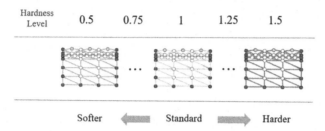

Fig. 7. Parameters for hardness

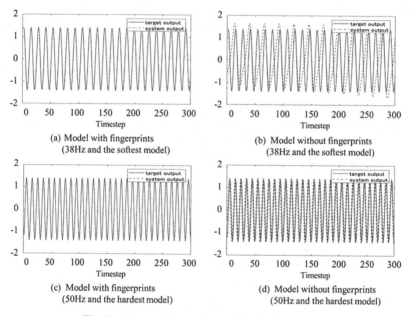

Fig. 8. Outputs of the softest and the hardest models

Figure 9 presents the comparison of the *MSE* values against inputs with different frequencies. The model with fingerprints has smaller errors up to approximately 110 Hz, on the other hand the model without fingerprints generates greater errors from 40 Hz. The results show that fingerprint structures make better performance for responding to higher frequencies. The study of Maeno et al. reported that Meissner corpuscles are regularly

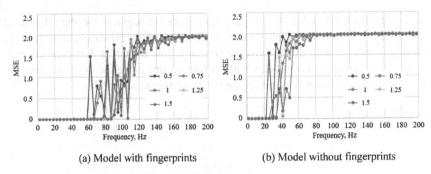

(a) Model with fingerprints   (b) Model without fingerprints

Fig. 9. MSE for each frequency

located underneath the fingerprints [1]. Our results also justify this arrangement of tactile receptors for effectively receiving the physical stimuli given to the skin surface.

5   Conclusions

The study investigated the effect of human skin structure focusing on the hardness and the existence of fingerprints from the point of morphological computation. We constructed a model that mimicked the skin of a human finger by connecting springs with mass points by referring to the actual skin structure and the physical parameters.

To verify the performance of the skin models with different structures, two experiments were conducted. The first experiment let the models learn the time series data. The multiplication of sinusoidal waves was given as inputs, and we validated that the proposed skin model properly contributed to the learning of time series data.

In the second experiment, the frequency response against inputs with different frequencies was studied by using simple sinusoidal waves. The models with different skin hardness were prepared, and their performance was verified. The results presented that the model with fingerprints could respond to higher frequency inputs than the model without fingerprints. Furthermore, we showed that the harder models were able to respond better to physical inputs having higher frequencies.

From these results, we can summarize that the existence of fingerprints in the skin enhances the tactile perception against physical stimuli having different frequencies. In the next work, we will study the relation between the physical structure of a finger skin and the location of four different tactile receptors, which have different response characteristics against physical stimuli.

Acknowledgment. The authors express gratitude towards Dr. Kohei Nakajima for the discussion about the reservoir computing. We also thank Dr. Helmut Hauser for sharing the implementation codes about the morphological computation. This work was supported by JSPS KAKENHI Grant Nos. 18H05473 and 18H05895.

References

1. Maeno, T., Yamada, D., Sato, H.: Analysis on geometry of human epidermal ridges. Trans. Jpn. Soc. Mech. Eng. Part C **71**(701), 245–250 (2005). https://doi.org/10.1299/kikaic.71.245

2. Müller, V.C., Hoffmann, M.: What is morphological computation? On how the body contributes to cognition and control. Artif. Life **23**, 1–24 (2017). https://doi.org/10.1162/ARTL_a_00219
3. Dambre, J., Verstraeten, D., Schrauwen, B., Massar, S.: Information processing capacity of dynamical systems. Sci. Rep. **2**, 514 (2012). https://doi.org/10.1038/srep00514
4. Pfeifer, R., Iida, F., Gomez, G.: Morphological computation for adaptive behavior and cognition. Int. Congr. Ser. **1291**, 22–29 (2006). https://doi.org/10.1016/j.ics.2005.12.080
5. Maass, W., Natschläger, T., Markram, H.: Real-time computing without stable states: a new framework for neural computation based on perturbations. Neural Comput. **14**, 2531–2560 (2002). https://doi.org/10.1162/089976602760407955
6. Nakajima, K., Hauser, H., Li, T., Pfeifer, R.: Information processing via physical soft body. Sci. Rep. **5**, 10487 (2015). https://doi.org/10.1038/srep10487
7. Nakajima, K., Hauser, H., Li, T., Pfeifer, R.: Exploiting the dynamics of soft materials for machine learning. Soft Robot. **5**(3), 339–347 (2018). https://doi.org/10.1089/soro.2017.0075
8. Nakajima, K., Li, T., Hauser, H., Pfeifer, R.: Exploiting short-term memory in soft body dynamics as a computational resource. J. R. Soc. Interface **11**, 20140437 (2014). https://doi.org/10.1098/rsif.2014.0437
9. Appeltant, L., Soriano, M.C., Van der Sande, G., Danckaert, J., Massar, S., et al.: Information processing using a single dynamical node as complex system. Nat. Commun. **2**, 468 (2011). https://doi.org/10.1038/ncomms1476
10. Hauser, H., Ijspeert, A.J., Füchslin, R.M., Pfeifer, R., Maass, W.: Towards a theoretical foundation for morphological computation with compliant bodies. Biol. Cybern. **105**, 355–370 (2011). https://doi.org/10.1007/s00422-012-0471-0
11. Hauser, H., Ijspeert, A.J., Füchslin, R.M., Pfeifer, R., Maass, W.: The role of feedback in morphological computation with compliant bodies. Biol. Cybern. **106**, 595–613 (2011). https://doi.org/10.1007/s00422-012-0516-4
12. Boyd, S., Chua, L.: Fading memory and the problem of approximating nonlinear operators with Volterra series. IEEE Trans. Circuits Syst. **32**(11), 1150–1161 (1985). https://doi.org/10.1109/TCS.1985.1085649
13. Yamanaka, Y., Yaguchi, T., Nakajima, K., Hauser, H.: Mass-spring damper array as a mechanical medium for computation. In: Kůrková, V., Manolopoulos, Y., Hammer, B., Iliadis, L., Maglogiannis, I. (eds.) ICANN 2018. LNCS, vol. 11141, pp. 781–794. Springer, Cham (2018). https://doi.org/10.1007/978-3-030-01424-7_76
14. Maeno, T., Kobayashi, K., Yamazaki, N.: Relationship between the structure of human finger tissue and the location of tactile receptors. JSME Int. J. Ser. C **41**(1), 94–100 (1998). https://doi.org/10.1299/jsmec.41.94

Time Series Clustering with Deep Reservoir Computing

Miguel Atencia[1]([⊠]) [iD], Claudio Gallicchio[2] [iD], Gonzalo Joya[1] [iD],
and Alessio Micheli[2] [iD]

[1] Universidad de Málaga, Campus de Teatinos, 29071 Málaga, Spain
{matencia,gjoya}@uma.es
[2] Department of Computer Science, University of Pisa,
Largo B. Pontecorvo, 3, 56127 Pisa, Italy
{gallicch,micheli}@di.unipi.it

Abstract. This paper proposes a method for clustering of time series, based upon the ability of deep Reservoir Computing networks to grasp the dynamical structure of the series that is presented as input. A standard clustering algorithm, such as k-means, is applied to the network states, rather than the input series themselves. Clustering is thus embedded into the network dynamical evolution, since a clustering result is obtained at every time step, which in turn serves as initialisation at the next step. We empirically assess the performance of deep reservoir systems in time series clustering on benchmark datasets, considering the influence of crucial hyper-parameters. Experimentation with the proposed model shows enhanced clustering quality, measured by the silhouette coefficient, when compared to both static clustering of data, and dynamic clustering with a shallow network.

Keywords: Clustering · Time series · Echo State Networks · Reservoir Computing

1 Introduction

Cluster analysis can be described as the *discovery* of categories into data where class labels are not available or simply data is not known to be organised in classes [1], thus clustering is an unsupervised learning algorithm. Numerous methods, notoriously k-means, have been proposed to deal with clustering. In particular, clustering of time series introduces several critical issues. First of all, the series to be clustered may have different lengths, or may even be regarded as infinite, which is usual in the context of signal processing, e.g. audio or video sequences. Also, time series usually contain temporal dependencies of arbitrary length that cannot be captured by selecting fixed-length windows of data. Finally, casting a sequence into a vector misses the temporal information

This work is partially supported by the Spanish Ministry of Science and Innovation through Project TIN2017-88728-C2-1-R, and the Universidad de Málaga.

I. Farkaš et al. (Eds.): ICANN 2020, LNCS 12397, pp. 482–493, 2020.
https://doi.org/10.1007/978-3-030-61616-8_39

that emerges from the ordering: simply put, the values of the series at different moments in the past have varying relevance for the prediction of the future value. One way to summarise all these difficulties is the fact that computing simply the Euclidean distance between the series samples is not a good measure of whether the series are alike. For instance, a small phase shift of the *same* series would produce completely different values, while preserving significant dynamical features. Therefore, it is not obvious how to compare two sequences, and a critical issue is the choice of similarity measure of time series. Much work has been recently dedicated to the topic of clustering of time series [2], but there is still a significant margin for improvement, where this work aims to contribute.

The paradigm of Reservoir Computing (RC) has emerged in the last two decades (see e.g. [11] and references therein), being characterised by a reduction of weight adaptation, which is the usual meaning of learning in conventional machine learning algorithms. In particular, Echo State Networks (ESNs) [10] comprise a set of hidden units or neurons (the reservoir), linked by recurrent connections that have feedback loops, but the weights of connections are fixed at the beginning and remain constant. Only weights in the output or *readout* layer are adjusted by a fitting algorithm, which is usually very simple, even linear. Since ESNs are dynamical systems that evolve through time, they are often used to deal with prediction of time series. Applications of ESNs to classification and clustering have also been proposed [12,14], but much remains to be done in this direction. In a previous work [4], a method for time series clustering was proposed by embedding a conventional clustering algorithm during the evolution of an ESN. In this work we further explore this topic by using a deep RC architecture [7], which has been shown to improve the memorisation abilities of standard reservoir networks [5], enabling multiple time-scales and multi frequency representations of the driving input signals [7–9]. Hierarchical reservoir architectures go beyond the dynamical properties of shallow reservoirs by implementing a pool of diversified (fading) memories of the driving input time series. Here we aim at empirically exploring the impact of such diversified pool of dynamics in the context of time series clustering.

The rest of this paper is structured as follows. Deep RC is introduced in Sect. 2, which also presents the standard shallow reservoir neural networks methodology as a sub-case. The proposed algorithm for time series clustering is formally described in Sect. 3, and then demonstrated on benchmark datasets in Sect. 4, thus providing an experimental validation of the method. Finally, some conclusions and directions for further research are presented in Sect. 5.

2   Deep Reservoir Computing

Reservoir Computing (RC) denotes a class of Recurrent Neural Networks in which the parameters of the recurrent hidden layer, the reservoir, are left untrained after initialisation. Deep RC extends this line of research considering hierarchical organisations of the reservoir architectures, with the Deep Echo State Network (DeepESN) model [7] being a representative of the approach.

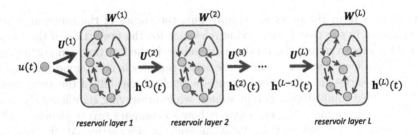

Fig. 1. Deep reservoir architecture.

The dynamical component of a DeepESN is organised into a stacked composition of L reservoir layers. The external input signal drives the dynamics of the first layer, while each successive layer is driven by the activation of the previous layer in the stack. The state of the i-th reservoir layer at time step t, denoted by $\mathbf{h}^{(i)}(t)$ is computed by means of the following state update equation[1]:

$$\mathbf{h}^{(i)}(t) = (1 - \alpha^{(i)})\mathbf{h}^{(i)}(t-1) + \alpha^{(i)}\tanh\left(\mathbf{U}^{(i)}\mathbf{x}^{(i)}(t) + \mathbf{W}^{(i)}\mathbf{h}^{(i)}(t-1)\right), \quad (1)$$

where $\alpha^{(i)}$, $\mathbf{U}^{(i)}$ and $\mathbf{W}^{(i)}$ respectively indicate the leaking rate constant, the input weight matrix and the recurrent weight matrix for layer i in the deep reservoir architecture. Besides, $\mathbf{x}^{(i)}(t)$ indicates the driving input time series for layer i, which, for the first layer corresponds to the external input, i.e. $\mathbf{x}^{(i)}(t) \equiv u(t)$, which in this paper is considered as a one dimensional signal. For successive layers, the driving signal is the state of the preceding layer, i.e. $\mathbf{x}^{(i)}(t) \equiv \mathbf{h}^{(i-1)}(t)$ for $i > 1$. The hierarchical architecture of the deep reservoir is shown in Fig. 1. As initial condition, the state of each layer is set to a zero vector, i.e. $\mathbf{h}^{(i)}(0) = \mathbf{0}$ for all i. Noteworthy, when the reservoir architecture contains a single layer (i.e., $L = 1$) Eq. 1 reduces to the state update equation of standard (shallow) reservoirs [10,11].

The values in the weight matrices $\mathbf{U}^{(i)}$ and $\mathbf{W}^{(i)}$ are left untrained after initialisation under stability constraints expressed by the Echo State Property in [6]. For practical usage, this implies a random initialisation of the weight values, e.g. from a uniform distribution on $[-1, 1]$, followed by a re-scaling. In particular, the weights in $\mathbf{W}^{(i)}$ are scaled to control its effective spectral radius (the maximum among the eigenvalues in modulus), a hyper-parameter of the model indicated as $\rho^{(i)}$. Moreover, the input weight matrix for the first layer, i.e. $\mathbf{U}^{(1)}$, is re-scaled to have a maximum absolute weight value ω_{in}, which acts as input scaling hyper-parameter. The weight matrices $\mathbf{U}^{(i)}$ for layers $i > 1$ are scaled similarly by a value ω_{il}, which is an inter-layer scaling hyper-parameter.

While in standard DeepESNs settings (in supervised learning contexts) the reservoir is coupled with a readout layer, in this paper we limit to consider only the network's states for the purposes of time series clustering.

---

[1] Bias terms are dropped to ease the notation.

Algorithm 1. Dynamic clustering through evolution of the RC model.

Require: Dataset of n time series $\mathbf{u}_j$ with lengths l_j, $j = 1 \ldots n$.
Ensure: k centroids

1: Initialise weight matrices $\mathbf{U}^{(i)}$, $\mathbf{W}^{(i)}$, $i = 1 \ldots L$, and replicate n identical instances

2: Initialise all instances states $\mathbf{h}^{(i)}(0) = 0$, $i = 1 \ldots L$
3: **for** $t = 1$ to $\max_j l_j$ **do**
4:     **for** $j = 1$ to n **do**
5:         **if** $t \leq l_j$ **then**
6:             Update the corresponding ESN instance by Eq. (1)
7:         **end if**
8:     **end for**
9:     **if** $t = 1$ **then**
10:        Initialize centroids
11:     **else**
12:        Set initial centroids to centroids resulting from step $t - 1$
13:     **end if**
14:     Build the dataset $\mathbf{Y}(t)$ of n reservoir states, where $\mathbf{Y}_{i.}(t) = \left(\mathbf{h}^{(1)}, \ldots \mathbf{h}^{(L)} \right)$
15:     Compute centroids at step t from clustering of dataset $\mathbf{Y}(t)$
16: **end for**

---

3   Clustering with Deep Echo State Networks

The proposed algorithm for clustering of time series can be described as the sequential clustering of the states of a set of RC models. See a formal description in Algorithm 1. One reservoir architecture is built and evolved receiving as input each one of the time series within the data set, but all these reservoirs have the same values for all weights. Note that this means that if a total number of N neurons compose the reservoir, and there are n series in the dataset, clustering is performed on a matrix sized $N \times n$ **at each time step** t of the evolution of the networks. Arguably, the reservoirs allow for storing long-term dependencies on data that are lost if only the series samples themselves are used. For explanatory purposes, we consider that each basic clustering process is performed by the well-known k-means algorithm, but any iterative partition clustering method can be embedded, as long as the initial centroids of the clustering can be freely fixed. This is necessary because the key aspect of the proposed *dynamical* algorithm is that the centroids are initialised at time t with the result of the clustering at time $t - 1$. The final result of each dynamic procedure is the clustering at the end of the time series. Contrarily to common usage, no readout layer performing supervised learning is included.

Algorithm 1 describes the application of a deep RC model to clustering of a time series. Note that the standard shallow model is recovered simply by setting $L = 1$, i.e. a fully connected single layer. The notation of line 14 represents that a single vector is formed with all units in the reservoir, simply by concatenating neurons belonging to each layer. An alternative clustering can be designed by using for clustering only the units of a layer. In this way, L independent clustering results can be obtained from the same deep architecture. We analyse below the performance of these three modalities: shallow ESN, deep ESN considering the full reservoir, and each one of the layers of the deep architecture.

4   Experimental Results

In this section we aim at exploring the behaviour of RC neural networks with respect to the clustering of time series. To that end, we apply the Algorithm 1 described in the previous Sect. 3 to two datasets artificially built as described in Sect. 4.1, following the experimental settings reported in Sect. 4.2. The results for both shallow and deep reservoir architectures are presented in Sects. 4.3 and 4.4, respectively on the two datasets used.

4.1   Data

Two different time series datasets are built for the evaluation of the proposed clustering method. The first one is constituted by different versions of the Multiple Superimposed Oscillator (MSO), which has already used as a challenging benchmark for learning with ESNs [9,15]. The second dataset results from the evaluation of mathematical formulae with stochastic components, leading to different synthetic modes (SMs), and has been proposed in the context of time series similarity queries [3].

MSOs are sums of sinusoidal functions:

$$s(t) = \sum_{i=1}^{n} \sin(\varphi_i t) \tag{2}$$

where the frequencies φ_i are assigned the following values: $\varphi_1 = 0.2$, $\varphi_2 = 0.331$, $\varphi_3 = 0.42$, $\varphi_4 = 0.51$, $\varphi_5 = 0.63$, $\varphi_6 = 0.74$, $\varphi_7 = 0.85$, $\varphi_8 = 0.97$, $\varphi_9 = 1.08$, $\varphi_{10} = 1.19$, $\varphi_{11} = 1.27$, $\varphi_{12} = 1.32$. In our experiments, each series is built by, first, randomly setting a value for $n \in \{1, 4, 8, 12\}$ and then building a series by $u(t) = s(t + T)$ where T is a uniform random variable. Finally, we obtain a dataset comprising 160 series of 500. A realisation of these series for each value of n is shown in Fig. 2. The difficulty of this task is that it requires to properly separate input time series with different frequency content, a known challenge for standard RC system.

In contrast to the oscillatory nature of the MSOs, SM time series result from the composition of simple linear functions. Time series are extracted by selecting one from the following 6 types:

$$
\begin{aligned}
s(t) &= 30 + 2\,R_t \\
s(t) &= 30 + 2\,R_t + A\,\sin 2\pi t/T \\
s(t) &= 30 + 2\,R_t + G_t\,t \\
s(t) &= 30 + 2\,R_t - G_t\,t \\
s(t) &= 30 + 2\,R_t + I_{\{t>K\}}\,t \\
s(t) &= 30 + 2\,R_t - I_{\{t>K\}}\,t
\end{aligned}
\tag{3}
$$

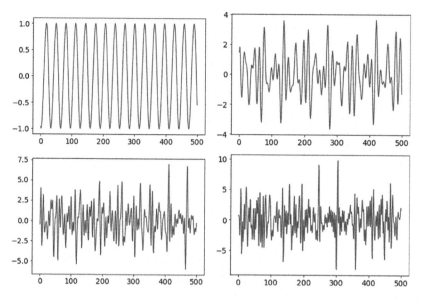

Fig. 2. Example realisations of multiple superimposed oscillators for $n \in \{1, 4, 8, 12\}$.

where A, T, K, and each R_t, G_t are uniform distributions (over different intervals), and I_S is the indicator function of the set S. In the experiments, each one of these synthetically generated data will constitute the external input to the reservoir system (i.e., to the first layer in the deep setting), with $u(t) = s(t)$. We create a total of 180 independent series of length 100, chosen randomly from the six modes defined in Eq. (3). In Fig. 3 a realisation of each type is shown for illustration purposes. Here the challenge is to properly represent a variety of input signals with heterogeneous behaviours.

In order to establish a baseline, a conventional clustering algorithm has also been performed on data, considered as standard vectors. In other words, all the series belonging to a dataset are stacked together yielding a large matrix X, and then k-means is applied to the rows of X. This procedure is called "static" clustering in this paper, to distinguish it from the proposed algorithm that is executed during the dynamical evolution of the reservoir neural network.

4.2 Experimental Settings

In order to apply the proposed algorithm to the datasets described in the previous section, shallow and deep reservoir architectures are built, with the total number of recurrent units being 100 in both cases. For the DeepESN, these 100 units are structured forming 10 layers with 10 units each, i.e., $L = 10$. For the shallow ESN case, the 100 recurrent units are organised in one single layer, i.e., $L = 1$. Preliminary experimentation revealed that results were strongly dependent on the choice of hyper-parameters. Therefore, an exhaustive cross-validation was performed in order to determine optimal settings of the four

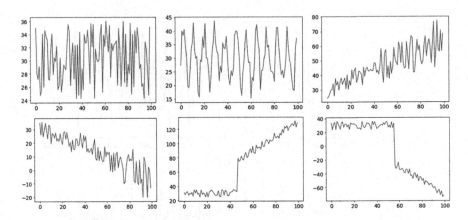

Fig. 3. Example realisations of synthetic modes for each class of Eq. (3).

hyper-parameters that are considered most important: spectral radius ρ, leaking rate α, input scaling ω_{in}, and inter-layer scaling ω_{il} (the last one, only for deep reservoirs). Hyper-parameters are chosen from values shown in Table 1, leading to 192 possible settings. To simplify the construction, all layers share the same spectral radius for the self-connection (recurrent) matrices, the same leaking rate, and the same inter-layer scaling. The number of clusters is set to $k = 10$ for all experiments.

For each experiment, the goodness of the clustering is measured by the silhouette coefficient [13]: a value between -1 and 1 that can be roughly considered as the probability that a particular data instance belongs to the assigned cluster. Then, this value is averaged for all data, so the closer the value to 1, the more compact the clustering. For each model, and for each one of the hyper-parameter combinations, 100 runs are performed on the same dataset with different, independent weight initialisations of the reservoir architectures, as well as centroid initializations of the k-means method (at $t = 1$), to account for stochastic fluctuations due to initialisation of network weights and cluster centroids.

Table 1. Values of hyper-parameters used in the experiments with both tasks. All combinations are generated leading to 192 hyper-parameter sets.

Spectral radius	ρ	0.6	0.9	1.2	1.5
Leaking rate	α	0.5	0.7	0.9	
Input scaling	ω_{in}	0.5	1	1.5	2
Inter-layer scaling	ω_{il}	0.5	1	1.5	2

4.3   Clustering of Multiple Superimposed Oscillators

In order to ascertain the relation between the dynamical behaviour of the network and the clustering results, under different combinations of hyper-parameters, we apply the described algorithm to the MSOs data. Both the shallow and deep architecture are implemented and, besides, as mentioned above, for the deep architecture the clustering may be performed by using either the whole reservoir or each one of the layers independently. Finally, the silhouette coefficient is computed and the hyper-parameters that led to the best result for each one of the architectures are recorded. The results are summarised in Table 2, which also reports the corresponding values of the hyper-parameters.

Table 2. Best results for each architecture and layer, measured by the silhouette coefficient, with $k = 10$, for the MSO task. For each result, the values of the corresponding hyper-parameters are shown.

Architecture	Clustering	silh	ρ	α	ω_{in}	ω_{il}
Static	Data vector	0.12				
Shallow 100	Full reservoir	0.44	0.60	0.90	2.00	
Deep 10×10	Full reservoir	**0.84**	1.50	0.70	0.50	2.00
Deep 10×10	Layer 1	0.90	1.50	0.50	0.50	1.00
Deep 10×10	Layer 2	0.91	1.50	0.50	1.00	0.50
Deep 10×10	Layer 3	0.92	1.50	0.50	0.50	0.50
Deep 10×10	Layer 4	0.92	1.50	0.70	0.50	0.50
Deep 10×10	Layer 5	0.96	1.50	0.70	1.50	0.50
Deep 10×10	Layer 6	0.94	0.60	0.50	2.00	0.50
Deep 10×10	Layer 7	0.94	1.50	0.70	0.50	0.50
Deep 10×10	Layer 8	0.96	1.20	0.50	1.50	1.00
Deep 10×10	Layer 9	**0.98**	1.50	0.70	1.50	0.50
Deep 10×10	Layer 10	0.96	1.20	0.50	2.00	1.50

The analysis of results in Table 2 shows, first of all, that a conventional clustering considering the series as a standard vector does not provide a satisfactory performance, measured in terms of the silhouette coefficient. We interpret that this is due to the fact that casting a sequence into a vector misses the temporal information that is contained in the ordering. The clustering performed on the states of the shallow architecture with 100 neurons, as described in Sect. 3, considerably improves with respect to the vectorized data, but it is still outperformed by the the deep architecture. Remarkably, the deep network (full reservoir setting) almost doubles the performance of the shallow counterpart, indicating a substantially improved ability to represent input series with multiple frequency content. Moreover, in the deep architectural organisation, a differential behaviour

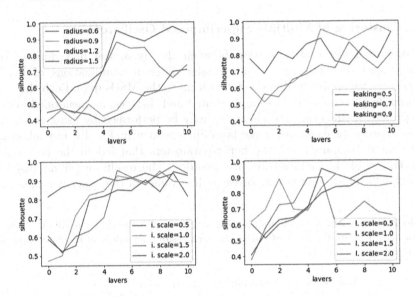

Fig. 4. Silhouette coefficient for increasing layer depth on the X-axis, for different values of spectral radius (top, left), leaking rate (top, right), input scaling (bottom, left), and interlayer scaling (bottom, right) on the task MSO. For each plot, the other three hyper-parameters are as in the penultimate row of Table 2.

is observed when layering is taken into account in the clustering: deeper layers (farther from input) exhibit increasing silhouette coefficient, evidencing a more complex dynamics that is grasping information about the temporal input features. Beside the best result obtained by each architecture in Table 2 it is indicated the hyper-parameter set that led to such result.

As a final investigation on the clustering performance of the ESN under the influence of different choices of hyper-parameters, we plot in Fig. 4 the silhouette coefficients obtained by each layer, where clustering on the full reservoir is represented as layer 0. Starting from the configuration that achieved the global maximum, namely the shown in the penultimate row of Table 3, each hyper-parameter is iterated along the possibilities in the considered range (shown in Table 1). Observing for instance the influence of the spectral radius in the top left plot, looking at the graph for the value 1.5, it is hardly surprising that the maximum is achieved by level 9, since this particular hyper-parameter combination was precisely selected by this feature. It is though more interesting that a general increasing trend is apparent, instead of a random distribution with a peak at level 9 that could have resulted from overfitting. Also, a stronger and more consistent influence of spectral radius and leaking rate compared to the scaling hyper-parameters is observable, which is coherent with the general knowledge on dynamics of reservoir computing.

4.4   Clustering of Synthetic Modes

A similar set of experiments has been performed on data coming from the SM task as defined in Eq. (3), covering the same combinations of hyper-parameters as in Table 1. In this way, cross-validation results, shown in Table 3, allow to select optimal hyper-parameter settings for each architecture. Clustering with reservoir networks is again obviously advantageous with respect to the baseline static clustering, even for the shallow network. Also in this case we observe the beneficial effect of layering, although albeit less pronounced than in the previous MSO case. In this respect, results indicate that even in a case in which a shallow reservoir network is able to achieve an excellent clustering performance, a deep reservoir architecture is still (slightly) advantageous (and adding more layers improves, though not greatly, the achieved results).

Table 3. Best results for the SM task with each architecture and layer, measured by the silhouette coefficient, with $k = 10$. For each result, the values of the corresponding hyper-parameters are shown.

Architecture	Clustering	silh	ρ	α	ω_{in}	ω_{il}
Static	Data vector	0.57				
Shallow 100	Full reservoir	0.90	0.60	0.90	2.00	
Deep 10×10	Full reservoir	**0.91**	0.60	0.70	2.00	1.00
Deep 10×10	Layer 1	0.96	0.60	0.70	2.00	1.00
Deep 10×10	Layer 2	0.95	1.50	0.50	1.50	2.00
Deep 10×10	Layer 3	0.95	1.50	0.50	2.00	1.00
Deep 10×10	Layer 4	0.93	0.90	0.90	1.00	2.00
Deep 10×10	Layer 5	0.94	1.20	0.50	1.00	1.00
Deep 10×10	Layer 6	0.94	1.20	0.50	2.00	0.50
Deep 10×10	Layer 7	0.95	1.50	0.70	0.50	2.00
Deep 10×10	Layer 8	0.95	1.50	0.70	1.00	1.50
Deep 10×10	Layer 9	0.95	1.20	0.50	1.50	1.00
Deep 10×10	Layer 10	**0.97**	1.20	0.50	1.50	1.00

It is also remarkable that, for the SM dataset, several results had to be discarded because they provided meaningless results. For instance, in some cases all reservoir states converged to zero or saturated to one, regardless of the input. Then, the corresponding series were all assigned to a single cluster leaving most other clusters depopulated. When this occurred, the silhouette coefficient was approximately one yet this could not be considered as a satisfactory clustering. This phenomenon can be attributed to an insufficient excitation of the network due to the information provided by the input becoming negligible, and deserves further exploration in future works.

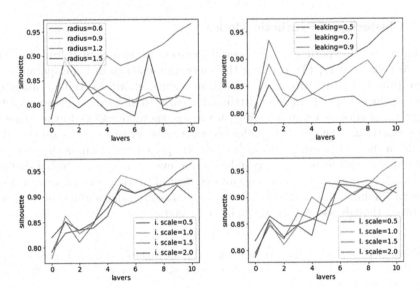

Fig. 5. Silhouette coefficient for increasing layer depth on the X-axis, for different values of spectral radius (top, left), leaking rate (top, right), input scaling (bottom, left), and interlayer scaling (bottom, right) on the task SM. For each plot, the other three hyper-parameters are as in last row of Table 3.

The interrelations of layer depth and each hyper-parameter setting are illustrated by Fig. 5. As observed in the graphs of the bottom row, results are better for deeper layers regardless the value of the scaling hyper-parameters. Although this trend is also visible for the optimal combination of hyper-parameters in the plots of spectral radius and leaking rate, for other settings a more erratic behaviour remains to be explained.

5   Conclusions

In this work we have implemented a clustering algorithm on the states of reservoir computing architectures along their dynamical evolution. The results suggest that this idea contributes to grasp the temporal features of a time series, which are lost when the series is formulated as a static vector. When comparing shallow to deep reservoir algorithms, it was observed that the latter presented an enhanced capability to provide a good clustering, as measured by the silhouette coefficient. The fact that this effect was more evident for series with multiple oscillations reinforces the notion that layered recurrent architectures are naturally most suitable to deal with several time scales by developing diversified fading memories in the different layers.

Looking ahead to future developments, an interesting direction is to explore extensions in the context of supervised problems. Interestingly, in cases in which data with class labels are available, such supervision information could be used to drive the clustering, for instance by exploiting output feedback connections from the output to the reservoir units. This could be useful in real-world problems of time series classification, e.g. for medical diagnosis from ECG data. Remarkably, our algorithm can deal with series of variable length, simply by stopping evolution when input is finished, whereas a conventional clustering method must be applied on a rectangular matrix, which cannot be formed from variable-length rows. In light of such considerations, extensive applications to real-world problems are also planned as future works.

References

1. Aggarwal, C.C., Reddy, C.K.: Data Clustering: Algorithms and Applications. CRC Press, Cambridge (2014)
2. Aghabozorgi, S., Seyed Shirkhorshidi, A., Ying Wah, T.: Time-series clustering - a decade review. Inf. Syst. **53**, 16–38 (2015)
3. Alcock, R.J., Alcock, R.J., Manolopoulos, Y.: Time-series similarity queries employing a feature-based approach. In: 7th Hellenic Conference on Informatics, pp. 27–29 (1999)
4. Atencia, M., Stoean, C., Stoean, R., Rodríguez-Labrada, R., Joya, G.: Dynamic clustering of time series with echo state networks. In: Rojas, I., Joya, G., Catala, A. (eds.) IWANN 2019. LNCS, vol. 11507, pp. 73–83. Springer, Cham (2019). https://doi.org/10.1007/978-3-030-20518-8_7
5. Gallicchio, C.: Short-term memory of deep RNN. In: 26th European Symposium on Artificial Neural Networks (ESANN), pp. 633–638. i6doc.compubl (2018)
6. Gallicchio, C., Micheli, A.: Echo state property of deep reservoir computing networks. Cogn. Comput. **9**(3), 337–350 (2017)
7. Gallicchio, C., Micheli, A., Pedrelli, L.: Deep reservoir computing: a critical experimental analysis. Neurocomputing **268**, 87–99 (2017)
8. Gallicchio, C., Micheli, A., Pedrelli, L.: Design of deep echo state networks. Neural Netw. **108**, 33–47 (2018)
9. Gallicchio, C., Micheli, A., Pedrelli, L.: Hierarchical temporal representation in linear reservoir computing. In: Esposito, A., Faundez-Zanuy, M., Morabito, F.C., Pasero, E. (eds.) WIRN 2017 2017. SIST, vol. 102, pp. 119–129. Springer, Cham (2019). https://doi.org/10.1007/978-3-319-95098-3_11
10. Jaeger, H., Haas, H.: Harnessing nonlinearity: predicting chaotic systems and saving energy in wireless communication. Science **304**(5667), 78–80 (2004)
11. Jaeger, H., Lukoševičius, M., Popovici, D., Siewert, U.: Optimization and applications of echo state networks with leaky-integrator neurons. Neural Netw. **20**(3), 335–352 (2007)
12. Koprinkova-Hristova, P., Alexiev, K.: Echo state networks in dynamic data clustering. In: Mladenov, V., Koprinkova-Hristova, P., Palm, G., Villa, A.E.P., Appollini, B., Kasabov, N. (eds.) ICANN 2013. LNCS, vol. 8131, pp. 343–350. Springer, Heidelberg (2013). https://doi.org/10.1007/978-3-642-40728-4_43
13. Rousseeuw, P.J.: Silhouettes: a graphical aid to the interpretation and validation of cluster analysis. J. Comput. Appl. Math. **20**(C), 53–65 (1987)
14. Tanisaro, P., Heidemann, G.: Time series classification using time warping invariant echo state networks. In: 2016 15th IEEE International Conference on Machine Learning and Applications (ICMLA), pp. 831–836 (2016)
15. Wierstra, D., Gomez, F.J., Schmidhuber, J.: Modeling systems with internal state using evolino. In: GECCO 2005 - Genetic and Evolutionary Computation Conference, pp. 1795–1802. ACM Press, New York (2005)

ReservoirPy: An Efficient
and User-Friendly Library
to Design Echo State Networks

Nathan Trouvain[1,2,3] , Luca Pedrelli[1,2,3] , Thanh Trung Dinh[1,2,3] ,
and Xavier Hinaut[1,2,3(✉)]

[1] INRIA Bordeaux Sud-Ouest, Talence, France
xavier.hinaut@inria.fr
[2] LaBRI, Bordeaux INP, CNRS, UMR 5800, Talence, France
[3] Institut des Maladies Neurodégénératives,
Université de Bordeaux, CNRS, UMR 5293, Bordeaux, France

Abstract. We present a simple user-friendly library called *ReservoirPy* based on Python scientific modules. It provides a flexible interface to implement efficient Reservoir Computing (RC) architectures with a particular focus on Echo State Networks (ESN). Advanced features of *ReservoirPy* allow to improve up to 87.9% of computation time efficiency on a simple laptop compared to basic Python implementation. Overall, we provide tutorials for hyperparameters tuning, offline and online training, fast spectral initialization, parallel and sparse matrix computation on various tasks (MackeyGlass and audio recognition tasks). In particular, we provide graphical tools to easily explore hyperparameters using random search with the help of the *hyperopt* library.

Keywords: Reservoir Computing · Echo State Networks · Offline learning · Online learning · Hyperparameter optimization · Parallel computing · Sparse matrix computation · Toolbox

1 Introduction

Reservoir Computing (RC) [10,14] is a paradigm to train Recurrent Neural Networks (RNN), while not as popular as fully trained neural networks typically used in Deep Learning. It is attractive given the good performance/computation cost ratio, and it is even at the state-of-the-art for several timeseries tasks [10]. Echo State Networks (ESN) [8] is the most well known instance of Reservoir Computing paradigm. While programming a basic ESN is relatively easy – requiring a hundred lines of code for the MackeyGlass timeseries prediction task[1] – having a complete customizable ESN framework error-prone and including hyperparameter optimization requires more effort. Therefore, we want to provide new users

---

[1] See for instance the minimal version of Mantas Lukoševičius saved at https://mantas.info/code/simple_esn or reproduced in *examples* directory of *ReservoirPy*: https://github.com/neuronalX/reservoirpy/tree/master/examples.

© Springer Nature Switzerland AG 2020
I. Farkaš et al. (Eds.): ICANN 2020, LNCS 12397, pp. 494–505, 2020.
https://doi.org/10.1007/978-3-030-61616-8_40

or regular ones an easy to handle and flexible library for Echo State Networks, and more generally extensible to Random RNN-based methods. While it is still in active development, it already includes several useful and advanced features, such as various methods for offline and online learning, parallel computation, and efficient sparse matrix computation. Importantly, we provide integrated graphical tools to easily perform what is usually time-consuming for each new task: explore the influence of various hyperparameters (e.g. spectral radius, input scaling, ...) on the performance of a given task. Moreover, we would like to emphasize the educational aspects of *ReservoirPy*, simple to manage for beginners, and for experts it is easy to build more complex architectures like deep or hierarchical reservoirs [4,11].

A decade ago, some integrated libraries were available, like *Oger*[2] in Python language, or *aureservoir* [7] in C++. Several projects on ESNs can be found on Github[3]. However, there is currently no equivalent library to Oger. Existing Python libraries either use specific frameworks such as PyTorch, or custom implementations. In order to have a general, flexible and easily extendable programming library for RC, which encourages collaboration and educational purposes, we developed *ReservoirPy*. Indeed, reservoir computing is an intuitive way to dive into the processing of timeseries with RNNs; compared to less intuitive training methods used in Long Short Term Memory (LSTM) for instance.

Moreover, we provide visualisation methods for hyperparameter exploration that ease this dive into reservoirs for newcommers, and which is insightful for experts. Several members of our team and students already used it for different tasks and purposes (e.g. to build Computational Neuroscience models and Human-Robot Interaction modules [6,9,12]), it is now time to share it more extensively.

2   The *ReservoirPy* library

2.1   Features Summary

ReservoirPy can be accessed here: https://github.com/neuronalX/reservoirpy The library provides several features:

- general features: **washout, input bias, readout feedback, regularization coefficient,** ...;
- custom or general **offline or online training methods** (e.g. other methods available in *scikit-learn*)
- save and load of ESNs in a readable structure;
- **parallel computation** of reservoir states for independent timeseries (with *jolib* library);
- **sparse matrix** computation (using scipy.sparse);
- **fast spectral initialization** [5];
- tools for easy **hyperparameter exploration** (with *hyperopt* [3]).

---

[2] Oger is no longer maintained; archived at https://github.com/neuronalX/Oger.
[3] See for instance https://github.com/topics/echo-state-networks.

Several tutorials and demos are provided (see Sect. 5.4), along with a documentation. *Nota Bene*: In the following when we say *"train the reservoir"* we mean *"train the readout (i.e. output weights) of the reservoir"*; the internal recurrent connections of the reservoir are always kept fixed throughout the paper.

2.2   Precisions on Online Learning Feature

Alongside with offline learning, *ReservoirPy* also provides the ability to perform online (incremental) learning. Given a sequence of inputs, online learning allows to train the reservoir sequentially on each time step, avoiding storing all data in memory and making matrix inversion on large matrices. Thus, online learning proposes a lighter approach to train reservoir with less computational demand while still achieving compatible level of accuracy. More importantly perhaps, online incremental learning methods are crucial for computational neuroscience models [12] and developmental experiments in cognitive science (developmental psychology, robotics, ...) [6,9]. Current implementation of online learning in *ReservoirPy* is based on FORCE learning method [13], and resides in a separate class: `ESNOnline`. More details on FORCE can be found in Supplementary Material.

3   Getting Started with *ReservoirPy*

In this section, we introduce how to use basic features of *ReservoirPy*.

3.1   Requirements

Basic ReservoirPy (requirements.txt): numpy, joblib, scipy, tqdm. Advanced features to use notebooks and hyperperameters optimization (examples.txt, requirements.txt): hyperopt, pandas, matplotlib, seaborn, scikit-learn. Installation instructions are given in Supplementary Material.

3.2   Prepare Your Dataset

```
1 data = np.loadtxt('MackeyGlass_t17.txt').reshape(-1, 1)
2 # inputs and teachers for training and testing
3 x_train, y_train = data[0:train].T, data[1:train+1]
4 x_test, y_test = data[train:train+test], data[train+1:train+test+1]
```

3.3   Generate Random Matrices

The `mat_gen` module contains functions to create new input, feedback and internal weights matrices, control spectral radius, modify sparsity and add bias.

```
1    from reservoirpy import mat_gen
2    W = mat_gen.generate_internal_weights(...)
3    Win = mat_gen.generate_input_weights(...)
4    # optionnaly, generate a feedback matrix Wfb
```

3.4   Offline Training

Set a Custom Offline Reservoir. ESN can be created using various parameters, allowing to set the leaking rate `leak_rate`, the regularization coefficient value `regularization_coef`, feedback between outputs and the reservoir, an activation function for feedback, or a reference to a Scikit-Learn linear regression model (respectively `lr`, `ridge`, `Wfb`, `fbfunc` and `reg_model` arguments).

```
1 from reservoirpy import ESN
2 esn = ESN(leak_rate, W, Win, input_bias, regularization_coef, ...)
3 # Additional parameters: Wfb, fbfunc, reg_model, use_raw_input
```

Train and Test the Reservoir. The `train` method can handle a sequence of inputs to train a readout matrix `Wout`, using various linear regression methods. The `run` method can then output the readout values from any sequence of inputs. Internal states generated by the reservoir during both processes are returned by all functions. `wash_nr_timesteps` argument also allows to consider only the states generated after a warmup phase for training, ensuring to use only dynamics generated from the input itself and not the initial zero state.

Inputs should be lists of time series. Each time series will be used to compute the corresponding internal states. Between each time series, the internal states of the reservoir are reinitialized, or can be reset to particular values.

```
1 # training
2 states_train = esn.train(inputs=[x_train,], teachers=[y_train,],
3                          wash_nr_timesteps=100)
4 # testing
5 out_pred, states_pred = esn.run(inputs=[test_in,], reset_state=False)
6 print("Root Mean Squared error:")
7 print(np.sqrt(np.mean((out_pred[0] - y_test)**2)) / test_len)
```

3.5   Online Learning

A custom reservoir needs to be instantiated for online learning. Then, the reservoir can be trained and tested in the same way as for offline learning. `alpha_coef` is needed to initialize $P(0)$, where P is used in Eqs. (1) and (2) in Supplementary Material. More information on `alpha_coef` can be found in the FORCE learning paper. `Wout` needs to be initialized in the online version, because the modification of the weights starts since the beginning of the training. `Wout` could be initialized with null matrix.

```
1 from reservoirpy import ESNOnline
2 Wout = ... #initializaton of Wout
3 esn = ESNOnline(... alpha_coef, Wout, ...) # other parameters are the same
```

4   A Tutorial to Explore Visually Hyperparameters

4.1   Random-Search vs. Grid-Search

Setting a reservoir is easy, but training it optimally (or with good enough performance) requires some expertise. Novices and experts' first reaction is to tune parameters by hand, in order to get "some insights" on the influence of parameters. Many users will try grid-search to find which hyperparameters produce a good performance. Indeed, grid-search can be useful to have a global understanding on the influence of hyperparameters. However, in the following we show that this can be done with random exploration as well, especially if you get help from some graphical tools, such as the one we provide in *ReservoirPy*.

More importantly, as Bergstra et al. show [2], grid-search is *suboptimal* compared to random search. Indeed, as shown in Fig. 1, grid-search undersamples the hyperparameter space compared to random-search. This undersampling comes from the fact that grid-search repeatedly tests the same values for one given hyperparameter while changing other hyperparameters. Therefore, grid-search "looses" time (i.e. useful samples) when changing values of unimportant hyperparameters while keeping fixed important hyperparameters. Consequently, random-search obtains better results by sampling more values of important hyperparameters.

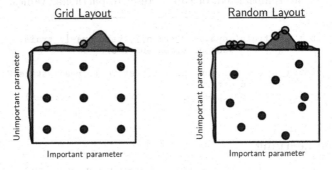

Fig. 1. Why *random search* is better than *grid search*? With *random search* one is able to obtain more samples from the *important parameters*, because with *grid search* one undersamples the space by repeatedly sampling the same values for *important parameters*. Image from [2].

4.2   Integrated Graphical Toolbox

In order to make hyperparameters optimisation more efficient and less time-consuming, we integrate a simple toolbox in *ReservoiPy*. It relies on the widely used *hyperopt* [3] and *Matplotlib* Python libraries. This toolbox provides users with research management and visual tools adapted to the exploration of hyperparameters spaces of ESN. We will present these tools through a minimalist experiment with random search, over a regression task with Mackey-Glass time series (see also Subsect. 5.4). For this tutorial we will use the famous Mackey-Glass task in the RC community: the aim is to perform chaotic timeseries prediction.

4.3   Set the Experiment

The first step consists of defining an *objective* function, based on the parameters we want to explore. This function describes the experiment the user wants to perform. Within this function, the model is instantiated, trained and tested using the parameters yielded by the optimization algorithm. The function should then return a quantitative evaluation of the subsequent model performances when receiving a combination of parameters and input data.

In this example, the objective function returns to *hyperopt* the mean-squared error (MSE) over the testing set, which is the required loss metric for *hyperopt* optimisation. In addition to the loss metric, any other metric can be added in the returned dictionary, by inserting another named item storing its value. Additional metrics can give significant insights on how hyperparameters influence the final results of the model. For the sake of the example we added the root mean-squared error (RMSE) as an additional metric. The codomain of loss functions should preferentially be $\mathbb{R}_+$ and they should have a reachable local or global minimum within the range of explored parameters. If these conditions are not reached, the trials results may be hard to analyse, and show no interesting properties. In this case, the range of parameters defined should be considered as sub-optimal. Additional metrics functions codomain should be $[0; 1]$. Otherwise, the visualisation tool will normalize the results by default to ensure that the figure is readable, which may cause substantial loss of information and add bias when interpretation the figure.

We call one *hyperparameter (hp) combination* (or *hp configuration*) the set of hyperparameters passed to the objective function: the result returned will be represented by one point of data in Fig. 2. During a hp search, the hp combinations should preferably be computed and averaged on several reservoir instances: i.e. it is preferable that the objective function returns the average loss obtained from different reservoir instances for the same set of hyperparameters instead of the loss for one single reservoir instance. As the performance varies from one reservoir instance to another, averaging over 5 or 10 instances is a good compromise between representativeness of results and overall computation time. In the example depicted in Fig. 2, we set `instances_per_trial` to 10. In case only one instance is used, the resulting performance of the hp configuration could not be trusted. In any case, one should not trust blindly to the best hp combination found by *hyperopt*, but rather take the 1 or 2% best configurations and think of it as a range of values for which hyperparameters are optimal. Additionally, this procedure provides more robustness to the parameters found.

```
1    def objective(train_d, test_d, config, *, iss, N, sr, leak, ridge):
2    # the empty starred expression is mandatory in objective function
3    # definition. It separates hyperopt keyword arguments (right)
4    # and required arguments (left).
5
6        # unpack train and test data, with target values.
7        x_train, y_train = train_d # proprocessing could be done here
8        x_test, y_test = test_d     # if parametric
9
10       # train and test an 'insts' number of ESN
11       # This value can be extrated from the config
12       insts = config["instances_per_trial"] # = 10
13
14       mses = []; rmses = [];
15       for i in range(insts):
16           W = ...; Win = ...; reservoir = ...;
17           reservoir.train(inputs=[x_train], teachers=[y_train])
18           outputs, _ = reservoir.run(inputs=[x_test])
19           mses.append(mse(outputs[0], y_test))
20           rmses.append(sqrt(mse(outputs[0], y_test)))
21
22       # return a dictionary of averaged metrics.
23       # The 'loss' key is mandatory when using hyperopt.
24       return {'loss': np.mean(mses)
25               'rmse': np.mean(rmses)}
```

4.4 Define the Parameters Spaces

The next step is to declare the exploration space of parameters inside a JSON structured file, named *configuration file*. This convention allows to keep track of all the parameters used for each exploration, and to uniquely identify every experiments. It is important when doing random search explorations that all choices of parameter ranges are detailed and saved to make the experiments fully reproducible (e.g. define parameters that are kept constant like the number of neurons N in our example). The configuration file has the following structure, and should always begin with an unique experiment name:

```
1    {   "exp": "hyperopt-mackeyglass-1",
2        "hp_max_evals": 1000,
3        "hp_method": "random",
4        "instances_per_trial": 10,
5        "hp_space": {
6            "N": ["choice", 300],
7            "sr": ["loguniform", 1e-6, 10],
8            "leak": ["loguniform", 1e-3, 1],
9            "iss": ["choice", 1.0],
10           "ridge": ["loguniform", 1e-8, 1] }     }
```

Not all parameters are tested at the same time. To maximize the chance to obtain interesting results, we advise to keep some parameters constant. This will minimize the number of covariant interactions, which are difficult to analyse (e.g. spectral radius sr, leak-rate leak and input scaling iss are often interdependent). In this example, only spectral radius, leaking rate and regularization coefficient (respectively sr, leak and ridge) are set with an active exploration space. Other fields are used to configure the *hyperopt* module, setting the optimization algorithm – random search in this case – and the number of trials – one thousand. For example, these parameters could also set the number of initial random trials of *hyperopt* (`n_startup_jobs`) when using the TPE (Tree-Parzen Estimator) Bayesian optimizer (see [3] for more details). All these parameters are defined accordingly to *hyperopt* conventions.

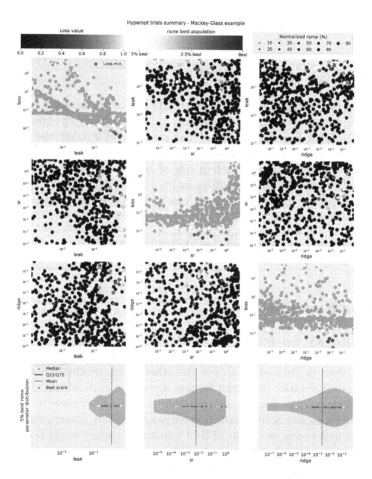

Fig. 2. An example of figure obtained after 1000 trials over Mackey-Glass time series. The random search was performed on spectral radius (sr), leaking rate (leak) and regularization parameter (ridge). MSE and RMSE are displayed as evaluation metrics. Each trial point represent the averaged evaluation metrics over 10 sub-trials. Each sub-trial was performed on the same parameters combination within each trial, but with different ESN instances (e.g. different random weights initialization).

4.5 Launch the Trials

Then, we call the `research` function to run the experiment. The function will call *hyperopt* algorithm and automatically save the results of each trial as JSON structured files in a report directory. Objective function is passed as argument, with the dataset and the paths to configuration files and report directory.

```
1   best = research(loss_ESN, dataset,
2                   config="examples/mackeyglass-config.json",
3                   report="examples/report")
```

4.6 Display the Results

After the end of the random search, all results can be retrieved from the report directory and displayed on a scatter plot, using the `plot_opt_results` function (Fig. 2). This function will load the results and extract the parameters and additional metric the user wants to display, specified with the `params` and `metric` arguments. Other parameters can be used to adjust the figure rendering, for instance by removing outliers or switching scales from logarithmic to linear. More details about Fig. 2 and a more complex example can be found in Supplementary Material.

```
1   fig = plot_opt_results("examples/report/hpt-mg"),
2   params=["sr", "leak", "ridge"], metric="rmse")
```

5 Demo Experiments

In this section, we provide applications on three tasks to showcase a selection of features. The first task is the well-known Mackey-Glass task: chaotic timeseries prediction (used in Subsects. 5.4). For the other tasks, we chose more computationally expensive tasks (bird and human audio recognition tasks) in order to better demonstrate the gain in computation time (used in Subsects. 5.1, 5.2 and 5.3). We used a canary song annotation corpus (we call it *Canary* dataset in the following) which contains about 3.5 h of annotated canary songs (i.e. 1,043,042 MFCC frames), with 41 target classes. The speech recognition corpus TIMIT [1] is composed by 5.4 h of spoken audio characterized by 5040 multidimensional time series with a total of 1,944,000 time steps.

5.1 Parallel Computations

If the ESN is provided with a sequence of independent inputs during training or running (for example for an independent sequence classification task), the reservoir internal states can be computed in parallel. The parallel computation can be enabled by setting the `workers` parameters to a value >1 in the `train` and `run` methods. The `backend` parameter also allows to seamlessly control the module used for parallel computation by the *joblib* package. To ensure minimal performance overhead across all hardware environments, we recommend users to keep the default *threading* backend.

```
1  # setting workers at -1 will use all available threads/processes
2  # for computation. Backend can be switched to any value proposed
3  # by joblib ("threading","multiprocessing", "loki"...)
4  states_train = esn.train(..., workers=-1, backend="threading")
```

5.2   Sparse Matrix Computation

In order to address applications characterized by medium/big datasets, the state computation of the network is implemented considering sparse matrix operations. Here, we show the improvement in terms of efficiency obtained by the sparse computation of the network's state on two audio datasets, the *Canary* and *TIMIT* datasets. Table 1 shows the time spent (in seconds) by the network in the state computation on Canary and TIMIT datasets by using parallelization and sparse recurrent matrices with 1000 units and 10% of sparsity. Interestingly, the sparse computation allows the network to significantly improve the efficiency. In particular, it obtains an improvement of 19.00% and 77.50% in terms efficiency w.r.t. the dense computation on Canary and TIMIT tasks, respectively. Overall, by combining the parallel and the sparse approach, the network obtains a very good improvement spending of 38.81% and 87.87% in terms of efficiency w.r.t. the baseline case on Canary and TIMIT tasks, respectively.

Table 1. Comparison in terms of efficiency considering parallelization and sparse recurrent matrices for the state computation of the network on Canary and TIMIT datasets by using 1000 units and 10% of sparsity, with and without parallel computation enabled. Performance was measured with an *Intel Core i7-8650U*, 1.90 GHz with 8 cores using the Canary dataset, and with an *Intel Core i5*, 2.7 GHz with 2 cores using TIMIT dataset. The percentage of improvement is indicated by taking the *Dense – Serial* case as baseline.

Task	Dense – Serial	Dense – Parallel	Sparse – Serial	Sparse – Parallel
Canary	621 s (-)	442 s (28.82%)	503 s (19.00%)	380 s (38.81%)
TIMIT	849 s (-)	627 s (26.15%)	191 s (77.50%)	103 s (87.87%)

5.3   Fast Spectral Initialization

In the RC context, the recurrent weights are typically initialized by performing the spectral radius through eigenvalues computation. This can be expensive when the application needs large reservoirs or a wide model selection of hyperparameters. A very efficient initialization approach to address these cases is called Fast Spectral Initialization (FSI) [5]. Here, we compare the Python implementation of the FSI approach integrated in this library with the typical methods

Table 2. Comparison in terms of efficiency among FSI, eigen-sparse and eigen-dense by using 1000, 2000 and 5000 recurrent units and 10% of sparsity. Performance was measured with an *Intel Core i5*, 2.7 GHz with 2 cores.

Units	FSI	Eigen – Sparse	Eigen – Dense
1000	0.042 s	0.319 s	1.341 s
2000	0.226 s	1.475 s	7.584 s
5000	1.754 s	21.238 s	128.419 s

based on eigenvalues computation in sparse (**eigen – sparse**) and dense (**eigen – dense**) cases typically used to initialize recurrent weights. Table 2 shows the time (in seconds) spent by FSI, eigen-sparse and eigen-dense considering 1000, 2000 and 5000 recurrent units and 10% of sparsity. As expected, FSI obtains an extremely better efficiency w.r.t. the typical initialization approaches which is progressively enhanced when the number of units increases.

5.4   Online Learning

To demonstrate that online training with FORCE learning method is competitive, we trained a reservoir and evaluated it on the Mackey-Glass task with FORCE learning (with and without feedback). In addition, results are compared with the offline learning case. Surprisingly, online learning method obtains slightly better result than offline learning (Table 3).

Table 3. Comparison of online learning and offline learning on Mackey-Glass task. For each cell: mean (± standard deviation) averaged on 30 reservoir instances. Hyperparameters are the same as the best results for the experiment performed in Sect. 4.6 with $sr = 0.5$, `leak` $= 0.6$ and `ridge` $= 0.02$. Normalized Root Mean Square Error (NRMSE).

Method	NRMSE (10^{-3})
Online learning (with feedback)	3.47 (±0.09)
Online learning (without feedback)	4.39 (±0.26)
Offline learning	6.06 (±1.67)

6   Conclusion

We presented the *ReservoirPy*: a simple and user-friendly library for training Echo State Networks, and soon more models of Random Recurrent Neural Networks. It provides a balance between a flexible tool, based on pure Python library using only scientific libraries, and a computational effective one (parallel implementation, sparse matrix computations, ...), without the burden of a complex framework such as TensorFlow or PyTorch.

The library includes several features that enables to computations more efficient. By using sparse and parallel computations we showed computation time improvement from 38.8% to 87.9% depending on the dataset and the CPU. Moreover, we provided a tutorial to explore efficiently hyperparameters with a graphical tools.

7   Supplementary Material

Supplementary material can be accessed at https://github.com/neuronalX/Trouvain2020_ICANN.

References

1. Garofolo, J, et al.: Timit acoustic-phonetic continuous speech corpus. Linguistic Data Consortium LDC93S1 (1993)
2. Bergstra, J., Bengio, Y.: Random search for hyper-parameter optimization. J. Mach. Learn. Res. **13**(Feb), 281–305 (2012)
3. Bergstra, J., Yamins, D., Cox, D.D.: Hyperopt: a Python library for optimizing the hyperparameters of machine learning algorithms. In: Proceedings of 12th SciPy Conference (2013)
4. Gallicchio, C., Micheli, A., Pedrelli, L.: Deep reservoir computing: a critical experimental analysis. Neurocomputing **268**, 87–99 (2017)
5. Gallicchio, C., Micheli, A., Pedrelli, L.: Fast spectral radius initialization for recurrent neural networks. In: Oneto, L., Navarin, N., Sperduti, A., Anguita, D. (eds.) INNSBDDL 2019. PINNS, vol. 1, pp. 380–390. Springer, Cham (2020). https://doi.org/10.1007/978-3-030-16841-4_39
6. Hinaut, X., Spranger, M.: Learning to parse grounded language using reservoir computing. In: IEEE ICDL-EpiRob, August 2019
7. Holzmann, G.: Efficient C++ library for analog reservoir computing neural networks (echo state networks). http://aureservoir.sourceforge.net (2007–2008)
8. Jaeger, H.: The "echo state" approach to analysing and training recurrent neural networks. Technical report 148, GNRCIT GMD, Bonn, Germany (2001)
9. Juven, A., Hinaut, X.: Cross-situational learning with reservoir computing for language acquisition modelling. In: IJCNN (2020)
10. Lukoševičius, M., Jaeger, H.: Reservoir computing approaches to recurrent neural network training. Comput. Sci. Rev. **3**(3), 127–149 (2009)
11. Pedrelli, L., Hinaut, X.: Hierarchical-task reservoir for anytime POS tagging from continuous speech. In: IJCNN (2020)
12. Strock, A., Hinaut, X., Rougier, N.P.: A robust model of gated working memory. Neural Comput. **32**(1), 153–181 (2020)
13. Sussillo, D., Abbott, L.: Generating coherent patterns of activity from chaotic neural networks. Neuron **63**(4), 544–557 (2009)
14. Verstraeten, D., Schrauwen, B., d'Haene, M., Stroobandt, D.: An experimental unification of reservoir computing methods. Neural Netw. **20**(3), 391–403 (2007)

Robotics and Neural Models
of Perception and Action

Adaptive, Neural Robot Control – Path Planning on 3D Spiking Neural Networks

Lea Steffen[(⊠)], Artur Liebert, Stefan Ulbrich, Arne Roennau,
and Rüdiger Dillmannn

FZI Research Center for Information Technology, Karlsruhe, Germany
{steffen,liebert,stefan.ulbrich,roennau,dillmann}@fzi.de

Abstract. Safe, yet efficient, Human-robot interaction requires real-time-capable and flexible algorithms for robot control including the human as a dynamic obstacle. Even today, methods for collision-free motion planning are often computationally expensive, preventing real-time control. This leads to unnecessary standstills due to safety requirements. As nature solves navigation and motion control sophisticatedly, biologically motivated techniques based on the Wavefront algorithm have been previously applied successfully to path planning problems in 2D. In this work, we present an extension thereof using Spiking Neural Networks. The proposed network equals a topologically organized map of the work space, allowing an execution in 3D space. We tested our work on simulated environments with increasing complexity in 2D with different connection types. Subsequently, the application is extended to 3D spaces and the effectiveness and efficiency of the used approach are attested by simulations and comparison studies. Thereby, a foundation is set to control a robot arm flexibly in a workspace with a human co-worker. In combination with neuromorphic hardware this method will likely achieve real-time capability.

Keywords: Cognitive robotics · Neural motion control · Spiking Neural Networks · Wavefront algorithm

1 Introduction

Nowadays, robots are crucial for the production in several major industries. Until recently, robots were applied isolatedly, enabling work with exclusively predefined paths. As product individualization and diverse product needs increase, the production moves away from repetitive high precision tasks evolving into more complex processes. Additionally, the demand for human-robot interaction requires flexible and real-time capable robot control, considering humans as dynamic obstacles, to meet safety precautions. State-of-the-art algorithms following the Sense-Plan-Act cycle do not meet these requirements. Nature's sophisticated manner of fast and reactive motion control has been an inspiration to scientists for decades. Hence, it is not a new idea to use Artificial Intelligence (AI), and more precisely, Artificial Neural Networks (ANN), to solve path

© Springer Nature Switzerland AG 2020
I. Farkaš et al. (Eds.): ICANN 2020, LNCS 12397, pp. 509–520, 2020.
https://doi.org/10.1007/978-3-030-61616-8_41

planning [9] and also motion planning problems [23] for robotics. However, it is still an active field of research as well in navigation [19] as in motion control [3,4,18]. Algorithms creating collision-free motions as the A* algorithm [12], Rapidly Exploring Random Trees [16] (RRT) and the Wavefront Algorithm [15] already exist but are far from realtime-capable on conventional hardware due to extensive computing times caused by high complexity.

The fundamental concept of path planning, motion control and navigation in humans is formed by the *Place Cells* [14] discovered in 1971 by O'Keefe. These cells are located in the hippocampus. If an organism enters a particular location, the respective place cells fire simultaneously. The location responsible for this impulse is called *Place Field*. Place Cells depict the environment as a cognitive map [21], which is resistant to rotation and changes in lightning, and therefore not relying on visual input. ANNs, are usually applied to model an artificial system for robotic control but recently, also Spiking Neural Networks (SNN) are used [1]. A major advantage is their massive parallelism, but to benefit from it, dedicated hardware, referred to as neuromorphic, is needed to compute the underlying differential equations efficiently. Neuromorphic hardware has already been an active research topic for years, as shown by the development of SpiN-Naker [6]. However, as of recently, companies like Intel (Loihi [2]) and IBM (TrueNorth [13]) have also invested in this technology.

Neural adaptations of the Wavefront algorithm using SNNs have been applied successfully to path planning problems in 2D [8]. In this work, we present an extension of this approach where the network represents a topologically organized map of the navigational space of a robot cell in 3D. This system forms the basis of a reactive real-time capable technique to control a robot arm flexibly considering humans and, in general, static as well as dynamical obstacles.

2   Related Work

Already in 1995, a Hopfield-type ANN has proven as effective for path planning and obstacle avoidance [7]. A biologically plausible alternative is presented in [22], whereby random exploration is used to learn the state space. However, there is a lack of neural path planning algorithms in 3D as up until now neural path planning has mostly been applied to 2D surroundings. Our method is based on the work of Qu et al. [8], a mathematically profound technique using SNNs. Nonetheless, there are several related methods employing a similar network architecture. [11,17,24] cover a wide spectrum from simplified to complex and biologically plausible neuron models. Furthermore, they differ in how the membrane potential is determined, weight adaptation and path calculation.

Most methods introduced in this section rely on Spike-time-dependent Plasticity (STDP), a neurobiological process that regulates the strength of synaptic connections in the brain [10]. If an incoming spike into a neuron occurs immediately before the neuron's own spike, STDP amplifies the respective synapse's weight. If the incoming spike into a neuron occurs immediately after its own spike, the synapse responsible for the incoming signal gets weakened. The process thus reinforces the relevance of the inputs potentially responsible for the excitation of the postsynaptic neuron. As a consequence, such inputs will have a higher impact on the postsynaptic neuron in the future.

In [17], Ponulak et al. introduce an approach for parallel path planning using the Wavefront algorithm and neural plasticity. The neurons of the applied SNN are organized as a 2D topological map and represent biological Place Fields. In this method, the environment has to be learned before path planning is executable. Hence, an initial exploration phase creates a cognitive map of the surroundings by strengthening neurons which represent nearby locations through STDP. Afterwards, a *neural wave*, travelling the entire network, is initiated by activating the neuron representing the target location. Synapses are strengthened by anti-Hebbian STDP [5]. As the wave travels from the goal to the start position and anti-Hebbian STDP strengthens weights in the opposite direction, the optimal path can be determined by retracing the strongest synapses from the start to the target neuron. The network's architecture and synaptic connections are similar to our approach, but everything else is not. In particular, the calculation of the membrane voltage, and how synaptic connections are altered is different. Our approach and [8] determine the optimal path by following the parent of every neuron. In [17] the path is found by following the strongest synapse weights, which are a result of learning with STDP.

Another method for neural path planning based on Place Cells and cognitive maps was presented in [24]. Also here, impulses travel wave-like through a 2D network. The unique feature of this work is an additional same-sized network, referred to as the *occupancy map*. Synaptic connections, between a neuron of the main network and the occupancy grid are only established if they cover the same part of the environment. These connections are either inhibitory, in case of an obstacle, excitatory in case of a robot or neutral for empty spaces. Learning, and thus updating the synaptic weights is achieved by STDP. The similarities of this method and our work lie in the network architecture. They differ through the application of an occupancy grid and STDP as the learning rule in [24].

A scale-free navigational approach for planning by neural waves was introduced in [11]. The navigational space is represented by a topological graph where exciting synapses connect neurons of the free space representing portions of the surrounding which are close to each other. Neurons representing obstacles are isolated. What distinguishes this technique the most is that each neuron is excited periodically. The target neuron is excited with a higher frequency than the others, influencing their respective frequencies. The optimal path emerges along the phase-shifted frequencies.

3   Methodology

The core idea of our approach is mostly based on the work of [8]. However, our work differs to [8] in several ways. The nature of the network is merely outlined mathematically in [8], hence we used our own implementation to generate a neural representation of the environment but kept in line with the mathematical features of [8]. Furthermore, it is not stated in [8] how neighbor neurons are determined. We solved this issue initially with Euclidean vector metric to ensure an easy transition from 2D to 3D environments. As we managed to reduce the generation time by using a direct mapping we replaced the Euclidean vector metric with that. To boost the performance even more, we used precise instead of equidistant time steps. The time steps are adapted to the occurrence of spikes, thus the network is only simulated if spikes are emitted. The method of [8] uses the differential equation in Eq. (7) to calculate the internal activity of every neuron in every single time step. Hence, even intern activities of neurons which have not had an input yet are calculated resulting in $U(t) = 0$. In our work we assigned the value of neurons which had no input yet to zero. Another aspect that differs from the method of [8] is that in their method the simulation iterates over every single neuron in every single time step. In contrast, we delete neurons which have already spiked which reduces the simulation time massively. Finally, we want to emphasize the most important difference, that there is no execution on 3D environments in [8].

3.1 Network Architecture and Synaptic Connections

The network's finite set of neurons is called N. Every neuron $i \in N$, used for our system is a modified pulse-coupled neuron. We will describe their specific features in more detail in Sect. 3.2. Our algorithm operates on a discrete topologically organized map which is arranged as a 2D or 3D grid with solely local lateral connections among neurons. The synaptic weight between the neuron i and j is called ω_{ij} and is corresponding to the Euclidean distance of the neurons. Hence $\omega_{ij} = \sqrt{2}$ if i and j are diagonally connected and $\omega_{ij} = 1$ if i and j are crosswise connected. As all weights are symmetrical, $\omega_{ij} = \omega_{ji}$, the system with its synaptic connections corresponds to an undirected graph. While neurons representing free space are connected to their neighbors, neurons representing obstacles are isolated. Two network structures are possible, the Manhattan method and the Chamfer Method. The former only considers direct neighbors, in contrast to the latter, which additionally takes diagonal neighbors into account. It is noteworthy that, in 3D, the diagonal connections are alongside two axes, meaning they run on the convex hull of the 'cube' between two neurons.

3.2 Neural Features and Information Processing

Every neuron i has a set of neighbors R_i which is expressed by $R_i = \{j \in N, j$ is connected to $i\}$. This set can be separated into two subsets $R_i^r = \{j \in R_i \mid \omega_{ij} = \sqrt{2}\}$ and $R_i^l = \{j \in R_i \mid \omega_{ij} = 1\}$. R_i^l contains every neighbor connected crosswise to i and R_i^r holds all diagonal neighbors of i. A neuron i is said to fire at time $T \geq 0$, if $\exists \epsilon \geq 0$ such that

$$Y_i(t) = \begin{cases} 0, & \text{if } T - \epsilon \leq t < T \\ 1, & \text{if } t = T \\ 0, & \text{if } T < t \leq T + \epsilon \end{cases} \tag{1}$$

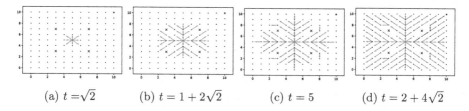

(a) $t = \sqrt{2}$ (b) $t = 1 + 2\sqrt{2}$ (c) $t = 5$ (d) $t = 2 + 4\sqrt{2}$

Fig. 1. Expansion of a neural wave in the network at different stages from the initiation in (a) to the termination in (d). The start neuron is marked in green while the target neuron and the resulting path are indicated in blue and obstacles are marked by an x. The parameter t states the number of time steps passed since the wave's onset. The time is unit less as explained in Sect. 4. (Color figure online)

The firing time is t^i_{fire}. The output function $Y_i(t)$ and neurons' output Y_i are explained in more detail later on.

To describe the internal neural activity, we need to introduce an additional concept. The first neighbor of neuron i that fires is denoted as R^F_i. It is referred to as the *pseudo parent neuron* of i. If a spike emitted by i is a direct consequence of the stimulation from R^F_i the pseudo parent becomes the *parent neuron* R^P_i of neuron i. However, if another neighbor j spikes after the initial pseudo parent R^F_i causing an earlier firing event of neuron i, then j is called the new pseudo parent neuron R^F_i. The entirety of every potential parent of a neuron i at time t is called the *changing set* $\xi(t, i)$. This set is time-dependent, at first it contains every neighbor of i. When t approaches t^i_{fire} the changing set $\xi(i, t)$ empties.

Auxiliary fields are needed to describe the internal activity $U_i(t)$ of a neuron i. The linking field $L_i(t)$ and feeding field $F_i(t)$ of each neuron are expressed as

$$L_i(t) = f(Y_{r^1}, \cdots, Y_{r^k}, t) = \begin{cases} 0, & \text{if } t < t^{R^F_i}_{fire} \\ 1, & \text{else} \end{cases} \tag{2}$$

$$F_i(t) = -g(\omega_{ir^1}, \cdots, \omega_{ir^k}, t)U_i(t) \tag{3}$$

where $\omega_{ir^1}, \cdots, \omega_{ir^k}$ are linking strengths from neuron i to every k neighbors. The internal activity of each neuron determines if a spike is emitted and can be solved via an initial value problem

$$\begin{cases} \frac{dU_i(t)}{dt} = F_i + CL_i = -g(\omega_{ir^1}, \cdots, \omega_{ir^k}, t)U_i(t) + CL_i, & \text{for } t \geq t^{R^P_i}_{fire} \\ U\left(t^{R^P_i}_{fire}\right) = 0 \end{cases} \tag{4}$$

where C is a positive constant and $g(\cdot)$ is a function which uses connection weights from neighboring neurons and the time as an input. It has a positive output. The function g can be depicted as

$$g_i(\omega_{ir^1}, \cdots, \omega_{ir^k}, t) = \begin{cases} 0, & \text{if } t < t^{R^F_i}_{fire} \\ \mu(\omega_{ij}), & \text{if } t \geq t^j_{fire} \text{ for a } j \in \xi(i, t) \end{cases} \tag{5}$$

where $\mu(\omega_{ij})$ is given by

$$\mu(\omega_{ij}) = \frac{B}{\omega_{ij}} = \begin{cases} B, & \text{if } j \in R^l \\ \frac{B}{\sqrt{2}}, & \text{if } j \in R^r \end{cases} \qquad (6)$$

In this case, B is also a positive constant. The particularity of the system is that if the parent of neuron i changes, the intern activity U_i of i is reset to 0 and the process of solving the changed differential equation starts all over again.

The final differential equation for the internal activity $U_i(t)$ for a neuron i results from this derivation and is expressed as

$$\begin{cases} U_i(t) = 0, & \text{if } 0 \le t < t_{fire}^{R_i^F} \\ U_i(t) = 0, & \text{if } t = t_{fire}^{j} \text{ for any } j \in \xi(i,t) \\ \frac{dU_i(t)}{dt} = -\mu(\omega_{iR_i^P})U_i(t) + C, & \text{if } t \ge t_{fire}^{R_i^P}. \end{cases} \qquad (7)$$

Since the membrane potential behaviour of a neuron has been described, the next step is to formulate the process of spiking.

It requires a output function $Y_i(t)$ of a neuron i which has the time t as input and compares the internal activity $U_i(t)$ of a neuron i with its threshold function $\theta_i(t)$ at time t as follows

$$Y_i(t) = \text{Step}(U_i(t) - \theta_i(t)) = \begin{cases} 1, & \text{if } U_i(t) \ge \theta_i \\ 0, & \text{else} \end{cases} \qquad (8)$$

The threshold function $\theta_i(t)$ is expressed as

$$\theta_i(t) = \begin{cases} A_{init}, & \text{if } t < t_{fire}^{R_i^F} \\ A_{ij}, & \text{if } t_{fire}^{j} \le t < t_{fire}^{i}, \ j \in \xi(i,t) \\ V_\theta, & \text{if } t \ge t_{fire}^{i} \end{cases} \qquad (9)$$

for all i, where A_{init} and V_θ are real-valued, positive constants. V_θ is set to be a very large value, such that every neuron will not spike a second time, once they have already spiked. A_{ij} is expressed as

$$A_{ij} = \begin{cases} A^r, & \text{falls } j \in R_i^r \\ A^l, & \text{falls } j \in R_i^l \end{cases} \qquad (10)$$

where A^r and A^l are also real-valued, positive constants. A_{ij} describes the changing value of the threshold which depends on the type of connection of i to its neighbor j.

The fundamental difference to a pulse coupled neural network (PCNN) [20] lies in the structure of the threshold function. In modified PCNN (MPCNN) the threshold function can receive simulated inputs from neighboring neurons, which can then artificially change their value. This is not possible with PCNN. The presented neuron model is described in its entirety from the output function, the threshold function, the linking- and feeding fields, g, μ and the final form of the differential Eq. (7). However, a special case has to be considered here. If more than one neuron fires at the same time $t_{fire}^{R_i^P}$, the neuron with the lowest connection strength is selected as the parent neuron R_i^P.

3.3   Expansion of the Neural Wave and Path Calculation

In order to generate a neural wave in the network, its origin, the initial start neuron which represents the robot cell, referred to as *start*, must be declared. This is done by raising the internal current of the neuron in question, such that $U_{start}(0) > A_{init}$. This excites its neighbors activating the neural wave, impulses forwarded by the neurons via spikes. Four stages of a neural wave expansion in an environment with four dot obstacles is visualized in Fig. 1. Here, the start neuron is marked in green and the target neuron as well as the resulting path in blue. In Fig. 1(a), the artificially altered membrane potential of the start neuron surpasses a threshold starting the wave expansion in all directions generating a vector field. The wave is terminated when the target neuron is reached, as shown in Fig. 1(d). During this process, each neuron stores internally its *parent*. Finally, the path is determined by following the stored parent-child connections from the start neuron to the target neuron.

4   Evaluation and Simulation

For all experiments presented in this section, the necessary parameters are chosen as follows:

$$A_{init} = 0,5 \qquad\qquad V_\theta = 20$$
$$B = 1 \qquad\qquad A^r = \sqrt{2}C\left(1 - e^{-1}\right)$$
$$C = 10 \qquad\qquad A^l = C\left(1 - e^{-1}\right)$$

The thresholds A^r and A^l were chosen such that the time the wave needs to travel from neuron to neuron corresponds to the Euclidean distance of the neurons. It is hence unit less. The other constants are chosen such that the three conditions from the mathematical analysis of the proposed model hold [8]. The naming of Table 1 and 2 is uniform. *Generation time* refers to the amount of time (in seconds), needed to construct the 2D or 3D network, the neural representation of the environment. *Simulation time* is the time necessary to simulate the wave and calculate the optimal path through the network.

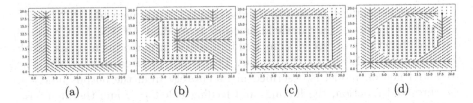

| | (a) | (b) | (c) | (d) |

Fig. 2. 2D environments with different complexity. In (a), the obstacle is formed like a rectangle and is placed on the upper border. In (b), an obstacle shaped like a horseshoe is enclosing the start position. In (c), a square- and in (d) a circle-shaped obstacle are placed in the center.

4.1   Experiments in 2D Environments

All experiments presented in this section are carried out on 2D maps, thus they are quite similar to the results of [8]. However, these tests provide a basis for the more advanced results of Sect. 4.2 and 4.3. The experiments carried out on 2D maps are all performed on a network connected by the Chamfer method. 2D Experiments regarding the Manhattan method are neglected due to triviality. In Fig. 2(d) four experiments in different 2D environments are shown. It is obvious that in each one of them the optimal path (marked in blue) was found. It is noticeable that mostly lateral connections are used in Fig. 2(a) and Fig. 2(c) as the optimal path is alongside axis. Diagonal connections are solely applied to get around the corners. A more balanced combination of lateral and diagonal connections is necessary for the optimal path in Fig. 2(b) and 2(d). Furthermore, it can be seen that the neural wave, displayed by red vectors did not reach all free neurons as the expansion of the wave is terminated immediately when the target neuron is found.

Details about the experimental results are provided in Table 1. The simulation on the map displayed in Fig. 2(c) requires the least amount of time as the majority of neurons could be discarded by the algorithm. In contrast to that, the performance shown in Fig. 2(a) is quite bad even though many neurons could be ignored here due to a huge obstacle as well. This can be explained by the fact

Table 1. All results of this table were obtained on a 2D grid connected by the Chamfer method. The respective environments are visualized in Fig. 2.

	Rectangle	Horseshoe	Square	Circle
Generation time	1.93 s	2.38 s	1.71 s	2.49 s
Simulation time	26.04 s	22.72 s	14.56 s	15.80 s
Start neuron	(3, 18)	(8, 10)	(1, 1)	(2, 2)
Target neuron	(17, 18)	(3, 10)	(18, 18)	(17,1 7)
Path length	42	27	32	26

that the length of the optimal path also influences the simulation time. These results lead to three conclusions about the general performance of our system. The generation time, the time needed to generate a neural representation of a map, increases with more complex obstacles. The simulation time on the other hand decreases if the number of neurons representing obstacles rises. This is not surprising as a large amount of obstacles decreases the neurons which need to be considered by the algorithm. Lastly, the simulation time is also related to the size of the resulting vector field.

4.2 3D Experiments with the Manhattan Method

Networks connected via the Manhattan method are visualized in Fig. 3(a), (b), (c) and (d). The results of these experiments are shown in Table 2. All grids of Fig. 3, also the once covered in Sect. 4.3, have the size $12 \times 12 \times 12$. The map of Fig. 3(a) is completely free of obstacles and serves as a basis for comparisons. The optimal path is of length 33 and changes its direction twice. In Fig. 3(a) a wall, parallel to the x-y plane, is inserted. Even though the length of the optimal path does not change from Fig. 3(a) to (b), the generation time increases and the simulation time decreases. The second observation can be explained by the fact that neurons representing obstacles are neglected by the algorithm. In (c) a second wall, parallel to the first one, is added extending the optimal path to 55 steps. The last experiment regarding the Manhattan method is carried out on a 3D map with a sphere located at the center, as shown in (d).

The data of Table 2 shows that the generation time does not always increase with complexity. If many neurons are removed, the algorithm does not need to determine all their values and neighbors. As the generation times are all within 3.7 s to 4.36 s they show only minor variations.

The worst simulation time, 0.71 s, is obtained in (a), the map without any obstacles. This is because while simulation, the wave could expand over the entire network meaning vectors needed to be calculated for every neuron. In contrast, the shortest simulation time of 0.51 s was achieved in (c). The neural wave only expanded over a subset of the network's neurons. It is remarkable that this simulation time was achieved even though the optimal path of (c) is the longest. However, the length of the optimal path does have a great influence on the simulation time as a short optimal path terminates the expansion of the wave. This effect is noticeable in (c) and the last column of Table 2.

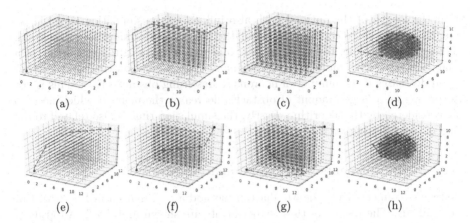

Fig. 3. The $12 \times 12 \times 12$ network includes 1728 neurons. The networks of (a), (b), (c) and (d) apply the Manhattan, whereby (e), (f), (g) and (h) the Chamfer method. All obstacles are marked in red and the optimal path is visualized in green. The networks (a) and (e) consist only of free space while the environment of (b) and (f) embody a wall. In (c) and (g) two walls are present and the obstacle in (d) and (h) is a sphere. For all experiments, except (d) and (h), the start neuron is (0, 0, 0) and the target neuron is (11, 11, 11). (Color figure online)

Table 2. Results about experiments on a 3D grid connected by the Manhattan vs the Chamfer method. The first three rows correspond to Fig. 3(a), (b), (c) and (d) while the results of the last three rows belong to Fig. 3(e), (f), (g) and (h).

		None	Wall	2 walls	Sphere
Manhattan	Generation time	4.02 s	4.36 s	4.0 s	3.7 s
	Simulation time	0.71 s	0.62 s	0.51 s	0.53 s
	Path length	33	33	55	21
Chamfer	Generation time	5.5 s	5.36 s	5.43 s	5.12 s
	Simulation time	7.34 s	6.79 s	10.59 s	4.78 s
	Path length	16	16	33	12

4.3   3D Experiments with the Chamfer Method

The experiments displayed in Fig. 3(e), (f), (g) and (h) are connected by the Chamfer method. Hence the network including 1728 neurons is not only connected with lateral but also diagonal synapses. Information about time and path length for those tests is given in the lower half of Table 2. The most obvious difference between the results with the Manhattan method and the Chamfer method (see Table 2) is the length of the optimal path. For the map of Fig. 3(a) and (e) as well as Fig. 3(b) and (f), the optimal path is reduced by half. Also the other experiment show a significantly shorter optimal path if the network is connected via the Chamfer method. The effect on the computation time, even though it was expected, is less desirable. Comparing the results of Table 2 shows that the generation time is increased by ca 20% while the simulation time rises massively. In some cases, the simulation time is increased by factor 10. This is simply because each neuron has up to 12 synapses more due to the Chamfer method.

In Fig. 3(e), a map with no obstacles, the approach only finds a poor solution. This observation can be explained as the synaptic connections of the Chamfer model in 3D were intentionally chosen to resemble those in 2D. For (e) the resulting path would be improved if the synaptic connections would go along the 3D diagonal. However, in cases where the optimal path is approximately along the 2D-diagonals the opposite is true. As an extension of the network to embody both diagonals for distant neurons would decelerate computations two potential solutions exist. Firstly, this issue is easily overcome with an increased number of neurons, as the approximation of the optimal path would improve. Secondly, it is possible to switch between connection types by simply changing the neighborhood definition without adversely affecting the performance.

5   Discussion

The progress with spiking neurons has resulted in a model that can be used effectively for robot path planning. MPGNN are a strong simplification of the biological basis. By eliminating superfluous influences and neuronal properties, the computing time is greatly reduced. This neuron model is effectively tailored to the problem of path planning and accordingly delivers results efficiently without being hindered by disturbing factors. If a target neuron can be reached from the start neuron, the optimal path is found without exception. Although the system does not yet achieve real time, neuromorphic hardware still promises a significant improvement in this respect. It was found that the generation time hardly depends on the type of obstacle, but on the number of neurons and, above all, the type of connection. In general, it was shown that the MPGNN-based model can be successfully used for motion planning in 3D.

Acknowledgments. The research leading to this paper received funding as the project *NeuroReact* from the Baden-Württemberg Stiftung under the research program *Neurorobotik*.

References

1. Bing, Z., Meschede, C., Röhrbein, F., Huang, K., Knoll, A.: A survey of robotics control based on learning-inspired spiking neural networks. Front. Neurorobot. **12**, 35 (2018)
2. Davies, M., et al.: Loihi: a neuromorphic manycore processor with on-chip learning. IEEE Micro **38**(1), 82–99 (2018)
3. De Momi, E., Kranendonk, L., Valenti, M., Enayati, N., Ferrigno, G.: A neural network-based approach for trajectory planning in robot-human handover tasks. Front. Robot. AI **3**(JUN), 34 (2016)

4. Ewerton, M., et al.: Learning trajectory distributions for assisted teleoperation and path planning. Front. Robot. AI **6**, 89 (2019)
5. Feldman, D.: The spike-timing dependence of plasticity. Neuron **75**(4), 556–571 (2012)
6. Furber, S., Galluppi, F., Temple, S., Plana, L.: The SpiNNaker project. Proc. IEEE **102**(5), 652–665 (2014)
7. Glasius, R., Komoda, A., Gielen, S.C.: Neural network dynamics for path planning and obstacle avoidance. Neural Netw. **8**(1), 125–133 (1995)
8. Qu, H., Yang, S., Willms, A., Yi, Z.: Real-time robot path planning based on a modified pulse-coupled neural network model. Trans. NN **20**(11), 1724–1739 (2009)
9. Janglová, D.: Neural networks in mobile robot motion. Int. J. Adv. Robot. Syst. **1**(1), 15–22 (2004)
10. Jost, J.: Temporal correlation based learning in neuron models. Theory Biosci. **125**(1), 37–53 (2006)
11. Khajeh-Alijani, A., Urbanczik, R., Senn, W.: Scale-free navigational planning by neuronal traveling waves. PLoS ONE **10**(7), e0127269 (2015)
12. Koenig, S., Likhachev, M.: Incremental A*. NIPS2001, pp. 1539–1546 (2002)
13. Merolla, P.A., et al.: A million spiking-neuron integrated circuit with a scalable communication network and interface. Science **345**(6197), 668–673 (2014)
14. O'Keefe, J., Dostrovsky, J.: The hippocampus as a spatial map. Preliminary evidence from unit activity in the freely-moving rat. Brain Res. **34**(1), 171–175 (1971)
15. Pal, A., Tiwari, R., Shukla, A.: A focused wave front algorithm for mobile robot path planning. In: Corchado, E., Kurzyński, M., Woźniak, M. (eds.) HAIS 2011. LNCS (LNAI), vol. 6678, pp. 190–197. Springer, Heidelberg (2011). https://doi.org/10.1007/978-3-642-21219-2_25
16. Polyakova, M., Rubin, G., Danilova, Y.: Method for matching customer and manufacturer positions for metal product parameters standardization. In: AIP, vol. 1946 (2018)
17. Ponulak, F., Hopfield, J.: Rapid, parallel path planning by propagating wavefronts of spiking neural activity. Front. Comp. Neurosci. **7**, 98 (2013)
18. Qureshi, A., Simeonov, A., Bency, M., Yip, M.: Motion planning networks (2019)
19. Raković, M., Savić, S., Santos-Victor, J., Nikolić, M., Borovac, B.: Human-inspired online path planning and biped walking realization in unknown environment. Front. Neurorobot. **13**, 36 (2019)
20. Subashini, M., KumarSahoo, S.: Pulse coupled neural networks and its applications. Expert Syst. Appl. **41**(8), 3965–3974 (2014)
21. Tolman, E.C.: Cognitive maps in rats and men. Psychol. Rev. **55**(4), 189 (1948)
22. Weber, C., Triesch, J.: From exploration to planning. In: Kůrková, V., Neruda, R., Koutník, J. (eds.) ICANN 2008. LNCS, vol. 5163, pp. 740–749. Springer, Heidelberg (2008). https://doi.org/10.1007/978-3-540-87536-9_76
23. Zeller, M., Sharma, R., Schulten, K.: Motion planning of a pneumatic robot using a neural network. IEEE Control Syst. **17**(3), 89–98 (1997)
24. Zennir, M., Benmohammed, M., Boudjadja, R.: Spike-time dependant plasticity in a spiking neural network for robot path planning. In: AIAI, vol. 1539 (2015)

CABIN: A Novel Cooperative Attention Based Location Prediction Network Using Internal-External Trajectory Dependencies

Tangwen Qian[1,2], Fei Wang[1(✉)], Yongjun Xu[1], Yu Jiang[1,2], Tao Sun[1,2], and Yong Yu[2]

[1] Institute of Computing Technology, Chinese Academy of Sciences, Beijing, China
{qiantangwen,wangfei,xyj,jiangyu,suntao}@ict.ac.cn
[2] University of Chinese Academy of Sciences, Beijing, China
yuyong171@mails.ucas.edu.cn

Abstract. Nowadays, large quantities of advanced locating sensors have been widely used, which makes it possible to deploy location-based service (LBS) enhanced by intelligent technologies. Location prediction, as one of the most fundamental technologies, aims to acquire possible location at next timestamp based on the moving pattern of current trajectories. High accuracy of location prediction could enrich and increase user experience of various LBSs and brings lots of benefits to service providers. Lots of state-of-the-art research try to model spatial-temporal trajectories based on recurrent neural networks (RNNs), yet fails to arrive at a practical usability. We observe that there exists two ways to improve through attention mechanism which performs well in computer vision and natural language processing domains. Firstly recent location prediction methods are usually equipped with single-head attention mechanism to promote accuracy, which is only able to capture limited information in a specific subspace at a specific position. Secondly, existing methods focus on external relations between spatial-temporal trajectories, but miss internal relations in each spatial-temporal trajectory. To tackle the problem of model spatial-temporal patterns of mobility, we propose a novel Cooperative Attention Based location prediction network using Internal-External trajectory dependencies correspondingly in this paper. We also design and perform experiments on two real-world check-in datasets, Foursquare data in New York and Tokyo cities. Evaluation results demonstrate that our method outperforms state-of-the-art models.

Keywords: Attention · Internal-external relations · Spatial-temporal trajectory · Location prediction

1 Introduction

Nowadays, large quantities of various sensors (e.g., GPS-devices, radar system, electronic toll collection, infrared distance meter, etc.) are deployed to track

© Springer Nature Switzerland AG 2020
I. Farkaš et al. (Eds.): ICANN 2020, LNCS 12397, pp. 521–532, 2020.
https://doi.org/10.1007/978-3-030-61616-8_42

persons or vehicles, which makes a variety of location data accumulate steadily. Fusing different kinds of location data for one object is the key to improve relevant technologies in complex application scenarios. Location prediction, as one of the most fundamental technologies, aims to acquire possible location at next timestamp based on the moving pattern of current trajectories. In last decades, it has already been applied broadly ranging from city management to personal services. High accuracy of location prediction is fundamental to enrich and increase user experience of various LBSs and brings lots of benefits to service providers [10,11]. Therefore, the task to design best location prediction model for various situations has attracted the attention of both academy and industry.

According to the architecture, existing location prediction methods can be roughly divided into two categories: pattern-based and model-based. Pattern-based methods [1,5,8] extract spatial-temporal patterns (e.g., sequential patterns, frequent patterns) from historical movements firstly, which are used to predict next location. Although pattern-based methods are commonly used, it's non-trivial to discover meaningful patterns which are important to the performance [12]. Therefore, model-based methods [2,3,6,7], such as Markov model and Recurrent Neural Network (RNN), are introduced to tackle this problem. These model-based methods leverage sequential statistical models to capture the transition regularities of movements. At present, RNN-based methods achieve a state-of-the-art performance.

However, trajectories are too complex in some of the real-world scenarios. In these scenarios, on one hand the sensing procedure could be sheltered or disturbed, on the other the persons or vehicles with malicious purpose might try to forge location data and avoid being tracked. Therefore, relying on only short-range patterns or transition regularities might cause the huge error in prediction and crash down the LBS systems. When we try to solve the challenge with RNN, we observe that the receptive field of RNN is weak in capturing long-range dependency due to how it models and optimizes. Hence until now, many scholars continue to improve RNN-based methods to get better results in different ways, such as, replacing basic RNN with long short-range memory (LSTM) or gated recurrent neural networks (GRU) and adopting the encoder-decoder architectures. However, the fundamental constraint of sequential computation remains.

To overcome the constraints, recently scholars equip RNN with attention mechanism to improve the ability of modeling sequence context, which is proved to perform well in computer vision and natural language processing domains. Yet we observe that there still exists two ways to improve. Firstly recent location prediction methods are usually equipped with single-head attention mechanism to promote accuracy, which is only able to capture limited information in a specific subspace at a specific position. Secondly, existing methods focus on external relations between spatial-temporal trajectories, but miss internal relations in one spatial-temporal trajectory.

Inspired by above observations, we proposed CABIN, a novel **C**ooperative **A**ttention **B**ased location prediction network using **I**nternal-**E**xternal trajectory dependencies in this paper. Firstly, we transformed raw sparse trajectory data into dense feature representation with a spatial-temporal feature disentangling module. Secondly, we constructed our method based on pure attention, which is able to seize not only external but also internal relations of each spatial-temporal trajectory. Finally, we designed a cooperative attention module to effectively filter the current trajectory features with the historical spatial-temporal mobility pattern from different representation subspaces at different positions. We conducted thorough experiments on two public check-in datasets of the real world, results showed that our method reaches a new state-of-the-art result in location prediction task.

Our main contributions are summarized as follows:

- We introduced a novel complete Transformer network through introducing a spatial-temporal feature disentangling module, which is a pure attention-based Transformer network to predict next location based on historical and current trajectories.
- We proposed a new cooperative attention module and added it to traditional Transformer network to filter current trajectories based on historical ones, which is able to capture trajectory information from different representation subspaces at different positions.
- We evaluated our methods through extensive experiments on two public check-in real-world datasets. Experimental results demonstrate that acc@1 of our method improves nearly 4.79% and 9.62% than the state-of-the-art methods on the two datasets.

The rest of the paper is organized as follows. In Sect. 2, we introduce related work of pattern-based methods, model-based methods and Attention mechanism. Then our proposed method are detailed in Sect. 3. We conduct comparative experiments and perform extensive analysis of experimental results in Sect. 4. Finally, we introduce future work and conclude our paper in Sect. 5.

2   Related Work

2.1   Pattern-Based Methods

Pattern-based methods extract patterns (e.g., sequential patterns, frequent patterns) from the law of historical movements first, and then use them to predict the next location. Cheng et al. [1] focus on personalized point-of-interest (POI) recommendation in location-based service and fuse matrix factorization with geographical and social influence. WhereNext [8] is a classical pattern-based method, building a decision tree named T-pattern Tree, which is learned from the discovered patterns. The tree is then used to acquire the best matching path to predict the next location. Periodica [5] is another one classical pattern-based method. It uses reference spot to capture the reference location, and then uses a probability model to characterize the periodic behaviors. During the process of automatic pattern discovery, manual intervention is needed to judge effectiveness, which is time-consuming and inefficient.

2.2 Model-Based Methods

Model-based methods are introduced to tackle inherent problems of pattern-based methods, and obtain a better performance than pattern-based in general. Many methods have been proposed, such as hidden Markov models (HMM) [7] and Recurrent Neural Network (RNN) based models [2,6]. Hidden Markov Model (HMM) [7] is first used to model user's historical trajectories, and then we predict the next probable location by this trained HMM model. Meanwhile, a Spatial Temporal Recurrent Neural Networks model (ST-RNN) [6] is proposed to model the spatial and temporal contexts, and achieve the state-of-the-art results in the location prediction task. Until now, RNN-based methods are the most popular. Hence many scholars continue to improve the RNN-based method to get better results in recent years, such as, DeepMove [2] replaces basic RNN with more powerful GRU and extends GRU with attention mechanisms to get a higher performance. Although RNN is designed to tackle timing problem and performs well in sequence modeling, it is still weak and time-consuming in capturing long-range dependency due to its modeling and optimization mechanism.

2.3 Attention Mechanism

Attention mechanisms induce conditional distributions over hidden feature representation to compose a weighted normalized vector for feature importance evaluation. It is widely used in many fields, for examples, image classification, recommendation system, machine translation and location prediction. Armed with attention mechanism, deep learning models obtain a boosting performance and improvement on interpretability through visualizing attention matrix. For RNN-based model, attention mechanism strengthens the ability in capturing the long-range dependencies to some extent. Following the tremendous success of attention mechanism, several variant have been proposed. Among them, self-attention is extremely powerful in modeling the inherent relation between different elements in one sequence, making it suitable to perform feature combination and pattern exploration. Building on pure self-attention, Transformer [9] is firstly proposed to address the translation tasks in Natural Language Processing (NLP). In this paper, we adapt Transformer with cooperative attention module to model the mobility patterns in trajectory data.

3 Proposed Method

As shown in Fig. 1, Our method consists of two core parts, Spatial-Temporal Feature Disentangling and Attention-based Model. In former, we introduced a spatial-temporal feature disentangling module to enable Transformer network to capture spatial and temporal information from trajectories. In latter, we equipped pure attention-based Transformer network with cooperative attention module to acquire the internal and external historical and current patterns of mobility from different representation subspaces at different positions. Due to that we trained our method in an end-to-end manner, hand-crafting features are no longer needed.

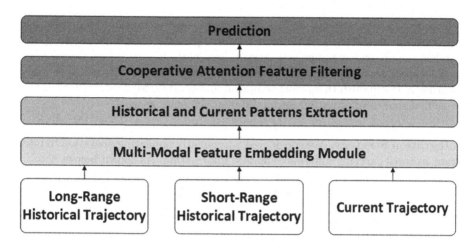

Fig. 1. Architecture of our model.

3.1 Spatial-Temporal Feature Disentangling

An embedding module is needed to transform high dimensional discrete raw features into low dimensional dense representation, which is more semantic expressing and computable. There are multiple factors that may exert influence on mobility transitions, such as exact time of day and location. It is necessary to integrate all these meaningful information together to describe target objects' movements. Therefore, we designed a spatial-temporal feature disentangling module to jointly embed the spatial-temporal features into dense representations.

Embedding Strategy. In RNN, the recurrence mechanism endows model with auto-regressive essence, making it naturally temporal perceptive. However, in pure attention-based Transformer, in order to make the model to use the order of the sequence, positional encoding is added to inject some information about the relative or absolute position of the token in the sentence. In vanilla Transformer, the positional encoding is designed as below:

$$PE_{(pos,2i)} = sin(pos/10000^{2i/d_{model}}) \tag{1}$$

$$PE_{(pos,2i+1)} = cos(pos/10000^{2i/d_{model}}) \tag{2}$$

where pos is the position and i is the dimension. d_{model} is the dimensionality of input and output. More details could be found in Transformer [9].

Considering spatial-temporal trajectories have natural time attribute which is more accurate to express the position of the input token, we replaced position encoding with temporal feature encoding in CABIN. The procedure of embedding temporal feature is as follows. Firstly, we divided temporal feature into two parts, workday and weekend. The workday is denoted as $\{0, 1, ..., 23\}$, and the weekend is denoted as $\{24, 25, ..., 47\}$. Secondly, we translated temporal feature into one-hot vectors. And finally, we mapped the high dimensional sparse one-hot vectors to low dimension dense representation.

The spatial information is the carrier of semantics in mobility of trajectories. In order to distinguish them from temporal information, we used another matrix to embed spatial information into a different semantic space.

Integration Strategy. We considered a frequently appearing operation to integrate features carrying different semantic information. As shown below:

$$x_{vanilla} = E_{spatial} + E_{temporal} \qquad (3)$$

the $E_{spatial}$ and $E_{temporal}$ separately denote the dense representation after embedding of spatial and temporal features. The "add" operation assumes that these two features have same dimension. However, this is not always the case. In location prediction problem settings, input features are specific in two aspects. 1) spatial and temporal information express different meanings, which makes it inappropriate to embed them into the same hidden space. 2) The capacity of semantic space that spatial and temporal information require is vastly different, because the range of temporal information is limited in a small number of positive integers.

Simply adding these two different embeddings may confuse the model and be harmful for further feature extraction. So here we replaced the "add" operation with the "concatenate" operation. As stated below:

$$x = Concat(E_{spatial}, E_{temporal}) \qquad (4)$$

3.2   Attention-Based Model

The original trajectories are divided into history ones and current ones. Seizing the patterns of mobility from trajectory data is the key to accurately predicting next location. Lots of state-of-the-art research try to equip RNN with single-head attention, which captures limited external relations between trajectories in a specific subspace at a specific position. To overcome the shortage, our method equipped pure attention-based Transformer network with cooperative attention module to seize the internal and external historical and current patterns of mobility from different representation subspaces at different positions.

Historical and Current Patterns Extraction. Transformer [9], a new network architecture, eschews recurrence and relies entirely on attention mechanism to draw global dependency between features in different positions. The most appealing strength of Transformer is that it breaks down the auto-regressive assumption to obtain the ability of highly parallel computation and one-hop feature correlation: input elements interact with each other simultaneously without regard to their distance. As a powerful model, Transformer is firstly designed to address the translation tasks in Natural Language Processing (NLP). Recently, it is proved that the architecture and capacity of Transformer makes it suitable to process massive data, such as images and videos. Considering that attention mechanism is suitable to catch internal and external spatial-temporal patterns of mobility, we designed our method based on Transformer with encoder-decoder architecture.

Each layer in Transformer Encoder module is composed of two sub-layers, multi-head self-attention mechanism (MA) and position-wise feed-forward network (FFN). And a residual connection is employed around each of the two sublayers, followed by layer normalization (LN). After N layer's feature extraction, we obtained the output O_{TE}^N as final historical pattern representations, here the right corner mark TE denotes the "Transformer Encoder".

Each layer in Transformer Decoder module is composed of three sub-layers, masked multi-head self-attention mechanism (MMA), multi-head self-attention mechanism (MA), and position-wise feed-forward network (FFN). Similar to Transformer encoder, a residual connection is employed around each of the two sublayers, followed by layer normalization (LN). The difference lies in the mask mechanism. The mask signal is designed to ensure that the prediction for current trajectory point depends only on previous trajectory points. After N layer's feature extraction, we obtained the output O_{TD}^N as final current pattern representations, here the right corner mark TD denotes the "Transformer Decoder".

Cooperative Attention Feature Filtering and Prediction. We designed a cooperative attention feature filtering module, which adapts multi-head attention, to effectively filter the current trajectory features with the historical spatial-temporal mobility pattern from different representation subspaces at different positions. Cooperative attention module regards the output of Transformer encoder, i.e. O_{TE}^N, as historical pattern representations, the output of Transformer decoder, i.e. O_{TD}^N as current movements representations.

The cooperative attention module is formulated as below:

$$MultiHead(Q, K, V) = Concat(head_1, ..., head_h)W^O \tag{5}$$

$$head_i = Attention(QW_i^Q, KW_i^K, VW_i^V) \tag{6}$$

$$Attention(Q, K, V) = softmax(\frac{QK^T}{\sqrt{d_k}})V \tag{7}$$

where h denotes the number of parallel attention layers, We got the historical patterns filtered by current features as below:

$$O_{CA} = MultiHead(O_{TE}^N, O_{TD}^N, O_{TD}^N) \tag{8}$$

where the right corner mark "CA" denotes "cooperative attention".

After multi-head attention module, we obtained the probability of each POI at next time under the given historical and current trajectory as below:

$$Prob = softmax(O_{CA}) \tag{9}$$

4   Experiments

We conducted a series of experiments and compared our method, CABIN, with LSTM, DeepMove, DeepMove* (a variety of DeepMove), and CABIN* (a variety of CABIN) on two public Foursquare check-in datasets.

4.1   Dataset

In our experiments, we followed the datasets, preprocessing of datasets and data splitter setting as same as previous related work as described in [2,4]. We evaluated our model on two public Foursquare check-in datasets [13], which is collected in New York (NYC) and Tokyo (TKY) from Foursquare API for about 10 months, ranging from Apr. 2012 to Feb. 2013. Each of them contains 8 columns of data (i.e. User ID, Venue ID, Venue category ID, Venue category name, Latitude, Longitude, Time zone offset in minutes and UTC time). Here we used former 3 columns because the others carry more textual information than spatial and temporal information. In this paper, we only considered modeling trajectory data and leave this textual information to our future work.

We segmented the original trajectories into several sessions based on the time interval between two neighbor records. We chose 72 h as the default time interval threshold. Further, we filtered out the sessions with record less than 5 and users with session less than 5. In following experiments, for each user, we take the first 80% check-in data as the training set, the other 20% data as the evaluation set. The overall statistics of original and processed datasets is shown in Table 1.

Table 1. The overall statistics of datasets.

Dataset	Type	Raw	Cleaned
NYC	Users	1083	935
	Locations	38333	13962
TKY	Users	2293	2108
	Locations	61858	21395

4.2   Baselines

To evaluate the performance of our method, we compared CABIN with several representative methods for location prediction:

- LSTM [3]: Long short-term memory is an adaptive version of vanilla recurrent neural network. Equipped with gated mechanism, LSTM is more effective in modeling longer sequence. It represents a class of auto-regressive methods.
- DeepMove [2]: It's a state-of-the-art method for next location prediction. It adapts the ST-RNN with a historical attention module.

- DeepMove*: It's a variety of DeepMove, replacing single attention module with multi-head attention.
- CABIN*: It's a variety of our method, discarding cooperative attention mechanism.

4.3 Analysis

Overall Performance. The overall performance comparison on two public check-in datasets evaluated by $acc@k, ADE@k$ are illustrated in Table 2.

Table 2. Results for NYC and TKY dataset. The results with the best performance are marked in bold.

Dataset	Method	acc@1	acc@5	acc@10	ADE@1	ADE@5	ADE@10
NYC	LSTM	0.1557	0.3432	0.4068	4760.1629	1589.4411	1054.3837
	DeepMove	0.1839	0.3959	0.4480	3780.7436	1156.7545	768.2902
	DeepMove*	0.1958	0.3981	0.4532	3722.8963	1149.0330	765.6733
	CABIN*	0.1970	0.4092	0.4699	3630.3077	1129.0954	728.4006
	CABIN	**0.2016**	**0.4103**	**0.4764**	**3584.3926**	**1081.0376**	**674.9032**
TKY	LSTM	0.1426	0.3024	0.3624	6108.5688	2556.6697	1799.951
	DeepMove	0.1565	0.3168	0.3772	6030.0399	2157.6815	1437.6740
	DeepMove*	0.1594	0.3235	0.3836	5915.9244	2109.9256	1383.7364
	CABIN*	0.1618	0.3337	0.3956	5893.2292	2090.1591	1371.0090
	CABIN	**0.1640**	**0.3339**	**0.3982**	**5868.6996**	**2071.2962**	**1363.8166**

We can see that **CABIN*** and **CABIN** both outperforms all baselines in all evaluation metrics. Moreover, compared with the state-of-the-art **DeepMove**, our method **CABIN** gains a relative performance of 9.62% acc@1 in NYC dataset, and 4.79% acc@1 in TKY dataset. From evaluation results, we can conclude that multi-head self-attention models and cooperative attention mechanism both give obvious advantage to our method. The former succeeds in capturing external and internal mobility patterns simultaneously, while the latter is able to draw global dependency between historical and current spatial-temporal information effectively. **CABIN*** has poor results compared to **CABIN**, which suggests that there cooperative attention mechanism indeed seizes the relation between historical and current spatial-temporal trajectories.

In general baselines, **DeepMove**, as an adaption of recurrent neural network, equipped with a single historical attention module, shows a boosting performance compared with a vanilla **LSTM**, which suggests that there indeed exists historical mobility periodicity and that attention mechanism can promote the performance in seizing spatial-temporal contexts. **DeepMove*** performs better than vanilla **DeepMove** in both two datasets due to the powerful ability of multi-head attention, which captures trajectory information from different representation subspaces at different positions.

Time Consumption The time consumption comparison results are presented in Table 3. We chose two frequently-used standards to evaluate the time consumption: 1) training time spent on every epoch. 2) the number of epoch when model converges.

Table 3. Time consumption of different methods. "evaluation" denotes evaluation standards. "time" denotes training time per epoch (min). "converge" denotes the number of epoch when model converges.

Dataset	Evaluation	LSTM	DeepMove	DeepMove*	CABIN*	CABIN
NYC	Time(min)	0.583	70.921	5.058	7.794	9.277
	Converge(epoch)	19	20	22	16	17
TKY	Time(min)	1.568	216.955	16.147	22.330	28.928
	Converge(epoch)	26	29	22	16	18

It is clear that **LSTM** has advantage of high training speed among all methods, this is because it is a simple model without encoder-decoder architecture and attention mechanism. **DeepMove** uses recurrent models with time-consuming point-wise product-based attention mechanism to model long trajectory sequence, resulting in an extremely slow training process and relatively slow convergence.

Compared with **DeepMove**, **CABIN** is much time-saving mainly due to replacing point-wise product-based attention with scaled dot-product based attention. To prove the aforementioned point, we carried out comparative experiment between **DeepMove** and **DeepMove***. The only difference between **DeepMove** and **DeepMove*** is that the former uses point-wise product-based attention, while the latter replaces it with multi-head attention based on scaled dot-product attention. And the **DeepMove*** has a sharp drop in time consumption compared with **DeepMove**.

We can also see that **CABIN** is nearly two times of time consumption compared with **DeepMove***, this is because **CABIN** uses more than one module armed with attention mechanisms. To prove the aforementioned point, we carried out comparative experiment between **CABIN** and **CABIN***. We can see **CABIN*** costs less time and epochs due to that it uses no cooperative-attention module compared to **CABIN**.

Feature Disentangling Module Analysis. To validate the rationality of our spatial-temporal feature disentangling module, we conducted experiments with vanilla feature embedding, whose feature embedding adopts positional encoding and "add" integration strategies. The results are shown in Table 4. We can see that the performance of our spatial-temporal feature disentangling module is almost the same to the vanilla feature embedding in both NYC and TKY datasets. We inferred that the reason of the phenomenon is that the regular loss of location prediction models focuses only on next location, ignoring the temporal

Table 4. Results for NYC and TKY dataset. The results with the best performance are marked in bold.

Dataset	Method	acc@1	acc@5	acc@10	ADE@1	ADE@5	ADE@10
NYC	Ours vanilla	0.2012	0.4002	0.4659	3585.1205	1120.7728	728.6527
	Ours	**0.2016**	**0.4103**	**0.4764**	**3584.3926**	**1081.0376**	**674.9032**
TKY	Ours vanilla	**0.1645**	0.3319	0.3927	5869.0309	2089.3468	1393.8850
	Ours	0.1640	**0.3339**	**0.3982**	**5868.6996**	**2071.2962**	**1363.8166**

information. Due to that, the spatial-temporal trajectory can be viewed from two aspects with no difference, one is original spatial-temporal sequence, the other is ordered temporal sequence. Our spatial-temporal feature disentangling module captures the inner relation of both spatial and temporal from the aspect of original spatial-temporal trajectory, while vanilla feature embedding module captures just temporal relations from the aspect of ordered temporal sequence.

In a nutshell, our method, **CABIN**, is far more efficient than **DeepMove**. Although it is not as far as **DeepMove*** in time consumption, it costs less epochs to reach a higher accuracy. What's more, the evaluation in two real-world datasets show that **CABIN** is with good robustness.

5   Conclusion

In this paper, we focused on next location prediction problem, which is of tremendous importance for advanced location-based services. We proposed CABIN, a novel Cooperative Attention Based location prediction network using Internal-External trajectory dependencies, which enjoys two novel characteristics compared to previous methods: 1) Cooperative attention module is able to capture trajectory information from different representation subspaces at different positions, which is better and faster than single point-wise product attention. 2) Our method predicts more accurately and efficiently than existing RNN-based methods proved by experimental results on real-world datasets.

Considering that the check-in data is relatively sparse, we plan to extend the problem into other area, such as datasets of dense trajectory like T-drive taxi datasets, to improve our method robustly.

Acknowledgment. This work is partially supported by NSFC No. 61902376 and NSFC No. 61702487. This work is also financially supported by National Key Research and Development Program of China No. 2018YFC1407400.

References

1. Cheng, C., Yang, H., King, I., Lyu, M.R.: Fused matrix factorization with geographical and social influence in location-based social networks. In: Proceedings of the Twenty-Sixth AAAI Conference on Artificial Intelligence, 22–26 July, Toronto, p. 2012. Canada, Ontario (2012)

2. Feng, J., et al.: Deepmove: predicting human mobility with attentional recurrent networks. In: Proceedings of the 2018 World Wide Web Conference on World Wide Web, WWW 2018, Lyon, France, 23–27 April 2018, pp. 1459–1468 (2018)

3. Graves, A.: Supervised sequence labelling with recurrent neural networks. Stud. Comput. Intell. Springer, **385** (2012)

4. Hang, M., Pytlarz, I., Neville, J.: Exploring student check-in behavior for improved point-of-interest prediction. In: Proceedings of the 24th ACM SIGKDD International Conference on Knowledge Discovery & Data Mining, KDD 2018, London, UK, 19–23 August 2018, pp. 321–330 (2018)

5. Li, Z., Ding, B., Han, J., Kays, R., Nye, P.: Mining periodic behaviors for moving objects. In: Proceedings of the 16th ACM SIGKDD International Conference on Knowledge Discovery and Data Mining, Washington, DC, USA, 25–28 July 2010, pp. 1099–1108 (2010)

6. Liu, Q., Wu, S., Wang, L., Tan, T.: Predicting the next location: a recurrent model with spatial and temporal contexts. In: Proceedings of the Thirtieth AAAI Conference on Artificial Intelligence, 12–17 February 2016, Phoenix, Arizona, USA, pp. 194–200 (2016)

7. Mathew, W., Raposo, R., Martins, B.: Predicting future locations with hidden Markov models. In: The 2012 ACM Conference on Ubiquitous Computing, Ubicomp '12, Pittsburgh, PA, USA, 5–8 September 2012, pp. 911–918 (2012)

8. Monreale, A., Pinelli, F., Trasarti, R., Giannotti, F.: Wherenext: a location predictor on trajectory pattern mining. In: Proceedings of the 15th ACM SIGKDD International Conference on Knowledge Discovery and Data Mining, Paris, France, June 28 - July 1 2009, pp. 637–646 (2009)

9. Vaswani, A., Shazeer, N., Parmar, N., Uszkoreit, J., Jones, L., Gomez, A.N., Kaiser, L., Polosukhin, I.: Attention is all you need. In: Advances in Neural Information Processing Systems 30: Annual Conference on Neural Information Processing Systems 2017, 4–9 December 2017, Long Beach, CA, USA, pp. 5998–6008 (2017)

10. Wang, F., Xu, Y., Zhang, H., Zhang, Y., Zhu, L.: 2flip: a two-factor lightweight privacy-preserving authentication scheme for VANET. IEEE Trans. Veh. Technol. **65**(2), 896–911 (2016)

11. Wang, F., Xu, Y., Zhu, L., Du, X., Guizani, M.: LAMANCO: a lightweight anonymous mutual authentication scheme for n -times computing offloading in iot. IEEE Internet Things J. **6**(3), 4462–4471 (2019)

12. Wu, R., Luo, G., Shao, J., Tian, L., Peng, C.: Location prediction on trajectory data: a review. Big Data Min. Analytics **1**(2), 108–127 (2018)

13. Yang, D., Zhang, D., Zheng, V.W., Yu, Z.: Modeling user activity preference by leveraging user spatial temporal characteristics in LBSNs. IEEE Trans. Syst. Man Cybern. Syst. **45**(1), 129–142 (2015)

Neuro-Genetic Visuomotor Architecture for Robotic Grasping

Matthias Kerzel[(✉)], Josua Spisak, Erik Strahl, and Stefan Wermter

Knowledge Technology, Department of Informatics, University of Hamburg,
Hamburg, Germany
{kerzel,6spisak,strahl,wermter}@informatik.uni-hamburg.de
http://www.knowledge-technology.info,
https://www.inf.uni-hamburg.de/en/inst/ab/wtm/

Abstract. We present a novel, hybrid neuro-genetic visuomotor architecture for object grasping on a humanoid robot. The approach combines the state-of-the-art object detector RetinaNet, a neural network-based coordinate transformation and a genetic-algorithm-based inverse kinematics solver. We claim that a hybrid neural architecture can utilise the advantages of neural and genetic approaches: while the neural components accurately locate objects in the robot's three-dimensional reference frame, the genetic algorithm allows reliable motor control for the humanoid, despite its complex kinematics. The modular design enables independent training and evaluation of the components. We show that the additive error of the coordinate transformation and inverse kinematics solver is appropriate for a robotic grasping task. We additionally contribute a novel spatial-oversampling approach for training the neural coordinate transformation that overcomes the known issue of neural networks with extrapolation beyond training data and the extension of the genetic inverse kinematics solver with numerical fine-tuning. The grasping approach was realised and evaluated on the humanoid robot platform NICO in a simulation environment.

Keywords: Bio-inspired visuomotor learning · Neuro-robotic models · Genetic algorithms · Hybrid neural networks

1 Introduction

We present a novel neuro-genetic architecture for robotic grasping with a humanoid platform. The architecture, depicted in Fig. 1, leverages the strength of two different bio-inspired approaches (neural networks and genetic algorithms) in a modular architecture that allows developing, training and evaluating each module independently. The architecture addresses the challenge that neural end-to-end approaches for learning a direct mapping from visual input to motor commands become challenging to analyse with increasing task complexity. In case of

The authors gratefully acknowledge partial support from the German Research Foundation DFG under project CML (TRR 169).

I. Farkaš et al. (Eds.): ICANN 2020, LNCS 12397, pp. 533–545, 2020.
https://doi.org/10.1007/978-3-030-61616-8_43

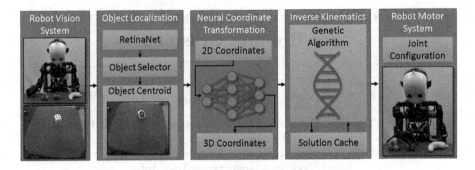

Fig. 1. Hybrid neuro-genetic visuomotor architecture.

a failed grasp, there are competing error hypothesis: 1) the object was not recognised or located incorrectly in the visual input; 2) the object's location in the two-dimensional visual input is not correctly transformed into the robot's three-dimensional reference frame and 3) the inverse kinematics computation failed to compute the suitable joint configuration to reach for the object. Our proposed neuro-genetic architecture complements previous work on end-to-end visuomotor learning [8,10] by allowing to analyse and monitor each of these steps separately and thus affording explainability and transparency. The proposed architecture consists of three modules: two neural modules localise a graspable object in the robot's field of view and transform the position of the object in the robot's two-dimensional camera image into three-dimensional coordinates. A third module based on a genetic algorithm computes a joint configuration for grasping the object.

The *object localisation* uses the neural object detection network RetinaNet [14] with a ResNet50 backbone pre-trained on ImageNet. The architecture is a fast and reliable single-stage image detector that achieves state-of-the-art results on the COCO dataset. RetinaNet outputs bounding boxes of objects. In a scene with multiple objects, an object selector submodule selects the object to be grasped based on the object classifications.

The neural *coordinate transformation* module transforms the position of the centroid of the target object in the robot's camera image to a 3d coordinate in the robot's reference frame. The architecture is based on a multi-layer perceptron. We introduce a novel spatial-oversampling method to improve transformation accuracy by compensating known issues of neural networks with extrapolation beyond known data points [20].

The *inverse kinematics* (IK) solver transforms the 3d-coordinates into a joint configuration using a combination of a genetic algorithm and a numerical approach. Especially for humanoid robots, genetic IK solvers have advantages over classical approaches. Humanoid robots, do not have the classical 6-DOF-design of industrial robots but mimic the joint limits of humans. Genetik IK solvers can handle these constraints better than classical approaches. The constraints lead to unreachable positions, where a genetic IK can compute a best-possible solution [19] which we further optimise with gradient-based Sequential Least SQuares Programming. The novel architecture offers separate and well-controllable training and evaluation options: The object detector is trained on a large, existing image dataset while the coordinate transformation is trained with data from a virtual environment. We implemented and evaluated the approach on the humanoid robot NICO [9] in the V-REP[1] simulation environment, see Fig. 4.

Our main contributions are 1) A neuro-genetic visuomotor architecture that combines the advantages of neural and genetic approaches. 2) A novel spatial-oversampling method that overcomes inaccuracies in neural networks for spatial visuomotor tasks caused by extrapolation beyond known data points.

2   Background and Related Work

2.1   Visuomotor Frameworks for Object Grasping

Visuomotor frameworks for object grasping solve three subtasks: they locate an object in the sensory input of the robot, transform this location to the reference frame of the robot and solve the inverse kinematic calculation to enable the robot to reach for the object. Classical frameworks consist of independent modules, often applying analytical solutions to coordinate transformations, which require accurate localisation of the robot and the object in a common reference frame, e.g., [12]. Neural approaches utilise different learning strategies ranging from supervised end-to-end learning [10,13] to deep reinforcement learning, see [16] for an overview. Many Approaches take inspiration from biology and human development, e.g., [7]. However, these systems are difficult to analyse [8]. In contrast to approaches that employ an evolutionary algorithm to optimise a visuomotor neural network [18], our system uses a neural network and an evolutionary algorithm in separate modules, allowing easier analysis of each module.

2.2   Neural Object Detectors

Object detectors locate and classify objects in an image. Two-stage architectures [5] use one network to generate region proposals and a second network to classify these proposals. To reduce redundant computations, single-stage models realise proposal generation and classification with a shared network [17], called backbone. Retinanet [14] uses a deep residual network (Resnet [6]) and a Feature Pyramid Network (FPN) for this purpose. The Resnet's feature maps are connected to regression and classification subnetworks that output object bounding boxes and class labels.

---

[1] https://www.coppeliarobotics.com/.

2.3 Inverse Kinematics Solvers

Once an object is located in the robot's reference frame, the visuomotor framework calculates an inverse kinematics solution, a joint configuration that moves the end effector of a robotic arm into a grasping pose. While analytical solutions are feasible for a low number of degrees of freedom (DoFs), numerical methods are often used to solve the inverse kinematics for industrial arms and robots. Most commonly, iterative models, like the Jacobian approach, are applied [1]. Humanoid robots with constrained joints can not reach all possible poses. In this case, iterative models tend to follow the gradient into local minima, resulting in suboptimal outcomes. Purely neural approaches can overcome this issue, but require a large amount of training data and can suffer from relatively high errors. Daya et al. [3] attributes this to the non-linearity of the robotic kinematic systems. Köker et al. [11] combine neural and genetic approaches to overcome this issue. Genetic and particle-swarm algorithms use a pool of IK solutions that are iteratively improved by random changes (mutation) and exchange of partial solutions (crossing over). These algorithms are well-suited to find the best possible solution in a given time for a humanoid robot [19].

3 Methodology

The neuro-genetic visuomotor architecture consists of three main modules, as shown in Fig. 1. 1) the *Object Localisation* is realised with the neural object detector RetinaNet [14]; in case of multiple detected objects, the *Object Selector* arbitrates which object to grasp. 2) The *Neural Coordinate Transformation* generates the robot-centric 3d-coordinates based on the position of the detected object in the visual input. 3) Finally, the *Inverse Kinematics* generates a joint configuration to move the robot's hand to the 3d-coordinates and into a grasping position that is then executed by the robot's motor system.

3.1 Object Localisation

RetinaNet [14] with a ResNet-50 backbone pretrained on the Imagenet dataset is used for object detection. The network takes RGB images as input and outputs bounding boxes and classifications for found objects. A Keras implementation[2] is used. In the case of multiple objects in the robot's visual input, an *Object Selector* arbitrates between objects based on the objects' class labels. From the bounding box of the selected object, the centroid is computed.

3.2 Neural Coordinate Transformation and Spatial Oversampling

The *Coordinate Transformation* is a multi-layer perceptron (MLP) that regresses from the 2d-coordinates of the object's centroid in the robot's visual input to 3d-coordinates in the robot's reference frame. Both the two input and the three

---

[2] https://github.com/fizyr/keras-retinanet.

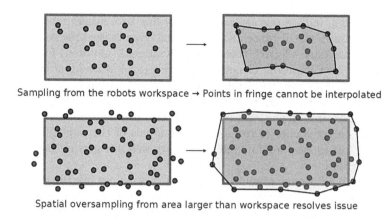

Sampling from the robots workspace → Points in fringe cannot be interpolated

Spatial oversampling from area larger than workspace resolves issue

Fig. 2. Top: When only using samples from the workspace of the robot to train a neural network for coordinate transformation, there are areas of the workspace that require extrapolation from known samples, which can cause inaccuracies. Bottom: By using training samples from beyond the robot's workspace (spatial oversampling), larger parts of the workspace can be covered by interpolation.

output coordinates are scaled to the range of $[-1, 1]$. The hyperparameters of the architecture result from automated hyperparameter optimisation. The input layer is followed by three dense layers with 30 units. The ReLU activation function is used for the hidden layers and the sigmoid function for the output layer. We developed a novel spatial oversampling strategy for training the *Coordinate Transformation*. Neural networks excel at interpolating between known data points, but they can not reliably extrapolate beyond these points [20]. This issue causes problems when training a neural network with randomly sampled points from a robot's workspace: random sampling will not completely cover the outer areas of the workspace and lead to inaccuracies of the trained model. However, by extending the sampling area beyond the workspace, a larger part of the workspace can be covered, as shown in Fig. 2. The module is trained independently of the object detector; its training pairs of 2d and 3d-coordinates are generated in a simulation environment where exceeding the robot's workspace can easily be realised.

3.3   Genetic Inverse Kinematics Solver

Genetic algorithms model the evolutionary selection process on a population of individuals, modelled by their chromosomes [15]. Chromosomes can be affected by mutations, some individuals can become an elite and get special treatment, and there are niches of populations, which are isolated from the rest. All these principles are implemented in the genetic inverse kinematics solver. Each chromosome represents a joint configuration of the robot's arm. In each iteration of the algorithm, individuals are ranked according to a fitness function. In our case, this measures the distance and orientation error toward the goal pose. The fittest individuals are selected; their randomly altered (mutated) form the population of the next iteration. Genetic algorithms excel at avoiding local minima but lack an effective way to further optimise into these minima. For this purpose, we use gradient-based Sequential Least SQuares Programming (SLSQP) to minimise the error on the local minima. As this is computationally expensive, we optimise only the elite of the n-best individuals of the population. SLSQP tends to get lost in local minima but works very well if it gets initialised via the genetic algorithm.

To take full advantage of multiple processing cores, we use the genetic niche concept, running one evolutionary niche on every available CPU, like on an isolated island. This uses multiple cores effectively as there is minimal management overhead.

4   Experiments and Results

The evaluation leverages one of the main advantages of the modular architecture; each module can be analysed separately. We report the evaluation of the neural *Coordinate Transformation* with a focus on the effect of the spatial oversampling strategy and the *Genetic Inverse Kinematics Solver*. For the object detector RetinaNet [14], we refer to the results published by Lin et al. and assume that objects on a non-cluttered desk can be correctly classified and localised.

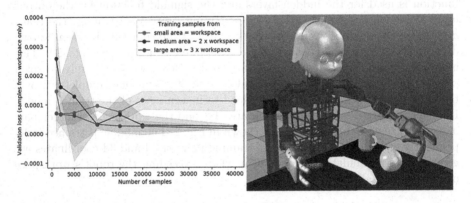

Fig. 3. Left: Validation loss computed on the actual workspace of the robot for different sampling areas and dataset sizes. Right: NICO in a virtual training environment.

4.1   Experimental Setup: NICO Robot and Simulation Environment

Our approach is realised and evaluated on a virtual version of NICO, the Neuro Inspired COmpanion [9], a child-sized humanoid. We use the V-REP environment with a physics engine shown in Fig. 3, where NICO is seated at a children's desk with several objects in its 40 × 60 cm workspace. In contrast to previous work [4,8,10], where end-to-end grasping approaches were realised on the physical NICO by using its ability to place the training object, we chose a virtual environment as the spatial oversampling can be realised more efficiently. Moreover, our architecture allows a fully decoupled training of the vision component (trained on real-world images) from the coordinate transformer (trained in a virtual environment), avoiding the so-called sim-to-real gap. To gather the training data for the coordinate transformer, a visually salient grasping object is moved through NICO's workspace and the extended workspaces, respectively. The object's 3d position, as well as a visual image from the perspective of the robot, is recorded. As the grasping object has a clear contrast to the background, a simple colour-based object detector is used to determine the centroid of the object in the visual image for purposes of gathering training data.

4.2   Neural Coordinate Transformation

The *Neural Coordinate Transformation* creates a link between the vision and the motoric modules by transforming the position of an object in the visual input to 3d-coordinates. Extrapolation beyond known data points can be problematic for neural networks. Preliminary experiments show that despite a good overall accuracy, the points at the fringes of the workspace are pulled towards the centre, as shown in Fig. 4 To address this systematic bias, samples from outside the robot's workspace were used. While the workspace is limited to an area of 40 × 60 cm, two different spatial oversampling strategies were evaluated by sampling from wider areas of about two and three times the original workspace. Forty thousand samples were collected from each area.

Hyperparameter Optimisation. Hyperparameters were optimised independently for all three sampling conditions using Hyperopt [2]. Samples from each area were split into 75% training and 25% validation data. Table 1 shows the ranges and results for the parameters: number of layers (2 or 3), optimiser (adadelta or adam with learning rates 0.01,0.001 and 0.0001), neurons per layer (20, 30 or 40), dropout (0 or 0.2), batch size (5, 10 and 15) and the number of epochs (100, 150 and 200). While the hyperparameter optimisation was performed for all three sampling areas independently, the validation loss was calculated only for samples from the robot's actual workspace area for all three networks. The resulting hyperparameters are shown in Table 1. Optimisation was performed for 100 trials for each condition. We notice that the larger areas have a lower learning rate and use three layers instead of two.

Spatial Oversampling Comparison and Evaluation. All sampling strategies were evaluated with individually optimised hyperparameters. Figure 3 shows averaged results for 1000 to 40000 samples taken from the original workspace and the two larger areas. Each experiment was repeated with ten-fold cross-validation with a split of 90% test and 10% validation data. The validation loss is computed on the actual workspace of the robot (60 cm × 40 cm) for all

Table 1. Hyperparameter optimisation: range of parameters and results for all three area sizes. *The learning rate was only adjusted for the adam optimiser.

Hyperparameter	Range	Large area	Medium area	Small area
Batch size	5, 10, 25	10	5	15
Dropout	0, 0.2	0	0	0
Learning rate*	0.01, 0.001, 0.0001	0.001	0.001	0.01
Optimiser	adam, adadelta	adam	adam	adam
Number of layers	2, 3	3	3	2
Units per layer	20, 30, 40	30	40	40
number of epochs	100, 150, 200	200	100	200

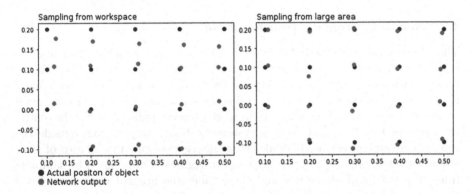

Fig. 4. Actual (blue) and computed (red) positions by the neural coordinate transformation in NICO's 60 cm × 40 cm workspace. Left: The best model trained with samples from the workspace. Points near the fringe converge towards the middle. Right: The best model trained with spatial oversampling from a three-times larger area. (Color figure online)

sampling areas and dataset sizes. One could assume that using only samples only from this workspace, against which the model is validated, yielded the best result. However, we observe that at 5000 samples, taking more samples from the original workspace stops to improve the result. Instead of using samples from outside the workspace (spatial oversampling) results in a lower loss. The best averaged MSE over ten trials of 1.55E−05 (SD 5.07E−06) is achieved with 40000 samples from the largest area, which is negligible for the grasping task.

4.3   Genetic IK

Based on previous work [10] we estimate the accuracy that NICO requires for grasping: we define errors in position < 10 mm and errors in orientation with a sum of < 20° as a successful trial. This accuracy range is sufficient for grasping, as the robot's hand has an opening of around 40 mm. As we limited the joints on

NICO for human-like movements, the genetic IK needs larger populations and larger numbers of generations, causing possible run time issues. However, good Human-Robot Interaction requires a result in a time that enables interaction; we used the options of 1 s, 2.5 s and 4 s with the hyperparameters optimised for these time constraints. The algorithm has run on a Linux server with an Intel Xeon CPU E5–2630, v4 by 2.20 GHz with a maximum use of 8 cores. On a Dell laptop with an Intel i7-9750H CPU, we see very similar running times, so the running time is representative for standard pc environments. Storing past solutions in a cache and ending the calculations after the specified accuracy is reached can further speed up the algorithm.

Table 2. Optimised hyperparameters for genetic algorithm for different time goals. TPE optimiser, 1000 trials

Time goal	Range	1s goal	2.5s goal	4s goal
Population size	4–50	4	8	4
Number of generations	4–50	4	4	16
Number of elites	1–8	2	2	2
Mutation rate	0–1	0.18	0.36	0.36
Orientation weight	0–1	0.516	0.449	0.27
Max. iterations (SLSQP)	10–1000	880	820	740

Hyperparameter Optimisation. The hyper-parameters (population size, number of generations, mutation rate, number of elites) were optimised to ensure a balance of run time and accuracy using a Tree Parzen Estimator (TPE) with the goal to deliver the results 1) with a position error of less than 10 mm and 2) with an additive orientation error of fewer than 20° (0.349 rad) and 3) and appropriate computing time. We optimised for the three variants 1, 2.5 and 4 s to compare the results. The calculation times are all adequate for Human-Robot Interaction, but a lower value would enhance the robot's responsiveness in a Human-Robot Interaction scenario. Table 2 shows the standard parameters for population size, number of generations, number of elites, mutation rate, orientation weight and the maximum number or SLSQP iterations. Furthermore, the orientation weight, which controls the ratio in the fitness function between position accuracy and orientation accuracy. In the results of the hyper-optimisation, we see that the population size and the number of generations are the main factors to decrease computing times; nonetheless, different strategies are possible. For the 2.5 s goal, the optimiser locked in for a high population and a low number of generations, while it went for a high number of generations strategy for the four seconds goal.

Table 3. Results of three different hyperparamter sets tuned for running times of 1 s, 2.5 s, 4, an pure SLSQP optimisation and finetuned hyperparameters

Algorithm and parameter set	ga(1s)	ga(2.5s)	ga(4s)	SLSQP
Position error (m) (mean)	2.778×10^{-4}	1.627×10^{-4}	2.161×10^{-5}	1.557×10^{-3}
Orientation error (rad) (mean)	1.507×10^{-1}	1.077×10^{-1}	8.912×10^{-2}	5.47×10^{-1}
Time (s) (mean)	0.817	1.72	2.91	0.241
Error rate	0.115	0.078	0.057	0.528

Evaluation. We generated 1000 samples with the forward kinematics in the robot's workspace on the table to ensure all generated positions are reachable. With these samples, we tested our three different parameter sets for a calculation goal time of 1 s, 2.5. and 4 s. Furthermore, an optimisation using the SLSQP without the genetic algorithm (max of 100000 iterations). Table 3 shows the results. The more calculation time is invested for the genetic algorithm, the better the accuracy. The results for the SLSQP show that the optimiser performs poorly without the genetic algorithm.

We choose a compromise between speed and accuracy with the 2.5 s model (average calculation time 1.72 s). Figure 5 shows the position errors, orientation errors, and the calculation time for this parameter set. The red lines mark our success definitions. Figure 6 shows a visualisation of the position and orientation rotation errors depending on the position in the workspace. While the position accuracy is relatively uniform with some patches of higher error near the fringes, the orientation accuracy improves in the top right area while it decreases in the lower-left area. We attribute this tendency to the kinematics of the robot. While its hand can reach all positions in the workspace, it can not do so everywhere with the desired rotation, which increases the difficulty of finding solutions in these areas.

4.4   Discussion on the Hybrid Neuro-Genetic Approach

Comparing the results from the neural coordinate transformation and the genetic inverse kinematics solver, we see two tendencies: The neural approach's accuracy diminishes towards the fringes of the workspace. This error can, however, be mostly be compensated through spatial oversampling. In contrast, the orientation accuracy of the inverse kinematics solver changes along a diagonal axis, which we attribute to the kinematic constraints of the robot. This detailed analysis is possible because of the modular nature of the architecture. In a neural end-to-end learning approach, an alternative hypothesis, which we can rule out, would be an imbalance in the training data, with more or better samples towards the upper right region.

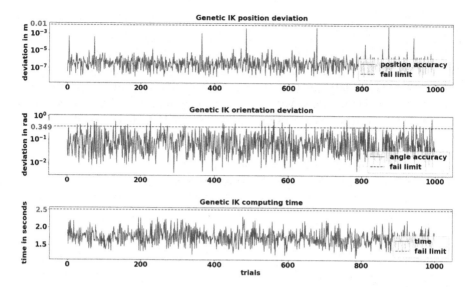

Fig. 5. Position error, orientation error and running time for 1000 random positions in the robot's workspace on the table.

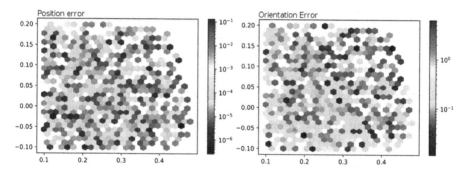

Fig. 6. Position (left) and orientation (right) error of the genetic inverse kinematics solver in relation to the position in the robot's workspace. The orientation errors are higher in the lower-left area.

5   Conclusion

Our main contribution is a neuro-genetic visuomotor architecture for robotic grasping that leverages the strength of neural networks while compensating their possible shortcomings through hybridisation with a genetic algorithm. While neural networks excel at object detection and, due to spatial oversampling, also achieve good results on coordinate transformation, a genetic inverse kinematics solver in combination with a numerical optimisation is used to address the inaccuracy of neural approaches for humanoid kinematics. The modularity of the architecture allows attributing inaccuracies to different modules and, in our case, to the robot's human-like joint angle limitation. An added advantage of the decoupled neural modules is that the object detector can use pretrained models or existing datasets, while the coordinate transformation is trained in simulation. We also contribute a novel spatial oversampling method that avoids extrapolation beyond known data points for the spatial task of coordinate transformation, thus increasing the accuracy. We evaluate the neural coordinate transformation and the genetic inverse kinematics solver in a simulation environment; in future work, we will implement the architecture on a physical robotic platform and compare its performance to related approaches. We show that our novel neuro-genetic architecture combines the advantages of the two approaches and yields an additive error that is appropriate for robotic grasping.

References

1. Aristidou, A., Lasenby, J.: Inverse kinematics: a review of existing techniques and introduction of a new fast iterative solver. Technical report. Cambridge University Engineering Department (2009)
2. Bergstra, J., Yamins, D., Cox, D.: Making a science of model search: hyperparameter optimization in hundreds of dimensions for vision architectures. In: 30th International Conference on Machine Learning (ICML 2013), pp. 115–123 (2013)
3. Daya, B., Khawandi, S., Akoum, M.: Applying neural network architecture for inverse kinematics problem in robotics. J. Softw. Eng. Appl. 3(03), 230 (2010)
4. Eppe, M., Kerzel, M., Griffiths, S., Ng, H.G., Wermter, S.: Combining deep learning for visuomotor coordination with object identification to realize a high-level interface for robot object-picking. In: IEEE-RAS International Conference on Humanoid Robots (Humanoids), pp. 612–617 (2017)
5. Girshick, R., Donahue, J., Darrell, T., Malik, J.: Rich feature hierarchies for accurate object detection and semantic segmentation. In: IEEE Conference on Computer Vision and Pattern Recognition, pp. 580–587 (2014)
6. He, K., Zhang, X., Ren, S., Sun, J.: Deep residual learning for image recognition. In: Proceedings of the IEEE Conference on Computer Vision and Pattern Recognition, pp. 770–778 (2016)
7. Jamone, L., Natale, L., Nori, F., Metta, G., Sandini, G.: Autonomous online learning of reaching behavior in a humanoid robot. Int. J. Humanoid Rob. 9(03), 1250017 (2012)
8. Kerzel, M., Eppe, M., Heinrich, S., Abawi, F., Wermter, S.: Neurocognitive shared visuomotor network for end-to-end learning of object identification, localization and grasping on a humanoid. In: Proceedings of the 9th Joint IEEE International Conference on Development and Learning and on Epigenetic Robotics (ICDL-EpiRob), pp. 19–24, September 2019
9. Kerzel, M., Strahl, E., Magg, S., Navarro-Guerrero, N., Heinrich, S., Wermter, S.: NICO - Neuro-Inspired COmpanion: a developmental humanoid robot platform for multimodal interaction. In: IEEE International Symposium on Robot and Human Interactive Communication (RO-MAN), pp. 113–120. IEEE (2017)
10. Darvishi Boloorani, A., Samany, N.N., Mirzaei, S., Bahrami, H.A., Alavipanah, S.K.: Remote sensing and GIS for dust storm studies in Iraq. In: Al-Quraishi, A.M.F., Negm, A.M. (eds.) Environmental Remote Sensing and GIS in Iraq. SW, pp. 333–375. Springer, Cham (2020). https://doi.org/10.1007/978-3-030-21344-2_14

11. Köker, R.: A genetic algorithm approach to a neural-network-based inverse kinematics solution of robotic manipulators based on error minimization. Inf. Sci. **222**, 528–543 (2013)
12. Leitner, J., Harding, S., Förster, A., Corke, P.: A modular software framework for eye-hand coordination in humanoid robots. Front. Robot. AI **3**, 26 (2016)
13. Levine, S., Finn, C., Darrell, T., Abbeel, P.: End-to-end training of deep visuomotor policies. J. Mach. Learn. Res. **17**(1), 1334–1373 (2016)
14. Lin, T.Y., Goyal, P., Girshick, R.B., He, K., Dollár, P.: Focal loss for dense object detection. In: 2017 IEEE International Conference on Computer Vision (ICCV), pp. 2999–3007 (2017)
15. Marsland, S.: Machine Learning: An Algorithmic Perspective, 2nd edn. Chapman & Hall/CRC, United States (2014)
16. Quillen, D., Jang, E., Nachum, O., Finn, C., Ibarz, J., Levine, S.: Deep reinforcement learning for vision-based robotic grasping: a simulated comparative evaluation of off-policy methods. In: 2018 IEEE International Conference on Robotics and Automation (ICRA), pp. 6284–6291. IEEE (2018)
17. Ren, S., He, K., Girshick, R., Sun, J.: Faster R-CNN: towards real-time object detection with region proposal networks. In: Advances in Neural Information Processing Systems, pp. 91–99 (2015)
18. Savastano, P., Nolfi, S.: A robotic model of reaching and grasping development. IEEE Trans. Auton. Mental Dev. **5**(4), 326–336 (2013)
19. Starke, S., Hendrich, N., Magg, S., Zhang, J.: An efficient hybridization of genetic algorithms and particle swarm optimization for inverse kinematics. In: 2016 IEEE International Conference on Robotics and Biomimetics (ROBIO), pp. 1782–1789. IEEE (2016)
20. Trask, A., Hill, F., Reed, S.E., Rae, J., Dyer, C., Blunsom, P.: Neural arithmetic logic units. In: Advances in Neural Information Processing Systems, pp. 8035–8044 (2018)

From Geometries to Contact Graphs

Martin Meier[(✉)], Robert Haschke, and Helge J. Ritter

Neuroinformatics Group, CITEC, Bielefeld University, Bielefeld, Germany
{mmeier,rhaschke,helge}@techfak.uni-bielefeld.de

Abstract. When a robot perceives its environment, it is not only important to know what kind of objects are present in it, but also how they
relate to each other. For example in a cleanup task in a cluttered environment, a sensible strategy is to pick the objects with the least contacts
to other objects first, to minimize the chance of unwanted movements
not related to the current picking action. Estimating object contacts in
cluttered scenes only based on passive observation is a complex problem.
To tackle this problem, we present a deep neural network that learns
physically stable object relations directly from geometric features. The
learned relations are encoded as contact graphs between the objects. To
facilitate training of the network, we generated a rich, publicly available
dataset consisting of more than 25000 unique contact scenes, by utilizing
a physics simulation. Different deep architectures have been evaluated
and the final architecture, which shows good results in reconstructing
contact graphs, is evaluated quantitatively and qualitatively.

Keywords: Physical reasoning · Graph generation · Robotics

1 Introduction

Having knowledge about the relations of objects is important for everyday activities. For example, when taking a plate from a stack of dishes, we intuitively pick
the one that is on top of the stack, since it has only contact with one of the
other objects in the stack. This, for humans intuitive, knowledge is also crucial
in the robotic domain when manipulation actions have to be planned and carried
out. One way of specifying this knowledge that allows to infer relations between
objects and their mutual contacts is in terms of a contact graph. To generate
a contact graph, two major strategies can be distinguished. Either an agent
actively explores its environment, for example by pushing objects around and
track changes in their movements, or passively by capturing a snapshot of the
environment and using an analysis pipeline to extract contact information based
on rules. In this setting, the snapshot would be, for example, a 3D point cloud
from a depth sensor. This point cloud needs to be further processed to extract

The research reported in this paper has been supported by the German Research
Foundation DFG, as part of Collaborative Research Center 1320 "EASE - Everyday
Activity Science and Engineering". The research was conducted in subproject R05.

© Springer Nature Switzerland AG 2020
I. Farkaš et al. (Eds.): ICANN 2020, LNCS 12397, pp. 546–555, 2020.
https://doi.org/10.1007/978-3-030-61616-8_44

segments from it, which in turn have to be fitted to object models, to finally infer contact information from these objects by reproducing them in a virtual environment, e.g. a physics simulation, and extract their mutual contacts from the simulation. Alternatively, object hypotheses can also be generated by means of a neural network [11].

By creating a contact graph from object geometries and a set of predefined rules the work presented in [10] follows the latter, rule based line of approaches to generate a contact graph. They propose a formalism to generate motion plans from a sequence of transitions in this graph. Rosman and Ramamoorthy [13] used SVMs to segment point clouds into objects based on geometric separability and generated rule based relations between these objects. In [1], the authors pursue the idea of active exploration. They use contact graphs to plan planar pushing actions of a robot to arrange boxes in a desired pattern. Here the contact graph is constructed by letting the robot actively move the boxes around and register contacts between them. The work presented in [15] used a learned representation of contact events in a manipulation sequence that was carried out by human demonstrators and successfully applied it to a real robot.

Exploiting relational properties of data has recently been of major interest in the machine learning and robotics community. The authors in [4] used graphs constructed from spatial relations between objects in a classification task to predict actions performed by humans. The input graphs here are constructed based on prior knowledge. In [6], the authors used the graph structure in the underlying datasets with graph convolutional layers to facilitate semi supervised classification. They were able to outperform different graph clustering methods. The model presented in [2] introduced the term of interaction networks. These networks are able to predict future states in a 2D physics simulation by learning from object properties an their physical relations expressed in graph structures. By using the kinematic tree of different robots directly as an input graph to a network, the authors in [14] were able to learn physics based controllers for different robots. Exploiting the underlying graph structure of data also gained interest in the area of activity recognition. In [17], a networks was presented which is able to reconstruct the relations between different team members in a game of volleyball from video sequences. Here, the prediction of the relations is formulated by optimizing multiple cross entropies to obtain the most probable relations. The work in [12] internally uses a graph structure to keep track of activity descriptions over time when trying to estimate when and where in a video an actions has taken place.

In this paper, we present a neural network that is able to infer complex contact graphs only from geometric properties of physically stable object configurations. This extends rule-based approaches such as [10,13], that rely on geometry alone, e.g. without considering the embedding in a physical situation with gravity and friction. We include such physical information through the way our training data set is generated, relying on the power of deep neural nets to implicitly extract the resulting correlations between physics and geometry for constructing accurate contact predictions. In our setting, we do not have a-priori knowledge of the underlying graph structure, but we want to predict it given physical realistic geometric object configurations. We decided on an approach similar to [17], to let the network generate contact hypotheses. To this end, we created a novel dataset[1] of physically realistic object relations and corresponding contact graphs and evaluated different network architectures to facilitate contact graph generation from single examples.

Since one of the most tedious tasks when generating a dataset is acquiring high quality label information, we will describe our approach to automatically generate object relations and corresponding contact graphs in the following section. After that we lay out the design decisions for the network architectures we chose and evaluate them.

2   Data Generation and Preprocessing

To generate a sufficiently large dataset for training a neural network and also to obtain ground truth data, we employed the open source robot simulation gazebo [7]. The goal of our network is to realize a mapping:

$$\hat{\mathbf{A}} = f(\mathbf{F}, \theta) \tag{1}$$

where θ denote the network weights, $\mathbf{F}$ is a $n \times d$ matrix of input features (cf. below) and $\hat{\mathbf{A}}$ an estimate of the true contact graph $\mathbf{A}$, represented in the form of an undirected binary adjacency matrix of size $n \times n$ to accommodate contacts between up to n objects ($n = 10$ in our simulations).

To this end, we randomly generated scenes which contain between six and ten objects. Each scene is generated as the result of a physical process, modeling how an initially random configuration of physical objects above a planar support surface ("ground") comes to rest under its natural dynamics and the influence of gravity. Therefore, each of these objects is initialized with a randomized 6D position in space and random size along its x, y and z dimension. Mean and upper/lower bound of the uniformly distributed initialization values are shown in Table 1. We chose a smaller z dimension compared to x and y to assure that one dimension is small enough to be easily graspable by a robotic manipulator, so that the dataset could possibly be used in future experiments. Having one smaller dimension is also a common feature in most household objects, for example books or various kind of storage boxes for food. The friction between the simulated objects is set to a rather high value in simulation, a real world analogy would be bricks made of clay, to facilitate reaching a stable state in a shorter period of time by reducing unwanted sliding motions. The density of each object is also set to a value similar to bricks with $2\frac{g}{cm^3}$.

It is important to note that the objects are initialized above the ground and in a consecutive fashion to prevent an overlap of objects during initialization. If two objects are initialized in an overlapping or penetrating state, physics simulators

---

[1] Dataset is available at https://pub.uni-bielefeld.de/record/2943056.

Table 1. Mean and upper/lower bound of the uniformly distributed initialization parameter of generated objects. Position and size are in meters while the orientation is given in Euler xyz angles.

Property	X	Y	Z
Position	$0.0 \pm 0.1\,\mathbf{m}$	$0.0 \pm 0.1\,\mathbf{m}$	$0.4 \pm 0.1\,\mathbf{m}$
Orientation	$\pi \pm \pi\,\mathbf{rad}$	$0.0 \pm 0.1\,\mathbf{rad}$	$\pi \pm \pi\,\mathbf{rad}$
Size	$0.25 \pm 0.15\,\mathbf{m}$	$0.125 \pm 0.05\,\mathbf{m}$	$0.05 \pm 0.01\,\mathbf{m}$

tend to estimate extremely high forces and the simulated scene has a high chance to "explode", being in an unrecoverable state afterwards.

To obtain a stable state in the simulation, after initializing the objects, we let the simulation run for 15 s at a rate of 1000 simulation steps/second and evaluated the object movements afterwards. If the center of none of the objects moves further than $0.1\,mm$ in any direction within 100 simulation steps, we recorded ten simulation steps consisting of object locations and contact pairs between objects. These contact pairs were accumulated over the ten simulation steps. Accumulating contacts over multiple steps was necessary due to unstable contacts generated by the simulation. An example for a stable configuration, e.g. no object is moving, of ten objects is shown in Fig. 1. Although the objects are not moving, not all contacts are recognized during all time steps, for example the contact between object two and six is not present in each of the four consecutive frames of the simulation shown in Fig. 1. This is due to the technique of simulation engines to add small noise internally to all object states, to avoid running into numerical instabilities. Recording ten consecutive steps proved to be sufficient to collect all contact pairs between objects. We ran simulations for nearly a week and were able to gather 25116 samples of training data, consisting of object locations and their pairwise contacts.

From the recorded samples of contacts, we generate the binary object adjacency matrices $\mathbf{A}$ by checking if there exists a contact for a given object pair within the recorded ten simulation steps. If this is the case, we set the corresponding element in the adjacency matrix to 1, 0 otherwise. Contacts between objects and the ground plane in the simulation were omitted, since most of the objects have contacts with the ground and these connections would be over represented compared to object-object contacts.

As our object features we used shape (3D elongation along x, y, z object edges), spatial position (3D) and orientation (represented as quaternions with 4 parameters). By having at most ten objects, we obtain a 10×10 feature matrix $\mathbf{F}$ consisting of object features × the number of objects. Since we generated the scenes with a varying number of objects, rows with a higher row index have a higher probability to consist only of zeroes. To circumvent this bias and to augment the dataset, we applied random permutations to the rows of the feature matrix $\mathbf{F}$ and the same permutations to the rows and columns of the corresponding adjacency matrix $\mathbf{A}$, to preserve the symmetry of $\mathbf{A}$. We applied

32 permutations to each pair $\{\mathbf{F}, \mathbf{A}\}$ which, together with the original pair, leads to a total of 828828 training samples.

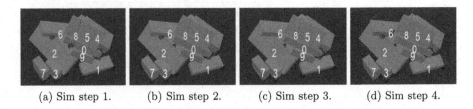

(a) Sim step 1.   (b) Sim step 2.   (c) Sim step 3.   (d) Sim step 4.

Fig. 1. Contacts calculated by the physics simulation for a stable configuration of ten objects. Contacts between objects are depicted as blue spheres. During four consecutive simulation steps, not always the same contacts are calculated. This is due to numerical instabilities and added noise by the simulation engine.

3   Learning Contact Relations

The goal of this work is to learn a mapping from a set of physical object configurations to a binary adjacency matrix that indicates their mutual contacts. To this end, the natural idea is to express our learning problem as a multi-label classification task and use binary cross entropy

$$\mathcal{L}(\mathbf{A}, \hat{\mathbf{A}}) = -\frac{1}{n * n} \sum_{i=1}^{n} \sum_{j=1}^{n} (a_{ij} \log \hat{a}_{ij} + (1 - a_{ij}) \log(1 - \hat{a}_{ij})) \qquad (2)$$

as loss function, where a_{ij} are the elements of $\mathbf{A}$ and $\hat{a}_{ij}$ are the elements of the predicted adjacency matrix $\hat{\mathbf{A}}$. We also investigated using Focal Loss [8] and reconstruction with *mean squared error* as losses, but these did not lead to better results than binary cross entropy, details are in the next section.

Since our generated dataset contains, on average, 20% positive entries in the adjacency matrices while the remaining 80% entries are zero, it is not sensible to use a straightforward accuracy metric to evaluate our model, because the dataset is not sufficiently balanced. Therefore, we are using the *Area under the ROC curve* (AUC) as metric in the following evaluation [3]. Here, *ROC* is the receiver operating characteristic, which is defined by the ratio of the true positive rate to the true negative rate of a classifier.

To obtain a network architecture which is able to reconstruct an adjacency matrix from our dataset and to ensure it learns some kind of dense representation, we performed a reverse ablation study. Since we have a 100 dimensional output with sigmoid activation to match the binary cross entropy loss, we want the second to last layer to contain less neurons than the output, to facilitate the learning of a denser representation than the original input. We started with a single hidden layer with 64 neurons and ReLU (rectified linear unit) activation, and successively added hidden layers of increasing size with ReLU activation to the model, while keeping the 64 unit layer always as the second to last layer, to enforce the learning of a dense representation in this layer. The final reconstruction of the adjacency matrix from the last layer is done by applying a threshold of 0.5 to the output of the sigmoid units, to obtain binary values. Since our dataset contains more than 800k samples, we followed the idea to increase the batch size instead of decreasing the learning rate [16], to facilitate faster training. Starting from a batch size of 64, we double the batch size every 20 epochs up to a final batch size of 2048. All trainings have been carried out using the Adam optimizer [5]. From the 800k samples, 20% were kept from training to perform the evaluation. Table 2 shows the seven deep architectures we tested. The table is read column wise. For example, if the network has four hidden layers, the first hidden layer has 192 ReLU units and the network achieved a final AUC score of 0.8425. As can be seen in the table, the AUC score increases with each additional hidden layer until it reaches a plateau at five hidden layers. We therefore decided to do a thorough evaluation on a network with five hidden layers with 256-192-128-96-64 units.

Table 2. Evaluation of different deep architectures. The table is read column wise. For example, a network with three hidden layers has the architecture of input-128-96-64-output and a validation AUC score of 0.8164 after training.

# hidden layers	1	2	3	4	5	6	7
Units in first hidden layer	64	96	128	192	256	384	512
AUC score		0.6623	0.7393	0.8146	0.8425	0.8629	0.8653	0.8647

4   Evaluation

We evaluated the selected model in a 5-fold cross validation. The AUC score reaches a final value of $\mu = 0.8564, \sigma = 0.007$, with a minimum of 0.8495 and a maximum of 0.8709, the training progress is shown in Fig. 2. The increase in AUC score reaches a plateau around epoch 60, where the batch size is increased to 512. As a comparison, using focal loss with these settings leads to a final AUC score of 0.7719. This could be due to the fact that focal loss is tailored towards shaping the underlying binary cross entropy towards rewarding very rare occurring features, which could be too extreme in the dataset at hand. Using mean squared error as the loss function leads to a final AUC score of 0.8146.

We further evaluated the impact of our dataset augmentation to the achievable AUC score. To this end, we started with the original dataset and successively doubled the number of permuted samples, which are added to the training set. The results are shown in Table 3. Here we can see that the augmentation proves to be beneficial for the task. Especially the comparison of no permutation to one

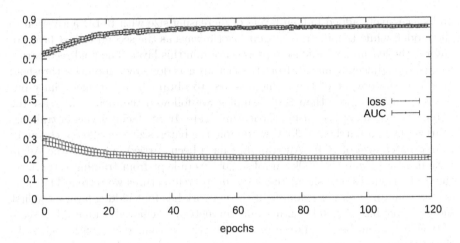

Fig. 2. Results of a 5-fold cross validation using the proposed model from Sect. 3. Starting from an initial batch size of 64, the batch size is doubled every 20 epochs. The values shown are mean and standard deviation for AUC score and loss at the end of each epoch, for the evaluation sets of the five runs.

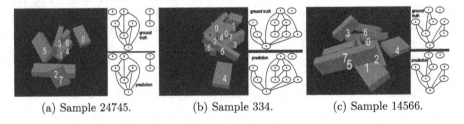

(a) Sample 24745.   (b) Sample 334.   (c) Sample 14566.

Fig. 3. Example scenes from the dataset where our network achieved perfect results. Each panel shows a screenshot of the scene and the corresponding contact graphs.

is a strong hint that it is important to permute the feature matrices to reduce the bias which originates from possible empty feature vectors. Also in this case, the gain from adding more permutations becomes neglectable around 64 permutations, which is a good indicator that our chosen settings of 32 is a good trade-off between training duration and achieved AUC score. To get a qualitative insight into the results of our trained model, we randomly selected successful reconstructions of contact graphs and the corresponding scenes from our dataset as well as reconstructions that partially failed, i.e. contain missing or wrong links between objects. The successful reconstructions are shown in Fig. 3. Here the prediction contact graph always matches the ground truth. The partially failed examples are shown in Fig. 4. Here it can be seen that our model has problems with corner to surface contacts, for example between objects 7 and 0 in the left panel, 8 and 7 in the center panel and 7 and 9 in the rightmost panel. Also, edge to surface contacts seem to be slightly over estimated in some cases, there is a

Table 3. Evaluation of the dataset augmentation in terms of added permutations to the dataset. The initial increase in performance is compelling in the lower numbers of permutations but reaches a plateau around 64, using the proposed network architecture.

Permutations	0	1	2	4	8	16	32	64	128	256
AUC score	0.6647	0.7503	0.7693	0.7805	0.8177	0.8253	0.8511	0.8532	0.8534	0.8506

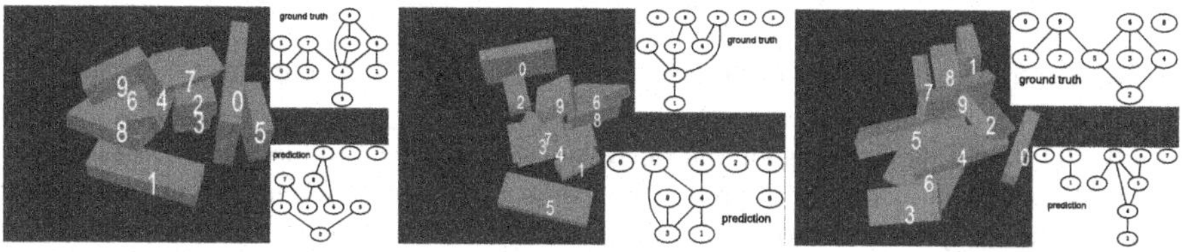

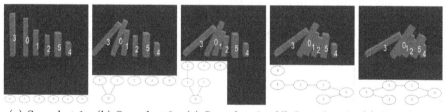

    (a) Sample 23710.   (b) Sample 414.   (c) Sample 327.

Fig. 4. Example scenes from the dataset where our network partially failed to reconstruct the contact graph. In the top right of each panel, the ground truth contact graph is shown. The reconstruction is in the lower right. For discussion please refer to the text.

  (a) Snapshot 1. (b) Snapshot 2. (c) Snapshot 3. (d) Snapshot 4. (e) Snapshot 5.

Fig. 5. Example for a manually constructed "domino" sequence. In the beginning, six objects are arranged in a straight line. The leftmost object is tilted to initiate tipping over the other objects. The corresponding contact graph generated by our neural network is shown at the bottom of each panel.

non existing contact added between object 8 and 1 in the rightmost panel and between object 5 and 4 in the central panel.

We further investigated the behavior of our model in a successively changing simulation. To this end, we manually constructed a scene that resembles a domino effect, as shown in Fig. 5. We pushed the leftmost box to tip over the remaining five boxes and took snapshots of the object poses when other blocks started to fall over. The resulting contact graphs are shown at the bottom of each panel. The graphs represent the sequence of the blocks contacting their neighbors and create a chain that connects all blocks, eventually.

Additionally, we investigated the activations in the last hidden layer in our network. Figure 6 shows the same TSNE [9] embedding of activations for each sample in our dataset, colored with respect to two different properties in our

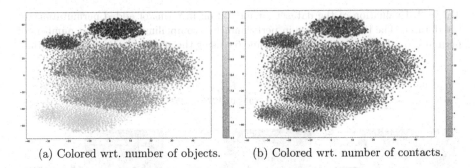

(a) Colored wrt. number of objects.   (b) Colored wrt. number of contacts.

Fig. 6. 2D TSNE embedding of the activations in the last hidden layer. This figure shows the same embedding colored with respect to two different properties of our dataset. The left panel is colored based on the number of objects in the input feature while the right panel is colored wrt. the number of contacts in the input feature.

dataset. In the left panel, the embedded activations are colored according to the number of objects in the input feature. Here clear clusters are visible, where the yellow color at the bottom of the figure indicates six objects in the input while the dark blue at the top indicates ten objects.

The right panel is colored according to the number of contacts in the output contact graphs. Here only a slight tendency is visible, the lighter coloring at the bottom indicates less contacts. This correlates with the number of objects in the left panel, since samples with less objects have a tendency to also have less contacts.

5   Conclusion

We considered the task of predicting contact graphs from object configurations through a deep neural network and presented a dataset which represents rich physical contact situations. We compared network architectures of different depths for solving this task, considering it as a multi-label classification task from geometric object features to the elements of an adjacency matrix that describes the contact graph. We showed that for the resulting, unbalanced multi-label classification task with our dataset, an optimization based on binary cross entropy is superior to least squares or focal loss in term of the respective AUC score and present typical examples and TSNE embeddings to provide some insight into the properties of the network solution. The used input representation is well tailored to become part of a point cloud processing pipeline leading from a depth map of a cluttered arrangement of 3D objects to a high-level contact representation of their physical configuration. Such a pipeline can enable a recording of rich contact episodes and help to guide every day manual actions of robots in unstructured environments.

References

1. Anders, A.S., Kaelbling, L.P., Lozano-Perez, T.: Reliably arranging objects in uncertain domains. In: 2018 IEEE International Conference on Robotics and Automation (ICRA), pp. 1603–1610. IEEE (2018)
2. Battaglia, P., et al.: Interaction networks for learning about objects, relations and physics. In: Advances in neural information processing systems, pp. 4502–4510 (2016)
3. Chawla, N.V.: Data mining for imbalanced datasets: an overview. In: Maimon O., Rokach L. (eds) Data Mining and Knowledge Discovery Handbook. pp. 875–886. Springer, Boston, MA (2009). https://doi.org/10.1007/978-0-387-09823-4_45
4. Dreher, C.R., Wächter, M., Asfour, T.: Learning object-action relations from bimanual human demonstration using graph networks. IEEE Robot. Autom. Lett. 5(1), 187–194 (2019)
5. Kingma, D.P., Ba, J.: Adam: a method for stochastic optimization. arXiv preprint arXiv:1412.6980 (2014)
6. Kipf, T.N., Welling, M.: Semi-supervised classification with graph convolutional networks. arXiv preprint arXiv:1609.02907 (2016)
7. Koenig, N., Howard, A.: Design and use paradigms for gazebo, an open-source multi-robot simulator. In: 2004 IEEE/RSJ International Conference on Intelligent Robots and Systems (IROS). 3, pp. 2149–2154. IEEE (2004)
8. Lin, T.Y., Goyal, P., Girshick, R., He, K., Dollár, P.: Focal loss for dense object detection. In: Proceedings of the IEEE international conference on computer vision, pp. 2980–2988 (2017)
9. Maaten, L., Hinton, G.: Visualizing data using t-SNE. J. Mach. Learn. Res. 9(Nov), 2579–2605 (2008)
10. Najafi, E., Shah, A., Lopes, G.A.: Robot contact language for manipulation planning. IEEE/ASME Trans. Mechatron. 23(3), 1171–1181 (2018)
11. Qi, C.R., Yi, L., Su, H., Guibas, L.J.: Pointnet++: deep hierarchical feature learning on point sets in a metric space. In: Advances in neural information processing systems, pp. 5099–5108 (2017)
12. Rashid, M., Kjellstrom, H., Lee, Y.J.: Action graphs: weakly-supervised action localization with graph convolution networks. In: The IEEE Winter Conference on Applications of Computer Vision, pp. 615–624 (2020)
13. Rosman, B., Ramamoorthy, S.: Learning spatial relationships between objects. Int. J. Robot. Res. 30(11), 1328–1342 (2011)
14. Sanchez-Gonzalez, A., et al.: Graph networks as learnable physics engines for inference and control. In: International Conference on Machine Learning, pp. 4470–4479 (2018)
15. Scherzinger, S., Roennau, A., Dillmann, R.: Contact skill imitation learning for robot-independent assembly programming. In: IEEE International Conference on Intelligent Robots and Systems, pp. 4309–4316. IEEE (2019)
16. Smith, S.L., Kindermans, P.J., Ying, C., Le, Q.V.: Don't decay the learning rate, increase the batch size. arXiv preprint arXiv:1711.00489 (2017)
17. Wu, J., Wang, L., Wang, L., Guo, J., Wu, G.: Learning actor relation graphs for group activity recognition. In: Proceedings of the IEEE Conference on Computer Vision and Pattern Recognition, pp. 9964–9974. IEEE (2019)

Sentiment Classification

Structural Position Network for Aspect-Based Sentiment Classification

Pu Song[1,2], Wei Jiang[3], Fuqing Zhu[1(✉)], Yan Zhou[1,2], Jizhong Han[1], and Songlin Hu[1,2]

[1] Institute of Information Engineering, Chinese Academy of Sciences, Beijing, China
{songpu,zhufuqing,zhouyan,hanjizhong,husonglin}@iie.ac.cn
[2] School of Cyber Security, University of Chinese Academy of Sciences, Beijing, China
[3] Department of Energy Internet, State Grid Corporation of China, Beijing, China
wei-jiang@sgcc.com.cn

Abstract. Aspect-based sentiment classification aims to discriminate the polarity of each aspect term for a given sentence. Previous works mainly focus on sequential modeling and aspect representations. However, the syntactical information and relative structural position of aspect in sentence are neglected, resulting in some irrelevant contextual words as clues during the identification process of aspect sentiment. This paper proposes a structural position network (SPNet) based on bidirectional long short-term memory (LSTM) for further integrating syntactical information. Specifically, we first utilize the dependency tree to represent the grammatical structure of the aspect in sentence. Then, a structural weighted-layer is applied after LSTM. In this situation, the syntactically relevant context is formulated. Besides, the sequential position is combined to reduce the impact of noise caused by imperfect grammatical analysis tools. SPNet not only significantly improves the ability of encoding syntactical information and word dependencies, but also provides a tailor-made representation for different aspect in a sentence. On three public ABSC datasets, SPNet produces a competitive performance compared with some existing state-of-the-art methods.

Keywords: Aspect-based sentiment classification · Structural position · Noise

1 Introduction

Aspect-based (also mentioned as "aspect-level" or "target-based" in some works) sentiment classification (ABSC) aims to discriminate the polarity of each aspect term for a given sentence. The input of ABSC task is a sentence with several given aspects, while the output is a multi-way sentimental classes (*i.e.*, negative, neutral, or positive) on each aspect. For example, in the sentence "*Great **food** but the **service** was dreadful!*", there are two aspect term, "**food**" and "**service**". The sentiment polarities are *positive* and *negative*, respectively.

© Springer Nature Switzerland AG 2020
I. Farkaš et al. (Eds.): ICANN 2020, LNCS 12397, pp. 559–570, 2020.
https://doi.org/10.1007/978-3-030-61616-8_45

Fig. 1. The examples of position encoding and noise. Aspect of a) is "**waiting**", the b) is "**food**". Marks of green are relative descriptors to "**waiting**", the reds are noise (not all listed) to "**food**".

The main challenge of ABSC is the relationship capture between aspect term and context. Ever since attention mechanism is successfully applied to machine translation [14], recurrent neural network (RNN) based model with attention mechanism has become dominant in ABSC. For example, attention based RNN is utilized in [1,6,13,21,25,27] for measuring the relatedness between aspect and sentence, providing a significant performance.

However, several researches have pointed out that the sequential structure may exist some limitations for hierarchically structured natural language [8,18,19,24], especially in ABSC task. Some works [1,11,12] hold a imperfect idea that opinion word with closer sequential position is more likely to be the actual descriptor of the aspect. For example, in "*The food$_{pos}$ is so good and so popular that waiting$_{neg}$ can really be a nightmare.*", the first aspect "food" will benefit from closer "*good*". While another term "**waiting**" may ignore the further but relevant opinion word "*nightmare*", resulting an incorrectly predicting of *positive* due to closer "*popular*". It has been argued that attention mechanism is not a ideal method to tackle the problem of sequential modeling in [22,26].

It seems to be imperative of exploiting syntactical information for modeling word dependencies. Figure 1 a) shows that the sentiment of "**waiting**" could be easily recognized by the corresponding governor in dependency tree. Indeed, there has been several exploring and attempts. The attention score is weighted by syntactical constraints in [5], while graph convolutional network (GCN) [9] is built over dependency tree to enhance the representation of aspect term in [26]. Nevertheless, both of above strategies do not overcome the drawbacks of sequential modeling. **And most importantly, the noise caused by parsing tools or the limitations of dependency grammar is amplified in the models containing hard-coded dependency-tree, and has not received enough attention.** We can observe from Fig. 1 b), the aspect "food" has two descriptors with *one* structural distance, "*great*" and "*dreadful*", but "*dreadful*" is related to "service". Therefore, the noise of dependency tree parsed by automated tools is an additional interference for predicting "**food**".

To tackle the two problems mentioned above, a structural position network (SPNet) is proposed based on bidirectional long short-term memory (Bi-LSTM). Specifically, SPNet firstly encodes relative structural position to inputs rather than hard coding into framework. The inputs about word dependencies are exploited to obtain the distance of context in parsing tree by Bi-LSTM, further generating the sentence representations with rich syntactical information. In order to reduce the impact of noise caused by grammatical analysis, the sequential position information, which is the natural order of sentence, is also encoded to combine with structural position. As shown in Fig. 1 b), if the sequential position is considered, model will quickly exclude the distant *"dreadful"* of *four* positions and capture the *"great"* of *one* positions for aspect **"food"**. Therefore, sequential position is well suitable for complementing structural position.

Then, a structural-weighted layer is adopted following Bi-LSTM for attention mechanism to capture the syntactical constraints more accurately. The reutilization of structural information will make the model give priority to structural position of context. The model would utilize the sequential position to distinguish the sentiment polarity only if there are several opinion words with different sentiment which have the same distance in dependency tree. Finally, SoftMax function is adopted on the output of attention-layer to predict sentiment polarity for the given aspect.

The main contributions of this paper are summarized as below:

- A well-designed network based on Bi-LSTM is proposed to integrate the structural and sequential position information into sentence representations, further modeling the hierarchical structure of sentence and enhancing the robustness of the model.
- A structural weighted layer is designed to further make use of structural information, avoiding the model getting caught up in structure and sequence conflicts.
- The proposed embedding strategy of structure is scalable for some other sequence based framework (*e.g.*, RAM [1] and PBAN [4]). Experimental results demonstrate the effectiveness and scalability.

2 Methodology

In this section, we will describe the proposed SPNet in detail. The overview of SPNet architecture is shown in Fig. 2. The input is a pair of sentence and aspect term, while the output is sentiment class of the aspect term. The set of sentiment labels is {*positive, neural, negative*}.

2.1 Embedding

The embedding of aspect and sentence are encoded separately. Our sentence embedding consists of three-fold (*i.e.*, lexical feature, syntactic structure and sequential position), as shown in the left bottom of Fig. 2. Lexical feature is the pre-trained general embedding, denoted as $G = (g_1, ..., g_n), g_i \in \mathbb{R}^{d_g}$. Syntactic structure is represented by relative structural position of words in dependency tree to aspect term. While the aspect embedding is only composed of general embedding, denoted as $A = (a_1, ..., a_t)$, where t is the length of aspect term.

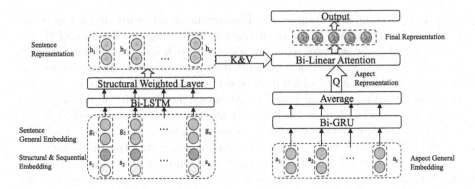

Fig. 2. The overview of the proposed SPNet architecture.

Calculation of Structural Position and Sequential Position. Inspired by the position encoding used in [4,24], we define a structural index sequence illustrated in Fig. 1. We can observe from Fig. 1 b), for the sentence *"Great **food** but the **service** was dreadful"*, the relative structural position of context for "**food**" is $st = [1, 0, 3, 3, 2, 1]$. However, for the aspect "**service**", the relative structural position of context is $st = [3, 2, 2, 0, 2, 1]$. Let the index of current aspect term be "0", and the others are set to the shortest path length in dependency tree to current aspect.

Sequential position can be calculated by the following equation. Suppose that the location of aspect is from j to $j + t$, where t is the length of aspect. The illustration has been shown in Fig. 1.

$$seq_i = \begin{cases} j - i & \text{if } i < j, \\ 0 & \text{if } j \le i < j + t, \\ i - j - t + 1 & \text{if } j + t \le i. \end{cases} \tag{1}$$

The two sequences of structural position st and sequential position seq will be transformed to continuous representations by looking up from the corresponding embedding matrixes $\mathbf{W}^{st} \in \mathbb{R}^{d_{st} \times n}$ and $\mathbf{W}^{seq} \in \mathbb{R}^{d_{seq} \times n}$, respectively. Here, we employ d_{st} and d_{seq} as the denotations of structural and sequential embedding dimension, respectively. And "n" is the max length of sentence. Matrixes $\mathbf{W}^{st}$ and $\mathbf{W}^{seq}$ are initialized randomly and updated during training.

Sentence Embedding. The sentence embedding is obtained as follows:

$$E = [G; \ st \otimes \mathbf{W}^{st}; \ seq \otimes \mathbf{W}^{seq}], \tag{2}$$

where $\otimes$ denotes the "looking-up" operation, and ";" denotes vector concatenation. After the two kinds of position indexes are encoded to embedding, the embedding could be exploited to model the hierarchical structure of sentence without too much noise. As shown in Fig. 1, the embedding could not only recognize the correct descriptors *"nightmare"* for **"waiting"** by closer structural position, but also could distinguish out the noise *"dreadful"* for **"good"** by distant sequential position.

2.2   Word Representation

We use a Bi-LSTM to extract the features of contexts from the sentence embedding which contains structural and sequential information. The hidden state $h_i^* \in \mathbb{R}^{2d_h}$ is calculated as follows:

$$h_i^* = [\overrightarrow{LSTM}(e_i); \; \overleftarrow{LSTM}(e_i)], i \in [1, n], \tag{3}$$

where $e_i \in \mathbb{R}^{d_g + d_{st} + d_{seq}}$ denotes the embedding of words in sentence.

Structural Weighted Layer. The model benefits from the embedding with structural and sequential positions, while the conflicts between structure and sequence cannot be handled. To tackle this problem, a structural weighted layer is designed between Bi-LSTM and attention layer. The vectors generated by Bi-LSTM are edited to exploit syntactic information besides structural embedding again. Specifically, if the word is closer to aspect, its vector will multiply a higher coefficient. The distance between aspect and word is defined to the shortest path length in dependency tree. This intuitive measure can make the model pay more attention on structural information. The priority strategy adopted by model is that sequential position should be utilized to distinguish the sentiment polarity only if there are opposite opinion words which have the same distance to current aspect in dependency tree.

Precisely, the weight coefficient w_i of st_i length and structural-weighted vector h_i are respectively calculated as follows:

$$w_i = 1 - \frac{st_i}{n}, \; i \in [1, n], \tag{4}$$

$$h_i = [w_i \cdot h_i^*; \; \frac{st_i}{n}], \; i \in [1, n], \tag{5}$$

where n is the length of sentence. $h_i \in \mathbb{R}^{2d_h+1}$ is the final structural weighted vector. Inspired by [1], h_i also concatenate $\frac{st_i}{n}$ to the tail of representation for memorizing the weight coefficient of each word. The h_i vectors will be transferred to attention layer as key K and value V.

Aspect Representation. Aspect term embedding is fed into the bidirectional gated recurrent unit (Bi-GRU) [2] to exact the feature of current aspect, which is calculated as follow:

$$h_i^a = [\overrightarrow{GRU}(e_i); \; \overleftarrow{GRU}(e_i)], \; i \in [1, n], \; h_i^a \in \mathbb{R}^{2d_h}. \tag{6}$$

The reason of choosing GRU but not LSTM for extracting aspect is that GRU with fewer parameters converges more easily for short aspect. Then, the final representation of aspect is calculated by the following formula:

$$\overline{h^a} = \frac{\sum_{i=1}^{n} h_i^a}{n}, \ \overline{h^a} \in \mathbb{R}^{2d_h}. \tag{7}$$

The aspect representation $\overline{h^a}$ is applied as a query Q for the attention layer, as shown in the right middle of Fig. 2.

2.3   Bi-linear Attention

An attention layer is adopted to calculate the final representation $fr \in \mathbb{R}^{2d_h+1}$ of the input pair (sentence, aspect) as follows:

$$fr = \sum_{i=1}^{n} \alpha_i h_i, \tag{8}$$

where α_i is the score of context word i for current aspect. The α_i is calculated by following:

$$\alpha_i = SoftMax(\tanh(h_i^T \mathbf{W}_m \overline{h^a} + b_m)), \tag{9}$$

where $\mathbf{W}_m \in \mathbb{R}^{(2d_h+1) \times 2d_h}$ is the weight matrixes and b_m is the bias.

2.4   Output and Model Training

Finally, we feed the fr to a non-linear layer, and compute the probability distribution as follows:

$$\hat{y} = SoftMax(\mathbf{W}_z(\tanh(\mathbf{W}_r fr + b_r)) + b_z), \tag{10}$$

where $\mathbf{W}_z \in \mathbb{R}^{2d_h \times |C|}$ and $\mathbf{W}_r \in \mathbb{R}^{2d_h \times (2d_h+1)}$ are the weight matrixes, $|C|$ is the total number of labels in sentiment set (i.e., 3in our experiment), b_r and b_z are the bias terms, and $\hat{y} \in \mathbb{R}^{|C|}$ is the probability distribution of labels.

The model is trained in the supervised learning by minimizing loss function term as much as possible. In this paper, we employ the cross-entropy loss function with a l_2 regularization listed as follows:

$$L(\theta) = -\sum_{i}^{D} y_i \log \hat{y}_i + \frac{\lambda}{2}||\theta||^2, \tag{11}$$

where λ is regularization hyper-parameter, θ denotes all the parameters, D is the training set, y is the ground truth and $\hat{y}$ is the probability distribution of labels.

Table 1. Statistics of the three datasets.

Datasets		#Positive	#Neural	#Negative	Total
LAPTOP(L)	Train	994	464	870	2,328
	Test	341	169	128	638
REST(R)	Train	2,164	637	807	3,608
	Test	728	196	196	1,120
TWITTER(T)	Train	1,561	3,127	1,560	6,248
	Test	173	346	173	692

3 Experiment

3.1 Datasets

The proposed SPNet model is evaluated on three benchmark datasets as shown in Table 1. The first two datasets (LAPTOP and REST) are from SemEval 2014 [17], containing the reviews of the laptop and restaurant domain, respectively. A few examples labeled the "conflict" are removed from datasets as same as [1]. The third dataset (TWITTER) contains the tweets built by [3]. All datasets are three-way (*i.e.*, negative, neutral, or positive) classification data.

3.2 Experimental Settings and Evaluation Protocol

We initialize the general embedding by GloVe vectors (300-dim) [16]. To reduce the risk of over-fitting, dropout with 0.1 probability is applied on the ultimate representation fr. The hidden states dimension d_h is set to 200. The hyper-parameters d_{st} and d_{sep} are both 50. We employ the cross-entropy loss function with a l_2 regularization whose λ is equal to 10^{-5}. Adam with the learning rate 0.001 is adopted to update the parameters. We adopt accuracy (Acc) and macro-f1 (F1) as the evaluation protocol in our experiments.

3.3 Baselines

We compare the proposed SPNet model with several typical or state-of-the-art methods, listed as below:

- **MemNet** [21]: Multiple attention layers are stacked over the word embedding for selecting more abstractive evidences from the context. And the output vector in last attention layer is used to predict the sentiment polarities.
- **RAM** [1]: GRU is utilized to connect multiple layers of attention, where each layer contains the aggregation of previous representation, contexts and aspect features.
- **AOA** [6]: The attention score is calculated by attention-over-attention method inspired by the strategy in machine translation community.

566   P. Song et al.

Table 2. Experimental results (%) comparisons on three datasets. The results with symbol "*" are obtained from the paper of ASGCN-DT, others are reproduced by ourselves. The bold is the best performance comparing with baselines.

Models		LAPTOP		REST		TWITTER	
		Acc	F1	Acc	F1	Acc	F1
Baselines	MemNet*	70.64	65.17	79.61	69.64	71.48	69.90
	RAM	74.06	70.05	80.42	70.52	70.81	69.00
	AOA*	72.62	67.52	79.97	70.42	72.30	70.20
	PBAN	74.55	71.68	81.05	71.33	71.75	69.40
	TNet-LF*	74.61	70.14	80.42	71.03	72.98	71.43
	ASGCN-DT*	74.14	69.24	80.86	72.19	71.53	69.68
Scalability	RAM+	75.89	72.26	81.63	72.96	71.96	70.18
	PBAN+	75.98	72.62	81.74	73.07	72.40	71.26
Ablation	SPNet-PE	73.74	68.78	80.14	68.73	72.11	70.61
	SPNet-SE	75.07	70.75	81.43	72.69	72.04	70.31
	SPNet-SW	74.76	69.96	81.07	71.50	71.75	69.20
SPNet	SPNet(SY)	74.84	70.87	81.83	72.63	**73.62**	**72.33**
	SPNet full	**76.18**	**72.37**	**82.10**	**73.32**	72.85	71.14

- **TNet-LF** [11]: The context preserving transformation (CPT) is proposed to consolidate word representation and target representation in TNet-LF. And the contexts are fed into convolutional neural network for sentiment classification.
- **PBAN** [4]: The relative sequential position between context and aspect is formulated, where the position information is integrated into embedding. The bidirectional attention is designed to learn sentence representation.
- **ASGCN-DT** [26]: The directional dependency trees are applied to build GCN to improve the representation of aspect.

We reproduce the code of RAM and PBAN, while the rest experimental results are obtained from [26]. In order to evaluate the performance brought by syntactical information, a model named SPNet(SY) without sequential position embedding is also designed. d_{st} is set to 100.

3.4 Main Results

The experimental results comparisons are shown in Table 2 on three datasets LAPTOP, REST and TWITTER. SPNet provides a significant improvement over all the baselines on LAPTOP and REST, and also achieves a competitive result on TWITTER. The performance on TWITTER only has a slightly lower accuracy and F1 than TNet. But the SPNet(SY) produces the best performance on TWITTER, outperforming all the baselines. In particular, compared with the current state-of-the-art dependency-based method ASGCN-DT (a carefully-designed model with GCN), SPNet could still achieve +2.75%, +1.53% and +1.85% improvements on LAPTOP, REST and TWITTER, respectively. There may be two reasons for the improvements. The first is that SPNet could utilize both structural and sequential position embedding to learn richer syntactical information without introducing too much noise than other models. The second is that SPNet could handle the conflicts of structure and sequence since the reutilization of structural position make SPNet pay more attention to structure. Specifically, the improvement on TWITTER which is considered to be ungrammatical sentences shows that the syntactical information is still effectiveness to TWITTER.

The reason why SPNet is inferior to SPNet(SY) on TWITTER may be the irregularity of colloquial tweets. Sequential position could not provide the effective information and also shrinks the dimension of structural embedding, further demonstrating the effectiveness of the structural information from the side.

3.5 Ablation Study

To investigate the impact of each component in SPNet (*e.g.*, structural embedding, sequential embedding and structural weighted layer), we compare full SPNet with a set of ablation experiments as shown in the *3*-rd group of Table 2. After removing the position embedding (named SPNet-PE), a sharp fall in both of ACC and F1 are observed, demonstrating that the integration of structural and sequential information into inputs is crucial for the outstanding performance. When we remove the structural position embedding (named SPNet-SE), the experimental results are obviously decreased, showing that the structural information is significant for sequence-based model understanding the syntactic structure.

By comparing the results of SPNet and SPNet-SW which removes the structural weighted layer, we observe that the performance of SPNet-SW drops significantly on all three datasets. It could be inferred that SPNet-SW is stuck in the conflicts between structure and sequence. On REST and LAPTOP, compared with SPNet(SY), SPNet is more robust due to encoding the sequential position.

3.6 Scalability Study

To further evaluate the scalability of our method, we reproduce the experiments of RAM and PBAN, and append the structural and sequential embedding (PBAN already contains sequential position embedding). The results are shown in the *2*-nd group of Table 2 (named RAM+ and PBAN+). We can observe the significant improvements on all three datasets, demonstrating that the structural and sequential embedding could improve the ability of modeling hierarchical structure in sentence without too much noise. Besides, it also reveals the scalability of our method for other models to obtain a more excellent performance.

3.7 Case Study

Several examples from the testing set are picked to present a case study of RAM, PBAN and SPNet model. Specifically, we visualize the attention weights

Table 3. Visualization of attention scores from RAM, PBAN and SPNet.

Models	Aspect	Attention visualization	Label	Prediction
RAM	Waiting	The food is so good and so popular that waiting can really be a nightmare	Negative	Positive$_\times$
	Usb ports	This laptop has only 2 usb ports, and they are both on the same side	Negative	Neural$_\times$
PBAN	Waiting	The food is so good and so popular that waiting can really be a nightmare .	Negative	Negative$_\checkmark$
	Usb ports	This laptop has only 2 usb ports, and they are both on the same side	Negative	Neural$_\times$
SPNet	Waiting	The food is so good and so popular that waiting can really be a nightmare	Negative	Negative$_\checkmark$
	Usb ports	This laptop has only 2 usb ports, and they are both on the same side	Negative	Negative$_\checkmark$

on the sentence to obtain an intuitive understanding of SPNet for comparison in Table 3. As illustrated in the first example, "The food is ... nightmare.", it contains two aspect terms and multiple descriptors which is difficult to align the aspects with the corresponding relevant words for attention-based models. SPNet and PBAN predict the label correctly for "**waiting**" by focusing on the relevant word "*nightmare*" even far away from aspect , while RAM fails to predict. For the second example, "This laptop ... side.", it can be observed that the phrase "*only* 2" of implicit expression is arduous to obtained high score. SPNet could recognize it correctly and give an accurate classification. However, both of RAM and PBAN cannot handle the implicit semantics.

Our SPNet successfully handles both of the above two examples, implying that the proposed model could learn the rich syntactical information from the inputs with structural position. Specifically, the correct prediction on the first example shows that SPNet are capable of capturing long-range information, and the second demonstrates that SPNet could handle several implicit semantics.

4   Related Work

Traditional methods mainly train a sentiment classifier by building a sentiment lexicon or other hand-coded features, such as [7,10,23]. Due to the inefficiency of manual feature refinement, neural network architectures, which can learn features automatically, are widely applied for ABSC task. It is a crucial problem for early works that long distance dependencies are difficult to be captured [3,20]. To tackle above problem, attention mechanism is applied to model aspect-context relatedness in recent years [1,4,13,15,21,25,27].

However, the deficiencies of sequence model and lack of explanation for syntactical constraints have given rise to the attention of researchers [18,24]. In [3], dependency parsing is utilized to build adaptive recursive neural network, and further incorporating the sentiment information to the aspect node. In [19], dependency tree is proved the effectiveness for ABSC task. In [26], GCN is constructed by dependency tree to enhance the aspect representation. Syntactical information integrated to model could account for word dependencies, while the hard-coding applications could not tackle the drawbacks of sequence modeling well and carry too much noise caused by imperfect tools. Therefore, the attention-based models is mostly superior to dependency-based models.

Inspired by [4,24], we realize that the dependency tree should not be hard coded into the model, but rather as inputs learned by model. Therefore, the SPNet is proposed to encode structural and sequential position, so that the model could utilize the rich syntactical information to recognize the dependencies between aspect and contexts without too much noise.

5   Conclusion

In this paper, we propose structural position network (SPNet) for ABSC task. Different from previous existing dependency-based models, SPNet handles the structural information as inputs but not hard coding into framework. Therefore, SPNet has the fewer noise caused by parsing tools than other dependency-based models. In order to further reduce the impact of noise, we also encode the sequential position to embedding. Besides, the structural weighted layer is designed to utilize the structural information more intuitional. Finally, experimental results on three public datasets demonstrate the effectiveness and scalability of our method.

Acknowledgement. This research is supported in part by the Beijing Municipal Science and Technology Project under Grant Z191100007119008.

References

1. Chen, P., Sun, Z., Bing, L., Yang, W.: Recurrent attention network on memory for aspect sentiment analysis. In: Proceeding of EMNLP, pp. 452–461 (2017)
2. Cho, K., et al.: Learning phrase representations using RNN encoder-decoder for statistical machine translation. Proc. EMNLP, 1724–1734 (2014)
3. Dong, L., Wei, F., Tan, C., Tang, D., Zhou, M., Xu, K.: Adaptive recursive neural network for target-dependent twitter sentiment classification. In: Proceeding of ACL, pp. 49–54 (2014)
4. Gu, S., Zhang, L., Hou, Y., Song, Y.: A position-aware bidirectional attention network for aspect-level sentiment analysis. In: Proceeding of COLING, pp. 774–784 (2018)
5. He, R., Lee, W.S., Ng, H.T., Dahlmeier, D.: Effective attention modeling for aspect-level sentiment classification. In: Proceeding of COLING, pp. 1121–1131 (2018)

6. Huang, B., Ou, Y., Carley, K.M.: Aspect level sentiment classification with attention-over-attention neural networks. In: Thomson, R., Dancy, C., Hyder, A., Bisgin, H. (eds.) SBP-BRiMS 2018. LNCS, vol. 10899, pp. 197–206. Springer, Cham (2018). https://doi.org/10.1007/978-3-319-93372-6_22

7. Jiang, L., Yu, M., Zhou, M., Liu, X., Zhao, T.: Target-dependent twitter sentiment classification. In: Proceeding of ACL, pp. 151–160 (2011)

8. Kim, Y., Denton, C., Hoang, L., Rush, A.M.: Structured attention networks. Proc. ICLR (2017)

9. Kipf, T.N., Welling, M.: Semi-supervised classification with graph convolutional networks. In: Proceeding of ICLR (2017)

10. Kiritchenko, S., Zhu, X., Cherry, C., Mohammad, S.: NRC-canada-2014: detecting aspects and sentiment in customer reviews. In: Proceeding of SemEval, pp. 437–442 (2014)

11. Li, X., Bing, L., Lam, W., Shi, B.: Transformation networks for target-oriented sentiment classification. Proc. ACL, 946–956 (2018)

12. Li, X., Lam, W.: Deep multi-task learning for aspect term extraction with memory interaction. In: Proceeding of EMNLP, pp. 2886–2892 (2017)

13. Liu, J., Zhang, Y.: Attention modeling for targeted sentiment. In: Proceeding of EACL, pp. 572–577 (2017)

14. Luong, M.T., Pham, H., Manning, C.D.: Effective approaches to attention-based neural machine translation. Proc. EMNLP, 1412–1421 (2015)

15. Ma, D., Li, S., Zhang, X., Wang, H.: Interactive attention networks for aspect-level sentiment classification. Proc. IJCAI, 4068–4074 (2017)

16. Pennington, J., Socher, R., Manning, C.: Glove: global vectors for word representation. In: Proceeding of EMNLP, pp. 1532–1543 (2014)

17. Pontiki, M., Galanis, D., Pavlopoulos, J., Papageorgiou, H., Androutsopoulos, I., Manandhar, S.: SemEval-2014 task 4: aspect based sentiment analysis. In: Proceeding of SemEval, pp. 27–35 (2014)

18. Shen, Y., Tan, S., Sordoni, A., Courville, A.: Ordered neurons: integrating tree structures into recurrent neural networks. In: Proceeding of ICLR (2019)

19. Tai, K.S., Socher, R., Manning, C.D.: Improved semantic representations from tree-structured long short-term memory networks. Proc. ACL-CoNLL, 1556–1566 (2015)

20. Tang, D., Qin, B., Feng, X., Liu, T.: Effective LSTMs for target-dependent sentiment classification. In: Proceeding of COLING, pp. 3298–3307 (2016)

21. Tang, D., Qin, B., Liu, T.: Aspect level sentiment classification with deep memory network. Proc. EMNLP, 214–224 (2016)

22. Tang, J., et al.: Progressive self-supervised attention learning for aspect-level sentiment analysis. Proc. ACL, 557–566 (2019)

23. Titov, I., McDonald, R.: Modeling online reviews with multi-grain topic models. In Proceedings of the 17th international conference on World Wide Web, pp. 111–120 (2008)

24. Wang, X., Tu, Z., Wang, L., Shi, S.: Self-attention with structural position representations. Proc. EMNLP-IJCNLP, 1403–1409 (2019)

25. Wang, Y., et al.: Attention-based LSTM for aspect-level sentiment classification. In: Proceeding of EMNLP, pp. 606–615 (2016)

26. Zhang, C., Li, Q., Song, D.: Aspect-based sentiment classification with aspect-specific graph convolutional networks. Proc. EMNLP-IJCNLP, 4560–4570 (2019)

27. Zhou, Y., Huang, L., Guo, T., Han, J., Hu, S.: A span-based joint model for opinion target extraction and target sentiment classification. In: Proceeding of IJCAI, pp. 5485–5491 (2019)

Cross-Domain Sentiment Classification Using Topic Attention and Dual-Task Adversarial Training

Kwun-Ping Lai[(⊠)], Jackie Chun-Sing Ho[(⊠)], and Wai Lam[(⊠)]

The Chinese University of Hong Kong, Hong Kong, People's Republic of China
{kplai,wlam}@se.cuhk.edu.hk,
jackieho@link.cuhk.edu.hk

Abstract. Cross-domain sentiment classification aims at transferring the knowledge of the source domain with rich annotation resource to the scarcely labeled target domain or even without labels. Existing models fail to automatically capture simultaneously the three related topics, namely sentiment-only topic, i.e. containing domain-independent sentiment words or pivots in literature, domain-only topic, i.e. containing domain-specific words, and function word topic containing such as stop words. We propose a two-stage framework for tackling this problem. The first stage consists of a topic attention network specialized in discovering topics mentioned above. The second stage utilizes the learned knowledge from the first stage for learning a sentiment classification model with the consideration of context. A new sentiment-domain dual-task adversarial training strategy is designed and utilized in both stages. Experiments on a real-world product review dataset show that our proposed model outperforms the state-of-the-art model.

Keywords: Cross-domain sentiment classification · Artificial neural network · Dual-Task Adversarial Training

1 Introduction

Sentiment classification is an important task in natural language processing. It focuses on automatically understanding people's emotional tendency. Specifically, it aims at finding the overall sentiment polarity of the given text, either in positive or negative polarity. Researchers started to tickle this problem from early 2000 [17]. This problem can be solved by applying the supervised learning algorithm provided that there are sufficient amount of labeled data. However, labeled data may not be easily obtained for some unpopular domains. Therefore, researchers propose the cross-domain sentiment classification task which

The work described in this paper is substantially supported by a grant from the Asian Institute of Supply Chains and Logistics, the Chinese University of Hong Kong.

I. Farkaš et al. (Eds.): ICANN 2020, LNCS 12397, pp. 571–583, 2020.
https://doi.org/10.1007/978-3-030-61616-8_46

aims at transferring the knowledge learned from the source domain with abundant labeled data to the target domain with only few or even no labeled data. It requires the model having a less dependent relationship to the domain-specific information of the labeled domain. This makes the problem challenging due to the domain discrepancy.

Researchers propose the pivot-based method [5,13,21] which focuses on identifying general keywords carrying sentiment information, known as pivots in literature, (e.g. the word "good" or "bad") based on the corresponding learned weights. This also improves the interpretability of the model.

However, the pivot-based approach is not working well in the situation that the source and the target domain share few overlapping pivot features. Besides exploiting pivot words, Li et al. [12] proposes a new model which also considers words that carry domain-dependent sentiment information (they call them non-pivot words). The model consists of P-net and NP-net that identify pivots and domain-dependent sentiment words respectively. Manshu and Bing [14] propose a model considering dis-pivots, which have different sentiment polarities across domains, by using external knowledge. However, these models ignore some important related topics such as domain-only topic which can assist the training of domain classifier. A good domain classifier is important for obtaining pivots by domain adversarial training [7].

In this paper, we propose a **T**opic **A**ttention and dual-**T**ask **A**dversarial training model (TATA) with two-stage framework for solving the CDSC problem. The first stage using the topic attention model aims at discovering three related topics: i) the sentiment-only (SO) topic, i.e. domain-independent sentiment words, or pivots in literature, ii) the domain-only (DO) topic, i.e. domain-specific words and iii) the function word (FW) topic such as stop words. It is achieved by utilizing topic attention queries, and using the sentiment-domain dual-task adversarial training solving the optimization direction unalignment problem. Specifically, SO topical words contribute to the sentiment classification task only while DO topical words contribute only to the domain classification task. FW topical words contribute neither the sentiment nor the domain classification task. The second stage utilizes the learned knowledge from the first stage to capture the contextualized sentiment related information for the final sentiment polarity prediction.

2   Related Work

Domain adaptation concerns learning a model on a novel domain from labeled data mostly in other domains. The feature mismatch between the source and the target domain can be overcome by learning a share feature space across domains. Selection of pivots, i.e. domain-independent features, thus poses an important research problem. Traditional methods rely on manual selection based on a predefined measure, such as frequency [3], mutual information [2,16] and pointwise mutual information [4], which may have limited accuracy. In recent years, due to the success of deep learning technique, researchers revisit the problem and apply neural network models to tackle it. The deep learning model is well known for automatically extracting useful features. Yu and Jiang [20] use two auxiliary tasks to learn sentence embeddings with CNN to capture the sentiment polarity. He et al. and Qu et al. [9,18] propose the model learning domain invariant features by minimizing the domain discrepancy. Ganin et al. [6,7] propose the DANN using a simple and effective Gradient Reversal Layer that keeps features invariant across domains, while Ajakan et al. [1] propose a shallow version of it with in-depth theoretical justification. Li et al. [13] make use of memory networks to improve interpretability of the model, enabling identification and direct visualization of pivots. Besides pivots, Zhang et al. [21] combine external aspect information for predicting the sentiment.

3   Model Description

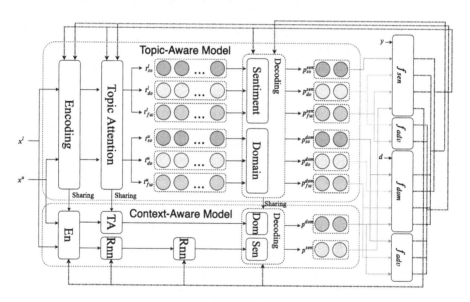

Fig. 1. Diagram depicting the proposed framework.

3.1   Problem Setting

There are two given domains, namely the source domain D_s and the target domain D_t. For each domain, we have two sets of data: i) the labeled data $L = \{x_i^l, y_i^l\}|_{i=1}^{n_L}$ and ii) the unlabeled data $U = \{x_j^u, d_j\}|_{j=1}^{n_U}$ where n_L and n_U are the number of labeled and unlabeled data respectively, and d_j is the augmented domain membership label. Therefore, the source domain and target domain can be written as $D_s = \left\{ L_s = \{x_i^{l,s}, y_i^s\}|_{i=1}^{n_{L_s}}, U_s = \{x_j^{u,s}, d_j^s\}|_{j=1}^{n_{U_s}} \right\}$ and

$D_t = \left\{ L_t = \{x_i^{l,t}, y_i^t\}|_{i=1}^{n_{L_t}}, U_t = \{x_j^{u,t}, d_j^t\}|_{j=1}^{n_{U_t}} \right\}$ respectively. We set all d_*^s to 0 and all d_*^t to 1. The objective of CDSC is to find out a best mapping function f so that given the training data set $T = \{L_s, U_s, \mathbf{x}^{l,t}, U_t\}$, the predicted label of the target domain labeled data $\bar{\mathbf{y}}^{l,t} = f(\mathbf{x}^{l,t})$ is as close to the actual label $\mathbf{y}^{l,t}$ as possible.

3.2   Overview of the Model

Our proposed topic attention and dual-task adversarial training model, as depicted in Fig. 1, consists of two stages: i) it discovers three related topics using a topic-aware model, ii) it captures contextualized sentiment information using a context-aware model. Three topics are: i) sentiment-only (SO) topic, ii) domain-only (DO) topic, and iii) function word (FW) topic. For SO and DO topic, they only carry the information related to either sentiment polarity or domain membership. For example, the word "good" or "bad" carry positive or negative sentiment polarity but do not carry any domain information. It means that people can not distinguish whether these words are coming from a particular domain as they are general enough to be used in any domains. Therefore, they should be grouped under SO topic. On the contrary, the word "essay" or "author" carry domain information related to books domain and do not contain any sentiment information. People cannot distinguish the sentiment polarity of the review containing these words only. Therefore, they should be grouped under DO topic. For FW topic, the topical word does not carry any information related to sentiment polarity or domain membership. Stop words are good examples.

In the first stage, the topic-aware model identifies topical words by utilizing topical queries learned during the training process. The topical query magnify the weighting of corresponding topical words to capture the representation of the topic for each review. The model generates one topic representation for each topical query. To help the topical query focusing on its corresponding words, we apply the sentiment-domain dual-task adversarial training exploiting the intrinsic feature of each topic. Specifically, the dual tasks are sentiment classification and domain classification with a customized training strategy. Let us take SO topic as an example, it can distinguish the sentiment polarity but cannot discriminate the domain membership. Therefore, the prediction of the sentiment polarity generated by SO topic representation should be as close to the true sentiment label as possible, which can be achieved by minimizing the cross-entropy loss. For the prediction of the domain membership, it should be close to even probability prediction, i.e. (50%, 50%), in the best case representing the indistinguishable domain membership. It is achieved by applying the concept of domain adversarial training [7]. We design a new adversarial training strategy by introducing an additional loss function to solve the optimization direction unalignment problem. Details are presented in the Dual-Task Adversarial Training subsection. For DO topic, we apply the sentiment adversarial training. Similarly, we apply both sentiment and domain adversarial training for FW topic.

In the second stage, the context-aware model utilizes the knowledge learned from the first stage by sharing the encoding layer and classification layer of the topic-aware model. The context of the review is captured by the bidirectional LSTM [10] layer. To maintain the domain invariance, we also apply the domain adversarial training in this stage. The sentiment prediction generated by the sentiment decoder is considered as the final output.

3.3 Data Preprocessing

Each review x is pre-processed to contain a fixed number of sentence k_c and a fixed number of word k_w. The exceeding sentences or sentence words are removed. Following the settings of [12], the short review is zero padded. Therefore, each review can be represented as $x = \{c_i\}|_{i=1}^{k_c}$ and $c_i = \{w_{i,j}\}|_{j=1}^{k_w}$ where c_i is the ith sentence of the review and $w_{i,j}$ is the jth word of the sentence c_i.

3.4 Topic-Aware Model

The model has two inputs: i) the labeled data $x^{l,s}$ is used for the sentiment classification task, and ii) the unlabeled data x^u is used for the domain classification.

Encoding Layer. Each word $w_{i,j}$ of the input is mapped to its corresponding embedding vector $w_{i,j}^E$ by the embedding matrix $E \in \mathbb{R}^{n_w \times d_e}$ where n_w is the number of distinct words and d_e is the dimension of the word embedding. The word vector is then projected to the word latent space to form the projected word vector $h_{i,j}^w$:

$$h_{i,j}^w = \tanh(W_w w_{i,j}^E + b_w)$$

where W_w and b_w are model parameters.

Topic Attention Layer. The weight of each word corresponding to each topic is estimated by the corresponding topical query vector q_k, which is randomly initialized and learned by the model during the training process. They are used to identify the important word regarding each topic by fulfilling specific contribution to the sentiment or domain classification task. The weight $\alpha_{i',j',k}$ of the word $w_{i',j'}$ corresponding to the kth topic is calculated as follows:

$$\alpha_{i',j',k} = \frac{m_{i',j'} e^{q_k^\top h_{i',j'}^w}}{\sum_{i=1}^{k_c} \sum_{j=1}^{k_w} m_{i,j} e^{q_k^\top h_{i,j}^w}} \times n_m$$

where $m_{i,j}$ is the word-level indicator indicating whether the (i, j)th position is a word or a padding. $m_{i,j}$ is 1 for words while it is 0 for paddings. n_m is the number of non-padding words: $n_m = \sum_{i=1}^{k_c} \sum_{j=1}^{k_w} m_{i,j}$. The topical representation vector t_k corresponding to the kth topic is the weighted sum of projected word vectors $h_{*,*}^w$: $t_k = \sum_{i=1}^{k_c} \sum_{j=1}^{k_w} \alpha_{i,j,k} h_{i,j}^w$. The outputs of the topic attention layer are three topical representation vectors.

Decoding Layer. This layer consists of two decoders, namely the sentiment decoder and the domain decoder for classifying the sentiment polarity and the domain membership respectively. The topical representation vector is projected to the sentiment and domain latent space. Finally, the probabilities of the sentiment polarity and the domain membership are calculated by passing the semantic projected vector to a softmax function:

$$p_k^{sen} = \text{softmax}(W_{sen}t_k^l + b_{sen})$$

$$p_k^{dom} = \text{softmax}(W_{dom}t_k^u + b_{dom})$$

where t_k^l is kth topical representation of the labeled input data $x^{l,s}$ while t_k^u is for the unlabeled input data x^u.

Dual-Task Adversarial Training. The topic attention layer generates three outputs for every single input, i.e. $t_{so}^l, t_{do}^l, t_{fw}^l$, representing the information captured by the corresponding topic from the labeled data $x^{l,s}$. These three topical representations are then passed to the sentiment decoder to obtain three predictions regarding the sentiment polarity. On the other hand, three topical representations of the unlabeled data x^u are passed to the domain decoder to obtain three domain membership predictions. Therefore, there are 6 predictions for every single pair of input.

We first consider the three predictions generated using the labeled data. There are two objectives for the sentiment classification task, i) to train a sentiment classifier, and ii) to maintain the intrinsic properties of each topic. To achieve the first objective, we introduce the first pair of the loss function, namely the classification loss which estimate the performance of the sentiment and the domain classification task. The sentiment classification loss is calculated using the predicted probability against the true label as follows:

$$L_k^{sen} = -\frac{1}{b}\sum_{i=1}^{b}\left(y_i \ln p_{i,k,1}^{sen} + (1 - y_i)\ln p_{i,k,0}^{sen}\right)$$

where $p_{i,k,l}^*$ is the predicted probability of the lth class by the kth topic given the ith training data, y_i is the binary number indicating the sentiment polarity, and b is the batch size. Similarly, the domain classification loss is used in the domain classification task. We apply the sentiment classification loss function to all three outputs to obtain $L_{so}^{sen}, L_{do}^{sen}$ and L_{fw}^{sen}, and then we update the parameters of sentiment decoder by minimizing these losses. To achieve the second goal, we divide three topics into two groups: i) task-aligned group, and ii) adversarial group. The member of the task-aligned group shares the same optimization direction with the decoder while the member of the adversarial group has a different direction. SO topic is the member of the task-aligned group as it captures sentiment related information, while DO topic and FW topic are members of the adversarial group as they capture non-sentiment information. For the task-aligned group, its related parameters are trained using the sentiment loss L_{so}^{sen} with the standard back propagation to update the topic attention layer and the encoding layer. To handle different optimization directions between parameters of the decoder and inner layers of related to the adversarial group, we introduce a new pair of adversarial loss functions which are designed to have a minimum value when the predicted probability is (50%, 50%) (it means that the classifier completely fails to make a decision), and attain a maximum value when the prediction is either (100%, 0%) or (0%, 100%). We use the following adversarial loss function:

$$f_{adv}(p) = |p_0 - 0.5| + |p_1 - 0.5|$$

The sentiment adversarial loss of the kth topic is computed as follows:

$$L_k^{sen\text{-}adv} = \frac{1}{b} \sum_{i=1}^{b} f_{adv}(p_{i,k}^{sen})$$

Similarly, the domain adversarial loss is calculated using the predicted probability from the unlabeled data. We compute the sentiment adversarial loss for every member of the adversarial group and update the related parameters using back propagation based on these losses. Specifically, we compute $L_{do}^{sen\text{-}adv}$ and $L_{fw}^{sen\text{-}adv}$, and update the topic attention layer and the encoding layer based on them. We name this training strategy as sentiment adversarial training. Note that we do not update the sentiment decoder using the sentiment adversarial loss as they have a different optimization direction. This completes the training strategy for the sentiment classification task.

For the domain classification task, we use similar technique. The domain classification loss is defined as follows: $L_k^{dom} = -\frac{1}{b} \sum_{i=1}^{b} \left(d_i \ln p_{i,k,1}^{dom} + (1 - d_i) \ln p_{i,k,0}^{dom} \right)$, where d_i is the binary number indicating the domain membership. We first compute the domain classification losses, $L_{so}^{dom}, L_{do}^{dom}$ and L_{fw}^{dom}, corresponding to three topics of the unlabeled data x^u. We update parameters of the domain decoder based on these losses. The task-aligned group has DO topic while the adversarial group has SO topic and FW topic for domain classification task. Next, we update the topic attention layer and encoding layer using L_{do}^{dom} as DO topic shares the same training direction with the domain decoder. Finally, we compute the domain adversarial loss of each member of the adversarial group: $L_k^{dom\text{-}adv} = \frac{1}{b} \sum_{i=1}^{b} f_{adv}(p_{i,k}^{dom})$, to obtain $L_{so}^{dom\text{-}adv}$ and $L_{fw}^{dom\text{-}adv}$. We update the topic attention layer and encoding layer based on these losses.

The L2 regularization loss is applied to the sentiment and domain decoder to prevent the overfitting problem. The L2 regularization loss is the sum of the square of all parameters of the corresponding decoder: $L_{sen\text{-}reg} = \gamma \left(||W_{sen}||_2^2 + |b_{sen}|^2 \right)$, $L_{dom\text{-}reg} = \gamma \left(||W_{dom}||_2^2 + |b_{dom}|^2 \right)$, where γ is the regularization parameter.

3.5   Context-Aware Model

The input also includes the labeled data $x^{l,s}$ and the unlabeled data x^u. The model reuses the encoding layer, the topic attention layer and two decoders trained from the topic-aware model to obtain its knowledge. Note that the topic attention layer is only used for obtaining the representation of the unlabeled data x^u and only the topical representation of SO topic t^u_{so} is selected.

Bi-LSTM Layer. We employ the bidirectional LSTM [10,19] to capture the context of the sentence. The projected word vectors of each sentence $h^c_i = [h^w_{i,1}, h^w_{i,2}, ..., h^w_{i,k_w},]$ are passed to the bi-LSTM layer to obtain the individual contextualized sentence representation c_i:

$$c_i = \text{bi-LSTM}(h^c_i, m_i)$$

We use the final state vector of the forward and backward LSTM layer and take the average of these two vectors to obtain c_i. To remove the effect of padding words, we also pass the mask vector $m_i = [m_{i,1}, m_{i,2}, ..., m_{i,k_w}]$ to the layer for ignoring paddings. Contextualized sentence representations of the review $c = [c_1, c_2, ..., c_{k_c}]$ are passed to the bi-LSTM layer again to obtain the final sentiment representation of the review $r^l = \text{bi-LSTM}(c, m^c)$, where $m^c = [m^c_1, m^c_2, ..., m^c_{k_c}]$ is the sentence mask vector indicating whether the sentence is empty of not. m^c_i is zero if the whole sentence are paddings, otherwise it is one.

Decoding Layer. The sentiment and the domain representation vector are passed to the sentiment and the domain decoder respectively to obtain predictions of the sentiment polarity p^{sen} and the domain membership p^{dom}.

Model Training. The training of the domain-aware model is a simplified version of training the topic-aware model. It generates one single pair of outputs given a single pair of inputs. We use the same strategy of handling the outputs generated by SO topic in the topic-aware model. The sentiment classification loss is used to update the sentiment decoder and all layers before it. The domain classification loss is used to update the domain decoder only. The domain adversarial loss is used to update the topic attention layer and the encoding layer. The L2 regularization loss is applied to both sentiment and domain decoder.

4   Experiments

4.1   Experiment Settings

We use the Amazon review dataset [2] for the evaluation of our proposed framework. The Amazon review dataset is a common benchmark for sentiment classification. The dataset consists of various domains with thousands of labeled and unlabeled data. We use four most common domains, namely Books, DVD, Electronics, and Kitchen. We conduct experiments on 12 crosses generated by these four domains. For each domain, we follow the data setting in [12] having 5600 training data and 400 validation data. The unlabeled data size is described in Table 1. Note that there is no testing data listed in the table as the training data and the validation data of the target domain are treated as the testing data.

Table 1. Statistics of the Amazon review dataset including the number of training, validation and unlabeled data for each domain

Domain	# Training	# Validation	# Unlabeled
Books	5600	400	9750
DVD	5600	400	11843
Electronics	5600	400	17009
Kitchen	5600	400	13856

4.2 Implementation Details

We set the maximum number of sentences k_c and the maximum number of words per sentence k_w to 20 and 25 respectively. We use the word2vec embedding [15] which is publicly available[1]. To prevent the model from overfitting the source domain, we do not further train the word embeddings. The word embedding dimension d_e is 300 and the dimension of the word latent space is also 300. The parameter of the network is initialized using Glorot uniform [8]. We set the regularization parameter to 0.005. For training, we use the Adam optimizer [11]. We train the sentiment classifier using the batch of 100 for labeled data. For training domain classifier, we use a batch size of 200 having 100 from the source unlabeled data and 100 from the target unlabled data. 56 batch samples of the unlabeled data are selected randomly for every epoch for joint training with the labeled data. We use two Adam optimizers to handle the corresponding losses. Classification losses and L2 regularization losses are handled by a scheduling optimizer with a scheduling function $\beta e^{\frac{-p}{10}}$ controlling the maximum learning rate, where p is the current epoch and β is the maximum learning rate. Adversarial losses are controlled by a slow optimizer with a learning rate of $\frac{\beta}{10}$ without scheduling. We clip the gradient with the norm greater than 2.

For training the topic-aware model, we set the maximum learning rate β to 0.002. We train the model for 10 epochs, i.e. $p = \{0, 1, ..., 9\}$. We save the model having a highest validation score for initializing the second stage.

For training the context-aware model, we set the learning rate to 0.001. The model is adapted for two epochs. Next, the model is fine-tuned for three epochs and the epoch with a highest validation score is used for final testing.

---

[1] Word2vec is available in https://code.google.com/archive/p/word2vec/.

4.3 Model Comparison

Models for performance comparison are listed as follows:

- SFA [16]: It is a linear method, which aims at aligning non-pivots and pivots by spectral feature alignment.
- DANN [7]: It is based on the adversarial training. DANN performs domain adaptation on the representation encoded in a 5000-dimension feature vector of the most frequent unigrams and bigrams between domains.
- CNN-aux [20]: It is based on the CNN and makes use of two auxiliary tasks to help inducing sentence embeddings.
- AMN [13]: It learns domain-shared representations based on memory networks and adversarial training.
- HATN [12]: It uses two networks to extract pivots and non-pivots, and predict the sentiment polarity based on them.
- TATA: It is the proposed framework

Results are presented in Table 2. We use the classification accuracy as the metric for performance measurement. Note that we follow exactly the data settings of HATN [12], so we directly quote the result in their paper. To make a fair comparison, we remove the external knowledge used by HATN such as the white list of the part-of-speech tags and the black list of words. Results of HATN shown in Table 2 are re-run results after removing the external knowledge.

The proposed framework achieves the best average accuracy of 86.34%, which is a 0.46% improvement of the previous state-of-the-art model, i.e. HATN. Specifically, it obtains the best accuracy score in 9 test cases out of 12 test cases. The result demonstrates the effectiveness of our proposed framework.

Table 2. Sentiment classification accuracy based on the Amazon review dataset

Source	Target	SFA	DANN	CNN-aux	AMN	HATN	TATA
Books	DVD	0.8285	0.8342	0.8442	0.8562	0.8698	**0.8783**
Books	Electronics	0.7638	0.7627	0.8063	0.8055	0.8508	**0.8592**
Books	Kitchen	0.781	0.779	0.8338	0.8188	0.8662	**0.8678**
DVD	Books	0.802	0.8077	0.8307	0.8453	0.878	**0.8835**
DVD	Electronics	0.76	0.7635	0.8035	0.8042	0.8478	**0.8555**
DVD	Kitchen	0.775	0.7815	0.8168	0.8167	**0.8652**	0.8562
Electronics	Books	0.7235	0.7353	0.7738	0.7752	0.8355	**0.8405**
Electronics	DVD	0.7593	0.7627	0.7907	0.8053	**0.8412**	0.8348
Electronics	Kitchen	0.865	0.8453	0.8715	0.8783	0.8972	**0.9045**
Kitchen	Books	0.7397	0.7417	0.7847	0.7905	0.839	**0.8518**
Kitchen	DVD	0.7567	0.7532	0.7907	0.795	0.8257	**0.8408**
Kitchen	Electronics	0.8538	0.8553	0.8673	0.8668	**0.8895**	0.8882
Average		0.784	0.7852	0.8178	0.8215	0.8588	**0.8634**

4.4 Topic Words Analysis

To analyze the knowledge learned by each topic, we extract top 30 words with the highest overall weighting from the testing data. We select the cross DVD → Electronics. The result is presented in Table 3. We observe that the quality of topic words is quite high. The model focuses on verbs, adjectives and adverbs for SO topic. It focuses on nouns for DO topic. For FW topic, most of them are stop words. The result shows that the proposed dual-task adversarial training is effective for helping the model to identify suitable knowledge for each topic.

Table 3. Top 30 words of learned topics for the testing data of DVD → Electronics

Topic	Top 30 words
Sentiment-only	Barely finest poorly solid worst wasted waste comfortably superior excellent pleasantly perfectly allowed save decent saved disappointment fastest terrible trash favorite strongest flawlessly best precious horrible rarely hardest dull fooled
Domain-only	Earphone tablet headphone armband earphones modulator device headphones adapter headset usb transmitter film earbuds pda macbook lcd receiver firmware microsoft stylus function chipset adapters module handset motherboard interface sensor connector
Function word	Are is were was be for becomes been appears by currently this may towards the now at gets become being getting due according became s than seems within toward considered

5   Conclusion

We present a novel framework composed of two models, namely the topic-aware model and the context-aware model, for tackling cross-domain sentiment classification. It is capable of capturing three topics which help the knowledge transfer from the source domain to the target domain. We also propose a dual-task adversarial training to overcome the optimization direction unalignment between parameters of the adversarial group and the decoder. Extensive experiments show that our framework outperforms the state-of-the-art model.

References

1. Ajakan, H., Germain, P., Larochelle, H., Laviolette, F., Marchand, M.: Domain-adversarial neural networks. In: NIPS 2014 Workshop on Transfer and Multi-task learning: Theory Meets Practice (2014)
2. Blitzer, J., Dredze, M., Pereira, F.: Biographies, bollywood, boom-boxes and blenders: domain adaptation for sentiment classification. In: Proceedings of the 45th annual meeting of the association of computational linguistics, pp. 440–447 (2007)

3. Blitzer, J., McDonald, R., Pereira, F.: Domain adaptation with structural correspondence learning. In: Proceedings of the 2006 Conference on Empirical Methods in Natural Language Processing, pp. 120–128 (2006)
4. Bollegala, D., Mu, T., Goulermas, J.Y.: Cross-domain sentiment classification using sentiment sensitive embeddings. IEEE Trans. Knowl. Data Eng. **28**(2), 398–410 (2015)
5. Cui, X., Coenen, F., Bollegala, D.: TSP: learning task-specific pivots for unsupervised domain adaptation. In: Ceci, M., Hollmén, J., Todorovski, L., Vens, C., Džeroski, S. (eds.) ECML PKDD 2017. LNCS (LNAI), vol. 10535, pp. 754–771. Springer, Cham (2017). https://doi.org/10.1007/978-3-319-71246-8_46
6. Ganin, Y., Lempitsky, V.: Unsupervised domain adaptation by backpropagation. In: Proceedings of the 32nd International Conference on International Conference on Machine Learning, pp. 1180–1189 (2015)
7. Ganin, Y., et al.: Domain-adversarial training of neural networks. J. Mach. Learn. Res. **17**(1), 2030–2096 (2016)
8. Glorot, X., Bengio, Y.: Understanding the difficulty of training deep feedforward neural networks. In: Proceedings of the Thirteenth International Conference on Artificial Intelligence and Statistics, pp. 249–256 (2010)
9. He, R., Lee, W.S., Ng, H.T., Dahlmeier, D.: Adaptive semi-supervised learning for cross-domain sentiment classification. In: Proceedings of the 2018 Conference on Empirical Methods in Natural Language Processing, pp. 3467–3476 (2018)
10. Hochreiter, S., Schmidhuber, J.: Long short-term memory. Neural Comput. **9**(8), 1735–1780 (1997)
11. Kingma, D.P., Ba, J.: Adam: A method for stochastic optimization. arXiv preprint arXiv:1412.6980 (2014)
12. Li, Z., Wei, Y., Zhang, Y., Yang, Q.: Hierarchical attention transfer network for cross-domain sentiment classification. In: Thirty-Second AAAI Conference on Artificial Intelligence, pp. 5852–5859 (2018)
13. Li, Z., Zhang, Y., Wei, Y., Wu, Y., Yang, Q.: End-to-end adversarial memory network for cross-domain sentiment classification. In: Proceedings of the Twenty-Sixth International Joint Conference on Artificial Intelligence, IJCAI-17, pp. 2237–2243 (2017)
14. Manshu, T., Bing, W.: Adding prior knowledge in hierarchical attention neural network for cross domain sentiment classification. IEEE Access **7**, 32578–32588 (2019)
15. Mikolov, T., Sutskever, I., Chen, K., Corrado, G.S., Dean, J.: Distributed representations of words and phrases and their compositionality. In: Advances in Neural Information Processing Systems, pp. 3111–3119 (2013)
16. Pan, S.J., Ni, X., Sun, J.T., Yang, Q., Chen, Z.: Cross-domain sentiment classification via spectral feature alignment. In: Proceedings of the 19th International Conference on World Wide Web, pp. 751–760 (2010)
17. Pang, B., Lee, L., Vaithyanathan, S.: Thumbs up?: sentiment classification using machine learning techniques. In: Proceedings of the ACL-02 Conference on Empirical Methods in Natural Language Processing-Volume 10, pp. 79–86 (2002)
18. Qu, X., Zou, Z., Cheng, Y., Yang, Y., Zhou, P.: Adversarial category alignment network for cross-domain sentiment classification. In: Proceedings of the 2019 Conference of the North American Chapter of the Association for Computational Linguistics: Human Language Technologies, Volume 1 (Long and Short Papers), pp. 2496–2508 (2019)
19. Schuster, M., Paliwal, K.K.: Bidirectional recurrent neural networks. IEEE Trans. Signal Process. **45**(11), 2673–2681 (1997)

20. Yu, J., Jiang, J.: Learning sentence embeddings with auxiliary tasks for cross-domain sentiment classification. In: Proceedings of the 2016 Conference on Empirical Methods in Natural Language Processing, pp. 236–246 (2016)
21. Zhang, K., Zhang, H., Liu, Q., Zhao, H., Zhu, H., Chen, E.: Interactive attention transfer network for cross-domain sentiment classification. In: Proceedings of the AAAI Conference on Artificial Intelligence, pp. 5773–5780 (2019)

Data Augmentation for Sentiment Analysis in English – The Online Approach

Michał Jungiewicz$^{(\boxtimes)}$ ⓘ and Aleksander Smywiński-Pohl ⓘ

Department of Computer Science, AGH University of Science and Technology,
Krakow, Poland
{mjungiew,apohllo}@agh.edu.pl
https://www.agh.edu.pl

Abstract. This paper investigates a change of approach to textual data augmentation for sentiment classification, by switching from offline to online data modification. In other words, from changing the data before the training is started to using transformed samples during the training process. This allows utilizing the information about the current loss of the classifier. We try training with examples that maximize, minimize the loss, or are randomly sampled. We observe that the maximizing variant performs best in most cases. We use 2 neural network architectures, 3 data augmentation methods, and test them on 4 different datasets. Our experiments indicate that the switch to the online data augmentation improves the results for recurrent neural networks in all cases and for convolutional networks in some cases. The improvement reaches 2.3% above the baseline in terms of accuracy, averaged over all datasets, and 2.25% on one of the datasets, but averaged over dataset sizes.

Keywords: Neural networks · Data Augmentation · Natural language processing · Sentiment classification

1 Introduction

The advent of deep learning has already shown some stunning results in multiple different fields. It began mostly with image processing but soon arrived at computational linguistics [17].

One of the challenges in training the modern neural networks is the shortage of data and especially the one that is labeled. The cost of labeling is usually high and rises with the complexity of the task at hand. One of the ways of dealing with this problem is the techniques of data augmentation (DA). We are observing the rise of interest in augmenting data of different kinds – from images to texts.

Data augmentation involves replicating the original data automatically. We perform certain transformations on the data. These modifications must not change the meaning of the data. For example, if we flip an image of number 6 vertically, we will get 9.

© Springer Nature Switzerland AG 2020
I. Farkaš et al. (Eds.): ICANN 2020, LNCS 12397, pp. 584–595, 2020.
https://doi.org/10.1007/978-3-030-61616-8_47

The gist of this paper is to test a change of approach to data augmentation for sentiment analysis. The switch is from the offline DA to online DA (Sect. 5). Offline means augmenting the dataset before training a classifier, and the online approach involves augmenting the dataset while training a model. We compare these approaches to DA solving sentiment classification on 4 different datasets. We deal with short texts only. We use recurrent and convolutional networks (RNN and CNN).

2 Related Work

This literature review deliberately focuses on the augmentation of textual data. We are aware that there are a lot of papers on augmenting other kinds of data, but for the sake of this article, it is more useful to focus on texts.

One of the most similar works to ours is called EDA: Easy Data Augmentation Techniques [25]. We use this method as one of the DA techniques, and we describe it in more detail in Sect. 3.2. Wei and Zou also use both CNN and RNN architectures. We do the same in this paper. We use their idea to experiment on parts of datasets. We also use a similar set of datasets. The main difference between our work and EDA is that we investigate the switch of the approach – from offline to online. Besides, to our knowledge, no one has investigated this kind of transition yet.

Another set of two papers focus on contextual augmentation. The first one presents a technique to replace words using their paradigmatic relations [15]. Sosuke Kobayashi trains a bi-directional language model that predicts words at certain positions. The second paper builds on top of this idea [27]. But as a language representation model, the Chinese research group uses BERT. They retrofit BERT to preserve the label of a phrase. Both of the papers show the results of using CNN and RNN architectures. At least according to the authors of [27], their model outperforms Kobayashi's model, and it gives around 2% improvement of accuracy on average upon baseline.

Recently a research group from IBM has published a paper on data augmentation for text classification [6]. They call their method LAMBADA, which stands for language-model-based data augmentation. They leverage pre-trained GPT-2 model [22] to synthesize new labeled data. Their model outperforms other DA approaches like EDA.

Jonathan Quijas presented research on DA as his master thesis [21]. The author tests shuffling, noise injection, and padding. Claude Coulombe also experiments with multiple different techniques: textual noise, spelling errors, synonyms replacement, paraphrases generation (with regexes), paraphrases generation (using syntax trees), and back-translation [8]. He uses RNN, multi-layer perceptron (MLP) and XGBoost, but doesn't use CNN. The best variant overall is MLP with 2 hidden layers and regex paraphrase generation.

Abulaish and Sah propose an approach that leverages n-grams and LDA techniques to identify class-specific phrases [5]. They use CNN. The authors state that augmented corpus has lower variance and better validation accuracy. They perform their experiments on four Amazon's review datasets.

3 Data Augmentation Methods

We use different types of transformations on the texts, which are otherwise called data augmentation techniques. These methods appear in the literature or are available as parts of public data augmentation libraries.

3.1 BERT Replacement

The first data augmentation method that we use is based on BERT [9]. To apply this method we use the nlpaug library [16]. We provide the details of its configuration.

We use bert-base-uncased model – it is a pretrained model [3]. Its training architecture has the following characteristics: 12 layers, 768 hidden states, and 12 attention heads, which totals to 110 million parameters. We use substitution as the action type. We use the following punctuation marks ? ! . , ” ’ as stop words. Aug_p is the percentage of words that we replace. We deliberately lower this value from 0.3 to 0.1, because we observe that the transformations make more sense when we restrict their number. We leave the rest of the parameters to their default values.

This method substitutes a word feeding surrounding words to BERT language model to choose the most suitable word for transformation [16]. It does not perform any kind of more sophisticated processing like, for example, conditional BERT contextual augmentation proposed in [27].

3.2 EDA: Easy Data Augmentation Techniques

The second method is called Easy Data Augmentation [25]. It's authors use it and test it on solving the text classification task on multiple datasets.

The method uses four simple but robust types of transformations: Synonym Replacement, Random Insertion, Random Swap, and Random Deletion. The authors randomly choose one of these types and perform it on a sentence in a dataset. They say that the method improves the effectiveness of both convolutional and recurrent neural networks.

The authors of EDA try their method on both the whole original datasets as well as their parts. According to their paper, EDA gives improvements comparing with training the models without augmentation. They show larger gains for smaller parts of the datasets.

For parameters of EDA, we use the values suggested in the original paper. Number of generated sentences per one original sentence ($n_{aug} = 4$) and the percent of words in a sentence that are changed ($\alpha = 0.1$). The α parameter has the same meaning as the above aug_p parameter, but we keep the original names that the methods' authors propose. The only modification we make to the original code is that we do not use the preprocessing, which removes special characters. We observe that in our case, it is better to leave these characters.

3.3 WordNet Synonym Replacement

Finally, the last method we use is replacing words with their synonyms taken from WordNet [4,18,19]. To achieve this we use a Python library nlpaug [16].

We follow the default approach for replacing the synonyms, customizing only the list of stop words. We use the following punctuation marks ? ! . , " ' as stop words – the same as for BERT. We use the default values for all other parameters. The most important ones are $aug\_min = 1$ and $aug\_p = 0.3$. Aug_min means the minimum number of synonyms replaced in a sentence. Aug_p is the percentage of words replaced.

4 The Baseline

Baseline solutions are based on convolutional and recurrent neural network architectures used by Sosuke Kobayashi in his experiments and implementation [2,15,24].

The convolutional architecture has filters of size {3, 4, 5} and word embeddings following the work of Yoon Kim [13]. The concatenated output of all the filters is passed through a maximum pooling layer. This output goes into a two-layer feed-forward network with ReLU, followed by the softmax function. The recurrent architecture has a single layer LSTM and word embeddings. The output of the LSTM goes into an output affine layer with the softmax function. Both of the neural network types are trained with stochastic gradient descent [7] (SGD) and optimized by Adam [14].

Both for the baselines and all solution variants described in Sect. 5, we use the above architectures and the following hyperparameters. We use early stopping when there is no improvement on the validation set for 10 epochs. We deliberately use no dropout. This is because data augmentation can be considered as a kind of regularization for training neural networks. We want to separate these two kinds of regularization to have clearer conclusions on the effect of DA. We also use the suggested values for the learning rate (0.001), the word embedding unit size (256), and the batch size (64). Word embeddings are randomly initialized, as in Kobayashi's work. We do not use any pre-trained model for them.

5 Solution Variants: The Online and Offline Approach

We use the offline and online approaches. The offline approach consists of applying data augmentation methods before training a neural network. With the use of these methods, we obtain a larger dataset that contains both original and transformed data. We use this dataset for training the neural network. The online approach, on the other hand, uses the original dataset as the training input to the neural network. The input is not augmented, but the online approach changes the samples while training the model. We might leverage different methodologies to choose which transformation to use, when, and how often. This work proposes taking into account the current loss of the classifier, following the works of [12] and [10].

This work focuses mostly on comparing the online and offline approaches. To get a fair comparison, we use the same types of transformations (augmentations) while testing the offline and online approaches. We describe these approaches in detail in Sect. 5.

First of all, we have the baseline variants. We present their results in Sects. 6.2 and 6.3. After the baseline, we present the offline variants of augmentation (OFFLINE). It means that the datasets are augmented before training of a neural network. For all online variants, we use the probability $p = 0.5$. This is the probability with which we choose transformed batch (or sentence) instead of the original batch (or sentence). In each case, transformed sentences come from one of the DA methods described in Sect. 3. BERT stands for BERT augmentation, EDA for augmentation of the same name and WN for WordNet augmentation. These sentences are the same for each of the offline variants and their online counterparts. This allows for a fair comparison. For online variants, we use suffixes. MAX suffix means we transform the mini-batch so that it maximizes the current loss of the classifier. MIN analogously minimizes the loss, and RAND forms a batch by randomly sampling from the given sentences. Furthermore, we use the S suffix when we decide to transform sentences individually, rather than to decide for the whole mini-batch.

Below we describe the offline and online variants in detail:

1. GENERATING EXAMPLES WITH ONE OF THE DATA AUGMENTATION METHODS
   We use one of the methods: {BERT, EDA, WN} (see Sect. 3). With each of the methods for each sentence in the original dataset, we generate 4 transformations (augmentations). We use the same transformations, both with offline and online approaches.

2. OFFLINE VARIANTS
   For the offline variants, we use all sentences – original and transformed – as the training sets. We choose a validation set and a test set for each dataset. These datasets are not augmented in any case. We use the same data for testing in both offline and online scenarios. The same holds for the validation set.

3. ONLINE VARIANTS
   For the online variants, we use the original data for training. We do not use the transformed examples as the input data. Instead, we use them to replace the original sentences while training a neural network. We propose two strategies for replacing the sentences and show their mechanisms below:
   - SINGLE strategy (S suffix)
     While training with SGD, we execute the following procedure on each mini-batch (see Algorithm 1):
   - BATCH strategy (without the S suffix)
     While training with SGD, we execute this procedure on each mini-batch (see Algorithm 2):

Algorithm 1. Procedure for transforming each mini-batch using the SINGLE strategy. For the whole training, we choose one of the modes: {MAX, MIN, RAND}.

Input: A mini-batch that contains multiple sentences
Output: Transformed mini-batch
1: **for each** sentence S in mini-batch **do**
2:      $random\_number \leftarrow generate(0.0, 1.0)$
3:      **if** $random\_number < p$ **then**
4:          **for each** augmentation A of sentence S **do**
5:              $loss \leftarrow compute\_loss\_for\_sentence(A)$
6:          **end for**
7:          choose augmentation that gives min/max loss
                or choose randomly, depending on mode
8:      **else**
9:          leave original sentence
10:     **end if**
11: **end for**

Algorithm 2. Procedure for transforming each mini-batch using the BATCH strategy. For the whole training, we choose one of the modes: {MAX, MIN, RAND}.

Input: A mini-batch that contains multiple sentences
Output: Transformed mini-batch
1: $random\_number \leftarrow generate(0.0, 1.0)$
2: **if** $random\_number < p$ **then**
3:      **for each** sentence S in mini-batch **do**
4:          **for each** augmentation A of sentence S **do**
5:              $loss \leftarrow compute\_loss\_for\_sentence(A)$
6:          **end for**
7:          choose augmentation that gives min/max loss
                or choose randomly, depending on mode
8:      **end for**
9: **else**
10:     leave original batch
11: **end if**

6   Training and Evaluation

6.1   Datasets

We use 4 different datasets to compare the offline and online approaches. Customer Reviews (CR), Multi-Perspective Question Answering Corpus (MPQA), and the Stanford Sentiment Treebank in its two variants: 5-label (SST-1) and 2-label (SST-2). On all of these datasets, we perform sentiment classification (Table 1).

Table 1. Statistics of the datasets used in this paper according to [1].

	Classes	Av. sentence length	Dataset size	Vocab. size
CR	2	19	3775	5340
MPQA	2	3	10606	6246
SST-1	5	18	11855	17836
SST-2	2	19	9613	16185

CR contains customer reviews of products (digital cameras, DVD players, mp3 players, etc). The problem lies in predicting the sentiment of a review [11]. From MPQA, we use the opinion polarity detection subtask [26]. It contains mostly very short phrases. The text fragments are taken from news articles from a wide variety of sources. We predict whether an utterance is positive or negative. Stanford Sentiment Treebank comprises positive and negative processed reviews from Rotten Tomatoes – a website for movie reviews [20,23]. It has two versions. One that contains 5 different labels: (very positive, positive, neutral, negative, very negative), and the other that contains 2 labels: (positive, negative).

6.2 Results Averaged over Datasets

We present the results of all variants described in Sect. 5 in Fig. 1. For each dataset, we split it into the test, validation, and training part. The charts show the accuracy on the test set, that is not used in the training of the neural network. We use the validation part for early stopping (see Sect. 4). The validation set is not augmented in any case. In each case – so for each variant on each dataset – we run the experiment 10 times using 10 different seeds of random number generator and average the results. The Fig. 1 shows the accuracies averaged over all 4 datasets. We also run our experiments using only some parts of the training data (half and quarter). We use both neural network architectures: convolutional (CNN) and recurrent (RNN).

The results shown in Fig. 1 lead us to multiple different conclusions. The first finding is that in all cases, the best variant uses some kind of data augmentation. It means that in all cases, data augmentation improves the baseline. However, the level of improvement varies. On the other hand, not all variants of DA improve the baseline.

The second finding is that for CNN for two dataset sizes, one of the online variants wins, and for one size an offline variant wins. These are WN-MAX-S, WN-MAX, and EDA for full datasets, halves, and quarters respectively. On the other hand, for RNN for all dataset sizes, the best variant is one of the online variants: WN-MAX-S, EDA-MAX-S, and EDA-MAX.

It is also interesting to observe the results for different online variants: MAX, RAND, and MIN. In most cases, MAX variants perform best, then RAND and MIN are the worst. This pattern is visible both for CNNs and RNNs. This

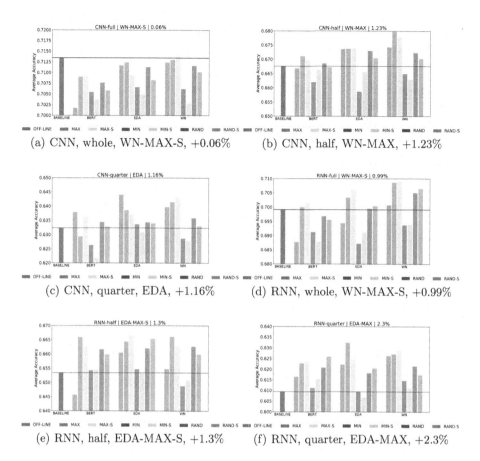

Fig. 1. Results of accuracy for CNN and RNN, averaged over all datasets. We show the neural network architecture, size of datasets, the winning variant and it's difference with the baseline. Baseline shown in grey, offline variants in magenta, max in green, min in blue, random in red. (Color figure online)

confirms that maximizing the loss improves the results more probably than minimizing or choosing at random.

It is interesting that for RNN the online MAX variants improve the offline variants in all cases. However, for CNNs online MAX variants improve offline DA in most of the cases, but not in all of them.

At least in our set of experiments, EDA and WordNet augmentation tie for first place in this "competition". They both win in 3 out of 6 cases. The biggest improvement upon the baseline comes from EDA-MAX and reaches 2.3%. This improvement comes from RNN trained on quarters of the datasets.

Finally, there is also a general tendency that DA improves the results better for smaller dataset sizes. It does not exactly hold for CNNs, but it holds perfectly for RNNs.

Table 2. Results per dataset. CNN is shown on the top and RNN on the bottom. Results averaged over three dataset sizes {full, half, quarter}. The best variant per dataset shown on the bottom.

	CR		MPQA		SST-2		SST-1	
BASELINE	76.3%		79.94%		75.52%		36.68%	
BERT	76.99%	0.69%	78.67%	1.27%	75.41%	0.11%	36.44%	0.25%
MAX	75.94%	0.36%	79.59%	0.35%	75.38%	0.14%	37.01%	0.33%
MAX-S	76.52%	0.23%	79.58%	0.36%	75.8%	0.27%	36.81%	0.12%
MIN	75.93%	0.36%	78.74%	1.2%	74.75%	0.77%	36.41%	0.28%
MIN-S	76.11%	0.18%	78.82%	1.12%	74.4%	1.12%	36.2%	0.48%
RAND	76.31%	0.02%	79.83%	0.11%	75.21%	0.32%	36.72%	0.04%
RAND-S	76.11%	0.19%	79.45%	0.49%	75.43%	0.09%	36.43%	0.25%
EDA	**77.13%**	0.83%	80.44%	0.5%	76.25%	0.73%	36.74%	0.06%
MAX	77.04%	0.74%	79.52%	0.42%	76.68%	1.16%	36.71%	0.02%
MAX-S	76.6%	0.3%	79.4%	0.54%	76.36%	0.83%	37.01%	0.32%
MIN	76.21%	0.09%	79.09%	0.85%	74.99%	0.53%	36.23%	0.46%
MIN-S	76.09%	0.2%	79.53%	0.41%	74.89%	0.64%	36.33%	0.36%
RAND	76.49%	0.19%	80.44%	0.5%	75.54%	0.02%	36.67%	0.01%
RAND-S	76.27%	0.02%	80.05%	0.11%	75.45%	0.07%	36.59%	0.09%
WN	76.69%	0.39%	80.26%	0.32%	76.34%	0.82%	36.88%	0.2%
MAX	76.6%	0.3%	80.35%	0.41%	**76.83%**	1.3%	**37.47%**	0.78%
MAX-S	76.43%	0.14%	**81.03%**	1.09%	76.62%	1.09%	37.22%	0.54%
MIN	75.35%	0.95%	79.97%	0.03%	74.93%	0.59%	36.38%	0.3%
MIN-S	75.39%	0.91%	79.7%	0.24%	74.65%	0.87%	36.07%	0.62%
RAND	76.15%	0.14%	80.68%	0.74%	75.69%	0.17%	36.77%	0.09%
RAND-S	75.97%	0.32%	79.82%	0.12%	75.6%	0.08%	37.06%	0.37%
best:	EDA		WN-MAX-S		WN-MAX		WN-MAX	
BASELINE	73.91%		78.34%		73.9%		35.43%	
BERT	74.88%	0.97%	77.37%	0.97%	73.76%	0.14%	33.95%	1.48%
MAX	74.72%	0.81%	79.12%	0.78%	75.04%	1.14%	36.28%	0.85%
MAX-S	75.08%	1.17%	79.03%	0.69%	74.4%	0.5%	36.51%	1.08%
MIN	74.31%	0.41%	78.24%	0.11%	73.58%	0.32%	34.75%	0.68%
MIN-S	74.55%	0.64%	78.33%	0.01%	73.57%	0.33%	34.56%	0.87%
RAND	74.73%	0.83%	79.27%	0.93%	74.23%	0.33%	35.65%	0.22%
RAND-S	74.57%	0.66%	79.08%	0.74%	74.87%	0.97%	35.64%	0.21%
EDA	74.55%	0.64%	79.99%	1.64%	74.56%	0.66%	34.52%	0.91%
MAX	**75.22%**	1.32%	79.74%	1.39%	75.06%	1.16%	**36.65%**	1.23%
MAX-S	75.06%	1.16%	79.4%	1.06%	75.18%	1.28%	36.63%	1.2%
MIN	73.71%	0.19%	78.5%	0.16%	73.29%	0.61%	34.68%	0.75%
MIN-S	73.46%	0.45%	78.61%	0.27%	73.29%	0.61%	34.76%	0.67%
RAND	74.63%	0.72%	79.47%	1.13%	74.51%	0.61%	35.36%	0.07%
RAND-S	74.38%	0.47%	79.87%	1.53%	74.53%	0.63%	36.04%	0.62%
WN	74.42%	0.51%	79.71%	1.37%	74.99%	1.09%	35.11%	0.32%
MAX	74.19%	0.28%	**80.59%**	2.25%	**75.79%**	1.89%	36.34%	0.92%
MAX-S	74.25%	0.34%	80.5%	2.16%	75.6%	1.7%	36.36%	0.94%
MIN	73.43%	0.48%	79.53%	1.19%	73.81%	0.09%	34.18%	1.24%
MIN-S	73.74%	0.17%	79.49%	1.15%	73.28%	0.62%	34.27%	1.16%
RAND	74.28%	0.37%	80.27%	1.93%	74.92%	1.02%	35.74%	0.32%
RAND-S	74.07%	0.16%	79.93%	1.58%	74.95%	1.05%	35.55%	0.12%
best:	EDA-MAX		WN-MAX		WN-MAX		EDA-MAX	

6.3   Results per Dataset

Table 2 shows the results per dataset. In each case, we average the results from three different sizes of a dataset: {full, half, quarter}. These results come from the same runs as those from Sect. 6.2. We run each variant 10 times for 10 different seeds of random number generator and average the results.

For all datasets at least one of the variants of DA is above the baseline. As for the winners in each "competition" (CNN and RNN). We have 1 offline variant and 3 online variants for CNN. These are EDA, WN-MAX-S, and WN-MAX 2 times. For RNN, there are 4 online DA winners. These are 2 WN-MAX and 2 EDA-MAX.

Two DA variants are always above the baseline. These are WN-MAX and WN-MAX-S. Multiple variants are above the baseline in all cases but one. These include EDA, WN, BERT-MAX-S, EDA-MAX, EDA-MAX-S, and WN-RAND.

The overall two biggest improvements above the baseline come from WN-MAX and WN-MAX-S on the MPQA dataset with RNNs – these are 2.25% and 2.16% respectively. The biggest improvement for CNNs is 1.3%, and it comes from WN-MAX-S on the SST-2 dataset.

7   Conclusions

At least for this set of experiments on sentiment classification, the online max approach improves DA for RNNs. However, for CNNs, the case is not that clear. Improvement occurs in most of the CNN cases, but not all, and it is smaller than for RNN. Among the three tested DA methods, WordNet and EDA perform better than BERT. It is worth noting that BERT is not used here for the downstream task, which is sentiment classification, but for DA itself. As for the results per dataset (Sect. 6.3) the online approach wins in all of them for RNNs and in most of them for CNNs. Our work also confirms the finding of Wei and Zou that DA tends to give better improvements with the decreasing size of a dataset.

The improvements over the baseline reach 2.3% in accuracy for the results averaged over datasets and 2.25% on one of the datasets but averaged over dataset sizes. We use 2 neural network architectures and 3 data augmentation methods on 4 different datasets, and repeat each variant 10 times. Our research indicates that, at least for RNN, the switch to online DA can help. All of this gives a solid basis for further research in this field.

Acknowledgment. This work was supported by the Polish National Centre for Research and Development – LIDER Program under Grant LIDER/27/0164/L-8/16/NCBR/2017 titled "Lemkin – intelligent legal information system". We used the computational resources of the Prometheus computer of the PLGrid infrastructure for the experiments described in this paper.

We are grateful to Krzysztof Wróbel for his inspirational idea and to Agnieszka Jungiewicz for her remarks.

References

1. Harvard Kim CNN implementation. https://github.com/harvardnlp/sent-conv-torch
2. Sosuke Kobayashi's data augmentation implementation. https://github.com/pfnet-research/contextual_augmentation
3. Transformers: State-of-the-art Natural Language Processing for TensorFlow 2.0 and PyTorch. https://github.com/huggingface/transformers
4. WordNet online. https://wordnet.princeton.edu
5. Abulaish, M., Sah, A.K.: A text data augmentation approach for improving the performance of CNN. In: 2019 11th International Conference on Communication Systems & Networks (COMSNETS), pp. 625–630 (2019)
6. Anaby-Tavor, A., et al.: Do not have enough data? Deep learning to the rescue! In: AAAI, pp. 7383–7390 (2020)
7. Bottou, L.: Large-scale machine learning with stochastic gradient descent. In: Lechevallier Y., Saporta G. (eds.) Proceedings of COMPSTAT'2010, pp. 177–186. Springer, Heidelberg (2010). https://doi.org/10.1007/978-3-7908-2604-3_16
8. Coulombe, C.: Text data augmentation made simple by leveraging nlp cloud apis. arXiv preprint arXiv:1812.04718 (2018)
9. Devlin, J., Chang, M.W., Lee, K., Toutanova, K.: BERT: pre-training of deep bidirectional transformers for language understanding. In: Proceedings of the 2019 Conference of the North American Chapter of the Association for Computational Linguistics: Human Language Technologies, Volume 1 (Long and Short Papers), pp. 4171–4186. Association for Computational Linguistics, Minneapolis, Minnesota, June 2019. https://doi.org/10.18653/v1/N19-1423
10. Fawzi, A., Samulowitz, H., Turaga, D., Frossard, P.: Adaptive data augmentation for image classification. In: 2016 IEEE International Conference on Image Processing (ICIP), pp. 3688–3692. IEEE (2016)
11. Hu, M., Liu, B.: Mining and summarizing customer reviews. In: Proceedings of the Tenth ACM SIGKDD International Conference on Knowledge Discovery and Data Mining, pp. 168–177. ACM (2004)
12. Jungiewicz, M., Smywiński-Pohl, A.: Towards textual data augmentation for neural networks: synonyms and maximum loss. Comput. Sci. **20**(1) (2019). https://doi.org/10.7494/csci.2019.20.1.3023
13. Kim, Y.: Convolutional neural networks for sentence classification. In: Proceedings of the 2014 Conference on Empirical Methods in Natural Language Processing (EMNLP), pp. 1746–1751. Association for Computational Linguistics (2014). https://doi.org/10.3115/v1/D14-1181
14. Kingma, D.P., Ba, J.: Adam: a method for stochastic optimization. CoRR abs/1412.6980 (2015)
15. Kobayashi, S.: Contextual augmentation: data augmentation by words with paradigmatic relations. In: Proceedings of the 2018 Conference of the North American Chapter of the Association for Computational Linguistics: Human Language Technologies, Volume 2 (Short Papers), pp. 452–457. Association for Computational Linguistics (2018). https://doi.org/10.18653/v1/N18-2072
16. Ma, E.: nlpaug: data augmentation for NLP. https://github.com/makcedward/nlpaug. version 0.0.8 beta
17. Manning, C.D.: Computational linguistics and deep learning. Comput. Linguist. **41**(4), 701–707 (2015)

18. Miller, G.: WordNet: An Electronic Lexical Database. MIT Press, Cambridge (1998)
19. Miller, G.A.: Wordnet: a lexical database for English. Commun. ACM **38**(11), 39–41 (1995)
20. Pang, B., Lee, L.: A sentimental education: sentiment analysis using subjectivity summarization based on minimum cuts. In: Proceedings of the 42nd Annual Meeting on Association for Computational Linguistics, p. 271. Association for Computational Linguistics (2004)
21. Quijas, J.K.: Analysing the effects of data augmentation and free parameters for text classification with recurrent convolutional neural networks. The University of Texas, El Paso (2017)
22. Radford, A., Wu, J., Child, R., Luan, D., Amodei, D., Sutskever, I.: Language models are unsupervised multitask learners. OpenAI Blog **1**(8), 9 (2019)
23. Socher, R., et al.: Recursive deep models for semantic compositionality over a sentiment treebank. In: Proceedings of the 2013 Conference on Empirical Methods in Natural Language Processing, pp. 1631–1642 (2013)
24. Tokui, S., Oono, K., Hido, S., Clayton, J.: Chainer: a next-generation open source framework for deep learning. In: Proceedings of Workshop on Machine Learning Systems (LearningSys) in the Twenty-Ninth Annual Conference on Neural Information Processing Systems (NIPS), vol. 5, pp. 1–6 (2015)
25. Wei, J., Zou, K.: EDA: easy data augmentation techniques for boosting performance on text classification tasks. In: Proceedings of the 2019 Conference on Empirical Methods in Natural Language Processing and the 9th International Joint Conference on Natural Language Processing (EMNLP-IJCNLP), pp. 6383–6389. Association for Computational Linguistics, Hong Kong, China, November 2019
26. Wiebe, J., Wilson, T., Cardie, C.: Annotating expressions of opinions and emotions in language. Lang. Res. Eval. **39**(2), 165–210 (2005). https://doi.org/10.1007/s10579-005-7880-9
27. Wu, X., Lv, S., Zang, L., Han, J., Hu, S.: Conditional BERT contextual augmentation. In: Rodrigues, J.M.F., et al. (eds.) ICCS 2019. LNCS, vol. 11539, pp. 84–95. Springer, Cham (2019). https://doi.org/10.1007/978-3-030-22747-0_7

Spiking Neural Networks I

Dendritic Computation in a Point Neuron Model

Alexander Vandesompele$^{(\boxtimes)}$, Francis Wyffels, and Joni Dambre

IDLab-AIRO, Electronics and Information Systems Department,
Ghent University - Imec, Ghent, Belgium
`alexander.vandesompele@ugent.be`

Abstract. Biological neurons possess elaborate dendrites that perform elaborate computations. They are however ignored in the widely used point neuron models. Here, we present a simple addition to the commonly used leaky integrate-and-fire model that introduces the concept of a dendrite. All synapses on the dendrite have a mutual relationship. The result is a form of short term plasticity in which synapse strengths are influenced by recent activity in other synapses. This improves the ability of the neuron to recognize temporal sequences.

Keywords: Spiking neural networks · Dendritic computation · Point neuron model

1 Introduction

Biological neurons are 3-dimensional structures consisting of a cell body (soma), an axon and dendritic arborization. The variety in dendritic tree morphology among neurons has always suggested a role for dendrites in the functionality of the neuron. Over the past decades, thanks to new optical stimulation methods and recording techniques [1,8,9], it has become clear that dendrites are not merely passive electrical components. Instead, they are found to integrate inputs in a nonlinear fashion [3,11,13] and participate actively in computations [2,10,12].

While dendrites are function critical, they are often not taken into account when simulating spiking neural networks. Especially in the machine learning context, point neuron models such as the leaky-integrate-and-fire (LIF) model are widely used. As suggested by their name, point neuron models ignore the existence of dendrites and mimic the integration of all inputs on the neuron soma. They are popular because they seem to be a good trade-off between capturing biological neuron behaviour and computational complexity. Li et al. [6] formulated a synaptic current in order to integrate dendritic nonlinearity into a point neuron model. This current was based on electrophysiological recordings and neuronal simulations. The addition of the current resulted in computational abilities such as direction selectivity.

© Springer Nature Switzerland AG 2020
I. Farkaš et al. (Eds.): ICANN 2020, LNCS 12397, pp. 599–609, 2020.
https://doi.org/10.1007/978-3-030-61616-8_48

In a study by Branco et al. [3], dendrites were observed to be sensitive to the sequence of synaptic inputs. Different sequences of the same inputs result in different somatic response magnitudes. The underlying mechanism was observed to rely on NMDA receptor activation, causing synapses to differentially influence each other, dependent on the relative timing of their activations. In this work, we investigate the extension of the computational LIF neuron model to mimic this dendritic functionality. Synapses are enabled to influence each other, based on the relative timing of activation. We investigate the impact of this extension on the capacity of the neuron to discriminate spatiotemporal inputs.

2 Materials and Methods

2.1 Network Structure

We consider networks that consist of an input layer, an output layer and an inhibitory layer (see Fig. 1). The input layer is fully connected to the output layer, and both consist of only excitatory neurons. The output layer connects to the inhibitory layer with a one-to-one connectivity. The inhibitory layer consists of inhibitory neurons and implements lateral inhibition across the output layer (see Fig. 1). Weights from the input to the output layer are uniformly drawn from [0, 0.5]. Inhibitory neurons are activated by a single input spike and connect to excitatory neurons with weight magnitude of 5, resulting in fairly strong inhibition. This network architecture implements a winner-take-all (WTA) mechanism.

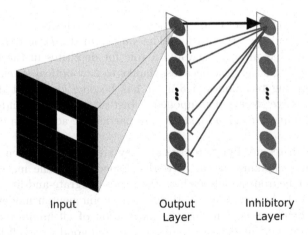

Input   Output   Inhibitory
          Layer   Layer

Fig. 1. Network architecture. Inputs are connected to the excitatory output layer in an all-to-all fashion. Lateral inhibition between excitatory neurons is implemented with an inhibitory layer.

2.2 Neuron Model

Neurons are of type leaky integrate-and-fire (LIF). In the absence of input spikes, the neuron membrane potential (u) change is described by a simple differential equation:

$$\tau_{\text{leak}} \frac{du}{dt} = -(u - u_{\text{rest}}) \tag{1}$$

With τ_{leak} the membrane time constant. Upon input spike arrival, the membrane potential is increased by amount w, the synaptic efficacy. If the membrane potential u reaches a threshold value of u_{thres}, an output spike is sent to all outgoing synapses and u is reset to the resting potential u_{rest} and insensitive to excitatory input for a refractory period T_{refr} (see Table 1 for an overview of parameter values).

To implement inter-synaptic influencing and STDP, a synaptic trace (x) keeps track of recent synaptic activity. Each synapse has a synaptic trace that decays exponentially:

$$\tau_{\text{x}} \frac{dx}{dt} = -x \tag{2}$$

with τ_{x} the decay time constant. Every time a presynaptic spike arrives at the synapse, the synaptic trace is set to 1. The value of x thus indicates recent synaptic activation.

Table 1. Simulation parameters.

Parameter	Value
u_{rest}	$-65\,\text{mV}$
u_{thres}	$-63\,\text{mV}$
T_{refr}	$30\,\text{ms}$
τ_{leak}	$10\,\text{ms}$
τ_{x}	$8\,\text{ms}$
η	0.05

2.3 Synaptic Relations

To mimic dendritic functionality, we introduce a synaptic relation (r) between every pair of synapses. The efficacy of a synapse is then determined by both the synaptic weight and the recent activity of other synapses with which it has a non-zero synaptic relation r (Fig. 2). Upon spike arrival, the synaptic efficacy w_i of synapse i is computed as:

$$w_i = w_{\text{proper,i}} + w_{\text{sr}} \tag{3}$$

$$w_{sr} = \sum_{j=0}^{N} r_{i,j} x_j \tag{4}$$

with w_{proper} the synaptic weight, and w_{sr} the contribution of synaptic relations. $r_{i,j}$ is the magnitude of the synaptic relation between synapse i and j. The synaptic trace (x) is a variable that decays exponentially to 0, hence $r_{i,j} x_j$ will be small except if a spike recently arrived in synapse j. As the efficacy of a synapse can now change transiently, the term w_{sr} implements a form of short term plasticity induced by recent presynaptic activity.

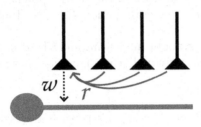

Fig. 2. Synaptic efficacy is influenced by both the synaptic weight (black, dotted arrow) and the synaptic relations (red, solid arrows). (Color figure online)

2.4   Learning Rule

The magnitude of the proper weights can be learned using a form of spike-time dependent plasticity (STDP). When a neuron is caused to fire, it's incoming synaptic weights are updated. All weights are depressed except if a presynaptic spike immediately preceded the postsynaptic spike (see Fig. 3). Using this learning rule, a synapse that does not contribute to spike generation is systematically depressed. Note that if a neuron never fires, it weights will remain static. The positive weight change (potentiation) is given by ηx with η the learning rate and x the synaptic trace. In case of depression, a negative weight change of fixed magnitude $(\eta/2)$ is applied.

Winner-take-all (WTA) mechanisms are long thought to be present in biological networks. In combination with STDP, WTA networks achieve unsupervised feature learning [4,5,7]. Here, a WTA mechanism is implemented with lateral inhibition provided by the inhibitory layer. Hence, output neurons compete for input patterns and activation of the winning neuron is reinforced through the STDP update.

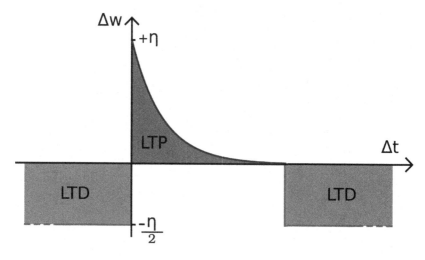

Fig. 3. STDP learning rule. Synaptic weights updates (Δw) are positive (ηx) if the postsynaptic spike shortly follows the presynaptic spike and negative otherwise. $\Delta t = t_{\text{post}} - t_{\text{pre}}$. LTP = long term potentiation, LTD = long term depression.

3   Results

3.1   Direction Sensitivity

To illustrate the impact of the proposed dendritic mechanism, the reaction of two neurons to two input sequences is compared. The neurons differ only in synaptic relations, which were hand-tuned to increase sensitivity for either the first sequence or the second sequence. The first sequence consist of 5 inputs that fire subsequently with a 5 ms interval. The second sequence is the same as the first, but in reversed temporal order. Figure 4 plots the membrane potential of the two neurons. As can be seen from the membrane potential response, the short term plasticity introduced by inter-synaptic relations causes neurons to be sensitive for the order in which inputs arrive.

3.2   Random Sequences

Random sequences are used to assess the increased capacity of temporal sequence discrimination. The input population consists of 16 neurons. One hundred random input sequences were generated, with each input neuron firing once per sequence and fixed inter-spike times (Fig. 5A). Output layers with random synaptic relations (uniformly sampled from [0, 0.5]) are compared to output layers without synaptic relations. Due to strong lateral inhibition only one output

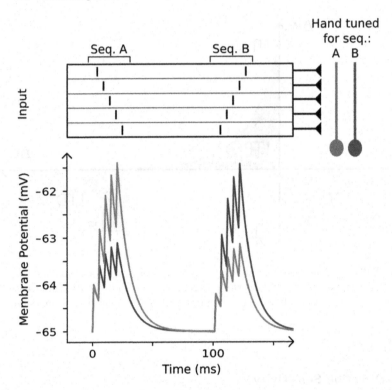

Fig. 4. Inter-synaptic relations cause temporal sensitivity. **Top panel:** Two input sequences are given to two output neurons. The output neurons differ only in inter-synaptic relations. **Bottom panel:** Response of the membrane potentials. The spiking threshold was set high to prevent spiking.

neuron fires in response to an input sequence (see Fig. 5B). As a metric for discrimination capacity, the fraction of neurons in the output layer that is activated by at least one of the input sequences is used. The output layer size is varied from ten up to one hundred neurons. Regardless of the output layer size, the presence of short term plasticity induced by synaptic relations, increases variation in activated output neurons (Fig. 5C).

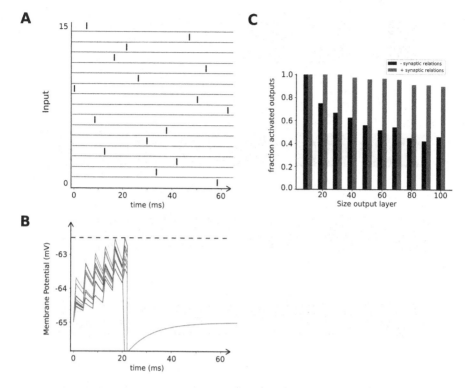

Fig. 5. Discrimination of random sequences without learning. **Panel A:** Example input sequence. **Panel B:** Example response of 10 competing output neurons to the sequence pictured in panel A. Dashed line indicates firing threshold. **Panel C:** Fraction of output neurons activated by at least one input sequence, for different output layer sizes.

3.3 Synaptic Relations Improve Unsupervised Learning

To test the learning capacities of spatiotemporal sequences, we stimulate an output layer of 50 neurons with inputs consisting of a moving pixel on a four by four grid (see Fig. 1). Every time step, the pixel moves to an adjacent tile with a 10% probability of changing direction. During the training phase the output layer receives continuous input while weights are updated according to the STDP rule. During the test phase, the learning updates are halted and the response to continuous input is recorded, in order to establish the receptive field of the output neurons.

Training is repeated for two categories. In the first, all synaptic relations have the same magnitude and hence do not contribute to input discrimination. In the second category, synaptic relations are drawn uniformly from $[0, 0.5]$.

When all synaptic relations are identical, receptive fields develop only as a consequence of the STDP-based weight learning. Figure 6A shows the spatiotemporal receptive fields for a selection of 3 output neurons. The top panel plots the location of the moving pixel, for each time the output neuron was triggered

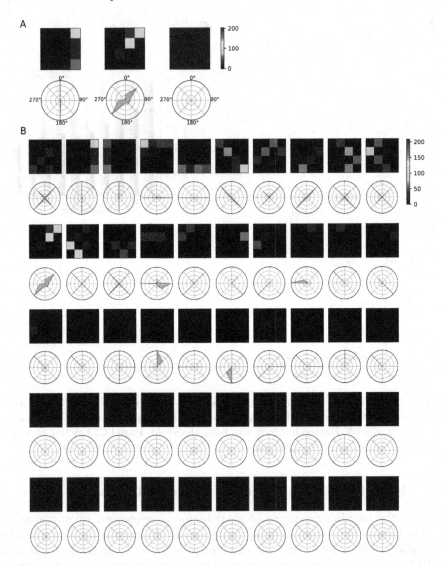

Fig. 6. Spatiotemporal receptive fields of output neurons with **identical synaptic relations**. **A:** Location (top) and direction (bottom) of moving input pixel on moment of neuron activation, for a selection of output neurons. **B:** Spatiotemporal receptive fields for all output neurons, sorted by activity magnitude.

during test run. The bottom panel indicates the direction in which the pixel was moving. Some neurons develop a spatially confined receptive field. The left-most depicted neuron is sensitive for both upwards (0°) and downwards (180°) movement in the rightmost column. The middle neuron is mainly activated by movement along the diagonal 45°–225° axis, but to a lesser extent also to other directions on that location. Other neurons, like the third shown, are never

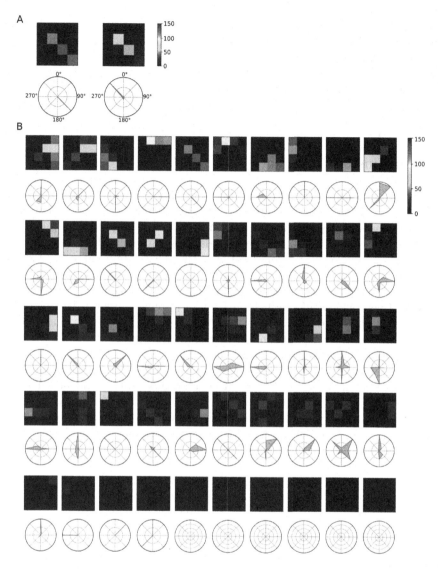

Fig. 7. Spatiotemporal receptive fields of output neurons with **randomized synaptic relations**. **A:** Location (top) and direction (bottom) of moving input pixel on moment of neuron activation, for a selection of output neurons. **B:** Spatiotemporal receptive fields for all output neurons, sorted by activity magnitude.

activated as they are always inhibited by other output neurons that win the competition. Figure 6B shows the receptive fields of all 50 output neurons. Less than half of the neurons form meaningful receptive fields. Note that most frequently active neurons are sensitive for at least 2 opposing directions of movement.

Figure 7 shows the result for the second category, with randomized synaptic relations. It is clear from Fig. 7B that more output neurons have developed meaningful receptive fields. This can be explained by the increased direction sensitivity of output neurons. Figure 7A shows two output neurons that have a similar spatial receptive field, however they are sensitive for movement in the opposite direction. The addition of random synaptic relations hence enabled neurons to discriminate inputs based on their temporal order. Indeed, most of the active output neurons have a single dominant direction to which they are sensitive.

4 Conclusions

The computations performed by dendrites are known to be crucial for biological neurons. in this work we present a simple method to include some of the observed functionality into a point neuron model, commonly used in spiking network simulations. Inclusion of synaptic relations results in a form of short term plasticity that makes the neuron sensitive to the precise temporal order of inputs. This increases the capacity of a neuron to discriminate between spatiotemporal inputs, as exemplified by directional sensitivity. This capacity, also observed in biological neurons, should be helpful for interpreting temporal data. This can be useful at the input level, for instance when dealing with video data, but it can also be useful for neurons in more downstream layers, as they continuously receive sequences of inputs from other neurons.

In this work, the magnitude of the synaptic relations have been sampled in a random fashion, whilst in biological neurons this value would be related to the spatial adjacency of synapses on the dendritic arbour. In further work, we will explore the use of distance based relationships. In addition, it may also be interesting to apply an unsupervised learning rule, similar to the STDP used in this work, to adjust the synaptic relations based on the inputs provided to the network.

Acknowledgment. This research has received funding from the European Union's Horizon 2020 Framework Programme for Research and Innovation under the Specific Grant Agreement No. 785907 (Human Brain Project SGA2).

References

1. Anselmi, F., Ventalon, C., Bègue, A., Ogden, D., Emiliani, V.: Three-dimensional imaging and photostimulation by remote-focusing and holographic light patterning. Proc. Nat. Acad. Sci. **108**(49), 19504–19509 (2011)
2. Bittner, K.C., Milstein, A.D., Grienberger, C., Romani, S., Magee, J.C.: Behavioral time scale synaptic plasticity underlies CA1 place fields. Science **357**(6355), 1033–1036 (2017)
3. Branco, T., Clark, B.A., Häusser, M.: Dendritic discrimination of temporal input sequences in cortical neurons. Science **329**(5999), 1671–1675 (2010)
4. Ferré, P., Mamalet, F., Thorpe, S.J.: Unsupervised feature learning with winner-takes-all based STDP. Front. Comput. Neurosci. **12**, 24 (2018)

5. Kohonen, T.: Self-organized formation of topologically correct feature maps. Biol. Cybern. **43**(1), 59–69 (1982). https://doi.org/10.1007/BF00337288

6. Li, S., Liu, N., Zhang, X., McLaughlin, D.W., Zhou, D., Cai, D.: Dendritic computations captured by an effective point neuron model. Proc. Nat. Acad. Sci. **116**(30), 15244–15252 (2019)

7. Masquelier, T., Guyonneau, R., Thorpe, S.J.: Competitive STDP-based spike pattern learning. Neural Comput. **21**(5), 1259–1276 (2009)

8. Packer, A.M., Peterka, D.S., Hirtz, J.J., Prakash, R., Deisseroth, K., Yuste, R.: Two-photon optogenetics of dendritic spines and neural circuits. Nat. Methods **9**(12), 1202 (2012)

9. Packer, A.M., Roska, B., Häusser, M.: Targeting neurons and photons for optogenetics. Nat. Neurosci. **16**(7), 805 (2013)

10. Schmidt-Hieber, C., et al.: Active dendritic integration as a mechanism for robust and precise grid cell firing. Nat. Neurosci. **20**(8), 1114 (2017)

11. Stuart, G.J., Sakmann, B.: Active propagation of somatic action potentials into neocortical pyramidal cell dendrites. Nature **367**(6458), 69–72 (1994)

12. Takahashi, N., Oertner, T.G., Hegemann, P., Larkum, M.E.: Active cortical dendrites modulate perception. Science **354**(6319), 1587–1590 (2016)

13. Wang, S.S.H., Denk, W., Häusser, M.: Coincidence detection in single dendritic spines mediated by calcium release. Nat. Neurosci. **3**(12), 1266–1273 (2000)

Benchmarking Deep Spiking Neural Networks on Neuromorphic Hardware

Christoph Ostrau$^{(\boxtimes)}$ ⓘ, Jonas Homburg ⓘ, Christian Klarhorst, Michael Thies, and Ulrich Rückert

Technical Faculty, Bielefeld University, Bielefeld, Germany
costrau@techfak.uni-bielefeld.de

Abstract. With more and more event-based neuromorphic hardware systems being developed at universities and in industry, there is a growing need for assessing their performance with domain specific measures. In this work, we use the methodology of converting pre-trained non-spiking to spiking neural networks to evaluate the performance loss and measure the energy-per-inference for three neuromorphic hardware systems (BrainScaleS, Spikey, SpiNNaker) and common simulation frameworks for CPU (NEST) and CPU/GPU (GeNN). For analog hardware we further apply a re-training technique known as hardware-in-the-loop training to cope with device mismatch. This analysis is performed for five different networks, including three networks that have been found by an automated optimization with a neural architecture search framework. We demonstrate that the conversion loss is usually below one percent for digital implementations, and moderately higher for analog systems with the benefit of much lower energy-per-inference costs.

Keywords: Spiking neural networks · Neural architecture search · Benchmark

1 Introduction

Diverse event-based neuromorphic hardware systems promise the accelerated execution of so called spiking neural networks (SNN), also referred to as the third generation of neural networks [14]. The most prominent representatives of this class of hardware accelerators include the platforms Braindrop [16], BrainScaleS [22], DYNAPs [15], Loihi [5], SpiNNaker [8] and Truenorth [1]. With the diversity of hardware accelerators comes a problem for potential end-users: which platform is suited best for a given spiking neural network algorithm, possibly respecting inherent resource requirements for embedding in mobile robots or smart devices. Usually, this question is answered by evaluating a set of benchmarks on all qualified systems, which measure the state-of-the-art and quantify progress in future hardware generations (see e.g. [4])). Here, we face two major challenges with neuromorphic hardware. First, there is no universal interface to all hardware/software simulators despite some projects like PyNN [6]. Second,

© Springer Nature Switzerland AG 2020
I. Farkaš et al. (Eds.): ICANN 2020, LNCS 12397, pp. 610–621, 2020.
https://doi.org/10.1007/978-3-030-61616-8_49

there are quite a few promising network models and learning strategies, but still "the" algorithm for spiking neural networks is missing. One recent system overarching network is the cortical microcircuit model [2,13]. A follow-up publication [21] shows, how this benchmark has driven platform specific optimization that, in the end, improves the execution of various networks on the SpiNNaker platform confirming the value of benchmarks. However, it is also an example of a platform specific implementation to reach maximal performance on a given system.

One commonly agreed application for spiking neural networks is the conversion of conventionally trained artificial neural networks (ANN) to rate-based SNNs [7]. Although this is not using SNNs in their most efficient way, it is a pragmatic approach that is suitable to be ported to different accelerators, independent of their nature. In this work, we use this approach for evaluating five distinct networks, either defined by hardware restrictions, by already published work, or by employing neural architecture search (NAS) with Lamarck_ML [11] to optimize the network topology. We evaluate these networks on Brain-ScaleS, Spikey [20], and SpiNNaker as well as the CPU simulator NEST [9] and the CPU/GPU code-generation framework GeNN [25]. Furthermore, we use a retraining approach with neuromorphic hardware-in-the-loop (HIL) proposed in [23] to unlock the full potential of the analog neuromorphic hardware systems. Section 2 outlines the target systems, the software environment, and the used methods. Section 3 presents the results, including neuron parameter optimization, and accuracy along with energy measurements for all target platforms.

2   Methods

In the following we introduce all target systems and the software environment as well as the methodology followed.

2.1   Target Systems and Software

All target systems in this work support the simulation or emulation of leaky integrate-and-fire neurons with conductance-based synapses, although especially analog systems are limited to specific neuron models. **NEST** is a scaleable software simulator suited to simulate small as well as extensive networks on compute clusters. It is used in version 2.18 [12] executed with four threads on an Intel Core i7-4710MQ mobile processor. **GeNN** [25] is a code generation framework for the simulation of SNNs. In its current release version $(4.2.1)$[1], it supports generating code for a single-threaded CPU simulation or for graphics processing units (GPU) supporting NVIDIA CUDA. Networks are evaluated on a NVIDIA GeForce 1080 TI GPU; runtimes are measured for networks without recording any spikes due to the overhead of getting spikes back from GPU, which effectively stops the simulation at every time step and copies the data between GPU

---

[1] Here, we use the most recent GeNN from github (end of April 2020).

and CPU. For this publication we make use of single precision accuracy and all simulators use a time step of 1 ms. However, NEST is using an adaptive time-step to integrate the neuron model. The fully digital many-core architecture **SpiNNaker** [8] comes in two different sizes, which are both used in this work. The smaller SpiNN3 system is composed of four chips; the larger SpiNN5 board consists of 48 chips. A single chip comprises 18 ARM968 general purpose CPU cores, with each simulating up to 255 `IF_cond_exp` neurons. The system runs in real-time, simulating 1 ms of model time in 1 ms wall clock time. SpiNNaker is used with the latest released software version 5.1.0 using PyNN 0.9.4. Finally, we make use of two mixed-signal (analog neural circuits, digital interconnect) systems: First, the **Spikey** system [20] supports the emulation of 384 neurons with 256 synapses each. The emulated neuron model is subject to restricted parameter ranges (e.g. four bit weights, limited time constants) with some parameters prescribed by the hardware (e.g. the membrane capacitance). The system runs at a speedup of 10,000, therefore taking only 0.1 ms to emulate 1 ms of model time. Second, Spikey's successor **BrainScaleS** [22] shares many of Spikey's properties. Most notably is the now fully parameterizable neuron model, as well as the usage of wafer-scale integration, combining 384 accessible HICANN chips on a single wafer for a full system. Each chip implements 512 neuron circuits with 220 synapses each, where up to 64 circuits can be combined to form a single virtual neuron, allowing more robust emulations and a higher synapse fan-in.

While all of these platforms formally support the **PyNN** API [6], the supported API versions differ between simulators impeding the portability of code. **Cypress**[2] [24] is a C++ framework abstracting away these differences. For NEST, Spikey and SpiNNaker the framework makes use of their PyNN interfaces, however, for BrainScaleS and GeNN a lower-level C++ interface is used. Furthermore, the proposed networks studied below are part of the **S**piking **N**eural **A**rchitecture **B**enchmark **Suite**[3] (SNABSuite) [17,18], which also covers benchmarks like low-level synthetic characterizations and application-inspired (sub-)tasks with an associated framework for automated evaluation.

Energy measurements have been taken with a Ruideng UM25C power meter (SpiNNaker, Spikey), with a PeakTech 9035 for CPU simulations, or with the NVIDIA `smi` tool. There is no possibility for remote energy measurements on the BrainScaleS system. Thus, the values have been estimated from the number of pre-synaptic events using published data in [23].

2.2   Converting DNNs to SNNs

This work is based on the idea of [3,7], where a pre-trained artificial neural network is converted into a SNN. In this case, we train several multi-layer perceptrons that differ in size to classify MNIST handwritten digits. The training uses standard batch-wise gradient-descent in combination with error back-propagation. The conversion method exploits that the activation curve of a LIF

---

[2] https://github.com/hbp-unibi/cypress.

[3] The code for this and other work can be found at https://github.com/hbp-unibi/SNABSuite.

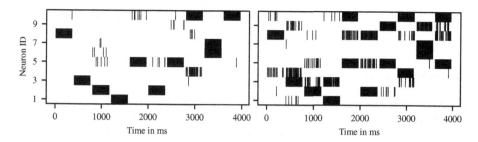

Fig. 1. Output spikes for converted networks. Left: Output spikes of a network that has been trained using a softmax layer as the last layer. Right: The same network trained with only ReLU activation functions.

neuron resembles the ReLU activation curve, such that float (analog) values of the ANN become spike rates in the SNN. All weights of the ANN are normalized to the maximal weight of the full network, and then scaled to a maximal value either given by restrictions of the hardware platform (e.g. 4 bit weights on Spikey/BrainScaleS) or determined by parameter optimization (see below for details). Similarly, other parameters of the SNN are found by extensive parameter tuning or are fixed due to hardware constraints. Neuron biases are not easily and efficiently mapped to SNNs, which is why we set all bias terms to zero in the training process of the ANN. In contrast to [7], we found that using a softmax layer as the last layer in the ANN for training does not necessarily decrease the performance of the SNN. However, using soft-max will lead to an increased number of spikes for all rejected classes (cf. Fig. 1).

As the Spikey platform is very limited in size and connectivity, the smallest and simplest network (referred to as *Spikey network*) consists of a single hidden layer with 100 neurons and no inhibitory connections. Spikey requires separation of excitation and inhibition at the neuron level and consists of two separate chips with limited connectivity between them. Thus, we only used positive weights and achieved the best performance using a hinge loss, which increases the weights for the winner neurons and decreases weights for the second place neuron only. Due to the acceleration factor of Spikey and BrainScaleS, communication bandwidth limits the usable spike rates. Too high rates (input as well as inter-neuron rates) will inevitably lead to spike loss that would reduce the performance of the network. This naturally restricts the parameter space to be evaluated. Still, there is a significant performance loss when applying the conversion process for analog systems. Perfect conversion requires that every synapse with the same weight and every neuron behaves in the same way, referring to identical activation curves. On analog systems, however, we have to deal with temporal noise perturbing the membrane voltage, trial-to-trial variation and analogmismatch between circuits [19]. As shown in [24], such a hardware network will perform at roughly 60–70% accuracy compared to a simulator, even after platform specific parameter tuning. [23] proposed to train the pre-trained neural network again while replacing the outputs of the ANN with spike rates recorded from hardware employing back-propagation to train a device specific network. All details can be found in Fig. 7 of [23].

2.3   Neural Architecture Search (NAS)

Lamarck_ML[4] [11] is a modular and extensible Python library for application driven exploration of network architectures. This library allows to define a class of network architectures to be examined and operations to modify and combine those architectures. These definitions are then used by a search algorithm to explore and evaluate network architectures in order to maximize an objective function. For this work, the limitations of the neuromorphic hardware systems compared to state-of-the-art processing units are the leading motivation for the applied restrictions. The applied layer types are limited to fully connected layers which may be arranged in a nonsequential manner resulting in an acyclic directed graph structure. To preserve the structural information of a single neural network in the exploration process, a meta graph is created to contain the current network and the meta graph of the networks which were involved in creating it. This process is unbounded and accumulates structural information over several generations in the meta graph. To forget unprofitable information, the meta graph is designed to dismiss structural information that has not been used in the last five exploration steps. One exploration step consists of combining the meta graph of two network architectures and sampling a new path in this meta graph in order to create an improved architecture. A new architecture is created by sampling a path based on the quality of its best architecture and amending it with elements that have not been examined before.

The exploration procedure is performed by a genetic algorithm configured with a generation size of 36 network architectures of which 20 are selected based on an exponential ranking to create new architectures for the next generation. This next generation is created with an elitism replacement scheme that preserves the best two network architectures of the previous generation. In total 75 generations have been created in the NAS to find an architecture that achieves at least 97% evaluation accuracy. Above this threshold, an architecture is defined to be better if it requires less than 100 neurons for increasing the accuracy by 1%.

3   Results

The first two parts of this section present the parameter tuning process used for the converted SNNs. Details of four different networks are shown, the smallest one was defined by the restrictions of the Spikey platform, while the remaining networks were picked from the neural architecture search. The final part gathers the results for all networks including one model taken from literature.

---

[4] https://github.com/JonasDHomburg/LAMARCK_ML. .

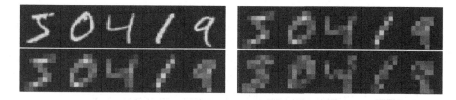

Fig. 2. Visualization of the down-scaled and converted images. The top left row shows the first five images of the MNIST training data set. The bottom left row shows down-scaled images using 3×3 average pooling. The top right row represents the conversion to spikes and back to analog values. The bottom right row shows differences between down-scaled and converted images scaled up by a factor of 10.

3.1 The Spikey Network and Parameter Optimization

This is the simplest network used in this work. As described above, it is motivated by the hardware restriction of the Spikey neuromorphic hardware system and uses a $89 \times 100 \times 10$ layout which requires images to be scaled down using 3×3 average pooling (cf. Fig. 2). These restrictions limit the test-accuracy of the pre-trained network to only 90.13%. This serves as the baseline for the following optimizations of the most relevant SNN parameters.

- The **maximal weight** determines the incoming activity per neuron. If chosen too high, the neuron operates in its non-linear and saturating range near the maximum output frequency.
- The **leakage/membrane time constant** describes the time window in which the neuron integrates incoming input. Too small values would require high frequencies for encoding analog values while higher numbers lead to saturation effects.
- The **sample presentation time** increases accuracy with higher values, which in turn require more energy and time.
- A higher **frequency range of input pixels** improves the pixel approximation accuracy, but is subject to saturation of neurons.

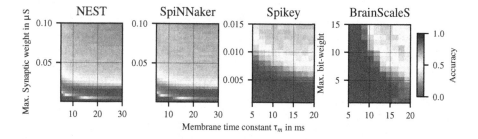

Fig. 3. Sweep over the maximal input frequency. Weights for BrainScaleS are set via low level digital weights (0 to 15).

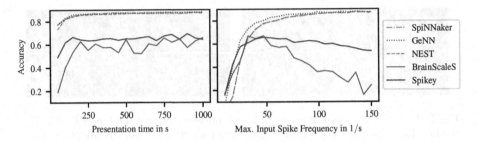

Fig. 4. Sweep over the sample presentation time (left) and the maximal input frequency (right)

Figure 3 shows parameter sweeps over the two most essential neuron parameters for the training set. The images show large areas of high relative accuracy for the analog platforms. On the simulated platforms, one can see the discussed effects of saturating neurons at high weights/time constants. Here, the area of high relative accuracy is rather narrow. Therefore, careful parameter tuning has to be done.

Taking a look at the most relevant conversion parameters, Fig. 4 shows the accuracy in relation to the sample presentation time and the maximal spike input frequency. First, simulating more than 200 ms will result in minor improvements only. Analog platforms converge a bit slower (which is partially caused by different neuron parameters used in the simulation), and the benefits of using presentation times larger than 200 ms are minor again. However, prolonged presentation times can cancel out some of the temporal noise on membrane voltages and synapses. Second, all platforms gain significantly from frequencies larger than 40 Hz. However, due to communication constraints in the accelerated analog platforms, the accuracy decreases for values above 60 Hz. Here, two bandwidth restrictions may play a major role: input spikes are inserted into the digital network using FPGAs. Any spike loss is usually reported by the respective software layer. However, on the wafer, there might be additional loss in the internal network, which is not reported. Output rates of hidden and ouput layers are a second source of potential spike loss which is only partially reported for the Spikey system (by monitoring spike buffers), but happens silently on the BrainScaleS system. The Spikey system reports full buffers for larger frequencies, which is why we assume that this is the major cause for spike loss on both systems.

To reach a high efficiency on larger systems, it is crucial to fully utilize them. Therefore, we used several parallel instances of the same network each classifying a separate portion of the data. In our setup this is controlled by choosing the batch size: a smaller batch size leads to more independent batches processed in parallel and thus effectively reduces processing time and energy per inference. This also avoids idle cores contributing to the energy calculation. These system-specific variations in batch size have negligible effects on the classification accuracy. On SpiNNaker, the hardware size and the required number of processor cores per network instance determine the parallelism. On GeNN, the

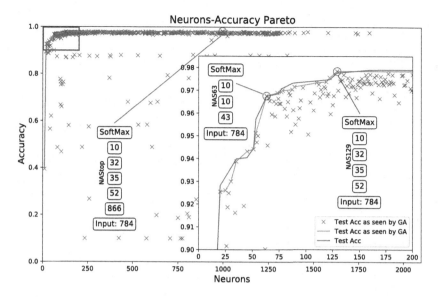

Fig. 5. Results of the optimization process. Highlighted are three candidates networks at the pareto front with their respective network layout.

working memory required to compile the GPU code is the determining factor. The latter is a limitation caused by using separate populations per layer, which could be merged to possibly lead to an increased parallelism of the networks, but not necessarily to increased efficiency. Only the Spikey system executes batches sequentially to avoid full spike buffers.

3.2 NAS Optimized Networks

The optimization process was driven by two major goals: to reach an accuracy larger than 97% and at the same time to reduce the network size in terms of the number of neurons. Results in Fig. 5 reveal, that this not necessarily leads to networks with a single hidden layer. Furthermore, the sequential neural networks outperformed all evaluated non-sequential architectures. We have chosen three candidates on the pareto-front for evaluation on neuromorphic hardware:

- the network with the highest evaluation accuracy (*NAStop*, 97.71%)
- the optimal network with the best trade-off (*NAS129*, 97.53%)
- a small network with still sufficient accuracy (*NAS63*, 96,76%)

3.3 Benchmark Results

Table 1 collects the results for all target platforms. Most striking is the energy efficiency of the analog platforms, which is two orders of magnitude higher compared to other simulators. Furthermore, HIL training recovers most of the

Table 1. Results from all converted networks. Highlighted are the best values per converted network. [†] Reduced number of neurons per core from its default 255 to 200 and [×] further reduced to 180 together with a slowed-down simulation (factor 2).

Platform	Accuracy in %	Conversion Loss in %	Wall clock time in ms	Energy per Inference in mJ	Batchsize
Spikey Network (ANN accuracy: 90.13%)					
Spikey	65.33	24.80	350	0.21	2500
Spikey HIL	84.99	5.14	350	0.21	100
BrainScaleS	61.65	28.43	900	0.33	10000
BrainScaleS HIL	83.87	6.56	900	0.36	10000
SpiNN3	88.41	1.72	264000	79	480
SpiNN5	88.40	1.73	23100	61	42
NEST	88.98	1.15	70542	316	2500
GeNN CPU	89.11	1.02	5070	10	10000
GeNN GPU	88.87	1.26	2623	21	100
NAS63 (ANN accuracy: 96,76%)					
SpiNN3	96.04	0.63	368500	109	670
SpiNN5	96.04	0.63	30800	80	56
NEST	96.37	0.30	217252	952	10000
GeNN CPU	96.29	0.38	16659	31	10000
GeNN GPU	96.32	0.35	17881	145	160
NAS129 (ANN accuracy: 97,53%)					
SpiNN3	96.86	0.67	458700	138	834
SpiNN5	97.25	0.28	38500	105	70
NEST	97.10	0.43	263134	1247	10000
GeNN CPU	97.42	0.11	20436	38	10000
GeNN GPU	97.34	0.19	18495	153	200
NAStop (ANN accuracy: 97,71%)					
SpiNN3[†]	96.80	0.91	918500	353	1670
SpiNN5[†]	97.42	0.29	82500	288	150
NEST	97.35	0.36	907869	4004	10000
GeNN CPU	97.53	0.18	96324	173	10000
GeNN GPU	97.51	0.20	21355	196	265
Network from [7] (ANN accuracy of 98.84%)					
SpiNN3[×]	97.83	1.01	2750000	1021	2500
SpiNN5[†]	98.77	0.07	104500	407	190
NEST	98.82	0.02	3061562	13869	10000
GeNN CPU	98.86	-0.02	314049	587	10000
GeNN GPU	98.85	-0.01	26632	293	280

conversion losses found for these platforms (despite the four bit weight accuracy). Larger networks have not been evaluated either due to size restrictions, or because combined spike rates of input pixels are too high to get any reasonable results. The SpiNNaker system, in both variants, performs on the same efficiency level as a CPU/GPU implementations although its technology is much older (130 nm vs. 22 nm CPU vs. 16 nm GPU). Furthermore, there is less than one percent loss in accuracy due to the conversion in almost all cases. However, for the large networks the system was performing at its limits, and we had to reduce the maximal number of neurons per core. Of course, this can be mitigated by further reducing the number of neurons per core or slowing down the system with respective negative impacts on the energy per inference. Interesting differences have been found for NEST: in some cases the accuracy is a bit lower, but the energy per inference is one order higher than for the GeNN CPU simulation. The latter is mainly due to the more accurate integrator employed by the NEST simulator (especially the adaptive time step in the integrator), which is also responsible for the significant energy gap between the two CPU simulators NEST and GeNN. Furthermore, the multi-threaded execution of NEST does not reduce the computation time compared to GeNN. With the increase of network complexity there is next to no increase in GPU execution time, indicating that despite parallelization of the networks, the GPU is still not utilized fully for the smaller networks (there are 3969-86,760 simultaneously simulated neurons for the GPU depending on the network). Still, for the larger networks, the GPU implementation is the fastest simulation available.

The last network in Table 1 is taken from [7], as the network weights are published within the respective repository. The layout is $784 \times 1200 \times 1200 \times 10$, and thus it is significantly larger. The results show that the SpiNN3 system still operates at its limits (as reported by the software stack) despite the used slow-down. The other platforms show nearly the same accuracy with next to no loss in the conversion process. Concerning the energy per inference, the larger SpiNNaker platform is slightly better than the CPU implementation, with the GPU being the most efficient platform.

4   Conclusion and Outlook

We have demonstrated the capability of all target platforms to simulate converted deep neural networks. The loss in the conversion process is negligible in many cases, and for analog platforms Spikey and BrainScaleS we successfully employed retraining to reach high accuracy. Furthermore, we calculated the used energy-per-inference, quantifying the efficiency vs. accuracy trade-off of analog platforms. The digital SpiNNaker platform is highly efficient if fully utilized despite the rather old chip manufacturing process, demonstrating the suitability for efficient large-scale simulations. If primarily simulation time at highest accuracy for not too large networks needs to be optimized, GeNN's GPU backend allow fast and efficient simulation of SNNs. The approach used in this work is not the most efficient way of using spiking neural networks. However, the rate-coding applied here can be replaced with a more efficient time-to-first-spike (TTFS) encoding, using only a few spikes with much faster response times, which has recently been demonstrated on analog hardware [10]. Therefore, the results from this work must be seen as a conservative measure for the relative efficiency of SNNs on neuromorphic hardware. Furthermore, we did not make use of convolutional networks, because these currently cannot be mapped well to neuromorphic hardware. For the future of our benchmark suite we plan to include both: networks using TTFS encoding and convolutions. This will allow us to test more challenging data-sets with larger and more complex networks.

Funding/Acknowledgment. The research leading to these results has received funding from the European Union Seventh Framework Programme (FP7) under grant agreement no 604102 and the EU's Horizon 2020 research and innovation programme under grant agreements No 720270 and 785907 (Human Brain Project, HBP). It has been further supported by the Cluster of Excellence Cognitive Interaction Technology "CITEC" (EXC 277) at Bielefeld University, which is funded by the German Research Foundation (DFG). Furthermore, we thank the Electronic Vision(s) group from Heidelberg University and Advanced Processor Technologies Research Group from Manchester University for access to their hardware systems and continuous support and James Knight from the University of Sussex for support regarding our GeNN implementation.

References

1. Akopyan, F., et al.: TrueNorth: design and tool flow of a 65 mW 1 million neuron programmable neurosynaptic chip. IEEE Trans. Comput.-Aided Design Integr. Circuits Syst. **34**(10), 1537–1557 (2015). https://doi.org/10.1109/TCAD. 2015.2474396
2. van Albada, S.J., et al.: Performance comparison of the digital neuromorphic hardware SpiNNaker and the neural network simulation software NEST for a full-scale cortical microcircuit model. Front. Neurosci. **12**, 291 (2018). https://doi.org/10. 3389/fnins.2018.00291
3. Cao, Y., Chen, Y., Khosla, D.: Spiking deep convolutional neural networks for energy-efficient object recognition. Int. J. Comput. Vision **113**(1), 54–66 (2014). https://doi.org/10.1007/s11263-014-0788-3
4. Davies, M.: Benchmarks for progress in neuromorphic computing. Nat. Mach. Intell. **1**(9), 386–388 (2019). https://doi.org/10.1038/s42256-019-0097-1
5. Davies, M., et al.: Loihi: a neuromorphic manycore processor with on-chip learning. IEEE Micro **38**(1), 82–99 (2018). https://doi.org/10.1109/MM.2018.112130359
6. Davison, A.P.: PyNN: a common interface for neuronal network simulators. Front. Neuroinform. **2**(January), 11 (2008). https://doi.org/10.3389/neuro.11.011.2008
7. Diehll, P.U., et al.: Fast-classifying, high-accuracy spiking deep networks through weight and threshold balancing. In: Proceedings of the International Joint Conference on Neural Networks 2015-September (2015). https://doi.org/10.1109/IJCNN. 2015.7280696
8. Furber, S.B., et al.: Overview of the SpiNNaker system architecture. IEEE Trans. Comput. **62**(12), 2454–2467 (2013). https://doi.org/10.1109/TC.2012.142
9. Gewaltig, M.O., Diesmann, M.: NEST (neural simulation tool). Scholarpedia **2**(4), 1430 (2007)

10. Göltz, J., et al.: Fast and deep neuromorphic learning with time-to-first-spike coding (2019). https://doi.org/10.1145/3381755.3381770
11. Homburg, J.D., Adams, M., Thies, M., Korthals, T., Hesse, M., Rückert, U.: Constraint exploration of convolutional network architectures with neuroevolution. In: Rojas, I., Joya, G., Catala, A. (eds.) IWANN 2019. LNCS, vol. 11507, pp. 735–746. Springer, Cham (2019). https://doi.org/10.1007/978-3-030-20518-8_61
12. Jordan, J., et al.: NEST 2.18.0 (2019). https://doi.org/10.5281/ZENODO.2605422
13. Knight, J.C., Nowotny, T.: GPUs outperform current HPC and neuromorphic solutions in terms of speed and energy when simulating a highly-connected cortical model. Front. Neurosci. 12(December), 1–19 (2018). https://doi.org/10.3389/fnins.2018.00941
14. Maass, W.: Networks of spiking neurons: the third generation of neural network models. Neural Netw. 10(9), 1659–1671 (1997). https://doi.org/10.1016/S0893-6080(97)00011-7
15. Moradi, S., et al.: A scalable multicore architecture with heterogeneous memory structures for dynamic neuromorphic asynchronous processors (DYNAPs). IEEE Trans. Biomed. Circuits Syst. 12(1), 106–122 (2018). https://doi.org/10.1109/TBCAS.2017.2759700
16. Neckar, A., et al.: Braindrop: a mixed-signal neuromorphic architecture with a dynamical systems-based programming model. Proc. IEEE 107(1), 144–164 (2019). https://doi.org/10.1109/JPROC.2018.2881432
17. Ostrau, C., et al.: Comparing neuromorphic systems by solving sudoku problems. In: Conference Proceedings: 2019 International Conference on High Performance Computing & Simulation (HPCS). IEEE (2019). https://doi.org/10.1109/HPCS48598.2019.9188207
18. Ostrau, C., et al.: Benchmarking of neuromorphic hardware systems. In: Proceedings of the Neuro-Inspired Computational Elements Workshop. Association for Computing Machinery (ACM) (2020). https://doi.org/10.1145/3381755.3381772
19. Petrovici, M.A., et al.: Characterization and compensation of network-level anomalies in mixed-signal neuromorphic modeling platforms. PLoS ONE, 9(10) (2014). https://doi.org/10.1371/journal.pone.0108590
20. Pfeil, T., et al.: Six networks on a universal neuromorphic computing substrate. Front. Neurosci. 7(7 FEB), 11 (2013). https://doi.org/10.3389/fnins.2013.00011
21. Rhodes, O., et al.: Real-time cortical simulation on neuromorphic hardware. Philos. Trans. R. Soc. A: Math. Phys. Eng. Sci. 378(2164), 20190160 (2020). https://doi.org/10.1098/rsta.2019.0160
22. Schemmel, J., et al.: A wafer-scale neuromorphic hardware system for large-scale neural modeling. In: Proceedings of 2010 IEEE International Symposium on Circuits and Systems, pp. 1947–1950 (2010). https://doi.org/10.1109/ISCAS.2010.5536970
23. Schmitt, S., et al.: Neuromorphic hardware in the loop: training a deep spiking network on the BrainScaleS wafer-scale system. In: 2017 International Joint Conference on Neural Networks (IJCNN), pp. 2227–2234. IEEE (2017). https://doi.org/10.1109/IJCNN.2017.7966125
24. Stöckel, A., et al.: Binary associative memories as a benchmark for spiking neuromorphic hardware. Front. Comput. Neurosci. 11(August), 71 (2017). https://doi.org/10.3389/fncom.2017.00071
25. Yavuz, E., et al.: GeNN: a code generation framework for accelerated brain simulations. Sci. Rep. 6(2015), 18854 (2016). https://doi.org/10.1038/srep18854

Unsupervised Learning
of Spatio-Temporal Receptive Fields
from an Event-Based Vision Sensor

Thomas Barbier[1]([⊠]) [ID], Céline Teulière[1]([⊠]) [ID], and Jochen Triesch[1,2]([⊠]) [ID]

[1] Université Clermont Auvergne, CNRS, SIGMA Clermont, Institut Pascal,
63000 Clermont-Ferrand, France
{thomas.barbier,celine.teuliere}@uca.fr
[2] Frankfurt Institute for Advanced Studies, Frankfurt, Germany
triesch@fias.uni-frankfurt.de

Abstract. Neuromorphic vision sensors exhibit several advantages compared to conventional frame-based cameras including low latencies, high dynamic range, and low data rates. However, how efficient visual representations can be learned from the output of such sensors in an unsupervised fashion is still an open problem. Here we present a spiking neural network that learns spatio-temporal receptive fields in an unsupervised way from the output of a neuromorphic event-based vision sensor. Learning relies on the combination of spike timing-dependent plasticity with different synaptic delays, the homeostatic regulations of synaptic weights and firing thresholds, and fast inhibition among neurons to decorrelate their responses. Our network develops biologically plausible spatio-temporal receptive fields when trained on real world input and is suited for implementation on neuromorphic hardware.

Keywords: Event-based vision · Unsupervised learning · Receptive field · Neuromorphic engineering · Spiking neural network · Spike timing-dependent plasticity

1 Introduction

Biological vision systems learn to make sense of their environments without much external supervision. Mimicking such unsupervised learning abilities in technical systems may pave the way for vision systems that do not require millions of manually labelled training examples, but that can learn in a much more

This work was sponsored by a public grant overseen by the French National Agency as part of the "Investissements d'Avenir" through the IMobS3 Laboratory of Excellence (ANR-10-LABX-0016) and the IDEX-ISITE initiative CAP 20–25 (ANR-16-IDEX-0001). Financial support was also received from Clermont Auvergne Metropole through a French Tech-Clermont Auvergne professorship. JT acknowledges support from the Johanna Quandt foundation.

© Springer Nature Switzerland AG 2020
I. Farkaš et al. (Eds.): ICANN 2020, LNCS 12397, pp. 622–633, 2020.
https://doi.org/10.1007/978-3-030-61616-8_50

autonomous fashion. How biological vision systems learn to see without supervision is still poorly understood, however. While fundamental mechanisms of neuronal and synaptic plasticity have been identified, there is still no model that could explain the development of vision in terms of these basic mechanisms. One hurdle to building such models is scale. Simulating detailed large-scale spiking neural network models of, e.g., the primate visual system on conventional (super-)computers is prohibitively expensive. This has led to growing interest in neuromorphic approaches that mimic principles of neural information processing and learning in hardware and can be vastly more energy efficient compared to conventional computing paradigms.

Event-based cameras are inspired by the mammalian retina and represent a great starting point for creating biologically inspired artificial vision systems. They offer very high temporal resolution (of the order of μs) and low data rates. Importantly, they operate in a fully asynchronous way, i.e., there are no clearly defined image "frames". This necessitates to drastically change the design of the vision system. Spiking neural networks (SNNs) are the asynchronous analog to conventional neural networks, which makes them ideally suited for unsupervised learning from an event-based camera.

Here, we propose a SNN model to learn spatio-temporal receptive fields from the output of a neuromorphic event-based vision sensor in an unsupervised fashion. The network combines three unsupervised learning mechanisms: spike timing-dependent plasticity, a homeostatic regulation of neuronal firing thresholds, and a multiplicative synaptic normalization to prevent unbounded growth of synapses. A simple fast inhibition scheme decorrelates neural responses and effectively prevents multiple neurons from developing identical receptive fields. We show that our network learns motion-sensitive receptive fields in an unsupervised fashion and that the learned receptive fields qualitatively resemble receptive fields observed in visual cortex.

2   Related Work

There have been various previous attempts at solving classification and recognition tasks using SNNs fed with event data. The works fall into two main categories. The first are spiking convolutional neural networks inspired by their frame-based counterparts. Most of the time these are transformations of successful deep learning convolutional neural networks and use a form of supervised training [13,16,20]. The second category uses spike timing-dependent plasticity (STDP) to train an SNN in an unsupervised way [1,5,7,8,12]. For example, Akolkar et al. [1] demonstrate the possibility to learn visual receptive fields (RFS) in an event-driven framework. However, their attempt is limited to learning purely spatial RFs without any time dependence, i.e. they do not consider the encoding of image motion.

The primate visual system uses specific populations of neurons tuned to different motion directions and velocities to estimate object motion. Some work has been done on bio-inspired ways of sensing motion using event-driven data.

Specifically, Tschechne et al. [19] have proposed a model using filters with spatio-temporal tuning to compute the optical flow of a scene. Haessig et al. [6] have proposed a spiking neural network implemented on IBM's TrueNorth neurosynaptic system inspired by the Barlow & Levick method for optical flow estimation. Orchard et al. [10] have created a motion sensing SNN using synaptic delays. Each neuron is designed to detect a specific motion direction and speed. The main limitation is that the delays and orientations for the whole population need to be set by hand. Hopkins et al. [7] also describe motion estimation via synapses with delays, but do not consider learning. Most recently, Paredes-Vallés et al. [11] have proposed a framework for learning motion sensitive receptive fields from an event-based camera via a form of STDP in an unsupervised fashion. Their work is most closely related to ours, but there are a number of differences. First, the depression part of their STDP rule does not require presynaptic input spikes to arrive shortly after a postsynaptic spike, which is an important feature of biological STDP. Second, they use a convolutional network architecture, which enforces the development of identical receptive fields in all parts of the visual field. This prevents the receptive fields at different locations from adapting to systematic differences in the statistics of optical flow signals across the visual field as is common, e.g., during ego motion. Finally, our implementation is fully event-based, which makes it well-suited for implementation on neuromorphic hardware.

3   Methods

3.1   Spiking Neural Network

We designed our spiking neural network to couple efficiently with an event-based camera. We use the sensor as our input layer and the second layer comprises a set of spiking neurons, each connected to a specific region of the event-based camera via weighted synapses which define the neuron's receptive field. If one of the camera's pixels records an event, the neurons connected to it will receive an excitatory input depending on the strength of the synapse. In order to differentiate ON and OFF events, neurons are connected with at least two synapses to a pixel, one for each event polarity. Furthermore, we allow pixels to connect to the spiking neurons with different synaptic delays (described below), to enable the development of motion tuning.

We chose the well-known Leaky-Integrate and Fire (LIF) point neuron model. $V(t)$ denotes the neuron's membrane potential at time t. Updates of $V(t)$ are only performed upon receiving an event. More precisely, an input event from a pixel i creates an excitatory post-synaptic potential, which increases the membrane potential according to the strength of the corresponding synapse $w_i(t)$. If the neuron's membrane potential exceeds a threshold V_θ, the neuron "spikes" and its membrane potential returns to the resting value, which we define to be zero. Between the arrival of successive synaptic inputs to the neuron at times t and $t + \Delta t$, the membrane potential exponentially decays back to its resting value with the membrane time constant τ_m. Taken together, $V(t)$ evolves according to:

$$\tilde{V}(t + \Delta t) = V(t)e^{\frac{-\Delta t}{\tau_m}} + w_i(t) \tag{1}$$

$$V(t + \Delta t) = \begin{cases} \tilde{V}(t + \Delta t) : \tilde{V}(t + \Delta t) < V_\theta \\ 0 : \tilde{V}(t + \Delta t) \geq V_\theta \, . \end{cases} \tag{2}$$

When the neuron is inhibited (see Sect. 3.4 below), however, its membrane potential is not updated for the duration of the inhibition.

3.2 Synaptic Delays and Spike Timing-Dependent Plasticity

To allow for the learning of motion sensitive receptive fields, each pixel of the event-based camera can be coupled to an LIF neuron via D synapses with different delays. Therefore, a neuron can receive, e.g., the same on-event from the same pixel at D different times. Similarly, it can simultaneously receive events having occurred at different pixels at different times and therefore be sensitive to image motion. Having signals with multiple delays from the same sensor is a very common motif in biological motion vision circuits. In fact, it is the classic idea behind the Reichardt detector, also known as Hassenstein-Reichardt detector model [3].

Synaptic weights adapt according to a simple STDP model. In STDP, the sign and magnitude of a synaptic weight change depend on the relative timing of pre- and post-synaptic spikes. In the most common form of STDP, presynaptic spikes arriving shortly before a postsynaptic spike will lead to a long-term potentiation (LTP) of the synapse, while the reverse timing leads to long-term depression (LTD). We use a symmetric interpretation, where each presynaptic spike is paired with the last postsynaptic spike, and each postsynaptic spike is paired with the last presynaptic spike. In our implementation of LTP, as soon as a neuron spikes, its synaptic input connections will increase depending on the timing of the last input they received. Each synapse undergoes an instantaneous change in weight depending on an exponential relationship between the time difference between the timestamp t_i of the last input arriving at synapse i and the time of the postsynaptic spike $t_s > t_i$:

$$\Delta w_i^{\text{LTP}} = A_{\text{LTP}}\, e^{\frac{-|t_i - t_s|}{\tau_{\text{LTP}}}}, \tag{3}$$

with A_{LTP} and τ_{LTP} controlling, respectively, the height and duration of the potentiation window. Any input spike arriving after a postsynaptic spike $(t_i > t_s)$ leads to depression of the synaptic weight:

$$\Delta w_i^{\text{LTD}} = -A_{\text{LTD}}\, e^{\frac{-|t_s - t_i|}{\tau_{\text{LTD}}}}, \tag{4}$$

where A_{LTD} and τ_{LTD} control, respectively, the height and duration of the depression window. Note that in this formulation, multiple presynaptic spikes can interact with the last postsynaptic spike to induce depression. Synapses whose weight would become negative due to LTD are set to zero. The STDP rule applies equally to all synapses with different time delays. The relevant time difference

$|t_s - t_i|$ is always the one between the *arrival* of the presynaptic spike (potentially delayed with respect to the time it was generated) and the moment of the postsynaptic spike.

3.3   Threshold Adaptation and Synaptic Normalization

Homeostatic regulation of firing rates is a common feature of neural circuits allowing stable activity levels [17]. To avoid the necessity to fine-tune the neuron's firing thresholds we use a homeostatic regulation to enforce a certain target firing rate $S^* = 0.75$ spikes s^{-1}. The threshold is adapted automatically every second depending on the difference between an estimate of the recent spike rate $S(t)$ and the desired S^* as:

$$\Delta V_\theta = A_\theta \left(S(t) - S^* \right), \tag{5}$$

where A_θ is a scalar parameter controlling the rate of change of the spike threshold. To estimate the recent spike rate $S(t)$, we store the number of spikes that occurred during each of the last 10 s in a 10-element ring buffer $S_i(t)$, $i = 1, \ldots, 10$. The spike rate $S(t)$ is estimated as $S(t) = 0.1 \times \sum_{i=1}^{10} S_i(t)$.

To avoid unbounded growth of synaptic weights we use a simple weight normalization mechanism, which normalizes the weights projecting to a single neuron in a multiplicative fashion. Different groups of synapses onto the same neuron are normalized separately. Each neuron receives inputs from two channels (for on and off events) and D synaptic delays from a pixel array of width W and height H. This amounts to a total number of $2 \times D \times W \times H$ synapses per neuron. The synapses from the same channel and the same synaptic delay form a synapse group, i.e., each synapse group comprises $W \times H$ synapses and there are $2D$ such groups. After every spike of the neuron, all input synapses of all synapse groups are multiplicatively rescaled such that the L_2 norms of the weights of each group equal a parameter λ, chosen empirically. This separate normalization of different synapse groups ensures that on- and off-channels and the different synaptic delays all contribute equally to activating the neuron. Such multiplicative re-scaling of the efficacies of groups of synapses could be the result of a local competition for synaptic building blocks such as neurotransmitter receptors [18].

3.4   Lateral Inhibition

We use a simple lateral inhibition mechanism to facilitate the learning of diverse receptive fields tuned to different orientations, phases, and movement directions and speeds. In the network, N neurons are connected to the same set of input pixels as shown in Fig. 1a. Such neurons are linked by inhibitory connections. When one neuron spikes, it immediately inhibits the other $N - 1$ neurons from firing for a fixed duration $T_I = 8$ ms. This prevents neurons which receive input from the same region of the sensor from firing at roughly the same time, which would imply similar synaptic weight updates and lead to similar receptive fields.

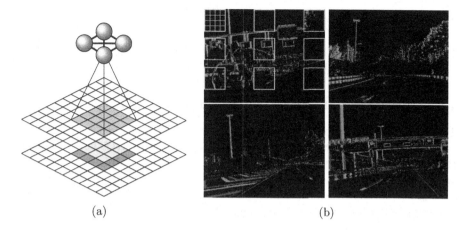

(a)   (b)

Fig. 1. (a) Groups of $N = 4$ neurons are connected to the same patch of input pixels providing On (green) and Off (red) events. The neurons are linked by inhibitory connections (blue). A neuron can be connected to pixels of its receptive field by D synapses with different delays to gain localised motion sensing properties (not shown). (b) Examples of input events from the driving sequence. The first example indicates the locations of neurons' receptive fields across the 9 different regions. (Color figure online)

3.5 Coupling of the Event-Based Camera to the Network

The input to the network comes from the DAVIS346B [4], a DVS sensor of 346×260 pixels. It is known that inputs from different parts of the visual field have different statistical properties. An optimal representation of the visual inputs must take into account such effects [15]. To explore statistical differences of visual inputs across the sensor array, we divided the pixel array into 9 different regions (compare Fig. 1b). We offseted the three bottom regions because of the car's dashboard being visible in some of the driving sequences. Each region is subdivided into 16 smaller input tiles of 10×10 pixels, giving $9 \times 16 = 144$ tiles (see Fig. 1b). Each input tile projects to $N = 100$ neurons connected by inhibitory synapses (compare Fig. 1a and Sect. 3.4 on lateral inhibition). The 16 neurons of the same region and slice N share the same synaptic weights. This implies a network size of $14,400$ neurons but only 900 learned receptive fields. Each neuron receives inputs from $2 \times D \times 100$ synapses corresponding to the 2 event polarities, D time delays, and $W \times H = 100$ input pixels. For $D = 1$, this amounts to $2\,880\,000$ input synapses for the entire network. The event-based spiking neural network simulation was implemented in C++ as a DV-software module. Running on a standard Intel Core i5-8365U CPU @1.60 GHz without particular optimization, the network showed near real-time performance.

4   Results

To demonstrate the learning abilities of our approach we tested different network configurations on both natural and synthetic visual input.

4.1   Development of Orientation-Tuned Receptive Fields

To test the network's ability to develop diverse orientation-tuned receptive fields as observed in visual cortex, we used sequences from the DDD17: DAVIS Driving Dataset [2]. It features many hours of driving recorded on freeways, highways and in cities. Fig. 1b shows 4 examples of short time slices of events. The data set features various types of visual inputs such as cars, traffic signs, poles, trees, buildings, safety barriers, road markings, etc.

Table 1. Parameters used for the learning.

A_{LTP} (mV)	A_{LTD} (mV)	τ_{LTP} (ms)	τ_{LTD} (ms)	τ_m (ms)	V_θ (mV)	A_θ	S^* (spikes.s^{-1})	T_I (ms)	λ
0.077	0.021	7	14	18	30	4	0.75	8	4

Table 1 lists the parameters used in our spiking neural network. Changes in parameters specific to one test will be mentioned in the text. In a first experiment we focused on the spatial structure of the learned receptive fields and we thus considered a network without multiple synaptic delays (i.e., $D = 1$). The initial synaptic weights were drawn randomly from a uniform distribution. Figure 2 shows examples of learned receptive fields in the 9 visual regions after 60 min of training on driving sequences alternating between highway, freeway and cities. Green/red pixels represent synapses transmitting On/Off events, respectively. The weight strength is represented by the color intensity. Yellow areas indicate regions where the neuron is sensitive to both On and Off events.

The receptive fields of simple cells in primary visual cortex are well described by Gabor functions. To test the biological plausibility of our learned receptive fields, we fitted Gabor functions to them. 93% of receptive fields obtained a good fit (sum of squared errors ≤5). Example fits are shown in Fig. 2b. They exemplify that filters of different orientation and scale are learned. Figure 2c shows the histograms of fitted Gabor orientations for each of the 9 visual regions. Horizontal and vertical orientations are over-represented, resembling the oblique effect in visual perception [9]. Each region exhibits very different receptive field characteristics including orientation preferences, as seen in Fig. 2c. The constant flow of objects from the center to the edges of the sensor generated by the car's forward motion is reflected in the preferred orientations of each visual region.

To test the importance of the lateral inhibition mechanism, we studied the effect of disabling it in Fig. 3. Each column in Fig. 3a represents the receptive fields of 4 neurons connected to the same input patch after learning without

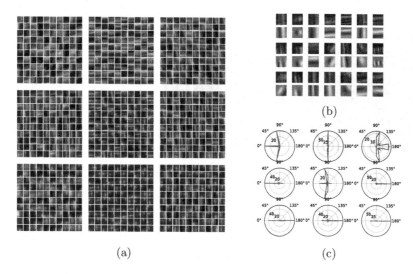

(a)   (c)

Fig. 2. (a) Receptive fields learned for the 9 visual regions. (b) Selected examples of learned receptive fields (rows 1, 3 and 5) and corresponding Gabor fits (rows 2, 4 and 6) showing tuning to different orientations and scales. (c) Histogram of the network's receptive field orientations obtained from the fitting of Gabor functions for each of the visual regions. (Color figure online)

lateral inhibition. Even though the receptive field initialisation was different, all 4 neurons have learned very similar receptive fields. In contrast, the lateral inhibition leads to more diverse receptive fields (Fig. 3b). Figure 3c quantifies this effect by showing box plots of the distributions of all pairwise squared Euclidean distances between the receptive fields learned at the same location. Inhibition greatly improves the diversity of receptive fields.

4.2   Development of Motion Tuned Receptive Fields

To test the network's ability to develop motion tuned receptive fields, we introduced synapses with $D = 3$ different time delays of 0, 10, and 20 ms. We also changed to a complete tiling of the DVS array instead of the 9 visual regions and disabled synaptic weight sharing. We first tested the motion learning capacity in a controlled setting using synthetic stimuli. We generated a simple sequence showing 4 vertical bars moving horizontally at predefined speeds of 420, 210, 140 and 105 pixels per second across the pixel array. The video was recorded at a framerate of 1200 frames per second and then converted to events using the Open Event Camera Simulator, ESIM [14]. A snapshot of the events can be seen in Fig. 4a. We used a very high (not biologically realistic) starting threshold $V_\theta = 700$ mV to compensate for the extra synapses as well as a lower target spiking rate of $S^* = 0.15$ spikes s^{-1}, which is sufficient in this sequence of fewer events. All other parameters were as in Table 1.

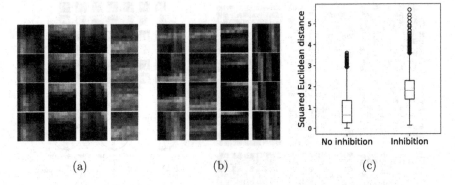

(a)   (b)   (c)

Fig. 3. Lateral inhibition diversifies receptive fields. Examples of 16 neurons' receptive fields learnt without (a) and with (b) lateral inhibition. All neurons in a column receive the exact same inputs from the event sensor, but start with a different random initialisation of their synaptic weights. (c) Boxplot of the squared Euclidean distances between synaptic weights of neurons receiving similar inputs with and without lateral inhibition.

The speed of the bars influences the number of events produced, which means that neurons should have different threshold values to appropriately fit the input. To accommodate this problem, we first set the neurons' thresholds to a high value to prevent spiking. The threshold adaptation described in Sect. 3.3 then decreases the threshold until a neuron starts spiking and its receptive field will adapt to the input. With the delays between the synapses being fixed at 10 ms, we expected to see a consistent shift in the receptive fields corresponding to the different synaptic delays. For instance, for the fastest bar the expected shift was $10\,\mathrm{ms} \times 420\,\mathrm{px\,s^{-1}} = 4.2\,\mathrm{px}$. Indeed, after exposing the network to about 50 repetitions of the vertical inputs, we obtained the receptive fields in Fig. 4b matching the expected shifts, even though the expected displacement could go down to a fraction of a pixel.

Next, we investigated the network's ability to develop motion tuned receptive fields for natural input by training it on the driving sequence of Fig. 1b. We were particularly interested in systematic differences in tuning properties across the visual field reflecting typical optic flow patterns occurring during driving. We chose a higher starting membrane potential threshold of $V_\theta = 150$ mV. Learned spatio-temporal receptive fields across the entire sensor array are shown in Fig. 5. Only one out of four neurons per location (compare Fig. 3) is shown. The receptive fields of some regions of the sensor are enlarged in Fig. 5b. Overall, a large variety of receptive fields tuned to different orientations, motion directions, and speeds have been learned. Importantly, we observe systematic differences in tuning properties across different parts of the visual field. In particular, the left and right regions of the network have mostly learned vertically tuned receptive fields, whereas the top and bottom parts have developed horizontally tuned receptive fields (compare pink, blue, and orange regions). This is consistent with

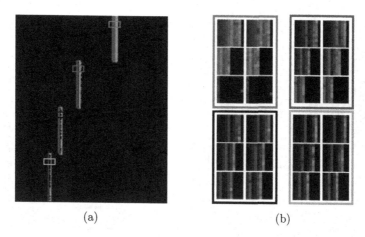

(a)   (b)

Fig. 4. Motion sensitive receptive fields develop from STDP with multiple synaptic delays. (a) On and off events recorded by the DV-software visualisation GUI for 4 vertical bars moving at speeds of 420, 210, 140 and 105 px/s (top to bottom). (b) Receptive fields of pairs of neighboring neurons receiving the 4 vertical bars as input (arranged by decreasing speed from top left to bottom right). Each neuron has 3 groups of input synapses with delays of 0, 10, and 20 ms (top to bottom). The expected displacements of the 4 bars during 10 ms are 4.2, 2.1, 1.4 and 1.05 pixels, which matches the horizontal shifts of receptive field structures for different synaptic delays.

the expected statistics of the sensory input. The left and right regions of the data sequence contain many poles, trees, and buildings, which due to the motion of the car will generate vertically aligned event patterns moving horizontally. In contrast, the top and bottom parts contain bridges, highway panels, and road markings, generating mostly horizontally aligned event patterns moving vertically. Furthermore, the shifts between receptive fields of different synaptic delays reflect the average speed of objects passing through that region of the sensor. We find that bigger shifts in outer regions and smaller shifts in inner regions (compare top and bottom part of orange region), corresponding to large optic flow in the periphery and small optic flow in the center. This reflects the dominant optic flow pattern expected from forward ego motion.

5   Discussion

We have presented a spiking neural network that learns motion-sensitive receptive fields from the input of an event-based camera in an unsupervised fashion. Motion tuning arises from spike timing-dependent plasticity (STDP) with multiple synaptic delays combined with homeostatic mechanisms and a simple lateral inhibition scheme to diversify tuning properties. The mechanisms used are all biologically inspired, but were not intended as accurate models of biological reality. Among the biggest idealizations are the instantaneous lateral inhibition to

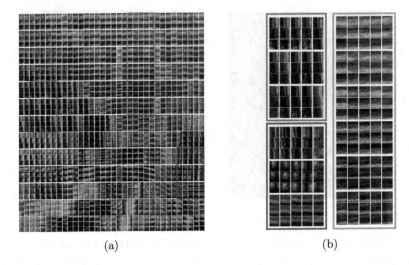

(a)   (b)

Fig. 5. (a) Motion tuned receptive fields learned across the entire field of view. Each receptive field has three sub-fields (arranged vertically) corresponding to different synaptic delays. Every second row of neurons has been removed in the figure to limit display size. (b) Enlarged view of marked groups of receptive fields in (a). See text for details.

decorrelate responses of neurons with overlapping receptive fields and the group-wise normalization of synaptic inputs. The latter could be biologically plausible, however, if the different groups of synapses were considered to reside on separate dendritic branches [18]. This seems plausible for synapse groups with short vs. long delays, which could correspond to inputs to more proximal vs. more distal dendritic branches, respectively. Similarly, On an Off channel inputs could also be sorted to different dendritic branches or regions during development based on their correlations.

Our work suggests a number of avenues for future research. First, we would like to extend our approach to active binocular vision, considering the simultaneous learning of disparity representations and vergence eye movements in a fully spiking implementation. Second, scaling up our approach to more complex spiking neural networks using neuromorphic hardware is an exciting topic for future research.

References

1. Akolkar, H., Panzeri, S., Bartolozzi, C.: Spike time based unsupervised learning of receptive fields for event-driven vision. In: IEEE International Conference on Robotics and Automation. IEEE, May 2015
2. Binas, J., Neil, D., Liu, S.C., Delbruck, T.: Ddd17: end-to-end DAVIS driving dataset, November 2017. https://arxiv.org/abs/1711.01458
3. Borst, A.: Models of motion detection. Nat. Neurosci. **3**(1), 1168 (2000)

4. Brandli, C., Berner, R., Yang, M., Liu, S.C., Delbruck, T.: A 240 × 180 130 dB 3 μs latency global shutter spatiotemporal vision sensor. IEEE J. Solid-State Circuits **49**(10), 2333–2341 (2014)
5. Diehl, P.U., Cook, M.: Unsupervised learning of digit recognition using spike-timing-dependent plasticity. Front. Comput. Neurosci. **9** (2015)
6. Haessig, G., Cassidy, A., Alvarez, R., Benosman, R., Orchard, G.: Spiking optical flow for event-based sensors using IBM's TrueNorth neurosynaptic system. IEEE Trans. Biomed. Circuits Syst. **12**(4), 860–870 (2018)
7. Hopkins, M., Pineda-García, G., Bogdan, P.A., Furber, S.B.: Spiking neural networks for computer vision. Interface Focus. **8**(4), 20180007 (2018)
8. Kheradpisheh, S.R., Ganjtabesh, M., Thorpe, S.J., Masquelier, T.: STDP-based spiking deep convolutional neural networks for object recognition. Neural Netw. **99**, 56–67 (2018)
9. Li, B., Peterson, M.R., Freeman, R.D.: Oblique effect: a neural basis in the visual cortex. J. Neurophysiol. **90**(1), 204–217 (2003)
10. Orchard, G., Benosman, R., Etienne-Cummings, R., Thakor, N.V.: A spiking neural network architecture for visual motion estimation. In: IEEE Biomedical Circuits and Systems Conference (BioCAS), October 2013
11. Paredes-Valles, F., Scheper, K.Y.W., Croon, G.C.H.E.D.: Unsupervised learning of a hierarchical spiking neural network for optical flow estimation: from events to global motion perception. IEEE Trans. Pattern Anal. Mach. Intell. **42**, 2051–2064 (2018)
12. Paulun, L., Wendt, A., Kasabov, N.: A retinotopic spiking neural network system for accurate recognition of moving objects using NeuCube and dynamic vision sensors. Front. Comput. Neurosci. **12**, 13 Pages (2018). Article no: 42
13. Perez-Carrasco, J.A., Serrano, C., Acha, B., Serrano-Gotarredona, T., Linares-Barranco, B.: Spike-based convolutional network for real-time processing. In: IAPR International Conference on Pattern Recognition. IEEE, August 2010
14. Rebecq, H., Gehrig, D., Scaramuzza, D.: ESIM: an open event camera simulator. In: Conference on Robot Learning, October 2018
15. Rothkopf, C.A., Weisswange, T.H., Triesch, J.: Learning independent causes in natural images explains the spacevariant oblique effect. ICDL 2009. IEEE 8th International Conference on Development and Learning, pp. 1–6, January 2009
16. Stromatias, E., Soto, M., Serrano-Gotarredona, T., Linares-Barranco, B.: An event-driven classifier for spiking neural networks fed with synthetic or dynamic vision sensor data. Front. Neurosci. **11**, 17 Pages (2017). Article no: 350
17. Tien, N.W., Kerschensteiner, D.: Homeostatic plasticity in neural development. Neural Dev.**13**(1), 7 Pages (2018)
18. Triesch, J., Vo, A.D., Hafner, A.S.: Competition for synaptic building blocks shapes synaptic plasticity. Elife **7**, e37836 (2018)
19. Tschechne, S., Sailer, R., Neumann, H.: Bio-inspired optic flow from event-based neuromorphic sensor input. In: El Gayar, N., Schwenker, F., Suen, C. (eds.) ANNPR 2014. LNCS (LNAI), vol. 8774, pp. 171–182. Springer, Cham (2014). https://doi.org/10.1007/978-3-319-11656-3_16
20. Zhao, B., Ding, R., Chen, S., Linares-Barranco, B., Tang, H.: Feedforward categorization on AER motion events using cortex-like features in a spiking neural network. IEEE Trans. Neural Netw. Learn. Syst. **26**(9), 1963–1978 (2015)

Spike-Train Level Unsupervised Learning Algorithm for Deep Spiking Belief Networks

Xianghong Lin[✉] and Pangao Du

College of Computer Science and Engineering, Northwest Normal University,
Lanzhou 730070, China
linxh@nwnu.edu.cn

Abstract. Deep spiking belief network (DSBN) uses unsupervised layer-wise pre-training method to train the network weights, it is stacked with the spike neural machine (SNM) modules. However, the synaptic weights of SNMs are difficult to pre-training through simple and effective approach for spike-train driven networks. This paper proposes a new algorithm that uses unsupervised multi-spike learning rule to train SNMs, which can implement the complex spatio-temporal pattern learning of spike trains. The spike signals first propagate in the forward direction, and then are reconstructed in the reverse direction, and the synaptic weights are adjusted according to the reconstruction error. The algorithm is successfully applied to spike train patterns, the module parameters are analyzed, such as the neuron number and learning rate in the SNMs. In addition, the low reconstruction errors of DSBNs are shown by the experimental results.

Keywords: Deep spiking belief networks · Unsupervised learning · Spike neural machines · Reconstruction error

1 Introduction

Deep learning uses an architecture with many layers of trainable parameters and has demonstrated outstanding performance in machine learning applications [1]. Deep neural networks (DNNs) are trained end-to-end by using optimization algorithms usually based on backpropagation mechanism. Spiking neural networks (SNNs) are the third generation artificial neural networks, which are biologically-inspired computational models and more efficient for spatio-temporal information processing than the traditional neural networks based on spike rate encoding [2, 3]. SNNs have also shown promising performance in a number of pattern recognition tasks [4]. However, the performance of directly trained deep SNNs is not as good as traditional DNNs. A major reason is that SNNs are not differentiable, but differentiable activation functions are fundamental for using error backpropagation. Due to the complex hierarchical structure and implicit nonlinear mechanism, the formulation of efficient deep learning methods for deep SNNs based on spike train encoding is difficult and remains an important problem in the research area. Therefore, using greedy layer-wise pre-training algorithm to train the deep networks is an approach that is worth exploring.

© Springer Nature Switzerland AG 2020
I. Farkaš et al. (Eds.): ICANN 2020, LNCS 12397, pp. 634–645, 2020.
https://doi.org/10.1007/978-3-030-61616-8_51

Deep belief networks (DBNs) are a type of multi-layer networks initially developed by Hinton et al. [5]. They efficiently use greedy layer-wise unsupervised learning. The layer-wise method stacks pre-trained, single-layer learning modules known as restricted Boltzmann machines (RBMs). The representation layer in an RBM is restricted from having lateral connections. This enables the learning algorithm to optimize the representation by making use of independence assumptions among the representation units, given a particular input state. The RBMs are trained in a layer-wise fashion by contrastive divergence (CD) method, which approximates a maximum-likelihood learning algorithm. Unlike backpropagation, the CD update equations do not use derivatives. The pre-trained hierarchy is fine-tuned by backpropagation if labeled data are available.

Traditional DBNs have successfully been employed in many areas such as visual processing [6, 7], audio processing [8], time series forecasting [9], and protein folding [10]. With the continuous in-depth study of this theory, some researchers have proposed spike-based DBN model which is called deep spike belief network (DSBN), and other researchers have innovated in this research theory and obtained new research results. The first DSBN was introduced by O'Connor et al., in which a DBN is converted to a network of leaky integrate-and-fire neurons for MNIST image classification [11]. This work is then extended to develop a noise robust DSBN and as well as conforming to hardware constraints by Stromatias [12]. Neftci uses stochastic integrate-and-fire neurons instead of the memoryless stochastic units in a standard RBM [13]. This shows that in the context of a particular type of spiking network, a variant of STDP can approximate CD. Based on the traditional CD learning algorithm, Fatahi et al. proposes a new CD learning algorithm using frequency encoding from the perspective of encoding neural information [14]. However, these methods require a lot of calculations and are not easy to understand, so it is need to develop the simple and efficient unsupervised learning algorithm for DSBN.

In this paper, we propose a new layer-wise pre-training algorithm that uses unsupervised multi-spike learning rule to train DSBN. The rest of this paper is organized as follows. In Sect. 2 we introduce the network structure and spike train error. In Sect. 3 we introduce the unsupervised layer-wise pre-training algorithm for DSBN. In Sect. 4 we mainly carry out the experiments of spike train patterns for SNMs and reconstruction error analyze for the DSBNs. The conclusions are presented in Sect. 5.

2 Network Structure and Spike Train Error

2.1 The Structure of DSBN

The spike neural machine (SNM) is the basic module of DSBN. The structure of SNM is shown in Fig. 1, which is composed of two layers of spiking neurons. The bottom layer is the visible layer and the top layer is the hidden layer. The visible layer has N neurons, and the hidden layer has M neurons. The layers in the SNM are completely symmetrically connected, but there is no connection between the units of the same layer.

The DSBN is composed of several SNM module stacks. As shown in Fig. 2, the first layer is the visible layer as the data input. The remaining layers are all set as hidden layers for feature extraction. The last layer is spike output layer. From the visible layer,

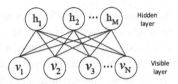

Fig. 1. The SNM module structure

every two layers in the network form an SNM module. The output spike trains of the former module are the input spike trains of the latter module.

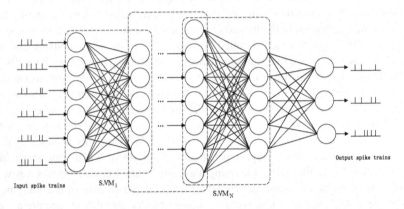

Fig. 2. The structure of DSBN

2.2 Spike Train Error Computation

The discrete spikes are used to form a spike train. Therefore, it is assumed that the discrete spikes are generated by a spiking neuron in the time interval $\Gamma = [0, T]$, and then spike train $s = \{t^f \in \Gamma : f = 1, \ldots, F\}$ can be formally represented as:

$$s(t) = \sum_{f=1}^{F} \delta(t - t^f) \tag{1}$$

where F is the number of spikes, $\delta(.)$ represents the Dirac delta function, $\delta(t) = 1$ if $t = 0$ and $\delta(t) = 0$ otherwise.

In order to facilitate calculation, it is necessary to transform discrete spike train into a continuous function. We can choose a specific smoothing function h, the convolution of spike train s is represented as:

$$\tilde{s}(t) = s(t) * h(t) = \sum_{f=1}^{F} h(t - t^f) \tag{2}$$

Through the convolution calculation, the spike train can be interpreted as a specific neural physiological signal, such as neuronal postsynaptic potential or spike firing intensity function [15]. Using Eq. (2), we can define the inner product of spike trains s_i and s_j on the $L_2(\Gamma)$ space as follows [16]:

$$F(s_i, s_j) = \langle \tilde{s}_i(t), \tilde{s}_j(t) \rangle_{L_2(\Gamma)} = \sum_{m=1}^{F_i} \sum_{n=1}^{F_j} \int_\Gamma h(t - t_i^m) h(t - t_j^n) dt = \sum_{m=1}^{F_i} \sum_{n=1}^{F_j} \kappa(t_i^m, t_j^n)$$

(3)

where kernel function κ is the autocorrelation of the smoothing function h, $\kappa(t^m, t^n) = \int_\Gamma h(t - t^m) h(t - t^n) dt$.

The error function indicates the deviation between the reconstructed spike train and the input spike train. The goal of the spike train learning is that the reconstructed spike train eventually is the same as the input spike train by adjusting the synaptic weights. In this experiment, the spike train error function in the network is computed by the inner products of spike trains. s_v^r and s_v^a are the reconstructed spike train and actual input spike train in the visible layer of SNM respectively. The instantaneous reconstruction error function $E(t)$ is defined as:

$$E(t) = \frac{1}{2} \sum_{v=1}^{N} [\tilde{s}_v^a(t) - \tilde{s}_v^r(t)]^2$$

(4)

According the Eq. (4), the total reconstruction error function E in the time interval $\Gamma = [0, T]$ can be expressed as:

$$E = \int_0^T E(t) dt = \frac{1}{2} \sum_{v=1}^{N} \int_0^T [\tilde{s}_v^a(t) - \tilde{s}_v^r(t)]^2 dt$$

$$= \frac{1}{2} \sum_{v=1}^{N} \left[F(s_v^a, s_v^a) - 2F(s_v^a, s_v^r) + F(s_v^r, s_v^r) \right]$$

(5)

where $F(s_i, s_j)$ is the inner product of the spike trains. That is, the learning error of the spike neurons can be converted into the inner product of the two spike trains [17].

3 Unsupervised Learning Algorithm for DSBN

3.1 Multi-spike Learning Rule of SNM

The spike train learning process of the SNM module is divided into two parts, the forward propagation process and the reverse reconstruction stage. In the process of forward propagation, the visible layer is equivalent to the input layer of the network, and the hidden layer is equivalent to the output layer. Input spike trains are generated randomly by a homogeneous Poisson process, and then the network is running to obtain the output spike trains of the hidden layer. In the reverse reconstruction stage, spike trains of the hidden layer are used as the input spike trains to calculate the reconstruction spike trains of the visible layer, and then the synaptic weights between the visible layer and the hidden layer are updated according to the weight adjustment rule, and repeat this process. In the process of adjusting the synaptic weights, we use the original input spike trains and the reconstruction spike trains for comparison, without using external labels, so this is an unsupervised learning process. This process is shown in Fig. 3.

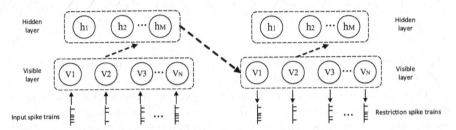

Fig. 3. Spike trains learning process of the SNM

We will derive the synaptic weight adjustment rule that is applicable to our network. Inspired by [18], we derive the proposed rule from the common Widrow-Hoff (WH) rule. The WH rule is described as:

$$\Delta w_i = \eta x_i (y_d - y_o) \tag{6}$$

where η is a positive constant referring to the learning rate, x_i, y_d and y_o refer to the input, the desired output and the actual output, respectively.

Note that because the WH rule was introduced for the traditional neuron models such as perceptron, the variables in the WH rule are regarded as real-valued vectors. In the case of spiking neurons, the input and output signals are described by the timing of spikes. Therefore, a direct implementation of the WH rule does not work for spiking neurons. So we need to convert to the input-output spike trains.

In the Sect. 2.2, we know that the spike trains are represented formally by sums of Dirac delta functions. In the reverse reconstruction stage, the input spike trains are the output spike trains of the hidden layer, the desired output spike trains are the original input spike trains of the visible layer, and the actual output spike trains in the visible layer obtained after reconstruction. Thus, we use s_h, s_v^a, s_v^r instead of input, desired and output spike trains, respectively. These spike trains are described as:

$$\begin{cases} s_h = \sum_g \delta(t - t_h^g) \\ s_v^a = \sum_m \delta(t - t_a^m) \\ s_v^r = \sum_n \delta(t - t_r^n) \end{cases} \tag{7}$$

The products of Dirac functions are mathematically problematic. To solve this difficulty, we apply an approach called spike convolution in Eq. (2). Unlike the offline supervised learning methods used in [17, 18], the synaptic weights are updated according to the entire actual and desired output spike trains after running of the network, which require spike convolution on all the spike trains of the input, actual and desired output. In this paper, we use online learning mode to adjust the synaptic weight, so we only convolve the input spike trains. In this case, the learning rule becomes:

$$\Delta w_{hv}(t) = \eta[s_v^a(t) - s_v^r(t)]\tilde{s}_h(t) \tag{8}$$

where $\tilde{s}_h(t)$ is a unique continuous function using the convolution operator to convert the discrete spike train, the double exponential convolution kernel is used in our work. This is an online learning rule, which adjusts the synaptic weight between neurons when the visible neuron fires a reconstruction spike or an original input spike during the running process.

3.2 Layer-Wise Pre-training of DSBN

Using the online learning rule of SNMs, the layer-wise pre-training algorithm refers to train each SNM in the DSBN. We train all SNMs to complete network's training tasks. The algorithm is described as follows:

Algorithm: Layer-wise Pre-training Algorithm

Input: input spike trains of visible layer, layer number L, simulation duration T
Output: output spike trains of hidden layer, synapse weight w

---

1. Initialization: randomly generate synaptic weight matrix w
2. for each SNM module do
    // the forward propagation process
3.   for $t <= T$ do
4.   for $h = 1...M$ do
5.   Calculate the output spike trains of the hidden layer
6.   end for
7. $t = t + \Delta t$
8.   end for
    // the reverse reconstruction stage
9.   for $t <= T$ do
10.   for $v = 1...N$ do
11.   Calculate the reconstructed spike trains of the visible layer
12.   if visible neuron v fires
13. $w(t) = w(t) + \Delta w(t)$
14.   end if
15.   end for
16. $t = t + \Delta t$
17.   end for
18. end for

---

4 Simulation Experiments

In the simulation experiments, the neuron model in the DSBNs use the spike response model (SRM) [19]. In SRM, the time constant of the spike response function is $\tau = 5$

ms, the time constant of the refractory period function is $\tau_R = 50$ ms, the excitation threshold $\theta = 1.0$ and absolute refractory period $t_{ref} = 1.0$ ms, the range of synaptic weights between adjacent neurons is [0, 0.8]. The simulation time of the network is 100 ms, and the time step is $\Delta t = 0.1$ ms. We set the learning rate $\eta = 0.001$. Each input spike train is generated randomly according to the Poisson process with rates of 50 Hz. The maximum number of reconstruction is 500.

4.1 Spike Train Learning of SNM Module

In this section, we will verify the performance of the above unsupervised learning algorithm through spike train learning experiments for the SNM module. It mainly analyzes the variation of the error between input spike trains and reconstructed spike trains during the learning process, so as to evaluate the accuracy and learning efficiency of the algorithm, and provide a factual basis for applying the algorithm to the DSBNs. In the SNM module, it contains 25 visible neurons, and 15 hidden neurons.

Figure 4 shows the changes in the learning and reconstruction error of the spike trains. Figure 4(a) shows the spike trains of the original input in the visible layer, the vertical axis shows the number of input neurons and the total of 25, the horizontal axis shows the simulation duration, and the points in the figure represent whether the neurons emit spike at each time. Figure 4(b) shows the first reconstruction of the SNM module, and the network's learning of the spike trains in the visible layer. It can be seen that learning spike trains of all neurons are chaotic. Figure 4(c) represents output spike trains of SNM after 100 reconstruction. We can see that these spike trains are basically close to the original input spike trains. Figure 4(d) represents the reconstruction error change curve of the network in the reconstruction process. From the curve change, it can be seen that at the beginning of the network, the error is very large, close to 14, indicating that the difference between spike trains after the first reconstruction and original input spike trains is large. However, the error began to decrease gradually, indicating that the reconstruction spike trains have begun to approach the original spike trains. When the number of network reconstruction is between 0 and 30, the error of network reconstruction decreases rapidly, which indicates that the error converges rapidly in this period. In the later reconstruction, the downward trend of error is more moderate. After 70 learning epochs, the error curve becomes smoother, the spike trains after network reconstruction gradually approaches the original input spike trains of visible layer, but it is difficult to approach 0, and the error remains between 2.5 and 3.5 all the time, indicating that although the reconstructed spike trains continues to approach original spike trains, it cannot be completely consistent.

Figure 5 shows the learning results of spike trains with learning rates 0.0001, 0.0005, 0.001, 0.003 and 0.005. Figure 5(a) shows the learning error of different learning rates. We can see that the learning error decreases at first, then increases when the learning rate reaches 0.001, so the suitable learning rate is 0.001. For example, when the learning rates are 0.0001, 0.0005 and 0.003, the corresponding errors are 3.55, 2.89 and 2.88 respectively. Figure 5(b) shows the learning epoch when the error reaches the minimum value. When the learning rates are 0.0001 and 0.003, the average learning epoch is larger, and the average learning epoch is relatively smaller when the learning rates are 0.0005, 0.001 and 0.005. For example, when the learning rates are 0.0001 and 0.001, the average learning epochs are 373.2 and 254.3 respectively.

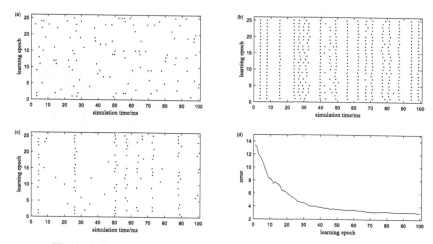

Fig. 4. Spike train learning performance and reconstruction error curve.

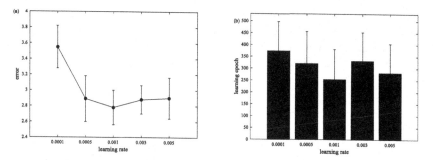

Fig. 5. The learning results of spike trains with different learning rates.

Figure 6 shows the learning results of spike trains with different numbers of neurons in the visible layer. The number of visible neuron increases from 10 to 50 with an interval of 10. Figure 6(a) shows the learning error different numbers of neurons in the visible layer. When the number of neurons in the hidden layer is 60, as the number of neurons in the visible layer increases, the reconstruction error exhibits certain fluctuations. The minimum reconstruction error is reached when the number of neurons in the visible layer is 40, and the maximum reconstruction error is when the number of neurons in the visible layer is 20. Figure 6(b) shows the learning epoch when the error reaches the minimum value. When the number of neurons in the visible layer is 40, the average number of iteration needed for the algorithm to achieve the best learning effect is 331, the average number of iteration is the least. When the number of neurons in the visible layer is 30, the number of iteration needed is 433, the average number of iteration is the most.

Figure 7 shows the learning results of spike trains with different numbers of neurons in the hidden layer. The number of hidden neuron increases from 10 to 50 with an interval of 10. Figure 7(a) shows the learning error different numbers of neurons in the hidden

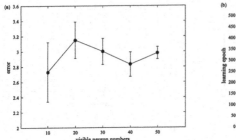
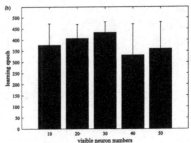

Fig. 6. The learning results of spike trains with different numbers of neurons in the visible layers

layer. When the number of neurons in the visible layer is 60, as the number of neurons in the hidden layer increases, the reconstruction error decrease first and then increase. The minimum reconstruction error is reached when the number of neurons in the hidden layer is 30, and the maximum reconstruction error is when the number of neurons in the hidden layer is 50. Figure 7(b) shows the learning epoch when the error reaches the minimum value. When the number of neurons in the hidden layer is 20, the average number of iteration needed for the algorithm to achieve the best learning effect is 307, the average number of iteration is the least. When the number of neurons in the hidden layer is 10, the number of iteration needed is 394, the average number of iteration is the most.

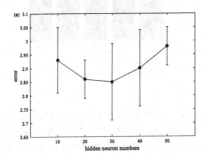
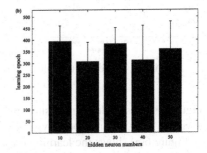

Fig. 7. The learning results of spike trains with different numbers of neurons in the hidden layers.

4.2   DSBN Reconstruction Error Analysis

We use layer-wise pre-training algorithm to analyze the reconstruction error of spike train in DSBN. We build a four layer DSBN, including visible layer and three hidden layers. The number of neurons in each layer are 60, 48, 36, 24, respectively. Therefore, we can divide it into three SNMs. The input spike trains of visible layer are generated by the spike coding method. Output spike trains of the former SNM hidden layer are the input spike trains of the latter SNM visible layer. Running the network, we got the reconstruction error curve of DSBN.

Figure 8(a) represents the error change curve of the first SNM in the reconstruction process. From the curve change, it can be seen that at the beginning of the network, the error is very large, close to 70, which indicating that the difference between the spike train after the first reconstruction and the original input spike trains is large. Then, the error began to decrease gradually, it shows that the reconstruction spike trains has begun to approach original spike trains. When the number of network reconstructions is between 0 and 15, the error of network reconstruction decreases rapidly, which indicates that the error converges rapidly in this period of time. In the later reconstruction, the downward trend of error is more moderate. After 30 epochs, the error curve becomes smoother, the spike trains after network reconstruction gradually approaches the original input spike trains of visible layer. The minimum error value is 3.52. Figure 8(b) represents the error change curve of the second SNM in the reconstruction process. This SNM input spike trains are the first SNM hidden layer output spike trains. Because the weight matrix is randomly generated, the reconstruction error at the beginning is larger than 21. As the number of iterations increases, the error gradually decreases. The minimum error value is 3.15. Figure 8(c) represents the error change curve of the third SNM in the reconstruction process. This SNM input spike trains are the second SNM hidden layer output spike trains. We can see that during the initial training, the error is relatively small, As the number of iterations increases, the reconstruction error decreases to 2.32.

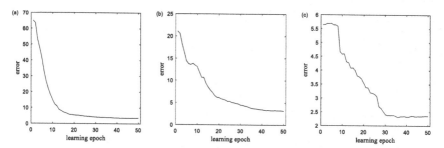

Fig. 8. DSBN layer-wise pre-training reconstruction error curve

We build a new DSBN to test layer-wise pre-training algorithm, the network also including visible layer and three hidden layers. The number of neurons in each layer is 40, 80, 60, 30, respectively. Therefore, we divide it into three SNMs. After layer-wise pre-training, we got the reconstruction error of each SNM, as is shows in Fig. 9. Figure 9(a), (b), (c) represent the error decline curves of the three SNMs, respectively. These curves are the same as the error decline curve in Fig. 8, we can see that at the beginning of the reconstruction, the error is relatively large, and the error decreases quickly. In the later reconstruction, the downward trend of error is more moderate. This is indicating that the reconstruction spike trains is close to original input spike trains of visible layer.

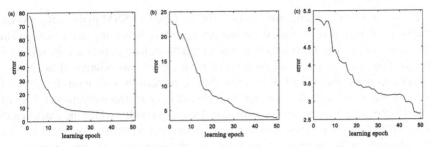

Fig. 9. A new DSBN layer-wise pre-training reconstruction error curve

5   Conclusions

In this paper, we present a spike-train level unsupervised learning algorithm for DSBN layer-wise pre-training, which can implement the complex spatio-temporal pattern learning of spike trains. In each SNM module of DSBNs, the visible input spike trains propagate to hidden layer and then the output spike trains are obtained through the reverse reconstruction process, and the synaptic weights are adjusted according to the proposed online learning rule. This pre-training algorithm was tested on different learning processes, such as the learning performance of the spike trains and the analysis of network structure change which includes the number of neurons in the visible layers and the hidden layers. The experimental results show that the proposed algorithm has the high accuracy and efficiency for learning spike train patterns.

References

1. Schmidhuber, J.: Deep learning in neural networks: an overview. Neural Netw. **61**, 85–117 (2015)
2. Ghosh-Dastidar, S., Adeli, H.: Spiking neural networks. Int. J. Neural Syst. **19**(4), 295–308 (2009)
3. Wang, X., Lin, X., Dang, X.: Supervised learning in spiking neural networks: a review of algorithms and evaluations. Neural Netw. **125**, 258–280 (2020)
4. Kasabov, N., Feigin, V., Hou, Z.-G., et al.: Evolving spiking neural networks for personalised modelling, classification and prediction of spatio-temporal patterns with a case study on stroke. Neurocomputing **134**, 269–279 (2014)
5. Hinton, G.E., Osindero, S., Teh, Y.-W.: A fast learning algorithm for deep belief nets. Neural Comput. **18**(7), 1527–1554 (2006)
6. Lee, H., Grosse, R., Ranganath, R., et al.: Unsupervised learning of hierarchical representations with convolutional deep belief networks. Commun. ACM **54**(10), 69–95 (2011)
7. Mleczko, W.K., Kapuściński, T., Nowicki, R.K.: Rough deep belief network - application to incomplete handwritten digits pattern classification. In: Dregvaite, G., Damasevicius, R. (eds.) ICIST 2015. CCIS, vol. 538, pp. 400–411. Springer, Cham (2015). https://doi.org/10.1007/978-3-319-24770-0_35
8. Kang, S., Qian, X., Meng, H.: Multi-distribution deep belief network for speech synthesis. In: IEEE International Conference on Acoustics, Speech and Signal processing, pp. 8012–8016. IEEE (2013)

9. Kuremoto, T., Kimura, S., Kobayashi, K., et al.: Time series forecasting using a deep belief network with restricted Boltzmann machines. Neurocomputing **137**, 47–56 (2014)
10. Jo, T., Hou, J., Eickholt, J., et al.: Improving protein fold recognition by deep learning networks. Sci. Rep. **5**, 17573 (2015)
11. O'Connor, P., Neil, D., Liu, S.-C., et al.: Real-time classification and sensor fusion with a spiking deep belief network. Front. Neurosci. **7**, 1–13 (2013)
12. Tavanaei, A., Maida, A.S.: Studying the interaction of a hidden Markov model with a Bayesian spiking neural network. In: IEEE 25th International Workshop on Machine Learning for Signal Processing, pp. 1–6. IEEE (2015)
13. Neftci, E., Das, S., Pedroni, B., et al.: Event driven contrastive divergence for spiking neuromorphic systems. Front. Neurosci. **8**, 1–14 (2014)
14. Fatahi, M., Shahsavari, M., Ahmadi, M., et al.: Rate-coded DBN: an online strategy for spike-based deep belief networks. Biol. Inspired Cogn. Arch. S2212683X18300173 (2018)
15. António, R.C., Park, I., Príncipe, J.C.: Inner products for representation and learning in the spike train domain. Stat. Signal Process. Neurosci. Neurotechnol., 265–309 (2010)
16. Paiva, A.R., Park, I., Príncipe, J.C.: A reproducing kernel Hilbert space framework for spike train signal processing. Neural Comput. **21**(2), 424–449 (2009)
17. Lin, X., Wang, X., Hao, Z.: Supervised learning in multilayer spiking neural networks with inner products of spike trains. Neurocomputing **237**, 59–70 (2017)
18. Mohemmed, A., Schliebs, S., Matsuda, S., et al.: SPAN: spike pattern association neuron for learning spatio-temporal spike patterns. Int. J. Neural Syst. **22**, 1250012 (2012)
19. Gerstner, W., Kistler, W.M.: Spiking Neuron Models: Single Neurons, Populations, Plasticity. Cambridge University Press, New York (2002)
20. Yu, Q., Tang, H., Tan, K.C., et al.: Precise-spike-driven synaptic plasticity: learning hetero-association of spatiotemporal spike patterns. PLoS ONE **8**(11), e78318 (2013)
21. Tavanaei, A., Ghodrati, M., Kheradpisheh, S.R., et al.: Deep learning in spiking neural networks. Neural Netw. **111**, 47–63 (2019)
22. Lin, X., Shi, G.: A supervised multi-spike learning algorithm for recurrent spiking neural networks. In: Kůrková, V., Manolopoulos, Y., Hammer, B., Iliadis, L., Maglogiannis, I. (eds.) ICANN 2018. LNCS, vol. 11139, pp. 222–234. Springer, Cham (2018). https://doi.org/10.1007/978-3-030-01418-6_22

Spiking Neural Networks II

Modelling Neuromodulated Information Flow and Energetic Consumption at Thalamic Relay Synapses

Mireille Conrad and Renaud B. Jolivet[(✉)][iD]

Department of Nuclear and Corpuscular Physics,
University of Geneva, Geneva, Switzerland
{mireille.conrad,renaud.jolivet}@unige.ch

Abstract. Recent experimental and theoretical work has shown that synapses in the visual pathway balance information flow with their energetic needs, maximising not the information flow from the retina to the primary visual cortex (bits per second), but instead maximising information flow per concomitant energy consumption (bits of information transferred per number of adenosine triphosphate molecules necessary to power the corresponding synaptic and neuronal activities) [5,10,11]. We have previously developed a biophysical Hodgkin-Huxley-type model for thalamic relay cells, calibrated on experimental data, and that recapitulates those experimental findings [10]. Here, we introduce an improved version of that model to include neuromodulation of thalamic relay synapses' transmission properties by serotonin. We show how significantly neuromodulation affects the output of thalamic relay cells, and discuss the implications of that mechanism in the context of energetically optimal information transfer at those synapses.

Keywords: Brain energetics · Information theory · Energetic optimality · Neuromodulation

1 Introduction

The brain consumes an inordinate amount of energy with respect to its size. It is responsible for about 20% of the whole body baseline energy metabolism at rest, while representing usually only 2% of its mass [9]. Over the last couple of years, attempts at theoretically or experimentally determining an energetic budget for the brain have all pointed to synapses as the locus where most of brain energy is being spent [7], with estimates putting their share of the brain's signalling energy budget at roughly 60% [1,9,13]. A better understanding of

This work was supported by grants from the Swiss National Science Foundation (31003A_170079), the European Commission (H2020 862882 IN-FET), and the Australian Research Council (DP180101494) to RBJ. MC is enrolled in the Lemanic Neuroscience Doctoral School.

© Springer Nature Switzerland AG 2020
I. Farkaš et al. (Eds.): ICANN 2020, LNCS 12397, pp. 649–658, 2020.
https://doi.org/10.1007/978-3-030-61616-8_52

brain energetics is essential because abnormal energy metabolism is an early hallmark of numerous pathologies of the central nervous system [9], and because neuroenergetics offers a lens through which one can easily address the complex heterocellular complexity of the brain [4,12,13].

Synapses are also the locus where electrophysiological 'information' is transmitted from neuron to neuron, and Shannon's information theory [18] has been used to great effectiveness in neuroscience, to measure information flow at synapses, in neural networks, or between different brain areas [9,15,16].

Given that synapses are a key mechanism in interneuronal communication and appear by all estimates to be responsible for a large fraction of the brain's energy consumption, it is natural to think that they would be reliable information transmission devices. A large body of experimental evidence, however, shows that synapses can be remarkably unreliable. For instance, the release probability for presynaptic vesicles is often measured to be in the few tens of percents for cortical neurons [3,8]. Similarly, action potential transmission at thalamic relay synapses, which relay information from sensory modalities to the primary sensory cortices, can be astonishingly low (see references in ref. [10]).

Recently, we have shown that this apparent paradox can be resolved when considering the energetic optimality of information transmission. In other words, synapses and neurons maximise the energetic efficiency of information transfer, measured in bits of information transferred through a synaptic connection, or from the input to the output of a cell, per number of adenosine triphosphate molecules necessary to power this synaptic or neuronal activity [5]. In particular, we have shown that this trade-off between information flow and concomitant energetic consumption can explain low release probability at cortical synapses [9], and action potential transmission characteristics in the visual pathway, at thalamic relay synapses between retinal ganglion cells and thalamic relay neurons [10], as well as at the next synapse in that pathway, the synapse that thalamic relay cells form on layer 4 spiny stellate cells in the primary visual cortex [11].

In parallel to experiments, we have developed biophysical Hodgkin-Huxley-type models of these systems, all carefully calibrated on experimental data (see refs. [10,11] for further details). Here, we resume our study of these questions at thalamic relay synapses to investigate neuromodulation of these synapses' transmission properties by serotonin. The next section introduces the Hodgkin-Huxley-type model and the newly experimentally-calibrated model of neuromodulated synaptic input.

2 Mathematical Model of Information Transmission and Concomitant Energy Consumption in Thalamic Relay Cells

2.1 Hodgkin-Huxley Formalism

We have previously published an experimentally calibrated biophysical single-compartment model of the Hodgkin-Huxley-type for thalamic relay cells [10].

Briefly, the model is written as follows: The Hodgkin-Huxley formalism describes the dynamics of the membrane voltage V as:

$$C_m \frac{dV}{dt} = -\sum_j i_j - i_{Hold} - i_{syn},$$ (1)

with C_m the membrane capacitance, i_j the intrinsic currents, i_{Hold} an experimentally injected holding current (see ref. [10] for further details) and i_{syn} the synaptic currents. Following Bazhenov and colleagues [2], the intrinsic currents include a leak current i_L, a potassium leak current i_{KL}, an A-type potassium current i_A, a T-type low threshold calcium current i_T, an h-current i_h, a fast sodium current i_{Na} and a fast potassium current i_K. All the intrinsic currents have the same general form:

$$i = gm^M h^N (V - E),$$ (2)

where for each current i, g is the maximal conductance, $m(t)$ is the activation variable, $h(t)$ is the inactivation variable, E is the reversal potential, and M and N are the number of independent activation and inactivation gates.

The intracellular calcium dynamics is defined by:

$$\frac{dCa_i^{2+}}{dt} = -\frac{1}{\tau_{Ca}}(Ca_i^{2+} - Ca_{i,0}^{2+}) - A\, i_T,$$ (3)

with $Ca_{i,0}^{2+} = 2.4\,10^{-4}$ mM, the baseline intracellular calcium concentration, and $A = 5.18\,10^{-5}$ mM cm^2 ms^{-1} μA^{-1}, a constant. The time dependence for m and h is defined by:

$$\frac{dx}{dt} = \alpha_x(1 - x) - \beta_x x,$$ (4)

where x stands for either h or m.

We refer the interested reader to ref. [10] for all further details of the model, and for a detailed description of experimental and calibration procedures.

2.2 Modelling Synaptic Input, Synaptic Depression and Neuromodulation

In order to model the strong paired-pulse depression and neuromodulation that is known to happen at thalamic relay synapses, we use the formalism introduced by Tsodyks and Markram [20].

First, a sequence of binarized input action potentials is generated with a temporal resolution $\Delta t = 3$ ms. In order to generate sequences with the same temporal statistics than recorded *in vivo*, we use sequences recorded *in vivo* (available from ref. [10]) to calculate the non-Poissonian *in vivo* inter-spike interval distribution. From this distribution, we calculate the cumulative distribution function of inter-spike intervals, and in turn, use that cumulative distribution function to generate synthetic binary sequences.

Each input is then used to trigger an AMPA and a NMDA conductance with the generic form:

$$g(\delta t) = A\left(\exp(-\delta t/\tau_{\text{rise}}) - \exp(-\delta t/\tau_{\text{decay}})\right), \tag{5}$$

with τ_{rise} and τ_{decay} some time constants, δt the time elapsed since the input action potential and A an amplitude. Consecutive contributions are summed up.

In each case, the effective amplitude A of the triggered conductance is modulated by synaptic depression. To model this, we use a slight adaptation of the Tsodyks-Markram model [20], whereby the amplitude of the conductance is given by:

$$A_{n+1} = A_n\left(1 - U\right)\exp(-\Delta t/\tau_{\text{rec}}) + AU\left(1 - \exp(-\Delta t/\tau_{\text{rec}})\right), \tag{6}$$

with U and τ_{rec} some parameters. Fitting that model on experimental data from ref. [10] yields $U = 0.7$ and $\tau_{\text{rec}} = 620\,\text{ms}$ (to be described in details somewhere else). These parameters predict a paired-pulse depression of ~ 0.4 for consecutive pulses at $100\,\text{ms}$ interval, in excellent agreement with what was observed in electrophysiological recordings [10]. Additionally, that procedure yields $\tau_{\text{rise}} = 0.75\,\text{ms}$ and $\tau_{\text{decay}} = 2\,\text{ms}$ for the AMPA conductance, and $\tau_{\text{rise}} = 9\,\text{ms}$ and $\tau_{\text{decay}} = 22\,\text{ms}$ for the NMDA conductance, and a ratio between the peak amplitudes of the NMDA and AMPA conductances of 0.1.

Thus, i_{syn} (see Eq. 1) is given by:

$$i_{syn} = -g_{\text{AMPA}}(V - E_{\text{excitatory}})$$
$$- g_{\text{NMDA}}\left(\frac{9.69}{1 + 0.1688\,e^{-0.0717\,V}}\right)(V - E_{\text{excitatory}}), \tag{7}$$

with $E_{\text{excitatory}} = 0\,\text{mV}$, the reversal potential of AMPA and NMDA receptors. The additional term in the description of the NMDA conductance is added to describe the nonlinear I-V relation of NMDA receptors due to the Mg^{2+} block [10]. In each case, g_{AMPA} and g_{NMDA} are determined by the procedure mentioned above combining Equations (5) and (6). An example of what that procedure yields can be observed in the top two panels of Fig. 1 below.

Activation of serotonin receptors at thalamic relay synapses modulates the release probability of presynaptic vesicles. Specifically, the release probability is reduced and while this tends to lead to smaller postsynaptic potentials (PSPs), it makes consecutive PSPs more similar to each other in amplitude. The literature and preliminary experimental data (courtesy of D. Attwell, E. Engl and J.J. Harris) show that the presence of serotonin receptor agonists experimentally lead to reduced paired-pulse depression with the ratio of consecutive PSPs at $100\,\text{ms}$ interval to be about ~ 0.8 (instead of ~ 0.4 in control conditions). This can be easily achieved in the model presented here by changing the value of the parameter U to 0.2, yielding an elegant and simple framework to study the effect of neuromodulation at thalamic relay synapses. An example of what that procedure yields can be observed in Fig. 2 below and can be directly compared with the results in Fig. 1.

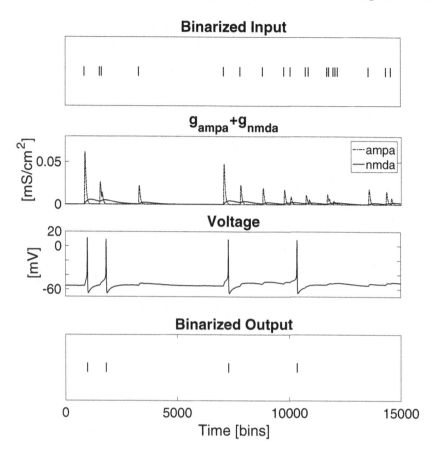

Fig. 1. Model dynamics in absence of neuromodulation ($U = 0.7$). **Top row:** Binarized input sequence at time resolution $\Delta t = 3$ ms. Input action potentials are generated at approximately 20 Hz and their temporal dynamics follows experimental data recorded *in vivo* in rodents, i.e. their inter-spike interval distribution matches the inter-spike interval distribution observed *in vivo*. **Second row:** The dynamics of the AMPA and NMDA conductances with parameter values for amplitudes, time constants and synaptic depression derived from experimental recordings and following the Tsodyks-Markram model [20]. With $U = 0.7$, synaptic conductances display significant depression. A paired-pulse depression of ~0.4 is predicted in these circumstances (consecutive pulses at 100 ms interval), matching what was observed in electrophysiological recordings [10]. **Third row:** Dynamics of the membrane voltage of the thalamic relay cell predicted in response to the input sequence. **Bottom row:** Binarized output sequence at time resolution $\Delta t = 3$ ms. The thalamic relay cell model only produces 4 output action potentials in response to the top input sequence (the average output frequency is ~4 Hz). In general, those are synchronous with the first input following a relatively long silent period.

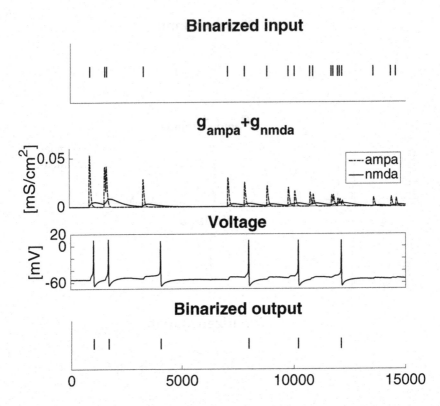

Fig. 2. Model dynamics with strong neuromodulation by serotonin ($U = 0.2$). **Top row:** Binarized input sequence at time resolution $\Delta t = 3$ ms. Input action potentials are generated at approximately 20 Hz and their temporal dynamics follows experimental data recorded *in vivo* in rodents. This is the same sequence as in Fig. 1. **Second row:** The dynamics of the AMPA and NMDA conductances with parameter values for amplitudes, time constants and synaptic depression derived from experimental recordings and following the Tsodyks-Markram model [20]. With $U = 0.2$, synaptic conductances display much less depression than in Fig. 1. A paired-pulse depression of ~0.8 is predicted in these circumstances (consecutive pulses at 100 ms interval), matching what was observed in preliminary electrophysiological recordings. **Third row:** Dynamics of the membrane voltage of the thalamic relay cell predicted in response to the input sequence. **Bottom row:** Binarized output sequence at time resolution $\Delta t = 3$ ms. The thalamic relay cell model now produces 6 output action potentials in response to the top input sequence. That output sequence is significantly different than the one at the bottom of Fig. 1.

2.3   Information Flow and Neuroenergetics

In order to assess information flow at the modelled feed-forward synapse, we collect the binarized input and output sequences with a temporal resolution of $\Delta t = 3$ ms (see Fig. 1 top and bottom panels). We then apply the so-called direct method by Strong *et al.* [19] to compute the *mutual information* between those input and output sequences, similar to what has been done in [16] and [10]. A detailed description of how to use this method and others for the analysis of spike trains can be found in ref. [15]. Note also that it is possible to use the so-called *transfer entropy* to measure information flow between neurons [17], instead of the mutual information as we do here. We refer the reader to refs. [6,11] for a comparative discussion of these measures in a context similar to the one discussed here.

The energy consumption in thalamic relay cells in this scenario arises from presynaptic activity and from the generation of output action potentials. Transport of ions across membranes during neural activity leads to the activation of the Na, K-ATPase electrogenic pump, which consumes adenosine triphosphate (ATP) molecules to maintain and reestablish normal ionic gradients [1,9,13]. It is thus possible to compute the energetic cost of neuronal activity (number of ATP molecules consumed in response to that activity) using biophysics as described in [1,10,11].

3 Modulation of Transmission Properties by the Neuromodulator Serotonin

Figure 1 shows typical data generated by the model in the scenario corresponding to the control experimental situation described in ref. [10], i.e. with strong paired-pulse depression ($U = 0.7$). Strong depression is apparent in the second panel from the top, where each input action potential following the first action potential after a long period of silence only evokes a much reduced conductance. As a result, the model, like the cells it is based on, tends to generate outputs only when two input action potentials come in close succession to each other (this is not always the case, however, as a single input action potential can be seen to trigger an output spike at time bin 7000). While the model receives input action potentials at a frequency of $\sim$20 Hz, it generates output action potentials at only $\sim$4 Hz.

Figure 2 shows typical data generated by the model in the scenario corresponding to application of serotonin, i.e. with weak paired-pulse depression ($U = 0.2$). The binary input sequence is the same as the one used in Fig. 1. Weak depression is apparent in the second panel from the top, where each input action potential triggers in average smaller conductances, but with amplitudes more evenly distributed over time. A comparison between Figs. 1 and 2 reveals that even though the model is driven in both cases by the same binary input sequence, the voltage trajectory of the cell is very significantly affected by changing the value of U, and the binary output sequence of the cell is now largely different. These results suggest that neuromodulation at these synapses could have a significant effect on the quantity and type of information that reaches the primary visual cortex.

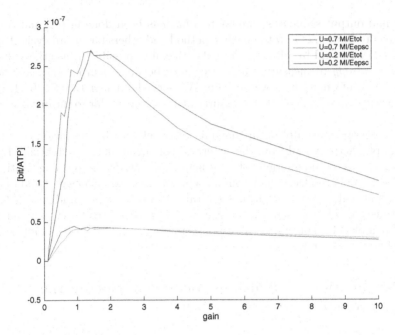

Fig. 3. Energetic optimality of information transfer at thalamic relay synapses. Mutual information (bits/sec) divided by concomitant energetic costs (ATP/sec), factoring the cost of reverting ionic flows across the cellular membrane resulting from the activation of postsynaptic receptors (top curves), or resulting from the activation of postsynaptic receptors and from the generation of action potentials (bottom curves). The parameter U is chosen to be either $U = 0.7$ to match control experimental conditions or $U = 0.2$ to model the application of serotonin receptor agonists. An overall gain factor is applied to the synapse with gain = 1 matching the experimental physiological gain in control conditions. The curves reveal the presence of an optimum at, or slightly above, gain = 1 [10]. Shifting from $U = 0.7$ to $U = 0.2$ appears to shift the peak of each curve slightly to the right, and to slightly broaden the peak.

We then tested whether this type of neuromodulation affects the energetic optimality of information transmission at these synapses. To this end, we ran simulations varying the overall gain of the thalamic relay synapse and measured the mutual information between the input and output sequences [10,11] using the direct method [19]. We additionally computed the equivalent energetic budget using standard biophysical methods developed in ref. [1]. We observed that, while changing the value of U does affect absolute values, the energetic consumption (measured in ATP/sec) associated with the generation of postsynaptic potentials, or with the generation of postsynaptic potentials *and* action potentials, scales more or less linearly with the gain of those synapses, whatever the value of U (not shown). This matches what has been observed elsewhere [9–11]. We also observed that, while changing the value of U does affect absolute values, information flow across the relay synapse (measured in bits/sec) scales sigmoidally with the gain of those synapses (not shown). Again, this matches what has been observed elsewhere [9–11].

We then computed in each scenario the ratio of information flowing through the synapse to the concomitant energy consumption necessary to power the synaptic and neuronal activity of the thalamic relay neuron. Preliminary results displayed in Fig. 3 show that this results in curves with a relatively well-defined energetic optimum for information transmission, whether $U = 0.7$ or 0.2, and whether the energy budget includes the cost of postsynaptic potentials alone (top curves), or also includes the cost of postsynaptic potentials and action potentials (bottom curves). In all cases, the energetic optimum stood at, or close to, gain $= 1$, the physiological gain of the synapse in control conditions. This is in excellent accordance with experimental findings and a previous version of this model (driven by experimentally-recorded conductances). Despite its significant effect on the actual output sequences generated by the thalamic relay neuron, neuromodulation (shifting from $U = 0.7$ to $U = 0.2$) only appears to shift the peak of each curve slightly to the right, and to slightly broaden said peak.

4   Discussion

Here, we have introduced a carefully-calibrated *mechanistic* [14] model of synaptic depression and neuromodulation by serotonin at thalamic relay synapses. We have described how to build and calibrate such a model using experimental data, and together with the work in ref. [10], we have established that it qualitatively, and to some extent quantitatively, captures the behaviour of biological thalamic relay neurons, in particular here, with respect to modelling *in vivo*-like synaptic inputs, including their modulation by serotonin.

The results presented here suggest that neuromodulation by serotonin does not very significantly affect the energetic optimality of information transmission at thalamic relay synapses. The fact that neuromodulation does not very strongly affect the position of the peak in the information over energy curves, and the fact that this peak sits at the experimentally observed physiological gain for those synapses (gain $= 1$), reinforces the notion that this principle might be a relatively generic design principle in the brain. This model thus also contains *normative* (energetic) aspects [14]. It is our contention that synaptic activity has evolved under, and is to an extent shaped by, energetic constraints [5,9–11].

Neuromodulation does, however, very significantly affect what output sequences are sent out to the primary visual cortex in response to a given input sequence. In other words, it appears to change the encoding of visual information. Our model thus opens now the possibility to systematically investigate what kind of input sequences will maximise under different circumstances information flowing from the retina to the primary visual cortex.

References

1. Attwell, D., Laughlin, S.B.: An energy budget for signaling in the grey matter of the brain. J. Cereb. Blood Flow Metab. **21**(10), 1133–1145 (2001)

2. Bazhenov, M., Timofeev, I., Steriade, M., Sejnowski, T.J.: Cellular and network models for intrathalamic augmenting responses during 10-Hz stimulation. J. Neurophysiol. **79**(5), 2730–2748 (1998)
3. Branco, T., Staras, K., Darcy, K.J., Goda, Y.: Local dendritic activity sets release probability at hippocampal synapses. Neuron **59**(3), 475–485 (2008)
4. Coggan, J.S., et al.: A process for digitizing and simulating biologically realistic oligocellular networks demonstrated for the neuro-glio-vascular ensemble. Front. Neurosci. **12**, 664 (2018)
5. Conrad, M., Engl, E., Jolivet, R.: Energy use constrains brain information processing. In: Technical Digest - International Electron Devices Meeting, pp. 11–3 (2018)
6. Conrad, M., Jolivet, R.B.: Comparative performance of mutual information and transfer entropy for analysing the balance of information flow and energy consumption at synapses (2020, Submitted)
7. Engl, E., Jolivet, R., Hall, C.N., Attwell, D.: Non-signalling energy use in the developing rat brain. J. Cereb. Blood Flow Metab. **37**(3), 951–966 (2017)
8. Hardingham, N.R., Read, J.C., Trevelyan, A.J., Nelson, J.C., Jack, J.J.B., Bannister, N.J.: Quantal analysis reveals a functional correlation between presynaptic and postsynaptic efficacy in excitatory connections from rat neocortex. J. Neurosci. **30**(4), 1441–1451 (2010)
9. Harris, J.J., Jolivet, R., Attwell, D.: Synaptic energy use and supply. Neuron **75**(5), 762–777 (2012)
10. Harris, J.J., Jolivet, R., Engl, E., Attwell, D.: Energy-efficient information transfer by visual pathway synapses. Curr. Biol. **25**(24), 3151–3160 (2015)
11. Harris, J.J., Engl, E., Attwell, D., Jolivet, R.B.: Energy-efficient information transfer at thalamocortical synapses. PLOS Comput. Biol. **15**(8), e1007226 (2019)
12. Jolivet, R., Coggan, J.S., Allaman, I., Magistretti, P.J.: Multi-timescale modeling of activity-dependent metabolic coupling in the neuron-glia-vasculature ensemble. PLoS Comput. Biol. **11**(2)(2015). https://doi.org/10.1371/journal.pcbi.1004036
13. Jolivet, R., Magistretti, P.J., Weber, B.: Deciphering neuron-glia compartmentalization in cortical energy metabolism. Front. Neuroenergetics **1** (2009). https://doi.org/10.3389/neuro.14.004.2009
14. Levenstein, D., et al.: On the role of theory and modeling in neuroscience (2020). https://arxiv.org/abs/2003.13825v2
15. Panzeri, S., Senatore, R., Montemurro, M.A., Petersen, R.S.: Correcting for the sampling bias problem in spike train information measures. J. Neurophysiol. **98**(3), 1064–1072 (2007)
16. Reinagel, P., Reid, R.C.: Temporal coding of visual information in the thalamus. J. Neurosci. **20**(14), 5392–5400 (2000)
17. Schreiber, T.: Measuring information transfer. Phys. Rev. Lett. **85**(2), 461 (2000)
18. Shannon, C.E.: A mathematical theory of communication. Bell Syst. Tech. J. **27**(3), 379–423 (1948)
19. Strong, S.P., Koberle, R., Van Steveninck, R.R.D.R., Bialek, W.: Entropy and information in neural spike trains. Phys. Rev. Lett. **80**(1), 197 (1998)
20. Tsodyks, M.V., Markram, H.: The neural code between neocortical pyramidal neurons depends on neurotransmitter release probability. Proc. Natl. Acad. Sci. **94**(2), 719–723 (1997)

Learning Precise Spike Timings
with Eligibility Traces

Manuel Traub[1] , Martin V. Butz[1] , R. Harald Baayen[2] ,
and Sebastian Otte[1(✉)]

[1] Neuro-Cognitive Modeling Group, University of Tübingen,
Sand 14, 72076 Tübingen, Germany
sebastian.otte@uni-tuebingen.de
[2] Quantitative Linguistics, University of Tübingen,
Wilhelmstr. 19, 72074 Tübingen, Germany

Abstract. Recent research in the field of spiking neural networks
(SNNs) has shown that recurrent variants of SNNs, namely *long short-
term SNNs* (LSNNs), can be trained via error gradients just as effective
as LSTMs. The underlying learning method (e-prop) is based on a formalization of eligibility traces applied to *leaky integrate and fire* (LIF)
neurons. Here, we show that the proposed approach cannot fully unfold
spike timing dependent plasticity (STDP). As a consequence, this limits
in principle the inherent advantage of SNNs, that is, the potential to
develop codes that rely on precise relative spike timings. We show that
STDP-aware synaptic gradients naturally emerge within the eligibility
equations of e-prop when derived for a slightly more complex spiking
neuron model, here at the example of the Izhikevich model. We also
present a simple extension of the LIF model that provides similar gradients. In a simple experiment we demonstrate that the STDP-aware LIF
neurons can learn precise spike timings from an e-prop-based gradient
signal.

Keywords: Eligibility traces · Recurrent neural networks ·
Backpropagation through time · Spike timing dependent plasticity

1   Introduction

Spike timing dependent plasticity (STDP) is assumed to be a fundamental learning principle in the brain [5]. It is considered a prerequisite for developing temporal codes in which precise relative spike timings are key, thus going beyond
plain rate coding. Accordingly, STDP is based on temporal correlations between
presynaptic and postsynaptic neural activities. Indeed, it has been shown that
such a Hebbian-like form of synaptic plasticity is at play in the visual cortex of
primates [8].

Recently, (non-supervised) STDP based learning rules were successfully
applied to train deep (non-recurrent) convolutional SNNs for image recognition [10,13]. In terms of effectiveness, though, supervised back-propagation-like

© Springer Nature Switzerland AG 2020
I. Farkaš et al. (Eds.): ICANN 2020, LNCS 12397, pp. 659–669, 2020.
https://doi.org/10.1007/978-3-030-61616-8_53

approaches seem to be more promising [11], even though spiking neurons are not differentiable per se, such that an error gradient signal can only be approximated.

Recently, it has been shown that even *back-propagation through time* (BPTT) [14] can be applied for training recurrent SNNs [1]. Bellec et al. demonstrated that SNNs, specifically a variant that is called *long short-term SNN* (LSNN), for the first time can reach the performance of the well-known LSTM [7]. Moreover, the mathematical approach of learning in SNNs has led to the derivation of a biologically plausible learning rule called *e-prop*, which approximates BPTT [2] by means of a formalization of *eligibility traces*.

Bellec et al. established a link between e-prop and (biological) synaptic plasticity [3,4]. It appears, however, that STDP can only fully arise within eligibility trace-based learning, when the neuron model provides a negated gradient signal in the case when a presynaptic spike arrives too late, i.e., shortly after a postsynaptic spike. This does not happen in the LIF model proposed in [3], cf. Sect. 4 for further details.

The contributions of this paper are as follows. We show that STDP emerges within e-prop when it is derived using a more complex neuron model, which adequately incorporates a refractory period. This is exemplarily shown for the Izhikevich model [9]. Moreover, we present an adjustment of the basic LIF model used in LSNNs in order to produce the same STDP behavior within the e-prop framework.

2   Background

Experimental data suggests that the brain solves the *temporal credit assignment problem* by combining local eligibility traces, which maintain information about individual synapses' activation histories, with neuromodulator-based reward signals [6]. The e-prop algorithm [2] adapts this principle by factorizing the error gradients from BPTT into a sum of products between local eligibility traces and online learning signals.

$$
\begin{aligned}
\frac{dE}{dw_{i,j}} &= \sum_t L_j^t e_{i,j}^t \\
&= \sum_t \frac{dE}{dz_j^t} e_{i,j}^t
\end{aligned}
\tag{1}
$$

Here, the learning signal (L_j^t) represents the global error information of the post-synaptic spike, whereas the eligibility trace ($e_{i,j}^t$) captures the local information available at the synapse. z_j^t refers to the (spiking) output of neuron j at time step t.

The eligibility trace is furthermore a product of pre- and postsynaptic information, but does not include any error gradient information:

$$
e_{i,j}^t = \frac{\partial z_j^t}{\partial \mathbf{s}_j^t} \boldsymbol{\epsilon}_{i,j}^t
\tag{2}
$$

Specifically, it is the product of a *pseudo derivative*, replacing the non-existing derivative of the spiking function $\partial z^t_j / \partial s^t_j$ and the presynaptic activity flow accumulated within an eligibility vector $\epsilon^t_{i,j}$. The latter is computed forward through time:

$$\epsilon^t_{i,j} = \epsilon^{t-1}_{i,j} \frac{\partial s^t_j}{\partial s^{t-1}_j} + \frac{\partial s^t_j}{\partial w_{i,j}} \tag{3}$$

where s^t_j refers to the current state of a neuron containing, for instance (depending on the model), its action potential and possibly further adaptive parameters.

3   STPD with Izhikevich Neurons

The Izhikevich neuron [9] is a precise, but computationally cheap model of a biological neuron that uses two parameterizable differential equations. It is particularly more complex than the simple LIF model, but, more importantly, explicitly models the refractory period of the neuron.

3.1   Izhikevich Model and Eligibility Trace

The dynamics of the Izhikevich neuron are described with the following differential equations.

$$v' = 0.04v^2 + 5v + 140 - u + I \tag{4}$$

$$u' = 0.004v - 0.02u \tag{5}$$

Here v is the membrane voltage and u is a recovery variable, which controls the refractory period of the Izhikevich neuron. I is the current input to the neuron.

Once the membrane voltage crosses $30\,\mathrm{mV}$, a spike is emitted and v and u are reset as described in Algorithm 1.

In order to derive an eligibility trace for Izhikevich neurons, the Eqs. (4) and (5) have to be modeled in discrete time steps, and also the reset has to be modeled within the new equations. To accomplish this built-in reset, the variables $\tilde{v}^t_j$ and $\tilde{u}^t_j$ are introduced, replacing v and u in the standard equations.

$$\tilde{v}^t_j = v^t_j - (v^t_j + 65)z^t_j \tag{6}$$

$$\tilde{u}^t_j = u^t_j + 2z^t_j \tag{7}$$

Algorithm 1. Izhikevich neuron reset

---

if $v < 30mv$ **then**

$\quad v \leftarrow -65mV$

$\quad u \leftarrow u + 2$

end if

Here the binary variable z_j^t, resets $\tilde{v}_j^t$ and $\tilde{u}_j^t$ after a spike of neuron j at time step t. Now v and u can be computed in discrete time steps using Euler integration with a constant step size of δt.

$$v_j^{t+1} = \tilde{v}_j^t + \delta t(0.04(\tilde{v}_j^t)^2 + 5\tilde{v}_j^t + 140 - \tilde{u}_j^t + I_j^t) \tag{8}$$

$$u_j^{t+1} = \tilde{u}_j^t + \delta t(0.004\tilde{v}_j^t - 0.02\tilde{u}_j^t) \tag{9}$$

The hidden state of Izhikevich neurons is then defined as a two-dimensional vector containing v_j^t and u_j^t.

$$\mathbf{s}_j^t = \begin{pmatrix} v_j^t \\ u_j^t \end{pmatrix} \tag{10}$$

To finally derive the eligibility vector (3), the derivative of the next hidden state s_j^{t+1} by the current state s_j^t has to be computed. This state derivative can be expressed in the following form of a 2×2 matrix.

$$\frac{\partial \mathbf{s}_j^{t+1}}{\partial \mathbf{s}_j^t} = \begin{pmatrix} \frac{\partial v_j^{t+1}}{\partial v_j^t} & \frac{\partial v_j^{t+1}}{\partial u_j^t} \\ \frac{\partial u_j^{t+1}}{\partial v_j^t} & \frac{\partial u_j^{t+1}}{\partial u_j^t} \end{pmatrix} \tag{11}$$

The partial derivatives can be further simplified by taking into account that z_j^t is a binary variable.

$$\frac{\partial v_j^{t+1}}{\partial v_j^t} = 1 - z_j^t$$
$$+ 0.08\delta t(v_j^t - (v_j^t + 65)z_j^t)(1 - z_j^t)$$
$$+ 5\delta t(1 - z_j^t)$$

$$= 1 - z_j^t + 0.08\delta t v_j^t(1 - z_j^t)$$
$$+ 5\delta t(1 - z_j^t) \tag{12}$$

$$= (1 - z_j^t)(1 + (0.08v_j^t + 5)\delta t)$$

$$\frac{\partial v_j^{t+1}}{\partial u_j^t} = -\delta t \tag{13}$$

$$\frac{\partial u_j^{t+1}}{\partial v_j^t} = 0.004\delta t(1 - z_j^t) \tag{14}$$

$$\frac{\partial u_j^{t+1}}{\partial u_j^t} = 1 - 0.02\delta t \tag{15}$$

Given this state derivative, the eligibility vector is computed in the following two-dimensional vector, which contains a voltage eligibility value in the first row and a refractory eligibility value in the second row:

$$\epsilon_{i,j}^{t+1} = \frac{\partial \mathbf{s}_j^{t+1}}{\partial \mathbf{s}_j^t} \cdot \epsilon_{i,j}^t + \frac{\partial \mathbf{s}_j^{t+1}}{\partial \theta_{ji}^{rec}} \tag{16}$$

where

$$\epsilon_{i,j,v}^{t+1} = (1 - z_j^t)(1 + (0.08v_j^t + 5)\delta t)\epsilon_{i,j,v}^t \\ - \delta t \epsilon_{i,j,u}^t + \delta t z_i^t \tag{17}$$

$$\epsilon_{i,j,u}^{t+1} = 0.004\delta t(1 - z_j^t)\epsilon_{i,j,v}^t + (1 - 0.02\delta t)\epsilon_{i,j,u}^t \tag{18}$$

Here the recovery eligibility value $\epsilon_{i,j,u}^t$ approximates an exponential filter of the voltage eligibility. The voltage eligibility itself is a function of the neuron's action potential that also accumulates presynaptic spikes and gets dampened by its exponential average (by the recovery eligibility).

Another insight from the equations is that, whenever the postsynaptic neuron spikes, the voltage eligibility vector is reset to the negative recovery eligibility vector.

In order to derive the final eligibility trace, a pseudo-derivative for the Izhikevich neuron is defined as follows:

$$h_j^t := \gamma \, \exp\left(\frac{\min(v, 30) - 30}{30}\right) \tag{19}$$

where γ is a damping factor.

With this pseudo-derivative, the neuron spike z_j^t derived by the hidden state $\mathbf{s}_j^t$ is then defined as:

$$\begin{pmatrix} \frac{z_j^t}{v_j^t} \\ \frac{z_j^t}{u_j^t} \end{pmatrix} \stackrel{\text{def}}{=} \begin{pmatrix} h_j^t \\ 0 \end{pmatrix} \tag{20}$$

The eligibility trace then simplifies to the pseudo-derivative times the voltage eligibility vector.

$$\begin{aligned} e_{i,j}^{t+1} &= \frac{\partial z_j^{t+1}}{\partial \mathbf{s}_j^{t+1}} \cdot \epsilon_{i,j}^{t+1} \\ &= \begin{pmatrix} h_j^{t+1} & 0 \end{pmatrix} \begin{pmatrix} \epsilon_{i,j,v}^{t+1} \\ \epsilon_{i,j,a}^{t+1} \end{pmatrix} \\ &= h_j^{t+1} \epsilon_{i,j,v}^{t+1} \end{aligned} \tag{21}$$

3.2 Experimental Results

In the following evaluation, our goal was to inspect the evolution of the derived eligibility traces. Two Izhikevich neurons were weakly connected by a synapse and received random inputs to simulate behavior within a greater network. To specifically investigate the influence of the eligibility trace on the gradient, a constant positive learning signal was used. The gradient was calculated based on (1).

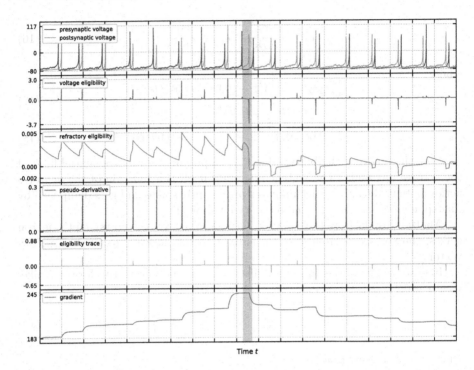

Fig. 1. Simulation of two connected Izhikevich neurons that exhibit a positively rewarded STDP behavior followed by a negatively rewarded one. As a result, a gradient computed with a constant positive learning signal increases during positively rewarded STDP and decreases during negatively rewarded STDP.

In the simulation shown in Fig. 1, first an artificial strengthening STDP behavior is introduced by using an overall lower random input current to the output neuron. To ensure that an output spike (postsynaptic neuron) fires shortly after an input spike (presynaptic neuron) we steadily increased the random input current for the output neuron after the input neuron spiked. In the second part of the simulation this behavior is reversed (presynaptic spike before postsynaptic spike) in order to produce a weakening STDP behavior, as shown in Algorithm 2. Here $U(\alpha, \beta)$ represents a random variable drawn uniform from the interval (α, β) and t_{z_i}, t_{z_o} are the spike times for the last input or output spike.

As can be seen in the diagram, the desired STDP behavior of the synapse is clearly reflected within the gradient, which for the first half of the simulation increases, and then decreases. The eligibility trace and the eligibility vector also reflect the introduced STDP behavior. They have only positive values during the STDP strengthening phase, but they also take on negative values during the STDP weakening phase.

Algorithm 2. Izhikevich e-prop simulation

if $t < T \cdot 0.45$ then
    $I_i^t \leftarrow U(1, 15)$
    $I_o^t \leftarrow U(1, 5)$
    if $t_{z_i} > t_{z_o}$ then
        $I_o^t \leftarrow U(0, 1)(t - t_{z_i})$
    end if
else
    $I_i^t \leftarrow U(1, 5)$
    $I_o^t \leftarrow U(1, 15)$
    if $t_{z_o} > t_{z_i}$ then
        $I_i^t \leftarrow U(0, 1)(t - t_{z_o})$
    end if
end if

4 STDP with LIF Neurons

While our experimental results confirm the desired general tendency to reflect full STDP behavior in gradients based on the eligibility traces of Izhikevich neurons, plain LIF neurons do not show this behavior. We now detail the reason for this lack and introduce negative eligibilities to induce effective connection weakening.

4.1 LIF Model

Considering the definition of the dynamics of the LIF neuron

$$v_j^{t+1} = \alpha v_j^t + I_j^t - z_j^t v_{thr} \tag{22}$$

Equation (22) shows the action potential dynamics of a LIF neuron in discrete timesteps, as defined in [2]. The neuron integrates over the weighted sum of incoming spikes I_j^t; $\alpha < 1$ controls the leakage. Once a LIF neuron spikes, its action potential is reset by subtracting the value of the spike threshold.

A neuron spike is modeled by the Heaviside step function. The neuron is prohibited from spiking during a fixed refractory period after the last spike.

$$z_j^t = \begin{cases} 0, & \text{if } t - t_{z_j} < \delta t_{ref} \\ H(v_j^t - v_{thr}), & \text{otherwise} \end{cases} \tag{23}$$

Here (23) t_{z_j} represents the most recent spike time of neuron j and δt_{ref} denotes the length of the refractory period.

Seeing that also the *pseudo derivative* (24) is set to zero during this refractory period:

$$h_j^t := \begin{cases} 0, & \text{if } t - t_{z_j} < \delta t_{ref} \\ \gamma \max(0, 1 - |\frac{v_j^t - v_{thr}}{v_{thr}}|), & \text{otherwise} \end{cases}, \tag{24}$$

no weakening STDP based gradients can unfold in the e-prop equations using standard LIF neurons.

4.2 STDP-LIF Model and Eligibility Trace

Whereas an STDP influenced gradient cannot be observed with the standard equations for LIF or adaptive LIF (ALIF) neurons within an LSNN [1], by slightly modifying the original LIF formulation from (22), a clear STDP based eligibility trace emerges.

In order to compute such an eligibility trace reflecting the STDP behavior of the synapse connecting two LIF neurons, the LIF equation has to be slightly altered into, what we from now on will refer to, an STDP-LIF neuron:

$$v_j^{t+1} = \alpha v_j^t + I_j^t - z_j^t \alpha v_j^t - z_j^{t-\delta t_{ref}} \alpha v_j^t \tag{25}$$

Instead of using a soft reset at a fixed threshold, in (25) the STDP-LIF neuron is hard reset to zero whenever it spikes, and whenever its refractory period ends. Since the reset now does include the voltage v_j^t as a factor, the spike is now included in the hidden state derivative

$$\frac{\partial v_j^{t+1}}{\partial v_j^t} = \alpha - z_j^t \alpha - \alpha z_j^{t-\delta t_{ref}} \tag{26}$$

$$= \alpha(1 - z_j^t - z_j^{t-\delta t_{ref}})$$

and hence also in the computation of the eligibility trace

$$\epsilon_{i,j}^{t+1} = \frac{\partial \mathbf{s}_j^{t+1}}{\partial \mathbf{s}_j^t} \cdot \epsilon_{i,j}^t + \frac{\partial \mathbf{s}_j^{t+1}}{\partial \theta_{ji}^{rec}} \tag{27}$$

$$= \alpha(1 - z_j^t - z_j^{t-\delta t_{ref}})\epsilon_{i,j}^t + z_i^t$$

$$e_{i,j}^{t+1} = \frac{\partial z_j^{t+1}}{\partial \mathbf{s}_j^{t+1}} \cdot \epsilon_{i,j}^{t+1} \tag{28}$$

$$= h_j^{t+1} \epsilon_{i,j}^{t+1}$$

As a result, the eligibility trace is reset after a spike and after the refractory period.

This reset behavior allows us now to create an eligibility trace that reflects the STDP behavior of its synapse by using a constant negative pseudo-derivative during the refractory period and otherwise leave the neuron dynamics unchanged.

$$h_j^t := \begin{cases} -\gamma, & \text{if } t - t_{z_j} < \delta t_{ref} \\ \gamma \max(0, 1 - |\frac{v_j^t - v_{thr}}{v_{thr}}|), & \text{otherwise} \end{cases} \tag{29}$$

As a result, any incoming spike during the refractory period produces a negative eligibility trace that persists for the time of the refractory period and has a negative influence on the gradient.

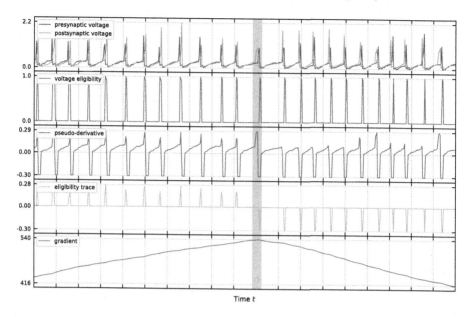

Fig. 2. Simulation of two connected LIF neurons that exhibit a positively rewarded STDP behavior followed by a negatively rewarded one. As a result, a gradient computed with a constant positive learning signal increases during positively rewarded STDP and decreases during negatively rewarded STDP.

4.3   Experimental Results

The STDP influenced gradient is shown in Fig. 2, in which two connected STDP-LIF neurons are simulated similarly to the Izhikevich neuron simulation in Algorithm 2. Strengthening and weakening STDP events can be clearly identified in the eligibility trace, directly influencing the resulting gradient. Thus, by the above simple modifications of the LIF model, one can derive eligibility traces for STDP-LIF neurons that reflect the STDP behavior of the underlying synapse.

Since the gradient calculation using eligibility traces in combination with a back-propagated learning signal (1) is mathematically equivalent to normal BPTT, it follows that BPTT itself facilitates STDP behavior.

4.4   Learning Precise Timing

In a simple additional experiment we evaluated the performance of STDP-LIF neurons in comparison to standard LIF neurons by learning an LSNN with 16 hidden neurons, one input neuron, and one output neuron to approximate a function based on the timing of the input spike. In this experiment the LSNN receives Poisson distributed spikes from the input neuron with an average spike rate of 25 Hz. The supervised target signal for the leaky readout neuron is then

$$v_{target}^t = \frac{1}{1 + t - t_{in}} \tag{30}$$

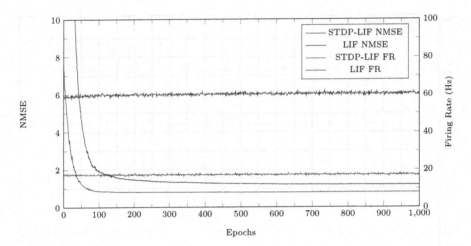

Fig. 3. Spike timing test: STDP-LIF neurons manage to learn a simple function based on the inputs spike timing efficiently, while standard LIF neurons produce a lager error by approximating the function using a high firing rate. Graphs are averaged over 100 independent runs each.

In this equation, t_{in} is the spike time of the most recent input spike. A good approximation of (30) can be learned when the input spikes are just forwarded to the readout neuron, which can in turn approximate the shape of the function via its readout decay.

In the simulation, the spike threshold v_{thr} for each neuron was set to 0.5 and the LSNN was trained over 1 000 epochs using a batch size of 16 and an initial learning rate of 0.003, which is decayed every 100 epochs by multiplying it with 0.7. The network was trained with Adam [12] and no further regularization was used.

As can be seen in Fig. 3, the STDP-LIF neurons quickly manage to suppress the hidden connections and only forward the input spikes to the readout neuron, while the LIF neurons on the other hand produce a lager error by approximating the function with a high firing rate.

5   Conclusion

In this paper we showed that STDP emerges within eligibility trace-based gradient signals in SNNs, given that the neuron model is sufficiently detailed. Specifically, it is crucial that the refractory period of postsynaptic neurons is taken into account. While this is not the case for regular LIF neurons, we demonstrated that by including eligibility traces derived from the well-known Izhikevich model, the gradient signal induces STDP behavior. The standard LIF model can also be refined such that it provides STDP. Equipped with STDP-aware gradient signals, we showed that learning precise spike timings becomes possible.

Seeing the recent advances in applying (recurrent) SNNs successfully, we will evaluate these mathematical insights very soon to harder benchmark problems like handwriting or speech recognition (TIMIT) and expect to achieve similar performances. The observed effect of reduced firing rates when using STDP-aware gradients could be particularly interesting for neuromorphic hardware implementations, in which sparse spiking behavior effectively benefits energy consumption.

References

1. Bellec, G., Salaj, D., Subramoney, A., Legenstein, R., Maass, W.: Long short-term memory and learning-to-learn in networks of spiking neurons. In: Advances in Neural Information Processing Systems, pp. 795–805 (2018)
2. Bellec, G., Scherr, F., Hajek, E., Salaj, D., Legenstein, R., Maass, W.: Biologically inspired alternatives to backpropagation through time for learning in recurrent neural nets. arXiv preprint arXiv:1901.09049 (2019)
3. Bellec, G., et al.: Eligibility traces provide a data-inspired alternative to backpropagation through time (2019)
4. Bellec, G., et al.: A solution to the learning dilemma for recurrent networks of spiking neurons. bioRxiv p. 738385 (2019)
5. Caporale, N., Dan, Y.: Spike timing-dependent plasticity: a Hebbian learning rule. Annu. Rev. Neurosci. **31**, 25–46 (2008)
6. Gerstner, W., Lehmann, M., Liakoni, V., Corneil, D., Brea, J.: Eligibility traces and plasticity on behavioral time scales: experimental support of neoHebbian three-factor learning rules. Front. Neural Circuits **12**, 53 (2018)
7. Hochreiter, S., Schmidhuber, J.: Long short-term memory. Neural Comput. **9**(8), 1735–1780 (1997). https://doi.org/10.1162/neco.1997.9.8.1735
8. Huang, S., et al.: Associative Hebbian synaptic plasticity in primate visual cortex. J. Neurosci. **34**(22), 7575–7579 (2014)
9. Izhikevich, E.M.: Simple model of spiking neurons. IEEE Trans. Neural Netw. **14**(6), 1569–1572 (2003)
10. Kheradpisheh, S.R., Ganjtabesh, M., Thorpe, S.J., Masquelier, T.: STDP-based spiking deep convolutional neural networks for object recognition. Neural Netw. **99**, 56–67 (2018)
11. Kheradpisheh, S.R., Masquelier, T.: S4NN: temporal backpropagation for spiking neural networks with one spike per neuron. arXiv preprint arXiv:1910.09495 (2019)
12. Kingma, D.P., Ba, J.L.: Adam: a method for stochastic optimization. In: 3rd International Conference for Learning Representations abs/1412.6980 (2015)
13. Mozafari, M., Kheradpisheh, S.R., Masquelier, T., Nowzari-Dalini, A., Ganjtabesh, M.: First-spike-based visual categorization using reward-modulated STDP. IEEE Trans. Neural Netw. Learn. Syst. **29**, 6178–6190 (2018)
14. Werbos, P.: Backpropagation through time: what it does and how to do it. Proc. IEEE **78**(10), 1550–1560 (1990). https://doi.org/10.1109/5.58337

Meta-STDP Rule Stabilizes Synaptic Weights Under *in Vivo*-like Ongoing Spontaneous Activity in a Computational Model of CA1 Pyramidal Cell

Matúš Tomko[1(✉)], Peter Jedlička[2,3], and L'ubica Beňušková[1]

[1] Centre for Cognitive Science, Department of Applied Informatics, Faculty of Mathematics, Physics and Informatics, Comenius University in Bratislava, Mlynská dolina, Bratislava, Slovakia
matus.tomko@fmph.uniba.sk
[2] Faculty of Medicine, ICAR3R - Interdisciplinary Centre for 3Rs in Animal Research, Justus-Liebig-University, Giessen, Germany
[3] Frankfurt Institute for Advanced Studies, Frankfurt am Main, Germany

Abstract. It is widely accepted that in the brain processes related to learning and memory there are changes at the level of synapses. Synapses have the ability to change their strength depending on the stimuli, which is called activity-dependent synaptic plasticity. To date, many mathematical models describing activity-dependent synaptic plasticity have been introduced. However, the remaining question is whether these rules apply in general to the whole brain or only to individual areas or even just to individual types of cells. Here, we decided to test whether the well-known rule of Spike-Timing Dependent Plasticity (STDP) extended by metaplasticity (meta-STDP) supports long-term stability of major synaptic inputs to hippocampal CA1 pyramidal neurons. For this reason, we have coupled synaptic models equipped with a previously established meta-STDP rule to a biophysically realistic computational model of the hippocampal CA1 pyramidal cell with a simplified dendritic tree. Our simulations show that the meta-STDP rule is able to keep synaptic weights stable during ongoing spontaneous input activity as it happens in the hippocampus *in vivo*. This is functionally advantageous as neurons should not change their weights during the ongoing activity of neural circuits *in vivo*. However, they should maintain their ability to display plastic changes in the case of significantly different or "meaningful" inputs. Thus, our study is the first step before we attempt to simulate different stimulation protocols which induce changes in synaptic weights *in vivo*.

Keywords: Synaptic plasticity · Metaplasticity · Meta-STDP · Computational model · CA1 pyramidal cell

1 Introduction

Hippocampal CA1 pyramidal cells are crucially involved in processes associated with a learning and memory. That includes working memory [1–3], temporal processing of

© Springer Nature Switzerland AG 2020
I. Farkaš et al. (Eds.): ICANN 2020, LNCS 12397, pp. 670–680, 2020.
https://doi.org/10.1007/978-3-030-61616-8_54

information [4], and several others. CA1 pyramidal cells are the major excitatory cells of the CA1 region of hippocampus.

Synaptic plasticity is believed to be a key neural mechanism behind major types of memory. It represents the ability of neurons to strengthen and weaken synaptic weights or synaptic transmission depending on input/output activity. The most studied forms of long-term synaptic plasticity are long-term changes in synaptic weights referred to as long-term potentiation (LTP) and long-term depression (LTD) [5] as it is reviewed for instance in the paper of Martin et al. [6], which states: "activity-dependent synaptic plasticity is induced at appropriate synapses during memory formation and is both necessary and sufficient for the encoding and trace storage of the type of memory mediated by the brain area in which it is observed" [6].

So far, several models of synaptic plasticity have been introduced [7]. The meta-STDP rule of synaptic plasticity [8] used in our project is the nearest-neighbor implementation of the STDP rule [9], which is extended by metaplasticity [10]. The prefix "meta" points to the fact that synaptic plasticity itself is regulated by various mechanisms and thus manifests its higher-order character. One of the important factors of metaplasticity is the dependence of the outcome of synaptic plasticity upon the previous history of firing of the postsynaptic neuron [10]. This idea was used by Benuskova and Abraham [8] in modifying the classical STDP rule. Due to the use of metaplasticity, the amplitudes of LTP and LTD become dynamic and change their actual values depending on the previous postsynaptic activity [8]. The meta-STDP rule has already been successfully used in modeling studies of heterosynaptic plasticity in the hippocampal granule cells [8, 11]. Heterosynaptic plasticity means that stimulation of one input pathway leads to synaptic changes not only of the stimulated pathway (homosynaptic plasticity) but also of the neighboring unstimulated pathway, which receives only the spontaneous activity. The computational model of granule cell endowed with this meta-STDP rule was able to reproduce the experimental results of synaptic plasticity observed in these neurons. Among other things, ongoing spontaneous activity simulated in the model proved to be a key factor influencing the magnitude of homo-LTP and hetero-LTD. The phenomenon of spontaneous activity affecting the magnitude of synaptic changes was previously demonstrated experimentally by Abraham et al. [12]. As in hippocampal granule cells, homosynaptic and heterosynaptic plasticity has also been observed in CA1 pyramidal cells.

In this work, we applied the meta-STDP synaptic plasticity to a realistic compartmental model of CA1 pyramidal cell with reduced morphology. Our aim was to simulate the effects of ongoing spontaneous activity [13, 14] on the long-term stability of synaptic weights in the hippocampus. After optimization of model parameters and parameters of the meta-STDP rule, the result of this process was the achievement of dynamically stable synaptic weights.

2 Methods

2.1 Computational Model of CA1 Pyramidal Cell

In creating of our model, we were inspired by a previously published model from Cutsuridis et al. [15], which is available online in the ModeDB database under accession

No. 123815, and which we used in our previous study [16]. However, we have extended the morphology since this model did not contain the side dendritic branches where the majority of excitatory inputs is located in the real cell especially in the proximal and medial parts of the dendritic tree [17]. Basal dendrites in the stratum oriens (SO) were modeled by two thicker proximal sections, followed by 2 thinner distal sections. We added another 2 distal sections while maintaining the same parameters as the original distal sections. An apical trunk 400 μm long in the stratum radiatum (SR) consisted of 3 interconnected sections, which decreased in thickness with increasing distance from the soma. We attached one section to the center of each section of the apical trunk, representing thin oblique dendrites. A dendritic tuft in the stratum lacunosum-moleculare (SLM) was represented by two dendrites, each consisting of 3 sections with gradually decreasing thickness. We have kept this part unchanged [15]. The original model also contained an axon, which we also preserved. The structure of the model and typical somatic responses are shown in the Fig. 1.

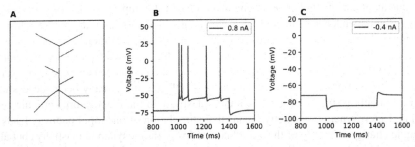

Fig. 1. Morphology and typical somatic responses of the model. (**A**) The reduced morphology of the model captures all essential parts of the dendritic tree of CA1 neurons. (**B**), (**C**) The typical somatic responses of the model to the positive and negative somatic current injections.

Passive and active properties of our model were adapted from the full-morphology model of CA1 pyramidal cell presented in the paper of the Migliore et al. [18] which is accessible in the ModelDB database (accession No. 244688). All apical and basal sections have uniformly distributed sodium current, a delayed rectifier K+ current (Kdr), a dendritic A-Type K+ current (KA), a hyperpolarization-activated cation current (Ih), tree types of Ca2+ currents (CaL, CaN, CaT), and two types of calcium-activated K+ currents (KCa and Cagk). The somatic section has the same set of currents. However, a dendritic A-Type K+ current is exchanged for a somatic A-Type K+ current and a somatic M-Type K+ current (KM) is included. The axonal section contains a sodium current, a delayed rectifier K+ current, and M-Type and A-Type K+ currents. Each section containing calcium current contains a simple calcium extrusion mechanism. The peak conductivity of Ih and KA were calculated separately for each section according to its distance from the soma. Similarly, the equilibrium potential of the passive current (e_pas) was calculated for each section [18].

2.2 Model Synaptic Inputs

Excitatory synapses are modeled using NEURON [19] built-in synapse class *Exp2Syn*. Synaptic conductivity is expressed using a two-state kinetic scheme described by two exponential functions:

$$g(t) = w\left(e^{-\frac{t}{\tau_2}} - e^{-\frac{t}{\tau_1}}\right) \tag{1}$$

where w is the synaptic weight, $\tau_1 = 0.5$ ms is the rise time constant, and $\tau_2 = 3$ ms is the decay time constant [15]. The synaptic weight is modified according to the meta-STDP plasticity rule (see below).

Each synapse received a train of presynaptic spikes that were generated by independent spikes generators. In NEURON it is taken care of by the built-in process *NetStim*. Presynaptic spikes sequence delivered to one synapse consisted of a combination of random and periodic spike trains. We have chosen this strategy because we can thus simulate the theta activity that is a prominent state of the hippocampal network [20], plus the random spikes.

2.3 Synaptic Plasticity Rule

To model synaptic plasticity, we used the meta-STDP rule with the nearest neighbor implementation. In this implementation, each presynaptic spike is paired with two time-closest postsynaptic spikes. One occurring before the presynaptic spike and the other occurring after the presynaptic spike. The choice of this pairing scheme is related to the fact that it is biologically relevant, as it agrees with the Bienenstock-Cooper-Munro (BCM) theory [21] as shown by Izhikevich and Desai [22]. The weight change is calculated as:

$$w(t + \Delta t) = w(t)\left(1 + \Delta w_p - \Delta w_d\right) \tag{2}$$

where Δw_p is positive weight change and Δw_d is negative weight change.

The positive weight change (potentiation) occurs when the presynaptic spike precedes the postsynaptic spike. On the other hand, weakening of the weight (depression) occurs when the postsynaptic spike precedes the presynaptic spike. It is formulated as:

$$\Delta w_p(\Delta t) = A_p exp\left(-\frac{\Delta t}{\tau_p}\right) \Delta t > 0 \tag{3}$$

$$\Delta w_d(\Delta t) = A_d exp\left(\frac{\Delta t}{\tau_d}\right) if \ \Delta t < 0 \tag{4}$$

where $\Delta t = t_{post} - t_{pre}$, A_p and A_d are potentiation and depression amplitudes, respectively, τ_p and τ_d are decay constants for the time windows over which synaptic change can occur. Parameter t_{post} represents the instant of time at which the local voltage on the postsynaptic dendrite, where a synapse is located, exceeds the threshold of -30 mV.

Amplitudes of LTP/LTD in the meta-STDP are dynamically changed as a function of a previous temporal average of soma spiking θ_S:

$$A_p(t) = A_p(0)\left(\frac{1}{\theta_S(t)}\right) \tag{5}$$

$$A_d(t) = A_d(0)\theta_S(t) \tag{6}$$

$$\theta_S(t) = \alpha\langle c\rangle_\tau = \frac{\alpha}{\tau}\int_{-\infty}^{t} c(t')\exp\left(\frac{-(t-t')}{\tau}\right)dt' \tag{7}$$

where $A_p(t)$ and $A_d(t)$ are amplitudes for potentiation and depression at time t, and α is a scaling constant. $A_p(0)$ and $A_d(0)$ are initial values at time 0. The term $<c_\tau>$ expresses the weighted temporal average of the postsynaptic spike count, with the most recent spikes entering the sum with bigger weight than the previous ones [8]. The source code of *Exp2Syn* endowed with the meta-STDP rule is available on ModelDB database under accession number 185350. The simulations were performed with the NEURON simulation environment (version 7.7.2) [19] embedded in Python 2.7.16.

3 Results

When stabilizing the model, we worked with parameters from two groups. On the one hand, it was the number of synapses, the distribution of synapses on the dendrites and their initial weight values. The second group were the parameters of synaptic plasticity and metaplasticity. We analyzed the simulation results from both perspectives at the same time, but we always modified only one selected parameter. All these parameters were optimized by trial and error.

3.1 Number of Synapses, Distribution of Synapses and Initial Weights

We started with an initial number of synapses of 600, which we uniformly randomly distributed to the dendritic tree, maintaining the ratio of synapses on the individual branch parts according to Table 3 from the paper of Megías et al. [17]. The total number of excitatory synapses impinging on a single CA1 neuron was estimated to be about 30 000. Their relative representation on individual parts of the dendritic tree is as follows: 38.3% on the stratum oriens distal dendrites, 0.8% on the stratum oriens proximal dendrites, 0.9% on the stratum radiatum thick medial dendrites, 7.1% on the stratum radiatum thick distal dendrites, 47.1% on the stratum radiatum thin dendrites, 1.6% on the stratum lacunosum-moleculare thick dendrites, 1.4% on the stratum lacunosum-moleculare medial dendrites, and 2.8% on the stratum lacunosum-moleculare thin dendrites [17]. The number of synapses in individual layers were: stratum oriens – 240 (40%), stratum radiatum – 330 (55%), and stratum lacunosum-moleculare – 30 (5%).

The meta-STDP synaptic plasticity rule requires the model cell to fire as is the case *in vivo*. Our goal was to achieve an output firing frequency of about 2 Hz, which was also observed *in vivo* [23]. We decided to generate the initial synaptic weights from the normal distribution, while we experimentally found suitable parameters of the normal distribution, namely $\mu = 0.000165$ and $\sigma = 0.000015$. For any randomly generated initial synaptic weights from the normal distribution thus defined, the meta-STDP rule ensured that the synaptic weights were dynamically stable during ongoing spontaneous activity and at the same time the output frequency was around 2 Hz. This result is important because even in *in vivo* experiments, the stable baseline is measured for some time before applying the stimulation protocol [12]. We also experimented with the lognormal distribution of initial weights, which was observed in several *in vitro*, *-ex vivo*, and *in vivo* studies [24]. Our unpublished results suggest that the meta-STDP rule is able to maintain dynamically stable weights generated from the lognormal distribution.

When generating weights from the normal distribution with the indicated parameters and simulating spontaneous activity for 20 min, 3 groups of synapses were formed at the end of the simulation. The first group consisted of synapses, the final weights of which were more or less the same as the initial ones (change in weights ±5%). The second group consisted of synapses that were attenuated, and their final weights were approximately 50% lower than the initial ones. The last group consisted of synapses with weight changes between 5–50%. It should be noted here that in each group there were synapses with different initial weights and from different parts of the dendritic tree. At this point, we asked ourselves the question of whether synapses, whose weights have significantly decreased as a result of spontaneous activity, are necessary to stabilize the entire system. We decided to remove them, reducing the total number of synapses to 391. Thus, the resulting number of synapses in individual layers is as follows: stratum oriens – 158 (40.4%), stratum radiatum – 203 (51.9%), and stratum lacunosum-moleculare – 30 (7.6%) As we can see from the results, the percentage of synapses within each layer was maintained as in [17]. Due to the removal of synapses, we increased all initial weights by 20% in order to maintain cell firing which is necessary to activate synaptic plasticity and metaplasticity in our meta-STDP rule.

3.2 Synaptic Plasticity Parameters

In evaluating the stability of synaptic plasticity and metaplasticity parameters, we monitor the evolution of depression and potentiation amplitudes and the evolution of the integrated spike count scaled by alpha over time (Eq. 7). The integrated spike count is important because the amplitudes are adjusted based on it. This mechanism represents metaplasticity. In simulations, it is crucial that its value oscillates around the value 1. Values higher than one results in increased depression and weakened potentiation. Conversely, values less than one yield potentiation to be attenuated and depression enhanced. Slight oscillations around 1 will ensure dynamically stable amplitudes and thus the entire system. The free parameters are mainly alpha and the average time constant τ for the postsynaptic spike count (Eq. 7). The following proved to be the most suitable parameter values: $A_p(0) = 0.0001$, $A_d(0) = 0.0003$, $\tau_p = 20\,\text{ms}$, $\tau_d = 20\,\text{ms}$, $\tau = 100000\,\text{ms}$, and $\alpha = 500$. The following figures show the results of potentiation and depression amplitudes (Fig. 2) and integrated spike count θ_S scaled by alpha (Fig. 3) for any typical simulation.

3.3 Results of Simulations

After simulating spontaneous activity for 20 min, we achieved dynamically stable synaptic weights in all layers. The figures (Fig. 4, 5, 6 and 7) show the results for any simulation with the best parameters of the meta-STDP plasticity rule for the period of 20 min.

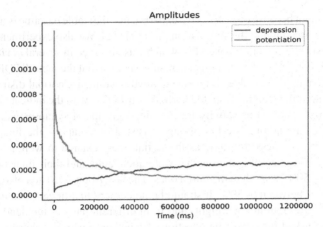

Fig. 2. The CA1 pyramidal cell model depression and potentiation amplitudes were stabilized after a short transitory period with employed meta-STDP rule.

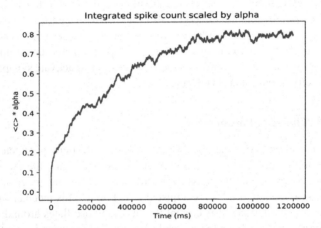

Fig. 3. Evolution of the integrated spike count scaled by alpha with employed meta-STDP rule applied to the synapses of the CA1 pyramidal cell model.

The results document that the weights are stable on average in all layers of the dendritic tree of the CA1 pyramidal cell model endowed with the meta-STDP synaptic plasticity rule.

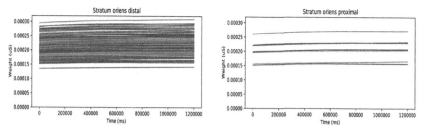

Fig. 4. Evolution of synaptic weights in the distal stratum oriens (left) and the proximal stratum oriens (right) of the CA1 pyramidal cell model. The x-axis denotes time in ms and the y-axis denotes values of synaptic weights.

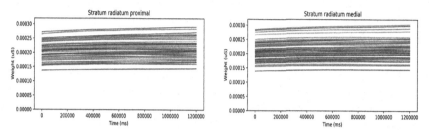

Fig. 5. Evolution of synaptic weights in the proximal stratum radiatum (left) and the medial stratum radiatum (right) of the CA1 pyramidal cell model. The x-axis denotes time in ms and the y-axis denotes values of synaptic weights.

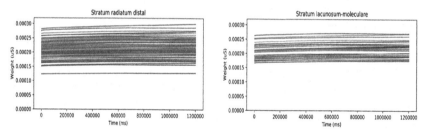

Fig. 6. Evolution of synaptic weights in the distal stratum radiatum (left) and the stratum lacunosum moleculare (right) of the CA1 pyramidal cell model. The x-axis denotes time in ms and the y-axis denotes values of synaptic weights.

4 Discussion

Computational studies that model synaptic plasticity *in vivo* neglect the fact that *in vivo* neurons exhibit an ongoing spontaneous spiking in the neural circuits [14]. The first synaptic plasticity theory that explicitly took into account ongoing neuronal activity was the BCM theory [21]. A key element of this BCM theory is a whole-cell variable termed the modification threshold, the tipping point at which the presynaptic activity either leads to long-term depression (LTD) or long-term potentiation (LTP) of synaptic efficacy. A second key element is the theory's postulate that the average ongoing level of

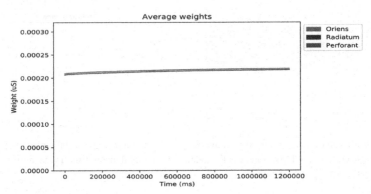

Fig. 7. Evolution of synaptic weights average in the stratum oriens, radiatum, and lacunosum-moleculare of the CA1 pyramidal cell model. The x-axis denotes time in ms and the y-axis denotes values of average synaptic weights.

spontaneous activity dynamically sets the position of the LTD/LTP tipping point in such a way that potentiation is favored when the postsynaptic cell firing is low on average and, vice versa, depression is favored when the postsynaptic activity is high on average. The BCM model has been used to account for experimental findings of experience-evoked plasticity in the developing visual [21] and adult somatosensory cortices *in vivo* [25]. The proposal of a modifiable plasticity threshold foreshadowed the concept of metaplasticity [10], developed to account for the abundant experimental evidence that prior neural activity can change the state of neurons and synapses such that the outcome of future synaptic plasticity protocols is altered.

Here we study how key components of learning mechanisms in the brain, namely spike timing-dependent plasticity and metaplasticity, interact with spontaneous activity in the input pathways of the CA1 neuron model.

In this study we optimized the synaptic model parameters to achieve the long-term stability of synaptic weights under *in vivo*-like conditions mimicking ongoing spontaneous activity as recorded in neuronal circuits [20]. Each synapse received an independent spike train input consisting of periodic spikes corresponding to theta activity and random spikes corresponding to random background activity. Average frequency of spikes in the one spike train was ~8 Hz. During the 20-min simulation of spontaneous activity, the individual synaptic weights and synaptic plasticity parameters are dynamically stable. These results provide a good basis for experimenting with synaptic plasticity stimulation protocols and ultimately for modeling the synaptic plasticity observed in CA1 pyramidal cells *in vivo*.

In our previous study [16], we used a model from Cutsuridis et al. [15]. Using HippoUnit tests [26], we tested and compared the latter model and our currently used model. As a result, our model achieved better results than the Cutsuridis model [15], which is more excitable (data not shown/paper in preparation). The consequence of the higher excitability of the Cutsuridis model was that at the beginning of each simulation there was a significant increase in the integrated spike count function θ_S and at the same time a decrease in the weights [16]. In our current model, the weights are dynamically stable from the beginning of the simulation (Fig. 4, 5, 6 and 7) and the integrated spike count function θ_S saturation occurs gradually (Fig. 3). By adding side branches, we have ensured that experimentally observed non-linear summation of synaptic inputs occurs on these branches, resulting in dendritic spikes.

In summary, we have modified existing compartmental model of the CA1 pyramidal cell by adding the side dendrites, synapses, and by implementing synaptic plasticity rule, namely the meta-STDP rule. Our model exhibits realistic input-output spontaneous activity as neurons *in vivo*. During ongoing spontaneous activity, synapses should not change their weights. This has been achieved after manual optimization of synaptic model parameters. Next, we intend to implement several of synaptic plasticity protocols which were experimentally studied for CA1 pyramidal cells.

References

1. Lee, I., Jerman, T., Kesner, R.: Disruption of delayed memory for a sequence of spatial locations following CA1- or CA3-lesions of the dorsal hippocampus. Neurobiol. Learn. Mem. **84**, 138–147 (2005). https://doi.org/10.1016/j.nlm.2005.06.002
2. Lee, I., Kesner, R.P.: Differential contribution of NMDA receptors in hippocampal subregions to spatial working memory. Nat. Neurosci. **5**, 162–168 (2002). https://doi.org/10.1038/nn790
3. Lee, I., Kesner, R.P.: Differential contributions of dorsal hippocampal subregions to memory acquisition and retrieval in contextual fear-conditioning. Hippocampus. **14**, 301–310 (2004). https://doi.org/10.1002/hipo.10177
4. Hoang, L.T., Kesner, R.P.: Dorsal hippocampus, CA3, and CA1 lesions disrupt temporal sequence completion. Behav. Neurosci. **122**, 9–15 (2008). https://doi.org/10.1037/0735-7044. 122.1.9
5. Hughes, J.R.: Post-tetanic potentiation. Physiol. Rev. **38**, 91–113 (1958). https://doi.org/10. 1152/physrev.1958.38.1.91
6. Martin, S.J., Grimwood, P.D., Morris, R.G.M.: Synaptic plasticity and memory: an evaluation of the hypothesis. Annu. Rev. Neurosci. **23**, 649–711 (2000). https://doi.org/10.1146/annurev. neuro.23.1.649
7. Mayr, C.G., Partzsch, J.: Rate and pulse based plasticity governed by local synaptic state variables. Front. Synaptic Neurosci. **2**, 33 (2010). https://doi.org/10.3389/fnsyn.2010.00033
8. Benuskova, L., Abraham, W.C.: STDP rule endowed with the BCM sliding threshold accounts for hippocampal heterosynaptic plasticity. J. Comput. Neurosci. **22**, 129–133 (2007). https:// doi.org/10.1007/s10827-006-0002-x
9. Markram, H., Lübke, J., Frotscher, M., Sakmann, B.: Regulation of synaptic efficacy by coincidence of postsynaptic APs and EPSPs. Science **275**, 213 (1997). https://doi.org/10. 1126/science.275.5297.213
10. Abraham, W.C.: Metaplasticity: tuning synapses and networks for plasticity. Nat. Rev. Neurosci. **9**, 387 (2008). https://doi.org/10.1038/nrn2356
11. Jedlicka, P., Benuskova, L., Abraham, W.C.: A voltage-based STDP rule combined with fast BCM-Like metaplasticity accounts for LTP and concurrent "heterosynaptic" LTD in the dentate gyrus in vivo. PLoS Comput. Biol. **11**, e1004588–e1004588 (2015). https://doi.org/ 10.1371/journal.pcbi.1004588
12. Abraham, W.C., Logan, B., Wolff, A., Benuskova, L.: "Heterosynaptic" LTD in the dentate gyrus of anesthetized rat requires homosynaptic activity. J. Neurophysiol. **98**, 1048–1051 (2007). https://doi.org/10.1152/jn.00250.2007
13. Frank, L.M., Brown, E.N., Wilson, M.A.: A comparison of the firing properties of putative excitatory and inhibitory neurons from CA1 and the entorhinal cortex. J. Neurophysiol. **86**, 2029–2040 (2001). https://doi.org/10.1152/jn.2001.86.4.2029

14. Deshmukh, S.S., Yoganarasimha, D., Voicu, H., Knierim, J.J.: Theta modulation in the medial and the lateral entorhinal cortices. J. Neurophysiol. **104**, 994–1006 (2010). https://doi.org/10. 1152/jn.01141.2009

15. Cutsuridis, V., Cobb, S., Graham, B.P.: Encoding and retrieval in a model of the hippocampal CA1 microcircuit. Hippocampus **20**, 423–446 (2010). https://doi.org/10.1002/hipo.20661

16. Tomko, M., Jedlička, P., Beňušková, Ľ.: Computational model of CA1 pyramidal cell with meta-STDP stabilizes under ongoing spontaneous activity as in vivo. In: Kognícia a umelý život 2019. Vydavateľstvo Univerzity Komenského, Bratislava (2019)

17. Megías, M., Emri, Z., Freund, T.F., Gulyás, A.I.: Total number and distribution of inhibitory and excitatory synapses on hippocampal CA1 pyramidal cells. Neuroscience **102**, 527–540 (2001). https://doi.org/10.1016/S0306-4522(00)00496-6

18. Migliore, R., et al.: The physiological variability of channel density in hippocampal CA1 pyramidal cells and interneurons explored using a unified data-driven modeling workflow. PLoS Comput. Biol. **14**, e1006423–e1006423 (2018). https://doi.org/10.1371/journal.pcbi. 1006423

19. Hines, M.L., Carnevale, N.T.: The NEURON Simulation Environment. Neural Comput. **9**, 1179–1209 (1997). https://doi.org/10.1162/neco.1997.9.6.1179

20. Buzsáki, G.: Theta oscillations in the hippocampus. Neuron **33**, 325–340 (2002). https://doi. org/10.1016/S0896-6273(02)00586-X

21. Bienenstock, E.L., Cooper, L.N., Munro, P.W.: Theory for the development of neuron selectivity: orientation specificity and binocular interaction in visual cortex. J. Neurosci. Off. J. Soc. Neurosci. **2**, 32–48 (1982). https://doi.org/10.1523/JNEUROSCI.02-01-00032.1982

22. Izhikevich, E.M., Desai, N.S.: Relating STDP to BCM. Neural Comput. **15**, 1511–1523 (2003). https://doi.org/10.1162/089976603321891783

23. Mizuseki, K., Buzsáki, G.: Preconfigured, skewed distribution of firing rates in the hippocampus and entorhinal cortex. Cell Rep. **4**, 1010–1021 (2013). https://doi.org/10.1016/j.celrep. 2013.07.039

24. Buzsáki, G., Mizuseki, K.: The log-dynamic brain: how skewed distributions affect network operations. Nat. Rev. Neurosci. **15**, 264–278 (2014). https://doi.org/10.1038/nrn3687

25. Benusková, L., Diamond, M.E., Ebner, F.F.: Dynamic synaptic modification threshold: computational model of experience-dependent plasticity in adult rat barrel cortex. Proc. Natl. Acad. Sci. U. S. A. **91**, 4791–4795 (1994). https://doi.org/10.1073/pnas.91.11.4791

26. Sáray, S., et al.: Systematic comparison and automated validation of detailed models of hippocampal neurons. bioRxiv. 2020.07.02.184333 (2020). https://doi.org/10.1101/2020.07. 02.184333

Adaptive Chemotaxis for Improved Contour Tracking Using Spiking Neural Networks

Shashwat Shukla$^{(\boxtimes)}$, Rohan Pathak, Vivek Saraswat, and Udayan Ganguly

Department of Electrical Engineering, IIT Bombay, Bombay, India
shashwat.shukla@iitb.ac.in

Abstract. In this paper we present a Spiking Neural Network (SNN) for autonomous navigation, inspired by the chemotaxis network of the worm Caenorhabditis elegans. In particular, we focus on the problem of contour tracking, wherein the bot must reach and subsequently follow a desired concentration setpoint. Past schemes that used only klinokinesis can follow the contour efficiently but take excessive time to reach the setpoint. We address this shortcoming by proposing a novel adaptive klinotaxis mechanism that builds upon a previously proposed gradient climbing circuit. We demonstrate how our klinotaxis circuit can autonomously be configured to perform gradient ascent, gradient descent and subsequently be disabled to seamlessly integrate with the aforementioned klinokinesis circuit. We also incorporate speed regulation (orthokinesis) to further improve contour tracking performance. Thus for the first time, we present a model that successfully integrates klinokinesis, klinotaxis and orthokinesis. We demonstrate via contour tracking simulations that our proposed scheme achieves an 2.4x reduction in the time to reach the setpoint, along with a simultaneous 8.7x reduction in average deviation from the setpoint.

Keywords: Spiking Neural Network · Navigation · C. elegans

1 Introduction

The worm Caenorhabditis elegans (C. elegans) is a model organism for neurobiology as it displays fairly sophisticated behavior despite having only 302 neurons. One such behavior of interest is chemotaxis: the ability to sense chemicals such as NaCl and to then move in response to the sensed concentration. The worm prefers certain concentrations of NaCl as it associates them with finding food, with these concentrations thus acting as setpoints for the worm. This ability to search for and follow the level set (which is an isocontour in 2D) for a particular setpoint concentration is called contour tracking, and has been observed experimentally in the worm [9]. Remarkably, the worm is able to track contours

---

S. Shukla and R. Pathak—Equal contribution.

I. Farkaš et al. (Eds.): ICANN 2020, LNCS 12397, pp. 681–692, 2020.
https://doi.org/10.1007/978-3-030-61616-8_55

in a highly resource-constrained manner with just one concentration sensor and a small number of neurons. Contour tracking is also an important function for autonomously navigating robots, and it is thus of interest from an engineering standpoint to study the small yet efficient chemotaxis circuit of C. elegans. The emergence of energy-efficient nanoscale Neuromorphic hardware [4] motivates mapping these compact chemotaxis circuits onto Spiking Neural Networks (SNNs) in order to instantiate autonomously navigating robots operating under severe resource and energy constraints.

One of the strategies that the worm uses is called klinokinesis, wherein the worm makes abrupt turns away from its current direction. Klinokinesis requires the worm to compare the current sensed concentration with past samples to estimate the concentration gradient along its path of motion. It turns away when it is above the setpoint and senses a positive gradient, or if it is below the setpoint and senses a negative gradient. It thus corrects its path so that it is always moving towards the setpoint. A model for the sensory neurons used to compute temporal derivatives was proposed in [1]. Santurkar and Rajendran added motor neurons to the model from [1] to propose an SNN for klinokinesis [10]. They also demonstrated hardware compatibility with standard CMOS circuitry. However, their SNN required external currents to operate correctly and thus was not an autonomous solution. Shukla, Dutta and Ganguly resolved this problem by designing SNNs for the rate-coded logic operations required by the klinokinesis circuit and ensuring correctness of operation [11]. Furthermore, they incorporated an additional sub-circuit to allow the worm to escape local extrema, reduced the response latency of the SNN by incorporating anticipatory control and demonstrated feasibility on nanoscale neuromorphic hardware.

An important limitation of klinokinesis is that it only uses the sign of the gradient and not its magnitude. Thus while klinokinesis ensures that the worm is always moving towards the setpoint, it does not ensure that it takes the shortest path. By definition, the direction with the highest gradient magnitude corresponds to the path of steepest ascent or descent. Indeed, the worm is known to align itself along (or against) the gradient via gradual turns in a process called klinotaxis. The worm performs klinotaxis by estimating the spatial gradient in the direction perpendicular to its current path by comparing concentration values to the left and right of its head while moving in a snake-like sinusoidal motion, using this estimate to gradually correct its path. Izquierdo and Lockery proposed a mechanistic model for gradient ascent using klinotaxis and learned model parameters via evolutionary algorithms [8]. Izquierdo and Beer subsequently attempted to map this model onto the connectome of the worm [7] (Fig. 1).

The first important contribution of this paper is to build upon the gradient ascent circuit in [8] to develop a novel adaptive klinotaxis circuit that can be autonomously configured to perform gradient ascent, gradient descent, and disabled upon reaching the setpoint. Second, we implement this adaptive klinotaxis circuit with spiking neurons and then integrate it with the klinokinesis SNN from [11]. It is important to note that these strategies serve complementary roles, with

(a)

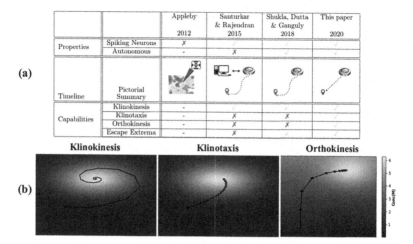

		Appleby 2012	Santurkar & Rajendran 2015	Shukla, Dutta & Ganguly 2018	This paper 2020
Properties	Spiking Neurons	✗	✓	✓	✓
	Autonomous	-	✗	✓	✓
Timeline	Pictorial Summary				
Capabilities	Klinokinesis	-	✓	✓	✓
	Klinotaxis	-	✗	✗	✓
	Orthokinesis	-	✗	✗	✓
	Escape Extrema	-	✗	✓	✓

(b)

Fig. 1. (a) Timeline and comparison of this paper with past literature. (b) Gradient ascent to illustrate navigation mechanisms. Left: The bot makes abrupt turns to correct its path by using only the sign of the gradient, and thus takes a circuitous route to the peak. Center: The bot gradually corrects its path to align with the direction of steepest ascent and thus takes a much shorter route to the peak. Also note the sinusoidal motion of the bot. Right: This plot is only to visualize orthokinesis. Note that the arrows become denser close to the peak, depicting how the bot slows down near the setpoint and regions with large gradients.

klinokinesis allowing for rapid turns to ensure that the worm always moves closer to the setpoint, and klinotaxis allowing the worm to gradually optimize its path [5,6]. Indeed, the worm is known to use klinokinesis and klinotaxis in tandem [5]. However, in the context of contour tracking, it is important to understand how klinotaxis and klinokinesis can work together. In particular, the worm must align with the gradient until it reaches the setpoint and must subsequently move perpendicular to the gradient to follow the setpoint contour, thus requiring the worm to change its behavior based on how close it is to the setpoint. This problem was previously encountered in work by Skandari, Iino and Manton who proposed a non-adaptive, non-spiking model that attempts to extend Lockery's work to perform contour tracking [12]. Their simulations show that their network for reaching the setpoint and their network for subsequently following the contour are incompatible with each other, leading to a failure in tracking contours near regions with large gradients. The adaptive nature of our klinotaxis circuit allows us to address this important problem. Furthermore, the gradual nature of klinotaxis steering leads to large deviations from the setpoint while following the desired contour, a problem that we are able to address by also including the klinokinesis circuit to enable faster turns. Our circuit thus allows us to seamlessly integrate the benefits of both these navigation strategies.

We also incorporate orthokinesis in our SNN model, wherein the bot can also regulate its speed as a function of sensed concentration [3]. This allows it to slow down near the setpoint and near regions with large gradients, leading to a further reduction in deviations from the setpoint while following the desired contour. To the best of our knowledge, this is the first circuit model that successfully integrates klinokinesis, klinotaxis and orthokinesis.

2   Proposed Algorithm

2.1   Adaptive Klinotaxis

Klinotaxis is the mechanism whereby, as the worm moves along its sinusoidal trajectory, it compares the values of sensed concentrations in one half-cycle to those in the next half-cycle, and then changes its course based on this information. Klinotaxis has typically been studied in the context of gradient ascent, wherein the worm will bias its motion towards the side which is better aligned with the local gradient direction, thus gradually aligning with the gradient and performing steepest ascent, and thus allowing the worm to reach the peak faster. Crucially, if the worm had two spatially separated concentration sensors, then it could compare the values from these sensors to estimate the gradient direction, which is called tropotaxis. However, the worm only has one concentration sensor, thus requiring it to use its own body motion to sample to the left and right of its path, as it does with its sinusoidal motion. Such a setting is of great interest for highly resource constrained bots that are too small to carry two bulky sensors and where the spatial separation between sensors is too small to enable tropotaxis. In this paper, we enable our bot to not only perform gradient ascent, but also enable gradient descent and the ability to switch off the klinotaxis mechanism entirely. Furthermore, this change in behavior is affected autonomously based on sensed concentration, and we thus call this adaptive klinotaxis.

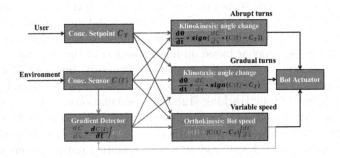

Fig. 2. Block diagram for the full network.

The gradient detector and klinotaxis blocks are depicted in Fig. 3(a). Like the worm, our bot has a single concentration sensor whose output at time t is the sensed concentration $C(t)$. This $C(t)$ is used to compute an adaptive difference-estimate for the gradient, $I_{ad}(t)$, given as:

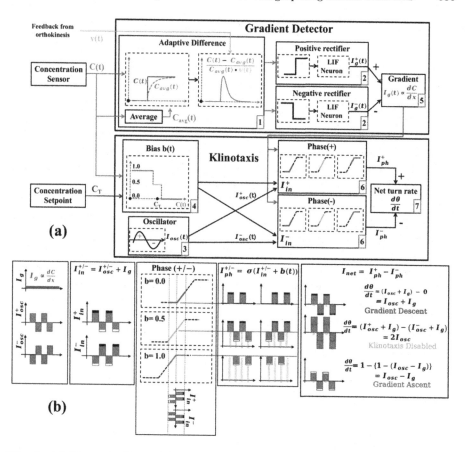

Fig. 3. (a) Network diagram for the gradient detector and klinotaxis blocks. The gradient detector functions by computing a temporal estimate for the gradient: $C(t) - C_{avg}(t)$, which is normalized by $C_{avg}(t)$ to make this estimate scale-invariant. It is further divided by $v(t)$ to convert the temporal derivative to a spatial derivative ($\frac{dC}{dt} = v(t) \cdot \frac{dC}{dx}$). This spatial derivative is then rate-coded using two sparsely firing leaky-integrate-and-fire neurons, with the refractory periods acting as saturating non-linearity. (b) Signal flow through the klinotaxis block. The bias shifts the piecewise linear sigmoidal response curve to the left or right, while the sum of currents from the oscillator and gradient detector, $I_{ph}^{\pm}(t)$, is the input to these shifted response curves. For $b = 0.0$: The positive parts of the input are retained and thus the turning rate increases with $I_g(t)$. Thus the bot turns slower when aligned against the gradient - gradient descent. For $b = 0.5$: Both the positive and negative parts of the input are retained and the effect of $I_g(t)$ is cancelled out. Thus the bot's turning rate is independent of the gradient - klinotaxis disabled. For $b = 1.0$: Effectively, the negative parts of the input are retained and thus the turning rate decreases with $I_g(t)$. Thus the bot turns slower when aligned along the gradient - gradient ascent.

$$I_{ad}(t) = \frac{C(t) - C_{avg}(t)}{C_{avg}(t) \cdot v(t)} \tag{1}$$

Here $C_{avg}(t)$ is the sensed concentration averaged over the past 10 s, and thus $C(t) - C_{avg}(t)$ is an estimate for the temporal derivative $\frac{dC}{dt}$. This is dynamically scaled by $\frac{1}{C_{avg}(t)}$ to allow the gradient detector neurons to effectively utilize available signaling bandwidth and to make its response invariant to the average concentration, allowing our bot to operate in environments where the concentrations can vary over many orders of magnitude. This is thus a simple but important modification to the static scaling used in [7,8,10,11]. This is in turn scaled by $\frac{1}{v(t)}$ to convert the temporal derivative to a spatial derivative, in line with $\frac{dC}{dx} = \frac{1}{v(t)} \cdot \frac{dC}{dt}$. This requires the existence of a feedback loop which gives the sensory neurons access to the bot's velocity, as depicted in Fig. 2. Note that such divisive gain modulation has also been observed in neurons in-vivo [2,13]. Also note that while operating with a constant speed, as was the case in [10,11], the temporal and spatial gradients are linearly proportional to each other and thus there was no need for such speed-dependent scaling in past work.

The positive and negative parts of this signal given are respectively denoted by $I_{ad}^+(t) = I_{ad}(t) \cdot \delta(I_{ad}(t) > 0); I_{ad}^-(t) = I_{ad}(t) \cdot \delta(I_{ad}(t) < 0)$, where $\delta(.)$ is a delta-function which is 1 if the input condition is true and is 0 otherwise. Next, $I_{ad}^+(t)$ and $I_{ad}^-(t)$ are respectively fed into neurons N_+ and N_-, noting that $I_{ad}(t)$ was encoded this way using two neurons because neurons can only have positive firing rates. We model N_+ and N_- as leaky integrate-and-fire (LIF) neurons with respective membrane potentials V_+ and V_- which evolve as:

$$C_G \frac{dV_+}{dt} = I_{ad}^+(t) - \frac{V_+(t)}{R_G} \; ; \; C_G \frac{dV_-}{dt} = I_{ad}^-(t) - \frac{V_-(t)}{R_G} \tag{2}$$

Here C_G and R_G are respectively the membrane capacitance and resistance. The neurons N_+ and N_- fire when V_+ and V_- respectively cross the firing threshold V_T, and the membrane voltage is then reset to 0 for the duration of the refractory period. The spike-trains of N_+ and N_- are convolved with the kernel $\kappa(t) = e^{\frac{-t}{\tau_1}} - e^{\frac{-t}{\tau_2}} \; ; \; \tau_1 > \tau_2$ to generate the respective output currents $I_g^+(t)$ and $I_g^-(t)$. This is an instance of rate-coding wherein $I_g^\pm(t)$ increases with $I_{ad}^\pm(t)$. However this mapping is non-linear due to the refractory period, and crucially, $I_g^\pm(t)$ saturates for large values of $I_{ad}^\pm(t)$. The refractory period and parameters of $\kappa(t)$ are chosen so that this maximum value of $I_g^\pm(t)$ is 1, a fact that will be used in the klinotaxis circuit. Apart from this non-linear response, the other advantage of using spiking neurons is that unlike analog neurons they are not always on and are thus much more energy-efficient. Finally, the rate-coded gradient estimate is given as $I_g(t) = I_g^+(t) - I_g^-(t)$.

Having discussed the gradient detector circuit, we now proceed to describe the klinotaxis circuit. The first component is the oscillator current $I_{osc}(t)$ with time period T_{osc}, which is used to generate two oscillatory signals with opposite phases as: $I_{osc}^+(t) = I_{osc}(t)$ and $I_{osc}^-(t) = -I_{osc}(t)$. The second component is the bias function which determines the mode of operation of the klinotaxis circuit and is denoted by $b(t)$. The third input, $I_g(t)$, comes from the gradient detector discussed above. Output from these three blocks is fed to the two non-linear "phase" blocks, denoted by "Phase($\pm$)" in Fig. 3. These phase blocks are the most important part of the circuit, yielding output currents $I_{ph}^{\pm}(t)$. The net turning rate $\frac{d\theta(t)}{dt}$ due to klinotaxis is given by the scaled difference in output of these two phase blocks, where $\theta(t)$ is the bot's steering angle. We choose the convention wherein a positive change in θ will correspond to turning clockwise.

$$I_{osc}(t) = I_{osc}^{+}(t) = -I_{osc}^{-}(t) = \sin(\frac{2\pi t}{T_{osc}}) \tag{3}$$

$$b(t) = \begin{cases} 1.0 ; & (C_T - C(t)) > \varepsilon \\ 0.5 ; & |C(t) - C_T| < \varepsilon \\ 0.0 ; & (C(t) - C_T) > \varepsilon \end{cases} \tag{4}$$

$$I_g(t) = I_g^{+}(t) - I_g^{-}(t) \tag{5}$$

$$I_{ph}^{\pm}(t) = \sigma(\alpha \cdot I_{osc}^{\pm}(t) + \beta \cdot I_g(t) + b(t)) \tag{6}$$

$$\frac{d\theta(t)}{dt} = w_m \cdot (I_{ph}^{+}(t) - I_{ph}^{-}(t)) \tag{7}$$

To understand (4), observe that if we wish to reach the setpoint concentration C_T to within a tolerance ε, it is straightforward to see that we want $b(t) = 1.0$ (gradient ascent) for $C(t) < (C_T - \varepsilon)$, $b(t) = 0.0$ for $C(t) > (C_T + \varepsilon)$ (gradient descent), and $b(t) = 0.5$ (disable klinotaxis) for $|C(t) - C_T| < \varepsilon$. By disabling klinotaxis close to the setpoint, we allow klinokinesis to seamlessly take over, allowing the bot to follow the setpoint contour using klinokinesis as demonstrated in [11]. These mechanisms thus serve complementary roles, with klinotaxis used to reach the setpoint, and klinokinesis to subsequently follow the setpoint contour. In (6), the non-linear response of the phase blocks, $\sigma(x)$ (for input x), is equal to 0 for $x < 0$, x for $0 < x < 1$, and 1 for $x > 1$. Thus it increases linearly between 0 and 1 and saturates outside this range. While we have used this piecewise-linear form for $\sigma(x)$ in subsequent analysis, we have used a smoother and more biologically feasible approximation in our final contour tracking simulations, given as $\sigma(x) \approx 0.5 \cdot (1 + \tanh(2 \cdot x - 1))$. Also note that α, β and w_M are positive scaling constants.

We now proceed to describe the adaptive klinotaxis mechanism for the half-cycle from 0 to $T_{osc}/2$. We will first do this for $b = 1.0$, corresponding to gradient ascent. In this half-cycle $I_{osc}^{+}(t)$ is positive and thus $\sigma(1 + \alpha \cdot I_{osc}^{+}(t)) = 1$, meaning that $I_{ph}^{+}(t)$ saturates to 1. On the other hand, as $I_{osc}^{-}(t)$ is negative during this cycle, $\sigma(1 + \alpha \cdot I_{osc}^{-}(t)) = 1 + \alpha \cdot I_{osc}^{-}(t)$ and thus $I_{ph}^{-}(t)$ lies in the linear region. Note that these are approximate statements that ignore the contribution from $I_g(t)$. While it can be verified that these statements are exact for $\frac{T_{osc}}{2\pi} \sin^{-1}(\frac{\beta}{\alpha}) < t < \frac{T_{osc}}{2}$ (by noting that both $I_g(t)$ and $I_{osc}(t)$ have maximum amplitude of 1), they will be assumed for the entire half-cycle for ease of analysis. We are thus interpreting $\beta \cdot I_g(t)$ as a small perturbation to the output. We then have $\frac{d\theta(t)}{dt} = 1 - (1 + \alpha \cdot I_{osc}^{-}(t) + \beta \cdot I_g(t)) = \alpha \cdot (-I_{osc}^{-}(t)) - \beta \cdot I_g(t) = \alpha \cdot I_{osc}(t) - \beta \cdot I_g(t)$.

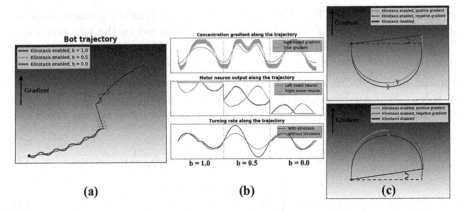

Fig. 4. (a) Path of the bot over five oscillator cycles for the three choices of b. Note how the trajectory bends towards, does not bend, and bends away from the steepest gradient direction respectively for $b = \{1.0, 0.5, 0.0\}$. (b) Timeplots for system variables over a representative cycle, one for each choice of b. The top plot shows that the rate-coding estimate is indeed able to follow the true gradient. The middle plot shows the difference in clipping of left $(I_{ph}^+(t))$ and right $(I_{ph}^-(t))$ motor neurons, for choices of b. The bottom plot shows how the gradient changes the turning rate vis-a-vis the zero-gradient case. Note that there is no skew for $b = 0.5$, while the skews for $b = 0.0$ and $b = 1.0$ are precisely opposite to one another. (c) Trajectory of the bot performing gradient ascent for a half-cycle, with and without klinotaxis enabled. Top: The bot is initially aligned against the gradient and is turning clockwise. Bottom: The bot is initially aligned along the gradient and is turning anticlockwise. The green and red parts of the curves respectively correspond to sensing positive and negative gradients, making the bot turn slower and faster respectively. In both cases the axis of motion is initially perpendicular to the gradient and at the end of the half-cycle this axis has rotated clockwise towards the gradient direction when klinotaxis is enabled. (Color figure online)

Thus we see that for $b = 1.0$ the bot turns slower when aligned along the gradient $(I_g(t) > 0)$ and turns faster when aligned against the gradient $(I_g(t) < 0)$. The bot's net motion is thus biased and it tends to align along the gradient, thus performing gradient ascent. This is depicted in Fig. 4(c) wherein the turning rate is higher and lower respectively for the red part $(I_g(t) < 0)$ and green part $(I_g(t) > 0)$ of the trajectories.

Next, we consider gradient descent with $b = 0.0$. In the first half-cycle $I_{osc}^-(t)$ is negative and thus $\sigma(0 + \alpha \cdot I_{osc}^-(t)) = 0$, and thus $I_{ph}^-(t)$ saturates to 0. On the other hand, as $I_{osc}^+(t)$ is positive during this cycle, $\sigma(0 + \alpha \cdot I_{osc}^+(t)) = \alpha \cdot I_{osc}^+(t)$ and thus $I_{ph}^+(t)$ lies in the linear region. Again, treating $\beta \cdot I_g(t)$ as a perturbation that only affects the non-saturated phase, we have $\frac{d\theta(t)}{dt} = (\alpha \cdot I_{osc}^+(t) + \beta \cdot I_g(t)) - 0 = \alpha \cdot I_{osc}(t) + \beta \cdot I_g(t)$. Thus we see that for $b = 0.0$ the bot turns faster when aligned along the gradient $(I_g(t) > 0)$ and turns slower when aligned against the gradient ($I_g(t) < 0$). The bot's net motion is thus biased and it tends to align against the gradient, thus performing gradient descent.

Finally, we discuss the case of disabling klinotaxis by setting $b = 0.5$. Furthermore, we choose hitherto unspecified constants as $\alpha = 0.4$ and $\beta = 0.1$. For all time t we then have that $|0.1 \cdot I_g(t) \pm 0.4 \cdot I_{osc}(t) + 0.5| < 0.1 + 0.4 + 0.5 = 1$, recalling that by design, both $I_g(t)$ and $I_{osc}(t)$ have a maximum magnitude of 1. Thus for $b = 0.5$, neither $I_{ph}^+(t)$ nor $I_{ph}^-(t)$ saturate and both lie in the linear region. We then have $\frac{d\theta(t)}{dt} = (\alpha \cdot I_{osc}^+(t) + \beta \cdot I_g(t) + 0.5) - (\alpha \cdot I_{osc}^-(t) + \beta \cdot I_g(t) + 0.5) = \alpha \cdot (I_{osc}^+(t) - I_{osc}^-(t)) = 2\alpha \cdot I_{osc}(t)$. Thus in this case, $I_g(t)$ has no effect on the turning rate of the bot and hence the klinotaxis mechanism stands disabled. We note that the amplitudes of $\alpha = 0.4$ and $\beta = 0.1$ respectively for the oscillatory and gradient terms were chosen such that they sum up to 0.5. This was done to maximize the dynamic range of input in the linear output regime, while also not allowing this input to saturate. Also note that the larger value of 0.4 was chosen for the oscillatory component to ensure that the bot swerves to the left and right with a large enough amplitude and thus samples it local environment, despite the modulatory effect of the gradient term. At the same time, the amplitude of 0.1 for the gradient term is large enough to ensure that it does have a sufficiently large modulatory effect to enable klinotaxis. In summary, the turning rate in the first half-cycle is given as:

$$\frac{d\theta}{dt} = \begin{cases} w_M \cdot (\alpha \cdot I_{osc}(t) + \beta \cdot I_{grad}(t)) \; ; \; b = 0.0 \\ w_M \cdot 2\alpha \cdot I_{osc}(t) \; ; \; b = 0.5 \\ w_M \cdot (\alpha \cdot I_{osc}(t) - \beta \cdot I_{grad}(t)) \; ; \; b = 1.0 \end{cases} \tag{8}$$

It can be verified that in the next half-cycle from $T_{osc}/2$ to T_{osc}, we get the same expression for $\frac{d\theta}{dt}$ as given in (8), but now with a negative sign. Thus the bot turns clockwise in one half-cycle and anti-clockwise in the next. Note also that it suffices to describe one full-cycle as the same mechanism recurs over time.

2.2   Klinokinesis

Klinokinesis is a course correction algorithm, wherein the worm turns around when it senses that it is moving away from the desired setpoint concentration. This happens in two cases: when it senses $\frac{dC(t)}{dt} > 0$, $C(t) > C_T$ or if $\frac{dC(t)}{dt} < 0$, $C(t) < C_T$. Note that this requires computing an AND operation over the sensed gradient and concentration values for which we use the SNN developed in [11]. While klinokinesis allows for rapid corrections to the bot's path and is thus well suited to closely following the contour once it is reached, it is not capable of finding the shortest path to the setpoint as it only uses the sign of the gradient and does not seek out the direction of *steepest* descent, thus motivating the inclusion of the complementary mechanism of klinotaxis.

2.3   Orthokinesis

We incorporate orthokinesis to reduce overshoot whilst following the setpoint contour using klinokinesis. We describe the bot's speed in discrete-time for ease of understanding, while noting that it is straightforward to convert this to continuous-time. For discrete time $1, ..., t-1, t, ...$, the bot speed is given as:

$$v[t] = v_c + \frac{k \cdot v[t-1] \cdot |C[t] - C_T|}{a + \left| \frac{\mathrm{d}C[t-1]}{\mathrm{d}x} \right|} \tag{9}$$

Here v_c is a constant that ensures that the worm continues to move along the setpoint contour despite the second term going to 0 close to C_T. Furthermore, the second term is proportional to $v[t-1]$ as a means of enforcing continuity in the values of $v[t]$. The term $|C[t] - C_T|$ is included so that the worm slows down close to the setpoint. Thus by allowing the worm to slow down near the setpoint concentration, we enable improved contour tracking. We would also like the bot to slow down near regions with high gradient magnitudes so that it does not overshoot the setpoint. This is ensured by including $\frac{\mathrm{d}C[t-1]}{\mathrm{d}x}$ in the denominator, which is the output of the gradient detector in the previous time step. Finally, k is a constant scaling factor while a is a constant that ensures that the denominator is never 0.

3   Results and Conclusions

The algorithms are visually compared in Fig.5(a). Note that the bot was started from the same starting point and initial angle in all three plots. Using only klinokinesis (left), the bot takes a long route to reach the setpoint and exhibits large overshoots around the setpoint contour. Adding klinotaxis (middle) allows the bot to reach the setpoint using a much faster route while also reducing setpoint deviation. Adding orthokinesis (right) further reduces the setpoint deviation.

We now define the Time to Reach Ratio (TRR) of an algorithm A for a setpoint C_T as the time taken to first reach C_T using A divided by the time to first reach C_T using klinokinesis. Clearly, the TRR also depends on the particular concentration landscape, starting point and initial angle. Here we consider the aggregated TRR obtained by averaging the TRR over 10 landscapes, 10 starting points for each landscape and 10 initial angles for each tuple of landscape and starting point. Also note that the TRR for klinokinesis will trivially be 1.0. The second metric is adopted from [10,11] to quantify the deviation from the setpoint once the bot has reached the contour. This metric is the average deviation ratio from setpoint (ADR), defined as $ADR = \frac{1}{T-T_0} \int_{T_0}^{T} \frac{|C(t)-C_T|}{C_{max}-C_{min}} dt$, where T_0 is the first time that the bot reaches C_T, T is the total simulation time, C_{max} and C_{min} are respectively the maximum and minimum concentrations values on the landscape. Thus the ADR measures the time-averaged ratio of the absolute deviation to the landscape concentration range. We report the aggregated ADR by averaging over the same set of configurations as for the aggregated TRR.

The algorithms are benchmarked using these two metrics in the left panel of Fig. 5(b). We find that there is a drastic reduction in the TRR, by a factor of 2.6, due to the inclusion of klinotaxis, implying that the bot reaches the setpoint faster. Remarkably this improvement is achieved despite the bot's effective

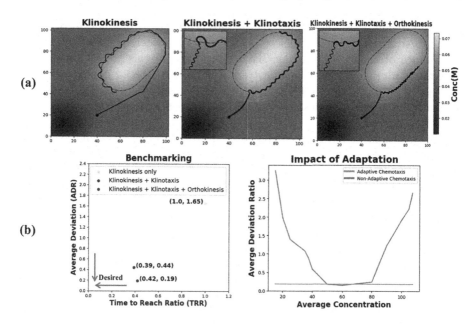

Fig. 5. (a) The dotted line in all three contour tracking plots is the setpoint contour corresponding to $C_T = 55\,\text{mm}$. (b) Left: Benchmarking with TRR and ADR. Right: Impact on ADR of dividing by $C_{avg}(t)$ while computing the gradient estimate. (Color figure online)

speed being reduced by a factor of roughly 7.5 by moving along a sinusoidal path instead of a straight line. As expected, a second effect of this reduced effective velocity is that the inclusion of klinotaxis also reduces the ADR, by a significant factor of 3.8. The TRR is slightly larger with the inclusion of orthokinesis as the bot slows down near the setpoint. However we observe a larger reduction in ADR, demonstrating that orthokinesis can adaptively trade-off speed for a significant reduction in setpoint overshoot. The TRR and ADR respectively reduced by a factor of 2.4 and 8.7 by including both klinotaxis and orthokinesis (w.r.t just klinokinesis). Also note that the standard deviation of the TRR for both the "klinokinesis + klinotaxis" and "klinokinesis + klinotaxis + orthokinesis" algorithms were found to be 0.05. The standard deviation of the ADR for "klinokinesis only", "klinokinesis + klinotaxis" and "klinokinesis + klinotaxis + orthokinesis" algorithms were respectively found to be 0.34, 0.08 and 0.04.

In the right panel of Fig.5(b), we quantitatively demonstrate the drastic improvement in robustness of chemotaxis due to the inclusion of $C_{avg}(t)$ in the denominator of (1). We plot the ADR for the "klinokinesis + klinotaxis + orthokinesis" algorithm as a function of average landscape concentration. Without adaptive scaling (red), the ADR is comparable to that with adaptive scaling (green) in a narrow range of average concentration, but degrades rapidly away from this optimal range. Similar plots were also obtained for the "klinokinesis only" and "klinokinesis + klinotaxis" algorithms. This shows that previously proposed chemotaxis algorithms in the literature (that did not incorporate dynamic scaling) are not robust to concentration rescaling, highlighting the importance of the novel dynamic scaling proposed in this paper. Finally, we refer the reader to [10] for a demonstration of the SNN-based klinokinesis-only strategy achieving lower ADR compared to PID control while also being significantly more energy efficient, with these results holding transitively for the schemes proposed here.

In conclusion, we have presented a scale-invariant, adaptive chemotaxis algorithm using spiking neurons that successfully combines klinotaxis, klinokinesis and orthokinesis. This allows us to perform robust, resource constrained and energy efficient contour tracking while achieving state-of-the-art performance.

References

1. Appleby, P.A.: A model of chemotaxis and associative learning in C. elegans. Biol. Cybern. **106**(6–7), 373–387 (2012). https://doi.org/10.1007/s00422-012-0504-8
2. Bastian, J.: Gain control in the electrosensory system: a role for the descending projections to the electrosensory lateral line lobe. J. Comp. Physiol. A **158**(4), 505–515 (1986). https://doi.org/10.1007/BF00603796
3. Benhamou, S., Bovet, P.: How animals use their environment: a new look at kinesis. Animal Behav. **38**(3), 375–383 (1989)
4. Dutta, S., Kumar, V., Shukla, A., Mohapatra, N.R., Ganguly, U.: Leaky integrate and fire neuron by charge-discharge dynamics in floating-body MOSFET. Sci. Rep. **7**(1), 8257 (2017)
5. Iino, Y., Yoshida, K.: Parallel use of two behavioral mechanisms for chemotaxis in Caenorhabditis elegans. J. Neurosci. **29**(17), 5370–5380 (2009)
6. Itskovits, E., Ruach, R., Zaslaver, A.: Concerted pulsatile and graded neural dynamics enables efficient chemotaxis in C. elegans. Nat. Commun. **9**(1), 2866 (2018)
7. Izquierdo, E.J., Beer, R.D.: Connecting a connectome to behavior: an ensemble of neuroanatomical models of C. elegans Klinotaxis. PLoS Comput. Biol. **9**(2), e1002890 (2013)
8. Izquierdo, E.J., Lockery, S.R.: Evolution and analysis of minimal neural circuits for Klinotaxis in Caenorhabditis elegans. J. Neurosci. **30**(39), 12908–12917 (2010)
9. Luo, L., Clark, D.A., Biron, D., Mahadevan, L., Samuel, A.D.: Sensorimotor control during isothermal tracking in Caenorhabditis elegans. J. Exp. Biol. **209**(23), 4652–4662 (2006)
10. Santurkar, S., Rajendran, B.: C. elegans chemotaxis inspired neuromorphic circuit for contour tracking and obstacle avoidance. In: 2015 International Joint Conference on Neural Networks (IJCNN), pp. 1–8. IEEE (2015)
11. Shukla, S., Dutta, S., Ganguly, U.: Design of spiking rate coded logic gates for C. elegans inspired contour tracking. In: Kůrková, V., Manolopoulos, Y., Hammer, B., Iliadis, L., Maglogiannis, I. (eds.) ICANN 2018. LNCS, vol. 11139, pp. 273–283. Springer, Cham (2018). https://doi.org/10.1007/978-3-030-01418-6_27
12. Skandari, R., Iino, Y., Manton, J.H.: On an analogue signal processing circuit in the nematode c. elegans. In: 38th Annual International Conference of the IEEE Engineering in Medicine and Biology Society (EMBC), pp. 965–968. IEEE (2016)
13. Vestergaard, M., Berg, R.W.: Divisive gain modulation of motoneurons by inhibition optimizes muscular control. J. Neurosci. **35**(8), 3711–3723 (2015)

Text Understanding I

Test Understanding I

Mental Imagery-Driven Neural Network to Enhance Representation for Implicit Discourse Relation Recognition

Jian Wang[1,2], Ruifang He[1,2(✉)], Fengyu Guo[1,2(✉)], and Yugui Han[1,2]

[1] College of Intelligence and Computing, Tianjin University, Tianjin, China
{jian_wang,rfhe,fengyuguo,yghan}@tju.edu.cn
[2] Tianjin Key Laboratory of Cognitive Computing and Application, Tianjin, China

Abstract. Implicit discourse relation recognition is an important sub-task in discourse parsing, which needs to infer the relation based on proper discourse comprehension. Recent studies on cognitive learning strategies have suggested that using mental imagery strategy will foster text comprehension, which could effectively improve the capability of learners' reading. Therefore, we propose a novel **M**ental **I**magery-driven **N**eural **N**etworks (**MINN**) to enhance representation for implicit discourse relation recognition. It employs the multi-granularity imagery vectors generated by the arguments to capture the deeper semantic information of discourse at different scales. Specifically, we 1) encode the different granularities of arguments (i.e., phrases, sentences.) and generate the corresponding imagery vectors as mentally imagining images of text content; 2) fuse the argument representations and imagery vectors as sequence representations; 3) further adopt self-attention to mine the important interactions between the sequence representations to infer the discourse relations. Extensive experimental results on the Penn Discourse TreeBank (PDTB) show that our model achieves competitive results against several state-of-the-art systems.

Keywords: Implicit discourse relation recognition · Mental imagery-driven neural network · Self-attention mechanism

1 Introduction

Discourse relation recognition is a fundamental task in natural language processing (NLP), which connects linguistic units such as clauses and sentences to form coherent semantics. Implicit discourse relation recognition remains a challenge due to the absence of discourse connectives [15]. Improving implicit discourse relation recognition benefits to many downstream tasks such as machine translation, question answering and so on.

The existing neural network-based models have achieved great success in this task, which mainly includes: 1) Basic neural networks [12,20] can learn the dense vector representations of discourse arguments, which can capture the

© Springer Nature Switzerland AG 2020
I. Farkaš et al. (Eds.): ICANN 2020, LNCS 12397, pp. 695–707, 2020.
https://doi.org/10.1007/978-3-030-61616-8_56

semantic information to some extent. Many studies use attention neural networks [6,11] to capture the significant information of discourse. Although those methods selectively extract important words from the arguments, they ignore much deeper interactions between the arguments. 2) The further approaches considering the interaction information between the arguments exploit semantic interaction-based neural network to learn the argument representation, which obtain more abundant interaction clues [2,7]. However, they neglect the different semantic information in the argument representations with different granularities. 3) Multi-granularity neural networks [1,3,17] enhance the argument representations at different scales. They capture the richer semantic information by mining more fine-grained argument representations, thereby enhancing the ability of discourse relation recognition. Yet, most of them only concentrate on text itself, which maybe insufficient for precise semantic understanding.

From the perspective of cognitive theory, Leutner2007 [8] found that mentally imagining images of text content were often spontaneously used when learners read a discourse. It seems to be a reasonable learning strategy when these mentally imagining images are helpful for comprehension, but are not provided in the discourse. For our task, people have to mentally transform the textual information into pictorial information which fosters the deeper discourse understanding. Moreover, different text spans could generate the corresponding mentally imagining images which promote the discourse comprehension together. Thus, there are the following aspects to be considered: 1) sequence information of different text spans and their mentally imagining images; 2) different importance of the new sequences and their interaction. We give an example for further explanation (Fig. 1):

Arg1: All you have to do is eat a big pizza, and then go to bed.
Arg2: You'll have weird dreams, too.

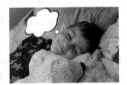

    (a) eat a big pizza   (b) go to bed   (c) have weird dreams

Fig. 1. The phrase images in *Arg1* and *Arg2*

The real discourse relation of the example is Temporal relation. If only focusing the literal information of this argument pair, the discourse relation might be recognized as Contingency or Temporal relation due to the existing of the phrases pairs ("eat a big pizza", "have weird dreams"), ("go to bed", "have weird dreams"). It is an ambiguity issue influencing implicit discourse relation recognition.

Therefore, we propose a mental imagery-driven neural network to enhance representation for implicit discourse relation recognition. Particularly, we make

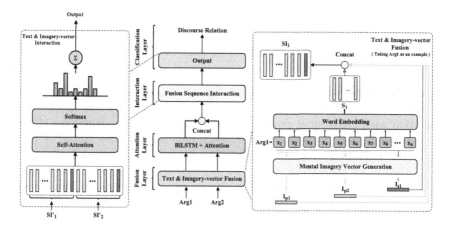

Fig. 2. Overview of the MINN framework

an attempt to generate the corresponding imagery vectors based on the different granularity of argument representations, so as to foster the discourse comprehension for improving the recognizing performance. In summary, the main contributions of this paper are as follows:

1) Propose a mental imagery-driven neural network to enhance representation for our task from the perspective of cognitive learning strategy;
2) Generate the relevant mental imagery vectors based on the representations of different text spans (i.e., phrases and sentences.), which mimic the process of imaging the discourse content;
3) Fuse the text and the mental imagery vectors of discourse arguments, and utilize self-attention to capture the deeper semantic interactions of them;
4) Extensive experimental results on the PDTB show that our model achieves the competitive results against several state-of-the-art systems.

2   The Proposed Model

Implicit discourse relation recognition is usually formalized as a classification problem. As shown in Fig. 2, we will introduce our model in detail.

2.1   Fusion Layer

The goal of the fusion layer is to obtain new fusing argument representations, including the textual information and the mentally imagining image vectors of discourse.

Word Embedding. We transform the original words into the distributed representation, which is a simple projection layer by lookup table operations according to the indexes. We choose the word embeddings pre-trained from Google News to obtain the text representation of arguments: S_1 and S_2.

Mental Imagery Vector Generation. In order to imitate the cognitive learning strategy, we utilize the AttnGAN [19], which is a fine-grained text to image generation with attentional generative adversarial networks, to process the discourse arguments and obtain the corresponding intermediate states of image generation as mental imagery vectors. The attentional generative network of AttnGAN has m generators $(G_0, G_1, ..., G_{m-1})$, which take the hidden states $(h_0, h_1, ..., h_{m-1})$ as input and generate image vectors (i.e., mental imagery vectors) of small-to-large scales $(\hat{x}_0, \hat{x}_1, ..., \hat{x}_{m-1})$ as follows:

$$
\begin{aligned}
h_0 &= F_0(z, F^{ca}(\bar{e})), \\
h_i &= F_i(h_{i-1}, F_i^{attn}(e, h_{i-1})), \\
\hat{x}_i &= G_i(h_i).
\end{aligned}
\tag{1}
$$

where, z is a noise vector usually sampled from a standard normal distribution. $\bar{e}$ is a global sentence vector, and e is the matrix of word vectors. F^{ca} represents the Conditioning Augmentation [21] that converts the sentence vector $\bar{e}$ to the conditioning vector. F^{ca}, F_i^{attn}, F_i and G_i are modeled as neural networks. F_i^{attn} is the attention model at the i-th stage of the AttnGAN and defined as:

$$
\begin{aligned}
F^{attn}(e, h) &= (c_0, c_1, ..., c_{N-1}), \\
c_i &= \sum_{i=0}^{T-1} \beta_{j,i} e_i', \\
\beta_{j,i} &= \frac{exp(s_{j,i}')}{\sum_{k=0}^{T-1} exp(s_{j,k}')}, \\
s_{j,i}' &= h_j^T e_i'.
\end{aligned}
\tag{2}
$$

where, h is the image features from the previous hidden layer. $\beta_{j,i}$ indicates the weight the model attends to the i-th word when generating the j-th sub-region of the image.

Specifically, given two arguments and their phrases, we feed them into AttnGAN, respectively, and then AttnGAN could generate the argument-level and phrase-level mental imagery vectors: $I_s^1, \{I_{p_1}^1, ..., I_{p_n}^1\}, I_s^2$ and $\{I_{p_1}^2, ..., I_{p_m}^2\}$, where the $I_{p_k}^1$ and $I_{p_l}^2$ represent the k-th and l-th mental imagery vectors of the phrases, and the p_n and p_m indicate the total number of phrases in $Arg1$ and $Arg2$, respectively.

Text and Imagery-Vector Fusion. After the two steps (Word Embedding and Mental Imagery Vector Generation), we obtain the text representation of discourse arguments: S_1 and S_2, and their argument-level and phrase-level mental imagery vectors: $I_s^1, \{I_{p_1}^1, ..., I_{p_n}^1\}, I_s^2$ and $\{I_{p_1}^2, ..., I_{p_m}^2\}$. In order to reflect the sequential connections of the phrases, we sequentially concatenate the text and mental imagery representation to receive the new fusion representations SI_1 and SI_2, defined as:

$$SI_1 = [S_1, I_{p_1}^1, ..., I_{p_n}^1, I_s^1]$$
$$SI_2 = [S_2, I_{p_1}^2, ..., I_{p_m}^2, I_s^2]$$

$$(3)$$

Finally, these fusion representations are fed into the attention layer.

2.2 Attention Layer

We choose the bidirectional Long Short-Term Memory network (BiLSTM) to learn the semantic information of the final fusion representations. First, we use the fusion representations SI_1 and SI_2 as the input of BiLSTM, and then adopt the attention mechanism to capture important information including imagining image clues of discourse content, defined as:

$$M = tanh(H), \tag{4}$$

$$\alpha = softmax(w^T M), \tag{5}$$

$$r = H\alpha^T. \tag{6}$$

where $H \in \mathbb{R}^{l_t \times d}$ is the matrix consisting of output vectors, l_t is the sum of the three parts: the sizes of words in the argument, the number of phrase-level imagery vectors and argument-level imagery vectors. d is the dimension of the word, w is a parameter vector. The new representation r of the argument is formed by a weighted sum of the output vectors. Thereby, we can obtain the fusion representation SI_1' and SI_2', which contains sequence information and attention weights.

2.3 Interaction Layer

How to capture the interaction information is essential for discourse relation recognition. Self-attention mechanism is a special case of the attention mechanism that relates elements at different locations in a single sequence by computing the attention between each pair of tokens of the sequence [18], which is very flexible to model the long-range and local dependencies. Therefore, we intend to utilize self-attention mechanism to capture the interaction information of the fused sequences concatenated by arguments and their corresponding mental imagery vectors. The self-attention mechanism is defined as:

$$Attention(Q, K, V) = softmax(\frac{QK^T}{\sqrt{d_k}})V \tag{7}$$

where, the $Q, K, V \in \mathbb{R}^{l_a \times d_k}$ represent queries matrix, keys matrix and values matrix, respectively. The initial values of Q, K, and V are all the fused sequence vector, l_a is the length of the fused sequence vector. The d_k is the dimension of the fused sequence vector, which equals the dimension of word embeddings d. Thereby, we can obtain a more abstract vector, which containing important interaction information.

2.4   Classification Layer

Finally, the final fusion representations are fed to the output layer. For our classification task, the outputs are the probabilities of different discourse relations, which is computed by the softmax function, which is defined as follows:

$$y = f(W_f\hat{y} + b_f). \tag{8}$$

where f is the softmax function, $W_f \in \mathbb{R}^{l_t \times d}$, $b_f \in \mathbb{R}^c$ are the weights and bias term respectively, and c denotes the number of relation class.

The training objective is to minimize the cross entropy of the predicted and the true label distributions, defined as:

$$\mathcal{L} = -\sum_{j=1}^{C} y_j log(\hat{y}_j) \tag{9}$$

where y is the one-hot representation of the ground-truth relation; $\hat{y}$ is the predicted probabilities of relations; C is the number of relation class.

3   Experiments

3.1   Datasets

The Penn Discourse Treebank 2.0 (PDTB) [16] is a benchmark corpus for our task, which is annotated on 2,312 Wall Street Journal articles. PDTB has three levels of senses: Level-1 class, Level-2 type, and Level-3 subtypes. The top level consists of four major semantic classes: Comparison, Contingency, Expansion, and Temporal. For each class, the second level of types is defined to further refine the semantics of the class levels. Following the settings of Bai2018 [1], we use two splitting methods of PDTB dataset. The first is PDTB-Lin [10], which uses section 2–21, 22 and 23 as training, dev and test sets respectively. The second is PDTB-Ji [4], which uses sections 2–20, 0–1, and 21–22 as training, dev and test sets respectively. According to Ji2015 [4], five relation types have few training instances and no dev and test instance. Removing the five types, there remain 11 s level types in the PDTB-Ji dataset.

3.2   Experimental Settings

In this section, we will introduce the related parameter settings. The word embeddings are 300-dim word2vec [13] pre-trained from Google News. We use Adam optimization to optimize the loss function, and set the enhanced word embeddings by using 300-dim pre-trained from ELMo [14]. The dropout for

BiLSTM and word embeddings are set to 0.3, the numbers of BiLSTM layer is 3, and the number of epochs is 100. The length of the sentence is 100 and the learning rate is 0.001. We use the StanfordNLP to obtain the phrases of arguments and the maximum number of phrases for each argument is 5.

3.3 Compared Models

Discourse Argument Representation

Lin2009 [10] used the context of the two arguments, word pair information, as well as the arguments' internal constituent and dependency parses.

Ji2015 [4] computed distributed meaning representations for each discourse argument by composition up the syntactic parse tree.

Zhang2015 [20] proposed pure neural networks with three different pooling operations with only one simple convolution layer on the top of word vectors to learn shallow representations.

Liu2016 [11] combined attention mechanisms and external memory to focus on specific words that helps determine discourse relations.

Lan2017 [6] designed an attention based neural network for learning discourse relation representation.

Argument Pair Interaction

Chen2016 [2] proposed a Gated Relevance Network (GRN) and incorporated both the linear and non-linear interactions between word pairs.

Lei2017 [7] devised the Simple Word Interaction Model (SWIM) to learn the interactions between word pairs.

Multi-granularity Argument Representation

Qin2016 [17] adopted context-aware character-enhanced embeddings to address implicit discourse relation recognition task.

Bai2018 [1] employed different grained text representations, including character, subword, word, sentence, and sentence pair levels.

Besides, we also design the four ablation models stack layer by layer to compare with our model:

Baseline. We encode two discourse arguments by 3-layer BiLSTM and utilize the self-attention to obtain the interactions, and finally stack the softmax function to predict the discourse relation.

+Phrase Imagery-vector. Based on Baseline, we utilize the text representations and the corresponding generated phrase imagery vectors of the arguments as the inputs of the softmax.

+Sentence Imagery-vector. We adopt the generated phrase and sentence imagery vectors to enhance argument representations together.

+ELMo. We utilize pre-trained ELMo vector to enrich the argument representations, and finally feed them to the softmax function to recognize discourse relations.

3.4   Results and Discussion

To effectively validate the effectiveness of our model, we perform binary (one-versus-other), 4-way classification on the top level classes, and 11-way classification on the second types.

Table 1. F_1 scores (%) of different comparison systems and ablation models Binary and 4-way classification.

Model	Comp.	Cont.	Exp.	Temp.	4-way
Zhang2015	33.22	52.04	69.59	30.54	–
Ji2015	35.93	52.78	–	27.63	–
Chen2016	40.17	54.76	-	31.32	–
Liu2016	39.86	54.48	70.43	**38.84**	46.29
Lan2017	40.73	**58.96**	72.47	38.50	47.80
Lei2017	40.47	55.36	69.50	35.34	46.46
Bai2018	**47.85**	54.47	70.60	36.87	51.06
Baseline	32.32	49.53	65.91	34.86	46.36
+Sentence Imagery-vector	39.15	52.05	68.05	35.16	47.96
+Phrase Imagery-vector	41.15	53.36	69.66	36.70	50.83
+ELMo(Ours)	44.35	55.26	**73.55**	37.04	**52.64**

Table 2. Accuracy (%) of different comparison systems and ablation models on 11-way classification.

Model	PDTB-Lin	PDTB-Ji
Lin2009	40.20	–
Ji2015	–	44.59
Qin2016	43.81	45.04
Bai2018	45.73	48.22
Baseline	40.60	43.60
+Sentence Imagery-vector	42.72	44.18
+Phrase Imagery-vector	45.44	47.35
+ELMo(Ours)	**46.16**	**49.24**

Binary and 4-way Classification. To be consistent with previous work, we first show the F_1 scores of the reported state-of-the-art systems and the ablation methods on the binary and 4-way classification in Table 1.

4-way Classification. For the comparison systems, the F_1 score of our model is higher than that of the other systems. This is because the fusing representations we utilized not only remain the global-level textual information of discourse, but also introduce the multi-granularity mental imagining image clues to enhance the semantic understanding of discourse.

Binary Classification. Our model achieves the best F_1 score on Expansion relation. The main reason might be that the arguments with Expansion tend to be a textual narrative which could generate the richer imagery vectors to further enhance the argument representations. In addition, the performance of our model on Contingency relation is not satisfying, which is caused by no complicated inference in the mentally imagining images of argument content.

11-way Classification. We perform 11-way classification on the second level of PDTB. Our model achieves state-of-the-art performance, i.e., 46.16% and 49.24%, in the two splitting methods, as shown in Table 2. It also shows the results of ablation models in term of accuracy, and we make the following observations:

1) Overall: Fusing the multi-granularity imagery vectors could improve the performance of implicit discourse relation recognition, which is consistent with the process of human-like cognitive learning. Additionally, the accuracy of the model without ELMo is 47.35% on the PDTB-Ji, which is comparable to the accuracy of using ELMo. This demonstrates that our model takes advantage of the mentally imagining image clues to understand the sentence semantics from a novel aspect, which is different from ELMo only focusing on the contextual information of the text itself.
2) Sentence Imagery-vector: The accuracy values on the PDTB-Lin and PDTB-Ji are 42.72% and 44.18%, higher than those of Baseline, respectively. It indicates that sentence-level imagery vectors, containing the imagining scene of a whole sentence, bring the relevant semantic clues to promote the discourse understanding.
3) Phrase Imagery-vector: Our model gains 3.75% improvement than the Baseline on the accuracy of PDTB-Ji. Compared with introducing the sentence-level imagery vectors, the performance of the model with phrase-level imagery vectors increases 3.17%. The reason may be that phrase-level imagery vectors as fine-grained representations contain richer semantic information with time series and contextual cues, which are important for argument analysis.
4) ELMo: The model with ELMo achieves 1.89% improvement than that of the phrase-level imagery vectors on the accuracy of PDTB-Ji. It verifies that ELMo, as pre-trained contextualized word embeddings, can make the embeddings contain more contextual information which is beneficial to the task.

Impact of Mental Imagery Vector
To verify the effectiveness of imagery vectors, we visualize the self-attention weight of the arguments with different phrases out of the example in Sect. 1, as shown in Fig. 3. The darker patches indicate higher correlations of the vectors. We can obtain the following observations:

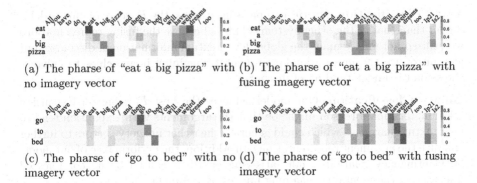

(a) The pharse of "eat a big pizza" with no imagery vector

(b) The pharse of "eat a big pizza" with fusing imagery vector

(c) The pharse of "go to bed" with no imagery vector

(d) The pharse of "go to bed" with fusing imagery vector

Fig. 3. Visualization of self-attention with fused sequences.

1) Seen from Fig. 3(a), without fusing imagery vectors, the model has a high correlation between the phrases "eat a big pizza" and "have weird dreams", which might be recognized as Contingency relation directly. As a comparison, Fig. 3(b) shows that the model fusing imagery vectors reduces the attention of the phrase "have weird dreams". This demonstrates that only considering the shallow features of argument may suffer the problem of fuzziness, and fusing imagery vectors could relieve this issue to some extent. Similarly, the model shifts the higher attention from the phrase "eat a big pizza" to the phrase "have weird dreams" for the phrase "go to bed", as shown in Fig. 3(c) and Fig. 3(d) respectively.

2) In general, if we only consider the shallow features of arguments, the phrase "have weird dreams" has a high correlation with "eat a big pizza" than that with "go to bed", which may indicate the example as Contingency relation. Furthermore, the model shifts the focus of the phrase "eat a big pizza" to "go to bed", so as to identify the Temporal relation of the example, after fusing the imagery vectors into our model. This demonstrates that fusing imagery vectors could help understand the discourse arguments more deeply.

4   Related Work

After the release of PDTB2.0, there are many studies on implicit discourse relation recognition, and we demonstrate the mainly related work as follows:

4.1   Discourse Relation Recognition

How to model the discourse arguments and how to incorporate their semantic interactions are the core factors of implicit discourse relation recognition. To this end, the neural network-based models are roughly divided into:

Basic Discourse Argument Representation Many original studies based on CNN or RNN learned the low-dimensional dense vector of arguments, which could capture semantic information to some extent [12,20]. Liu2016 [11] combined attention mechanisms and external memory to focus on specific words that helped determine discourse relations. Although these approaches could capture the important information with indicative clues to some extent, they neglect the semantic interactions between the arguments.

Discourse Argument Pair Interactions The approaches comprehensively considered the interaction information of argument pairs based on the attention or gate mechanism [2,7]. Lei2017 [7] demonstrated that word-weighted averaging can encode argument representation which can be incorporated with word pair information efficiently. However, the discourse is composed of different granularity units with different semantics, these models ignore the features of different granularity text spans and the effective interaction clues between them.

Multi-granularity Semantic Information Recently, many researches have learned the different semantic information of different granularity of arguments [1,3,17]. Dai2018 [3] introduced a paragraph-level neural network that model inter-dependencies between discourse units as well as discourse relation continuity and patterns, and predicted a sequence of discourse relations in a paragraph. Bai2018 [1] proposed a model that fused text representations of different granularity, including characters, subwords, words, sentences, and sentence pairs. Despite the richer features they obtained, they only concentrate on the text content itself which is insufficient to identify implicit discourse relation recognition.

4.2   Cognitive Learning Inspiration

Some studies of cognitive learning strategy [5,9] illustrate that learner may construct "images" for understanding by mentally imagining images of text content when reading a discourse, which is a reasonable learning strategy since images are helpful for the discourse comprehension. Inspired by this strategy, we propose the mental imagery-driven neural network to enrich the argument representations for recognizing implicit discourse relations. And we learn from the methods of generating images in the text-image generation task [19,21] to generate the imagery vectors (the intermediate states of image generation).

To our knowledge, this is the first attempt to generate the imagery vectors to enhance the semantic understanding of arguments, which also brings a new idea for implicit discourse relation recognition.

5   Conclusion

As a complex text processing task, implicit discourse relation recognition needs the deeper analysis of the arguments. We propose a mental imagery-driven neural network to enhance representation for the task. To imitate the cognitive learning strategy, we mentally transform the textual clues into pictorial information for avoiding the issues about ambiguity and fuzziness of arguments. We construct the corresponding mental imagery vectors in the light of the multi-granularity arguments (i.e., phrases, sentences), which could be helpful for the semantic understanding of discourse. And then we integrate the text content and the mentally imagining images to capture the contextual information, so as to infer the discourse relation effectively. The experimental results on the PDTB demonstrate the effectiveness of our model.

Acknowledgments. We thank the anonymous reviewers for their valuable feedback. Our work is supported by the National Natural Science Foundation of China (61976154), and the Tianjin Natural Science Foundation (18JCYBJC15500).

References

1. Bai, H., Zhao, H.: Deep enhanced representation for implicit discourse relation recognition. In: Proceedings of the 2018 COLING, pp. 571–583 (2018)
2. Chen, J., Zhang, Q., Liu, P., Qiu, X., Huang, X.: Implicit discourse relation detection via a deep architecture with gated relevance network. In: Proceedings of the 2016 ACL, pp. 1726–1735 (2016)
3. Dai, Z., Huang, R.: Improving implicit discourse relation classification by modeling inter-dependencies of discourse units in a paragraph. In: Proceedings of the 2018 NAACL, pp. 141–151 (2018)
4. Ji, Y., Eisenstein, J.: One vector is not enough: entity-augmented distributional semantics for discourse relations. Trans. ACL **3**, 329–344 (2015)
5. Kosslyn, S.M.: Image and Brain: The Resolution of the Imagery Debate. MIT press, Cambridge (1996)
6. Lan, M., Wang, J., Wu, Y., Niu, Z.Y., Wang, H.: Multi-task attention-based neural networks for implicit discourse relationship representation and identification. In: Proceedings of the 2017 EMNLP, pp. 1299–1308 (2017)
7. Lei, W., Wang, X., Liu, M., Ilievski, I., He, X., Kan, M.Y.: Swim: a simple word interaction model for implicit discourse relation recognition. In: Proceedings of the 2017 IJCAI, pp. 4026–4032 (2017)
8. Leutner, D., den Elzen-Rump, V., Leopold, C.: Self-regulated learning from science texts. In: Prenzel, M. (ed.) Studies on the Educational Quality of Schools. The Final Report on the DFG Priority Programme, pp. 221–238 (2007)
9. Leutner, D., Leopold, C., Sumfleth, E.: Cognitive load and science text comprehension: effects of drawing and mentally imagining text content. Comput. Hum. Behav. **25**(2), 284–289 (2009)
10. Lin, Z., Kan, M.Y., Ng, H.T.: Recognizing implicit discourse relations in the Penn discourse treebank. In: Proceedings of the 2009 EMNLP, pp. 343–351 (2009)
11. Liu, Y., Li, S.: Recognizing implicit discourse relations via repeated reading: neural networks with multi-level attention. In: Proceedings of the 2016 EMNLP, pp. 1224–1233 (2016)
12. Liu, Y., Li, S., Zhang, X., Sui, Z.: Implicit discourse relation classification via multi-task neural networks. In: Proceedings of the 2016 AAAI, pp. 2750–2756 (2016)
13. Mikolov, T., Chen, K., Corrado, G., Dean, J.: Efficient estimation of word representations in vector space. arXiv preprint arXiv:1301.3781 (2013)

14. Peters, M., et al.: Deep contextualized word representations. In: Proceedings of the 2018 NAACL, pp. 2227–2237 (2018)
15. Pitler, E., Louis, A., Nenkova, A.A.: Automatic sense prediction for implicit discourse relations in text. In: Proceedings of the AFNLP, pp. 683–691 (2009)
16. Prasad, R., et al.: The Penn discourse treebank 2.0. In: Proceedings of the 2008 LREC (2008)
17. Qin, L., Zhang, Z., Zhao, H.: Implicit discourse relation recognition with context-aware character-enhanced embeddings. In: Proceedings of the 2016 COLING, pp. 1914–1924 (2016)
18. Vaswani, A., et al.: Attention is all you need. In: Proceedings of the 2017 NIPS, pp. 5998–6008 (2017)
19. Xu, T., et al.: AttnGAN: fine-grained text to image generation with attentional generative adversarial networks. In: Proceedings of the 2018 CVPR, pp. 1316–1324 (2018)
20. Zhang, B., Su, J., Xiong, D., Lu, Y., Duan, H., Yao, J.: Shallow convolutional neural network for implicit discourse relation recognition. In: Proceedings of the 2015 EMNLP, pp. 2230–2235 (2015)
21. Zhang, H., et al.: StackGAN: text to photo-realistic image synthesis with stacked generative adversarial networks. In: Proceedings of the 2017 ICCV, pp. 5907–5915 (2017)

Adaptive Convolution Kernel for Text Classification via Multi-channel Representations

Cheng Wang[1](✉) and Xiaoyan Fan[2]

[1] School of Information Engineering, East China Jiaotong University, Nanchang 330013, China
Wangcheng.me@gmail.com
[2] School of Software, East China Jiaotong University, Nanchang 330013, China

Abstract. Although existing text classification algorithms with LSTM-CNN-like structures have achieved great success, these models still have deficiencies in text feature representation and extraction. Most of the text representation methods based on LSTM-like models often adopt a single-channel form, and the size of convolution kernel is usually fixed in further feature extraction by CNN. Hence, in this study, we propose an Adaptive Convolutional Kernel via Multi-Channel Representation (ACK-MCR) model to solve the above two problems. The multi-channel text representation is formed by two different Bi-LSTM networks, extracting time-series features from forward and backward directions to retain more semantic information. Furthermore, after CNNs, a multi-scale feature attention is used to adaptively select multi-scale feature for classification. Extensive experiments show that our model obtains competitive performance against state-of-the-art baselines on six benchmark datasets.

Keywords: Multi-channel representation · Adaptive kernel · Text classification

1 Introduction

In recent years, deep learning model has made remarkable achievements in computer vision [1, 2] and speech recognition [3], and gradually began to be applied to the field of natural language processing. Text classification is a fundamental task for natural language processing [4]. For text classification, the key is how to capture the sequence characteristics between different time steps [5–7]. Because the long short-term memory network (LSTM) can deal with the text sequence with temporal relation well, LSTM models are widely used in NLP field [8–10]. However, the researchers found that there are serious shortcomings in using only LSTM to encode the target sequence. For example, when LSTM encodes the information at the current time, it can only contain the information before the current time, and cannot pay more attention to the information after the current time.

At the same time, due to the success of convolutional neural network (CNN) in the field of image processing, it is naturally introduced into the field of natural language processing (NLP) [11, 12]. Thanks to CNN model's powerful ability to capture spatial features, researchers have successfully applied it to text classification model [13–15],

© Springer Nature Switzerland AG 2020
I. Farkaš et al. (Eds.): ICANN 2020, LNCS 12397, pp. 708–720, 2020.
https://doi.org/10.1007/978-3-030-61616-8_57

and the core idea of which is to describe the relative relationship between words in spatial position through CNN model. But its disadvantage is that the traditional convolutional neural network has low matching degree between convolution kernel window size and target sequence length due to the unreasonable setting of convolution window size, which leads to low accuracy of classification [11, 16]. Although there are various depth network models combining LSTM and CNN in the future, they still failed to solve the above problems [17–19].

And in the traditional text classification models based on deep learning, there were usually two kinds of word vector processing for text representation: the one was already pre-trained word vector such as Glove [20] and the another one was randomly initialized word vector (such as embedding layer) and then training with the whole model. But generally speaking, they both had advantages and disadvantages. The advantage of directly loading the pre-trained word vector is that its sematic information is relatively rich, but the dimension of vector is limited by the original size of dimension; the advantage of random initialization is that the dimension can be adjusted according to the needs, but it may be limited by the amounts of text datum, which may ultimately lead to the word vector cannot accurately represent the semantic information of the phrase, leading to poor classification accuracy. In this paper, hence, we used these two methods for word representation, so as to combine the advantages of the two models.

To sum up, in order to overcome these problems 1) that the traditional LSTM model cannot encode the information before and after the current time simultaneously, 2) and the problem of low matching between the convolution kernel width and the target words. In this paper, an Adaptive Convolutional kernel size via Multi-Channel Feature Representation of text classification algorithm is proposed. In this model, BiLSTMs are used to extract temporal features in both forward and backward directions to generate new multi-channel text feature representation by using two types of word embeddings. Then, multi-scale CNN network is integrated into attention mechanism to further realize the purpose of convolution kernel self-adaptive, followed by classification. The experimental results show that this algorithm can obtain a competitive performance, especially on long text datasets.

The main contributions of this paper are as follows:

- In this paper, based on BiLSTM, we propose a new way to represent text feature. We use BiLSTM to extract the temporal features from the original text representation which are represented by two different types of word vectors, so that the model can take into account the semantic information before and after the current time simultaneously. And different from the traditional feature fusion methods, we adopt a multi-channel text feature representation method (inspired by image feature extraction), in order that multi-level semantic features can be obtain.
- In order to solve the problem of low matching degree between convolution kernel size and target sequence length in traditional CNNs, multi-scale feature attention mechanism is used. Through this design consideration, the model can adaptively select appropriate combination of features for text classification.
- In the experiment of real-life datasets, we evaluate and analyze the performance of ACK-MCR. Experiment shows that ACK-MCR can obtain a competitive result compared with the state-of-the-art baselines.

2 Related Work

In recent years, convolutional neural network, recurrent neural network and their combinations have made great development in the field of computer vision [1, 2] and speech recognition [3] areas, so they have become a research hotspot to transfer various technologies to the field of NLP [13, 15, 21–23].

Text Classification Based on Deep Learning

[13] used CNN model to classify text, they took as CNN input two channels with different word vector representations, and added convolution kernels of various sizes to extract multi granularity phrase features, and finally classified text. [15] proposed a CNN model based on dense connection for text classification. This model changes the sequential connection mode in traditional CNN convolutional network to dense connection based on skip connection technology, so as to extract the text feature representation with different particle sizes. [21] represented a weighted recurrent neural network W-RNN to solve the problem of semantic constraints in sparse representation text classification method, which can fully extract text serialization semantic information.

Text Classification Based on Attention Mechanism

[22] utilized the SAMF- BiLSTM model to solve the problem of emotional information missing due to the restriction of feature vector length in emotional classification task. The method models the existing linguistic knowledge and sentiment resources in sentiment analysis tasks to form different feature channels, and uses self-attention mechanism to enhance the sentiment information. [23] adopted an Attention-Gated Convolutional Neural Network (AGCNN) for sentence classification, which generates attention weights from the feature's context windows of different sizes by using specialized convolution encoders. [24] applied a hierarchical architecture (ATT-LSTM) model based on LSTM for question-answer classification. The model connects the continuous hidden states of the previous time steps to the current time steps, and applies the attention mechanism to these hidden states. It not only effectively captures the local features, but also helps to learn the long-distance correlation in an input sequence. [25] proposed a BiLSTM model based on attention mechanism for the classification task of text relationship. [26] recently proposed a revolutionary pre-trained language representation model BERT, which is designed to pre-train deep bidirectional representations from unlabeled text by jointly conditioning on both left and right context in all layers. And after that, many variant models based on BERT have been proposed.

In this model, attention mechanism is introduced into Bi-LSTM to capture the most important semantic information in sentences, so as to avoid the complex feature engineering in traditional work and achieve better results in this task.

3 Method

3.1 Overview

The architecture of our proposed model is shown in Fig. 1. The left panel is the model of an intuitive view while the right shows more technical details. The model begins with a text sequence input $x_1, x_2, \cdots, x_l$, and forms multi-channel text feature representation through two completely different BiLSTM networks. And then multi-scale features are obtained by convolutional blocks with various kernel sizes. The multi-channel feature representation enables the model to capture more semantic information from a global perspective while retaining the richness of text feature, because it has two types of word embeddings and uses a multi-channel feature representation method (similar to feature maps in image processing). Next, convolutional blocks are applied to compose convolutional features with different granularity sizes. In order to select task-friendly convolutional features, an attention mechanism is presented to find these multi-scale feature maps through the two steps: feature ensemble ($F_{ensem}(\cdot)$) and feature reweight ($F_{reweight}(\cdot)$). A final representation is then generated for text classification.

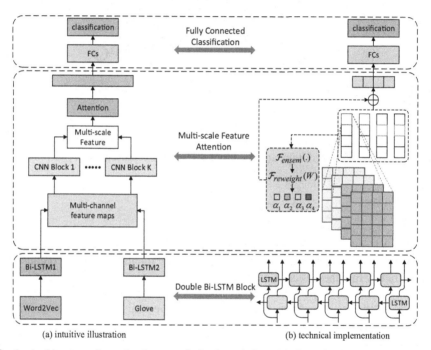

(a) intuitive illustration (b) technical implementation

Fig. 1. Architecture of our adaptive convolution kernel via multi-channel representation. (a) Intuitive illustration of how the model completes the entire workflow. (b) Technical implementation shows the detail of the model, including the formation of multi-channel features and adaptive process of convolution kernel.

3.2   Multi-channel Representation

Motivated by image processing [27–29], in order to capture more semantic information from a global perspective and obtain richer features of text, we proposed a multi-channel text representation method in this work. We feed two different types of word embeddings (glove and word2vec) to two BiLSTM networks respectively. In Fig. 2, the left is a

BiLSTM network and the right is the same, but different weights. In each time step, the left network is fed with glove word embedding and the right word2vec.

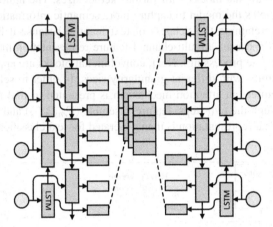

Fig. 2. Multi-channel representation. The left panel is a BiLSTM network with glove embedding and right word2vec embedding.

Let x_i^g, $x_i^w \in \mathbb{R}^d$ be the $d-$ dimensional word vector of the $i-th$ word in a text with two types of word embeddings and the input text can be represented as two matrixes:

$$X^g = [x_1^g, x_2^g, \cdots, x_l^g] \in \mathbb{R}^{l \times d}$$
$$X^w = [x_1^w, x_2^w, \cdots, x_l^w] \in \mathbb{R}^{l \times d} \tag{1}$$

where l is the number of words in a sequence.

After X^g and X^w are fed into the two BiLSTM networks, the model will output the encoding vectors of each time step. Different from other traditional feature combinations which crudely fuse these vectors of each output time step together, the proposed method vertically stacks the output vectors in the same direction in each BiLSTM network into a feature matrix in order. After this, we can obtain 4 feature maps containing different levels of semantic information, namely multi-channel representation.

Specifically, for a text sequence of length l, after processing by two BiLSTM networks, we can obtain the output of each direction in each BiLSTM network, namely: $\vec{y}_1^g \cdots \vec{y}_l^g, \overleftarrow{y}_1^g \cdots \overleftarrow{y}_l^g, \vec{y}_1^w \cdots \vec{y}_l^w$ and $\overleftarrow{y}_1^w \cdots \overleftarrow{y}_l^w$. Next, we stack these four outputs separately in order to obtain the final multi-channel feature representation. It can be written as follow:

$$\overrightarrow{\mathcal{H}}_{1:l}^g = \vec{y}_1^g \oplus \vec{y}_2^g \cdots \oplus \vec{y}_l^g$$
$$\overleftarrow{\mathcal{H}}_{1:l}^g = \overleftarrow{y}_1^g \oplus \overleftarrow{y}_2^g \cdots \oplus \overleftarrow{y}_l^g$$
$$\overrightarrow{\mathcal{H}}_{1:l}^w = \vec{y}_1^w \oplus \vec{y}_2^w \cdots \oplus \vec{y}_l^w \tag{2}$$
$$\overleftarrow{\mathcal{H}}_{1:l}^w = \overleftarrow{y}_1^w \oplus \overleftarrow{y}_2^w \cdots \oplus \overleftarrow{y}_l^w$$

where $\overrightarrow{\mathcal{H}}_{1:l}^g, \overleftarrow{\mathcal{H}}_{1:l}^g, \overrightarrow{\mathcal{H}}_{1:l}^w, \overleftarrow{\mathcal{H}}_{1:l}^w \in \mathbb{R}^{l \times d}$ represent the four feature maps and $\oplus$ is concatenation operation.

3.3 Multi-scale Feature Attention

Convolutional Blocks. After going through the previous stages, we can obtain the multi-channel text feature representation:

$$X_{Multi} = [\vec{H}^g_{1:l}, \overleftarrow{H}^g_{1:l}, \vec{H}^w_{1:l}, \overleftarrow{H}^w_{1:l}] \in \mathbb{R}^{4 \times l \times d} \tag{3}$$

Then, the model takes X_{Multi} as input to the multi-scale convolutional network. In the convolutional network, the model will convolve the input features X_{Multi} with different kernels which also has different window sizes s(such as $s = 2, 3, 4, 5$) to capture semantic information on adjacent spaces of a text sequence, followed by k convolution features with various granularity sizes. It can be expressed as follow:

$$c_i = \mathcal{F}(\mathcal{W}_k, X_{Multi})$$
$$C = [c_1, c_2, \cdots, _k] \tag{4}$$

where $\mathcal{F}(\cdot)$ is a composite function consisting of three cascaded operations: a basic 2d-convolutional operation, a batch normalization (BN) [30] and a rectified linear unit (ReLU) [31]. The $i-$ th convoluted feature c_i are produced by receiving preceding multi-channel features maps X_{Multi} with learnable weights $\mathcal{W}_k \in \mathbb{R}^{4 \times s \times d}$, and these features indicate the responses of multi-scale $n-$ grams (e.g. unigram, bigram, trigram).

Notice that, we use zero padding to both two sides of each channel of the input X_{Multi} to ensure that the resulting feature maps has the same shape as the input. For example, we pad $\mathbf{0} \in \mathbb{R}^{4 \times 1 \times d}$ above X_{Multi} when $s = 2$; and pad $\mathbf{0}$ above X_{Multi} and below X_{Multi} when $s = 3$.

Traditional CNN models usually perform max-pooling operation on the previous feature maps and concatenate the pooling results, finally followed by multiple fully connected classification layers. Although this method can also obtain good results, it is easy to fall into the problem of low matching between the window size of and the target sequence length. Inspired by [15], we use attention mechanism between convolutional feature maps to equip the model with the ability to adapt the window size, which is crucial for language processing.

Through multi-scale convolutions, a lot of feature maps are produced. However, how to effectively utilize these features (maybe some are redundant) [15] is still a key issue. And then, we present an attention mechanism to select the appropriate combination of different scale feature maps for text classification.

Adaptive Convolution Kernels. The attention mechanism consists of two main parts: feature ensemble and feature reweight, as shown in Fig. 3. For the feature ensemble, we use a parametric-matrix-based fusion to merge them,

$$s_i = \mathcal{F}_{ensem}(i) = \sum_{i=1}^{k} w_i \odot c_i$$
$$S = s_1 + s_2 + \cdots + s_k \tag{5}$$

where $\odot$ is the Hadamard product (i.e., element-wise mul-tiplication), w_i are the learnable weights that adjust the degrees affected by each feature maps respectively.

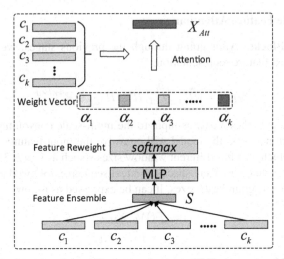

Fig. 3. Multi-scale Attention. It contains two main steps: (1) Feature ensemble and (2) Feature reweight

After obtaining S, we will use them as input to produce attention weights in order to adaptively reweight the feature maps from different scales. And then, we define the final representation X_{Att} and attention weights α_i as follow:

$$X_{Att} = \sum_{i=1}^{k} c_i \cdot \alpha_i$$

$$\sum_{i=1}^{k} \alpha_i = 1, \quad \forall \alpha_i, \ 0 \le \alpha_i \le 1 \tag{6}$$

where α_i are attention weights. Notice that, feature maps produced by different kernels have correspondence to the scale of features.

The attention weights are generated as follow:

$$\alpha_i = \frac{\exp(MLP(S)_i)}{\sum_{i=1}^{k} \exp(MLP(S)_i)} \tag{7}$$

where MLP is a multi-layer perceptron.

After being processed by the attention module, the final feature representation $X_{Att} \in \mathbb{R}^l$ is generated, which will be fed into the classification layers.

3.4 Output Layer

For the classification tasks, the output X_{Out} is the whole representation of the input text sequence. And then it is passed to a softmax classifier layer to predict the label $\hat{y}$:

$$\hat{y} = \arg\max(softmax(W \cdot X_{Out} + b)) \tag{8}$$

A reasonable training objective to be minimized is the categorical cross-entropy loss. The loss is calculated as a regularized sum:

$$\mathcal{J}(\theta) = -\frac{1}{m}\sum_{i=1}^{m} t_i \log(y_i) + \lambda \, ||\theta||^2 \tag{9}$$

where $\mathbf{t} \in \mathbb{R}^m$ is the one-hot represented ground truth, $\mathbf{y} \in \mathbb{R}^m$ is the estimated probability for each class by softmax, m is the number of target classes, and λ is the coefficient of $L2-$ regularization. Training is done by stochastic gradient descent over shuffled mini-batches.

4 Experiments

4.1 Datasets

The proposed model is evaluated on six public datasets: AG, Yelp_F, Yelp_P, SST-2, TREC and MR. Summary statistics of the datasets are listed in Table 1.

Table 1. Summary statistics for the datasets. Length means the truncated sentence length and CV means there is no standard train/test split and thus 10-fold cross validation is conducted.

	Dataset	Classes	Length	Train	Test
Short text	SST-2	2	45	6920	1821
	TREC	6	20	5452	500
	MR	2	45	10662	CV
Long text	AG	4	60	120k	7600
	Yelp_F	5	300	650k	50k
	Yelp_P	2	150	560k	38k

4.2 Word Embeddings

In order to enhance the feature expression of text, we take as input two different types of word embeddings. The first is the Glove embedding trained by [20] on 6 billion tokens of Wikipedia 2014 and Gigaword5. Words are initialized by randomly sampling from uniform distribution in $[-0.5, 0.5]$, if not appear in the set of pre-trained words. And the second is the Word2vec embedding which is only an embedding layer in this model. Finally, these two types word embeddings will be trained along with all the weights of the model to improve the performance of classification.

4.3 Hyper-parameter Settings

Because the maximum length of text in different data sets is different, we set a truncation length for each datasets, as shown in Table 1. The dimensions of the two types of word embeddings are glove 300 and word2vec 200. And we set the hidden units of the both two BiLSTM to 200, the units of FC layers to 256, the learning rate to 0.003 with SGD optimizer. We use 128 convolutional filters each for window size 2,3,4,5. For regularization, we apply Dropout [32] operation with dropout rate of 0.6 for the BiLSTM layer and 0.5 for the FC layers, and we also use l2 with coefficient 0.01 over the parameters.

4.4 Baselines and Main Results

We benchmark the following baseline methods for sentence-level classification.

- DSCNN [33], Dependency Sensitive Convolutional Neural Networks, this model first uses LSTM for building textual representations and subsequently extracting features with convolutional operators.
- VeryDeep-CNN* [12], A CNN based model, by increasing the number of convolutional layers (up to 29 layers) to capture the dependencies between long sequences.
- CNN [34], The earliest model to introduce CNN to the field of natural language processing, which uses only one convolutional layer for classification.
- FastText [35], A simple but fast shallow neural network classifier.
- WE, A classification model similar to FastText.
- MCTC-dense [6], This model uses different temporal filters of convolution, which vary in size, to capture different contextual features.

The main results are listed in Table 2. In the task of short text, compared with the other five models, our model has the best effect on the data set TREC, with an accuracy 98.8%, which is 3.4% higher than the second-best model DSCNN. It can be seen that simply relying on a single LSTM for feature extraction and then classifying by CNN does not solve the problem of the lack of text semantics and kernel adaption. At the same time, the accuracy of ACK-MCR on the dataset MR is also slightly higher than other models, especially on FastText and WE up to nearly 6%. And on the dataset SST-2, ACK-MCR is also close to the other five models. On long text, the proposed model is better than the other five models, and its accuracy is improved by 1.9%, 0.2% and 0.8% respectively compared with the corresponding second-best. It is clearly that, contrasted with the classic CNN model, the accuracy of ACK-MCR on three datasets is higher than 3%, which shows that single CNN model has no ability to capture the long-distance text feature. For the Very-Deep CNN model, simply increasing the depth of the convolutional layer does not effectively improve the feature extraction capability of the model, and finally obtains a high classification accuracy, especially on long text.

Table 2. Classification accuracy on several popular standard benchmarks.

Short text	MR	SST-2	TREC	Long text	AG	Yelp_F	Yelp_P
DSCNN	81.5%	89.1%	95.4%	VeryDeep-CNN*	91.3%	64.7%	95.4%
CNN	81.5%	87.2%	93.6%	CNN	91.6%	61.0%	93.5%
FastText	75.0%	83.0%	89.7%	FastText	91.5%	60.4%	93.9%
WE	74.3%	82.5%	89.2%	WE	91.1%	58.3%	93.1%
MCTC-dense	80.5%	86.1%	93.0%	MCTC-dense	92.2%	65.7%	96.2%
ACK-MCR	82.1%	87.9%	98.8%	ACK-MCR	94.5%	66.2%	96.8%

4.5 Multi-channel and Attention Analysis

In order to verify the reliability of the multi-channel feature representation method and convolution kernel adaptive design proposed in this paper, we carry out an experimental analysis on a series of derivative models of ACK-MCR.

As shown in Fig. 4, the proposed model ACK-MCR integrating multi-channel feature representation and convolution kernel adaptation is better than the other two derived models. From the perspective of multi-channel feature representation, although the ACK-SCR and ACK-MCR have both introduced adaptive kernel design, the latter are significantly better than the former in accuracy. While ACK-SCR incorporates adaptive kernel technology, it uses a sing-channel representation method, which results in lower accuracy than MCR. Hence, it can be concluded that the two techniques proposed in this paper can improve the accuracy of text classification.

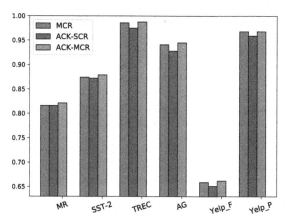

Fig. 4. The results of derivative models. **MCR** means that the model only uses multi-channel representation, and performs max-pooling after convolution, followed by classification. The different between **ACK-SCR** and **ACK-MCR** is reflected in that **ACK-SCR** uses only on fused channel for feature representation.

5 Conclusion

In this paper, we propose a BiLSTM-CNN model equipped with adaptive convolution kernel and multi-channel representations for text classification. Through BiLSTM, the model can extract features from a global perspective, while multi-channel feature maps can also express richer semantic information. By multi-scale feature attention, the model can adaptively select the appropriate combination of convolution kernels to improve the matching degree with the target sequence. And finally, the model shows a competitive performance on six benchmark datasets.

Acknowledgements. This work was supported partly by the National Science Foundation of China under Grants No.61967006 and No.61562027, the project of Jiangxi Provincial Department of Education under Grants No. GJJ180321.

References

1. Zhang, L., Lin, L., Liang, X., He, K.: Is faster R-CNN doing well for pedestrian detection? In: Leibe, B., Matas, J., Sebe, N., Welling, M. (eds.) ECCV 2016. LNCS, vol. 9906, pp. 443–457. Springer, Cham (2016). https://doi.org/10.1007/978-3-319-46475-6_28
2. Garg, R., Vijay Kumar, B.G., Carneiro, G., Reid, I.: Unsupervised CNN for single view depth estimation: geometry to the rescue. In: Leibe, B., Matas, J., Sebe, N., Welling, M. (eds.) ECCV 2016. LNCS, vol. 9912, pp. 740–756. Springer, Cham (2016). https://doi.org/10.1007/978-3-319-46484-8_45
3. Chiu, C.C., Sainath, T.N., Wu, Y., et al.: State-of-the-art speech recognition with sequence-to-sequence models. In: IEEE International Conference on Acoustics, Speech and Signal Processing (ICASSP), pp. 4774–4778. IEEE (2018)
4. Collobert, R., Weston, J., Karlen, M., Kavukcuoglu, K., Kuksa, P.: Natural language processing (almost) from scratch. J. Mach. Learn. Res. **12**(1), 2493–2537 (2011)
5. Lee, J.Y., Dernoncourt, F.: Sequential Short-Text Classification with Recurrent and Convolutional Neural Networks (2016)
6. Xu, J., Zhang, C., Zhang, P., Song, D.: Text classification with enriched word features. In: Geng, X., Kang, B.-H. (eds.) PRICAI 2018. LNCS (LNAI), vol. 11013, pp. 274–281. Springer, Cham (2018). https://doi.org/10.1007/978-3-319-97310-4_31
7. Yao, D., Bi, J., Huang, J., Zhu, J.: A word distributed representation based framework for large-scale short text classification. In: Proceedings of International Joint Conference on Neural Networks (2015)
8. Ding, Z., Xia, R., Yu, J., Li, X., Yang, J.: Densely connected bidirectional LSTM with applications to sentence classification. In: Zhang, M., Ng, V., Zhao, D., Li, S., Zan, H. (eds.) NLPCC 2018. LNCS (LNAI), vol. 11109, pp. 278–287. Springer, Cham (2018). https://doi.org/10.1007/978-3-319-99501-4_24
9. Nowak, J., Taspinar, A., Scherer, R.: LSTM recurrent neural networks for short text and sentiment classification. In: Rutkowski, L., Korytkowski, M., Scherer, R., Tadeusiewicz, R., Zadeh, L.A., Zurada, J.M. (eds.) ICAISC 2017. LNCS (LNAI), vol. 10246, pp. 553–562. Springer, Cham (2017). https://doi.org/10.1007/978-3-319-59060-8_50
10. Bai, X.: Text classification based on LSTM and attention. In: Thirteenth International Conference on Digital Information Management (ICDIM), pp. 29–32. IEEE (2018)
11. Zhang, X., Zhao, J., LeCun, Y.: Character-level convolutional networks for text classification. In: NIPS, pp. 649–657 (2015)

12. Conneau, A., Schwenk, H., Barrault, L., Lecun, Y.: Very deep convolutional networks for natural language processing. In: EACL (2017)
13. Yin, W., Schütze, H.: Multichannel variable-Size convolution for sentence classification. In: Proceedings of the Nineteenth Conference on Computational Natural Language Learning (2015)
14. Johnson, R., Zhang, T.: Effective use of word order for text categorization with convolutional neural networks. arXiv preprint arXiv:1412.1058 (2014)
15. Wang, S., Huang, M., Deng, Z.: Densely connected CNN with multi-scale feature attention for text classification. In: IJCAI, pp. 4468–4474 (2018)
16. Wang, J., Wang, Z., Zhang, D., Yan, J.: Combining knowledge with deep convolutional neural networks for short text classification. In: IJCAI, pp. 2915–2921 (2017)
17. Lin, Z., et al.: A structured self-attentive sentence embedding. In: ICLR (2017)
18. Tao, C., Feng, R., Yulan, H.: Improving sentiment analysis via sentence type classification using BiLSTM-CRF and CNN. Expert Syst. Appl. **72**(15), 221–231 (2017)
19. Sainath, T.N., Vinyals, O., Senior, A.W., Sak, H.: Convolutional, long short-term memory, fully connected deep neural networks. In: Proceedings of the 2015 IEEE International Conference on Acoustics, Speech and Signal Processing, pp. 4580–4584. IEEE, Piscataway (2015)
20. Pennington, J., Socher, R., Manning, C.D.: Glove: global vectors for word representation. In: EMNLP, vol.14, pp. 1532–1543 (2014)
21. Wang, D., Gong, J., Song, Y.: W-RNN: news text classification based on a weighted RNN. arXiv preprint arXiv:1909.13077 (2019)
22. Li, W., Qi, F., Tang, M., et al.: Bidirectional LSTM with self-attention mechanism and multi-channel features for sentiment classification. Neurocomputing **387**, 63–77 (2020)
23. Liu, Y., Ji, L., Huang, R., et al.: An attention-gated convolutional neural network for sentence classification. Intell. Data Anal. **23**(5), 1091–1107 (2019)
24. Xia, W., Zhu, W., Liao, B., et al.: Novel architecture for long short-term memory used in question classification. Neurocomputing **299**, 20–31 (2018)
25. Zhou, P., Shi, W., Tian, J., et al.: Attention-based bidirectional long short-term memory networks for relation classification. In: Proceedings of the 54th Annual Meeting of the Association for Computational Linguistics (vol. 2: Short papers), pp. 207–212 (2016)
26. Devlin, J., Chang, M.W., Lee, K., et al.: Bert: pre-training of deep bidirectional transformers for language understanding. arXiv preprint arXiv:1810.04805 (2018)
27. Cheng, D., Gong, Y., Zhou, S., et al.: Person re-identification by multi-channel parts-based CNN with improved triplet loss function. In: Proceedings of the IEEE Conference on Computer Vision and Pattern Recognition, pp. 1335–1344 (2016)
28. Ruder, S., Ghaffari, P., Breslin, J.G.: Character-level and multi-channel convolutional neural networks for large-scale authorship attribution. arXiv preprint arXiv:1609.06686 (2016)
29. Xu, K., et al.: Mixup-based acoustic scene classification using multi-channel convolutional neural network. In: Hong, R., Cheng, W.-H., Yamasaki, T., Wang, M., Ngo, C.-W. (eds.) PCM 2018. LNCS, vol. 11166, pp. 14–23. Springer, Cham (2018). https://doi.org/10.1007/978-3-030-00764-5_2
30. Ioffe, S., Szegedy, C.: Batch normalization: accelerating deep network training by reducing internal covariate shift. In: ICML (2015)
31. Nair, V., Hinton, G.E.: Rectified linear units improve restricted boltzmann machines. In: ICML, pp. 807–814 (2010)
32. Hinton, G.E., Srivastava, N., Krizhevsky, A., Sutskever, I., Salakhutdinov, R.R.: Improving neural networks by preventing co-adaptation of feature detectors. arXiv preprint arXiv:1207.0580 (2012)
33. Zhang, R., Lee, H., Radev, D.R.: Dependency sensitive convolutional neural networks for modeling sentences and documents (2016)

34. Kim, Y.: Convolutional neural networks for sentence classification. In: EMNLP, pp. 1746–1751 (2014)
35. Joulin, A., Grave, E., Bojanowski, P., et al.: Bag of tricks for efficient text classification. arXiv preprint arXiv:1607.01759 (2016)

Text Generation in Discrete Space

Ting Hu$^{(\boxtimes)}$ and Christoph Meinel

Hasso Plattner Institute, University of Potsdam, Potsdam, Germany
{ting.hu,meinel}@hpi.de

Abstract. Variational AutoEncoders (VAEs) are applied to many generation tasks while suffering from posterior collapse issue. Vector Quantization (VQ) is recently employed in VAE model on image generation, which could get rid of the posterior collapse problem and show its potentiality for more generation tasks. In this paper, the VQ method is applied to VAE on text generation. We elaborately design the model architecture to mitigate the index collapse issue brought in by VQ process. Experiments show that our text generation model can achieve better reconstruction and generation performance than other VAE based approaches.

Keywords: Text generation · Vector quantization · Variational autoencoder

1 Introduction

Text generation is important for many Natural Language Processing (NLP) tasks, such as machine translation, dialogue system, and text summarization. In general, there are two classes of approaches to generate text, Generative Adversarial Networks (GANs) [4] and Variational AutoEncoders (VAEs) [10]. GANs generally suffer from training instability, while VAEs seem promising in generating coherent texts, therefore leading to a wide range of applications [11,21,22].

Although VAE models achieve lots of success in many generation tasks, they still suffer from the "posterior collapse" problem which limits its wider potential applications. Recently proposed VQ-VAE-2 model [18] that combines Vector Quantization (VQ) with VAE, is capable of getting over posterior collapse and achieves state-of-the-art performance in image generation, which makes us wonder how VQ method can benefit VAE model in text generation task.

In this paper, we apply the VQ approach to VAE model to generate texts. However, we encounter the problem of "index collapse", which has a negative impact on the performance of text generation model. [8,19] propose several strategies to mitigate the issue, while requiring complicated network parameters update mechanism. We propose that the index collapse issue can be drastically alleviated through well-designed network architecture, and good text reconstruction and generation results will be achieved.

The rest of this paper is organized as follows: After discussing related work in Sect. 2, Sect. 3 introduces VQ-VAE model and our strategy to mitigate the index

© Springer Nature Switzerland AG 2020
I. Farkaš et al. (Eds.): ICANN 2020, LNCS 12397, pp. 721–732, 2020.
https://doi.org/10.1007/978-3-030-61616-8_58

collapse issue. This is followed by experiments and conclusion. We summarize our main contributions as:

- Apply Vector Quantization VAE to text generation task.
- Significantly alleviate the index collapse issue accompanying with Vector Quantization process.
- A comprehensive evaluation of several VAE based text generation models through both traditional and recently proposed metrics.

2   Related Work

Variational AutoEncoder [10] is one type of generative models of which the goal is to generate data similar to real data. The model consists of an encoder parameterized by ϕ and a decoder parameterized by θ. The encoder inferences the distribution of latent variables z, conditioned on real data x. Latent variables z are supposed to be some unobservable intrinsic factors determining samples. The decoder, usually called generative network, reconstructs input data according to the distribution of latent variables. The whole VAE model works to maximize the marginal log-likelihood $\log p_\theta(x)$, which can be achieved by maximizing its Evidence Lower BOund (ELBO):

$$L(\theta, \phi; x) = E_{q_\phi(z|x)}[\log p_\theta(x|z)] - D_{KL}(q_\phi(z|x)||p_\theta(z)). \qquad (1)$$

The first term in $L(\theta, \phi; x)$ is the log probability of the reconstruction of input conditioned on latent variables z, with z sampled from posterior distribution $q_\phi(z|x)$. The second term is the negative KL divergence between $q_\phi(z|x)$ and prior distribution $p_\theta(z)$, which works as a regularizer, keeping the posterior close to the prior distribution. In general, $p_\theta(z)$ is assumed to be standard Gaussian distribution.

The first VAE model for text generation is proposed by [1]. They identify the "posterior collapse" problem, that the decoder tends to depend less on latent vectors and turns to be a strong auto-regressive model, that is, intrinsic latent information is not efficiently encoded into the latent variables. KL cost annealing and word dropout strategies are employed in alleviating the issue. Then [25] replaces the decoder of VAE with a dilated Convolution Neural Network (CNN) to control the tradeoff between decoder contextual capacity and latent information dependence. [9] attributes the problem to the gap between the marginal log-likelihood and its ELBO, and proposes semi-amortized VAE (SA-VAE), which uses conventional VAE to initialize model parameters and run stochastic variational inferences to refine them. These methods manage to enhance the decoder's dependence on latent information but accompanied by a decline in generation quality.

As another category of generative models, GANs also attract much research attention. GANs consist of a generator G and a discriminator D, where D is trained to distinguish real data from fake data, while G is trained to generate data that is real enough to fool D. Since generation is conducted during adversarial training, GANs fail to shed light on the latent information distribution as VAEs do. This naturally leads to the idea, how about combining these two types of models together. [13] proposes Adversarial AutoEncoder (AAE), in which besides the encoder-decoder architecture, an extra discriminator is used to distinguish whether the latent vector is originated from a specific prior distribution. Adversarial Regularized AutoEncoder (ARAE) [26] employs an additional adversarial network to learn the posterior distribution, where the generator generates latent vectors, and the discriminator distinguishes whether given vectors are real or fake. Considering that these two models comprise the basic encoder-decoder structure, we include them in the scope of discussion in this paper.

3   Vector Quantization Variational AutoEncoder

Different from VAE model, where an input sentence is encoded into a latent vector approximating standard Gaussian distribution, the core idea of VQ-VAE [16] is to encode a sentence into a discrete latent vector, of which distribution is approximated by a prior model.

The architecture of VQ-VAE is illustrated in Fig. 1, consisting of an encoder E, a decoder D, and a latent embedding dictionary e. A bidirectional LSTM is adopted as the encoder, with input sequence $x = [x_1, x_2, \ldots, x_n]$ of length n, and produces a sequence of hidden states $E(x) = [h_1, h_2, \ldots, h_n]$. The latent embedding dictionary can be defined as $e = \{e_j\}_{j=1}^{K}$, where K denotes the number of embedding vectors. Then Vector Quantization is performed, that each hidden state h_i is mapped to an embedding vector e_k through nearest-neighbor lookup, where

$$k = argmin_j ||h_i - e_j||_2^2. \tag{2}$$

Hence, $E(x)$ can be represented as a discrete latent vector $d = [d_1, d_2, ..., d_n]$, where $d_i, i \in [1, n]$ refers to the discrete index k corresponding to hidden states h_i. The decoder, a unidirectional LSTM, is then expected to reconstruct x, with a sequence of embedding vectors $z(e) = [e_{d_1}, e_{d_2}, ..., e_{d_n}]$ as input. Since each $e_{d_i}, i \in [1, n]$ is used as the step-wise input of the decoder, the problem of posterior collapse can be effectively avoided through such a decoding mechanism.

However, the Vector Quantization process described above is non-differentiable. To backpropagate the gradient, a straight-through gradient estimation strategy [16] can be used. To be specific, the gradient of the loss with respect to the decoder input is regarded as the gradient of the loss with respect to the encoder output. Hence, the training objective of VQ-VAE is as follows [16]:

$$L = \log p(x|D(z(e))) + ||sg[E(x)] - e||_2^2 + \beta||E(x) - sg[e]||_2^2 \tag{3}$$

where "sg" denotes stop gradient operator, $D(z(e))$ denotes the decoder output, β is the weight hyper-parameter.

Moreover, with such a structure, the model is merely capable of reconstructing input sequence. How to obtain novel discrete latent vectors as the input of

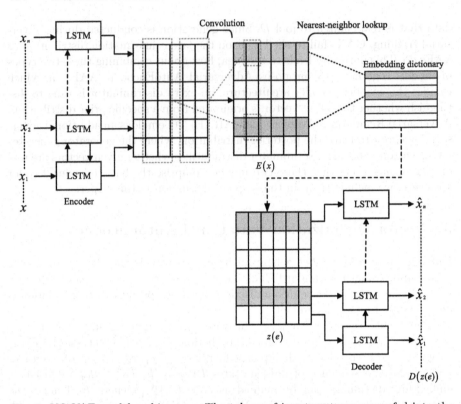

Fig. 1. VQ-VAE model architecture. The tokens of input sentence x are fed into the LSTM encoder, producing a sequence of hidden states, on which a two-dimensional convolution operation is performed. The transformed hidden states are substituted by their respective nearest neighbors in the embedding dictionary and then used as the input of the decoder targeting at reconstructing the input. In other words, the input sentence is encoded into a discrete latent vector, where each element is the index of the nearest neighbor of each hidden state, which is called Vector Quantization process.

decoder is to be considered. The straight forward solution is to employ a prior model to learn the distribution of discrete latent vectors and generate novel discrete vectors for the decoder to generate texts. As strong auto-regressive models, both Recurrent Neural Network [15] and Transformer [23] can be the candidate. Experiments show that the Transformer model is outperformed by RNN, which can be explained that learning discrete latent vectors distribution is similar to training a language model, while self-attention and positional encoding mechanism in Transformer are inefficient to incorporate significant word-level context to language modeling and result in worse language modeling performance [24].

Besides all these considerations, we encounter "index collapse" issue accompanying the Vector Quantization process. Index collapse indicates that after training VQ-VAE model, the number of distinct discrete indexes occurring in all discrete latent vectors is far less than the embedding dictionary size K, namely a low utilization ratio. The issue has further influenced the training of the prior model, ultimately leads to poor generation quality. Several methods are proposed to alleviate the issue. [8] comes up with two strategies to make more efficient use of embedding vectors: divide encoder output into smaller slices corresponding to several distinct sliced embedding dictionaries; project encoder output into one smaller subspace. [19] uses soft Expectation Maximization (EM) algorithm as the training strategy to train VQ-VAE. [7] introduces improved semantic hashing technique to propagate gradients through discrete representation. These methods either make the network structure more complex or back-propagate the gradient in more sophisticated manners.

Since [6] verifies that hidden states of RNN tend to form clusters. And based on the observation that the Vector Quantization process is similar to clustering, we analyze that the index collapse phenomenon arises because the information in hidden states is insufficiently extracted for clustering. In order to combine more information across different time steps and different dimensions of hidden states, we apply a two-dimensional convolution neural network to the output of the encoder as plotted in Fig. 1, which dramatically raise the utilization ratio of discrete indexes (embedding vectors). In the best case, the utilization ratio can reach 100% indicating the vanishing of the index collapse issue and good generation quality is achieved.

4 Experiments

In this section, we follow the work of [2] and compare VQ-VAE with other VAE related text generation models on two datasets.

4.1 Datasets

The first dataset is Stanford Natural Language Inference (SNLI) corpus, which is a collection of sentence pairs labeled as entailment, contradiction, and neural. We ignore these labels and collect all different sentences with the 5000 most common words in the dataset, resulting in 500k distinct sentences. Among these sentences, 10k sentences are randomly chosen for testing, and others are used for training.

The second dataset is Quora Kaggle challenge dataset, which contains 400k sentence pairs with labels indicating whether they are duplicate questions. We ignore labels and fetch all separate sentences, hold out 10k sentences as test set and others are used as training set.

In experiments, sentences in both datasets are tokenized by Stanford CoreNLP [14] and then lowercased. For SNLI dataset, the vocabulary size is 5k and the maximum sentence length is 20. For Quora Kaggle challenge dataset, the vocabulary size is truncated to 20k and the maximum sentence length is set to 25.

4.2 Models

Models compared with VQ-VAE are VAE, AAE [13] and ARAE [26]. In VAE model, KL cost annealing and word dropout are employed as [1]. For ARAE, we use the implementation provided by [26]. For a fair comparison, all models have the same architecture of one-layer LSTM encoder and decoder. The hidden state is 256-dimensional and word embedding is 300-dimensional with Glove embedding initiation. The latent vector is of size 64. Models are trained up to 30 epochs with a batch size of 100 and a learning rate of 10^{-3}.

Besides these common settings among models, the specific component of VQ-VAE is set as follows. Embedding vectors are of size 64, initialized by uniform distribution. And the prior model is one-layer LSTM with 128-dimensional hidden states. The weight parameter β and the embedding dictionary size K are finetuned for different datasets.

4.3 Metrics

For all models trained by given datasets, we evaluate them in two aspects: reconstruction and generation [2].

For reconstruction, only the encoder-decoder component of each model is used. After training, we take sentences in test set as encoder input and take the decoder output as reconstructed sentences. Metrics BLEU [17], ROUGE [12], and Fréchet Distance(FD) [5] are computed between the encoder input and reconstructed sentences. BLEU and ROUGE evaluate sentence-level reconstruction, and FD measures corpus-level reconstruction quality. FD is firstly used to measure image generation quality through measuring the distance of generated data distribution and real data distribution. When employing FD to sequence distribution, we use a pre-trained general sentence embedding model InferSent [3] to encode each sentence into a 4096-dimensional vector, therefore FID is used to refer to FD below.

For generation, the decoder of different models is used as the generative model, and random sentences are generated based on their corresponding generation mechanism, respectively. Forward cross-entropy [2], Reverse cross-entropy and FID are used as evaluation metrics. Forward cross-entropy evaluates the quality of generated sentences, computed by

$$E_{p_{data}(x)}[-\log p_G(x)], \tag{4}$$

where $p_{data}(x)$ denotes the real data distribution, and $p_G(x)$ denotes the distribution of generated sentences. In order to approximate $p_G(x)$, for each text generation model, we take 100k generated samples to train one RNN language model and evaluate on test set. Reverse cross-entropy measures the diversity of generated texts, calculated by

$$E_{p_G(x)}[-\log p_{data}(x)]. \tag{5}$$

We use Wikipedia corpus to train an RNN language model to estimate $p_{data}(x)$, and evaluate on this model using 10k sentences generated from each model.

Table 1. Evaluation results for different models on SNLI dataset. LM stands for language model. ↑ means higher is better, ↓ means lower is better. The reverse score lower than that of real data indicates mode collapse occurs.

Model	Generation			Reconstruction		
	Forward ↓	Reverse ↓	FID ↓	BLEU ↑	ROUGE ↑	FID ↓
Real data	1.842	3.567	0.353			
LM	1.876	3.691	0.353			
VAE	2.131	**2.985**	0.533	0.622	**0.880**	0.329
ARAE	**1.943**	3.494	0.421	0.037	0.175	0.361
AAE	3.246	3.468	1.785	0.114	0.505	0.567
VQ-VAE	1.975	3.622	**0.374**	**0.636**	0.866	**0.293**

FID is capable of capturing both quality and diversity of generated sentences by computing the distance between the distribution of real sentence embeddings and that of generated sentence embeddings [20].

4.4   Results and Analysis

As discussed before, the utilization ratio of embedding vectors after training is crucial for generation performance. In our implementation, when encountering the index collapse issue, the maximum utilization ratio can only reach 20%, which deprives the model of the capability of generating coherent sentences, in this case, the evaluation results are not listed below. Once the two-dimensional convolution neural network is employed, β could vary in a considerably wide range, meanwhile, maintain utilization ratio to be 100%, much higher than other strategies [8], and the model generates coherent sentences.

For SNLI dataset, comparisons of different models on multiple evaluation metrics are summarized in Table 1. For VQ-VAE model, weight β is set to 10.0 and the embedding dictionary size K is 1000. For generation diversity, VAE, ARAE, and AAE obtain lower reverse cross-entropy than real data, which signifies mode collapse [2], that is, models generate a limited diversity of samples. VQ-VAE achieves the lowest FID and slightly higher reverse cross-entropy than real data, indicating the highest diversity in generated sentences. In terms of generating quality, though outperformed by ARAE, VQ-VAE still gets a better result than other methods in forward cross-entropy, which suggests its capability of generating high-quality texts. With regard to reconstruction, good performances in metrics BLEU and ROUGE indicate that VQ-VAE is good at sentence-to-sentence reconstruction. And its lowest FID score shows its ability to reconstruct the whole data distribution. In conclusion, VQ-VAE outperforms other models, considering both generation and reconstruction evaluation metrics.

For Quora Kaggle challenge dataset, generation and reconstruction performance of different models are listed in Table 2. For VQ-VAE model, weight β

Table 2. Evaluation results for different models on Quora Kaggle challenge trainset. LM stands for language model. ↑ means higher is better, ↓ means lower is better. The reverse score lower than that of real data indicates mode collapse occurs.

Model	Generation			Reconstruction		
	Forward ↓	Reverse ↓	FID ↓	BLEU ↑	ROUGE ↑	FID ↓
Real data	2.013	2.791	0.232			
LM	2.669	2.852	0.267			
VAE	3.100	3.664	0.474	0.387	0.685	0.288
ARAE	**2.732**	**2.620**	0.324	0.043	0.144	0.489
AAE	3.148	3.743	0.363	0.046	0.211	0.342
VQ-VAE	2.735	2.938	**0.278**	**0.553**	**0.783**	**0.190**

is set to 5.0 and the embedding dictionary size K is 2048. Regarding generation, ARAE gets the best generation quality in terms of forward cross-entropy. Nevertheless, its lower reverse cross-entropy than real data indicates that mode collapse occurs. In contrast, VQ-VAE gets a comparative forward cross-entropy to ARAE and its lowest FID indicating that VQ-VAE can generate both high-quality and diverse texts. For reconstruction, VQ-VAE outperforms other methods on all metrics. To summarize, VQ-VAE performs better than other models on Quora Kaggle challenge dataset.

We attribute the superior reconstruction performance and decent generation capability of the VQ-VAE model to introducing Vector Quantization process. Other VAE related models manage to deal with the contradiction between latent information dependence and generation capability, where the former indicates good reconstruction results while the latter is on the contrary. In the VQ-VAE model, more information is encoded into the latent vector through the embedding dictionary, which makes it easier to reconstruct the input. And the generation task is transferred to the prior model, which learns the distribution of discrete latent vectors and generates novel ones. As a result, VQ-VAE outperforms other models in terms of comprehensive performance.

Table 3. Example of discrete latent vectors and their corresponding sentences on Quora Kaggle challenge trainset. Two instances of index repetition and two instances of index swap are shown.

Operation	Discrete latent vectors and sentences
Index repetition	[1243, 1084, 863, 1559, **629**, 225, 1537, 1705]
	how can one learn to become a beginner?
	[1243, 1084, 863, 1559, **1559**, 225, 1537, 1705]
	how can one learn free as a beginner?
	[1243, 308, 1349, 624, **851**, 1307, 501, 570]
	how do I improve my spoken English?
	[1243, 308, 1349, 624, **624**, 1307, 501, 570]
	how do I improve English spoken English?
Index swap	[278, 308, **385**, 2001, 1734, **1395**, 266, 50]
	when do we use instagram?
	[278, 308, **1395**, 2001, 1734, **385**, 266, 50]
	when do use instagram use?
	[1003, 10, **372**, 901, 612, **1274**, 1624, 1294]
	what are the advantages of presence?
	[1003, 10, **1274**, 901, 612, **372**, 1624, 1294]
	what are google's advantages of the same?

4.5 Discussion

According to the model architecture, due to the existence of two-dimensional convolution layer, each discrete index in the discrete latent vector could correspond to wider-range local information rather than merely token-wise information. It will be interesting to know what discrete indexes indicate and how they interact with one another. Several discrete latent vectors and their corresponding decoded sentences are displayed in Table 3. We implement index repetition and index swap in discrete latent vectors. If one index corresponds to one word or one phrase, the same word or phrase should appear after index repetition, while the results turn out to be different. The phenomenon demonstrates that although each index represents some local information across words, the order of latent indexes still matters. Regarding index swap, we exchange the value of two latent indexes, and the corresponding sentences turn to be merely partially changed. If we regard index repetition and index swap as errors occurring in the decoding process, then it can be said that the VQ-VAE model is, to some degree, capable of correcting decoding errors rather than accumulating errors as other autoregressive models do, which indicates its robustness.

We list some generated sentences from different models in Table 4. For SNLI dataset, we randomly select five sentences containing the word "standing" from the generated results of each model. For Quora dataset, five sentences beginning

Table 4. Generated sentences from different models containing the word "standing" for SNLI dataset, and beginning with the word "what" for Quora Kaggle challenge trainset. Models tend to produce higher-quality sentences on SNLI dataset, of which sentence structure and pattern are relatively simpler.

	SNLI
VAE	young man wearing a headscarf are standing
	a boy is standing in the backyard
	the person is standing behind his high camera
	two couple standing in front of the water
	a man and girl standing next to a green beach
ARAE	two women are standing beside the building
	here in the picture the woman is standing by the bus
	the man is standing
	a very small dog standing in front of a large sun
	a japanese group of people are standing and laugh
AAE	a man in black is standing in the middle of the street
	child in a blue shirt is standing on a bridge
	a man is standing on a rock wall
	there's a woman is standing in the living room
	someone in a black shirt and black pants is standing.
VQ-VAE	the man is standing with his family
	the people are standing around the beach
	three women are standing outside performing
	the young men are standing on the sidewalk
	the woman is standing on a tree with paper flags
	Quora
VAE	what should i prepare to setting a server?
	what does it mean in president and?
	what is integer greatest problem?
	what should i use free about aging idea?
	what is the advantages to having military?
ARAE	what does a girl look like for her interviews?
	what is the best logic to predict a future?
	what are the oldest computer science fiction?
	what is the best thing to do not on quora?
	what are some of the best ways to learn java?
AAE	what is the idea thing like unix?
	what is the greatest will and damage math rate?
	what can i do for gixxer overpopulation?
	what are the countries like a simplilearn?
	what are the brothers to bliss?
VQ-VAE	what is the best way to learn german?
	what is your favorite metallica policy?
	what is subprime analysis?
	what are some of the best hindi movies to watch?
	what is the best place to live in the united states?

with the word "what" are randomly picked up for each model. To some extent, each model could generate coherent sentences and it's difficult to distinguish the quality and diversity of generated sentences from different models only by observation, which makes it necessary to use evaluation metrics.

5 Conclusion

In this paper, we apply Vector Quantization to Variational AutoEncoder on text generation task. For the index collapse issue that follows, we elaborately design the model architecture and drastically alleviate it. Experiments on two datasets show that our model outperforms other VAE based text generation models on reconstruction and generation. We also take a deeper analysis of the interpretable meaning of discrete latent vectors, that each discrete index corresponds to some local semantic information, which endows the model with robustness.

For future work, we want to further improve the performance of the model on text generation, for example, through hierarchical discrete latent vectors. Additionally, introducing a conditional signal to guide topic-specified text generation could be interesting.

References

1. Bowman, S.R., Vilnis, L., Vinyals, O., Dai, A., Jozefowicz, R., Bengio, S.: Generating sentences from a continuous space. In: Proceedings of The 20th SIGNLL Conference on Computational Natural Language Learning, Berlin, Germany, pp. 10–21. Association for Computational Linguistics, August 2016. https://doi.org/10.18653/v1/K16-1002
2. Cífka, O., Severyn, A., Alfonseca, E., Filippova, K.: Eval all, trust a few, do wrong to none: comparing sentence generation models. arXiv preprint arXiv:1804.07972 (2018)
3. Conneau, A., Kiela, D., Schwenk, H., Barrault, L., Bordes, A.: Supervised learning of universal sentence representations from natural language inference data. arXiv preprint arXiv:1705.02364 (2017)
4. Goodfellow, I., et al.: Generative adversarial nets. In: Advances in Neural Information Processing Systems, pp. 2672–2680 (2014)
5. Heusel, M., Ramsauer, H., Unterthiner, T., Nessler, B., Hochreiter, S.: GANs trained by a two time-scale update rule converge to a local Nash equilibrium. In: Advances in Neural Information Processing Systems, pp. 6626–6637 (2017)
6. Hou, B.J., Zhou, Z.H.: Learning with interpretable structure from RNN. arXiv preprint arXiv:1810.10708 (2018)
7. Kaiser, L., Bengio, S.: Discrete autoencoders for sequence models. arXiv preprint arXiv:1801.09797 (2018)
8. Kaiser, L., et al.: Fast decoding in sequence models using discrete latent variables. arXiv preprint arXiv:1803.03382 (2018)
9. Kim, Y., Wiseman, S., Miller, A.C., Sontag, D., Rush, A.M.: Semi-amortized variational autoencoders. arXiv preprint arXiv:1802.02550 (2018)
10. Kingma, D.P., Welling, M.: Auto-encoding variational Bayes. arXiv preprint arXiv:1312.6114 (2013)

11. Li, P., Lam, W., Bing, L., Wang, Z.: Deep recurrent generative decoder for abstractive text summarization. arXiv preprint arXiv:1708.00625 (2017)
12. Lin, C.Y.: ROUGE: a package for automatic evaluation of summaries. In: Text Summarization Branches Out, pp. 74–81 (2004)
13. Makhzani, A., Shlens, J., Jaitly, N., Goodfellow, I., Frey, B.: Adversarial autoencoders. arXiv preprint arXiv:1511.05644 (2015)
14. Manning, C.D., Surdeanu, M., Bauer, J., Finkel, J.R., Bethard, S., McClosky, D.: The Stanford CoreNLP natural language processing toolkit. In: Proceedings of 52nd Annual Meeting of the Association for Computational Linguistics: System Demonstrations, pp. 55–60 (2014)
15. Mikolov, T., Karafiát, M., Burget, L., Černocký, J., Khudanpur, S.: Recurrent neural network based language model. In: Eleventh Annual Conference of the International Speech Communication Association (2010)
16. van den Oord, A., Vinyals, O., et al.: Neural discrete representation learning. In: Advances in Neural Information Processing Systems, pp. 6306–6315 (2017)
17. Papineni, K., Roukos, S., Ward, T., Zhu, W.J.: BLEU: a method for automatic evaluation of machine translation. In: Proceedings of the 40th Annual Meeting of the Association for Computational Linguistics, pp. 311–318 (2002)
18. Razavi, A., Oord, A.v.d., Vinyals, O.: Generating diverse high-fidelity images with VQ-VAE-2. arXiv preprint arXiv:1906.00446 (2019)
19. Roy, A., Vaswani, A., Neelakantan, A., Parmar, N.: Theory and experiments on vector quantized autoencoders. arXiv preprint arXiv:1805.11063 (2018)
20. Semeniuta, S., Severyn, A., Gelly, S.: On accurate evaluation of GANs for language generation. arXiv preprint arXiv:1806.04936 (2018)
21. Shen, X., Su, H., Niu, S., Demberg, V.: Improving variational encoder-decoders in dialogue generation. In: Thirty-Second AAAI Conference on Artificial Intelligence (2018)
22. Su, J., Wu, S., Xiong, D., Lu, Y., Han, X., Zhang, B.: Variational recurrent neural machine translation. In: Thirty-Second AAAI Conference on Artificial Intelligence (2018)
23. Vaswani, A., et al.: Attention is all you need. In: Advances in Neural Information Processing Systems, pp. 5998–6008 (2017)
24. Wang, C., Li, M., Smola, A.J.: Language models with transformers (2019)
25. Yang, Z., Hu, Z., Salakhutdinov, R., Berg-Kirkpatrick, T.: Improved variational autoencoders for text modeling using dilated convolutions. In: Proceedings of the 34th International Conference on Machine Learning, vol. 70, pp. 3881–3890. JMLR. org (2017)
26. Zhao, J.J., Kim, Y., Zhang, K., Rush, A.M., LeCun, Y., et al.: Adversarially regularized autoencoders. In: ICML, pp. 5897–5906 (2018)

Short Text Processing for Analyzing User Portraits: A Dynamic Combination

Zhengping Ding[1,2], Chen Yan[1,2], Chunli Liu[1,2], Jianrui Ji[1,2], and Yezheng Liu[1,2(✉)]

[1] School of Management, Hefei University of Technology, Hefei 230009,
Anhui, People's Republic of China
liuyezheng@hfut.edu.cn
[2] Key Laboratory of Process Optimization and Intelligent Decision Making,
Ministry of Education, Hefei 230009, Anhui, China

Abstract. The rich digital footprint left by users on the Internet has led to extensive researches on all aspects of Internet users. Among them, topic modeling is used to analyze text information posted by users on websites to generate user portraits. For dealing with the serious sparsity problems when extracting topics from short texts by traditional text modeling methods such as Latent Dirichlet Allocation (LDA), researchers usually aggregate all the texts published by each user into a pseudo-document. However, such pseudo-documents contain a lot of irrelevant topics, which is not consistent with the documents published by people in reality. To that end, this paper introduces the LDA-RCC model for dynamic text modeling based on the actual text, which is used to analyze the interests of forum users and build user portraits. Specifically, this combined model can effectively process short texts through the iterative combination of text modeling method LDA and robust continuous clustering method (RCC). Meanwhile, this model can automatically extract the number of topics based on the user's data. In this way, by processing the clustering results, we can obtain the preferences of each user for deep user analysis. A large number of experimental results show that the LDA-RCC model can obtain good results and is superior to both traditional text modeling methods and short text clustering benchmark methods.

Keywords: Topic model · User portraits · Short texts · Dynamic combination

1 Introduction

In recent years, user analysis has been a productive area of research. This is mainly due to the large number of users who leave their digital footprints on social platforms. To make full use of the user's various text information to build a comprehensive and accurate user portrait, more researchers have adopted the topic-based portrait method. For instance, Blei et al. proposed a Latent Dirichlet allocation (LDA) algorithm for text analysis, which is also one of the most well-known topic modeling algorithms [1]. However, with the rise of social conversations, the text messages left by users on the Internet are getting shorter and shorter. If such short text data is directly applied to the LDA model,

© Springer Nature Switzerland AG 2020
I. Farkaš et al. (Eds.): ICANN 2020, LNCS 12397, pp. 733–745, 2020.
https://doi.org/10.1007/978-3-030-61616-8_59

it will encounter serious sparse problems. To solve these problems, Yan et al. learned the topic by directly modeling the generation of co-occurrence patterns (i.e., double words) in the entire corpus [2]. Kar et al. used a hierarchical Poisson-Dirichlet process (PDP) for text modeling to analyze short texts and study social networks [3]. The most common method currently is to merge all the text of the same user into one fixed pseudo document. Unfortunately, such a processing method not only cannot keep the subject originally described in each short document but also does not conform to the interests of the user in reality. Inspired by Zuo et al. [4], we propose a topic model for user portraits, which is used to improve the quality of the topics extracted from the data of the forum, thereby facilitating the portrait of the user preferences. We introduce a clustering method to reduce the problem of sparsity and obtain the final result by iterating. Specifically, we propose the LDA-RCC model which exploits the idea of dynamic text modeling. First, all short texts published by the same user are aggregated into a pseudo-document. The topic is obtained by the LDA algorithm and the clustering algorithm is used to cluster short texts. Since the similarity of the subject described by a document is high in reality, to comply with the actual situation, we aggregate similar short texts into a pseudo document as the input of the next cycle. When the clustering results are stable, we summarize the extracted topics in words. Then we analyze the user's preference for these aspects [5]. Our work mainly has the following aspects: First, we propose a new topic model for user portraits and introduce a clustering method when performing topic modeling. This treatment for short documents is more in line with the actual situation. Secondly, we verify that the result of the proposed topic model has higher quality and can better solve the problem of data sparsity to make more precise and accurate user portraits.

The rest of this article is arranged as follows. In the second section, we review the literature on user portraits, topic modeling, and short text processing. In the third part, we describe the mechanism of the proposed topic model in detail and describe how to use the results of the topic model to make user portraits. In the fourth part, we introduce the experimental results and compare the quality of the topics and the accuracy of the user portrait obtained by the proposed model. In the last part, we explain the significance of this research and describe future research directions.

2   Related Work

The focus in marketing management is to understand the consumer, and the most important thing to understand the consumer is to collect available data and build user profiles [6]. Since Cooper first proposed the concept of user portraits [7], researchers have carried out in-depth research on user portraits from various aspects, such as using web log information [8], using questionnaires to collect information and conduct psychological analysis [9]. Sumner et al. used LIWC to examine the language of 537 Facebook users and introduced more open citations for semantic analysis [10]. Schwartz and others applied the method of differential language analysis. They distinguished users from topics and psychological attributes based on texts posted by 75,000 users on Facebook [11]. In the analysis of users, topic models are beginning to emerge. Puranam et al. used topic models to analyze menu information to obtain the impact of government regulations on users [12]. Liu et al. applied text mining with latent Dirichlet allocation (LDA) and analyze user sentiment [13].

Similarly, many researchers have also proposed a topic-based portrait method, which extracts topics from user-published text to obtain user preferences to further study behavioral preferences and characteristics in a specific area. Michelson et al. Extracted topics from Twitter. They used a textual knowledge base to disambiguate Twitter and finally built a user portrait based on the frequency of entity classification [14]. Abel and others adopted a user portrait method based on topic tags and user entities [15]. Liu et al. calculated the user's interest topics and built a portrait model that incorporated the user's interest through the Dirichlet model. But when the information published by the user is too little or the number of users' fans is not enough, the accuracy of mining user interests is poor [16]. It is precisely because of the large number of short text data sets emerging in social media that it becomes increasingly important to mine useful topics from them. Wang et al. proposed a sparseTM model. They randomly selected subsets of words and defined topics on these subsets, then built models based on the uncertainty of probability [17]. Weng et al. used the LDA method to refine the topics and built a relationship network between Twitters based on the extracted topics. To deal with Twitter's sparseness, they merged all the Twitter posts made by users into pseudo-documents [18]. However, in reality, an article will not describe multiple unrelated topics. Similarly, Hong et al. proposed several schemes to train a basic topic model on the aggregated text to achieve better results [19]. Unlike non-parametric hierarchical Bayesian models, Cheng et al. learned the topic of short texts by directly modeling the biterms in the entire corpus [20]. Phan et al. proposed the idea of obtaining external knowledge to make data richer and easier to process [21]. Yin et al. proposed a folded Gibbs sampling algorithm called DMM, which can not only extract topics hidden in short texts but also cluster short documents [22]. Since users' comments on the website are short texts, we adopted the idea of clustering. We not only find topics from short documents by constructing pseudo-documents that are closer to real documents but also introduce a clustering algorithm to obtain user preferences.

3   Proposed Approach

In this section, we describe the proposed user portrait method in detail. Figure 1 summarizes the system steps used to obtain the user portrait on the car-home website in this study. We first perform data cleaning, which is essential for generating a meaningful topic model. Then we take the approach of iterating until the result is stable. We aggregate each user's short texts into lengthy pseudo-documents before training the standard topic model in the first loop. We next conduct topic modeling on the forum information and get the topic each word belongs to. After statistical analysis, we get the short documents -Topic(DT) matrix which describes the probability that each short document belongs to each topic. We consider each row of the matrix as a vector describing the short text. Then, we use a robust continuous clustering method (RCC) to cluster the short texts of each user. We aggregate the short texts in the same cluster into new lengthy pseudo-documents as a new input for the second loop. The difference in two times of clustering results is measured by normalized mutual information score (NMI-score).

The loop terminates while the NMI-score is stable. As shown in the figure, the same preferences are expressed in the same color. The darker the color of user preference clustering results, the stronger the user preference in this aspect. To visualize and analyses the user's preference, we make the word cloud based on their reviews on the forum.

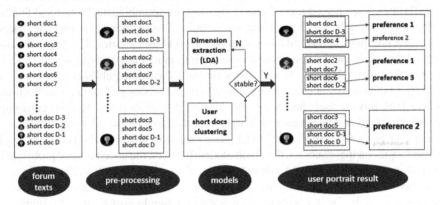

Fig. 1. Short document analytic techniques.

3.1 Pre-processing Text

To avoid the interference of noisy words, we first perform data cleaning for topic modeling. We removed non-textual data, such as URL addresses, and emoticons that are not meant for topic modeling. Then we introduce a car dictionary to tokenize the text. This operation can divide the text into atomic elements while introducing a car dictionary so that car-related terms are not separated [23]. Then we eliminate stop words that are useless for topic modeling. However, comments which are too short are not valuable for analysis, we delete short text that contains fewer than five words. After pre-processing, we consider the result as texts used for statistical analysis.

3.2 User Preference Extraction

The LDA algorithm is used to analyze online forum texts. LDA model is a generative probabilistic model for collections of discrete data such as text corpora. Formally, the terms in the LDA model are defined as follows:

T is the number of total topics.

U is the number of total users while I_u is the number of total short documents of user u.

$D = \sum_{u=1}^{U} I_u$ is the number of total short documents.

A corpus is a collection of D documents, each one indexed by $\{1, 2, ..., D\}$.

A word is the basic unit of discrete data, defined as an element from a vocabulary indexed by $\{1, ..., V\}$.

We aggregate each user's short texts into lengthy pseudo-documents. Then we get M pseudo-documents while at this time M = U. The terms we define are as follows:

$|J_u^l|$ denotes the index of a pseudo-document of user u while J_u^l is the clustering of I_u sample labels of user u in the iteration $l (l \in \{1, 2, \ldots, L\})$.

$M^l = \sum_{u=1}^{U} |J_u^l|$ is the number of total pseudo-documents in the iteration l and M^l changes continuously during iteration.

The pseudo-document m^l is a sequence of N_{m^l} words denoted by $w = \left\{ w_1, \ldots, w_n, \ldots, w_{N_{m^l}} \right\}$, where w_n is the n-th word in the pseudo-document.

LDA algorithm makes no assumptions about the structure or grammar properties of texts. As a result, each document can be considered as a probability distribution of topics and each topic k_t can be considered as a probability distribution of words in forum texts. Figure 2 shows how the LDA model finds topics where α and β are hyperparameters that obey the Dirichlet distribution. Parameters θ represent the polynomial distribution association relationship between each pseudo-document and T topics. Parameters ϕ represent the polynomial distribution association relationship between each topic and N_{m^l} words. For each word in pseudo-document m^l, we sample z from the polynomial distribution θ and sample w from the polynomial distribution ϕ. We repeat this process $\sum_{m=1}^{M^l} N_{m^l}$ times and form pseudo-document m^l. The shadow part in Fig. 2 for the variable represents observable variables, whereas non-shadows parts for the variables represent latent variables. The box represents repeated sampling and the number of sampling times is written in the lower right corner. By learning parameter θ and ϕ of each pseudo-document, we can get information about which topics the author usually concerns. The results are shown in three matrices:

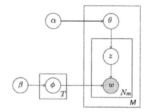

Fig. 2. Graphical model of LDA.

1. M^lT, a $M^l \times$ T matrix, where M^l is the number of pseudo-documents in the iteration l. M^lT matrix describes the probability of which topic each pseudo-document belongs to.
2. VT, a V × T matrix, where V is the number of unique words used in the forum information. VT matrix describes the probability which topic each unique word belongs to.
3. DT, a D × T matrix, where D is the number of short documents. DT matrix describes the probability which topic each short document belongs to.

3.3 User Interest Aggregation

However, the aggregated results cannot describe user preferences in detail. On the one hand, it is more realistic to classify and aggregate many similar short texts published by users. Therefore, each row of the DT matrix is considered as a T-dimensional vector describing the short text. We cluster these vectors to get clusters containing one or more vectors. The greater the amount of short text contained in a cluster, the stronger the user's preference for this aspect. On the other hand, compared to Weng et al. making each document correspond to a twitterer [18], we make multiple similar pseudo-documents correspond to a user through clustering. This is equivalent to analyzing multiple long texts published by users with similar preferences, which is more conducive to get detailed and realistic portraits of users.

We choose the Robust Continuous Clustering (RCC) algorithm in which the number of clusters does not need to be known. In the previous section, we obtain the DT matrix and each pseudo-documents can be considered as a probability distribution of topics. The input is denoted by $d_{u,i_u} = [p_{d_{u,i_u},k_1}, \ldots \ldots, p_{d_{u,i_u},k_T}]$ where p_{d_{u,i_u},k_t} is the probability that the short document d_{u,i_u} of user u describes the topic k_t and $i_u \in \{1, 2, \ldots, I_u\}$. In the RCC model, p_{d_{u,i_u},k_t} has a unique representative. By optimizing these representatives we obtain the final result. In the final result, these representatives come together to show the potential clustering structure in the data. Therefore, it is not necessary to know the number of clusters in advance [24]. In all short documents posted by user u, similar short documents will be clustered into a cluster.

3.4 User Portrait Discovery

The LDA algorithm loops through sampling until it stabilizes, so the results of each time are different. When we only aggregate all the short texts of the users into a single document to run the model, the clustering results are very rough. Although the LDA model will have different results in each loop, most short texts describing similar topic distributions will still be clustered into the same cluster. But there are still a few short documents that will be affected. Through the iteration, we can not only get more detailed results but also can determine the final attribution of short texts in different clusters in the results of each iteration. Therefore, we aggregate all the short documents of user u in the same cluster into a pseudo-document. Then we get new M^l pseudo-documents while at this time $M^l \geq U$. We continue to use the LDA and RCC model to get results. We normalize the mutual information to measure the similarity of this and previous clustering results. Mutual Information (MI) is a measure of the similarity between two labels of the same data. The entropy of the two clustering results of user u in the iteration l and l-1(l > 1) is $H(J_u^l)$ and $H(J_u^{l-1})$:

$$H\left(J_u^l\right) = \sum_{j_u^l=1}^{|J_u^l|} \frac{|j_u^l|}{I_u} \log\left(\frac{|j_u^l|}{I_u}\right) \tag{1}$$

$$H\left(J_u^{l-1}\right) = \sum_{j_u^{l-1}=1}^{|J_u^{l-1}|} \frac{|j_u^{l-1}|}{I_u} \log\left(\frac{|j_u^{l-1}|}{I_u}\right) \tag{2}$$

where j_u^l is a cluster of user u in the iteration l and j_u^{l-1} is a cluster of user u in the iteration l-1. The mutual information between J_u^l and J_u^{l-1} is defined as

$$MI\left(J_u^l, J_u^{l-1}\right) = \sum_{j_u^l=1}^{\left|J_u^l\right|} \sum_{j_u^{l-1}=1}^{\left|J_u^{l-1}\right|} P\left(j_u^l, j_u^{l-1}\right) \log\left(\frac{P\left(j_u^l, j_u^{l-1}\right)}{\frac{\left|j_u^l\right|}{I_u} \frac{\left|j_u^{l-1}\right|}{I_u}}\right) \tag{3}$$

where

$$P\left(j_u^l, j_u^{l-1}\right) = \frac{\left|J_u^l \cap J_u^{l-1}\right|}{I_u} \tag{4}$$

Normalized Mutual Information (NMI) is a normalization of the MI score to scale the results between zero and one which represents no mutual information and perfect correlation respectively. The NMI-Score is:

$$NMI\left(J_u^l, J_u^{l-1}\right) = \frac{MI\left(J_u^l, J_u^{l-1}\right)}{\sqrt{H\left(J_u^l\right)H\left(J_u^{l-1}\right)}} \tag{5}$$

Normalized Mutual Information (NMI) is a commonly used indicator in machine learning algorithms and we stipulate that when the calculation result of each user is greater than 0.6, the user's preference can be considered to have stabilized. Then we use cosine similarity to measure the similarity between short documents in the same cluster. We suppose that d_{u,i_u} and d'_{u,i_u} are the topic distributions of two short documents in the same cluster. The similarity between them is

$$Similarity\left(d_{u,i_u}, d'_{u,i_u}\right) = \frac{\sum_{t=1}^{T} p_{d_{u,i_u},k_t} p'_{d_{u,i_u},k_t}}{\sqrt{\sum_{t=1}^{T}\left(p_{d_{u,i_u},k_t}\right)^2 \sum_{t=1}^{T}\left(p'_{d_{u,i_u},k_t}\right)^2}} \tag{6}$$

When the similarity value between short documents in a cluster is greater than 0.8, we consider the clustering result is stable and stop iterating.

4 Experimental Results

4.1 Dataset

The dataset used in the experiment is crawled by visiting the user detail information page on the car-home website (https://www.autohome.com.cn). In the ten months from April 2018 to January 2019, we obtained a total of 1,040,768 comments from 89,491 users. Users are at different ages and distribute throughout China. The vast majority of comments contain less than 80 words, which is considered as short texts. Figure 3 is a histogram showing the number of users and the total amount of short text posted by a user. Among a total of 1,040,768 texts published by 89,491 users, users with a total of short texts which contain words less than 10 accounts for 63.28% of all users. Figure 4 shows the statistics of the number of short texts and the number of words contained in the short texts. We find that 996 users publish a large number of short texts containing more words. So we choose them as the dataset.

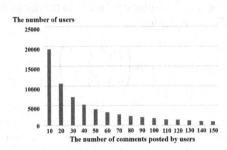

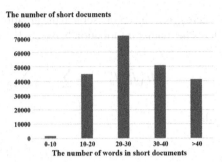

Fig. 3. Statistics of the comments posted.   **Fig. 4.** The number of words in texts.

4.2   User Preference Extraction Results

We set 30 topics in the model. We name a topic by looking for a logical connection of two words on the same topic. After identifying the candidate topic name, we further tested it using logical connections to other words in the top distribution list. Table 1 shows all topic names and keywords related to these topics. The remaining topic names are "Exterior and feel", "Company brand", "Relatives and friends", "Style", "Second-hand car", "Ask for mutual assistance", "Widget sound", "Purchase experience", "Subjective feelings", "Business administration", "Purchasing time and quantity", "Maintenance time and kilometers", "Riders", "Software", "Air conditioner", "Manufacturer", "Drive type", "Suggestions", "Oil maintenance", "Transmission type".

4.3   User Preference Clustering Results

As described above, each row of the DT matrix we obtained is considered as a vector describing the probability which topic each short document belongs to. We cluster these vectors and we calculate the NMI-score of the clustering results of this iteration and the last iteration starting from the second generation. We also calculate the similarities between short documents in the same clusters to measure the similarity of them. When the NMI-score of each user is greater than 0.6 and all the similarities are greater than 0.8, it can be considered that the user's preference has stabilized and the iteration is terminated. Based on the stable clustering results, we make his preference word cloud map for each user. Figure 5 shows the word cloud describing the preferences of each user. The greater the number of short texts describing the user's preference, the bigger and bolder the preference word appears in the word cloud.

4.4   Comparative Analysis

Clustering Results Analysis. Figure 6 shows six short documents of each of the three classes in the preference clustering results of user *u*. Each topic in the stacked bar chart is displayed in a different color, and its length represents the magnitude of the probability. It can be seen from cluster A that the topic probability distributions of these short texts are similar. However, in clusters B and C, the color distribution is different from that in cluster A. This shows that the short documents in different clusters have different topic

Table 1. Name of topics of short documents.

Topic	Words
配件(Accessories)	钥匙(Key) 座椅(Seat) 后备箱(Trunk) 后视镜(Rearview Mirror) 仪表盘(Dashboard)
购买方式与价格 (Purchase way and price)	价格(Price) 优惠(Discount) 销售(Sales) 贷款(Loan) 便宜(Cheap)
地点(Place)	北京(Peking) 天津(Tianjin) 地方(Place) 上海(Shanghai) 工作地点(Workplace)
自驾游(Self-driving travel)	自驾(Self-driving) 生活(Life) 漂亮(Pretty) 不错(Nice) 游记(Travel Notes)
能源与技术(Automotive energy)	电池(Battery) 充电(Charging) 能源(Energy) 续航(Endurance) 燃油(Fuel)
改装零件(Modified parts)	车轮(Wheels) 改装(Modification) 大灯(Headlights) 原厂(Original) 喇叭(Horn)
油耗(Fuel consumption)	公里(Kilometer) 速度(Speed) 市区(Urban) 燃油(Fuel) 驾驶(Driving)
论坛交流(Forum exchange)	车主(Owner) 帖子(Post) 水军(Astroturfers) 图片(Picture) 回复(Repeat)
故障(Malfunction)	声音(Sound) 发动机(Engine) 抖动(Jitter) 故障(Failure) 检查(Check)
驾驶规则(Driving regulations)	停车(Stop) 违章(Violate) 举报(Report) 事故(Accident) 车道(Driveway)

Fig. 5. Word cloud of user preference for three users.

distributions. The topic distribution of short documents is different between clusters while it is similar in the same cluster.

Topic Quality Comparison. We use coherence as an index to measure the quality of the topic and compare four cases [25]. Topic coherence is used to identify flawed topics that do not rely on references outside of training data. We first input short texts directly into the LDA model without aggregating. Then we aggregate short texts by users. Each user corresponds to a pseudo-document and is used as input to the LDA model. We then adopted the DMM algorithm, which is an algorithm that processes short texts to obtain topics and can cluster short texts. Finally, we use the LDA-RCC model to obtain the text topic and perform user portraits. We select the first 10 words to calculate the coherence

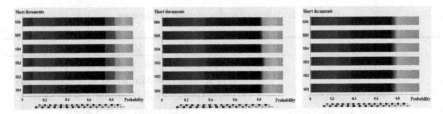

Fig. 6. Topic distribution of short documents in cluster A, B, C of user u.

value of each topic corresponding to the topic extraction task. To be consistent with the LDA-RCC algorithm, we set all algorithms to the same number of topics when making comparisons, and set α to 50/K and $\beta = 0.01$ which are defined in Sect. 3.2. The results of the topic comparison are shown in Table 2.

Table 2. The coherence values of three algorithms.

Topic Number	LDA (with short texts)	LDA (with pseudo-documents)	DMM	LDA-RCC
20	−198.2602	−157.9289	−136.4822	−81.6170
30	−196.3452	−156.1905	−134.6653	−77.6984
40	−195.7384	−155.0746	−114.8646	−81.6295
50	−193.2462	−151.5630	−122.5287	−82.0068

Table 2 shows the comparison of coherence values for each algorithm. As shown in the table, LDA-RCC achieves the best performance in each case. LDA remains stable across all topic number settings. When we use the LDA algorithm to process short texts, we find that the topic quality is poor, and the coherence value is around −200. When we aggregate the text into pseudo-documents according to users, the quality of the topic improved, and the coherence value was around −150. When we aggregate short texts published by a user into multiple pseudo-documents based on similarity, the quality of the topic is significantly higher. This shows that this processing method is not only in line with the actual situation, but also can achieve better results. Compared with the DMM algorithm, the quality of the topics obtained by the LDA-RCC combined model is also improved. This shows that compared with short text clustering algorithms, the combined model can still get better topics. This finding shows that the LDA-RCC algorithm can achieve better performance on the quality of topics.

User Portrait Comparison. Subfigures a, b, c, d in Fig. 7 respectively show user portraits obtained by four users using two methods. The word cloud generated by the LDA-RCC method is on the left, and the word cloud generated by the DMM algorithm is on the right. As shown in the figure, the word cloud generated by the LDA-RCC method is denser and can show more information to the user. In Fig. 7(a), the DMM algorithm analysis shows that the user prefers "Oil", "Power", "Engine", "Sound", and "Wheels".

It can be seen that the user's biggest preference is related to "oil". In the results of the LDA-RCC algorithm, "Oil maintenance" also accounts for the largest proportion, but we use malfunction to summarize the words "Engine". Also in Fig. 7(b), we find that "power" in the user portrait obtained by the DMM algorithm also accounts for the largest proportion. "Oil" and "Forum" are also shown in the user portraits obtained by the LDA-RCC algorithm. However, "Power" accounts for the largest proportion on the right while "Forum exchange" accounts for the largest proportion on the left. This is because power describes too much due to rough division. In Fig. 7(c), we can see that "Sound", "oil" and "Driving" are highlighted in the DMM algorithm, which corresponds to the user portrait obtained by the LDA-RCC algorithm. However, "Exterior and feel" is directly ignored, and the proportion of "Accessories" is small, which indicates that the results of the DMM algorithm are not detailed. As shown in Fig. 7(d), "Oil" accounts for a large proportion of the DMM algorithm results. "Place" and "driving regulations" are more important while they are not highlighted. In summary, the DMM algorithm is relatively rough for user portraits, while the LDA-RCC algorithm is more accurate for user portraits.

Fig. 7. Comparison results of the two algorithms.

5   Conclusions and Future Work

In this paper, we design a new algorithm for processing short text for user portraits. Our experiments demonstrate the superiority of the LDA-RCC algorithm over many existing benchmarks which is the basis for large but unstructured online reviews [26]. Then we use the results of the topic model to analyze and portrait users to make accurate user portraits. However, the difficulty of obtaining forum data makes us only able to analyze users of the Autohome website. The introduced clustering algorithm may also affect the running time of the model. In future research, we consider other clustering algorithms to explore better accuracy and higher performance.

References

1. Blei, D.M., Ng, A.Y., Jordan, M.I., Lafferty, J.: Latent Dirichlet allocation. J. Mach. Learn. Res. **3**, 993–1022 (2003)
2. Yan, X., Guo, J., Lan, Y., Cheng, X.: A biterm topic model for short texts. In: Proceedings of the 22nd International Conference on World Wide Web, pp. 1445–1456 (2013)
3. Lim, K.W., Chen, C., Buntine, W.: Twitter-network topic model: a full Bayesian treatment for social network and text modeling. arXiv preprint arXiv:1609.06791 (2016)
4. Zuo, Y., et al.: Topic modeling of short texts: a pseudo-document view. In: Proceedings of the 22nd ACM SIGKDD International Conference on Knowledge Discovery and Data Mining, pp. 2105–2114 (2016)
5. Liu, J., Toubia, O.: A semantic approach for estimating consumer content preferences from online search queries. Market. Sci. **37**, 930–952 (2018)
6. Thomaz, F., Salge, C., Karahanna, E., Hulland, J.: Learning from the Dark Web: leveraging conversational agents in the era of hyper-privacy to enhance marketing. J. Acad. Mark. Sci. **48**(1), 43–63 (2019). https://doi.org/10.1007/s11747-019-00704-3
7. Amato, G., Straccia, U.: User profile modeling and applications to digital libraries. In: Abiteboul, S., Vercoustre, A.-M. (eds.) ECDL 1999. LNCS, vol. 1696, pp. 184–197. Springer, Heidelberg (1999). https://doi.org/10.1007/3-540-48155-9_13
8. Nasraoui, O., Soliman, M., Saka, E., Badia, A., Germain, R.: A web usage mining framework for mining evolving user profiles in dynamic web sites. IEEE Trans. Knowl. Data Eng. **20**, 202–215 (2007)
9. Zhou, M.X., Wang, F., Zimmerman, T., Yang, H., Haber, E., Gou, L.: Computational discovery of personal traits from social multimedia. In: IEEE International Conference on Multimedia and Expo Workshops (ICMEW), pp. 1–6. IEEE (2013)
10. Sumner, C., Byers, A., Shearing, M.: Determining personality traits and privacy concerns from facebook activity. Black Hat Brief. **11**, 197–221 (2011)
11. Schwartz, H.A., et al.: Personality, gender, and age in the language of social media: The open-vocabulary approach. PLoS One **8**, e73791 (2013)
12. Puranam, D., Narayan, V., Kadiyali, V.: The effect of calorie posting regulation on consumer opinion: a flexible latent Dirichlet allocation model with informative priors. Market. Sci. **36**, 726–746 (2017)
13. Liu, X., Burns, A.C., Hou, Y.: An investigation of brand-related user-generated content on Twitter. J. Advert. **46**, 236–247 (2017)
14. Michelson, M., Macskassy, S.A.: Discovering users' topics of interest on Twitter: a first look. In: Proceedings of the Fourth Workshop on Analytics for Noisy Unstructured Text Data, pp. 73–80 (2010)
15. Abel, F., Gao, Q., Houben, G.-J., Tao, K.: Analyzing user modeling on Twitter for personalized news recommendations. In: Konstan, Joseph A., Conejo, R., Marzo, José L., Oliver, N. (eds.) UMAP 2011. LNCS, vol. 6787, pp. 1–12. Springer, Heidelberg (2011). https://doi.org/10.1007/978-3-642-22362-4_1
16. Liu, Q., Niu, K., He, Z., He, X.: Microblog user interest modeling based on feature propagation. In: 2013 Sixth International Symposium on Computational Intelligence and Design, pp. 383–386. IEEE (2013)
17. Wang, C., Blei, D.M.: Decoupling sparsity and smoothness in the discrete hierarchical Dirichlet process. In: Advances in Neural Information Processing Systems, pp. 1982–1989. (2009)
18. Weng, J., Lim, E.-P., Jiang, J., He, Q.: Twitterrank: finding topic-sensitive influential Twitterers. In: Proceedings of the third ACM International Conference on Web Search and Data Mining, pp. 261–270 (2010)

19. Hong, L., Davison, B.D.: Empirical study of topic modeling in Twitter. In: Proceedings of the First Workshop on Social Media Analytics, pp. 80–88 (2010)

20. Cheng, X., Yan, X., Lan, Y., Guo, J.: Btm: Topic modeling over short texts. IEEE Trans. Knowl. Data Eng. **26**, 2928–2941 (2014)

21. Phan, X.-H., Nguyen, L.-M., Horiguchi, S.: Learning to classify short and sparse text & web with hidden topics from large-scale data collections. In: Proceedings of the 17th International Conference on World Wide Web, pp. 91–100 (2008)

22. Yin, J., Wang, J.: A Dirichlet multinomial mixture model-based approach for short text clustering. In: Proceedings of the 20th ACM SIGKDD International Conference on Knowledge Discovery and Data Mining, pp. 233–242 (2014)

23. Xu, C., Zhang, H., Lu, B., Wu, S.: Local community detection using social relations and topic features in social networks. In: Sun, M., Wang, X., Chang, B., Xiong, D. (eds.) CCL/NLP-NABD -2017. LNCS (LNAI), vol. 10565, pp. 371–383. Springer, Cham (2017). https://doi.org/10.1007/978-3-319-69005-6_31

24. Shah, S.A., Koltun, V.: Robust continuous clustering. Proc. Natl. Acad. Sci. **114**, 9814–9819 (2017)

25. Mimno, D., Wallach, H., Talley, E., Leenders, M., McCallum, A.: Optimizing semantic coherence in topic models. In: Proceedings of the 2011 Conference on Empirical Methods in Natural Language Processing, pp. 262–272 (2011)

26. Feldman, R., Sanger, J.: The Text Mining Handbook: Advanced Approaches in Analyzing Unstructured Data. Cambridge University Press, Cambridge (2007)

A Hierarchical Fine-Tuning Approach Based on Joint Embedding of Words and Parent Categories for Hierarchical Multi-label Text Classification

Yinglong Ma[1]([✉]), Jingpeng Zhao[1], and Beihong Jin[2]

[1] School of Control and Computer Engineering, North China Electric Power University,
Beijing 102206, China
yinglongma@ncepu.edu.cn
[2] Institute of Software, Chinese Academy of Sciences, Beijing 100190, China
beihongjin@iscas.cn

Abstract. Many important classification problems in real world consist of a large number of categories. Hierarchical multi-label text classification (HMTC) with higher accuracy over large sets of closely related categories organized in a hierarchical structure or taxonomy has become a challenging problem. In this paper, we present a hierarchical fine-tuning deep learning approach for HMTC, where a joint embedding of words and their parent categories is generated by leveraging the hierarchical relations in the hierarchical structure of categories and the textual data. A fine tuning technique is applied to the Ordered Neural LSTM (ONLSTM) neural network such that the text classification results in the upper levels are able to help the classification in the lower ones. The extensive experiments were made over two benchmark datasets, and the results show that the method proposed in this paper outperforms the state-of-the-art hierarchical and flat multi-label text classification approaches, in particular the aspect of reducing computational costs while achieving superior performance.

Keywords: Text classification · Multi-label classification · Word embedding · Hierarchical fine tuning

1 Introduction

As the number of textual documents drastically increases, many important classification problems in real world consist of a large number of categories. These categories are usually very similar, and further organized into a hierarchical structure or taxonomy. The typical examples of large hierarchical text repositories are web directories (e.g., The Open Directory Project/DMOZ[1]), medical classification schemes (e.g., Medical Subject Headings[2]), the library and patent classification scheme[3], and the Wikipedia

---

[1] https://www.dmoz-odp.org/.
[2] https://meshb.nlm.nih.gov/treeView.
[3] https://www.loc.gov/aba/cataloging/classification/.

© Springer Nature Switzerland AG 2020
I. Farkaš et al. (Eds.): ICANN 2020, LNCS 12397, pp. 746–757, 2020.
https://doi.org/10.1007/978-3-030-61616-8_60

topic classifications[4], etc. Text classification (TC) is to automatically classify textual data into categories so that information system users can more easily retrieve, extract, and manipulate information to recognize latent patterns and discover knowledge. It is generally treated as a supervised machine learning problem, where we can train a model from several examples and further utilize this model to classify a previously unseen piece of text. In the last decades, the traditional TC tasks have been widely used in many applications such as automatic email categorization and spam detection, etc., but they generally work well in problems with only two or a small number of well-separated categories and are inadequately in cases where there are a large number of classes and attributes to cope with [1]. The text classification problem with higher accuracy over large sets of closely related categories is inherently difficult [2], which has become a challenging task.

Hierarchical multi-label text classification (HMTC) [3] is towards structured text classification problem with a large number of usually very similar categories in a hierarchical structure, where a text piece must correspond to one or more nodes of a taxonomic hierarchy. Each category corresponds to a node in the hierarchy, and all categories are closely related in terms of the hierarchical structure. Currently, some flat classifiers ignore the hierarchical structure by "flattening" it to the leaf nodes level for multi-label text classification, and therefore are subject to the problems similar to the traditional TCs. Undoubtedly, the hierarchical structure information is crucial for building efficient HMTC algorithms to improve text classification accuracy in case that a large number of categories/classes and attributes need to be handled.

Recently, HMTC typically has two main kinds of approaches [2, 3], namely local and global approaches. The local approaches create a unique classifier for each node/each parent node/each level in the taxonomy, while global approaches create a single classifier for the entire taxonomy. First, the state-of-the-art of local approaches for HMTC is HDLTex [4], which shows superior performance over traditional non-neural-based models with a top-down structure. However, it has relatively higher computation cost and suffers from the problem of tremendous parameter variables possibly causing parameter explosion (similar to other local approaches). On the other hand, the state of the art of global approaches for HMTC is based on a unified global deep neural network model [5], in which a unified global deep neural-based text classifier (HATC) that relieves the problem of model parameter explosion. Unfortunately, HATC generally suffers from the inherent disadvantage of global approaches: the classifier constructed is not flexible enough to cater for dynamic changes to the category structure [6]. Second, many experimental observations including HATC and HDLTex have illustrated that the accuracy of many HMTC approaches are not always better than that of some flat classifiers [2, 7]. Just similar to the work in [5], we argue that the inherent information residing in a category hierarchy/taxonomy, e.g., semantic association between different levels in the hierarchy, should be carefully analyzed, and HMTC should be fine-tuned with the aid of these inherent information for classification with high accuracy. At last, most of existing approaches for HMTC often use some neural network models such as CNN and LSTM, etc. These models are often suitable for learning a chain structure on the text, but they are difficult to deal with the hierarchically structured text, especially for the situation

---

[4] https://en.wikipedia.org/wiki/Portal:Contents/Categories.

where smaller units (e.g., phrases) are nested within larger units (e.g., clauses). So some new models should be adopted to actually cater for the hierarchically structured text for HMTC.

In this paper, aiming at the problems mentioned above, we present a hierarchical fine-tuning deep learning approach for HMTC, which is an HMTC local approach. A joint embedding approach of words and parent categories are utilized by leveraging the hierarchical relations in the hierarchical structure of categories and the textual data. A fine tuning technique is applied to the neural network called Ordered Neural LSTM (ONLSTM) [8] such that the text classification results in the upper levels should contribute to the classification in the lower ones. The extensive experiments were made over two benchmark datasets, and the results show that the method proposed in this paper is very competitive with the state-of-the-art hierarchical and flat multi-label text classification approaches at significantly lower computational cost while maintaining higher performance.

This paper is organized as follows. Section 1 is the Introduction. In Sect. 2, we discuss the related work about HMTC. In Sect. 3, we briefly give the overview of our HMTC approach, and described how the words and parent categories are jointly embedded and how the fine tuning is made in details. In Sect. 4, extensive experiments were made over two benchmark textual datasets in comparison with the state-of-the-art multi-label approaches for illustrating the effectiveness and efficiency of our approach. Section 5 is the conclusion.

2   Related Work

The key problem of HMTC is how to make better use of the hierarchical relationship of categories to improve classification performance [3]. Deep learning based text classification approaches [9–12] have achieved surpassing performance in comparison to the previous machine learning algorithms [13, 14] in text classification.

In the last decades, HMTC has mainly covered two aspects [2, 3]: local approaches and global approaches. The typical global HMTC approaches [15–18] are mostly based on the specific flat model, and rely on the static, human curated features as input. A single classification model is built on the training set, which is usually relatively complex [3, 6]. The whole hierarchical structure of categories is considered in one run of the classification algorithm. The advantage of learning a single global model for all categories is that the total parameter scale of the global classification model is usually much smaller than that of all local models learned by any local classification method. However, because the number of training data per category in a lower level is much smaller than that in an upper level, the discriminant features for the parent categories may not be discriminant in the subcategories. In this situation, it is usually difficult for the global approaches to use different feature sets in different levels of categories. In addition, the global classifiers constructed may not be flexible enough to cater for changes to the hierarchical structure of categories [3, 6].

The typical local HMTC approaches [19–23] often use the hierarchy structure to build classifiers based on local information of the hierarchy. In the top-down manner, the local HMTC approaches can be subdivided into three subgroups according to the way of using local information in the training phase: local classifier per node (LCN), local classifier per parent node (LCPN) and local classifier per level (LCL). LCN trains a binary classifier for each child node, LCPN trains a multi-class classifier for each parent node, and LCL trains a multi-class classifier for the entire hierarchy level. What the top-down local approaches adopt is essentially a strategy for avoiding category-prediction inconsistencies across class levels during the testing phase when a local hierarchical classifier is used [3]. The disadvantage of local approaches is that the error propagates of classification from the higher level categories to the lower level categories. When the classifiers go deeply into the hierarchy, error propagation will cause more and more significant performance degradation [24].

What is most similar to our work is the work in HDLTex [4], HATC [5] and HFT-CNN [25]. Both approaches HDLTex and HATC successfully achieve the better performance outperforming most of existing multi-label classification methods. HDLTex builds a separate neural network (either CNN or RNN) at each parent node to classify its children/subcategories. It needs numerous parameter variables over 5000 million, and consumes higher computation cost. HATC is an end-to-end global natural attention based model, which sequentially predicts the category labels of the next level based on a variant of an attention mechanism [26]. It only needs about 34 million parameters for learning. HFT-CNN uses a fine tuning technique is used to make the data in the upper levels contribute to categorization in the lower levels. However, we believe that the performance of HFT-CNN will be greatly improved if some hierarchical word representations with excellent performance such as FOREST [27] and ONLSTM [8], can be used to learn word representation in a hierarchy for HMTC. In contrast to the three approaches, our approach uses the ONLSTM instead of CNN or LSTM because ONLSTM cates for capturing the hierarchical information of textual data. Our approach presents a new joint embedding based on both words and parent categories instead of simple word embedding. Furthermore, we use a fine tuning technique to utilize the joint embedding of words and category labels for ensuring that the text classification results in the upper levels contribute to the classification in the lower ones.

The contributions of this paper are as follows.

- We propose a joint embedding method of words and parent categories.
- We present a hierarchical fine-tuning ONLSTM model for HMTC.
- The extensive experiments were made over two benchmark datasets, and the results show that the method proposed in this paper outperforms the state-of-the-art hierarchical and flat multi-label text classification approaches at significantly lower computational cost while maintaining high interpretability.

3 The Proposed Approach

3.1 Overview of Approach

In this paper, our HMTC approach deals with tree structure in the hierarchy or taxonomy in which there is a parent-child relationship between the upper and lower levels. A parent category contains many children subcategories, while a subcategory has only one parent category. The overall process of our HMTC approach is shown in Fig. 1. W means to transfer the ONLSTM training parameters of the upper level training to the adjacent lower level ONLSTM. c_i is the category label of level i, which can be obtained by mapping the probability distribution of the output of softmax layer to its corresponding semantic words. The notation $\oplus$ indicates that the parent category label of the upper level prediction is concatenated with its corresponding text.

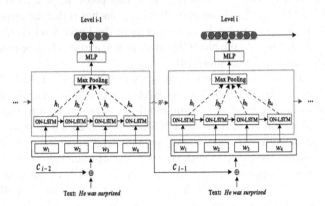

Fig. 1. An overview of our proposed approach.

Specifically speaking, we first concatenate the predicted parent category label with its corresponding text. The concatenated text is further represented in the same vector space by using word embedding matrix [28–30]. What is worth noting that there is no need to embed the parent category label for the first level since the first level does not have a parent category label. Then, the vector representation of the joint embedded parent category label and text is put into the deep learning model for training. The deep learning model we used in this paper consists of two parts: the ONLSTM models and a multi-layer perceptron (MLP). In the course of model training, we transfer the parameters of ONLSTM trained in the upper level to the lower level, and then finely tune these parameters of ONLSTM to make sure that the parameters in the upper level are supposed to contribute to more accurate classification in the adjacent lower level. The same process is repeated until the bottom level categories are trained.

3.2 Joint Embedding of Words and Category Labels

In a hierarchy of taxonomic categories, a parent category contains one or more subcategories, while a subcategory belongs to only one parent category. There is the conceptual inclusion relationship between a parent category and all its child categories: the text belonging to the subcategory must also belong to the parent category.

In this section, we use the method of joint embedding of parent category labels and textual words to incorporate conceptual inclusion relationship into the text classification process. Specifically, we first extract the corresponding parent category labels of each text in the text preprocessing stage, and then stitch it together with the corresponding text. The parent category and text are embedded in the same space.

Formally, suppose we are given a collection T of n texts and a collection C of categories corresponding to the n texts, where $T = (x_1, x_2, \ldots, x_n)$, $C = ((c_{11}, c_{12}, \ldots, c_{1k})$, $(c_{21}, c_{22}, \ldots, c_{2k}), \ldots (c_{n1}, c_{n2}, \ldots, c_{nk}))$, where x_n represents the n-th text, and c_{nk} represents the k-th level label of the n-th text. The text representation is obtained by concatenating the text with its corresponding parent category label, which can defined in Eq. (1), where the text representation $z_{i,j}$ is obtained by concatenating the i-th text x_i in the text set and its corresponding $(j-1)$-level label $c_{i,j-1}$, the $(j-1)$-level label represents the parent category label of the j-level label, and $\oplus$ is a concatenation operation.

$$z_{i,j} = \begin{cases} x_i, & if \ level \ j = 1 \\ c_{i,j-1} \oplus x_i, & if \ 1 < j \le k \end{cases} \tag{1}$$

3.3 Hierarchical Fine-Tuning

Hierarchical fine tuning refers to transferring the training parameters of some layers in the classification model of the upper level category to the corresponding layer in the classification model of the lower level category for training according to the hierarchy of categories [25, 31]. Because of the high correlation between the target task and the pre-training task in the hierarchical text classification task, the hierarchical fine tuning can be used to make full use of the information of the parent training in the subcategory training process to improve the classification performance. The parameters of parent category training model can be used as initialization parameters of child category training model, which can not only acquire prior knowledge, but also accelerate convergence [32]. We transfer the ONLSTM parameters from the upper level to the lower level for training, and then fine-tune the parameters of ONLSTM. Here, we only fine tune between adjacent layers, and repeat this process from the top level to the bottom of the hierarchy. When the dataset is large enough, it can accelerate the convergence. If the dataset is small, it can improve the classification accuracy more effectively.

3.4 Learning Based on ONLSTM

A natural sentence can usually be expressed as a hierarchical structure that we call grammatical information. The ONLSTM model extends the LSTM model and can learn hierarchical structures naturally in the process of training [8]. Its model structure is shown in Fig. 2. In the LSTM, updates between neurons are independent of each other and unrelated, and the ONLSTM has made changes to the LSTM units by adding two gates: master forget gate $\tilde{f}_t$ and master input gate $\tilde{i}_t$, which use a new activation function *cumax* to control the information to be stored and forgotten based on the state of the neurons. By introducing such a gate mechanism, the renewal rules of interdependence among neurons are established, and the order and hierarchical differences among neurons therefore can be made.

After obtaining the text representation $z_{i,j}$ through the above steps, we will convert it into semantic vector w through word embedding. In addition, in the following, we will use w_t^j to represent all text representations of the j-th level label at time t. Finally, we will

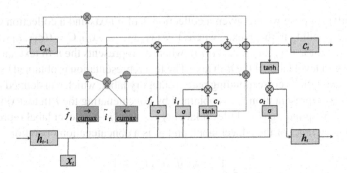

Fig. 2. The ONLSTM structure.

extract the syntactic structure information in the word vector representation w_t^j through ONLSTM to obtain the text representation.

$$h_t^j = \text{ONLSTM}^j \left(w_t^j, h_{t-1}^j, W_{on-lstm}^{j-1} \right) \tag{2}$$

Where is the training process of the ONLSTM layer in the classification model of the j-th level label, h_t^j is the hidden state vector of input sequence at time t. $W_{on-lstm}^{j-1}$ is the weight parameter of ONLSTM network when classifying $j - 1$ level categories. The weight parameters of the ONLSTM layer trained on the upper level is transferred to the ONLSTM layer of the adjacent lower level as initialization parameters.

3.5 Multi-layer Perceptron (MLP)

Finally, a two-layer multi-layer perceptron is employed to enhance the expressive power of neural networks and predicts the probability distribution over classes at level j:

$$d_j = \tanh\left(W_1 h_T^j + b_1 \right) \tag{3}$$

$$y_j = \text{softmax}\left(W_2 d_j + b_2 \right) \tag{4}$$

The parameters of the network are trained to minimize the cross-entropy of the predicted distributions $\hat{y}$ and true distributions y.

$$L(\hat{y}, y) = -\sum_{n=1}^{N} \sum_{c=1}^{C^j} y_n^c \log \hat{y}_n^c \tag{5}$$

Where y_n^c is the ground-truth label; $\hat{y}_n^c$ is prediction probabilities; N denotes the number of training samples and C^j is the number of categories at level j.

4   Experiments

4.1   Datasets

We evaluate our method on two widely-studied datasets for multi-label classification: Web of Science (WOS) and DBpedia. Web of Science (WOS) dataset was created by [4], which contains 46985 documents, 7 parent categories and 134 subcategories. Compared to WOS, the DBpedia dataset was first used in [12] for flat text classification. [5] uses the DBpedia ontology to construct a dataset with a three-level taxonomy of classes. The processed DBpedia contains 381,025 documents in total. Details of these two datasets are shown in Table 1.

Table 1. Dataset description.

	WOS	DBpedia
Level 1 categories	7	9
Level 2 categories	134	70
Level 3 categories	–	219
Number of documents	46985	381025

4.2 Hyperparameters

For WOS, we use a 300 dimensional pre-training word vector trained by the GloVe tool as our pre-trained word embeddings, which does not participate in model training. We add an ONLSTM with 500 hidden units and 0.25 dropout, then add a full connection layer with 500 units, a 0.5 dropout layer, and a batch normalization layer in turn. The last layer is a fully connected layer whose number of units is set to the category number. We use the standard Adam optimizer [33] with the learning rate of 0.001 to optimize all the trainable parameters. If the validation accuracy is no longer improved after 3 epochs, we reduce the learning rate to 0.1 times. The batch size is set to 64. In addition, we employ early stopping to select the best model. For DBpedia, other hyperparameters are exactly the same as WOS, with the exception that the hidden layer size of ONLSTM is 300.

We implemented our approach, and the source code was uploaded to the GitHub website[5].

4.3 Empirical Results

Analysis for Classification Accuracy
In this paper, the classification accuracy is evaluated from two perspectives. One perspective is to evaluate the accuracy at each level, which refers to the classification performance of each level when we provide the true parent class to the classifier while predicting the next class. However, this is not desirable because during inference we should not have access to the correct parent category. So, the other perspective is the overall accuracy, which refers to the accuracy of text classification at the last level, but true parent categories are not provided in advance in the process of classification at each level. That is,

---
[5] github.com/masterzjp/HFT-ONLSTM.

in the process of hierarchical classification, the required parent categories come from the classification results of the algorithm at the upper level. The flat algorithm does not deal with the middle levels in the hierarchy, but only considers the classification of the last level, so the result of each flat algorithm is only overall accuracy.

The information in Table 2 is from the comprehensive results of our approach and HDLTex [4] and HATC [5], which shows the classification accuracy comparison. We made comparison against the current state-of-the-art flat classifiers such as FastText [34], Bi-directional LSTM with max/mean pooling [29, 35] and the Structured Self-attentive classifier [36]. Of course, the state-of-the-art hierarchical multi-label classifiers including HDLTex and HATC were compared to our approach.

Table 2. Comparison of experimental results.

		DBpedia				WOS		
		l_1	l_2	l_3	Overall	l_1	l_2	Overall
Flat classifiers	FastText				86.20			61.30
	BiLSTM/Maxpool				94.20			77.69
	BiLSTM/Meanpool				94.68			73.08
	Struc. self-attention				94.04			77.40
Hierarchical classifiers	HDLTex	99.26	97.18	95.5	92.10	90.45	84.66	76.58
	HATC	99.21	96.03	95.32	93.72	89.32	82.42	77.46
	Our method	**99.43**	**97.54**	**97.36**	**95.16**	**90.92**	**86.65**	**82.62**

In Table 2, the classification experiments were made over two data sets DBpedia and WOS, where the columns corresponding to l_1, l_2 and l_3 are the classification accuracy at the first, second and third levels when providing the real category of text in the upper level. The column *Overall* refers to the classification accuracy of the last level labels of text without providing real parent categories, that is, the parent categories used in the classification process is the parent categories predicted by the classifier itself. Because the flat classifier does not deal with the middle levels in the category hierarchy, we only consider the classification accuracy of the last level as the overall accuracy for the flat classifiers.

In Table 2, we can find that our approach is very competitive against the classification accuracy, compared to all the state-of-the-art classifiers. Our classification model is not only superior to the state-of-the-art flat classification models, but also superior to the state-of-the-art HMTC models. Through a more detailed analysis from Table 2, we can see that in the hierarchical classification model, the difference between the classification accuracy of our model and the other two models continually increases level by level, which indicates that our classification method outperforms the state-of-art HMTC approaches.

Analysis for Training Parameters

Table 3 shows the comparison between the state-of-the-art HMTC models (e.g., HDL-Tex for local HMTC and HATC for global HMTC) and our classification model in terms of model parameters. Smaller number of parameters often means lower computational complexity. Because our model is a level-by-level local HMTC model, the number of parameters is obtained by adding all the parameters of each level classification model together. The parameters of each level include both the parameters participating in training and the parameters not participating in training.

Table 3. Number of parameters.

Model	Number of parameters/million	
	DBpedia	WOS
HDLTex	5000	
HATC	34	
Our method	140	

From Table 3, we can see that the total parameters of HDLTex are much larger than those of HATC and our model, while the total parameters of HATC are the smallest. However, although local approaches often have more parameters due to more training models required, the number of parameters required in our local HMTC approach is very close to the number of HATC parameters. It is currently the least number of parameters required in the current local HMTC approaches.

5   Conclusion

In this paper, we propose a local hierarchical multi-label text classifier with less parameters and superior performance. We employ both the joint embedding of text and parent categories and hierarchical fine-tuning technique to make full use of the hierarchical relationship between categories. It reduces computational costs while achieving superior performance.

In the future work, we will study the HMTC classification method with more complex hierarchical structure, e.g., hierarchy with directed acyclic graph, and the sentence-based embedding models like BERT for HMTC.

Acknowledgments. This work is partially supported by the National Key R&D Program of China under granted (2018YFC0830605, 2018YFC0831404).

References

1. Koller, D., Sahami, M.: Hierarchically classifying documents using very few words. In: Proceedings of International Conference on Machine Learning (ICML 1997), pp. 170–178, Morgan Kaufmann Publishers Inc., San Francisco (1997)

2. Stein, R., Jaques, P., Valiati, J.: An analysis of hierarchical text classification using word embeddings. Inf. Sci. **471**, 216–232 (2019)
3. Silla, C., Freitas, A.: A survey of hierarchical classification across different application domains. Data Min. Knowl. Disc. **22**(1–2), 31–72 (2011)
4. Kowsari, K., Brown, D., Heidarysafa, M., et al.: HDLTex: hierarchical deep learning for text classification. In: Proceedings of the 16th IEEE International Conference on Machine Learning and Applications, pp. 364–371 (2017)
5. Sinha, K., Dong, Y., et al.: A hierarchical neural attention-based text classifier. In: Proceedings of the 2018 Conference on Empirical Methods in Natural Language Processing, pp. 817–823 (2018)
6. Sun, A., Lim, E.: Hierarchical text classification and evaluation. In: Proceedings 2001 IEEE International Conference on Data Mining, pp. 521–528 (2001)
7. Tsatsaronis, G., Balikas, G., et al.: An overview of the BioASQ large-scale biomedical semantic indexing and question answering competition. BMC Bioinformatics **16**(1), 138 (2015)
8. Shen, Y., Tan, S., Sordoni, A., et al.: Ordered neurons: Integrating tree structures into recurrent neural networks. In: Proceedings of the 7th International Conference on Learning Representations (2019)
9. Alexis, C., Holger, S., et al.: Very deep convolutional networks for text classification. In: Proceedings of the 15th Conference of the European Chapter of the Association for Computational Linguistics, pp. 1107–1116 (2017)
10. Lai, S., Xu, L., et al.: Recurrent convolutional neural networks for text classification. In: Proceedings of the 29th AAAI conference on artificial intelligence, pp. 2267–2273 (2015)
11. Zhou, P., Qi, Z., Zheng, S., et al.: Text classification improved by integrating bidirectional LSTM with two-dimensional max pooling. In: Proceedings of the 26th International Conference on Computational Linguistics, pp. 3485–3495 (2016)
12. Zhang, X., Zhao, J., LeCun, Y.: Character-level convolutional networks for text classification. In: Proceedings of the 29th Annual Conference on Neural Information Processing Systems, pp. 649–657 (2015)
13. Cortes, C., Vapnik, V.: Support-vector networks. Mach. Learn. **20**(3), 273–297 (1995)
14. Han, X., Liu, J., Shen, Z., Miao, C.: An optimized k-nearest neighbor algorithm for large scale hierarchical text classification. In: Proceedings of the Joint ECML/PKDD PASCAL Workshop on Large-Scale Hierarchical Classification, pp. 2–12 (2011)
15. Cai, L., Hofmann, T.: Hierarchical document categorization with support vector machines. In: Proceedings of the thirteenth ACM international conference on Information and knowledge management, pp. 78–87 (2004)
16. Chen, Y., Crawford, M., Ghosh, J.: Integrating support vector machines in a hierarchical output space decomposition framework. In: IEEE International Geoscience & Remote Sensing Symposium IEEE, vol. 2, pp. 949–952 (2004)
17. Gopal, S., Yang, Y.: Recursive regularization for large-scale classification with hierarchical and graphical dependencies. In: Proceedings of the 19th ACM SIGKDD International Conference on Knowledge Discovery and Data Mining, pp. 257–265 (2013)
18. McCallum, A., Rosenfeld, R., Mitchell, T., Ng, A.: Improving text classification by shrinkage in a hierarchy of classes. In: Proceedings of the 15th International Conference on Machine Learning, vol. 98, pp. 359–367 (1998)
19. Bennett, P., Nguyen, N.: Refined experts: improving classification in large taxonomies. In: Proceedings of the 32nd International ACM SIGIR Conference on Research and Development in Information Retrieval, pp. 11–18 (2009)
20. Bi, W., Kwok, J.: Mandatory leaf node prediction in hierarchical multilabel classification. IEEE Trans. Neural Networks Learn. Syst. **25**(12), 2275–2287 (2014)

21. Jin-Bo, T.: An improved hierarchical document classification method. New Technol. Libr. Inf. Serv. **2**(2), 56–59 (2007)
22. Li, W., Miao, D., Wei, Z., Wang, W.: Hierarchical text classification model based on blocking priori knowledge. Pattern Recog. Artif. Intell. **23**(4), 456–463 (2010)
23. Weigend, A., Wiener, E., Pedersen, J.: Exploiting hierarchy in text categorization. Inf. Retrieval **1**(3), 193–216 (1999)
24. Liu, T., Yang, Y., et al.: Support vector machines classification with a very large scale taxonomy. ACM SIGKDD Explor. Newsl. **7**(1), 36–43 (2005)
25. Shimura, K., Li, J., Fukumoto, F.: HFT-CNN: learning hierarchical category structure for multi-label short text categorization. In: Proceedings of the 2018 Conference on Empirical Methods in Natural Language Processing, pp. 811–816 (2018)
26. Dzmitry, B., Kyunghyun, C., Yoshua, B.: Neural machine translation by jointly learning to align and translate. In: Proceedings of the 3rd International Conference on Learning Representations (2015)
27. Yogatama, D., Faruqui, M., Dyer, C., Smith, N.A.: Learning word representations with hierarchical sparse coding. In: Proceedings of International Conference on Machine Learning (ICML 2015), pp. 87–96 (2015)
28. Bengio, Y., et al.: A neural probabilistic language model. J. Mach. Learn. Res. **3**, 1137–1155 (2003)
29. Collobert, R., Weston, J.: A unified architecture for natural language processing: deep neural networks with multitask learning. In: Proceedings of the 25th International Conference on Machine Learning, pp. 160–167 (2008)
30. Turian, J., Ratinov, L., Bengio, Y.: Word representations: a simple and general method for semi-supervised learning. In: Proceedings of the 48th Annual Meeting of the Association for Computational Linguistics, pp. 384–394 (2010)
31. Banerjee, S., Akkaya, C., et al.: Hierarchical transfer learning for multi-label text classification. In: Proceedings of the 57th Annual Meeting of the Association for Computational Linguistics, pp. 6295–6300(2019)
32. He, K., Girshick, R., Dollar, P.: Rethinking imagenet pre-training. In: Proceedings of the IEEE International Conference on Computer Vision, pp. 4917–4926 (2019)
33. Kingma, D., Ba, J.: Adam: a method for stochastic optimization. In: Proceedings of the 3rd International Conference on Learning Representations (2015)
34. Joulin, A., et al.: Bag of tricks for efficient text classification. In: Proceedings of the 15th Conference of the European Chapter of the Association for Computational Linguistics, pp. 427–431 (2017)
35. Lee, J., Dernoncourt, F.: Sequential short-text classification with recurrent and convolutional neural networks. In: Proceedings of the 15th Conference of the North American Chapter of the Association for Computational Linguistics: Human Language Technologies, pp. 515–520 (2016)
36. Lin, Z., Feng, M., et al.: A structured self-attentive sentence embedding. In: Proceedings of the 5th International Conference on Learning Representations (2017)

Text Understanding II

Test Understanding II

Boosting Tricks for Word Mover's Distance

Konstantinos Skianis[1]([✉]), Fragkiskos D. Malliaros[2], Nikolaos Tziortziotis[3], and Michalis Vazirgiannis[4]

[1] BLUAI, Athens, Greece
skianis.konstantinos@gmail.com
[2] Paris-Saclay University, CentraleSupélec, Inria, France
fragkiskos.malliaros@centralesupelec.fr
[3] Jellyfish, Orsay, France
ntziorzi@gmail.com
[4] École Polytechnique, Palaiseau, France
mvazirg@lix.polytechnique.fr

Abstract. Word embeddings have opened a new path in creating novel approaches for addressing traditional problems in the natural language processing (NLP) domain. However, using word embeddings to compare text documents remains a relatively unexplored topic—with Word Mover's Distance (WMD) being the prominent tool used so far. In this paper, we present a variety of tools that can further improve the computation of distances between documents based on WMD. We demonstrate that, alternative stopwords, cross document-topic comparison, deep contextualized word vectors and convex metric learning, constitute powerful tools that can boost WMD.

Keywords: Word mover's distance · Word embeddings · Text classification

1 Introduction

Measuring distance between documents has always been a key component in many natural language processing tasks, such as document classification [2], machine translation[38], question answering [3] and text generation [5]. Nevertheless, the task can present various difficulties, making it not trivial; whether two documents are similar or not, is not always clear and may vary from application to application.

Following a naive, but effective in many cases, assumption, previous similarity measures that make use of the vector space model [29], were treating words in a document as if they were independent to each other. On the contrary, the distributional hypothesis [13], stated that words that co-occur in similar contexts and frequently, tend to have similar meanings and share common semantics.

With the rise of neural networks and deep learning methods in the natural language processing community [1,6], word embeddings [22] have had a huge

© Springer Nature Switzerland AG 2020
I. Farkaš et al. (Eds.): ICANN 2020, LNCS 12397, pp. 761–772, 2020.
https://doi.org/10.1007/978-3-030-61616-8_61

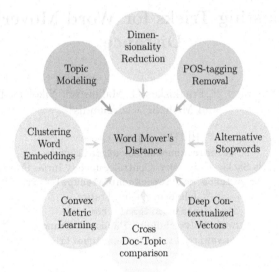

Fig. 1. Areas and tools that could be utilized to boost Word Mover's Distance.

impact in numerous tasks. Apart from constituting the most popular input for CNNs [18] and LSTMs [15], word embeddings have been used to compute similarity between documents that might not carry any identical words.

Succeeding the idea of using Earth Mover's Distance to measure document distance [33], Kusner et al. [19] presented *Word Mover's Distance* (WMD), a method for measuring the dissimilarity between two text documents as the minimum amount of distance that the embedded words of one document need to travel to reach the embedded words of another document. Moving forward, a supervised version of Word Mover's Distance has been introduced [14], which employs metric learning techniques when label knowledge exists. Their approaches have shown unprecedented results in the task of text classification via k nearest neighbor ($k$nn).

Although Word Mover's Distance is a powerful method for comparing two text documents, it can fall into the case where a word is very common and thus not contributing to measuring the distance. Moreover the exact computation of WMD scales at $\mathcal{O}(n^3)$, making it prohibitive for large collections of documents with big vocabularies. Kusner et al. [19] addressed this problem with a much faster variant, the *Relaxed WMD*, which is a lower bound of the exact WMD.

As WMD consists of multiple components, several improvement suggestions can be done. We observe that many tools can be of service, such as: a) dimensionality reduction, where some of the dimensions are actually useful, or dropping the number of dimensions may help as well making the computation faster; b) POS-tagging removal, where we care mainly about nouns and verbs; c) testing alternative stopwords and which stopwords to remove; d) topic modelling, adding words that belong in the same topic; e) clustering word embeddings; f)

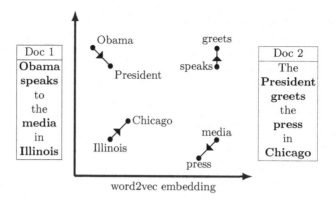

Fig. 2. An illustration of the Word Mover's Distance by [19]. The distance between the two documents is given by the minimum cumulative distance that all the words in Doc 1 need to travel in order to reach the words of Doc 2.

cross doc-topic comparison, adding neighbour words; g) contextualized vectors, like the recently introduced ELMo [24]; h) metric learning, assuming we want to add label information. An illustration of the components is shown in Fig. 1.

In this work, we have focused on testing alternative stopwords, cross document-topic comparison, deep contextualized word vectors and convex metric learning, by examining how they can further improve the performance of text categorization based on the WMD. Our approach is summarized as follows.

- First, by selecting specific *stopwords*, we observe that they play a significant role in the distance computation process.
- Next, utilizing *cross document-topic comparison*, we aim to make the comparison of two documents more meaningful by employing additional neighbour words.
- Finally, in order to boost the supervised version of WMD (S-WMD), we apply two state-of-the-art convex metric learning algorithms, namely *Large Margin Nearest Neighbors* (LMNN) [35], as well as *Maximally Collapsing Metric Learning* (MCML) [11].

Roadmap. In Sect. 2 we introduce the background and related work needed for the rest of paper. Next, in Sect. 3 we present our focused contribution on boosting Word Mover's Distance and Supervised Word Mover's Distance. Our experiments and results follow in Sect. 4. Finally, in Sect. 5 we conclude our study and present future work directions.

2 Background and Related Work

Let's assume that we have access to a word2vec [22] embedding matrix $X \in \mathbf{R}^{n \times m}$ for a finite size vocabulary of n words. $x_i \in \mathbf{R}^m$ represents the embedding of the i-th word in a m-dimensional space.

Word Mover's Distance. Word Mover's Distance tries to embody the semantic similarity between individual word pairs into the document distance metric. Let d and d' be the nBOW representation of two documents, and $T \in R^{n \times n}$ be a flow matrix where $T_{ij} \geq 0$ denotes how much of word i in d travels to word j in d'. More precisely, the distance between word i and word j becomes $c(i, j) = ||x_i - x_j||_2$. By $c(i, j)$ we point to the cost associated with "traveling" from one word to another. To transform d entirely into d' we ensure that the entire outgoing flow from word i equals d_i, i.e. $\sum_j T_{ij} = d_i$. Formally, the minimum cumulative cost of moving d to d' given the constraints is provided by the solution to the following linear program:

$$\text{minimize} \quad \sum_{i,j=1}^{n} T_{ij} c(i, j)$$

$$\text{subject to:} \quad \sum_{j=1}^{n} T_{ij} = d_i \quad \forall i \in \{1, \ldots, n\} \tag{1}$$

$$\sum_{i=1}^{n} T_{ij} = d'_j \quad \forall j \in \{1, \ldots, n\},$$

where $T_{ij} >= 0$ denotes how much of word i in d travels to word j in d'.

In Fig. 2 we present a schematic illustration of the Word Mover's Distance, between two documents "Obama speaks to the media in Illinois" and "The President greets the press in Chicago".

Relaxed Word Moving Distance (RWMD). Although WMD is powerful, it comes with a high complexity. Thus the authors in [19] relaxed the WMD optimization problem by removing one of the two constraints. If just the second constraint is removed, the optimization becomes:

$$\text{minimize} \quad \sum_{i,j=1}^{n} T_{ij} c(i, j)$$

$$\text{subject to:} \quad \sum_{j=1}^{n} T_{ij} = d_i \quad \forall i \in \{1, \ldots, n\}. \tag{2}$$

RWMD, which can be seen as an approximation of WMD, is much faster, making it more efficient for large documents.

Topics in Word Embeddings. In terms of utilizing topics, Das et al. [7] introduced Gaussian Latent Dirichlet Allocation, a method for topic modeling on word embeddings, treating the document as a collection of word embeddings and topics itself as multivariate Gaussian distributions in the embedding space. Later, the authors of [23] presented a novel document similarity measure based on the definition of a graph kernel between two pairs of documents. By representing each document as a graph-of-words, various approaches were able to model these relationships and then determine how similar two documents are by using a modified shortest-path graph kernel [21, 27]. Skianis et al. [31] clusters the word vectors and extracts topics from the embedding space. The work by Kim et al. [17] utilizes Word Mover's Distance to identify related words when no direct matches are found between a query and a document. In recent work, a topical distance approach [36] was attempted using word embeddings, by iteratively picking words from a vocabulary that closes the topical gap between documents.

Table 1. A sample of the most popular stopword lists available. The first three are integrated in well-known Python NLP libraries (versions of tools are mentioned inside parenthesis).

List	#	Description
nltk (3.2.2)	153	Van Rijsbergen (1979) [34] and Porter (1980) [25]
spaCy (2.0.9)	305	Improved list from [32] words: former, beside, done, whither, sometimes
Gensim (3.7.1)	337	Same as spaCy (Improved list from [32] words: thick, computer, cry, system, bill
SMART	571	SMART (System for the Mechanical Analysis and Retrieval of Text) Information Retrieval System developed at Cornell University in the 1960s
ROUGE	598	Extended SMART list used in ROUGE 1.5.5 Summary Evaluation Toolkit extra words: reuters, ap, news, tech, index, 3 letter days of the week and months
Terrier	733	Terrier Retrieval Engine
ATIRE	988	Puurula (2013) [26]

Metric Learning. Metric or distance learning is a field covering both supervised and unsupervised techniques [37]. As an extension of Word Mover's Distance, Supervised Word Mover's Distance [14] was presented, a method which utilized Neighborhood Component Analysis (NCA) [12] along with word embeddings and documents labels. While S-WMD is powerful, its loss function is nonconvex and is thus highly dependent on the initial setting of A and w.

Apart from NCA, there exists a plethora of popular methods for generalized Euclidean metric learning. Information-Theoretic Metric Learning (ITML) [8] learns a metric by minimizing a KL-divergence subject to generalized Euclidean distance constraints.

3   Boosting WMD and S-WMD

Our work is focused on studying the contribution of the following three tools in the computation of WMD: vocabulary trimming with stopword removal, cross document-topic comparison and convex metric learning methods. In the next paragraphs, we present in detail each of those tools.

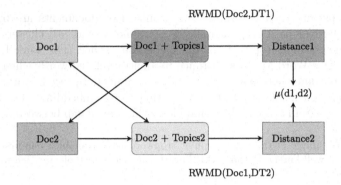

Fig. 3. Cross document-topic comparison schematic. With Topics we refer to neighbor or centroid words. DT1 stands for adding Doc1 words with Topics1.

3.1   Alternative Stopwords

In the natural language processing domain, stop words are generally the most common words in a language. For plenty of natural language processing tasks, these words are normally filtered out, making the vocabulary's size of the text set to be analyzed smaller. More specifically stopword removal is advised for text classification (or categorization) and caption generation, but not for tasks like machine translation, text summarization and language modeling.

Vocabulary pruning can help us to get rid of insignificant words, making the Relaxed WMD faster, while producing a better comparison between documents. In this way, we can make the "travel cost" needed from one document to another cheaper, faster and more effective, as the remaining words are the actual words that contribute to the meaning. Stopwords are in general category independent and thus the first that one could consider irrelevant. In recent work [30], stopword removal has been studied especially for topic modelling.

Nevertheless, there is no single universal list of stopwords used by all natural language processing tools, and indeed not all tools even use such a list. In the Word Mover's Distance paper, Kusner et al. [19] used the stopword list provided by the SMART system [28], composed of 571 words. [32] introduced another stopword list for English, with 339 words. Later, Puurula [26] created a new stopword list with 988 words (ATIRE). Along the study of this paper, we found more than 10 different stopword lists that are currently being used across many NLP tasks. Our goal is to examine how a different stopword list can affect the distance computation.

In Table 1 we present a sample of the most popular stopword lists used in the NLP community, as well as some integrated in well-known Python libraries.

3.2   Cross Document-Topic Comparison

Words that compose documents are sometimes not adequate to indicate the topics covered. Following this intuition, we augment the word space of each

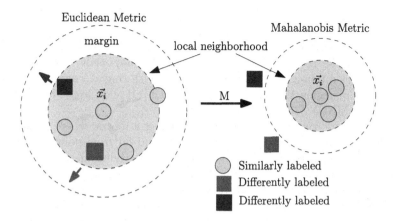

Fig. 4. An illustration of the LMNN algorithm [35]. In text, documents of the same class are pushed together in order to be closer and those of different class to be further away.

document by adding neighbors of each word. That way, the documents become more descriptive and carry more specific information. Our initial approach is to apply $k$nn search for each word in a document. Then, we either add these words' vectors, or create a centroid of the word's neighbors, adding it as a "topic-word".

Nevertheless, looking for the nearest neighbors of each word inside the global word vector space for every document is expensive. Thus, we apply clustering in the word vector space beforehand, and then search for the nearest neighbors of each word in the topic that the word belongs to. Here we introduce the concept of "topic-words", which we refer to either neighbors or centroids of a word's neighbors. In our settings, we have used hard k-means clustering. After extracting these "topic-words", we cross compare with the Relaxed Word Mover's Distance approach. Finally, we quantify the distance as the mean of the previous two RWMD distances. Our proposed scheme is shown in Fig. 3.

3.3 Deep Contextualized Word Representations

Recent work by [24] introduced ELMo, a novel type of deep contextualized word representations. These vectors represent internal states of a deep bidirectional language model (biLM), which is pre-trained on a large text corpus. In their work, the vectors used are derived from a bidirectional LSTM that is trained with a coupled language model (LM) objective. Essentially, for every word there is a vector every time it is found around a context.

In our work, we replace Google's pretrained vectors with ELMo, to test how it can affect measuring distances. This is expected, as ELMo is proved to boost many diverse NLP tasks, even with a simple averaging without any fine-tuning. To the best of our knowledge, our work is the first to incorporate deep contextualized word representations as an input for distance computation.

3.4   Convex Metric Learning

We extend our work in supervised settings, similarly to Supervised WMD [14]. Here, we propose to replace the Neighborhood Component Analysis method, which includes a non-convex cost function [12] with convex ones. These are the Maximally Collapsing Metric Learning (MCML) [11] and Large Margin Nearest Neighbors (LMNN) [35].

Both methods carry the property of learning a metric where points in the same class are simultaneously near each other and far from points in the other classes. As the $k$nn rule relies heavily on the underlying metric (a test input is classified by a majority vote amongst its k nearest neighbors), it is a good indicator for the quality of the metric in use. We present a schematic illustration of LMNN in Fig. 4. Similarly labeled text documents are pushed together in order to be closer and those differently labeled tend to be further away.

Maximally Collapsing Metric Learning (MCML). Maximally Collapsing Metric Learning (MCML) [11] was introduced as a linear learning algorithm for quadratic Gaussian metrics (Mahalanobis distances) used in supervised classification tasks. The method is based on the simple geometric intuition that a good metric is one under which points in the same class are simultaneously near each other and far from points in the other classes. A convex optimization problem is formulated, whose solution generates such a metric by trying to collapse all instances within the same class to a single point, while pushing other class instances infinitely far away.

Large Margin Nearest Neighbors (LMNN). Later, Large Margin Nearest Neighbors (LMNN) [35] came along, a metric that encourages inputs with similar labels to be close in a local region, and inputs of different labels to be farther by a large margin. LMNN is an algorithm to learn a Mahalanobis metric specifically to improve the error of $k$nn classification.

4   Experiments

Datasets. We evaluate in the context of $k$nn classification on six document categorization tasks:

1. BBCSPORT: articles between 2004–2005;
2. TWITTER: set of tweets labeled with sentiments 'positive', 'negative', or 'neutral';
3. RECIPE: set of recipes labeled by their region of origin;
4. OHSUMED: collection of medical abstracts;
5. CLASSIC: sets of sentences from academic papers, labeled by publisher name;
6. REUTERS: classic news labeled by news topics [4].

Table 2. Datasets' statistics.

Dataset	#docs	Voc	Avg	$|y|$
BBCSPORT	517	13,243	117	5
TWITTER	2,176	6,344	9.9	3
RECIPE	3,059	5,708	48.5	15
OHSUMED	3,999	31,789	59.2	10
CLASSIC	4,965	24,277	38.6	4
REUTERS	5,485	22,425	37.1	8

Table 3. Comparison in $k$nn test error (%) to LSI, WMD and S-WMD. Blue shows best results in unsupervised methods and bold indicates best result for a dataset.

		BBCSPORT	TWITTER	RECIPE	OHSUMED	CLASSIC	REUTERS
	LSI	4.30 ± 0.60	31.70 ± 0.70	45.40 ± 0.50	44.20	6.70 ± 0.40	6.30
	WMD	4.60 ± 0.70	28.70 ± 0.60	42.60 ± 0.30	44.50	2.88 ± 0.10	3.50
Unsupervised Cross	Stopword RWMD	4.27 ± 1.19	27.51 ± 1.00	43.98 ± 1.40	44.27	3.25 ± 0.50	5.25
	All, 5nn	6.00 ± 1.34	29.23 ± 1.09	42.52 ± 1.18	46.73	3.18 ± 0.44	6.26
	All, 5nn, Mean	4.00 ± 1.55	28.58 ± 2.29	42.53 ± 0.67	43.90	3.08 ± 0.62	5.76
	k-means, 5nn	5.91 ± 2.65	28.56 ± 1.20	42.23 ± 1.15	46.50	2.98 ± 0.66	4.71
	k-means, 5nn, Mean	3.82 ± 1.72	28.50 ± 1.51	41.95 ± 1.04	44.05	3.08 ± 0.51	4.57
	ELMo (avg)	6.36 ± 1.24	27.51 ± 1.03	40.66 ± 1.15	68.31	**1.15 ± 0.26**	6.30
Supervised	S-WMD (NCA)	2.10 ± 0.50	27.50 ± 0.50	39.20 ± 0.30	**34.30**	3.20 ± 0.20	3.20
	LMNN	**1.73 ± 0.67**	28.86 ± 2.22	40.88 ± 1.88	39.59	2.76 ± 0.30	4.02
	MCML	2.45 ± 1.27	**27.15 ± 1.36**	**38.93 ± 1.24**	42.38	3.56 ± 0.49	**2.92**

Table 2 shows statistics for the training datasets[1], including the number of inputs (docs), vocabulary size (Voc), the average number of unique words per document (Avg), and the number of classes $|y|$.

Setup. For comparison purposes, we use the train/test splits provided by [19]. Datasets are pre-processed by removing all words in the SMART stop word list [28], except TWITTER. We make use of the pre-trained version of word embeddings [22]., known to the NLP community as word2vec, offering more than three million words/phrases (from Google News), trained using the skip-gram approach [22]. Words that do not exist in word2vec, are removed. As alternative stopwords, compared to SMART, we use another stopword list [32], consisting of 339 words, which is used in popular libraries like Gensim[2] and spaCy[3]. In k-means clustering we set a $k = 500$ clusters. In all our proposed methods we use the Relaxed WMD (RWMD) instead of WMD, so that we can scale as well to larger datasets with higher vocabularies.

Results. We evaluate our approaches against WMD [19], LSI [9], and Supervised WMD [14]. We remind that we compare to state-of-the-art distance based methods. The effectiveness of the learned metrics is assessed by the $k$nn classification error.

Table 3 demonstrates results of our proposed "bag-of-tricks" to boost Word Mover's Distance. Our unsupervised approaches achieve superior results in four out of six datasets. Stopword removal with alternative resources can assist the embeddings and reach the Supervised WMD accuracy in the case of the TWITTER dataset. As expected, removing unnecessary stopwords can help WMD significantly, especially in small size documents.

---

[1] https://github.com/mkusner/wmd.

[2] https://radimrehurek.com/gensim/.

[3] https://spacy.io/.

Next, adding neighbors of words that exist in a document, can further enhance the "topical" expression and thus result in better distance computation. We observed that, by incrementing a document with words that are close in the word embedding space, we achieve better accuracy than traditional WMD or LSI approach in most cases. Utilizing prior clustering in word vectors can further boost neighbor words that belong in semantically closer clusters or groups, especially in very small or very large document sizes.

We see that in three datasets, using ELMo as vectors reduced the $k$nn classification error dramatically, with its expressive contextualized power. In the remaining datasets ELMo failed to drop the error, a fact that can be explained since we followed a simple average process over the layers and no fine-tuning was performed. Moreover, we observe that ELMo's worst performance was in OHSUMED, maybe due to big number of classes and specialization of the medical abstracts.

Last, we observe that trying convex metric learning techniques boost the performance of the categorization task in four out of six datasets. As expected, supervised methods yield superior results, with MCML being the best in three datasets. In fact, simple convex loss metric learning resulted in better accuracy, while non-convex NCA can be less stable and accurate due to local minima.

5   Conclusion and Future Work

In this paper, we presented effective and efficient boosting tricks for improving Word Mover's Distance speed and accuracy. We empirically pointed out a number of possible adjustments for the existing WMD, such as stopword removal, cross document-topic comparison, deep contextualized word representations and new metric learning methods. Calibrating those four components (three unsupervised and one supervised), we managed to achieve lower error in the task of text categorization compared to the original WMD and its supervised counterpart.

Measuring similarity between two documents that share words, appearing in different context, can make comparison harder. Thus, the problem of polysemy should also be addressed. In order to address that, topical word embeddings [20] can be applied. Thus, a "topical" WMD, based on topics rather than documents alone, would be a promising direction step. Fine-tuning ELMo or BERT [10] for distance computation can be a future direction. Moreover, we plan to fully examine non-Linear Metric Learning methods, like Gradient Boosting LMNN or χ^2-LMNN [16] for the supervised version of WMD. Finally, we would like to examine new metrics for measuring distance between text documents, using methodologies from computational geometry.

References

1. Bengio, Y., Ducharme, R., Vincent, P., Jauvin, C.: A neural probabilistic language model. J. Mach. Learn. Res. **3**(Feb), 1137–1155 (2003)

2. Bigi, B.: Using Kullback-Leibler distance for text categorization. In: Sebastiani, F. (ed.) ECIR 2003. LNCS, vol. 2633, pp. 305–319. Springer, Heidelberg (2003). https://doi.org/10.1007/3-540-36618-0_22

3. Brokos, G.I., Malakasiotis, P., Androutsopoulos, I.: Using centroids of word embeddings and word mover's distance for biomedical document retrieval in question answering. In: Proceedings of the 15th Workshop on Biomedical Natural Language Processing (2016)

4. Cachopo, A.M.d.J.C.: Improving methods for single-label text categorization. Instituto Superior Técnico, Portugal (2007)

5. Chen, L., et al.: Adversarial text generation via feature-mover's distance. In: Advances in Neural Information Processing Systems (2018)

6. Collobert, R., Weston, J.: A unified architecture for natural language processing: Deep neural networks with multitask learning. In: Proceedings of the 25th International Conference on Machine Learning, pp. 160–167. ACM (2008)

7. Das, R., Zaheer, M., Dyer, C.: Gaussian LDA for topic models with word embeddings. In: Proceedings of the 53rd Annual Meeting of the Association for Computational Linguistics and the 7th International Joint Conference on Natural Language Processing (Volume 1: Long Papers). Association for Computational Linguistics (2015)

8. Davis, J.V., Kulis, B., Jain, P., Sra, S., Dhillon, I.S.: Information-theoretic metric learning. In: Proceedings of the 24th International Conference on Machine Learning, pp. 209–216. ACM (2007)

9. Deerwester, S., Dumais, S.T., Furnas, G.W., Landauer, T.K., Harshman, R.: Indexing by latent semantic analysis. J. Am. Soc. Inf. Sci. 41(6), 391 (1990)

10. Devlin, J., Chang, M.W., Lee, K., Toutanova, K.: Bert: pre-training of deep bidirectional transformers for language understanding. In: NAACL 2019, (2019)

11. Globerson, A., Roweis, S.T.: Metric learning by collapsing classes. In: Advances in Neural Information Processing Systems, pp. 451–458 (2006)

12. Goldberger, J., Hinton, G.E., Roweis, S.T., Salakhutdinov, R.R.: Neighbourhood components analysis. In: Advances in Neural Information Processing Systems, pp. 513–520 (2005)

13. Harris, Z.S.: Distributional structure. Word 10(2–3), 146–162 (1954)

14. Huang, G., Guo, C., Kusner, M.J., Sun, Y., Sha, F., Weinberger, K.Q.: Supervised word mover's distance. In: Advances in Neural Information Processing Systems, pp. 4862–4870 (2016)

15. Johnson, R., Zhang, T.: Supervised and semi-supervised text categorization using lstm for region embeddings. In: Proceedings of the 33rd International Conference on International Conference on Machine Learning - Volume 48, ICML 2016, pp. 526–534. JMLR.org (2016). http://dl.acm.org/citation.cfm?id=3045390.3045447

16. Kedem, D., Tyree, S., Sha, F., Lanckriet, G.R., Weinberger, K.Q.: Non-linear metric learning. In: Advances in Neural Information Processing Systems, pp. 2573–2581 (2012)

17. Kim, S., Fiorini, N., Wilbur, W.J., Lu, Z.: Bridging the gap: Incorporating a semantic similarity measure for effectively mapping pubmed queries to documents. J. Biomed. Inform. 75, 122–127 (2017)

18. Kim, Y.: Convolutional neural networks for sentence classification. In: Proceedings of the 2014 Conference on Empirical Methods in Natural Language Processing, EMNLP 2014, 25–29 October 2014, Doha, Qatar, A meeting of SIGDAT, a Special Interest Group of the ACL, pp. 1746–1751 (2014). http://aclweb.org/anthology/D/D14/D14-1181.pdf

19. Kusner, M.J., Sun, Y., Kolkin, N.I., Weinberger, K.Q.: From word embeddings to document distances. In: ICML (2015)
20. Liu, Y., Liu, Z., Chua, T.S., Sun, M.: Topical word embeddings. In: AAAI, pp. 2418–2424 (2015)
21. Malliaros, F.D., Skianis, K.: Graph-based term weighting for text categorization. In: 2015 IEEE/ACM International Conference on Advances in Social Networks Analysis and Mining (ASONAM), pp. 1473–1479. IEEE (2015)
22. Mikolov, T., Chen, K., Corrado, G., Dean, J.: Efficient estimation of word representations in vector space. In: ICLR Workshop (2013)
23. Nikolentzos, G., Meladianos, P., Rousseau, F., Stavrakas, Y., Vazirgiannis, M.: Shortest-path graph kernels for document similarity. In: Proceedings of the 2017 Conference on Empirical Methods in Natural Language Processing, pp. 1890–1900 (2017)
24. Peters, M.E., et al.: Deep contextualized word representations. In: Proceedings of NAACL (2018)
25. Porter, M.F.: An algorithm for suffix stripping. Program **14**(3), 130–137 (1980)
26. Puurula, A.: Cumulative progress in language models for information retrieval. In: Proceedings of the Australasian Language Technology Association Workshop 2013 (ALTA 2013), pp. 96–100 (2013)
27. Rousseau, F., Vazirgiannis, M.: Graph-of-word and TW-IDF: new approach to ad hoc IR. In: Proceedings of the 22nd ACM International Conference on Information & Knowledge Management, pp. 59–68. ACM (2013)
28. Salton, G.: The smart retrieval system–experiments in automatic document processing (1971)
29. Salton, G., Wong, A., Yang, C.S.: A vector space model for automatic indexing. Commun. ACM **18**(11), 613–620 (1975)
30. Schofield, A., Magnusson, M., Mimno, D.: Pulling out the stops: rethinking stopword removal for topic models. In: Proceedings of the 15th Conference of the European Chapter of the Association for Computational Linguistics: Volume 2, Short Papers, vol. 2, pp. 432–436 (2017)
31. Skianis, K., Rousseau, F., Vazirgiannis, M.: Regularizing text categorization with clusters of words. In: Proceedings of the 2016 Conference on Empirical Methods in Natural Language Processing, pp. 1827–1837 (2016)
32. Stone, B., Dennis, S., Kwantes, P.J.: Comparing methods for document similarity analysis. TopiCS, DOI 10 (2010)
33. Tao, J., Cuturi, M., Yamamoto, A.: A distance between text documents based on topic models and ground metric learning. In: The 26th Annual Conference of the Japanese Society for Artificial Intelligence (2012)
34. Van Rijsbergen, C.J.: Information retrieval (1979)
35. Weinberger, K.Q., Saul, L.K.: Distance metric learning for large margin nearest neighbor classification. J. Mach. Learn. Res. **10**(Feb), 207–244 (2009)
36. Witt, N., Seifert, C., Granitzer, M.: Explaining topical distances using word embeddings. In: Database and Expert Systems Applications (DEXA), 2016 27th International Workshop on. pp. 212–217. IEEE (2016)
37. Yang, L., Jin, R.: Distance metric learning: a comprehensive survey, vol. 2, no. 2. Michigan State University (2006)
38. Zhang, M., Liu, Y., Luan, H.B., Sun, M., Izuha, T., Hao, J.: Building earth mover's distance on bilingual word embeddings for machine translation. In: AAAI, pp. 2870–2876 (2016)

Embedding Compression with Right Triangle Similarity Transformations

Haohao Song, Dongsheng Zou$^{(\boxtimes)}$, Lei Hu, and Jieying Yuan

College of Computer Science, Chongqing University, Chongqing 400044, China
{songhaohao2018,dszou,hulei,yuanjyyy}@cqu.edu.cn

Abstract. Word embedding technology has promoted the development of many NLP tasks. However, these embeddings often require a lot of storage, memory, and computation, resulting in low efficiency in NLP tasks. To address the problem, this paper proposes a new method for compressing word embeddings. We sample a set of orthogonal vector pairs from word embedding matrix in advance. Then these vector pairs are fed into a neural network sharing weights (i.e., Siamese network), and low-dimensional forms of the vector pairs are obtained. We get two vector triplets by adding the subtraction results of the vector pairs, respectively, which can be regarded as two triangles. The neural network is trained by minimizing the mean square error of the three internal angles between the two triangles. Finally, we extract its shared body as a compressor. The essence of this method is the right triangle similarity transformation (RTST), which is a combination of manifold learning and neural networks. It is distinguishable from other methods. The orthogonality in right triangles is beneficial to the compressed space construction. RTST also maintains the relative order of each edge (vector norm) in triangles. Experimental results on semantic similarity tasks reveal that the vector size is 64% of the original, while the performance is improved by 1.8%. When the compression rate reaches 2.7%, the performance drop is only 1.2%. Detailed analysis and ablation study further validate the rationality and the robustness of the RTST method.

Keywords: Word embedding · Dimensionality reduction · Binarization

1 Introduction

Word embeddings are commonly used as a starting point in neural-based natural language processing (NLP) models. Neural word embeddings encapsulate the linguistic information of words in continuous vectors. Since the word embedding model was proposed, the study for word embedding has never stopped [4,15–17]. As of now, according to whether the context is considered, word embedding models can be divided into two categories: context-independent embeddings and contextualized embeddings. In context-independent embedding models, each word is

© Springer Nature Switzerland AG 2020
I. Farkaš et al. (Eds.): ICANN 2020, LNCS 12397, pp. 773–785, 2020.
https://doi.org/10.1007/978-3-030-61616-8_62

assigned a vector representation with linguistic information (e.g., semantic information), which does not change with the context. Word2Vec [15] and GloVe [16] are representative methods in this category; Unlike the former, each word representation obtained with contextualized embedding models is a result calculated from a function of the entire input sentence. e.g., ELMo [17] and BERT [4].

These embeddings generally require several gigabytes of memory. However, such resource requirements are sometimes inappropriate. i). For low-resource devices, the NLP applications running on them commonly follow the client/server architecture: clients send data to servers, and servers calculate and return the results. Such an architecture relies heavily on real-time networks, and has the risk of privacy disclosure. Localizing NLP applications can solve this problem. However, the resources required for word embeddings cannot be provided by low-resource devices; ii). Efficiency is critical for NLP tasks, especially for clustering tasks. The text clustering tasks often use a similarity measure matrix. Because word embeddings are real-valued and high-dimensional, each element in the matrix requires a lot of calculation, resulting in low efficiency of NLP tasks. Compression for word embeddings can solve or alleviate the problems. The compressed vectors can be low-dimensional and binarized, which only take up a small amount of memory. It allows NLP applications to be localized into low-resource devices. Because smaller vectors require less calculation, compression is very beneficial to improve the efficiency of NLP tasks.

The compression for context-independent embeddings is more suitable than that of the contextualized ones. In terms of compression complexity, there are two problems to be solved in contextualized embedding compression: context-independent embedding compression and context function compression. It is quite difficult to achieve both without performance loss. From the perspective of computational complexity, each word representation in contextualized models requires context function calculation, which is computationally expensive, and the context-independent embeddings only require to be indexed.

In this paper, we introduce a new compressing context-independent word embedding method. Our inspirations come from the understanding of space transformation in matrix theory. The orthogonal basis is defined as: in the n-dimensional space where the inner product is defined, an orthogonal basis is a group of vectors containing n vectors, and the vectors in the group are mutually perpendicular. An n-dimensional orthogonal basis can uniquely determine an $\mathbb{R}^n$ space. All vectors in this $\mathbb{R}^n$ space can be obtained by a linear combination of the orthogonal basis. Therefore, from the perspective of spatial transformation, embedding compression can be regarded as: *considering the spatial distribution of the data, look for an orthogonal basis transformation from the original space to the target subspace to use fewer dimensions to represent the original data.* Solving such a transformation is difficult:

1. Finding an orthogonal basis from millions of high-dimensional word embeddings requires massive computation.
2. How to integrate data distribution information into the orthogonal basis transformations?

A promising way to alleviate both problems is to use many orthogonal vector pairs to approximate the orthogonal basis, and to fuse data distribution by reasonably sampling for orthogonal vector pairs. Siamese networks are one kind of neural networks with two inputs and two outputs, where the inputs go through the same operations. We use a Siamese network to compress orthogonal vector pairs. Its output vector pairs are expected to maintain the orthogonal relationship, so that to minimize information loss. The sharing structure in Siamese networks learns how to compress a word embedding. We extract this part as our compressor.

Simply supervising orthogonality invariance between vector pairs is not enough, because the Siamese networks do not consider the vectors' norms, which may destroy their relative magnitude order. Figure 1 depicts this case. To maintain the relative invariance of the vector norms, we calculate the subtraction results of the orthogonal vector pairs and add them into these pairs. The composed triples can be regarded as **right triangles**, where each vector represents one edge. The training objective for Siamese networks is to maintain the invariance of the three internal angles of both triangles accordingly. Behind this is the principle and properties of **triangle similarity transformations**: two triangles are similar if they have two pairs of corresponding angles that are congruent; corresponding sides are all in the same proportion if two triangles are similar. We learn a compressor with right triangle similarity transformations (RTST), which can be regarded as a combination of manifold learning and neural networks.

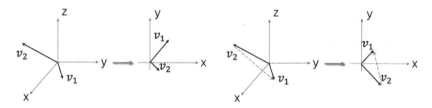

Fig. 1. Only orthogonal vector pair transformations can destroy the relative order of vector norms.

To adapt the limited memory and computing power of low-resource devices, We also use the threshold truncation function to extend the binarization capability for the RTST method. Because the word embeddings after binarization take up less memory and their calculation speed can be faster.

We evaluate the quality of the learned binary representations with extensive experiments. It is observed that the inferred memory-efficient codes successfully maintain the semantic features contained in the continuous embeddings. In many downstream tasks (e.g., sentiment analysis), these codes also perform quite well.

Contributions. This paper proposes a novel compressing word embedding method. It reduces the hardware threshold of NLP tasks while improving the efficiency. The experimental results reveal that the construction of subspace based on right triangle similarity transformations can help original word vectors evolve in encoding semantic information in real-valued space, and outperform autoencoder [21] in almost all tasks in binary space. Source code is available at github.com/songs18/rtst.

2   Related Work

Related work for compressing word embeddings can be divided into 3 categories: dimensionality reduction [19], precision limitation [13] and the combination of both [21]. Some other work cannot be simply divided into these categories. Chen et al. [3] and Shu et al. [20] use the linear combinations of a set of basis vectors to represent each word. These basic vectors require less memory compared to the original embeddings. Faruqui et al. [5] transforms original vectors into sparse overcomplete representations by increasing vector size first and then binarize them. These produced vectors are binarized and high-dimensional. The product quantization method is used to binarize word vectors on document classification tasks [11]. Li et al. [12] proposes a compression method for ELMo in dependency parsing tasks, which uses a variational information bottleneck method to nonlinearly compress these embeddings. However, this method does not solve the compression problem of the context function. The problem of binarizing word embeddings considered in this paper is also related to semantic hashing [9]. This paper is the first to use right triangle similarity transformations to compress word embeddings.

3   Methodology

We use bold uppercase and lowercase letters as matrices and vectors, respectively. The compressing word embedding problem is formulated as follows: given a word embedding matrix $\mathbf{X} \in \mathbb{R}^{d \times |\mathcal{V}|}$, we aim to learn a matrix $\mathbf{Y} \in \mathbb{R}^{r \times |\mathcal{V}|}$ and $\mathbf{B} \in \{\pm 1\}^{r \times |\mathcal{V}|}$ with semantic information. In $\mathbf{X}$, $\mathbf{Y}$ and $\mathbf{B}$, each column $\mathbf{x}_i$, $\mathbf{y}_i$ and $\mathbf{b}_i$ are one-word embedding. $\mathbb{R}$ represents real-valued numbers. $|\mathcal{V}|$ is the number of words in a vocabulary $\mathcal{V}$. d stands for original word vector dimensionality and r is the compressed space dimensionality.

3.1   Preparation: Obtaining Right Triangle Vector Triples

Since one vector in the vector triples is the calculation result of the remaining two vectors, we only need to obtain the orthogonal vector pairs. The orthogonality of two vectors means that their cosine similarity score is 0, so we can obtain orthogonal vector pairs by this rule. The time complexity is $\mathcal{O}\left(n^2\right)$ for calculating the cosine similarity scores of all possible word vector pairs. It is impractical since n is often over 100k. To solve this problem, we propose two methods:

i). **Heuristic Method.** Considering the limitation of word collocation, two word vectors with different parts of speech are likely to possess a lower score, and further filtering will increase the hit rate of orthogonality. *e.g.*, the cosine similarity score of verb 'stove' and noun 'ventre' is 0.00069.[1] We first divide the words into sets according to parts of speech, then sample the sets, and finally calculate the cosine similarity scores for words with different parts of speech.

ii). **Constructive Method.** This method randomly samples some word embeddings. For one n-dimensional vector, it generates a pairing vector: it randomly generates $n-1$ numbers and calculates the nth component of the random vector according to the rule of the cosine similarity score of two vectors is 0.

The constructive method is simple, but the introduction of random vectors disrupts the approximation for data distribution. In the experiments of this paper, we use the heuristic method.

3.2 Compressing Word Embeddings with Siamese Network

Architecture. In the Siamese network of RTST, inputs are orthogonal vector pairs and outputs are compressed counterparts. The sharing body is a single hidden layer neural network, which is defined as:

$$\mathbf{y}_k = \tanh(\mathbf{W}\mathbf{x}_k + \mathbf{bias}) \tag{1}$$

where $\mathbf{x}_k$ and $\mathbf{y}_k$ are original vector and the compressed result, respectively, and **bias** is a bias vector. Before fed into the network, the input $\mathbf{x}_k$ is clipped to be within $[-1, 1]$. The range of $\mathbf{y}_k$ is $[-1,1]$ and each element $\mathbf{b}_{km}$ of the binary vectors $\mathbf{b}_k$ is also binarized to -1 or 1:

$$\mathbf{b}_{km} = \begin{cases} -1, & \text{if } \mathbf{y}_{km} < t \\ 1, & \text{otherwise} \end{cases} \quad m \in [1, r] \tag{2}$$

where t is the truncation value obtained from grid search and m is the element index. Depending on whether to use Eq. 2, RTST can produce two types of embeddings: real-valued (*real*) or binary-valued (*bin*). For the latter, not only can they be used like real-valued vectors, but they can also use pure bit-wise operations in downstream tasks. e.g., the binary codes with Hamming distance are competent for information retrieval tasks. So we can further divide *bin* into *bin-real* and *bin-bin* based on whether real-valued calculation is used. In the remainder of this paper, we will demonstrate bit-wise operations where necessary. Figure 2 summarizes this architecture.

---

[1] Word vectors are from glove.6B.300d.txt file [16].

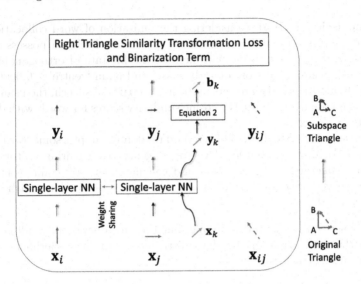

Fig. 2. Siamese network architecture used to compress word embeddings. The architecture is based on right triangle similarity transformations.

Objective Function. Taking $\mathbf{x}_i$ and $\mathbf{x}_j$ as inputs, we can obtain a right triangle by adding the third edge $\mathbf{x}_{ij}$, which is the result of $\mathbf{x}_i$-$\mathbf{x}_j$. The counterpart triangle in the target subspace can be constructed with $\mathbf{y}_i$, $\mathbf{y}_j$ and $\mathbf{y}_{ij}$ in the same way. The similarity transformation loss ℓ_{sim} for $\mathbf{x}_i$ and $\mathbf{x}_j$ is defined as:

$$\ell_{sim}(\mathbf{x}_i, \mathbf{x}_j) = \ell_{\angle A}(\mathbf{x}_i, \mathbf{x}_j) + \ell_{\angle B, \angle C}(\mathbf{x}_i, \mathbf{x}_j) \tag{3}$$

$$\ell_{\angle A}(\mathbf{x}_i, \mathbf{x}_j) = (\cos \langle \mathbf{x}_i, \mathbf{x}_j \rangle - \cos \langle \mathbf{y}_i, \mathbf{y}_j \rangle)^2 \tag{4}$$

$$\ell_{\angle B, \angle C}(\mathbf{x}_i, \mathbf{x}_j) = \frac{1}{2} \times ((\cos \langle \mathbf{x}_i, \mathbf{x}_{ij} \rangle - \cos \langle \mathbf{y}_i, \mathbf{y}_{ij} \rangle)^2 \\ + (\cos \langle \mathbf{x}_j, \mathbf{x}_{ij} \rangle - \cos \langle \mathbf{y}_j, \mathbf{y}_{ij} \rangle)^2) \tag{5}$$

Interestingly, the cosine similarity function is sensitive to orthogonality ($\cos' x = \sin x$, $\sin x$ gets maximum at $\frac{\pi}{2}$), so the combination of orthogonal vector pairs and cosine similarity can help train our model. Seeing that tanh's output range is $[-1,1]$ and $(-1)^2 = (1)^2 = 1$, our binarization term is defined as:

$$\mathcal{T}_{bin}(\mathbf{y}_i, \mathbf{y}_j) = \frac{\frac{1}{r}\sum_{m=1}^{r} \mathbf{y}_{im}^2 + \frac{1}{r}\sum_{m=1}^{r} \mathbf{y}_{jm}^2}{2} \tag{6}$$

where r is the dimensionality of target subspace. Obviously, we hope to minimize similarity transformation loss and maximize the binarization term (equivalent to minimizing quantization error). We denote the orthogonal vector pairs obtained in Sect. 3.1 as $\mathbf{X}_o$ and the global objective function to minimize is:

$$\mathcal{L} = \sum_{<\mathbf{x}_i, \mathbf{x}_j> \in \mathbf{X}_o} \log(\ell_{sim}(\mathbf{x}_i, \mathbf{x}_j)) - \log(\mathcal{T}_{bin}(\mathbf{y}_i, \mathbf{y}_j)) \tag{7}$$

Note that the RTST method does not use any task related information, and it can be applied to other compression fields without modifications.

4 Experiments

We run the proposed method on pre-trained embeddings and evaluate the compressed embeddings on various NLP tasks. These tasks can be divided into two categories. One is intrinsic, which includes semantic similarity and word analogy, and the other is extrinsic, including document/question classification and sentiment analysis. Besides, several ablation experiments are performed to validate the effectiveness of each component in the model.

4.1 Experimental Setup

Pre-trained Continuous Embeddings. We conduct experiments on GloVe [16] and fasttext [1]. GloVe embeddings have been trained on 42B tokens of Common Crawl data with 400k words. Fasttext embeddings are trained from public Wikipedia with 2.5M words, which has better quality than GloVe due to considering sub-word information. Word embeddings in experiments are 300-dimensional and are downloaded from their corresponding websites. In practice, we observe that GloVe satisfies the orthogonality better than fasttext. The difference of orthogonality satisfaction results in a slight performance decrease of RTST on downstream tasks. Used embeddings are based on different methods (derivation of skip-gram for fasttext, matrix factorization for GloVe) and they have different satisfactions for orthogonality. This illustrates the conditions and effects of the method.

Training Details. The Siamese network is trained with mini-batch stochastic gradient descent with learning rate 0.01, epoch 2, batch size 64, 2M orthogonal vector pairs for GloVe and 4M for fasttext due to unsatisfied orthogonality. Compressed vectors of 3 sizes are produced: 64, 128 and 256. t in Eq. 2 is selected from -0.99 to 0.99 (0.01 interval) to make about 50k untrained right triangles possess smallest internal angle error.

Evaluation

Semantic Similarity. This task is to compute Spearman's rank correlation coefficient between the similarity scores attributed by humans and the scores computed with word vectors. For real-valued vectors, the metric is the cosine similarity. For binary vectors, the metric is the Sokal&Michener similarity function [18] (bit-wise):

$$sim\left(\mathbf{v}_1, \mathbf{v}_2\right) = \frac{\text{XNOR}\left(\mathbf{v}_1, \mathbf{v}_2\right)}{len\left(\mathbf{v}_1\right)} \tag{8}$$

MEN [2], RW [14], SimLex [10], SimVerb [7], WordSim [6] are used in this task.

Word Analogy. Word analogy is to find the word d in questions like "a is to b as c is to d". If the nearest neighbor of $\mathbf{v}_b - \mathbf{v}_a + \mathbf{v}_c$ is $\mathbf{v}_d$, word analogy is correct, otherwise false. The score reported in this task is proportion of correct analogies. For binary vectors, we follow [21] to replace + with OR bitwise operator and - with AND NOT operator because in binary space adding or subtracting bits do not make sense. The dataset used in this task is [15] (Sem. and Syn.).

Text Classification. The evaluation on text classification tasks follows the protocol in [8,22]: given a bag-of-words representation of a text, predict the assigned label. In this task, we use a single hidden layer neural network. Its input weights are initialized with the compressed embeddings, and they are fixed during training so that the classification accuracies only depend on the vectors used to initialize the neural network. The datasets used can be divided into three tasks: document classification (AG-News and DBpedia), question classification (Yahoo Answers) and sentiment analysis (Amazon and Yelp reviews, both polarity and full). Each dataset is split into a training and a test file, and the same training and test files are used for all word embedding models. Figure 4 depicts the results of text classification.

Comparative Methods. Our method has dimensionality reduction and binarization functions. Two methods are used for comparison. i). Original Embeddings. For GloVe and fasttext, the compressed word embeddings (64, 128 and 256) are compared with the corresponding original 300-dimensional embeddings. Under the condition of orthogonal satisfaction (GloVe), to evaluate the robustness of our method, compressed word embeddings are also compared with several different low-dimensional (50, 100, 200 and 300) original word embeddings (reported in Fig. 3); ii). Autoencoder. Autoencoder [21] learns binarized embeddings by using the Heaviside step function on the implicit variable of autoencoder. In [21], the encoder and decoder share weights, and the weights are updated only by gradient backward propagation of the decoder. To date, autoencoder has established the latest and best baseline on binarized embeddings.

4.2 Experimental Results and Analysis

Table 1 reports the performances of compressed embeddings on semantic similarity and word analogy tasks.

Performances on Real. On the compression for GloVe, the best scores on semantic similarity and word analogy are obtained with 256-dimensional vectors (Table 1). For semantic similarity tasks, the compressed vectors achieve absolute improvements of **1.5%, 0.8%, 2.6%, 2.8%** and **3.2%** over original GloVe vectors on MEN, RW, SimLex, SimVerb and WS353, respectively, with 85.3% size. 128-dimensional compressed embeddings sometimes outperform 300-dimensional original ones. e.g., 23.1% against 22.7% on SimVerb and 61.5% against 60.1% on WS353. Figure 3 further demonstrates the advantages of compression: the

Table 1. Semantic similarity results and word analogy scores for word vectors produced with Siamese network (SN) in three scenarios (training data is nonorthogonal for fasttext, while GloVe is orthogonal). The performances of vectors produced with autoencoder (AE) [21] and original vectors (*raw*) are also reported.

		Fasttext						GloVe					
		raw	*real*	*bin-real*		*bin-bin*		*raw*	*real*	*bin-real*		*bin-bin*	
				SN	AE	SN	AE			SN	AE	SN	AE
MEN		76.4						73.8					
	256	–	76.1	70.5	**71.8**	70.5	**72.2**	–	**75.3**	**70.5**	67.2	70.5	**70.6**
	128	–	71.8	62.6	**65.3**	62.6	**66.1**	–	72.3	**65.7**	61.1	**65.8**	62.5
	64	–	64.4	54.4	**55.9**	54.4	**58.6**	–	62.3	**54.6**	32.3	**54.6**	43.0
RW		48.7						41.2					
	256	–	47.1	42.0	**42.2**	42.0	41.0	–	42.0	**39.9**	33.9	39.9	**40.0**
	128	–	43.6	**37.9**	33.3	**37.8**	34.6	–	39.2	**36.8**	36.0	**36.8**	35.8
	64	–	38.4	**32.1**	26.7	**32.1**	29.6	–	32.2	**30.4**	19.8	**30.4**	25.8
SimLex		38.0						37.1					
	256	–	37.5	**34.7**	32.9	**34.7**	33.3	–	**39.7**	38.5	34.8	**38.5**	36.7
	128	–	33.9	**27.2**	26.0	**27.2**	26.1	–	34.9	**30.1**	29.8	30.1	**31.1**
	64	–	28.6	**23.3**	20.1	**23.3**	20.0	–	28.6	**27.9**	13.3	**27.9**	18.5
SimVerb		25.8						22.7					
	256	–	25.2	**22.8**	20.7	**22.8**	21.1	–	**25.5**	24.6	21.5	**24.6**	22.4
	128	–	23.2	**20.2**	16.8	**20.2**	16.6	–	23.1	**20.5**	17.7	20.4	16.8
	64	–	18.6	**17.9**	13.3	**17.9**	13.9	–	16.6	**16.4**	7.3	**16.4**	11.6
WS353		73.2						60.1					
	256	–	**73.8**	68.4	64.0	**68.4**	65.7	–	63.3	**60.5**	52.2	**60.5**	57.6
	128	–	69.1	**59.5**	58.8	**59.5**	57.9	–	61.5	**57.6**	52.3	**57.6**	55.6
	64	–	59.1	**53.3**	43.5	**53.3**	45.3	–	52.9	**52.0**	18.0	**52.0**	26.6
Sem. analogy		63.8						77.4					
	256	–	59.7	19.8	**26.9**	10.8	**17.3**	–	75.4	50.1	**51.4**	**37.6**	33.9
	128	–	55.8	9.5	**9.7**	7.2	**8.6**	–	64.6	**26.0**	18.8	**21.2**	10.6
	64	–	39.4	**4.8**	2.3	**5.5**	3.1	–	38.4	**9.4**	5.0	**9.8**	3.0
Syn. analogy		67.0						67.0					
	256	–	63.7	28.4	**35.3**	21.8	**30.8**	–	64.4	**45.9**	45.3	**38.8**	37.0
	128	–	60.2	13.5	**13.7**	16.5	**17.3**	–	57.5	**27.5**	17.3	**27.5**	16.4
	64	–	42.3	**4.3**	3.9	**8.6**	6.9	–	37.1	**11.0**	4.1	**14.8**	3.9

produced vectors with Siamese network perform better than original ones on almost all datasets and dimensions except for RW and SimVerb from 64 to 100 dimensions, which indicates that *Siamese network with right triangle similarity transformations can help word vectors evolve in encoding semantic information most of the time.* The above comparisons for the experimental results are scattered. To get a brief conclusion, we can also calculate the average scores of several dimensions from the data of Table 1 or Fig. 3 with Fisher's transformation method [21]. Limited to the number of pages, these scores are not shown in detail. However, we can cite some comparative results. e.g., in the match between the SN 128-dimensional and the original 200-dimensional (Fig. 3), the RTST win by 1.8% with 64% size. However, 256-dimensional vectors have accuracy drops of 2% and 2.6% on word analogy tasks. Thinking of an 85.3% compression ratio, the performance decreases are following expectation. In text classification tasks, the performances of 256-dimensional *real* are near-lossless with absolute differences ∼0.3% (Fig. 4); As training data are not applied equitably to fasttext, the performances of compressed vectors are inferior to their competitors on three tasks. e.g., for 256-dimensional embeddings, 47.1% against 48.7% on RW, 59.7% against 63.8% on Sem. and 84.1% against 84.5% on Amazon polarity.

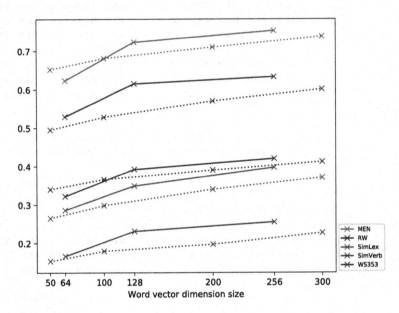

Fig. 3. Semantic word similarity results for vectors produced with Siamese network (solid line) and naive GloVe algorithm (dashed line).

Performances on Bin-Real. Compared with *real*, *bin-real* has a higher compression ratio. *e.g.,* 256-bit vectors are 32 times smaller than 256-dimensional *real*, reaching 2.7% relative to original vectors. A higher compression ratio also means the sharp collapse of representation space, which results in a slight performance decrease. Table 1 and Fig. 4 report it. In general, 256-bit GloVe vectors degrade performances by 1.2% on average (aggregated with Fisher's transformation) on semantic similarity tasks and ∼1.9% on text classification tasks. The accuracy decreases are more on word analogy tasks, reaching the same conclusion as autoencoder [21]. This can be explained by the fact of the finiteness of representation space. Compared with autoencoder [21], the advantages of Siamese network based on right triangle similarity transformations are obvious: the latter achieves better scores in **39** out of **42** tasks and this is especially true for the 64-bit version of GloVe on semantic word similarity tasks, where the absolute superiorities are between **9.1%** and **34%** depending on the dataset.

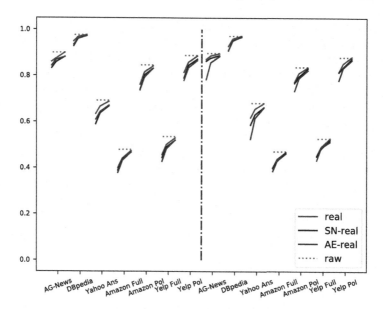

Fig. 4. Text classification accuracies for *real* (real), *bin-real* of Siamese networks (SN-real) and *bin-real* of autoencoder (AE-real). Original embeddings (raw) are also reported. The break points of each polyline represent 64, 128 and 256-dimensional. The left part is on fasttext and the right is on GloVe (training data is nonorthogonal for fasttext, while GloVe is orthogonal).

Performances on Bin-Bin. Binary vectors can be utilized with mere bitwise operations. On semantic word similarity tasks, the performances of *bin-bin* and *bin-real* are very similar, with absolute differences ~0.1%, which in turn exhibits near performances to original vectors. In word analogy tasks, the result space based on Hamming distance contains only $|dimensions + 1|$ unique values, so it is difficult to distinguish the target word from vocabulary. Experimental results show word analogy is not suited to evaluate binary vectors, which is consistent with autoencoder [21].

4.3   Ablation Study

Table 2. The role of orthogonality.

Vector pairs angle	0	0.05	0.10	0.15	0.20
real	**48.4**	46.1	46.4	45.6	47.2
bin-real	**43.5**	40.7	40.0	38.8	41.3

Table 3. The influence of the 3rd edges

Dataset	MEN	RW	SimLex	SimVerb	WS353
real	+2.6	+1.4	+1.9	+3.4	+1.6
bin-real	+1.7	+2.6	+1.2	+2.3	+2.3

The Role of Orthogonality. To evaluate the role of orthogonality in RTST, we sample vector pairs with different angles (cosine angle) from GloVe to train models. The comprehensive performances of compressed 128-dimensional word embeddings in 5 datasets are reported in Table 2 (Fisher's transformed average scores). The one with orthogonal vector pairs obtains the best performances. This describes that orthogonality plays an important role in helping models compress word embeddings.

The Influence of the Third Edges. We compare the performances of compressed 128-dimensional word embedding with and without the third edges. The experimental results are reported in Table 3. '+' represents the performance improvement brought by the third edges. The absolute improvement is between 1.2% and 3.4%. This indicates that constructing right triangles with the subtraction results of vector pairs can improve the learned semantic representations.

5   Conclusion

This paper presents a novel method of compressing word embeddings using the right triangle similarity transformations. Extensive experiments verify the effectiveness and rationality of the RTST method. From an academic point of view, the RTST incorporates manifold learning ideas in machine learning and neural networks. It is a supplement to the existing research on word embedding compression. From the application perspective, the RTST can be applied to 3 scenarios. The generated memory-efficient word embeddings are near-lossless.

References

1. Bojanowski, P., Grave, E., Joulin, A., Mikolov, T.: Enriching word vectors with subword information. TACL **5**, 135–146 (2017)
2. Bruni, E., Tran, N., Baroni, M.: Multimodal distributional semantics. J. Artif. Intell. Res. **49**, 1–47 (2014)
3. Chen, T., Min, M.R., Sun, Y.: Learning k-way d-dimensional discrete codes for compact embedding representations. In: Proceedings of ICML, pp. 853–862 (2018)
4. Devlin, J., Chang, M.W., Lee, K., Toutanova, K.: BERT: pre-training of deep bidirectional transformers for language understanding. In: Proceedings of NAACL: Human Language Technologies. ACL (2019)
5. Faruqui, M., Tsvetkov, Y., Yogatama, D., Dyer, C., Smith, N.A.: Sparse overcomplete word vector representations. In: Proceedings of ACL, vol. 1, pp. 1491–1500 (2015)
6. Finkelstein, L., et al.: Placing search in context: the concept revisited. ACM Trans. Inf. Syst. **20**, 116–131 (2002)
7. Gerz, D., Vulic, I., Hill, F., Reichart, R., Korhonen, A.: SimVerb-3500: a large-scale evaluation set of verb similarity. In: Proceedings of EMNLP, pp. 2173–2182 (2016)
8. Grave, E., Mikolov, T., Joulin, A., Bojanowski, P.: Bag of tricks for efficient text classification. In: Proceedings of EACL, Valencia, Spain, vol. 2, pp. 427–431, April 2017

9. Hansen, C., Hansen, C., Simonsen, J.G., Alstrup, S., Lioma, C.: Unsupervised neural generative semantic hashing. In: Proceedings of SIGIR, Paris, France, pp. 735–744, July 2019

10. Hill, F., Reichart, R., Korhonen, A.: SimLex-999: evaluating semantic models with (genuine) similarity estimation. Comput. Linguist. **41**(4), 665–695 (2015)

11. Joulin, A., Grave, E., Bojanowski, P., Douze, M., Jégou, H., Mikolov, T.: Fast-Text.zip: compressing text classification models. CoRR abs/1612.03651 (2016)

12. Li, X.L., Eisner, J.: Specializing word embeddings (for parsing) by information bottleneck. In: Inui, K., Jiang, J., Ng, V., Wan, X. (eds.) Proceedings of EMNLP, pp. 2744–2754. ACL (2019)

13. Ling, S., Song, Y., Roth, D.: Word embeddings with limited memory. In: Proceedings of ACL, vol. 2 (2016)

14. Luong, T., Socher, R., Manning, C.D.: Better word representations with recursive neural networks for morphology. In: Proceedings of the Seventeenth Conference on Computational Natural Language Learning, Sofia, Bulgaria, pp. 104–113, August 2013

15. Mikolov, T., Sutskever, I., Chen, K., Corrado, G.S., Dean, J.: Distributed representations of words and phrases and their compositionality. In: Proceedings of NIPS, pp. 3111–3119 (2013)

16. Pennington, J., Socher, R., Manning, C.D.: GloVe: global vectors for word representation. In: Proceedings of EMNLP, pp. 1532–1543 (2014)

17. Peters, M.E., et al.: Deep contextualized word representations. In: Walker, M.A., Ji, H., Stent, A. (eds.) Proceedings of NAACL, pp. 2227–2237. ACL (2018)

18. Sokal, R.R., Michener, C.D.: A statistical method for evaluating systematic relationships. Univ. Kansas Sci. Bull. **38**, 1409–1438 (1958)

19. Raunak, V., Gupta, V., Metze, F.: Effective dimensionality reduction for word embeddings. In: Proceedings of the 4th Workshop on Representation Learning for NLP, pp. 235–243 (2019)

20. Shu, R., Nakayama, H.: Compressing word embeddings via deep compositional code learning. In: Proceedings of ICLR (2018)

21. Tissier, J., Gravier, C., Habrard, A.: Near-lossless binarization of word embeddings. In: Proceedings of AAAI, pp. 7104–7111 (2019)

22. Zhang, X., Zhao, J.J., LeCun, Y.: Character-level convolutional networks for text classification. In: Proceedings of NIPS, pp. 649–657 (2015)

Neural Networks for Detecting Irrelevant Questions During Visual Question Answering

Mengdi Li[✉], Cornelius Weber, and Stefan Wermter

Department of Informatics, University of Hamburg,
Vogt-Koelln-Str. 30, 22527 Hamburg, Germany
{mli,weber,wermter}@informatik.uni-hamburg.de
http://www.informatik.uni-hamburg.de/WTM

Abstract. Visual question answering (VQA) is a task to produce correct answers to questions about images. When given an irrelevant question to an image, existing models for VQA will still produce an answer rather than predict that the question is irrelevant. This situation shows that current VQA models do not truly understand images and questions. On the other hand, producing answers for irrelevant questions can be misleading in real-world application scenarios. To tackle this problem, we hypothesize that the abilities required for detecting irrelevant questions are similar to those required for answering questions. Based on this hypothesis, we study what performance a state-of-the-art VQA network can achieve when trained on irrelevant question detection. Then, we analyze the influences of reasoning and relational modeling on the task of irrelevant question detection. Our experimental results indicate that a VQA network trained on an irrelevant question detection dataset outperforms existing state-of-the-art methods by a big margin on the task of irrelevant question detection. Ablation studies show that explicit reasoning and relational modeling benefits irrelevant question detection. At last, we investigate a straight-forward idea of integrating the ability to detect irrelevant questions into VQA models by joint training with extended VQA data containing irrelevant cases. The results suggest that joint training has a negative impact on the model's performance on the VQA task, while the accuracy on relevance detection is maintained. In this paper we claim that an efficient neural network designed for VQA can achieve high accuracy on detecting relevance, however integrating the ability to detect relevance into a VQA model by joint training will lead to degradation of performance on the VQA task.

Keywords: Visual question answering · Irrelevant question detection · Multimodality · Deep neural networks

1 Introduction

Visual question answering (VQA) [3] is an important multimodal task in the field of artificial intelligence in recent years. Given an image and a natural language

© Springer Nature Switzerland AG 2020
I. Farkaš et al. (Eds.): ICANN 2020, LNCS 12397, pp. 786–797, 2020.
https://doi.org/10.1007/978-3-030-61616-8_63

question about the image, the task is to provide an accurate natural language answer. This task has received significant interest from researchers because it not only can be utilized to examine the development of multimodal and cross-modal technologies [6], but also has great potentials in real-world application scenarios [8].

Despite significant progress in recent years, the majority of conducted research focuses on improving accuracy on current hand-curated VQA datasets [3,7,10], in most of which questions are relevant to corresponding images by default. When given an irrelevant question to an image, current state-of-the-art models would still produce an answer with a high probability score rather than predict that the question is irrelevant and cannot be answered correctly. Obviously, it is not what we expect for an intelligent VQA system. On the one hand, this situation shows that current VQA models do not truly understand visual information of images and what questions are asking about. On the other hand, producing answers to irrelevant questions would be a harm to user experience and mislead users by conveying misinformation that premises in questions are all correct.

More formally, irrelevant questions in the context of VQA can be defined by premises [15], which are facts implied by questions. For instance, the question "What's the black cat on the table doing?" implies the presence of a black cat, a table, and that the cat is on the table. Mahendru et al. [15] categories premises into three classes of order. The first-order premises mean the presence of objects (e.g. a cat). The second-order premises reflect attributes of objects (e.g. a black cat) and the third-order premises are about relations and interactions between objects (e.g. a cat on a table). Once there is at least one false premise in a question, the question should be classified as an irrelevant question to the paired image. In the previous example, if there is a dog instead of a cat, or the cat is under the table in the image, the question is irrelevant to the image. In this case, if a VQA model still gives an answer like "sleeping", misinformation that there is "a black cat on the table" in the image would be conveyed to the asker.

Current approaches treat the VQA task as a multiclass classification problem. Given a question $q \in Q$ and an image $v \in V$, a VQA model is expected to give the ground truth answer $a^* \in A$ with the highest classification score

$$\hat{a} = \underset{a \in A}{\operatorname{argmax}}\, p_\theta(a|v, q), \tag{1}$$

where $\hat{a}$ is the predicted answer, and θ are the parameters of the trained model. The task of irrelevant question detection can be defined as a binary classification task. For a question-image pair (q, v), the task is to classify whether the question q is relevant to the image v.

Works of Ray et al. [16] and Mahendru et al. [15] are most related to ours. Ray et al. [16] firstly introduce the problem of irrelevant question detection in the context of VQA. They construct a dataset named VTFQ (Visual True and False Question) by showing annotators with images paired with randomly selected questions and asking them to annotate whether the question is relevant to the corresponding image or not. Mahendru et al. [15] propose a premise extraction pipeline to automatically extract premise information from questions. In their paper, they give a formal definition of question premises and classify premises into mentioned three orders according to their complexity. A new dataset named QRPE (Question Relevance Prediction and Explanation) is constructed by them for the task of irrelevant question detection based on premises of questions. This dataset encompasses more and ambiguous examples in comparison to the VTFQ dataset, which makes it more challenging. Several different methods have been proposed for detecting question relevance in these works. Their experimental results indicate that methods based on image captioning models have the best performance on this task. Thought both of these papers briefly mention the benefits of integrating relevance detection to existing VQA systems, less attention has been devoted to relations between the relevance detection task and the VQA task.

In this paper, we have a hypothesis that the abilities required for detecting irrelevant questions are similar to those required for answering visual questions. In contrast to answering visual questions, judging whether a question is relevant to an image also requires a model to have a thorough and comprehensive understanding of both images and questions. To achieve this task, a model has to acquire information about classes of objects, colors, relative locations, counts, etc. Based on this hypothesis, using an end-to-end network architecture designed for the VQA task for detecting irrelevant questions is a more natural approach, in contrast to existing best-performing methods [15,16] which utilize separated image captioning models and MLP networks. In this work, we investigate the possibility of solving the task of irrelevant question detection with a neural network designed for the VQA task.

To integrate the ability to detect irrelevant questions into a VQA model, a straight-forward idea is training a VQA model jointly on a dataset containing both relevant cases and irrelevant cases by treating answers of irrelevant cases as "irrelevant". However, interference between these two tasks is still unclear when jointly training them together. Therefore we conduct several experiments to investigate this issue. We expect the performance of the joint model on both of two tasks could be boosted based on our hypothesis. Our main contributions are as follows:

1. We find that the task of irrelevant question detection could be solved well by a neural network designed for the VQA task.
2. We set a new baseline accuracy on the QRPE dataset.
3. We find that the task of irrelevant question detection benefits from iterative reasoning and relational modeling.
4. We find that jointly training a VQA model on extended VQA data containing irrelevant cases impairs the accuracy on the VQA task while the performance on the task of irrelevant question detection is maintained.

2   Model

We choose the Multimodal Relational reasoning (MuRel) network [5], one of the current state-of-the-art models on the VQA task, as our basic model.

Explicit iterative reasoning and relational modeling abilities distinguish MuRel from other networks. Two components associated with iterative reasoning and relational modeling in the network are the MuRel cell and the pairwise module. It has been shown that visual features fed into a VQA model play an important role in VQA performance [2,9]. MuRel uses the Bottom-up features [2] to represent images. An object detector Faster R-CNN [17] is used to extract region feature vectors to generate the Bottom-up features of images. A pretrained skip-thought encoder [12] is used for the question features extraction.

MuRel cell takes visual features and question features as inputs and produces updated visual features. The MuRel cell could be invoked several times to update visual features interactively. A pairwise module is an element of the MuRel cell. It obtains region features and coordinates of regions to model relations between them. An efficient bilinear fusion module [4] is used as the multimodal fusion strategy to combine visual and language information. A running process of the MuRel cell with the pairwise module is formalized as

$$\{s_i^t\} = MuRelCell(\{s_i^{t-1}\}, \{b_i\}, q), \tag{2}$$

where $t \in \{1, ..., T\}$ is the step number of the current process, s_i^t represents the updated representation of region i, b_i is the coordinate of region i and q is the representation of the input question. In the first step of the process (when $t = 1$), $s_i^0 = v_i$ exists, where v_i is the feature of region i of the visual features provided by the Bottom-up features. After the last step of this process, when $t = T$, all s_i^T are aggregated together to provide a single vector s, which is then fused with question features q to produce a probability distribution $\hat{y}$ over all possible answers. This process can be formalized as

$$\hat{y} = B(s, q, \Theta_c), \tag{3}$$

where Θ_c are trainable parameters of the classifier.

We term MuRel2 the MuRel relational reasoning network trained for relevance detection with a binary classifier. The network architecture of MuRel2 is illustrated in Fig. 1. The network is applied to the task of irrelevant question detection. Inputs of MuRel2 are Bottom-up features of images and question features extracted by a skip-thought encoder. Labels of "relevant" and "irrelevant" in irrelevant question detection datasets are treated as two answers and correspond to two output neurons. Cross entropy loss is calculated to supervise the learning process.

3 Validation of MuRel2

3.1 Dataset

We use the QRPE dataset[1] [15] to evaluate the MuRel2 model and compare it against other approaches on the task of irrelevant question detection.

---

[1] https://virajprabhu.github.io/qpremise/dataset/.

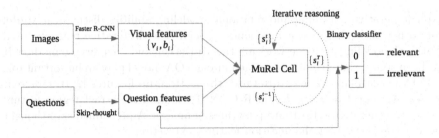

Fig. 1. Illustration of the network architecture of MuRel2.

The QRPE dataset is curated automatically based on the MSCOCO [14], Visual Genome [13] and VQA v2 dataset [7]. First-order and second-order premises are firstly extracted from questions through a semantic tuple extraction pipeline used in the SPICE metric [1] for evaluating the quality of image captions. For first-order premises, irrelevant images for a question are selected by checking the absence of the appropriate class label in the MSCOCO annotations. For second-order premises, images that contain a matching object but a different attribute to the question premise according to annotations of Visual Genome are determined as irrelevant images. To ensure that the irrelevant image is similar enough to the relevant image, the one with the closest visual distance to the relevant image has been selected from irrelevant candidate images. In the end, every question in the QRPE dataset is paired with a relevant image and an irrelevant image. Compared to the VTFQ dataset, which is the first dataset for the task of irrelevant question detection, the QRPE dataset is balanced in the label space, larger and constructed in finer granularity.

The training set of the QRPE dataset contains 35,486 irrelevant question-image pairs which are generated from the training set of the VQA v2 dataset. The test set of the QRPE dataset contains 18,425 irrelevant question-image pairs which are generated from the validation set of the VQA v2 dataset. Based on the order of the false premise, irrelevant cases can be divided into a first-order part and a second-order part. The number of irrelevant question-image pairs in the QRPE dataset is shown in Table 1.

Table 1. Number of irrelevant question-image pairs in the QRPE dataset.

Split	Overall	First-order	Second-order
Training set	35,486	32,939	2,547
Test set	18,425	17,096	1,329

3.2   Experimental Setup

Matching the experimental setup of existing methods we compare, we randomly select 90% of the training set of the QRPE dataset for training and the rest for validation. To avoid bias resulting from random division, we train 5 models independently and report the average accuracy of them on the test set as final results. All MuRel2 models are trained from scratch on the QRPE dataset. We performed some preliminary study for training strategy and critical hyperparameters. We observed that overfitting problems can easily arise when inappropriate learning rates applied. Finally, a similar learning scheduler as [5] with different settings is used in our training. We begin with a learning rate of $5e-6$, linearly increasing it at each epoch till it reaches $2e-5$ at epoch 6. Then we decrease the learning rate by a factor of 0.25 every 2 epochs from epoch 8 to epoch 14, at which we stop training. In our experiments, the batch size is set to 80, and experiments are conducted on $2 \times$ NVIDIA Geforce 1080 TI.

3.3   Comparison to State-of-the-Art Approaches

We compare MuRel2 against state-of-the-art approaches on the QRPE dataset. The goal of this experiment is to evaluate whether a well-performing network designed for the VQA task can solve the task of irrelevant question detection well.

QC-Sim, PC-Sim, and QPC-Sim [15] are existing best-performing approaches on the QRPE dataset. QC-Sim uses an image captioning model NeuralTalk2 [11] pretrained on the MSCOCO dataset to automatically generate natural language descriptions for images. An LSTM network is used to encode both the generated image captions and corresponding questions into vector representations. Then, question and caption representations are concatenated and fed into an MLP network to predict the relevance between questions and images. PC-Sim and QPC-Sim are variants of QC-Sim. PC-Sim uses automatically generated image captions and premises extracted from questions for relevance prediction. QPC-Sim considers all the three sources, including questions, premises, and captions, for relevance prediction, and achieved the highest overall accuracy.

Results of MuRel2 in Table 2 are achieved when the number of reasoning steps is set to 3 and the pairwise module is not used. Figure 2 shows the training curves of MuRel2 under this setting. The figure indicates that the model converges soon. After 8 epochs, an evaluation accuracy of around 90% is reached. We can notice that from epoch 8 on, the evaluation loss starts to increase slightly, which indicates that the model tends to overfit. A comparison of accuracy between MuRel2 and other approaches on the overall and two splits of the test set of the QRPE dataset is shown in Table 2.

Results of QC-Sim, PC-Sim, and QPC-Sim are reported in their original paper [15]. The accuracy on the test set would be 50% if chosen at random since every question in the test set of QRPE is paired with a relevant and an irrelevant image. From Table 2, we can see that MuRel2 outperforms existing best performing approaches by a big margin (over 10%) both on the overall

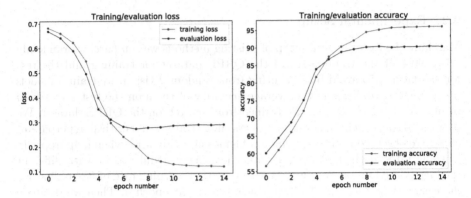

Fig. 2. Training curves of MuRel2 on the QRPE dataset.

Table 2. Comparison of accuracies on the QRPE dataset.

Models	Overall	First-order	Second-order
QC-Sim	74.35	75.82	55.12
PC-Sim	75.05	76.47	56.04
QPC-Sim	75.35	76.67	55.95
MuRel2	**86.62**	**88.13**	**67.02**

test set and each split divided according to the order of false premises. We can conclude from this experiment that a network architecture designed for the VQA task can solve the task of irrelevant question detection well.

3.4   Ablation Study

In this part, we investigate the effects of multi-step reasoning and relational modeling on irrelevant question detection. Their contributions to the VQA task have been well proven [5]. In Table 3, we compare four MuRel2 models with different settings. To ensure comparability, we train them following the same experimental setup. The setting "Pairwise" means whether the pairwise module is used and the setting "Iter." means whether iterative reasoning is used. In our experiments, the number of reasoning steps is set to 3 when iterative reasoning is used.

The results in Table 3 show that a MuRel2 model with iterative reasoning but without the pairwise relational module achieves the best overall performance and the highest accuracies on both the first-order and second-order part. The first three rows of Table 3 show that both iterative reasoning and relational modeling contribute to MuRel2 network's performance on the QRPE dataset, which is consistent with their benefits on the VQA task. However, comparing row 3 and row 4, we find adding the pairwise module to a model with iterative reasoning results in a loss of accuracy. We observed that the distance between training and evaluation loss curves increases when the pairwise module is used in this case, thus a possible explanation for this situation is using the iterative reasoning process and the pairwise module together leads to overfitting.

Table 3. Accuracies in the ablation study of MuRel2.

Pairwise	Iter.	Overall	First-order	Second-order
✗	✗	85.64	87.20	65.69
✓	✗	86.15	87.84	64.35
✗	✓	**86.62**	**88.13**	**67.02**
✓	✓	86.16	87.72	66.27

4   Joint Training

In this part, we investigate the idea of integrating the ability to detect irrelevant questions into a VQA model by joint training a VQA model on a training set containing also irrelevant cases. For handling irrelevant cases, the model treats answers of irrelevant cases as a special answer "irrelevant". Based on our hypothesis that abilities required for detecting irrelevant questions are similar to those required for answering visual questions, we expect that training data for these two tasks could benefit each other by joint training. The approach to joint training the MuRel network on an extended VQA dataset containing irrelevant cases is illustrated in Fig. 3.

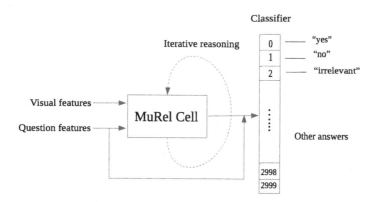

Fig. 3. Illustration of the approach to joint training the MuRel network on an extended VQA dataset containing irrelevant cases.

4.1 Dataset

In extended training sets, irrelevant cases are annotated with answer "irrelevant" for fitting VQA networks. In our experiments, we construct extended training sets based on the VQA v2 dataset, which is the most widely used VQA dataset. The VQA v2 dataset contains 443K, 214K, and 453K question-image pairs for training, evaluation, and testing respectively. We denote the training set of the VQA v2 dataset as $VQAv2$ in our experiments. We assume that all questions in the VQA v2 dataset are relevant to their corresponding images since human annotators are instructed to ask questions about the image that can be answered. First, we add 90% of irrelevant question-image pairs in the training set of the QRPE dataset to $VQAv2$ to build an extended training set $VQAv2 + QRPE$. The reason why we only select 90% of irrelevant cases is to match the training setting in Sect. 3 for fair comparisons on the test set of the QRPE dataset. In $VQAv2 + QRPE$, irrelevant cases account for 6.7% of all cases. To investigate the impact of different proportions of irrelevant cases, we construct another training set by adding all irrelevant cases in the training set of both the QRPE dataset and the VTFQ dataset. We denote this training set as $VQAv2 + QRPE + VTFQ$, of which irrelevant cases account for 9.0%.

For $VQAv2$, 3000 most frequent answers are selected as candidate answers. The top two most frequent answers are "yes" and "no", both of which occur over 80K times in the training set. Following them are answers "1" and "2", both of which occur over 10K times.

For $VQAv2 + QRPE$ and $VQAv2 + QRPE + VTFQ$, the special answer "irrelevant" is included in the 3000 candidate answers. In these two training sets, counts of the answer "irrelevant" are 31938 and 44024 respectively, which matches the numbers of irrelevant cases in them. Thus, in both of these two training sets, the answer "irrelevant" ranks between "no" and "1". The count of answer "irrelevant" is about half the count of answer "yes" and in the same order of magnitude as some other frequent answers.

4.2 Experimental Setup

For experiments on joint training, we use a MuRel network with a pairwise module and a 3-step iterative reasoning process, because this setting achieves the best performance on the VQA v2 dataset. We adopt the same learning schedulers with the original MuRel model [5] trained on the VQA v2 dataset. The starting learning rate is set to $1.5e-4$ with a batch size of 160. Models are trained for 25 epochs. Our experiments are conducted on $4 \times$ NVIDIA Geforce 1080 TI. We train all models on different training sets following the same experimental setup to ensure comparability.

4.3 Results

Three MuRel models are trained on $VQAv2$, $VQAv2 + QRPE$, $VQAv2 + QRPE + VTFQ$ respectively and evaluated on the validation set of the VQA v2 dataset at every epoch. Checkpoints with the highest top 1 accuracy on the validation set are selected and tested on the *test-dev* split of the VQA v2 dataset for comparison. Scores of accuracy in Table 4 are calculated by the evaluation metric of the VQA Challenge[2] for all questions, "yes/no" questions, "number" questions, and other questions that are neither answered "yes/no" nor number.

Table 4. Resulting accuracies on the *test-dev* split of the VQA v2 dataset after joint training on different training sets

Training set	Yes/No	Num.	Other	All
$VQAv2$	82.70	48.32	**56.13**	**66.19**
$VQAv2 + QRPE$	**83.03**	47.95	54.79	65.64
$VQAv2 + QRPE + VTFQ$	82.91	**48.35**	54.69	65.59

From the accuracies shown in Table 4, we derive that jointly training a VQA model on training sets containing also irrelevant cases has a negative impact on its overall performance on the normal VQA data. As the proportion of irrelevant cases increases, the overall accuracy gradually decreases. We notice that the accuracy of "yes/no" questions can be improved when training on extended training sets.

We also test the MuRel model trained on $VQAv2 + QRPE$ on the test set of the QRPE dataset to see the impacts of joint training on the task of irrelevant question detection. To get the accuracy of this model on an irrelevant question detection dataset, we treat the answer of "irrelevant" as a prediction of irrelevance and other answers as a prediction of relevance. For a fair comparison, we take the same checkpoint that produces in scores in Table 4 for testing on the QRPE test set. The overall accuracy achieved by this MuRel model on the test set of QRPE is 86.24%. This accuracy is a bit higher than the accuracy of 86.16% achieved by the MuRel2 model with the same setting shown in row 4 of Table 3. It shows that joint training can maintain accuracy on the task of irrelevant question detection well.

To avoid degradation on the VQA task when jointly training a model on a training set containing data for both VQA and relevance detection, we would like to suggest an alternative architecture. In this architecture, network layers for processing features of images and questions are shared for two tasks, while the output layers are separated. When the network is trained on irrelevant cases, parameters in output layers for the VQA task are not updated. This separation procedure might avoid unexpected interference of those tasks and reduce the overfitting problem.

---

[2] https://visualqa.org/evaluation.html.

5   Conclusion

In this paper, we investigate networks designed for VQA on the task of irrelevant question detection. A multimodal relational network for VQA is used for experiments. We demonstrate that the network adapted as a binary classifier outperforms the existing state-of-the-art methods by a large margin on the task of irrelevant question detection. From the ablation study, we derive that the relevance prediction task has the same requirement for the reasoning ability and relational modeling ability as the VQA task has. We also investigate the idea of integrating the ability to detect irrelevant questions into a VQA model by training a VQA model on a training set containing also irrelevant cases. It is interesting that joint training leads to degradation of performance on the normal VQA data, while the accuracy on the task of irrelevant question detection is maintained compared with models trained for each specific task.

Future work may include building a larger and more difficult dataset for the task of irrelevant question detection. Though compared with the VTFQ dataset, the QRPE dataset is collected in a finer granularity by concerning different orders of false premises, it only contains irrelevant questions with false first-order and second-order premises and ignores irrelevant cases with false third-order premises concerning relations and interactions between objects. That makes current datasets unsuitable for the true challenges of the relevance detection task. In addition to the dataset building necessity, it is also promising to study methods of improving models' performance on the VQA task by taking advantage of the task of irrelevant question detection and vice versa. While we observed that jointly training a model on extended datasets containing also irrelevant cases leads to degradation of accuracy on the VQA task, we hypothesize that it may be possible to improve the performance by using other training methods, such as the method mentioned that shared layers are trained jointly while output layers are trained separately.

Acknowledgement. We gratefully acknowledge support from the China Scholarship Council (CSC) and the German Research Foundation (DFG) under project Crossmodal Learning (TRR 169).

References

1. Anderson, P., Fernando, B., Johnson, M., Gould, S.: SPICE: semantic propositional image caption evaluation. In: Leibe, B., Matas, J., Sebe, N., Welling, M. (eds.) ECCV 2016. LNCS, vol. 9909, pp. 382–398. Springer, Cham (2016). https://doi.org/10.1007/978-3-319-46454-1_24
2. Anderson, P., et al.: Bottom-up and top-down attention for image captioning and visual question answering. In: Proceedings of the IEEE Conference on Computer Vision and Pattern Recognition, pp. 6077–6086 (2018)
3. Antol, S., et al..: VQA: visual question answering. In: Proceedings of the IEEE International Conference on Computer Vision, pp. 2425–2433 (2015)

4. Ben-Younes, H., Cadene, R., Thome, N., Cord, M.: BLOCK: bilinear superdiagonal fusion for visual question answering and visual relationship detection. In: Proceedings of the AAAI Conference on Artificial Intelligence, vol. 33, pp. 8102–8109 (2019)
5. Cadene, R., Ben-Younes, H., Cord, M., Thome, N.: MUREL: multimodal relational reasoning for visual question answering. In: Proceedings of the IEEE Conference on Computer Vision and Pattern Recognition, pp. 1989–1998 (2019)
6. Fu, D., et al.: What can computational models learn from human selective attention? A review from an audiovisual unimodal and crossmodal perspective. Front. Integr. Neurosci. **14**, 10 (2020)
7. Goyal, Y., Khot, T., Summers-Stay, D., Batra, D., Parikh, D.: Making the V in VQA matter: elevating the role of image understanding in visual question answering. In: Proceedings of the IEEE Conference on Computer Vision and Pattern Recognition, pp. 6904–6913 (2017)
8. Gurari, D., et al.: VizWiz grand challenge: answering visual questions from blind people. In: Proceedings of the IEEE Conference on Computer Vision and Pattern Recognition, pp. 3608–3617 (2018)
9. Jiang, Y., Natarajan, V., Chen, X., Rohrbach, M., Batra, D., Parikh, D.: Pythia v0.1: the winning entry to the VQA challenge 2018. arXiv preprint arXiv:1807.09956 (2018)
10. Kafle, K., Kanan, C.: An analysis of visual question answering algorithms. In: Proceedings of the IEEE International Conference on Computer Vision, pp. 1965–1973 (2017)
11. Karpathy, A., Fei-Fei, L.: Deep visual-semantic alignments for generating image descriptions. In: Proceedings of the IEEE Conference on Computer Vision and Pattern Recognition, pp. 3128–3137 (2015)
12. Kiros, R., et al.: Skip-thought vectors. In: Advances in Neural Information Processing Systems, pp. 3294–3302 (2015)
13. Krishna, R., et al.: Visual Genome: connecting language and vision using crowdsourced dense image annotations. Int. J. Comput. Vision **123**(1), 32–73 (2017)
14. Lin, T.-Y., et al.: Microsoft COCO: common objects in context. In: Fleet, D., Pajdla, T., Schiele, B., Tuytelaars, T. (eds.) ECCV 2014. LNCS, vol. 8693, pp. 740–755. Springer, Cham (2014). https://doi.org/10.1007/978-3-319-10602-1_48
15. Mahendru, A., Prabhu, V., Mohapatra, A., Batra, D., Lee, S.: The promise of premise: harnessing question premises in visual question answering. arXiv preprint arXiv:1705.00601 (2017)
16. Ray, A., Christie, G., Bansal, M., Batra, D., Parikh, D.: Question relevance in VQA: identifying non-visual and false-premise questions. arXiv preprint arXiv:1606.06622 (2016)
17. Ren, S., He, K., Girshick, R., Sun, J.: Faster R-CNN: towards real-time object detection with region proposal networks. In: Advances in Neural Information Processing Systems, pp. 91–99 (2015)

F-Measure Optimisation and Label Regularisation for Energy-Based Neural Dialogue State Tracking Models

Anh Duong Trinh[1,2]([✉])(iD), Robert J. Ross[1,2](iD), and John D. Kelleher[1,3](iD)

[1] ADAPT Centre, Technological University Dublin, Dublin, Ireland
{anhduong.trinh,robert.ross,john.d.kelleher}@tudublin.ie
[2] School of Computer Science, Technological University Dublin, Dublin, Ireland
[3] Information, Communications and Entertainment Institute, Technological University Dublin, Dublin, Ireland

Abstract. In recent years many multi-label classification methods have exploited label dependencies to improve performance of classification tasks in various domains, hence casting the tasks to structured prediction problems. We argue that multi-label predictions do not always satisfy domain constraint restrictions. For example when the dialogue state tracking task in task-oriented dialogue domains is solved with multi-label classification approaches, slot-value constraint rules should be enforced following real conversation scenarios.

To address these issues we propose an energy-based neural model to solve the dialogue state tracking task as a structured prediction problem. Furthermore we propose two improvements over previous methods with respect to dialogue slot-value constraint rules: (i) redefining the estimation conditions for the energy network; (ii) regularising label predictions following the dialogue slot-value constraint rules. In our results we find that our extended energy-based neural dialogue state tracker yields better overall performance in term of prediction accuracy, and also behaves more naturally with respect to the conversational rules.

Keywords: Neural dialogue state tracking · Energy-based learning · F-measure optimisation · Label regularisation · Multi-label classification · Dialogue processing

1 Introduction

Task-oriented dialogue systems have a wide range of applications in the modern technology world. The performance of dialogue systems depends directly on the performance of their dialogue state tracking (DST) components, that are responsible for maintaining meaningful dialogue representations including user intents and dialogue context. Although the dialogue state tracker plays an essential role, it is far from perfect due to various factors [20].

Task-oriented dialogue systems are typically restricted in specific closed domains, and cast dialogue states as sets of slot-value pairs. Within this setting

© Springer Nature Switzerland AG 2020
I. Farkaš et al. (Eds.): ICANN 2020, LNCS 12397, pp. 798–810, 2020.
https://doi.org/10.1007/978-3-030-61616-8_64

the dialogue state tracking task can be interpreted as a multi-task classification problem, where tracking the value of each slot is by itself a classification task. This interpretation is applied for various public dialogue domains [3,19].

To date various deep learning approaches have been proposed to tackle the dialogue state tracking problem as a combination of individual tasks [10,17] or in a multi-task learning-based fashion [13]. Among multi-task learning-based approaches it is also common to treat the dialogue state tracking task as a multi-label classification problem [21]. While classic multi-label classification methods assume independence between class labels, more recent approaches tend to explore the role of label dependencies in the task, that casts the task itself as a structured prediction problem. From a practical point of view, structured prediction models have shown significant improvements in natural language processing. Particularly in the dialogue processing field, recent structured dialogue state trackers [14,15] demonstrate that accounting for label associations can boost the performance when used to supplement a classic deep learning approach. In these models the label dependencies are captured via an energy function that is implemented with a deep learning architecture in the so-called energy-based learning methodology [8].

Despite the fact that a structured prediction methodology has already improved multi-label classification models' performance, we argue that there is still room for improvement. In particular, multi-label classifiers do not naturally enforce strict restrictions on dialogue states such that each slot has only one activated value at any time during the conversation. Such restrictions can be thought of as additional constraints on the structured prediction task. In order to investigate this phenomenon we propose a modelling approach to improve energy-based neural dialogue state trackers focusing on: (i) revising and redefining the energy-based estimation of the dialogue states; and (ii) applying slot-value constraint rules via label regularisation. Furthermore we conduct a detailed error analysis on the impact of the mentioned points on the structured prediction performance.

We proceed by introducing the domains in which we work in a more detail before going on to detail the specifics of our contributed model and subsequent analysis.

2   Task-Oriented Dialogue Domains

The effectiveness of structured prediction is based on the assumption of dependencies between label classes. We base our work on the analysis of a series of well-known dialogue datasets that have moderate size and are limited to a single closed domain. The first two datasets we chose come from the second and the third dialogue state tracking challenge (DSTC2 & 3) competitions. The third dataset was created more recently with Wizard-of-Oz crowd-sourced data collection framework, and is named WOZ 2.0[1]. The details of these datasets are as follow:

---

[1] From here we simplify the name of this dataset to WOZ as in common practice.

- DSTC2 [3] is a restaurant information dataset that consists of spoken conversations. It includes 1612 dialogues for training, 506 dialogues for validation, and 1117 dialogues for testing. DSTC2 dialogue states consist of three subtasks: *Joint goals*, *Search methods*, and *Requested slots*; and among these the latter two have been solved with various machine learning and deep learning approaches. The most difficult task is *Joint goals*, which requires tracking the value of four informable slots: *food*, *price range*, *area*, and *name*. However the slot *name* is omitted from many works due to the lack of its appearance in the whole dataset.
- DSTC3 [4] is a spoken dialogue dataset in the tourism information domain. It contains 2286 dialogues in a complete set. The dialogue states are defined in the same way as the DSTC2 challenge. In this work we solve the *Joint goals* task of only four informable slots, *food*, *price range*, *area*, and *type*, as we omit other slots due to their extremely low appearance frequency in the data.
- WOZ [19] is a chat-based restaurant information dataset that shares the same ontology as DSTC2. The WOZ dataset includes 1200 dialogues in total, split into the training, validation, and test sets with a ratio 3:1:2. The WOZ data is collected in a Wizard-of-Oz chat environment, therefore it is cleaner than DSTC2. Subsequently the tracking results can be much higher. The WOZ dialogue state tracking task requires capturing the *Joint goals* of three slots (*food*, *price range*, and *area*), as well as the *Requested Slots*.

In all domains we focus on the most challenging task, *Joint goals*, and study the impact of label dependencies between informable slots in the tracking process.

To verify that interlabel dependencies are present, we investigated label dependencies of DSTC2 & 3 data with Pearson's chi-square test and related measurements [16]. The statistical test analysis shows that there exist dependencies between dialogue slots. In this work we conduct similar statistical tests for the WOZ dataset. We observe the associations between WOZ data slots with the Cramer's V coefficient as follow: *food – price range* 0.316; *food – area* 0.302; *price range – area* 0.180. The analysis indicates that there exist dependencies between the WOZ slots.

3   Energy-Based Dialogue State Tracker

Energy-based learning [8] focuses on exploiting the dependencies between different variables in the system. The classic concept of learning energy values is that the energy function should be trained to assign lower values to correct variable configurations, and higher energy for undesired variable configurations.

The architecture of an energy-based model is usually split into two components: a feature function $F(X)$, and an energy function $E(F(X), Y)$, where X and Y are input and output variables respectively. In the implementation of our energy-based dialogue state tracker we develop the feature function with a hierarchical recurrent neural network to transform dialogue data into meaningful high-dimensional representations, and the energy function with a deep learning network to estimate the goodness of fit between variables. We detail these below before discussing the learning and inference strategies.

3.1 Multi-task Recurrent Neural Feature Network

Our feature function network $F(X)$ is designed with a hierarchical recurrent neural network architecture to extract dialogue data in a fixed-size vector representations (Fig. 1). The architecture consists of three main elements:

- A bidirectional LSTM layer [7] for user input;
- An encoder for machine acts for the DSTC2 & 3 data, or a bidirectional LSTM layer for machine transcripts for the WOZ data. We parse the DSTC machine acts with the technique proposed by Henderson et al. [6];
- A LSTM layer to handle dialogue turns, that takes the output of the above two elements as the input and produces the vector representations of dialogues on a turn-based basis.

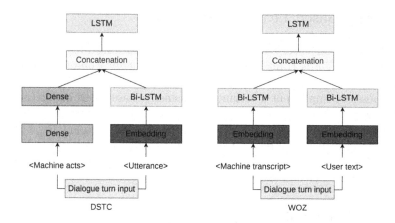

Fig. 1. Multi-task recurrent neural feature network for DSTC and WOZ datasets.

Following the practice of pretraining the feature network to achieve higher results [1], we pretrain our feature network with a multi-task learning method proposed by Trinh et al. [13]. The representations extracted with this feature network are in turn fed into the subsequent energy network.

3.2 Deep Neural Energy Network

Our energy network is developed based on the concept of the Structured Prediction Energy Network (SPEN) [1], that consists of two energy terms: local energy and global energy. It is formulated as follow:

– Energy function

$$E(F(X), Y) = E_{local}(F(X), Y) + E_{global}(Y) \tag{1}$$

– Local energy represents the relationships between input and label variables

$$E_{local}(F(X), Y) = \sum_{i=1}^{L} y_i W_i^\top F(X) \tag{2}$$

– Global energy calculates the associations between label variables

$$E_{global}(Y) = W_2^\top f(W_1^\top Y) \tag{3}$$

Here we use the tuple, $\theta = \{W, W_1, W_2\}$, to capture the energy trainable parameters, $f(\cdot)$ is a non-linearity function for the global energy, and L is the number of classes in the target.

This has been applied previously in other structured dialogue state trackers [14,15].

4   Energy-Based Learning Strategy

The training of an energy-based model involves learning functions such that the energy function is trained to assign minimal energy value for desired variable configurations, while giving higher energy to undesired configurations. For this purpose, we implement a variant of the energy-based learning methodology based on the Deep Value Networks [2], that use a F-measurement to evaluate the compatibility between variables. However, while this variant has been successfully applied to structured dialogue state tracking [14], it is not as we noted earlier well designed for the case of outputs where certain types of constraints on those outputs much be adhered to.

4.1   Ground Truth Energy

Initially Gygli et al. [2] propose to define the ground truth energy $E_{F_1}^*$ through the use of the dice coefficient F_1 measurement as the estimation for the fitness of the predicted labels and ground truth labels. This measurement was invented to evaluate discreet classification output, and now is modified to fit the dialogue state predictions as continuous variables, that also makes it differentiable for the training process. The ground truth dice coefficient F_1 is defined as:

$$E_{F_1}^*(Y, Y^*) = \frac{2(Y \cap Y^*)}{(Y \cap Y^*) + (Y \cup Y^*)} \tag{4}$$

where Y is the predicted labels, Y^* is the ground truth labels, $Y \cap Y^* = \sum_i \min(y_i, y_i^*)$ and $Y \cup Y^* = \sum_i \max(y_i, y_i^*)$ are extended for continuous output variables.

We argue that the sums $\sum_i \min(y_i, y_i^*)$ and $\sum_i \max(y_i, y_i^*)$ are in fact the lower and upper boundaries of these vectors, therefore they indicate the extreme values in all cases. In a multi-label classification task the differentiable F_1 metric can be defined in a more relaxed manner [18]:

$$E_{F_1}^*(Y, Y^*) = \frac{2 \sum_i y_i y_i^*}{\sum_i y_i + \sum_i y_i^*} \tag{5}$$

When comparing the two F_1 scores in Eqs. 4 and 5, it is not difficult to mathematically prove that

$$\sum_i \min(y_i, y_i^*) = \sum_i y_i y_i^*$$
$$\sum_i \min(y_i, y_i^*) + \sum_i \max(y_i, y_i^*) = \sum_i y_i + \sum_i y_i^* \tag{6}$$

given the fact that any ground truth label y_i^* can hold only the value 0 or 1.

However, we argue that Eq. 4 makes the differential process discontinuous based on the nature of the operations min and max. Therefore we propose to use Eq. 5 as the formula for the ground truth energy for our energy-based learning experiments. We retain the cross entropy loss function for the experiments:

$$L(E, E_{F_1}^*) = -E_{F_1}^* \log E - (1 - E_{F_1}^*) \log(1 - E) \tag{7}$$

where $E = E(F(X), Y)$ is the predicted energy, and $E_{F_1}^* = E_{F_1}^*(Y, Y^*)$ is the ground truth energy.

4.2   Label Regularisation

In order to apply the dialogue restriction, that requires assigning only one value to a slot at any time of the conversation, onto the dialogue state prediction, we propose a label regularisation term that would penalise the predictions that activate greater or fewer values than the number of activated values in the ground truth labels. We formulate this regularisation term as follow:

$$R(Y, Y^*) = \left(\frac{\sum_i y_i - \sum_i y_i^*}{\sum_i y_i^*} \right)^2 \tag{8}$$

where Y is the predicted output, and Y^* is the ground truth labels.

Our use of the term regularisation is based on its more general meaning and is fundamentally different from the L_2 or L_1 regularisation that instead penalise excessive parameter values.

Ultimately the objective function including the label regularisation term for training the energy network in our proposal is formulated as follow:

$$\mathcal{L} = L(E, E_{F_1}^*) + \alpha R(Y, Y^*)$$
$$= \left(-E_{F_1}^* \log E - (1 - E_{F_1}^*) \log(1 - E) \right) + \alpha \left(\frac{\sum_i y_i - \sum_i y_i^*}{\sum_i y_i^*} \right)^2 \tag{9}$$

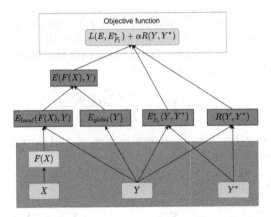

Fig. 2. The learning process of our energy-based dialogue state tracker.

where α is the regularisation coefficient.

The whole learning process is visualised in Fig. 2.

Overall, the redefinition of the objective function, that includes redesigning the ground truth energy and introducing the label regularisation, is a novel contribution to work on structured prediction dialogue state tracking.

5   Experiment Setup

As outlined above to achieve the best results the feature network should be pre-trained. Therefore we stage our experiments in two phases. Firstly, we train the feature network in a multi-task learning system where the target variables are assumed to be independent. We train the multi-tasks systems for each dataset five times with different weight initialisation and select the best one to extract dialogue features. Secondly, we train the energy network while freezing the feature network. The energy network is also trained five times, but the outcomes of the network are ensembled into an end prediction for evaluation. The performance of both the multi-task feature network and the energy network will be reported separately to show the improvement based on label dependencies that we aim to leverage.

As the DSTC2 and WOZ data are split into training, validation, and test subsets, we use them directly according to the purpose of these sets. Meanwhile, the DSTC3 data is provided in a single set, therefore we split it into five folds and trained our system with a cross validation technique.

6   Results and Discussion

We report the overall performance of both our multi-task feature system and energy-based system against the DSTC2 & 3 and WOZ data, and benchmark them against the state-of-the-art models in Table 1. The state-of-the-art models are selected if either they achieve the highest accuracy result or they are related to our work.

Table 1. Performances of the state-of-the-art and our dialogue state tracking systems on the DSTC 2 & 3 and WOZ data. The results for *Joint Goals* are reported with the Accuracy metric. The baseline models for DSTC2 & 3 were proposed during the competitions [3,4], and the baseline model for WOZ is the very first work on this dataset [10].

Model	DSTC2	DSTC3	WOZ
Globally-conditioned encoder (GCE) [11]	–	–	0.885
Hybrid system [17]	0.796	–	–
Multi-domain system [9]	0.774	0.671	–
Word-based system [6]	0.768	–	–
Global-locally self-attentive tracker (GLAD) [21]	0.745	–	0.881
Unsupervised RNN-based system [5]	–	0.646	–
Our work			
Energy-based system	0.774	0.651	0.875
Multi-task feature system	0.709	0.531	0.841
Baseline [3,4,10]	0.719	0.575	0.844

We find that the energy-based learning approach boosts the results on top of the multi-task learning methodology, up to 12% accuracy, across the datasets. That improvement strongly indicates that the impact of label dependencies in dialogue domains is significant.

Although our energy-based dialogue state trackers yield competitive results for the *Joint goals* task in all three datasets, they do not yet outperform the state-of-the-art performance seen for example in the globally-conditioned encoder (GCE) for WOZ [11], the hybrid system [17] for DSTC2, and the multi-domain system for DSTC3 [9]. However, none of the state-of-the-art systems model the label dependencies in an explicit manner when performing dialogue state tracking. Given that, we believe that their performance could be improved if structured prediction is applied, in particular with the energy-based learning methodology.

As our contributions are centred on the redefinition of the F_1 metric as well as regularising the label constraint rules for the energy-based model, we conduct an analysis of the effectiveness of these phenomena in the dialogue state tracking results. We also conduct an analysis on errors to emphasise the role of label regularisation in structured multi-label classification.

6.1   Improvement Based on F_1 Metric

To evaluate the improvement based on the redefinition of F_1 we benchmark our energy-based model during the development phase with the work done by Trinh et al. [14], which was developed based on the Deep Value Networks algorithm [2] (Table 2). Here we report our work in the development phase, that does not include the label regularisation, hence the performance is different from Table 1.

Table 2. Performances of the energy-based dialogue state trackers with different F_1 metrics on the DSTC 2 & 3 data. The results for *Joint Goals* are reported with Accuracy metric.

Energy-based DST model	DSTC2	DSTC3
Multi-label classification F_1 (this work)	0.769	0.642
Dice coefficient F_1 (Eq. 4) [14]	0.760	0.622

From this we can observe that by redefining the F_1 measurement the energy-based model achieves a slight improvement, that is approximately 1% accuracy for DSTC2 and 2% accuracy for DSTC3. We cannot compare the performance against the WOZ dataset, as it was not reported with the dice coefficient F_1 metric.

6.2   Effectiveness of Label Regularisation

The impact of label regularisation is reported in two types of analysis: the overall performance of our energy-based model before and after including the regularisation term, and the proportion of correct predictions over the total number of dialogue turns that follow the slot-value constraint rules with different thresholds.

With label regularisation we find that the overall performance of our energy-based trackers is not improved significantly (Table 3). The performance accuracy improvement across three datasets is less than 1%, that is small in comparison with the result differences seen between the multi-task feature system and the energy-based system, or when comparing with the achievement based on the F_1 measure redefinition.

Table 3. Performances of the energy-based dialogue state trackers with and without label regularisation on the DSTC 2 & 3 and WOZ data. The results for *Joint Goals* are reported with Accuracy metric.

Energy-based DST model	DSTC2	DSTC3	WOZ
With label regularisation	0.774	0.651	0.875
Without label regularisation	0.769	0.642	0.866

We conduct another analysis to evaluate the behaviours of our energy-based systems when tracking dialogue states with our regularisation (Table 4). In this analysis we set different threshold values, and consider a value activated if the predicted belief score of this value exceeds the threshold. Among the correct predictions we count the number of those predictions satisfying the slot-value constraint rules in task-oriented dialogue domains such that each slot has only one activated value at any moment. Finally we report the proportion of recorded numbers against the total number of dialogue turns in the datasets.

Table 4. Analysis of the label regularisation on the energy-based dialogue state tracking on the DSTC 2 & 3 and WOZ data. The results are reported with the proportion (%) of the correct predictions over the total number of dialogue turns, that follow the slot-value constraint rules.

Threshold	DSTC2		DSTC3		WOZ	
	+Reg	−Reg	+Reg	−Reg	+Reg	−Reg
0.5	76.1	75.6	65.0	63.9	87.2	86.1
0.7	73.7	72.8	64.6	62.4	85.7	83.8
0.9	63.4	59.6	62.8	59.3	80.9	78.7

We find that with different threshold values the energy-based systems with label regularisation consistently outperform those without the regularisation term. This finding indicates that the impact of label regularisation in the dialogue state tracking process is systematic. Not only can it improve the overall performance, but it also guides the system's prediction behaviour towards the requirement of specific domains.

6.3   Error Analysis

To our knowledge only one example of a comparative error analysis of dialogue state trackers was given by Smith [12]. In that analysis the author reports the error distributions of tracking models over three error types of possible deviations from the true joint goal for every turn in the dialogue. We find that these error types match our label regularisation analysis as such:

- Missing attributes (MA) is the error where the tracker fails to recognise a value for a slot despite it being present in data. In our scenario we interpret this as the label regulariser assigning the number of activated values less than the number of slots.
- Extraneous attributes (EA) is the error where the tracker classifies unnecessary values for a slot when they are not mentioned in the data. In our task it is similar to the situation when the number of activated values is bigger than the number of slots.
- False attributes (FA) is the error that occurs when the tracker assigns a false value to a slot. In this case the number of activated values satisfies the slot-value constraint rules that we apply, but the tracked dialogue state is wrong due to the false value.

The analysis results of error distributions are reported in Table 5, where we compare the behaviours of our energy-based dialogue state tracker with and without the label regularisation. We set the activated threshold 0.5 for the error analysis.

Table 5. Error distributions of the energy-based dialogue state trackers on the DSTC 2 & 3 and WOZ data. The results are reported with the proportion (%) of the number of errors with the respective type over the total number of incorrectly predicted turns.

Dataset	Label	#Turns	Error distributions		
			MA	FA	EA
DSTC2	+Reg	2235	436 (19.5%)	1283 (57.4%)	516 (23.1%)
	−Reg	2285	660 (28.9%)	919 (40.2%)	706 (30.9%)
DSTC3	+Reg	6532	1724 (26.4%)	3319 (50.8%)	1489 (22.8%)
	−Reg	6700	2144 (32.0%)	2533 (37.8%)	2023 (30.2%)
WOZ	+Reg	627	96 (15.3%)	399 (63.6%)	132 (21.1%)
	−Reg	672	226 (33.6%)	236 (35.1%)	210 (31.3%)

We observe that where the label regularisation is present, the error distributions move toward the FA error type, that indicates that the majority of errors still satisfy the slot-value constraint rules of the dialogue domains. Meanwhile the energy-based model without the label regularisation term produces more evenly distributed errors with a special case of the WOZ dataset. This finding outlines the effectiveness of the label regularisation term in the training process of our energy-based tracker.

In the comparative error analysis of Smith [12] the error distributions align with the difference in difficulty observed in tracking different slots. For example in the DSTC2 data the error distributions are relative to the order {*food* >> *area* >> *price range*}, that follows the setting of the ontology where the slot *food* has the biggest set of values, while the slot *price range* has the smallest one. However, we do not find this phenomenon in our error analysis. It can be explained that as we treat the dialogue state tracking task as a multi-label classification problem, we flatten the label set and make all the values of any slots equally important.

7   Conclusion

In this paper we demonstrated that an energy-based structured prediction methodology can be improved with additional constraint integration. We have examined this in the context of dialogue systems. By proposing to mathematically optimise the quality measurement, and regularise label classes, we demonstrated that our energy-based model's behaviours achieve a high level of satisfactory in a number of dialogue domains. We also provided a systematic analysis on the tracker's performance regarding the overall improvement, and in particular the error distributions. The error analysis is essential to understand the mechanism of dialogue state tracking process, subsequently it helps to improve future models.

We note that there are elements of the energy-based learning methodology that we can continue to develop. For the learning process of our energy-based model we see that including the label regularisation is not the only possible solution, instead, for example we can also regularise the constraint rules directly in the energy function formulation. On the other hand, the performance of our energy-based tracker can be boosted by an inference strategy where we apply the inference process multiple times to generate multiple alternative predictions and then apply a reranking process to select the best overall prediction as output.

Acknowledgements. This research was conducted with the financial support of Science Foundation Ireland under Grant Agreement No. 13/RC/2106 at the ADAPT SFI Research Centre at Technological University Dublin.

References

1. Belanger, D., McCallum, A.: Structured prediction energy networks. In: Proceedings of the 33rd International Conference on Machine Learning, vol. 48 (2016)
2. Gygli, M., Norouzi, M., Angelova, A.: Deep value networks learn to evaluate and iteratively refine structured outputs. In: Proceedings of the 34th International Conference on Machine Learning (2017)
3. Henderson, M., Thomson, B., Williams, J.D.: The second dialog state tracking challenge. In: Proceedings of the SIGDIAL 2014 Conference, pp. 263–272 (2014)
4. Henderson, M., Thomson, B., Williams, J.D.: The third dialog state tracking challenge. In: Proceedings of 2014 IEEE Workshop on Spoken Language Technology, pp. 324–329 (2014)
5. Henderson, M., Thomson, B., Young, S.: Robust dialog state tracking using delexicalised recurrent neural networks and unsupervised adaptation. In: Proceedings of 2014 IEEE Workshop on Spoken Language Technology, pp. 360–365 (2014)
6. Henderson, M., Thomson, B., Young, S.: Word-based dialog state tracking with recurrent neural networks. In: Proceedings of the SIGDIAL 2014 Conference, pp. 292–299 (2014)
7. Hochreiter, S., Schmidhuber, J.: Long short-term memory. Neural Comput. **9**(8), 1735–1780 (1997). https://doi.org/10.1162/neco.1997.9.8.1735
8. LeCun, Y., Chopra, S., Hadsell, R., Ranzato, M.A., Huang, F.J.: A tutorial on energy-based learning. In: Predicting Structured Data (2006)
9. Mrksic, N., et al.: Multi-domain dialog state tracking using recurrent neural networks. In: Proceedings of the 53rd Annual Meeting of the Association for Computational Linguistics, pp. 794–799 (2015)
10. Mrksic, N., O'Seaghdha, D., Wen, T.H., Thomson, B., Young, S.: Neural belief tracker: data-driven dialogue state tracking. In: Proceedings of the 55th Annual Meeting of the Association for Computational Linguistics (2017). https://doi.org/10.18653/v1/P17-1163
11. Nouri, E., Hosseini-Asl, E.: Toward scalable neural dialogue state tracking model. In: 32nd Conference on Neural Information Processing Systems (NeurIPS 2018), 2nd Conversational AI Workshop (2018)

12. Smith, R.W.: Comparative error analysis of dialog state tracking. In: Proceedings of the SIGDIAL 2014 Conference, pp. 300–309 (2014)

13. Trinh, A.D., Ross, R.J., Kelleher, J.D.: A multi-task approach to incremental dialogue state tracking. In: Proceedings of the 22nd Workshop on the Semantics and Pragmatics of Dialogue, SEMDIAL, pp. 132–145 (2018)

14. Trinh, A.D., Ross, R.J., Kelleher, J.D.: Capturing dialogue state variable dependencies with an energy-based neural dialogue state tracker. In: Proceedings of the SIGDial 2019 Conference, pp. 75–84 (2019)

15. Trinh, A.D., Ross, R.J., Kelleher, J.D.: Energy-based modelling for dialogue state tracking. In: Proceedings of the 1st Workshop on NLP for Conversational AI, pp. 77–86 (2019)

16. Trinh, A.D., Ross, R.J., Kelleher, J.D.: Investigating variable dependencies in dialogue states. In: Proceedings of the 23rd Workshop on the Semantics and Pragmatics of Dialogue, pp. 195–197 (2019)

17. Vodolan, M., Kadlec, R., Kleindienst, J.: Hybrid dialog state tracker with ASR features. In: Proceedings of the 15th Conference of the European Chapter of the Association for Computational Linguistics, EACL, vol. 2, pp. 205–210 (2017)

18. Wang, B., Li, C., Pavlu, V., Aslam, J.: Regularizing model complexity and label structure for multi-label text classification. In: Proceedings of KDD 2017, Halifax, Nova Scotia, Canada (2017)

19. Wen, T.H., et al.: A network-based end-to-end trainable task-oriented dialogue system. In: Proceedings of the 15th Conference of the European Chapter of the Association for Computational Linguistics, EACL, pp. 438–449 (2017)

20. Williams, J.D., Raux, A., Henderson, M.: The dialog state tracking challenge series: a review. Dialogue Discourse **7**(3), 4–33 (2016). https://doi.org/10.5087/dad.2016.301

21. Zhong, V., Xiong, C., Socher, R.: Global-locally self-attentive dialogue state tracker. In: Proceedings of the 56th Annual Meeting of the Association for Computational Linguistics, pp. 1458–1467 (2018)

Unsupervised Learning

Unsupervised Change Detection Using Joint Autoencoders for Age-Related Macular Degeneration Progression

Guillaume Dupont[1], Ekaterina Kalinicheva[1] (ID), Jérémie Sublime[1,2(✉)] (ID),
Florence Rossant[1] (ID), and Michel Pâques[3]

[1] ISEP, 10 rue de Vanves, 92130 Issy-Les-Moulineaux, France
{guillaume.dupont,ekaterina.kalinicheva,jeremie.sublime,
florence.rossant}@isep.fr
[2] LIPN - CNRS UMR 7030, 99 av. J-B Clément, 93430 Villetaneuse, France
[3] Clinical Imaging Center 1423, Quinze-Vingts Hospital, INSERM-DGOS Clinical
Investigation Center, Paris, France
mpaques@15-20.fr

Abstract. Age-Related Macular Degeneration (ARMD) is an eye disease that has been an important research field for two decades now. Researchers have been mostly interested in studying the evolution of lesions that slowly causes patients to go blind. Many techniques ranging from manual annotation to mathematical models of the disease evolution bring interesting leads to explore. However, artificial intelligence for ARMD image analysis has become one of the main research focus to study the progression of the disease, as accurate manual annotation of its evolution has proved difficult using traditional methods even for experienced doctors. Within this context, in this paper, we propose a neural network architecture for change detection in eye fundus images to highlight the evolution of the disease. The proposed method is fully unsupervised, and is based on fully convolutional joint autoencoders. Our algorithm has been applied to several pairs of images from eye fundus images time series of ARMD patients, and has shown to be more effective than most state-of-the-art change detection methods, including non-neural network based algorithms that are usually used to follow the evolution of the disease.

Keywords: Change detection · Unsupervised learning · ARMD

1 Introduction

Dry age-related macular degeneration (ARMD or AMD), a degenerative disease of the retina, is a main cause of irreversible visual loss. It is characterized by a centrifugal progression of atrophy of the retinal pigment epithelium (RPE),

This study has been approved by a French ethical committee (Comité de Protection des Personnes) and all participants gave informed consent.

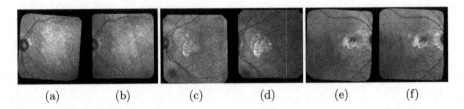

(a)   (b)   (c)   (d)   (e)   (f)

Fig. 1. 3 examples of pairs of images acquired 6 months apart. The GA corresponds to the bright areas. The green arrow in (f) shows a new lesion.

a cellular layer playing a key role in the maintenance of the photoreceptors. Blindness may occur when the fovea (the central part of the eye), is affected. The disease can be diagnosed and monitored using fundus images: ophthalmologists can observe pathologic features such as drusens that occur in the early stages of the ARMD, and evaluate the geographic atrophic (GA) progression in the late stages of degeneration (Fig. 1).

Automatic analysis of dry ARMD fundus images is of high medical interest and this has been an important research field for two decades, for diagnosis [15] or follow up [10,16] purposes. Imaging modalities are most often color eye fundus images [3,11,13], fundus autofluorescence (FAF) [6,12,16], and, to a lesser extent, confocal scanning laser ophthalmoscopy (cSLO) in infrared (IR), or optical coherence tomography (OCT) [5]. In this work, we use cSLO images in infrared (IR): this modality is comfortable to acquire for the patients, and has better resolution and contrast than color imaging, an older technology. Our goal is to detect the appearance of new atrophic areas and quantify the growth of GA from pairs of images acquired from follow-up exams and to ultimately propose predictive models of the disease progress.

Figure 1 shows 3 pairs of consecutive images, taken at 6 months interval. The lesions (GA) in the fundus and around the optical disk are the brighter areas. Monitoring the GA progression in these areas is obviously challenging because of the images quality: uneven light, saturation issues, illumination distortion between images, GA poorly contrasted with retinal structures interfering (vessel, optical disk), blur, etc. The difficulty also lies in the high variability of the lesions in terms of shape, size and number. The lesion boundary is quite smooth in some cases (c and d) and very irregular in others (a and b). At any time, new spots can appear (as shown by the green arrow between e and f) and older lesions can merge. All these defaults make the manual delineation task very complex, even for expert ophthalmologists.

In order to assess the disease progression, it is necessary to perform a differential analysis between consecutive images to get the lesion growth, so that the lesion growth can be modelled. In this paper, we propose a fully unsupervised differential analysis method based on a joint autoencoders. Our model does not require labeled images that are difficult to come by in quantity and quality high enough to train a supervised neural network. Our method is applied to pairs of images of a patient eye fundus time series and aims at efficiently segmenting medically significant changes between the two images: we are interested only in changes in the GA lesions, while meaningless differences and light artefacts should be ignored.

2   Related Works

The following works are most related to our proposed algorithm as they are unsupervised algorithm applied to various eye disease images, including ARMD: In [18], Troglio et al. published an improvement of their previous works realized with Nappo [19] where they use the Kittler and Illingworth (K&I) thresholding method. Their method consists of applying the K&I algorithm on random sub-images of the difference image obtained between two consecutive eye fundus images of a patient with retinopathy. By doing so, they obtain multiple predictions for each pixel and can then make a vote to decide the final class. This approach has the advantage that it compensates for the non-uniform illumination across the image, however it is rather primitive since it does not actually use any Machine Learning and rely on different parameters of the thresholding method to then make a vote. To its credit, even if it achieves a relatively weak precision, it is fully unsupervised like our method. In [13], the authors tackle a similar problematic to ours where they correct eye fundus images by pairs, by multiplying the second image by a polynomial surface whose parameters are estimated in the least-squares sense. In this way, illumination distortion is lessened and the image difference enhances the areas of changes. However, the statistical test applied locally at each pixel is not reliable enough to get an accurate map of structural changes.

Other works related with eye diseases take the different approach of segmenting lesions in individual images instead of looking for changes in pairs of images. In [11], Köse et al. proposed an approach where they first segment all healthy regions to get the lesions as the remaining areas. This approach also requires segmenting separately the blood vessels, which is known to be a difficult task. This method involves many steps and parameters that need to be supervised by the user. In [16], Ramsey et al. proposed a similar but unsupervised method for the identification of ARMD lesions in individual images: They use an unsupervised algorithm based on fuzzy c-means clustering. Their method achieves good performances for FAF images, but it performs less well for color fundus photographs. We can also mention the work of Hussain et al. [7] who proposed another supervised algorithm to track drusen progression for ARMD. It uses a U-Net to segment vessels and detect the optic disc to reduce the region of interest of drusen detection. After that, they detect the drusen using intensity ratio between neighbor pixels.

Other traditional Machine learning algorithms have also been used for GA segmentation such as random forest [3] or k-nearest neighbor classifiers [6]. Feature vectors for these approaches typically include intensity values, local energy, texture descriptors, values derived from multi-scale analysis and distance to the image center. Nevertheless, these algorithms are supervised: they require training the classifier from annotated data, which brings us back to the difficulty of manually segmenting GA areas.

Apart from medicine, change detection algorithms have been proposed for many different applications such as remote sensing or video analysis. In [1] the authors reveal a method combining principal component analysis (PCA) and K-means algorithm on the difference image. In [8], an architecture relying on joint auto-encoders and convolutional neural networks is proposed to detect non-trivial changes between two images. In [2] the authors propose an autoencoder architecture for anomaly detection in videos.

Finally, as we have seen that quite a few methods rely on segmentation first and change detection after. We can also mention a few noteworthy unsupervised segmentation algorithms used outside the field of medicine: Kanezaki et al. [9] used CNN to group similar pixels together with consideration of spatial continuity as a basis of their segmentation method. Finally, W-Nets using with a soft Normalized-Cut Loss are another option.

3   Data Description

In this section, we will provide some details on the data we used.

Our images were all acquired at the Quinze–Vingts National Ophthalmology Hospital in Paris, in cSLO with IR illumination. Patients have been followed-up during a few years, hence we have series of retinal fundus images, often for both eyes, showing the progression of the GA. The average number of images in each series is 13. We used 336 images from 15 patients time series taken between 2007 and 2019. All pictures are in grayscale and vary greatly in size, but the most common size is $650 * 650$ pixels.

As mentioned in the introduction, the images contain many imperfections such as blurs, artifacts and, above all, non-uniform illumination (see Fig. 2). All images were spatially aligned with i2k software[1]. Furthermore, all images are surrounded by black border that contain no useful information. These borders were removed from the segmentation area using a mask.

All images were preprocessed using a new method (not published yet) to reduce the light distortion within images series. This algorithm relies on an illumination/reflectance model and corrects all images of a serie with respect to a common reference image. Uneven illumination generally remains present in every processed image (Fig. 2) but the smooth illumination distortions are compensated. The calculus of the absolute value of the difference between two consecutive images demonstrates the benefit of this algorithm (Fig. 2, last column).

We used 3 different series of images to rate our proposed change detection method: they feature different characteristics in terms of disease progress, lesion

---

[1] https://www.dualalign.com/retinal/image-registration-montage-software-overview.php.

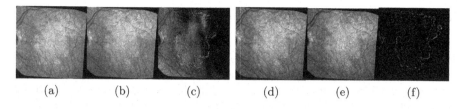

  (a)   (b)   (c)   (d)   (e)   (f)

Fig. 2. Illumination correction. The 3 images on the left represent the 2 original consecutive images and their raw difference in absolute value; On the right: the same images after illumination correction and the new difference.

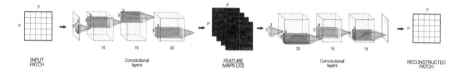

Fig. 3. Autoencoder architecture

shape and size. We developed several user-guided segmentation tools for ophthalmologists to build the validation images with the expected segmentation: These tools allowed them to provide a manual segmentation of some of our dataset images using techniques such as segmentation algorithms, local thresholdings and simple linear interpolation to draw the lesions borders. However, it is worth noting that the task remained long and tedious and couldn't be done for all images as on average, it took 13 min to process one single image. Finally, the binary change mask between two consecutive images was obtained by subtraction of the segmentation masks.

4   Proposed Algorithm

Our algorithm uses principles from previous remote sensing applications [8], where an unsupervised deep autoencoder was used to automatically detect meaningful changes between two satellite images with the goal of finding new constructions or changes in the landcover, all the while discarding seasonal changes.

In our paper, we use the common issues between satellite imaging and our medical ARMD eye fundus to adapt this deep learning algorithm: both types of images may suffer from lighting issues, noise issues, blurry elements, complex objects present in the images, various intervals between images, and most importantly the common goal of detecting only the changes from specific classes within the images.

While the problematic look similar, remote sensing and medical applications also have specific issues: medical images only have one channel, the textures are different, and the size and scale of both the images and objects to analyze is quite different. To account for these specificities, we had to modifiy their AE architecture as described in the next subsection.

4.1   Joint Autoencoder Architecture

As mentioned previously, our algorithm is based on autoencoders. Autoencoders [4] are a type of neural networks whose purpose is to make the output as close as possible to the input. The learnign process consists in an encoder part learning some meaningful representations of the original data and a decoder transforming them back into the original data: in a fully convolutional AE, a stack of convolutive layers is applied to the input image in order to extract feature maps (FM) which will then be used to reconstruct the input image.

Usually AEs with dense layers are used to perform a dimensionality reduction followed by a clustering or segmentation. However, in computer vision, fully convolutionnal AEs are prefered for their ability to extract textures. Examples of such networks include fully convolutional networks (FCNs) or U-Nets [17]. However, in our case we do not use pooling layers, and so we keep the same dimensions as the input and only the depth increases.

Our network (Fig. 3) is made of 4 convolutional layers in the encoder of size 16, 16, 32, 32 respectively, and in the same way of 4 convolutional layers of size 32, 32, 16, 16 respectively in the decoder side. We apply a batch normalization and a ReLU activation function at each step of the network except for the last layer of the encoder where we only add the L2 normalization, and also for the last layer of the decoder where we apply a Sigmoid function (see in Fig. 3).

4.2   Algorithm Steps

Our algorithm is made of four steps. We start by dividing the images into several patches. Then we build the joint autoencoder where it learns how to reconstruct the images, and after we tweak the method by learning the autoencoder to reconstruct not the image itself but the precedent or the future image. The neural networks will learn the changes caused by the non-uniform illumination or noise, but will fail on ARMD progression generating a high reconstruction error (RE), consequently making it possible to detect them. The next subsections will detail some of these steps:

Pre-training. Let us consider a series of M images representing the progression of ARMD in a patient's eye. Each image has the same number of N useful patches, and we sample $\left\lfloor \dfrac{N}{M} \right\rfloor$ of the patches from every image. This allows us to build a unique autoencoder AE that works for all pairs in the series, and to prevent overfitting. We also apply a gaussian filter to the patches in order to weight the pixels by giving more importance to the center of the patch in the RE calculus.

During the encoding pass of the AE, the model extracts feature maps of N patches of chosen samples with convolutional layers (Fig. 4), and then during the decoding pass, it reconstructs them back to the initial ones.

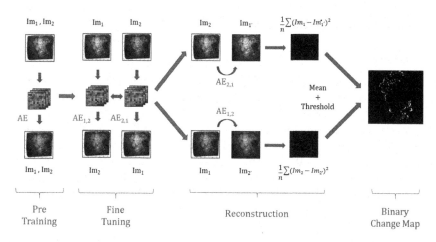

Fig. 4. Structure of the algorithm. *Example for series of two images Im_1 and Im_2 and n the number of patches.*

Fine-Tuning. For every consecutive pair $i, i+1$ with $i \in [\![1; M-1]\!]$ of images we are going to build two autoencoders initialized with the weights found in the pre-training part. On one hand $AE_{i,i+1}$ aims to reconstruct patches of Im_{i+1} from patches of Im_i and, on the other hand, $AE_{i+1,i}$ is going to reconstruct patches of Im_i from patches of Im_{i+1}.

The whole model is trained to minimize the difference between: the decoded output of $AE_{i,i+1}$ and Im_{i+1}, the decoded output of $AE_{i+1,i}$ and Im_i, and the encoded outputs of $AE_{i,i+1}$ and $AE_{i+1,i}$, see Fig. 4.

This joint configuration where the learning is done in both temporal directions, using joint backpropagation, has empirically proven to be much more robust than using a regular one-way autoencoder [8]. To optimize the parameters of the model, we use the mean squared error (MSE) of the reconstructed patches.

Reconstruction and Thresholding. Once the models are trained and stabilized, we perform the image reconstruction. For each pair, we note $Im_{i+1'}$ the reconstruction of Im_{i+1} from Im_i with $AE_{i,i+1}$ and likewiwse we note $Im_{i'}$ the reconstruction of Im_i from Im_{i+1} with $AE_{i+1,i}$. Then, we calculate the reconstruction error RE for every patch between Im_i and $Im_{i'}$ on one side and between Im_{i+1} and $Im_{i+1'}$ on another side. This gives us two images for each pair representing the average REs for $Im_{i'}$ and $Im_{i+1'}$, that we average to get only one. The model will easily learn the transformation of unchanged areas from one image to the other: changes in luminosity and blurring effects. At the same time, because the changes caused by the disease progression are unique, they will be considered as outliers by the model, and thus will have a high RE. Hence, we apply Otsu's thresholding [14] that requires no parameters and enables us to produce a binary change map (BCM) (Fig. 4).

5   Experimental Results

5.1   Experimental Settings

We chose to compare our methods presented in Subsect. 4.1 with 3 other methods, all on the preprocessed images. We applied all the methods to 3 of our series for which we have a ground truth.

The following parameters were chosen for all convolutional layers of our method: kernel size to 3, stride to 1 and padding to 1. Adam algorithm was used to optimize the models. We set the number of epochs to 8 for the pre-training phase and just 1 for the fine-tuning phase. For both phases, the learning rate was set to 0.0001 and the batch size to 100. Using trials and errors to determine the best parameters, we chose a patch size $P = 13$ and a value $\sigma = 12$ for the Gaussian filters.

The first method that we use for comparison is a simple subtraction of two consecutive images with an application of Otsu's thresholding on the result. The second comparison is a combination of principal component analysis (PCA) and K-means algorithm on the difference image proposed by Celik et al. in [1], and we apply it to medical images with blocks of size 5. To finish we take a Deep-Learning based approach [9] which uses CNN to group similar pixels together with consideration of spatial continuity. This work by Kanezaki et al. was initially made for unsupervised segmentation, consequently, we apply the algorithm to our images and then do the segmentation substractions to get binary change maps. The convolutive layers have the same configuration than for our network and we set the *minimum number of labels* to 3.

All algorithms were executed on an Nvidia GPU (RTX TITAN) with 64 GB of RAM and an Intel 9900k. It took about 20 min for a series of 8 frames with a patch size P of 13, with the execution time increasing with it.

5.2   Results

The results for patients 1, 3 and 5 are shown in Table 1, as well as Figs. 5 and 6 that we added for visual inspection purposes. Note that the scores presented in Table 1 are for the complete series (15 to 20 pairs per patient), while the scores schown in the Figures are for the individual couples of images used in each example.

When looking at Table 1, we can see that the simple difference coupled with Otsu thresholding achieves the best recall results on average, that there is no clear winner for the Precision, and that our proposed method on average has the best F1 Score. Note that we did not use Accuracy because of the strong class imbalance, with a large majority of "no change class" pixels leading to results over 95% of accuracy for all methods that were irrelevant.

Our interpretation of these results is the following: Otsu thresholding applied to the difference between two images has the best recalls because it detects most real change pixels. But the binary change map is also very noisy, corresponding to a high number of false positives (wrongly detected changes) which is confirmed

Table 1. Results and comparison of the different approaches. *It contains the means of the recall, the precision and the F1 score for each serie.*

Patient ID	Method	Recall	Precision	F1 score
001 *15 images*	Diff+Otsu	**0.68**	0.11	0.16
	Kanezaki	0.32	**0.29**	0.18
	Celik	0.48	0.28	**0.3**
	Our method	0.44	0.21	0.26
003 *5 images*	Diff+Otsu	**0.55**	0.1	0.17
	Kanezaki	0.2	0.27	0.07
	Celik	0.24	**0.33**	0.27
	Our method	0.29	0.28	**0.28**
005 *8 images*	Diff+Otsu	**0.46**	0.2	0.26
	Kanezaki	0.2	**0.43**	0.21
	Celik	0.26	0.37	0.28
	Our method	0.33	0.34	**0.32**
Total *(patients' mean)*	Diff+Otsu	**0.57**	0.14	0.2
	Kanezaki	0.24	**0.33**	0.15
	Celik	0.33	**0.33**	0.28
	Our method	0.35	0.28	**0.29**

by the very low precision score. This can also be observed on Fig. 5d which is an example of the high number of false positive detected using Otsu thresholding compared with the ground truth in Fig. 5c, or our method result in Fig. 5e.

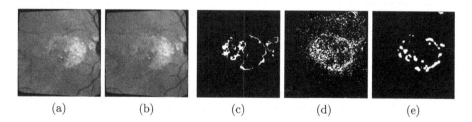

(a)	(b)	(c)	(d)	(e)

Fig. 5. Difference+Otsu thresholding VS our approach (AE) on patient 003. **a&b**-Images taken 3 months apart, **c**-groundthruth, **d**-difference with Otsu (F1 score = 0.26), **e**-our method (F1 score = 0.36).

In Fig. 6, we compare our approach with the 2 other algorithms relying on more advanced Machine Learning techniques. First we can see that like in Table 1, our approach gets the best F1-score for both patients and pairs of images. Then, we can see that Kanezaki et al. approach achieves over-segmentation in Fig. 6d and under-segmentation in Fig. 6j, which highlights that it is more difficult to parametrize and may require different parameters for each pair of image, which is not the case for both our approach and Celik et al. approach. Finally, regarding the comparison between Celik et al. approach and our proposed method, we can see from Figs. 6e, 6f, 6k and 6l, that also like in Table 1, Celik et al. approach achieves overall good results that are comparable to the ones of our method. However, in the same way that we have better F1-score and accuracy results, the visual results for our methods are also better as the changes we detect in the lesions are cleaner and overall less fragmented into very small elements compared with the ones found by Celik et al. approach. Furthermore, we can see that our method finds changes that are more in the peripheral areas of the lesions, while Celik et al. approach tends to find elements inside existing lesions (Fig. 6k) which are of lesser interest from a medical point of view.

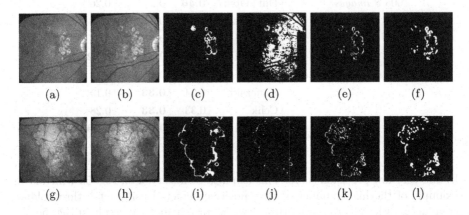

Fig. 6. Comparison of 3 methods on patients 001 (1st line) and 005 (2nd line): **a**-Patient 001 April 2017, **b**-Patient 001 October 2017, **c**-ground truth, **d**-Asako Kanezaki approach (F1 = 0.17), **e**-Turgay Celik approach (F1 = 0.43), **f**-our method (F1 = 0.43), **g**-Patient 005 October 2017, **h**-Patient 005 June 2018, **i**-ground truth, **j**-Asako Kanezaki approach (F1 = 0.15), **k**-Turgay Celik approach (F1 = 0.35), **l**-our method (F1 = 0.4).

Overall, we can conclude that both Otsu thresholding and Kanezaki's approach suffer from risks of over-segmentation detecting a lot of noise, or under-segmentation detecting nothing, both of which are impossible to exploit from a medical point of view. On the other hand, despite somewhat mild recall and precision scores, Celik approach and our method are visually much better at detecting meaningful changes in ARMD lesions structures. Moreover, we can see that our proposed method has a slightly higher F1-Score and finds structures that are visually better and more interesting from a medical point of view since they tend to be more at the border of existing lesions instead of inside them, and are also less fragmented.

6 Conclusion and Future Works

In this work, we have introduced a fully unsupervised deep learning new architecture that detects the evolution of ARMD lesions in eye fundus series of images. With a pre-cleaning of the series to remove as much lighting issues as possible, our proposed method is based on an auto-encoder architecture that can detect non-trivial changes between pairs of images, such as the evolution of a lesion, while discarding more trivial changes such as lighting problems or slight texture changes due to different image angles. Our proposed method was applied to 3 real sets of images, and was compared with 3 methods from the state of the art. Despite mild F1-Score results due to various issues, our method has shown to give good enough results for a fully unsupervised algorithm and to perform better than the other methods from the state of the art, and may prove useful to assist doctors in properly detecting the evolution of ARMD lesions by proposing a first raw segmentation of the evolution.

In our future works, we plan on working on an approach that can work on full time series rather than pairs of images. This would require both better lighting correction algorithms as well as more accurate ground-truth but may lead to more interesting models to predict the evolution of ARMD.

References

1. Celik, T.: Unsupervised change detection in satellite images using principal component analysis and k-means clustering. IEEE Geosci. Remote Sens. Lett. **6**(4), 772–776 (2009)
2. Chong, Y.S., Tay, Y.H.: Abnormal event detection in videos using spatiotemporal autoencoder. In: Cong, F., Leung, A., Wei, Q. (eds.) ISNN 2017. LNCS, vol. 10262, pp. 189–196. Springer, Cham (2017). https://doi.org/10.1007/978-3-319-59081-3_23
3. Feeny, A.K., Tadarati, M., Freund, D.E., Bressler, N.M., Burlina, P.: Automated segmentation of geographic atrophy of the retinal epithelium via random forests in AREDS color fundus images. Comput. Biol. Med. **65**, 124–136 (2015)
4. Hinton, G.E., Salakhutdinov, R.R.: Reducing the dimensionality of data with neural networks. Science **313**(5786), 504–507 (2006). https://doi.org/10.1126/science.1127647. http://science.sciencemag.org/content/313/5786/504
5. Hu, Z., Medioni, G.G., Hernandez, M., Hariri, A., Wu, X., Sadda, S.R.: Segmentation of the geographic atrophy in spectral-domain optical coherence tomography and fundus autofluorescence images. Invest. Ophthalmol. Vis. Sci. **54**(13), 8375–8383 (2013)
6. Hu, Z., Medioni, G.G., Hernandez, M., Sadda, S.R.: Automated segmentation of geographic atrophy in fundus autofluorescence images using supervised pixel classification. J. Med. Imaging **2**(1), 014501 (2015)
7. Hussain, M.A., Govindaiah, A., Souied, E., Smith, R., Bhuiyan, A.: Automated tracking and change detection for age-related macular degeneration progression using retinal fundus imaging, pp. 394–398, June 2018. https://doi.org/10.1109/ICIEV.2018.8641078

8. Kalinicheva, E., Sublime, J., Trocan, M.: Change detection in satellite images using reconstruction errors of joint autoencoders. In: Tetko, I.V., Kůrková, V., Karpov, P., Theis, F. (eds.) ICANN 2019. LNCS, vol. 11729, pp. 637–648. Springer, Cham (2019). https://doi.org/10.1007/978-3-030-30508-6_50

9. Kanezaki, A.: Unsupervised image segmentation by backpropagation. In: Proceedings of IEEE International Conference on Acoustics, Speech, and Signal Processing (ICASSP) (2018)

10. Köse, C., Sevik, U., Gençalioglu, O.: Automatic segmentation of age-related macular degeneration in retinal fundus images. Comput. Biol. Med. **38**(5), 611–619 (2008)

11. Köse, C., Sevik, U., Gençalioğlu, O., Ikibaş, C., Kayikiçioğlu, T.: A statistical segmentation method for measuring age-related macular degeneration in retinal fundus images. J. Med. Syst. **34**, 1–13 (2010)

12. Lee, N., Laine, A.F., Smith, R.T.: A hybrid segmentation approach for geographic atrophy in fundus auto-fluorescence images for diagnosis of age-related macular degeneration. In: 2007 29th Annual International Conference of the IEEE Engineering in Medicine and Biology Society, pp. 4965–4968. IEEE (2007)

13. Marrugo, A.G., Millan, M.S., Sorel, M., Sroubek, F.: Retinal image restoration by means of blind deconvolution. J. Biomed. Opt. **16**(11), 116016 (2011)

14. Otsu, N.: A threshold selection method from gray-level histograms. IEEE Trans. Syst. Man Cybern. Cybern. **9**(1), 62–66 (1979). https://doi.org/10.1109/TSMC.1979.4310076

15. Priya, R., Aruna, P.: Automated diagnosis of age-related macular degeneration from color retinal fundus images. In: 2011 3rd International Conference on Electronics Computer Technology, vol. 2, pp. 227–230. IEEE (2011)

16. Ramsey, D.J., Sunness, J.S., Malviya, P., Applegate, C., Hager, G.D., Handa, J.T.: Automated image alignment and segmentation to follow progression of geographic atrophy in age-related macular degeneration. Retina **34**(7), 1296–1307 (2014)

17. Ronneberger, O., Fischer, P., Brox, T.: U-Net: convolutional networks for biomedical image segmentation. In: Navab, N., Hornegger, J., Wells, W.M., Frangi, A.F. (eds.) MICCAI 2015. LNCS, vol. 9351, pp. 234–241. Springer, Cham (2015). https://doi.org/10.1007/978-3-319-24574-4_28

18. Troglio, G., Alberti, M., Benediksson, J.A., Moser, G., Serpico, S.B., Stefánsson, E.: Unsupervised change-detection in retinal images by a multiple-classifier approach. In: El Gayar, N., Kittler, J., Roli, F. (eds.) MCS 2010. LNCS, vol. 5997, pp. 94–103. Springer, Heidelberg (2010). https://doi.org/10.1007/978-3-642-12127-2_10

19. Troglio, G., Nappo, A., Benediktsson, J., Moser, G., Serpico, S., Stefánsson, E.: Automatic change detection of retinal images. In: Dössel, O., Schlegel, W.C. (eds.) World Congress on Medical Physics and Biomedical Engineering, vol. 25, pp. 281–284. Springer, Heidelberg (2010). https://doi.org/10.1007/978-3-642-03891-4_75

A Fast Algorithm to Find Best Matching Units in Self-Organizing Maps

Yann Bernard[1,2]([⊠]), Nicolas Hueber[1], and Bernard Girau[2]

[1] French-German Research Institute of Saint Louis, 68300 Saint-Louis, France
nicolas.hueber@isl.eu
[2] Université de Lorraine, CNRS, LORIA, 54000 Nancy, France
{yann.bernard,bernard.girau}@loria.fr

Abstract. Self-Organizing Maps (SOM) are well-known unsupervised neural networks able to perform vector quantization while mapping an underlying regular neighbourhood structure onto the codebook. They are used in a wide range of applications. As with most properly trained neural networks models, increasing the number of neurons in a SOM leads to better results or new emerging properties. Therefore highly efficient algorithms for learning and evaluation are key to improve the performance of such models. In this paper, we propose a faster alternative to compute the Winner Takes All component of SOM that scales better with a large number of neurons. We present our algorithm to find the so-called best matching unit (BMU) in a SOM, and we theoretically analyze its computational complexity. Statistical results on various synthetic and real-world datasets confirm this analysis and show an even more significant improvement in computing time with a minimal degradation of performance. With our method, we explore a new approach for optimizing SOM that can be combined with other optimization methods commonly used in these models for an even faster computation in both learning and recall phases.

Keywords: Self-Organizing Maps · Vector quantization · Dimensionality reduction

1 Introduction

Self-organizing maps (SOM) are widely used algorithms that feature vector quantization with dimensionality reduction properties. An explanation of how they work can be found in [11]. They are used in numerous fields like image processing, automatic text and language processing, and for visualization, analysis and classification of all kinds of highly dimensional datasets. Many applications examples are depicted in [3]. However, the amount of computations required by SOMs linearly increases with the number of neurons, the number of elements in the dataset and the dimensionality of the input, in both learning and recall phases. Therefore applying SOMs on datasets with huge numbers of elements

© Springer Nature Switzerland AG 2020
I. Farkaš et al. (Eds.): ICANN 2020, LNCS 12397, pp. 825–837, 2020.
https://doi.org/10.1007/978-3-030-61616-8_66

and with a high number of neurons to precisely represent the input induces a significant computational cost that may exceed some constraints such as real-time computation or low power consumption.

With the goal of reducing the required computational time of SOMs in mind, variants of the classical SOM algorithm have been developed. The most well-known SOM modification is the Batch Learning algorithm, as explained in [3]. Contrary to the classical online learning, the batch learning averages the modifications over multiple training vectors before updating the neurons weights. Similar efforts have been made in [4] or in [14]. However, all those variants are only focusing on reducing the convergence time of the SOM training. To the best of our knowledge, no work has been carried out to reduce the time required for each iteration. This can be partially explained by the highly parallel nature of the computations inside each iterations, in so far as when a fast real world implementation is required, parallel solutions are proposed, like the use of an FPGA substrate with each neuron having its own circuitry, as in [1] and in [6]. However, parallel solutions should not lead to a lack of effort in optimizing the algorithms, as the majority of SOM training is performed on CPU, and parallel hardware can be costly and difficult to program. Furthermore one can parallelise multiple iterations within an epoch instead of inside the iteration itself, and therefore can benefit from our improvements on parallel hardware.

A SOM training iteration consists of two major parts, a competitive part which searches the Best Matching Unit (or winner neuron), and a cooperative part which updates all the neurons weights proportionally to their distance with the BMU. In the classic SOM, both steps have the same algorithmic complexity (number of neurons multiplied by the dimensionality of the data) and take roughly the same time (depending on implementation details). In this paper we focus on improving the competitive part by reducing the number of neurons evaluated to find the BMU. This optimization also applies to the recall phase.

After a brief description of the standard SOM model in Sect. 2, Sect. 3 defines the proposed method to speed up the computation of BMU, before analyzing its computational complexity. The experimental setup is described in Sect. 4, and the corresponding results are discussed in Sect. 5.

2   Self-Organizing Maps

2.1   Vector Quantization

Vector quantization (VQ) is a lossy source coding technique in which blocks of samples are quantized together [15]. It consists in approximating the probability density of the input space (which is split in blocks of samples) with a finite set of prototype vectors. A prototype vector is often referred to as a codeword and the set of codewords as the codebook. Many VQ techniques exist such as k-means [12], self-organizing maps (SOM) [8], neural gas (NG) [13], growing neural gas (GNG) [5]. Algorithms such as NG or GNG present good performance in terms of minimization of the quantization error which is measured by the mean squared error. However this performance is often related to the creation in the network of a very large number of new prototypes and/or connections between prototypes, thus inducing a significant increase in computational cost. On the contrary SOM are based on a static underlying topology and a fixed number of codewords (neuron weight vectors). Moreover, in a SOM each prototype has an associated position in a map of a predefined topology (usually a 2D lattice). This spatial arrangement of the prototypes in the map makes it able to capture the topographic relationships (i.e. the similarities) between the inputs, in such a way that similar blocks of samples tend to be represented by spatially close neurons in the map. As a matter of fact, the SOM is a well-known and biologically plausible model of the topographical mapping of the visual sensors onto the cortex [16].

2.2 Kohonen SOM

The neurons of a Kohonen SOM [10] are spatially arranged in a discrete map that usually consists of a two-dimensional grid (see Fig. 1), or with hexagonal tiling. Each neuron n is connected the input and has a weight vector w_n, or codeword, whose dimension is equal to the size of the input vectors (or input dimension).

At the beginning of the learning algorithm, all codewords are initialized with random weights. The training of the SOM lasts several epochs. One epoch includes enough training iterations such that the whole training dataset has been used once for learning. For each training iteration, a training vector v is picked among the inputs. The best matching unit (BMU) g is then found, it corresponds to the neuron with the minimal distance (usually L^2) between w_g and v. Then the weights of all neurons are updated according to the following equation:

$$w_i(t+1) = w_i(t) + \epsilon(t) \cdot \Theta(\sigma(t), d_{i,g}) \cdot (v - w_i(t)) \tag{1}$$

where ϵ and σ are time functions (see below for details), and $d_{i,g}$ is the normalized distance between neuron i and the BMU in the map (not in the input space). Θ is a normalized centered Gaussian function with standard deviation σ.

Figure 1 illustrates how a SOM unfolds in the input space (here simply with 2D vector sizes): the codewords that are learned are shown as red points in the input space (from which random inputs are drawn, see blue points), and red links are showing the connections between the direct neighbouring neurons in the map.

$\sigma(t)$ is a parameter that influences the neighbourhood function. The higher it is, the more the BMU influences other neurons. In our experiments, we have set it to start at 0.5 and linearly decrease to a final value of 0.001, so that at the beginning of the training all neurons are significantly influenced by the BMU (unfolding the SOM), and at the end, nearly none except the BMU are (optimizing the quantization). $\epsilon(t)$ is the learning parameter, it starts at 0.6 and linearly decreases to a final value of 0.05. In our tests, we ran the SOM for 10 epochs.

An iterative batch version of SOM learning exists. Instead of using a single input vector at a time, the whole dataset (batch) is presented to the map before updating any weight [9]. This algorithm is deterministic, and the limit states of the prototypes depend only on the initial choices. However, this batch version is far less used than the above "on-line" learning version, and it can not be used in the applications where the dataset dynamically evolves. Therefore we will describe and discuss our efficient method to compute the BMU in the context of the standard on-line learning algorithm.

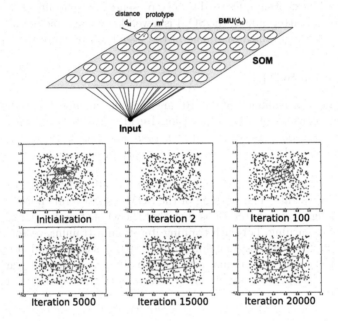

Fig. 1. Top: Typical SOM architecture. Bottom: A Kohonen SOM learning uniformly distributed random data in $[0,1]^2$.

3   Fast-BMU

3.1   Algorithm

We present here our new algorithm for searching the Best Matching Unit (BMU) in the SOM. It is traditionally determined by means of an exhaustive search by comparing all the distances between the input vector and the neurons weights. This method, while able to always find the correct minimum of the map, is computationally inefficient. The dimensionality reduction property of the SOM means that close neurons in the SOM topology represent close vectors in the input space. Therefore when an input vector is presented to the SOM, a pseudo-continuous gradient appears in the SOM when considering the distances between the neuron weights and the input vector whose minimum is located at the BMU.

In our algorithm we use this progressive reduction of distances to perform a discretized gradient descent to find the Best Matching Unit. The pseudo-code is

---

Algorithm 1 Particle

Input: *pos* : current position
Parameters: *values*: global table of distances, *eval*: global history of evaluations
Output: *bmu* : best matching unit's index

1: **if** *eval*(*pos*) is True **then**
2:     **return** *pos*
3: **end if**
4: *eval*[*pos*] ← True
5: Let *new_pos* take the index of the closest not evaluated neighbour to the input vector (ignoring neighbours *p* such that *eval*(*p*) =True)
6: **if** *values*[*new_pos*] ≤ *values*[*pos*] **then**
7:     **return** Particle(*new_pos*)
8: **end if**
9: **return** The index of the smallest value between *pos* and the returned indexes by execution of Particle() on all direct neighbours of *pos*.

---

shown in Algorithm 1, and illustrated in Fig. 2 (left). The algorithm starts at an arbitrarily selected position in the map. For this example let us consider that it starts at coordinates $(0,0)$ (top left corner). This neuron has two neighbours, one to the east $(1,0)$ and one to the south $(0,1)$. We evaluate the distances to the input vector of these three neurons to find the next step in the gradient descent. If the smallest distance is found where we are currently positioned, then we consider this is a local minimum. On the contrary if one of the neighbouring neurons gives the smallest distance, then the gradient descent goes in the direction of this particular neuron, that becomes the next selected position from which we repeat this process until we find a local minimum. In our example the smallest distance is measured for the eastern neuron in $(1,0)$. Thus the search process moves one step to the east, and this neuron has three neighbours, one to the south $(1,1)$, one to the east $(2,0)$ and one to the west that we come from (and thus we ignore it). We compare the three distances again, and move towards the lowest distance (south).

This process iterates until it reaches a local minimum at position $(6,5)$, where all neighbouring neurons have a higher distance to the input vector than the selected neuron. In order to ensure that the local minimum that has been found is the best one in the local neighbourhood, we then perform a search of the local space by continuing the gradient descent from all directly neighbouring neurons that are still unexplored. If this search finds a better local minimum, then this local minimum is considered as the BMU. This part of the algorithm aims at circumventing problems that may arise from the topology. In a grid topology for instance, we can only look at orthogonal axes. But sometimes, the gradient is oriented towards a diagonal direction, and by extending the search from a local minimum, we are able to still follow this gradient towards a potential BMU.

Another problem that can arise with the particle algorithm is edge effects. When mapping high dimensional data onto a 2D map, the map sometimes become twisted no gradient between the top left neuron and the bottom right

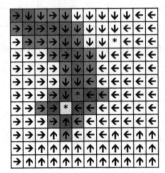 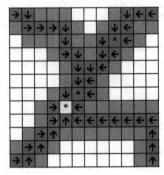

Fig. 2. Left: Example of the execution of one particle. Each cell represents one neuron. The arrow in each cell points towards the best neighbour (where a lower distance can be found). A star represents a local minimum. The green colored cells are the neurons who have been explored during the search, and the blue cells are the neurons whose distance to the input has been computed but that have not been explored by the algorithm. After having found a local minimum, new particles are created (in red) and continue the gradient descent by exploring the local neighbourhood. The cell in Yellow is the BMU, and the global minimum of the map. Right: Execution of the four particles. (Color figure online)

neuron. Imagine a net that is thrown onto a ball and nearly completely enveloping it: the shortest path between one corner of the net and the opposite corner of the net does not follow the mesh of the net. If in the learning phase, the particle ends up in the wrong corner of the SOM, it will find a terrible BMU and the following weight update will locally break the neighbourhood continuity, and create a negative feedback loop that will remove all dimensionality reduction properties from the SOM. Thankfully there is an easy way to avoid this, by simply starting 4 particles, one in each corner of the SOM, and selecting the smallest BMU found. This technique preserves the continuity of the SOM and makes the Fast-BMU algorithm more robust to local discontinuities in the gradient, especially at the beginning of the training process, when the map is not yet well unfolded. In the case where there is no clear gradient present in the SOM (typically when the SOM is randomly initialized before training), this algorithm will fail to find the correct BMU. However it is not a problem at the start of training as the neighborhood function will create a gradient by unfolding the SOM regardless of which neuron is initially selected. The result of a full Fast-BMU execution is shown in Fig. 2 (right).

3.2 Complexity Analysis

The execution time of the Fast-BMU algorithm depends on the shape and size of the neural map, and on the input vector. As our algorithm relies on the dimensionality reduction property of the SOM, we will hypothesise that there is always some kind of continuity in the neural map in our analysis, because if not, our algorithm would not work anyways. In order to estimate the complexity of our algorithm, we have to estimate the number of steps that each of the four particles takes before finding a potential Best Matching Unit (BMU). We assume that: 1) all particles follow paths that do not significantly differ from shortest XY paths until their destination (thus minimizing the number of steps), and 2) they do not stop early in some local minimum (thus maximizing the number of steps). We will call this kind of best-worst-case complexity: *Expected Complexity*. Let us consider that the BMU is located at position x, y of the SOM:

- The top left particle with coordinates $(0,0)$ needs x steps in the width dimension, and y steps in the height dimension in order to get to the BMU.
- Similarly, the top right particle with coordinates $(w, 0)$ will take $w - x$ steps for the width and y steps for the height.
- For the bottom left $(0, h)$, it will be x and $h - y$ steps.
- For the bottom right (w, h), it will be $w - x$ and $h - y$ steps.

To get the total number of steps for one execution, we sum the steps from all particles together as shown in Eq. 2:

$$\text{NbSteps} = (x + y) + (w - x + y) + (x + h - y) + (w - x + h - y) \quad (2)$$

The x and y cancel out, and the resulting number of steps only depends on the width and the height of the map. The total number of steps taken by our algorithm is consequently equal to $(2w + 2h)$. We can therefore derive Eq. 3, which defines the expected complexity of our algorithm.

$$\mathcal{EC}(w, h) = 2 \times (w + h) \times NbrEvalPerStep \quad (3)$$

with w, h the width and height of the SOM respectively and $NbrEvalPerStep$ the number of new distances to compute on each step of a particle. Its value depends on the topology. It is at most 3 with a grid (4 neighbours minus the neuron from the previous step) and also 3 with a hexagonal topology (6 neighbours minus the neuron from the previous step and 2 neurons that were neighbours of the previous neuron and consequently have already been evaluated).

From an analytical point of view, we can estimate that our Fast-BMU algorithm ($\mathcal{EC}(w, h) = 6(w + h)$ in the worst case in a standard grid configuration) is significantly faster than the current exhaustive search algorithm ($O(w, h) = wh$) when the number of neurons in the map is substantial. For instance, it is twice as fast with 24 by 24 SOMs, and 10 times faster with 120 by 120 SOMs. An experimental evaluation of the speed difference is reported in Sect. 5.

4   Experimental Setup

To evaluate the robustness of our algorithm with various kinds of data, we have selected 6 datasets aimed at being representative of the kind of data SOMs are usually trained on. For the 2D case, we have generated data with different properties (uniform distribution and a highly non-convex shape), for 3D data we use a uniformly distributed cube shape and the pixel color values of an image. For the high dimensional case, we consider an image compression application [2] with 10 by 10 sub-images as training vectors (100 pixels with 3 colors each, resulting in 300 dimensions), and the Free Spoken Digits Dataset [7] which uses soundwaves that we have reduced to 1000 dimensions.

Our algorithm is mostly designed for a 2 dimensional SOM, although adaptations to higher dimensions can be easily defined by just adapting the neighbourhood and the number of initial particles, even leading to possibly greater gains in computational cost. We tested it with a grid and a hexagonal shaped 2D topology, which are the most commonly used in SOM applications.

In order to evaluate the differences between all tested models, we used three metrics. The first one is the standard *Mean Squared Quantization Error* (MSQE) which estimates the Vector Quantization quality of the tested algorithm. The *Mean Squared Distance to Neurons* (MSDtN) which computes the average squared codeword distance between neurons and all of their direct neighbours. The lower this value is, the more closely related neighbouring neurons are, and the better the dimensional reduction property is. Numerous metrics exist in the SOM literature to estimate the topographical mapping of the SOM, but MSDtN has the advantage of being easy to compute, without parameters and only dependent on the neurons weights. For all metrics, lower is better.

$$\text{MSQE} = \frac{1}{V} \sum_{i=1}^{V} ||v_i - w_{\text{bmu}(i)}||^2 \tag{4}$$

$$\text{MSDtN} = \frac{1}{N} \sum_{i=1}^{N} \sum_{j=1}^{N} \begin{cases} ||w_i - w_j||^2, & \text{if dist}(i,j) = 1 \\ 0, & \text{otherwise} \end{cases} \tag{5}$$

With V the number of vectors in the dataset, v_i the weights of the ith vector of the dataset, and bmu(i) is the index of the neuron which is the best matching unit for the ith vector of the dataset. Similarly N is the number of neurons and w_i the weights of the ith neuron, while dist(i,j) is the number of links in the shortest path between neurons i and j in the neural map.

5   Results

In this section, we explore the differences in quality of learning and recall between the standard version and our fast version for the computation of the BMU in a SOM. We also look at the practical differences in the amount of computations required for the two versions and we compare it with the previously presented complexity analysis. Quality tests were performed on a 32×32 SOM (1024 neurons). For each combination of dataset and model (choice of topology and BMU algorithm), we ran 50 executions with different random seeds which affect the datasets that are generated, the initialization of the neuron weights (who are all randomly initialised with no pre-existing gradient) and the order in which the training vectors are presented. Results are shown in Table 1.

The algorithm column of the table shows the combination of BMU finding algorithm and topology that was used for training. The MSDtN (see Sect. 4) is calculated on the trained neurons weights. The MSQE_S (Standard) is the quantization error in the recall phase (after learning) when using the standard BMU algorithm. Comparing the different MSQE_S values for a standard version and a fast version gives an indication of the influence of the Fast-BMU algorithm

Table 1. Results with a 32 × 32 neurons SOM, averaged over 50 executions. The Algorithm column specifies with which algorithm and topology the SOM was trained, FastG and FastH stand respectively for Fast Grid and Fast Hexagonal. MSQE_S is the MSQE calculated with the standard (exhaustive) BMU algorithm whereas MSQE_F uses the Fast-BMU version. Differences of MSQE_S between different algorithms reflect the quality of the training phase. The mismatch is the proportion of BMU that are differently selected by the two algorithms.

Data	Algorithm	MSDtN	MSQE_S	MSQE_F	Mismatch
Square	Grid	1.94e−4	2.22e−4	2.22e−4	0%
	FastG	**1.93e−4**	2.23e−4	2.23e−4	0%
	Hex	2.39e−4	**2.12e−4**	**2.12e−4**	0%
	FastH	2.38e−4	2.15e−4	2.15e−4	0%
Shape	Grid	**1.38e−4**	1.40e−4	1.40e−4	>0%
	FastG	**1.38e−4**	1.40e−4	1.40e−4	>0%
	Hex	1.65e−4	**1.31e−4**	**1.31e−4**	>0%
	FastH	1.65e−4	**1.31e−4**	**1.31e−4**	>0%
Cube	Grid	**4.48e−4**	2.21e−3	2.50e−3	4.8%
	FastG	4.61e−4	2.25e−3	3.21e−3	9.8%
	Hex	5.29e−4	**2.09e−3**	**2.34e−3**	3.1%
	FastH	5.38e−4	2.11e−3	2.79e−3	7.6%
Colors	Grid	**1.15e−4**	8.64e−5	8.80e−5	4.4%
	FastG	1.19e−4	8.91e−5	9.08e−5	5.4%
	Hex	1.33e−4	8.29e−5	8.30e−5	0.4%
	FastH	1.35e−4	**8.26e−5**	**8.29e−5**	0.7%
Digits	Grid	2.02e−4	1.42e−2	1.49e−2	31.3%
	FastG	**1.93e−4**	1.44e−2	1.51e−2	32.2%
	Hex	2.29e−4	**1.41e−2**	**1.45e−2**	19.8%
	FastH	2.25e−4	1.42e−2	**1.45e−2**	13.3%
Image	Grid	**1.64e−4**	1.80e−3	1.83e−3	4.2%
	FastG	1.65e−4	1.82e−3	1.85e−3	4.4%
	Hex	1.97e−4	**1.75e−3**	1.77e−3	1.2%
	FastH	1.99e−4	**1.75e−3**	**1.76e−3**	1.2%

on training quality only, as it always selects the real BMU in the recall phase. The MSQE_F (Fast) metric measures the vector quantization error with the BMU selection done by the Fast-BMU algorithm. If the training was performed on the standard SOM, it gives an indication of the influence of the Fast-BMU algorithm on recall accuracy only; if it was trained on a Fast version, it represents the MSQE result of a SOM that only uses the Fast-BMU algorithm. The mismatch column gives the proportion of BMU that are selected differently by the two algorithms.

5.1   Experimental Results

We first observe that the distance between neurons after learning (MSDtN) is lower with the grid topology than with the hexagonal one, but this difference could be attributed to the different number of neighbours between the two topologies and therefore should only be used to compare the standard and Fast-BMU algorithms, and not topologies. We also remark that the Fast algorithm does not make any significant mismatch on the Square and Shape datasets, and therefore MSQE_S and MSQE_F have similar recall results on these datasets.

The mismatch percentages vary greatly between the datasets. From 0 to 6% for the Images and Colors Datasets, 3 to 10% for the Cube and 13 to 33% for the Spoken Digits dataset. Such differences could be explained by the distribution of the data in the datasets, as Images and Colors feature data that are closely related together. In pictures for instance, there are usually a few dominant colors with a lot of color gradients that make the continuities in the distribution easier to learn for the SOM, thus improving the performance of our Fast-BMU algorithm. The Spoken Digits dataset on the other hand has high mismatch values, which seems to indicate that a strong continuity in the neurons weights is not present after learning the SOM. The hexagonal topology also performs better with the Fast-BMU algorithm than the grid topology as mismatches are significantly lower with it. Finally the dimensionality of the dataset does not seem to play a key role here, as the Image dataset (300 dimensions) has lower mismatches than the Cube dataset (3 dimensions).

For the vector quantization part, the hexagonal topology leads again to the lowest error values. What is more surprising is that the Fast-BMU version has quantization results that are very similar to the standard version. Even with high mismatches (30% with Digits using a grid-based SOM) the MSQE is only around 5% higher, and even less when only training is compared. The only significantly higher MSQE values with Fast-BMU is with the Cube dataset where the algorithm selects quite bad BMU choices in the recall phase while being able to correctly train the SOM. In most cases, a difference in the topology of the SOM has more impact on the resulting MSQE than the use of the Fast-BMU algorithm.

5.2   Computational Gains

To evaluate the computational gains that are induced by the use of the Fast-BMU algorithm independently from implementation techniques, we compared the percentage of neurons that must be evaluated in order to find the BMU. The results are shown in Fig. 3. The standard SOM is evaluating all neurons by definition, so the percentage is always 100%. The complexity curve for Fast-BMU plots the function defined in Sect. 3.2. To obtain the Fast-measured curve, we ran tests with $n \times n$ SOM, where n is every even number between 10 and 50 (21 tests in total). Each test featured all datasets and all topologies (so 12 executions per test). With these results, we can observe significant improvements in the required computational time. Our algorithm is twice as fast with (16×16) SOMs, four times faster with 1000 neurons (32×32). The (50×50) SOM evaluates approximately 375 neurons per iteration, which is similar to the 400 neurons a standard (20×20) SOM has to evaluate. We can also observe that the complexity curve follows a similar shape to the measured curve, while overestimating the required number of evaluated neurons by approximately 75%.

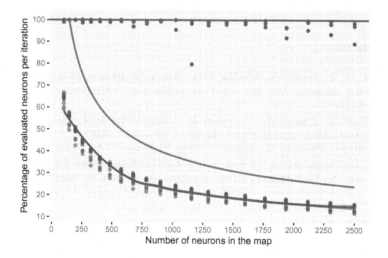

Fig. 3. Evaluation of performance gains with the number of neurons. All results were calculated on square maps. The blue line is the standard SOM, in green is the analytical value and in red the measured value. Additionally, the purple dots are the percentage of correct BMU in an execution on the Image dataset. (Color figure online)

6   Conclusion

We have presented a novel method to find the Best Matching Unit in Self-Organizing Maps by taking advantage of their ability to preserve their underlying topology within the codebook. Our algorithm is significantly faster to compute while performing barely worse than the standard approach in vector quantization. This result makes SOM with a high number of neurons a more viable solution for many applications. We expect future improvements of this algorithm, or new approaches to further reduce the computational cost of SOM by modifying the BMU searching algorithm. We also study how the Fast-BMU approach can reduce the bandwidth demands in a fully parallel implementation on a manycore substrate, where all neurons are simultaneously evaluated but the BMU selection uses the simple unicast propagation of particles instead of full broadcast-reduce schemes. Finally it must be pointed out that the computational gains offered by our Fast-BMU algorithm specifically rely on preservation of neighbourhood relations when mapping the input space onto the neural map. This property is not present when using more conventional VQ models such as k-means, so that the use of SOM could be extended to more applications where their specific mapping properties would not be useful for the application itself, but would induce potential computational gains out of reach for other models.

Acknowledgements. The authors thank the French AID agency (Agence de l'Innovation pour la Défense) for funding the DGA-2018 60 0017 contract. The code is available at github.com/yabernar/FastBMU.

References

1. Abadi, M., Jovanovic, S., Khalifa, K.B., Weber, S., Bedoui, M.H.: A scalable and adaptable hardware NoC-based self organizing map. Microprocess. Microsyst. **57**, 1–14 (2018)
2. Amerijckx, C., Legat, J.D., Verleysen, M.: Image compression using self-organizing maps. Syst. Anal. Modell. Simul. **43**(11), 1529–1543 (2003)
3. Cottrell, M., Olteanu, M., Rossi, F., Villa-Vialaneix, N.N.: Self-OrganizingMaps, theory and applications. Revista de Investigacion Operacional **39**(1), 1–22 (2018)
4. Fiannaca, A., Di Fatta, G., Rizzo, R., Urso, A., Gaglio, S.: Simulated annealing technique for fast learning of SOM networks. Neural Comput. Appl. **22**(5), 889–899 (2013). https://doi.org/10.1007/s00521-011-0780-6
5. Fritzke, B.: A growing neural gas network learns topologies. In: Advances in Neural Information Processing Systems, vol. 7. pp. 625–632. MIT Press (1995)
6. Huang, Z., et al.: A hardware-efficient vector quantizer based on self-organizing map for high-speed image compression. Appl. Sci. **7**(11), 1106 (2017)
7. Jackson, Z., Souza, C., Flaks, J., Pan, Y., Nicolas, H., Thite, A.: Jakobovski/free-spoken-digit-dataset: v1.0.8, August 2018
8. Kohonen, T.: Self-organized formation of topologically correct feature maps. Biol. Cybern. **43**(1), 59–69 (1982). https://doi.org/10.1007/BF00337288
9. Kohonen, T.: The self-organizing map. Neurocomputing **21**(1–3), 1–6 (1998)
10. Kohonen, T.: Essentials of the self-organizing map. Neural Netw. **37**, 52–65 (2013)
11. Kohonen, T., Honkela, T.: Kohonen network. Scholarpedia **2**(1), 1568 (2007)
12. MacQueen, J.: Some methods for classification and analysis of multivariate observations. The Regents of the University of California (1967)
13. Martinetz, T.M., Berkovich, S.G., Schulten, K.J.: Neural-gas network for vector quantization and its application to time-series prediction. IEEE Trans. Neural Netw. **4**(4), 558–569 (1993)

14. Oyana, T.J., Achenie, L.E., Heo, J.: The new and computationally efficient MIL-SOM algorithm: potential benefits for visualization and analysis of a large-scale high-dimensional clinically acquired geographic data. Comput. Math. Methods Med. **2012**, 14 (2012)
15. Vasuki, A., Vanathi, P.: A review of vector quantization techniques. IEEE Potentials **25**(4), 39–47 (2006)
16. Yin, H.: The self-organizing maps: background, theories, extensions and applications. In: Fulcher, J., Jain, L.C. (eds.) Computational Intelligence: A Compendium. Studies in Computational Intelligence, vol. 115. Springer, Heidelberg (2008). https://doi.org/10.1007/978-3-540-78293-3_17

Tumor Characterization Using Unsupervised Learning of Mathematical Relations Within Breast Cancer Data

Cristian Axenie[1,2(✉)] and Daria Kurz[3]

[1] Audi Konfuzius-Institut Ingolstadt Lab, Ingolstadt, Germany
cristian.axenie@audi-konfuzius-institut-ingolstadt.de
[2] Technische Hochschule Ingolstadt, Esplanade 10, 85049 Ingolstadt, Germany
[3] Interdisziplinäres Brustzentrum, Helios Klinikum München West,
Steinerweg 5, 81241 Munich, Germany
daria.kurz@helios-gesundheit.de

Abstract. Despite the variety of imaging, genetic and histopathological data used to assess tumors, there is still an unmet need for patient-specific tumor growth profile extraction and tumor volume prediction, for use in surgery planning. Models of tumor growth predict tumor size and require tumor biology-dependent parametrization, which hardly generalizes to cope with tumor variability among patients. In addition, the datasets are limited in size, owing to the restricted or single-time measurements. In this work, we address the shortcomings that incomplete biological specifications, the inter-patient variability of tumors, and the limited size of the data bring to mechanistic tumor growth models. We introduce a machine learning model that alleviates these shortcomings and is capable of characterizing a tumor's growth pattern, phenotypical transitions, and volume. The model learns without supervision, from different types of breast cancer data the underlying mathematical relations describing tumor growth curves more accurate than three state-of-the-art models. Experiments performed on publicly available clinical breast cancer datasets, demonstrate the versatility of the approach among breast cancer types. Moreover, the model can also, without modification, learn the mathematical relations among, for instance, histopathological and morphological parameters of the tumor and, combined with the growth curve, capture the (phenotypical) growth transitions of the tumor from a small amount of data. Finally, given the tumor growth curve and its transitions, our model can learn the relation among tumor proliferation-to-apoptosis ratio, tumor radius, and tumor nutrient diffusion length, used to estimate tumor volume. Such a quantity can be readily incorporated within current clinical practice, for surgery planning.

Keywords: Artificial neural networks · Breast cancer · Unsupervised learning · Prediction algorithms

© Springer Nature Switzerland AG 2020
I. Farkaš et al. (Eds.): ICANN 2020, LNCS 12397, pp. 838–849, 2020.
https://doi.org/10.1007/978-3-030-61616-8_67

1   Background

With 71888 new cases reported in 2018 in Germany, breast cancer represents 25% of all cancer types affecting the population [1]. Breast cancer assessment has transitioned to novel techniques including, mammography, Magnetic Resonance Imaging (MRI), ultrasound, and optical tools, which are becoming increasingly accessible and affordable [18]. Yet, when considering, for instance, Ductal Carcinoma In Situ (DCIS) [2] - a significant precursor to invasive breast cancer - typical mammogram diagnosis is not accurate (i.e. initial cancer cells typically classified as microcalcifications). This is usually caused by the limited understanding of DCIS growth [9,10], its phenotype which is determined by genomic/proteomic- and microenvironment-dependent stochastic processes [16,19], and its cell volume changes during proliferation and necrosis [6]. The current landscape shows that there is still an unmet need for patient-specific tumor characterization and tumor volume prediction, for use in surgery planning [4,7]. As there is a difference between, for instance, mammography and histopathology estimated sizes, the clinician cannot obtain a "fixed surgical size" of a tumor to be excised. This may contribute to over-treatment, including needless surgery. Only limited work has been done towards patient-calibrated modelling and predictions of tumor clinical progression [15] or patient-specific assessment of surgical volume [8]. Our work addresses this need and finds motivation in the following clinically-pertinent scientific questions:

- Can we use machine learning to extract breast tumor growth patterns that take into account patient variability and limited amount of data?
- Can we use machine learning to capture the peculiarities of tumor biology data by learning the underlying mathematical relations/functional dependencies of phenotypical transitions of cancer cells?
- Can we use machine learning to predict the volume of the breast affected by tumor (as for instance in DCIS) from limited and noisy timeseries of histopathologic data?

In the following sections we answer these motivating questions by demonstrating the capabilities of our model.

2   Materials and Methods

In the current section we describe the proposed Machine Learning system along with relevant state-of-the-art models. Additionally, an overview of the experimental datasets and models parametrization details complete the section.

2.1   Models of Tumor Growth

Various tumor growth models have been proposed and are used to make predictions in cancer treatments planning [11]. In this work, we chose three of the most representative and typically used ordinary differential equations (ODE) growth models, namely Logistic, von Bertalanffy, and Gompertz, described in Table 1.

Table 1. Tumor growth models in our study. Parameters: N - cell population size (or volume/mass thorough conversion [13]), α - growth rate, β - cell death rate, λ - nutrient limited proliferation rate, k - carrying capacity of cells.

Model	Equation
Logistic [21]	$\frac{dN}{dt} = \alpha N - \beta N^2$
Bertalanffy [23]	$\frac{dN}{dt} = \alpha N^\lambda - \beta N$
Gompertz [12]	$\frac{dN}{dt} = N(\beta - \alpha \ln N)$

2.2   Introducing the Learning Model

Our proposed solution is an unsupervised machine learning system based on latent space learning (i.e. Self-Organizing Maps (SOM) [14]) and temporal correlation learning (i.e. Hebbian Learning (HL) [3]) used in combination in order to extract underlying mathematical relations among correlated timeseries describing tumor growth. Note that, in principle, we can use any autoencoder type for latent space learning. In order to introduce our system, we provide a simple example in Fig. 1. Here, we consider data from a cubic tumor growth law (3rd powerlaw) describing the impact of sequential cytostatics dose density over a 150 weeks horizon in adjuvant chemotherapy of breast cancer [5]. The two input timeseries (i.e. the number of cancer cells and the irregular measurement index over the weeks) follow a cubic dependency, depicted in Fig. 1a.

Core Model. The input SOMs (i.e. 1D lattice networks with N neurons) are responsible to extract the distribution of the timeseries data, depicted in Fig. 1a, and encode timeseries samples in a distributed activity pattern, as shown in Fig. 1b. This activity pattern is generated such that the closest preferred value of a neuron to the input sample will be strongly activated and will decay, proportional with distance, for neighbouring units. The SOM specialises to represent a certain (preferred) value in the timeseries and learns its sensitivity, by updating its tuning curves shape. Given an input sample $s^p(k)$ from one timeseries at time step k, the network computes for each i-th neuron in the p-th input SOM (with preferred value $w_{in,i}^p$ and tuning curve size $\xi_i^p(k)$) the elicited neural activation as

$$a_i^p(k) = \frac{1}{\sqrt{2\pi}\xi_i^p(k)} e^{\frac{-(s^P(k)-w_{in,i}^P(k))^2}{2\xi_i^P(k)^2}}. \tag{1}$$

The winning neuron of the p-th population, $b^p(k)$, is the one which elicits the highest activation given the timeseries sample at time k

$$b^p(k) = \underset{i}{\operatorname{argmax}} \ a_i^p(k). \tag{2}$$

The competition for highest activation in the SOM is followed by cooperation in representing the input space. Hence, given the winning neuron, $b^p(k)$, the cooperation kernel,

$$h_{b,i}^p(k) = e^{\frac{-||r_i-r_b||^2}{2\sigma(k)^2}}. \tag{3}$$

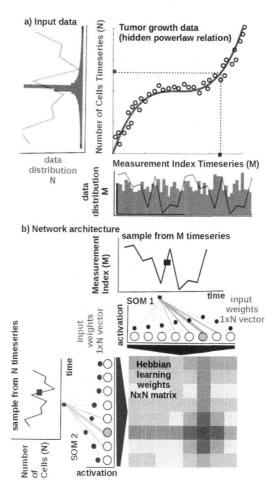

Fig. 1. Basic functionality: a) Tumor growth data resembling a powerlaw (i.e. number of cells vs. measurement index). Data from [5]. b) Basic architecture of the system: 1D SOM networks with N neurons encoding the timeseries (i.e. number of cells vs. measurement index), and a NxN Hebbian connection matrix coupling the two 1D SOMs that will eventually encode the relation between the timeseries, i.e. growth curve.

allows neighbouring neurons (i.e. found at position r_i in the network) to precisely represent the input sample given their location in the neighbourhood $\sigma(k)$ of the winning neuron. The neighbourhood width $\sigma(k)$ decays in time, to avoid twisting effects in the SOM. The cooperation kernel in Eq. 3, ensures that specific neurons in the network specialise on different areas in the input space, such that the input weights (i.e. preferred values) of the neurons are pulled closer to the input sample,

$$\Delta w^p_{in,i}(k) = \alpha(k)h^p_{b,i}(k)(s^p(k) - w^p_{in,i}(k)). \tag{4}$$

This corresponds to updating the tuning curves width ξ_i^p as modulated by the spatial location of the neuron in the network, the distance to the input sample, the cooperation kernel size, and a decaying learning rate $\alpha(k)$,

$$\Delta\xi_i^p(k) = \alpha(k)h_{b,i}^p(k)((s^p(k) - w_{in,i}^p(k))^2 - \xi_i^p(k)^2). \tag{5}$$

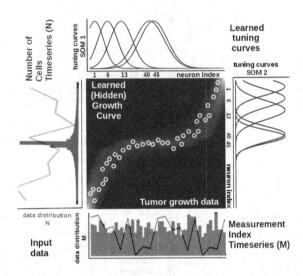

Fig. 2. Extracted timeseries relation describing the growth law and data statistics for the data in Fig. 1a depicting a cubic breast cancer tumor growth law among number of cells and irregular measurement over 150 weeks, data from [5]. Timeseries overlay on the data distribution and corresponding model encoding tuning curves shapes.

In order to describe of the process, let's consider learned tuning curves shapes for 5 neurons in the input SOMs (i.e. neurons 1, 6, 13, 40, 45) encoding the breast cancer cubic tumor growth law, depicted in Fig. 2. We observe that higher input probability distributions are represented by dense and sharp tuning curves (e.g.. neuron 1, 6, 13 in SOM1), whereas lower or uniform probability distributions are represented by more sparse and wide tuning curves (e.g. neuron 40, 45 in SOM1). Neurons in the two SOMs are then linked by a fully (all-to-all) connected matrix of synaptic connections, where the weights in the matrix are computed using Hebbian learning. The connections between uncorrelated (or weakly correlated) neurons in each population (i.e. w_{cross}) are suppressed (i.e. darker color) while correlated neurons connections are enhanced (i.e. brighter color), as depicted in Fig. 2. Formally, the connection weight $w_{cross,i,j}^p$ between neurons i,j in the different input SOMs are updated with a Hebbian learning rule as follows:

$$\Delta w_{cross,i,j}^p(k) = \eta(k)(a_i^p(k) - \overline{a}_i^p(k))(a_j^q(k) - \overline{a}_j^q(k)), \tag{6}$$

where

$$\overline{a}_i^p(k) = (1 - \beta(k))\overline{a}_i^p(k - 1) + \beta(k)a_i^p(k), \tag{7}$$

is a "momentum" like exponential decay and $\eta(k)$, $\beta(k)$ are monotonic (inverse time) decaying functions. Hebbian learning ensures that when neurons fire synchronously their connection strengths increase, whereas if their firing patterns are anti-correlated the weights decrease. The weight matrix encodes the co-activation patterns between the input layers (i.e. SOMs), as shown in Fig. 1b, and, eventually, the learned growth law (i.e. relation) given the timeseries, as shown in Fig. 2.

Self-organisation and Hebbian correlation learning processes evolve simultaneously, such that both the representation and the extracted relation are continuously refined, as new samples are presented. This can be observed in the encoding and decoding functions where the input activations are projected though w_{in} (Eq. 1) to the Hebbian matrix and then decoded through w_{cross}.

Parametrization and Read-Out. In all of our experiments data from tumor growth timeseries is fed to the system which encodes it in the SOMs and learns the underlying relation in the Hebbian matrix. The SOMs are responsible of bringing the timeseries in the same latent representation space where they can interact (i.e. through their internal correlation). In all our experiments, each of the SOM has $N = 100$ neurons, the Hebbian connection matrix has size NxN and parametrization is done as: $\alpha = [0.01, 0.1]$ decaying, $\eta = 0.9$, $\sigma = \frac{N}{2}$ decaying following an inverse time law. We use as decoding mechanism an optimisation method that recovers the real-world value given the self-calculated bounds of the input timeseries. The bounds are obtained as minimum and maximum of a cost function of the distance between the current preferred value of the winning neuron and the input sample at the SOM level.

2.3   Datasets

For experiments we used publicly available clinical cancer datasets (see Table 2).

Table 2. Description of the datasets used in the experiments.

Dataset	Data type	Data points	Experiment	Source
Breast carcinoma[a]	Fluorescence imaging	7	Tumor growth	[17]
Breast carcinoma[b]	Digital caliper	14	Tumor growth	[22]
Breast carcinoma[c]	Caliper	8	Tumor growth	[20]
DCIS phenotype	Immunohistochemistry	17	Tumor phenotype	[8]
DCIS volume	Histopathology	17	Tumor volume	[8]

[a] MDA-MB-231 cell line
[b] MDA-MB-435 cell line
[c] MCF-7, T47D cell lines

2.4 Procedures

In order to reproduce the experiments and figures, the MATLAB® code and copies of all the datasets are available on GITLAB[1].

For the tumor growth experiment: each of the three mechanistic tumor growth models (i.e. Logistic, Bertalanffy, Gompertz) and our model were presented the tumor growth data in each of the datasets (from [17,20,22]). When a dataset contained multiple trials, a random one was chosen.

For the tumor phenotype experiment our model was fed with timeseries of immunohistochemistry data and compared in accuracy against a mathematical model from [8].

For the tumor volume prediction experiment our model was fed with timeseries of histopathology data and compared in accuracy against a mathematical model and mammography data from [8].

Mechanistic Models Setup. Each of the state-of-the-art tumor growth models was implemented as ODE and integrated over the dataset length. We used a solver based on a modified Rosenbrock formula of order 2 that evaluates the Jacobian during each step of the integration. To provide initial values and the best parameters (i.e. $\alpha, \beta, \lambda, k$) for each of the four models the Nelder-Mead simplex direct search was used, with a termination tolerance of $10e^{-6}$ and upper bounded to 500 iterations. Finally, fitting was performed by minimizing the sum of squared residuals (SSR).

Our Model Setup. For our model the data was normalized (interval $[-1, 1]$) before training and de-normalized for the evaluation. The system was comprised of two input SOMs, each with $N = 50$ neurons, encoding the volume data and the irregular sampling time sequence, respectively. Both input density learning and correlation learning cycles were bound to 100 epochs.

3 Results

In the current section we introduce the results, discuss the findings, and demonstrate that our model can:

- extract breast tumor growth patterns that take into account patient variability and limited amount of data;
- learn the underlying mathematical relations/functional dependencies of phenotypical transitions of cancer cells;
- predict the volume of the breast affected by tumor (exemplified in DCIS) from limited and noisy timeseries of histopathologic data,

consistently with measurements in clinical setup.

---

[1] https://gitlab.com/akii-microlab/icann-2020-bio.

3.1 Tumor Growth Curve Extraction

In our first experiment, we explore the tumor growth curve prediction capability of our model across multiple breast cancer datasets. In all experiments, the state-of-the-art mechanistic models and our model were evaluated using Sum of Squared Errors (SSE), Root Mean Squared Error (RMSE), and Symmetric Mean Absolute Percentage Error (sMAPE). As our experiments demonstrate (Table 3), our model obtains superior accuracy in predicting the growth curve of the three types of tumors in three cell lines of breast cancer. Such a difference is supported by the fact that our model is a data-driven learning model that captures the peculiarities of the data and exploits its statistics to make predictions. The mechanistic models, on the other side, exploit biological knowledge and describe the dynamics of the physical processes, but fail in terms of versatility among tumor types.

Table 3. Evaluation of the tumor growth models.

Evaluation Metrics			
Dataset/Model	SSE	RMSE	sMAPE
Breast[a] *cancer* [17]			
Logistic	7009.6	37.4423	1.7088
Bertalanffy	8004.9	44.7350	1.7088
Gompertz	7971.8	39.9294	1.7088
Our model	119.3	4.1285	0.0767
Breast[b] *cancer* [22]			
Logistic	0.2936	0.1713	0.1437
Bertalanffy	0.2315	0.1604	0.1437
Gompertz	0.3175	0.1782	0.1437
Our model	0.0977	0.0902	0.0763
Breast[c] *cancer* [20]			
Logistic	3.0007	0.7071	1.0606
Bertalanffy	3.2942	0.8116	1.0606
Gompertz	3.1908	0.7292	1.0606
Our model	0.7668	0.3096	0.2615

[a] MDA-MB-231 cell line
[b] MDA-MB-435 cell line
[c] MCF-7, T47D cell lines

3.2 Learning the Phenotypical Transitions of Tumors

In order to demonstrate that our model can learn the mathematical relations describing the phenotypical transitions of tumors, we considered the study of 17

DCIS patients in [8]. In typical cancer phenotypic state space, quiescent cancer cells (Q) can become proliferative (P) or apoptotic (A). Non-necrotic cells become hypoxic when oxygen drops below a threshold value. Hypoxic cells can recover to their previous state or become necrotic [15]. Here we only focus on a 3-state sub-model (i.e. P, Q, A states). The transitions among theses sates are stochastic events generated by Poisson processes. Our model was fed with timeseries of raw immunohistochemistry and morphometric data for each of the 17 tumor cases (see [8], Tables S1 and S2) as following: cells cycle time τ_P, cells apoptosis time τ_A, proliferation index PI and apoptosis index AI. Using this input the system has to infer the mathematical relations for α_P, the mean Q - P transition rate, and α_A, the Q - A transition rate, respectively (see Fig. 3). Their analytical form is:

$$\alpha_P = \frac{\frac{1}{\tau_P}(PI + PI^2) - \frac{1}{\tau_A}AIPI}{1 - AI - PI}, \alpha_A = \frac{\frac{1}{\tau_A}(AI - AI^2) + \frac{1}{\tau_P}AIPI}{1 - AI - PI} \tag{8}$$

Looking at the learnt mathematical relation describing the quiescent (Q) to apoptosis (A) and quiescent (Q) to proliferation (P) state transitions of cancer cells in Fig. 3, we can see that our model is able to accurately recover the correct underlying mathematical function with respect to ground truth (clinically extracted and modelled Eq. 8 from [15]): for Q to A transition $SSE = 0.398$, $sMAPE = 0.131$, $RMSE = 0.153$ and for Q to P transition $SSE = 0.750$, $RMSE = 0.210$, $sMAPE = 0.172$, respectively. Note that our system had no prior knowledge of the data distribution or biological assumptions, it simply learnt from the data the underlying relations using the neural processing described in section Materials and methods.

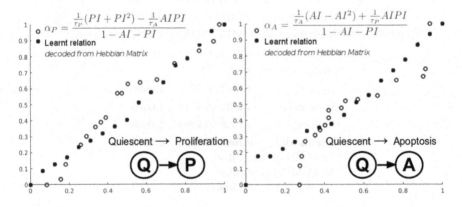

Fig. 3. Learning cancer cells phenotypical states transitions mathematical relations.

3.3   Prediction of Tumor Volume

In this section, we demonstrate that our model, without modification from the other experiments, can provably predict the surgical size of a tumor from pathology data on an individual patient basis.

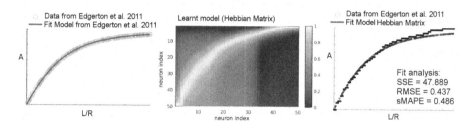

Fig. 4. Upper panel: Modelled relation among A - the ratio of cell apoptosis to proliferation rates, L - the nutrient diffusion penetration length across tumor surgical volume, and R - the geometric mean tumor surgical radius, corresponding to Eq. 9 on data from [8]. Middle panel: The learnt curve as visible in our model's neural weight matrix (i.e. Hebbian connection matrix). Lower panel: Evaluation of the learnt relation against the analytical (ground truth) model in Eq. 9. *In the Hebbian matrix brighter tones code higher values, darker tones lower values.*

Modelling surgical volume aims to elucidate the extent of the volume of tissue that must be surgically removed in order to (1) increase patient survival and (2) decrease the likelihood that a second or third surgery, or even (3) determine the sequencing with chemotherapy. We assessed this capability by demonstrating that our model can learn the dependency between histopathological and morphological data, such as nutrient diffusion penetration length within the breast tissue (L), ratio of cell apoptosis to proliferation rates (A) and radius of the breast tumor (R), in an unsupervised manner, from DCIS data of [8] (see Table 2). More precisely, the authors postulated that the value of R depends upon A and L following a "master equation":

$$A = 3\frac{L}{R}\left(\frac{1}{tanh(\frac{R}{L})} - \frac{L}{R}\right) \tag{9}$$

Its predictions, the study shown, are consistent with published findings that nearly 80% of in-situ tumors identified by mammographic screenings. Compared to ground truth, (Eq. 9) our model was capable of extracting an accurate depiction of the growth pattern with $SSE = 47.889$, $RMSE = 0.437$ and $sMAPE = 0.486$, respectively. Remarkably, despite the lack of prior knowledge about the data and biological constraints, the model learned the growth curve and inferred the tumor evolution (see decoded relation in Fig. 4). Our model is consistent with pathological/mammographic features predictions in [8] (Table 2). Our belief is that measuring such parameters at the time of initial biopsy, pathologists could use our model to precisely estimate the tumor size and thus advise the surgeon how much tissue (surgical volume) is to be removed.

4   Conclusion

There is a significant unfulfilled need for more accurate methods to assess the volume of a clinically diagnosed breast cancer before planning surgery or therapy. Tackling this need, we proposed a versatile unsupervised learning system that is able to extract breast tumor growth patterns that take into account patient variability and limited amount of data from 3 different breast cancer cell lines and overcome 3 state-of-the-art models. In a second experiment, using the same computational substrate, our model learned the underlying mathematical relations describing the phenotypical transitions of the cancer cells, consistent with clinical data. Finally, our model predicted the volume of the breast affected by tumor from limited and noisy timeseries of histopathologic data from 17 cases of DCIS. This suite of experiments prove the versatility of the model and propose it as a candidate for more accurate assessment of surgical volume, which could improve the success of complete excision of breast tumors.

References

1. W.G.: Germany Cancer Statistics (2018). https://gco.iarc.fr/today/data/factsheets/populations/276-germany-fact-sheets.pdf. Accessed 15 Apr 2020
2. Burstein, H.J., Polyak, K., Wong, J.S., Lester, S.C., Kaelin, C.M.: Ductal carcinoma in situ of the breast. New Engl. J. Med. **350**(14), 1430–1441 (2004)
3. Chen, Z., Haykin, S., Eggermont, J.J., Becker, S.: Correlative Learning: A Basis for Brain and Adaptive Systems, vol. 49. Wiley, Hoboken (2008)
4. Collins, L.C., Tamimi, R.M., Baer, H.J., Connolly, J.L., Colditz, G.A., Schnitt, S.J.: Outcome of patients with ductal carcinoma in situ untreated after diagnostic biopsy: results from the Nurses' Health Study. Cancer **103**(9), 1778–1784 (2005)
5. Comen, E., Gilewski, T.A., Norton, L.: Tumor growth kinetics. Holland-Frei Cancer Med., 1–11 (2016). https://doi.org/10.1002/9781119000822.hfcm054
6. Cristini, V., Lowengrub, J.: Multiscale Modeling of Cancer: An Integrated Experimental and Mathematical Modeling Approach. Cambridge University Press, Cambridge (2010)
7. Dillon, M.F., et al.: Needle core biopsy characteristics identify patients at risk of compromised margins in breast conservation surgery. Mod. Pathol. **21**(1), 39–45 (2008)
8. Edgerton, M.E., Chuang, Y.L., Macklin, P., Yang, W., Bearer, E.L., Cristini, V.: A novel, patient-specific mathematical pathology approach for assessment of surgical volume: application to ductal carcinoma in situ of the breast. Anal. Cell. Pathol. **34**(5), 247–263 (2011)
9. Franks, S., Byrne, H., King, J., Underwood, J., Lewis, C.: Modelling the early growth of ductal carcinoma in situ of the breast. J. Math. Biol. **47**(5), 424–452 (2003). https://doi.org/10.1007/s00285-003-0214-x
10. Franks, S., Byrne, H., Underwood, J., Lewis, C.: Biological inferences from a mathematical model of comedo ductal carcinoma in situ of the breast. J. Theoret. Biol. **232**(4), 523–543 (2005)
11. Gerlee, P.: The model muddle: in search of tumor growth laws. Cancer Res. **73**(8), 2407–2411 (2013)

12. Gompertz, B.: On the nature of the function expressive of the law of human mortality, and on a new mode of determining the value of life contingencies. In a Letter to Francis Baily, Esq. FRS & C. Philos. Trans. Roy. Soc. London **115**, 513–583 (1825)

13. Kisfalvi, K., Eibl, G., Sinnett-Smith, J., Rozengurt, E.: Metformin disrupts crosstalk between g protein-coupled receptor and insulin receptor signaling systems and inhibits pancreatic cancer growth. Cancer Res. **69**(16), 6539–6545 (2009)

14. Kohonen, T.: Self-organized formation of topologically correct feature maps. Biol. Cybern. **43**(1), 59–69 (1982)

15. Macklin, P., Edgerton, M.E., Thompson, A.M., Cristini, V.: Patient-calibrated agent-based modelling of ductal carcinoma in situ (DCIS): from microscopic measurements to macroscopic predictions of clinical progression. J. Theoret. Biol. **301**, 122–140 (2012)

16. Marx, J.: How cells cycle toward cancer. Science **263**(5145), 319–322 (1994)

17. Rodallec, A., Giacometti, S., Ciccolini, J., Fanciullino, R.: Tumor growth kinetics of human MDA-MB-231 cells transfected with dTomato lentivirus, December 2019. https://doi.org/10.5281/zenodo.3593919

18. Román, M., Sala, M., Domingo, L., Posso, M., Louro, J., Castells, X.: Personalized breast cancer screening strategies: a systematic review and quality assessment. PloS One **14**(12), e0226352 (2019)

19. Smith, J., Martin, L.: Do cells cycle? Proc. Nat. Acad. Sci. **70**(4), 1263–1267 (1973)

20. Tan, G., et al.: Combination therapy of oncolytic herpes simplex virus HF10 and bevacizumab against experimental model of human breast carcinoma xenograft. Int. J. Cancer **136**(7), 1718–1730 (2015). https://doi.org/10.1002/ijc.29163, https://onlinelibrary.wiley.com/doi/abs/10.1002/ijc.29163

21. Verhulst, P.F.: Notice sur la loi que la population suit dans son accroissement. Corresp. Math. Phys. **10**, 113–126 (1838)

22. Volk, L.D., Flister, M.J., Chihade, D., Desai, N., Trieu, V., Ran, S.: Synergy of nab-paclitaxel and bevacizumab in eradicating large orthotopic breast tumors and preexisting metastases. Neoplasia **13**(4), 327-IN14 (2011)

23. Von Bertalanffy, L.: Quantitative laws in metabolism and growth. Q. Rev. Biol. **32**(3), 217–231 (1957)

Balanced SAM-kNN: Online Learning with Heterogeneous Drift and Imbalanced Data

Valerie Vaquet$^{(\boxtimes)}$ and Barbara Hammer

Machine Learning Group, Bielefeld University, 33501 Bielefeld, Germany
{vvaquet,bhammer}@techfak.uni-bielefeld.de

Abstract. Recently, machine learning techniques are often applied in real world scenarios where learning signals are provided as a stream of data points, and models need to be adapted online according to the current information. A severe problem of such settings consists in the fact that the underlying data distribution might change over time and concept drift or change of the feature characteristics have to be dealt with. In addition, data are often imbalanced because training signals for rare classes are particularly sparse. In the last years, a number of learning technologies have been proposed, which can reliably learn in the presence of drift, whereby non-parametric approaches such as the recent model SAM-kNN [10] can deal particularly well with heterogeneous or priorly unknown types of drift. Yet these methods share the deficiencies of the underlying vanilla-kNN classifier when dealing with imbalanced classes. In this contribution, we propose intuitive extensions of SAM-kNN, which incorporate successful balancing techniques for kNN, namely SMOTE-sampling [1] and kENN [9], respectively, into the online learning scenario. Besides, we propose a new method, Informed Downsampling, for solving class imbalance in non-stationary settings with underlying drift, and demonstrate its superiority in a number of benchmarks.

Keywords: Online learning · Concept drift · Class imbalance

1 Introduction

Recently, there is a growing demand for machine learning techniques in all areas of the industry, startups, service providers, and everyday smart devices including IoT. Many of these novel domains build on considerable amounts of data, which are often collected as a stream of data e.g. by heterogeneous and possibly mobile sensors, as well as all types of explicit and implicit feedback by humans. There is a potential for these techniques to reshape quality control in factories, the analysis of online web applications, personalization of products, individualization of medical support and diagnostics, and numerous more applications. Further, facing today's growing issues around the topic of mobility, online learning will play an important role in intelligent mobile apps, individualized support and diagnostics, and the development of self-driving vehicles [11,12].

© Springer Nature Switzerland AG 2020
I. Farkaš et al. (Eds.): ICANN 2020, LNCS 12397, pp. 850–862, 2020.
https://doi.org/10.1007/978-3-030-61616-8_68

However, when building online learning applications, there are two major challenges. First, the data streams underlying concepts might change over time due to drift in the observed environment, such as a change in lighting in the setting of self driving vehicles [10]. Drift can also be caused by the sensors themselves, as sensors might fail or slowly degrade, or they might be caused by changed demands and expectations of customers. Challenges like these are commonly summarized as learning with drift, and they require learning technologies, which are capable of dealing with the stability-plasticity dilemma of machine learning, i.e. reacting to novel data while preserving learned information, provided it is still valid [2]. While numerous approaches have been proposed such as active drift detection methods or ensemble techniques [8], only few technologies can deal with heterogeneous drift or drift with priorly unknown characteristic, since model meta-parameters are often related to a specific drift strength or type [10].

Second, imbalanced data provides an additional challenge to many classifiers, since they are tailored to optimize the overall accuracy rather than the F-measure or another more balanced evaluation scheme. Imbalanced classes often occur in practice: Consider, for example, the setting of quality control in a factory, where the ratio of defective items that need to be rejected from further manufacturing is fairly small in most applications. Frequently, classifiers tend to assign novel samples to the majority class for the sake of optimizing the overall accuracy; specific technologies have been proposed to deal with this setting in particular in classical batch processing [4,14].

While there is extensive research conducted in the separate areas of online learning on data streams with underlying drift, and batch learning on imbalanced data sets, there is a need for technologies, which can reliably learn in the presence of imbalanced data sets and heterogeneous drift in the data. There do exist a few technologies, which address imbalanced and drifting data [5,14,16], yet these are not based on non-parametric methods and hence not optimum if dealing with heterogeneous drift. Quite a few online learning technologies address the challenge of imbalanced data, including suitable weighting in ensemble technologies, resampling, or bagging [4–7,13,15,16]. A comparative study [16] evaluated the performance of different approaches dealing with imbalanced online learning. Next to the recursive least square adaptive cost perceptron (RLSACP) [7], and an online multi-layer-perceptron [6], the authors investigate particularly promising ensemble models, including an ensemble of extreme learning machines called ESOS-ELM [13], and oversampling-based online bagging [15]. In the study, RLSACP and online MLP are modified by integrating a forget function and suitable weighting for the observed class imbalance into the underlying cost function. The study performs experiments with different drift types of concept drift. Overall, the OOB model detector obtains the highest classification scores. On some of the real drift data sets, this can be slightly improved by a combination of the algorithm with an active drift detection technique [16]. Yet, these models do not refer to non-parametric methods, which have turned out particularly flexible for heterogeneous drift [10].

In this contribution, we focus on a recent, particularly efficient non-parametric learner for online classification, SAM-kNN [10], which demonstrates a stable performance in the setting of online learning with different types of drift, but has been proposed in the context of balanced classes so far. Being based on kNN classification, it shares the deficiencies of the latter when dealing with class imbalance. We propose intuitive extensions of this model, which enable an efficient learning in the presence of imbalanced data. The resulting model is capable of dealing with both, real and virtual drift with different characteristics. We show that these extensions provide superior performance as compared to state-of-the-art methods for learning for streaming data with class imbalance [16].

This paper is organized as follows: After giving definitions for concept drift and class imbalance, we describe the SAM-kNN classifier, and summarize two popular batch models for learning imbalanced data, SMOTE and kENN, in Sect. 2. Section 3 introduces a family of balanced SAM-kNN learners, which are based on these batch technologies, and a new intuitive data processing method, which is inspired by the memory-structure of SAM-kNN. Section 4 and 5 present and discuss experimental evaluations. Section 6 gives a conclusion.

2 Fundamental Concepts

Online Learning

We focus on supervised learning from imbalanced data streams. For online learning as compared to classical batch processing, instead of having all data available at the beginning of the learning procedure, data with the corresponding labels are arriving as a stream of length T:

$$S = (x_t, y_t)_{t=1}^{T}, x_t \in X, y_t \in Y, t = 1, \dots T \tag{1}$$

With input set X and output classes Y. Online learning incrementally infers a model h_t at any time step t. This new set-up requires online evaluation methods, as an evaluation by applying a train test split is not possible. One technique to solve this issue is the application of the interleaved train test error (ITTE).

$$E(S) = \frac{1}{T} \sum_{t=1}^{T} \mathbb{1}(h_t(x_t), y_t) \tag{2}$$

The utilization of the ITTE ensures an evaluation at any chosen time step t, i.e. it evaluates the capability of the learner to rapidly adapt to the current data.

Concept Drift

The classical assumption of data being i.i.d. in batch learning is often violated when learning from data streams. The underlying distribution P_t changes with time t due to external factors as a change in the weather condition, or internal causes as a weakening of sensors. Formally concept drift occurs if

$$\exists t_0, t_1 : P_{t_0}(X, Y) \neq P_{t_1}(X, Y) \tag{3}$$

Imbalanced Data

In batch learning, imbalanced data constitute a well known problem, i.e. the classes have a significantly different frequency. Evaluation measures need to take this into account in the sense that the classifier's performance metrics puts the same weight to all classes. This can be achieved by considering the class-wise recalls

$$\text{recall} = \frac{TP}{TP + FN} \tag{4}$$

where the abbreviations refer to the true positives/negatives of the considered class, or accumulating this in the geometric mean (gmean)

$$\text{gmean} = \sqrt{\frac{TP}{TP + FN} \cdot \frac{TN}{TN + FP}} \tag{5}$$

As this is defined on batches only, we can use it for evaluation purposes wither referring to all already observed data or, in the case of known drift, for all homogeneous regions where no drift is present.

SAM-kNN Model

The Self Adjusting Memory (SAM) model for the k nearest neighbor algorithm (kNN), in the following abbreviated as SAM-kNN, combines a weighted kNN classifier with an intelligent memory structure to store the relevant temporal context as well as concepts in the previous data stream, which are still relevant [10]. Mode precisely, it consists of the following main ingredients:

(i) The short term memory (**STM**) keeps the most recent m examples of the data stream:

$$M_{STM} = \{(x_i, y_i) \in \mathbb{R}^n \times \{1, \dots, c\} | i = t - m + 1, \dots, t\} \tag{6}$$

The STM is dynamically adapted in size m based on the ITTE of a logarithmic number of potential window sizes. In this way, data points which were collected before a drift happened are discarded from the STM.

(ii) The long term memory (**LTM**) stores information, which has been discarded from the STM, but which is still relevant. To guarantee consistency, a robust and parameterless strategy has been proposed in the work [10] how to decide, which data points are still relevant. The LTM is compressed by kmeans clustering if the size becomes too big. We refer to the LTM as the set

$$M_{LTM} = \{(x_i, y_i) \in \mathbb{R}^n \times \{1, \dots, c\} | i = 1, \dots, p\} \tag{7}$$

Details can be found in [10].

(iii) The combined memory (CM) is the union of both memories:

$$M_{CM} = M_{STM} \cup M_{LTM} \tag{8}$$

In the prediction phase, the output of the kNN classifier on the memory with the best performance over the last $m = |M_{STM}|$ time steps is chosen as output for the SAM-kNN model.

Balancing Techniques

For batch learning, there exists a variety of methods dealing with class imbalance. Two main principles are algorithm-level and data-level methods. The first one is modifying the classification algorithm, the latter is directly changing the data set.

Synthetic Minority Over-sampling Technique (**SMOTE**) [1] is a data-level method for learning from imbalanced data. In order to generate additional minority class examples, for each minority point, the k nearest neighbors are found. Of all those neighbors, the ones belonging to the minority class are selected. A random new point is generated on each line between the example and the neighbors of the same class.

The algorithm-level solution k exemplar based nearest neighbor (**kENN**) [9] is modifying the kNN classifier. The basic idea is to give more importance to certain minority class examples, which are referred to as positive pivot instances (PPI). These points are expanded to a Gaussian ball. The challenge is to chose only those points for which a ball will not cause false positives (details can be found in [9]). In the classification step, the distances calculated by the kNN algorithm are adapted according to the computed exemplar balls:

$$adapted\_dist(t, x) = \begin{cases} dist(t, x) - x.radius & \text{if } x \text{ is a PPI} \\ dist(t, x) & \text{otherwise} \end{cases} \tag{9}$$

3   Balanced SAM-kNN

While SAM-kNN provides superior results for streaming data, it has not yet been evaluated and adapted to imbalanced settings. Here, we propose and evaluate modifications of SAM-kNN classifier which account for imbalanced data streams. The following changes are included:

Evaluation of Performance: We replace the ITTE, which is used to evaluate the performance of the algorithm on a window and memory structure, with a time decayed version of the gmean. This is based on the time-decayed recall of class c:

$$\text{recall}_{c,t} := \lambda \text{recall}_{c,t-1} + (1 - \lambda)\mathbb{1}(h_t(x_t), y_t)$$

This class-wise time-decayed gmeans can be accumulated over all yet observed classes. By applying the metric to all internal procedures of the SAM classifier, all classes are weighted equally.

Besides, we ensure that the memory structures used in SAM-kNN are balanced, as follows:

Balanced SAM-kNN-SMOTE: Periodically every 25 times steps, and whenever the STM is adapted, balancing according to SMOTE sampling is done.

Balanced SAM-kENN: The same is done based on kENN.

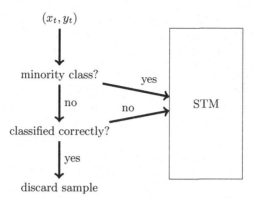

Fig. 1. Visualization of the informed downsampling procedure.

Informed Downsampling: Both proposed versions balance the memory structures by applying a balancing technique as an extra step. However, it is possible to obtain a balanced STM by modifying the training step of SAM-kNN instead of applying SMOTE or kENN computations as an extra step. In online learning, we know whether a data point is misclassified by the current model before performing the update step since in prequential evaluation each sample is first used for testing and afterwards for updating the model. This information can be used to implement a more informed balancing procedure, which we dub informed downsampling (ID). As indicated in Fig. 1, all correctly classified majority class samples are discarded, since they are not introducing crucial new information. Misclassified majority class points and minority samples are used to update the STM. While the update with minority points balances the memory, misclassified majority points need to be considered since they add new information. Especially when the distribution changes due to a drift, this consideration of majority points is crucial for a good classification performance. In this way, we obtain a more balanced class distribution without losing valuable information. An additional advantage of this approach is its computational efficiency.

4   Experiments with Known Drift

We follow the comparative study [16] and evaluate the learning models on the artificial data sets SINE1 and SEA, where the type of drift is known. We compare the extensions of SAM-kNN with the performance to the method oversampling-based online bagging (OOB) [15], since this method obtained the best results in comparison to alternatives as reported in [15].

Artificial Data Sets: All data sets contain a stream of length 3000 with an imbalance ratio of $\frac{1}{9}$. For both concepts, we evaluate the models on a version with abrupt drift at $t = 1500$ and a gradual drift, which occurs in the time from $t = 1500$ to $t = 2000$. The SINE1 samples are uniformly drawn from $[0, 1] \times [0, 1]$

while for the three dimensional SEA samples each dimension is sampled from the interval $[0, 10]$. Only the first two dimensions are relevant for the classification. Detailed descriptions of the data sets are given in Table 1.

Table 1. Artificial SINE1 and SEA concepts.

$P(Y|X)$ drift:

Data	Class 0		Class 1 (minority)	
	Old concept	New concept	Old concept	New concept
SINE1	$x_2 - \sin(x_1) \geq 0$	$x_2 - \sin(x_1) < 0$	$x_2 - \sin(x_1) < 0$	$x_2 - \sin(x_1) \geq 0$
SEA	$x_1 + x_2 > 7$	$x_1 + x_2 > 13$	$x_1 + x_2 \leq 7$	$x_1 + x_2 \leq 13$

$P(X|Y)$ drift:

Data	Class 0		Class 1 (minority)	
	Old concept	New concept	Old concept	New concept
SINE1	$x_2 - \sin(x_1) \geq 0$	$x_2 - \sin(x_1) \geq 0$	$x_2 - \sin(x_1) < 0$ $P(x_1 < 0.5) = 0.9$	$x_2 - \sin(x_1) < 0$ $P(x_1 < 0.5) = 0.1$
SEA	$x_1 + x_2 > 7$	$x_1 + x_2 > 7$	$x_1 + x_2 \leq 7$ $P(x_1 < 5) = 0.9$	$x_1 + x_2 \leq 7$ $P(x_1 < 5) = 0.1$

$P(Y)$ drift:

Data	Class 0		Class 1 (minority)	
	Old concept	New concept	Old concept	New concept
SINE1	$x_2 - \sin(x_1) \geq 0$ $P(y) = 0.1$	$x_2 - \sin(x_1) < 0$ $P(y) = 0.9$	$x_2 - \sin(x_1) < 0$ $P(y) = 0.9$	$x_2 - \sin(x_1) \geq 0$ $P(y) = 0.1$
SEA	$x_1 + x_2 > 7$ $P(y) = 0.5$	$x_1 + x_2 > 13$ $P(y) = 0.1$	$x_1 + x_2 \leq 7$ $P(y) = 0.5$	$x_1 + x_2 \leq 13$ $P(y) = 0.9$

For each of the artificial experiments we compare the performance of the different classifiers on the new concept. More precisely, we compute the averaged class recalls and gmean for the new concept, i.e. for the data sets with abrupt drift starting at $t = 1500$, and for the ones with gradual drift at $t = 2000$. In the following section, the results for the OOB classifier are taken from [16].

Experimental Results: The results of the experiments are summarized in Table 2. For real drift, even the basic implementation of balanced SAM-kNN outperforms the OOB classifier. Further performance improvements are obtained by integrating SMOTE and kENN and, in particular, balanced SAM-kNN+ID. These observations indicate that the SAM-kNN architecture adapts quickly to novel concepts and that all implemented balancing techniques improve the minority class classification score.

Facing virtual $P(X|Y)$ drift on the SINE1 data set, the basic implementation of the SAM-kNN classifier obtains worse results than the OOB model. Balancing techniques SMOTE and kENN accelerate SAM-kNN to a better performance

Table 2. Results of experiments on the SINE1 and SEA concepts with $P(Y|X)$ drift.

Data set	Model	recall 0	recall 1	gmean
SINE1	OOB	**0.942 ± 0.009**	0.033 ± 0.012	0.102 ± 0.022
SINE1	Balanced SAM-kNN	0.922 ± 0.122	0.436 ± 0.177	0.606 ± 0.230
SINE1	Balanced SAM-kNN+SMOTE	0.906 ± 0.117	0.602 ± 0.213	0.714 ± 0.239
SINE1	Balanced SAM-kENN	0.923 ± 0.114	0.525 ± 0.215	0.664 ± 0.249
SINE1	Balanced SAM-kNN+ID	0.800 ± 0.170	**0.684 ± 0.243**	**0.726 ± 0.242**
SINE1g	OOB	0.995 ± 0.002	0.027 ± 0.010	0.093 ± 0.028
SINE1g	Balanced SAM-kNN	**0.969 ± 0.021**	0.405 ± 0.133	0.618 ± 0.096
SINE1g	Balanced SAM-kNN+SMOTE	0.964 ± 0.022	0.462 ± 0.138	0.660 ± 0.098
SINE1g	Balanced SAM-kENN	0.934 ± 0.034	0.558 ± 0.167	0.714 ± 0.099
SINE1g	Balanced SAM-kNN+ID	0.808 ± 0.069	**0.737 ± 0.114**	**0.769 ± 0.080**
SEA	OOB	0.966 ± 0.008	0.287 ± 0.014	0.525 ± 0.012
SEA	Balanced SAM-kNN	**1.000 ± 0.000**	0.368 ± 0.073	0.601 ± 0.079
SEA	Balanced SAM-kNN+SMOTE	0.999 ± 0.001	0.419 ± 0.093	0.640 ± 0.091
SEA	Balanced SAM-kENN	0.990 ± 0.008	0.515 ± 0.119	0.706 ± 0.103
SEA	Balanced SAM-kNN+ID	0.981 ± 0.011	**0.597 ± 0.139**	**0.757 ± 0.106**
SEAg	OOB	0.974 ± 0.008	0.282 ± 0.032	0.506 ± 0.034
SEAg	Balanced SAM-kNN	**0.997 ± 0.002**	0.296 ± 0.083	0.537 ± 0.081
SEAg	Balanced SAM-kNN+SMOTE	0.993 ± 0.003	0.465 ± 0.123	0.674 ± 0.088
SEAg	Balanced SAM-kENN	0.967 ± 0.015	0.538 ± 0.102	0.717 ± 0.068
SEAg	Balanced SAM-kNN+ID	0.954 ± 0.013	**0.656 ± 0.067**	**0.789 ± 0.053**

than OOB on the data set with underlying abrupt drift. We cannot observe this effect on the SINE1g data set, as we report a much higher gmean score for the OOB model here. This is probably due to the fact, that the OOB classifier has time to adjust to the new concept as the evaluation metric is computed on the data points which are collected after the drift is completed. In contrast, the obtained scores for balanced SAM-kNN with SMOTE and kENN are stable for the data set with abrupt and gradual drift. This indicates that our model adapts quickly to the drift which is to be expected due to the automatic size adaption of the STM. The balanced SAM-kNN version with informed downsampling performs best over all data sets. This observation aligns with the idea behind the model. Since only misclassified majority data points are added to the STM, the dense areas of the data set are efficiently downsampled.

On the SEA concepts, we observe a weaker performance of OOB. Thus, the basic version reaches higher gmean values over both drift speeds. These results can be improved by applying the balancing techniques. Again, we obtain the highest gmean values for balanced SAM-kNN+ID, which confirms our prior observation.

Finally, we conducted experiments on the data sets with underlying $P(Y)$ drift. The results are shown in Table 4. For all versions of this experiment, we observe better results for the balanced SAM-kNN based models than for the OOB classifier. Besides, the obtained gmean scores are relatively close for the basic implementation, as well as for the balancing techniques SMOTE and kENN. This observation might be explained by the construction of the LTM which is balanced and thus gives a good input for the underlying kNN classifier. It seems, that the balanced SAM-kNN+ID model needs time to adjust to the new class imbalance ratio as it scores significantly higher scores for the experiments on the gradual data

Table 3. Results of experiments on the SINE1 and SEA concepts with $P(X|Y)$ drift.

Data set	Model	recall 0	recall 1	gmean
SINE1	OOB	0.985 ± 0.004	0.696 ± 0.020	0.817 ± 0.013
SINE1	Balanced SAM-kNN	$\mathbf{0.999 \pm 0.001}$	0.594 ± 0.068	0.769 ± 0.044
SINE1	Balanced SAM-kNN+SMOTE	$\mathbf{0.999 \pm 0.001}$	0.707 ± 0.085	0.839 ± 0.054
SINE1	Balanced SAM-kENN	0.995 ± 0.002	0.750 ± 0.075	0.863 ± 0.048
SINE1	Balanced SAM-kNN+ID	0.958 ± 0.011	$\mathbf{0.907 \pm 0.039}$	$\mathbf{0.932 \pm 0.030}$
SINE1g	OOB	0.988 ± 0.003	0.802 ± 0.034	0.884 ± 0.021
SINE1g	Balanced SAM-kNN	$\mathbf{1.000 \pm 0.000}$	0.613 ± 0.093	0.777 ± 0.101
SINE1g	Balanced SAM-kNN+SMOTE	0.995 ± 0.002	0.700 ± 0.092	0.830 ± 0.090
SINE1g	Balanced SAM-kENN	0.997 ± 0.001	0.771 ± 0.119	0.869 ± 0.114
SINE1g	Balanced SAM-kNN+ID	0.961 ± 0.022	$\mathbf{0.913 \pm 0.130}$	$\mathbf{0.931 \pm 0.109}$
SEA	OOB	0.919 ± 0.010	0.477 ± 0.031	0.657 ± 0.021
SEA	Balanced SAM-kNN	$\mathbf{0.997 \pm 0.001}$	0.693 ± 0.076	0.828 ± 0.076
SEA	Balanced SAM-kNN+SMOTE	0.988 ± 0.003	0.763 ± 0.094	0.864 ± 0.085
SEA	Balanced SAM-kENN	0.934 ± 0.030	$\mathbf{0.968 \pm 0.085}$	0.948 ± 0.082
SEA	Balanced SAM-kNN+ID	0.972 ± 0.010	0.955 ± 0.084	$\mathbf{0.960 \pm 0.083}$
SEAg	OOB	0.943 ± 0.018	0.345 ± 0.027	0.552 ± 0.022
SEAg	Balanced SAM-kNN	$\mathbf{0.999 \pm 0.001}$	0.591 ± 0.066	0.765 ± 0.069
SEAg	Balanced SAM-kNN+SMOTE	0.990 ± 0.005	0.641 ± 0.064	0.793 ± 0.069
SEAg	Balanced SAM-kENN	0.943 ± 0.011	0.841 ± 0.058	0.890 ± 0.041
SEAg	Balanced SAM-kNN+ID	0.942 ± 0.008	$\mathbf{0.963 \pm 0.042}$	$\mathbf{0.951 \pm 0.037}$

sets. In choosing the memory for the kNN classifier during the prediction phase, there might be confusion on which memory to consider (Table 4).

5   Experiments for Real World Data

In addition to the performance evaluation on artificial data, we examine the performance of the different implementations of the balanced SAM-kNN on a real world data set which was part of the comparative study [16] and used to evaluate the SAM-kNN classifier [10]. The data set contains measurements of weather conditions in the time between 1949–1999 on the Offutt Air Force Base in Bellevue, Nebraska. Each sample consists of eight features such as pressure, wind speed, and temperature. The labels are rain/no rain. The data set contains 5698 minority (rain) and 12461 majority (no rain) instances [3].

In our experiments, we compare the performance of the basic balanced SAM-kNN classifier with the implementations applying balancing strategies. Therefore, we run the models on versions of the weather data set with different imbalance ratios and measure the time decayed gmean with a decay factor of 0.995 for each model. To obtain data streams with various imbalance ratios, we randomly remove minority points.

The results for the experiments with the original imbalance ratio, a ratio of 0.2, and of 0.1 are shown in Fig. 2. We report similar gmean values of around 0.6 for the models in the experiments on the original data set. Overall, the balanced SAM-kNN+ID and SAM-kENN seem to perform slightly better. Applying the algorithms to a more severe imbalanced data set with a ratio of 0.2, the performance drops with a different severity for the implementations. While we observe a slight drop of the time decayed gmean for the model with informed downsampling, the strongest decline can be observed for the basic implementation. Comparing the kENN balancing technique with SMOTE, we note lower results for the latter.

Table 4. Results of experiments on the SINE1 and SEA concepts with $P(Y)$ drift.

Data set	Model	recall 0	recall 1	gmean
SINE1	OOB	0.699 ± 0.014	0.992 ± 0.002	0.832 ± 0.008
SINE1	Balanced SAM-kNN	0.885 ± 0.080	0.955 ± 0.073	0.917 ± 0.048
SINE1	Balanced SAM-kNN+SMOTE	$\mathbf{0.934 \pm 0.062}$	0.965 ± 0.048	0.948 ± 0.037
SINE1	Balanced SAM-kENN	0.932 ± 0.038	0.973 ± 0.023	$\mathbf{0.952 \pm 0.028}$
SINE1	Balanced SAM-kNN+ID	0.726 ± 0.065	$\mathbf{0.996 \pm 0.010}$	0.849 ± 0.038
SINE1g	OOB	0.709 ± 0.002	0.989 ± 0.002	0.835 ± 0.001
SINE1g	Balanced SAM-kNN	0.968 ± 0.028	0.925 ± 0.072	0.944 ± 0.043
SINE1g	Balanced SAM-kNN+SMOTE	0.979 ± 0.016	0.940 ± 0.055	0.958 ± 0.039
SINE1g	Balanced SAM-kENN	$\mathbf{0.980 \pm 0.007}$	0.941 ± 0.054	$\mathbf{0.959 \pm 0.040}$
SINE1g	Balanced SAM-kNN+ID	0.911 ± 0.039	$\mathbf{0.997 \pm 0.036}$	0.952 ± 0.040
SEA	OOB	$\mathbf{0.945 \pm 0.006}$	0.515 ± 0.016	0.689 ± 0.010
SEA	Balanced SAM-kNN	0.713 ± 0.125	0.976 ± 0.046	0.830 ± 0.061
SEA	Balanced SAM-kNN+SMOTE	0.797 ± 0.085	0.982 ± 0.034	$\mathbf{0.883 \pm 0.043}$
SEA	Balanced SAM-kENN	0.735 ± 0.060	0.981 ± 0.028	0.848 ± 0.053
SEA	Balanced SAM-kNN+ID	0.713 ± 0.093	$\mathbf{0.983 \pm 0.033}$	0.834 ± 0.052
SEAg	OOB	0.951 ± 0.012	0.484 ± 0.032	0.675 ± 0.022
SEAg	Balanced SAM-kNN	$\mathbf{0.974 \pm 0.027}$	0.873 ± 0.145	0.916 ± 0.100
SEAg	Balanced SAM-kNN+SMOTE	0.968 ± 0.016	0.910 ± 0.119	0.933 ± 0.089
SEAg	Balanced SAM-kENN	0.818 ± 0.032	$\mathbf{0.982 \pm 0.042}$	0.895 ± 0.034
SEAg	Balanced SAM-kNN+ID	0.915 ± 0.028	0.974 ± 0.043	$\mathbf{0.943 \pm 0.036}$

The observed behavior can be confirmed when considering a more severe imbalance ratio of 0.1. While balanced SAM-kNN+ID keeps gmean values between 0.5 and 0.6, the observations for the basic implementation stay below 0.2 for most of the time. Again, we report better results for the kENN based version than for the SMOTE based version. To summarize, our results confirm that our prior observations in the artificial experiment hold for real world data.

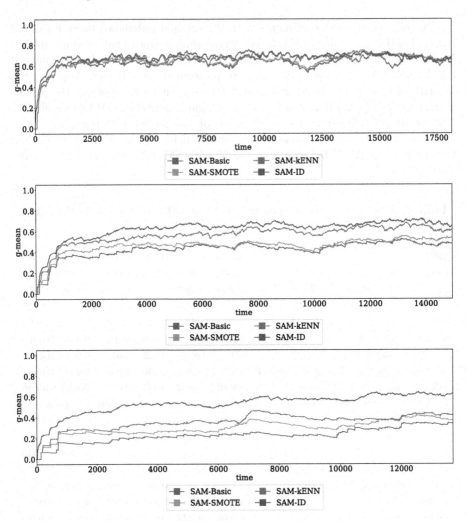

Fig. 2. Results of the experiment on the original weather data set (top) and imbalance ratio 0.2 (middle), and 0.1 (bottom).

6 Conclusion

This paper proposes methods to add robustness to the SAM-kNN model when facing imbalanced data streams. Next to basic modifications, we implement balancing by applying the known batch learning techniques SMOTE and kENN. Besides, we propose the informed downsampling heuristic.

Our artificial experiments, covering multiple types of drift, show that for some scenarios, even the basic version of balanced SAM-kNN without further balancing methods obtains higher results than the OOB classifier. Throughout the experiments, the balanced SAM-kNN model family obtains good results.

Particularly the results on data streams with underlying real drift, which is the most severe type, prove the effectiveness of the proposed model. Especially balanced SAM-kNN+ID, which is a very efficient approach in comparison to SAM-kNN+SMOTE and SAM-kENN, demonstrates high classification results. These findings were confirmed by our study of a real world data set.

Acknowledgment. Funding in the frame of the BMBF project TiM, 05M20PBA, is gratefully acknowledged.

References

1. Bowyer, K.W., Chawla, N.V., Hall, L.O., Kegelmeyer, W.P.: SMOTE: synthetic minority over-sampling technique. J. Artif. Intell. Res. **16**, 321–357 (2002)
2. Ditzler, G., Roveri, M., Alippi, C., Polikar, R.: Learning in nonstationary environments: a survey. IEEE Comput. Intell. Mag. **10**(4), 12–25 (2015). https://doi.org/10.1109/MCI.2015.2471196
3. Elwell, R., Polikar, R.: Incremental learning of concept drift in nonstationary environments. IEEE Trans. Neural Netw. **22**, 1517–1531 (2011). https://doi.org/10.1109/TNN.2011.2160459
4. Fernández, A., García, S., Galar, M., Prati, R.C., Krawczyk, B., Herrera, F.: Learning from Imbalanced Data Sets. Springer, Cham (2018). https://doi.org/10.1007/978-3-319-98074-4
5. Ferreira, L.E.B., Gomes, H.M., Bifet, A., Oliveira, L.S.: Adaptive random forests with resampling for imbalanced data streams. In: International Joint Conference on Neural Networks, IJCNN 2019 Budapest, Hungary, 14–19 July 2019, pp. 1–6. IEEE (2019). https://doi.org/10.1109/IJCNN.2019.8852027
6. Ghazikhani, A., Monsefi, R., Sadoghi Yazdi, H.: Online neural network model for non-stationary and imbalanced data stream classification. Int. J. Mach. Learn. Cybern. **5**(1), 51–62 (2013). https://doi.org/10.1007/s13042-013-0180-6
7. Ghazikhani, A., Monsefi, R., Sadoghi Yazdi, H.: Recursive least square perceptron model for non-stationary and imbalanced data stream classification. Evolving Syst. **4**, 119–131 (2014). https://doi.org/10.1007/s12530-013-9076-7
8. Gomes, H.M., Read, J., Bifet, A., Barddal, J.P., Gama, J.: Machine learning for streaming data: state of the art, challenges, and opportunities. SIGKDD Explor. **21**(2), 6–22 (2019). https://doi.org/10.1145/3373464.3373470
9. Li, Y., Zhang, X.: Improving k nearest neighbor with exemplar generalization for imbalanced classification. In: Huang, J.Z., Cao, L., Srivastava, J. (eds.) Advances in Knowledge Discovery and Data Mining, pp. 321–332. Springer, Heidelberg (2011)
10. Losing, V., Hammer, B., Wersing, H.: KNN classifier with self adjusting memory for heterogeneous concept drift. In: 2016 IEEE 16th International Conference on Data Mining (ICDM), pp. 291–300, December 2016. https://doi.org/10.1109/ICDM.2016.0040
11. Losing, V., Yoshikawa, T., Hasenjäger, M., Hammer, B., Wersing, H.: Personalized online learning of whole-body motion classes using multiple inertial measurement units. In: International Conference on Robotics and Automation, ICRA 2019, Montreal, QC, Canada, 20–24 May 2019, pp. 9530–9536 (2019). https://doi.org/10.1109/ICRA.2019.8794251
12. Ma, J., Alippi, C., Yang, L.T., Ning, H., Wang, K.I.: Introduction to the IEEE CIS TC on smart world (SWTC) [society briefs]. IEEE Comput. Intell. Mag. **13**(1), 7–9 (2018). https://doi.org/10.1109/MCI.2017.2773739

13. Mirza, B., Lin, Z., Liu, N.: Ensemble of subset online sequential extreme learning machine for class imbalance and concept drift. Neurocomputing **149**, 316–329 (2015). https://doi.org/10.1016/j.neucom.2014.03.075. Advances in Neural Networks, Advances in Extreme Learning Machines
14. Napierala, K., Stefanowski, J.: Types of minority class examples and their influence on learning classifiers from imbalanced data. J. Intell. Inf. Syst. **46**(3), 563–597 (2015). https://doi.org/10.1007/s10844-015-0368-1
15. Wang, S., Minku, L.L., Yao, X.: A learning framework for online class imbalance learning. In: 2013 IEEE Symposium on Computational Intelligence and Ensemble Learning (CIEL), pp. 36–45, April 2013. https://doi.org/10.1109/CIEL.2013.6613138
16. Wang, S., Minku, L.L., Yao, X.: A systematic study of online class imbalance learning with concept drift. IEEE Trans. Neural Netw. Learn. Syst. **29**(10), 4802–4821 (2018). https://doi.org/10.1109/TNNLS.2017.2771290

A Rigorous Link Between Self-Organizing Maps and Gaussian Mixture Models

Alexander Gepperth$^{(\boxtimes)}$ and Benedikt Pfülb

University of Applied Sciences Fulda, Leipzigerstr. 123, 36037 Fulda, Germany
{alexander.gepperth,benedikt.pfuelb}@cs.hs-fulda.de
https://www.hs-fulda.de/

Abstract. This work presents a mathematical treatment of the relation between Self-Organizing Maps (SOMs) and Gaussian Mixture Models (GMMs). We show that energy-based SOM models can be interpreted as performing gradient descent, minimizing an approximation to the GMM log-likelihood that is particularly valid for high data dimensionalities. The SOM-like decrease of the neighborhood radius can be understood as an annealing procedure ensuring that gradient descent does not get stuck in undesirable local minima. This link allows to treat SOMs as generative probabilistic models, giving a formal justification for using SOMs, e.g., to detect outliers, or for sampling.

Keywords: Self-Organizing Maps · Gaussian Mixture Models · Stochastic Gradient Descent

1 Introduction

This theoretical work is set in the context of unsupervised clustering and density estimation methods and establishes a mathematical link between two important representatives: Self-Organizing Maps (SOMs, [1,10]) and Gaussian Mixture Models (GMMs, [2]), both of which have a long history in machine learning. There are significant overlaps between SOMs and GMMs, and both models have been used for data visualization and outlier detection. They are both based on Euclidean distances and model data distributions by prototypes or centroids. At the same time, there are some differences: GMMs, as fully generative models with a clear probabilistic interpretation, can additionally be used for sampling purposes. Typically, GMMs are trained batch-wise, repeatedly processing all available data in successive iterations of the Expectation-Maximization (EM) algorithm. In contrast, SOMs are trained online, processing one sample at a time. The training of GMMs is based on a loss function, usually referred to as *incomplete-data log-likelihood* or just log-likelihood. Training by Stochastic Gradient Descent (SGD) is possible, as well, although few authors have explored this [9]. SOMs are not based on a loss function, but there are model extensions [4,7] that propose a simple loss function at the expense of very slight

© Springer Nature Switzerland AG 2020
I. Farkaš et al. (Eds.): ICANN 2020, LNCS 12397, pp. 863–872, 2020.
https://doi.org/10.1007/978-3-030-61616-8_69

differences in model equations. Lastly, GMMs have a simple probabilistic interpretation as they attempt to model the density of observed data points. For this reason, GMMs may be used for outlier detection, clustering and, most importantly, sampling. In contrast to that, SOMs are typically restricted to clustering and visualization due to the topological organization of prototypes, which does not apply to GMMs.

1.1 Problem Statement

SOMs are simple to use, implement and visualize, and, despite the absence of theoretical guarantees, have a very robust training convergence. However, their interpretation remains unclear. This particularly concerns the probabilistic meaning of input-prototype distances. Different authors propose using the Best-Matching Unit (BMU) position only, while others make use of the associated input-prototype distance, or even the combination of all distances [6]. Having a clear interpretation of these quantities would help researchers tremendously when interpreting trained SOMs. The question whether SOMs actually perform density estimation is important for justifying outlier detection or clustering applications. Last but not least, a probabilistic interpretation of SOMs, preferably a simple one in terms of the well-known GMMs, would help researchers to understand how sampling from SOMs can be performed.

1.2 Results and Contribution

This article aims at explaining SOM training as Stochastic Gradient Descent (SGD) using an energy function that is a particular approximation to the GMM log-likelihood. SOM training is shown to be an approximation to training GMMs with tied, spherical covariance matrices where constant factors have been discarded from the probability computations. This identification allows to interpret SOMs in a probabilistic manner, particularly for:

- outlier detection (not only the position of the BMU can be taken into account, but also the associated input-prototype distance since it has a probabilistic interpretation) and
- sampling (understanding what SOM prototypes actually represent, it is possible to generate new samples from SOMs with the knowledge that this is actually sanctioned by theory).

1.3 Related Work

Several authors have attempted to establish a link between SOMs and GMMs. In [8], an EM algorithm for SOMs is given, emphasizing the close links between both models. Verbeek et al. [14] emphasizes that GMMs are regularized to show a SOM-like behavior of self-organization. A similar idea of component averaging to obtain SOM-like normal ordering and thus improved convergence was previously demonstrated in [11]. An energy-based extension of SOMs suggesting a close relationship to GMMs is given in [7], with an improved version described in [4]. So far, no scientific work has tried to explain SOMs as an approximation to GMMs in a way that is comparable to this work.

2   Main Proof

The general outline of proof is depicted in Fig. 1. We start with a description of GMMs in Sect. 2.1. Subsequently, a transition from exact GMMs to the popular Max-Component (MC) approximation of its loss is described in Sect. 2.2. Then, we propose a SOM-inspired annealing procedure for performing optimization of approximate GMMs in Sect. 2.3 and explain its function in the context of SGD. Finally, we show that this annealed training procedure is equivalent to training energy-based SOMs in Sect. 2.4, which are a faithful approximation of the original SOM model, outlined in Sect. 2.5.

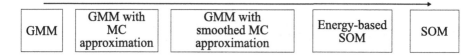

Fig. 1. Outline of main proof.

2.1   Default GMM Model, Notation and GMM Training

Gaussian Mixture Models (GMMs) are probabilistic latent-variable models that aim to explain the distribution of observed data samples $X = \{\boldsymbol{x}_n\}$. It is assumed that samples generated from a known parametric distribution, which depends on parameters θ and unobservable latent variables $Z = \{\boldsymbol{z}_n \in \mathbb{R}^K\}$, $z_{nk} \in \{0, 1\}$ and $\sum_k z_{nk} = 1$. The *complete-data probability* reads

$$p(X, Z) = \prod_n^N \prod_k^K \left[p_k(\boldsymbol{x}_n) \right]^{\pi_k z_{nk}} \tag{1}$$

where mixture components $p_k(\boldsymbol{x}_n)$ are modeled as multi-variate Gaussians, and whose parameters are the centroids $\boldsymbol{\mu}_k$ and the positive-definite covariance matrices Σ_k (both omitted from the notation for conciseness). $p_k(\boldsymbol{x}_n)$ represents the probability of observing the data vector $\boldsymbol{x}_n$, if sampled from mixture component k. The number of Gaussian mixture components K is a free parameter of the model, and the component weights π_k must have a sum of 1. Since the latent variables are not observable, it makes sense to marginalize them out by summing over the discrete set of all possible values $\mathcal{Z} = \{\boldsymbol{e}_j | j = 1 \ldots K\}$, giving

$$p(X) = \prod_n \sum_{z_n \in \mathcal{Z}} \prod_k p_k(\boldsymbol{x}_n)^{\pi_k z_{nk}}. \tag{2}$$

Taking the logarithm and normalizing by the number of samples (N) provides the *incomplete-data log-likelihood*, which contains only observable quantities and is, therefore, a suitable starting point for optimization:

$$\mathcal{L} = \frac{1}{N} \sum_{n=1}^{N} \log \sum_{k} \pi_k p_k(\boldsymbol{x}_n). \tag{3}$$

Concise Problem Statement

When training GMMs, one aims at finding parameters $\boldsymbol{\mu}_k$, Σ_k that (locally) maximize Eq. (3). This is usually performed by using a procedure called Expectation-Maximization (EM, [2,5]) which is applicable to many latent-data (mixture) models. Of course, a principled alternative to EM is an approach purely based on batches or SGD, the latter being an approximation justified by the Robbins-Monro procedure [12]. In this article, we will investigate how SGD optimization of Eq. (3) can be related to the training of SOMs.

Respecting GMM Constraints in SGD

GMMs impose the following constraints on the parameters π_k, $\boldsymbol{\mu}_k$ and Σ_k:

- weights must be normalized: $\sum_k \pi_k = 1$
- covariance matrices must be positive-definite: $\boldsymbol{x}^T \Sigma_k \boldsymbol{x} \geq 0 \, \forall \, k, \boldsymbol{x}$

The first constraint can be enforced after each gradient decent step by setting $\pi_k \to \frac{\pi_k}{\sum_j \pi_j}$. For the second constraint, we consider diagonal covariance matrices only, which is sufficient for establishing a link to SOMs. A simple strategy in this setting is to re-parameterize covariance matrices Σ_k by their inverse (denoted as precision matrices) $\mathbf{P}_k = \Sigma^{-1}$. We then re-write this as $\mathbf{P}_k = \mathbf{D}_k \mathbf{D}_k$, which ensures positive-definiteness of $\mathbf{P}, \Sigma$. The diagonal entries $\boldsymbol{s}_k$ of Σ_k can thus be re-written as $s_{ki} = d_{ki}^{-2}$, whereas $\boldsymbol{d}_k$ are the diagonal entries of $\mathbf{D}_k$.

2.2   Max-Component Approximation

In Eq. (3), we observe that the component weights π_k and the conditional probabilities $p(\boldsymbol{x})$ are positive by definition. It is, therefore, evident that any single component of the inner sum over the components k is a lower bound of the entire inner sum. The largest of these K lower bounds is given by the maximum of the components, so that it results in

$$\mathcal{L} = \frac{1}{N} \sum_{n=1}^{N} \log \sum_{k} \pi_k p(\boldsymbol{x}_n) \leq \hat{\mathcal{L}} = \frac{1}{N} \sum_{n} \log \max_k \left(\pi_k p(\boldsymbol{x}_n) \right)$$

$$= \frac{1}{N} \sum_{n} \max_k \log \left(\pi_k p(\boldsymbol{x}_n) \right). \tag{4}$$

Equation (4) displays what we refer to as *Max-Component approximation* to the log-likelihood. Since $\hat{\mathcal{L}} \leq \mathcal{L}$, we can increase $\mathcal{L}$ by maximizing $\hat{\mathcal{L}}$. The advantage of $\hat{\mathcal{L}}$ is that it is not affected by numerical instabilities the way $\mathcal{L}$ is. Moreover, it breaks the symmetry between mixture components, thus, avoiding degenerate local optima during early training. Apart from facilitating the relation to SOMs, this is an interesting idea in its own right, which was first proposed in [3].

Undesirable Local Optima

GMMs are usually trained using EM after a k-means initialization of the centroids. Since this work explores the relation to SOMs, which are mainly trained from scratch, we investigate SGD-based training of GMMs without k-means initialization. A major problem in this setting are undesirable local optima, both for the full log-likelihood $\mathcal{L}$ and its approximation $\hat{\mathcal{L}}$. To show this, we parameterize the component probabilities by the precision matrices $\mathbf{P}_k = \Sigma_k^{-1}$ and compute

$$
\begin{aligned}
\frac{\partial \mathcal{L}}{\partial \boldsymbol{\mu}_k} &= \mathbb{E}_n \left[\mathbf{P}_k \left(\boldsymbol{x}_n - \boldsymbol{\mu}_k \right) \gamma_{nk} \right] \\
\frac{\partial \mathcal{L}}{\partial \mathbf{P}_k} &= \mathbb{E}_n \left[\left((\mathbf{P}_k)^{-1} - (\boldsymbol{x}_n - \boldsymbol{\mu}_k)(\boldsymbol{x}_n - \boldsymbol{\mu}_k)^T \right) \gamma_{nk} \right] \\
\frac{\partial \mathcal{L}}{\partial \pi_k} &= \pi_k^{-1} \mathbb{E}_n \left[\gamma_{nk} \right]
\end{aligned}
\tag{5}
$$

whereas $\gamma_{nk} \in [0, 1]$ denote standard GMM responsibilities given by

$$
\gamma_{nk} = \frac{\pi_k p_k(\boldsymbol{x}_n)}{\sum_k \pi_k p_k(\boldsymbol{x}_n)}.
\tag{6}
$$

Degenerate Solution. This solution universally occurs when optimizing $\mathcal{L}$ by SGD, and represents an obstacle for naive SGD. All components have the same weight, centroid and covariance matrix: $\pi_k \approx \frac{1}{K}$, $\boldsymbol{\mu}_k = \mathbb{E}[\mathbf{X}]$, $\Sigma_k = \text{Cov}(\mathbf{X}) \; \forall k$. Since the responsibilities are now uniformly $1/K$, it results from Eq. (5) that all gradients vanish. This effect is avoided by $\hat{\mathcal{L}}$ as only a subset of components is updated by SGD, which breaks the symmetry of the degenerate solution.

Single/Sparse-Component Solution. Optimizing $\hat{\mathcal{L}}$ by SGD, however, leads to another class of unwanted local optima: A single component k^* has a weight close to 1, with its centroid and covariance matrix being given by the mean and covariance of the data: $\pi_{k^*} \approx 1$, $\boldsymbol{\mu}_{k^*} = \mathbb{E}[\mathbf{X}]$, $\Sigma_{k^*} = \text{Cov}(\mathbf{X})$. For $\hat{\mathcal{L}}$, the gradients in Eq. (5) stay the same except for $\gamma_{nk} = \delta_{nk^*}$ from which we conclude that the gradient w.r.t. $\mathbf{P}_k$ and $\boldsymbol{\mu}_k$ vanishes $\forall k$. The gradient w.r.t. π_k does not vanish, but is δ_{kk^*}, which disappears after enforcing the normalization constraint (see Sect. 2.1). A variant is the sparse-component solution where only a few components have non-zero weights, so that the gradients vanish for the same reasons.

2.3   Annealing Procedure

A simple SOM-inspired approach to avoid these undesirable solutions is to punish their characteristic response patterns by an appropriate modification of the (approximate) loss function that is maximized, i.e., $\hat{\mathcal{L}}$. We introduce what we call *smoothed Max-Component log-likelihood* $\hat{\mathcal{L}}^\sigma$, inspired by SOM training:

$$\hat{\mathcal{L}}^\sigma = \frac{1}{N} \sum_n \text{max}_k \left(\sum_j g_{kj} \log \left(\pi_j p(\boldsymbol{x}_n) \right) \right). \tag{7}$$

Here, we assign a normalized coefficient vector $\boldsymbol{g}_k$ to each Gaussian mixture component k. The entries of $\boldsymbol{g}_k$ are computed in the following way:

- Assume that the K Gaussian components are arranged on a 1D grid of dimensions $(1, K)$ or on a 2D grid of dimensions $(\sqrt{K}, \sqrt{K})$. As a result, each linear component index k has a unique associated 1D or 2D coordinate $\boldsymbol{c}(k)$.
- Assume that the vector $\boldsymbol{g}_k$ of length K is actually representing a 1D structure of dimension $(1, K)$ or a 2D structure of dimension $(\sqrt{K}, \sqrt{K})$. Each linear vector index j in $\boldsymbol{g}_k$ has a unique associated 1D or 2D coordinate $\boldsymbol{c}(j)$.
- The entries of the vector $\boldsymbol{g}_k$ are computed as

$$g_{kj} = \exp\left(-\frac{\left(\boldsymbol{c}(j) - \boldsymbol{c}(k) \right)^2}{2\sigma^2} \right) \tag{8}$$

and subsequently normalized to have a unit sum. Essentially, Eq. (7) represents a convolution of $\log \pi_k p_k(\boldsymbol{x})$, arranged on a periodic 2D grid with a Gaussian convolution filter, resulting in a smoothing operation. The 2D variance σ in Eq. (8) is a parameter that must be set as a function of the grid size so that Gaussians are neither homogeneous, nor delta peaks. Hence, the loss function in Eq. (7) is maximized if the log probabilities follow an uni-modal Gaussian profile of variance σ, whereas single-component solutions are punished.

It is trivial to see that the annealed loss function in Eq. (7) reverts to the non-annealed form Eq. (4) in the limit where $\sigma \to 0$. This is due to the fact that vectors $\boldsymbol{g}_k$ approach Kronecker deltas in this case with only a single entry of value 1. Thereby, the inner sum in Eq. (7) is removed. By making σ time-dependent in a SOM-like manner, starting at a value of $\sigma(t_0) \equiv \sigma_0$ and then reducing it to a small final value $\sigma(t_\infty) \equiv \sigma_\infty$. The result is a smooth transition from the annealed loss function Eq. (7) to the original max-component log-likelihood Eq. (4). Time dependency of $\sigma(t)$ can be chosen to be:

$$\sigma(t) = \begin{cases} \sigma_0 & t < t_0 \\ \sigma_\infty & t > t_\infty \\ \sigma_0 \exp(-\tau t) & t_0 < t < t_\infty \end{cases} \tag{9}$$

where the time constant in the exponential is chosen as $\tau = \log \frac{\sigma_0 - \sigma_\infty}{t_\infty - t_0}$ to ensure a smooth transition. This is quite common while training SOMs where the neighborhood radius is similarly decreased.

2.4   Link to Energy-Based SOM Models

The standard Self-Organizing Map (SOM) has no energy function that is minimized. However, some modifications (see [4,7]) have been proposed to ensure the existence of a C^∞ energy function. These energy-based SOM models reproduce all features of the original model and use a learning rule that the original SOM algorithm is actually approximating very closely. In the notation of this article, SOMs model the data through K prototypes $\boldsymbol{\mu}_k$ and K neighborhood functions g_k defined on a periodic 2D grid. Their energy function is written as

$$\mathcal{L}_{SOM} = \frac{1}{N} \sum_n \min_k \sum_j g_{kj} \|\boldsymbol{x}_n - \boldsymbol{\mu}_j\|^2, \tag{10}$$

whose optimization by SGD initiates the learning rule for energy-based SOMs:

$$\boldsymbol{\mu}_k(t+1) = \boldsymbol{\mu}_k + \epsilon g_{ki^*}(\boldsymbol{x} - \boldsymbol{\mu}_k) \tag{11}$$

with the Best-Matching Unit (BMU) having index i^*. In contrast to the standard SOM model the BMU is determined as $i^* = \mathrm{argmax}_i \sum_j g_{ik}\|\boldsymbol{x} - \boldsymbol{\mu}_i\|$. The link to the standard SOM model is the observation that for small values of the neighborhood radius $\sigma(t)$ the convolution vanishes and the original SOM learning rule is recovered. This is typically the case after the model has initially converged (sometimes referred to as "normal ordering").

2.5   Equivalence to SOMs

When writing out $\log \pi_k p_k(\boldsymbol{x}) = -\sum_j \frac{d_{kj}^2}{2}(\boldsymbol{x}_j - \boldsymbol{\mu}_{kj})$, tying the variances so that $\boldsymbol{d}_{kj} = d \,\forall\, j$ and fixing the weights to $\pi_k = \frac{1}{K}$ in Eq. (7) we find that the energy function Eq. (10) becomes

$$\hat{\mathcal{L}}^\sigma = \frac{1}{N} \sum_n \max_k \left(\sum_j g_{kj}\left(-\log K - \frac{d^2}{2}\|\boldsymbol{x}_n - \boldsymbol{\mu}_j\| \right) \right) \tag{12}$$

$$= \frac{d^2}{2N} \sum_n \min_k \sum_j g_{kj}\|\boldsymbol{x}_n - \boldsymbol{\mu}_j\| + \mathrm{const.} \tag{13}$$

In fact Eq. (7) is identical to Eq. (10), except for a constant factor that can be discarded and a scaling factor defined by the common tied precision d^2. The minus sign just converts the max into a min operation, as distances and precisions are positive. The annealing procedure of Eq. (9) is identical to the method for reducing the neighborhood radius during SOM training as well.

Energy-based SOMs are a particular formulation (tied weights, constant spherical variances) of GMMs which are approximated by a commonly accepted method. Training energy-based SOMs in the traditional way results in the optimization of GMMs by SGD, where training procedures are, again, identical.

3   Experiments

This section presents a simple proof-of-concept that the described SGD-based training scheme is indeed practical. It is not meant to be an exhaustive empirical proof and is, therefore, just conducted on a common image dataset. For this experiment, we use the MADBase dataset [13] containing 60 000 grayscale images of handwritten arabic digits in a resolution of 28×28 pixels. The number of training iterations $T = 24\,000$ with a batch size of 1, as it is common for SOMs. We use a GMM with $K = 25$ components, whose centroids are initialized to small random values, whereas weights are initially equiprobable and precisions are uniformly set to $d^2 = 5$ (we found that precisions should initially be as large as possible). We set $t_0 = 0.3\,T$ and stop at $t_\infty = 0.8\,T$ (proportional to the maximum number of iterations). σ_0 starts out at 1.2 (proportional to the

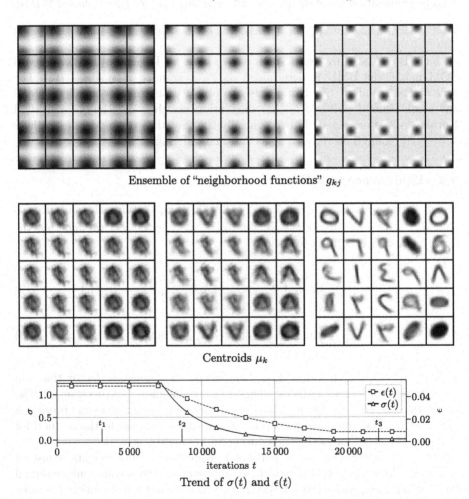

Ensemble of "neighborhood functions" g_{kj}

Centroids μ_k

Trend of $\sigma(t)$ and $\epsilon(t)$

Fig. 2. Visualization of GMM evolution at three points in time during training (from left to right: iterations $t_1 = 3\,120$, $t_2 = 8\,640$ and $t_3 = 22\,080$).

map size) and is reduced to a value of 0.01. The learning rate is similarly decayed to speed up convergence, although this is not a requirement, with $\epsilon_0 = 0.05$ and $\epsilon_\infty = 0.009$. In Fig. 2, three states of the trained GMM are depicted (at iteration $t_1 = 3120$, $t_2 = 8\,640$ and $t_3 = 22\,080$).

We observe from the development of the prototypes that GMM training converges, and that the learned centroids are representing the dataset well. It can also be seen that prototypes are initially blurred and get refined over time, which resembles SOMs. No undesired local optima were encountered when this experiment was repeated 100 times.

4   Discussion

Approximations. The approximations on the way from GMMs to SOMs are Eq. (4) and the approximations made by energy-based SOM models (see [8] for a discussion). It is shown in [3] that the quality of the first approximation is excellent, since inter-cluster distances tend to be large, and it is more probable that a single component can explain the data.

Consequences. The identification of SOMs as special approximation of GMMs allows for the performance of typical GMM functions (sampling, outlier detection) with trained SOMs. The basic quantity to be considered here is the input-prototype distance of the Best-Matching Unit (BMU) since it corresponds to a log probability. In particular, the following consequences were to be expected:

– **Outlier Detection.** The value of the smallest input-prototype distance is the relevant one, as it represents $\hat{\mathcal{L}}$ for a single sample, which in turn approximates the incomplete-data log-likelihood $\mathcal{L}$. In practice, it can be advantageous to average $\hat{\mathcal{L}}$ over several samples to be robust against noise.
– **Clustering.** SOM prototypes should be viewed as cluster centers, and inputs can be assigned to the prototype with the smallest input-prototype distance.
– **Sampling.** Sampling from SOMs should be performed in the same way as from GMMs. Thus, in order to create a sample, a random prototype has to be selected first (since weights are tied no multinomials are needed here). Second, a sample from a Gaussian distribution with precision 2 and centered on the selected prototype along all axes needs to be drawn.

4.1   Summary and Conclusion

To our knowledge, this is the first time that a rigorous link between SOMs and GMMs has been established, based on a comparison of loss/energy functions. It is thus shown that SOMs actually implement an annealing-type approximation to the full GMM model with fixed component weights and tied diagonal variances. To give more weight to the mathematical proof, we validate the SGD-based approach to optimize GMMs in practice.

References

1. Cottrell, M., Fort, J.C., Pagès, G.: Two or three things that we know about the Kohonen algorithm. In: Proceedings of ESANN 1994, pp. 235–244 (1994)
2. Dempster, A.P., Laird, N.M., Rubin, D.B.: Maximum Likelihood from Incomplete Data Via the EM Algorithm, vol. 39. Wiley Online Library (1977). https://doi.org/10.1111/j.2517-6161.1977.tb01600.x
3. Dognin, P.L., Goel, V., Hershey, J.R., Olsen, P.A.: A fast, accurate approximation to log likelihood of Gaussian mixture models. In: Proceedings of IEEE International Conference on Acoustics, Speech and Signal Processing, ICASSP, vol. 3, pp. 3817–3820 (2009). https://doi.org/10.1109/ICASSP.2009.4960459
4. Gepperth, A.: An energy-based SOM model not requiring periodic boundary conditions. Neural Comput. Appl. (2019). https://doi.org/10.1007/s00521-019-04028-9
5. Hartley, H.O.: Maximum likelihood estimation from incomplete data. Biometrics 14, 174–194 (1958)
6. Hecht, T., Lefort, M., Gepperth, A.: Using self-organizing maps for regression: the importance of the output function. In: 23rd European Symposium on Artificial Neural Networks, Computational Intelligence and Machine Learning, ESANN - Proceedings, pp. 107–112 (2015)
7. Heskes, T.: Energy functions for self-organizing maps. Kohonen Maps 303–315 (1999). https://doi.org/10.1016/b978-044450270-4/50024-3
8. Heskes, T.: Self-organizing maps, vector quantization, and mixture modeling. IEEE Trans. Neural Netw. 12(6), 1299–1305 (2001). https://doi.org/10.1109/72.963766
9. Hosseini, R., Sra, S.: Matrix manifold optimization for Gaussian mixtures. In: Advances in Neural Information Processing Systems, pp. 910–918 (2015)
10. Kohonen, T.: The self-organizing map. Proc. IEEE 78(9), 1464–1480 (1990)
11. Ormoneit, D., Tresp, V.: Averaging, maximum penalized likelihood and Bayesian estimation for improving Gaussian mixture probability density estimates. IEEE Trans. Neural Netw. 9(4), 639–650 (1998). https://doi.org/10.1109/72.701177
12. Robbins, H., Monro, S.: A stochastic approximation method. Ann. Math. Stat. 22(3), 400–407 (1951). https://doi.org/10.1214/aoms/1177729586
13. Sherif, A., Ezzat, E.S.: Ahdbase. http://datacenter.aucegypt.edu/shazeem/
14. Verbeek, J.J., Vlassis, N., Kröse, B.J.: Self-organizing mixture models. Neurocomputing 63, 99–123 (2005). https://doi.org/10.1016/j.neucom.2004.04.008

Collaborative Clustering Through Optimal Transport

Fatima Ezzahraa Ben Bouazza[1,2(✉)], Younès Bennani[1], Guénaël Cabanes[1], and Abdelfettah Touzani[2]

[1] LIPN-UMR 7030 CNRS, Université Sorbonne Paris Nord, Paris, France
{fatima.bouazza,younes.bennani,guenael.cabanes}@lipn.univ-paris13.fr
[2] LAMA-FSDM, Université Sidi Mohamed Ben Abdellah, Fez, Morocco
{fatima.bouazza,abdelfettah.touzani}@usmba.ac.ma

Abstract. Significant results have been achieved recently by exchanging information between multiple learners for clustering tasks. However, this approaches still suffer from a few issues regarding the choice of the information to trade, the stopping criteria and the trade-of between the information extracted from the data and the information exchanged by the models. We aim in this paper to address this issues through a novel approach propelled by the optimal transport theory. More specifically, the objective function is based on the Wasserstein metric, with a bidirectional transport of the information. This formulation leads to a high stability and increase of the quality. It also allows the learning of a stopping criteria. Extensive experiments were conducted on multiple data sets to evaluate the proposed method, which confirm the advantages of this approach.

Keywords: Collaborative clustering · Optimal transport · Prototype-based approaches

1 Introduction

Clustering is one of the main opining frameworks in Machine Learning [11]. There is a very large number of approaches of unsupervised clustering algorithms and choosing between several clustering results is often problematic. In addition, most algorithms are sensitive to the initial condition and the chosen parameters. This issue is often addressed by the intervention of an expert able to choose the most adapted algorithms, the parameters that will work best based on the nature of each data set, and the quality indexes relevant to the domain. Making this kind of decision requires a deep knowledge of the data to be analyzed and the available algorithms and indexes [19]. Furthermore, even with a good expert having a decent knowledge of both the data and the algorithms, it is still difficult to make the right choices when it comes to clustering.

One of the most popular solution to address this type of problem is to combine between different results coming from several algorithms. The idea behind is to

© Springer Nature Switzerland AG 2020
I. Farkaš et al. (Eds.): ICANN 2020, LNCS 12397, pp. 873–885, 2020.
https://doi.org/10.1007/978-3-030-61616-8_70

exchange information between several learners in order to increase the quality of the clusters [6]. Based on this idea, several approaches have been proposed, where one seeks to aggregate the information between different algorithms to either form a global consensus or find a local minimum for each learner, i.e. learn from other learners.

Collaborative clustering are one of the most popular algorithms that consists to learn from distant learners, it was introduced as a fuzzy clustering framework based on the fuzzy C-Means algorithm named Collaborative Fuzzy Clustering (CoFC) [12], where the main idea is to exchange different type of information between multiple sites. The framework can be divided into two principal steps:

Local Step: Each algorithm aims to cluster the data locally, to get a partition of the data set and their prototypes (this will be more formally explained in the following sections).

Learning Step: The algorithms aim to exchange the results obtained locally in order to improve the quality of each learner.

Several other approaches have been proposed to develop this idea, like CoEM in [1] and CoFKM [2] and collaborative EM-like algorithm [10] based on Markov Random Fields. Another popular algorithm of collaborative clustering was developed based on Self-Organization Maps (SOMs) [8] by adding a sort of penalized term either for horizontal collaboration or for vertical collaboration to the SOMs objective function, also they took the same principle to the collaborative clustering using the Generative Topographic Maps (GTM) [7] with a modification on M-step in the EM algorithm. Unlike SOMs, this approach came to make the collaboration more smoothed by eliminating the requirement of the same number of clusters an replaced by the same number of neurons which could be in same cases more restraining than the number of clusters.

A recent work have been done to develop the collaborative clustering and make it more flexible [17]. It consist to make the collaboration between different algorithms without fixing a unique number of clusters for all of the collaborators. The advantage of this approach is that different families of clustering algorithms can exchange information in a collaborative framework. Nevertheless, one of the most important issue in collaborative clustering is to find the optimal trade-off between the information gathered from the data and the information received from the other models, as well as detecting the right time to stop the collaboration in order to avoid a decrease of the local quality [14].

In this paper, we propose a novel approach of unsupervised learning from other models. It is based on optimal transport metrics in order to benefit from this mathematical formalism and improve the process of information exchange between the different algorithms. In this case, the collaboration (i.e. the exchange of information between models) is formalised as a bi-directional transport of information. The rest of the paper is organized as follow. The formalism of is discussed in Sect. 2. In Sect. 3 we introduce our novel framework of collaborative clustering using optimal transport theory. In Sect. 4 we investigate experimentally and discuss the quality of the approach. Finally we give a conclusion and some perspective work in Sect. 5.

2   Background

Optimal Transport (OT) has known a successful results in machine learning after its relaxation to a distribution problem [13] using linear program connecting a pair distributions.

More formally, given two measures defined on two different spaces, the OT problem find coupling γ defined as a joint probability over the product of the two spaces. In this paper, we focus on the discrete measures due to the nature of our problem. However, we refer to the book of Villani [18] for more details on the continuous case and more mathematics studies.

Definition: Let Ω be an arbitrary space with D a metric on that space, and $P(\Omega)$ the set of the probability measures on Ω. For $p \in [1, \infty[$ and a probability measures μ and ν in $P(\Omega)$, the p-Wasserstein distance [18] is given by:

$$W_p(\mu, \nu) = \left(\inf_{\gamma \in \Pi(\mu,\nu)} \int_{\Omega^2} D(x,y)^p d\pi(x,y) \right)^{\frac{1}{p}} \tag{1}$$

where $\Pi(\mu, \nu)$ is the set of the probability measures on Ω^2 and their marginals are μ and ν.

We consider here only the discrete version, represented by empirical measures. Formally, let $X_s = \left\{x_i^s \in \mathbb{R}^d\right\}_{i=1}^{i=N_s}$ and $X_t = \left\{x_i^t \in \mathbb{R}^d\right\}_{i=1}^{i=N_t}$ be two families of points in Ω and their empirical measures are $\mu_s = \frac{1}{N_s} \sum_{i=1}^{N_s} \delta_{x_i^s}$ and $\mu_t = \frac{1}{N_t} \sum_{i=1}^{N_t} \delta_{x_i^t}$ respectively defined as a uniform sums of Dirac, the OT problem consist on finding an optimal coupling γ as a joint probability between μ_s and μ_t over $X_s \times X_t$ by minimizing the cost of the transport w.r.t on some metric. This problem is based on two main elements: the matrix M of the pairwise distances between the elements of X_s and X_t raised to the power p which as a cost parameter and the transportation polytope $\Pi(\mu_s, \mu_t) = \left\{\gamma \in \mathbb{R}_+^{N_s \times N_t} \mid \gamma \mathbf{1} = \mu_s, \gamma^T \mathbf{1} = \mu_t\right\}$. This problem admits a unique solution γ^* and defines a metric called the *Wasserstein distance* on the space of the probability measures as follow:

$$W(\mu_s, \mu_t) = \operatorname*{argmin}_{\gamma \in \Pi(\mu_s,\mu_t)} <M, \gamma> \tag{2}$$

where $< .,. >$ is the Frobenius dot product.

The Wasserstein distance has been very useful recently especially in machine learning like domain adaptation [3] metric learning, clustering [4] and multi-level clustering [9]. The particularity about this distance is that it takes into account the geometry of the data using the distance between the samples, which explains its efficiency. On the other hand, in terms of computation the success of this distance is also comes back to Cuturi [4] who introduced an algorithm based on entropy regularization which going to present.

Even though, the Wasserstein distance has known a significant success but in therm of computation the objective function has always suffered from a very slow convergence which pushed Cuturi to propose a smoothed objective function by adding a term of entropic regularization that was introduced in [16] and applied to optimal transport in [13] because the primal objective function suffer from a very slow convergence. using the following objective function

$$\gamma^* = \operatorname*{argmin}_{\gamma \in \Pi(\mu_s, \mu_t)} \; <M, \gamma> -\frac{1}{\lambda} E(\gamma) \tag{3}$$

where $E(\gamma) = -\sum_{i,j}^{N_s, N_t} \gamma_{ij} \log(\gamma_{ij})$ and $\lambda > 0$ some fixed.

Thanks to this regularized version of optimal transport they obtained a less parse solution, more smoother and stable than the original problem and also this formulations allows to solve the problem of optimal transport using Sinkhorn-Knopp matrix Scaling algorithm.

3   Proposed Approach

3.1   Motivation

Classical collaborative algorithm is based on two step, the first one consist to cluster the data locally, and the second one consist to influence the local clusters by the other prototypes of other learners basing on some neighborhood function. Although there is many studies on this algorithm, it still requires many restrictions to ensure the convergence, eventually the same dimension, or the same data in each Learners, the same number of clusters in each learner which make the methods very limited comparing to the real data.

On the other hand optimal transport theory has shown a significant result in term of transfer learning [3] and the comparison of distribution. Based on this idea we had the intuition of comparing the distribution between learners to choose the right model, and use a transport plan to minimize the transfer of knowledge.

In this section we detail the proposed approach and how this well defended theory will improve the learning quality in two case of collaboration: where the models are trained is the same representation space with different instances, or were the models are trained in different representations of the same instances.

3.2   The Algorithm

The main goal of the proposed approach is to improve the mechanism of learning from other model by ensuring the stability of the process, and make sure that exchange of information will converge without an over-fitting.

Let consider r collaborator $X^1, .., X^r$ where each one is represented by a distribution $\mu^v = \frac{1}{n} \sum \delta_{x_i^v}$ where $x_i^v \in \mathbb{R}^{d^v}$.

Local View Learning. We seek in local step to find discrete distribution ν^v of the centroids $C^v = \{c_1^v, .., c_{k^v}^v\}$ that represents the local clusters of each sets. To effectuate this, we compute the optimal transport between μ^v and ν^v basing on the following objective function:

$$\min_{l_{ij}^v, c_j^v} \sum_{ij} l_{ij}^v \|x_i^v - c_j^v\|^2 - \frac{1}{\lambda} E(l_{ij}^v) \tag{4}$$

Subject to: $\sum_{j=1}^{k^v} l_{ij}^v = \frac{1}{n^v}$ and $\sum_{i=1}^{n^v} l_{ij}^v = \frac{1}{k^v}$

It should be noticed that resolving 4 is equivalent to a Llody's problem when $d = 1$ and $p = 2$ without any constraints on the weights. This is why to resolve this problem we alternate between computing the Sinkhor-Matrix to assign instances the closet cluster and updating the centroids.

Algorithm 1 detailed the computation of the local objective function 4, proceeding similarly to k-means. The advantage about clustering the data using the Wasserstein distance its allows to get soft assignment of the data contrary to classic k-means which means that $l_{ij} = [0, \frac{1}{n}]$ instead of $l_{ij} = \{0, \frac{1}{n}\}$. Besides, the penalty term based on the entropy regularization will guarantee a solution with higher entropy which means more stability of the algorithm and the instances will be assigned uniformly.

Algorithm 1: Local view algorithm

Input   : $X^v = \{x_i^v\}_{i=1}^n \in \mathbb{R}^{d^v}$ Data of the vth model.
   The number of clusters k^v
   The entropic constant λ

Output: The OT matrix $L^v = \{l_{ij}^v\}$ and the centroids $C^v = \{C_j^v\}_{j=1}^{k^v}$

Initialize k^v, random centroids $c^v(0)$ with the distribution $\nu^v = \frac{1}{k^v} \sum_{j=1}^{k^v} \delta_{c_j}$;
$t=0$;

while *not converge(clusters not stable)* **do**

   Compute the OT matrix(Sinkhorn matrix)
   $L^v(t) = \{l_{ij}^v\} 1 \le i \le n, 1 \le j \le k^v$;

   $$L^v(t) = \min_{L^v \in \Pi(\mu^v(t), \nu^v(t))} W_\lambda^2(\mu^v(t), \nu^v(t));$$

   Update the distribution centroids $c_j^v(t+1)$:

   $$c_j^v(t+1) = \sum_i l_{ij}^v x_i^v \quad 1 \le j \le k^v;$$

   $t = t + 1$;

end

return L^v *and* $\{c_j^v\}_{j=1}^{k^v}$

Learning from Other Models. The global step aims to create an exchange plane between the learners so each model can improve its local clustering.

The learning distant step could be seen as a two simultaneous phases. The first phase aims to create an interaction plan based on Sinkhorn-matrix distance which compares the local distribution of each algorithm to the others. The idea behind this phase is to allowed to each learner to choose the right model which means that the algorithm will also learn the order of the learning.

After the construction of the transport plan using the Sinkhorn algorithm, the algorithm will learn to choose for each learner, the right distant model to learn from. The second phase consist to exchange the knowledge to improve local quality of each learner basing on the locale prototypes. More precisely, we are looking to transport the prototypes to influence the location of the local prototypes to increase the local quality of each learner.

Considering the same notation above, the objective function of the proposed algorithm will be defined as follow:

$$
\min_{l_{ij}^v, c_j^v} \sum_{ij} l_{ij}^v \|x_i^v - c_j^v\|^2 + \sum_{v'=1, v' \neq v}^{r} \alpha_{v',v} \sum_{jj'} l_{jj'}^{v,v'} \|c_j^v - c_{j'}^{v'}\|^2 - \frac{1}{\lambda}(E(l_{ij}^v) + E(l_{jj'}^{v,v'}))
$$

(5)

where the first term consists to cluster the data locally, and the second term called the learning distant term it consists to influence the local centroids distribution by the centroids distributions distant. The $\alpha_{v',v}$ is a non-negative coefficients proportional to the diversity between learners.

Algorithm 2 explains the computation steps of our proposed approach and shows how we learn to choose the right collaborator to learn from at each iteration basing on Sinkhorn comparisons between the distributions. And how we alternate between influencing the local centroids basing the confidence coefficient relative to the chosen collaborator and its local centroids distribution and update of the centroids relative to local instances until getting better clusters.

It should be pointed out that in each iteration, each collaborator chooses successively the learners to exchange information with, based on the Sinkhorn matrix distance. More accurately, in each iteration, each model exchanges information with the collaborator having the median similarity between the two modelled distributions, computed with the Wasserstein metric. If this exchange increases the quality of the model (using Davis-Bouldin index [5]), the centroids of the model are updated. Otherwise, the selected collaborator is removed from the list of possible learners and the process is repeated with the remaining learners, until the quality of the clusters stops increasing.

4   Experiments

4.1   Experimental Protocol

In order to experimentally test the proposed algorithm, we first proceeded with a data pre-processing in order to create the local subsets. The idea is to split each

---

Algorithm 2: Collaborative learning algorithm

Input : $X^v = \{x_i^v\}_{i=1}^n \in \mathbb{R}^{d^v}$, $v \in \{1, .., r\}$

The number of clusters k^v

The entropic constant λ

The matrix of the confidence coefficient $\{\alpha_{v,v'}\}_{v,v'=1}^{v,v'=r}$

Output: The OT matrix $L^v = \{l_{ij}^v\}_{v=1}^{v=r}$ and the centroids $C^v = \{c_{ij}^v\}_{v=1}^{v=r}$

t=0;

while *not converge (clusters not stable)* **do**

    for $v = 1, ..., r$ **do**

        Get the centroids distributions ν^v by computing **algorithm1**

        for $v' = 1, ..., r$ **do**

            Compute the OT matrix (Sinkhorn matrix)

            $L^{v,v'}(t) = \left\{l_{jj'}^{v,v'}(t)\right\} 1 \le j \le k^v, 1 \le j' \le k^{v'};$

$$L^{v,v'}(t) = \min W_\lambda^2(\nu^v(t), \nu^{v'}(t));$$

        end

        chosen collaborator = median$(L^{v,v'}(t))$ for $1 \le v' \le r$;

        Exchange the information:

$$L^v(t) = \min_{L^v \in \Pi(\mu^v(t), \nu^v(t))} W_\lambda^2(\nu^v(t), \nu^{v'}(t));$$

$$c_j^v(t+1) = \alpha_{v,v'} \sum_{j'} l_{jj'}^{v,v'} c_j^{v'} \quad 1 \le j \le k^v;$$

        Update the distribution of the centroids $c_j^v(t+1)$ by **algorithm 1**

    end

    $t = t + 1;$

end

return $\{L^v\}_{v=1}^{v=r}$ and $\{C^v\}_{v=1}^{v=r}$

---

chosen data set to 10 subsets, that share the same instances but represented with different features in each subset, selected randomly with replacement. Considering the notation above, each subset X^v will be represented by the distribution μ^v that will be considered as the input of Algorithm 1 to get the distribution of the local centroids ν^v. Algorithm 2 is then applied to influence the location of the local centroids by the centroids of the distant learners without having access to their local data.

We therefore applied Algorithm 1 on local data, then the coefficient matrix α were computed based on a diversity index between the collaborators [14]. This coefficient is used to control the importance of the terms of the collaboration. Algorithm 2 in trained 20 times in order to estimate the mean quality of the collaboration and a 95% confidence interval for the 20 experiments.

The experimental results were compared with SOMs-collaborative [7]. Both approaches were trained on the same subsets and on the same local model, a 3×5 map, with the parameters suggested by the authors of the algorithm [7].

Table 1. Some characteristics of the experimental real-world data-sets

Datasets	#instances	#Attributes	#Classes
Glass	214	9	7
Spambase	4601	57	6
Waveform-noise	5000	40	3
WDBC	569	30	2

4.2   Experiments Results

In this section we evaluate our approach on several data sets described in Table 1. We chose two internal indexes to evaluate the quality of the clusters: the Davis Bouldin (DB) index [5] and the *Silhouette* index [15]. Moreover, since the original data are labeled, we choose to evaluate the experiments results with an external index: the Adjusted Rand Index (ARI) [19]. The BD index evaluates the quality of unsupervised clustering based on the compactness of clusters and a separation measure between clusters. The lower the value of DB index, the better the quality of the cluster. We also used the *Silhouette* index, which is based on the measurement of the difference between the average of the distance between the instance x_i and the instances belonging to the same cluster and the average distance between the instance x_i and the instances belonging to other clusters, a *Silhouette* value close to 1 means that the instances are assigned to the right cluster. The ARI measures the agreement between two partitions, one provided from the proposed algorithm and the second one provided from the labels. The values of ARI are between 0 and 1 and the quality is better when the value of ARI is close to 1.

Table 2. Values of the different quality indexes before and after collaboration for each collaborator built from the Spambase data set.

Models	DB		ARI		Silhouette	
	Before	After	Before	After	Before	After
collab1	0,583	0.565	0.045	0.137	0.415	0.532
collab2	0.751	0.690	0.086	0.136	0.392	0.452
collab3	0.555	0.495	0.043	0.135	0.543	0.788
collab4	1.436	0.578	0.073	0.118	0.315	0.631
collab5	0.714	0.459	0.057	0.136	0.507	0.717
collab6	1.067	0.706	0.058	0.139	0.287	0.578
collab7	1.183	1.099	0.157	0.144	0.304	0.312
collab8	0.722	0.511	0.101	0.143	0.505	0.470
collab9	0.707	0.503	0.036	0.136	0.435	0.555
collab10	1.370	0.418	0.069	0.132	0.202	0.755

Table 3. Average values ($\pm CI_{95\%}$) of the different quality indexes before and after the collaboration for each data set over 20 executions.

Models	DB		ARI		Silhouette	
	Before	After	Before	After	Before	After
Glass	1.028 ± 0.23	0.608 ± 0.18	0.155 ± 0.04	0.237 ± 0.01	0.335 ± 0.02	0.552 ± 0.04
Spambase	0.903 ± 0.20	0.481 ± 0.12	0.072 ± 0.02	0.135 ± 0.004	0.390 ± 0.06	0.579 ± 0.09
Waveform	2.481 ± 0.15	1.701 ± 0.20	0.179 ± 0.02	0.218 ± 0.02	0.078 ± 0.008	0.1083 ± 0.01
WDBC	0.734 ± 0.17	0.437 ± 0.09	0.219 ± 0.05	0.439 ± 0.13	0.483 ± 0.02	0.566 ± 0.05

Results are shown in Table 3. As one can see, the proposed approach gives in general good results at improving results after collaboration based on the BD index. In the same way, the average *Silhouette* values after the collaboration is closer to 1. In addition, the results achieved on the ARI index indicate that the average external quality of each data set is increasing after the knowledge exchange between learners. This is expected, of course, because the proposed algorithm evaluates the quality gain based on the DB index at each iteration so that it learns whether or not the collaborator can benefit from this collaboration.

In addition, we chose one data set (due to page limitation) to detail the effect of the proposed algorithm on each collaborator. Table 2 shows the values of different quality indexes of each collaborator built from Spambase data set, and confirm that the quality does increase the quality of most collaborators in the process.

4.3 Comparison with Others Collaborative Approaches

In this section we compare the proposed approach 2 to a popular collaborative algorithm based on Self-Organized-Maps (SOMs) [8].

In order to start with the same local models, both collaborative approaches are applied on the same subsets and each local collaborator start with the same 5×3 SOMs. The approaches are compared using the Silhouette index because it gives better results for the method of the state-of-the-art comparing to other indexes. As shown in Tables 4, 5, 6 and 7, the results obtained with the proposed approach, in comparison to the state-of-the-art, are globally better for this index. One can note that, for some collaborators, the quality of the collaboration leads to very similar results in both cases, despite very different quality before collaboration. However, the OT-based collaboration provides a much more stable quality improvement over the set of collaborators. This can be explained by the fact that the mechanism of the SOMs-based collaborative algorithms is constrained by the neighbourhood functions. In addition, it was built for a collaboration between two collaborators, then extended to allows multiple collaborations, unlike the proposed approach where each learner exchange information with all of the others at each step of the collaboration.

Table 4. Comparison of SOMs-based and OT-based collaborative approaches, starting with SOMs local models, using the *Silhouette* index for the Glass data set. The average values $(\pm CI_{95\%})$ is computed over 20 executions.

Models	SOMs	SOMs-coll	Gain	OT-coll	Gain
collab1	0.088	0.240	0.152	0.240	0.152
collab2	−0.009	−0.009	0.000	0.131	0.140
collab3	−0.036	−0.036	0.000	0.156	0.192
collab4	0.395	0.395	0.000	0.340	−0.055
collab5	−0.008	0.320	0.329	0.320	0.329
collab6	0.070	0.070	0.000	0.102	0.032
collab7	0.222	0.257	0.034	0.253	0.031
collab8	0.410	0.410	0.000	0.439	0.029
collab9	0.073	0.183	0.110	0.223	0.150
collab10	−0.053	−0.051	0.001	0.003	0.056
Average	0.115	0.177	0.063	0.221	0.106
$\pm CI_{95\%}$	±0.10	±0.10	±0.06	±0.07	±0.06

Table 5. Comparison of SOMs-based and OT-based collaborative approaches, starting with SOMs local models, using the silhouette index for the Spambase data set. The average values $(\pm CI_{95\%})$ is computed over 20 executions.

Models	SOMs	SOMs-coll	Gain	OT-coll	Gain
collab1	0.224	0.483	0.260	0.346	0.122
collab2	0.038	0.080	0.042	0.124	0.086
collab3	−0.137	−0.137	0.000	0.005	0.142
collab4	−0.308	−0.091	0.216	−0.103	0.205
collab5	−0.101	−0.028	0.073	0.052	0.153
collab6	−0.039	0.036	0.075	0.153	0.192
collab7	−0.035	−0.035	0.000	0.087	0.122
collab8	0.314	0.524	0.210	0.511	0.197
collab9	−0.260	−0.069	0.191	0.023	0.283
collab10	0.041	0.041	0.000	0.114	0.073
Average	−0.026	0.035	0.106	0.131	0.158
$\pm CI_{95\%}$	±0.12	±0.12	±0.06	±0.11	±0.03

It must be highlighted that for this experiences we trained the proposed algorithm on SOMs model instead of Sinkhorn K-Means, which illustrates the capability of the approach to work on different families of prototype-based models.

Table 6. Comparison of SOMs-based and OT-based collaborative approaches, starting with SOMs local models, using the silhouette index for the Waveform data set. The average values $(\pm CI_{95\%})$ is computed over 20 executions.

Models	SOMs	SOMs-coll	Gain	OT-coll	Gain
collab1	0.025	0.030	0.006	0.064	0.039
collab2	0.036	0.036	0.000	0.062	0.026
collab3	0.070	0.070	0.000	0.069	-0.001
collab4	0.043	0.047	0.003	0.064	0.021
collab5	0.054	0.058	0.004	0.069	0.015
collab6	0.063	0.063	0.000	0.067	0.004
collab7	0.026	0.026	0.000	0.063	0.037
collab8	0.040	0.044	0.004	0.067	0.027
collab9	0.031	0.038	0.007	0.065	0.034
collab10	0.025	0.032	0.007	0.063	0.038
Average	0.043	0.045	0.003	0.065	0.024
$\pm CI_{95\%}$	± 0.01	± 0.009	± 0.01	± 0.05	± 0.01

Table 7. Comparison of SOMs-based and OT-based collaborative approaches, starting with SOMs local models, using the silhouette index for the WDBC data set. The average values $(\pm CI_{95\%})$ is computed over 20 executions.

Models	SOMs	SOMs-coll	Gain	OT-coll	Gain
collab1	0.233	0.233	0.000	0.244	0.011
collab2	0.185	0.208	0.024	0.211	0.026
collab3	0.246	0.303	0.057	0.401	0.155
collab4	0.015	0.074	0.059	0.126	0.111
collab5	0.102	0.182	0.080	0.341	0.239
collab6	0.240	0.278	0.038	0.334	0.094
collab7	0.298	0.337	0.039	0.445	0.147
collab8	0.125	0.125	0.000	0.323	0.198
collab9	0.202	0.213	0.011	0.367	0.165
collab10	0.110	0.123	0.013	0.236	0.126
Average	0.175	0.204	0.032	0.303	0.127
$\pm CI_{95\%}$	± 0.05	± 0.05	± 0.01	± 0.06	± 0.04

5   Conclusion

To summarise, we proposed a novel approach of knowledge exchange between different learners based on optimal transport theory, where the main goal is to increase the local quality of each model and guaranty the stability of the process.

Compared to the most used prototype-based collaborative approaches of the state of the art, our approach is based on strong and well defended theory that became increasingly popular in the field of machine learning. Besides, its strength is highlighted by good experimental results both for artificial and real data-sets.

There are several possible perspectives to this work. On the short term, we are working to improve the approach in order to learn the confidence coefficient at each iteration, according to the diversity and the quality of the collaborators. This could be based on comparisons between the sub-sets' distributions using the Wasserstein distance. It would lead us to another extension where the interaction between collaborators is modelled as graph in a Wasserstein space, which would allow the construction of a theoretical proof of convergence.

References

1. Bickel, S., Scheffer, T.: Estimation of mixture models using co-EM. In: Gama, J., Camacho, R., Brazdil, P.B., Jorge, A.M., Torgo, L. (eds.) ECML 2005. LNCS (LNAI), vol. 3720, pp. 35–46. Springer, Heidelberg (2005). https://doi.org/10.1007/11564096_9
2. Cleuziou, G., Exbrayat, M., Martin, L., Sublemontier, J.H.: CoFKM: a centralized method for multiple-view clustering. In: 2009 Ninth IEEE International Conference on Data Mining, pp. 752–757. IEEE (2009)
3. Courty, N., Flamary, R., Tuia, D.: Domain adaptation with regularized optimal transport. In: Calders, T., Esposito, F., Hüllermeier, E., Meo, R. (eds.) ECML PKDD 2014. LNCS (LNAI), vol. 8724, pp. 274–289. Springer, Heidelberg (2014). https://doi.org/10.1007/978-3-662-44848-9_18
4. Cuturi, M., Doucet, A.: Fast computation of Wasserstein barycenters. In: ICML, pp. 685–693 (2014)
5. Davies, D.L., Bouldin, D.W.: A cluster separation measure. IEEE Trans. Pattern Anal. Mach. Intell. **2**, 224–227 (1979)
6. Forestier, G., Wemmert, C., Gançarski, P.: Collaborative multi-strategical classification for object-oriented image analysis. In: Workshop on Supervised and Unsupervised Ensemble Methods and Their Applications in conjunction with IbPRIA, pp. 80–90 (2007)
7. Ghassany, M., Grozavu, N., Bennani, Y.: Collaborative clustering using prototype-based techniques. Int. J. Comput. Intell. Appl. **11**(03), 1250017 (2012)
8. Grozavu, N., Bennani, Y.: Topological collaborative clustering. Aust. J. Intell. Inf. Process. Syst. **12**(2) (2010)
9. Ho, N., Nguyen, X.L., Yurochkin, M., Bui, H.H., Huynh, V., Phung, D.: Multilevel clustering via Wasserstein means. In: ICML, pp. 1501–1509 (2017)
10. Hu, T., Yu, Y., Xiong, J., Sung, S.Y.: Maximum likelihood combination of multiple clusterings. Pattern Recogn. Lett. **27**(13), 1457–1464 (2006)
11. Kotsiantis, S., Pintelas, P.: Recent advances in clustering: a brief survey. WSEAS Trans. Inf. Sci. Appl. **1**(1), 73–81 (2004)
12. Pedrycz, W.: Collaborative fuzzy clustering. Pattern Recogn. Lett. **23**(14), 1675–1686 (2002)
13. Peyré, G., Cuturi, M., et al.: Computational optimal transport. Found. Trends® Mach. Learn. **11**(5–6), 355–607 (2019)

14. Rastin, P., Cabanes, G., Grozavu, N., Bennani, Y.: Collaborative clustering: how to select the optimal collaborators? In: 2015 IEEE Symposium Series on Computational Intelligence, pp. 787–794. IEEE (2015)

15. Rousseeuw, P.J.: Silhouettes: a graphical aid to the interpretation and validation of cluster analysis. J. Comput. Appl. Math. **20**, 53–65 (1987)

16. Schwarzschild, K.: Sitzungsberichte preuss. Akad. Wiss **424** (1916)

17. Sublime, J., Matei, B., Cabanes, G., Grozavu, N., Bennani, Y., Cornuéjols, A.: Entropy based probabilistic collaborative clustering. Pattern Recogn. **72**, 144–157 (2017)

18. Villani, C.: Optimal Transport: Old and New, vol. 338. Springer, Heidelberg (2008). https://doi.org/10.1007/978-3-540-71050-9

19. Wu, J., Xiong, H., Chen, J.: Adapting the right measures for k-means clustering. In: SIGKDD, pp. 877–886. ACM (2009)

Author Index

Printed in the United States
By Bookmasters